Century of Innovation:

A History of
European and American
Theatre and Drama
Since 1870

Century of Innovation:

A History of
European and American
Theatre and Drama
Since 1870

OSCAR G. BROCKETT

Indiana University

ROBERT R. FINDLAY

University of Kansas

Prentice-Hall, Inc., Englewood Cliffs, New Jersey

Library of Congress Cataloging in Publication Data

BROCKETT, OSCAR GROSS.
　　Century of innovation.

　　Bibliography:
　　1. Theater—History—20th century.　2. Drama—20th
century—History and criticism.　I. Findlay, Robert R.,
joint author.　II. Title.
PN2189.B64　　　792′.09　　　72-5425
ISBN 0-13-122747-5

Century of Innovation:
A History of European and American Theatre and Drama Since 1870

OSCAR G. BROCKETT AND ROBERT R. FINDLAY

Printed in the United States of America

10　9　8　7　6　5　4　3　2　1

PRENTICE-HALL INTERNATIONAL, INC., *London*
PRENTICE-HALL OF AUSTRALIA, PTY. LTD., *Sydney*
PRENTICE-HALL OF CANADA, LTD., *Toronto*
PRENTICE-HALL OF INDIA PRIVATE LIMITED, *New Delhi*
PRENTICE-HALL OF JAPAN, INC., *Tokyo*

PRENTICE-HALL SERIES IN THEATRE AND DRAMA

Oscar G. Brockett

CONSULTING EDITOR

Contents

Preface

There are at least two major theatrical traditions (Oriental and Western) and perhaps other lesser ones. This book concentrates on one segment of one tradition: the Western mode from the advent of the "modern" era (around 1870) until the early 1970s as seen in several European countries and the United States. Within those limits, coverage is further restricted to those persons and events either most characteristic of an era or of greatest significance in later times.

Both theatrical and dramatic practice are treated here as integral parts of a whole which would be incomplete were either omitted. Some attention is given to the climate of ideas and societal factors which have influenced theatre and drama, to dramaturgy and dramatists, to theoreticians and theatrical practitioners (directors, actors, and designers), and to audiences. But the overall concern has been to trace those changes in outlook and practice which lie behind our present situation.

No one can write a book of this scope without drawing heavily from the work of others. Our indebtedness is deep and only imperfectly indicated by the Bibliography given at the end of the text. We would like as well to acknowledge with gratitude the assistance given by William Kuhlke, Brooks McNamara, Richard Schechner, James Walton, Robert and Christine Asch, Ronald Willis, James Lauricella, Clyde Sumpter, John Scott, and David Flemming. We owe a special debt of thanks to our students who over the years have provided stimulation and new insights. To our wives, Lenyth Brockett and Lenore Findlay, we are grateful for assistance, encouragement, and forbearance. Credits for photographs are acknowledged in the captions accompanying the illustrations.

O.G.B.
R.R.F.

Century of Innovation:

A History of
European and American
Theatre and Drama
Since 1870

The First Stirrings,
1850-1870

If we accept the usual dating (from the appearance of Henrik Ibsen's prose plays in the 1870s), "modern" drama is now approximately one hundred years old. During that time it has undergone many and drastic changes, as movement has succeeded movement—realism, naturalism, symbolism, expressionism, surrealism, epic, absurdism, to name only the most prominent. Furthermore, the development has been complicated by contradictions and inconsistencies within the movements and within the work of individual authors. Still, it is this almost kaleidoscopic change that one must try to bring into focus if the development is to be clarified.

Today, when we are in concerted retreat from the realistic mode, it is sometimes difficult to remember that it was realism which ushered in the modern era or that realism itself was a product of mid-nineteenth-century demands that every field of knowledge become more sensitive to the needs of the time. The urge was so insistent and was met so well that the nineteenth century brought more far-reaching changes in almost every field than did any other time since the Renaissance. It was in these years that the bases were laid for almost all that has happened since. In art, the immediate result was realism, but the seeds of many later movements were also sown at this time.

~ I ~

To understand realism, it is necessary to consider, at least briefly, the socio-economic and political forces out of which it grew. First, during the nineteenth century individual industry was largely superseded by the factory. This change, usually summed up in the term Industrial Revolution, was made possible by a series of inventions, the most important of which was the steam engine (1769), since its potential as a source of motive power prompted so many others. Among them, the most significant were the power loom, perfected in 1785, which made possible the first factories, and the steamboat (1807) and locomotive (1812), both of which made the moving of industrial materials and products increasingly efficient. As the potentials of these new inventions were realized, "cottage" industry was made obsolete by factories. Second, the establishment of factories required the displacement of large numbers of persons, since workers had to live close to their jobs. Thus, one social consequence of industrialization was urbanization. Third, with urbanization came a host of problems, most easily seen in the slums which the industrial towns spawned.

Unfortunately, the problems created by industrialization and urbanization came at just the time when governments were least disposed to deal with them, for memories of the French Revolution haunted Europe throughout the first half of the nineteenth century and governments sought to insure that such an event would not recur. Thus, they failed to distinguish between legitimate demands for social reforms and revolutionary politics.

Politicians were clearly wrong in thinking they could turn the clock back to a time before the American and French revolutions had proclaimed a new social philosophy. These revolutions were based, in large part, upon a then-radical doctrine—"All men are created free and equal"—and thus they challenged the centuries-old tradition of the monarchical government of a society organized hierarchically into a small privileged and hereditary nobility, a somewhat larger politically underprivileged but economically favored middle class, and a socially, economically, and politically deprived working class (by far the majority). The new doctrine proclaimed the masses equal to those who had formerly been ranked above them in every way. Although the masses had more to gain from a revolution than did any other group, they were completely unprepared through education or tradition to exercise power judiciously. Thus, it is not surprising that during the French Revolution the masses were manipulated by those who had seized power. In the nineteenth century, this "reign of terror" was cited as the inevitable result of giving power to the masses.

When Napoleon was defeated in 1815, monarchy was restored in France and reactionary governments were established there and in other countries throughout Europe. In most countries, voting rights were reserved for property owners, thus effectively disenfranchising most of the working class. Since it benefitted most from the emerging industrialization and urbanization, the middle class was little inclined to favor changes designed to better the conditions of the workers. Thus, a kind of impasse was reached under which those most needing help were wholly dependent upon the benevolence of their rulers. But those in power were suspicious of any proposal for reform on the ground that any concessions would only encourage new demands and ultimately lead to rebellion. It is not surprising, therefore, that this "hard line" eventually led to the very thing that rulers most feared, new revolutions, since violence seemed the only weapon left the workers. Scarcely a country in Europe escaped. The first wave of uprisings came in 1830 and a second, more intense one between 1845 and 1850. Although most revolts were put down, by 1850 it had become evident that more democratic political systems were needed and that a host of pressing problems were crying out for solution. It was no doubt this recognition that led dramatists in the late nineteenth century for the first time to treat the problems of the lower classes with the seriousness formerly reserved for the middle and upper classes.

The increased awareness of serious problems brought in its wake widespread disillusionment with the past, a disillusionment that encompassed literature and drama as well as economics and politics. Romanticism, the dominant mode of the early nineteenth century, fell victim to the new outlook. In some ways, this rejection of romanticism seems unfair, for almost all the romantic writers were democratic in their sympathies. In romantic dramas, the antagonistic characters were apt to be rulers or aristocrats and the protagonists rebels or common men. The corrupt use of power (either economic or political) was a constant theme both in romantic drama and melodrama. Still, these potentially controversial views were usually submerged under incidents which glorified the human spirit and its ability to survive all hardships or which showed the incorruptibility of true virtue. Stories were usually drawn from other places and times (often some remote past) or they dealt with current problems only by implication. In melodrama, the virtuous characters were always triumphant, thus implying that God or Providence watches over human affairs and insures justice, while in romantic drama, in which the heroes often met death, some inscrutable or unavoidable fate seemed to determine the outcome. In either case, the outcome was made to appear outside human control. Such drama seemed rather to encourage endurance than a search for solutions. As it became clear in the political and economic realms that patience under adversity was not sufficient, the ideals encouraged by romantic drama and melodrama ceased to exert any strong appeal for those who favored change.

Attitudes change slowly, but by the mid-nineteenth century enough persons were questioning the past to provide a sympathetic audience for radically new ideas. Perhaps the most fundamental new demand was that the scientific method be applied to social problems. This call was set forth most persuasively by Auguste Comte (1798–1857) in his *Positive Philosophy* (5 vols., 1830–42) and *Positive Polity* (4 vols., 1851–54). Comte classified all knowledge according to decreasing simplicity and generality—mathematics, astronomy, physics, chemistry, biology, and sociology—each resting on the results of those that preceded it. The list also indicates the order in which each has been reduced to precise method—that is, the order in which each became a true science in the sense of exact knowledge. Since the phenomena of social life are so complex, it seemed only natural to Comte that sociology should be the last of the sciences to develop. Furthermore, as the apex of the sciences, sociology is the study for which all the others exist, since in Comte's scheme knowledge is valued only insofar as it contributes to "the science of society." For Comte, sociology was still emerging, and he proclaimed the great task of his age to be the application of precise observation, hypothesis, and analysis (that is, the scientific method) to social phenomena so that the causes of problems might be determined and the effects controlled. Thus, Comte believed that science could provide answers to the problems then plaguing man.

Comte's ideas were reenforced and new ones added by Charles Darwin (1809–82) in his *The Origin of Species* (1859), often said to be the most important work of the nineteenth century. Darwin set out to explain how the various species came into existence and how and why they changed. His explanation had two essential parts. First, he argued that all life forms have evolved from a common ancestry. This idea was not original, having often been suggested since the time of the Greeks, but Darwin, unlike his predecessors, supplied an immense amount of evidence to support his contention. Second, he argued that evolution is to be explained by a process of natural selection (the ability of a particular species to adapt to environmental circumstances, leading to the "survival of the fittest"). Reduced to its essentials, Darwin's theory explains all biological phenomena in terms of heredity (factors transmitted to an individual at birth) and environment (those forces to which the individual is subjected after birth).

The implications of Darwin's theories are many, although he did not see all of them himself. First, the role of God or Divine Providence (which had played such a large part in earlier thought) is greatly reduced, perhaps even eliminated. The story of creation as given in the Bible (at least if interpreted literally) is contradicted by Darwin's view that all life forms have evolved from a common ancestry. Furthermore, if causality can be reduced to heredity and environment, the intervention in human affairs by Divine Providence seems unlikely. Insofar as God retains a place in the Darwinian universe, it is as the original creator of matter, everything having evolved through a natural process in which divine intervention is unnecessary.

Second, if all causality is natural and can be explained by hereditary and environmental factors, then it can be apprehended through the five senses. Any "sixth" sense is to be distrusted unless its intuitions can be verified by scientific observation. Attention thus is diverted from the metaphysical or supernatural to the natural realm and to those things which can be directly observed here and now.

Third, in such a scheme, man's place in the universe is seriously altered, for he becomes an accidental product of a natural process and a species to be studied scientifically like any other biological phenomenon. As some critics of the late nineteenth century observed, man had been absorbed into nature as just another animal, rather than, as in earlier views, being treated as somehow superior, or an exception, to animalistic nature. More important, the scheme of causality summed up in "heredity and environment" makes of man a victim of circumstances rather than the architect of his own fate, since an individual has no control over his heredity or his early environment. The implications of this view (perhaps the most far-reaching of all) are enormously significant for morality. Can a man be blamed for his actions if they are determined by forces over which he has no control? Taken to its logical extreme, this view means that whatever a man does he must do. Many alterations in legal doctrine and moral values during the past century can be traced to the gradual acceptance of these views. In drama, they opened up the possibility (even the necessity) of treating sympathetically behavior formerly considered to be willful villainy.

Fourth, the inevitability of change suggested by Darwin's theory contributed much to the idea of progress. If all life forms, including humans, have evolved from some infinitesimal grain of matter, movement from simplicity to complexity and from lower to higher forms seems inevitable. This encourages the notion that progress is also inevitable. It was not long before Darwin's purely biological study was applied to cultural change. Consequently, since the late nineteenth century it has been usual to treat cultural phenomena as subject to an evolutionary process in which simplicity inevitably precedes and leads to complexity. This "cultural Darwinism," although of extremely questionable validity, is now so pervasive as to go almost unnoticed.

The idea of inevitable progress was an important ingredient in optimism about the ability of science to speed progress. The systematic application of scientific method to specific problems led to the enormous advances in technology upon which so much of modern life rests, while the ability to solve these "engineering" problems further reenforced faith in science to speed progress.

But is was not merely technology that developed so rapidly during the nineteenth century. It soon became clear that more knowledge had to be accumulated in many fields before they could become truly useful in the march toward progress. Thus, almost all the physical, biological, and social sciences made enormous leaps during the nineteenth century and, as specialized knowledge grew, many were subdivided to form new branches of learning. Psychology was separated from philosophy, of which it had always been considered a branch, to become a science in its own right. Anthropology, archeology, and geology were transformed by the knowledge and methods learned through intensive field studies. Furthermore, the new knowledge accumulated in these three fields destroyed the traditional belief that the world was only six thousand years old. Combined with Darwin's theory, it cast additional doubt on the story of creation as given in Genesis. A conflict between science and religion arose which has never been fully resolved. Gradually, science was cast in the role of skeptic challenging all received knowledge and the accumulated beliefs of centuries.

Because of the dramatic increases in specialized knowledge, optimism over the potentialities of science was partially realized. At the same time, however, the same advances began to undermine optimism. It is clear that mid-nineteenth-century enthusiasts had an oversimplified view of the problems that faced society and of the potentialities of science to solve them. This enthusiasm was gradually dissipated as it became clear that technology, although it solved many problems, created as many difficulties as it met. Furthermore, the newly emerging sciences, rather than providing definitive answers as had been anticipated, opened up new mysteries and made it seem even more unlikely that man could fully comprehend, synthesize, and utilize sensibly all the knowledge needed to solve human problems. Thus, the original optimism of the mid-nineteenth century eventually gave way to a more subdued, sometimes even a pessimistic, view.

It is also likely that mid-nineteenth-century enthusiasts did not comprehend the implications for morality of their faith in science. Pragmatists argued that nothing can be considered true unless verified by scientific investigation. But the application of scientific method to ethical systems merely demonstrates that values are inevitably subjective and incapable of scientific verification. Thus, while science depends upon precise knowledge, morality is always relative. Most champions of science in the nineteenth century were conventionally moral and few questioned the values of their day. Consequently, the results of a thoroughgoing scientific view were not fully evident during their lifetimes. But as the faith that undergirded the old morality was destroyed by new knowledge and new attitudes, no new faith appeared to replace the old. The continuing search for a set of values capable of commanding widespread commitment and of serving as a basis for action is one of the major characteristics of the modern era and one of the most pervasive influences on modern drama.

In the mid-nineteenth century it was enthusiasm over the potentialities of science that prevailed, inspiring many to seek ways of making all knowledge immediately relevant to the needs of the time. In art and literature, the result was realism. But those who embraced the new outlook could not entirely escape the past, and today the early realists often seem more nearly romantics than realists. It was to be many years before the ideals of realism were fully achieved. The years between 1850 and 1870 saw the first steps, if not the full development of the new mode.

II

It was in France that realism was first proclaimed a distinct style. The earliest reference to it is found in a letter published in 1853 by Jules-Husson Champfleury (1821–89), a leading novelist and critic. By 1863, the theoretical bases of realism had been thoroughly set forth and debated in such periodicals as *Réalisme* (founded in 1856), *Le Présent, L'Artiste, La Revue de Paris,* and *Le Figaro.* Advocates of the movement agreed upon the following points: (1) realism provides a truthful representation of the real world; (2) it is based upon direct observation of contemporary life and manners; and (3) the author must be impersonal in his attitude toward his subject matter.

Opponents of realism brought many charges against it, among which the most common were: (1) in avoiding the ideal, realism limits itself to the ugly and trivial; (2) it emphasizes external detail only; (3) it is completely materialistic; and (4) it emphasizes sensualism and fatalism and is morally indifferent or positively immoral in its outlook.

The conflict ultimately turns on opposing views of the nature and function of art. The detractors obviously believed that art should, either directly or implicitly, idealize human experience and provide a positive and moral picture of human destiny. The supporters saw art as a reflection of life as seen through direct observation and without any "prettyfying." To the charge of immorality, they answered that truth is the highest form of morality, that idealization only falsifies, and that such distortion is truly immoral. They further responded that, if the audience did not like what was represented in art it should blame the society which had created the conditions portrayed rather than the author who reported them.

This controversy is, of course, a perennial one. Almost any drastic new direction in art, whether toward or away from realism, is usually met with cries of outrage. Nonrealistic movements in the theatre (such as expressionism or absurdism) have been declared hoaxes perpetrated on the public by untalented men with sinister motives, while trends toward greater realism are usually declared morally degenerate, primarily because previously taboo subject matter and behavior are brought onto the stage. The outcries against realism are usually accompanied by a demand for censorship. Looking back on the realistic plays of the nineteenth century from the perspective of today, it is difficult to understand the outrage they aroused. It can perhaps be better appreciated if one remembers the response of the 1960s to the introduction of nudity on the stage.

It was almost entirely the "moral tone" of plays which aroused hostility in the late nineteenth century, for even the most "romantic" of critics and producers accepted and admired the reproduction on stage of external reality, so long as it was not sordid or ugly. Thus, there are two strains of realism in the nineteenth century: (1) romantic realism, in which dramas with idealized subjects are mounted in extremely detailed and historically accurate settings and costumes; and (2) true realism, in which plays based on nonidealized contemporary subjects are presented in settings designed to show the significant interaction of environment with character and action. It is only natural that romantic realism should develop first, for it was merely the culmination of trends that began in the Renaissance.

It is in the picture-frame stage—perfected in Italy in the sixteenth and seventeenth centuries—that the origins of romantic realism are to be found. Originally, it too was a radical departure, for it was quite unlike the stages of Greece, Rome, or Medieval Europe.

In Greece and Rome, stage setting had consisted largely of a permanent architectural façade as a scenic background for all plays. While this façade may have been altered slightly from play to play by *periaktoi* or other small scenic pieces, the basic visual effect always remained much the same. The stage was a place where performances occurred rather than where particular locales were represented.

In the medieval theatre, space was treated as cosmic. In the most typical of arrangements, a number of small scenic units were erected on a long unframed platform. At one end, a unit symbolized Heaven, and at the other, a unit symbolized Hell. Between these two a number of other units stood for various earthly places. Thus, Man operated between Heaven and Hell, and, through the simultaneous representation of the entire universe, the stage was made all-inclusive in its scope. Thus, space was conceived as infinite.

In the Renaissance, both classical and medieval practices were rejected. Instead, settings represented a single place depicted by the illusion of perspective painting. If more than one set was used, these were presented successively rather than simultaneously and entire settings rather than small scenic units were changed. This unitary approach was further emphasized by the development of the proscenium arch to frame the picture. Before the end of the seventeenth century, this picture-frame stage had become standard throughout Europe.

From the beginning, the picture-frame stage was essentially realistic, since it sought to create the illusion of a single place. Nevertheless, illusionism underwent several changes between the seventeenth and mid-nineteenth centuries. Originally, perspective settings were arranged symmetrically with the vanishing point at the center back, but in the eighteenth century, angle perspective, which permitted asymmetrical arrangements, became common and was considered more realistic because it was less formal. Until the late eighteenth century, settings usually depicted some generalized place. That is, settings were not meant to show a specific location but to capture the essence of a type of place—a garden, a prison, a palace—since art was thought to be concerned with universals rather than particulars and time and place to be of secondary concern to human nature, which is the same in all times and all places. Thus, drama, both in its settings and characterizations, concentrated on the timeless rather than the topical. This generalized approach to place, while illusionistic in the sense that it used representational means to depict idealized backgrounds, led to the use of stock settings which could be employed for many plays. Effects were gained almost entirely through painting, for the basic elements of all settings were side wings, backdrops, and overhead borders. Seldom were steps, platforms, and other three-dimensional units used. Furthermore, furniture was not brought onto the stage unless absolutely required by the action. Thus, the illusion of reality operated within rather strict limits.

The late eighteenth century brought an increase in particularity, and it was the culmination of this trend in the nineteenth century that created "romantic realism." The new trend built on several growing interests. One of these was the picturesque, or "local color." For example, at Drury Lane in London such productions as *The Wonders of Derbyshire* (1779) showed actual places in England, and *Omai, or a Trip Around the World* (1785) depicted various places where Captain Cook had stopped on his way around the world. This kind of "travelogue" remained popular through most of the nineteenth century. The melodramas of the early nineteenth century also exploited "local color." For example, René Guilbert de Pixérécourt (1773–1844), "the father of melodrama," often set his plays in unusual places and included local festivals as an excuse for showing native dances performed in colorful costumes. This use of particularizing detail was received enthusiastically, so long as it did not pass over into the sordid.

Interest in the picturesque was paralleled by a concern for the historical past. Until the end of the eighteenth century, the desire to achieve universality had discouraged attempts to depict specific times and places. But the emerging concept that events are determined in part by when and where they occur brought drastic changes in the eighteenth and nineteenth centuries. At first there were no readily available sources of information about the architecture and dress of the past, but antiquarian research began to flourish about 1775 and the results were soon seen on the stage. One of the first productions to seek complete accuracy in every detail was of

Coronation scene from Schiller's *The Maid of Orleans* as presented at the Court Theatre, Berlin, in 1801. The setting, by Karl Friedrich Schinkel, was one of the first anywhere to use detailed historical accuracy. This scene also required about 200 actors. (From Weddigen's *Geschichte der Theater Deutschlands*, 1904.)

Schiller's *The Maid of Orleans,* staged in Berlin in 1801. In England, Shakespeare's *King John* at the Covent Garden Theatre in 1823 was the first production in which all the costumes were historically authentic. In France, it was the romantic playwrights, Victor Hugo and Alexandre Dumas *père,* who insisted most on the need for accuracy in costumes and settings.

Antiquarianism was slow in winning universal acceptance, however, although instances of its use increased steadily from the late eighteenth century onward. In England, William Charles Macready, between 1837 and 1843, was probably the first to use historical accuracy consistently. The movement reached its climax in the work of Charles Kean (1811–68) at the Princess's Theatre in London between 1850 and 1859. Although Kean's repertory was made up almost entirely of melodrama and poetic drama, he applied standards of absolute accuracy in every detail of setting, costumes, and properties. Beginning with *Macbeth* in 1853, he provided the audience with a printed list of the authorities he had consulted in his search for authenticity.

Accompanying the movement toward accuracy of local and historical details was another which emphasized realism in special effects. Although this interest can be traced back to medieval times, it had since then been exploited primarily in such minor dramatic forms as pantomime and opera. In the early nineteenth century, melodrama brought it into full-length dramas, and from there it spread to other forms. For example, Pixérécourt's *Daughter of the Exile* showed a flood uprooting trees, inundating the stage, and carrying the heroine away on a plank, and his *Death's Head* culminated in the foiling of a plot as a volcanic eruption engulfs the stage and kills the villain. This kind of device became ever more popular. At midcentury, the plays of Dion Boucicault were exploiting all the potentialities of the stage in such effects as ghosts rising and disappearing through the floor, the destruction of houses by fire and of steamboats by explosions, and a host of others designed to create a maximum of sensation and suspense. In the 1850s, Charles Kean was using similar effects for such poetic dramas as Byron's *Sardanapalus,* which reached its climax in the destruction of a palace by fire.

Beginning in the early nineteenth century, moving panoramas and dioramas—scenes painted on continuous lengths of cloth and moved across the stage by means of turning spools—made it possible to stage episodes in which characters or objects (such as boats or carriages) seemed to travel

Elaborate setting for Byron's *Sardanapalus,* "The Hall of Nimrod,"
designed by E. Lloyds for Charles Kean in the 1850s.
(Courtesy Victoria and Albert Museum.)

Cross-section of a stage, showing the treadmills and moving panorama used in staging a horse race. The man at the upper right controls the speed of the treadmills. (From *L'Illustration,* March 14, 1891.)

enormous distances without leaving the stage. Before the end of the century, this type of moving scenery was to be coupled with treadmills set into the stage floor so that such events as the chariot race in *Ben Hur* could be staged convincingly. Panoramas and dioramas were also used in poetic drama. When Macready staged *Henry V* in 1839 he replaced Chorus's speech at the beginning of Act III, in which the movement of the English army is described, with a moving diorama which showed the voyage from Southampton to Harfleur.

Everyday life as the audience knew it was also brought onto the stage. As early as the 1730s, domestic tragedy had popularized the serious treatment of ordinary characters, and in the nineteenth century melodrama continued to exploit this interest. Settings for such plays were at first composed of the usual wings and drops, but eventually this way of depicting domestic interiors became unsatisfactory. Consequently, the box set, with three walls and a ceiling, was developed to simulate ordinary rooms. It is impossible to say when the box set appeared. The first tentative steps were probably taken in the late eighteenth century, and fully developed box sets can be found in most European countries by 1825, although they were not introduced into England until the 1830s. The box set was not to win universal acceptance, however, until the end of the nineteenth century.

Once the box setting was introduced, an increasing number of realistic touches were inevitable. Since a setting which simulates a real room looked bare if left unfurnished, it was only natural that it would eventually be fitted out with furniture, carpets, and other paraphernalia. Mme. Vestris (1797–1856) in the 1830s and 1840s is said to have furnished her settings as though they were real rooms, even though her repertory for the most part was restricted to light comedy and musical drama. In Paris in 1846, *Pierre Fevrier* created a sensation with its real furnishings and its decorated floor cloth, simulating black-and-white marble squares, the first attempt in France to make the floor an integral part of the stage design.

The introduction of gas lighting around 1820 also made illusion more complete. It was now possible to get as much light on the stage as desired, difficult when lighting had depended on oil lamps and candles. Furthermore, it was possible to control intensity by regulating the supply of gas. By 1850, the "gas table," an early form of controlboard, made it possible for one person to control all lights from one central location. The limelight and the carbon arc, both in use for theatrical purposes by the 1840s, made it possible to project strong beams of light onto the stage to simulate moonlight, sunlight, rainbows, and other special lighting effects. Equipped with housings, lenses, and reflectors, the limelight and carbon arc were the prototypes of spotlights. Even in their early forms, they made the simulation of sunrises, sunsets, lightning, storms, and other weather conditions convincing.

By 1850, then, illusionism was highly developed and accepted as a standard for which all theatrical production should aim. Thus, the realists' demands that closely observed detail be reproduced onstage was easily met. Still, the illusionism typical of theatres in 1850 had many limitations so far as the realists were concerned.

First, spectacle was largely extraneous to the dramas it accompanied. It provided picturesque and often sensational backgrounds, but the events and characters were not integrally related to it. For example, the addition of historically accurate costumes, realistic sound effects, and elaborate settings does not make *King Lear* realistic; it merely adds illusionistic embellishments to a nonrealistic drama. Similarly, in melodrama the hero is not good nor the villain evil because of hereditary or environmental factors; the settings and special effects merely serve to maximize sensational events rather than to illuminate character.

Second, spectacle was almost never sordid. The unpleasant was glossed over or transformed into painless picturesqueness. Consequently, the seamy side of life was kept firmly concealed.

Third, for the most part scenic designs were still realized through painted, two-dimensional settings. Steps, platforms, and other actualistic details, except for the occasional use of furniture, had not yet become common. Thus, realistic details were literally illusions created by paint.

The primary distinction between this incipient realism and true realism is to be found in the relationship of character and event to stage environment. In true realism, agents act as they do because in large part they are products of specific hereditary and environmental influences. Once this relationship is accepted, setting must be treated as a major cause of action, for the environment which has shaped character and event must be depicted so as to show the relationship. Thus, spectacle must be made an integral part of the action it accompanies; it must become environment rather than picturesque background.

By 1850, the theatre was equipped to stage realistic dramas and the demand for truly realistic plays was beginning to be felt. Still, it would be a long time before a fully developed realistic drama would emerge.

III

Since it was in France that the theory of realism evolved, it is probably not surprising that there also the first conscious school of realistic drama was attempted. While there had been realistic plays before this time—perhaps even as early as certain of Euripides' works and including such recent outstanding precursors as Büchner's *Woyzeck* (1836) and Hebbel's *Maria Magdalena* (1844)—these were for the most part isolated from any clearly defined movement. On the other hand, in France playwrights were seeking to embrace realism even as its tenets were being promulgated in such periodicals as *Réalisme* and *Le Présent*. In this, precedence should perhaps

The actress Sarah Bernhardt, early in her career, as the courtesan Marguerite Gautier in *Camille* by Dumas *fils*.

go to Alexandre Dumas *fils* (1824–95). His first play, *Camille,* written before realism as a conscious mode had appeared, now seems a residue of the romantic movement. Nevertheless, it was denied production for three years (written in 1849, it was not produced until 1852), in large part because it treated sympathetically the heroine, modeled on a well-known "kept woman" of the time. While many plays had featured the "prostitute with a heart of gold," they had normally placed the scene in some remote past and further distanced the story through poetic diction and other devices. Dumas, however, had set his story in contemporary Paris and had simulated everyday conversation in his dialogue. Consequently, both the subject and its handling were considered scandalous in the mid-nineteenth century, although today they appear contrived and conventionally moralistic.

Camille is the least realistic and the least characteristic of Dumas's plays, however, and it remained for *The Demi-Monde* (1855) to establish the path he was to take thereafter. In *The Demi-Monde,* Dumas treats the same kind of characters and the same milieu as in *Camille* but now unsympathetically. Whereas *Camille* shows the kept woman falling in love and nobly renouncing her lover when her past threatens his family's reputation, *The Demi-Monde* depicts a kept woman, Suzanne, coldly seeking to conceal her past and to gain respectability by marrying an unsuspecting dupe. Her foil, Olivier, has been her friend, but when he discovers her intentions, he shows no mercy in thwarting her. No doubt considered an admirable character in the nineteenth century, Olivier today seems self-righteous in his rigid application of a double standard, for though he has participated as fully as has Suzanne in the *demi-monde,* he feels perfectly comfortable in returning to the world of respectability which he so firmly denies her. *The Demi-Monde* established the thrust of Dumas's later work: the serious treatment of contemporary social issues. For example, in *A Question of Money* (1857) he inquires whether a man has the right to use trickery in order to gain an enormous return on his investments, while in *The Illegitimate Son* (1858) he shows the problems faced by illegitimate children in a world which refuses them all rights.

In dramatizing these subjects, Dumas created characters reasonably like those to be met in real life, made them speak dialogue which simulated the conversational mode, and placed them in drawing rooms furnished like those of the day. Thus, on the surface, his plays fulfilled most of the demands made by the realists. If they ultimately fell short of the realistic ideal, it was because of two outstanding elements in his plays: didacticism and ingenuity. That Dumas was both conscious and proud of these characteristics can be seen from a statement in an open letter, "To M. Sarcey": "I realize that the prime requisites of a play are laughter, tears, passion, emotion, interest, curiosity: to leave life at the cloak room; but I maintain that if, by means of all these ingredients, and without minimizing one of them, I can exercise some influence over society; if, instead of treating effects I can treat causes; if, for example, while I satirize and describe and dramatize adultery, I can find means to force people to discuss the problem, and the law-maker to revise the law, I shall have done more than my part as a poet, I shall have done my duty as a man. . . . We need invent nothing; we have only to observe, remember, feel, coordinate, restore. . . . As for basis, the real; as for facts, what is possible; as for means, what is ingenious; that is all that can be rightfully asked of us."

Dumas's didacticism is seen in the way he structured his plays to demonstrate the correctness of his own views about the social problems he treated. It was this characteristic that led critics to label his works *pièces à thèse* ("thesis plays"). Furthermore, Dumas became increasingly less objective. In the late plays especially, a character (the *raisonneur*) voices Dumas's own ideas about the problem under discussion. Consequently, while Dumas followed the realists' injunction to treat contemporary problems, he was never entirely objective in his presentation. Dumas was also no rebel against society. Rather, he sought to better the social conditions of his day by inculcating higher moral standards and by remedying social injustices. The sanctity of the home and family was his constant theme, and his position on most issues was beyond reproach. Thus, Dumas seldom offended conventional moral standards and consequently, except with *Camille,* he did not create the storms of protest that Ibsen's plays were to raise.

Dumas's ingenuity in handling his subjects also cause his plays to fall short of the realistic ideal, for they all too clearly rely on the kinds of complications, fortunate discoveries, and other devices inherited from the "well-made play" as perfected by Eugène Scribe (1791–1861), author of more than three hundred pieces for the theatre. One of the most successful playwrights who has ever lived (in terms of favorable audience response aroused during his lifetime), Scribe owed much of his success to his skill in manipulating events to create suspense and excitement. Each act usually built to some startling reversal just before the curtain. This concern for plot usually took precedence over depth of characterization or thought, although Scribe played on contemporary attitudes so skillfully that the lack of depth was not always evident at the time. Scribe also used devices (such as the fortunate arrival of letters or persons) that were later to be much overworked. Nevertheless, nothing happens in his plays that has not been carefully prepared for, although the expected outcome is usually avoided in favor of some surprising twist which has been foreshadowed but not emphasized.

Today Scribe's well-made-play formula is usually treated derisively, although it provided Dumas, and later Ibsen, with a basic method. Dumas gave it somewhat greater profundity but retained its typical devices. It was this ingenuity in plotting and in building suspense that made Dumas's plays seem contrived and which led to the charge that he, like Scribe, subordinated issues to dramatic effect. And it was this dependence upon contrivance which raised major doubts about Dumas's commitment to the realistic mode and his understanding of the realistic ideal. It would remain for Ibsen to transform the content and refine the devices of the well-made play until both seemed truly realistic.

Nevertheless, it was probably the very things that raised doubts about Dumas's commitment to realism—his extreme didacticism and his Scribean ingenuity in plotting—that made him so successful. His conventional and dedicated moralizing and his commitment to entertainment made him entirely acceptable to audiences of his time, so much so that by 1870 he seemed so conventional that he had been absorbed into the mainstream of the day.

A more orthodox practitioner of the realistic mode was Émile Augier (1820–89), who began his career in 1844 with verse drama but in the 1850s turned to writing prose plays about problems of his time. His first work in the new vein was *The Son-in-Law of M. Poirier* (1854), written in collaboration with Jules Sandeau and based on Sandeau's novel, *Sacs et Parchemins*. Considered one of the best comedies of manners of the nineteenth century, *The Son-in-Law of M. Poirier* reflects the contemporary conflict between the aristocracy and the newly rich, middle-class entrepreneurs. Representatives of each side are treated both sympathetically and satirically, for each is certain that his class is superior. In a somewhat sentimental resolution, the wife is able to reconcile her husband, a nobleman, and her father, a rich bourgeois.

Augier's next play, *Olympe's Marriage* (1855), is his most militant play and the one which most resembles Dumas's works. Intended as an answer to *Camille,* it shows the horrible outcome of a marriage between a former courtesan and an aristocrat. While Augier continued to write plays about contemporary problems, after 1855 he adopted a balanced, common-sense view of the issues and was always careful to represent all sides fairly and to avoid demonstrating a correct solution, as Dumas typically did.

In *Youth* (1858), Augier treated the evils of city life; in *The Impertinents* (1861), he explored the enormous power of men who run newspapers and the uses to which they put it; in *Giboyer's Son* (1862), he examined the dangers of the clergy meddling in politics; and in *Madame Caverlet* (1876), he considered problems relating to divorce.

The faults that marred Dumas's works are less evident in Augier's plays. Like Dumas, Augier absorbed Scribe's lessons, although he managed to make the devices of the well-made play less obvious. He was also able to mask his didacticism in his balanced view of problems. Still, like Dumas, Augier succeeded with contemporary audiences because he remained within the bounds of conventional morality and because his technical brilliance kept his plays entertaining. Consequently, Augier occupies something of a middle ground between Scribe and the fully developed realism of Ibsen.

Thus, it was through the plays of Dumas and Augier that realism first made itself felt. Not only were they the major serious dramatists of their time in France, they were popular throughout Europe.

Scene from Robertson's *Caste* at the Prince of Wales' Theatre in 1879.
(Courtesy Enthoven Collection, Victoria and Albert Museum.)

The French experience was repeated in miniature in England, where early realism is represented primarily by the work of one playwright, Thomas William Robertson (1829–71). After writing a number of plays in the traditional vein, Robertson adopted more realistic methods in the 1860s and dealt with subjects from contemporary life in *Society* (1865), *Ours* (1866), *Caste* (•1867), *Play* (1868), and *School* (1869). In these plays, Robertson developed the action as much through detailed stage business as through dialogue. So carefully did he integrate setting, costumes, and properties with character and action that his plays scarcely exist without their stage environment. In printing, the stage directions consume as much space as does the dialogue.

Perhaps the best of Robertson's plays is *Caste,* in which the heroine, Esther Eccles, is menaced not by a villain but by the snobbery of the hero's (George D'Alroy's) family. Melodramatic devices are everywhere in evidence, but they are now put to new use—to support Robertson's theme of the evils of the caste system. Unfortunately, Robertson had no successors in England and twenty years were to pass before the direction in which he pointed was followed by other English authors.

In addition to Dumas, Augier, and Robertson, other dramatists might be cited as incipient realists, but the basic picture would be altered little. It is merely important to note that between 1850 and 1870 a few dramatists made the first conscious attempts at realism. Though they did not write completely realistic plays, they paved the way for those who were to follow them in the 1870s.

~ IV ~

Between 1850 and 1870 theatrical practices also began to alter in directions that, when fully developed, would characterize the modern era. It is unlikely that at the time the implications of the innovations were fully appreciated, for it would be many years before they were clearly evident.

Many significant changes stemmed from the gradual abandonment of the repertory system. Until the nineteenth century the number of theatres was small even in cities. During most of the eighteenth century, for example, two theatres devoted to drama were sufficient to meet the demand in both Paris and London. By 1860, however, the theatregoing public was sufficiently large to support thirty theatres in both cities. In the eighteenth century, it was necessary for theatres to change their bills almost nightly in order to keep the small potential audience returning. As audiences began to increase in the nineteenth century, theatre buildings were enlarged and the evening's bill was extended in order to attract a cross-section of the population. A typical evening's offerings included a full-length play followed by a short farce, musical drama, or pantomime; between the acts of the dramatic pieces were interlarded variety acts. This incidental entertainment ranged through songs and dances, trained animals, acrobats, and freaks.

These attempts to attract a large audience led to a coarsening of theatrical fare. The theatres that escaped this trend were for the most part such state-subsidized companies as France's Comédie Française. By 1850 this calculated appeal to mass tastes had led many critics to declare that the theatre had ceased to be a medium for serious ideas.

The attempt by each theatre to attract all segments of the population was eventually abandoned as urbanization opened up alternatives. As potential audiences increased, it became possible for theatres to survive with patrons drawn from one segment of the population. Consequently, around 1850 theatres began to cater to restricted audiences. Most dramatic theatres dropped incidental entertainment from the evening's bill as music halls and theatres featuring variety and vaudeville attracted audiences that favored these forms. Dramatic theatres for a time continued to offer a full-length play and a short afterpiece, but it became increasingly common to perform the short play as a curtain raiser so that latecomers would not miss any part of the main piece. By 1900, it was a common, though not universal, practice to eliminate the curtain raiser, leaving the full-length play as the total offering. Producers also began to specialize in classics, light comedy, or melodrama, thus further fragmenting audiences.

The creation of specialty houses was very important in the development of modern theatre, for it made possible the presentation of avant-garde plays for limited but appreciative audiences, whereas under the old system, works of such limited appeal would probably have been denied a hearing.

Increased audiences also led to a reduction in the number of plays included in the repertories of individual theatres. In the eighteenth century, when it was usual to change the bill nightly, a theatre usually had from fifty to seventy-five plays in its active repertory. As audiences increased in the nineteenth century, popular pieces had to be played for extended runs in order to meet the demand. By 1830 some popular melodramas were running up to 150 consecutive nights in London, and by the 1850s Charles Kean was playing some of his Shakespearean productions for more than one hundred nights. This trend accelerated during the last half of the century.

The long run was also encouraged by increased production costs, for when it became necessary to provide specially designed settings and costumes for plays, costs were inflated far beyond those of the eighteenth century, when most productions used stock scenery and the fashionable dress of the day. The astronomical rise in costs during the nineteenth century made it necessary to run a production longer if the original investment was to be recovered.

Once the principle of the long run was accepted, other changes followed. Obviously, if a single production consumes more than one hundred nights, the number of plays needed to fill a season is considerably fewer than was required in the eighteenth century. Furthermore, if each production is to be played as long as it attracts an audience, the season must be planned with extended runs in mind. Thus, after 1850 managers began to present series of plays (each for an extended run) instead of a constantly changing repertory. Only when a play failed, or in order to fill out a season, was the older form of repertory used. In London, the Bancrofts, among the leading managers of the day, produced only thirty plays in the twenty-one-year period between 1865 and 1886. While this number may be lower than the average—the Bancrofts were more successful than most of their competitors—it suggests the trend then underway.

Such changes probably affected the actor more than any other person in the theatre. From the beginning of the commercial theatre in the Renaissance until the late nineteenth century, actors were normally employed for the season or longer. Under the long run, this arrangement was no longer economical, for often not all actors in a company were required for a production. So long as the bill had been rotated often, the workload was evened out over a period of time. But when productions were played for several months without interruption, some actors were left idle while others were working, even though all were under contract and had to be paid whether or not they were performing. Consequently, in the late nineteenth century, some managers began to restrict their companies to a nucleus of actors, those that would be usable no matter which plays were performed. To these, they added others as needed for individual productions. In this way the run-of-the-play contract came into existence; it became typical around 1900 when the single-play company had largely superseded permanent companies.

A degree of continuity persisted, nevertheless, because a number of managers took long-term leases on theatres and produced plays year after year, even though they changed their actors often or even from play to play. This practice, common until World War I, gave an air of stability to the theatre even after the repertory system was dead. Continuity now depended most upon the producer.

The repertory system was also undermined by improvements in transportation made during the nineteenth century, for the steamboat and the railroad made travel increasingly easier. By 1825, starring actors had begun to tour, making brief appearances with local companies. The monetary returns and the increased fame (partially attributable to the rapid development of popular journalism in the nineteenth century) made starring tours attractive. Soon the mania for stars was universal. After 1850 not even foreign language was a bar. Rachel, Adelaide Ristori, Sarah Bernhardt, Tommaso Salvini, Fannie Janauschek, and others played throughout the world.

By the 1860s the network of railroads was sufficiently extensive that full productions, complete with actors, scenery, costumes, and properties, were beginning to tour. Such productions, usually mounted with considerable care, made it increasingly difficult for local companies to survive. The full effects were not to be felt until after 1870, but thereafter the decline was so rapid that almost all local companies had disappeared by 1900. The theatre was then concentrated in major cities and the provinces were almost totally dependent upon touring companies for entertainment.

Other significant changes in the nineteenth century led to the emergence of the director as the dominant artistic force in the theatre. It is inaccurate to say, as some have, that the director is of modern origin. Someone has always taken responsibility for transferring scripts to the stage. The greater importance of the director in modern times is attributable to his increased authority and responsibility.

Prior to the modern era, plays were normally staged by the manager or an actor in the company, usually called the "acting manager" or "stage manager." His authority and responsibility, however, were limited by a number of conditions. Many of these involved the actor. The members of a company were employed according to "lines of business" (that is, according to the types of roles they were equipped to play), such as heroes in comedy and tragedy, low-comedy roles, old men, and so on. Casting, then, was largely a matter of matching the line of business with the character type.

Once a part was assigned it remained the actor's (except under unusual circumstances) as long as he was in the company. An actor was expected to know all roles assigned to him from the fifty to seventy-five plays which made up the company's repertory, although, with so many roles, it was difficult for actors to be letter-perfect in all parts. Therefore, one important skill was the ability to extricate oneself gracefully from the inevitable difficulties that arose because of inadequate rehearsals. Actors were assumed to be competent in their lines of business and to need little help beyond establishing exits and entrances or with difficult stage business. Furthermore, perhaps because of poor lighting, it had become traditional for actors to play almost all scenes well forward on the stage, where movement was largely restricted to trading off the emphatic position. Since almost no furniture was used before the mid-nineteenth century, actors usually stood in a semicircle near the front of the stage.

Despite all the problems he faced, the actor considered stage business, line readings, and movement to be more his responsibility than the director's. To him, interference reflected upon his competence.

The director's responsibility for costumes, scenery, and other aspects of a production was also restricted. While he probably consulted with the technicians in each area, he acted primarily as an advisor. There was as yet little attempt to achieve unity of effect through the careful coordination of all elements. Thus, the director's job was considerably more restricted in scope than it now is.

The need for more centralized and autocratic control over production began to be evident early in the nineteenth century, for, as productions grew in complexity, it became clear that someone was needed to coordinate all the elements if they were to be fully effective. For the most part, however, theatrical personnel were loathe to give up authority to anyone, and so it was only slowly that the director extended his powers.

The path to be taken by the modern director was laid out by a few pioneers. In the 1760s and 1770s, David Garrick (1717–79), working at the Drury Lane Theatre in London, staged a number of productions in which he assumed command of all elements of production and achieved results far superior to those of his contemporaries. At the Weimar Court Theatre in Germany, Johann Wolfgang von Goethe (1749–1832) between 1798 and 1805 created the most perfect ensemble to be found anywhere prior to the modern era. Backed up by the ruler of Weimar, Goethe required absolute obedience from his company. He dictated line readings and gestures, marked off the stage into squares to facilitate blocking, composed each scene with care for pictorial values, and sometimes beat out tempos with a baton to achieve the desired rhythmical effects. Everything was shaped to create an ideal beauty rather than everyday realism. His theatre became so famous that his actors were in demand throughout Germany, and the acting style developed in this theatre, known as Weimar classicism, was widely transmitted. This semi-rhetorical approach was to be one of the major deterrents to realistic acting in Germany. Goethe's principal legacy was this acting style, for his directing methods were adopted by few others.

Goethe's countryman, Ludwig Tieck (1773–1853), also advocated unity in theatrical production. He was unable to put his ideas into practice, however, until 1841, when his health was already beginning to fail. In that year, William IV of Prussia summoned Tieck to Potsdam to stage experimental productions, some of which were later moved to the large state theatre in Berlin. Tieck simplified stage settings and concentrated attention upon the actors, from whom he sought an intense psychological realism. He exerted full control over each element of his productions and coordinated all to achieve a unified effect. His productions of Sophocles' *Antigone* (1841) and Shakespeare's *A Midsummer Night's Dream* (1843) were among the most admired of the century. Because he sought to de-emphasize spectacle, Tieck was considered a reactionary, and when ill health forced him to retire his methods were rapidly abandoned.

In France, Pixérécourt insisted upon directing his own sensational melodramas, for he saw quite correctly that their full effect could be realized only through careful rehearsal. He attributed his great success to his directing as much as to his writing. His example was followed by Victor Hugo, Alexandre Dumas *père,* and a number of other French dramatists, although few of his successors took their responsibilities as seriously as did Pixérécourt.

In England, W. C. Macready, manager of Covent Garden from 1837 to 1839 and of Drury Lane from 1841 to 1843, exerted considerable con-

Scene from Macready's production of Shakespeare's *Henry V* at Covent Garden Theatre in 1839. (From Scharf's *Recollections,* 1839.)

trol over all aspects of his productions. Said by some to be the first English director in the modern sense, Macready probably failed to achieve wider recognition as a pioneering director because of his short career in management. Nevertheless, his methods were adopted and extended by Charles Kean, who, because of work done between 1850 and 1859, has been credited with much that Macready began. Kean's enormous success is explained in large part by the consistently high quality of his productions, achieved primarily through infinite care for detail.

All of these directors were concerned essentially with the classics or melodrama and thus were contributors to romantic realism. A lesser number of pioneers were concerned with plays of contemporary life. Dumas *fils* credits Adolphe Montigny (1805–80), director of the Gymnase Théâtre in Paris, with taking the first significant steps toward realism in directing. Beginning around 1853, Montigny placed a table downstage center in order to prevent the actors from forming themselves into the traditional semi-circle. Next, he put chairs around the table, seated the actors, and made them speak to each other, rather than to the audience, as had been typical in the past. Finally, he furnished his settings like real rooms and placed items, such as cigar boxes and handkerchiefs, about the stage to motivate movement from one place to another. His success encouraged others to adopt his methods. In this way, directing began to progress along lines suggested by realistic doctrine.

In England, the movement toward true realism is most associated with Squire Bancroft (1841–1926), his wife Effie Wilton Bancroft (1839–1921), and Tom Robertson at the Prince of Wales' Theatre between 1865 and 1871. Managing the theatre alone at first (she did not marry Squire Bancroft until 1867), Miss Wilton intended to present a repertory of light comedies and burlesques. It was largely by accident that she accepted Robertson's play, *Society,* in 1865, thus beginning an association which lasted until Robertson's death in 1871.

Not only did Robertson write the major plays presented by the Bancrofts, he also directed them. Robertson worked with the actors of the Bancroft troupe on every detail of their performances, seeking to substitute understatement for bravura acting and to emphasize ensemble effects. Casting was done without regard for the traditional lines of business. The company had no stars, even the Bancrofts often appearing in small roles. The Bancrofts wholeheartedly accepted the box setting and firmly anchored performances behind the proscenium arch. Their settings were fitted out exactly like comparable rooms in real life. Characters were asked to do such homely tasks as lighting fires, heating water, making tea, serving and drinking it. It was this detailed attention to routine domestic business that led critics to dub the Robertson-Bancroft approach the "cup-and-saucer" school of acting.

By 1870, the position of the director was in a state of transition.

Several persons had demonstrated that superior results could be achieved through the greater centralization of power, but the full potentialities of the new approach were seldom realized because several practices still thwarted the desire for unified production. Among these perhaps the most important was the star system. Although a few theatres did not depend upon stars, most did and most built their productions around popular performers. As stars, actors were able to defy a director in various ways. Many refused to wear anything that they considered unflattering and in this way often spoiled the effect created by the costumes of other players. Most insisted on supplying their own costumes. Many also refused to subordinate themselves to ensemble effects, arguing that the public wished them to stand out.

Another tradition which militated against unity was the almost universal practice of recruiting supernumeraries off the streets as needed. A member of the company was paid to find "extras," rehearse them, see that they were outfitted and that they appeared on stage when needed. Usually a different group appeared each night. This impromptu handling of crowd scenes jarred harshly with the polish evident in the stars' major scenes.

Thus, the director was still handicapped by a lack of funds to hire supernumeraries permanently and a lack of control over autocratic stars. These difficulties would have to be overcome before the director could assume the role he was to fill in the modern theatre.

The years between 1850 and 1870 were rich in beginnings but deficient in mature achievements. Advanced thinkers had voiced their deep-felt dissatisfaction with the theatre and had set forth new theoretical bases for its reform. A few playwrights had attempted to make the drama more sensitive to the needs of the time and many innovations had been made in theatrical practices.

In 1870, however, the repertory was still largely composed of romantic dramas, melodramas, farces, and other minor forms. The dominant theatrical mode was romantic realism. True realism, still very much an avant-garde movement, had made little impression on the general public.

It is doubtful that many theatregoers in 1870 suspected that they were on the threshold of a new era. This is understandable, for it was to be another twenty years before there was any significant meshing of truly realistic writing with truly realistic theatrical method. During the years between 1870 and 1890, Ibsen and the naturalists were to write plays so outrageous to the general public that most were denied production by official censors. At the same time, Saxe-Meiningen was capturing universal acclaim for his staging, although he essentially continued the traditions of romantic realism. It was not until the late 1880s that André Antoine was to bring the two strands together by applying Saxe-Meiningen's methods to the plays of Ibsen and the naturalists.

Wagner and Saxe-Meiningen: Unified Production and The Regisseur

In the 1870s significant steps were taken toward the modern theatre, for in that decade Ibsen began to write his prose plays, the French naturalists came to the fore, the Meiningen Players burst upon the world, and Wagner opened his Festspielhaus in Bayreuth. These occurrences did not transform the theatre overnight, but they focused attention upon concepts and practices that were to triumph in the future. Of the innovations, changes in the theory and practice of stage production gained acceptance most readily, for essentially they extended tendencies already accepted. As innovators, Wagner and Saxe-Meiningen are the key figures, for Wagner's conception of unity was to inspire almost every subsequent theatrical reformer, while Saxe-Meiningen's productions demonstrated the enormous artistic gains to

*Wagner and
Saxe-
Meiningen:
Unified
Production
and The
Regisseur*

be achieved by an all-powerful director or *regisseur*. But, while Wagner and Saxe-Meiningen must be granted precedence in the trend toward unified production, other directors (especially Henry Irving, Victorien Sardou, and Augustin Daly) were working along parallel lines. Consequently, between 1870 and 1890 the *regisseur* made his presence felt almost everywhere. In these years, nevertheless, the director used his talents primarily to achieve complete illusion in productions of traditional plays. Thus, at the time romantic realism benefitted most from the new developments.

~~~ I ~~~

Richard Wagner (1813–83) knew the theatre from childhood, for his step-father, three sisters, and one of his brothers worked in it. His own theatrical interests took a musical turn, leading him when only eighteen to write his first opera, *Die Feen*. He then was employed as chorus master at the Wurzburg Opera and when only twenty-one became conductor at the Magdeburg Opera. His first wide recognition came with *Rienzi*, first performed at Dresden in 1842. His fame was extended through *The Flying Dutchman* (1843), *Tannhauser* (1845), and *Lohengrin* (1850).

Much of Wagner's life was spent in violent controversy—political, personal, and artistic. Because of his part in the Revolution of 1848 he was forced to live in exile for twelve years, and throughout his career he voiced political views considered revolutionary by many. He was a man of contradictions, his democratic sentiments contrasting sharply with his autocratic treatment of others, his strong personal attachments alternating with betrayals of friends, and his taste for illusionism subverting his idealistic vision of drama. To many, Wagner seemed an egomaniac and conscienceless monster, but to others he was little less than a Messiah.

Wagner's influence on the modern theatre stems largely from his theoretical writings, especially *Opera and Drama* (1852) and *The Purpose of Opera* (1871). Much of what he wrote was provoked by his opposition to Italian composers, who had dominated the operatic form since its origin in the late sixteenth century. Italian domination was so extensive that until the early nineteenth century most opera houses of Europe imported Italian singers and designers to make their productions more attractive. The Napoleonic conquests in the early nineteenth century, however, aroused strong nationalistic sentiments, and local traditions began to be prized over foreign importations. In Germany, the Teutonic past and the concept of Germany as a nation began to exert strong attractions. Folktales, legends, and histories were compiled, printed, studied, and utilized as the basis for literary and dramatic works, and in 1871 the Germanic states were united in a federation. As these interests developed, the Italian opera troupes were dismissed (the last at Dresden in 1832) and replaced with German 29 personnel.

Wagner's concern for the Teutonic past is clearly seen in his operas *Die Meistersinger* (1867) and *Der Ring des Nibelungen* (in four parts, 1869–76). But he not only used Teutonic subjects, he sought to replace the Italianate operatic form with one more suitable to German tastes. When Wagner began writing, Italian opera was essentially a collection of showpiece arias separated by passages of recitative (necessary to make the story intelligible but treated as a mere appendage to the arias). Wagner obliterated the distinction between aria and recitative, making the melodic line continuous and eliminating the elaborate songs which focused attention on the opera star's virtuosity at the expense of overall dramatic effect.

In addition to Italianate opera, Wagner's dislikes extended to realism in drama. He argued that the poet is a mythmaker rather than a retailer of domestic intrigues—that, while drama must be a reflection of life, it should seek to portray an ideal world through the expression of the inner impulses and aspirations of the community as embodied in its racial myths. (It was this element in Wagner's work that made him seem to the Nazis the supreme composer.) To Wagner, the ideal realm is left behind as soon as spoken dialogue begins to replace the sung lyric. For him, therefore, the ideal work consisted of Teutonic myth (or at least mythlike stories) embodied in a union of drama and music, something like a blending of Shakespeare and Beethoven, in which drama is "dipped in the magic fountain of music" to create and preserve ideality.

More important to the modern theatre, however, were Wagner's ideas about theatrical production. His objection to spoken drama was based in large part upon its impreciseness—its vulnerability to the whim of actors. He considered musical drama much superior because the dramatist-composer can control performance through indications of melody, tempo, volume, and rhythm. In this way he dictates intonation, speed of playing, variations in intensity, and so on, whereas the writer of spoken drama must depend upon actors to make these important interpretive decisions.

Above all, Wagner is significant for his conception of the *Gesamtkunstwerk* ("unified art work") in which all elements of composition and production are fused. If this synthesis of the arts (later critics often used the term "synthetic art" to denote Wagner's ideal) is to be achieved, the same person must compose both words and music and must control all of the elements of stage production when the work is presented. Wagner demanded that control over all artistic functions in the theatre be placed in the hands of one man, a kind of universal genius—a role in which he did not hesitate to cast himself. It is primarily from this demand for artistic unity and its corollary—the all-powerful director or *regisseur*—that Wagner's enormous influence on the modern theatre stems.

Wagner was not content to remain a theoretician, however, and throughout his life sought the means of implementing his ideas. While his operas could exemplify his conception of music-drama, without production they were only partial embodiments of the master art work he envisioned. Wagner eventually sought a theatre of his own, for he believed that conditions in the opera houses of his day made it impossible for him to achieve his ideal. His dream was realized with the building of the Bayreuth Festspielhaus.

Plans for this theatre took shape over many years. The basic idea was probably suggested as early as 1841 by Karl Friedrich Schinkel (1781–1841), a leading German architect and scene designer. In 1864 Gottfried Semper (1803–79) did considerable work on the plans and these were later reworked by Wilhelm Neumann. When the theatre was built, primary credit went to Otto Bruckwald as architect, and to Karl Brandt, a leading stage technician of the day. Wagner's opera house was originally planned for Munich, but dissension led to its transfer to the small town of Bayreuth. The cornerstone was laid in 1872 and the theatre was formally opened in 1876. The fame of the Bayreuth Festival soon made this theatre well known throughout the world, and its innovations began to exert considerable influence on theatre architecture.

The principal architectural innovations at the Festspielhaus were in the auditorium's design. Wagner's democratic sentiments led him to build a "classless" theatre which departed markedly from traditional opera houses with their tiers of boxes and the consequent segregation of the audience. The auditorium was fan-shaped (about 100 feet deep, narrowing from 115 feet at the rear to about 50 feet at the front) with thirty rows of stepped seats rising rather sharply from front to back. The rows were not broken by aisles, each row giving onto an exit at either end. The main part of the auditorium seated about 1,345 persons, while a small box at the rear (intended originally for Wagner and his friends) seated about one hundred, and a balcony above it about three hundred persons. A uniform price was charged, since all seats were considered equally good for seeing and hearing.

If the auditorium was innovative, the stage was traditional. The floor raked up toward the back and provisions were made for seven sets of wings

The auditorium and stage of the Festspielhaus at Bayreuth. The setting on stage is for *Parsifal*, as designed by Max Bruckner. (From *Le Théâtre*, 1899.)

on either side to be shifted by chariot-and-pole mechanisms under the stage, the traditional European method since the seventeenth century. The major innovation was the installation of jets which permitted the use of steam to serve as a curtain masking scene changes or to provide atmospheric effects, such as fog and mist. Several workshops, storage rooms, and rehearsal rooms were included in the building.

Two features of the theatre are of special significance in Wagner's approach to production: the hidden orchestra pit and the double proscenium. The pit was sunken and a part of it extended under the stage for a distance of 17 feet. A curved wall at the front hid the pit from the spectators and reflected sound toward the stage. This pit and the two proscenium arches created a "mystic chasm" between the world of reality (the auditorium) and the world of ideality (the stage).

The limitations of Wagner's vision are most evident in the productions given at Bayreuth during his lifetime, for visually they differed little from those seen elsewhere. Although Wagner wished to raise his audience to the ideal plane, he sought to do so by creating a total illusion. To increase illusionism, he made a number of innovations. He would not permit the musicians to tune their instruments in the pit; also, no applause was permitted during the performance nor any curtain calls at the end. To emphasize the distinction between the real and ideal worlds, he darkened the auditorium during performances, concentrating all attention on the stage. (It had been traditional since the Renaissance to leave the lights on in the auditorium during performances.) These innovations, made in the name of ideality, were to serve equally well in realistic and naturalistic productions, which Wagner denounced. Wagner's scenery and costumes were also realistic and historically accurate in detail, differing in no significant way from those in use elsewhere. He used such devices as moving panoramas (to depict a journey in *Parsifal*) and a dragon with scales, movable eyes, and a mouth that opened and shut (in *Siegfried*). One of Wagner's scene designers was Max Bruckner, who also painted Saxe-Meiningen's sets.

Thus, despite his antirealistic theories, Wagner aimed at total illusionism. His productions differed most from other productions of the day because Wagner's dramas incorporated specific demands for mood and atmosphere which required a more complete synchronization of music, lighting, scenery, and acting than was typical at that time.

Wagner's reliance on illusionism was a result of his ultimate concern—the audience's experience. For Wagner, the purpose of the master art work was to unify and give meaning to a whole culture through a communal experience. By creating total illusion on the stage, he hoped to provide a sensual atmosphere so overpowering that it would induce in the audience "that spiritualized state of clairvoyance wherein the scenic representation becomes the perfect image of real life." Thus, Wagner sought to arouse an irresistible empathic response. From this aim stemmed one of Wagner's most important influences on the modern stage: the notion that the success of a production is determined by its ability to engage the audience's emo-

32

*Wagner and
Saxe-
Meiningen:
Unified
Production
and The
Regisseur*

tions and to draw it into the world of the play. This idea cannot, of course, be credited solely to Wagner, but he was one of its chief popularizers; its significance is evident since it has dominated modern theatrical practice. Only in recent years have Wagner's notions been seriously challenged. Almost all twentieth-century producers were to accept Wagner's notion that the finest theatrical art results from a synthesis of all the arts in a totally unified work. This view was reenforced by Adolphe Appia (whose inspiration came primarily from Wagner) and Gordon Craig (whose writings repeat many of Wagner's concepts), until recently considered the two major theoreticians of the modern theatre.

Wagner was also to influence those who sought to make of art a substitute for religion, for his ideal music-drama was intended to provide a mystical vision of human destiny, one capable of bringing meaning to an otherwise limited existence. As faith declined under the impact of scientism, it became increasingly common to seek in art a substitute for religion. The symbolists, expressionists, Artaudians, and many others in the modern era have viewed the theatre as an instrument for the salvation of mankind.

Wagner was also to be a source of inspiration to those in the late nineteenth century who sought to counteract the growing influence of realism and naturalism, for on the surface his ideas run directly counter to realistic doctrine. Still, his own productions fall clearly into the mainstream of romantic realism, and his most influential ideas—the need for unity and the master artist—are equally applicable to all artistic modes. Thus, Wagner's theories were eventually assimilated by practically all movements without regard for his own stylistic preferences.

~ II ~

While the Bayreuth Festival Theatre was under construction, another troupe destined to exert a lasting influence—the Meiningen Players—came to the fore. Virtually unknown prior to 1874, when it played a six-week season in Berlin, this company from the small duchy of Saxe-Meiningen soon became world-famous for its productions, which demonstrated forcefully the validity of Wagner's demand for unity.

The Meiningen Players was not a new organization in 1874. Theatrical performances had been given in Meiningen as early as 1781, and the Court Theatre, home of the troupe, had been opened in 1831. The company was insignificant, however, until Georg II (1826–1914), the duke of Saxe-Meiningen, assumed control over it in 1866. Before becoming ruler, Georg II had received a broad education and had traveled widely. He had studied at the universities of Bonn and Leipzig, had received extensive art training (always one of his consuming interests), had seen Charles Kean's Shakespearean productions in London, Tieck's productions in Berlin, and the finest companies of Paris, Vienna, and elsewhere. He was also much involved in the political and social life of his time. Unlike his father, Georg II was much in favor of German unification; it was this difference of views that motivated Prussia (the chief advocate of unification) to invade Saxe-Meiningen and force Bernhard II (who leaned toward an alliance with Austria) to abdicate in favor of his son. When Germany was united in 1871, Georg II, like other rulers of individual German territories, retained his position as head of his state.

As ruler of the duchy of Saxe-Meiningen, Georg II had the Court Theater, as a state-supported institution, under his jurisdiction and, when he came to power in 1866, he set out immediately to improve its repertory and the quality of its productions. Until 1870 the duke's direct participation in production was limited, and primary responsibility fell to Friedrich von Bodenstedt (1819–92) as *Intendant* (chief administrative officer). Bodenstedt did not work well with actors, however, and the many disputes which arose prompted Georg II to retire Bodenstedt with a pension. From 1870 until 1895, Saxe-Meiningen held the title of *Intendant* himself and employed a director (or *regisseur*) to work under him and to implement his plans. From 1870 to 1873, Karl Grabowski served as *regisseur,* but he too proved unsatisfactory.

The great period of the Meiningen Players came during the years 1873–91, when Ludwig Chronegk (1837–91) was director. Chronegk made his debut in Berlin in 1856 as an actor. At Meiningen, where he

Sketch by the Duke for a scene in Schiller's *Fiesko*. (From *Theatre Arts,* 1930.)

34

*Wagner and
Saxe-
Meiningen:
Unified
Production
and The
Regisseur*

joined the company in 1866, he was a dedicated but not outstanding comedian. Consequently, his appointment as *regisseur* was greeted with surprise and skepticism by the troupe. Nevertheless, he worked extremely well with the duke, who, though excellent in his conceptions, was largely ignorant of stage terminology and of precise means to achieve his wishes. The eminently practical Chronegk, on the other hand, was able to translate the duke's ideas into concrete terms. They also got along well because both were strict disciplinarians and indefatigable workers.

The company was really presided over by a directorate which, in addition to Saxe-Meiningen and Chronegk, included Ellen Franz (1839–1923), the duke's third wife, an actress in the company before their marriage in 1873 (as the morganatic wife of the ruler she held the title, Helene, Baroness von Heldburg). The baroness assumed primary responsibility for the repertory, and it was she who proposed the plays and adapted the texts as required. She also took as her special concern the actors' stage speech.

It was Chronegk who convinced the duke that the company should perform outside of Meiningen. Georg II was very skeptical at first but eventually agreed. The first essay came in 1874, when a four-week season was planned for Berlin; the troupe was so successful that the run was extended to six weeks. The company returned to Berlin in 1875 and 1876 and then began to perform in other cities. Gradually the tours became longer, eventually extending from six to eight months. The last tour was made in 1890. By that time, the company had played in thirty-eight cities in Germany, Austria, Czechoslovakia, Holland, England, Switzerland, Russia, Poland, Belgium, Denmark, and Sweden. A tour of America was planned but canceled because of Chronegk's illness.

The tours were almost entirely under Chronegk's supervision. He made all the arrangements and traveled with the troupe. The duke saw only three of his company's performances outside of Meiningen. When Chronegk died, the tours were abandoned and thereafter the troupe played only in its home theatre.

During the years between 1874 and 1890 the Meiningen Players was the most admired company in the world. Their success, however, was not owing to any new aim, for the duke, like most producers of his day, sought to create a perfect illusion of reality. Furthermore, his repertory differed little from that of other major producers. Outside of Meiningen, the company performed forty-one plays, the majority of which were either classics or recent plays in the poetic vein. The greatest success of the company was Shakespeare's *Julius Caesar; The Winter's Tale* and *Twelfth Night* also figured prominently in the repertory. Next to Shakespeare's, Schiller's plays —*Wilhelm Tell, The Maid of Orleans,* the Wallenstein trilogy, *Fiesko,* and *The Robbers*—were the most popular. Somewhat lesser success came with Molière's *The Imaginary Invalid* and Grillparzer's *Esther* and *The Ancestress.* Saxe-Meiningen did not content himself with standard favorites, however, for he championed the works of Heinrich von Kleist (1777–1811) —*The Battle of Arminius, Kathy of Heilbronn,* and *The Prince of Homburg*

*Wagner and
Saxe-
Meiningen:
Unified
Production
and The
Regisseur*

The company gave only minor attention to plays in the realistic vein. José Echegaray's *The Great Galeoto,* an Ibsenesque play about the power of gossip to ruin lives, was given seven performances. The most daring production came in 1886–87 with Ibsen's *Ghosts,* a play which Saxe-Meiningen admired and for which he officially decorated Ibsen. But, though he could present the play within his own duchy, he was able to perform it only twice elsewhere because of censorship. Overall, however, it seems clear that the duke's tastes ran to drama in the romantic vein.

In theatrical practice, Saxe-Meiningen built upon the work of Charles Kean and his German imitator, Friedrich Haase, director of the Leipzig Municipal Theater. Nevertheless, Georg II went considerably beyond his predecessors.

At Meiningen, exhaustive research preceded the designing of costumes, settings, and properties. Although by this time Jakob Weiss's monumental history of costume (published between 1856 and 1872) had been completed, Saxe-Meiningen found it only partially satisfactory. Weiss had merely divided each century into thirds and defined the characteristic features of dress within those divisions; Saxe-Meiningen insisted upon distinguishing national differences within Weiss's time segments. Consequently, his costumes were the most authentic ever seen on the German stage.

Accuracy in costuming was further insured by forbidding actors to tamper with their costumes. In most theatres of the day, stars assumed the right to alter their garments if unflattering and actresses insisted upon wearing crinoline petticoats under dresses of any period. In his dual capacity as ruler of the state and as *Intendant* of the theatre, Saxe-Meiningen could demand and gain obedience. In order to avoid misunderstandings, he gave each actor a drawing of his costume and detailed instructions about how each article was to be worn.

Georg II also insisted upon authentic materials rather than the usual cheap substitutes, which were available only in a limited range of colors and patterns. If he could not find satisfactory materials locally, he imported them from Italy or France and often had them manufactured to his specifications. Furthermore, he insisted upon authentic chain mail, armor, and weapons (such as swords, halberds, and axes). This demand for accuracy extended to furniture and properties as well and often led to having articles manufactured to order. As the influence of the Meiningen troupe increased, a number of theatrical supply houses were founded in Germany to meet the new demand for authentic costumes, armor, furniture, and properties.

The duke designed all of the costumes, scenery, and properties. His artistic talent, however, was in drawing and, as he once observed, he was criticized adversely whenever he used color. Perhaps this accounts for the many comments by reviewers on the garishness of his settings. On the other hand, these reactions may merely reflect the duke's departure from traditional practice, under which designers depended primarily upon pastel

Sketch by the Duke for a scene in Schiller's *Maria Stuart*. (From *Theatre Arts,* 1930.)

colors and the manipulation of line, light, and shadow rather than masses of saturated color. Traditionally the actor had played against a light background, but Saxe-Meiningen made the background darker than the actor.

Georg II also sought greater unity and illusion in scene design. He attempted to make both the overhead masking and the stage floor integral parts of the picture. Most designers had ignored the stage floor, the scenery stopping abruptly, leaving the boards clearly visible even in exterior settings. Saxe-Meiningen used fallen trees, rocks, hillocks, steps, platforms, and even a stuffed horse to disguise the stage floor and make it a part of the setting. He abandoned sky borders in favor of foliage, banners, arches, beams, or other illusionistic devices to mask the overhead space. Since he believed that symmetrical balance appeared contrived and artificial, he favored irregularly shaped and asymmetrical settings. He was especially careful about proportion so that the scale would not be destroyed if an actor moved close to the backdrop. He sought also to blend imperceptibly the painted details with the three-dimensional elements. Saxe-Meiningen's settings illustrate well the then-current movement away from painted to actualistic details. His architectural settings relied heavily on steps, platforms, and box sets; his exteriors normally included hillocks, rocks, or similar features. All were made sturdily so as not to appear flimsy when used by actors.

The duke's enormous care for detail extended to the acting as well. The company was composed primarily of young performers or of those who had not achieved fame. There were no stars. Occasionally guest actors performed with the troupe, but they were called "honorary members" and

37

*Wagner and
Saxe-
Meiningen:
Unified
Production
and The
Regisseur*

were required to comply with the company's working procedures. Saxe-Meiningen also abandoned the practice of using as supernumeraries persons not regularly employed in the company. It is partially for this reason that the Meiningen company came to be known above all for its effective crowd scenes. Any actor not cast in an important role was required to appear as a supernumerary. In rehearsing mob scenes, Saxe-Meiningen divided the performers into small groups, each under the charge of an experienced actor, who was partially responsible for training those under him. Each member of a crowd was treated as an individual and assigned specific actions and lines. The small groups were rehearsed individually and then as a unit. Thus, both enormous variety and unusual unity were achieved. The crowds were also made to appear larger than they were by the effective use of settings. Saxe-Meiningen typically placed his crowds in restricted spaces, forcing them off into the wings and creating the effect of a crowd so large that all its members could not be seen. He also used diagonal, hesitating, and conflicting movement to achieve effects of agitation and confusion. The contrast with the usual crowd scenes of the time was both startling and impressive.

Perhaps above all, the success of the company can be attributed to its rehearsal methods. The duke rehearsed a play until he considered it ready and refused to set a performance date until he was satisfied with the results. This approach was possible for at least two reasons. First, the duke's position as ruler of the state gave him firm control over both the actors and the company's finances. Second, the troupe had considerably more time in which to rehearse than did most companies, for the town of Meiningen was so small (the population was about eight thousand) that the theatre was open only twice a week during a season of six months.

Rehearsals were normally held in the evening after the duke's state duties were over. They began about 5 or 6 p.m. and lasted until midnight. Each play was rehearsed from the beginning with full settings, furniture, and properties and with costumes that simulated those to be worn in performance. From the beginning, actors were also required to act and not merely to walk through their parts. The duke did not make a promptbook (*Regiebuch*) in advance but worked out scenes as he went along. If there were problems, different approaches to a scene were tried. This often required rearranging a setting or the furniture. While this was time-consuming, it permitted the actors to take part in almost every decision and it also permitted them to become thoroughly familiar with their roles and at home in the scenic environment. The final result was a remarkable ensemble effect. Once a production was ready, a promptbook was made. Chronegk edited twenty-eight of the promptbooks and published them under the title, *The Repertory of the Saxe-Meiningen Court Theatre, Official Edition*.

The enormous impact of the Meiningen troupe stemmed in large part from its ability to realize more fully than had any previous company the then-current ideal of absolute illusion. As a result, it exerted considerable influence on the theatre of the late nineteenth century. It became obvious that the Meiningen Players' power was ultimately attributable to its director's assumption of absolute control over all the elements of production. Thus, the Meiningen troupe validated Wagner's demand for unity in production; because he assumed full artistic control, Saxe-Meiningen has traditionally been considered the first director in the modern sense and one of the founders of the modern theatre. Through its example, the Meiningen company became an inspiration for a new generation of theatrical innovators. Stanislavsky, Antoine, and others achnowledged their deep debt to Saxe-Meiningen. Furthermore, such established producers as Henry Irving were reenforced in their resolve to pursue practices not unlike those of the Meiningen troupe. The Meiningen Players also strengthened romantic realism as a theatrical mode and hastened the trend away from painted to three-dimensional details, a trend that continued until World War I.

Obviously, most producers did not have the authority, time, or financial resources to adopt completely Saxe-Meiningen's methods. Nevertheless, he established an ideal toward which to strive. Perhaps even more important, his productions attracted sufficient attention to gain acceptance for trends long underway and for practices soon to be considered standard.

~~~ **III** ~~~

</div>

Although Saxe-Meiningen was undoubtedly more successful than other producers of his day in achieving the illusion of reality through centralized control over all theatrical means, he was by no means the only practitioner of unified production. Several directors were working along parallel lines, many in total ignorance of the Meiningen troupe. Since the trend toward increased realism and unity merely intensified practices already underway, it was probably inevitable that it would be taken over and perfected by producers in several countries. Many instances could be cited, but it should be sufficient to look briefly at a few key figures: Henry Irving in England, Victorien Sardou in France, and Augustin Daly in the United States. The failure of these men to make as great an impact as Saxe-Meiningen is explained in part by the conditions under which they worked but also by their divided appeal: Irving was better known as an actor than as a director, while both Sardou and Daly were among the most successful playwrights of their time.

In England, Henry Irving (1839–1905) most nearly captured the Meiningen spirit. Born John Henry Brodribb, Irving began his career as an actor in the English provinces in 1856. He came to London in 1866 and performed with several companies before being employed in 1871 as

From the 1870s until his death, Irving enjoyed the reputation of
being England's finest serious actor. His first outstanding success came in
1871 as Mathias in *The Bells* (an adaptation by Leopold Lewis of *Le Juif
Polonais* by Erckmann-Chatrian), a short melodrama in which a man
under hypnosis confesses to the murder of a Jewish peddler. In 1874, his
Hamlet ran for 200 nights, a new record for a Shakespearean drama.
Thereafter, Irving's position was secure. Despite his enormous reputation,
Irving never won complete acceptance of the critics. He distorted many
vowel sounds, walked (as one critic put it) like a man trying to get over
a plowed field hastily, and interpreted many roles eccentrically. Nevertheless,
he was a master of stage business and by-play that clarified motivations and
thoughts and his emotional intensity moved audiences deeply. Although
Irving is now usually considered a Shakespearean actor, he excelled in only
one role, Shylock, which he rendered sympathetically. He was at his best
in melodrama, especially in such works as Boucicault's *Louis XI* and
Bulwer-Lytton's *Richelieu*. His position as head of his profession was recognized in 1895 when he was knighted, the first English actor to receive this
honor.

Irving's reputation depended as much upon his skill as a director as
upon his acting, since for twenty years (1878–98) he managed the Lyceum
Theatre and staged the productions in which he performed. As a manager,
Irving built upon the work of Macready and Charles Kean, both of whom
had conceived their productions with an eye for overall effect. Both also
had gained control over all the elements of production and had contributed
significantly to romantic realism in England. Their influence on Irving was
reenforced by the Meiningen Players, who appeared in London in 1881.
The strong impact of the Meiningen troupe is suggested by several changes
made by Irving almost immediately after seeing them, although it is impossible to establish any causal connection.

Irving's practices paralleled those of Saxe-Meiningen in many ways.
First, he was concerned with historical accuracy in scenery and costumes
and often employed archeologists either as consultants or as designers. For
example, Sir Lawrence Alma-Tadema (1836–1912), one of the foremost
archeologists of his day, assisted Irving with the costumes and scenery for
Cymbeline (1896) and *Coriolanus* (1901). Nevertheless, Irving was never
as insistent on accuracy as were Saxe-Meiningen and Charles Kean, and he
often deviated from accuracy for the sake of theatrical effectiveness. Irving's
costumes, however, are said to have marked an advance over those used by
Kean, who, though a stickler for accuracy in some respects, is said to have
placed minor characters in armor made of zinc and tinsel or in glazed
cotton instead of more expensive materials. Irving supposedly applied a
uniform standard to all costumes and thus achieved greater unity.

Irving employed a staff of fine designers. Hawes Craven (1837–1910)
and Joseph Harker (1855–1927), his principal scenic artists, were perhaps

*Wagner and
Saxe-
Meiningen:
Unified
Production
and The
Regisseur*

Irving's first important production after remodelling his theatre and seeing the work of Saxe-Meiningen. Note the extensive use of three-dimensional units for this final scene of Shakespeare's *Romeo and Juliet*. (From *The Illustrated London News,* 1882.)

the finest of their day, and their work was often supplemented with designs commissioned from outstanding painters of the period (for example, Edward Burne-Jones designed the settings for Irving's production of Tennyson's *King Arthur* in 1895). Thus, while Irving was not, like Saxe-Meiningen, an artist himself, he displayed considerable artistic judgment in his choice of designers.

Second, Irving liberally employed three-dimensional details in settings. In 1881 he remodeled his stage, removed the grooves, and leveled the floor. Instead of the old wing-and-groove arrangement, which had required that most of the scenery be set up parallel to the front of the stage, Irving now began to use "free plantation," which permitted much greater flexibility and more asymmetrical arrangement of settings. It also required a greatly enlarged stage crew. Irving employed about 135 stagehands, whom he rehearsed as carefully as he did his actors. Irving's first important production after these changes was *Romeo and Juliet* (1882), in which he made extensive use of steps, platforms, and other three-dimensional and practical elements. After this time, columns, pediments, and a variety of other actualistic details increasingly replaced the traditional painted decor.

Third, Irving is said to be the first English director to make an art of stage lighting. Great potential had long been available in gas and the gas table, for together they provided an enormous range in intensity and complete control over it. With few exceptions, however, these possibilities had been little explored. Irving set out to make full use of light as one element in stage design and scenic illusion. He broke up the footlights and borderlights into short sections, each equipped with different color filters and each controlled separately. Thus, he could mix colors and control intensity more efficiently than had his predecessors. Critics almost always commented on his lighting, often terming it arbitrary and distracting because each moment had been contrived for its beauty and effectiveness, but always acknowledging its power and its departure from typical practices of the past. Irving was also the first English producer regularly to darken the auditorium during performances so as to concentrate all attention on the stage and to insure that his effects would not be ruined by light from the auditorium. His lighting crew, which consisted of about thirty men, was rehearsed with a care equal to that bestowed on the actors.

Fourth, Irving controlled and coordinated all of the elements of his productions. He was an indefatigable worker, spending countless hours attaining the ends he desired. Ultimately the impact of his productions depended upon a totality of effect rather than upon individual elements.

Nevertheless, Irving's productions fell short of Saxe-Meiningen's for several reasons. He did not have as much time to spend on rehearsals. His was a commercial organization dependent entirely on box-office receipts for its income. The company played a full season, appearing nightly through most of the year, leaving relatively little time for daily rehearsals. Furthermore, if a production failed to attract an audience, Irving had to replace it quickly.

Unlike Saxe-Meiningen, Irving's productions were built around stars, especially himself and Ellen Terry (1847–1928), his leading lady from 1879 until he retired. On stage from childhood, Miss Terry had performed with Charles Kean's company and later in the provinces. She retired from 1868 to 1875 to "set up housekeeping" (as she put it) with Edward Godwin (1833–86), an architect and artist. From this union Gordon Craig, destined to be one of the major theoreticians of the modern theatre, was born in 1872. Upon returning to the stage in 1875, Miss Terry played at first with the Bancrofts and then joined Irving. After Irving retired, she managed the Imperial Theatre in London for a time, giving Gordon Craig one of his first opportunities to try out his innovative ideas. She seldom appeared after 1907, although she did not completely retire until 1925. In addition to Irving and Miss Terry, there was always a group of young actors of considerable ability and box-office appeal. Many achieved their first real fame with Irving, but none rivaled the two stars. Among those who played with the troupe were Johnston Forbes-Robertson, John Martin-Harvey, and William Terriss, all later to be major stars of the English stage.

Irving also fell short of Saxe-Meiningen in his crowd scenes, although he was more effective than most of his contemporaries. Nevertheless, he could not afford to rehearse these scenes as fully as did the Meiningen company or to hire so many supernumeraries as permanent members of his troupe.

Irving's greatest successes came in the 1880s. The relative failure of *Macbeth* in 1888 marked the beginning of a decline which was hastened by Irving's failing health after 1896. Nevertheless, Irving's most lavish productions were given in the 1890s, the zenith being reached with *Henry VIII* in 1892. He withdrew from management in 1898 but continued to act at the Lyceum until 1902. In addition to performing in London, Irving also undertook many tours with his company, making eight visits to America after 1883, thus extending his influence to the United States as well.

Like Saxe-Meiningen, Irving expended his efforts almost entirely on the classics, poetic drama, and melodrama. He raised romantic realism to new heights in England and demonstrated that the theatre of his day was capable of achieving almost any effect it wished. It was for his failure to devote that potential to vital contemporary drama that George Bernard Shaw chided Irving so severely in the 1890s.

In France, prior to Antoine, whose work with realistic drama did not begin until 1887, there was no strong figure who sought to establish the director as the major artistic force in the theatre. The trend toward actualistic detail in staging, however, was everywhere evident. Even the Comédie Française, the most conservative troupe in Paris, succumbed to the trend. In 1876, it staged Erckmann-Chatrian's *My Friend Fritz* in a farmyard setting which included a pump from which real water flowed and a tree from which real cherries were picked and eaten; in one scene real food and drink were served and consumed by the actors. It is not surprising, then, that other less tradition-bound companies should embrace similar devices wholeheartedly.

Perhaps the man who most nearly epitomized the theatre of the late nineteenth century was Victorien Sardou (1831–1908), not only the most popular playwright of the era but also the director who perfected romantic realism in France. As a writer, Sardou was Scribe's true successor. He once stated that he had trained himself by reading the first acts of Scribe's plays and then working out the remainder by himself. In his maturity, he wrote the obligatory scene of a play first and then arranged everything else accordingly. Thus, he shaped characters and ideas to lead to a high dramatic point and sacrificed depth for suspense and theatrical effectiveness.

Also like Scribe, Sardou wrote almost every kind of play—vaudevilles, melodramas, satirical comedies, historical spectacles—a total of about seventy works. His early successes were comedies, such as *A Scrap of Paper* (1860) and *Our Intimates* (1861), or mild satires on contemporary life, such as *The Family Benoiton* (1865). Several of his plays were written as vehicles for Sarah Bernhardt; the best of these were *Fedora* (1882) and *Tosca* (1887).

Let's Get a Divorce (1880) illustrates well those qualities in Sardou's plays that so offended Shaw. The play takes as its point of departure an attempt to legalize divorce in France. In the first act, a number of characters display their attitudes toward marriage and divorce in a manner not unlike Shaw's. But Sardou merely uses this beginning as a prelude to farce. The husband convinces his wife that the divorce law has been passed and that she is now free to divorce him and marry her would-be lover. To celebrate the occasion, he whisks her away to a restaurant, thus raising the jealousy of the suitor, now made to accept the role that the husband has formerly filled. The final part of the play is taken up with the suitor's pursuit of the husband and wife, who are treated by everyone they encounter as though they were engaged in an illicit affair. Eventually the wife decides that she prefers her husband to her lover. Divorce, in the first act seemingly a subject for serious consideration, is lost sight of in the farcical bustle. Nevertheless, *Let's Get a Divorce* is a thoroughly entertaining play. It was with such works that Sardou attained and held his position as France's most popular dramatist.

But it is Sardou's historical spectacles, especially *Patrie!* (1869), *Hatred* (1874), and *Theodora* (1884), that best display his range of talents, for not only did he create in them authentic milieus but he staged them so effectively that he must be considered one of France's leading directors of the late nineteenth century. In these historical plays, Sardou worked out every aspect of setting, properties, and costumes so thoroughly that they became vivid recreations of the past. *Hatred* was probably the

43

Wagner and Saxe-Meiningen: Unified Production and The Regisseur

Scene from Sardou's *Patrie!* as staged by the author in 1869. The settings are by Cambon. (From a contemporary engraving.)

most lavish of the productions. Set in Siena during the Middle Ages, it required seven sets. The armor alone cost 120,000 francs and the total production cost approximately 400,000 francs, a monumental sum at that time for a nonoperatic production.

Even those who disliked Sardou praised these spectacles. Antoine later stated that one might dream of recreating them, and Zola, the leader of the naturalists, voiced his admiration for Sardou's impeccable creation of specific historical milieus. Nevertheless, Sardou did not make a lasting impression as a director, probably because he did not manage a company and because his directing was overshadowed by his playwriting. Still, it was in these spectacles that romantic realism reached its peak in France.

In America, the man who most nearly achieved Saxe-Meiningen's ideal was Augustin Daly (1836–99), critic, playwright, manager, and director. Daly began his career as a critic in 1857 and during the next ten years wrote for a number of newspapers in New York. He turned to playwriting in 1862 with *Leah the Forsaken* (adapted from Salomon Hermann von Mosenthal's *Deborah,* a German melodrama written in 1850), the success of which brought him several commissions to adapt other foreign plays. It was not until 1867 that he wrote an original work, *Under the Gaslight,* a thrilling melodrama and the first to use the suspenseful device of binding the hero to a railroad track.

Counting both original work and adaptations, Daly is credited with about ninety plays, primarily melodramas and comedies. (There is considerable evidence to suggest that much of the writing was actually done by others.) For adaptations, he turned most frequently to the plays of Sardou and Dumas *fils,* although the works of both were considerably altered in the process. Of his original works, the majority of which were written early in his career, the most significant is *Horizon* (1871), often considered important in the development of American realism, since it contrasts the values of easterners and westerners and treats the Indian as villain rather than as "noble savage." Nevertheless, Daly's legacy to modern playwriting was small.

It was as a director that Daly made his primary contributions to the modern theatre. From 1867 until his death he was a director and manager. He controlled a series of theatres in New York but his major work was done at Daly's Theatre, his company's home from 1879 until his death in 1899.

Daly's work as a director paralleled Irving's, except that Daly's repertory was heavily weighted toward modern comedy and melodrama. Although he produced some of Shakespeare's comedies and a few classics, his company's success was won primarily with recent plays. In directing, however, Daly used methods not unlike those being employed by Irving at the same time. He assumed control over every element of production and insisted upon his right to coach actors in their interpretations, stage business, and blocking. He abandoned the practice of casting according to lines of business, using actors as he thought their capabilities warranted.

45

*Wagner and
Saxe-
Meiningen:
Unified
Production
and The
Regisseur*

Like Saxe-Meiningen, Daly voiced his dislike for stars. Thus, it is ironical that many of his young performers deserted him for the starring circuit (among them Agnes Ethel, Fanny Davenport, and Clara Morris), and that eventually his productions were built around four principal actors: Ada Rehan (1860–1916) and John Drew II (1853–1927) as leading players, and James Lewis (1840–96) and Mrs. G. H. Gilbert (1822–1904) as character actors. Miss Rehan especially won international fame as a star and is still considered by many to have been the finest Katherine (in *The Taming of the Shrew*) of all time. But, if Daly capitulated to the demand for stars, he retained his control over them and shaped their performances to fit his own conceptions of the plays in which they appeared.

Like Saxe-Meiningen, Daly insisted upon accuracy in settings, properties, and costumes. Every detail was worked out with care and all were coordinated for maximum effect. In this way, Daly created the finest ensemble that had yet been seen in America. If he fell short of Saxe-Meiningen's achievement, it was largely because the pressures of commercial management did not always permit him to work as he liked.

Like Irving and Saxe-Meiningen, Daly took his company on tour in other countries and helped to publicize the effectiveness of the *regisseur*. His company first played in England in 1884 and returned often thereafter. His success was so great that in 1892 a theatre bearing his name was opened in London. He also toured Germany in 1886 and played in Paris a number of times.

Daly's significance in the modern theatre lies in two areas: first, his work as a *regisseur* helped to establish the director as the major figure in the theatre. Not only did he provide a strong example for Americans, his foreign tours served to reenforce the influence of such figures as Saxe-Meiningen and Irving. Second, he contributed to the final phase of romantic realism, in which essentially traditional plays were mounted in actualistic settings and authentic costumes.

～ IV ～

Although the emergence of the *regisseur* was one of the most significant developments of the late nineteenth century, other lesser innovations contributed to the new ideal as well. Among these were the technological solutions to problems raised by the trend toward three-dimensionality in settings and properties. Those who played pioneering roles in this search include two Americans: Edwin Booth and Steele Mackaye.

Edwin Booth (1833–93), now remembered primarily as one of America's greatest actors, was among the first to devise new methods of

Backstage at Booth's Theatre, New York,
in 1870. Note the elevator traps and
the use of stage braces.
(From *Appleton's Journal,* 1870.)

scene shifting. Booth's efforts are now often overlooked, perhaps because
only about ten years of his long career (mostly spent as a touring star)
were devoted to theatrical management. From 1863 to 1867 he headed the
Winter Garden Theatre in New York, the destruction of which motivated
Booth to build his own theatre, one designed especially to fit his needs. The
result was Booth's Theatre, opened in 1869. Here until 1874 Booth staged
the most lavish productions yet seen in New York and proved himself an
incipient *regisseur* in the manner of Charles Kean. His desire for authenticity led him to many innovations in stage architecture. Booth was probably
the first producer in modern times to use a level stage floor. He also broke
the floor into a series of elevator traps powered by water-driven rams.
Using these, stagehands could set up heavy scenic pieces beneath the stage
and then raise them noiselessly to stage level. This arrangement permitted
Booth to use heavy set pieces and to shift them in a matter of seconds.
Booth's Theatre was also the first in New York to have a stage house
sufficiently tall to permit drops to be flown out of sight without being rolled
or folded.

Unfortunately Booth's poor business sense brought him to financial
ruin in 1874 and he lost control of his theatre. Nevertheless, his brief tenure
set a high standard for his successors, and his theatre foreshadowed the
many innovations that would be engendered by the need to cope more
efficiently with increasingly cumbersome scenery.

Booth's pioneering efforts were considerably extended by Steele
Mackaye (1842–94), one of the most inventive men ever to work in the
American theatre. Like Booth, Mackaye had an inadequate grasp of busi-

ness affairs and consequently every scheme he advanced ended in financial disaster. It is probably for this reason that his innovations had so little lasting effect, for they carried with them the taint of impracticality. Nevertheless, Mackaye is an undisputed pioneer in the attempt to devise a new technology for theatrical production.

After studying in France and England, Mackaye returned to the United States in the early 1870s and until about 1890 was associated with a series of theatres in New York: St. James', Union Square, Madison Square, and the Lyceum. It was at the Madison Square Theatre, opened in 1879, that Mackaye's first important invention was unveiled. Here he installed two stages, one above the other, inside an elevator shaft 114 feet deep. The stages, each 31 feet by 22 feet, could be moved to any of three locations—basement, stage level, or attic—thus permitting entire settings to be changed while another scene was in progress at stage level. One stage could replace the other in 40 seconds. This is the first known example of an entire stage mounted as an elevator.

Mackaye seems to have recognized the drawbacks of this arrangement (the relationship of the two stages could not be altered) for he continued to invent new devices. He applied for a patent on a stage that could move in any direction—forward, backward, diagonally, sideways—although he did not build one. He also invented an adjustable proscenium so that the size of the stage opening could be altered, a system for projecting moving clouds, a curtain of light, folding chairs for spectators, and many other devices too numerous to mention. For the Chicago Exposition of 1893 he designed his most ambitious project, a "spectatorium" with twenty-five

Sectional plan of the Madison Square Theatre, opened by Mackaye in 1879. Note the two stages, one above the other, mounted in a large elevator shaft. The orchestra can be seen in the balcony above the proscenium arch. (From *The Scientific American,* April 5, 1884.)

48

*Wagner and
Saxe-
Meiningen:
Unified
Production
and The
Regisseur*

stages, on which he intended to portray Columbus's voyage to the new world and the subsequent development of American history. These movable stages would have constituted the most elaborate arrangement ever devised, but, though the surviving plans show that Mackaye's ideas were feasible, a financial crisis prevented their completion.

Mackaye's experiences seem unfortunate, for it is clear that he was a visionary who saw the implications of many trends and anticipated ways of meeting them. In the tradition of the nineteenth century, he sought to solve problems through technology. Unfortunately, the financial means required to develop an extensive technology were not available to him.

Booth and Mackaye were not the only persons of the time interested in theatre technology. In the same year that Mackaye's Madison Square Theatre opened, the new Opera House in Budapest was also completed. Its stage was divided into three sections, each mounted on hydraulic rams. Essentially an extension of the solution used by Booth (although it should be noted that others besides Booth had used sinking traps to move scenery), it merely enlarged the traps until together they included almost all of the stage floor. As in Booth's Theatre, the sections moved only between the basement and stage level. Consequently, the innovations made at the Budapest Opera House were less revolutionary than were Mackaye's. In the 1880s inventors in other countries also began to set forth schemes not unlike those of Mackaye, but none was carried out until the end of the century. It was to remain for the Germans, especially in the state-owned theatres after 1896, to develop stage machinery and technology most fully.

Extensive theatrical technology had to await the development of electricity as a motive force. Electricity came into the theatre in the 1840s with the carbon arc, used to produce strong beams of light for special effects, but it was not until Edison invented the incandescent lamp in 1879 that it became a major medium for stage lighting. David Belasco maintains that the California Theatre in San Francisco was lighted by electricity in 1879 (others have questioned this); the Savoy Theatre in London was lighted entirely by electricity in 1881; and electricity was installed in the Stadttheater in Brunn, Austria, in 1882, in the Bijou Theatre in Boston in 1882, in the Residenztheater in Munich in 1883, and in the Paris Opera House in 1886. The change from gas to electricity was rapid, especially after two disastrous fires attributed to gas—at the Opéra Comique in Paris and the Exeter Theatre in England—took hundreds of lives in 1887. By 1900 almost every major theatre in the world had changed to electricity, although some older producers such as Irving clung to gas to the ends of their careers.

Controlboards were available for use with electricity from the beginning, thus making it extremely flexible. The board installed in the Residenztheater in Munich in 1883 had twenty-nine circuits, each of which could be set at twenty-five different grades of intensity. Furthermore, several circuits could be coupled and controlled by a single lever. This theatre also

used a system whereby cylinders could be rotated to place one of three 49
different colors between the lamps and the stage, thus providing considerable
control over the hue of the light.

*Wagner and
Saxe-
Meiningen:
Unified
Production
and The
Regisseur*

Interest in electricity developed rapidly. It was sufficiently great by
1881 that an international exhibition of electrical and technical equipment
was held in Paris. An experimental theatre was built there to demonstrate
the use of electricity for stage lighting. This exhibition subsequently became
an annual one held in a different country each year, thus helping to
acquaint persons all over the world with new advances.

Nevertheless, the use of electricity as a motive force was not exploited
until the end of the nineteenth century. Only after its potentials were
realized did elevator stages, revolving stages, and other complex machinery
become common.

V

Other changes involved acting. Traditionally actors had learned their trade
while serving an apprenticeship in a resident company. Occasionally an
actor entered the theatre as a star, but usually he began as a "utility" performer of innumerable small parts. Gradually he discovered his strengths
and as he gained experience tended to specialize in a "line of business." In
Europe, where state-subsidized theatres were common, conservatories had
been founded as an adjunct to the state troupes. The oldest of these was
established in 1786 by the Comédie Française, but most were founded in
the nineteenth century. In these schools, leading actors taught a limited
number of pupils through the method of imitation. The student prepared
a scene, performed it, watched his teacher demonstrate improvements, and
then imitated his teacher. This method ultimately differed little from the
apprentice system, since it was based primarily upon observation, trial, and
error.

These systems of actor training were reasonably effective so long as
there were many resident companies which changed their bills sufficiently
often to give actors many opportunities to learn. But when touring companies began to replace resident companies and when the long run displaced the nightly change of bill, the beginning actor lost his major
opportunity for training, since producers of long runs or touring shows
wished to employ actors who were already experienced. This pinch was
felt on the continent as well, for the conservatories reached only a few
actors and the training was oriented toward the classical repertory at a time
when contemporary plays were becoming increasingly popular. Thus, the
need for some new kind of training arose.

50

Wagner and
Saxe-
Meiningen:
Unified
Production
and The
Regisseur

Despite this need, both the apprentice system and the early schools tended merely to enshrine received ideas and techniques. Given the scientific bent of the nineteenth century, however, it was probably inevitable that an attempt would be made to reduce actor training to a precise method. The result was the Delsarte system.

Although now the object of considerable disdain, the Delsarte system was the best known in the world in the late nineteenth century, and it still —though generally unrecognized—exerts considerable influence on actor training. In keeping with the nineteenth century's interests, its founder, François Delsarte (1811–71), set out to demonstrate that the laws of stage expression are discoverable and can be formulated as precisely as mathematical principles. Delsarte began to set forth his approach in 1839 and continued to enlarge on it throughout his life. He attracted many disciples, among them Mackaye, who studied with Delsarte in France.

Delsarte sought to analyze emotions and ideas and to determine how they are outwardly expressed. Using his analyses as a basis, he then sought to show the actor how to communicate precisely whatever he wished. The ill-repute of the system today stems from two sources: Delsarte's schematized explanation of human behavior, and the mechanized performances encouraged by Delsarte's disciples.

Delsarte had a penchant for dividing everything into three parts. Consequently, for him human experience and behavior can be divided into the physical, mental, and emotional-spiritual, and these three aspects can be related in turn to each action, thought, and emotion. He also divided and subdivided the body into parts and related each to the physical, mental, or emotional-spiritual realms. Eventually he arrived at an elaborate scheme whereby he sought to describe how the feet, legs, arms, torso, head, and every other part of the body are to be used in communicating particular emotions, attitudes, or ideas. Thus, the primary weakness of the system stemmed from its questionable analysis of human behavior. Once accepted, however, it almost inevitably led to a set of prescribed stances and gestures, which became increasingly mechanized as the system was disseminated by Delsarte's disciples. Eventually it became so mechanical that a strong reaction set in against it.

Nevertheless, the basic elements of Delsarte's training are still used, probably because his was the first attempt to make training systematic. In the eighteenth century, several persons had sought to analyze human emotions and relate them to facial expression or to analyze vocal characteristics and reduce them to systems of notation. But Delsarte was the first to synthesize past efforts and to build from fundamentals. Thus, his training began with exercises designed to induce bodily relaxation, good posture, proper breathing, and easy vocal production—to train the actor as an instrument. He then went on to the mental aspects of acting, under which he included the analysis of texts to be interpreted. He taught students to paraphrase passages and to search out the underlying ideas and feelings.

As a final goal, he sought to enlarge and encourage his students' spiritual attributes, for to Delsarte it was these that made the difference between mere competence and greatness. While today one hears little about the actor's spiritual traits, the other basic parts of Delsarte's system are familiar ones.

Mackaye brought the Delsarte system to New York in the 1870s. At each of his theatres he established an actor-training program, the most important of which was that at the Lyceum Theatre in 1884–85, for this became the American Academy of Dramatic Art, the most prestigious acting school in America until after World War II. A number of Mackaye's pupils founded still other schools, the most important of which were the Emerson School of Oratory and the Curry School of Expression.

The Delsarte system was adopted throughout Europe as well. For example, it became the basis of training at the London Academy of Music (now the London Academy of Music and Dramatic Art), the oldest still operative acting school in England. In the first decade of the twentieth century, as emphasis began to shift from external appearance to internal motivation, the Delsarte system began to decline in popularity, but it still holds an important position in the history of actor training and in nineteenth-century attempts to apply scientific principles to the arts. Furthermore, it complemented the efforts of *regisseurs* and technicians, since all were seeking to discover means whereby actualistic effects could be achieved with precision and at will.

~ VI ~

The period between 1870 and 1890, then, brought to the fore the *regisseur*, who controlled every aspect of a production and shaped them to attain a unified effect. In this development, Wagner was the major theoretician and Saxe-Meiningen the principal practitioner. Lesser exponents were at work in almost every country in the Western world.

The primary aim of *regisseurs* in these years was the creation of an illusion more complete than any previously attained. Not only did this require that the actor subordinate his will to the director's, but that all elements be brought under his control. This led to greater care for detail in scenery, costume, properties, and lighting and to the increased use of three-dimensional elements in settings. Attempts to arrange the stage more "naturally" led to the abandonment of wings set in grooves. The stage floor was leveled and machinery for moving heavy pieces began to be introduced. These trends, only beginning to be evident in 1890, would not be completed until World War I.

*Wagner and
Saxe-
Meiningen:
Unified
Production
and The
Regisseur*

Many companies were as yet unaffected by the standards set by Saxe-Meiningen, Irving, Daly, and others. For example, at the Comédie Française the acting company was still self-governing and members of the troupe assumed responsibility in turn for making up the bills, while the directing duties rotated each week. Thus, since no one could enforce a decision not agreed upon by all, the kind of effect attained by Saxe-Meiningen was achieved only rarely.

Furthermore, the trend toward actualistic detail was by no means universal. Many producers still used painted decors almost entirely, even though they sought a realistic effect. Even those directors who favored three-dimensional units usually combined them with painted details. The disparity was often all too evident.

Most directors, even the *regisseurs,* were still restricting themselves to traditional drama. For the most part, Shaw's analysis of the theatre of his day was correct: it was given over to plays from the past or to "Sardoodledom," and major talents, such as those of Irving and Ellen Terry, were often expended on worthless plays while significant modern works were denied a hearing. By 1890, however, both new plays and new producers were beginning to open paths that would alter Shaw's analysis by merging significant recent drama with innovative theatrical practices.

The New Drama,
1870-1890

Between 1870 and 1890, while Wagner and Saxe-Meiningen were popularizing innovations in theatrical practice, a new drama was also gaining recognition. The key figures were Henrik Ibsen, often called "the father of modern drama," and Emile Zola, the principal advocate of naturalism. Ibsen not only created a drama of social significance which served as a rallying point for the realists, he wrote many symbolic plays which were equally inspiring to nonrealists. Zola sought to make drama an objective reflection of life and an instrument of social change. His theoretical views were more significant than his plays, but he articulated ideals which many sought to embody. Other dramatists, among them, Becque, Strindberg, Bjornson, and Anzengruber, also helped to shape a realistic drama and to pave the way for its wider acceptance in the 1890s.

Henrik Ibsen (1828–1906) began his playwriting career in 1850 with *Cataline,* a work based on the story of the Roman rebel but considerably influenced by the European revolutions of 1848–49. Although technically immature, *Cataline* nevertheless has considerable strength because it concentrates on the hero's inner conflict rather than upon the struggle between Cataline and the state. Ibsen's friends, much impressed by the work, paid to have it published when it failed to win production. Ibsen's next play, *The Warrior's Barrow* (1850), a one-act drama about the Vikings' encounter with Christianity in Sicily, fared somewhat better, being presented at the Christiania Theatre for three performances.

At this time, Ibsen was also writing prose essays and poems, and these, along with his two plays, brought him to the attention of Ole Bull, world-famous violinist and fiery patriot. Bull was then seeking to promote nationalism in Norway, where artistic life was still Danish even though Norway had seceded from Denmark in 1814 and had since enjoyed relative autonomy under the rule of Sweden. For example, Norway's foremost theatre at this time had a Danish director, actors, and repertory. In an attempt to counter this situation, Bull established a Norwegian theatre at Bergen, on the west coast of Norway, and in 1851 he offered Ibsen a position as stage manager and later as resident playwright there.

Ibsen spent six years in Bergen. During this time he obtained a grant to study theatrical practices in Denmark and Germany and from this opportunity learned much about staging techniques, scenic practices, stage machinery, and business management. Then in 1857 he accepted the post of artistic director of the Christiania Norwegian Theatre (established in 1852). Already in severe financial straits, it declined further under Ibsen's direction and closed in 1862. Ibsen then served as literary advisor to the Christiania Theatre, but in 1864 left Norway for a long, self-imposed exile.

A few points about Ibsen's early career are worthy of special note. First, from his considerable practical experience as stage manager, director, and playwright he gained first-hand knowledge of the theatre. Second, he learned much about playwriting. Although the Bergen Theatre was designed to encourage nationalism in drama, the repertory was largely foreign. During Ibsen's six years at Bergen, 145 plays were produced; of these, seventy-five were by French authors, twenty-one by Scribe. From these works he absorbed many of the techniques of the well-made play. Third, by the time Ibsen left Norway in 1864 he had written nine plays of his own and had completed his apprenticeship as a dramatist.

Since Ibsen was employed during most of this time as a resident playwright in Norwegian theatres, it is not surprising that all but two of his early dramas, *Cataline* and *Love's Comedy,* are based on Norwegian history,

Ibsen's *Love's Comedy,* produced by Den Nationale Scene, Bergen, Norway, 1918.
(From Bergens Teatermuseum.)

legend, fairytales, and sagas. For the most part they are in verse and resemble the romantic drama of the early nineteenth century. Nevertheless, they already revolve around the problem which dominated Ibsen's work throughout his career: the conflict between duty to self and duty to others. In the early, as in most of the later plays, the characters pursue goals that are sometimes personal, sometimes political; but happiness usually escapes them because in their strivings they either sacrifice integrity or tread others underfoot. Consequently, even if the immediate goal is gained, the sense of fulfillment is missing. Ibsen was to change his method and draw on new sources, but his central concerns never altered.

Of the early plays, the best are *The Vikings at Helgeland* (1858) and *The Pretenders* (1864). The former is based on Icelandic sagas and, like many of Ibsen's works, shows how past errors become a nemesis in the present. The main interest lies in the portrait of Hjordis, daughter of an Icelandic chieftain and wife of Gunnar. In her youth, she loved Sigurd, who, though he returned her love, withdrew in favor of Gunnar, his closest friend. Now Hjordis has come to believe that Sigurd's betrayal has stifled her development as a human being. Hardened to any appeal, she ruthlessly and successfully pursues Sigurd's destruction as an act of retribution.

In *The Pretenders,* Ibsen turned to Norwegian history of the thirteenth century. The principal interest lies in the contrast between the two main characters, King Haakon, who sets out to unite the Norwegian people, and Earl Skule, his chief opponent and rival for power. Haakon achieves his goal in large part because he is completely confident in the rightness of his cause and his ability to accomplish his goal. He sees himself as destined by fate to unite his country. Earl Skule, on the other hand, is an extremely complex man, far more intellectually gifted than Haakon, but one whose potential is subverted by doubt and reflection. When he appropriates Haakon's "great idea" and proclaims himself king, he fears his own spiritual impotence even more. Eventually Earl Skule, like Macbeth, faces his final battle with a shred of greatness; though he cannot live for Haakon's great idea, he willingly dies for it. Like Shakespeare's history plays, *The Pretenders* transcends its localized subject through its powerful characterizations and its perceptions about human motives and conflicts. It was Ibsen's first play to be presented outside of Scandinavia.

Before leaving Norway, Ibsen had written one other play that gave some indication of future directions in his work. *Love's Comedy* (1862) treats the relationship between the young poet Falk and Svanhild, whom he intends to marry. They believe that they are approaching marriage with their eyes open, fully aware of all the pitfalls into which their married acquaintances have fallen. Eventually, however, Svanhild weds the wealthy and practical Gulstad, who convinces the couple that their love would be destroyed by marriage. Although written in verse, the play seems far removed from Ibsen's historical and folklorist materials and looks forward to the prose plays of the 1870s. As might be expected, the play was assaulted as bitter, immoral, and lacking in good taste.

By the time Ibsen left Norway he had tired of nationalism in drama. Perhaps he felt too restricted by it, but he may have withdrawn because the battle had been won, for while the Norwegian Theatre closed in 1862, by 1865 the regular theatre in Christiania had rid itself of all Danish personnel and was fully Norwegian. But Ibsen himself was also progressing beyond provincialism to more philosophical concerns and between 1864 and 1868, while living in Rome, he wrote two of his most important early plays, *Brand* (1866) and *Peer Gynt* (1867).

Originally conceived as an epic poem, *Brand* became a lengthy, virtually unstageable, five-act tragedy in verse. Pastor Brand believes himself to be God's chosen instrument for moral regeneration on earth, and devotes himself to his task with unflinching piety and strength of will, making no concessions to human weakness. Like Kierkegaard, Brand takes as his creed All or Nothing. His God is not the soft, merciful, benevolent diety of Christianity, but the unswerving, wrathful, stern Jehovah of the Old Testament, and in His name Brand demands that human love, comfort, and weakness be suppressed. Brand's mother dies without his blessing because even at the end she is unwilling to renounce her worldly goods and give them for the glorification of God; his young son Alph dies because Brand refuses to accept the doctor's advice to take the boy south to warmth and sunshine; his wife dies after he forces her to give away all of Alph's possessions. But Brand steadily gains followers, and the civil authorities, in order to keep his favor, offer their assistance in building a great new church. Brand accepts, but on the day of the church's dedication he concludes that he has compromised his principles and leads his followers out onto the icy mountains. When he is unable to feed them, they turn on him, stone him, and leave him with only a mad gypsy girl as attendant. In visions that come to him, Brand is asked to turn to God's mercy, and, as an avalanche sweeps down to destroy him, a voice cries out, "He is the God of Love." Thus, Brand dies not as a martyr for God but as a victim of his own sterile perfectionism. The ending has been called inconsistent, since it seems to void most of the criticism of society and human behavior voiced earlier in the work. But it did not seem so to Ibsen's contemporaries, with whom it was enormously popular—almost a devotional book for the younger generation. It was Ibsen's first truly successful publication and the income from it (along with a small pension) allowed him to work as he wished thereafter.

Peer Gynt was a suitable sequel to Brand, for it shows the opposite side of the coin. Unlike Brand, Peer is the eternal compromiser, always self-indulgent and accepting of life as it is, taking as his motto "To thine own self be—enough." Peer tries many vocations, travels throughout the world, and undergoes a multitude of strange adventures. Finally he returns to Norway, where he encounters the Button Moulder, whose duty it is to melt down for buttons all those who have failed to realize their potential as human beings. When Peer protests that he has not been truly bad, the Button Moulder replies, "Why, that's precisely the rub; you're no sinner at all in the higher sense." Peer has failed because of his very mediocrity— he is neither supremely good nor bad—for he has never really discovered his true self. Threatened with extinction, he is saved at the last moment by his childhood sweetheart, Solveig, now grown old waiting for his return. Thus, as in Brand, love is the great redeemer. But, as in Brand, the ending perhaps denies most of the points made by Ibsen earlier in the play.

Peer Gynt was greeted with considerable hostility, for it was interpreted as a satire on the Norwegian character, especially because in the recent Dano-Prussian War Norway had declined to become involved. Eventually, however, this poetic drama with its fairytale atmosphere, fantasy, and satire was to become one of Ibsen's most popular works. Today, it is the only one of Ibsen's early works still regularly produced.

After completing Peer Gynt, Ibsen left Italy for Germany, where he was to make his home for the next twenty years. In Dresden he completed The League of Youth (1869), his most light-hearted play and one which foreshadowed the realistic works to come. Written in prose, it is Scribean in its techniques and in its skillful use of misunderstanding and farce. A satire on politics and on politicians who change alliances for the sake of expediency, it became a popular success in theatres throughout Europe.

Ibsen's last work in the romantic vein was Emperor and Galilean (1873), "a world historical drama" about the conflict in fourth-century Byzantium between paganism and Christianity. In this two-part, ten-act philosophical piece, Ibsen focuses upon the emperor Julian and his quest for an idea worthy of his dedication. Here Ibsen adopts an Hegelian view of progress: out of a conflict between two antithetical views comes a synthesis in which the two are reconciled. Julian at first vacillates between

Christianity and paganism, eventually choosing the latter. Although he sees that his choice serves for the moment only to strengthen Christianity, he persists in championing paganism, for he is convinced that only through the struggle can the "third empire" emerge. He believes that though eventually both emperor and Galilean will succumb, their ruin will lead to a fusion of flesh (paganism) and spirit (Christianity). Ibsen always considered this play his masterpiece in which he had presented "a positive theory of life." Few critics have concurred in Ibsen's judgment. *Emperor and Galilean* is, nevertheless, a watershed play. As the thirteenth of Ibsen's twenty-five dramas, it marks the midpoint in his writing career in several ways. It is the last of Ibsen's obviously philosophical works, the last of his romantic plays, the end of his poetic vein. From this time on, Ibsen was to write in prose and about contemporary subjects.

The plays which immediately followed are Ibsen's most consciously realistic dramas and consequently contrast sharply with his previous work. Ibsen's realistic phase is usually said to include the eight dramas written between 1877 and 1890—*Pillars of Society, A Doll's House, Ghosts, An Enemy of the People, The Wild Duck, Rosmersholm, Lady from the Sea,* and *Hedda Gabler*. But within this grouping there is much variety.

The first three plays, those which made the greatest impression on the public, may be viewed as one unit within the larger category. Of these, *Pillars of Society* (1877) is a tentative essay, for it still creaks under Scribean machinery not yet sufficiently refined. Ibsen's principal character, Consul Bernick, enjoys a position of great prominence and seeming security in the community. The play shows how his past deeds, through which Bernick has gotten rid of all those who endangered him, come to light and destroy him. A play of considerable power, it nevertheless seems overly contrived and has never ranked high among Ibsen's works.

A Doll's House (1879) shows considerable advance over its predecessor. It deals with the suppression of a woman under the hypocrisy of a respectable marriage. Before the play opens, Nora Helmer, unaware of the law, has forged her father's signature in order to borrow money from the disreputable Nils Krogstad so that she may take her husband to Italy where he can recuperate from a critical illness. When the play opens, her husband, Torvald, has recovered and is a respected bank manager. The family, which includes two small children, seems the epitome of happiness and respectability and Nora is thoroughly submerged in her "doll's world." Scarcely has the play begun, however, before the past begins to catch up with Nora, as Krogstad attempts to blackmail her. Though frightened, Nora is convinced that Torvald will praise her for her initiative in saving his life. But when he learns of her actions, Torvald, concerned only with the threat to his position, denounces Nora as monstrous and declares her unfit to rear his children. Horrified, Nora realizes that she has always been treated as a plaything rather than as a partner. She leaves both husband and children, determined to achieve her potential as a human being.

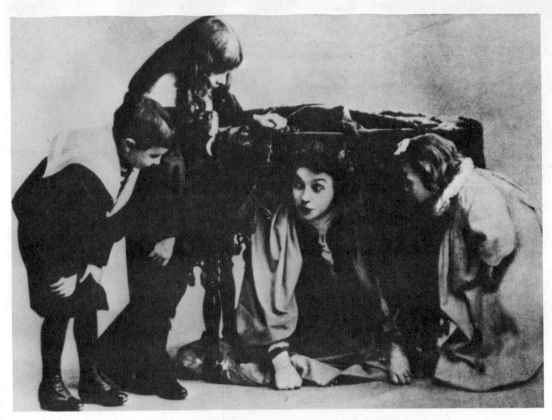

Gabrielle Réjane as Nora in Ibsen's *A Doll's House* in the 1890s at the
Théâtre du Vaudeville. (From *Le Théâtre,* 1900.)

A Doll's House is now considered the first important modern drama,
both because of qualities within the work and because of the powerful
impression it made on the public consciousness. That a woman would
leave her husband and children was considered scandalous and shocking.
Many producers refused to present it unless the ending was changed to
make Nora stay with Torvald. Ibsen even wrote an alternate ending when
it became clear that in no other form would the play be produced. *A Doll's
House* soon became a rallying point, much to Ibsen's chagrin, for the
feminists, who interpreted it as a propagandistic statement on their behalf.

In *A Doll's House,* Ibsen has advanced in technique beyond *Pillars of
Society* but still has not eliminated all the weaknesses. The confrontation
scene between Nora and Helmer is perhaps the major flaw, for here Nora
suddenly becomes a *raisonneur* not unlike those found in the works of
Dumas *fils.* Though she has led an extremely sheltered life, she now displays
great insights into human behavior and becomes an eloquent spokesman
for wives as partners rather than as playthings. 59

Scene between Regina and Engstrand in Ibsen's *Ghosts,* produced in 1890 by Den Nationale Scene, Bergen, Norway. (From Bergens Teatermuseum.)

In *Ghosts* (1881), Ibsen's realistic form reached its perfection. More than any other drama of the late nineteenth century, it came to represent the new trends and it was the play that traditionalists most deplored. The storm raised by *A Doll's House* was as nothing in comparison with that created by *Ghosts,* into which Ibsen introduced the taboo subject of syphilis.

It is often said that Ibsen wrote *Ghosts* in response to the critics of *A Doll's House* and in it sought to show the results of a marriage maintained for the sake of appearances even though love and respect are lacking. Many years before the play begins, Mrs. Alving has married Captain Alving to escape her oppressive upbringing, even though she does not love him. This is her initial error, for her inability to provide love and understanding causes him to turn to others and eventually to a life of debauchery. She then resolves to leave him, but is persuaded not to by Pastor Manders, who thinks only of maintaining the façade of respectability. It is implied that Mrs. Alving was in love with Manders, and that he could not face the scandal that would have resulted had she left her husband for him. Mrs. Alving remains with the captain and thereafter devotes her life to covering up his misadventures—she buys off a servant who is pregnant by the captain, and sends away her son, Oswald, so that he will not know about his father's conduct. When Alving dies of syphilis, she builds an orphanage in his honor to allay any gossip.

All of this has occurred before the curtain rises. In the first act,
Oswald has returned home for the dedication of the just-completed orphanage, Mrs. Alving's final attempt to put the past to rest before turning to
a new life of peace and fulfillment with her son. But "ghosts" are not so
easily laid to rest, and a series of events destroys her plans. Oswald begins to
display signs of the disease from which his father has died, although he does
not suspect what is wrong with him, and he forms a liaison with the servant
girl, Regina, who in actuality is the captain's illegitimate daughter and
thus Oswald's half-sister. Furthermore, on Pastor Mander's advice, Mrs.
Alving has not insured the orphanage, since this might be interpreted as a
lack of faith in God, and when the orphanage burns down there are no
funds to rebuild it. Oswald's efforts in fighting the fire bring on a new
attack of his disease and, fearing that he is losing his mind, he asks his
mother to give him the poison which he has provided her if he should go
mad. Seeking to quiet him, she promises to respect his wishes. At the end of
the play, he becomes little more than a babbling idiot, begging his mother
to give him the sun. Mrs. Alving stands over him indecisively as the curtain
falls.

Everything that happens comes about because of "ghosts" from Mrs.
Alving's past: her own puritanical upbringing, her inability to leave her
husband, her lies to cover up his debauchery, her son's inheritance from his
father. When the play opens, Mrs. Alving considers herself an emancipated
woman who understands herself and her past and who has come to terms
with them. Thus, her sense of confidence and relief that the past is done
with contrasts sharply with her dilemma at the end. Whether or not she
gives Oswald poison, her world is destroyed—by the ghosts which she has
sought so valiantly to deny.

In *Ghosts,* Ibsen has suppressed most of the marks of the well-made
play. The action is almost entirely internal, being composed of a series of
psychological discoveries made by Mrs. Alving. It is so masterfully constructed that almost every line is significant, but the economy and lack of
obvious theatrical devices left many readers so puzzled that they declared it
totally lacking in dramatic action. It was the moral aspects of the play,
however, that were considered most outrageous. Ibsen was declared per-
verted in his attempt to drag drama down into the sewer. In almost no
country could *Ghosts* be licensed for production. Probably because no
license was required, the first production was given in America in 1882 by
a Dano-Norwegian company touring midwestern cities.

In his first three realistic plays, Ibsen established the pattern that he
was to use thereafter. He deliberately limits the scope of his action, concentrating upon a few characters caught in toils of their own making. He
carefully lays out the past so that character and environment are the major
determinants of incidents. Each play treats only the end of a long chain of
events, all interconnected but whose significance is unclear until the past
recoils on the present and creates crisis and catastrophe. Most of the plays

occur in a single room, although occasionally an additional setting or two may be used. Above all, the emphasis is upon psychological conflict, external action being only a response to or a stimulus for internal struggle. The dialogue is a very precise prose which seems completely realistic, even though each speech is carefully tailored and essential. Economy is the key. Nothing is included which does not have a use. The overall effect is one of naturalness.

Ibsen's next two plays, *An Enemy of the People* and *The Wild Duck,* form a transition to a new phase. The first was probably motivated by Ibsen's anger over the response to *Ghosts,* and for this reason, is his most polemic play. In *An Enemy of the People* (1882), Ibsen uses as his main character Dr. Thomas Stockmann, whose uncompromising honesty runs head-on into the desire of others to cover up unpleasant facts. Stockmann is a medical officer in charge of the municipal baths, which have brought the town its wealth and reputation as a health spa. It was he who first discovered the medicinal value of the springs and it is he who now discovers that they have been polluted by wastes from a tannery. When he declares that the baths must be closed, he meets quiet but steady resistance from the leaders of the community; and when he insists upon announcing his findings at a town meeting, he is denounced and ostracized from the community. At the end, Stockmann declares: "The strongest man in the world is he who stands most alone."

In some ways, *An Enemy of the People* is an extension of the mode introduced by *A Doll's House* and *Ghosts,* but its very bitterness and uncompromising tone perhaps motivated Ibsen to seek in his next play to reestablish an equilibrium by showing a quite different side to his demand for truth at all costs. Thus, *The Wild Duck* (1884) is as harsh toward the shortsighted idealist as *An Enemy of the People* is toward the self-serving majority. In the latter play, Dr. Stockmann declares: "All who live on lies must be exterminated like vermin." But in *The Wild Duck,* Dr. Relling, Ibsen's *raisonneur,* says: "Rob the average man of his life-illusion, and you rob him of his happiness at one stroke."

In *The Wild Duck,* the well-meaning, idealistic Gregers Werle sets out to expose the lies which surround the lives of the Ekdal family, unable to perceive that they are happy in their illusions. Fifteen years before the play begins, Gina, then a servant, has had an affair with Gregers's father. She then marries Hjalmar Ekdal and shortly afterward has a child, Hedwig, whom Hjalmar accepts as his own. (The play never entirely settles the question of Hedwig's paternity but it is implied that Old Werle is her natural father.) At the time of the marriage, Hjalmar is also set up in a photographic shop by Old Werle. Gregers has a romanticized notion of Hjalmar's character, based upon schoolboy memories, and believes that Hjalmar could make a significant contribution to society if he would only free himself from the lies that surround him. Consequently, Gregers reveals what he knows about Gina's past and declares that Hedwig is not Hjalmar's child. Gina seems unconcerned, but Hjalmar is deeply affected and Hedwig, not understanding why he has rejected her, feels it necessary to prove her love for him. She takes a pistol into the attic where the wild duck is kept, apparently with the intention of sacrificing it as her most prized possession. Instead, however, she kills herself. Gina and Hjalmar are reconciled. Little has been changed except that Hedwig's death now offers Hjalmar new grounds for self-pity and another excuse for not getting ahead. Gregers never fully comprehends why his great plan has failed.

The Wild Duck is Ibsen's most satiric play. Many have seen in it a repudiation by Ibsen of his earlier work. More probably it was intended as a message to his militant followers, who considered him to be a social reformer rather than an artist. But it marked a change from his previous plays, for it placed considerable emphasis upon a central symbol, here the wild duck, a device that he was to develop more fully thereafter.

Ibsen next moved away from problems of social import to studies of individual characters and moral dilemmas set within a realistic framework but treated with mystical and symbolic overtones. *Rosmersholm* (1886), for example, centers upon two characters, Pastor Johannes Rosmer and Rebecca West. Long before the play opens, Rebecca has come to Rosmersholm to care for Rosmer's invalid wife, Beata. A thoroughly emancipated woman, Rebecca sees in Rosmer the possibilities of greatness if only his spirit can be freed from traditionalism and the joylessness of Christianity. She considers Beata the major block to her plans and, by insinuating that she is having an affair with Rosmer, encourages Beata to commit suicide in the mill race.

A production of *Rosmersholm* at the Schiller-Theater, Berlin, in 1901. (From the Deutsche Akademie der Künste zu Berlin.)

Under Rebecca's influence, Rosmer gives up his duties as a pastor to seek spiritual freedom through politics and an ethically based government. But, while he has thrown off many restraints, he is still haunted by images of "white horses" (which in this play serve much the same function as does the past in *Ghosts*). Rosmer fears that he may have been responsible for Beata's death—that she may have misinterpreted his relationship with Rebecca—but he determines to shut out the past and to marry Rebecca. Meantime, however, Rebecca has been as influenced by Rosmer as he by her, for she has absorbed much of his moral outlook. Eventually she confesses her part in Beata's death and declares that it is now impossible for her to marry Rosmer. She concludes, "The Rosmer view of life ennobles but it kills happiness." Realizing that only death is left, Rebecca and Rosmer throw themselves into the mill race as "white horses" clatter over the bridge above them. Here the emphasis is upon the crisis within Rebecca and Rosmer. Their dilemma is not so much social as moral and the overall effect is that of a detailed study of two complex beings whose world extends beyond the natural into the supernatural realm.

In *Hedda Gabler* (1890), the supernatural element is largely absent. In many ways it is much closer to *Ghosts* than to *Rosmersholm* but it lacks the explicit concern with social problems which most audiences saw in *Ghosts*. Consequently, its interest lies above all in its central character. Hedda, like Rebecca West, is an emancipated woman, but instead of using her potential she has hidden under the mask of respectability as the wife of a pedantic professor. Unable to adjust, she stands outside the life around her, observing ironically and unhappily. When Eilert Lovborg, with whom she might have found happiness, returns, she plays upon his self-destructive tendencies and slyly encourages him to commit suicide with one of her dueling pistols, once the property of her father and used in the play as a symbol of Hedda's freedom of will and revolt against her present situation. Lovborg botches the job and Hedda, because of her part in his death, is threatened with subjection to the cunning Judge Brack. At last Hedda asserts her will and kills herself with the remaining dueling pistol.

The emphasis upon symbols and irrational forces in the plays beginning with *The Wild Duck* does not constitute a sharp break with past practice, for all of Ibsen's plays after *Pillars of Society* share many common qualities. All are set within a realistic framework and are given detailed environments; all use a late point of attack, careful preparation, the logical ordering of events, and prose dialogue. Even the illogical elements in the later plays may be viewed as partially realistic, for they are never presented as actually existing forces but only as perceptions by the characters—in other words, they may be merely figments of the characters' imaginations. Similarly, even the most realistic plays make considerable use of symbolism. *Ghosts,* for many critics the epitome of realistic drama, uses symbols as complex as those in most of the later works. For example, the burning of the orphanage, on one level a completely realistic event, is highly symbolic, for it shows the impossibility of covering up the past. The titles of Ibsen's plays are in themselves symbolic, suggesting as they do the deeper meaning to be found beneath the realistic surfaces. Similarly, this symbolic element connects even the realistic prose works with Ibsen's early poetic dramas, for though he gave up writing in verse, he never gave up his search for equivalent means of expression. Through symbolism and the careful juxtaposition of contrasting elements, he was able to imply relationships among seemingly unlike objects and behavior so as to enlarge metaphorically the range of suggestion, association, and meaning and thus create a new type of "poetry" through strictly controlled prose diction.

The mystical element is especially prominent in Ibsen's last works, *The Master Builder* (1892), *Little Eyolf* (1894), *John Gabriel Borkman* (1896), and *When We Dead Awaken* (1899), sometimes called the "visionary" plays. They were to be as powerful influences on the nonrealistic drama of the 1890s as the plays of the 1870s and 1880s were on realistic works.

The Master Builder combines the internal subtleties of *Brand* with the external features of *Ghosts* and thus synthesizes the two earlier strands of his work. Its central figure is the aging "master builder," Halvard Solness, who has risen from humble beginnings to preeminence in his field. He recognizes that his young assistant Ragnar considers himself worthy to replace him and uses several devices to suppress Ragnar's talent. Solness realizes that he has paid dearly for his success, not only with his own happiness but with that of others, particularly that of his wife, Aline. His success has been made possible in part by the destruction of his wife's family home by fire. To Aline the loss is so great that she becomes ill and while she is incapacitated, her children die. Aline, who, according to Solness, was meant to build human beings just as he was meant to build houses, is now little more than a living corpse. Solness has come to believe that "the troll within him" unconsciously willed the fire and that he is responsible for his wife's condition.

This is the situation when the play opens. Then, Hilda Wangel, a charming and mysterious young woman, arrives and reminds Solness that ten years earlier, when she was only thirteen, he had promised to come and take her away. Since he did not come she has arrived to collect "either my kingdom or your life." She and Solness have much in common and she plays upon his pride in his work. She urges him to regain once more the spirit she knew when he climbed to the top of a church steeple to crown with a wreath his completed work. When Solness says that he no longer builds churches but homes for human beings, she urges him to return to the heights. Solness has added a spire to the house which he is just completing for his wife and when it is finished Hilda persuades him to crown it. As she stands below waving, he falls to his death. Hilda ecstatically cries out, "My—my Master Builder."

On the literal level, the play is the story of an aging man who falls in love with a young girl and, in attempting to prove his virility, dies. This level of the play is developed much as is the story in *Ghosts*. But the symbolic level is extremely complex and not always clear. The deeper inner drama concerns Solness's despair over his sense of guilt—over his "sickly conscience," as he puts it. On the realistic level, Hilda is a beautiful, spirited, and charming young woman, but on the symbolic level she is a kind of spirit who weaves her way into Solness's confidence and leads him to retribution. She appears to represent some higher authority.

Underneath both the symbolism and the realism, Ibsen pursues the same questions that lie behind practically all of his dramas: How can a man retain his own integrity without destroying the happiness of others? How can one be true to oneself and to others simultaneously? It is possible to achieve any worthwhile goal without trampling underfoot other human beings? Does success always become mere sackcloth and ashes because it must be won by sacrificing others? In *Ghosts,* the forces at work seem to be entirely those of heredity and environment, but in *The Master Builder* supernatural elements are introduced. Both Solness and Hilda speak of the "trolls" within them, and Solness sees himself at war with God, who he says has decreed his success and has taken away his children and his wife's love so that nothing can distract him from building churches; but Solness has defied God, and has turned to building homes for men. His final act, the crowning of a human dwelling, is perhaps the act of supreme defiance and one for which he is punished. Although the supernatural forces may be only figments of Solness's mind, in the drama they are active powers. Thus, *The Master Builder* depicts human destiny as far more complex than does *Ghosts.*

In Ibsen's last three works these mysterious forces are further extended, reaching a peak in his final play, *When We Dead Awaken* (1899), Ibsen's most symbolic and puzzling drama. In it, Arnold Rubek, a world-famous sculptor, feels his powers gone. In a sanitarium where he has come to rest, he encounters Irene, who years before posed for the work that made him famous. Irene believes that she has been spiritually dead since the moment when Rubek rejected her love. Rubek sees in her the possibility of his own artistic resurrection, but Irene tells him, "There is no resurrection. . . . When we dead awaken we realize that we have never lived." Rubek is determined to disprove her statement, and with Irene, he sets out to climb a mountain, only to be swallowed up by an avalanche. But in physical death they experience a spiritual release from the pains of a living death.

Shortly after completing *When We Dead Awaken,* Ibsen suffered a stroke from which he never fully recovered. He lived for another six years, but never wrote again. He died in May 1906, aged seventy-eight, honored the world over as the principal architect of modern drama.

No dramatist since Ibsen has exerted so wide an influence, perhaps because his work contained so many seeds later cultivated by others. Above all, it was his realistic strain that was admired. In the early years he was usually evaluated in one of two ways: as a writer whose works are exercises in moral persuasion (a view championed by George Bernard Shaw), or as a writer whose ideas are worthless (or commonplace) but whose technical skill is immense. In both cases, the plays of the 1870s and 1880s were considered to represent the "real Ibsen" while both the early and late plays were viewed as aberrant. It was probably for this reason that for a time in the twentieth century, Ibsen came to seem old-fashioned, for the social problems about which he wrote were no longer relevant.

But Ibsen's realistic plays make up only about one-quarter of his total output, and even they are not entirely realistic. All of Ibsen's plays are filled with ambiguities which suggest a multitude of interpretations. It is perhaps this which made Ibsen's works so attractive to the symbolists and other nonrealistic writers. The late plays, especially, suggest that human destiny is influenced by forces which extend beyond heredity and environment and that the analysis and control foreseen by the naturalists were doomed to failure because they were based on a too-restricted view of causality. Today Ibsen is valued for his deep psychological insights, his symbolism, his concealed poetry, and his great technical mastery. But perhaps Ibsen's greatest influence has stemmed from his unflinching belief that drama is a medium of serious ideas and a search for truth. Ibsen was always concerned with the bases of human happiness and insisted upon cutting through taboos and hypocrisies. Even if he did not find the answers he sought, he insisted upon asking the questions, often those most embarrassing and disturbing. To him, drama was not merely entertainment but a confrontation with human problems. The stylistic modes in which he presented confrontation varied, but both the modes and the questions were to shape the avant-garde in drama for many years to come.

~ **II** ~

While Ibsen was writing his realistic works, a new movement—usually called naturalism—was underway in France. Far less productive in significant plays than was Ibsen, it was much more self-conscious about the theoretical bases of drama. The primary spokesman for naturalism was Émile Zola (1840–1902), disciple of Comte and advocate of a scientific and useful art.

Although Zola's main interest lay in the novel, he sought to reform the theatre, which he declared to be fifty years behind the novel. To Zola the theatre seemed a victim of worn-out conventions—the "last citadel of falsehood." In the prefaces to his plays (particularly that to *Thérèse Raquin*) and in his essays (collected in 1881 under the title *Naturalism in the Theatre*), Zola declared the traditional theatre an exemplar of untruth, an institution dying of pomposity, unreality, and platitudes. He proclaimed: "Either the theatre will die or it will become modern and naturalistic." Zola did not conceive of naturalism as one movement coexisting with others, but rather as an all-embracing attitude to which every art must submit or perish.

For Zola, the enemy was not romanticism but the well-made play as practiced by Scribe, Sardou, Augier, and Dumas *fils*. He objected strenuously to the traditional arrangement of exposition, intrigue, complications, and satisfying resolution. He also objected to the typical treatment of the protagonist in the well-made play, since it led to the distortion of psychology in order to create sympathy and to reward the character at the end of the play.

Zola's ideas about the proper approach to art were heavily influenced by Claude Bernard's *Introduction to Experimental Medicine* (1865), a study of the effects of environment on the functioning of the bodily organs and of changes in body chemistry upon behavior. In *The Experimental Novel* (1881), Zola sought to apply Bernard's method to literature. He compared the writer to the doctor, who seeks the causes of a disease so that it may be cured, not glossing over infection but bringing it out into the open where it can be examined. Similarly, the writer should seek out social ills and reveal them so that they may be corrected. It was probably this analogy between pathology and art that led the naturalists so often to choose subjects from the more debased aspects of human behavior. It also led Zola to demand that the writer be as objective as the scientist: "There should not be any school or formula anymore; there is only life itself, a great field where each may study and create as he wishes."

Nevertheless, Zola recognized that subjectivity is inevitable. He once defined art as "a corner of life seen through a temperament," by which he probably meant that the artist's own personality dictates in large part what subjects he chooses to treat. But Zola does not allow subjectivity much scope. For him, the subject and characters represent something akin to the scientific hypothesis; once established, they should be permitted to interact according to "the inevitable laws of heredity and environment," and the results should demonstrate the truth of scientific observation. It is only fair to point out, however, that Zola always admired the simplicity of French classical drama, especially that of Racine, and that he emphasized elemental forces both within man and in nature. Thus, his three primary requirements for literature were truth, simplicity, and grandeur (the last to be achieved through an inevitability not unlike the concept of Fate in Greek and French classical tragedy). He advocated a type of play that would avoid the involved complications and startling reversals typical of nineteenth-century drama and that would depict with utter simplicity human beings caught in the coils of fate (or overpowering hereditary and environmental forces).

It was in the techniques then being used by dramatists that Zola saw the greatest danger to truth, for they tended to distort life for the sake of theatrical effect: "The word *art* displeases me: it contains I do not know what ideas of necessary arrangement." Because truth was for Zola something which is discoverable only through the scientific method, he demanded that art must work analogously. His knowledge of life told him that truth is not revealed in a series of complications leading to crisis and resolution, but in a more haphazard collection of events which create a texture and sense of direction. Thus, in the name of truth, he suggested that a play should be "a fragment of existence" without apparent beginning, middle, or end: "Instead of imagining an adventure, complicating it, preparing stage surprises, which from scene to scene will bring it to a final conclusion, one simply takes from life the history of a being, or of a group of beings, whose acts one faithfully records." By couching his literary demands in scientific terms, however, Zola seemed to suggest that the distinctions between art and science should be obliterated. Ultimately, it was probably the innate contradiction of a "scientific art" that brought naturalism into bad repute.

The application of naturalistic theory to literature had many results. The emphasis upon heredity and environment made of man a victim of forces beyond his control; even his "will" became merely an impulse dictated by background and experience. The naturalist eschewed any concern for beauty, and to establish his emancipation from the tendency to idealize he concentrated on man in the throes of avarice, lust, fear, and anger. Still, he sought to avoid passing judgment on the behavior he presented, arguing that he merely recorded social conditions. Nevertheless, his work, despite claims of objectivity, always implied criticism, for seldom could he mask his conviction that vice, crime, infidelity, and other social ills required that changes be made in society.

Despite its often pessimistic view of human behavior, naturalism as a movement tended to be optimistic, for its ultimate aim was the improvement of society, a goal which most naturalists considered feasible. By altering environment, man would ultimately be improved, and art, because of its effectiveness as persuasion, was considered a powerful tool for disseminating truth that would lead to the betterment of mankind.

Many demands made by the naturalists seem excessive for a play of normal length. But Zola thought the theatre well suited to naturalism if properly applied. He argued that descriptive passages in novels could be eliminated in drama because settings, costumes, properties, and stage business constitute "a continual description more exact and more striking than the descriptions of any novel." Spectacle provides a visible environment which illuminates character and action: ". . . scenery is, in short, the surroundings where the characters are born, live, and die."

Nevertheless, naturalism made its greatest impact on the novel, perhaps necessarily so, since it was much more compatible with the novel than with the drama. In the novel the hereditary and environmental factors which influence behavior can be explored at much greater length than on the stage, where time and scope are limited. Furthermore the novelist may develop his subject as he sees fit without having to depend upon other artists, perhaps not wholly sympathetic ones, to complete his work.

Naturalistic tendencies had been evident in the French novel since early in the nineteenth century. Honoré de Balzac (1799–1850), in a series of novels published under the collective title *The Human Comedy,* had treated man's limitations, aspirations, and struggles with societal and hereditary forces; Stendhal (1783–1842) had combined intensive psychological portraiture with keen observation of social and political forces in such novels as *The Red and the Black* (1831) and *The Charterhouse of Parma* (1839); Gustave Flaubert (1821–80) had provided microscopic analyses of contemporary life in such novels as *Madame Bovary* (1857) and *Sentimental Education* (1869); and the brothers Goncourt—Edmond (1822–96) and Jules (1830–70)—had brought the true scientific spirit to the novel with their near-clinical studies of pathological cases, as in *Renée Mauperin* (1864). It was upon this tradition that Zola built. Somewhat in the manner of Balzac, he wrote a cycle of twenty novels, *The Rougon-Macquarts,* in which he traced the history of a single family over a long period of time and created a startlingly detailed picture of nineteenth-century life.

As in the novel, several tentative attempts at naturalism in drama had been made prior to Zola's efforts. Balzac had tried his hand in two works, *The Stepmother* (1848) and *Mercadet* (1851), both cited by Zola as good beginnings. Nevertheless, *The Stepmother* seems little more than a melodrama. It tells of a woman who has married an old man so that she may acquire his money and then marry a younger one. But when the lover begins to prefer the stepdaughter, the two women fight for him with drugs, poison, stolen letters, and threats of blackmail. The daughter finally commits suicide by taking a poison known to have been in the possession of her stepmother. Accused of murder, the older woman is about to be arrested when the daughter arouses herself enough to exonerate her. The old man is on the verge of insanity as the curtain falls. Although the events are exaggerated, the setting is modern, there is no sympathetic character or *raisonneur,* and all the agents are drawn with crude power. The Goncourts also tried their hands at playwriting with *Henriette Maréchal* (1863), a failure, and *The Country in Danger* (1873), for which no producer could be found until 1889. *The Revolt* (1870) by Villiers de l'Isle Adam anticipated the situation developed more skillfully by Ibsen in *A Doll's House,* and Alphonse Daudet's *L'Arlesienne* (1872) treated a peasant who loves a young girl so much that when she comes to prefer a jockey he commits suicide. None of these plays, however, made a great impression.

In assessing the progress already made toward naturalism, Zola also praised Dumas *fils* for his treatment of social problems but declared that in his works the preacher had killed the observer. He admired Sardou for his minute recreations of specific milieus, but labeled his subjects and techniques false. Since no one had taken all the steps required to create a naturalistic drama, Zola himself sought to fill the need, and his dramatization of his own novel *Thérèse Raquin* became the first important landmark in naturalist drama. Produced in 1873, it received a chilly reception from both critics and audiences and was withdrawn after nine performances.

Thérèse Raquin is not the loosely structured "fragment of existence" that Zola champions in his theoretical essays. Part of the problem may be explained by the necessity of reducing a novel to stage length, for what in the original seems to develop leisurely and naturally has in the drama become hasty and melodramatic. The first act shows the environment—the world of lower-middle-class shopkeepers—in which Thérèse lives with her husband, the sickly Camille Raquin, and his mother. Life has been tolerable until Thérèse falls in love with Laurent, a painter friend of Camille. When the second act opens, Thérèse and Laurent have murdered Camille during a boating excursion on the Seine and made it appear an accident. In the third act, the lovers are married with the blessing of Mme. Raquin, with whom they will live. Not until their wedding night does the cold-bloodedness of their deed strike them. Their mutual recriminations are overheard by Mme. Raquin, who suffers a paralytic stroke. Throughout the fourth act she glares at them as they go about their barely tolerable lives. In the fifth act, the old woman regains the use of one hand and after beginning to write out a message on the kitchen table suddenly stops. Near the end of the play she regains her speech and says to Thérèse and Laurent: "I want to watch you pay for your crime . . . in this room where you robbed me of my happiness. I want to watch remorse tearing you like beasts." Thérèse and Laurent, now hating each other, take poison and die at the old woman's feet.

Zola has managed to rid his play of much that is typical of works by Dumas *fils*. No problem is presented; there is no *raisonneur* or even a sympathetic role. The characters are neither glamorous nor villainous. Still, the chief fault lies in the characterizations, for neither Thérèse nor Laurent seems capable of planning or executing a murder, especially one done in cold blood rather than in a moment of passion. The play also abounds in coincidences and contrivances not unlike those typical of melodrama. For example, Mme. Raquin enters at just the right moment to overhear Thérèse and Laurent admit their guilt and her stroke keeps her from revealing her knowledge; her recovery also seems contrived for theatrical effect. The play plods along in the same key most of the way, providing little variety. The poetic justice of the ending is scarcely what one would expect from an author who decried conventional resolutions. His own claim—"the denouement was the mathematical result of the proposed problem"—is clearly exaggerated. Zola is most successful in creating an environment—a lower-middle-class room that serves as bedroom, parlor, and kitchen. Hung with drab wallpaper and cluttered with cardboard

Production of the adaptation of Zola's novel *The Dram Shop,*
at the Porte-Saint-Martin, Paris, in 1900. Despite the naturalistic detail,
note that much of the setting is painted rather than three-dimensional.
(From *Le Théâtre,* 1900.)

haberdasher's boxes, it was, according to Zola, "a setting in perfect accord with the occupations" of the characters, one in which "they might not play but *live*."

In addition to *Thérèse Raquin,* Zola wrote four other plays: *Madeleine,* a short drama composed in 1865 but not produced until 1889 and then for a single performance; *The Rabourdin Heirs,* a satirical farce inspired by Jonson's *Volpone* and given seventeen performances in 1874; *The Red Button,* a play without any trace either of satire or of social purpose, performed seven times in 1878; and *Renée,* based on the second volume of his Rougon-Macquart series and performed thirty-eight times in 1887. In addition, a number of his novels and short stories were adapted for the stage. The best of these are the five attributed to William Busnach (although Zola seems to have taken an unacknowledged hand in the work). Especially noteworthy are *The Dram Shop* (which ran for 300 performances in 1879–80) and *Nana* (given 100 times in 1881). A number of other adaptations were made without Zola's cooperation. These include Léon Hennique's version of a short story, *Jacques Damour* (1887), and Raoul de Saint-Arroman and Charles Hugot's adaptation of the novel *Earth* (1902). For the most part, however, both Zola's own plays and the adaptations made by others are characterized by melodramatic action and inadequate characterizations. Consequently, they are almost always inconsistent with Zola's expressed ideals. Their primary contributions were made through spectacle—the painstaking recreation of specific environments.

Thus, by the 1880s, it was clear that, while Zola might provide leadership as a critic, effective drama would have to come from another source. Nevertheless, Zola remained naturalism's strongest advocate, so much so that even today it is impossible to discuss the movement without thinking first of him.

～ III ～

Ironically, it was Henri Becque (1837–99), always contemptuous of Zola, who raised naturalistic drama in France to its peak. Perhaps because he refused to align himself with the movement, his achievement is often overlooked. Becque's output was small—six full-length plays and approximately the same number of short pieces—and even then only two of his works can be considered significant. He began his career conventionally enough with the libretto for an opera, *Sardanapole* (1867), and a vaudeville, *The Prodigal Son* (1868). His first serious drama, *Michel Pauper* (1870), was a strange mixture of passionate romanticism with occasional sprinklings of brutal realism. It concerns an inventor who has discovered a means of crystallizing diamonds from coal. Throughout the play, he is tortured by the deceit of his wife. At the conclusion, as he lies dying, his repentant wife returns; Michel, believing that she intends to steal his secret, leaves his bed to protect his treasure and dies at her feet. The play was a distressing failure on the stage.

A year later, Becque experienced another setback with *The Emancipation,* a thesis play somewhat in the manner of Dumas *fils.* The heroine, Emma, retires to the country to escape the brutality of her husband and there falls in love with de la Rouvre, a man whose marital life has been as unhappy as her own. Emma's husband arrives with a mistress, who turns out to be the former wife of de la Rouvre. Emma decides to divorce her husband and marry de la Rouvre, not because, like Ibsen's Nora, she is exerting her independence, but because she can no longer endure the tortures of the brute to whom she is married.

Becque was much embittered by his failures and gave up writing for a time. His next play, however, was to be his masterpiece—*The Vultures,* produced by the Comédie Française in 1882 after having been refused by practically every other theatre in Paris. That this conservative group should have accepted the play is surprising, but it may be explained by its belief that Becque would revise the play as requested. Certainly he was pressed to change the work, and the play probably suffered in production because of the troupe's dissatisfaction with the script. It was given only three performances by them.

The Vultures shows few traces of the well-made play. The first act serves as a kind of prologue, for here the characters and environment are

Scene from Becque's *The Vultures,* as it was produced in 1903 at the Kleines Theater, Berlin. (From Deutsche Akademie der Künste zu Berlin.)

presented with scarcely a hint of what is to come; it provides preparation but no foreshadowing. This is the analytical method, thoroughly developed by novelists prior to this time, in which environment and characters, out of which everything else grows, are established without emphasizing story.

The first act of *The Vultures* shows the prosperous and happy Vigneron family: the father, a man who has made his way in the world; his wife; and his four children, Blanche (engaged to a man of good family), Judith (who studies music and is much flattered by her teacher), Marie (the most intelligent of the three daughters), and Gaston (the overindulged son). Several persons arrive for a party: Mme. de Saint-Genis and her son (engaged to Blanche), Merckens (Judith's music teacher), Teissier (Vigneron's business partner), and Bourdon (Vigneron's lawyer). In the midst of the party, a doctor enters and announces that Vigneron, who has been called away earlier, has died of a stroke. Becque has done nothing to prepare the audience for this occurrence; as in life, death has come without warning.

The remainder of the play shows the effects of this death on the family, especially as the "vultures" begin to prey upon them. Teissier and Bourdon connive in order to get as much of the fortune for themselves as possible; the young music teacher, Merckens, laughs at Judith when she suggests that she might teach music to support the family; Mme. de Saint-Genis breaks off her son's engagement to Blanche, even though she knows that Blanche is pregnant by him; Gaston joins the army rather than face up to his family's problems.

Ultimately Marie sacrifices her happiness to save her sisters and mother. Teissier, at least forty years her senior, proposes at first that she become his mistress and, when she refuses, his wife. She accepts. Ironically, Bourdon now connives with the family against Teissier to see that half of the old man's fortune is settled on Marie. There is no denouement in the conventional sense. The last episode shows a creditor trying to collect a debt already paid. Teissier, after exposing him, remarks to Marie: "You have been surrounded by rascals since your father's death." Here is Darwin's law of "survival of the fittest" worked out in dramatic form: at first it is the family who is preyed upon by those most fit (Teissier, Bourdon, and others); in the end it is the young girl Marie who, now the fittest, preys upon the old man Teissier to allow her family to survive.

Becque's victims awaken sympathy but are not drawn sentimentally. With the exception of Marie, all are too naïve to cope with the world, and the sympathetic hero is conspicuously absent. The "vultures" are not villainous so much as merely lacking in compassion. They believe it their duty to look after their own interests. The ending is neither sentimental nor grandly tragic. It is unobtrusive, especially when compared with those of Dumas *fils* or Sardou. The overall effect is pessimistic. *The Vultures* was not revived until 1897 and even then provoked protests against its frankness and cynicism.

Becque's next play, *The Woman of Paris* (1885), is a mordant comedy of worldly individuals who have accepted as a matter of course the materialistic values of the society in which they live. The opening scene sets the tone. It shows a woman arguing with a man, who in typical husbandly fashion is accusing her of being unfaithful to him. At the climax of the

Becque's *La Parisienne* at the Théâtre Antoine in 1904. Réjane, at center, played Clotilde, while Antoine, at right, played La Font. (From *Le Théâtre,* 1904.)

argument, she cautions him, "Take care, here comes my husband." DuMesnil, the husband, is entirely happy and, if aware of Clotilde's infidelity, chooses not to notice it. Her lover, Lafont, is an accepted part of the household and DuMesnil's close friend. He occupies Clotilde's time and permits DuMesnil to devote himself to writing books on the political economy of France. Clotilde is a frivolous, extravagant, amoral young society woman who sins with complete freedom of conscience.

As the play develops, it becomes clear that Clotilde is being untrue to Lafont. She has calculatingly entered into an affair with Simpson, whose political influence can gain DuMesnil the appointment in the Ministry of Finance that he so desires. In the final act, the appointment has been gained, Simpson and Clotilde have broken off, and Lafont has returned to the household. The happiness and smooth relationships of the opening act are reestablished. Since there has been no crisis, there is no need for resolution. There is no moment of reproof for Clotilde. She is treated neither as heroine nor as villain, merely as the amoral product of her environment. Overall, it is a strong comment on the society of the time, but this conclusion must be reached by the audience, for it is not emphasized within the play either by a *raisonneur* or by any other character. A situation is presented, but not commented upon. It is a true "fragment of existence" presented dispassionately.

Unfortunately, *The Woman of Paris* was Becque's last work of any importance. He worked for fourteen years on a long play, *The Puppets,* a sequel to *The Vultures,* concerned with the Parisian world of finance, but eventually lost interest in it and declined to complete it. Thus, Becque's contributions were virtually over by 1885.

Although Zola looked everywhere for a dramatist who could achieve in the theatre what Balzac and Flaubert had in the novel, he never suggested Becque. Of this slight, Becque remarked, "The dog barks, and the caravan passes." There were two major areas of disagreement between Zola and Becque. In his *Souvenirs,* Becque speaks of drama as "the art of elimination." In this he recognized what Zola never fully grasped: that art is by nature selective, even when it seeks to create the impression of photographic reality. For Becque, elimination meant reducing a work to absolute essentials. Not a speech or moment should be superfluous. Every element must contribute to the effect of vivid life, yet nothing should remain which does not contribute vitally to the whole. Zola suggests that there is no real difference between what happens in life and what should be put on the stage. Becque insisted upon a distinction. He saw the dramatist's task as that of concealing selection while enhancing the illusion that there has been no selection—that reality is being presented whole.

The second point of disagreement grows out of the first. Zola made scenic environment significant. None of Becque's settings acts as an environment. They are the traditional salons of Dumas *fils* and Augier—a door at the rear and two side entrances. Perhaps this is so because Becque concentrated on the upper middle class rather than, as was typical of the naturalists, the lower classes.

But if Zola did not recognize Becque's importance, the second wave of naturalists did. Those dramatists who came to the fore after Antoine offered them a home in 1887 tended to honor Becque along with Zola. But in the 1880s, naturalism in drama remained for Zola a still-to-be-realized ideal, while Becque, frustrated by his failure to win recognition, ceased to be productive.

～ IV ～

If Ibsen and the French naturalists were the major innovators in the 1870s and 1880s, others were also contributing to the new ideal. Among these the most important was the Swedish playwright August Strindberg (1849–1912), for ultimately his overall influence on modern drama was to be second only to that of Ibsen. Like Ibsen's, Strindberg's career may be divided into several stages—historical-romantic, realistic-naturalistic, and visionary-expressionistic. Strindberg began writing plays about 1870 and for the next dozen years treated subjects drawn primarily from Swedish history, as in *The Freethinker* (1870), *Master Olaf* (1872), *The Secret of the Guild* (1880), and *Sir Bengt's Wife* (1882). But it was with his realistic plays that Strindberg won his first wide fame.

Although a number of realistic traits can be discerned in Strindberg's work from the beginning, they did not become dominant until the late 1880s. In this transition one crucial influence was Zola's essays, with which Strindberg became familiar as early as 1883. Strindberg seems to have had Zola's theories clearly in mind when he wrote his major realistic-naturalistic

Strindberg's *Comrades,* produced by the author himself at the Intimate Theatre, Stockholm, in 1910. (From Drottningholms Teatermuseum.)

works: *The Father* (1887), *Miss Julie* (1888), *Comrades* (1888), and *Creditors* (1888). In a letter about *The Father*, Strindberg declared: "The young Frenchmen are still trying to find the formula, but I have found it."

The Father was also provoked in part by Ibsen's plays. Strindberg thought *A Doll's House* advocated feminism and exalted women, creatures he considered to be man's enemy, ones from whom he could not escape and with whom he was forever trapped in a love-hate relationship. He saw *Ghosts* as an attack on Captain Alving, who could no longer defend himself from his wife's accusations. In his own play, he presented a side of the story not told by Nora and Mrs. Alving.

In *The Father,* the Captain (he is given no other name) struggles with his wife, Laura, over the upbringing of their only child, a daughter. Just as he is about to win the argument by insisting upon his legal right to make decisions, the Captain is stopped by his wife's hints that he may not be the child's father. Thereafter Laura gradually and deliberately isolates him from others by insinuating that he is losing his mind. Furthermore, she provokes him into throwing a lighted lamp at her, an act which she uses to support her allegations. Eventually the broken Captain is put into a strait-jacket by his old and trusted nurse as she croons to him comfortingly (thus demonstrating still further the duplicity of women).

In many respects *The Father* falls far short of the naturalistic ideal. For example, it is severely lacking in objectivity, since it so clearly seeks to arouse sympathy for the Captain and antipathy for the female characters. Furthermore, there is almost no concern for heredity and environment, for what the characters do is not explained by their pasts and the setting is almost irrelevant. Nevertheless, it is linked to the naturalistic movement in other ways. For example, it fulfills Zola's demand for straightforwardness and simplicity, for it makes little use of the characteristic devices of the well-made play. (In this respect, it parallels Becque's *The Vultures*.) Furthermore, a sense of fate is achieved through characters who are engaged in the Darwinian struggle for the "survival of the fittest."

The Father demonstrates clearly the major difference between the naturalism of Zola and that of Strindberg: a divergence in the scientific interests which provide the focus for their works. Zola's methods are derived from Bernard's *Introduction to Experimental Medicine* and may be summarized as a concern for the power of external and physical forces over human behavior, whereas Strindberg was most influenced by inquiries being made by Charcot and Bernheim into hypnotism and the power of suggestion and thus his concerns are summed up in the interplay of minds in a struggle for dominance. In "The Battle of the Brains," an essay published in 1887, Strindberg states: "Dr. Charcot assumes the possibility of suggestion only in hypnotized hysterics; Dr. Bernheim goes somewhat further and admits that all who may be hypnotized are susceptible to suggested ideas. . . . I seem to have found that suggestion is only the stronger brain's struggle with and victory over the weak and that this procedure is applied unconsciously in everyday life. . . . " In another essay published at the same time, "Psychic Murder," Strindberg adds: "The struggle for power has, from being purely physical (prison, torture, death), gradually developed into a more psychological battle, but a no less cruel one. . . ." Thus, both Zola and Strindberg thought their work to be grounded in the scientific experiments of the day but they differed markedly in their choice of subjects. Consequently, Zola's works have a more realistic surface, whereas Strindberg's, poised as they are on the edge of irrationality, often seem to depart considerably from the naturalist ideal.

The Father dramatizes the conditions described in Strindberg's two essays, for the characters embody the struggle for dominance and survival, while Laura uses suggestion as her major psychological weapon in her successful attempt to destroy her husband. As a result, the characters seem more nearly personifications of principles than of individuals. It is not surprising, therefore, that Zola did not quite approve of the play, even though he supplied a preface when the play was published in France in 1888. Though he acknowledged the play's power, he found the characters insufficiently grounded in their milieu.

Perhaps it was this verdict which made Strindberg seek in his next play, *Miss Julie,* to adhere more closely to Zola's ideas. Like *The Father, Miss Julie* dramatizes the struggle between two wills, but it also develops complex characters who have been shaped by multiple hereditary and environmental forces. Miss Julie, the daughter of a declining aristocrat and a man-hating mother, vacillates between masculine assertiveness and feminine flirtatiousness and eventually allows herself to be seduced by the butler, Jean, with whom she then plans to run away after robbing her father. But when the count unexpectedly returns, Jean quickly reverts to subservience and, no longer able to act himself, he declares that the only path open to Julie is suicide. Now under the power of Jean's suggestions, Miss Julie in a trancelike state does as she is told. The action is loosely organized, complex, and seemingly spontaneous; the blunt dialogue has the quality of everyday speech. *Miss Julie* more nearly fulfills the naturalist ideal than do any of Zola's own plays.

In the preface to this play, Strindberg also set down his ideas about stage presentation. He declares his preference for a small stage and a small auditorium so that exaggeration may be avoided; he asks that foot-lights be abolished since they cast unnatural shadows on the actors' faces; he requests actors to use less makeup than is usual; and, while recognizing the unlikelihood that actors of his day will play scenes with their backs to the audience, he begs them at least not to play every crucial scene downstage center. He adds: "To make a real room on the stage, with the fourth wall missing, and a part of the furniture placed back towards the audience, would probably produce a disturbing effect at present." In the stage directions for the play, Strindberg requests that the rear wall be placed diagonally and demands that all furnishings and properties (including pots and pans) of his kitchen setting be real and that none be painted on the walls. He also replaces the usual act breaks with pantomimes, dances, and monologues, so that the action may be continuous and the effect cumulative.

Strindberg's next play, *Creditors,* resembles *The Father* in its treatment of characters and setting (since heredity and environment are unimportant) and *Miss Julie* in its concentrated form. Like both of the earlier plays, it dramatizes the struggle for dominance and the battle of the sexes, and it demonstrates the power of suggestion. There are only three characters—Tekla, Gustav (her first husband), and Adolf (her present husband)—and three scenes—the first between Gustav and Adolf, the second between Adolf and Tekla, and the final one between Gustav and Tekla. Gustav has come to see that Tekla is a vampirish creature who destroys her victims after she has absorbed their substance and he decides to make her repay the psychological debts she owes. This he does by gaining dominance over Adolf's will and leaving Tekla deserted.

In both *Miss Julie* and *Creditors,* Strindberg uses an abbreviated form. This brevity becomes even more extreme in the three short plays which he wrote in 1888–89: *Pariah, The Stronger,* and *Simoom.* In these "quarter of an hour" plays the action is reduced to a single scene. The best known is *The Stronger,* in which only one of the two characters speaks. Nevertheless, in her monologue Mrs. X manages to convey an enormous amount of psychological information which shows how she, by adapting to circumstances, has been able to defeat the other woman, Mlle. Y, an actress, who has believed herself the stronger because of her relationship with Mrs. X's husband. Again the conflict is essentially one of wills in a struggle for power.

In 1892, Strindberg wrote six long one-act dramas which he later grouped together under the common title "Plays from Cynical Life": *Debit and Credit, The First Warning, Playing with Fire, Mother Love, Before Death,* and *The Bond,* all of which show some indebtedness to naturalism. Of these perhaps the best is *The Bond,* based in part on Strindberg's own divorce proceedings of 1891. Set in the carefully re-created milieu of the courtroom, it at first establishes a tone of complete objectivity but soon passes over into partisan defense of the male. Eventually, however, the wife is shown to be a victim of forces beyond her control and to that degree is exonerated. The title refers to that tie—a child—which prevents the husband and wife from ever being completely separated so that they are doomed to remain bound together in a love-hate relationship.

By the time these plays were written, however, Strindberg had already begun to lose interest in naturalism. As early as 1889—in his essay "On Modern Drama and Modern Theatre"—he had contrasted the "great naturalism" of Zola with the "small naturalism" of Becque, whose *The Vultures* he denounced for its photographic realism: "This is the objective which is so beloved by those who lack subjectivity, by those devoid of temperament, the soulless, as they shall be called." Thus, it is not surprising that he, with his compelling interests in internal impulses which border on the irrational,

should eventually turn away from naturalism altogether. In the mid-1890s
many circumstances, not the least of which was a bout with insanity,
forced Strindberg to give up writing plays for a time. When he resumed,
his work took an entirely new direction—toward expressionism—one which
was to have a pervasive influence on the modern theatre. But even this
new direction is foreshadowed by the psychological elements in his realistic
plays. As Strindberg himself stated: "To me falls the task of bridging the
gap between naturalism and supra-naturalism by proclaiming that the
latter is only a development of the former." Nevertheless, prior to 1900,
his work served primarily to strengthen the trends begun by Ibsen and Zola.

Two other writers—Bjornson and Anzengruber—deserve mention, for
though today they have faded into obscurity, at one time they were considered among the foremost dramatists of their day and major contributors
to the new school of writing.

Bjornstjerne Bjornson (1832–1910) was Ibsen's closest rival in Norway
and throughout most of his life a respected friend. Bjornson was as outgoing
as Ibsen was retiring. Probably for this reason, he was more readily accepted
by his countrymen and was often lauded at Ibsen's expense. In fact,
Bjornson often seemed to succeed where Ibsen so clearly failed. It was
under the former's management in 1865 that the Christiania Theatre
entered a period of great productivity as a Norwegian institution after the
Christiania Norwegian Theatre had gone bankrupt under Ibsen's leadership. As a playwright, Bjornson's work paralleled and in many instances
anticipated Ibsen's. Probably because of his essential optimism, however, he
failed to develop significantly and his drama eventually suffered. Nevertheless, during the last part of the nineteenth century, Bjornson was
considered by many Ibsen's equal or superior as a playwright.

Like Ibsen, Bjornson began writing plays based on Norwegian history,
sagas, and legends. These early works include *Between the Battles* (1857),
King Sverre (1861), and *Sigurd the Bastard* (1862). In 1865, he turned
to the realistic vein, anticipating Ibsen by several years. In *The Newly
Married Couple* (1865), he treated, still in a light tone and with a happy
ending, the problem of a young man who finds that his life is being
encumbered by a wife who is unable to escape the childlike restrictions set
by her parents. While the play is resolved happily, it introduces the problem
that was to be treated more seriously by Ibsen in *A Doll's House.* Bjornson
returned to this realistic mode in 1874 with two plays, *The Editor,* in which
he lays bare the weaknesses of journalism in his day, and *A Bankruptcy,*
in which he attacks dishonest contemporary commercial practices.

Bjornson's most controversial play, *The Gauntlet* (1883), like some of Ibsen's works, was considered too bold for production. It explores the problem of a double standard of morality. In it, Alfred Christensen has had an affair, but, while repentant, declares himself unwilling to pardon his fiancée, Svava Riis, were she in the same position. Horrified by this double standard, Svava is torn between her love for Alfred and her intellectual desire to break off the marriage. Her mother agrees with her view but suggests that social life would have to be abandoned altogether if it were widely adopted. Bjornson fails to provide any answer, but he poses a question that was coming increasingly to the fore in his day, as women began to rebel against subservience to men.

After his realistic period, Bjornson, like Ibsen, turned increasingly to mysticism. In Bjornson's case, man's relation to God became an important subject. *Beyond Human Might I* (1883) was the first of the new type. In it, Pastor Sang comes to believe that he has been given the power to work miracles and has much evidence to support his view. But his bedridden wife sets her will against his and, unable to cure her, he dies when he realizes how limited his power is. *Beyond Human Might II* (1895) uses four characters from the earlier play and explores problems relating to capital and labor, arguing against superstition and for rational planning. It goes beyond anything found in Ibsen's work in its inclusion of two abstract allegorical figures, Credo and Spera, who represent faith and hope for the future.

In his final years, Bjornson seems to have regretted much of the social change that had come about with greater freedom for women. In *Laboremus* (1901), he denounces in the central figure, Lydia, the kind of aggressive individualism for which she stands, while in *When the Vineyards Are in Blossom* (1909), he deplores the Ibsenian new woman by showing a middle-aged husband turning to a young woman for the love he has been denied by his emancipated wife.

Bjornson's play *Laboremus,* produced at the Berliner Theater in 1901. Note the great detail used to create the illusion of a real room.
(From *Le Théâtre,* 1902.)

A scene from Anzengruber's *The Farmer Forsworn,* written in 1871. This production took place in Vienna in 1892. (From Osterreichische Nationalbibliothek.)

If Bjornson no longer enjoys his former reputation, it is probably for good reasons. First, his treatment of subjects was more topical and local than was Ibsen's. His characters and situations, being less universal, do not wear well because they seem too deeply rooted in specific times and places. Second, Bjornson tended to view life too optimistically. For example, in *The Bankruptcy,* the character used to represent dishonesty in business is converted and espouses standards based on high ethical values. Even in his most controversial play, *The Gauntlet,* Bjornson does not take a position and leaves his audience to reach whatever conclusions it wishes. Ibsen refused his audiences this luxury and sought to make them face the implications of the situations. Bjornson lacked Ibsen's puritanism; he was always humane and forgiving, even when dealing with characters he disliked or situations he deplored. The qualities that encouraged nineteenth-century acceptance of Bjornson (his optimism and his willingness for audiences to retain their old standards) eventually made his work seem shallow in comparison with Ibsen's. Nevertheless, at the time he probably did more to gain acceptance for the new drama than did Ibsen, who tended to alienate rather than attract the popular audience.

The Austrian playwright Ludwig Anzengruber (1839–89) is of interest primarily for his use of peasant materials and dialect to create a kind of realism not found in the plays of his more famous contemporaries. Anzengruber probably came to write this type of play as a natural extension of his work as a strolling actor playing for rural and peasant audiences.

Many of Anzengruber's works are in the tradition of the Viennese folk play, making extensive use of music, rapid change of scene, and loose structure. But his more important plays are in the realistic vein. In *The*

Kirchfeld Priest (1870), he tells the story of a young idealistic minister who arouses the hostility of both dogmatic churchmen and local dignitaries. They use his employment of an attractive young girl as a servant to slander him and eventually to remove him from his church. Anzegruber's most famous play is *The Fourth Commandment* (1877), which shows youth downtrodden by their elders and held in sway by the biblical fourth commandment. Set in the city, the play treats moral decay in Viennese life in a manner which might please the most demanding of naturalists. Anzengruber enjoyed little reputation in his own lifetime, but when naturalism came to the fore in Germany after 1890, his plays were honored as significant forerunners of the movement.

VI

The years between 1870 and 1890, then, brought the first major contributions to modern drama. For the most part they fall into the realistic or naturalistic vein, although other styles were foreshadowed. But while modern drama was introduced, it did not gain full acceptance immediately. It was still very much the avant-garde, appreciated and supported by a few in the vanguard of taste, but more often deplored as depraved or undramatic by the masses. What most struck the popular mind was the seeming attack on traditional morality and standards of decency. No play epitomized so well for the public these supposed aims as did *Ghosts.* Along with a few naturalistic dramas, it seemed to many an attempt to lower the theatre to the level of pathology.

Despite the general disapproval of plays such as *Ghosts,* audiences in the 1880s were becoming more tolerant of works in the new vein, so long as they did not depart too drastically from accepted moral standards and did not treat subjects considered unfit for public discussion. As in most periods, the plays that were at first scorned gradually gained an audience as familiarity with the methods and aims of the new movement grew. For example, Daudet's *L'Arlesienne* was a complete failure when first produced in 1872. The public did not understand it and Daudet was advised by critics to confine himself to novels and short stories. When the play was revived in 1885, however, it was a marked success. That Becque's *The Vultures* was presented by the Comédie Française is also significant, even if the play was not well received.

Still, many plays could not be presented, for they were considered too immoral to be licensed. Among these was *Ghosts,* but it was by no means alone. Thus, some of the most significant new plays were denied a hearing. Furthermore, many of the plays that were presented did not fare well because they were produced as if they were romantic dramas and without regard for the special demands made by naturalism and realism. The new drama awaited the new producer. Avant-garde plays were to find their champion in André Antoine, and his Théâtre Libre was to show how previously taboo subjects could be presented for appreciative audiences. Through his work, significant new theatrical methods were to be meshed with significant new drama.

The Independent
Theatre
Movement

4

By the late 1880s both a new drama and new theatrical methods had emerged in Europe. The new drama was being performed only rarely, however, while the new theatrical methods were being applied for the most part to traditional plays. Many of the most effective dramas had been denied production because they were considered offensive or immoral. Thus, the potential of both new plays and methods had not been realized. It remained for André Antoine to merge the new drama with new theatrical means. His "independent theatre" became the inspiration for others throughout Europe. Among those he inspired, the most important were Otto Brahm in Berlin and J. T. Grein in London. The new theatres provided an incentive as well for several new playwrights, among them

Porto-Riche, Curel, Brieux, Hauptmann, and Shaw. With the barriers breached, the modern theatre began to flourish by 1900.

~~~ I ~~~

In 1887 André Antoine (1858–1943) must have appeared an unlikely candidate for the role of theatrical reformer. He had had no formal education to speak of, although as a bookseller's clerk he had read widely. In the 1870s he had sometimes served as a supernumerary actor at the Comédie Française and had attempted unsuccessfully to gain entrance to the Conservatoire, France's major training school for actors. After five years in the army, Antoine had returned to Paris in 1883 and had become a clerk at the Paris Gas Company. He continued in this position until his work with the Théâtre Libre prompted him to resign in 1887.

That Antoine founded the Théâtre Libre was largely accidental. In 1886 he had joined the Cercle Gaulois, one of the many amateur theatrical groups in Paris. Headed by a retired army officer, Krauss, who also owned the theatre building in which it performed, the Cercle Gaulois was very conservative both in its theatrical methods and its choice of plays. Seeking to enliven the group, Antoine in early 1887 suggested that the Cercle produce a bill of plays by new playwrights. The other members were unenthusiastic but agreed to sponsor a bill if Antoine would make the arrangements. He accepted eagerly and soon acquired four plays: *A Prefect* by Arthur Byl, *The Cockade* by Jules Vidal, Paul Alexis's *Mademoiselle Pomme*, and Leon Hénnique's dramatization of Zola's *Jacques Damour*. The Cercle Gaulois became increasingly reluctant, however, especially about *Jacques Damour,* since Zola was considered a very controversial figure, and eventually withdrew its sponsorship of the program. Antoine, refusing to give up, persuaded Krauss to rent him the theatre, although he secured it for only one performance. All of the work of the production fell on Antoine. He even borrowed the necessary furniture from his mother and transported it by handcart across Paris.

Since he could not use the Cercle Gaulois's name, Antoine had to find another. He eventually settled on the Théâtre Libre (or "Free Theatre," an adaptation of Victor Hugo's epigraph, A Theatre Set Free). Paul Alexis, who wrote a daily column for a Parisian newspaper, publicized the program and other journals printed notices of the plays. Zola, who attended the dress rehearsal, was sufficiently impressed to return for the opening (on March 30, 1887) with a group of friends and critics. The audience was lukewarm to two of the plays, hissed one, and responded favorably only to *Jacques Damour,* in which Antoine played the title role. Nevertheless, the total effort received considerable favorable notice in the newspapers.

87

Invitation and program for the first bill of plays presented by the Théâtre Libre on March 30, 1887.

Antoine had not intended to continue the Théâtre Libre, but, encouraged by his friends and by critics, he decided to prepare another bill, presented in May 1887. Émile Bergerat's *Bergamesque Night,* a long verse play written to be performed in *commedia dell' arte* style, and Oscar Méténier's *In the Family,* a one-act naturalistic piece, were chosen. Although not all critics liked the plays, almost all were impressed by the productions. On the strength of the response, Antoine resigned his position with the gas company and set out to make the Théâtre Libre a permanent organization.

Scene from Méténier's *In the Family,* as it was produced on the second bill of plays offered by the Théâtre Libre, May 1887.

The Théâtre Libre began its first full season in the fall of 1887. It was at this time that Antoine decided to run the theatre by subscription, primarily because he needed to raise capital. Of greater importance ultimately, however, this arrangement, under which the theatre was a private organization open only to members, permitted the presentation of plays that otherwise might have been refused a license. It was this device which was to be adopted by later imitators throughout Europe and which gained a hearing for many plays previously banned.

The Théâtre Libre, an avant-garde organization roughly comparable to an off-off-Broadway theatre in America in 1970, provided opportunities for authors who would not have been able to place their works elsewhere. During its existence it presented a total of sixty-two programs composed of 184 plays. At least sixty-nine authors, several of whom went on to become important figures in the French theatre, had their initial productions there. Antoine's actors were for the most part amateurs, although many aspired to professional status. With Antoine's coaching, several became sufficiently accomplished to be hired by other theatres. In fact, the Théâtre Libre eventually became a victim of its own success, for after 1893 it was progressively weakened by the steady defection of authors and performers to established theatres.

During its existence, the Théâtre Libre occupied three different out-of-the-way theatres, all small (the first seated 343 and none more than 800). Each season it gave a series of bills (an average of about seven each year), most composed of one-act plays, although some included full-length works. Until 1890–91 each bill was given for only one performance; even at the height of its popularity no bill was performed for more than three nights, and one of these was for an invited, nonpaying audience. Consequently, the group's income was always inadequate. Nevertheless, Antoine insisted upon the highest standards of production, and debts increased annually. When Antoine left the Théâtre Libre in 1894 he owed more than 100,000 francs. The group struggled on until April 1896 (under the direction of Paul Larochelle) and then closed permanently.

Antoine exerted untold influence upon the theatre both in France and elsewhere. His fame was spread abroad through articles about his work and through tours by his company. In 1888 the troupe played in Brussels and later in Germany, Holland, Italy, and England. Antoine's influence was exerted in three ways: through the "independent theatre" concept, through his production methods, and through the plays and authors that he introduced.

It is difficult to overestimate the importance of the "independent theatre" concept. Although many realistic and naturalistic plays had been written by 1887, they had not received an adequate hearing because of conservative producers and censors. It was Antoine who showed others how to skirt the censor by playing only for "private" audiences. He also demonstrated that it was possible to make an enormous impact through playing for an audience too restricted in numbers to interest commercial producers. When the significance of his innovations became apparent, other independent theatres were formed in France and elsewhere. As a result, before 1900 audiences almost everywhere had become aware of the new drama and in many places were becoming sufficiently tolerant to sanction it in formerly conservative theatres. Since Antoine's time, the independent theatre, or some variation on it, has remained the major device for trying out radical innovations in writing and production. Practically all avant-garde theatres are lineal descendants of the Théâtre Libre.

Antoine also was instrumental in reshaping staging practices, although, like many reformers, Antoine invented little. In one sense, he merely marks the culmination of nineteenth-century trends, for almost every ingredient of his work had been anticipated by someone else. But the components had been applied only sporadically or in isolation from each other. Thus, Antoine synthesized many earlier practices and perfected the theatrical mode appropriate to the realistic and naturalistic plays of his time. In many respects his methods differed little from those of Saxe-Meiningen, Irving, or Daly, but he transformed such methods by applying them to plays which truly needed actualistic staging. Thus, he made the transition from romantic realism to naturalism.

Antoine was concerned with realism in staging from the very beginning of his work with the Théâtre Libre, but his concern seems to have increased after the summer of 1888, when he witnessed performances by Irving's company in London and by Saxe-Meiningen's in Brussels. He admired Irving's use of three-dimensional scenic pieces and came back to Paris determined to adopt the "free plantation" method of handling scenery, not then accepted in France. He declared that no theatre in Paris could stage Shakespeare without reducing the needed settings by half. He was also determined to abandon the practice of painting details (often even furniture) on walls. Antoine was even more impressed by the Meiningen troupe, above all by its ensemble effects and its handling of crowd scenes. Thus, after 1888 Antoine attempted to achieve a complete illusion of reality. This aim influenced every aspect of his productions.

For scenery, Antoine insisted upon new flats for each new production, since the sagging canvas on old ones destroyed illusion. More important, he insisted upon specially designed settings for each play because he considered the setting to be an environment which necessarily differs in each play. In creating a set, Antoine sought first to imagine the locale as it would be in real life. He furnished rooms completely, including bric-a-brac and other details. According to his own testimony, it was only after he was satisfied with every detail that he decided which wall to remove for stage use. Sometimes furniture remained along the curtain line, which was always treated as an invisible—but inviolable—fourth wall. For Curel's *The Fossils* (1892), which is set in a single room, Antoine created three different settings, each showing the room from a different angle.

The properties were numerous and as real as Antoine could obtain. The most famous example is the real carcasses of beef used in Fernand Icre's *The Butchers,* staged in 1888. (It is perhaps only fair to note that Antoine later declared the carcasses to have been a last-minute addition prompted by the bare appearance of the set.) For *Old Heidelberg,* Antoine bought the contents of a student's room and transferred them to the stage. It is important to recognize that, since Antoine sought to make his settings as real as possible, it was probably much easier and cheaper to fit them out with real objects than to employ scenic artists sufficiently skilled to create convincing replicas.

In lighting, Antoine sought to approximate the direction of the supposed source: sun, moon, lamps, windows, doors, and so on. He objected to footlights because of their unnatural direction and shadows. Perhaps the most famous example of his search for realism through light is Leon Hénnique's *Death of the Duc d'Enghien* (1888), in which a council of war was lighted entirely by lanterns resting on the table around which the actors sat.

The same care extended to acting. In his pamphlet, *The Théâtre Libre* (1890), Antoine severely criticized the training of actors then given at the Conservatoire (France's foremost training academy for actors) because it taught students that "the stage voice" must be quite different from the voice used in real life and because it required exaggerated enunciation in which the subtleties of normal conversational exchange were eliminated. He also charged that all students were trained to use the same basic gestures and movements. He acknowledged that this training might be adequate for standard works from the past, but he declared it wholly inappropriate to realistic plays of present-day life. In contrast, he demanded that his actors seek "to live" rather than "to act" on stage. To prevent them from "playing to" the audience, he often required them to turn their backs to the auditorium. In voice, he always sought the conversational tone. Antoine's aim was to create the impression of real people in real places taking part in real actions—and seemingly unaware of the audience's presence.

Antoine worked hard to achieve the kind of ensemble he had seen in the Meiningen troupe. He produced few plays that required crowds, but these he staged with extreme care. Despite his limited resources, he was by his own account able to assemble a crowd of 500 persons for J. H. Rosny's *Nell Horn* in 1891 and almost as many for the Goncourts' *The Fatherland in Danger* in 1889. According to Antoine, the storming of the employer's home in the fourth act of Hauptmann's *The Weavers* (in 1893) was so convincing that the spectators rose from their seats in fright.

Antoine's efforts to reform the theatre extended to the audience as well. He believed that the spectator must be compelled to forget that he is in a theatre and be affected as though watching a real event. To encourage this attitude, he darkened the auditorium and discouraged both actors and audience from acknowledging the presence of the other during performances. The proscenium always served as a fourth wall through which sight and sound emerged but which was otherwise treated as an unbreachable barrier. As Jean Jullien put it: "The front of the stage must be a fourth wall, transparent for the public, opaque for the player."

Understandably, Antoine was not always successful in achieving his aims. He was often severely criticized by those who could not see all of the action because of various obstructions (furniture along the curtain line, the backs of the actors, the crowds which often completely hid major characters, and so on) or because they could not hear when actors spoke upstage, were drowned out by sound effects and crowds, or were too intent on being natural to project sufficiently. Furthermore, Antoine sought to make almost all plays equally realistic, regardless of their literary style. Thus, while Antoine perceived that realistic plays demanded a new production style, he was not fully aware that the new style was not suited to all new plays.

Nevertheless, Antoine's influence was tonic. He did not completely transform the French theatre, but the notoriety which surrounded his work focused attention on his methods and made spectators aware of shortcomings in other theatres. In turn, this awareness prompted producers to mount their offerings with greater care. As its actors and methods were absorbed into other theatres, the Théâtre Libre ceased to seem innovative. By 1900 Antoine's methods had become commonplace, although they were not always applied with Antoine's care for detail. Thus, when Jacques Copeau set out to found his theatre in 1913, it was against Antoine that he felt it necessary to rebel. While acknowledging the theatre's indebtedness to Antoine, Copeau declared that by 1913 Antoine's methods had been so widely adopted that they had become as conservative and restrictive as those which the Théâtre Libre had overthrown. Almost all historians acknowledge that Antoine set the tone of the French theatre from the 1890s until World War I.

Antoine also exerted considerable influence on French drama by introducing and nurturing new talent. Eclectic in taste, he presented plays of many types. Perhaps because of his production style, Antoine made his greatest impression with naturalistic works. Despite his continual disclaimers of allegiance to naturalism, he was almost universally considered a champion of realistic and naturalistic drama. There are probably many reasons why this is so. First, it seems clear that Antoine considered illusionism to be the goal of production and thus he imposed realistic standards on drama. Second, most of the plays he presented were those which could not find other outlets, either because they were refused by other theatres or because they were unacceptable to the censor. Since the more romantic and poetic plays seldom ran into trouble with the censor, Antoine felt a special obligation to realistic writers. Furthermore, the notoriety aroused by some of the naturalistic plays tended to attract others of the same type. Third, after 1890 a number of other independent theatres were founded in Paris and,

The final scene from Antoine's production of Ibsen's *The Wild Duck* at the Théâtre Libre. (From a contemporary lithograph.)

since the most important of them opposed realism and naturalism, they attracted authors of nonrealistic plays. For these and perhaps other reasons, the Théâtre Libre has come to be associated almost entirely with the triumph of realism and naturalism in the French theatre.

Not only did Antoine introduce new French plays, he began in 1888 a policy of presenting significant foreign works not previously seen in France. The first was Leo Tolstoy's *The Power of Darkness,* a play that had been forbidden production in Russia and which Augier, Dumas *fils,* and Sardou thought unsuitable for the Parisian theatre. It outraged conservative theatregoers especially because of one scene in which a small child, born of adulterous parents, is murdered onstage (a variant version in which the child is murdered offstage is now better known). Tolstoy's play was followed by Strindberg's *The Father,* Ibsen's *Ghosts* and *The Wild Duck,* Hauptmann's *The Weavers,* and others. The production of *Ghosts* set off a debate in the French Senate and prompted an investigation into the need for stricter censorship, fortunately not enacted. These productions of foreign plays served to acquaint the Parisian public with significant trends in other countries.

Despite Antoine's desire to be eclectic, the Théâtre Libre was considered the home of *comédie rosse,* a type of play inaugurated in 1887 with *The Serenade* by Jean Jullien (1854–1919). *Rosserie* was a descriptive term applied to naturalistic plays which treat base and ignoble characters who assume a façade of respectability and in which the playwright, with callous and bitter irony, draws aside the cloak of respectability to reveal the ugly and bestial underneath. The critic Filon described *rosserie* as "a sort of vicious ingenuousness, the state of soul of people who never had any moral sense and who live in impurity and injustice like a fish in water." Many writers of *comédie rosse,* like the playwrights of the 1960s, deliberately sought to shock, offend, and even to alienate audiences.

The Serenade is a good example of *rosserie.* In it, a young tutor, Maxime Champenet, carries on an affair with Nathalie Cottin, the wife of a rich Parisian jeweler. Cottin, upon becoming suspicious, confronts them. Maxime is quick to admit his indiscretions but it soon becomes apparent that he is also having an affair with Cottin's young daughter, Geneviève. This shocks both Cottin and his wife, and when it is revealed that Geneviève is pregnant, Cottin demands that Maxime marry her, though she is promised to another man. Maxime reluctantly consents. As the party moves off to luncheon, the problems seemingly resolved, Mme. Cottin moves close to Maxime and whispers invitingly, "Sit by me—son-in-law!" Such a situation obviously provides material for comedy, but Jullien tends to make it distasteful, for Cottin is not a blundering, foolish, or insensitive bourgeois but a kind and basically good man who loves his family and is deeply injured by the indiscretions of his wife and daughter. Thus, he is worthy of pity. But Jullien forces the audience to laugh at Cottin and his predicament. The result is a kind of perverse humor. The other characters, although largely unprincipled, are the ones who win, thus reversing traditional poetic justice.

Jullien, the acknowledged leader of the second generation of naturalists, holds a place second only to Zola as a spokesman for the movement. In *The Living Theatre* (1892), Jullien's famous phrase, "A play is a slice of life," echoes Zola's statement that a play should be "a fragment of existence." But Jullien was not a slavish follower of Zola, for the second part of Jullien's cry, now seldom recalled—"A play is a slice of life put on the stage with art"—indicates his dissatisfaction with Zola's scientific pretensions. Jullien argued that the dramatist, while seeking to create an objective portrait of life, should never do so at the expense of dramatic interest or the arousal of emotion. Nevertheless he accepted Zola's demand that subjects be drawn from real life and that the techniques of the well-made play be abandoned: "The denouement is only an arbitrary interruption of the action which leaves the spectator free to speculate about what goes on beyond; our purpose is not to create laughter but thought."

In addition to Zola, other strong influences on the younger naturalists were Ibsen, Strindberg, and Becque. Jullien seems to have borrowed both his style and technique from Becque, although he unfortunately lacked both the insight and the sensitivity of his mentor.

But if Jullien's *Serenade* was the first of the *comédies rosses,* it was by no means the last or the most extreme. Many of the plays were too strong even for the Théâtre Libre's tolerant audiences. Perhaps the play which outraged them most was August Linert's *Christmas Story,* in which a child is killed and his body thrown to the pigs while Christmas carols play in the background.

Not all of Antoine's dramatists wrote *comédies rosses* (or what critics came to call the "genre Théâtre Libre"). In fact, the three who were to be of greatest importance—Porto-Riche, Curel, and Brieux—never wrote this type. Each of them had strong individualizing qualities and each was considerably more conservative than were the writers of *comédie rosse.* Perhaps for this reason they were eventually able to find an audience far more extensive than that commanded by the Théâtre Libre.

Georges de Porto-Riche (1849–1930) began his career by writing several poetic plays (none of which was produced) and verse, all in the romantic vein. His first play to reach the stage, *Françoise's Luck,* was produced by Antoine in 1888. It revolves around Marcel, a husband approaching middle age, and his wife, Françoise. Bored with marital life, Marcel seeks to renew an old affair, but Françoise's delicate and subtle handling of her husband wins him back. This play introduces what was thereafter to be Porto-Riche's principal preoccupation: the power of passion. Porto-Riche recognized his strength and when he published a collection of his works he entitled it *Theatre of Love.* In almost all of his plays, the characters are driven to misery by emotions, centering around love, which they do not fully understand; the subtle psychological play of conflicting desires is almost always the focus of the action.

By far the most effective of Porto-Riche's plays is *Infatuated* (1891), presented not by Antoine but as a vehicle for Gabrielle Réjane (1857–1920), one of the finest actresses of the day. *Infatuated* treats the emotional struggle of a middle-aged physician, Etienne Feriaud, who resents being distracted from his research by the demands of his wife, Germaine. He feels so guilty about putting his work before his wife's happiness, however, that when she threatens to be unfaithful to him with a former lover, Pascal, Etienne says to him, "If you love my wife, make her happy. I give her to you." In the end the couple are reconciled, although not in the traditional mode of sentimental drama. When Germaine prepares to leave, Etienne calls her back; she warns him that he is certain to be unhappy if she stays, but Etienne, wishing her to remain though aware that she speaks the truth, replies, "What difference does that make?" As in all of Porto-Riche's plays, the plot of *Infatuated* is simple. Interest is centered on subtle shadings of psychological responses and upon the highly polished though seemingly natural dialogue. Restraint was Porto-Riche's hallmark.

François de Curel (1854–1929) made his debut as a playwright at the

Théâtre Libre in 1892 with *The Other Side of a Saint*. Antoine chose the play not because it was the best available but because he recognized that no one else would produce it. Although the audience treated the play unkindly, Curel never ceased to voice his gratitude for Antoine's faith in him. *The Other Side of a Saint* tells the story of Julie, who after nineteen years returns from a convent which she entered because in a fit of jealousy she had attempted to kill Jeanne, who had married her lover. Now he has died and Julie seeks to steal away Jeanne's beloved daughter. But when Julie learns that the dead man has left an affectionate note addressed to her, she decides that she must return to the convent as the only place where she can find peace. The real interest resides in the psychological portrait of the protagonist.

Curel's most famous play, *The Fossils,* was produced by Antoine only a few months after *The Other Side of a Saint.* Here deep psychological analysis is allied with the theme of a decaying aristocracy (to which Curel himself belonged). It shows Robert de Cantemelle, the young ducal heir, who upon learning that he has only a few months to live tries to provide for the preservation of the family line. He declares that he has had a son by Hélène, once his mother's protégée (in reality the child was sired by Robert's father). The family decides to adopt the infant and to legitimize it through a marriage between Robert and Hélène. After the marriage, Hélène, fearing that the child will be taken from her, begs to be allowed to take him away with her after Robert dies. The duke, unwilling to permit this, reveals the truth, for the family's continuation is more precious to him than the happiness of his wife and son.

Curel went on writing until the end of his life. His plays were accorded mixed receptions, for Curel seems to have cared little for pleasing an audience and refused to employ commonly accepted dramatic techniques for the sake of greater effectiveness. He is very much better at establishing situations than at resolving actions. His work is devoid of sensationalism— unless his psychological revelations may be termed such. It also combines qualities often considered antagonistic: the real with the unreal, the poetic with the prosaic, the straightforward with the near-allegorical. The plays appear to make considerable use of symbolism, but it is often difficult to tell if Curel does so intentionally, for he makes few dramatic points with symbols. Of Curel's later plays, one of the most interesting is *The Dance Before the Mirror* (1914), in which a man and woman doubt whether their love will last. The man kills himself at the moment when he sees true love mirrored in the woman's eyes, for he prefers to die at the peak of happiness rather than risk the death of love.

The most famous of the trio was Eugène Brieux (1858–1932), in part because in 1911 he was declared by Shaw to be the most important dramatist then living in western Europe. Brieux won recognition first with *Blanchette,* presented by Antoine in 1892, although an earlier work, *Household of Artists,* had been produced at the Théâtre Libre in 1890 without attracting attention. Brieux is Dumas *fils*'s true successor, for like Dumas he was concerned with specific social problems and wrote with a thesis in mind. Consequently, most of his plays now seem outdated, for they are tied too closely to social conditions of a past time. His targets were numerous. In *The Philanthropists* (1896) he attacked fashionable philanthropy on the grounds that it is futile to give charity without love; in *The Three Daughters of M. Dupont* (1897) he treated loveless marriages arranged for social reasons; in *Racing Results* (1898) he chose gambling as his focus; in *The Deserter* (1904) he explored the evils of divorce; in *The Substitutes* (1901) he chided mothers for letting their babies be reared by wet nurses; in *Maternity* (1903) he launched a bitter attack upon a society which refuses to permit birth control; and in *The May Bugs* (1906) he treated the problems of free love.

   Damaged Goods (1902) probably best illustrates Brieux's penchant for preaching. In it, Georges Dupont discovers on the eve of his marriage that he has syphilis; after being treated by an incompetent doctor he believes that he is cured and marries; a child (infected by the disease) is born; when the wife discovers the truth she is saved only by the help of the *raisonneur*, a doctor, who suggests that a permanent cure may be brought about. *Damaged Goods* also demonstrates how much tolerance had increased since *Ghosts* was written in 1881, for Brieux's play treats the subject of venereal disease much more explicitly than did Ibsen's but failed to raise the ire that greeted *Ghosts*.

   Brieux's best play is probably *The Red Robe* (1900), an indictment

Scene from Act II of the original production of Brieux's *The Red Robe,* performed in 1900 at the Théâtre du Vaudeville. (From *Le Théâtre,* 1900.)

of the French judicial system. In it, a Basque peasant is falsely accused of murder, but the prosecutor, Mouzon, realizing that to gain promotion he must obtain convictions, sets out to win the case at any cost. To manipulate the peasant, he reveals to him that his wife has been unfaithful, a secret which he had promised the wife never to disclose. When the wife realizes that Mouzon has set her husband against her, she stabs the prosecutor to death. It is a powerful play which generates considerable pity for the victims of a system more concerned with personal advancement than with justice.

Jullien, Porto-Riche, Curel, and Brieux are only a few of the many dramatists introduced by Antoine, though these four are sufficient to suggest the crucial role played by the Théâtre Libre. Thus, both in repertory and production, Antoine had by 1894 set in motion currents that would profoundly influence the future. But, though he left the Théâtre Libre in that year, Antoine's career was not yet over. After touring South America, he returned to Paris, where in 1897 he established his own professional company, the Théâtre Antoine. Here he continued to work until 1906, when he was named director of the Odéon, France's second state theatre. This appointment signals the acceptance of Antoine's methods, for it gave semiofficial recognition to his leadership. At the Odéon, Antoine was to encounter new problems—staging the classical repertory. How he met these challenges will be treated later.

Antoine is clearly one of the most important figures of the modern theatre. Scarcely a significant theatrical leader of the next generation remained unaffected by him, although many of those who had begun with him at the Théâtre Libre put their experience to work in ways quite unlike Antoine's. Among the most important were Lugné-Poë, Gémier, and Dullin. The most immediate effect of Antoine's work, however, was the triumph of new theatrical methods and the acceptance of naturalistic drama. By 1900, Antoine's was the dominant mode, although many directors and writers were actively rebelling against it. The French theatre had been permanently affected by the work of an amateur troupe working on the fringes of the established theatre.

~~ II ~~

Antoine's effect was tonic not only for the French stage but for that of other countries as well. In some instances, the results were negligible, but in others they were to be revolutionary.

One short-lived effort was initiated by Strindberg in Copenhagen, where he had gone in 1887 to attend the first production of *The Father*. Encouraged by his reception there, Strindberg decided to found a company modeled on the Théâtre Libre. For it, he wrote his three "quarter of an hour" plays, which were staged by his group—the Experimental Theatre—in March 1889. That the venture was then abandoned may be attributed to several reasons: Strindberg was not a good administrator; financial support was inadequate; the press was antagonistic; and Strindberg was by now almost completely estranged from his wife, Siri von Essen, the company's principal actress and director.

Although Strindberg now returned to Sweden, he did not give up his dream of a theatre, and in 1892, in anticipation of a company that never materialized, he wrote his "Plays from Cynical Life," works often likened to the *comédies rosses* of the Théâtre Libre. Thus, though Strindberg's theatrical ambitions ended in frustration, they cannot be counted complete failures since they motivated the writing of several plays.

But if the independent theatre movement did not profoundly affect Scandinavia, quite the contrary may be said of Germany. Since Hebbel's death in 1863, Germany had produced no significant drama; for the most part new works took the form of pseudopoetic plays influenced by Schiller, chauvinistic dramas engendered by German unification in 1871, or imitations of Augier and Dumas *fils*.

During the 1880s considerable dissatisfaction with this situation developed. One result was the formation of Jungstdeutschen ("Youngest Germans"), the chief spokesmen for whom were the brothers Julius and Heinrich Hart (who edited a short-lived periodical *Waffengange* in Berlin), Michael Georg Conrad (founder of the literary review *Society* in Munich), and Karl Bliebtreu (author of a widely read pamphlet, *Revolution in Literature*). All of these men demanded a new art based upon reality and upon subjects chosen from life among the peasant and working classes.

Of still greater influence was another loosely organized society, Durch ("Through"), founded in Berlin in 1886 by Conrad Custer. Among its members were the poet Arno Holz, the Hart brothers, and Gerhart Hauptmann (then unknown but destined to be the leading dramatist of the new school). Holz, the principal spokesman for the group, reflected Zola's ideas but went even further by taking issue with Zola's seeming subjectivism in defining art as life "seen through a temperament." Holz declared, "Art equals nature minus x," the "x" representing the artist's subjectivity and the limitations of his medium. Thus, for Holz the greatest artist is inferior to the poorest photographer. Consequently, according to Holz, the writer's major problem is to overcome the limitations of "art" and to attain "truth." Seeking to implement his ideas, Holz, in collaboration with Johannes Schlaf, wrote a series of narrative pieces, under the title *Papa Hamlet,* about life in the Berlin slums. Later they turned to drama with *The Happy Family* (1890), in which a drunken father returns home laden with Christmas gifts and falls into a stupor as his youngest child dies in the same room. It is one of Germany's most determinedly naturalistic plays.

The greatest influence upon the German radicals, however, was Ibsen, who by the late 1880s was the most renowned dramatist in Europe, although his plays were seldom seen in the theatre. Ibsen had made his home in Germany since the late 1860s and a number of his plays had been performed there. (*Pillars of Society* had been produced in Berlin in 1879 and *A Doll's House* in 1880, although with the altered, "happy" ending.) But few of Ibsen's prose plays had been widely produced, and *Ghosts* was forbidden by the censor.

Like its drama, Germany's theatre was also conservative. Wagner's and Saxe-Meiningen's efforts were admired and imitated, but their influence served primarily to strengthen romantic realism. In Berlin, Saxe-Meiningen's methods were being applied at the Deutsches Theater, founded in 1883 by Adolf L'Arronge (1838–1908) and Ludwig Barnay (1842–1924), who sought to counteract the trend toward the long run and the effects of outmoded theatrical practices. Its acting company was headed by Josef Kainz (1858–1910) and Agnes Sorma (1865–1927), destined to become two of Germany's leading performers. Both Barnay and Kainz had worked in the Meiningen company and sought to re-create the spirit of that troupe in their own. Although its productions were soon considered the finest in Berlin, the Deutsches Theater's repertory was made up primarily of standard works. It did seek to perform some avant-garde plays, but was forced by the censor to retreat.

As elsewhere, then, there had been no significant meshing of new dramatic modes with new theatrical practices. In Germany, as in France, change began only with the establishment of an "independent theatre," the Freie Bühne ("Free Theatre"), founded in Berlin in 1889, two years after the opening of the Théâtre Libre.

The actress Agnes Sorma in the title role of *Nora* (the happily-ended German version of Ibsen's *A Doll's House*) in the 1890s. (From the Deutsche Akademie der Künste zu Berlin.)

Though the Freie Bühne was inspired by the Théâtre Libre, it differed from it in many respects. First, it was founded by design rather than by accident. Second, it was run by a group. Its elected president and dominant figure was Otto Brahm (1856–1912), a drama critic, but he was advised and assisted by a governing council of ten members, an arrangement which differed markedly from Antoine's autocratic control of the Théâtre Libre. Third, it employed professional actors altogether. Consequently, it worked around the schedules of other Berlin theatres and presented its offerings on Sunday afternoons at the well-equipped Lessing Theater and with actors employed at the Lessing Theater, the Deutsches Theater, and the Berliner Theater (which Barnay headed after leaving the Deutsches Theater in 1887). Fourth, the major emphasis was upon the plays, with lesser concern for production.

The Freie Bühne resembled the Théâtre Libre primarily in being organized as a private theatre club to avoid censorship. In Berlin the number of subscribers numbered 360 even before the first production and by the end of the first year had nearly tripled. Each subscriber received a copy of the society's periodical, entitled *Free Stage,* which contained critical discussions of the plays produced by the group, the texts of other new plays, and essays on various literary, dramatic, and philosophical topics.

The Freie Bühne's principal work was done between 1889 and 1891. It opened in September 1889 with *Ghosts,* chosen because Brahm believed that Ibsen was the "pathfinder of the new dramatic art." The play also set the radical tone of the enterprise, which went on to produce the Goncourts' *Henriette Maréchal,* Tolstoy's *The Power of Darkness,* Zola's *Thérèse Raquin,* Becque's *The Vultures,* and Strindberg's *The Father* and *Miss Julie.* Among the German works were Anzengruber's *The Fourth Commandment,* Holz's and Schlaf's *The Happy Family,* and Arthur Fitger's *By Divine Right.*

The Freie Bühne's one great discovery, however, was Gerhart Hauptmann (1862–1946). Like Ibsen's, Hauptmann's career spans a period of approximately fifty years and is extremely diverse. He wrote approximately thirty plays, in addition to novels, epic poems, lyrics, and autobiographical and travel works. By the early twentieth century, he was Germany's most respected playwright (in 1912 he was awarded the Nobel Prize in literature), although toward the end of his life he fell into disfavor because of his passivity under the Nazis.

Hauptmann began his career as a confirmed naturalist but soon began to oscillate between realistic and symbolic works, a pattern he was to continue through the rest of his life. Consequently, he wrote some of Germany's most naturalistic and some of its most symbolic plays. Hauptmann's original reputation, however, was won with naturalistic works.

Before Sunrise, presented by the Freie Bühne in 1889, is usually considered the first important modern German drama. In it, Hauptmann deals with a Silesian farm family who have become wealthy from the

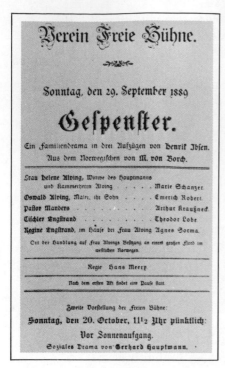

Program for Ibsen's *Ghosts,* the first production of the Freie Bühne, 1889. At the bottom is an announcement of the forthcoming production of Hauptmann's first play, *Vor Sonnenaufgang* (Before Sunrise), scheduled for the following month. (From the Deutsche Akademie der Künste zu Berlin.)

discovery of coal deposits under their land. The new-found wealth, however, has led only to drunken debauchery and viciousness, except in the daughter, Helene, who falls in love with a young social worker, Alfred Loth, a student of conditions among the miners. But after Loth becomes more fully aware of the terrifying conditions under which Helene lives and begins to wonder whether she can escape her heredity, he decides that he must give her up. Now without hope, Helene kills herself. The play is simple in structure and style, free from any of the typical devices of the well-made play or of the pseudo-classical drama. It is now admired especially for exactness of dialect and usage according to social level.

In several ways Hauptmann seems in *Before Sunrise* to have carried naturalistic doctrine beyond credibility—although perhaps not for audiences of his day. For example, he seems to believe that the tendency toward alcoholism is inherited and even shows an alcoholic three-year-old child. He further seems to approve of Loth's desertion of Helene on the grounds of her poor heredity. Despite any shortcomings, *Before Sunrise* astounded audiences when it was first produced. To many, Hauptmann appeared the redeemer of German drama, while to others he represented all that was most odious in the new trends.

Hauptmann's most famous play, *The Weavers* (1892), is considered by many critics the finest of all naturalistic dramas. In it, he deals with the futile uprising, in which his own family had participated, of Silesian weavers in 1844. The background is the Industrial Revolution at the time when

Poster for Hauptmann's *The Weavers*. (From the Deutsche Akademie der Künste zu Berlin.)

machine weaving is beginning to make cottage industry unprofitable. The weavers in Hauptmann's play are those who work at home, securing thread from an employer and then selling their cloth to him. When the play opens, their income has been so reduced that they are on the verge of starvation. Their employer maintains that he pays as well as he can considering the competition from the factories which are springing up elsewhere. Eventually the weavers revolt but, though at the end of the play they have not yet been suppressed, it is clear that their action is futile, for the tide of industrialization cannot be stemmed.

Conditions in Germany had improved so little by the 1890s that Wilhelm II, the emperor of Germany, considered the play highly provocative. When it was refused a license for production at the Deutsches Theater, it was performed by the Freie Bühne, revived especially for this purpose.

One of the most striking features of *The Weavers* is the absence of an individual protagonist. The focus shifts from act to act, with the result that the weavers as a group become the protagonist. There is no strong central action; rather the overall effect is cumulative—misery creates an ever-increasing desperation which eventually explodes into violence, much of it senseless. In the opening act, the near-starving weavers stand in line to show their week's work and are bullied into accepting whatever they are offered. The second act, set in the household of Old Baumert, exposes the conditions under which the weavers live. Among other incidents, Old Baumert becomes physically ill after eating flesh (that of a dog) for the first time in two years. In the third act, Baumert's nephew, Jaeger, puts courage into the weavers, and in the fourth act they loot the elegant home of Dreissiger, their employer. The final act takes place in the room of another weaver, Old Hilse, who refuses to join the revolt. The weavers now set out to destroy the power looms, the ultimate enemy, but are met by soldiers. They drive the soldiers back but a stray bullet kills Old Hilse as he sits working at his loom. Thus, at the end, although the weavers have seemingly repulsed the attack, Old Hilse's death is indicative of the true outcome.

Throughout the play, it is clear that Hauptmann's sympathies lie with the weavers, almost all of whom are depicted as decent people desiring to live upright, moral lives but who have been degraded to the level of animals by the conditions under which they live. He tends to make villains of the employers and heroes of the workers, although it is social, political, and economic conditions which entrap workers and employers alike. Nevertheless, Hauptmann clearly is not objective in Zola's sense. But, it is for precisely this reason that the play fulfills so well another demand made by naturalism—that art should be a weapon for social reform. The play generates enormous sympathy for the weavers and makes the need for better economic and social planning emotionally convincing. It is probably this compelling human interest which has kept the play, unlike most naturalistic dramas, fresh and powerful.

Hauptmann's difficulties in obtaining a license for *The Weavers* seem to have prompted him to write *The Beaver Coat* (1893), one of the few comedies to come out of the naturalist movement, a singularly humorless movement in its determination to serve society through truth. *The Beaver Coat* is a satiric thrust at the Prussian outlook, which had attempted to suppress *The Weavers*. When the Freie Bühne circumvented the ban, Kaiser Wilhelm canceled his box at the Deutsches Theater, the organization which had planned to present the play and which gave considerable aid to the private production. Analogously, *The Beaver Coat* shows Prussianism defeated by seeming compliance with its rules. Hauptmann takes as his dupe von Wehrhahn, a bullying, stupid, militaristic Prussian, and lets him be thoroughly outwitted by Frau Wolff, an amoral washerwoman who, in league with her equally disreputable husband, steals a beaver coat and then so befuddles the judge, von Wehrhahn, that he ends by lauding her honesty. It ranks only slightly lower than *The Weavers* in critical esteem.

In 1893, Hauptmann wrote his first nonrealistic play—*The Assumption of Hannele*—although the departure from naturalism is only partial. It treats an adolescent girl, wretchedly neglected and mistreated, whose death becomes almost euphoric through visions of heaven. Everything in it

Scene from the original production of Hauptmann's *The Beaver Coat* in 1893 at the Deutsches Theater, Berlin. Lucie Höflich, left, played Frau Wolff and Albert Steinrück, right, the magistrate Wehrhahn. (From the Deutsche Akademie der Künste zu Berlin.)

can be explained realistically—the visions are those of a girl brought up on notions of an eternally happy afterlife and nowhere is it implied that they are to be interpreted objectively. Still, the emphasis has shifted toward the poetic and away from the realistic.

In 1895, Hauptmann's *Florian Geyer* treated the same material used by Goethe in *Goetz von Berlichingen*—the Peasants' Revolt of the sixteenth century. Hauptmann was probably seeking to rival Goethe, universally considered Germany's greatest literary figure. The play was a wretched failure. It seems likely that this failure motivated Hauptmann's next play, *The Sunken Bell* (1896), a completely symbolic drama. A verse tragedy, it is filled with echoes of Goethe's *Faust,* of fairytales, and of a number of other works by Hauptmann's predecessors. It tells the story of a bell maker whose masterpiece is destroyed when it falls.

From this time on Hauptmann alternated realistic and symbolic works and his defection from realism increased as time went by. With the possible exceptions of *Rose Bernd* (1903) and *The Rats* (1911), Hauptmann never again recaptured his strength of the 1890s. Most of Hauptmann's drama after 1911 is mediocre. Much of it, as in *The Bow of Odysseus* (1914) and the tetralogy on the house of Atreus (1940–44), is based on classical mythology given a modern turn.

Although Hauptmann's subjects and methods changed, two basic qualities in his work remained constant—great compassion, and sensitivity to human suffering. Unlike Ibsen's central figures, Hauptmann's protagonists are almost always passive; they fall not because of their own mistakes, but because they are victims of forces beyond their control. Thus, rather than becoming heroic, they are merely pitiable (though sympathetic) creatures.

It was Hauptmann, nevertheless, who heralded the rejuvenation of German drama in the 1890s, and with his plays the Freie Bühne made its greatest impact. In fact, the Freie Bühne succeeded so well that at the end of its second season (1890–91) it discontinued regular programs. As Brahm stated: "It lies in the nature of the experiment that its greatest victory is its end." The society was not abandoned altogether, however, for when the need arose, as it did in the case of *The Weavers* in 1892, it was temporarily revived.

In 1894, when L'Arronge retired as head of the Deutsches Theater, Brahm was appointed to that post, in which he remained until 1904. While director of his own troupe, he staged not only new plays but works by Shakespeare, Lessing, Schiller, and other writers of the past. He sought to reform the traditional staging of these works by making them "come to life by utilizing . . . the new naturalistic art of acting," and by proving that modern realism and "the style of classical drama are not mutually exclusive." Unfortunately, the classics which he staged in this "natural" manner were failures, and the considerable reputation of the theater was based almost entirely on modern realistic works. Still, Brahm was instrumental in ridding the German stage of artificiality.

The Freie Bühne inspired a number of other independent theaters in Germany and Austria. Some of these, such as the Deutsches Bühne and Fresko-Bühne in Berlin and Max Halbe's Intimes Theater in Munich, were not very successful, but a large number of student groups, particularly in Berlin, Munich, and Vienna, gained considerable success with plays by Ibsen, Goethe, Schiller, and Anzengruber.

Undoubtedly the most significant outgrowth of the Freie Bühne was the *Volks* ("people's") theatres organized in the 1890s. Most of these were established by the socialists, whose leaders were concerned with raising the cultural standards of the working classes. The most important of these theatres were founded in Berlin. The first, the Freie Volksbühne, was organized in 1890 by Bruno Wille, Julius Turk, and Wilhelm Bolsche, all members of the Socialist-Democratic party. A second group, the Neue Freie Volksbühne, was founded in 1892 by Wille when he came into conflict with members of the original organization.

The Freie Volksbühne began operations with a membership of six hundred. Like the Freie Bühne, its performances were given on Sunday afternoons at regular theatres. Its repertory consisted of plays considered especially relevant to the working classes: Ibsen's *Pillars of Society* and *Ghosts,* Hauptmann's *Before Sunrise* and *The Weavers,* Zola's *Thérèse Raquin,* and similar dramas. Season tickets were distributed by lot and at a very nominal cost. This scheme was so successful that by 1908 the membership had grown to twelve thousand. When it became clear that there was a large potential audience, a number of commercial theatres began to give Sunday matinees, making it difficult for the Volksbühne to assemble strong casts for their own productions.

To combat the new threat, the Neue Freie Volksbühne began in 1905 to make arrangements for its members to see certain productions in commercial theatres at a slight additional cost over the regular subscription fee. Soon it was possible for members to choose between large numbers of special Sunday matinees offered by regular theatres.

By 1914 the two *Volksbühnen* had amalgamated and had a membership of fifty thousand. They now decided to build their own theatre and maintain their own company. Opened in 1915, the theatre, with its revolving stage, cyclorama, scenic projectors, adjustable proscenium, and workshops, was one of the best equipped in the world. The Berlin *Volksbühnen* were imitated elsewhere, most effectively in Vienna, where the Workmen's Theatre was founded in 1895.

Perhaps the greatest contribution of the people's theaters came from their encouragement of persons who had not normally attended the theater to take an interest in thoughtful and entertaining plays, both new and old. Their repertories included works by Shakespeare, Schiller, Goethe, Ibsen, and Hauptmann, as well as those by lesser authors. It is partially owing to the work of the *Volksbühnen* that the German theatregoing audience has remained broadly based, for they were instrumental in educating audiences to appreciate and expect the best in theatrical entertainment.

III

In England, as in France and Germany, it was the independent theatre movement which rescued drama from stagnation. Although the theatre was flourishing, with Irving's company in the vanguard, no significant new playwrights had appeared after Robertson's death in 1871. The theatre was given over to revivals of "standard" dramas of the past, to foreign adaptations (especially of Sardou's works), and to inconsequential new English plays.

In the 1880s several critics began to voice their unhappiness with the situation: William Archer in *English Dramatists of Today* (1882) and *About the Theatre* (1886) stressed the wide chasm between Continental and English developments; Frank Harris published a series of articles in the *Fortnightly Review* about modern drama in England and on the Continent; and the novelist George Moore suggested the need for a free theatre like those then being established abroad. But, as elsewhere, the situation began to improve only slowly. The first steps paralleled those taken by Dumas *fils* and Augier.

England's equivalents of the two French authors were Henry Arthur Jones (1851–1929) and Arthur Wing Pinero (1885–1934), who, though often labeled followers of Ibsen, were highly successful adapters of the well-made play's techniques and conventional moralists in resolving their dramatic actions. They served more to pave the way for a new drama than to create it, for they titillated audiences without seriously questioning accepted values.

Before entering upon careers as serious playwrights, both Jones and Pinero had achieved fame in minor forms—Jones with melodrama and Pinero with farce. Jones's first success came in 1882 with *The Silver King* (written in collaboration with Henry Herman), which ran for 289 performances. His pioneering effort in social drama came in 1884 with *Saints and Sinners,* a work about the disparity between a man's religious profession and his actual deeds. For the most part, it too is a melodrama, with characters divided between good and evil who are justly rewarded or punished; it attacked philistinism and moral hypocrisy, although without subtlety. Jones went on to write a great many serious plays, including *The Dancing Girl* (1891), *The Case of Rebellious Susan* (1894), *The Liars* (1897), and *Mrs. Dane's Defense* (1900).

Jones's best play, although by no means his most popular, is *Michael and His Lost Angel* (1896), in which he treats an illicit sexual relationship. In Act I, the stiffly proper Reverend Feversham compels a young woman to confess her sin of passion before the entire congregation. In Act II, he himself falls in love with Audrie Lesden and becomes an adulterer, although because he has acted out of love he does not consider himself a sinner. As if afraid of what he has created, Jones begins to shift ground in Act III and makes Feversham confess before his congregation and leave the church. Feversham does not see Audrie again until she is brought to him shortly before she dies. Ultimately the play is partially unsatisfactory because Jones distorts character in order to preserve a moral position.

On the whole, it seems clear that Jones sincerely desired to write thoughtful dramas, for he attempted to present significant social and religious conflicts on the stage. But Jones was no rigorous thinker and his analyses of problems were not grounded in any firm philosophical outlook. Consequently, today his plays seem shallow. Nevertheless, there is no reason to doubt his commitment to the new drama. His work—his plays and his endorsement of Ibsen and the new drama in *The Renascence of the English Drama* (1895)—did much to win over the public.

Pinero's first true success came in 1885 with *The Magistrate,* a farce which is still played with success. After writing a few other farces, Pinero made his first foray into "unpleasant" drama in 1889 with *The Profligate.* But it was *The Second Mrs. Tanqueray* (1893) which was to be Pinero's most famous work and the one which was to make the new type a commercial success. In it, Paula Ray, a "woman with a past," has married Aubrey Tanqueray, a middle-aged widower with a grown daughter, Ellean.

When Ellean's suitor arrives to ask for her hand, he turns out to be a man with whom Paula has had an affair. Ellean learns why her suitor has left so discreetly, and Paula, realizing that all hope for happiness is gone, commits suicide. Thus, though there is an air of sophistication throughout most of the play, the ending conveys the message that no woman who has strayed can hope to find happiness in polite society. Furthermore, the play is clearly in the "well-made" tradition, depending as it does upon concealed information, fortunate arrivals, and startling reversals. Although Pinero is skillful in concealing the machinery, he depends almost entirely upon coincidence in developing the action. But to London audiences in the 1890s the play seemed startlingly new and shockingly daring.

The Second Mrs. Tanqueray was produced by George Alexander (1858–1918), who as manager of St. James's Theatre after 1891 sought to encourage English dramatists. In addition to Pinero's plays, he also presented those of Oscar Wilde and of several other new playwrights. *The Second Mrs. Tranqueray* also did much to establish the reputation of Mrs. Patrick Campbell (1865–1940), who was to be one of England's leading actresses.

Pinero's later works included *The Notorious Mrs. Ebbsmith* (1895), *Trelawney of the Wells* (1898), *The Gay Lord Quex* (1899), *Iris* (1901), *Letty* (1903), and *Mid-Channel* (1909). The last is one of Pinero's best plays. It treats a middle-aged couple who, having fallen into bickering,

George Alexander and Mrs. Patrick Campbell in the original production of Pinero's *The Second Mrs. Tanqueray,* 1893. (Courtesy Enthoven Collection, Victoria and Albert Museum.)

decide to part. When the wife discovers that her husband has been having an affair, she falls into one of her own. On her return home, she finds that though she is willing to forgive her husband, he cannot overlook her transgressions. Angrily he orders her from the house. Now defeated, she commits suicide. Although he did not write his last play, *A Cold June,* until 1932, Pinero's reputation declined steadily in his final years.

Between 1890 and 1910 Pinero was often labeled a disciple of Ibsen, a designation which infuriated Shaw. Consequently, Shaw championed Jones and denounced Pinero, perhaps because he rightly perceived that Pinero was a true descendant of Scribe rather than of Ibsen and was more concerned with theatrical effectiveness than with depth of thought. It may be Pinero's concern for effect, however, that has helped his plays weather better than have Jones's, which now seem hopelessly outdated.

The significance of Jones and Pinero lies in their popularization of trends which the public was unwilling to accept in the uncompromising form used by Ibsen and his followers. By casting seemingly shocking subjects in a mold palatable to Victorian audiences, Jones and Pinero gradually led spectators to accept the more strenuous Ibsenesque drama.

Above all, it was Ibsen who became a rallying point for champions of a truly serious drama. Ibsen was first brought to English attention by Edmund Gosse in an article published in 1873, just after Ibsen had completed *Emperor and Galilean.* This play was also the first of Ibsen's works to be translated into English—by Catherine Ray in 1876. Shortly afterward, William Archer began his series of translations of Ibsen's plays, the standard English versions until the mid-twentieth century. *Pillars of Society* was the first of Ibsen's plays to be produced in England (in a single morning performance in 1880). Significant production for Ibsen's plays was lacking, however, until 1889, when Janet Achurch (1864–1916) and her husband Charles Charrington presented *A Doll's House* at a private showing, the first of several productions of Ibsen's plays by Miss Achurch. In 1891, Shaw published his pamphlet *The Quintessence of Ibsenism,* in which he defined "Ibsenism" as a critique, in dramatic form, of conventional morality.

Still, progress toward winning acceptance for Ibsenesque drama was slow until the Independent Theatre gave it momentum. The motive force behind the Independent Theatre was J. T. Grein (1862–1935), a Dutchman then residing in London who sought to accomplish in England what Antoine had in France. The declared purpose of the Independent Theatre was "to give special performances of plays which have a literary and artistic rather than a commercial value." Like its Continental models, the Independent Theatre was organized on a subscription basis and thus was free from the censorship of the lord chamberlain, who licensed all plays to be presented for public consumption. It did little about mounting the plays, being concerned primarily with providing a hearing for otherwise unproduced plays. Like the Freie Bühne, it gave its productions on Sundays so as to have the use of regular theatres and the services of professional actors.

Winifred Fraser as Hedwig in Ibsen's *The Wild Duck*, presented by the Independent Theatre (at the Royalty Theatre) in 1894. (Courtesy Enthoven Collection, Victoria and Albert Museum.)

The Independent Theatre's first production (on March 13, 1891) was of Ibsen's *Ghosts,* a play which had been refused a license for public performance. It provoked a critical storm of almost unbelievable intensity and brought the organization and the drama publicity far beyond what they could ever have achieved through normal means. The second program, Zola's *Thérèse Raquin,* was greeted with almost as much abuse. The Independent Theatre continued its work until 1897, presenting a total of twenty-six programs, mostly of foreign works.

While the organization was extremely successful in making the English public aware of new trends in drama, it had not been founded solely to present Continental plays. Grein believed that the low state of English drama was attributable to the conservatism of producers and was convinced that he would be deluged with plays by frustrated English dramatists. He soon discovered, however, that no significant English plays were available. It was in response to Grein's desperate appeal that George Bernard Shaw (1856–1950) began his playwriting career. Shaw was to be the only major playwright launched by the Independent Theatre, but his discovery alone guarantees the group a place in history.

By the time Shaw began to write plays he was almost forty years old and had tried his hand at many undertakings. Born in Ireland, in 1876 he moved to London where he began his literary career with five novels written between 1879 and 1883. After 1885 he turned primarily to criticism —of music, art, and letters—which he wrote for such periodicals as *Pall Mall Gazette, The Star,* and *The Saturday Review.* He also became a firm believer in socialism and in 1884 was a founding member of the Fabian Society, whose goal was the transition to socialism through gradual reform. Shaw's commitment to Fabianism heavily influenced much of his drama.

Shaw believed that if drama is to be significant, it must lead the audience to right action. It was this belief that made him praise Brieux so fulsomely and downgrade Shakespeare (partially on the grounds that he does not demand social or ethical improvement). He also disliked the well-made plays of Scribe and Sardou because they sacrifice truth to dramatic expediency. (Nevertheless, Shaw's own plays often depend on devices popularized by the well-made play.) He championed Ibsen because he was not a "mere artist" (Shaw's favorite pejorative), but a practical man seeking to reform the world through drama.

Despite Shaw's demands for utilitarianism, his own plays do not provide practical solutions to specific problems—they merely illuminate the problems and expose the paradoxes. His fundamental revelations tend to be more philosophical than practical. A few concepts tend to dominate his work: the Life Force and the Superman (both derived from the philosophy of Henri Bergson, who taught that through man an inscrutable "life force" is constantly working to evolve the "superman"), and Fabian socialism (which led him to champion economic and political reforms). The Fabians believed that the superior individual must lead lesser ones, and rejected the idea that the opinion of the majority should serve as a basis for action. To Shaw, leadership should be determined by intelligence and common sense rather than by birth, wealth, social position, or popularity. He championed the gradual solution of human problems, which will be eliminated only when the Superman has fully evolved. For the moment, Shaw saw the prospect for limited progress only, although each person should recognize "that to save himself, he must save the race." Better living conditions and education, therefore, can free man from immediate petty concerns and assist in the more rapid achievement of the ultimate goal—a world of Supermen who have risen above selfish preoccupations through rational power. Thus, correcting wrongheaded notions, shaking prejudices and convictions, and arousing skepticism are devices which can hasten progress, and it was with such devices that Shaw sought to serve mankind, although his aims are not equally evident in all his plays.

Fortunately, Shaw had as keen an eye for what is entertaining as he did for what is philosophically striking. He was firmly rooted in the nineteenth-century tradition of melodrama and the well-made play and, no matter how often he denounced it, he utilized that tradition in creating his own highly effective dramatic works.

The play which launched Shaw's career as a dramatist, *Widower's Houses* (1892), allegedly was begun in 1885 in collaboration with William Archer. Abandoned for a time, it was completed by Shaw at Grein's urging. Conventionally constructed, it ostensibly attacks slum landlordism but actually explodes the self-righteous and romantic notions of the protagonist,

Harry Trench. Upon discovering that the father of his fiancée, Blanche Sartorious, derives his income from slum rentals, Trench refuses to accept any of the money, although the couple will thereby have to lead an economically deprived existence. His idealism ultimately crumbles when Sartorious demonstrates that Trench's own meager funds are derived from slum property. Trench then joins Sartorious and Lickcheese, Sartorious's former rent collector, in a scheme which will greatly increase their income. Shaw is obviously primarily interested in exposing the unthinking philistinism of "respectable" people who condemn other, more practical persons without acknowledging their own involvement in exploiting the weak and poor. Thus, he suggests that the clear-sighted Sartorious is perhaps more admirable, and certainly more practical, than those who denounce him. Trench comes to see the world in a much less ideal light and is reconciled to it, but by no stretch of the imagination can Shaw be said to have suggested a practical solution to the problem of slum landlordism.

Shaw's later plays, of which there are more than fifty, continue to puncture popular beliefs. *Arms and the Man* (1894) attacks romantic notions of love and war. In *Candida* (1895), a wife decides to stay with her husband, a popular, spellbinding preacher, rather than to run away with her apparently naïve poet, Marchbanks, not because she fears scandal but because her husband needs her more than does the self-sufficient writer. Thus Shaw seems to argue that to be needed is more compelling than romantic attachment. In *The Devil's Disciple* (1897), set in the American Revolution, the seemingly irresponsible Dick Dudgeon becomes a saintly individual through his purely instinctive sense of right. Conversely, the Reverend Anthony Anderson, the man whom Dudgeon by chance is forced to impersonate and in whose guise he is sentenced to the gallows, changes from a nonviolent pastor to a man of action, taking up arms and leading a band of men to victory, effecting a last-minute rescue of Dudgeon from the gallows. Here Shaw is concerned with the paradox of human nature and suggests that in moments of crisis men act instinctively, according to their true temperaments and without regard for the roles they have been forced to play by society's conventions. In all of these early plays, Shaw manages to trick expectancy through carefully prepared-for but unforeseen developments. The resulting dramatic effectiveness probably explains why these early plays still are produced more frequently than are most of Shaw's later works, except for *Major Barbara* and *Pygmalion*, which tend to return to the early methods.

Many critics have pointed to the loosening of structure in Shaw's plays beginning with *Caesar and Cleopatra* (1899). Thereafter, he moved away from a dependence on the devices of the well-made play and toward greater concern for ideas and the means most appropriate for transmitting them. His philosophical preoccupation with the Life Force now came to the fore and was powerfully embodied in *Man and Superman* (1903). Shaw himself preferred another of his works on the same theme, *Back to*

Shaw's *Caesar and Cleopatra* at the Royal Court Theatre.
At right is Forbes-Robertson, for whom Shaw wrote the role.
(From *Play Pictorial*, 1907.)

Methuselah (composed of five plays written in 1919–20), in which he traces the whole history of mankind and suggests that either man must embrace the doctrine of Creative Evolution or perish. Despite Shaw's preference for this work, critics have generally found it tedious and dramatically inferior to *Man and Superman*.

Between 1900 and 1910, Shaw wrote several plays which he labeled "disquisitory" because they are essentially explorations of varying views about specific problems. *Getting Married* (1908), for example, treats marriage and divorce as seen by various characters, each of whom represents a specific point of view. Similarly, *Misalliance* (1910) explores the relationships of parents and children.

Among Shaw's most popular plays of the period between 1900 and 1915 are *Major Barbara* (1905) and *Pygmalion* (1913). In *Major Barbara,* a young woman has joined the Salvation Army so that she may save souls, but she eventually discovers that the body and the mind must be fed first. She comes to accept that her father, a munitions manufacturer who provides education and a high standard of living for his workers, is to be more admired than is the Salvation Army with its prolongation of the status quo by dispensing charity which preserves the body without doing anything to improve man's lot. In *Pygmalion*, Shaw takes as his premise that class distinctions are perpetuated by dialects which could be eliminated by the proper use of phonetics. He chooses an illiterate flower girl, Eliza Doolittle, as his heroine and shows how she is trained by Professor Higgins until she is accepted as a duchess. This Cinderella story is probably Shaw's most widely known work, in part because it served as the basis for the enormously popular musical comedy *My Fair Lady* (1956).

Among Shaw's later works, the most important are *Heartbreak*

House (1919) and *Saint Joan* (1923). *Heartbreak House* is Shaw's least characteristic work, for it is a symbolic drama about Europe and the conditions which brought about World War I (which was underway while Shaw was writing the play). To Captain Shotover's shiplike home (the ship of state) Shaw brings a number of characters, who represent the new financier, the purposeless woman, the conservative, and other types. The play is suffused with nostalgia for a worthwhile something which is vanishing and hope for a better future. Shaw seems both to condemn the moral helplessness of the characters and to admire their courage. It is an indictment of the past and a demand for a better future. *Saint Joan,* written at the time when Joan of Arc had at last been canonized by the church, explores the meaning of sainthood. Shaw concludes that Joan can be made a saint largely because she no longer represents any threat. According to Shaw, a saint is always so upsetting to his own age that he must be destroyed. He makes Joan ask, "How long, oh Lord, how long [will it be before the world is able to accept its saints]?"

All of Shaw's best work had been done by 1923. He continued to write until the time of his death, but such works as *The Apple Cart* (1929), *The Simpleton of the Unexpected Isles* (1935), and *In Good King Charles' Golden Days* (1939) are pale reflections of his former glory.

Granville Barker, Lillah McCarthy, and George Bernard Shaw rehearsing Shaw's *Androcles and the Lion* at the St. James' Theatre in 1913. (Courtesy Enthoven Collection, Victoria and Albert Museum.)

Few dramatists have believed so firmly in the power of dialectic to bring about progress. It is Shaw's commitment to the idea of progress which no doubt prevented him from acknowledging the darker side of human nature and made him gloss over obstacles to human perfection. Thus, it is probably fortunate that he chose comedy as a medium. Since optimism is almost inherent in the comic form, its presence in Shaw's plays is far more acceptable than it would be had he written serious drama, in which his optimism might have appeared shallow. Because Shaw believed that the dispersal of ignorance is the key to happiness, his dramatic actions are most usually constructed by establishing the prejudices about his subject then prevalent in society (usually treated sympathetically in the opening scenes) and then gradually undermining them and proving them false; since the new perceptions remove the bases for conflict, the actions can then be resolved harmoniously.

Shaw's works differ considerably from those of most realists and naturalists, with whom he allied himself, since most of them saw human problems in the most serious, even gloomy, light. Although Shaw considered himself a realist, that estimate must be qualified, for if he usually wrote with the "fourth wall" in mind and rarely permitted his characters to transgress it, he had no patience with attempts to transfer nature directly to the stage or to recreate milieus in all their details. His statement about Charles Dickens applies equally well to himself: Shaw declared that Dickens combined a "mirror-like exactness of character-drawing with the wildest extravagance of humorous expression and grotesque situation." In writing dialogue, Shaw was never hobbled by any theory that it must approximate real conversation. Although his characters are distinguishable by peculiarities of speech, all are articulate and most are masters of the witty, well-turned phrase. Thus, Shaw's is a superrealism in which the essence of life is captured by sharpening and exaggerating carefully chosen elements.

Shaw always billed himself as a thinker rather than as a dramatist. He emphasized this role by writing numerous essays and by prefacing many of his dramas with lengthy discussions which develop ideas parallel or analogous to those dramatized in the plays they accompany. But it is not as a thinker that Shaw will be remembered, but as a playwright who used thought as a basis for dramatic conflict.

In the 1890s Shaw's drama was still sufficiently unusual that to most spectators it was either puzzling or outrageous. Furthermore, many of his subjects were considered unsuitable for public consumption. Consequently, Shaw was not acceptable in the commercial theatre until after 1900. By World War I his fame was assured and today he is recognized as the dominant figure in modern English drama.

After the demise of the Independent Theatre in 1897, Shaw and other playwrights were aided by a new organization, the Incorporated Stage Society, founded in 1899 through the efforts of the banker Frederick

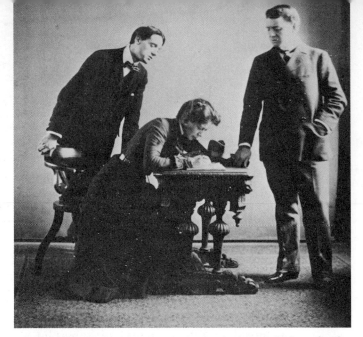

Scene from Shaw's *Mrs. Warren's Profession* in its original production
in 1902 at the New Lyric Club by the Incorporated Stage Society.
(Courtesy Enthoven Collection, Victoria and Albert Museum.)

Whelen. Like the Independent Theatre, the Stage Society produced recent
and experimental British and foreign plays which were otherwise unlikely
to receive public performances. Like those of the Independent Theatre, its
performances were given on Sundays so that professional actors might
appear in them. By 1914 the membership had grown to fifteen hundred and
Monday matinees had been added.

The Stage Society helped the English to keep abreast of the latest
developments both at home and abroad and encouraged new and experimental playwrights. Its first production was of Shaw's *You Never Can Tell,*
and it later gave the first performances of his *Candida, Mrs. Warren's
Profession,* and *Man and Superman.* In all, it produced ten of Shaw's plays.
It also gave first hearings to Harley Granville Barker, St. John Hankin,
Somerset Maugham, and Arnold Bennett, authors who were to make
important contributions to the English stage. In addition, such foreign
dramatists as Tolstoy, Gorky, Chekhov, Turgenev, Brieux, Curel, Hauptmann, and Ibsen were represented. The organization continued until 1939,
by which time it had presented more than two hundred programs.

The Incorporated Stage Society was not the only successor to the
Independent Theatre, although no other lasted so long or made so significant a contribution. Among the other groups were: the Pioneers, founded
in 1905, which introduced the work of John Masefield; the New Century
Theatre, which presented classical as well as new plays; and the Play
Actors' Society, founded in 1907 by members of the Actors' Association,
a theatrical union.

IV

In the years between 1887 and 1900 the major battle over the new drama was fought and, for the most part, won. The opponents had not yet vacated the field and the gains were not yet consolidated, but after 1900 acceptance was to come rapidly.

Many of the gains of these years were only of immediate importance, but others provided permanent lessons. For example, the "independent theatre" as a device for introducing new plays and production methods has been used down to the present. The label has not always been the same but the principle has varied little, whether the theatres have been called "art," "little," avant-garde, or off-off-Broadway. Whenever the established theatres have become insufficiently responsive to new demands, the answer has been found in some variation on Antoine's Théâtre Libre.

The independent theatres of the late nineteenth century did not introduce a great number of important new dramatists, but Shaw, Hauptmann, and Brieux are sufficient to justify their existence. Furthermore, the groups provided a platform for drama which deserved a hearing even if it could not command the mass audiences which most commercial theatres sought.

It was also in the independent theatres, especially Antoine's, that naturalistic production techniques were first consistently applied to create a unified style for naturalistic plays. Unfortunately, Antoine tended to use the same basic style for all plays, whether naturalistic or romantic. It may be for this reason that the 1890s saw both the peak and the decline of naturalism, for once naturalistic methods were applied to plays of various styles its limitations began to be evident. Furthermore, many of the plays which were given their first hearing at this time were so extreme that they set off a reaction against naturalism in general. To many, the *comédies rosses* came to be seen as the quintessential form of naturalism, although such plays were probably aberrant. Nevertheless, after 1890 dramatists began to display a greater concern for selection and arrangement for dramatic effect. Even the spokesmen for naturalism began to defect. As early as 1891, Jullien began to abandon *comédie rosse* in *The Sea,* which freely mingled fantasy and realism. Later he was to attack Antoine for producing the very kind of play that had made him famous. Even Zola underwent a change during the last decade of his life. Though he never gave up his faith in science or ceased to champion naturalism, he found the techniques he had formerly advocated no longer adequate to express the growing idealism of his final works, a number of which are near-mythic and symbolic. Just before he died, Zola turned once more to dramatic composition, but now instead of "fragments of existence," he composed six opera librettos—written in poetic prose and set to music by Alfred Bruneau—

three of which were produced in Paris: *Messidor* in 1897, *The Hurricane* in 1901, and *The Infant King* in 1905. In this final phase, Zola seems much more nearly related to Wagner than to Becque.

Hugh Allison Smith has argued that naturalism declined in France because it was foreign to the Frenchman's love for logic, order, and clarity. Similarly, it has been argued that naturalism was foreign to the German's penchant for philosophical drama based upon clearly defined premises. The English never embraced naturalism (or even a thoroughgoing realism). But probably the principal reason for the decline of naturalism was the growing skepticism about scientism, which had preached utopianism and had been the instigator of naturalism. Regardless of the reason, by 1900 naturalism as a conscious movement was largely over. Thereafter it was gradually absorbed into the more viable realistic mode.

But naturalism was to leave a powerful legacy. Its concern for concrete environment established the idea that each play must be performed in a setting designed especially for it. Even those who rejected naturalism came to expect an appropriate "artistic environment" for each play. A large proportion of modern drama has continued to emphasize the integral relationship of character and action to heredity and environment. Furthermore, naturalism's concern for society's ills has remained a significant ingredient of much drama.

Many ramifications of the developments after 1887 were not yet evident in 1900, but the public had become conscious of Ibsenesque and naturalistic drama and of new production methods. Furthermore, they were beginning to accept the new trends, largely because popularizers had adapted the original ideas to the tastes of conservative audiences. Once-radical departures were soon to be absorbed into the mainstream.

Anti-Realist Alternatives

5

The 1890s saw the wide acceptance of realism and naturalism, but it also brought significant alternatives to the realistic mode. From the beginning, realism had had its detractors, not only among conservative critics and playgoers but among a new generation of dissidents who rejected the objective and scientific view of human destiny then being proclaimed. At first the dissidents attracted few adherents, but gradually their voices were heard and realism's supremacy was challenged just as it seemed triumphant. The most important protest came from the symbolists in France, but lesser assaults were mounted elsewhere. Taking their inspiration from Poe, Baudelaire, Wagner, and other sources, such writers as Mallarmé, Maeterlinck, Claudel, and Jarry, and such producers as Fort and Lugné-Poë, made an impact in France second only to Antoine's. In England, the art-for-art's-sake movement, especially through Wilde, gained a grudging hearing, and in Germany, Nietzsche and von Hofmannsthal contributed to a neoromanticism. By 1900, a viable alternative to realism had been established.

~ | ~

Even as realism was being promulgated in the 1850s, there were many who believed that it was capable of revealing only one part of truth—that which can be perceived by the five senses—whereas its more significant aspects are found in mystery and myth, in shimmering, dreamlike figures rather than in the flesh-and-blood, material world. Consequently, many began either to look inward to the subjective, psychological, and irrational nature of man, or outward to the mysterious forces beyond the control or comprehension of man. Such individuals advocated a drama composed of images and symbols and a theatre in which line, color, and mood would replace illusionistic re-creations of real places. Just as the naturalists sought to make of theatre a social weapon, the antirealists sought to make of it a religion.

The antirealists in France found their inspiration in diverse sources, but especially in the works of Poe, Baudelaire, and Wagner. Edgar Allan Poe (1809–49) came to French attention during the 1850s through the translations made by the poet Charles-Pierre Baudelaire (1821–67). Poe's influence was felt in several ways. First, he had declared it a heresy in criticism to demand that literature be didactic. He pronounced poetry valuable in itself without any need of moral or social lessons to justify its existence. Second, he placed great stress upon correctness of language, meter, and structure, and his own poetry displayed a remarkable musical gift. His standards are best epitomized in such poems as "The Bells," in which no message is conveyed and in which sound is manipulated to create near-musical impressions. Third, and perhaps most important, Poe stressed the mysterious and macabre—especially in his short stories, in which forces beyond those of heredity and environment seem to control destiny. These aspects of Poe's work made of him almost a patron saint for those French writers who sought to counteract the realistic outlook.

Although he had been writing for some time, it was as the translator of Poe's works after 1852 that Baudelaire first became widely known. His first article on Poe appeared in the *Revue de Paris* in 1852, just at the time when the critical foundations of realism were being laid. Between 1852 and 1865 Baudelaire translated a number of Poe's stories and essays (but only one poem, "The Raven"). His fame as a translator of Poe's works led the

Revue des Deux Mondes to publish some of Baudelaire's own poems in 1855. As a result, he became notorious almost overnight. When his collection *The Flowers of Evil,* now among the most admired poems of the nineteenth century, was published in 1857, he and the publisher were prosecuted for obscenity, heavily fined, and six of the poems suppressed. For several generations, *The Flowers of Evil* was to be a byword for depravity, morbidity, and obscenity in literature. Baudelaire's remaining years were spent in growing pessimism, and in 1867 he died in almost complete obscurity.

Baudelaire's output was small. He spent most of his mature life writing those poems which make up *The Flowers of Evil,* but it was in part this perfectionism which recommended him to the symbolists. He was fascinated by the irrational forces which distort and destroy man and he affronted many readers by flouting his "evil" and making of it a judgment on man. For him, to write poetry was to "cultivate one's hysteria," but out of his delving into his own psyche he reached a kind of universal view of mankind and succeeded in being a moralist while simultaneously conveying a sense of ecstacy at being in the throes of evil. The symbolists were attracted by his depiction of human nature as mysterious and irrational, by his impeccable literary style, and by his rebellion against accepted standards of decency and against the demand that poetry be utilitarian.

Baudelaire also made a number of pronouncements about poetic method that were to be widely quoted. He believed that the writer works through a kind of irrational and mystical grasp of truth but that the very nature of his intuitions makes it impossible to express them directly—man walks in a "forest of symbols" which speak to him in words he cannot quite understand. Therefore, the writer can communicate only obliquely through a system of "correspondences," which suggest but do not directly express his vision. "From the world of the senses the poet takes the material in which to forge a symbolic vision of himself or of his dream."

It was also Baudelaire who through an article published in 1861 first called attention in France to Wagner's theories. Around 1870, interest in Wagner began to increase as Eduard Schuré, Villiers de l'Isle-Adam, and others began to write about him, but it was the outpouring of eulogies which followed Wagner's death in 1883 that made the greatest impact. Edouard Dujardin's *Revue Wagnérienne* (published from 1884 to 1888) was to serve as an outlet for much of the writing by the then-emerging symbolists. Nevertheless, few of Wagner's French admirers had any clear conception of his ideas, for his major theoretical works were not available in French, and they tended to substitute their own conceptions for his. Among Wagner's ideas, those with which the symbolists were most familiar were his rejection of realism, his conception of art as myth, his fusion of music and poetry, his quasi-religious view of the mission of art, and his synthesis of all the arts into a master art work.

The diverse antirealistic forces converged in the mid-1880s to create a conscious movement, symbolism, launched in 1885 with a "manifesto" written by Jean Moréas. Adherents of the new movement included Stephane Mallarmé, Paul Valery, Claude Debussy, René Ghil, Gustave Kahn, Charles Morice, and others.

Mallarmé (1842–98) soon became the recognized leader of the symbolists, although their opinions were often widely divergent. He began writing about 1860 and early in his career composed two dramas, *Hérodiade* (begun in 1864, left uncompleted as a drama, and later rewritten as a poem) and *The Faun* (1865), a short poetic drama, which after its rejection by the Comédie Française he reshaped into the poem "The Afternoon of a Faun." Mallarmé then abandoned the dramatic form, although many of his later works include dramatic elements. He never abandoned his interest in the theatre, however, and his theoretical and critical writings exerted considerable influence upon it.

Mallarmé was thoroughly familiar with the drama of his day. As critic for *La Dernière Mode* in the mid-1870s, he commented on almost every play then to be seen in Paris, including those of Dumas *fils,* Augier, Sardou, and Zola. He deplored the limitation of drama to the realistic mode and sought to encourage what he considered a higher form. His ideas on the drama found their fullest expression in the criticism which he wrote for *La Revue Independante* in the 1880s and in his essays of the 1890s.

For Mallarmé, drama is essentially a sacred and mysterious rite which, through dream, reverie, allusion, and musicality, evokes the hidden spiritual meaning of existence. The theatre is a kind of secular religious experience in which both actor and audience participate and in which the mystery of the universe is revealed and celebrated; it is concerned with man rather than with particular men. Like Baudelaire, Mallarmé believed that the poet must suggest rather than describe and that poetic images should be ambiguous so that reality is cloaked in mystery. He declared: "To name an object is to do away with three-quarters of the enjoyment of a poem, which is derived from the satisfaction of guessing little by little; to suggest it, that is the illusion. It is the perfect handling of the mystery that constitutes the symbol: to evoke an object little by little in order to show a state of mind or inversely to choose an object and to disengage from it a state of mind by a series of unriddlings."

For Mallarmé, poetic language and imagery took precedence over all else. He objected strenuously to Wagner's elevation of music above poetry and argued that in poetry music must be a part of the structure. He also took issue with Wagner's conception of the theatre as a synthesis of all the arts, declaring instead that, although the constituent arts should interact and reenforce each other, they should always remain under the dominance of poetry. Because spectacle was being overemphasized in the theatre of his day, Mallarmé called for the "detheatricalization of the theatre" and for a "dematerialized" stage. He wished to reduce all the theatre arts to the bare essentials needed to support the written word. Thus, he often seems close to advocating a closet drama. At times he also favors a coterie audience: he once proposed a theatre in which there would be only one actor (the poet), who would recite his works for an audience of not more than twenty-four persons.

Not all symbolists agreed with Mallarmé's ideas, but nearly all were affected by them. His view of drama—as an evocation of the mystery of existence through poetic and allusive language, performed with only the most essential and atmospherically appropriate theatrical aids, for the purpose of creating a quasi-religious experience—was to set the tone for the antirealistic works of the 1890s.

A number of dramatists may be considered forerunners of the symbolist school, but perhaps the most important of these was Philippe Villiers de l'Isle-Adam (1838–89), an aristocrat who traced his lineage back to the Crusades and who numbered among his ancestors many illustrious figures. In all of his work he opposed the light of dream to the darkness of common sense and took pride in an idealism that the vulgar crowd could not understand. He was thoroughly contemptuous of science and progress; to him, art was a path to an ideal realm beyond the access of materialism.

The symbolists were most attracted to Villiers de l'Isle-Adam's *Axel* (1885–86), the action of which is set in a cloister. Each of the characters represents a different ideal—the religious, the occult, the worldly, the passionate—and the drama is largely a struggle between these ideals. Axel, the hero, rejects the whole illusion that is life, for "infinity alone is not a deception." Sara, who originally desires life passionately, finds her fulfillment in Axel and accepts his standard. Since life is an illusion and infinity the only truth, they give up life willingly to become one with truth, and they commit suicide at the moment of marriage so that they may escape into Being rather than exist in a state of Becoming. The play uses many of the trappings of romanticism, especially in its spectacle, in which a kind of opulent splendor parallels the exalted plane of the action. It is written in an elevated diction—a poetic prose which makes no concessions to the conversational mode so dear to the realists.

Villiers de l'Isle-Adam wrote a number of other plays which either uphold the ideal or satirize materialism. Ignored through most of his career, he only began to attain recognition in the years immediately preceding his death. All the symbolists of the 1890s paid homage to him, however, and considered themselves his disciples.

In the 1890s symbolism burgeoned. But, though the playwrights were many in number, only two—Maeterlinck and Claudel—were to be of lasting importance. During that decade Maeterlinck was considered the leading antirealistic dramatist of France, while Claudel was virtually unknown. As Maeterlinck's reputation declined after 1910, however, Claudel's increased until today he stands preeminent among symbolist playwrights.

Maurice Maeterlinck (1862–1949) was born in Belgium and educated as a lawyer. In 1886 he went to Paris where he came under the influence of the emergent symbolist movement. At first he confined himself to poetry, but in 1889 he turned to drama with *Princess Maleine,* an action-filled tragedy of blood reminiscent of the Jacobean plays of Webster and Ford. *Princess Maleine,* based on a story by the brothers Grimm, tells of the destruction of Maleine by the wicked queen. The plot is episodic, the characters seemingly motiveless puppets, the dialogue repetitious and full of pauses. Nevertheless, with this play Maeterlinck achieved fame overnight when Octave Mirbeau, one of the most influential critics of the day, praised it as more tragic and significant than *Macbeth* or *Hamlet.*

During the 1890s Maeterlinck was looked upon as the semiofficial dramatist of the symbolist school, for it was his plays *The Intruder* (1890), *The Blind* (1890), and *Pelléas and Mélisande* (1892) that most nearly embodied the symbolist ideal. During these years Maeterlinck also made a number of theoretical statements which are helpful for understanding his dramatic method. About literature in general, he wrote: "Great poetry, if we observe it closely, is made up of three principal elements: first, verbal beauty; then the contemplation and passionate portrayal of what actually exists about us and within us, that is to say, nature and our sentiments; and, finally, enveloping the whole work and creating the atmosphere proper to it, the idea which the poet forms of the unknown in which float about the beings and things which he evokes, the mystery which dominates them, judges them, and presides over their destinies. I have no doubt that this last is the most important element." Maeterlinck also championed a "static theatre," in which the surface dialogue and action is unimportant but in which the unspoken—the language of silence—addresses the soul: "I have grown to believe that an old man, seated in his armchair, waiting patiently, with his lamp beside him, giving unconscious ear to all the eternal laws that reign about his house . . . does yet live in reality a deeper, more human, and more universal life than the lover who strangles his mistress, the captain who conquers in battle, or 'the husband who avenges his honor.' "

Maeterlinck's one-act plays *The Intruder* and *The Blind* best illustrate his notion of "static drama." In *The Intruder,* a blind old man of nearly eighty years sits quietly throughout the play sensing what is lost on the others as they move about unaware that death is approaching to take his daughter, who has given birth to a child in the next room. There is little overt action; attention is focused on the intuitional movement of the old man's mind as he quietly awaits the inevitable. In *The Blind,* a number of sightless persons, who have gone to a forest on an outing, await the return of their leader, an old priest, who has gone to find water for them. When he does not come, they begin to move about anxiously and eventually discover that he has died almost at their feet. They cry out for help, but there is no one to hear them. The play has often been interpreted as an allegorical attack on the Church—insensible to humanity blindly seeking a path out of the wilderness.

By far the most famous symbolist play of the 1890s is *Pelléas and*

Mélisande, which centers around a triangular love affair not unlike that of Paolo and Francesca or Tristan and Isolde. The elder brother, Golaud, brings home his new bride, Mélisande, only to have her and his brother, Pelléas, fall hopelessly in love. Eventually Golaud kills Pelléas, and Mélisande dies after giving birth to a baby. But primary emphasis is placed not on this story but on the mood of mystery and fate which surrounds it.

The action progresses through a set of loosely defined symbols, the significance of which can only be suggested. Water plays some part in almost every scene. Mélisande is first discovered by a pool in the forest; later, she and Pelléas play by a fountain, in which she loses her wedding ring, by which they declare their love, and by which Pelléas is killed; they search for her lost ring in a grotto which can be approached only by a narrow path between two lakes; Pelléas and Golaud find bottomless pools of water under the castle; the sea is the only open space visible from the castle and the only avenue of escape; serving women seek to wash away stains from the castle steps with water. Light and darkness are also recurring motifs. The castle is surrounded by forests so dense that they are dark and impenetrable in contrast with the open sea and its light; the characters often sit in darkness or anxiously seek to find a pool of light; lamps refuse to stay lit. Height and depth are also imbued with significance. Mélisande sits in a tower and combs her hair which falls down to engulf Pelléas standing below as doves fly away from the tower never to return; Pelléas and Golaud go into the bowels of the castle to investigate the stench that arises from there; the numerous pools and fountains are all described as bottomless. Although it is impossible to assign definite meanings to each of these motifs, it is reasonably clear that with them Maeterlinck seeks to suggest the struggle of the characters as their desires for love, happiness, and openness are pitted against fate, misery, and deceit.

Several scenes in the play are connected with the main action only in a symbolic sense. In the opening scene, the women try to wash away stains from the castle steps; in a later scene, sheep are driven to slaughter and the boy Yniold seeks to secure a golden ball pinned beneath an enormous boulder. These scenes are almost allegorical in their symbolization of the human condition, but they add nothing to the development of the plot.

Characterization is also minimal. All the characters desire the good but are overcome by forces more powerful than themselves. At the end, Arkel, the old king, says of Mélisande: "She was a little being quiet and fearful, a poor mysterious being like us all. I shall never understand it all." And of the new-born child, he adds: "It is the poor little one's turn." Thus, although Maeterlinck may be rebelling against naturalism, his view of human destiny is as deterministic as Zola's. His characters are at the mercy of forces as destructive and far more mysterious than those of heredity and environment. His world is both unknowable and uncontrollable. The dialogue is extremely simple and repetitive, but these elements serve to emphasize the recurring motifs and the demand that the audience

look beneath the surface for more complex meanings. Nevertheless, one
must sympathize somewhat with critic Francisque Sarcey's caustic comment after seeing the play that it is difficult to be interested in a heroine who does not know where she has come from or where she is going and who repeats everything three times.

Maeterlinck eventually tired of the symbolist view. He began to make the transition about 1895, but a new direction was not fully evident until 1902, when he wrote *Monna Vanna.* It has often been charged that Maeterlinck at this time deliberately chose the direction which had been laid out by Edmond Rostand (1868–1918), whose poetic and romantic dramas had achieved the popular success which had been denied Maeterlinck.

Rostand began his playwriting career in 1894 with *The Romancers,* a delightful satire on the aspirations of young lovers. (It has been given renewed life in recent years through the popular musical *The Fantasticks.*) This was followed by *The Far-Away Princess* (1895), a more serious though still tender and lyrical play about a troubadour who makes a last journey to the court of the princess he loves and dies in bliss. But it was *Cyrano de Bergerac* (1897), written as a vehicle for Constant Coquelin (1841–1909), one of the great actors of France, which was to be Rostand's masterpiece. It tells the story of Cyrano, poet, lover, and faithful friend, whose great spirit is encased in an ugly body. Feeling that his love for Roxane is hopeless, he aids the handsome Christian to win her. He eventually dies with his love unspoken but with the awareness that Roxane has come to appreciate his worth. The overall sense is not one of sadness, however, but of courage and

The actor Coquelin as Cyrano at the Porte-Saint-Martin shortly before the turn of the century. (From *Le Théâtre,* 1900.)

integrity, of joy gained through unselfish love for others. The many-sided Cyrano is a role so challenging that actors have kept the play alive ever since.

The success of *Cyrano de Bergerac* led Sarah Bernhardt (1845–1923), the most famous French actress of her day, to commission Rostand to write a play for her. The result was *The Eaglet* (1900), the story of Napoleon's seventeen-year-old son, who wishes to restore his father's empire but who has neither the will nor the strength to carry through his plans. Its principal appeal lies in its evocation of fallen grandeur and strong pathos.

Rostand's last complete play, *Chantecler* (1910), is a two-leveled allegory which uses barnyard creatures to comment on the human condition. With its masterly verse, it is considered by many critics Rostand's most profound play, although it was not very successful in the theatre. Rostand's last years were so marred by ill health that he was unable to complete *The Last Night of Don Juan,* a work with many fine moments. In it, Don Juan has been given a ten-year reprieve from death, but at the end of that time, having learned nothing, is sentenced to eternity as a marionette in the Devil's puppet theatre.

Rostand was not a great dramatist, but through his adaptation of the ideas and devices of the symbolists he created a popular poetic drama where they had failed to do so. Ironically, his work has outlived that of most of his more ambitious contemporaries.

It was in Rostand's vein that Maeterlinck cast most of his later work. In *Monna Vanna,* the city of Pisa is threatened with destruction and to save it Monna Vanna agrees to give herself to the general of the besieging forces. He is so chivalrous, however, that later, when he is threatened with torture, she lies to save him and at the end of the play it appears that she will rescue and go away with him. Although a vague mysticism still clings to the play, it is secondary to the action.

Of Maeterlinck's later works, by far the most famous is *The Blue Bird* (1908), an allegory in which two children search for the blue bird (a symbol for happiness) and after a great number of adventures discover it in their own backyard. Despite its great scenic demands, it has been Maeterlinck's most enduring play in the theatre. Although the plays written after 1900 brought Maeterlinck a much wider audience, they are generally considered less important than the plays written during the 1890s. After World War I, Maeterlinck's reputation steadily declined.

As Maeterlinck lost in prestige, Paul Claudel (1868–1955) gained. Claudel began his literary career as a poet in Mallarmé's circle between 1887 and 1895. Eventually he came to consider Mallarmé's view spiritually empty and he rejected the symbolist outlook, although he retained many of its poetic methods. From Mallarmé, Claudel absorbed the notion that poetry is a revelation of the hidden wonder of the universe, that it links the visible and invisible planes of existence, and that language has the power to evoke and suggest ideas and emotions.

Maeterlinck's *The Blue Bird* at the Théâtre Réjane, Paris, in 1911. The scenery, by V.E. Egerov, was loaned by the Moscow Art Theatre, for which it was originally designed. (From *Le Théâtre, 1911.*)

Claudel began his playwriting career in 1889 with *The Golden Head* (published anonymously, as was much of his early work because of his career in the French diplomatic service). Like all of his plays, it shows the futility of man without God and the limitations of man when compared with spiritual infinity. *The Golden Head* is semiallegorical, for the characters represent various spiritual states and are more nearly elements in an inner struggle than agents of an external action.

Claudel ignored the demands of the theatre more fully than did any of his contemporaries. It is probably for this reason that none of his works was staged in the 1890s and that he is often passed over in discussions of symbolist drama. His first work to reach the stage was *The Tidings Brought to Mary* (first written in 1892 as *The Maid Violaine*), produced in 1912 by Lugné-Poë. Set in the Middle Ages, it consists of a prologue and four acts. In the prologue, the beautiful Violaine is about to marry Jacques Hury when she encounters Pierre de Creon, an architect on his way to Rheims to build a cathedral. He is a leper, however, and out of compassion she kisses him and with this act takes his curse upon herself. She gives up her fiancé to her sister and thereafter lives the life of an outcast. The four acts, which comprise the main action, show Violaine's complete submission to the will of God. There is no struggle; the focus is on the effect of her saintliness upon others, who eventually find peace, just as the focus in Christ's story is not upon his suffering but upon his impact. Like Claudel's other plays, *The Tidings Brought to Mary* illustrates that the value of life can be realized only in giving it away, for it is in submitting to God's will that man finds fulfillment. Claudel's theological message is cloaked in language of considerable beauty (the vigorous rhythm of Claudel's free verse has

Design for the program used for the first production of Claudel's
The Tidings Brought to Mary at the Théâtre de l'Oeuvre in 1912.

been compared to that of the Bible), its powerful moods, and its symbolic
indirection (so great that the dogma often entirely escapes the casual
reader). The play also shows Claudel's profound awareness of the spiritual
wasteland that surrounds man and of the human quest for some meaning
in life. Although Claudel's outlook may be called optimistic (in that he
provides an answer to man's quest), it is not facile, for he requires sacrifice,
self-denial, and acceptance of suffering.

But Claudel is no ascetic. He does not demand a retreat from life or
from physical love. Rather, for him physical passion is a primary means for
learning divine love, since God's love can best be comprehended as an
extension of human love. This aspect of Claudel's work is perhaps best seen
in *Break of Noon* (written in 1905 and first produced in 1916 by the
Groupe Art et Action), which centers upon Mesa, a young man who has
sought to give his soul to God by divorcing himself from life. It is through
his passion for Ysé, another man's wife, that he begins to understand love.
But he always holds something back, and it is not until they are surrounded
by Chinese revolutionaries bent on destroying all foreigners that he fully
comprehends that Ysé is an instrument of God's will through which he has

come to know the love of God. At the conclusion of the play, Mesa, mortally wounded, is forced to stand erect by Ysé, who bids him reach out his hand to heaven. In the darkness, only the hand is visible as Ysé, at Mesa's feet, cries out: "Remember me for one moment in this darkness. I was once your vine."

The same basic ideas inform all of Claudel's plays. Their combination of sympathetic awareness of human suffering and doubt, of Catholic dogma, rich texture of poetic language, symbol, and complex spectacle have made Claudel's work both admired and disliked. Since he often confused the uninitiated, his acceptance in the theatre came only after he gained a literary following. Although the plays began to appear sporadically in the theatre from 1912 onward, it was only after Jean-Louis Barrault's production in 1943 of *The Satin Slipper* (written between 1919 and 1924) that Claudel's essential theatricality was fully recognized. Claudel makes such great demands on the theatre that many of his works were long considered unstageable, and it was primarily through those post-World War II directors committed to "total theatre" that his plays found their proper theatrical expression. Claudel is not concerned with illusion or with psychological and sociological problems but with the symbolic exploration of those spiritual states which can best be expressed through visions, often reaching out to encompass enormous spaces and lapses of time. *The Satin Slipper* includes events that span a century and occur in Spain, Italy, Africa, America, and at sea. At one point, the hemispheres converse and at another the earth is represented as one bead on a rosary. Thus, it requires more than ordinary means and more than ordinary imagination to do Claudel's plays justice in the theatre. From the beginning, Claudel's following steadily increased. Today he is recognized as the greatest of the symbolist playwrights.

Claudel's *Break of Noon,* produced at the Théâtre Marigny in 1948.
Jean-Louis Barrault, at left, played Mesa.
(He had much to do with the revival of Claudel's works after World War II.)
Pierre Brasseur performed Amalric; Edwige Feuillère, Ysé;
and Jacques Dacqmine (right), De Ciz.

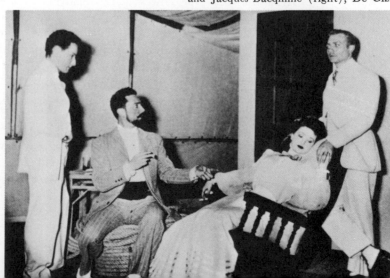

Like the naturalists, the symbolists did not prosper in the theatre until, taking their cue from Antoine, they accepted the principle of the "independent theatre." The first significant symbolist producer was Paul Fort (1872–1960), who in 1890 at the age of seventeen founded the Théâtre Mixte. After one program, Fort merged his group with the Théâtre Idéaliste (founded by Louis Germain but not yet operative), and still another transformation led to the Théâtre d'Art (the title usually associated with Fort's work). With his Théâtre d'Art, Fort produced seven bills between November 1890 and March 1892. After a lapse of several months, Fort, in cooperation with Lugné-Poë, began work on a production of *Pelléas and Mélisande* but withdrew before the play was presented. Thus, in 1893 the Théâtre d'Art came to an end and Fort retired permanently from the theatre at the age of twenty-one.

According to Fort, he founded his theatre to present works which had not been intended for the stage. His first program was composed entirely of recited poems, but the later ones turned to drama, although almost all included some nondramatic poetry. His repertory ranged through selections from the Bible and the *Iliad,* poems by Victor Hugo, Mallarmé, Poe, Theodore de Banville, and Arthur Rimbaud, and such plays as Shelley's *The Cenci,* Marlowe's *Doctor Faustus,* Maeterlinck's *The Intruder* and *The Blind,* Mme. Rachilde's *The Call of Blood,* and Quillard's *The Girl with the Severed Hands.* Most frequently an evening's bill included several offerings, for Fort attempted to provide considerable variety by combining the old and the new, the dramatic and the nondramatic. As a result, the evenings were often interminable; one program in December 1891 is said to have lasted until 5 a.m.

Fort was encouraged by Mallarmé and Verlaine, whose portraits graced *The Book of Art,* a small symbolist review which served as a program for the productions. The theatre was always financially shaky. Originally Fort went from door to door and sent out hundreds of handwritten letters soliciting subscriptions. He was never able to pay any of his authors, actors, or designers. For the most part, his actors were amateurs considerably out of their depth, but he also recruited a number of professionals—among them Marguerite Moreno, Suzanne Desprès, Berthe Bady, and Abel Tarride. The settings were by such leading symbolist painters as Paul Gauguin, Maurice Denis, Paul Sérusier, and Edouard Vuillard.

The motto of the Théâtre d'Art was "the word creates the decor." Quillard stated: "The decor ought to be a pure ornamental fiction which completes the illusion by color and line analogous with the drama. Most often some mobile draperies will suffice to give the impression of the infinite multiplicity of time and place. The spectator . . . abandons himself completely to the will of the poet and will see, according to his soul, some terrible or charming figures and imaginary lands where no one except himself can penetrate; the theatre will be what it ought to be: *a pretext for dream.*" The Théâtre d'Art's designers favored extremely simple settings, more ornamental and atmospheric than illusionistic. Their work was clearly influenced by the impressionists' use of clean color and by the carefully planned geometry of Japanese prints. For a recitation of Rimbaud's "The Drunken Boat," Ranson designed a four-leafed folding screen on which he painted a Japanese-style underwater garden. For *The Girl with the Severed Hands,* Maurice Denis used three scrim curtains and a gold-colored backdrop on which was painted angels and other figures like those on icons or as seen in the work of the "primitives." On the forestage, in front of the scrims, a reciter spoke (in a soft and monotonous voice) the passages which explained the changes of place. Behind the scrims, as in a vision, the silhouetted actors moved slowly and with dignity. For de Gourmont's *Théodat,* the setting was made up of a single backdrop, gold in color, on which were glued seven thousand red lions (all cut out with scissors). Occasionally, the background was completely unadorned. For a reading of Mallarmé's translation of Poe's "The Raven," a drop made of gray wrapping paper was used (or at least that was the plan; a backstage employee of the theatre in which it was performed decided that the set was too plain, cut a square in the middle and inserted in it the portrait of a Napoleonic general!).

Fort attempted a multimedia production with *The Song of Songs of Solomon* (as adapted by Roinard). In each scene, projected light changed color and specially written music underscored the shifting moods. But, more startling, perfumes of varying odors (also supposedly paralleling the emotions) filled the auditorium as persons stationed in the boxes manned vaporizers. (After a time the mingled odors virtually overpowered the audience.)

Fort and his associates were more enthusiastic than accomplished, more ambitious in planning than scrupulous in execution. Much of the work was outrageously amateurish and intentions were often far from clear. Because of the novelty of Fort's approach and the often slipshod results, audiences divided themselves into two clearly defined camps: the ardent supporters, who overlooked all shortcomings, and the deriders, who found every production outrageous or hilarious. Almost every performance became an occasion for riotous confrontations. Of Fort's supporters, Jules Lemaître wrote: "A scattered insanity floats in the air. . . . The very young heads of schoolboys, ecstatic and illuminated, listen to the words of Maeterlinck. . . . [There is] an undercurrent of perversion and craziness." On the other hand, Francisque Sarcey, Paris's most influential critic, was often in a state of uncontrollable laughter. His prestige made him a special target of abuse for Fort's friends. On one occasion they set off firecrackers under his seat, and on another the young poet Saint-Pol-Roux hung by his hands from the balcony and threatened to fall on Sarcey's head if he did not stop laughing. Not all the detractors were amused, for Fort received an enormous number of letters threatening him with violence if he did not cease his productions.

Fort's career in the theatre was short. Nevertheless, when he retired he had made an impact on the French theatre of his day second only to Antoine's. His is the pioneering effort in all modern departures from realism. As Camille Mauclair said of him: "Without his taste for mad adventures, the Symbolist theatre would without doubt have remained in the limbo of theory for there was not a man of action among all those thinkers."

Still, there was always an element of preciosity and dilletantism in Fort's work, and it remained for Aurélien-Marie Lugné-Poë (1869–1940) to solidify the work that Fort had begun. Lugné-Poë had been present at the first production of the Théâtre Libre and had performed in Antoine's productions from 1888 to 1890 while still a student at the Conservatoire. But he shared an apartment with the young painters Pierre Bonnard (1867–1947), Maurice Denis (1870–1943), and Edouard Vuillard (1868–1940), all destined to become leading figures in the Parisian art world of the 1890s. Through them he became aware of symbolism and gradually abandoned the views which animated the Théâtre Libre. He began to act for Fort and eventually directed a number of plays for him.

In 1893, Fort and Lugné-Poë decided to cooperate on the premiere production of Maeterlinck's *Pelléas and Mélisande;* when Fort withdrew, Lugné-Poë succeeded him as the principal purveyor of symbolist drama in Paris. The opening of *Pelléas and Mélisande* (May 17, 1893) is usually considered the birth of the Théâtre de l'Oeuvre, although that name was not taken until after the production and even then was chosen more or less at random. Only later was the name elevated to become a kind of credo and to indicate Lugné-Poë's desire to make of the theatre a work of art (*une oeuvre d'art*). Although Lugné-Poë is usually given sole credit for the work of the Théâtre de l'Oeuvre, he received substantial assistance from Camille Mauclair, poet and critic, and Edouard Vuillard, who oversaw the settings.

The original Théâtre de l'Oeuvre continued until 1899 (Lugné-Poë later revived it), by which time it had presented fifty-one bills, most of them for only two or three performances but some for as many as twenty (though not consecutively). The group considerably extended its influence by touring in Belgium, Holland, Denmark, Norway, and England.

Lugné-Poë laid out two goals for the Théâtre de l'Oeuvre: to familiarize the public with great foreign dramas and to perform the plays of young symbolist playwrights. Among foreign authors, Ibsen was favored, and Lugné-Poë produced *Rosmersholm, An Enemy of the People, The Master Builder, Little Eyolf, Brand, Pillars of Society, Peer Gynt, Love's Comedy,* and *John Gabriel Borkman.* It was largely Lugné-Poë who made

Ibsen acceptable to French audiences and he was ultimately rewarded by being named Ibsen's agent in France. Other foreign plays presented at the l'Oeuvre included Hauptmann's *The Sunken Bell,* Oscar Wilde's *Salome,* Thomas Otway's *Venice Preserved,* Marlowe's *Edward II,* and Bjornson's *Beyond Human Might.* Lugné-Poë also staged adaptations of the Sanskrit dramas *Shakuntala* and *The Little Clay Cart.* Among the new French authors were Maeterlinck, Maurice Beaubourg, Henri de Régnier, Judith Cladel, Jean Lorrain, Auguste Villeroy, Pierre Quillard, Maurice de Faramond, Émile Verhaeren, and Alfred Jarry. Each program was preceded by a lecture designed to increase appreciation of the plays being given on that bill. In production Lugné-Poë continued Fort's ideals but was far more effective in implementing them because of greater care in rehearsal and increased efficiency in organization. With their polish, Lugné-Poë's productions made a greater impact than did Fort's.

Lugné-Poë, following the Théâtre d'Art's creed that the word creates the decor, restricted himself to simplified settings designed to create the proper atmosphere through color, line, and light. In *Pelléas and Mélisande* (with settings by Paul Voegler) there was no furniture or properties and the backdrops were painted in grayed tones. Footlights were abandoned and all light came from overhead. The action, all behind a scrim, appeared to be enveloped in a mist. Costumes were based on the paintings of the fifteenth-century artist Memling. The actors used a singsong delivery (often a chant) and angular, stylized gestures.

A similar style was used in all productions. In 1894, a critic wrote: "The most simple and sensible things take on a different appearance in passing through the mouth and gestures of the l'Oeuvre's actors under the direction of Lugné-Poë. They have a continual ecstatic air of perpetually being visionaries. As if hallucinatory, they stare before them far, very far, vaguely, very vaguely. Their voices are cavernous, their diction choppy. They seem to be attempting to give the air that they are fools." Despite much adverse criticism, Lugné-Poë held firm in his conception of the acting appropriate to symbolist plays, for he felt it necessary to divert attention from external realism to the mysterious inner and outer forces which control destiny.

It is now difficult to judge the effectiveness of the productions. It is clear that the symbolist mode was incomprehensible to many. As is usual with misunderstood artistic movements, symbolism was considered by many a subversive assault on public morality and the state. The premiere of Ibsen's *An Enemy of the People* attracted a large audience because the play was thought to advocate anarchy and because the lecturer for the evening was a well-known writer with anarchist views. There was a half-hour disturbance during the lecture and another demonstration during the performance when Dr. Stockmann proclaimed that the majority is always wrong. Police were in attendance to arrest known anarchists. The next scheduled production, Hauptmann's *Lonely Souls,* was forbidden because the translator was said to be an anarchist. Such troubles plagued the symbolist theatre throughout the 1890s.

Some critics, such as Octave Mirbeau and Catulle Mendes, supported the symbolists, but the majority, like Sarcey, derided them. Still, familiarity bred indulgence and after a time Sarcey wrote: "There was a time when I was overcome with laughter when the curtain went up to discover that green scrim behind which were the mute puppets of a vast marionette show. But we have come to the point where we are no longer astonished by the most nonsensical eccentricities."

But as such critics became reconciled to the peculiarities of symbolist productions, Lugné-Poë himself came to have increasing doubts about them and in 1897 he broke with the symbolists. He stated that, with the exception of Maeterlinck, no significant writer had emerged and that henceforth he intended to choose plays without reference to their origin or outlook. It seems likely that Lugné-Poë had also come to perceive that his approach was not truly suited to Ibsen's work, for in his statement of future policy, he declared: "l'Oeuvre has found itself engulfed by this movement [symbolism] despite the evident contradiction which exists between Ibsen's theatre and the Symbolist theories." Lugné-Poë's manifesto set off a bitter controversy in which the dramatists attacked him and defended themselves. The rift marked the disintegration of the movement. Maeterlinck was already turning in new directions and in 1898 Mallarmé, the principal theorist, died. By 1900, symbolism as a conscious movement was virtually over.

The Théâtre de l'Oeuvre continued its programs until 1899 but, no longer attracting the old coterie audience and unable to gain a new one, was then dissolved. Lugné-Poë gave occasional productions thereafter and reinaugurated regular performances in 1912.

The work of Lugné-Poë and Fort is of tremendous significance. It was to the antirealistic theatre what Antoine's was to the realistic. In some ways, their efforts are even more remarkable than Antoine's, for the Théâtre Libre essentially extended practices that had developed throughout the nineteenth century, whereas the Théâtre d'Art and the Théâtre de l'Oeuvre made a radical break with the past. In their work can be found the seeds of all the antirealistic experiments to come.

III

In addition to the symbolist playwrights, another dramatist of the 1890s— Alfred Jarry (1873–1907)—is of great importance, although his work was not fully appreciated until much later. Jarry's drama is related to that of the symbolists in being antirealistic and in being produced by Lugné-Poë at the Théâtre de l'Oeuvre. But Jarry's view of man was quite unlike that of his symbolist contemporaries. The moral topsy-turvydom of his world more nearly resembles that of the naturalistic *comédies rosses,* although he completely disregards naturalism's scientific logic and attempts to re-create specific environments. Jarry was virtually unique in his day.

Jarry's reputation is based almost entirely on one play, *Ubu Roi* (published and produced in 1896), a work begun in 1888 by Jarry and his schoolmates for puppets in their Théâtre des Phynances. (It has been argued that the original work was by one of Jarry's friends, but, even if true, Jarry elaborated the creation until it became his own.) *Ubu Roi* (*King Ubu*) is a grotesque and bitter comedy about which Jarry stated: "Once the curtain went up, I wanted the stage...to become like that mirror in the stories of Mme. Leprince de Baumont in which the vicious see themselves with bull's horns and a dragon's body.... [The public] is made up, as Catulle Mendes has so well expressed it, 'of eternal human imbecility, eternal lust, eternal gluttony, baseness of instinct which takes over completely; of decorum, virtue, patriotism, and the ideal of people who have dined well.'... The comic element must at the most be the macabre comedy of an English clown or a dance of the dead." Jarry shows in all its grotesqueness a world without human decency. The central figure, Ubu, is violent, stupid, totally devoid of moral scruple; he is the epitome of all that Jarry found inane and ugly in bourgeois society, of all that is monstrous and irrational in man. The action of the play shows how Ubu makes himself king of Poland and keeps his power by killing and torturing all those who oppose him; eventually he is chased from the country but promises to continue his exploits elsewhere.

At about the time his play was published, Jarry went to work for

Sketch made for the production of *Ubu Roi* given at the Théâtre Antoine in 1908 by Firmin Gémier, who had originated the role of Ubu in 1896. (From *Le Figaro,* February 16, 1908.)

Lugné-Poë at the Théâtre de l'Oeuvre, where he was in charge of publicity and had a hand in almost everything. Jarry urged the production of his two favorite dramas—*Peer Gynt* and *Ubu Roi*—and did an adaptation of Ibsen's play (presented with only minor success). Eventually Lugné-Poë also agreed to produce *Ubu Roi*.

On opening night, December 11, 1896, every literary faction in Paris was represented. Jarry himself—dressed in a baggy black suit and in a grotesque makeup—delivered the lecture which preceded the play. The setting was by Jarry, assisted by Bonnard, Vuillard, Toulouse-Lautrec, and Sérusier. Arthur Symons gives this description of it: "The scenery was painted to represent by a child's convention, indoors and out of doors, and even the torrid, temperate, and arctic zones at once. Opposite to you, at the back of the stage, you saw . . . against the sky a small closed window and a fireplace . . . through . . . which . . . trooped in and out these clamorous and sanguinary persons of the drama. On the left was painted a bed, and at the foot of the bed a bare tree, and snow falling. On the right were palm trees, about one of which coiled a boa constrictor. . . . A skeleton dangled from a gallows. Changes of scene were announced by . . . placard. A venerable gentleman in evening dress . . . trotted across the stage on the points of his toes between every scene and hung the new placard on a nail." For battles, two men represented the opposing armies, but for the slaughters Jarry bought forty life-sized wicker mannequins which were beheaded. To indicate that he was on horseback, Ubu wore around his neck a cut-out of a horse's head.

Firmin Gémier, then an actor at the Odéon, played Ubu. At a loss about how to portray such a character, Gémier was advised by Lugné-Poë to imitate Jarry's own speech and gestures (no inflection or nuance and equal stress on each syllable, even the silent ones, and a few monotonous, stylized, and jerky gestures). Gémier's costume made him appear pear-shaped and swollen; Jarry designed a mask for the character (which included a nose like an elephant's trunk), but Gémier did not wear it. When he spoke the play's opening line—"Merdre" (the French *merde* with an extra syllable, or in English, "shit-e")—the audience was thrown into an uproar that lasted for fifteen minutes. Such an obscenity on stage was unknown. Many spectators walked out; the rest quickly divided themselves into supporters and opponents of the play. Fist fights broke out. Finally Gémier restored order by improvising a dance and reclining on the prompter's box. The play proceeded until the next "merdre" was reached, when the uproar was renewed. This was the pattern for the entire evening. The play received only two performances. Of the production, William Butler Yeats (who was in the audience on opening night) wrote: "After S. Mallarmé, . . . after our own verse, . . . what more is possible? After us the Savage God." This remark is now considered prophetic, for the detached, mysterious world of the symbolists was to give way before the grotesque savagery of Jarry's vision.

Setting by Max Ernst for a production of Jarry's *Ubu Bound*
at the Comédie des Champs-Elysées, Paris, in 1937.

Jarry went on to write two more plays about Ubu, *Ubu Bound* (1900),
and *Ubu the Cuckold* (published in 1944), but these were not produced
during his lifetime. Nevertheless, he retained his interest in the theatre and
often wrote about it. He advocated eliminating both settings (since they
are neither natural nor entirely artificial) and acting in the traditional
sense. He preferred the mask to the actor's face because it captures the
eternal qualities of a character, and argued that lines should be delivered as
though the mask itself were speaking.

Jarry's own life was as bizarre as his work. He deliberately flouted
every standard of his day and sought to make himself into a character not
unlike those about whom he wrote. When he died in 1907, he appeared to
leave little trace. As a kind of memorial, Gémier revived *Ubu Roi* briefly
at the Théâtre Antoine in 1908. Following World War I, Jarry's reputation
began to grow as the surrealists proclaimed him one of their progenitors.
In 1927, Antonin Artaud and Roger Vitrac founded their short-lived
Théâtre Alfred Jarry. In 1945, Cyril Connolly dubbed Jarry "the Santa
Claus of the Atomic Age," and shortly thereafter Eugène Ionesco, Boris
Vian, Raymond Queneau, and others acknowledged their indebtedness to
Jarry by founding the mock-serious College of 'Pataphysics to explore what
Jarry at the beginning of the twentieth century had proclaimed a new
"science of 'pataphysics," or "the science of imaginary solutions," in which
contradictions are pushed beyond the limits of human understanding
without ever abandoning the pretense of reason. Jarry was to be virtually
a patron saint of the absurdists.

England contributed little to the nonrealistic theatre of the late nineteenth century, although several critics voiced views similar to those of the French symbolists. In England, this movement was usually called "art-for-art's-sake" or "aestheticism" because its adherents believed that art is valuable in itself and need not be useful or didactic.

The key figure in the English movement was Walter Pater (1839–94), who in his "Conclusion" to *Studies in the History of the Renaissance* (1873) set forth the doctrine which was to be followed by the "aesthetes." Pater declared: "Not the fruit of experience, but experience itself, is the end. A counted number of pulses only is given to us of a variegated, dramatic life. How may we see in them all that is to be seen in them by the finest senses? How shall we pass most swiftly from point to point, and be present always at the focus where the greatest number of vital forces unite in their purest energy? To burn always with this hard, gemlike flame, to maintain this ecstacy, is success in life." To Pater, that man is most successful who lives life most intensely, and it is art which most thoroughly distills human experience and makes it most nearly possible to "maintain this ecstacy," for "art comes to you professing frankly to give nothing but the highest quality to your moments as they pass, and simply for those moments' sake." Ultimately, Pater seems to urge that life itself should become a work of art, intensely hedonistic in purpose and completely oblivious to morality and utility.

Before the 1870s were over, Pater had attracted a number of followers who sought to implement his creed in their own lives. They adopted a kind of dandyism in dress and proudly proclaimed their indifference to the opinion of the masses. It was these aspects of the movement which most quickly captured public attention, so much so that they were extensively satirized in Gilbert and Sullivan's *Patience* (1881).

Oscar Wilde (1856–1900) soon became the movement's primary spokesman, achieving notoriety in part through his adoption of long hair, eccentric dress, and fondness for sunflowers and blue china. It is primarily in his critical writings that Wilde's views on art are evident. He declared: "As a method, Realism is a complete failure, and the two things that every artist should avoid are modernity of form and modernity of subject matter. . . . It is only the modern that ever becomes old-fashioned." He added: "The only beautiful things . . . are the things that do not concern us. As long as a thing is useful or necessary to us, or affects us in any way, either for pain or pleasure . . . it is outside the proper sphere of art." This attitude led him to emphasize form over content and to place great value on precise workmanship. Wilde praised purely decorative art for its "deliberate rejection of Nature as the ideal of beauty, as well as of the imitative method. . . ."

As early as 1906, the British designer Charles Ricketts began to experiment differently from his contemporaries in the use of stage space. This is a design for Oscar Wilde's *Salome,* produced at King's Hall, Covent Garden, April 1906.

In the twentieth century, such views were to produce abstract art, in which recognizable subject matter was avoided so that the artistic medium might be explored for its own intrinsic values rather than for its ability to represent natural objects.

Wilde's theoretical views are not always clearly evident in his dramas. He began his playwriting career with *Vera* (1880) and *The Duchess of Padua* (1883), works in the romantic tradition, but the plays for which he is now remembered all date from the 1890s. Of these, only *Salome* (1893) is closely related to the work of the French symbolists, perhaps because, according to Fort, it was written with the Théâtre d'Art in mind. It treats the perverse passion of Salome for John the Baptist, his refusal of her advances, her demand for his head from her stepfather, Herod, who has an erotic interest in her. To please Salome, Herod accedes to her wishes, but when she makes love to the severed head, he is so revolted that he orders his guards to crush her to death instantly. *Salome* breathes an atmosphere of decadence, in large part because of its images centered around passion, color, and changes in the moon. Banned in England, it was first produced in Paris in 1894, but it was to hold the stage primarily in Richard Strauss's operatic version.

Others of Wilde's plays—*Lady Windermere's Fan* (1892), *A Woman of No Importance* (1893), and *An Ideal Husband* (1895)—seem at first glance closely related to the works of Jones and Pinero, for they treat many

George Alexander as Jack Worthing in the original production of Wilde's *The Importance of Being Earnest*, 1895. (Courtesy Enthoven Collection, Victoria and Albert Museum.)

of the same themes, particularly the complications surrounding the "woman with a past." But Wilde writes with tongue-in-cheek and lets show the machinery of his plays, largely derived from the well-made-play tradition. He is more interested in the witty turn of phrase and in entertaining an audience than in ideas or social problems.

It was only when he abandoned the pseudo-problem play that he wrote his most successful work, *The Importance of Being Earnest* (1895), one of the most skillful plays in the English language. Here he parodies the stories, sentiments, and devices of traditional comedy. The discovery at the end of the play sums up much of the parody, for in it Jack Worthing is shown to be Lady Bracknell's long-lost nephew, left in a handbag at a railroad station as a baby by an absent-minded nurse. This revelation provides him with the family he has needed in order to marry Lady Bracknell's daughter and also proves that his real name is Ernest, a name which Gwendolyn has declared absolutely essential for her husband. The epigrammatic inversion of ordinary sentiments creates a topsy-turvydom not unlike that of Gilbert and Sullivan's operettas.

Art-for-art's-sake did not make a deep impact on English drama. Its force was largely negated after 1895 when Wilde was sentenced to prison (for perjury, although behind this lay charges of sodomy). His conviction served as a kind of revenge on the "aesthetes" and their elitist conceptions of art and disdain for conventional behavior. But it is perhaps well to remember that artistic creeds have never prospered in England. Although all movements have made some impact on English writers, none has thrived. Like all the others, the art-for-art's-sake movement caught attention briefly and was then utilized as needed by the pragmatic English.

During the 1890s, Germanic writers also began to espouse many of the ideals already voiced by French symbolists and English aesthetes. In Germany and Austria, this movement, usually called neoromanticism, challenged the ugliness, dullness, and utilitarianism of naturalism and championed "beauty" and "life" (virtual watchwords). Like Pater, the neoromantics suggested that one should live for beauty alone, or that the highest of values is to be really alive and aware of vital forces at their most intense. Intuition was placed above reason, and all dogmas, conventions, and middle-class beliefs were proclaimed false. Baudelaire, Mallarmé, Maeterlinck, Wilde, and Ibsen (in his late plays) were significant influences on German literature in the 1890s. To these must be added Friedrich Nietzsche (1844–1900), one of the seminal thinkers of the nineteenth century.

Nietzsche wrote his first important work, *The Birth of Tragedy from the Spirit of Music* (1872), under the influence of Wagner, with whom he had become friendly in 1870. In it, Nietzsche explores the origins of Greek tragedy, not through a marshaling of historical evidence but through his own conceptions of the nature of man and of the significance of ritual and myth in ancient Greek society. He concludes that tragedy arose from the union of two conflicting human tendencies: the desire for clarity and order, and the wild, irrational urge toward disorder. He sees these two drives personified in the Greek art deities: Apollo and Dionysus. The dreamlike Apollonian spirit shields man against the terror of reality by providing illusions; in Greece, it led men to create the Olympian gods as a way of giving meaning to human life by making the gods themselves live it. The orgiastic Dionysian spirit, on the other hand, tears away the veil of illusion until it forces man to give up pride in his individuality and recognize his oneness with all of nature. As Nietzsche wrote: "Dionysiac art. . . . wishes to convince us of the eternal delight of existence, but it insists that we look for this delight not in the phenomena but behind them. It makes us realize that everything that is generated must be prepared to face its painful dissolution. It forces us to gaze into the horror of individual existence, yet without being turned to stone by the vision. . . . For a brief moment we become . . . the primal Being, and we experience its insatiable hunger for existence. Now we see the struggle, the pain, the destruction of appearances as necessary. . . . we become one with the immense lust for life and are made aware of the eternity and indestructibility of that lust. . . . we realize our great good fortune in having life—not as individuals, but as part of the life force with whose procreative lust we have become one."

According to Nietzsche, tragedy came into existence when the Apollonian spirit imposed order and harmony on the Dionysian vision; thus, tragedy is "a symbolizing of Dionysian wisdom by means of the expedients of Apollonian art." Nietzsche's notion of tragedy is bound up in his conception of immortality. He rejects the notion of an individual afterlife and argues instead that upon death we are absorbed into the natural cycle of existence. Thus, the tragic vision consists in accepting the necessity of one's own destruction and taking joy in it. Tragedy forces us to reaffirm the value of existence even in the jaws of death—"despite every phenomenal change, life is at bottom indestructibly joyful and powerful."

According to Nietzsche, great art requires a balance between the Dionysian and the Apollonian elements. When the Apollonian dominates—as it did in Greece in the late fifth century B.C. under the influence of Socrates and Euripides—tragedy declines, for rationalism glosses over the Dionysian vision. Similarly, he attributed the low state of drama in his own day to the reverence for science and progress. In Wagner's music-drama he saw the potentialities for a new golden age. (Nietzsche later denounced Wagner because he believed that Wagner was debasing his art in order to attract a popular audience to Bayreuth.)

The Birth of Tragedy has influenced almost all modern movements. First, its view that tragedy arose from Greek conceptions as embodied in myth and ritual undergirds all twentieth-century attempts to explain literature as mythic and ritualistic in origin and structure. Second, its denunciation of scientism and realism and its insistence upon looking behind physical phenomena for more profound truths has been significant in all modern antirealistic movements. Third, its conception of the Dionysian and Apollonian forces within man foreshadows Freud's conception of the human psyche. The Dionysian is roughly equivalent to the id, while the Apollonian encompasses the ego and superego. Furthermore, Nietzsche suggests that much human behavior may be seen as an attempt to gloss over the unpleasant and may be interpreted as signifying something quite different from surface appearance. Not only Freud, but Strindberg, O'Neill, and many other modern dramatists have voiced their admiration for Nietzsche's insights into human motives. Fourth, Nietzsche's description of the Dionsyian element—its dark, tortured, subterranean wisdom—has been echoed by many writers and theorists, perhaps most forcefully by Strindberg and Artaud.

Nietzsche's later writings were also to be extremely influential. In *Thus Spake Zarathustra* (1883–85), he declared, "God is dead." By this he meant that religion had lost so much of its potency that it can no longer serve as a basis for moral values. Nietzsche was the first major philosopher to declare Christianity bankrupt, although scientism had already laid the foundations for such a charge (since theological questions cannot be verified by scientific proof and since nineteenth-century thinkers declared all nonscientific knowledge invalid). Nietzsche's statement was for him merely a prelude to proposals about a sounder basis for morality. Nevertheless, the declaration was significant, for it is the loss of religious faith in the modern world which has removed the primary basis upon which judgments of value previously rested. Much of the twentieth century has been a search for a new system of values; with considerable regularity artistic creeds have been proclaimed and then abandoned as each new movement has come to seem as empty as the ones it sought to replace. "God is dead" was prophetic of the eventual conclusion that all systems of values are equally meaningless.

In *Beyond Good and Evil* (1886) and *The Genealogy of Morals* (1887), Nietzsche called for the "revaluation of all values." Here he argued that originally strength, courage, and wealth were considered virtues, but that Socrates and the Christians had labeled these same attributes evil and had substituted for them poverty, humility, and weakness. He saw this as a tyrannizing of the strong by the weak, who were reconciled to this world by the vision of some glorious afterlife. Thus, he charged that Christianity had given rise to a "slave morality," which in turn had engendered liberalism, socialism, and democracy, nineteenth-century decadence and its substitution of "domestic" tragedy for Dionysian wisdom. The product of this debased condition he called "the last man" and, as a countermeasure, he proclaimed the need for the *Uebermensch* ("superman"). Underlying Nietzsche's conception of the "superman" is his belief that the fundamental human drive is "the will to power," which in its purest state is the desire to gain power over oneself—a desire for perfection—but when thwarted and debased becomes the search to gain power over others. He demanded that man give up any hope for an afterlife and seek instead to perfect this one, for to master oneself and to use that mastery creatively (the essence of being a "superman") is the major challenge to mankind. The struggle to become a "superman" is the true Dionysian state and the opposite of Christianity. "The God on the Cross is a curse on life, a pointer to seek redemption from it. Dionysus cut to pieces is a *promise* of life: it is eternally reborn and comes back from destruction." Herein lies a stern challenge to much of nineteenth-century thought, especially to scientism, socialism, and the concept of progress. Nietzsche's views gave philosophical undergirding to the elitist art-for-art's-sake movement and its call for emancipation from conventions and traditional values, for he urged the superior individual to free himself from the "slave morality" of the common herd.

Ironically, it was only after Nietzsche became insane in 1889 that he gained a sizable following. In the 1890s he provided inspiration for writers rebelling against naturalism; later his works were to be quoted out of context and used to justify almost every conceivable position (the Nazis are especially notorious for popularizing the misconception that Nietzsche advocated a Nordic Superman who would rule over all inferior peoples). But these distortions are in themselves evidence of the continuing vitality of Nietzsche's work, for no other nineteenth-century philosopher has exerted such a potent spell on the twentieth century.

In the late nineteenth century, Nietzsche's influence mingled with that from several other sources to create neoromanticism. It was in Austria that neoromanticism most prospered, especially in the work of Hugo von Hofmannsthal (1873–1929), considered by many critics of the late nineteenth century to be the finest lyric poet since Goethe. As a dramatist, von Hofmannsthal's career falls into two parts—before and after 1900. In the early years, he wrote primarily short pieces, such as *The Fool and Death* (1893), *The Emperor and the Witch* (1895), and *The Adventurer and Singing Girl* (1899). *The Fool and Death* demonstrates that, despite his neoromanticism, von Hofmannsthal was no advocate of the aesthetic code. In it, Claudio, an aristocratic young aesthete, thinks of nothing but art and form. Confronted by Death, he protests that he has not yet lived. In response, a number of people (including his mother, a girl who loved him, and a friend) are summoned from the dead to show that he has not lived because he has failed to commit himself fully to anything. This play is also noted for its extraordinarily melodic and evocative poetry.

Although for a decade he had been hailed as the greatest author then writing in German, von Hofmannsthal around 1900 underwent a crisis during which he came to believe that words are meaningless. Although he passed beyond this belief, his work was never the same afterward. His next important drama, *Elektra* (1903), is his least characteristic work. Perhaps because he was working with Richard Strauss, who had recently set Wilde's *Salome* to music, von Hofmannsthal seems to have adopted the tone of Wilde's play, for he creates an essentially psychotic world. Elektra lives only for her revenge on Klytemnestra and Aegisthus and, when her mission is accomplished, she loses her reason for existing. Consequently, at the conclusion of her triumphal dance, she sinks lifeless to the earth. The poetry also differs markedly from that in von Hofmannsthal's earlier work, for it is dominated by images of carrion, corpses, snakes, dogs, and flies.

Most of von Hofmannsthal's later drama was written in collaboration with Strauss—as are *Die Rosenkavalier* (1911) and *Ariadne auf Naxos* (1912)—or was a reworking of earlier plays. Into the latter category fall *Venice Preserved* (1905), *Everyman* (1912), *The Great World Theatre* (1922), based on Spanish *autos sacramentales,* and *The Tower* (1922, 1927), based on Calderon's *Life Is a Dream.* Both *Everyman* and *The Great World Theatre* were to figure prominently in the Salzburg Festival, where they were mainstays of the annual programs.

In all of his work, von Hofmannsthal proves himself a poet of high quality. But there is little hope in his outlook, especially in his late work, which seems to give evil an increasingly dominant place. Toward the end of his life he came to believe that religion holds the only answer. But despite his growing pessimism, von Hofmannsthal continued to uphold certain basic human values. As Claude David said of him: "He defends a culture, he remains true to an art of moderation in an immoderate, violent epoch. As the troubles recede into the distance of history, his quiet light shines more and more brightly." Indeed, von Hofmannsthal's reputation has continued to grow as that of his neoromantic contemporaries has declined.

VI

By 1900, antirealism had established itself in almost every country, although far less firmly than had realism. Like the movements toward realism and naturalism, the tendency toward antirealism gained momentum only gradually. In the 1850s interest was aroused by Poe and Baudelaire and was further stimulated in the 1870s by Wagner, Nietzsche, and Pater, but it was not until the 1880s that it became widespread. The first significant response came in 1885 with the initiation of the symbolist school in France, but it was not until the 1890s that antirealist plays made an impact. Again, it was only after the formation of independent theatres, similar to those established by the naturalists, that the new drama was given a hearing on stage. It was in these theatres also that antirealistic production techniques were employed extensively for the first time in the modern era.

Few dramatists of significance emerged from the antirealist movement, but Maeterlinck, Claudel, Jarry, Wilde, and von Hofmannsthal constitute a respectable roster. Generally speaking, both in France and elsewhere the new attitudes found their most lasting expression in nondramatic writing. To a large degree, the antirealistic dramatists of the 1890s appealed to coterie audiences, especially to those who considered themselves superior to the masses favoring realistic illusionism. No doubt much of the work was precious, but then the majority of work by writers of any school must ultimately be judged inferior.

By 1900, self-conscious symbolists, aesthetes, and neoromantics were disappearing. All seem to have tired of the overuse of death and decay (a preoccupation which led many critics to label the antirealists "decadents"), of ineffable mystery, repetitious dialogue, and a general air of insubstantiality. But despite all shortcomings, antirealism had made a strong impact and had provided an alternative to the dominant realistic mode.

By 1900, doctrinaire realism was also considerably weakened. The decade between 1900 and 1910 was to be singularly devoid of strongly marked artistic movements. It was to be a period during which writers and directors borrowed freely from many sources, often seemingly contradictory ones, to create works which are neither clearly realistic nor clearly antirealistic. It was a time for consolidating gains from the past.

Innovation
and
Consolidation
in Drama,
1900-1915

6

Between 1875 and 1900 new directions in playwriting were firmly established by a few pioneers—most notably Ibsen, Becque, Hauptmann, Shaw, Maeterlinck, and Claudel. In comparison, the years between 1900 and 1910 were relatively unproductive, for this decade is characterized more by consolidation than innovation. Nevertheless, there were a few outstanding exceptions, among them Schnitzler and Wedekind, who embodied in their works many features of the revolutionary view of human psychology then being formulated by Sigmund Freud. Still more important were Strindberg's "dream" and "chamber" plays, for not only are they among the finest dramas of the period, they foreshadowed as well many of the most fertile experiments to come. Another outstanding achievement of the decade

149

*Innovation
and
Consolidation
in Drama,
1900–1915*

is the "Irish Renaissance," which reached its peak in the plays of Yeats, Lady Gregory, and Synge and in the productions of the Abbey Theatre.

With the exception of these few major figures, however, most of the dramatists of the era may more correctly be labeled disciples than innovators. In many instances, this second wave of writers won greater popular support than did their predecessors, who for the most part were unwilling to compromise with public taste. Perhaps because popularization brought a dilution of those qualities that made the originals distinctive, few dramatists of the second wave won lasting fame. Still, everywhere the new trends were evident. Italy, Spain, and America reflected them somewhat weakly, whereas England, France, and Germany supported them more fully. Everywhere there was a tendency to reach accommodations with romantic realism, the dominant style of the popular theatre, and with traditional moral values. Nevertheless, by 1915 most of the modes introduced after 1875 had won acceptance.

I

If turn-of-the-century playwriting was primarily devoted to consolidating previous gains, there was nevertheless at least one significant innovation— the introduction into drama of Freudian psychology, destined to be one of the most potent influences on virtually all subsequent thought and art.

During the last quarter of the nineteenth century, psychology for the first time began to be separated from philosophy and recognized as a branch of learning in its own right. The first important step was taken in 1879 when Wilhelm Wundt set up a laboratory in Leipzig for psychological experiments. At about the same time, Charcot and Bernheim in France were investigating hypnosis and the power of suggestion over human behavior. It was this pioneering work, especially that of Charcot, that first attracted the interest of Sigmund Freud (1856–1939), who, after completing his medical studies at the University of Vienna in 1881, had specialized in diseases of the nervous system, about which he wrote several treatises. He then went to study for a time with Charcot in Paris, and returned to Vienna to work with Josef Breuer on the use of hypnosis in the treatment of hysteria. With Breuer, Freud in 1895 published his first important work on psychoanalysis, *Studies in Hysteria*. Throughout the remainder of his life, Freud continued to extend and explicate his theories in articles and books, the most important of which are *The Interpretation of Dreams* (1900), *Three Contributions to the Theory of Sex* (1905), *General Introduction to Psychoanalysis* (1920), and *Civilization and Its Discontents* (1930).

Freud's work was revolutionary. Until his time, it was assumed that human beings are for the most part aware of what goes on in their own minds—in other words, that the level of consciousness is virtually the whole. Freud, on the contrary, argued that the mind is analogous to an iceberg, since only about one-eighth is above the surface. Thus, his originality lies primarily in the emphasis he placed on the unconscious (or subconscious).

Freud declared that personality is composed of three basic levels: (1) the *id* (which operates beyond conscious awareness), or reservoir of drives and impulses concerned with the preservation and propagation of life; (2) the *ego* (which operates on both the conscious and preconscious levels), or source of perception, cognition, and decision; and (3) the *superego* (which operates on the conscious level), or censor of the ego's functions. He argued that mental conflict—competition between urges and the superego—plays a central role in personality, both the healthy and the unhealthy. The normal mind finds satisfactory means of dealing with conflict, whereas the abnormal mind does not. An individual's personality is compounded of the accommodations reached among the three levels. But in all cases, unconscious processes exert dynamic pressure on consciousness and action.

Much of Freud's concern as a doctor was to discover the causes and remedies for abnormal behavior. Out of this work grew psychoanalysis, which sought to bring unconscious motives and repressed memories to the level of consciousness, so that disorders of the personality might be alleviated through therapy. As a diagnostic tool, Freud found dreams of enormous help, since in sleep the superego and ego are lulled, and suppressed urges come to the surface. In analyzing dreams, he discovered that fears and desires are seldom expressed directly but most often are masked behind symbols (for example, the male sexual organ might be symbolized in a knife or stick). He also found that in dreams events widely separated by time and place may become merged, that one person may fade into another, and that such transformations and substitutions require considerable and skillful interpretation.

So many of Freud's ideas have gained such widespread acceptance that it is sometimes difficult to appreciate how revolutionary they seemed at the turn of the century. Earlier views had usually emphasized man's rationality. Instinct, when discussed, was usually said to be an impulse which could be controlled by reason, or it was viewed as an urge toward the good, often subverted by circumstance. Freud not only argued that a large proportion of behavior is motivated by impulses we do not fully understand, but that the basic instincts are sexuality and aggressiveness (both considered highly unpleasant topics in Freud's day); the desire for good, which other periods had declared instinctual, Freud explained not as an inborn urge but as a censor built up during childhood through punishments and rewards (that is, the conscience, or superego, is a faculty superimposed on the mind by pressures from family and society).

Freud's theories were to have enormous significance for twentieth-century drama. First, his conception of the id and the preconscious aspects of the ego located within man's mind much of what in earlier periods had been considered supernatural, irrational, or demonic. Thus, he provided a scientific explanation for what had previously been considered suprahuman; this in turn made it possible to reach compromises between realistic and antirealistic modes in drama.

Second, Freud's view of personality prompted greater concern for the complexities of motivation in drama. In part, Freud's theories served merely to reenforce those of Darwin, since in both views motivations are explained by inborn temperament and environmental pressures. But Freud's views also prompted increased concern for the role of the unconscious in behavior. A number of playwrights were later to use a pseudopsychoanalytic approach in their plays by setting up aberrant behavior and then gradually revealing the causes behind it (usually some childhood trauma).

Third, sexual drives, previously almost taboo in drama, became increasingly important. Obviously, sexual implications are found in many plays prior to the late nineteenth century, but usually they are masked under farce or distanced through other devices. Direct and serious treatment of sex is seldom found prior to modern times. Furthermore, Freud's view that failure to find satisfactory channels for sexuality and aggressiveness leads to deviant behavior and violence undergirds much contemporary drama.

Fourth, nonrealistic dramatic modes were to be heavily influenced by Freud's emphasis upon the subconscious, the reservoir of basic drives which are suppressed through various strategies. The surrealists were to suggest that fundamental truth can only be intuited during dreamlike states, when the censorious conscious mind is lulled. Furthermore, many nonrealistic techniques—the telescoping or rapid shift in time and place, flashbacks, symbolic substitutions, transformations in identity or appearance of persons, places, or objects, organization through associational patterns, and so on—were said to be justified because they truthfully reflect psychological processes.

Fifth, Freud's view of the superego as a residue and censor of ideals makes values dependent on social pressures and personality rather than on any absolute source. Thus, moral truth becomes relative, mutable, and individual. Furthermore, Freud's notion that the superego censors the ego and the id suggests infinite possibilities for disparities between surface appearance and deeper realities, between "the mask" and "the face," between the varying roles we all assume. Consequently, truth becomes enormously complex (perhaps unknowable), for it is difficult to penetrate not only the masks of others but those of ourselves as well. Probably no other concept has so thoroughly permeated modern drama.

Freud's ideas were not wholly original, for many had been voiced long before he began his work. Furthermore, not all of those who later expressed similar views are directly indebted to him. But it was Freud who first

152

*Innovation
and
Consolidation
in Drama,
1900–1915*

formulated that unified conception of human personality that was to dominate twentieth-century thought. Many later psychologists were to attack various parts of his theory, but they succeeded only in making emendations rather than fundamental changes. His most important idea— the power of the subconscious over human behavior—has never been seriously challenged.

~~ II ~~

Even while Freud was formulating his ideas, a few dramatists were already utilizing similar notions in their plays. Among the most important were Schnitzler and Wedekind.

Arthur Schnitzler (1862–1931), like Freud (whom he knew), was a doctor in Vienna. One of his major interests was the treatment of neuroses through hypnosis, a subject on which he published a treatise. Also like Freud, he was deeply aware of unconscious motives, and these play a major role in many of his literary works. Schnitzler's outlook was essentially scientific, for he was a keen observer of surface detail and sensitive to subtle nuance, but he lacked the doctrinaire naturalist's naïve belief that science can correct society's ills. Like many of his Viennese contemporaries, Schnitzler was a skeptic, always pursuing knowledge while recognizing that apparent certainty may turn into utter falsity. This outlook is evident in his plays, in which characters, even while in the midst of happiness, sense its impermanence. This mingling of surface frivolity with an all-pervasive melancholy is one of the most characteristic features of Schnitzler's works.

Schnitzler's interest in psychology is most readily apparent in his novels and short stories. For example, his novella *Lieutenant Gustl* (1901) was one of the first literary works to use the stream-of-consciousness technique, while in the short story "Fraulein Else," the main character, having disrobed in the lobby of a hotel, gradually and unconsciously reveals what lies behind this act. Psychology also plays an important though less obvious role in Schnitzler's plays, especially *Anatol* (1893) and *Reigen* (1903). *Anatol* is composed of seven sketches, each dealing with a different love affair. Taken singly, they depict the hedonistic life of rather frivolous characters, but together they provide a more complex view: Anatol is always haunted by the ephemeral nature of happiness, but rather than trying to make it last or giving himself up to momentary joy, he unconsciously but deliberately destroys potentially meaningful relationships. Thus, it is his character as much as circumstance that determines the outcome of his affairs and creates the pervasive sense of world-weariness. *Reigen* (translated variously as *Round Dance, Hands Around,* and *La Ronde*) in its ten brief scenes

153

*Innovation
and
Consolidation
in Drama,
1900–1915*

shows a series of sexual encounters among characters who represent a cross-section of society: prostitute, soldier, housemaid, young gentlemen, wife, husband, young girl, poet, actress, and count. Each scene follows the same pattern—a discussion preparatory to copulation, a blackout (during which copulation presumably occurs), and an ensuing conversation. Although the subject is daring, there is nothing pornographic about its treatment. It shows that sexual drives are no respecter of persons and that there is an enormous difference between desire and love.

Schnitzler seldom strayed from his concern with the erotic, but in *Professor Bernhardi* (1912) he turned to anti-Semitism, a problem which was of personal concern to him as a Jew. It tells of the Jewish director of a large hospital, who, seeking to cheer the last moments of a girl who has committed suicide after being rejected by her lover, not only deceives her into thinking that her lover is returning but prevents a priest from administering the last rites. The case becomes an excuse for demanding major changes in the hospital's staff and policies; when the demands are refused, Professor Bernhardi is removed from his post and eventually sent to prison.

Schnitzler's worth has never been fully acknowledged, in large part because his preoccupation with sexual themes made him suspect to conservative critics, while to others his irony and wit seemed mere cynicism. Still others have viewed as a weakness his failure to condemn the imperfections he saw. Certainly Schnitzler was no wild-eyed reformer, nor had he any of the messianic qualities so apparent in the work of Wedekind and Strindberg. Though fully aware of man's flaws, he was content to record them with compassion and resignation. Undoubtedly Schnitzler restricted himself to a narrow range of topics, but within those limits he has seldom been excelled.

The work of Benjamin Franklin Wedekind (1864–1918)—so named by a father who had spent sixteen years in America following the Revolution of 1848—is difficult to evaluate, for it varies drastically in quality, often within a single work. Nevertheless, his preoccupation with sexual themes and his experiments with dramatic techniques make him worthy of study.

Wedekind admired Büchner (from whom he inherited his predilection for a rapid succession of short scenes and for mingling realistic and expressionistic modes), Nietzsche (as a result of which he declared that power and sex are man's primary urges and that it is only through sexual emancipation and other breaches of convention that man becomes free), and Strindberg (with whom he shared the notion of eternal conflict between male and female but which, unlike Strindberg, he considered a source of good). Wedekind combined all these influences (though he was not always able to blend them successfully) into a vision distinctively his own.

Although Wedekind's first play was completed in 1886, his significant work began with *Spring's Awakening* (1891), in which a series of unpleasant events stems from the unwillingness of adults to deal frankly with

154

*Innovation
and
Consolidation
in Drama,
1900–1915*

the subject of sex. Its sympathetic adolescents are held in bondage by caricatured parents and teachers (with such names as Baldbelly, Sunstroke, and Tongueclapper). Because her mother is too ashamed to talk to her about sex, Wendla becomes pregnant and later dies when her parents insist that she have an abortion. One young boy, Moritz, commits suicide because of his anxieties about sex, and another, Melchoir, urged by Moritz's ghost (who appears with his head under his arm) to do the same, is saved only by the appearance of the Man with a Mask, who restores Melchior's desire to live. *Spring's Awakening* is a strange mixture of naturalistic, burlesque, and symbolic scenes, although the total impression made on Wedekind's contemporaries was that of a determined antinaturalism. It was not performed until 1906, when Max Reinhardt presented it at the Kammerspiele in Berlin with Wedekind in the role of the Man with a Mask.

The principal character in *Earth Spirit* (completed in 1895, first performed in 1898) is Lulu, an archetypal figure whose age and origin are unknown but who has an insatiable appetite for life. In the prologue, an animal trainer introduces her in the guise of a snake. (She is at once the eternal woman and the omnipresent temptress.) During the course of this symbolic play about the power of lust to overwhelm love, Lulu takes and gets rid of three husbands. Although primarily serious, there is in it considerable humor in the dialogue and elements of farce in the ubiquitous hidden lovers. *Earth Spirit* is more stylistically unified than is *Spring's Awakening,* being more nearly expressionistic throughout. In its sequel, *Pandora's Box* (1904)—with one act each in German, French, and English —Lulu slides ever further into degradation and eventually is killed by Jack the Ripper. Forbidden a license, it was first seen at a private performance in Vienna in 1905.

Although the erotic element runs throughout Wedekind's work, there is as well a continuing concern for moral values, even if often depicted cynically. This strain is clearly evident in *The Marquis of Keith* (1900), in which Scholz, originally a morally upright man, allows himself, as a

A scene from the Kleines Theater production of Wedekind's *The Marquis of Keith* in 1905. The playwright himself, at right, played the title role. (From *Le Théâtre,* 1906.)

form of repentance after inadvertently being the cause of a death, to become the tool of the wholly amoral marquis (a title assumed by Keith). Just as Keith's monumental swindle is about to succeed, he is unmasked. Scholz then voluntarily enters a madhouse, while Keith agrees to leave town in return for 10,000 marks. The marquis consoles himself with the observation that "Life is a toboggan slide," with many reversals in its course.

Much of Wedekind's work is semiautobiographical, as in *King Nicolo, or Such Is Life* (1901). In this play, the king is driven from his throne by hypocritical moralists, becomes a performer (but is permitted to play only comic roles), then a playwright (although his tragedies are interpreted as parodies), and finally the court fool. Wedekind seems here to depict ironically both himself and the public he found unwilling to take him seriously.

Because of his subjects and his highly individualized style, Wedekind did not easily win acceptance. Many of his works were at first refused licenses for performance. But after 1900 the tide began to turn in his favor and by 1903–4 there were 149 performances of his plays in German theatres. Disliking much of what he saw, however, Wedekind himself turned more and more to acting, and thereafter until his death in 1918 divided his talents between writing and acting in his own works. (Wedekind also performed in cabarets. Brecht acknowledges a considerable influence on his work from Wedekind's songs and manner of performing them.)

Wedekind's dramas (of which he completed twenty-one) provide clear evidence of his genius, although it cannot be fully assessed since he never fully mastered the intricacies of dramatic form. Nevertheless, he was to be a major influence on the German expressionists, who were attracted both by his dramatic techniques and by his rebellion against conventional values. At the turn of the century, however, Wedekind made his greatest impact through his frank treatment of sex and his mixture of several stylistic modes within single works.

III

In international reputation and influence, August Strindberg (whose early career has already been discussed in Chapter III) was to be the most important of all those early writers who exploited the dramatic potential of the unconscious mind. Between 1892 and 1898 Strindberg underwent a mental and spiritual crisis, during which he wrote no plays. He now gave up his earlier interest in science and turned increasingly to Oriental religions and to the philosophy of Schopenhauer and Nietzsche. Then, in 1898,

Strindberg returned with renewed energy to dramatic writing and in less than a dozen years had composed thirty new plays.

Strindberg did not break altogether with the past, for his new works are clearly related to the earlier pieces. For example, in 1899 he returned to historical drama after a lapse of seventeen years, and more than one-third of his late plays treat historical subjects. Among the best are *Erik XIV* (1899), *Gustavus Vasa* (1899), *Queen Christina* (1903), and *The Nightingale of Wittenberg* (1903). The scope of Strindberg's historical writings is very broad, for not only do they range through Swedish subjects from the middle of the thirteenth to the beginning of the nineteenth century, they sometimes extend to "world" history. Although his dramatic techniques vary from play to play, all of the historical works, with the exception of *Charles XII* (1901), which passes over into expressionism, are basically realistic. Despite their considerable power, they have seldom been performed outside of Scandinavia.

Strindberg also did not abandon the realistic-naturalistic mode of *The Father* and *Miss Julie*. In one of the most powerful of his late plays, *The Dance of Death* (1901), he returned to the battle of the sexes and the struggle for domination as a major theme and clothed it in a form which links it directly to his earlier work. Here Edgar (a captain) and his wife Alice have been living for twenty-five years on an island fortress in an atmosphere of hatred and misery. Edgar remarks about his own behavior: "Life was so alien, so contrary, so cruel, right from my childhood, and people were so cruel that I became so too." Into this nightmarish relationship comes Kurt, the quarantine master, after fifteen years absence. At first Kurt seeks to rescue the couple from their misery, but soon he too is infected by their venom, and he forms an alliance with Alice, now determined to kill Edgar. In the second part of the play, Edgar appears to have outwitted Alice, but at the moment of triumph he dies of a stroke. At first exultant, Alice finally realizes that she must have loved Edgar despite the hatred which she still feels. In this play, Strindberg depicts, even more bitterly than in his earlier works, that "dance of death" which is the male-female, love-hate relationship.

But, powerful as are Strindberg's late historical and realistic plays, it is not upon them that his fame ultimately depends. Rather, it was the expressionistic works—the "dream" plays and the "chamber" plays—that set his drama apart from that of other writers of the time. The new direction is first found in *The Road to Damascus* (parts I and II, 1898; part III, c. 1901), an autobiographical work in which, as the title suggests, Strindberg relates his own progress to that of Saul of Tarsus. In *The Road to Damascus,* the protagonist step by step gives up all worldly things, including fame and womankind, and then, with nothing left to attach him to the world, enters a monastery (though not a sectarian one) to devote himself to a generalized humanitarianism. As one of the characters says: "You began life by accepting everything, and then went on to denying everything

A scene from Strindberg's *The Dance of Death*, produced at the Intimate Theatre in 1909. Strindberg's associate in founding the Intimate Theatre, August Falck, is at right in the role of Edgar. (Courtesy Drottningholms Teatermuseum.)

on principle. Now end your life by comprehending everything. Be exclusive no longer. Do not say: either–or, but: not only–but also. In a word, . . . Humanity and Resignation." Written just as Strindberg was emerging from his spiritual inferno, *The Road to Damascus* seeks to move beyond the preoccupation with such limited concerns as the battle of the sexes into a higher synthesis where an all-encompassing humanitarianism seeks to resolve the conflicts by putting them into a larger context. Here, as in most of his late works, Strindberg treats with great compassion alienated man, lost and rootless, seeking meaning in an incomprehensible universe, trying to reconcile the most disparate elements: lust and love, body and spirit, filth and beauty.

Of all the late plays, the best known and the most influential is *The Dream Play* (1902), for it sums up most of Strindberg's preoccupations and epitomizes the dramatic form which was to exert so much influence upon later nonrealistic dramatists, especially the German expressionists. In his preface to *The Dream Play,* Strindberg wrote: "The author has tried to imitate the disconnected but seemingly logical form of a dream. Anything may happen; everything is possible and probable. Time and space do not exist. On an insignificant background of reality, imagination designs and embroiders novel patterns, free fancies, absurdities and improvisations. The characters split, double, multiply, vanish, solidify, blur, clarify. But one consciousness reigns above them all—that of the dreamer; and before it there are no secrets, no incongruities, no scruples, no laws." Here Freud's conception of dream is given dramatic form.

Like Goethe's *Faust, The Dream Play* begins with a prologue in Heaven. Because of the wails from below, the god Indra decides to send down his Daughter to find out why men's lives are so unhappy. When she

158

*Innovation
and
Consolidation
in Drama,
1900–1915*

arrives, she discovers the Captain imprisoned in a castle which rests on a dunghill but has a chrysanthemum bud on top (thus symbolizing the human condition). She frees the Captain from the castle and they set out on the search to discover why men suffer.

The identities of the characters change often. The Captain becomes the Lawyer and the Poet, and Indra's daughter becomes the Lawyer's Wife. But in all guises there is only anguish. The situations also range through a cross-section of human experience: childhood, schooldays, young love, courtship, marriage, and so on. But here too disillusionment is universal. At last the Poet provides an explanation: the world is caught in a conflict between two urges, that of the spirit and that of the flesh; man suffers because, suspended between Heaven and Earth and incapable of resolving the conflict between the desire for spiritual transcendence and the desire to wallow in filth, he is eternally torn between two natural instincts.

The Daughter now wishes to return to Heaven, but in order to do so she must retrace her steps. Eventually she arrives back at the castle. She enters, and it bursts into flames as the chrysanthemum bud on top opens into full flower. The other characters cast into the fire all the things they have most valued. In this way, Strindberg seems to suggest that out of pain grows understanding and acceptance, but that happiness can be achieved only by freeing the spirit from all material chains.

The major source of unity in *The Dream Play* is thought, for it is Strindberg's conception of the human condition, rather than any cause-and-effect arrangement of incidents, that holds together the motifs, symbols, and allegorical devices. Ultimately, however, it was not Strindberg's vision but his techniques which were to be most influential, for through them he achieved fluidity of time and place, of identity and appearance, of idea and image.

It was not easy for Strindberg to find producers for his "dream" plays. Consequently, when he was approached by the young actor and director August Falck (1882–1938) about a plan for a theatre to be devoted entirely to his plays, he eagerly assented. Thus, the Intimate Theatre, with a company of only thirteen actors and a seating capacity of 161, came into being in 1907. At last Strindberg had at his disposal the kind of theatre for which he had longed since the late 1880s. By the time it closed in 1910, the Intimate Theatre had presented twenty-four of Strindberg's plays for a total of 1,025 performances in Stockholm and had toured Sweden, Norway, and Denmark. Perhaps more important, for the theatre Strindberg wrote five "chamber" plays: *Storm Weather* (1907), *The Burned House* (1907), *The Ghost Sonata* (1907), *The Pelican* (1907), and *The Black Glove* (1909). Of these, *The Ghost Sonata* is by far the best known.

As the title of the play suggests, *The Ghost Sonata* is constructed in part along musical lines. The first act is conceived as an allegro, the second as a largo, and the third as an andante. The action is a journey or search for an answer to the mystery of life. The Student (the creative man and

Interior of Strindberg's and Falck's Intimate Theatre in Stockholm, opened in 1907. The theatre seated only 161. It was here that Strindberg produced his "chamber" plays. (From Esswein, *August Strindberg*, 1909.)

saver of lives) is pitted against Old Hummel (the vampirish destroyer who sucks away the strength of others). As the drama unfolds, façades are stripped away to show what lies behind them. The action begins in front of a house and then moves indoors, just as it successively strips away the masks of the characters: the seeming benefactor turns out to be a murderer; the nobleman is shown to be a servant in disguise; the woman who once posed for a beautiful statue is now a mummy confined to a closet. In the final act, it appears for a moment that young love may be able to triumph over misery, but it gives way to the admonition that first comes "the labor of keeping the dirt of life at a distance." The Young Girl lacks the Student's spiritual fortitude, and, overwhelmed by the sinfulness of existence, dies when he seeks to help her face the truth. Now viewing death as a liberator, the Student prays to Buddha in the name of all mankind for patience to endure adversity. He then declares that the only hope for man lies in repentance: "No deed that we have wrought in anger can find in evil its atonement. Comfort him whom thou hast grieved, with goodness; this alone availeth. . . . Good is to be innocent." As the play ends, the room fades away and is replaced by a vision of the peaceful Island of the Dead.

In many ways, *The Ghost Sonata* resembles *The Dream Play,* but out of deference for the limited facilities of the Intimate Theatre, Strindberg avoids in his chamber plays the numerous shifts in time and place and the large casts found in the earlier dream plays. Nevertheless, there is still the same air of surreality in the magically charged events and a continuing use of semiallegorical devices to comment on the human condition.

By the time Strindberg died in 1912, his position as one of the major dramatists of the age was secure, even though opinion was still divided as

160

*Innovation
and
Consolidation
in Drama,
1900–1915*

to whether he should be viewed as a madman or as a visionary. Certainly, it is difficult to judge much of Strindberg's work, for at times his intentions are unclear and at others his messages are insufficiently embodied in dramatic action. But his vision of man as tortured and alienated was to attract many later writers, and his technical devices were to show others how psychological states and spiritual intuitions might be externalized. As the first dramatist to make extensive use of the unconscious, he was to be a major influence on subsequent playwrights. Although his works have never held a truly secure place in theatrical repertories, they have commanded deep and continuing respect from readers and above all from other writers.

~ IV ~

The years between 1900 and 1915 also saw a development of a quite different sort—the "Irish Renaissance," the manifestation of an aroused nationalistic spirit in literature. Since the seventeenth century Ireland had played an important part in the theatrical life of the British Isles: Dublin was long second only to London as a theatrical center, and many of Britain's most famous playwrights (including Congreve, Sheridan, Shaw, and Wilde) were born in Ireland. But the theatre in Ireland was essentially a branch of that in England rather than a truly native institution. Then, during the nineteenth century, as nationalism and the accompanying concern for things purely local and indigenous increased everywhere, Ireland began to deny its English heritage and to glorify the Celtic.

The first major step toward a native Irish drama was taken in 1899 with the formation of the Irish Literary Theatre by William Butler Yeats, Lady Augusta Gregory, George Moore, and Edward Martyn. Their major goals were: (1) "to build up a Celtic and Irish school of dramatic literature"; (2) "to bring upon the stage the deeper thoughts and emotions of Ireland"; (3) to insure "freedom to experiment"; (4) to disprove that Ireland is the "home of buffoonery and of easy sentiment" and to show it instead as the "home of an ancient idealism"; and (5) to place literature "outside all the political questions that divide us." For the most part, these were to remain the ideals of those who guided the subsequent dramatic and theatrical renaissance.

Between 1899 and 1902 the Irish Literary Theatre presented three programs (consisting of seven plays), of which only one was written in Gaelic, although all were Irish in subject and sentiment. It also published a periodical, *Beltaine,* to express and support its goals. But by 1902 it was evident that one faction within the group wished to enlarge the scope so as more nearly to approximate a Continental independent theatre, whereas another was interested only in Irish drama. Furthermore, there was by this time widespread dissatisfaction with the performances, for six of the seven productions had been given by English players, whose speech was ill-suited to the Irish idiom. Consequently, in 1902 the Irish Literary Theatre was dissolved.

Meanwhile, in 1899 W. G. Fay (1872–1947) and his brother Frank (1870–1931) had founded the Ormond Dramatic Society, which, with amateur actors, produced at irregular intervals programs composed mostly of farces. The Fays were extremely careful directors who refused to present any program until they thought it fully ready, and as a result soon won an enviable reputation in Dublin. A major change took place in their work beginning in 1901, when for the first time the Fays became aware of the pioneering work done in Norway by Ole Bull and in Paris by Antoine. As a result, they decided to revamp their repertory with the eventual goal of creating an Irish national theatre. Consequently, they began actively to seek Irish plays, and in April 1902 gave their first Irish program: *Dierdre* by "A. E." (George William Russell) and *Cathleen ni Houlihan* by Yeats. After rehearsing throughout the summer, they presented another program in November 1902 at the Samhain (All Hallow's) Festival in Dublin. As a result, they were invited by the Irish Literary Society of London to bring a program to England. Before doing so, however, the company was reorganized (in early 1903) and renamed the Irish National Theatre Society. Yeats was designated president.

The performance in London was a crucial one, for it sufficiently impressed Miss A. E. F. Horniman that in the following year she took a lease on the Mechanics' Institute Theatre in Dublin, had it remodeled, and gave it to the Irish players free of charge for six years, together with an annual subsidy. Thus, in 1904 the Abbey Theatre came into being, the first endowed theatre in any English-speaking country. Because of opposition from already established theatres, the Abbey was restricted to works written by Irishmen or on Irish subjects and foreign masterpieces in languages other than English. The theatre seated only 562 and the stage was only 15 feet deep. The troupe now set out to offer a different program each week for a season of ten months each year. It opened in December 1904 with a program composed prophetically of plays by Yeats, Lady Gregory, and Synge, for these were to be the Abbey's finest writers during its early history.

Overall, William Butler Yeats (1865–1939) is probably the single most important figure in the Irish Renaissance, for not only was he its major literary exponent, but he also provided leadership and championed standards of excellence which transcended patriotism and politics. To him, literature was superior to all factions and independent of time and place, since it distills experience and shapes ideals rather then merely reporting events from life and upholding local prejudice.

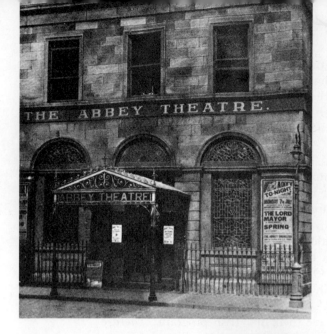

Exterior of the Abbey Theatre, Dublin, in the early twentieth century.

Widely traveled and thoroughly familiar with recent literary movements, Yeats was most attuned to the symbolist outlook, although never a strict adherent to it. Yeats disliked Ibsenian and Shavian plays, for he did not consider the ordinary man a fit subject for drama. He ignored the details of daily life and sought through ritualistic actions to arouse a sense of community among spectators and to enlarge their capacities for exalted experience—to make of them "temporary aristocrats" through the power of great emotions. According to Yeats, "tragedy must always be a drowning and breaking of the dykes that separate man from man." It "moves us by setting us to reverie, by alluring us almost to the intensity of trance."

The Yeatsian hero is a spiritual aristocrat motivated by an idealism which cannot be contained within normal limits. He acts according to a code independent of time and place, custom or law. He does not come to grief through hereditary or environmental forces but through an idealism which links him, no matter if he is a mythological or historical personage, with men of all times and places.

Above all, Yeats was a poet. His plays are written in blank verse for the most part, for he favored traditional verse forms so as to avoid over-personal expression. His imagery, both visual and auditory, helps to create great emotional intensity.

Yeats's playwriting career extended over more than forty years (from 1892 to 1938), during which time he wrote approximately thirty plays. His first, *The Countess Cathleen* (published in 1892, acted in 1899), tells how in the midst of a famine two Demon Merchants buy souls in exchange for the money needed for bread. To save her countrymen, Cathleen offers her own soul. In doing so, however, Cathleen follows the prompting of her own ideals rather than any sentimental notion of charity. Eventually the

Merchants are thwarted, for Heaven considers that such a soul as Cathleen's cannot be bought and sold. But Yeats is not interested merely in Irish folklore. Embedded in this mythical story is a rebuke to all of his countrymen who were selling their souls for material returns. Thus, Yeats sought through legend to suggest an eternal truth and to link it with the present.

After 1899 Yeats wrote a number of plays for the Irish Literary Theatre and the Abbey Theatre: *Cathleen ni Houlihan* (1902), *The King's Threshold* (1903), *The Hour Glass* (1903), *The Shadowy Waters* (1904), *On Baile's Strand* (1904), *Dierdre* (1906), *The Green Helmet* (1910), and others. Of these, perhaps the best are *The King's Threshold* and *On Baile's Strand.*

In *The King's Threshold,* Yeats depicts the role and power of poetry as greater than that of the state. He does so in a story about Seanchan, the master musician, who, after having been ousted from the King's council through the machinations of the "Bishops, Soldiers and Makers of the Law," sits at the King's threshold without food or drink. Most of the play is taken up with attempts to dissuade him, but, like Prometheus, he is unrelenting. Seanchan's pupils serve as a chorus, tracing his spiritual growth during his ordeal. Finally the King relents, for he comes to recognize that poetry is more enduring than earthly power. But, when Seanchan is given the crown, he places it once more on the King's head, for it is the poet's function to sing of greatness rather than to wield the scepter. (In a

Costume design by Charles Ricketts for a production of Yeats' *The King's Threshold* in 1904. A set of ancient costumes were built first for this play but used later for all of Yeats' and other ancient Irish pieces.

revision made in 1922, Yeats lets Seanchan die, and the play ends with a paean sung over the body by the chorus.)

In *On Baile's Strand,* Cuchulain (a typical Yeatsian hero with an ungovernable spirit) and Conchubar (a former hero now concerned only with ensuring political order) are treated as representatives of polar concepts. (As Yeats put it, Cuchulain is the burning sun, Conchubar the cold moon.) In the opening scene, Conchubar and his council seek to ensure lasting peace by inducing Cuchulain to swear that he will obey Conchubar's decrees. Though Cuchulain recognizes that this will make him subject to others rather than to his own will, he eventually agrees. But scarcely has he done so when a young stranger (who is now what Cuchulain must once have been) challenges Cuchulain to combat. Drawn to the youth, Cuchulain seeks to avoid the fight but cannot. Only after the duel does he discover that the young man he has killed is his son. Cuchulain now ends his life by walking into the waves as he seeks to strike off their heads. But in his defeat Cuchulain wins two victories: he escapes the oath that would have reduced him to vassaldom; and he remains the undefeated hero, though at the price of his own son's life. Unlike Yeats's earlier heroes, who ascend in greatness, Cuchulain descends from mythic freedom into human disillusionment. Nevertheless, he upholds the Yeatsian idea that true greatness cannot submit to those laws which govern ordinary mortals.

After 1910 Yeats ceased to write specifically for the Abbey's audiences and soon afterward came under the influence of the Japanese Noh drama. Consequently, his later plays differ considerably from the earlier ones. First, they are more concentrated. They each treat some polarity in human experience which involves a universally significant principle as seen at a decisive moment. Second, the action is always remote from everyday human experience. Time and setting are used symbolically, and the events are governed wholly by the universally valid choice being posed. Third, there are usually two principal characters, each of whom embodies a single passion, representative of one polar choice. Fourth, the diction is a rigidly controlled verse which makes extensive use of complex imagery. Fifth, the total result is to reduce each element to its essentials but to create such multilayered ideas, emotions, and spectacle that full comprehension of them requires intense concentration from the viewer or reader.

The late plays include *At the Hawk's Well* (1917), *The Only Jealousy of Emer* (1918), *Calvary* (1920), *A Full Moon in March* (1935), *The Herne's Egg* (1938), *Purgatory* (1938), *The Death of Cuchulain* (1938), and others. Of these, *At the Hawk's Well* may be taken as representative.

At the Hawk's Well was published in 1920 as one of *Four Plays for Dancers,* written under the influence of Noh drama. In it, Musicians act as a chorus and describe the action of the other characters. The scene is the Hawk's Well, the waters of which confer immortality but appear only for an instant. Set on a lonely promontory between earth and sky and between sea and land, the action occurs at sundown (the point between day and night). The polar characters are the Old Man and the Young Man

(Cuchulain), both of whom are determined to stay awake and keep their eyes firmly on the well so as not to miss the water when it appears. But the Old Man falls asleep, while Cuchulain's attention is turned aside at the crucial moment. Yeats suggests that immortality is not something won by quiet waiting like that of the Old Man (his name will not live on after him), but by the deeds of such as Cuchulain. Yet Cuchulain's is not an easy path. As his actions here suggest, he has more important things to do than stand and watch, for it is his urge to act in accordance with his impulses that makes him miss the water. But it is also this quality that will win him immortality, not because of magical waters but because of his own deeds. He is in a sense both hero and victim, for he can win immortality only through his mortality, though it is only such as he who can restore the broken bond between the natural and supernatural realms.

Yeats never won a wide following in the theatre, perhaps because his plays require a different kind of sensibility and greater concentration than that typical of the usual spectator. In the beginning he had high hopes for popular success, and he worked to discover the proper way to stage his plays. He experimented with acting styles and consulted on design with such outstanding artists as Charles Ricketts and Gordon Craig. But eventually Yeats resigned himself to a limited appeal. Near the end of his life he wrote: "What does it matter that it [tragic ecstasy] belongs to a dead art and to a time when a man spoke out of an experience and a culture that were not of his time alone, but held his time, as it were, at arm's length, that he might be a spectator of the ages. . . . What matter if the people prefer another art, I have had my fill." But if Yeats did not attract a wide popular following, he did win the respect of virtually all major critics and came to be recognized as one of the greatest modern poets of the English language. Furthermore, his work was to be central in practically all subsequent attempts to revive and reshape poetic drama.

As Yeats's experience suggests, there were from the beginning of the Irish Renaissance two conflicting dramatic ideals: the poetic-mythic and the realistic-domestic. Yeats was not alone in pursuing the first type, but he was by far the most important of those who did so. But it was with the second type that the Abbey was most successful, perhaps because it treated a world familiar to Irish audiences. Furthermore, the actors felt much more at home in it and thus gave more convincing performances.

Among those who wrote the second type of play, the most successful in the early years was Lady Augusta Gregory (1852–1932), like Yeats one of the Abbey's managing directors. Until about 1930, she was intimately concerned with the Abbey's affairs. In the period prior to 1915 she took primary responsibility for raising money, reading scripts, and encouraging new writers. Between 1908 and 1915 she also frequently supervised productions and directed a few plays herself.

Lady Gregory was in her way as devoted to legendary subjects as was Yeats. It was she who translated several of the ancient sagas and myths upon which Yeats drew. In turn, she was drawn into the theatre by Yeats and Edward Martyn. Most of her dramatic writing was done between 1902 and 1912, but she did not cease altogether until 1926. She was most at home in the one-act form and especially in peasant comedy. *The Spreading of the News* (1904), which shows how a passing remark is inflated as it passes from mouth to mouth, has remained a favorite. Similar pictures of Irish life are given in *Hyacinth Halvey* (1906), *The Rising of the Moon* (1907), *The Workhouse Ward* (1907), and many other plays.

Lady Gregory virtually invented the Irish folk-history play, based primarily on native oral traditions. Among her works of this type are *Kincora* (1905), a three-act epic drama about a figure comparable to the English King Alfred; *The White Cockade* (1905), a three-act comedy about James II's escape from Ireland; and *Dervorgille* (1907), a one-act tragedy about the woman whom legend blames for bringing the English into Ireland.

Only rarely did Lady Gregory venture into serious writing and then the effect was usually more pathetic than tragic, as in *The Gaol Gate* (1906) and *MacDonough's Wife* (1911). Toward the end of her career she wrote a few religious plays, such as *The Story Brought by Brigit* (1924) and *Dave* (1926).

Although she cannot be ranked in stature with Yeats, Lady Gregory was far more successful with the Abbey's audiences. (In fact, prior to 1910 the only authors whose works were really profitable financially were those of Lady Gregory and William Boyle, who wrote plays similar to hers.) Overall, Lady Gregory was probably the greatest stabilizing influence on the Abbey Theatre.

It remained for John Millington Synge (1871–1909), who from 1905 until his death served with Yeats and Lady Gregory as directors of the

The Abbey Theatre's production in 1906 of Lady Gregory's *Hyacinth Halvey.*
The actors are, left to right, W. G. Fay, Arthur Sinclair,
Frank Fay, J. A. O'Rourke, Brigit O'Dempsey, and Sara Allgood.

167

*Innovation
and
Consolidation
in Drama,
1900–1915*

Abbey, to bridge the gap between the two principal modes of writing. Synge came from the landed Protestant gentry of Ireland and was reared with a deep sense of sin. (His family was so puritanical that scarcely a member would attend the theatre, even after Synge became a director of the Abbey.) Educated at Trinity College, Dublin, he then studied music before settling in Paris (where he spent most of his time between 1894 and 1902) to teach English and to attend the Sorbonne. While in Paris he became interested in the Irish language and past. Yeats, whom he met in 1896, convinced him that he should go to live among the Irish peasants and write about their life. Consequently, beginning in 1898, Synge made a number of extended visits to the Aran Islands, Kerry, and other parts of Ireland. Out of these experiences, he gradually formulated the views which inform his plays and the language in which they are cast.

Synge usually treats life in one of two ways: as a struggle of the joyous, elemental urges to escape the repressions of a morality imposed by repressive religion, or as a struggle against (or acceptance of) mortality. As to the appropriate diction, Synge came to consider a near-Elizabethan dialect (which he found still preserved in some districts of Ireland) combined with Gaelic constructions and figures of speech to be that most suited to his needs, and from these elements he fashioned his own distinctive, lilting, poetic prose.

Synge began work on his first play, *When the Moon Has Set,* in 1900. It shows how a young man, after an encounter with an old woman now mad because when young she rejected love for religious reasons, convinces a nun to give up the veil to marry him. He declares: "The worst vice is slight compared with the guiltiness of a man or woman who defies the central order of the world. . . . The only truth we know is that we are a flood of magnificent life, the fruit of some frenzy of the earth." It was this rejection of conventional morality in favor of a more fundamental reality beyond intellect that made Synge the most controversial Irish playwright of his day.

The first of Synge's plays to be produced, *In the Shadow of the Glen* (1903), made him notorious. It shows a peasant seeking to punish his wife for flirting with a tramp (who represents for her all that lies beyond her narrow world). Pretending to die, he watches her make plans with the Tramp for the future. He then rises up and orders her from his cottage. Unrepentant, she is happy to go, for she knows that the Tramp will be waiting for her along the road. This dramatization of the conflict between a repressive life and the urge for joy and freedom infuriated many Irishmen, who declared Irish women incapable of adultery. Synge replied that his countrymen wished to see plays which praised all their virtues without "the plague spot of sex."

Riders to the Sea (first produced in 1904) illustrates Synge's second major concern: man face to face with his mortality. Many critics consider it the finest short play in the English language. Set in the kitchen of a

Scene from the 1906 production of Synge's *Riders to the Sea*, with, left to right, Brigit O'Dempsey, Sara Allgood, and Maire O'Neill.

cottage on the Aran Islands, it focuses on Maurya, who has lost her husband and five of her six sons to the sea. Despite her pleas, her last son sets off on a journey, and he too is lost. There is a sense of transcendence, nevertheless, for Maurya declares that there is now no more that the sea (here treated as an instrument of fate) can do to her. This play illustrates well Synge's method and helps to explain why he was more successful as a dramatist than was Yeats. Synge usually presents concrete contemporary situations but treats them in such a way that they seem timeless; consequently, the immediate world takes on mythic qualities with universal significance. Yeats, on the other hand, presents a remote past through which he seeks to suggest ideals for the present; as a result, his plays often achieve mythic grandeur but remain obscure as to their contemporary relevance.

Synge's other works include *The Well of the Saints* (1905), *The Playboy of the Western World* (1907), *The Tinker's Wedding* (1909), and *Dierdre of the Sorrows* (first produced in 1910). Of these, *The Playboy of the Western World* and *Dierdre of the Sorrows* are perhaps the best.

The Playboy of the Western World has as its central character Christy Mahon, a shy young man who thinks he has killed his domineering father. Fleeing to a strange village, he exaggerates his deed and wins the admiration of the villagers and the love of Pegeen Mike. When the supposedly dead father arrives, Christy is denounced by the villagers, and to regain their esteem he attacks his father again. But their repressions are such that the villagers cannot accept in actuality what they have romanticized in their minds, and they now treat Christy as a criminal instead of as a hero. When the father revives once more, now with new respect for his son, he promises to tell the whole world of the villagers' perfidy. Pegeen is left to moan the loss of the only "playboy of the western world." Few plays have elicited so stormy a response from audiences. Riots greeted the comedy nightly in Ireland (and later in America when the Abbey Theatre toured). One newspaper called *The Playboy* an "unmitigated, protracted libel upon Irish peasant men, and worse still upon Irish girlhood," and labeled the production squalid, the language barbarous, and the characters repulsive. Yeats and Lady Gregory defended Synge, although Lady Gregory thoroughly disliked the play because of its amorality.

Dierdre of the Sorrows was edited by Lady Gregory, Yeats, and Molly Allgood (the actress to whom Synge was engaged) after Synge's death. Based on Celtic legend, it tells how Dierdre, betrothed to King Conchubar, flees with Naisi. After seven years of bliss, they return to Ireland upon Conchubar's assurance that he has forgiven them. But when they arrive, Conchubar murders Naisi and seeks to carry away Dierdre, who, to prevent him, kills herself. The dramatic tension of the play, however, results from the disparity between Dierdre's all-encompassing and wholly satisfied love and Naisi's doubts that their love will prove lasting and sufficient. Thus, though Dierdre senses that death awaits them if they return to Ireland, she prefers to die rather than risk the loss of love.

Many years had to pass before Synge's worth was fully recognized. As Yeats said: "He was but the more hated because he gave his country what it needed." But Synge's reputation has continued to grow, and he is now considered by most critics to have been the finest playwright of the Irish Renaissance.

While Irish drama was gaining in stature, the Abbey Theatre was developing an ensemble of note. Nevertheless, its career was stormy. When formed in 1904, the company chose its repertory by democratic vote, for it was an actors' theatre. Then, in 1905 it was reorganized as a corporation with Yeats, Synge, and Lady Gregory as the directors. They reshaped it into a playwright's theatre. W. G. Fay, the former director, was now merely a paid employee, and several actors resigned. In 1907, Miss Horniman, believing Fay incapable of doing justice to Yeats's plays, insisted that B. Iden Payne be employed as artistic director. Largely ignored, Payne resigned after six months. Then, in 1908 Fay demanded greater authority over the company and, when refused, he resigned. A series of temporary directors followed, and in 1910 Miss Horniman withdrew her support. Under such circumstances, it is surprising that the company was able to build so enviable a reputation. But not only did it become a major force in Ireland's artistic life, it toured extensively in England, and in 1911, 1912, and 1914 played in America, where it was a significant influence on the "little theatre" movement.

By the time the Abbey Theatre visited America, however, it was already faltering. Many of its finest actors—including Dudley Digges and the Fays—had left, and its major writers had died, defected, or ceased to be productive. (Synge had died in 1909; several writers withdrew their plays following the controversy over *The Playboy of the Western World;* Yeats ceased to write specifically for the Abbey after 1910; and Lady Gregory virtually gave up playwriting after 1912.)

The years between 1910 and 1924 were especially trying ones for the

Abbey and much of the credit for holding it together goes to Lennox Robinson (1886–1958), who not only was one of the company's principal directors but a leading playwright of the new generation. Robinson began his playwriting career in 1908 with *The Clancy Name,* a study of pride in family reputation. John Clancy has committed murder and, though unsuspected, feels driven to confess despite his mother's repeated invocation of the family's reputation. Then, killed while rescuing a child from runaway horses, John dies a hero, and the Clancy name is saved. Though cynical, it is a well-constructed play with, in Mrs. Clancy, one truly fine characterization. Robinson also wrote a number of comedies, of which the best is *The Whiteheaded Boy* (1916). It shows the sacrifices made by a family for its favorite son, the lighthearted rogue Denis, who is accused of tampering with the affections of John Duffy's daughter. All is resolved happily when it is revealed that the pair are already married. Robinson was to continue for many years to be one of the guiding spirits, both as director and dramatist, of the Abbey.

By 1915, Ireland had for the first time been able to create a native dramatic tradition. Its progress was to be interrupted in 1916 when the struggle for national independence flared into open rebellion. But, as political stability returned in the 1920s, a measure of vitality was also to return to the drama.

~~ **V** ~~

Although Freud, Strindberg, Yeats, Synge, and others opened new paths between 1900 and 1915, they were exceptions. For the most part, dramatists of the period were imitative, capitalizing on trends already introduced by others. Because they served primarily to reenforce and popularize the work of their more innovative predecessors and contemporaries, they can be surveyed briefly, for in most countries—whether Italy, Spain, America, England, France, or Germany—the pattern was similar.

In Italy, the nineteenth century saw little vitality in playwriting, perhaps because of the general preoccupation with political and territorial unification, a goal finally achieved between 1861 and 1870. But unification did not end factionalism, for one group favored monarchy, the Church, and capitalism, while another championed democracy, freedom of conscience, and socialism. Furthermore, each region clung to its own dialect and customs, thus making the development of a national literature difficult. In the late nineteenth century, the most important regional centers were Milan, Turin, and Naples, and in each there grew up a school of dramatists. As elsewhere, the first important break with the past in drama took the form of realism (in Italy called *verismo*).

171

*Innovation
and
Consolidation
in Drama,
1900–1915*

The acknowledged leader of the Milanese school, Marco Praga (1862–1929), focused most often upon conflicts between men and women and especially upon the subordination of women to male values. Of his plays, which include *The Ideal Wife* (1890), *The Moral of the Fable* (1904), and *The Closed Door* (1913), perhaps the best is *The Virgins* (1889). It tells the story of Paolina, who lives with her two sisters and mother, an unprincipled woman who presents a mask of respectability but urges her daughters to give themselves to wealthy admirers in order to obtain jewels and fashionable clothes. Paolina, sickened by the hypocrisy of her family, is ecstatic when asked in marriage by Dario. But when, out of a desire to be completely honest, Paolina tells her fiancé about her background, he proposes that instead of his wife she become his mistress. Deeply wounded, Paolina refuses and so becomes a hopeless victim of the moral hypocrisy around her.

The most important of the Turin playwrights, Guiseppe Giacosa (1847–1906), is now remembered primarily as Puccini's librettist for *La Bohème* (1896), *Tosca* (1899), and *Madame Butterfly* (1903), but at one time was considered a disciple of Ibsen. His indebtedness to the Norwegian dramatist is perhaps most evident in *Rights of the Soul* (1894), which, like *A Doll's House,* traces a young wife's disillusionment. In this case, the wife, though attracted to her husband's cousin, has renounced him; but the husband, when he discovers that she has been tempted, orders her out of his house. When it is clear that rather than begging forgiveness she intends to go, he asks her to stay, but, now recognizing the "rights of the soul," she insists on pursuing her own life. Giacosa treated other social and domestic problems in such plays as *Unhappy Love* (1888), *Like Falling Leaves* (1900), and *The Stronger* (1904), but with results more nearly resembling those of Dumas *fils* than of Ibsen.

The most important of the Neapolitan writers was Roberto Bracco

Giacosa's comedy, *Like Falling Leaves*, produced at the Odéon, Paris, in 1910. (From *Le Théâtre*, 1910.)

Roberto Bracco's *The End of Love,* produced at the Bouffes-Parisiens, 1904, with Leonie Yahne as Anna and Krauss as the Count of Fontaneau. (From *Le Théâtre,* 1904.)

(1862–1943), most of whose plays, which include *A Woman* (1892), *The Unfaithful* (1894), *The End of Love* (1896), *Lost in Darkness* (1901), *Maternity* (1903), and *The Fools* (1921), mingled a thoroughgoing realism with deep human compassion. A characteristic work is *Don Pietro Caruso* (1895), in which a man spends his life shielding his daughter from reality only to discover that she has become the mistress of one of his friends. Similarly, *Nellina* (1908) draws a sympathetic portrait of a prostitute who struggles to hide her identity (and love) from her daughter, also a prostitute.

Related to the realists (or *veristi*), though never acknowledging any allegiance to the school, was the Sicilian writer Giovanni Verga (1840–1922), primarily a novelist. His most famous drama is *Cavalleria Rusticana* (*Rustic Chivalry,* 1884), a short naturalistic work which later served as the basis for Mascagni's opera. In it, Turridu, upon his return from military service, discovers that his sweetheart, Lola, has married Alfio, and, to make her jealous, he takes up with Santuzza, who becomes pregnant. When the play opens, Turridu has abandoned Santuzza, who, in revenge, reveals to Alfio that Turridu is now seeing Lola. The entire action transpires in the village square against the background of a festive Easter Sunday, during which a duel is fought offstage by Turridu and Alfio. The counterpoint between the joyful celebration of the Resurrection and the almost ceremonial demands of "rustic chivalry" creates a near-mythic quality.

As these examples indicate, the *veristi* were concerned primarily with the effects of social mores and ingrained custom on personal relationships. Seldom did they inquire into the ultimate societal forces which lay behind

172

Verga's *Cavalleria Rusticana,* produced by the Sicilian Company of Giovanni Grasso at the Théâtre de l'Oeuvre in 1908. Grasso himself is at right in the role of Turridu. (From *Le Théâtre,* 1908.)

the problems they depicted. Thus, they tended to show victims without suggesting hope that others might be saved from similar fates.

Despite the sizable output, Italy never offered a sympathetic reception to veristic drama. On the other hand, neoromanticism was welcomed more enthusiastically, although few writers in this vein are now remembered. By far the most important of the neoromantics was Gabriele D'Annunzio (1863–1938), who outdid the English aesthetes in his devotion to an amoral sensuality in which the goal of experiencing life at its most intense takes precedence over all else. In fact, D'Annunzio's reputation depended almost as much on his flamboyant personal life as upon his literary works.

The best known of D'Annunzio's plays is *La Giaconda* (1898), the story of a sculptor, Lucio, who finds his wife, Silvia, lacking in the inspiration provided by his model, Giaconda. The high point of the play comes in a confrontation between wife and model during which Silvia's hands are crushed as she seeks to save a statue from destruction by Giaconda, who has posed for it. But despite Silvia's sacrifice, Lucio leaves her, for the call of art overrides all other concerns.

Other plays by D'Annunzio include *The Dead City* (1898), *Francesca da Rimini* (1902), *Jorio's Daughter* (1904), and *La Piave* (1918). In each the central character is little more than a puppet, since he is controlled by a single, almost elemental urge, but the incidents are swept along by powerful poetic diction and passionate commitment. Many of D'Annunzio's

173

subjects were erotic, almost perverse, and consequently they seemed daring, almost scandalous. As time passed, both the author and his plays lost their appeal and today they seem more pretentious than significant. Nevertheless, in the period between 1900 and 1920 D'Annunzio was thought to be one of the world's major playwrights.

Although a number of competent Italian playwrights had emerged by 1915, none is now considered truly outstanding. No doubt the low state of playwriting is explained in part by theatrical conditions, which provided little incentive for serious dramatists. Since the only form that commanded wide popular support was opera, most dramatic troupes could maintain themselves only through constant touring. Standards of production were low, for everything was subordinated to the appeal of starring performers whose passionate, bravura style of acting tended to perpetuate earlier practices. Unlike many other countries, Italy produced no reformer capable of bringing about significant change.

The nearest equivalent to a reformer and certainly the finest Italian actress of the age was Eleanora Duse (1859–1924). On stage from the age of four, Duse had by 1878 become leading lady to Ernesto Rossi, one of Italy's major stars, with whom she toured widely. After playing in South America in 1885, Duse formed her own company, with which she appeared throughout the world for the next fifteen years. In 1897 Duse met D'Annunzio, with whom she fell in love and for whose recognition she was partially responsible. For Duse, D'Annunzio wrote five plays, three of which (*The Dead City, La Giaconda,* and *Francesca da Rimini*) were enormously successful. It was through them that D'Annunzio's fame was established in Europe.

Duse in the title role in *Francesca da Rimini* of Gabriel D'Annunzio. This was the original production of 1902 at the Constanzi Theatre, Rome. (From *Le Théâtre,* 1902.)

But it was as Ibsen's heroines—Nora, Rebecca West, Hedda Gabler, Mrs. Alving, Ella Rentheim, and Ellida Wangel—that Duse's great powers were seen to best advantage. To all her characterizations she brought enormous psychological insight and the capacity to seem completely different in each role. She relied entirely upon internal stimuli to produce the appropriate outward manner (she refused to use makeup). All critics remark upon her subtlety: she rendered "by means of only actual or possible external details the inmost idea." Thus, without any of the bravura, heroic diction, or flamboyance associated with starring performers of her day, Duse achieved results which were all that "modernists" could desire.

Like many other stars of her day, Duse also mounted her own productions. Her interest in updating theatrical practices is demonstrated by her invitation to Gordon Craig in 1906 to work with her on a production of *Rosmersholm*. Craig designed a drawing-room setting with a 30-foot-square window looking out on a red, green, and yellow landscape and used shafts of light through the window to encase the actors in an atmosphere of mysticism and fantasy. Duse sought to adapt her style of acting to the setting, but gave up after one performance. The other actors, who had been trained to play in Duse's quiet way, were likened by one reviewer to "stage hands who had walked on by mistake." Thereafter Duse seems to have relied upon her own taste as a guide in staging.

In 1913 ill health led Duse to retire, but financial reverses brought about by World War I forced her to return in the early 1920s. She died in Pittsburgh while on a tour of America. Although Duse too often devoted her great talent to inferior plays, she probably did more than any other actress of her time to win acceptance for the realistic mode, perhaps because she had the ability to make "the real poetic and the poetic real."

But the Italian theatre did not produce a leader who could lay out a path and inspire others to follow him. Lacking direction, it remained, with the exception of Duse, essentially derivative.

❧ VI ❧

Much the same pattern is found in Spain, which in the nineteenth century was still an agricultural nation dominated by the Church and the aristocracy. As yet virtually untouched by the Industrial Revolution, Spain was more backward than forward looking.

Nowhere was the conservatism more evident than in drama, for until 1850 the theatres of Madrid were, as in the sixteenth century, exploited as means of raising funds for charity. Virtually nothing was done to improve production facilities or acting companies. Then, the first important reorgani-

176

*Innovation
and
Consolidation
in Drama,
1900–1915*

zation in 250 years occurred. The exploitation for charity ceased, and a national theatre, the Teatro Espagñol, with reasonably up-to-date facilities and production methods, was created. Other theatres were classified into groups, each restricted to a specific range of dramatic types. In 1870, of Madrid's thirty-two theatres, only eight were devoted to regular drama. By then, minor houses had adopted the practice of offering an evening's bill made up of four distinct entertainments. Since each part could be seen separately, spectators were offered considerable flexibility in starting times, length of stay, and price of admission. The consequent increase in the popularity of minor houses made it difficult for the major theatres to retain audiences for full-length serious plays.

Under these conditions, it is not surprising that Spanish drama did not reach a high level. Still, it followed at a distance the major trends underway elsewhere. For example, the indebtedness to Ibsen of the first modern Spanish playwright of note, José Echegaray (1832–1916), is clearly evident in *The Son of Don Juan* (1892). Like *Ghosts,* upon which it is modeled, Echegaray's play closes with a young man calling for the sun as his mind deteriorates under the pressures of the hereditary disease. But unlike Ibsen, Echegaray makes his play sensational by focusing upon the libertine father and the disease rather than upon the mother's responses.

Today Echegaray is remembered primarily for *The Great Galeoto* (1881). Here the story concerns a young poet, Ernesto, a protégé of Don Julian and his wife Teodora. When gossip begins to circulate about Ernesto and Teodora, Don Julian at first ignores it and then becomes involved in a duel. Wounded, he is carried to Ernesto's apartment, to which Teodora has come to beg Ernesto not to fight the man who has challenged her husband. But Don Julian takes her presence as evidence of infidelity and he dies cursing them. Ernesto then slays Don Julian's killer, even though he realizes that no one can now ever kill the gossip.

Literary historians now usually treat Echegaray as a realist, but such a classification is a distortion. Most of his plays were "sword and cloak" dramas and even his most realistic works were written in verse. It would be more accurate to say that Echegaray was a traditionalist who in a few works demonstrated his admiration for Ibsen.

Of Echegaray's contemporaries, the best was Benito Pérez Galdós (1843–1920), far more important as a novelist than as a dramatist. Better than Echegaray at handling character and idea, Galdós never fully mastered dramatic form. Furthermore, his subjects were usually so peculiarly Spanish that they did not export well. Among the best of his works are *The Duchess of San Quintín* (1894), which shows the horror of a young noblewoman's relatives when she chooses to marry a vital commoner rather than a spiritless member of her own class; *The Condemned* (1894), a criticism of the Spanish clergy; *The Beast* (1896), a plea for a compromise between extremist political factions; and *Electra* (1900), in which a girl is driven into convent life, for which she is wholly unsuited.

Pérez Galdos' *Electra*, produced at the Porte-Saint-Martin (Paris) in 1904. (From *Le Théâtre*, 1902.)

In the 1890s new forces began to affect Spanish drama. In 1896 the independent theatre movement arrived when the Teatre Independent opened with a production of *Ghosts*. More important was the foundation in 1898 of the Teatre Intim by Adriá Gual (1872–1943), who for the next thirty years was to present a cross-section of world drama in production styles which reflected developments in Europe. It is perhaps significant that these theatres were located in Barcelona, always more attuned to foreign developments than was Madrid.

But for Spain the most important event of the 1890s was the Spanish-American War, for with Spain's humiliating defeat went the last vestiges of an empire and out of it rose a new movement, the Generation of '98, which sought to discover the real "soul of Spain" and to prescribe a cure for its ills. Agitation for reform affected every aspect of life. Symbolism was introduced into Spain in 1898 by the Nicaraguan poet Rubén Darío, after a stay in Paris. Darío did not write plays, however, and his art-for-art's-sake views were never very popular, but the techniques he championed were intermingled with patriotic fervor and taken over by a few dramatists.

The major playwrights of the years between 1898 and 1915 were Benavente, Martínez Sierra, and the Alvarez Quinteros. Jacinto Benavente y Martínez (1866–1954) was one of the most prolific dramatists of all times, having written more than three hundred works, which from the 1890s until his death kept the Spanish stage supplied with new plays of all types—short and long; romantic, realistic, sentimental; farce, comedy, drama, and history. So great was his variety that Benavente was often accused of mere pandering to public taste.

Of Benavente's realistic dramas, perhaps the most famous is *The Passion Flower* (1913), certainly his most violent work. In it, Acacia

177

178

*Innovation
and
Consolidation
in Drama,
1900–1915*

seems deeply to resent Estaban, the new husband of her mother, Raimunda. But gradually it becomes clear that Estaban and Acacia have conceived an overwhelming passion for each other. Estaban kills Acacia's fiancé and then Raimunda when she seeks to stop them from running away together. But Raimunda dies knowing that her daughter can never marry the man who has killed her own mother.

Benavente won his greatest international fame with *Bonds of Interest* (1907), in which the conflicts between materialism and love are embodied in *commedia dell' arte* characters and conventions. When Leandro and Crispin arrive penniless in a strange city, Crispin poses as Leandro's servant and promotes his marriage to Silvia, a young heiress. But pretended love becomes real and after many complications the two are united. Crispin thinks that it is the outward show of wealth that has forged these "bonds of interest," but Silvia and Leandro know that other bonds have been more powerful. Benavente has selected his characters to represent humanity in general, and at the end of the play he has Silvia say to the audience: "You have seen...how these puppets have been moved by...strings which were their interests, their passions, and all the illusions and petty miseries of their state. [But there is] something divine in our lives...which is eternal, and which shall not close when the farce of life shall close." This successful blending of convention, fantasy, high spirits, social criticism, and ideas found a ready audience almost everywhere and was long considered one of the modern theatre's major works.

Next to Benavente, Spain's best-known dramatist in the years after 1898 was Gregorio Martínez Sierra (1881–1947), now remembered primarily for *Cradle Song* (1911). Set in a convent, it shows the impact of a foundling on the nuns. In the first act, a baby is left at the gate; in later scenes she grows up and is married. There is little overt action but the quiet, sympathetic portrayal of the characters maintains and builds interest throughout. Similarly, *The Kingdom of God* (1916) shows three crucial periods in the life of its heroine: just before she becomes a nun; at a time when she is tempted by love; and, long afterward, as she works with a group of half-starved orphans. But Martínez Sierra did not always write about convent life. Typical of his more secular works is *A Dream of an August Evening* (1918), which centers around a young girl who feels discriminated against because she is denied the adventures to which boys can look forward. Then the wind blows a hat into her window and there begins an adventure which is equal to her fondest dreams. It was warm, human sentiment and skillfully maintained characterizations and moods which won Martínez Sierra a wide popular following, both at home and abroad. After 1916 he also directed the Teatro Eslava in Madrid, where he maintained a fine company and produced some of the best plays of Europe, many, including several by Shaw, in his own translations.

Somewhat similar in tone were the works of Serafín Alvarez Quintero (1871–1938) and Joaquín Alvarez Quintero (1873–1944), joint authors

of some 150 plays. A typical work is *The Merry Heart* (1906), in which
the coldly austere world of Donna Sacramento is gradually changed after
the arrival of her orphaned niece. Others of their plays are essentially
character studies, as in *The Lady of Alfáqueque* (1914) where a rascal
sponges off everyone but is tolerated because of his perfect manners. Only
occasionally did good-natured sentiment give way to a darker picture, as in
Malvaloca (1912). In it, two brothers, Salvador and Leonardo, are mend-
ing a cracked bell at a convent; Salvador seduces Malvaloca, but then
Leonardo falls in love with her and promises to mend her life as he has
the bell. Thus, even in their darker moments, the Alvarez Quinteros
celebrated the essential goodness of man.

As this brief survey indicates, Spanish dramatists in the years after
1880 were attuned to foreign developments and for the first time in almost
two hundred years began to win international recognition for Spanish
drama (Echegaray and Benavente were awarded Nobel Prizes). But for
the most part, their work was marred by sentimentality and conventionally
moral endings. Their achievement must be respected, especially in light of
what had gone before, but, in the context of world drama, they seem more
derivative than original.

179

*Innovation
and
Consolidation
in Drama,
1900–1915*

~ **VII** ~

In America, playwriting prior to 1915 was little influenced by foreign
developments, although a tentative realism emerged. The first American
play consciously cast in the realistic mode was *Margaret Fleming* (1891)
by James A. Herne (1839–1901). In it, a young "pillar of society" has
been carrying on an illicit relationship with a girl, who dies after giving
birth to his child. When the man's wife, Margaret Fleming, learns of the
affair, the shock causes her to lose her already weakened eyesight. Nevertheless, she takes the illegitimate child into her home to rear with her own
children, although she refuses to live with her husband. Ultimately there
is a reconciliation, but happiness has yet to be regained. The milieu is
re-created in great detail and the dialogue shows an unusual sensitivity to
the American idiom, but unfortunately the plot depends heavily upon
coincidence. Even though Herne avoided sensationalism, the play was
considered by commercial producers too outspoken for public performance
and it had to be presented privately. Well received critically by such realists
as William Dean Howells and Hamlin Garland, it was so unsuccessful with
the public that it brought Herne to the verge of financial ruin. Perhaps for
this reason, Herne's later plays, while realistic in setting and characterization, treat more conventional subjects. Thus, *Shore Acres* (1892), a senti-

180

*Innovation
and
Consolidation
in Drama,
1900–1915*

mental portrait of a man whom life has seemingly passed by but whose insight enables him to resolve a series of family crises, restored Herne's fortunes. It demonstrates well the type of realism that was to prevail in America until O'Neill's time—sentimental stories embedded in naturalistic detail.

It is this type of realism which William Gillette (1855–1937) exploited so successfully in such plays as *Secret Service* (1895), a melodrama about a Union spy among Confederate forces during the American Civil War. A mingling of love and adventure, it is set against a background re-created in infinite detail. The most famous scene is set in a telegraph office, where in the original production the actors tapped out messages in accurate Morse code on a working telegraph key. Such care for minutiae gave the action a sense of reality far in excess of that demanded by the subject. One of the finest actors of his day, Gillette approached performance much as he did playwriting—building up character out of many small concrete details. He argued that if an actor concentrates on re-creating reality moment by moment he can achieve at each performance a "sense of the first time" no matter how often he has played a role. Gillette's was a realism of surface detail applied to melodramatic subjects.

Another skillful playwright in the semirealistic vein was Clyde Fitch (1865–1909), author of some fifty plays of varying types. Today he is remembered primarily for three works: *The Girl with the Green Eyes* (1902), which shows the evil effects of jealousy on a marriage; *The Truth* (1906), about the unhappiness created by a congenital liar; and *The City* (1909), which shows the effect of city life on a family from a small town. All of these works demonstrate Fitch's great gift for characterization and compelling dramatic situation, but, though they begin by creating the conditions out of which a rigorous exploration of character and idea could develop, all degenerate into melodramatic devices and imposed happy endings.

Perhaps the most promising American dramatist of the early twentieth century was William Vaughn Moody (1869–1910), a poet and university professor. His play *The Great Divide* (1906) treats the conflict between the reserved, puritanical East (represented by Ruth Jordan) and the impulsive, lusty West (represented by Stephen Ghent); a near-rape is followed by an uneasy marriage, separation, and eventual reconciliation. The strength of the play lies in its characterization, finely wrought dialogue, and symbolic treatment of the American consciousness. But the action after the opening scene is not very compelling and the ending seems overly optimistic. To many critics, characterization and dialogue are more adroitly handled by Moody in *The Faith Healer* (1909). But this play was never popular with audiences, perhaps because the subject, a sympathetic treatment of faith healing, is a difficult one to present convincingly. Unfortunately, Moody's potential was never realized, for he died shortly after completing *The Faith Healer*.

Moody's play, *The Great Divide*, with Margaret Anglin as Ruth Jordan, the leading female role. The production was staged at the Princess Theatre, New York, in 1906. (From *The Theatre Magazine,* 1906.)

Edward Sheldon (1886–1946) also failed to live up to the promise shown in his early plays: *Salvation Nell* (1908), the story of a scullery maid turned Salvation Army lass who clings to her ne'er-do-well lover and eventually reclaims him; *The Nigger* (1909), in which a Southern governor discovers that his grandmother was a slave; and *The Boss* (1911), about a ruthless political leader. But even these rather sordid subjects were ultimately sentimentalized through happy endings. Consequently, Sheldon's later mode, first seen clearly in *Romance* (1913), in which an opera singer attracts and wins an idealistic young clergyman, does not mark a complete change.

Mrs. Fiske in Edward Sheldon's *Salvation Nell*, 1908. (From *The Theatre Magazine*, 1909.)

182

*Innovation
and
Consolidation
in Drama,
1900–1915*

As this brief survey suggests, several American playwrights prior to 1915 adopted lifelike dialogue and characterization and set their plays against actualistic backgrounds. But their addiction to melodrama, sentiment, and optimism undercut all attempts to explore the relationship among character, environment, and action, the essence of true realism.

The low state of American playwriting can be attributed in part to theatrical conditions, especially those relating to touring. After the 1870s the touring company gradually became the usual source of entertainment for most Americans, just as New York became virtually the only theatrical center. Out of this situation arose many problems, the most obvious of which involved booking. At first local managers had to go to New York and deal with many different producers to secure a season of traveling productions. But many producers failed to live up to their contracts, leaving local managers without attractions. These difficulties prompted the creation of booking agencies, which served as middlemen between local managers and producers. Since most agencies covered limited geographical areas, circuits, each controlled by an agency, gradually took shape and were fully established by the 1890s.

In 1896 a group of booking agents and theatre owners (Sam Nixon, Fred Zimmerman, Charles Frohman, Al Hayman, Marc Klaw, and Abraham Erlanger) saw the possibility of gaining control over the American theatre, for between them they already controlled theatres throughout the country. Consequently, they joined together to create what came to be called the Syndicate. They began by offering a full season of stellar attractions to any manager who would book exclusively through them, an offer welcomed by many, since it permitted them to deal with a single agent and to obtain outstanding productions. Now the Syndicate set out to eliminate all competition by gaining control over certain key routes, for rival productions could not tour if they were unable to perform in towns between major cities. In places where it could not acquire already existing theatres, the Syndicate built rival houses and booked into them outstanding productions at reduced prices until the competition was eliminated. New York producers who would not sign exclusive booking contracts were refused all engagements in the Syndicate's theatres, and actors who opposed them were "blackballed" (that is, the Syndicate would accept no production in which they appeared). By 1900, the Syndicate was in effective control of the American theatre. Now in a position to influence (if not dictate) play selection, it refused to book any production it thought incapable of attracting a mass audience. Furthermore, it favored productions featuring stars with large personal followings. Thus, strong pressures were exerted on the theatre to remain within the established and popular mold.

Of the Syndicate's members, by far the most important was Charles Frohman (1854–1915), for he was the only one directly concerned with theatrical production. Beginning as a program seller, he worked his way up to business manager and agent. In 1889 he became a producer and in 1893 opened the Empire Theatre in New York, where for many years he maintained a fine stock company and established the reputations of several stars. In 1896, he extended his activities to London, where he eventually controlled five theatres and supplied many new works to the Syndicate's American theatres. (Frohman was especially fond of J. M. Barrie's plays, which he was instrumental in popularizing.) At the height of his power, Frohman employed some 10,000 persons.

The Syndicate did not go unopposed. Some of the best actors of the day, including Minnie Maddern Fiske, James A. Herne, and James O'Neill, refused to work through it and were reduced to playing in minor theatres or in makeshift quarters. But it met a truly powerful opponent in David Belasco (c. 1854–1931), who during the first decade of the twentieth century became the most popular producer-dramatist in America.

Born in San Francisco, Belasco was on the stage from childhood and, by his own estimate, had written or adapted about one hundred plays and staged about three hundred by the time he left for New York in 1882. He then served as Steele Mackaye's stage manager for a time and collaborated with Henry C. DeMille on four very successful plays. After 1890 he continued to turn out such popular melodramas as *The Heart of Maryland* (1895), *The Girl of the Golden West* (1905), and *Rose of the Rancho* (1906). In 1902 Belasco acquired his own theatre and until 1928 was one of America's most successful producer-directors.

Above all, Belasco is now remembered for his naturalistic staging of romantic and melodramatic plays. With him, actualism reached its peak in America. For *The Governor's Lady* (1912), he re-created a Childs Restaurant on stage, and the Childs chain stocked it daily with food which was served and consumed on stage. For Eugene Walters's *The Easiest Way* (1909), he bought the contents of a boarding-house room, including the wallpaper, and had it transferred to the stage. The blizzard in *The Girl of*

David Belasco's *The Girl of the Golden West*, with Blanche Bates and Frank Keenan, in 1905. (From *The Theatre Magazine*, 1906.)

184

*Innovation
and
Consolidation
in Drama,
1900–1915*

the Golden West gave the effect of absolute fidelity, and the twelve-minute silent sequence in *Madame Butterfly* (1900), during which the passage of a night was shown by sunset, darkness, and dawn, was considered a marvel of stage lighting. Working in the tradition of Saxe-Meiningen and Daly, Belasco controlled every element of his productions and coordinated them with extreme care. Whatever one might think of Belasco's choice of plays, no one ever accused him of careless workmanship.

Belasco achieved all the qualities most admired by the Syndicate, but his refusal to sign an exclusive contract with it created a conflict that eventually led to a court battle. But by 1909 Belasco's productions were in such demand that the Syndicate finally accepted Belasco on his own terms. This marked the first significant break in the Syndicate's power. Its willingness to make such concessions, however, was prompted as well by the rise of the Shuberts (Sam, Lee, and Jacob J.), who, when the Syndicate closed its theatres to their productions in 1905, set out to create a rival chain. By this time many local managers were dissatisfied with the Sydicate's high-handed methods and welcomed the Shuberts as reformers. After 1910 the rivalry intensified, and the Syndicate ceased to be a major force after Frohman's death in 1915. Unfortunately, the Shuberts turned out to be as dictatorial as their rivals and kept effective control of the road until about 1956, when the government ordered them to sell many of their theatres.

In the years between 1896 and 1915, then, the power of businessmen over the American theatre served to discourage innovations in playwriting and production. New paths were laid out only tentatively and brought few notable results until after World War I.

❦ VIII ❦

In the years between 1900 and 1915, England produced a far larger number of forward-looking playwrights than did America, but most were either realists in the vein of Pinero and Jones or humorless disciples of Shaw. Perhaps the best were Barker and Galsworthy.

Harley Granville Barker (1877–1946) began his playwriting career in 1902 with *The Marrying of Ann Leete,* which, through the title character, suggested the need for England to revise its outmoded moral and social values. Born into the upper classes and destined to marry the dull, plodding Lord John Carp, Ann comes to realize that the mate best suited to her is John Abud, a gardener. Though her family is scandalized, she is firm in her resolution to marry without regard for convention. The story itself is of little importance, for Barker concentrates upon character, idea, and atmosphere.

185

*Innovation
and
Consolidation
in Drama,
1900–1915*

Barker's best play is *The Madras House* (1910), a loosely structured, satirical work in which a gallery of characters provides a cross-section of English society as seen against the background of the business world. The most original character is Constantine Madras, wife deserter turned Mohammedan, who seeks to convince the draper Huxtable, father of six daughters, of the advantages of polygamy and the segregation of the sexes. Contrasting with the irresponsible Constantine and the self-satisfied Huxtable is Constantine's idealistic son, Philip, who sees beyond the drapery establishment, of which he is part-owner, to suffering in the world at large. Out of a desire to aid humanity, he resolves to devote himself to politics, even though he recognizes that one man alone can do little to alter entrenched customs.

Like Shaw's, Barker's plays progress more through discussion than through overt physical action. His dialogue is always subtle and his characterizations psychologically sound. The chief weakness of his drama is its lack of emotional intensity. As one critic has put it, "His plays are like reminiscences of passionate things after emotion has cooled, or they are aloof and cynical."

John Galsworthy (1867–1933) had already established a reputation as a socially conscious novelist before turning to playwriting in 1906 with *The Silver Box,* a play about the inequities of the law. In it, two men steal, but the rich man's son, who has stolen a purse, is allowed to right his wrong with a check, while the servant, who steals a silver box, is sent to prison. Inequities of law and class privilege were Galsworthy's favorite subjects. He developed them again in *Justice* (1910), in which a weak-willed clerk is sent to prison for having forged a check so that he might elope to South America with the woman he loves. In prison he is placed in solitary confinement and in other ways treated in a manner wholly unsuited either to his crime or to his personality. The strong impression made by this play is credited with bringing about significant changes in England's penal code. Similar subjects were treated in *Loyalties* (1922) and *Escape* (1926).

Strife (1909) develops a different theme. Here the conflict is between management and labor. Both David Roberts, who represents the striking workers, and John Anthony, who represents the company's directors, are blind to any position but their own. Consequently, the workers starve while the company is on the point of collapse. Finally both men are deserted by their followers and they are left alone in their mutual defeat. Galsworthy weights the scales so evenly that it is impossible to decide between rival claims, although he appears to condemn both for extremeness.

All of Galsworthy's dramas demonstrate his deep concern for principle (perhaps more than for human beings) and depict characters as victims of a social system. The plots are well constructed, the characters keenly sketched, the dialogue natural. Galsworthy's chief fault lies in his inability to create any strong sense of universality. Furthermore, his preoccupation

The original production of Galsworthy's *Strife* at the New Theatre, London, in 1909. (From *Theatre Arts*, 1943.)

with objectivity leads to an austere intellectualism which undercuts deep emotional involvement. Unlike Shaw and Barker, who were consciously didactic, Galsworthy struggled to remain objective and to permit the audience to form its own opinions. Thus, his plays usually end with questions rather than with answers. But Galsworthy's faults became evident only with the passage of time. Until World War II, he was considered one of England's most significant playwrights.

A quite different view animates the plays of James M. Barrie (1860–1937), whose closely observed pictures of daily life are filtered through whimsy, sentiment, and optimism. Though often satirical, he is never bitter. These qualities won him a following far more extensive than that commanded by his pessimistic and uncompromising contemporaries. Today

James M. Barrie's *Peter Pan*, "The Pirate Ship," produced at the Duke of York's Theatre in 1904. (Courtesy Enthoven Collection, Victoria and Albert Museum.)

Barrie is probably best known for *Peter Pan* (1904), a glorification of childhood make-believe as seen in fantastic adventures involving pirates, Indians, and fairies. An element of fantasy is also evident in many of his plays for adults. In *Dear Brutus* (1917), for example, a sprite, Mr. Lob, allows the characters to experience what they believe circumstances have prevented them from becoming, but when the play ends nothing has really changed, for they learn that character determines destiny more than does external circumstance.

Most of Barrie's major works are rooted in character. *The Admirable Crichton* (1902) shows the well-ordered household of Lord Loam, in which the butler Crichton fulfills his function admirably but aloofly. Then, when the family is shipwrecked, Crichton emerges as the aristocrat, becomes the leader, and is about to marry one of Lord Loam's daughters when all are rescued. Back in London, the characters resume their old roles, for they accept the necessity of social convention. Several of the plays center around women. Perhaps the best is *What Every Woman Knows* (1908), which shows how the quiet but forceful Maggie forwards her husband's career so effectively that he is unaware of her assistance until he leaves her for another woman and comes to recognize how much he owes her. Barrie was extremely prolific until about 1920, after which he wrote little.

It was also during the period 1900–1915 that musical comedy was established as a separate genre, primarily by George Edwardes (1852–1915), manager of the Gaiety Theatre in London, where beginning in 1892 he presented such prototypical works as *In Town, The Shop Girl, San Toy,* and *The Geisha.* In them a sketchy plot provides excuses for songs, elabo-

George Edwardes' production of *San Toy* at Daly's Theatre, London, in 1899. The actress is Topsy Sinden. (Courtesy Enthoven Collection, Victoria and Albert Museum.)

188

*Innovation
and
Consolidation
in Drama,
1900–1915*

rate production numbers performed by beautiful chorus girls, and specialty acts like those seen in music halls and variety theatres. Many of Edwardes's productions were exported to America. Thus came into being a type that would eventually assume a major place in the modern repertory.

Between 1900 and 1915 the theatre in England remained, for the most part, in familiar paths, since it was dominated either by commercial producers or by actor-managers seeking to maintain the traditions of Macready, Kean, and Irving. The dominant figure was Herbert Beerbohm Tree (1853–1917), who, after entering the theatre in 1878 as an actor, became a manager in 1887. In 1897 he built Her Majesty's Theatre, which, with its repertory of Shakespeare's plays and melodramas, rapidly became the leading theatre of the day after Irving retired. With Tree, romantic realism reached its peak in England. In 1900, his production of *A Midsummer Night's Dream* featured a forest of three-dimensional trees, carpets of grass, real flowers, and live rabbits. It attracted more than 220,000 spectators. With such productions, Tree set the standard.

Tree should also be remembered for founding England's first important acting school when, in 1904, he began a course of training at his theatre. In 1905, the school was moved to new quarters and soon blossomed into the Royal Academy of Dramatic Art, from which many of England's finest actors were to come.

Tree was merely the most prominent of many actor-managers of the time: John Hare, Charles Wyndham, Madge and William Hunter Kendal, John Martin-Harvey, and others. They were the last of their breed, for

Scene from Beerbohm Tree's production of Shakespeare's
A Midsummer Night's Dream at Her Majesty's Theatre in 1900.
Titania's bower is seen at center. (Courtesy Enthoven Collection,
Victoria and Albert Museum.)

with World War I, the actor-manager system, which had dominated the English theatre for more than two centuries, was largely to end. But during the years between 1900 and 1914, they sought to maintain tradition by presenting a repertory which mingled the old and the new. Their tastes seldom extended beyond romantic realism, however, and consequently they did little to support new trends in drama. Only Martin-Harvey seems to have recognized the direction of change. After his considerable success in Reinhardt's production of *Oedipus Rex* in 1912, he made many attempts to alter his earlier techniques. But, for the most part, the English theatre remained rooted in the past.

~ IX ~

Between 1890 and 1915 France produced few dramatists of note other than Curel, Porto-Riche, Brieux, Maeterlinck, Claudel, and Rostand (all discussed in earlier chapters). Lesser playwrights reenforced the trends established by their more famous contemporaries, but added little that was new or lasting.

Among the writers of the realistic school, the best known are Lavedan, Hervieu, and Donnay. Henri Lavedan (1859–1940) is often compared to Curel, but he lacked that author's deep psychological insight. His most characteristic works are rather jaundiced pictures of fashionable life in Paris. In one of the most successful, *The Rakes* (1895), a couturier's studio and a well-known Parisian restaurant serve as backgrounds for the intrigues of decadent but fashionable pleasure seekers. In *The Taste for Vice* (1911), two young people pretend to be amoral because it is expected of them, but eventually discover their common pretense. Here as in all of Lavedan's work a sense of moral purpose can be perceived but it is subordinated to sensational elements. Consequently, he seems more interested in theatrical effect than realistic portraiture.

Paul Hervieu (1857–1915) is most clearly related to Dumas *fils* and Brieux, for his is essentially a drama of ideas. Many of his plays revolve around family life and the question of divorce. In the first of his dramas to win critical success, *The Pincers* (1895), a wife seeks a divorce and is refused; then, some years later, the husband proposes a separation, but now the wife refuses for the sake of her child, the son of the man for whom she had sought to divorce her husband. Somewhat similarly, in *Man-Made Law* (1897), a woman discovers that her husband is having an affair with Mme. d'Orcieu, mother of her son's fiancée. But when she tells M. d'Orcieu, he insists that she remain silent so that scandal can be avoided. Thus, the wedding is to proceed and the mother becomes a victim of the man-made

190

*Innovation
and
Consolidation
in Drama,
1900–1915*

law. During his lifetime, Hervieu enjoyed an enormous reputation, in part because of the classic simplicity of his plays, in which episodes and details are reduced to essentials and logic appears irrefutable. But the plays now seem monotonously similar for in all the characters and actions are constructed to illustrate preconceived ideas.

Maurice Donnay (1859–1945), like Porto-Riche, was concerned primarily with the power of love over human behavior. He first gained recognition with *Lovers* (1896), in which two young people, despite their mutual love, are forced to marry others but accept their fate as unavoidable. Perhaps Donnay's best play is *The Other Danger* (1902), the story of a woman who finds happiness for the first time only to renounce it when her daughter falls in love with the same man. Through Donnay's work runs the idea that happiness is fleeting but that life does not end merely because joy goes.

As in other countries, France's most popular drama was light in tone. Farce flourished, especially with Courteline and Feydeau. Many of the works of Georges Courteline (1861–1929) are based on the vagaries of army life, as in *Lidoire* (1891) and *High Spirits in the Squadron* (1895), or of the law, as in *The Policeman Has No Pity* (1899) or *Article 330* (1901); in all he gains unfailing effects by turning the characters' own arguments against them. His best play is *Boubouroche* (1893), a mixture of wit and gross brutality not unlike medieval farce. In most of his plays Courteline seems to view with bitter joviality the rather cowardly battles between human beings. Thus, behind his humor there is always a rather cynical commentary on mankind. Georges Feydeau (1862–1921), on the other hand, seems to have been content to extract the greatest possible humor from the exaggerated situations which he so masterfully engineered. His farce is a precision machine in which nonsensical situations are underlined by incongruous repartee. Among his masterpieces of drollery are *Hotel Paradiso* (1894), *A Flea in Her Ear* (1907), and *Look After Emily* (1908).

Feydeau's *A Flea in Her Ear* in its original production at the Théâtre des Nouveautés, 1907, with Germain as Victor Emmanuel, at left, and Milo de Meyer as Homénidès de Histangua. (From *Le Théâtre*, 1907.)

191

*Innovation
and
Consolidation
in Drama,
1900–1915*

Among the playwrights who kept the Boulevard theatres supplied with vehicles, the most popular was Sacha Guitry (1885–1957), who, as dramatist, actor, and director, was from 1910 to 1940 the undisputed master of the popular (or Boulevard) theatres. Among the best of his ninety plays are *The Night Watchman* (1911), *The Illusionist* (1917), and *When Do We Begin the Play?* (1935). He also composed a number of plays— among them *Deburau* (1918), *Pasteur* (1919), and *Béranger* (1920)— for his father, Lucien Guitry (1860–1925), one of the most popular actors of the period.

But the French public was not restricted to new and popular fare, for it was offered a steady diet of classics by the Comédie Française, which included in its ranks several of France's finest actors. Perhaps the best were Mounet-Sully (1841–1916), a man of exceptional good looks, fine voice, and emotional power; his brother, Paul Mounet (1847–1922), of only slightly lesser fame; Eugène Silvain (1851–1930), noted for his subtle and intelligent reading of verse; Julia Bartet (1854–1941), called "the Divine" because of her charm, exquisite tenderness, and flawless diction; and Eugénie Segond-Weber (1867–1945), outstanding impersonator of classical heroines. Despite its fine performers, the Comédie Française was very conservative, for the actors still controlled the company's policies and refused to delegate authority to a director. Thus, its brilliance depended more upon individuals than upon ensemble playing or mounting.

Several French actors of the period—most notably Coquelin, Réjane, and Bernhardt—became international stars. Constant-Benoît Coquelin (1841–1909) performed at the Comédie Française from 1860 to 1886, then toured widely in Europe and America, and managed his own company in Paris. He was noted for his superb technique, based on observation but sharpened and exaggerated through selection and emphasis. Though outstanding in Molière's major roles, he is noted above all for his Cyrano de Bergerac, especially created by Rostand to display Coquelin's talents to greatest advantage. Gabrielle Réjane (1857–1920) became a leading comic actress soon after making her debut in 1875. She never ventured into the classics, but in light and high comedy she was unrivaled. In addition to performing in Paris and managing her own company for a time, she appeared in London, New York, South America, and elsewhere before retiring in 1915. Sarah Bernhardt (1845–1923) was probably the best-known actress in the world from the 1870s until World War I. After 1862 she appeared sporadically at the Comédie Française, but as her fame grew after 1870 she began to tour, and left the troupe permanently in 1880. Then between international engagements she managed a series of theatres in Paris. At the height of her powers she was noted for her "voice like a golden bell," her slim figure, expressive dark eyes, and mastery of stage techniques. Among her finest roles were Phaedra, Camille, Rostand's L'Aiglon, and— written for her by Sardou—Fédora, Théodora, and Tosca. Almost a legend in her own time, she epitomized for many The Great Actress.

192

*Innovation
and
Consolidation
in Drama,
1900–1915*

Thus, in the years between 1900 and 1915 France did not produce many dramatists of the first rank, but it maintained a strong dramatic tradition, especially through its outstanding actors. The French also were relatively unaware of developments going on elsewhere and were not to be shaken out of their complacency until about 1910 (a development which will be discussed in the next chapter).

In central Europe, the picture was much the same as elsewhere—a number of second-rank dramatists reenforced the work of their more significant peers. In Germany, the most important of these writers were Sudermann, Halbe, and Hirschfeld.

Hermann Sudermann (1857–1928), long considered a powerful rival to Hauptmann, is now virtually forgotten. His first play, *Honor* (1889), produced only a few weeks after Hauptmann's *Before Sunrise,* was so successful that it tended to overshadow Hauptmann's work. It treats differing conceptions of honor among the upper-middle and lower classes and voices superficial social protest, but it uses many devices of the well-made play (including soliloquy and aside) and centers upon an unbelievably pure hero. Thus, it more nearly resembles the plays of Augier and Dumas *fils* than it does those of Ibsen and Hauptmann, but it was sufficiently advanced to seem daring while remaining within acceptable limits. Consequently, it won approval from an audience that denounced Hauptmann's play.

Sudermann's most popular work was *Die Heimat* (*Home,* usually played in English as *Magda,* 1893), which gave new direction to a character type—"the woman with a past"—already exploited by Hugo, Dumas *fils,* and others. The heroine, desiring emancipation from her puritanical home, makes a career for herself as a singer; when she gives birth to an illegitimate child, her father demands that she marry her lover, and when she refuses he dies of a stroke. *Die Heimat* was a favorite with actresses, including Bernhardt, Duse, and Mrs. Patrick Campbell. Sudermann went on to write many other plays but on the whole they served primarily to popularize the more rigorous paths laid out by others.

Unlike Sudermann, Max Halbe (1865–1944) sought for a stringent naturalism. His most famous play, *Youth* (1893), concerns Annchen, an illegitimate child, and her mentally retarded half-brother, who have grown up under the domination of their uncle, who urges Annchen to enter a convent so that she may save her sinful mother from purgatory. A cousin, Hans, arrives and he and Annchen begin a touching and passionate relationship. Deeply resentful, the half-brother attempts to kill Hans, but it is Annchen

Scene from Act IV of *Magda* by Sudermann,
produced at the Lyceum Theatre, London,
in 1896 with Mrs. Patrick Campbell (left)
in the title role.
(Courtesy Victoria and Albert Museum.)

who dies as she throws herself between them. In addition to naturalism, Halbe also championed the rights of the poor in such plays as *The Just World* (1897), which contrasts the misery of the Hugel family with the prosperity of the Grossman brothers.

Georg Hirschfeld (1873–1935) was especially adept at capturing the social texture of contemporary life. In *At Home* (1893), for example, the Doergens household, with its hardworking, tradesman father, selfish mother, depressed daughter, and ill-tempered son, is depicted in great detail. Hirschfeld's most famous play is *The Mothers* (1896), which develops the familiar theme that the poor are sacrificed to the rich. In it, a young composer, Robert, opposed in his career by his well-to-do father, leaves home to live in the slums with a working-class girl, Marie. When the father dies, Robert returns home with Marie. Although the family is kind to her, Marie realizes that she will be an impediment to Robert and, without telling him that she is pregnant, returns to the slums.

In Austria, the new trends were reenforced by Schönherr and Bahr. Karl Schönherr (1867–1943) was fascinated by the bitter aspects of life, which at times he treated with comic irony and at others with complete seriousness. Much of his work seems an extension of the folk-drama tradition of Anzengruber and his predecessors. One of his best plays in this vein is *Earth* (1908), in which an aging innkeeper, who will permit his son of fifty neither to marry nor to take over the inn, is told that he has little time to live. He orders a coffin and places it by his bed, from which throughout the winter he watches as his son is fought over by two women, one of whom emerges as the apparent victor when she becomes pregnant. But when spring comes, the old innkeeper, as if rejuvenated, rises from his bed and smashes the coffin and the hopes of the son and his would be wife. But Schönherr was not always so lighthearted. In *Carnival Folk* (1904), hunger drives a young boy to betray his father for a loaf of bread, and in *The Children's Tragedy* (1919) a mother's love affair ruins the lives of her three children.

Of all European dramatists, probably none was so adept at recognizing and capitalizing on new trends as was Herman Bahr (1863–1934). Originally attracted to naturalism, Bahr edited the Freie Bühne's periodical. Then in 1891 he denounced naturalism and shortly afterward came under the influence of symbolism. Thereafter he attempted almost every other form and style in his eighty plays of varying types. Ironically, his most famous work is a rather flimsy light comedy, *The Concert* (1909), in which a pianist, although he loves his wife, is constantly amorously involved with his female students. Aware of his predilections and the symptoms of a new attachment, the wife, in order to distract him, pretends to develop an interest in a student's husband. Her stratagem works, but at the end of the play we see the husband embark on a new affair. Bahr was certainly not a great playwright, but, through his plays and criticism, he was a major popularizer of new techniques and styles in Austria and Germany.

~ **XI** ~

As this survey suggests, by World War I the realistic-naturalistic mode pioneered by Ibsen and Zola had gained worldwide currency. Nevertheless, the most successful dramatists between 1900 and 1915 altered the rigorous standards of the pioneers as they reached accommodations with romantic realism, still the dominant force in the popular theatre. But no doubt it was this softening of realism and naturalism, through the inclusion of devices borrowed from the well-made play and melodrama and through concessions to traditional values and the desire for happy endings, that made audiences more receptive. Such compromises, nevertheless, won increased tolerance for Ibsen and other dramatists previously considered unacceptable. Thus, if the more rigorous drama did not wholly triumph, at least it gained ground.

Antirealism fared less well. A few playwrights, most notably D'Annunzio, won a wide popular following, but Yeats, Wedekind, and Strindberg were at first little appreciated and could only command a small audience. Perhaps the most important development of the years between 1900 and 1915, however, was the exploration by a few dramatists of the unconscious as explicated by Freud. In this way, the foundations for many future movements were laid even as the gains of the preceding period were being consolidated.

Forging a New Art of The Theatre

Although in every period its leading practitioners have considered the theatre an art (and often a business as well), the new wave of directors, designers, and playwrights at the end of the nineteenth century began to denounce their predecessors as misguided or tasteless perverters of the theatre's true mission. They proclaimed their intention to right the situation by transforming the theatre into an art worthy of taking its rightful place among the other arts. They discussed at length its nature, function, and elements, and through theory and practice sought to revitalize it. Adolphe Appia and Gordon Craig, through their theoretical works, provided a rationale for the new trends. Others sought through practice to find new solutions for problems of long standing. Some, such as William Poel and

Jacques Copeau, suggested a return to the bare platform stage; others, such as Maurice Pottecher and Percy Mackaye, sought to return the theatre to the people as in ancient Greece; some, like Georg Fuchs, suggested the need to abandon realism for a stylized, bas-relief stage; and still others, such as Reinhardt and Barker, sought answers in a wide-ranging eclecticism. In almost every country there was a self-conscious attempt to define the "art of the theatre" and to implement it, no matter how great the obstacles. Out of this search gradually emerged those views and practices which would shape the future.

The number of would-be reformers in the years between 1890 and 1915 was indeed extensive. Of these, many were concerned with limited or specialized problems. For example, several producers were preoccupied above all with seeking more effective ways of staging Shakespeare's plays, for they had come to believe that antiquarian settings on proscenium stages were inappropriate. Not only was the elaborate pictorial decor difficult to shift, the rhythm of the dramatic action was frequently broken by the waits required for scene changes. Attempts to find more adequate means led to numerous experiments.

Interest in Shakespearean staging was especially strong in Germany, where as early as the 1830s Ludwig Tieck made the first attempt in modern times to reconstruct an Elizabethan public theatre. In 1840, Karl Immermann, working in Dusseldorf, arranged the first stage intended especially for Shakespeare's plays by erecting back of the traditional proscenium a structure in two parts—a forestage surrounded by an architectural façade with doors at either side, and, at the rear, an inner stage, where pictorialized decors could be set up and changed. This solution was to influence all subsequent German experiments.

The next important attempt to create a *Shakespearebühne* ("Shake-

Immermann's Shakespearebühne,
Dusseldorf, begun in 1840.
(From a contemporary print.)

Klein's and Kilian's Shakespearebühne at the Munich Hoftheater in 1909–10. The production is of *Hamlet*; the design by Klein. (From *Stage Yearbook*, 1913.)

spearean stage") came in 1889 at the Hoftheater in Munich, where the general manager, Karl von Perfall, the stage manager, Jocza Savits, and the technical director, Karl Lautenschlager, mounted *King Lear* on a stage which, except in elaborateness, differed little from Immermann's. Theirs was a three-part arrangement, for to Immermann's two divisions they added a semicircular forestage forward of the proscenium arch. The façade of the architectural unit erected back of the proscenium and the settings used on the inner stage were more elaborate than in Immermann's arrangement, but the overall conception differed little. Another attempt along similar lines was made in 1909–10 at the same theatre by Julius Klein and Eugen Kilian. The principal improvements were the less ornate architectural façade and the more careful integration of the pictorial elements. All of these attempts had the virtue of permitting uninterrupted playing, but all suffered from a disconcerting combination of formal and representational modes. Nevertheless, they were widely publicized and imitated.

One of those influenced by the German experiments was André Antoine, who between 1904 and 1912 staged five of Shakespeare's plays in ways completely new to the French. Part of the novelty lay in the avoidance of the cuts and adaptations to which the plays had invariably been subjected in France. Knowing that the French considered the plays chaotic, Antoine sought to emphasize continuity and unity. His solution in the first production, *King Lear* (1904), was not unlike that used by Irving: a shallow forestage on which short, unlocalized scenes were played before a neutral curtain while large settings were erected and changed behind it. For *Julius Caesar* (1906), Antoine added a large architectural unit (a Roman arch) which framed both interior and exterior scenes, but otherwise used the earlier method. When he mounted *Coriolanus* (1910), however, he erected an elaborate scenic unit at each side, one representing Rome, the other Corioles; in a slightly raised inner stage at the rear, scenic elements were changed as needed. The result was a compromise between the simultaneous settings of the Middle Ages and the pictorial decors of the picture-frame stage. But the constant presence of Rome and Corioles functioned

197

Setting for *King Lear* as it was staged at the Théâtre Antoine in 1904.
(From *Le Théâtre,* 1904.)

symbolically to show the poles between which Coriolanus is pulled. Like his German contemporaries, however, Antoine could not resolve the disparity between convention and representation.

Meanwhile in England a far more drastic solution was being championed by William Poel (1852–1934). On the stage since 1876, Poel had from the beginning been interested in the problems of Shakespearean production and as early as 1881 had staged the first-quarto *Hamlet* on a bare stage. Poel's major experiments, however, date from 1893, when he staged *Measure for Measure* at the Royalty Theatre in London on a reconstructed Elizabethan public stage (facilitated by the rediscovery in the

William Poel's reconstruction of an Elizabethan theatre for his production in 1893 of Shakespeare's *Measure for Measure* at the Royalty Theatre. The scene is of Act II, 2. (Courtesy Enthoven Collection, Victoria and Albert Museum).

1880s of the drawing of the Swan Theatre made in 1596). A large forestage was backed by a two-leveled façade equipped with curtains which could reveal or conceal the interior, while two posts on the forestage supported the "heavens." Actors costumed in Elizabethan garments and seated on stools at either side simulated the audience of Shakespeare's day. Despite the attempt at authenticity, the result was "the image of an Elizabethan stage seen across that of a modern stage."

Between 1894 and 1905 Poel was supported and encouraged by the Elizabethan Stage Society, of which he was the guiding spirit. Under its auspices in 1895, Poel presented *A Comedy of Errors* at Gray's Inn, which, with its large hall built in Tudor times, permitted a much more authentic relationship between audience and performers than was possible in a conventional theatre. In 1896, he mounted productions of *Two Gentlemen of Verona* in the Merchant Taylor's Hall and of *Twelfth Night* in the hall of the Middle Temple. In addition to Shakespeare's plays, Poel presented several other older English works, among them Marlowe's *Doctor Faustus* and the first production in modern times of *Everyman*. He was to continue similar experiments throughout his life.

Although he did not always use the same solution, Poel is now remembered almost entirely for his attempts to reconstruct the Elizabethan public stage. He also popularized several conventions: dressing the actors in Elizabethan garments to reflect Shakespeare's own day rather than the historical epoch of the dramatic action; using costumed pages to draw the curtains of the inner stage and to arrange properties and furniture; and employing an onstage audience to emphasize the audience-actor relationships of the Elizabethan era. But Poel's major emphasis was upon continuity and rapidity both in action and speech. Although the productions did not generate widespread enthusiasm, they demonstrated the advantages of unbroken playing and of concentrating attention upon the actors.

Poel's methods were taken to America by his associate in the Elizabethan Stage Society, Ben Greet (1857–1936), who toured extensively in the United States between 1903 and 1914. They were also taken to France by Lugné-Poë in 1898, when, in imitation of Poel's production, he mounted *Measure for Measure* in the Cirque d'Eté in Paris. Attracting little attention, it generated no imitations.

Interest in the staging conventions of earlier times extended beyond the Elizabethan era. For example, Edward Godwin, Gordon Craig's father, simulated the conditions of the Greek theatre when in 1886 he staged John Todhunter's *Helen of Troy* at Hengler's Circus in London. Re-creations of the stage of classical Greece were not to be fully exploited, however, until Reinhardt mounted his productions of Greek plays some twenty-five years later.

The French stage of the seventeenth century was also reconstructed in several experiments, most notably those of Antoine at the Odéon. Believing that classical French drama is rooted in the era of its writing, Antoine

Antoine's production of Corneille's *The Cid* at the Odéon in 1907, an attempt to reproduce the original production of 1636. (Courtesy Bibliothèque de l'Arsenal, Paris.)

ignored the supposed period of the action and mounted the plays in seventeenth-century milieus. For Corneille's play *The Cid* in 1907, he sought to re-create the original production of 1636. Corneille's text became a play-within-a-play as Antoine surrounded it with the invented action of an onstage audience. Similarly, in 1909 he staged Racine's *Andromaque* in a setting which simulated a seventeenth-century drawing room with a courtier audience at either side.

All of these attempts may be viewed as another form of antiquarianism in which the historical accuracy of architecture and dress have been replaced by accuracy of past theatrical conditions. But such a judgment is not wholly adequate, for the experiments also point up the integral relationship between drama and the theatre for which it is written. As used by such men as Reinhardt, the theatrical conventions, architecture, and audience-performer relationships of the past would provide some of the most fruitful keys to stylization and the revitalization of the classics.

~~~ II ~~~

Meanwhile, all-embracing theories of theatrical production were being formulated by Adolphe Appia and Gordon Craig, destined to be the most powerful influences on the modern theatre. Although neither was extensively involved in theatrical production nor markedly successful when he was, together they formulated the theoretical bases upon which others would build. Working independently, they drew many of the same conclusions, but each also had distinctive ideas and developed along different lines.

Although long less famous than Craig, Appia began his work first. Born in Geneva, Adolphe Appia (1862–1928) was brought up in such a puritanical family that he did not see his first theatrical performance until he was nineteen years old. A music student, he came to his interest in theatre through Wagner's operas, which were long to be the greatest influence on him. But when he went to Bayreuth, he was deeply disappointed, for he considered the productions there completely misguided, and from the early 1880s he struggled to resolve the disparity between Wagner's theoretical statements and the staging of his operas. Almost all of Appia's early writing, beginning about 1891, was addressed to this problem.

His first important work, *The Staging of Wagnerian Music Drama* (1895), of which only 300 copies were printed, was little more than a pamphlet. It drew little notice, but nevertheless Appia elaborated his ideas in a full-length work, *Music and the Art of the Theatre* (1899), which also included nineteen of Appia's own designs for the Wagnerian operas. Since his next major book did not appear until 1921, Appia's views were long known primarily from these two early works.

The problem to which Appia first addressed himself was the cause of disunity in the Wagnerian productions at Bayreuth. He concluded that the primary deterrent was the disparity between the three-dimensional actor and the two-dimensional stage settings. Since he believed that the performer is the intermediary between dramatist and audience and that "scenic illusion is the presence of the living actor," Appia sought to harmonize all other elements with the performer. In his search, Appia was guided by principles already voiced by Wagner. Like Wagner, Appia believed that the goal of production is to create an ideal realm into which the spectator is drawn by an overpowering empathic experience. He also accepted the need for a unifying artistic force—the director—to control all of the elements of

Setting for Wagner's *Parsifal* at Bayreuth, shortly after the turn of the century. The attempt at illusionism is still apparent in this setting of two-dimensional cutouts. (From *Le Théâtre,* 1911.)

Appia's design for Wagner's *Parsifal,* 1895. (From Fondation Adolphe Appia, Berne.)

production so that the desired effect might be achieved. But Appia also believed that Wagner had violated his own theory when he used a multitude of realistic scenic details to express the ideal realm. It seemed to Appia that ideality could only be created through simplicity and suggestion. But Appia also thought these qualities had to be harmonized with the three-dimensional actor, and he established a hierarchy of means, with the actor first, followed by spatial arrangement, lighting, and painted flats.

The essential problem for Appia, then, lay in the relationship among the moving actor, the horizontal floor, and the vertical scenery. In past practice, the three had normally been treated as unrelated elements, for the flat, two-dimensional scenery usually stopped abruptly at the stage floor and was designed without concern for the presence of the living actor. Consequently, Appia conceived his designs in terms of space, volume, and mass; platforms, steps, and ramps provided transitions between scenery and floor and opportunities for the actor to move both horizontally and vertically. They also became rhythmical forces in the visual composition. His principal scenic elements (in addition to steps and platforms) were pillars, drapes, and walls—all free of nonessential details and conceived in three dimensions.

Appia's designs were rendered in black and white, for he thought in terms of light and shadow. He also recognized that even three-dimensional elements may appear flat under general illumination. Consequently, he called for multidirectional lighting with strong contrasts to emphasize mass, shape, and plasticity. For Appia, light was the visual element most analogous to music, which is capable of reflecting moment-by-moment changes in mood, tonality, and rhythm. Thus, he considered light the primary means of unifying and blending all the other visual elements into a harmonious whole.

Ultimately, Appia sought to create an absolute beauty through idealized elements. He completed the scheme which Wagner had envisioned but had failed to realize. Nevertheless, Appia did not escape altogether the realistic tenor of his times. Behind his work lies the fundamental assumption that illusion is impossible if there is any disparity between the perceived dimensions of performer and setting. This concern for three-dimensionality is a legacy of naturalism, one that was to be rejected by adherents of many subsequent movements.

Appia had hoped that his work would be read and heeded by Wagner's widow, who controlled the Bayreuth Festival, but, if conscious of it, she steadfastly ignored it. His first opportunity to implement his ideas did not come until 1903, when the Countess de Béarn invited him to mount a production at her private theatre in Paris. At first he planned to present portions of Wagner's *Tristan and Isolde* but eventually had to settle for scenes from Bizet's *Carmen* and Schumann's musical setting of Byron's *Manfred*. Appia hoped that the response to this program, which was highly favorable, would bring him other commissions; their failure to materialize was very disillusioning.

In 1906 a new phase in Appia's life began when he met Emile Jaques Dalcroze (1865–1950), next to Wagner the greatest influence on Appia's thought. Dalcroze, after completing his musical training, had by the 1890s achieved considerable fame as a composer and as a teacher at the Conservatoire in Geneva. Increasingly concerned about the inability of his students to master rhythm, a problem with which the teaching methods of the day did not help, he began experiments from which he gradually evolved "eurythmics," a system under which students were led to experience music kinesthetically by responding physically to the rhythms of musical compositions. Not only did they learn to move each arm and leg to a different rhythm or tempo, they were taught to express every rhythmical detail of a composition through some movement. After he became acquainted with Appia, Dalcroze expanded his system to include exercises designed to inject emotional values into stage postures and movement. Much of Dalcroze's work was to be assimilated by modern dance, and in many acting schools it played an important part in the physical training and in the integration of emotion with movement.

Under the influence of Dalcroze, Appia in 1909 made a series of drawings entitled "Rhythmic Spaces" which he considered suitable for Dalcroze's exercises. These were not carried out, perhaps because a more important project intervened. In 1910 two wealthy German manufacturers offered to build Dalcroze a school at Hellerau, a suburb of Dresden, and for it Appia, in collaboration with Alexander von Salzmann and Heinrich Tessenow, designed the auditorium, stage, and lighting. This was the first theatre built in modern times without a proscenium arch—that is, the first completely "open" stage. There was no separation (other than a sunken orchestra pit) of stage from auditorium, the walls and ceiling being continuous. Furthermore, the walls and ceiling were covered with transparent canvas behind which about three thousand lamps were installed to give indirect light and to avoid any sharp break between auditorium and stage. The theatre held about six hundred persons on steeply raked banks of seats.

Appia's design for Schiller's *The Diver*, 1910, a demonstration of what Appia referred to as "Rhythmic Space." (From Fondation Adolphe Appia, Berne.)

The major collaboration between Appia and Dalcroze came in 1913 when Gluck's *Orpheus and Eurydice* was staged at Hellerau. The sets, designed to enhance the choreographic movement, were among the most abstract of the period, for there were no representational details beyond those created by the formal arrangements of steps, platforms, and draperies as seen under the lighting which was used for both atmospheric and compositional purposes.

Design by Appia for *Orpheus and Eurydice,* Act II, "Entrance to the Underworld." (From Fondation Adolphe Appia, Berne.)

Photograph of the staging at Hellerau in 1913 of Appia's and Dalcroze's production of *Orpheus and Eurydice.*

When the war began in 1914, the school at Hellerau was closed and the intimate association between Appia and Dalcroze ceased. Still, the years with Dalcroze left a permanent mark on Appia, and in *The Work of Living Art* (1921), the fullest expression of his ideas, rhythm plays a key role. Over the years Appia's vision had become increasingly mystical and he now wrote of the theatre as a "cathedral" in which a union of body and soul creates an experience "lived in common with others." His hierarchy of elements and his ideas about light and three-dimensionality remained unchanged, but his notions about how these elements are to be fused had become more refined. Now placing much greater emphasis upon movement and rhythm, he declared, "Our body is the expression of space in time and time in space," and "movement brings about the meeting of Space and Time." He had also come to believe that the rhythm embedded in the text provides the key to every gesture and movement to be used on the stage and that the proper mastery of rhythm will unify all the spatial and temporal elements of a production into a harmonious and satisfying whole.

By the 1920s Appia began to gain his long-delayed recognition. In 1922 the International Theatre Exhibition in Amsterdam made his and Craig's work the focus of the collection of scenic designs from all over the world. Furthermore, at last he began to receive commissions for practical theatre work. Perhaps the most important of these came from Arturo Toscanini at La Scala opera house in Milan, where he assisted in staging *Tristan and Isolde* in 1923. Again, however, the results were disillusioning, for, although the acting and singing were praised, the simple, expressive settings were disliked by patrons accustomed to sumptuous mountings in the Italianate style. Furthermore, the stage personnel, rooted in traditional practices, resisted the changes that would have been required to do justice to Appia's settings and lighting. Still, Appia was almost immediately invited to Basel to stage Wagner's *Ring* cycle, a lifetime ambition. In 1924 *The Rhinegold* was favorably received, but in 1925 *The Valkyrie* led to such a virulent

Craig's design for the production of Ibsen's *The Pretenders,* staged in Copenhagen in 1926. (From *Theatre Arts,* 1929.)

campaign against Appia that the rest of the cycle was abandoned. In its place, Appia was asked to mount *Prometheus,* and, though well received, it was of little comfort to the thwarted Wagnerite. This was the end of Appia's practical work in the theatre and three years later he died, still not fully appreciated.

Gordon Craig (1872–1966) was a man of quite different temperament; as flamboyant as Appia was retiring, he achieved notoriety throughout Europe long before Appia's work was widely known. Thus, it was Craig who, prior to 1914, received sole credit for many of their common ideas.

The illegitimate son of Ellen Terry and Edward Godwin, an architect and scene designer, he was given the name "Craig" because Miss Terry liked its strength. In 1889 at the age of seventeen, Craig joined Irving's company, in which he remained for nine years. As an actor, his most significant performance came in 1897 when he played Hamlet.

By about 1890, Craig had become interested in art and early turned his attention to stage settings. His first attempts were in the romantic-realistic vein of Irving, and it was not until shortly before 1900, in a project for *Hamlet,* that a more stylized approach became evident. The first of his settings to reach the stage was for the Purcell Operatic Society's *Dido and Aeneas* in 1900. By 1903 he had designed seven productions (including Ibsen's *The Vikings at Helgeland* and Shakespeare's *Much Ado About Nothing* for his mother's company at the Imperial Theatre), more than he was to do during the remainder of his life. After 1903 he was involved in only five productions: *Venice Preserved* (in von Hofmannsthal's version) at Otto Brahm's Deutsches Theater in Berlin (1904); *Rosmersholm* for Eleanora Duse in Florence (1906); *Hamlet* at the Moscow Art Theatre (1912); *The Pretenders* at the Theatre Royal, Copenhagen (1926); and *Macbeth* in New York (1928).

Thus, most of Craig's practical work had been done before he turned to writing, but, as he was fond of remarking, "after practice comes theory." His influence was exerted above all through his writings—including *The*

Art of the Theatre (1905, translated into German in 1905 and into Dutch and Russian in 1906), *On the Art of the Theatre* (1911), *Towards a New Theatre* (1913), *The Theatre Advancing* (1919), and his periodical *The Mask* (published sporadically between 1908 and 1929)—and his drawings, most of which were not intended as designs to be realized in the theatre. Wherever he went controversy ensued, especially since he accused practically every major theatrical figure in Europe of plagiarizing his ideas. After 1905, Craig rapidly became known everywhere, by some as a visionary reformer, by others as a dangerous and impractical crank.

A disciple of Walter Pater, Craig was concerned with art-for-art's-sake and above all with winning recognition for the theatre as an independent art. Consequently, he rebelled against Wagner's conception of the theatre as a union of all the arts, for, according to Craig, "the Art of the Theatre is neither acting nor the play, it is not scene nor dance, but it consists of all the elements of which these things are composed: action, which is the very spirit of acting; words, which are the body of the play; line and colour, which are the very heart of the scene; rhythm, which is the very essence of dance." Craig refused to recognize any hierarchy among these elements, declaring instead that the theatre artist uses them all in his creative work, which is as pure and independent as that of the painter, sculptor, composer, or poet. Craig acknowledged the kind of theatre in which a craftsman-director, beginning with a literary text, coordinates the work of several other independent craftsmen, but he sought a higher form in which the master-artist, without the medium of a literary text, creates every element of a wholly autonomous art.

The purpose of this new theatre was to express an absolute beauty. According to Craig, art is not concerned with everyday appearance—with realism—but seeks to reveal the "spiritual universe of the imagination," the

Design for *Electra* by Gordon Craig, 1905. (From City of Manchester Art Gallery, *Exhibition of Drawings and Models... by Edward Gordon Craig, 1912.*)

A design by Craig for Yeats's play *The Hour Glass*.
(From Yeats's *Plays for an Irish Theatre,* 1911.)

mysterious, interior, and secret planes of being. Like the symbolists, Craig believed that this ideal beauty cannot be expressed directly but can only be revealed through suggestion and symbol, which he called "the visible sign of the idea." Consequently, he rejected both the realism of everyday life and historical accuracy. In their place he sought to put color, line, mass, light, movement, gesture, and sound—all chosen entirely for their evocative rather than for their representational powers.

Craig's influence was to be most heavily felt in design, perhaps because he conceived of the theatre primarily in visual terms. He argued that the public comes to see rather than to hear a play and that it is through sight that the imagination and intelligence are reached. Sometimes he spoke of a theatre of silence and he tended to write of the theatre in terms of movement, gesture, dance, and decor rather than words, music, and sound.

Craig's drawings show a marked predilection for right angles—strong vertical and horizontal lines—and almost an obsession with parallelism. The most notable feature, however, is the emphasis upon height and the resulting sense of grandeur. (It is this characteristic which has led many critics to declare that Craig's settings if built would be eight stories tall.) Like Appia, Craig was concerned most with volume and space—created by a few strong lines, devoid of realistic detail, and emphasizing the three-dimensionality and plasticity of stage and actor. Also like Appia, he used light both as a compositional element and as an atmospheric effect. But unlike Appia, who always thought in terms of light and shadow, Craig relied heavily on color to evoke the dramatic qualities of a scene. Similarly, he made considerable use of texture—often ones, such as heavy woven materials and metal, not normally used for scenery.

Perhaps Craig's favorite project was the mobile setting. Most of Craig's predecessors had conceived of scenery as entirely static (one set might replace another or alter in appearance under lighting, but it did not itself

208

One of Craig's experimental designs in which screens are employed.
(From *Stage Yearbook,* 1914.)

move). Craig experimented at length with screens out of which he hoped to create a setting which, by invisible means, could move in ways analogous to the actor and the lighting. He began his experiments in 1907, authorized Yeats to try them at the Abbey Theatre in 1911, and used them himself in his production of *Hamlet* at the Moscow Art Theatre in 1912.

Craig's screens were neutral in color so their appearance under light might be altered almost infinitely. In Moscow they were cream and gold; they also were to have been covered in different natural materials, such as metal and cork, but, because of weight, eventually had to be made like conventional flats and painted to simulate other textures. They were also supposed to glide from one position to another, transforming the scene without closing the front curtain, but so many difficulties arose that the curtain was closed to mask each change. Despite this setback, Craig continued his experiments with screens until the 1920s. Though never perfected, they did inspire the unit set (in which the same pieces are combined in various ways or transformed by the addition of curtains or set pieces), which was widely adopted throughout the world.

Although Craig's influence was greatest upon the visual elements, it was felt in other areas as well. Most of his controversial solutions arose from his unwillingness to assign a hierarchy to theatrical means. On the predominance of one or another element—playwriting, acting, scenic investiture— he blamed most faults of the past. Thus, he often denounced the dramatist, upon whom he blamed an overemphasis on the spoken word and a theatre of sermons and moral lessons. Similarly, he often blamed starring actors for the low state of theatrical art. To counteract their influence, perhaps the dominant one of Craig's youth, he made some of his most controversial statements. He argued that acting is not an art, since it is impossible to mold human beings into an artistic product, and because the actor's desire to aggrandize himself and to interject his own conceptions between those of the master artist and the audience make art impossible. Consequently, he

Craig's screens, as used in the production of *Hamlet* at the Moscow Art Theatre in 1912. (From *Moscow Art Theatre, 1898–1917*, 1955.)

suggested that ideally the master artist should use an *Uebermarionette,* a superpuppet without any ego but capable of carrying out all demands. No idea voiced by Craig aroused a greater storm. Perhaps significantly, Craig never sought to implement it. As a less controversial alternative, Craig suggested that the actor be trained as in the Oriental theatre so that conventionalized movement and gesture might express ideas, attitudes, and emotions. He also advocated the revival of masks. Again, he experimented with neither of these suggestions.

It should be clear, then, that Appia and Craig arrived at many of the same conceptions. Both considered the theatre an autonomous art and sought to redefine its elements and sources of unity. Both rejected realism in favor of suggestion, selection, and synthesis. Both sought three-dimensional plasticity and demanded an artist capable of welding the diverse elements into a harmonious whole. Both were idealists who with the theatre desired to create a pure beauty—for Appia one almost religious, for Craig one more nearly sensuous.

But there were also important differences. Appia's artist was to be primarily an interpreter of the composer-dramatist's work; Craig's was a full-fledged artist in his own right. Appia assigned a hierarchy to the theatrical elements; Craig refused to acknowledge any hierarchy. Appia thought in terms of successive settings (different settings for each locale); Craig sought a single setting capable of expressing the spirit of the entire work or of reflecting changes through mobility.

Appia and Craig were often denounced as impractical men who knew x

Appia and Craig were often denounced as impractical men who knew little of the workaday theatre and whose ideas were useless in practice. In some instances this judgment is probably correct, but they were visionaries and as such championed ideals and goals which practical theatre men of the period could not provide. Together they forced their contemporaries to reconsider the nature of the theatre as an art, its function in society, and its elements (both separately and in combination). They influenced the trend toward simplified decor, three-dimensional settings, plasticity, and directional lighting—toward evocation rather than literal representation. Theirs was a theatre of ideal beauty addressed to the imagination and the spirit. At first highly controversial, their theories were after World War I to prevail and to dominate both theory and practice until, following World War II, the newer ideas of Brecht and Artaud began to replace them. Even today, their power is still felt.

III

Between 1900 and 1910, a number of groups began to follow the path sketched out by Appia and Craig. Of these, one of the most significant was the Munich Art Theatre between 1908 and 1914. Although this theatre came into being through the efforts of many persons, it is now associated primarily with its principal spokesman, Georg Fuchs (1868–1949), a scholar and critic whose theoretical writings for a time ranked only slightly lower than those of Appia and Craig. Before the theatre opened, Fuchs had already published two books—*Stimulating the Style of Staging* (1891) and *The Stage of the Future* (1904)—and at the end of the first season he published another—*Revolution in the Theatre* (1909)—which described the work being done at the Munich Art Theatre.

Fuchs argued that the theatre architecture and decor of his day were relics of an earlier period (when the middle class had sought to rival the courts) and thus were rooted in outmoded social conditions. He declared that it is the true function of theatre to arouse an intense sense of community —an end impossible to achieve when the picture frame separates the audience from the spectator and when the fourth-wall convention is observed —and, adopting the slogan, "Retheatricalize the theatre," Fuchs set out to return the theatre to that function. His program, which required changes in almost every theatrical element, was for the most part implemented at the Munich Art Theatre.

The architect of the theatre, Max Littman (1862–1931), greatly admired Wagner and had already designed two theatres based on the Festspielhaus at Bayreuth, the Prinzregenten in Munich (1901), and the Schiller in Berlin (1906), before adapting it once more for the Art Theatre.

A cross-section of the Munich Art Theatre's auditorium and proscenium. (From *The Theatre Magazine,* 1912.)

The influence of Bayreuth was most evident in the auditorium, which was steeply raked and without a central aisle or boxes. There was also a sunken orchestra pit which could be covered over to create a forestage if desired. But the stage differed markedly from Wagner's. Although as at Bayreuth there was an inner proscenium, here it was sufficiently thick to contain a door below and a window or balcony above. These side structures, coordinated with an overhead bridge, could be moved on or off stage to alter the size of the proscenium opening or to serve as scenic elements. Behind this inner proscenium the stage floor was broken into sections, each mounted on an elevator which could be lowered into the basement to change settings or raised above the stage floor to create levels of varying heights. The stage was also equipped with four different cycloramas, which could be changed electrically.

The most controversial aspect of this theatre was the acting, which for the most part was confined to the plane outlined by the inner proscenium, while the area back of this plane was reserved for scenery or for crowd scenes. Thus, the actors often appeared to be in bas-relief. The aim, however, was to keep the performer close to the audience so as to establish a sense of community and to emphasize his plasticity by framing him against a simplified background.

The theatre's principal designer was Fritz Erler (1868–1940), who, like Fuchs, believed that, since the theatre is based on convention, decor must be stylized. Sometimes he used the adjustable proscenium as the principal scenic element; sometimes he used it in combination with other pieces, but often he employed it merely as a frame for the area behind it. Erler's effects were achieved primarily with simple forms, painted drops, and the play of colored light.

Like Appia and Craig, Fuchs believed that rhythm fuses all the elements of production. Unlike them, however, he placed the actor in front of the setting rather than within it and so tended to mute the three-dimensionality they so avidly sought. Still, as the work of the Munich Art Theatre became widely known, Fuchs's theories reenforced those of Appia and Craig and helped to establish the trend toward stylization in all theatrical elements.

But the popularization and synthesis of the new ideas owe most to Max Reinhardt (1873–1943). Born in Austria, Reinhardt began his career as an actor there before joining Otto Brahm's troupe at the Deutsches Theater in Berlin in 1894. From Brahm he learned much about ensemble playing, respect for a script, and care for the details of production. But Reinhardt also had to free himself from the naturalism to which Brahm was wedded.

His first important step away from naturalism came when he and several friends organized Sound and Smoke, a cabaret where after theatre hours they presented vaudeville sketches, popular entertainment, and short plays. In 1902 this cabaret was transformed into the Kleines Theater (Little Theatre), which featured such works as Wilde's *Salome,* Wedekind's *The Earth Spirit,* and Gorky's *The Lower Depths* (which ran for 400 performances). In 1903 Reinhardt left Brahm to become director of the Neues Theater, a large house which he ran in conjunction with the Kleines Theater. Here he presented Maeterlinck's *Pelléas and Mélisande* and *Sister Beatrice,* Euripides' *Medea,* Shaw's *Candida,* Shakespeare's *A Midsummer Night's Dream,* and other works of high quality.

When Brahm retired, Reinhardt in 1905 became director of the Deutsches Theater, where he was to remain until the 1930s. By 1906, he had given up the Neues and Kleines theaters, but in the same year he converted a dance hall next door to the Deutsches into a small theatre, the Kammerspiele (Chamber Theatre), seating 300 persons and with the stage only 3 feet from the first row. The Deutsches Theater, on the other hand, seated about one thousand, and, with its revolving stage, plaster skydome, and elaborate lighting system, was one of the best-equipped theatres in the world. Reinhardt was the first major producer to use this combination of large and small theatres, and it was he who virtually institutionalized experimentation. Prior to Reinhardt, most of the persistent experimentation had been done in small, coterie theatres. Reinhardt, on the other hand, made a place for experimentation within an established theatre by providing a small house for productions not likely to attract a large audience. This arrangement was eventually taken over by most of the state theatres in Germany, by the Moscow Art Theatre in Russia, and by educational theatres in America.

Within a few years, Reinhardt had won an international reputation. Not only was he frequently invited to direct at other theatres in Germany (he staged many productions at the Munich Art Theatre), but in other European countries as well. And as his fame spread, so did the acceptance of his outlook and theatrical methods.

To Reinhardt, the theatre was not a literary or moral institution

Setting for the throne room in Ibsen's *The Pretenders,*
as it was staged by Reinhardt at the Neues Theater, Berlin, ca. 1903–6.
The setting was one of several used in the play.
(From the Deutsche Akademie der Künste zu Berlin.)

designed to educate or guide mankind. Rather he saw it as establishing a
community among men through the arousal of shared emotion. Consequently, the major problem became how to make a play (regardless of
period, form, or style) meaningful to a contemporary audience. Reinhardt's
greatest contribution came from his recognition that no single method is
sufficient for staging all plays. Throughout history, producers in each era had
accepted a single method which was then applied in all productions. And,
despite the widespread experimentation after 1890, each director of Reinhardt's time had tended to settle on his own distinctive approach and to
harden it into an exclusive one. Reinhardt was the first to perceive that
each play represents a new problem to be solved in its own individual way.
Thus, unlike his contemporaries, he could embrace realism and naturalism
without denying the validity of antirealism. To him it was not a question
of choosing one over the other but of finding the approach most appropriate
to the particular play. Consequently, Reinhardt was the first true eclectic,
and he elevated eclecticism into an artistic creed. As a result, he was able
to appeal to an extremely wide range of tastes and to make an "art" theatre
popular for the first time in western Europe. But because he did not champion any particular school and because he seldom used extreme departures
from realism, he was often accused of charlatanism or of vulgarizing other
people's ideas. Even if the charge is true, he must still be given credit for
winning widespread acceptance for previously unpopular ideas and techniques.

Reinhardt's wide-ranging taste led him to present plays representative of almost every period, form, and style. In all he was concerned with establishing the proper relationship between performer and audience. He often voiced this concern in terms of intimacy. But by "intimacy" he obviously did not mean mere physical proximity, for some of his productions were presented in enormous halls or circuses; rather he meant that psychological relationship which makes dramatic values seem relevant to an audience. This search for meaningful contact between stage and auditorium took many forms.

In some instances Reinhardt sought to re-create the spatial arrangements in use when the play was written. Thus, he staged *Oedipus Rex* (1910) and the *Oresteia* (1911) in the Circus Schumann in Berlin, for he believed that in the circus could be found the nearest modern architectural equivalent of the Greek theatre. Similarly, for a production of *Hamlet* at the Deutsches Theater in 1910 he removed the first three rows of seats and extended a forestage into the auditorium to simulate an Elizabethan theatre. For *Sumurun* (1910), a pantomime based in part on the *Arabian Nights,* he borrowed devices from the Oriental theatre, most notably the *hanamichi,* or flower way, along which entrances were made through the auditorium. For another pantomime, *The Miracle,* based on a medieval legend about a nun whose place is taken by the Virgin, he converted the vast Olympia Hall in London into the nave of a cathedral so that the audience seemed to be watching a ritualized religious spectacle.

On the other hand, Reinhardt certainly did not seek in all his productions to simulate audience-actor relationships of the past. Many of his Shakespearean productions, among them *A Midsummer Night's Dream, The Merchant of Venice, Othello,* and *Henry IV,* were mounted on a revolving stage with "sculptural" settings, the appearance of which could be changed by varying the angle from which they were seen. In this way Reinhardt accomplished what the *Shakespearebühnen* had failed to do: provide an uninterrupted flow of scenes and satisfying backgrounds while avoiding the disparity between formalism and representationalism.

Sometimes Reinhardt sought to reach his audience by choosing a visual motif or idea as a focus around which to build an entire production. For

Reinhardt's production of *Oedipus Rex* at the Circus Schumann in Berlin, 1910. (From *Theatre Arts,* 1924.)

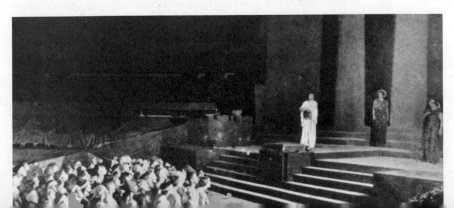

Model by Ernst Stern,
showing a revolving stage,
for one of Reinhardt's earliest
productions of Shakespeare's
A Midsummer Night's Dream
(he produced the play on at least
four different occasions) this one
at the Neues Theater in 1905.
(From the Österreichische
Nationalbibliothek.)

example, in Gozzi's *Turandot,* an eighteenth-century *commedia dell' arte* script set in China, settings and costumes were based on motifs taken from eighteenth-century European *chinoiserie,* for it seemed clear that the Oriental elements in the script were mere exotic embellishments seen through the European consciousness of its age. Such an approach through "stylization" not only made for unity, it also created a perspective through which an audience could enter more fully into the spirit of a work.

In choosing the approach to be used in a specific production, Reinhardt seems to have been guided in part by his designers. In the early years he used such painters as Arnold Bocklin, noted for his atmospheric effects, and Emil Orlik, addicted to Japanese compositions and coloration. But it is significant that Reinhardt's most important experiments were done in collaboration with a single designer, Ernst Stern (1876–1954). Not only was Stern sensitive to actor-audience spatial relationships, he was noted for his bold use of color, line, and mass to suggest the dominant mood of a piece. Though he always used recognizable pictorial elements in his settings, he simplified and stylized them in ways intended to evoke a powerful emotional response in the audience.

Much of Reinhardt's success came from his working methods, for he was a *regisseur* in the tradition of Saxe-Meiningen. Each department of his theatre was headed by a trusted associate who was responsible for its efficiency, and all supervisory personnel conferred regularly to ensure the coordination of the theatre's work with Reinhardt's desires. Thus, Reinhardt delegated considerable authority but remained undisputed master. Like the productions of Saxe-Meiningen, Reinhardt's made their mark in large part because of his care for detail and for the integration of all the elements into a unified whole.

As a director, Reinhardt made a promptbook, or *Regiebuch,* in which he worked out every detail of a production before rehearsals began. Consequently, he was often accused of using his actors as mere puppets, since he had decided in advance precisely what he wanted from each. Reinhardt's admirers responded that he was so sensitive that he knew exactly how to get the best from each of his actors. Regardless of the truth, his performers were usually ranked among the best of the time. Especially admired were Gertrude Eysolt (1870–1955), Alexander Moissi (1880–1935), Friedrich Kayssler (1874–1945), Max Pallenberg (1859–1934), Albert Bassermann (1867–1952), Werner Krauss (1884–1959), and Emil Jannings (1887–1950). In connection with the Deutsches Theater, Reinhardt also maintained an acting school where students were given systematic training in speech, posture, dance, gesture, elocution, and characterization.

By 1914, Reinhardt had largely won recognition for stylization. No doubt many of his departures from realism would today seem conservative, but he gradually led audiences to accept approaches which previously they had rejected. By World War I, Reinhardt had also established his working methods. While after the war he was to alter some details, his basic approach would not change.

~ IV ~

After 1900 the spirit of eclecticism began to be felt in almost every country. In some instances it came through Reinhardt's influence but in others it developed quite independently. Seldom, however, was it embraced so wholeheartedly or explored so fully as by Reinhardt.

In England, the eclectic ideal is best exemplified by Harley Granville Barker (1877–1946). After beginning his career in 1891 as an actor, Barker worked with Poel, served as both director and actor with the Incorporated Stage Society, and gained considerable prominence as a playwright. But his most important work was to begin in 1904 when he was invited by the manager of the Royal Court Theatre in London to assist John Vedrenne (1863–1930) in a production of *Two Gentlemen of Verona*. Barker accepted on the condition that he be permitted to present Shaw's *Candida* for a series of six matinees. Their success was so great that soon Vedrenne and Barker took full control of the theatre.

The Barker-Vedrenne management is of major significance. First, it virtually established George Bernard Shaw's reputation in the English theatre. Prior to this time Shaw's plays had, for the most part, been seen only in private performances, and the critical estimate had been that he was a polemicist rather than a dramatist. Then, in 1904 the overwhelming success of *John Bull's Other Island* at the Royal Court suddenly brought Shaw's plays into demand. But Shaw remained loyal to Barker and Vedrenne, who eventually produced eleven of his plays. Of the 946 performances given at the Royal Court, 701 were of Shaw's works. By 1907, Shaw's theatrical viability had been thoroughly established. Shaw also deserves credit for assisting the Royal Court in other ways. Since he directed his own plays, the majority of the repertory, he was the company's principal director. Furthermore, the notoriety which surrounded his works did much to keep the theatre in the public eye.

Second, the Royal Court presented a wide-ranging repertory. Next to Shaw the most popular playwright was Euripides, but the majority of the plays were by such "modernists" as Ibsen, Hauptmann, Maeterlinck, Schnitzler, Galsworthy, and Hankin. Thus, the Royal Court did much to acquaint the English public with the latest in drama.

Third, ensemble performance and careful (though simple) mounting were emphasized. Barker and Vedrenne had agreed never to spend more than 200 pounds in staging a play. Thus, major attention was concentrated on the acting. Barker favored understated playing (Shaw's desire for bravura was a frequent source of disagreement), a quiet, simple realism. Although the salaries were very low, the company included a number of dedicated performers—among them Louis Calvert, Florence Farr, Lillah McCarthy, Lewis Casson, Edmund Gwenn, Matheson Lang, Harcourt Williams, and Nigel Playfair—who were to be among England's most respected actors in the years to come. Barker also appeared in practically every production, and occasionally such stars as Ellen Terry, Mrs. Patrick Campbell, and Laurence Irving joined the troupe.

Fourth, the Royal Court's example as a repertory theatre dedicated to high artistic principles stimulated the revival of the repertory system outside of London. The first of the new groups was formed in 1908 by Miss A. E. F. Horniman in Manchester, and a second soon followed at Glasgow in 1909 under the direction of Alfred Waring. Then in 1911 the Liverpool Repertory Theatre, under the leadership of Basil Dean, was founded, and in 1913 Barry Jackson established the Birmingham Repertory Company. These were the pioneers in the fight to rescue the English provincial theatre from its almost total dependence upon touring companies from London. Their strength was such that the repertory system has continued in England to the present time.

Despite critical success, Barker and Vedrenne were constantly on the verge of financial disaster. Convinced that their dilemma was attributable to the out-of-the-way location of the Royal Court and its small size (it seated only 614), they gave up their lease in 1907 and moved to the Savoy, a much larger house in a more central location. But they soon discovered that there was not yet an audience of sufficient size to support the kind of theatre they desired, and they had to abandon their new home, although they continued to present plays from time to time at other theatres.

In 1910 an attempt was made to salvage the venture when Charles Frohman (with a financial guarantee from J. M. Barrie) installed it in his Duke of York's Theatre. But after seventeen weeks it was discontinued. In 1911 the Barker-Vedrenne partnership was dissolved and Shaw paid off its outstanding debts.

But Barker did not give up directing. Between 1912 and 1914 he mounted at the Savoy Theatre three Shakespearean productions—*A Winter's Tale* (1912), *Twelfth Night* (1912), and *A Midsummer Night's Dream* (1914)—which outraged conservatives and delighted the avant-garde. Most important, with these productions he synthesized practically all the experimentation with Shakespearean staging of the preceding two decades. His stage was divided into three parts: a wide forestage forward of the proscenium, a middle plane upstage of the proscenium, and a slightly raised inner stage. It combined the advantages of Poel's platform and the *Shakespearebühnen* but solved most of the problems that had plagued them. Like Poel's arrangement, Barker's stage permitted continuous playing but it avoided the sense of archeological reconstruction that had hampered Poel's work. Like the *Shakespearebühnen,* it was designed for scenery, but it avoided the disparity between the formal and the pictorial by using highly stylized decor and (by repeating the architectural features of the proscenium arch) making the frame of the inner stage seem a part of the theatre rather than a scenic element.

The extent of the innovations can best be seen in *A Midsummer Night's Dream,* which a few years earlier had been presented in London by Herbert Beerbohm Tree in settings which featured seemingly real trees and flowers, grass carpets, and live rabbits. Now, Barker's artists, Norman Wilkinson (1882–1934) and Albert Rutherston (1884–1953), represented the forest with stylized trees painted on a curtain which hung in folds and formed Titania's bower from streamers of brightly colored gauze suspended from a crown of flowers. To set them off from the mortals, the fairies were bronzed and restricted to puppetlike movement. Although Barker acknowledged his indebtedness to Craig, his settings were more decorative than three-dimensional. Still, his use of color and stylized forms was well suited to the conventionalized stage arrangement. With these productions Barker provided a major lesson in how to synthesize diverse approaches.

Barker took the same lesson to America in 1915, when, at the invitation of the New York Stage Society, he mounted *A Midsummer Night's Dream* and plays by Shaw and others. These were landmarks in American production. Shortly afterward Barker abandoned his career in the theatre and thereafter confined himself to the critical writing for which he is so justly famous.

Around 1910 eclecticism began to reach France, which, after the feverish activity of the 1890s, had virtually abandoned experimentation and had remained equally unaware of developments elsewhere. The first break in this isolationism came in 1909 when the Ballets Russes (to be discussed more fully in the next chapter) took Paris by storm. The exotic, colorful settings and energetic, masterful dancing of the Russian troupe made the French realize how far behind the rest of Europe they had fallen. This impression was confirmed in 1910 when Jacques Rouché (1862–1957) published *Modern Theatre Art,* a description of the work of Fuchs, Erler,

Barker's production of *A Midsummer Night's Dream*
at the Savoy Theatre in 1914. Titania's bower is seen at center.
(Courtesy Enthoven Collection, Victoria and Albert Museum.)

and Reinhardt in Germany, of Stanislavsky, Komissarzhevskaya, and Meyerhold in Russia, and the theories of Appia and Craig. Rouché also set forth a program of reform.

More important, Rouché decided to implement his suggestions at the Théâtre des Arts, which he ran from 1910 to 1913. In imitation of the Ballets Russes, he appointed a committee of artists (including Maurice Denis, Xavier Roussel, Maxime Dethomas, and Edouard Vuillard) to design settings, costumes, and properties, to advise on the actors' gestures and movement, and to assist in attaining visual unity. It is perhaps significant that the artists he chose had matured in the 1890s and that he ignored the newer painters of the fauvist and cubist schools. Understandably, the visual style reflected the tastes of the artists, especially that of Maxime Dethomas (1867–1929), the most successful of Rouché's designers. Rather than extreme stylization, they favored simplicity of line, elimination of unessential details, and subtle coloration. It seems likely, however, that, as Copeau charged, Rouché placed too much emphasis upon the visual elements at the expense of dramatic action. Nevertheless, it was Rouché who precipitated the revival of the French theatre. In 1913, he gave up the Théâtre des Arts to assume the direction of the Opéra, where he remained until 1936 and, with the assistance of Dethomas and the choreographer Serge Lifar, completely revitalized the repertory.

But by the time he left his theatre in 1913, Rouché had inspired others to take up the task of renovation. In 1912, Lugné-Poë revived his Théâtre

Scene from *Hamlet,* as staged at the l'Oeuvre in 1913 by Lugné-Poë and Gémier. The setting is by Variot. (From *Le Théâtre,* 1913.)

de l'Oeuvre (which he was to direct until 1929), where in the same year he presented *The Tidings Brought to Mary,* the first of Claudel's plays to reach the stage. In a statement about the settings, Jean Variot, the designer, acknowledged his indebtedness to the Munich Art Theatre. On either side of the stage he erected a fixed structure (to simulate the Art Theatre's inner proscenium) which, according to Variot, announced his theatricalist approach and warned the spectator not to expect realism. Behind these fixed pieces, he used a series of extremely stylized painted drops in conjunction with essential properties and furniture. In 1913, Variot designed the settings for *Hamlet* at the l'Oeuvre. Here he borrowed many of the conventions of the *Shakespearebühnen,* but, like Barker, managed to unify them. The forward part of the stage was surrounded by a permanent unit with a door at either side and a large arch at the back. This neutral architectural unit, further formalized by a pattern of heraldic devices painted on it, was supplemented with simple, evocative properties and set pieces. Variot's settings are among the most effective of the day.

After 1910, Antoine's productions also began to reflect a growing concern for stylization. For example, his directorial approach to Racine's *Esther* in 1913 was based on an eighteenth-century Gobelins tapestry. Not only did the setting reproduce the features of the tapestry, the gestures and attitudes of the actors were also modeled on it. In addition, the costumes—according to H. G. Ibels, who designed them—were made of coffee sacking and the details then painted on them. In 1914, for his final production at the Odéon—*Psyché* by Molière, Corneille, Quinault, and Lully—Antoine took as his point of departure the seventeenth-century courtier consciousness through which the classical myth has been filtered, and chose Versailles as a unifying image. Ignoring the stage directions in the script (which place the action on riverbanks, seashores, and in other spots), Antoine depicted places with mythological associations (such as the fountain of Neptune) in the gardens at Versailles and in every scene kept the palace visible in the distance. Costumes were based upon the mythologically oriented court entertainments of Louis XIV's time. Thus, Antoine was able to render the intermingled contexts of classical myth and seventeenth-century court life. According to all reviews, this was Antoine's finest production. Unfortunately, it also drove him into bankruptcy and he was forced to resign his position. Thereafter he gave up production but until his death was one of Paris's finest dramatic critics.

Perhaps the most important event in the French theatre of the time occurred in 1913, when the Théâtre du Vieux Colombier was founded by Jacques Copeau (1879–1949), who was to dominate the French theatre between the wars as thoroughly as Antoine had in the years between 1887 and 1914. By 1913, Copeau had served as dramatic critic and editor for several journals and had been initiated into the theatre in 1911 when Rouché produced his adaptation of Dostoevsky's *The Brothers Karamazov*.

In "An Essay on the Renovation of the Drama: the Théâtre du Vieux Colombier" (published in *La Nouvelle Revue Française* in September 1913), Copeau acknowledged his admiration for Rouché but deplored his emphasis upon decor and also declared his dissatisfaction with Antoine's realism. He proclaimed that the renovation of the drama depended, not on these two paths, but upon a return to the bare stage (*le treteau nu*), for only there can attention be focused fully upon the actor, who is the essence of the theatre and the "living presence" of the author.

For Copeau, the director's ultimate task is the transformation of a written text into a "poetry of the theatre" (that is, the translation of the script from a literary into a theatrical language, of which acting is the principal ingredient). He declared that the director should study a script until he comprehends every nuance, and then, with infinite care and purely theatrical means, re-create it on stage for an audience. Decor should be reduced to absolute essentials so that nothing will detract from the actor.

With the financial assistance and advice of several leading literary figures—André Gide, Jean Schlumberger, Gaston Gallimard, and Charles Pacquement—Copeau acquired an old, out-of-the-way theatre and converted it into the Théâtre du Vieux Colombier. After it was remodeled by Francis Jourdain (Louis Jouvet would remodel it along still different lines after the war), it had a forestage forward of an inner proscenium, but no machinery except for a set of curtains and asbestos hangings which could be moved on rods to effect rapid changes of locale. To these curtains were added only the most essential furniture and set pieces.

In the summer of 1913 Copeau assembled a company of young actors, including Charles Dullin, Louis Jouvet, Suzanne Bing, and Romain

Jacques Copeau and the company of the newly formed
Vieux-Colombier during the summer of 1913 prior
to the opening of the company's first season in Paris.
Copeau sits at the table discussing a text;
Charles Dullin sits at the far left;
Louis Jouvet is standing, second from right;
and Suzanne Bing is seated second from right.
(From *Le Théâtre,* 1913.)

Bouquet, and took them to the country to rehearse a repertory of diverse plays. The theatre opened in October 1913 with Heywood's *A Woman Killed With Kindness* and went on to present works by Molière, Shakespeare, and several modern playwrights. By May 1914, fifteen plays had been produced. Because of the war, the theatre was not to reopen until 1919.

In some respects, Copeau's theatre resembles Poel's platform stage, but Copeau adopted the bare stage out of esthetic conviction rather than from any desire to re-create the conditions of a past era. Furthermore, Copeau was dedicated to training the finest company of actors available anywhere, while Poel's performers were often second-rate and were not organized as a permanent company. Furthermore, Copeau was ultimately interested in the renovation of modern drama rather than in the presentation of any particular playwright's work. Above all, Copeau wished to serve the dramatist by the most scrupulous rendering of his text. His was an ascetic—almost religious—approach depending on a highly refined sensibility and requiring absolute dedication.

A Woman Killed with Kindness, the first production of the Vieux-Colombier, Paris, October 1913. (From *Le Théâtre,* 1913).

Of all the demands made in the years between 1890 and 1914 perhaps none was more persistent than the call for a theatre that would engender a sense of community among men, one that would recapture the spirit of ancient Greece and the Middle Ages. Even some of those who ran coterie theatres voiced this plea, and many tried to implement it through reforms in staging. But others interpreted it more literally and sought to return the theatre to the common man and to integrate it more fully into community life.

The notion of a "people's" theatre probably first took shape in France, where in 1895 at Bussang (a small village in eastern France) Maurice Pottecher, an actor and dramatist who had worked with the Théâtre Libre, initiated his Théâtre du Peuple. Annually thereafter until World War I the residents of Bussang, under Pottecher's guidance, mounted a new production each summer and eventually built their own outdoor theatre. Most of the plays were written by Pottecher, while the actors and other personnel were drawn from the community. As the fame of this theatre spread, other communities sought to follow its example. In 1899, a number of prominent writers proposed the formation of a people's theatre for Paris. Although nothing came of it, the idea did not die and in 1903 Romain Rolland, in *The People's Theatre,* suggested that each community should perform dramatizations of local and national history and through this means uplift and inspire the people of the present.

The idea soon spread to other countries. In England it was introduced by Louis N. Parker (1852–1944) when at Sherbourne in 1905 he staged a pageant which dramatized the community's past. Soon similar works were being written and performed all over England: at St. Albans in 1907, at Oxford in 1907, at Chester in 1910, and so on.

The pageant movement was to be especially strong in America. One of the first examples was seen in 1905 when George Pierce Baker staged an outdoor masque at Cornish, New Hampshire, to celebrate the twentieth anniversary of Augustus Saint-Gaudens's art colony. Hundreds of others were to follow. Most dramatized local history, but others were based on more remote themes: *A Pageant of the Italian Renaissance* (Chicago, 1909); *Robin of Sherwood* (New Haven, 1912); *A Pageant of the Thirteenth Century* (Columbia University, 1914). Many were extremely elaborate and required enormous casts. Perhaps the most ambitious of all was the *Pageant and Masque of Saint Louis* (1914) with its cast of 7,500 and its stage 1,000 feet long and 200 feet deep. In 1915, the American Pageant Association recorded sixty-three productions in twenty-three states. The major champion of such community efforts was Percy Mackaye (son of Steele Mackaye), who in such books as *The Playhouse and the Play* (1909), *The Civic Theatre* (1912), and *Community Drama* (1917) touted its merits. The movement reached its peak around 1915 and then slowly subsided.

A rehearsal of *Orpheus* by Gluck in the ancient Roman theatre at Orange in 1911. Reopened in 1894, this theatre influenced the development of summer festivals at Nimes, Arles, and Beziers. (From *Le Théâtre,* 1911.)

Intertwined with the people's theatre movement was another which championed outdoor playing. Many critics argued that the deterioration of drama had begun with the move indoors and they saw as a prerequisite to a renovation of drama the return to outdoor performances. Consequently, outdoor theatres began to be built throughout the world. By 1918, when he published *The Open-Air Theatre,* Sheldon Cheney could list numerous examples of three types of outdoor structures: the architectural (based on ancient Greek models); the nature theatre (which capitalized on some natural setting); and the garden theatre (a formal arrangement of shrubbery and hedges). He described theatres ranging from the Hearst Greek Theatre at Berkeley (1903), to the Harz Mountain Theatre in Germany (1903), to the Klampenborg Woods Theatre near Copenhagen (1910). Most of the outdoor theatres were used by amateur groups, but occasionally professionals played there. For example, during the early twentieth century Ben Greet virtually made a career of presenting Shakespearean drama and other classics out-of-doors for school, college, and community audiences.

The ancient Roman theatres were also refurbished and put back into use. In France, the theatre at Orange was reopened in 1894 and soon there were annual festivals at Nimes, Arles, and Beziers. It was out of such productions that the modern vogue for summer festivals was to grow.

In addition, the festival idea owes much to Wagner's Festspiel, initiated at Bayreuth in 1876, which, like the people's theatre, was intended to generate a sense of community. It was from the festival at Bayreuth that

Frank Benson's production of *Macbeth* at the Shakespeare Festival at
Stratford-on-Avon in 1910. Benson himself played Macbeth; Benson's wife,
Lady Macbeth. (From the Royal Shakespeare Theatre, Stratford-on-Avon.)

the Shakespeare Festival at Stratford-on-Avon took much of its inspiration.
Instituted in 1879, it provided short seasons of Shakespeare's plays annually.
At first a different company was invited to perform each year, but from
1886 until World War I the festival productions were for the most part
staged by Frank Benson (1858–1939). Educated at Oxford, Benson made
his professional debut in Irving's company in 1882. In the following year
he founded his own troupe, with which he toured for the remainder of
his career, presenting mostly Shakespearean drama and other English
classics. As the provincial theatre shrank, Benson became virtually the
only purveyor of Shakespeare outside of London. In the early years, his
style was modeled on Irving's, but after 1900 he simplified his staging
considerably, although he remained clearly within the limits of representationalism. Above all, Benson was noted for his strenuously athletic productions and for the training he gave to a whole generation of actors, the
"Bensonians," who were among the major Shakespearean actors of
twentieth-century England.

Also imbedded in the demand for a people's theatre was the notion
that drama should not be reserved for the few but made available to the
common man as well. It was out of this conviction that the *Volksbühnen* of
Germany and Austria were founded in the 1890s. Their success was so
remarkable that many other theatres began to present plays thought especially suitable to a working-class audience. But Germany was more fortunate than most countries, for (as a heritage from the time when it was
divided into many small independent states) it had state-subsidized theatres
in each sizable town. In America and most of western Europe, however,
the theatre had by 1900 shrunk to the major cities, from which companies

toured the latest hits to lesser towns. Not only was the theatre no longer community-based, it was increasingly restricted to diversionary entertainment.

In France the man most concerned with correcting these problems was Firmin Gémier (1869–1933). After beginning his career in 1892 as an actor with Antoine, Gémier went on to create the title role in *Ubu Roi* at the Théâtre de l'Oeuvre and to perform a wide range of characters in many theatres. (By 1917, he had performed an estimated two hundred roles.) In 1900, Antoine offered Gémier his first chance to direct and when Antoine moved to the Odéon in 1906 Gémier took control of the Théâtre Antoine, where he remained until 1922.

Gémier was deeply interested in social drama and a theatre for the people. In 1902 he directed *The Fourteenth of July,* written by Rolland to demonstrate his conception of works appropriate to a community effort, and in 1903 he staged the Festival of Vaud, a pageant (with a cast of 2,400) tracing the Swiss canton's history from the Middle Ages to the present.

But Gémier also dreamed of providing the people throughout France with the finest productions of the worthiest plays. To implement this idea, he established in 1911 his Théâtre Ambulant to bring on tour complex and spectacular productions from the Théâtre Antoine. Using thirty-seven trailers and eight steam-driven tractors, he traveled over the inadequate roads of outlying areas and at each stop erected an enormous tent inside which was set up a theatre, complete with comfortable seating and elaborate machinery. Although he was able to continue this venture for only two seasons, Gémier would after the war explore other means for realizing his dream.

For the most part, the people's theatre movement was abortive. For a time it seemed to flower, but after World War I it lost its idealistic fervor. Gradually its place was taken by local amateur groups who, for the most part, were content to perform the latest hits from the commercial theatre. Except in being community-based, these groups had little in common with their predecessors. But the dream of creating a truly popular theatre did not die and in the future it would reemerge periodically under new guises.

∼ VI ∼

If America wholeheartedly embraced pageantry, it remained impervious to most European movements. A number of beginnings were made but most were harbingers of things to come after the war rather than solid present achievements. The record up to 1915 can be summarized briefly.

The independent theatre movement, so effective in Europe, was attempted sporadically in America. The first trial came in 1891 when Chickering Hall in Boston was converted into a theatre for Herne's *Margaret Fleming,* a play thought by commercial producers too scandalous for public presentation. But despite a concerted attempt by such American realists as William Dean Howells and Hamlin Garland to make the enterprise permanent, it soon closed. Other short-lived independent theatres include New York's Criterion Independent Theatre (1897–1900) and Chicago's New Theatre (1906–7). None made a strong or lasting impression.

Between 1900 and 1910 a few independent producers (that is, ones not associated with the Syndicate) began to win recognition for major modern dramatists and more realistic acting. Among these, Minnie Maddern Fiske (1865–1932) and her husband Harrison Grey Fiske (1861–1942) are especially noteworthy for their productions of Ibsen's plays (including *A Doll's House, Hedda Gabler, Rosmersholm,* and *Pillars of Society*) and for their carefully staged productions at the Manhattan Theatre between 1901 and 1907. Mrs. Fiske was also instrumental in replacing bravura performance with psychologically realistic portraiture.

Ibsen's reputation and realistic acting also were enhanced by Alla Nazimova (1879–1945), a Russian actress who left a touring company to remain in America. After learning English in six months, she opened in 1906 in a repertory which included *Hedda Gabler* and *A Doll's House.* So great was her appeal that for many years her name was virtually synonymous with great acting.

Similarly, Arnold Daly (1875–1927) did much to establish Shaw's reputation in America. In 1903 his production of *Candida* achieved a run of 133 performances and in 1905 he mounted a two-month repertory of Shaw's work. But *Mrs. Warren's Profession* proved too heady for the authorities and Daly was prosecuted for presenting an immoral play. Although acquitted, Daly was eventually forced by adverse response to return to a more conventional repertory.

Beginning around 1910 the pace accelerated. Perhaps out of the interest engendered by the community drama movement, the Drama League of America, dedicated to the discussion and promotion of outstanding plays, was founded in 1910. Through its magazine, *Drama,* it kept its members, scattered throughout the United States, abreast of new developments and recommended plays for production and reading.

The concern for ideals and the increased knowledge of foreign developments were to lead by 1912 to the "little" or "art" theatre movement. By 1917 there were about fifty groups dedicated to presenting a series of plays for limited runs and with techniques borrowed (for the most part) from the European theatres. Determinedly anticommercial, they stated their goals in artistic terms. Most depended upon unpaid volunteers for personnel and upon subscribers for financial support (arrangements reminiscent of the European independent theatres). Among the most important of the groups were: the Chicago Little Theatre, run by Maurice Browne and his wife

Nazimova as Hilda Wangel and Walter Hampden, at right, as Solness in a production of Ibsen's *The Master Builder* in 1907 at the Bijou Theatre, New York. (From *The Theatre Magazine*, 1907.)

Ellen Van Volkenburg; the Toy Theatre of Boston, under the direction of Mrs. Lyman Gale; the Neighborhood Playhouse, established in New York by Irene and Alice Lewisohn; the Washington Square Players, in New York; the Provincetown Players, founded in Provincetown, Massachusetts, but soon moved to New York; and the Detroit Arts and Crafts Theatre. After the war, most of the little theatres took one of two paths: they either metamorphosed into semiprofessional or professional companies, or they were absorbed into the community theatre movement. Several were to make important contributions to the American theatre and, as a movement, the little theatres were instrumental in introducing and popularizing new ideas and practices.

The new spirit was also fostered by colleges and universities. Although plays had been presented by college students since Colonial days, course work in theatre was rare until 1903, when George Pierce Baker (1866–1935) initiated a class in playwriting at Radcliffe College. This course was later opened to students at Harvard University and in 1913 a workshop for producing plays was added. To these courses came several young men—among them Eugene O'Neill, S. N. Behrman, Sidney Howard, Robert Edmond Jones, Lee Simonson, Winthrop Ames, Samuel Hume, and Donald Oenslager—who were to be leaders in the postwar American theatre. Baker's innovation soon caught on elsewhere and in 1914 Thomas Wood Stevens (1880–1942) was able at the Carnegie Institute of Technology to inaugurate the first degree-granting program in theatre, an ambition denied Baker until he moved to Yale University in 1925. After the war, educational theatre was to burgeon.

The pace in the professional theatre also quickened around 1910. One of the most promising schemes—to build and maintain an "art" theatre with a permanent company and a repertory of the highest quality—was launched in New York, where in 1909 the New Theatre, with such advanced machinery as the revolving stage, was opened to much fanfare. To head this company the directors employed Winthrop Ames (1871–1937), who, after running the Castle Square Theatre in Boston from 1904 to 1907, had been abroad to study recent developments. Thus, he seemed ideally suited to the post. But the New Theatre was too large, was in an out-of-the-way location, and was surrounded by an aura of wealth which discouraged attendance by less affluent playgoers. Furthermore, instead of an ensemble, it featured such stars as E. H. Sothern and Julia Marlowe. Not surprisingly, it foundered after two seasons. In 1912, Ames opened his own carefully planned Little Theatre, where he presented a repertory of meticulously staged plays. But the 300-seat house proved too small to maintain itself in midtown Manhattan and had to be abandoned. Despite these setbacks, Ames was the most progressive of the prewar producers and was to maintain high standards for many years to come.

European companies also began to appear in America. In 1911–12 the Abbey Theatre toured the country to high critical praise for its ensemble acting and with considerable notoriety because of the riots precipitated by *The Playboy of the Western World.* In 1912, Ames imported Reinhardt's production of *Sumurun,* and in 1914 Sam Hume mounted the first exhibit of the "new stagecraft" seen in America. Besides designs by Bakst, Craig, and several of Reinhardt's artists, the exhibit also featured models of European theatres (including the stage machinery). After opening in Cambridge, Massachusetts, it was moved to New York, Chicago, Detroit, and Cleveland. In 1915, Barker came to New York at the invitation of the Stage Society to direct several productions, among them *A Midsummer Night's Dream* and works by Shaw. Perhaps most important, for Barker's production of *The Man Who Married a Dumb Wife* Robert Edmond Jones designed settings which are normally considered the first important native expression of the "new stagecraft" (as the European trends were called in America).

Overall, attempts to reform the theatre in America were few in number and, for the most part, isolated from one another. But together they provide a picture of the accelerating desire to establish a native version of the European "art" theatre. By 1915, the bases for more solid achievements had been laid.

～ VII ～

While the struggle to create a new theatre art was underway, so was the search for a new technology. The two often merged, for in many instances the new artistic demands could be met only through new technological means.

Many inventions were provoked by the need to make scene shifting more efficient, for three-dimensional settings made earlier means increasingly unsatisfactory. Sometimes the waits required for scene changes added as much as one hour to the playing time. The proposed solutions took many forms.

The mechanical means most widely adopted was the elevator (or sinking) stage, perhaps because it was a logical development of the sinking trap that had long been in use. In the 1880s there had been a few experiments with enlarging these traps to include sizable sections (or all) of the stage floor, but it was not until after 1900 that elevators came into wide use. Thereafter, stages were often divided into sections, each on a separate lift that could be lowered to the basement, used to raise scenic elements to stage level, or elevated above the stage to create platforms of varying heights. As the forestage came back into favor, it also became common to install an elevator forward of the proscenium; at stage level it could be used for acting and lowered it could serve as an orchestra pit. But, since the elevator had the disadvantage of being restricted to vertical movement, other, more versatile solutions were sought.

One of the most indefatigable inventors of the period was Karl Lautenschlager (1843–1906), who included among his interests the potential of electricity as a new technological force in the theatre. For the International Exhibition of Electricity, held in Munich in 1882, he demonstrated a theatre operated entirely with electricity. He was to be one of the pioneers in the use of electrical motors, an important element in the heavy new stage machinery. Lautenschlager was also much interested in facilitating the rapid playing of episodic works. In 1889 he helped to create the *Shakespearebühne* at Munich and in 1900 he redesigned the stage of the Oberammergau Passion Play to make it more efficient. But his most important contribution to continuous playing was the revolving stage (a device invented in Japan), which in 1896 he introduced into western Europe. First used at the Residenz Theater in Munich, it was not entirely satisfactory, but Lautenschlager and others continued to improve it. After 1900 it was installed in many leading theatres, among them the Deutsches Theater and the Moscow Art Theatre. But, like other solutions, the revolving stage had limitations, since it was restricted to circular movement and made the stage level the principal work area (thus creating both congestion and noise).

A third solution was sought in the rolling platform. At first, small wagons mounted on casters were employed to move heavy units on and off stage (a solution still in wide use), but in 1900 at the Royal Opera House in Berlin, Fritz Brandt (1846–1927) introduced large platforms moved on and off stage by means of wheels set in tracks. His arrangement permitted the mounting of entire settings offstage, but it was feasible only in theatres with considerable wing space. Furthermore, the noise created by changing scenery in the wings often interfered with performances. These drawbacks led Adolf Linnebach (1876–1963) to introduce a new solution at the

Dresden Schauspielhaus in 1914. Here the stage floor was divided into three sections, each of which could be raised to stage level by hydraulic lifts. When lowered to the basement, they could move horizontally in tracks to an area where scenery was mounted. At stage level, each could also move up or down stage in tracks. Thus, while one setting was in use, another could be raised behind it; when the scene ended, one setting sank as another rolled forward.

As Linnebach's work demonstrates, the solutions were sometimes combined. By 1914, almost every conceivable combination of elevator, revolving, and sliding stage had been proposed. The majority of this complex machinery was installed in Germany, for in countries without subsidized resident troupes the devices seemed useless, since most productions eventually toured to theatres where such machinery was not available. Consequently, the majority of theatres throughout the world continued to shift scenery manually, or with such supplementary means as small wagons and overhead battens. When realism began to decline, many critics declared that machinery was doomed to extinction, for it had been invented to handle naturalistic settings. But it was soon found that abstract arrangements of steps, platforms, and similar elements also benefitted from mobility, and revolving, sliding, and elevator stages continued to play a prominent role in European theatres.

Heavy machinery also encouraged the use of iron and other new structural materials which permitted changes in theatre architecture. Consequently, it now became possible to cantilever balconies and in this way to eliminate obstructions in sight lines. Aisles were also relocated to ensure seating at the spots most advantageous for seeing and hearing, and, in most theatres, boxes were eliminated, not only because they were badly located for seeing and hearing but because of the new concern for cultural democracy. Despite all changes, theatres remained wedded to the picture frame. A few small houses sought to bridge the barrier between auditorium and stage by adding forestages or steps, but, with a few exceptions, most notably in Appia's theatre at Hellerau, the proscenium remained intact.

Other innovations stemmed from the increased emphasis on lighting as a compositional and atmospheric effect. Although by 1900 electricity had been adopted almost everywhere, there had been few advances in practice over those developed with gas. Since wattages were low (100 was the maximum), the incandescent lamp was used primarily for footlights, borderlights, and striplights, or in groups of ten or twelve mounted in a single housing (a "bunchlight") for floods. Bright beams of light still required the carbon arc or limelight. Then, a series of improvements in the incandescent lamp made possible many changes. In 1907 the introduction of the tungsten filament made lamps up to 500 watts feasible and when gas-filled lamps replaced vacuum lamps in 1913, wattages of 750–1000 watts became available. In 1911, a concentrated filament made it possible to develop spotlights designed to use incandescent lamps. Thus, by 1914,

single-source floodlights were replacing bunchlights, and spotlights were
replacing arclights and limelights.

The demands for three-dimensionality, plasticity, and atmosphere led to many experiments with the direction, intensity, and color of light. Because of the unnatural direction, footlights came under increasingly heavy attack and in many theatres were abandoned. This did not create any serious problem so long as the action remained upstage of the proscenium, but, when directors began to utilize the forestage, new lighting positions had to be found. Thus began the practice of mounting instruments on the front of balconies or in the ceiling of the auditorium, although this was still a novelty in 1914. Similarly, lighting from the side, rear, or from above (to emphasize shape and dimension or for atmospheric effects) began to play a prominent role, and numerous devices for attaining color (dipped lamps, glass filters, silk reflectors) were tried.

The most ambitious lighting system of the period was designed around 1903 by Mariano Fortuny (1871–1949), who was concerned both with theory and with the means to implement it. He noted that in nature there are two kinds of light—direct and reflected—and declared that any acceptable system for the stage must simulate both. Direct light offered him little problem, for it could be supplied by carbon arcs and limelights, but his scheme for producing reflected light was elaborate indeed. To achieve it, he projected light onto panels of colored silk, from which it was reflected onto a neutral-toned, semispherical cyclorama, from which in turn it was reflected onto the stage. Because of its cost and inefficiency, the system was never fully developed. Nevertheless, it was to be influential, for Fortuny's division of light into direct and indirect (specific and general) and his analysis of the means required to attain satisfactory results laid the foundations for later practice. Furthermore, the neutral-toned cyclorama became standard in most theatres. In Germany, it often took the form of a fixed plaster dome (the *Kuppelhorizant*), but in other places it was more often made of cloth and mounted so that it could be raised out of sight when not in use. It served many purposes: its shape and height made it possible to abandon overhead borders; it created a sense of infinite space; and it provided an ideal surface for projections.

Projections began to make their appearance in the theatre in the 1890s. Appia wrote of their scenic possibilities, but in this period they were used almost entirely for clouds, for nonrealistic shapes, and for atmospheric effects.

A related development was the motion picture. Out of the desire to record visual reality, photography had taken shape in the nineteenth century. But despite its fidelity, photography still lacked one important ingredient—movement—and it was this which several men sought to supply. In 1894, Edison invented a device—the kinetoscope—whereby one person could view moving pictures through a peephole, and in 1895, moving pictures were for the first time projected onto a screen. These crude efforts were exploited primarily for their novelty and ability to record everyday occurrences. It was Georges Méliès (1861–1938) who first recognized the film's potential for fantasy, transformations, dissolves, and other effects impossible in more concrete media, although the significance of his work (done between 1896 and 1914) was not fully appreciated until much later.

Not until about 1903, with Edwin S. Porter's *The Great Train Robbery,* did films with connected plots begin to be popular. Soon, short dramatic episodes were being turned out by the hundreds. The film remained a novelty, however, until 1905, when the first "nickelodeon" (where one could see a twenty-minute show for five cents) was opened in Pennsylvania. This proved so successful that by 1909 there were eight thousand similar establishments in the United States. The early movie houses usually seated no more than one hundred, but soon they began to be enlarged and in 1914 the Strand Theatre, with seating for 3,300, was opened in New York. Meanwhile the film had also been growing in length and sophistication, and with D. W. Griffith's *The Birth of a Nation* in 1915 a new era began, for here was a full-length work of great power and emotional appeal. Technology had created a new art—one that was to threaten the very existence of the theatre, but also one that eventually would provide it with new means.

～ VIII ～

By 1914 comprehensive new theories of the theatre had been voiced by Appia, Craig, Fuchs, and Copeau and had been partially implemented by Poel, Reinhardt, Barker, Rouché, and others. Throughout this period the intense concern for theatre as an art is evident in the widespread inclusion of "art" in the titles of organizations. High idealism was omnipresent, even if the constant invocation of culture, beauty, and communion did at times suggest preciosity. No doubt such invocations were necessary in the fight to counteract the romantic-realistic mode and the commercialism of the day. Certainly the desire to regain for the theatre the respect it had commanded in ancient Greece was admirable.

But, despite the widespread discussion of a people's theatre and of the role of theatre in a community, most of the experimentation in these years remained avant-gardist. Without doubt, the majority of commercial producers and theatregoers preferred the "inartistic" realism which had triumphed at the end of the nineteenth century. Still, audiences were gradually becoming aware of the new theories and practices and, after the war, the stylized realism that Reinhardt favored would become the standard against which a new avant-garde would feel compelled to rebel. If in 1914 it had not yet won widespread popular acceptance, a new art of the theatre had nevertheless been forged.

The Russian Renaissance

8

Until the end of the nineteenth century, Russia remained on the periphery of European theatrical developments. It had exported plays occasionally, but its influence on the West had been slight. Between 1900 and 1917 this situation changed drastically as Russia became a center of experimentation. The Moscow Art Theatre, after beginning with productions in the manner of Saxe-Meiningen, developed its own style, marked by psychological realism and a keen sense of mood and atmosphere. Others, especially Meyerhold, Komissarzhevsky, Evreinov, and Tairov, began to experiment with nonrealistic modes. Such major Russian dramatists as Chekhov, Tolstoy, Gorky, and Andreyev, also came to the fore. In less than a quarter of a century, Russia had by 1917 moved from a position of obscurity to one of leadership.

For most westerners, even those of today, the Russian theatre scarcely existed before the formation of the Moscow Art Theatre in 1898. Nevertheless, it had been an accepted institution since about 1750, although its artistic development had been inhibited by bureaucratic organization and by censorship designed to ensure that it posed no threat to the government. Consequently, it was not until the nineteenth century that it began to produce dramatists of the first rank.

The first playwright with modernistic tendencies was Nikolai Gogol (1809–52), best known today for *The Inspector General* (1836). Set in a small provincial town, Gogol's comedy shows corrupt and ignorant officials thrown into a violent uproar by the rumor that an inspector from the capital is on his way to investigate their administration. When a stranger appears, they assume that it is the inspector traveling in disguise and obsequiously offer him favors and bribes. In actuality, he is a poor government clerk, Khlestakov, stranded for lack of funds. A rascal too, he takes advantage of the corruption to enrich himself before he departs. Scarcely has he gone when the Postmaster appears with an intercepted letter, written by Khlestakov to his friends, which reveals the truth. Before the officials can recover, the real inspector is announced and the curtain falls as the process begins again. There are no admirable characters; each is concerned only for his own welfare. All are drawn as grotesques or caricatures but with sufficient truth that many persons of the time considered the play a realistic rendering of provincial life or an attack on Russian officialdom. More important, it was a well-constructed comedy which provided actors with roles they could flesh out inventively. It soon became and remains a part of the standard repertory and is now almost universally considered to be the first realistic Russian comedy.

Gogol's play appeared at a propitious moment, for a number of actors were becoming increasingly interested in truth to life on the stage and it permitted them to demonstrate the strength of their methods. The most important of these actors was Mikhail Shchepkin (1788–1863), credited by Stanislavsky with establishing the basis for a genuine Russian dramatic art. His concern for close observation of life, careful preparation and rehearsal, and realistic portrayal of roles set an example for a whole generation of actors then beginning their careers. The combined examples of Gogol's writing and Shchepkin's acting did much to encourage the trend toward realism.

The movement toward realism was also encouraged after 1850 by a great upsurge of interest in social and political problems and by the growing demand for change which accompanied it. In 1850 Russia was still largely a feudal state with a rigid class structure under which nobles and aristorats owned most of the land and the peasants who cultivated it. Not until 1861 was serfdom abolished. The crown, while granting many reforms, was wary of moving too rapidly and oscillated between loosening and tightening governmental controls. Censorship of drama was so rigid that most major authors turned to the novel and other nondramatic forms. But virtually all serious writers of the late nineteenth century were united in the belief that literature should serve a humanizing or didactic role. This growing concern for contemporary life was reflected in an increased realism.

The trend toward realism in drama is best seen in the work of Turgenev, Pisemsky, Ostrovsky, and Tolstoy. Ivan Turgenev's (1818–83) *A Month in the Country* (written in 1850 but not produced until 1872) is one of the earliest and finest realistic plays in any language. It antedates the realistic dramas of Dumas *fils* and Augier and was written just as Ibsen was composing his first romantic work, *Cataline*. Like Chekhov's major works, Turgenev's drama is set on a remote country estate and emphasizes psychological relationships and inner struggles. The principal character is the landowner's young wife, Natalya, who leads a boring existence in which she innocently toys with Rakitin, a friend of the family. The arrival of a young tutor, Belyaev, serves as a catalyst which stirs up and reveals the submerged frustrations and desires of the other characters. Natalya, drawn to the tutor, almost unconsciously comes to view Vera, her young ward, as a rival, and arranges for her marriage to a coarse neighboring landowner. Vera, although naïve, recognizes what has happened and forces Natalya to examine her own motives. At the end, both Rakitin and Belyaev go away, leaving Natalya more alone than ever.

It is a play of cross-purposes, for each person against his will loves another who cannot return his affection. There are no villains; each person is essentially good but led into questionable deeds by feelings over which he has no control. Each is made sympathetic by revealing his inner suffering and motivations. *A Month in the Country* in mood and psychological subtlety is prophetic of Chekhov's work to come.

Just as Turgenev's work antedates the development of realism in the West, so Alexey Feofilaktovich Pisemsky's (1820–81) precedes naturalism. His play *A Bitter Fate* (1859), one of the earliest and finest examples of naturalistic drama anywhere, was the first serious drama in Russia to use a peasant as protagonist. The story is simple. The serf Anany, upon returning home after an absence of some time, discovers that his wife Yelizaveta has had an affair with the landowner and has borne him a child. Anany kills the baby and flees, but later gives himself up and is sent off to Siberia after humbly repenting. Its starkness, sense of inevitability, and lack of contrivance came nearer to realizing the naturalistic ideal as set forth by Zola than did any French play of the century. Like Turgenev, however, Pisemsky was primarily a novelist whose major creative energy was expended on nondramatic works.

Between 1846 and his death, Alexander Ostrovsky (1823–86), Russia's first professional playwright (in the sense of confining himself entirely to drama and making his living from it), wrote seventy-six plays which are usually considered the essence of Russian realism and the cornerstone of the Russian repertory. Ostrovsky's keen aural and visual sense led him to create closely observed characters and concrete environments. It is often said that he is the most Russian of all playwrights since his work is so deeply rooted in the speech, thought, and actions of the petty tradesmen and civil servants of his day.

Among Ostrovsky's best plays are *The Poor Bride* (1852) and *The Thunderstorm* (1860), both of which show the effects of social conditions on the lives of young women. In *The Poor Bride,* the young and attractive Marya is courted by several men but, because she has no dowry, eventually must marry a rich, debauched government official rather than the young man she loves. The early scenes are much like those of traditional comedies in which young lovers are kept apart by circumstances, but all romantic expectations are gradually shattered and at the end Marya has accepted her fate and reconciled herself to harsh reality. In *The Thunderstorm* the outcome is more tragic. Here, Katerina, a deeply religious young woman, is dominated by the mother of her weak husband. Against her will, she falls in love with a man who like herself is miserable under the oppression of a vicious uncle. While her husband is away, Katerina gives into temptation and is unfaithful. Her feeling of guilt is so intense, however, that in a thunderstorm, which she considers a threat from Heaven itself, she publicly confesses her guilt and then commits suicide. The thunderstorm is here used symbolically—as a parallel to the psychological storm within the characters and within the repressive society—much in the manner that Chekhov would later adopt in his plays.

In addition to his playwriting, Ostrovsky was active in the theatre in other ways. In 1865, he was one of the founders of the Artistic Circle, which provided training in the realistic manner for beginning and provincial actors. Furthermore, when his plays were produced he worked closely with actors and designers to achieve an illusion of reality. Near the end of his life he was appointed artistic director of the Maly Theatre in Moscow, but died before he could overcome bureaucratic interference with that theatre's productions. He also served as president of the Society of Russian Dramatic Writers and Opera Composers (founded in 1874), which gained increased payment for authors and encouraged excellence by establishing a prize for each season's best play. Ostrovsky was probably the most important single individual in the Russian theatre of the nineteenth century.

Toward the end of his life, the great novelist Leo Tolstoy (1828–1910) turned to playwriting. His first important drama, *The Power of Darkness* (1886), failing to pass the censor in Russia, received its premiere at Antoine's Théâtre Libre in 1888 (it was finally produced in Russia in 1895). In many ways *The Power of Darkness* is reminiscent of Pisemsky's *A Bitter Fate.* In it, the farmhand Nikita carries on an affair with Anisya, the second wife of Nikita's employer, Petr, and helps her to murder him.

After he marries Anisya he is bitterly unhappy and takes to drink, seduces Akulina, Petr's daughter by his first marriage, and at the urging of his wife and mother, kills the child that is born to them so that Akulina may be married off to an unsuspecting peasant. But at the engagement party Nikita is so overcome by guilt that he publicly confesses his crimes. Tolstoy's interests, however, were quite different from those of Pisemsky, who was content to tell his story without comment. Tolstoy, preoccupied with man's moral and spiritual aspirations, shows how Nikita, despite attempts to suppress his spiritual despair, comes to accept his guilt and attain a kind of heroism worthy of compassion.

Thus, despite many handicaps, Russia had by the late nineteenth century established a strong dramatic tradition. Next to censorship its greatest obstacle was probably antiquated theatrical conditions. Although there were many outstanding actors, rehearsal practices discouraged ensemble performances and encouraged individual virtuosity. Plays often received no more than three rehearsals and frequently director and actors did not even know what scenery would be used until opening night. In general there were only three kinds of settings in use: "Gothic" which served for all periods prior to the nineteenth century; "Gogolian" for Russian drama up to 1850; and "urban" for contemporary pieces. Furthermore, until 1882 the state theatres held a monopoly on theatrical production in Moscow and St. Petersburg. Since they were ruled over by political appointees who had few qualifications for their jobs beyond loyalty to the government, there was little concern in them for artistic excellence.

After the monopoly was rescinded in 1882, private theatres were instrumental in bringing some improvements. In Moscow, O. A. Korsh staged productions of high quality, and in St. Petersburg, Alexey Suvorin, a publisher and writer with important government connections, was able to present many plays—among them Tolstoy's *The Power of Darkness* and Pisemsky's *The Willful Ones*— which previously had been banned. By far the most important productions, however, were those mounted by Savva Mamontov, a railroad magnate, at first in his own mansion and after 1896 in his public opera house. He employed the best modern painters, costumers, and directors to present visually beautiful and esthetically satisfying productions. The venture soon proved too costly, however, and came to an end. But Mamontov's work long remained a standard and many of the artists who began their careers with him went on to work in other theatres. In the drive for improvement, the visits of the Meiningen troupe in 1885 and 1890 were also significant.

These fitful and uncoordinated efforts, however, made little impression on the Russian theatre as a whole. The general dissatisfaction seems to have come to a focus in the First All-Russian Conference of Theatre People, held in Moscow in 1897 and attended by theatrical personnel from all over Russia. Speakers blamed the sorry state of the theatre on the commercial motive, on the inadequate training of performers, on conventionalized staging, and on other factors. All were agreed that reform was needed. In less than a year the first important new step—the formation of the Moscow Art Theatre—had been taken. This new organization not only signaled a change in Russia but was destined to affect the theatre all over the world.

~ II ~

The Moscow Art Theatre was the creation of Vladimir Nemirovich-Danchenko (1858–1943) and Konstantin Stanislavsky (1863–1938). Nemirovich-Danchenko, born into the nobility, had been educated at Moscow University and was an established dramatist and journalist when in 1891 he became a teacher of acting at the Moscow Philharmonic Society. Here he soon came to feel that no training would be effective unless the theatres in which the students were to work changed their methods.

Stanislavsky (born Konstantin Alexeyev), son of a wealthy industrialist, received an excellent education. His interests early centered on the theatre and when he was sent to Paris on business took the opportunity to study at the Conservatoire and to attend innumerable performances. At this time he also took the name of Stanislavsky from a retiring Polish actor. Upon returning to Russia, he in 1888 became chairman of the Moscow Society for Arts and Letters, an organization which offered theatrical productions as a part of its program to bring together persons interested in the arts. Although this organization was bankrupt after two years, it continued to present one play a week for the Hunters' Club, which took over its premises. By 1898, Stanislavsky had had approximately ten years of experience as an actor and director working with a company composed of amateurs and professionals in a wide range of dramatic forms and styles.

But by 1897 both Nemirovich-Danchenko and Stanislavsky found their situations confining and they agreed to explore together the possibility of forming an organization that would permit them to work as they wished and which would seek to remedy the shortcomings then so evident in the major Russian theatres. Out of a meeting in June 1897 came the decision to found the Moscow Popular Art Theatre (a title later shortened to Moscow Art Theatre). Nemirovich-Danchenko was to be literary advisor and Stanislavsky production director. Eventually both men directed plays, Stanislavsky became one of the company's leading actors, and Nemirovich-Danchenko performed many of the managerial tasks.

The original company was made up of thirty-nine persons, many chosen from among Nemirovich-Danchenko's students and from the Society for Arts and Letters. Perhaps the best of these were Ivan Moskvin (1874–1946), Vassily Kachalov (1875–1948), Olga Knipper (1870–1959), and Maria Ghermanova (1884–1945). Rehearsals got underway in the summer

A scene from *Tsar Fyodor,* first production of the Moscow Art Theatre, 1898.
Victor Simov designed the setting, which was one of several used in the production.

of 1898 in a village about thirty miles from Moscow where the company
lived and worked together on a rigorous schedule.

In the early years of the Moscow Art Theatre Stanislavsky planned
every detail of his productions in advance. Armed with his production book,
he maintained a school-like discipline as he dictated to the actors precisely
what he wanted moment by moment. In later years he radically altered his
approach (often making almost no advance preparation in order to encourage creativity among the actors), but in the beginning his regimen had
the salutary effect of creating an artistic ensemble rapidly.

The first season of the Moscow Art Theatre opened on October 14,
1898, with Alexey Tolstoy's historical drama *Tsar Fyodor,* mounted with
infinite care for its sixteenth-century milieu. Director, designer, and actors
had visited monasteries, provincial villages, museums, and art galleries to
absorb a sense of the period and to copy, buy, or borrow authentic properties
and costumes. The designer, Victor Simov, created convincing replicas of
the Archangel Cathedral, the tsar's quarters in the Kremlin, and assorted
other intricate and detailed locales. The response was enthusiastic, although
some claimed that the production was merely an imitation of the Meininger's
methods and others declared that the welter of scenic detail made it difficult
to concentrate on the actors.

The company next performed Sophocles' *Antigone* and Shakespeare's
The Merchant of Venice in the same antiquarian mode. But interest began
to wane and the enterprise seemed in danger of collapse when it presented
as its fourth offering Chekhov's *The Sea Gull.* With this production, the
group brought to bear on a modern play all that it had learned through its
earlier work. The result was mutually beneficial, for in Chekhov the
Moscow Art Theatre found a contemporary dramatist whose plays were
attuned to their own creative aspirations, while Chekhov for the first time

found actors who were willing to discover and project the psychological nuances of his drama. This collaboration was so fruitful that eventually the Moscow Art Theatre adopted a sea gull as its emblem and was called "the House of Chekhov."

Despite its successes, the Moscow Art Theatre ended its first season with a sizable deficit. Saved by the generosity of a wealthy financier, Savva Morozov, and his friends, the company thereafter was able to support itself primarily from box-office receipts. Its new security led to the building of a permanent home for the company. Designed by F. O. Schechtel and opened in 1902, the new theatre seated 1,200. Its technical facilities, which included a revolving stage and the latest equipment for lighting, scenery, and costuming, were among the finest in the world. At this time the company was also enlarged to one hundred, and it settled into the pattern that was to be typical: the majority of its performances were of proven successes, while only three to five new works were mounted each year. The repertory, therefore, had considerable stability. This guaranteed the company a large degree of financial security and permitted it to mount new productions somewhat leisurely and with great care.

Of the Moscow Art Theater's contemporary authors the most important were Chekhov and Gorky. Anton Chekhov (1860–1904), son of a grocer and grandson of a serf, turned to writing in 1880 as a means of supporting himself and his family while he attended medical school. These early works were sketches, topical commentaries, parodies, and other short comic pieces. Upon receiving his medical degree in 1884, he decided to devote himself entirely to literature and soon attained considerable renown as a short story writer. His first long play, *Ivanov* (1887), was presented successfully in St. Petersburg in 1889 and his short farces, such as *The Boor* (1888), *The Proposal* (1888–89), and *The Wedding* (1889–90), were widely performed as curtain raisers.

But when *The Sea Gull* was first presented in 1896 by the Alexandrinsky Theatre in St. Petersburg it was a miserable failure because many of the actors had not bothered to learn their lines and because no one connected with the production seems to have had any idea of how to cope with this play, which differed so radically from the typical fare of the time. Chekhov was so discouraged that he had virtually decided to give up playwriting when the Moscow Art Theatre achieved its resounding success with *The Sea Gull*. He was then induced to let the company present *Uncle Vanya* (1897) in 1899 and went on to write two new works, *The Three Sisters* (1901) and *The Cherry Orchard* (1904), with the company in mind. His ties with the troupe were further cemented when in 1901 he married Olga Knipper, one of its leading actresses.

Today Chekhov's reputation rests primarily upon four plays produced by the Moscow Art Theatre: *The Sea Gull, Uncle Vanya, The Three Sisters,* and *The Cherry Orchard.* Each is set in rural Russia and treats the boredom and monotony of life among the landowning class; all show the

Chekhov's *The Cherry Orchard,* originally produced at the Moscow Art Theatre in 1904.

vast gulf between aspiration and accomplishment. *The Three Sisters* may be taken as typical. In it, Chekhov deals with the plight of the Prozoroff family, the children of a deceased officer in a provincial army post far from the gaiety and culture of Moscow, which for them symbolizes all that is missing from their lives. The sisters—Olga, Masha, and Irina—and their brother, Andrey, have been equipped by education and upbringing for sophisticated city life and are useless in their present surroundings. Olga has become a teacher; Masha, married to a dull schoolmaster, enters into an affair with Colonel Vershinin; Irina, after trying a civil service post, eventually agrees to marry Tusenbach, a man she does not love. Their plight is increased by Andrey's marriage to the insensitive Natasha, who gradually displaces them all from their home. In the last act, the army garrison, their one shield against the provincialism which surrounds them, is transferred, and Tusenbach is killed in a duel. Now more isolated than ever, the sisters, perhaps unconvincingly, resolve to find real purpose in their lives.

Although on the surface seemingly simple, Chekhov's plays are among the most complex in the modern repertory. In them all violent deeds and emotional climaxes occur offstage and the plays conclude before any full reversal has taken place. Thus, the action is muted, for it is kept in the background. In the foreground, the onstage action, is placed a plethora of seemingly trivial, commonplace occurrences. But these details are chosen and arranged with enormous care to give the effect of randomness while at the same time they constantly reveal character, mood, and idea. As a result, attention is concentrated not on events but on the texture of the life that surrounds and shapes the characters and upon their psychological responses. Since the characters, like most human beings, do not fully understand their own feelings and motives and since they seek to conceal as much as to reveal their emotions, it is in the seeming trivia, the nuances, the

243

subtext that underlies the dialogue that one must seek the revelations that constitute the dramatic action.

Chekhov does not create villains. All his characters are victims of conflicting forces; most try to act decently. What happens to each is a direct result of the kind of person he is. Thus, character and fate are essentially one. As a play progresses, Chekhov gradually strips his characters of their illusions and reveals the anxieties and inadequacies which lie beneath. But in all his revelations there is tolerance and compassion. At the same time, the spectator is sufficiently distanced from the characters to see them as both sympathetic and ridiculous. Thus, the pathetic and the comic are inextricably intertwined in a way that gives Chekhov's plays a flavor all their own.

Chekhov is also able to create an extraordinary sense of atmosphere, an almost concrete manifestation of environment. The dominant impression in all the plays is one of indolence and moral inertia. The spectator feels both sympathy for the characters' pointless lives and impatience with their inability to act. Thus, although Chekhov never comments directly upon the society of his time, much is implied.

Despite their surface naturalness, all of Chekhov's plays make considerable use of symbolism to enlarge meaning and to comment indirectly upon the action. In *The Cherry Orchard,* for example, the orchard, once productive and useful, is now merely decorative. Eventually it is bought by a former peasant, Lopakhin, who intends to cut it down and build villas for the middle class. But since the orchard also represents the aristocracy, it is used to suggest much about Russian society of Chekhov's time.

Chekhov's mosaiclike technique sometimes led the Moscow Art Theatre astray and he often complained about unnecessary and distracting details in the productions and about the failure to project the humor in his plays. Despite these complaints, however, it seems certain that it was this very care for detail and nuance (undoubtedly sometimes an overzealous one) that made the Moscow Art Theatre serve Chekhov so well. Through its productions, Chekhov assumed his rightful place as one of the world's great dramatists.

Maxim Gorky (Alexei Maximovich Peshkov, 1868–1936) supplied the Moscow Art Theatre with three plays, but only one of them, *The Lower Depths* (1902), remained in its repertory. Son of a paperhanger, Gorky was orphaned at the age of eight. With only five months of schooling, he was forced to earn his living by working as errand boy, baker, shipworker, and at dozens of other jobs. His one solace was reading, but through it he also developed a keen sense of the gap between the idealistic tone of what he read and the harsh realities of his own life. His first efforts at writing were published in 1892, and he became famous overnight in 1898 when his collected stories were printed. By 1900 he was looked upon as "a hero of the people." His first play, *The Petty Bourgeoisie* (or *Smug Citizens*) was staged by the Moscow Art Theatre in 1902, but it is on *The Lower*

Depths (produced later in the same year) that Gorky's fame as a dramatist most firmly rests.

245

The Russian Renaissance

The Lower Depths is set in a flophouse peopled with human wrecks. The slight story line centers around the thief Pepel and his love for Natasha, the sister of Vasilisa, wife of the brutal pawnbroker who owns the flophouse. Pepel carries on an affair with Vasilisa, who urges Pepel to kill her husband, which he eventually does but to save Natasha from the terrible life she leads rather than to satisfy Vasilisa. Around this center cluster the stories of the other characters: the locksmith Kleshch and his consumptive wife, Anna; the prostitute Nastya; the alcoholic actor; the baron who has been ruined by women and gambling; and various other victims of social conditions. Into this atmosphere of degradation comes Luka, a pilgrim, who tells them of hope and a bright future. For a time he rekindles their illusions, but after he leaves nothing has really changed. The only character not seduced by Luka's appeal is Satin, who believes in facing the truth courageously. Although no better off than the others, he argues that Luka's lies are designed to keep the poor and weak submissive. To Luka's deceptions, he opposes struggle and the fight to attain dignity. Thus, Luka and Satin represent polar positions—the deceptive path of religion, and the more difficult but realistic way of struggle for social and political reform. Within the play, however, Gorky does not favor one over the other and the action is sufficiently ambiguous that more than one interpretation of the author's intention is possible.

While staging *The Lower Depths,* Stanislavsky made his actors visit various flophouses in Moscow and study the behavior, surroundings, and

The Lower Depths by Gorky, produced originally by the Moscow Art Theatre in 1902. (From *Moscow Art Theatre, 1898–1917,* 1955.)

dress. These were re-created on stage with such care that spectators in the first few rows were said to fear being infected with vermin.

By the time the Revolution began in 1917, Gorky had written eight plays, most of which had been denied production because Gorky had participated in the uprising of 1905 and had subsequently been imprisoned and exiled. Aside from *The Lower Depths,* the best of these early dramas is *Enemies* (written in 1906 but not produced in Russia until 1933), a work which shows how workers and factory owners become increasingly polarized into class enemies. From the beginning Gorky was a firm supporter of the Communist cause, and after the Revolution he was eventually to become the acknowledged head of the literary profession in Russia. (The final stages of his career will be discussed in a later chapter.)

By the time Chekhov died in 1904 the Moscow Art Theatre was a secure and thriving institution. Its reputation had been made with sensitive and detailed productions of contemporary plays and with historically accurate mountings of older works. Thus, in many ways it had merely extended the work of Antoine and Saxe-Meiningen. This was, of course, an enormous achievement, especially in a country which had been so backward theatrically only six years earlier. But Stanislavsky was not entirely satisfied with his accomplishments, for he feared that too much emphasis had been placed upon concrete reality while the realms of fantasy and the spirit had been left unexplored. Consequently, he now began a series of experiments designed to enlarge the company's methods.

~~~ **III** ~~~

By the time of Chekhov's death, realism was beginning to lose much of its power, although it remained the dominant mode. Meanwhile, in the 1890s, a nonrealistic stream related to the symbolism of France, the aestheticism of England, and the neoromanticism of Germany had appeared. In Russia, these early nonrealists were usually called decadents, and like their European counterparts, from whom they drew much inspiration, their watchwords were inspiration, beauty, form, and art-for-art's-sake. In the 1890's the movement was characterized by revolt against almost all tradition and against social and utilitarian literature. After 1900, the tone changed and the movement came to be called symbolism. Now there was a turning away from Western influence and toward national concerns, especially after the Revolution of 1905 when political and social problems loomed large. Between 1905 and 1917 most of the major Russian writers paid allegiance to the symbolist outlook.

The new trends, which were evident in all the arts, came to a focus in the "World of Art" group, named for the periodical founded in St.

Petersburg in 1898 by Sergei Diaghilev (1872–1929). Each issue of the lavishly illustrated *World of Art* included reports from correspondents in Paris, Rome, Munich, and other European cities about literature, the visual arts, theatre, and music. Thus, it kept Russians abreast of the latest artistic developments throughout Europe. But it also began to explore the Russian past, especially icons and eighteenth-century painting, and issued a number of monographs on Russian art. This interest was to have considerable influence on scenic design. Although the magazine came to an end in 1904, the movement continued to serve as a rallying point for practically all modernist tendencies until the 1917 Revolution.

The World of Art group promoted the arts in many ways. It arranged exhibitions of paintings by such French artists as Degas, Renoir, and the late impressionists, and "Evenings of Contemporary Music" with works by Strauss, Debussy, Ravel, Scriabin, Stravinsky, Rachmaninov, and Prokofiev. Diaghilev also brought Russian art to the West. In Paris he mounted an exhibition of Russian painting in 1906, concerts of Russian music in 1907, and productions of Russian opera in 1908. But by far the greatest impact was made with a six-week season of ballet in 1909. The Ballets Russes, an overnight sensation, initiated intense interest both in ballet and in a new style of stage decoration.

The ballets which made such a deep impression in the West were also relatively new to Russia. In the last part of the nineteenth century, Russian ballet had been dominated by Marius Petipa (1822–1910), who not only placed great emphasis upon technical excellence (as a result of which Russian dancers came to be the finest in the world) but favored long story-telling works featuring pantomime and elaborate scenery and costumes in the romantic-realistic vein. Typical of these were *The Sleeping Beauty* and *Swan Lake,* with music by Tchaikovsky. After Petipa retired in 1903, leadership passed to Mikhail Fokine (1880–1942), who disliked the long ballets with involved plots and the conventionalized steps and poses which had resulted. Thus, he chose shorter subjects and sought in various ways to achieve novelty. Although he maintained the earlier strict training, he used this technical excellence inventively to achieve an overpowering sense of vitality. The dancers with whom he worked—including Nizhinsky, Pavlova, Karsavina, and Rubenstein—were probably the best in the world. When the Ballets Russes burst upon the European scene it was called the "Diaghilev miracle."

But the effect was not made by the dancing alone. Of equal (and for the theatre of greater) importance were the scenic designs. The major painters for the Ballets Russes at this time were Leon Bakst (1866–1924) and Alexandre Benois (1876–1960). Bakst's work was characterized by a kind of Oriental and barbaric spendor in which startling color combinations and decorative motifs were blended in fresh and original ways to create an overpowering sensual effect. Benois was perhaps much more versatile. His settings for *Armide's Pavilion* were praised for the delicacy

Leon Bakst's setting for *Tamar* at the Ballets Russes, 1912.
(From the souvenir program.)

with which he handled eighteenth-century motifs, but he was equally adept
at creating the Chinese background of *Le Rossignol* and the Russian folk
settings of *Petrouchka*. Other major designers were Alexander Golovin,
Nicolas Roerich, Mstislav Dobuzhinsky, and Natalie Goncharova.

There was nothing new in the technical means used by these designers,
for they relied on wings and drops. The novelty lay in the stylization
achieved through unusual coloration, compositions, and decorative motifs.
Many of the settings made considerable use of perspective painting, but it
was a forced perspective which did not seek to give a sense of reality or to
cheat the eye. Other settings, however, deliberately avoided perspective and
adopted the flatness typical of primitive painting, icons, or peasant and
folk art. No doubt this convention was also influenced by the tendency in
art nouveau at this time toward posterlike flatness. Mikhail Larionov and
Natalie Goncharova were especially fond of this technique. The stylization,
the deliberate avoidance of illusionism, the reveling in color and exotic
detail made a profound impression on audiences in 1909.

The effect was probably also due in large part to the care with which
settings, music, and choreography were coordinated. The creators of the

Ballets Russes were conscious of working to develop a *Gesamtkunstwerk* in the Wagnerian sense. All of those involved in a production worked together from the beginning. Not only did Bakst, Benois, and other designers provide settings, they often conceived the overall plot. For example, Bakst supplied the "books" for *Scheherazade, Tamar,* and *The Afternoon of a Faun,* while Benois conceived *Armide's Pavilion.* Stravinsky collaborated with Benois on *Petrouchka* and with Roerich on *The Rite of Spring.* In several instances, composers worked directly with Fokine and the designers.

The impact made by the Ballets Russes in 1909 was so intense that Diaghilev soon formed a permanent troupe to tour the major cities of western Europe. It was to exert significant influence both on ballet and scenic design until Diaghilev's death in 1929.

In the West, Diaghilev's designers are known almost exclusively for their work with ballet. In Russia, however, they are much more significant as the major stage designers of their era. They gradually displaced the old scene painters not only in the theatres primarily concerned with nonrealistic methods but in the Moscow Art Theatre and in other more conventional troupes.

But though the new movement was triumphant in ballet and design, it produced few dramatists of importance. The lack was not seriously felt, however, for it was filled by such foreign authors as Maeterlinck and Ibsen. Nevertheless, Russian authors were demanding changes and they supplied a theoretical foundation for them. In the fourth issue of *The World of Art*

Costume design, "The Beautiful Princess," by Bakst for the Ballets Russes' production in 1910 of Stravinsky's *The Firebird.* (From the Museum of Modern Art, New York.)

(in 1902), Valery Briussov (1873–1924), a leading "decadent" poet, launched an attack on the Moscow Art Theatre for its emphasis upon "faithfulness to life." He declared that, since the stage is based upon esthetic conventions, conscious stylization rather than realistic imitation is needed. Briussov was later to serve on the repertory committees of such champions of nonrealistic drama as Komissarzhevskaya and Meyerhold. Vyacheslav Ivanov (1866–1949), another symbolist, argued for a "theatre of congregate action" which through mythlike drama would provide something like a communal religious experience, a "temple theatre" in which spectators and performers would be united in a "common ecstasy." Sologub (Theodore Teternikov, 1863–1927) demanded that all barriers between the stage and auditorium be removed so that an "active audience" might assist in a "collective creation." Alexander Blok (1880–1921) was especially interested in *commedia dell' arte,* the conventions of which he utilized in several of his works, most notably in *The Little Show Booth* (1906), a play which was a favorite of Meyerhold and which initiated his work with *commedia.*

The impact of these demands was soon felt by the Moscow Art Theatre. Stanislavsky had always been interested in nonrealistic drama but around 1904 he began to feel the necessity of finding a place for it in the Moscow Art Theatre's repertory. Thus, in the season of 1904–5 he presented a bill of Maeterlinck's one-act plays (*The Intruder, The Blind,* and *Inside*). The results were so unsatisfactory, however, that he decided it would be necessary to explore new methods outside the confines of the regular program.

To head the new enterprise, he turned to Vsevelod Meyerhold (Karl Theodor Kasimir Meyergold, 1874–1940). After giving up law to enter the drama school of the Moscow Philharmonic Society, Meyerhold had studied with Nemirovich-Danchenko and had been one of the original members of the Moscow Art Theatre, in which he had played some eighteen roles before leaving in 1902. He had then formed (in association with Alexander Kosheverov) his own company, which had staged a repertory using methods not unlike those of the Moscow Art Theatre. By 1903, however, he had become intensely interested in the new nonrealistic trends and had begun his first directorial efforts in this vein. When Stanislavsky heard of these experiments he invited Meyerhold to take charge of the studio which he established in 1905.

From the beginning Stanislavsky and Meyerhold had differing views of the studio's goals. Stanislavsky seems to have viewed it as an evolutionary process whereby new means would gradually enlarge the old, whereas Meyerhold viewed it as a complete break with the past. No doubt Meyerhold was encouraged in this by Briussov, who had been appointed literary advisor to the group. Meyerhold set to work on Maeterlinck's *The Death of Tintagiles,* but Stanislavsky became increasingly disturbed by what he considered Meyerhold's tendency to make puppets of the actors by sub-

ordinating them to his directorial concept. The Revolution of 1905 delayed
the scheduled opening in October and shortly afterward it was canceled
altogether and the studio closed. Several productions had been planned and
much of the preliminary work had been done. Some of the scenic designs
are indicative of the direction Meyerhold was taking. For Hauptmann's
Schluck and Jau, an artist's studio was depicted by a huge canvas which
covered half stage; a royal bedchamber was indicated by an enormous
bed and canopy; in another scene several women costumed identically
embroidered on a single broad ribbon in perfect unison. Of the studio,
Briussov declared that the director's and designer's work was entirely successful but that the actors were unable to break away from the training
they had received in the parent company.

Although the studio was short-lived, it is significant for drawing the
battle lines which were to persist in the Russian theatre until the 1930s.
These are worth considering for they clarify much that was to come.
Stanislavsky's goals resembled those of Wagner: to create such an overpowering empathic response in the spectator that he would forget that he
is in a theatre. Meyerhold, on the other hand, was interested in exploring the
theatre as a means of expression quite apart from its ability to mesmerize
an audience or to create the illusion of reality. In 1922 Yevgeny Vakhtangov
explained the difference between the two: "For Meyerhold a performance
is theatrical when the spectator does not forget for a second that he is in
a theatre, and is conscious all the time of the actor as a craftsman who
plays a role. Stanislavsky demands the opposite: that the spectator become
oblivious to the fact that he is in a theatre and that he be immersed in the
atmosphere in which the protagonists of a play exist." The distinction is
important, for, although Stanislavsky throughout his life was to seek satisfying means through which to approach nonrealistic drama, he was seldom
content with the results, for all tended to disrupt or prevent the kind of
audience response that he found essential. Still, he remained conscious that
many of the plays he admired could not be staged entirely satisfactorily
through those means he employed with Chekhov's works. Consequently,
though in 1905 he closed the studio, he did not give up the search for new
methods.

Stanislavsky went on to stage Ibsen's *Brand,* Hamsun's *Drama of Life,*
Maeterlinck's *The Blue Bird,* and several other nonrealistic plays. One of
his most interesting experiments came in 1907 with Leonid Andreyev's
(1871–1919) *The Life of Man,* an allegorical drama. Andreyev began his
career as a realistic writer and achieved instantaneous success with a collection of stories published in 1901. After 1905 he adopted many of the devices
popularized by the symbolists, although he denied any allegiance to that
school. After turning to drama in 1906 he was to write some thirty plays
and for a time was the most popular of all Russian dramatists. After the
Revolution his reputation declined rapidly and today he is generally viewed
as a popularizer and vulgarizer of the symbolist trends of his time.

Scene from Andreyev's *The Life of Man* at the Moscow Art Theatre, as staged by Stanislavsky. Setting by V. E. Egerov. (From *Moscow Art Theatre, 1898–1917*, 1955.)

The Life of Man is more allegorical than symbolistic. The characters are given generic names: The Man, The Wife, and so on. At one side of the stage sits Someone in Gray who by the light of a candle reads aloud the story of Man's life as the scenes unfold on stage. Man is born, becomes an ambitious youth, marries, dreams of fortune in the midst of poverty; his dreams come true but the reality seems duller than the anticipation, for envy and wickedness now surround him; misfortunes come upon him as his son dies; he falls ill and helpless; then Someone in Gray blows out the candle.

For this production, Stanislavsky hung the stage in black velvet and on it outlined doors, windows, and other details in white rope. The characters were also dressed in black with details outlined in white. (In later scenes, as Man became successful, the white gave way to gold.) The black costumes seen against a black background made the actors blend into the setting; at times they were almost invisible and, since some portions of the body appeared to be isolated in space, there was a sense of distortion and impermanence. The actors spoke as though making reports. Stanislavsky was not satisfied with the results, for he felt it was impossible to create living characters in such an abstract play, and *The Life of Man* did not remain a part of the theatre's repertory.

In 1908 Stanislavsky became interested in the work of Gordon Craig and invited him to stage *Hamlet* at the Moscow Art Theatre. (It was not performed until 1912.) Although the association was not entirely a happy one, Craig did suggest some lessons for the company. Stanislavsky had always been dissatisfied with the disparity between the painted details of settings and the three-dimensional actors. Craig banished painted details and two-dimensional scenery in favor of three-dimensional screens which were shifted about to create the different locales. Still, the settings seemed overly abstract to Stanislavsky, and Craig's attempt to minimize the personal and subjective elements of acting eventually led to disagreements. Craig also emphasized the need to synthesize music, light, and architecture. Ultimately, however, he exerted more influence on Russian nonrealists than upon the Moscow Art Theatre.

By 1917, the Moscow Art Theatre had undertaken a great number of experiments with fragmentary scenery, directional lighting, and stylized acting. Still, Stanislavsky tended to be unhappy with deviations from illusionism and few nonrealistic productions remained in the repertory. He found it difficult to reconcile stylization with his conviction that great acting is synonymous with the creation of living characters—almost personalities—and that the audience must be made to forget that it is in a theatre. Thus, Stanislavsky continually strove for new means and was almost always disappointed by the results.

～ IV ～

It should also be remembered that at the center of Stanislavsky's concern was the actor rather than theatrical production. It was through his attempts to analyze and solve the actor's problems that he was to arrive at his "system," through which he was to exert his greatest influence on the modern theatre. When the Moscow Art Theatre was founded in 1898 there was no system, for, although always deeply interested in the actor's problems, Stanislavsky did not begin to give them serious attention until 1906. After experimenting with various approaches, he wrote down the first sketch of his system in 1909, one that was never published. When in that year he attempted to apply his ideas in his production of Turgenev's *A Month in the Country,* he met considerable opposition, although the success of the piece won over most of the skeptics. Its complete acceptance came following the production in 1911 of Tolstoy's *Redemption.* Consequently, it was decided that a new studio should be formed to train students in the system and to work out problems as they arose.

This new workshop (called the First Studio) was founded in 1911 and placed under the direction of Leopold Sulerzhitsky (1872–1916), originally a stagehand at the Moscow Art Theatre. Early in life, Sulerzhitsky had been a revolutionary and had served a prison sentence before being con-

Sulerzhitsky's production of *The Cricket on the Hearth* at the First Studio in 1914. It was with this and similar productions at the First Studio that Sulerzhitsky and the younger members of the Moscow Art Theatre company first experimented in depth with the Stanislavsky system.

verted to Tolstoy's conception of redemption through simplicity, nature, and love. To him the theatre had enormous potential for good if only it could reach the spectator's genuine emotions. He argued that the "theatre of spectacle" must be replaced by the "theatre of true feelings," and, believing that Stanislavsky's system provided the necessary means, he embraced it wholeheartedly and taught it at another dramatic school even before it had been fully accepted by the Moscow Art Theatre.

In the studio were a number of young men who were to be of considerable importance, among them Yevgeny Vakhtangov, Mikhail Chekhov, and Richard Boleslavsky. The theatre in which they worked was small, without footlights or an orchestra pit to separate actors and audience. It was designed to encourage the actors to be natural and to avoid any forcing of voice or gesture. The first production, of Herman Heijermans's *The Good Hope,* directed by Boleslavsky, was a considerable success, but the real triumph came in 1914 with Sulerzhitsky's adaptation of *The Cricket on the Hearth*. When Sulerzhitsky died, leadership passed to Yevgeny Vakhtangov (1883–1916), whose genius was first fully displayed in his staging of Henning Berger's *The Flood* in 1922. After the Revolution he was to be one of the most significant figures in the Russian theatre.

Thus, by 1917 the Stanislavsky system had been formulated and tested. Although it was to undergo later revisions, there would be no drastic alterations. The system was only gradually made available through print and thus was often imperfectly understood and misrepresented. Some aspects were set forth in Stanislavsky's *My Life in Art* (1924), but the details had to wait for *An Actor Prepares* (1936) and were not fully revealed in the West until after World War II when *Building a Character* (1949) and *Creating a Role* (1961) were finally published.

It is difficult and probably unfair to attempt a brief summary of so elaborate a system. Still, the main outlines can be sketched. Stanislavsky took it almost for granted that the actor's body and voice should be so thoroughly trained that they could respond efficiently to all demands and that the actor should be schooled in stage techniques so that he might project his characterization to an audience without any sense of contrivance. These "mechanics" of acting have often been played down by Stanislavsky's disciples perhaps because they were much less innovative than was his insistence that the actor find an "inner justification" for everything he does on stage so that he will not seem insecure and artificial. Many of the exercises created by Stanislavsky were designed to help the actor discover this inner justification. His "circle of attention" asks the actor to draw an imaginary circle about himself and to shut out all distractions so that he may concentrate wholly upon entering the world of the play. The actor can also use the "magic 'if'" to enter more fully into the character's being by saying, "If I were this character in this situation, I would. . . ." In this way, he relates the truth of life to the truth of drama and finds meaningful motivations for what he does. "Memory of emotion" is a further aid to be used if an actor has difficulty in developing an appropriate and sincere emotional response to a dramatic situation. Using this device, the actor seeks to recall some analogous situation from his own life which he then re-creates detail by detail until the emotional experience of that moment is evoked; the feeling may then be used in achieving the proper inner justification in the fictional event.

If the actor is not merely to play himself, however, he must be thoroughly aware of the "given circumstances" of the production, which are to be discovered in part through a detailed analysis of the play and the role and in part by understanding the directorial concept, the setting, costumes, and other limitations under which he must work. In this process he becomes aware of his character's "objective" in each scene and in the play as a whole so that he may work for appropriate emphasis and subordination. He must be aware of the play's major lines of action so that he can determine the "through line" which must be clarified and around which all else is built. By understanding the function of his role and those of his fellow actors in each scene, he can contribute to the overall ensemble effect, for he must seek to serve the dramatic action rather than to stand out from his fellow players. Above all, Stanislavsky demanded of his actors absolute dedication and the desire for continuing improvement.

These are Stanislavsky's basic points, although he made many others as well. Various parts of the system have been emphasized by Stanislavsky's disciples who have argued strenuously among themselves about the validity of conflicting interpretations. In America, it is the inner, psychological aspects of the system that have been emphasized at the expense of technical facility. It seems clear, nevertheless, that Stanislavsky sought to clarify and find a solution for each of the actor's problems and that he was concerned with everything from basic training through finished performance. Stanislavsky himself was never fully satisfied with his answers and he often cautioned others about trying to take over his system without allowing for differences in artistic needs and cultural backgrounds. Despite all shortcomings or misunderstandings, however, it has undoubtedly been thus far the most influential approach to acting in the twentieth century.

The major contributions of the Moscow Art Theatre had been made by 1917. It was to continue its work after the Revolution but it added little to its earlier achievements. Without denying the originality of Stanislavsky, he can probably best be viewed as the ultimate inheritor of the tradition of Saxe-Meiningen and Antoine, for his sensibilities were essentially formed in the late nineteenth century with its commitment to illusionism.

The other major innovators in the Russian theatre after 1900—Meyerhold, Komissarzhevsky, Evreinov, and Tairov—are more nearly allied with the tradition of Fort and Lugné-Poë. All were linked in part through Vera Komissarzhevskaya (1864–1910) for whom all worked. Komissarzhevskaya began her enormously successful career as an actress in 1891 and after working for several theatres and touring widely founded her own company in St. Petersburg in 1904. Here she sought to promote the new movements, declaring realism "uninteresting and unnecessary" and seeking in its place a "theatre of the spirit." In search of a sympathetic director, she employed Meyerhold in 1906 after he had been dismissed by Stanislavsky.

Their association was short-lived (it terminated at the end of 1907) for they proved to be incompatible. At about this time, Meyerhold read Georg Fuchs's *The Stage of the Future,* and its advocacy of a stylized relief stage seems to have influenced his work with Kommissarzhevskaya. For Maeterlinck's *Sister Beatrice* he employed a platform only 7 feet deep backed by a decorative screen. By greatly restricting the movement and gestures of the chorus of nuns he created a stage analogous to a bas-relief frieze from an ancient cathedral. The overall effect was of two-dimensionality.

Hedda Gabler, which had in most previous productions been treated with thoroughgoing realism, was staged similarly. Using a stage 33 feet wide and only 12 feet deep, Meyerhold sought through extreme stylization to project his conception of Hedda as cold, regal, and autumnal. The walls, sky, and much of the furniture were blue-green; other furniture was white and one large chair covered in white fur served as a kind of throne for Hedda. A tapestry and threads in other fabrics contained the autumnal tints. Each character was assigned a costume of distinctive color and without realistic detail; furthermore, each actor had certain characteristic poses to which he always returned. At times the actors conversed with each other across the wide stage, and in one scene Hedda and Lovborg looked straight ahead throughout. With the stylized setting, costume, gesture, and speech, Meyerhold hoped to make the spectator seek the inner rather than the outer reality.

Meyerhold soon found this rather static, two-dimensional approach unsatisfying, but in Blok's *The Fairground Booth,* with its use of *commedia dell' arte* conventions and grotesque human situations, he encountered a new inspiration which he was to develop more fully after leaving Komissarzhevskaya. For Wedekind's *Spring's Awakening* in 1907, Meyerhold tried still another experiment. Here he placed all the scenic elements needed for the eighteen scenes on stage at the same time and then through lighting isolated each as needed. While today this may seem commonplace, it was original at the time and was to be widely adopted since in episodic plays it permitted a rapid flow of scenes.

At this time Meyerhold seems to have placed primary emphasis upon directorial concepts embodied primarily in visual terms. Consequently, he was accused of treating the actor as a marionette and of ignoring the psychological aspects of acting. He used Komissarzhevskaya's great talent to little advantage, and, since the theatre had been built around her appeal, it is not surprising that they soon parted company.

Scarcely had Meyerhold left Komissarzhevskaya's theatre, however, when he was employed as a director in St. Petersburg's imperial theatres, veritable strongholds of tradition. Here he was to remain from 1908 until 1917. To reassure the patrons, Meyerhold published a statement in which he acknowledged his error in using Komissarzhevskaya's theatre for experiments and promising in the future to confine such work to studios. Although many of his productions were relatively conventional, others clearly were out of the ordinary. One of the most famous was of Molière's *Dom Juan,* presented in 1910 at the Alexandrinsky Theatre, in which he achieved a theatricality that was to be widely imitated. He removed the curtain and footlights and extended the forestage well into the auditorium. Candles and candelabra were used plentifully and the lights were left on in the auditorium through most of the performance. By now much interested in Oriental theatre, Meyerhold borrowed from it the convention of stage attendants and used them to arrange the stage, to carry on and off the needed properties, and to summon the audience with bells at the end of intermissions. A screen was set up on either side of the stage and costumed prompters were stationed there. The actors used balletic movement set to the accompaniment of Lully's music. This lighthearted production was a great favorite with both critics and spectators.

At the imperial theatres, Meyerhold staged both plays and operas. His production of *Tristan and Isolde* in 1909 offered him the occasion to become thoroughly acquainted with the writings of both Wagner and Appia. Fokine did the choreography for some of Meyerhold's operatic productions, and his usual designer for all his work was Golovin, who contributed much to the success of the Ballets Russes. Between 1908 and 1910 Meyerhold also published articles on Max Reinhardt and Gordon Craig, translated a Kabuki play, and staged one of Calderon's *autos*. Thus, his interests and knowledge continued to grow.

Between 1908 and 1917, however, Meyerhold's major experimentation occurred in the studios with which he was associated. When he began this outside activity he was requested by the imperial theatres to adopt a pseudonym, since otherwise he would be violating his contract. Thus, for all of his experimental work in the years between 1910 and 1917 he used the name "Dr. Dappertutto."

Meyerhold's first important studio work was done in 1910–11 at the Interlude House, a theatre which had been converted into a cabaret by linking the stage and auditorium with steps and by replacing the seats with restaurant tables and chairs. His first production here was *Columbine's Scarf*, an adaptation of Arthur Schnitzler's pantomime *The Veil of Pierrette*. It tells how Columbine, who has made a suicide pact with Pierrot, tries to avoid her bargain, but is eventually led by forces beyond her control to return to Pierrot's body and to her own death. Not only did Meyerhold use *commedia* figures and techniques, he combined them with elements of grotesque, which to him was not only a kind of exaggerated parody but an approach through which "the audience is continually led from the plane that it has guessed to another one that it does not expect." The whole production seemed to be controlled by the insistent rhythms of an orchestra, the leader of which fled through the auditorium when Columbine committed suicide as though acknowledging his own responsibility for her act. In many of his productions at Interlude House, Meyerhold sought to involve the audience in the action and scenes and dances were often staged among the tables.

From 1913 to 1917, Meyerhold controlled his own studio, where he experimented and published a journal, *The Love for Three Oranges*. Here he explored patterned movement based on squares, circles, rectangles, and other shapes; had his students improvise pantomimes to various musical rhythms; sought to utilize devices borrowed from the folk theatres of Japan, China, Spain, Italy, and France; experimented with completely nonrepresentational settings of the type he was to develop after the Revolution as "machines for acting"; and introduced uniform clothing for the actors. This list could be extended almost indefinitely but is sufficient to indicate Meyerhold's restless and persistent search for new and more expressive means. Without doubt he was the most dedicated experimenter in the Russian theatre between 1900 and 1917.

Although Meyerhold often reiterated that he was seeking to free the
actor from realism, his was essentially a director's theatre. He was not concerned with transposing a playwright's work faithfully to the stage. Rather,

he maintained the right of the director to use a script as material in his
own creative act, just as a painter might take his inspiration from a biblical
story. His creative urge led him both to seek new means and to explore the
limits of old ones. Scarcely an element escaped his attention. He borrowed
from older forms, other cultures, and contemporary sources; he experimented with the possibilities of movement and speech, with spatial relationships both on the stage and between actor and performer; he wished
to make the theatre more democratic and to involve the audience in the
creative act. His search was to continue and intensify after the Revolution.

Theodore Komissarzhevsky (1882–1954) grew up around the theatre
(his father was an opera star) and had studied architecture before becoming
scenic director for his sister's theatre at about the same time that Meyerhold
began his work there. He soon came into conflict with Meyerhold, who he
felt insisted upon fitting actors into scenery instead of fitting scenery to the
actors. When Meyerhold resigned, Komissarzhevsky became artistic director
of the theatre and shared directorial duties with Nikolai Evreinov and A.
Zonov, a former assistant to Meyerhold. But the theatre was unable to
survive a series of financial setbacks and was closed in 1909. Komissarzhevskaya then went on tour hoping to recover her fortunes and reopen her
theatre, but in 1910 she contracted smallpox and died.

Between 1910 and 1919 (when he emigrated to the West), Komissarzhevsky was involved in numerous theatrical endeavors: as director of the
Free School of Scenic Art from 1910 to 1919; as director with Evreinov
of the Gay Theatre in 1910–11; as resident director of the Moscow
Nezlobin Dramatic Theatre from 1910 to 1913; as director at the Maly
and Bolshoi theatres in Moscow, 1913–14; as artistic director of the Moscow
Opera House, 1914–19; as director of the Vera Komissarzhevskaya Memo-
rial Theatre, 1914–18; and as managing director and producer of the
Bolshoi Ballet and Opera, 1918–19. During his last year in Russia,
Komissarzhevsky was running four theatres and a school.

Like Meyerhold, Komissarzhevsky was opposed to realism and was
deeply interested in *commedia dell' arte* and in reinterpreting the classics.
But he disapproved of Meyerhold's subordination of the actor to the visual
elements just as he did of Stanislavsky's emphasis on realistic detail. He
believed that the director should leave the actor as free as possible, assist
him in finding the proper line of action (even work around inadequate or
incalcitrant actors if necessary), but always avoid dictating to him.

Above all he thought the director should serve the author. He declared
it necessary to study not only the script but all of an author's work and
outlook. Since each author differs from all others, so must the director's
approach differ with each. Consequently, Komissarzhevsky was the most
eclectic of Russian directors.

His eclecticism extended further than that of Reinhardt, however, for he adopted a working method best described as "internal eclecticism." Rather than choosing a historical period or single style for a play and then staying consistently within it, Komissarzhevsky believed that each character and action has its own qualities for which the director must find some meaningful visual metaphor that will set up the right associations for contemporary audiences. Thus, his productions often combined elements from many periods and styles, all artfully blended through Komissarzhevsky's impeccable taste.

Similarly, Komissarzhevsky recognized no fundamental differences among drama, ballet, and opera, and considered the best theatre to be a synthesis of the three. His students were trained in all these forms in order to create a "universal actor." His productions were always heavily influenced by music, for in each scene and character he sought an appropriate rhythm and tempo and he orchestrated speech, pause, gesture, movement, and lighting like a musical score to create strong moods and emotionally charged dramatic action.

Komissarzhevsky directed works from an extremely wide range of periods and forms. Gorchakov has called him "the most profound thinker of all the pre-Revolutionary innovators." His influence can be seen almost everywhere, especially in the work of Tairov and Vakhtangov.

For a time Komissarzhevsky shared directorial duties at his sister's theatre with Nikolai Evreinov (1879–1953) and later the two ran a theatre together. But Evreinov's major significance probably lies more in his theoretical views than in his practice. His basic outlook was set forth in a famous essay, "Apology for Theatricality," published in 1908. He argued that there is an innate human instinct for transformation which makes each person wish to become someone other than himself and to transform life into something more interesting and desirable. This theatrical instinct takes precedence over all esthetic concerns. "To make a theatre of life is the duty of every artist. . . . The stage must not borrow so much from life as life borrows from the stage." Through highly controlled acting, masks, nonrealistic scenery and lighting, the stage should show a life worth living to the fullest.

Sometimes Evreinov spoke of the theatre as therapeutic. In a passage that might have been written by Antonin Artaud, Evreinov declares that the theatre is "as it were a purgatory to which the soul is taken. . . . Acting gives a way out to the elemental forces of nature that have been hidden in the human soul under the organized structure of culture, the systems of rules in society, and the gloss of decency."

Out of these views he shaped his concept of "monodrama," through which he sought to transport the spectator inside the play as a direct participant by making him see everything from the viewpoint of the protagonist, the spectator's "alter ego." Thus, he made the acting, scenery, lighting, and other elements reflect the emotional state of the protagonist. These theories, set forth in *Monodrama* (1909) and *Theatre for Oneself*

(1915–17), have much in common with those of the German expressionists, while, according to Martin Esslin, one of the monodramas, *The Theatre of the Soul,* is a forerunner of absurdist drama.

Evreinov's concern for the audience led him to declare that the whole nineteenth century and its concern for realism had been erroneous, since it sought to imitate rather than to transform life and to separate audience and stage completely. To return the theatre to its rightful path, Evreinov turned for help to the past. Consequently, he staged two seasons of plays, in 1907–8 and 1911–12, at the "Old" or "Ancient Theatre." The first focused on plays of the Middle Ages and the second on works from the golden age of Spain. With each program he attempted to re-create not only stage conventions but the entire milieu. Audience as well as performers were represented and the relationship between them emphasized. Sometimes an itinerant acting company would be shown arriving, setting up its stage, costuming itself; then the audience would assemble; the play, presented as it would have been in that era (complete with characteristic incidental entertainment), would then be shown; afterward the audience dispersed and the actors packed up their belongings and went away. Evreinov was much interested in *commedia dell' arte,* conducting many experiments in this form in cooperation with K. Miklashevsky, a scholar who later wrote an important study of the form (published in the West as by Constant Mic). Evreinov was concerned above all with visual effect: "Words play but a subordinate role on the stage, and we hear more with the eyes than with the ears." His programs at the Ancient Theatre were great successes. Not only did they arouse interest in the theatre of other times, they served as well to reintroduce many theatrical conventions from the past onto the contemporary stage.

Evreinov was also associated with the cabaret theatres The Crooked Mirror and The Happy Theatre for Grown-up Children. Most of his pieces here were short parodies of those things he disliked in plays, operas, directing, and acting. One famous piece showed various directorial approaches to *The Inspector General,* while his *Vampuka* was both a parody of *Aida* and an attack on the banality of Italian opera in general. His work set the standard in sophisticated revues and sketches for many years.

Evreinov enriched Russian theatrical life in many ways. His theories of transformation opened up inquiries into the nature of the theatre and were especially influential on the Soviets, who turned his ideas in new directions in their own desire to transform society.

Amidst all this experimentation, Alexander Tairov (Alexander Jakovlevich Kornblit, 1885–1950) managed to find a niche all his own. In 1905 he abandoned his legal studies to enter the theatre and later that year joined Komissarzhevskaya's company, where he appeared in Meyerhold's productions. He left the troupe after becoming disillusioned with Meyerhold's tendency to subordinate the actor's creativity to his directorial image. For several years he led an itinerant existence as actor and director working in both realistic and stylized modes. In 1913 he was on the verge of giving up the theatre when he at last found an approach that seemed sound. At this time he also met and married Alice Koonen, who was to be the leading lady in his productions thereafter. In 1914 he opened the Kamerny (or Chamber) Theatre, which he was to run until 1949. By the time of the Revolution he had staged fourteen works of widely varying types.

Tairov believed that the theatre must remain free of all tendentiousness, for he considered it a completely autonomous activity, something roughly analogous to the sacred dances of an ancient temple. For him, the theatre merely serves to create and project imaginary emotions and inner images in satisfying esthetic form.

Tairov placed primary emphasis upon emotion-charged gesture, which he declared to be the true art of the theatre. He considered the actor the major creative artist in the theatre and sought performers who could dance, sing, speak, and improvise. To him the finest theatre would be that based on a scenario worked out collectively by the actors and filled out improvisationally by them in performance. He thought a poet should be required only for exceptional moments and that he should work directly with the performers. Thus, Tairov did not envision the theatre as a purveyor of literary works. But, since he had not yet perfected ideal actors, he considered it necessary to use already existing materials, but to reshape them as needed.

Tairov thought it the director's function to create the proper atmosphere for the actors' improvisations. According to him, a setting should resemble architecture rather than painting, for it must be three-dimensional if it is to be completely functional for movement. It need not resemble anything in real life but must be artistically appropriate to the specific play and provide "a keyboard for acting." Most of his sets were composed of steps, levels, and "sculptural" elements which seemed constantly to change appearance under skillfully manipulated lighting. To assist him, he employed some of the finest designers of his day, among them Natalie Goncharova, Alexander Yakovlev, and Alexandra Ekster.

Tairov considered music the purest art and he sought to make his productions approximate it by rhythmically fusing all the elements. A musical score was composed especially for each production. Dialogue was intoned and movement tended toward dance, since it was choreographed to be expressive and flowing. His was an antiliterary theatre which aimed to create a sense of deeply experienced beauty; it was smooth, polished, refined, and sensual.

The Kamerny opened in 1914 with a production of the Sanskrit drama *Shakuntala,* which Tairov had transformed into something like an opera-ballet. The brilliant compositions (sometimes pictorial, sometimes sculptural), the half-naked bodies, the processions, pantomimes, and subtle rhythms were greatly admired. Perhaps Tairov's most famous production in this period was *Famira Kifared* by Innokenty Annensky, a contemporary symbolist poet and classical scholar. For this treatment of a Greek mytholog-

Tairov's production of *Famira Kifared* by the symbolist poet Annensky at the Kamerny Theatre in 1914. The cubist designs for setting and costumes were by Alexandra Ekster. (From *The Art of the Kamerny Theatre, 1914–1934*, Moscow, 1935.)

ical theme, Tairov built his production around the clash between the Dionysian and Apollonian—the ecstatic and the calm—and two distinctive rhythms dominated all the elements. The cubist landscape designed by Alexandra Ekster was divided into two parts: the upper (or Apollonian-tragic) and the lower (or Dionysian-antic). Under the elaborate lighting, the sculptural forms of the setting and the painted half-nude bodies of the actors seemed in constant motion. Every part of the setting was employed, as satyrs wriggled along the broad steps or climbed into the cypress trees. As in all his productions, Tairov executed every detail faultlessly. Although he was sometimes accused of formalism, aestheticism, and antiintellectualism, no one ever suggested that he was amateurish.

~ **VI** ~

Thus, between 1900 and 1917 the Russian theatre was almost completely transformed. No longer backward, it was now one of the most experimental and fruitful theatres in the world. Its enormous range probably exceeded that of any nation at the time. Here can be found the seeds of developments still not fully realized and often considered of much more recent origin.

Despite its fruitfulness, the Russian theatre, with the exception of the Moscow Art Theatre and the Ballets Russes, was scarcely known in the West at this time. After World War I, the Russian theatre was to exert considerable impact in the West, but its prerevolutionary developments long remained little known and little appreciated.

New Modes of Perception: Expressionism, Futurism, Dadaism and Surrealism

9

The years between 1910 and 1925 were ones of violent contrasts. On the one hand an extreme chauvinism resulted in global war, while on the other the rejection of national policies led to civil wars and to skepticism about the civilization that had created such catastrophes. With questioning came the conviction that existing perceptions were mistaken, or overly restricted, and that the nature of truth and the modes of perceiving it should be reexamined. As a result, few eras have witnessed the launching of so many artistic movements, of which even the names of some—such as Orphism, rayonnism, and suprematism—are now unfamiliar. But others, among them cubism, expressionism, futurism, dadaism, and surrealism, not only won widespread acceptance but set in motion forces still being felt. On the surface, the diverse movements may seem to be distinct, at times even in conflict, but they were united in their skepticism about the past and in their attempts to redefine modes of perception and expression. They constitute the third wave—of which realism-naturalism and symbolism were the first two—of that experimentation in theatre and drama that had begun in the nineteenth century.

~~~ I ~~~

A common denominator among most of the movements which sprang up between 1910 and 1925 was skepticism about earlier modes of perception. Realism and naturalism had been based upon the assumption that reality can be discovered through the systematic application of scientific method to objective phenomena. The consequent tendency to ignore subjective elements led to an oversimplified view. On the other hand, the symbolists, aesthetes and neoromantics had sought truth in such vague abstractions as mystery, fate, beauty, and the ideal. Thus the realist-naturalist outlook came to seem overly materialistic and the symbolist view overly abstract. Both placed ultimate reality outside of man.

The subsequent movements were as deeply concerned about truth and reality as were their predecessors, but, finding the old definitions inadequate, they sought new ones. They were not antiscientific; rather they attempted to incorporate scientific discoveries into a more comprehensive vision of reality. That their versions of truth would eventually prove as ephemeral as those they replaced was inevitable.

Many of the new movements placed considerable emphasis upon the subconscious, perhaps because Freud's theories provided a semiscientific explanation for forces which the symbolists had relegated to the realm of fate, mystery, or the supernatural. Through the subconscious, the subjective and the objective worlds could be brought into a logical relationship which synthesized the views of both the realist-naturalists and the symbolists.

Freud's theories were given new dimensions by Carl Jung (1875–1961). At first a friend and disciple of Freud, Jung later concluded that Freud's conceptions were inadequate and, beginning in *Psychology of the Unconscious* (1912), he suggested several important changes. Jung argued that Freud's description of the mind's structure is incomplete, for to its three divisions should be added a fourth, the "racial unconscious." He posited that the human brain has acquired its particular structure in part through the necessity of dealing, generation after generation, with certain basic patterns of experience, and that, because of this structure, the brain responds more quickly to some stimuli (those Jung labels archetypal) than

266

*New Modes
of
Perception:
Expressionism,
Futurism,
Dadaism and
Surrealism*

to others. The racial unconscious is "nothing but a possibility...which from primordial time has been handed down to us in the definite form of mnemic images, or expressed in anatomical formations in the very structure of the brain. It does not yield innate ideas, but inborn possibilities of ideas." It incorporates "the psychic residua of numberless experiences of the same type." Jung declares that the racial unconscious is outside the reach of psychoanalysis, for "by no analytical technique can it be brought to conscious recollection, being neither repressed nor forgotten." Thus, Jung pushed the conception of the unconscious one step further than did Freud (who understandably accused Jung of passing over into mysticism) and suggests an explanation for psychological responses not accounted for by Freud.

Jung also objected to Freud's restriction of basic urges to sexuality and aggression and declared that additional drives are embedded in the racial experience. Furthermore, he disagreed with Freud's conception of symbols (for example, a knife for the male sexual organ). "The true symbol differs essentially from [a mere sign or symptom], and should be understood as the expression of an intuitive perception which can as yet neither be better apprehended nor expressed differently." For Jung, a symbol is not merely the substitution of one thing for another (for then it could easily be fully translated), but is the most direct expression possible. As does his conception of the racial unconscious, Jung's definition of symbol allies him with the nonrealists of the late nineteenth century.

Jung went on the declare that there are two basic kinds of art: that based on the personal unconscious and that based on the racial unconscious. Since the first is limited by the author's personal vision, the second is more significant since it captures (through archetype, myth, and symbol) experiences embedded in the racial unconscious. "The moment when the mythological situation appears is always characterized by a peculiar emotional intensity; it is as though chords in us were touched that had never resounded before, or as though forces were unloosed the very existence of which we had never even dreamed. . . . At such moments we are no longer individuals but the race." He further hypothesized that the most satisfying art in each age is that which reaches back into the racial unconscious to find those archetypes best suited to compensate for what is missing in the present.

Jung also was interested in primitive man (his social structures, mythology, and art) as a key to understanding the racial unconscious. His theories in turn helped to stimulate the interest—then just beginning—in African sculpture and other "primitive" art, which previously had been ignored or discounted but which thereafter would exert strong influence on Western art forms.

Jung's ideas about myth, symbol, and archetype were reenforced by those then being championed by cultural anthropologists. The scientific revolution of the nineteenth century gave rise to several new disciplines, among them anthropology, one branch of which was especially concerned with the cultural patterns of past societies. Out of this interest came J. G. Frazer's monumental *The Golden Bough,* a comparative study of myth and religion. In turn, his work was extended during the early twentieth century by the "Cambridge school" of classical anthropologists, who focused their study on Greece and Rome. Jane Ellen Harrison published studies on art and religion, F. M. Cornford on the ritual origins of comedy, Gilbert Murray on the ritual bases of tragedy, and A. B. Cook on the god-king as a ritual figure. This group, following in somewhat the same track as Nietzsche, promoted the idea that all art and drama originated in ritual and that myth is merely the residue of rite (that is, that myths are stories that grew up around rites, either to explain or to mask them, and that they survived the rites they accompanied). They sought to perceive patterns shared in common by myths and secular art forms and to reconstruct the rituals which lay behind the myths. They were to be extremely influential on later attempts to perceive ritualistic elements in all significant art.

The work of Nietzsche, Jung, and the classical anthropologists combined to promote interest in ritual, myth, and archetype as revelations of values more elemental than those of modern life. Not only did they offer support to the "community drama" movement of the early twentieth century, they argued forcefully for a reality that is more complex than surface appearance suggests. Therefore, they added new dimensions to the unconscious as conceived by Freud.

New developments in physics were to be even more far-reaching, since they were to permeate twentieth-century thought more fully. Beginning in 1905, Albert Einstein (1879–1955) published a number of articles and books in which he sought to amend Newtonian physics, in which physical laws were stated in terms of a fixed point of reference. Although his theory of relativity can only be fully explained through mathematical formulas and has probably never been consciously applied by artists and writers, it must be examined in broad outline since it constitutes the most revolutionary and precise statement of those perceptions of time and space that have influenced twentieth-century science and art.

Einstein sought to formulate a theory which would incorporate both spatial and temporal dimensions. Newtonian physics had depicted space as static and absolute because both time and point of view were treated as fixed; with Einstein space came to be seen as relative to a moving point of reference. Thus, to the three spatial dimensions he added the fourth dimension of time (in the form of movement). The faster the movement, the greater are the changes in perceived dimensions both of time and space.

Perhaps the most readily understandable examples of relativity are those involving astronomical phenomena. For instance, an observer on earth might see as simultaneous the events immediately around him and an explosion in space, even though in actuality the explosion may have occurred more than a century ago and the light rays from it only now be reaching this planet. But though Einstein saw mass, length, time, and simultaneity as relative, he never doubted the orderliness of the universe and he sought formulas that would harmonize the variables. Less scientifically oriented minds, however, were more aware of relativity itself (whether of eye-point or inner perception) and elevated it to a principle under which all perception is considered to be purely subjective. For many, the possibility of firm truth had vanished forever.

The changed conceptions of time and space were soon evident in artistic forms, especially in organizational patterns. For example, in painting, space had, since the Renaissance, been conceived as fixed, and objects had been depicted as viewed from a single eye-point at a specific instant in time. In fact, the entire logic of perspective painting was based on this convention, which was grounded in Newtonian physics. The first major break with tradition came in the late nineteenth century when Paul Cézanne began to include in one painting objects that could only be seen from different eye-points. But it was cubism (usually said to have begun in 1907 and to have reached its height just prior to World War I) that first systematically introduced into a single painting several points of view, no one of which had more authority than the others. This group of painters, of which Pablo Picasso and Georges Braque were the leading figures, sought to break down objects semigeometrically into cubes, spheres, cylinders, and cones, but also to provide several views of the same object simultaneously. Cubism represents an attempt to deal analytically with space and to incorporate the dimension of time into painting.

Similar innovations can be seen in drama. Whereas painting is essentially a space art, drama is primarily a time art (that is, composed of successive events which can be experienced only as they occur in sequence). Traditionally in drama, time has been treated as linear (events occur in orderly sequence from beginning to middle to end) rather than as simultaneous or random. Just as fixed space governed most painting, so the orderly sequence of time governed most drama. Consequently, most plays were unified through a cause-and-effect arrangement of incidents. Using this approach, the playwright sets up in the opening scenes all of the necessary conditions—the situation, the desires and motivations of the characters—out of which the later events develop. The story makes sense because of the sequential and causal relationship of events. Less often, dramatists had used thought to unify otherwise seemingly random incidents (as in Aristophanes' comedies and medieval morality plays). Here it was the logic of thesis and supporting evidence which related the incidents to one another.

It is a variation on the latter method that practically all nonrealistic dramatists have adopted, for most have organized their works around some central idea or motif. But the specific form that the organization takes depends in large part upon the assumptions made by the playwright about reality. Most dramatists prior to the modern period assumed that this is a logical universe ruled over by a just God. Thus, behind any apparent chaos was the notion of ultimate orderliness and justice. In such a world the logic of cause and effect was fundamental. But with symbolism the world became merely mysterious. In *Pelléas and Mélisande,* the characters are led to the slaughter like sheep but for reasons that are never clear, either to them or to the audience. There is sequence but no causality (that is, one event follows another but is not caused by it).

Pelléas and Mélisande illustrates a characteristic feature of modern art: the juxtaposition of elements whose relationships are left unexplored. The effect is discontinuous—the audience is provided with fragments from which it must assemble a whole and what it perceives depends upon its ability to supply missing connectives. The point can be illustrated with a short poem by Guillaume Apollinaire:

> Three lit gas jets
> The proprietor has lung trouble
> When you're finished we'll have a game of backgammon
> A conductor who has a sore throat
> When you come to Tunis I'll have you smoke some kiff
> It seems to rhyme.

These lines may evoke the experience of sitting in a Parisian cafe, but all the elements are independent, existing side by side. The sequence is unimportant, the connectives missing. Here are many of the qualities often criticized in modern art: abruptness, illogicality, obscurity. Because of these characteristics, many major modern plays would in earlier periods have been considered unfinished, inept, unacceptable. In fact, much that is praised in modern times would earlier have been considered pure amateurishness.

In the years between 1910 and 1925 such techniques as juxtaposition of disparate elements, discontinuity, multiple focus, and unity through theme or motif came into widespread use for the first time. Through these means of expression artists in all fields sought to capture the new modes of perception described in the work of Freud, Einstein, Jung, and others—the world of relativity and of the unconscious.

～ II ～

Of the movements which flourished between 1910 and 1925, the one most intimately connected with the theatre was expressionism, primarily a German phenomenon. "Expressionism" first gained currency in France around 1901 as a label to distinguish the kind of painting done by Van Gogh, Gauguin, and others from the works of the impressionists, who sought to capture the appearance of objects as seen under a certain light at a par-

270

*New Modes
of
Perception:
Expressionism,
Futurism,
Dadaism and
Surrealism*

ticular moment. In contrast, expressionism was thought to emphasize strong inner feelings about objects and to portray life as modified and distorted by the painter's own vision of reality. Thus, in expressionism truth or beauty was said to reside in the mind rather than (with impressionism) in the eye.

Around 1910 or 1911 expressionism as a term was introduced into Germany, where shortly afterward it was picked up by critics and popularized as a label for tendencies already under way both in literature and the visual arts. Since it was applied to almost any work that deviated from traditional modes, it is not surprising that under the banner of expressionism were grouped artists of widely differing outlooks and methods. Most of those who were later called expressionists were not aware of belonging to a movement and many denied having belonged to one.

Still, there were several points upon which most so-called expressionists agreed, for they were involved in a sociophilosophic movement as much as in an esthetic revolution. Most were opposed to realism and naturalism because those movements glorified science, which the expressionists associated with technology and industrialism, major tools of the materialistic society they deplored. They also disliked naturalism's emphasis on external appearance, which they considered an insignificant aspect of reality. On the other hand, the expressionists were equally contemptuous of neoromanticism because of its flight from contemporary social problems. Thus, although they were willing to accept as valid the realist-naturalist concern for modern problems and neoromantic antirealistic techniques, they found both earlier movements unsatisfactory in other respects.

The expressionists believed that fundamental truth is to be found within man—his spirit, his soul, his desires, his visions—and that external reality should be reshaped until it is brought into harmony with these inner attributes so that man's spirit may realize its highest aspirations. Thus, subjective urge was given primacy over objective appearance. As Kasimir Edschmid, a major advocate of expressionism, wrote: "We expressionists do not work as photographers but are overcome by visions. We...are concerned not with descriptions but lived experience. We do not reproduce but create."

That expressionism was not a wholly unified movement may be explained in part by the lack in Germany (unlike most European countries) of a single major artistic center. As a result, expressionists of various types formed themselves into loose groupings in several German cities. In the visual arts, the most important of these groups came to be called *Die Brücke* ("The Bridge") and *Der Blaue Reiter* ("The Blue Rider"). *Die Brücke,* which began in Dresden about 1905, was originally conceived as an international youth movement. Its manifesto (written by Ernst Kirchner in 1906) declared: "We call upon all youth to unite. We who possess the future shall create for ourselves a physical and spiritual freedom opposed to the values of the comfortably established older generation." Before it was dissolved around 1913, *Die Brücke* had become through its exhibitions an

271

*New Modes
of
Perception:
Expressionism,
Futurism,
Dadaism and
Surrealism*

important factor in establishing the reputations of many expressionist painters. *Der Blaue Reiter,* established in Munich in 1911, included artists from many fields, but its primary focus was the visual arts, and it too provided an outlet for new trends. Its leaders stated: "We wish to demonstrate by means of a *variety* of forms that the *inner wish* of the artist can be structured in many different ways." The Blue Rider was dissolved around 1913.

The most important group for literature and drama was that centered around the weekly review *Der Sturm (The Storm)*, founded in Berlin in 1910 by Herwarth Walden (1878–1941). *Der Sturm* rapidly became the leading organ for young writers; in 1912 Walden opened as well a gallery for visual artists, and in 1913 he introduced programs of readings and dramatic performances. As other groups broke up, *Der Sturm* became the most important showcase for expressionist art of all types. Walden's interests were not restricted to expressionism, however, for he also championed cubism and futurism, influences which were assimilated into German expressionism. Walden was to continue his work until 1929.

Although expressionism made its first major impact in the visual arts, it was soon recognized as a significant force in literature as well. Expressionist writing took diverse forms, in part because many authors sought merely to express a mystical grasp of the inner spirit, whereas others sought to transform man and society. Consequently, some historians have divided the expressionists into two basic groups: the mystics and the activists. At times, expressionism seems a variation on romanticism and nowhere more so than in its vision of man struggling to free his spirit from the limitations of material existence. Much of expressionist literature has a messianic tone, for it sought nothing less than the "regeneration of man." Transformation (*Wandlung*) is a key term in expressionist writing, and the creation of the "new man" was its almost universal goal. Since it set itself almost impossible tasks, it is not surprising that expressionism, like earlier movements of romantic extreme and extravagance, ended in disillusionment.

In addition to the messianic, there was often a more negative motif— the need to destroy materialism and all other trappings of the old society. In 1917, Ludwig Rubiner, in a passage that might well have been written in 1970, stated both the destructive and the utopian goals of expressionism: "Life has only moral purpose. . . . We want to bring, for one brief moment, intensity into human life: We want to arouse by means of heart-shaking assaults, terrors, threats, the individual's awareness of his responsibility in the community! . . . We are the scum, the offal, the despised. We are the holy mob. We do not want to work because work is too slow. . . . Progress does not exist for us. We believe in miracles. . . . For us destroyer is a religious concept, inseparable for us today from creator." Here is the activist view at its most extreme, but embedded in it there is as well the vision of a better world to come.

The expressionists were always vague about their specific goals, but

272

*New Modes
of
Perception:
Expressionism,
Futurism,
Dadaism and
Surrealism*

in essence they differed little from present-day utopians: they sought a world free from war, hypocrisy, and hate, where social justice and love would reign, where the artist might express himself without constraint, where the "new man" would be free from materialistic urges and would base his life on humanitarian principles. Such was the expressionist vision.

The drama that sought to embody this vision has a number of characteristic features. First, because it is "message"-centered, most expressionist drama is organized primarily through idea, theme, or motif rather than through a cause-and-effect relationship among incidents. The action in many plays takes the form of a search, pilgrimage, or "stations" on the road to martyrdom. Second, the central character, most often a Christ-like figure, is usually sacrificed to the materialism, hypocrisy, or callousness of the other characters, who epitomize various social attitudes and human types. Since the protagonist is often the only character to appear throughout the play, he may serve as a unifying element second only to thought. Furthermore, the events of the drama are sometimes given a strongly subjective bent because they are seen through the eyes of this central figure. Third, the dramatists typically seek to reduce each element to its essentials. Consequently, plots may be mere demonstrations of a thesis or argument, and characters entirely generic (the Husband, the Son, the Soldier, the Prostitute, the Minister, and so on). Dialogue is frequently reduced to one- or two-word sentences (the "telegraphic" style), and gesture and pantomime are usually chosen for their ability to evoke through succinctness some intense feeling. Fourth, distortion is evident in every element. Often events are bizarre (corpses rise from their graves, a man carries his head in a sack, groups of identical characters appear in unlikely places) in order to illuminate some point in the play's argument. Distortion is especially evident in the visual elements. Walls may lean inward to suggest oppression; trees may change into skeletons as precursors of death; characters may move mechanically to indicate dehumanization; color, shape, and size of objects may be distorted to emphasize departures from everyday reality. Light is often used to arouse a strong sense of mood, to give unusual coloration or to isolate characters in a void. Fifth, sharp contrasts are omnipresent. Dialogue often alternates between poetry and prose, idyllic passages and obscenities, telegraphic speeches and lengthy monologues. Realistic scenes may fade into "dream visions" and brutality into transcendental apotheoses. Sixth, the works are permeated with a sense of dreamlike fantasy and magic, sometimes ecstatic, sometimes frightening. Seventh, the overall impression is one of allegory clothed in nightmare or vision.

The influences on expressionist drama were numerous. They include the doctrine of democratic love and the free verse forms of Walt Whitman, the writings of Freud and Jung on the unconscious mind, and the dramas of Kleist, Grabbe, and Büchner. Another pervasive influence was Goethe's *Faust, Part II* with its dramatization of the search for spiritual fulfillment. (Long considered unstageable, it was given its first full-scale production in

273

*New Modes
of
Perception:
Expressionism,
Futurism,
Dadaism and
Surrealism*

1911 by Reinhardt.) In fact, some critics have labeled the entire expressionist outlook Faustian. But the most immediate influences were probably the dramas of Wedekind (a cycle of whose plays were staged by Reinhardt in 1911) and above all those of Strindberg, especially *To Damascus* and *A Dream Play*. By 1906, about thirty of Strindberg's plays were available in German translations, and Reinhardt alone staged seventeen of them. Between 1913 and 1915, more than one thousand performances of Strindberg's plays were given in Germany.

Although some critics call Wedekind and Strindberg the first of the expressionist playwrights, others grant that position to Oskar Kokoschka (1886–   ) because of two short works, *Sphinx and Strawman* and *Murderer the Women's Hope*, both written in 1907. The first of these has as characters Mr. Firdusi (a gigantic, revolving straw head with arms and legs), Mr. Rubberman (a contortionist), Female Soul, Death, Parrot, and several gentlemen. It translates inner states into visual images. For example, Firdusi is an intellectual, poet, and idealist (all head, a man of straw) who is eventually destroyed by his wife's infidelity. Overall, the play is concerned with the destructive relationships of men and women and the struggle between passion and spirit; it ends in moral chaos. As Death says: "A good strong faith is like blindness. It covers over unpleasant things, but those things never disappear." It was first staged by students at the Vienna School of Arts and Crafts in 1907, and later was enlarged into *Job* (1917). Similarly, *Murderer the Women's Hope* (which has as characters Man, Woman, and a Chorus of Men and Women) gives a savage view of the relationship between the sexes. But it is perhaps most remarkable for its extensive use of atmospheric lighting. It was first performed in Vienna in 1908 as part of an art exhibit.

Other critics have located the beginning of expressionist drama in the work of Carl Sternheim (1878–1942), certainly more important as a writer than Kokoschka, although his plays resemble the later expressionistic works primarily in their condemnation of bourgeois society and in their telegraphic dialogue. Sternheim seems to have taken over Wedekind's penchant for caricature and parody and to have developed it into a unified method. Most of Sternheim's plays present harshly satirical portraits of middle-class characters. (Eight of his comedies were published in 1922 under the collective title *Scenes from the Heroic Life of the Middle Classes*.) His best-known works are the plays of a trilogy which trace the fortunes of a single family (significantly named Maske). In the first play, *The Underpants* (1909), the wife of the petty clerk Maske loses her underpants in the street and acquires two would-be suitors as a result. They take lodgings in her home, and the opportunistic Maske welcomes the added income, for it permits him to improve his financial position and to start a family. Christian, the son born from this decision, becomes the millionaire hero of the next two plays, *The Snob* (1913) and *1913* (1914). In the former, Christian is able to marry the daughter of a count after being coached by his mistress, send-

274

*New Modes
of
Perception:
Expressionism,
Futurism,
Dadaism and
Surrealism*

ing his family out of the country, and passing himself off as the illegitimate son of a nobleman. When he succeeds, he deserts his mistress and pays his parents to stay out of the way. In *1913,* Christian struggles to thwart his daughter's plan to sell arms to the Dutch government. When all else fails, he joins the Catholic church, thus alienating the Dutch Protestants and canceling the negotiations. Like his expressionist contemporaries, Sternheim saw man as the barren and soulless victim of materialistic society. Also like them, he created characters who are little more than generic types and employed short, staccato dialogue resembling the expressionists' "telegraphic" style. But here Sternheim's affinity with expressionism ends. He can more rightly be considered a precursor than a member of the movement.

It was not until 1912 that the first true expressionist play—*The Beggar* by Reinhard Johannes Sorge (1892–1916)—was published. *The Beggar,* subtitled "a dramatic mission," was to be characteristic of the early phase (that is, up to about 1915) of expressionist drama, during which the primary emphasis was on the conflict between the older and younger generations and between established conventions and new values as seen from a highly subjective point of view. The central character of *The Beggar* is the Poet. The first act shows his failure to gain a hearing for his visionary plays. The second act shifts the focus to the struggle between the Poet and his Father, who in his obsession with machines represents the older generation's faith in science and technology. The Father, characterized as mad, is deliberately poisoned by the Poet, who also inadvertently kills his mother. In the final part of the play, the Poet finds release from despair through the Girl. Now free to devote himself to his art, he is overcome by ecstatic visions: "O consolation of lightning. . . . Illumination. . . . The lightning's consolation of pain. . . . SYMBOLS OF ETERNITY. . . . End! End! Aim and End!" With its emphasis upon the tortured visionary hero, Sorge's play, which won the newly established Kleist Prize, captured the imaginations of other young writers and became an inspiration for them. Like Sorge's, their works tended to focus on the struggle of the "new man," who (like the misunderstood genius of romantic drama a century earlier) longs for fulfillment despite the obstacles thrown up by the materialistic, hypocritical society which surrounds him.

The family relationship developed in Sorge's play is also treated in a drama by Walter Hasenclever (1890–1940), *The Son* (1914), in which the protagonist threatens to kill his father (who as a result dies of a stroke) because his freedom to experience life in all its glory is restricted by his puritanical and hypocritical parents. On the surface the events seem an extension of adolescent fantasies, but Hasenclever no doubt intended them to serve as a symbolic statement about the need to rid the world of those old values and social forms that stand in the way of the "new man."

With the coming of World War I, expressionism began to change, for the global conflict seemed to epitomize the results of those mistaken values and outmoded social forms against which its adherents had long

A post-World War II production of Hasenclever's *The Son,*
directed by Hans Schalla at the Schauspielhaus, Dusseldorf.
(Photo by Liselotte Strelow.)

been in revolt. A few expressionists supported their country and many
served in the army. A number (including Sorge) died in battle. Near the
end of 1914 several leading expressionists met in Weimar to discuss their
attitude toward the war, and thereafter their opposition to it increased.
Some fled to Switzerland to avoid direct involvement in the conflict and
to have greater freedom in opposing it. (In Zurich, several expressionists
became involved in the dadaist movement.) Many of those who remained
in Germany suffered deep psychological trauma. As a result of all these
experiences, dramatists increasingly abandoned personal concerns in favor
of warnings of impending universal catastrophe or of pleas for the reforma-
tion of man and society.

The direction of change can be seen in the plays of Hasenclever, who
after the subjective *The Son* turned to universal moral and political problems. One of his most outspoken antiwar plays is *Antigone* (1916), which,
according to Hasenclever, he wrote to "protest war and violence by clothing it in ancient garments. . . . The tragedy becomes a battle-cry against
the principle of power, manifested in Kreon and his followers. The
sacrificial death of Antigone signifies the triumph of ideas and at the same
time the redemption of a defenseless, misguided people." Hasenclever's play
begins with a herald proclaiming the end of an imperialistic war and the
safety of the city. But the people are still required by Kreon to give up
everything, including basic necessities, for the good of the state. ("Only
the strong will conquer the world.") When the people cry out for food,
Kreon's police beat them, and when Antigone champions their cause,
horsemen run down the citizens and drag away Antigone. So great is
Kreon's commitment to order that he instructs the commander of his troops

276

New Modes
of
Perception:
Expressionism,
Futurism,
Dadaism and
Surrealism

to burn the city if he should give the signal. When the play ends, Kreon has sacrificed everything: his family is dead, the city has been destroyed, the people are reduced to madness. Hasenclever's stage directions read: "Light in the arena. Corpses piled up. Bloody men with open wounds. Women, men with knives in their chests. Insane bleating. Multilated arms and legs. Children stumble about among the bodies." But Hasenclever does not permit the play to end on a wholly negative note, for as the mob storms the palace they are stopped by a Voice from the Grave: "People, fall to your knees. God has restored order." Kreon's dictatorial power has been destroyed, Antigone's regenerative love can now flourish. The message is clear: love is the only true path to happiness, but it cannot be effective until unjust and autocratic rulers are overthrown.

In *Humanity* (1918), Hasenclever extends his indictment to include not only misguided rulers but mankind in general. Most of the play's scenes illustrate the materialism, callousness, and degradation of society. Hasenclever seems to suggest that man is responsible for the world's ills and that his regeneration is the prerequisite for a regenerated society. *Humanity* also utilizes many characteristic expressionistic devices in their most extreme form. At the beginning of the play, the hero rises from his grave and is handed his head in a sack. Later the head is used as evidence against him when he is accused, tried, and condemned as his own murderer. The action takes place largely through pantomime, supplemented by dialogue reduced to one- and two-word sentences. Scenes are brief, shifting in rapid, dream-like fashion and lasting only long enough to make a point. Here everything is reduced to absolute essentials. (The five acts take up only about thirty pages in print.)

The outlook of Fritz von Unruh (1885–1970) seems to have undergone an even more drastic change, In his prewar plays, especially *Louis Ferdinand, Prince of Prussia,* von Unruh upholds militarism and the necessity of obedience to authority, but after serving in the army he had by late 1914 begun to denounce war. His *One Race (Ein Geschlecht,* published in 1918), one of the most powerful antiwar plays of the time, was written at the front and dedicated to his dead brother. The German title of von Unruh's play suggests several levels of meaning, for not only does it imply one race (or mankind), it also means a generation or a family, all of which are intended, for the play centers around the members of a family who not only represent von Unruh's generation but all mankind. The family is composed of three sons, a daughter, and a mother (significantly an authoritarian father figure is missing). Two of the sons are sentenced to death by the army, one for rape, the other for cowardice. The daughter refuses to give birth to children in such a world. The mother, who is extremely proud of her ancestry, is at first a firm supporter of the war, but eventually, having been made by her children to see the results of her misguided values, she snatches the staff from an army officer as an act of rebellion. At the end the only hope resides in the Youngest Son, who incites his comrades to storm "the barracks of violence." But like many expressionists, von Unruh after the war became disillusioned, as can clearly be seen in his sequel to *One Race, Place* (1920), in which the Youngest Son fails in his attempt to found an ideal society based on love; only in his personal life is he able to attain a measure of success.

In November 1918, widespread revolution in Germany overthrew the government and brought an end to the war. In some cities, communes were set up. In the attempts to establish new forms of government, expressionists played a major role. For a time it seemed that the expressionists' vision of a transformed society might be achieved, but the communes were soon suppressed. Furthermore, the harshness of the Versailles treaty (and the resultant economic hardship within the newly created German Republic) led to bitterness and a growing suspicion that mankind is beyond redemption.

Expressionism seems to have reached its peak in 1919. For example, in 1917 ten German-language expressionist periodicals were being published; in 1919 the number increased to forty-four; but by 1922 only eight were left. By 1924, expressionism had ceased to be a major force in German life. Nowhere is the movement from optimism to pessimism more evident than in the work of the two major expressionist playwrights, Kaiser and Toller.

Georg Kaiser (1878–1945), who has been called the finest German dramatist between Hauptmann and Brecht, was the first German playwright to win acceptance abroad after the war. (Anti-German sentiments in large measure explain why expressionism remained essentially a German movement.) Kaiser was undoubtedly the most rigorous thinker among the expressionists. He once declared, "Writing a drama means: thinking a thought through to its conclusion," and the dialectical approach suggested by this statement is always evident in his plays. Kaiser rejected the naturalists' belief in heredity and environment as the determinants of man's actions, just as he did the symbolists' belief in the role of a mysterious fate. Rather, he declared that man has freedom to choose and that he can regenerate himself if he can free himself from the weight of politics and materialism. Thus, most of Kaiser's mature works are dialectical demonstrations showing the awakening of the human will to act or attempts to overcome mechanizing and dehumanizing forces.

Kaiser wrote over sixty plays of various types and styles. His earliest works, *The Jewish Widow* (1911) and *King Cuckold* (1913), are satiric travesties of legendary subjects, the former of Judith and Holofernes, the latter of Tristan and Isolde. But it is upon his expressionistic works that Kaiser's fame rests. He first won wide critical acclaim with *The Burghers of Calais* (1912), based on a fourteenth-century story about six burghers who seek to save Calais from destruction by offering themselves as sacrifices to the English besiegers. Opposed to the war party who advocate fighting to the last man, Eustache de Saint-Pierre, Kaiser's "new man," commits

278

*New Modes
of
Perception:
Expressionism,
Futurism,
Dadaism and
Surrealism*

suicide in order to convince his fellow townsmen that it is more important to save the citizens than to uphold military honor.

Today Kaiser is remembered primarily for *From Morn to Midnight* (written in 1912) and the trilogy composed of *The Coral* (1917), *Gas I* (1918), and *Gas II* (1920). In *From Morn to Midnight*, it is the Cashier's pilgrimage or search that unifies the play. In the opening scene he is little more than an automaton, taking in and paying out money in a bank. Then he is jarred out of this daily routine by the appearance of the exotic, sensual Lady from Italy. Desiring her, he knows of only one path to fulfillment— through money—and so he stuffs his pockets and follows her. But when she turns out to be unattainable he is faced with a crisis: unable to go back and unfitted by his past to be anything more than a cog in the vast social machine, he determines to seek some deeper meaning in life than he has previously known. The remainder of the play is devoted to his search, which leads him through the family, social norms, sensuality, and religion. Finally, at a Salvation Army meeting, he comes to recognize that the road to fulfillment lies through the soul, but when he flings away his stolen money the supposedly repentant sinners fight like animals over it and the Salvation Lass, in whom he had perceived his soul mate, betrays him for the reward. Thus, even religion has succumbed to the materialistic urge. When officers come to seize him, the Cashier shoots himself and dies stretched out as if crucified. As with Christ, the world is not yet ready for the Cashier's message, but it has at least been shown the way.

From Morn to Midnight is a modern morality play, for, as the title suggests, it uses a day to symbolize the period of man's life, during which the Cashier-Everyman moves through the principal types of human experience. Because he is concerned with essences, Kaiser reduces the characters to generic types (or, to show the mechanization of life, merely to numerical designations) and archetypal situations. The action takes place in a dreamlike atmosphere where through distortion and condensation everything is charged with strangeness. Kaiser's message is summed up in the final line of the play (spoken by the Policeman when the lights go out), "There must be a short circuit in the main," which, though ostensibly referring to electricity, is a comment on a society which has short-circuited man's desire for spiritual fulfillment.

The Coral also treats a protagonist who gradually acknowledges the primacy of the soul. This time the hero is the Billionaire, who, after a childhood of misery and deprivation, has attained security as a man of enormous wealth. But his children, in whom all his hopes for the future reside, reject him because he has won his position by preying on the poor. Recognizing his error, he seeks to disrupt the materialistic forces with which he is surrounded. Like *From Morn to Midnight*, *The Coral* depicts the emergence of regenerated man. *Gas I* extends the concern to regenerated society. Here the protagonist is the Billionaire's Son, who, having inherited his father's industrial empire, enters into cooperative ownership with his workers of a plant whose principal product is gas, the very essence of industrialization. Consequently, when an explosion destroys the plant, the Billionaire's Son decides not to rebuild it but to lead his workers back to a simpler, more fulfilling life. But the Engineer, the spokesman for industrialization, is able to rally the workers behind him and during the ensuing riot the Billionaire's Son is killed. Like his father, he has had a vision of a regenerated world, and as he dies his daughter promises to carry on his fight.

Gas II centers around the Billionaire-Worker, to whom the daughter has given birth. But now Kaiser seems to have lost all hope of reclaiming man or society. In *Gas II* all industry has been placed under the control of the state and is more highly developed than ever before. Man has become a mere automaton in the service of a political machine. The Billionaire-Worker at first seeks to stop production of a deadly gas which is being made for use in war, but, when he sees that his efforts are hopeless, he hurls a bomb, thus setting off a series of cataclysmic explosions, which we are led to believe will destroy the entire human race. The final stage directions read: "In the mist-grey distance, sheaves of flaming bombs bursting together —vivid in self-extermination." Thus ended Kaiser's vision of regenerated man.

Thereafter Kaiser not only abandoned the expressionistic outlook but most of its techniques as well. In 1933 his plays were banned in Nazi Germany and in 1938 he fled to Switzerland. The most interesting of his later works is *The Raft of Medusa* (1943), which recalls his earlier outlook though not its techniques. It tells of a group of English children adrift on a raft after their boat has been sunk by a German submarine during World War II. When they throw overboard the smallest and weakest child because he takes up needed space and food, Allan, one of the older children, is so incensed that when a rescue plane arrives he refuses to return to a civilization so lacking in human values. Left alone on the raft, he is strafed by a German airplane and dies. Like Kaiser's earlier protagonists, Allan is a martyr to man's inhumanity, but Kaiser now holds out no hope for change.

The plays of Ernst Toller (1893–1939) reflect his own personal experiences and changing outlooks. A university student at the outbreak of World War I, Toller volunteered for military duty and served for more than a year at the front before being released in 1916 after suffering a physical breakdown. Now a confirmed pacifist, he took part in a strike of munitions workers in 1918 and was imprisoned. While waiting release he wrote *Transfiguration* (1918), subtitled *A Man's Wrestling,* his first major play. Alternating between realistic scenes and dream visions, *Transfiguration* shows events as seen through the eyes of Friedrich (easily identifiable with Toller himself), who during the course of the play is transformed from naïve chauvinist to militant rebel. Friedrich volunteers for the army and only begins to change after going on a patrol into no-man's-land, where in an abstracted dream-vision he sees skeletons hanging on barbed wire and

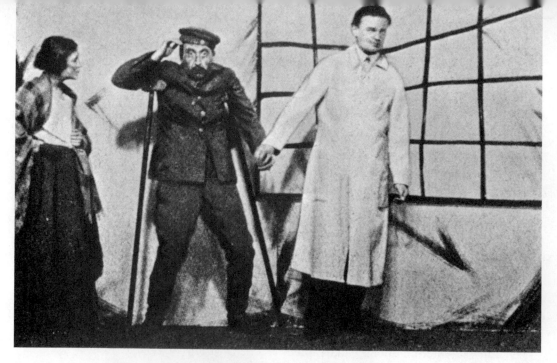

Scene from a production of Toller's *Transfiguration* at the Tribune Theater, Berlin, in 1919. Directed by Karlheinz Martin.

performing a dance of death. In the next scene, Friedrich, delirious in a field hospital, has similar visions, but now it is of hospital orderlies and a medical professor who symbolizes Death; through the wounded soldiers in the ward, the pointless anguish of war is externalized. Friedrich determines to oppose all war and when he is released he appeals to the masses to revolt against their leaders: "Go to the soldiers and tell them to beat their swords into ploughshares. Go to the rich and show them your heart, your heart that was once buried alive beneath their rubbish.... The castles—these you must destroy; destroy them laughing, the false castles of illusion."

The program of action laid out in this conclusion seemed near realization in 1918 when the rebellion of German workers brought the abdication of Kaiser Wilhelm and the cessation of hostilities. In the following year Toller became one of the leaders in a commune established in Munich following an uprising. Upon its suppression, he was sent to prison again, where he remained until 1924. While serving his sentence he wrote his two best-known plays, *Man and the Masses* (1920) and *The Machine Wreckers* (1922), both of which show a considerable decrease in optimism since *Transfiguration*, for both emphasize the wide gap between idealistic leaders and the fickle mob.

Man and the Masses revolves around the Woman, who seeks to help the working classes through a strike for peace and through a continuing fight against capitalism. But she seeks revolution through bloodless means,

281

*New Modes
of
Perception:
Expressionism,
Futurism,
Dadaism and
Surrealism*

for she believes that man can only be saved by humanitarian principles. Her outlook is opposed by the Nameless One, who is interested only in a victory over capitalism. He says: "The Masses count, not man. . . . Our cause comes first." To this, the Woman replies: "People come first. You sacrifice to dogmas." The Nameless One fans the frustration of the Masses into open rebellion, but when it is put down it is the Woman who is betrayed as the leader. Jailed and condemned to death, she is offered a chance to escape but refuses because it would mean killing her guard.

Man and the Masses is evidence of Toller's growing pessimism. Here the Masses are shown to be just as cruel and self-serving as those against whom they rebel. As the title is meant to suggest, the Masses can be saved only when they come to recognize the value of man (here epitomized in the Woman), for they cannot be transformed by adherence to some cause (this merely substitutes one type of mechanization for another) but only by humanitarian values. Still, Toller is not entirely pessimistic. At the end he shows two women squabbling over articles left in the Woman's cell. When the shots of the executioners ring out, they quietly replace the items and fall on their knees weeping, as one says: "Sister, why de we do such things?" The play obviously struck a sympathetic chord in contemporary audiences for it ran in Berlin for two years and was presented in theatres throughout Europe and America.

In *Man and the Masses* as in *Transfiguration,* Toller alternates realistic scenes with "dream visions." Furthermore, the characters are given only generic names, and the masses are treated as a chorus that speaks and acts as a unit. But in *The Machine Wreckers* Toller began to move toward greater concreteness. The story is based on actual historical events (the English Luddite rebellion which in the early nineteenth century sought to destroy weaving machines) and the characters are all given specific names and individualizing traits. Although the dialogue is often lyrical and all the elements are somewhat stylized, the overall effect more nearly resembles a modified realism than a full-blown expressionism. Nevertheless, the conflict is similar to that shown in *Man and the Masses.* The idealistic protagonist, Jimmy Cobbet, believes that the machine is an inevitable development and consequently that the problem is how to make it serve man, whereas John Wible, the radical proponent of violence, fans the workers' frustrations into open rebellion. In the final scene, Cobbet is beaten to death by the workers at the base of a machine they have destroyed, but then, realizing that Wible has been too cowardly to join them in the violence he has advocated, they begin to question his way. As the play ends, Wible's father-in-law kneels to kiss Cobbet's body, as he says, "We must be good to one another."

Following *The Machine Wreckers,* Toller seems to have become increasingly pessimistic. In *Hinkemann* (1924), the protagonist, a man who (symbolically) has lost his sexual organs in battle, comes to believe that all the lessons of the war have already been forgotten, for crassness and vulgarity are as rampant as ever beneath the outwardly changed façade of

282

*New Modes
of
Perception:
Expressionism,
Futurism,
Dadaism and
Surrealism*

the German state. Toller's last major work, *Hurrah, We Live!* (1927), is even more bitter. In it, a revolutionary, released after several years of imprisonment, discovers that all his old comrades have settled into comfortable lives and have forgotten the ideals for which they had fought. Believing that the world has gone mad, he commits suicide in despair. The play is prophetic, for Toller, after fleeing the Nazis, committed suicide in 1939 when World War II broke out. Although it is sometimes said that Toller was a mere propagandist, it is impossible to doubt his genuine anguish over a world seemingly bent on destroying all that is finest in humanity.

The disillusionment so evident in the works of Kaiser and Toller had by 1925 virtually brought expressionism to a close, although a residue persisted for a time, both in Germany and elsewhere. As late as 1930 the Austrian playwright Hans Chlumberg (1897–1930) achieved considerable success with *Miracle at Verdun,* in which 32 million war dead rise from their graves—much to the distress of the living, who would like to forget them.

Outside of Germany, expressionism probably reached its peak with *R.U.R.* (1921) by the Czechoslovakian dramatist Karel Čapek (1890–1938). *R.U.R.* depicts an almost wholly mechanized world in which men are served by Rossum's Universal Robots. When the robots seize power, it appears that the world is doomed to total dehumanization, but unexpectedly the stirring of love in two robots leads to an act of self-sacrifice and

Design by Feuerstein for a Czech production in 1921 of Karel Čapek's *R.U.R.*
(Courtesy Professor F. Cerny, Charles University, Prague.)

283

*New Modes
of
Perception:
Expressionism,
Futurism,
Dadaism and
Surrealism*

the hope of a new humanitarianism is reborn. Čapek does not seem to have been committed to expressionism, for it is inconsistently reflected in his other works. *The Insect Comedy* (1921) is perhaps related to expressionism in its exploration of various human philosophies through such insect behavior as the butterflies' hedonism and the dung beetles' materialism. Like the expressionists, Čapek also seems to have become increasingly pessimistic. *Adam the Creator* (1927), written with his brother Josef (1887–1945), shows the protagonist blowing the world to pieces out of horror at its mistakes. Ordered by God to refashion it, Adam does so only to discover that his new world is precisely like the one he has destroyed.

Although none seems to have been committed to the expressionist outlook, a number of American playwrights borrowed techniques from the German drama. The most obvious examples are Elmer Rice's *The Adding Machine,* Eugene O'Neill's *The Hairy Ape,* John Howard Lawson's *Processional,* and George S. Kaufman's and Marc Connelly's *Beggar on Horseback.* Indeed, the techniques became the currency of nonrealists everywhere. Perhaps the ultimate heirs of expressionism are those playwrights of the present day who, rebelling against materialism and hypocrisy, seek to discomfit the enemy with allegorical stories told through caricature, distortion, and the vision of regenerated man.

~~~ **III** ~~~

</div>

Expressionist drama was available to a reading public long before it was to be seen in the theatre, largely because the plays were denied licenses for production. The first public performance of expressionist drama did not come until 1916, when Hasenclever's *The Son* was presented at the German National Theatre in Prague (then a part of the Austro-Hungarian Empire). The first public performances in Germany were given in 1917, but by the end of 1918 only eight theatres had presented expressionist plays. Most of these programs were given for single or afternoon performances. Hasenclever's *Antigone* was banned after one showing.

In addition to these public performances, a few private showings (to avoid censorship) had been given for restricted groups. In 1917–18 Reinhardt instituted at the Deutsches Theater in Berlin a series of afternoon, private performances of works by Sorge, Kaiser, Goering, Kokoschka, von Unruh, and others. He also published a magazine, *Young Germany (Das Junge Deutschland)*, to accompany the plays.

Nevertheless, by the end of the war only a few expressionist plays had been produced in Germany. Furthermore, with a few exceptions, these had been staged rather traditionally. Thus, both the public presentation of

*New Modes
of
Perception:
Expressionism,
Futurism,
Dadaism and
Surrealism*

the plays and the development of theatrical techniques appropriate to them had to await the end of the war. Then, beginning in 1919, expressionist dramas suddenly came into vogue and a new style of production developed rapidly.

The most common notion in expressionistic drama was that the world of science and technology, of politics and traditional morality, is a nightmare —that those external appearances upon which the realists and naturalists had concentrated merely mask a horror that has distorted and is destroying man's spirit. Taking their clues from the plays, postwar directors and designers employed three basic approaches in staging: the realistic; the nightmarish; and the lyric-hymnic. The most characteristic approach is the second, for realistic scenes in expressionistic drama are relatively few in number, and the lyric-hymnic, usually reserved for visions of future perfection, steadily decreased as disillusionment set in. The dominant effect, however, was nonrealistic, for even when realism was used, it was usually intermingled with the nightmarish and consequently the overall effect was one of stylization and distortion.

It is sometimes said that expressionism depicts the world as seen through the eyes of the central character, but this is only partially true, for in many plays the protagonist does not appear in all scenes. Furthermore, even in those plays in which events are presented from the protagonist's subjective viewpoint, the audience must remain sufficiently detached to judge him and the events in which he takes part. Were the drama to become wholly subjective, the playwright's purpose would be subverted, for he wishes the audience to accept as valid his vision of the new man and the new world. In fact, the expressionists' greatest problem was how to avoid the purely aberrational while using a subjective approach to reveal and comment upon objective reality, for even in the most subjective scenes there is always an implied comparison between the stage world and the audience's world outside the theatre.

To project this subjective/objective vision, expressionist designers adopted a number of characteristic devices. First, like the dramatists, they often reduced scenic elements to essentials. Black drapes or a cyclorama were used to create the effect of a void, in which characters and set pieces appeared and disappeared like magic. This arrangement was especially appropriate in those highly episodic plays with readily shifting locales. Second, light was an integral part of design. It was used in part as a selective device, for it permitted the set pieces needed for several scenes to be mounted on the stage simultaneously and picked out by light as needed. It was especially useful in those plays in which one event faded into another as if being shifted through stream of consciousness. Through selective lighting, the frame of vision could be narrowed to show only the face of one person or extended to include the entire stage. Light was also used to create mood and atmosphere. Strongly contrasting light and shadow, extreme angles, light from the side, from overhead, or from the

An example of expressionism in design (by Ludwig Sievert for Brecht's *Drums in the Night*). Note that all vertical lines are distorted to diagonals and that the mood is thus tense and energetic.

rear, intense or unusual color—all could help to arouse that nightmarish atmosphere in which much of the action passed. (Probably no movement has done so much to develop the expressive powers of stage lighting.) Third, and perhaps most characteristic, distortion—in line, color, mass, proportion, and balance—was omnipresent. Diagonal lines, leaning walls, large blocks of bold color, enlarged furniture and properties, and various other exaggerating devices were used to project emotional qualities into objects and to achieve a sense of interpenetration between the physical and spiritual levels of existence.

Similarly, makeup and costume were more often used to reflect social roles, inner truth, or psychological states than to depict everyday appearance. The uniformity and mechanization of modern life were frequently suggested by dressing characters in identical clothing to create something like a uniform. Caricature was common: the bloated capitalist, the bemedaled general, the diseased seeker after carnal pleasure, the starving worker.

Acting did not seek to reproduce everyday behavior. In an "Epilogue to the Actor" appended to *The Seduction*, Paul Kornfeld advises: "Let him not be ashamed of the fact that he is acting. . . . The melody of a great gesture says more than the highest consummation of what is called naturalness. Let him think of the opera, in which the dying singer still gives forth a high C and with the sweetness of his melody tells more about death than if he were to crawl and writhe."

But the triumph of expressionistic theatrical techniques is especially associated with two directors, Fehling and Jessner. Jurgen Fehling (1885–1968) did his most important work for the Berlin Volksbühne (People's Theatre), which in 1915 had built one of the best-equipped theatres in Europe. Under the direction of Friedrich Kayssler, one of Reinhardt's finest actors, the Volksbühne promoted expressionist drama, perhaps because

Scene from Shakespeare's *Richard II*, directed by Jurgen Fehling, at the Berlin State Theatre in 1939. The abstract and suggestive setting was designed by Traugott Müller. (From Biedrzynski, *Schauspieler, Regisseure, Intendante.*)

of the movement's bias in favor of the workingman, to whom the theatre catered. (*Volksbühnen* flourished throughout Germany after 1918; by 1933 there were more than three hundred separate groups.) In the years immediately following the war, the Berlin Volksbühne presented plays by Strindberg, Toller, Kaiser, and other expressionists.

At the Volksbühne, Fehling won only moderate success as an actor but was catapulted to fame in 1921 as the director of Toller's *Man and the Masses*. For Fehling's production, Hans Strobach designed an extremely simple setting, essentially a single unit composed of a platform and steps enclosed by black curtains which could be used to reveal or conceal sections of the stage. For the "dream visions," caricature and distortion were used extensively. For example, the Man, perched on a fantastically high stool, recorded bids for war contracts in a giant ledger. When a new enterprise, a brothel disguised under the name War Convalescents' Home, was created, the bankers fox-trotted to music that sounded like the jingling of coins. Similarly, when the Nameless One gained control over the Masses, he led them in a wild dance which, set to the tune of a concertina and accompanied by constantly shifting colored lights, gave the impression of a witches' sabbath. Throughout the production, the Masses were used to create striking effects through movement and sound. One observer wrote of the "massive forms...clenched together like a single living creature.... Suddenly the base of the terrace was illuminated and figures were hissing like demons."

Fehling's production was considered revolutionary, in large part because, despite the many locales indicated in the script, virtually no scenery was used to indicate specific place. Although essential properties and furniture were used, major attention was paid to mood and atmosphere, created with shafts of light, music, and the choruslike Masses. It was perhaps the most abstract staging yet seen in Germany, but its powerful emotional impact vindicated Fehling's approach.

Setting for Jessner's production of *Richard III* at the Berlin State Theatre in 1919. (From Bab, *Das Theater der Gegenwart.*)

Because Fehling's reputation was made with expressionist drama, it is sometimes forgotten that he was one of Germany's most eclectic directors. His adaptability is perhaps best illustrated by his appointment under the Nazis to the directorship of the Berlin State Theatre, the most prestigious of Germany's subsidized companies.

While Fehling was making his reputation as a director of expressionist plays, Leopold Jessner (1878–1945) was becoming even better known for his application of expressionist techniques to the dramas of such authors as Shakespeare, Schiller, Hebbel, Hauptmann, Grabbe, and Wedekind. Like Reinhardt and Fehling, Jessner began his career as an actor and only later turned to directing. The attention attracted by his wartime productions at the Neues Schauspielhaus in Königsberg won him the directorship of the Berlin State Theatre, which he headed from 1919 to 1925.

Jessner used the same basic approach in almost all his productions, on most of which he worked with the designer Emil Pirchan (1884–1957). His favorite scenic device was a permanent arrangement of three-dimensional platforms and steps, the appearance of which could be disguised or altered through the addition of set pieces and properties and especially by curtains and lighting. Decorative detail was almost wholly abandoned. Thus, Jessner was a follower of Appia, although he used visual elements to achieve effects quite unlike those envisioned by Appia.

Perhaps Jessner's most famous production was of Shakespeare's *Richard III,* for which he used a permanent setting composed of steps and a platform backed by a wall pierced by a portal. Richard's rise to power was indicated by his progress upward on the levels and by the growing intensity of the red hue of costumes and lighting. Then, during the battle with Richmond, Richard was gradually forced to descend the stairs until he reached the bottom, where he was killed. As Richmond's strength grew, his color, pure white, began to dilute the red until at Richard's death the red was entirely washed away.

Setting by Emil Pirchan for the production of Wedekind's *The Marquis of Keith,* directed by Jessner in 1922. Upper and lower levels separated social classes. (From Bab, *Das Theatre der Gegenwart.*)

A similar approach (which many critics found overly schematized) was used by Jessner in all his productions. Levels and steps (soon known everywhere as *Jessnertreppen*) served not only to give variety to the playing but also as symbols of dominance or repression, as suggestions of varying levels of reality, and as reenforcements for rhythmic and kinetic effects. For example, in Wedekind's *The Marquis of Keith,* the somewhat fantastic scenes involving the dynamic though disreputable marquis and his friends were all staged on an upper level while those showing the docile middle class were confined to a lower level. For Grabbe's *Napoleon,* with its rapid shifts in time and place and its enormous scope, the upper level was used as a place where objects and figures appeared as if called up out of a void, into which they disappeared when no longer needed. Such productions did much to popularize what came to be called "space staging," since they used a permanent setting throughout and altered it merely by the addition of a few stylized set pieces and properties.

In Jessner's productions, light played an important role, for not only was it used to isolate scenes in space, it often reflected the emotional states of the characters. For example, Othello's jealousy might serve as motivation for the entire cyclorama to become green or his rage to make it red. Costumes also reflected emotional states, and the actors' rapid speech and movement often created a frenetic quality. Jessner's favorite actor was Fritz Kortner (1892–1970), who played for him Richard III, Macbeth, Gessler in *Wilhelm Tell,* and the Marquis of Keith.

Between 1919 and 1925 Jessner was one of the most famous directors in the world. But he seems to have fallen into a pattern and his approach soon came to seem monotonous. By the time he left Germany in 1933 his career was ended.

Films also served to gain acceptance for expressionist techniques throughout the world. Perhaps the most influential of all those made was

The Cabinet of Doctor Caligari (1920), directed by Robert Weine. Several important theatrical directors also made movies. For example, Karlheinz Martin filmed Kaiser's *From Morn to Midnight* in 1920 and Jessner directed Wedekind's *Earth Spirit* in 1922. These and many other films helped to bring expressionism to the attention of audiences who otherwise would have remained ignorant of it.

Expressionism in the theatre seems to have reached its peak during 1923. After that time audiences began to decline and critics to be bored with the plays. By the end of 1924 the movement was at a standstill. But its emphasis upon an inner vision and its development of techniques for projecting that vision made a strong and lasting impression. It would be modified by Brecht, the Bauhaus school, and others, through whom it would long remain a strong influence on theatre and drama.

IV

While expressionism was developing in Germany, other movements (in many respects paralleling it) had appeared elsewhere. Of these, futurism was the first to emerge. It was launched by the Italian poet Filippo Tommaso Marinetti (1876–1944) in an impassioned manifesto published on the front page of the Parisian newspaper *Le Figaro* in February 1909. Simultaneously Marinetti mailed hundreds of copies of his manifesto to important people throughout Italy. At first a literary movement, futurism was enlarged almost immediately to include the visual arts and music as well.

Like the expressionists, the futurists rejected the past and wished to transform man. But, whereas the expressionists associated the past with soul-destroying materialism and industrialism, the futurists, perhaps because for the most part they came from industrially backward Italy, deplored the veneration of the past as a barrier to progress. Consequently, the futurists glorified the energy and speed of the machine age and sought to embody them in artistic forms. In his manifesto, Marinetti wrote: "We declare that the world's splendor has been enriched by a new beauty: the beauty of speed. A racing motor car...is more beautiful than the *Victory of Samothrace*." (In one of his best-known poems, "My Pegasus," Marinetti declares that the racing car is the modern equivalent of the winged horse of ancient mythology.) He went on to say that cemeterylike museums and libraries are perhaps good enough for the old and dying, "but we will have none of it, we, the young, the strong, and the *living* Futurists." Like his heirs of more recent times, Marinetti proclaimed: "The oldest among us are thirty; we have, therefore, ten years at least to accomplish our task. When

Futurist production of a pantomime titled *Cocktail* by Marinetti at the Théâtre de la Madeleine, Paris, in 1927. (From Moussinac, *New Movement in the Theatre.*)

we are forty, let others, younger and more valiant, throw us into the waste basket like useless manuscripts."

The futurists so valued energy and aggressiveness that they were led to label war the supreme activity: "We wish to glorify War—the only health giver of the world—militarism, patriotism, the destructive arm of the Anarchist, the beautiful Ideas that kill, the contempt for women." In other words, the futurists' ideal man was an aggressive, masculine fighter who forges ahead with his eye squarely on the future, caring nothing for the past.

The futurists' pronouncements were publicized around the world. But they were not content with newspaper publicity. They were seeking to change attitudes about life itself and consequently they actively sought direct confrontations with audiences. (They seem to have been the first to do so.) From 1910 onward they gave performances (*serate*) during which they proclaimed their manifestoes, gave concerts, read poems, produced plays, and exhibited works of visual art—sometimes several of these simultaneously. Sometimes they moved about among the spectators, using various parts of a room sequentially or concurrently. Because of their militancy, they were soon considered the epitome of all that was new (and dangerous) in outlook and art. They especially outraged audiences with their demands that libraries and museums be destroyed as the first step toward creating a more dynamic future. They were welcomed by a few, but more often they were greeted by boos, barrages of fruit, or physical violence. On several occasions, the evenings ended in true riots. The futurists also became well known elsewhere—in France, England, Russia, and Germany—through exhibitions, writings, lectures, and demonstrations. As their ideas gained currency, they became important influences on other artistic movements of the time.

291

*New Modes
of
Perception:
Expressionism,
Futurism,
Dadaism and
Surrealism*

In their attempts to create art forms appropriate to a machine age, the futurists utilized various means. Marinetti and others created "picture-poems" (or what today would be called concrete poetry) out of type of varying size arranged in configurations designed to arouse sensations of movement, space, time, and sound. Others made kinetic sculptures in order to introduce the dimension of movement and energy into what had previously been a static form. Along with the cubists, the futurists invented the art of collage, an "assemblage" of fragments torn from newspapers, cloth, or prints, and thus made it possible to "paint" with any material. Some futurists also argued that modern utilitarian objects (such as wine racks and kitchen utensils) are more beautiful than the canvases or sculptures of the old masters and entered such articles in exhibitions.

In music, the futurists developed the notion of *bruitisme,* or dynamic sound. They argued that, since every movement produces sound, noise is a reflection of the volcanic soul of life. Therefore, they orchestrated the sounds of everyday existence (along with abstract noise) to form "musical" works more suitable to modern life than those created through traditional means. (Much of their work anticipates later developments in electronic music.) On one of their programs, the futurists included a "noise symphony" depicting "the awakening of the capital" through the sounds of pot covers, rattles, typewriters, and similar "instruments." *Bruitisme* was explained at length in *The Art of Noises* (1913) by Luigi Russolo (1885–1947), who also invented "noise organs" (or *intonarumori*) upon which he and others gave concerts.

As in other areas, the futurists did not think of theatre and drama in conventional terms, and beginning in 1911 they published a series of manifestoes demanding change. The first, "Manifesto of Futurist Playwrights" (1911), signed by Marinetti and nineteen others, is primarily a denunciation of contemporary practices and a call for innovation. The second, "The Variety Theatre" (1913), by Marinetti, is more positive in tone. It proclaims the variety theatre—music halls, nightclubs, and circus—superior to traditional theatre as a model for the drama of the future. But Marinetti does not encourage direct imitation; he merely wishes to capture the spirit and to adapt certain conventions of popular entertainments—especially the carefree and unselfconscious atmosphere, the rapid succession of disparate attractions, the interaction of performers and actors, the mingling of elements drawn from many media, and the overall dynamism of the performances. The ideas expressed here are brought into sharper focus in "The Futurist Synthetic Theatre" (1915), written by Marinetti, Emilio Settimelli, and Bruno Corra. They condemn traditional drama for being lengthy, analytic, and static, and propose in its stead a "synthetic" drama: "That is, very brief. To compress into a few minutes, into a few words and gestures, innumerable situations, sensibilities, ideas, sensations, facts, and symbols. . . . Our acts can also be moments only a few seconds long." To

292

*New Modes
of
Perception:
Expressionism,
Futurism,
Dadaism and
Surrealism*

such drama, which aims to capture the dynamism of modern life, they apply such adjectives as *simultaneous, alogical, unreal,* and *autonomous.*

It was in "synthetic drama" that the futurist ideal found its characteristic expression in the theatre. In 1915–16 futurist writers published seventy-six short plays (or *sintesi*), a large number of which were performed in several Italian cities during that season by acting companies headed by Gualtiero Tumiati, Ettore Petrolini, and others. This was perhaps the most concerted effort made anywhere to establish futurism in the theatre.

The *sintesi* varied widely in techniques and subjects. Some were distillations into a few moments of well-known plays, such as those by Shakespeare and Alfieri; they not only pointed up the futurists' claim that traditional drama devotes too much time to exposition and logical progression, they often parodied overused dramatic situations as well. Most writers of *sintesi,* however, ignored earlier practice and sought instead to capture the essence of some mood, situation, condition, or sensation. One of the briefest dramas is Francesco Canguillo's *Detonation* (1915), in which the curtain rises on a deserted road at night; after a period of silence, a gunshot is heard and the curtain falls. The great compression aimed at in many of the pieces can be clearly seen in *Sempronio's Lunch* (1915) by Bruno Corra and Emilio Settimelli: in five short scenes Sempronio moves through life from the age of five to the age of ninety as he eats under conditions and in places that vary with each time of life.

Some of the plays are very abstract. For example, Giacomo Balla's *Disconcerted States of Mind* (1916) calls for a white stage, on which four persons perform four disconnected scenes. In the first, each character is assigned a different number which he repeats twelve times; in the second, each repeats a different letter of the alphabet twelve times; in the third, each performs a different action (raising his hat, reading his newspaper, blowing his nose, looking at his watch); in the final part, each seeks to convey a different state (sadness, quickness, pleasure, denial). In each scene all four perform simultaneously and without taking any notice of each other. Somewhat greater unity is achieved in Marinetti's *Feet* (1915), in which the curtain is raised only far enough to reveal the actors' feet, which during the seven brief, disconnected scenes perform movements appropriate to distillations of typical conditions (partially conveyed by telegraphic dialogue), such as anxiety, violence, work, and various kinds of love.

Some of the plays seem to foreshadow the drama of Ionesco, as in Marinetti's *They Are Coming* (1915), in which furniture assumes greater importance than people and eventually moves offstage by itself, and in Umberto Boccioni's *The Body That Ascends* (1916), in which a body floats up the side of a building. Still others of the plays seek to involve the audience in the action, as in Corra and Settimelli's *Gray + Red + Violet + Orange* (1915), in which an onstage character accuses a spectator of murder, or in Canguillo's *Lights* (1919), in which the curtain goes up on complete darkness, thus provoking calls from the auditorium for lights

293

*New Modes
of
Perception:
Expressionism,
Futurism,
Dadaism and
Surrealism*

(begun by actors planted there, but hopefully leading others to join in) until answered by a blinding glare just as the curtain falls. A few works utilize concurrent actions. Marinetti's *Simultaneity* (1915), for example, depicts two different places in which parallel actions proceed at the same time—one relating to the life of a typical middle-class family, the other to that of a coquette. In *The Communicating Vases* (1916), Marinetti extends the settings and actions to three.

These examples should be sufficient to indicate that *sintesi* used many innovative techniques: extreme brevity, discontinuity, abstraction, alogicality, and simultaneity. In many, the place of the action is the stage itself; time is usually indefinite or severely telescoped; nonverbal sound and symbolic lighting are common; various media are intermingled. In almost every instance, clear-cut story, logical progression, and psychological characterization are minimized or ignored.

During World War I, the international influence of futurism rapidly waned, for the horrors of the war made the glorification of aggression seem perverse. Nevertheless, futurism was to remain a major artistic force in Italy until the 1930s and it was to regain some of its international prestige during the 1920s. After the war Marinetti and his followers continued to call for innovations: a theatre of touch, a theatre of smells, a theatre with variable air temperatures, and a "radiophonic" theatre. In 1918–19, Fedele Azari advocated and gave a performance of "aeriel theatre," in which airplanes were to be the performers.

During the 1920s there were several new attempts to create a futurist theatre. Between 1921 and 1924, Rodolfo DeAngelis toured throughout Italy with his Theatre of Surprise and his New Futurist Theatre in a repertory made up primarily of *sintesi*. Futurism was also promoted by Anton Guilio Bragaglia (1890–1960), one of Italy's most important postwar directors. Originally a member of the futurist movement, Bragaglia left it in 1913, perhaps because his interests were more eclectic than those of his associates, for he was sympathetic to practically all modern movements, most of which he publicized in Italy through his periodical *Cronache d'Attualita* (1916–22). He began directing plays around 1916, and from 1922 to 1936 ran the Teatro degli Independenti in Rome, where on a tiny stage he presented a wide-ranging program of works by Strindberg, Wedekind, Schnitzler, Jarry, Apollinaire, Maeterlinck, and Pirandello, in addition to those by futurists, whom he always supported enthusiastically.

Among the futurists of the postwar era, perhaps the most important in theatrical production were Depero and Prampolini. Fortunato Depero (1892–1960) worked in many forms but was especially interested in kinetic sculpture, a concern which heavily influenced his theatrical designs, for he sought to create settings and costumes capable of numerous transformations during a performance. He also sought complete unity between performer and background and consequently often used the same materials, colors, and shapes for both scenery and costumes. Furthermore, to achieve

The Merchant of Hearts, a pantomime staged by Enrico Prampolini
at the Théâtre de la Pantomime Futuriste, Paris, in 1927.
(From Moussinac, *New Movement in the Theatre.*)

this integration, he often distorted the human shape into mechanical,
floral, and geometrical forms. Most of his designs were done for ballet. In
1916–17, he designed settings and costumes for the Ballets Russes's production of Stravinsky's *Song of the Nightingale;* in 1918, in collaboration with
Gilbert Clavel, he presented a series of *Plastic Dances* with marionettes as
performers; and in 1924 he wrote and staged the ballet *Machine of 3000.*
But if Depero's work was small in volume, it nevertheless was extremely
influential.

The most important postwar futurist scenographer was Enrico
Prampolini (1894–1960), who in addition to designing more than one
hundred theatrical productions was a dramatist, director, and painter. His
"Futurist Scenography" (1915) and "Futurist Scenic Atmosphere" (1924)
are the most important futurist manifestoes relating to production. In these
works, Prampolini demands the abolition of the painted scene in favor of
a "dynamic stage architecture that will move." Instead of lighting the stage,
the scenic space itself should include luminous sources "coordinated
analogically with the psyche of each scenic action." Furthermore, "human
actors will no longer be tolerated. . . . Vibrations, luminous forms (produced
by electric currents and colored gases) will wriggle and writhe dynamically,
and these authentic actor-gases. . .will replace living actors. . . . The appearance of the human element on the stage shatters the mystery of the
beyond that must reign in the theatre, the temple of spiritual abstraction."
Thus, Prampolini saw the theatre as a polydimensional space in which
spiritual forces (represented by light and abstract forms) play out a drama

of semireligious significance. Prampolini called his stage "a center of spiritual abstraction for the new religion of the future."

Obviously such a vision is difficult to translate into actuality and Prampolini never fully succeeded in doing so. (In fact, his settings tend to be more two-dimensional than polydimensional.) Nevertheless, he sought to put his theories into practice. In 1925, his model for a "Magnetic Theatre" (a version of the theatre he describes in his manifestoes) won the Grand Prize in theatrical design at the International Exposition of Decorative Arts in Paris. Furthermore, he designed numerous productions, among them several for Bragaglia, and others for futurist programs given in Prague in 1921 and for a "mechanical ballet," *The Psychology of Machines* (1924) by Silvio Mix. His best-known work is probably that done in 1927 for his Théâtre de la Pantomime Futuriste in Paris, where he presented a series of dance-dramas, some of which combined living actors with abstract shapes and geometric marionettes while others eliminated human actors altogether, a trend taken even further in *Sacred Speed* (staged in Milan in 1928), in which the only dynamic elements were light and "noise music."

After 1930 interest in futurism rapidly declined. If it never became a major theatrical movement, it nevertheless pioneered innovations that would be revived in the 1950s and treated as original. In terms of subsequent developments, perhaps the most important of the innovations are: (1) the attempt to rescue theatrical art from a museumlike atmosphere; (2) direct confrontation and intermingling of performers and audiences; (3) the exploitation of modern technology to create multimedia presentations; (4) the use of simultaneity and multiple focus; (5) an antiliterary and alogical bias; and (6) the breaking down of barriers between the arts.

In addition to its long-range inheritors, futurism had more immediate heirs. In Soviet Russia it came to be associated with the idea of destroying old social forms and building a new society through modern technology. Consequently, many Russian artistic experiments sailed under the banner of futurism, even when they had little in common with Marinetti's views. In Germany many of the innovations were revived and extended by the Bauhaus. But, the immediate successor to futurism was dadaism, though more in techniques than in total outlook.

Scenery and costumes by Enrico Prampolini for the "mechanical ballet" *The Psychology of Machines* by Silvio Mix.

Although many individuals have billed themselves as its first practitioner, dadaism as a movement was launched in Switzerland in 1916. During World War I the mecca for those seeking to avoid the war was Zurich, and there the Cabaret Voltaire, run by the German poet Hugo Ball (1886–1927), served as headquarters for the circle of artists and writers who founded dadaism. In addition to Ball, other leaders of the movement were Richard Hulsenbeck (1892–), a German medical student who later became a Jungian psychoanalyst (Zurich was the home of Jung), Marcel Janco (1895–), a Roumanian artist who decorated the cabaret's interior and provided the settings for its programs, and Tristan Tzara (1896–1963), a Roumanian poet usually considered the movement's principal spokesman, who wrote its manifestoes (of which there were seven between 1916 and 1920) and who edited its periodical, *Dada,* from 1917 to 1920. The name *dada,* chosen at random from the dictionary (any name would have served as well), is baby talk in French for anything to do with horses.

Although it is often said that dadaism was wholly negative, it would probably be more accurate to describe it as grounded in a thoroughgoing skepticism engendered by disgust and horror for a world that could produce a global war. Since insanity seemed to them the world's true state, the dadaists sought in their actions to replace logic and reason with calculated madness and in their art to substitute discord and chaos for unity, balance, and harmony. In actuality, the dadaists, like the members of all movements, were concerned with truth. Finding past values wanting, they reached out for something more satisfying and stated the results in a few key words: spontaneity, complete freedom, all-inclusiveness. In one of his manifestoes, Tzara wrote: "Freedom: Dada Dada, Dada, a roaring of tense colors, an interlacing of opposites and of all contradictions, grotesques, inconsistencies; LIFE." To indicate their complete rejection of the past, they produced "antiartistic" paintings and poems, deliberately illogical works, rubbish collages, and noise music.

Although they totally rejected the futurists' glorification of war, the dadaists borrowed much from the earlier movement. Hulsenbeck, in his history of dadaism, declares that from the futurists they borrowed *bruitisme,* simultaneity, and collage. In addition, they engaged in direct confrontations with their public. All of these are clearly evident in the programs presented at the Cabaret Voltaire (a small room which seated from thirty-five to fifty persons at tables), where every "manifestation" was something of a collage, for it might be composed of lectures, readings, "sound poems," dances, concerts, visual art works, or plays. Furthermore, more than one event was usually going on simultaneously. For example, it was not unusual for several persons to recite separate poems at the same time, often to the accompani-

Samstag, den 14 April, abends 8¹, Uhr findet in den Räumen der GALERIE DADA, Bahnhofstrasse 19 (Eingang Tiefenhöle 12) unter der Leitung von HUGO BALL und TRISTAN TZARA als II. geschlossene Veranstaltung eine

STURM-SOIRÉE

statt

PROGRAMM:

I.

TRISTAN TZARA: Introduction.

HANS HEUSSER: „Prélude", „Mond über Wasser", gespielt vom Komponisten.

F. T. MARINETTI: „Die futuristische Literatur", gelesen von HUGO BALL.

W. KANDINSKY: „Fagott", „Käfig", „Blick und Blitz", gelesen von HUGO BALL

GUILLAUME APOLLINAIRE: „Rotsoge", „Le los du Douanier", lecteur F. GLAUSER.

BLAISE CENDRARS „Crépitements", lecteur F. GLAUSER.

MUSIQUE ET DANSE NEGRES exécutées par 5 personnes avec le concours de Mlles JEANNE RIGAUD et MARIA CANTARELLI. (Masques par M. JANCO).

H. S. SULZBERGER: „Cortège et fête", exécuté par le compositeur.

JACOB VAN HODDIS: Verse, rezitiert von EMMY HENNINGS.

HERWART WALDEN: August Macke †, Franz Marc †, August Stramm †, gelesen von F. GLAUSER.

HANS HEUSSER: „Burlesques turques", „Festzug auf Capri", gespielt vom Komponisten.

ALBERT EHRENSTEIN: Eigene Verse. Ueber Kokoschka.

III.

PREMIÈRE

„SPHINX UND STROHMANN"

Kuriosum von OSCAR KOKOSCHKA

Masken und Inscenierung von MARCEL JANCO.

Herr Firdusi — HUGO BALL
Herr Kautschukmann — WOLFG. HARTMANN
Weibliche Seele, „Anima" — EMMY HENNINGS
Der Tod — FREDERIC GLAUSER

Auskunft an der Kasse der Galerie. Billets nur auf den Namen lautend.

SAMSTAG, den 28. APRIL, abends 8½ Uhr
III. GESCHLOSSENE VERANSTALTUNG.

Program for the first dada soirée, on April 14, 1917, in Zurich. Oscar Kokoschka's *Sphinx and Strawman* was given its premiere performance.

ment of "music" made by screeching wheels, rattling keys, banging kitchen utensils, typewriters, or other instruments. Ball was especially fond of "sound poems"—that is, works composed of nonverbal vocal noises. Tzara favored "chance poems"—created by cutting sentences from newspapers, putting them in a hat, mixing them up and then drawing and reading them at random. Hulsenbeck was especially interested in African chants and dances, for which Janco designed full-body masks (as well as the other visual elements required by the programs). The first play performed by the group was Oskar Kokoschka's *Sphinx and Strawman*. (It is interesting to note that Kokoschka, Max Ernst, Yvan Goll, and several other expressionists were considered dadaists in these years.)

As the war drew to a close, the dadaists dispersed. For a brief time dada thrived in Germany. Hulsenbeck returned to Berlin, where during the uprisings he was appointed commissar of fine arts by the Communists. But the ultimate fate of dadaism in Berlin is probably best exemplified in Georg Grosz, who, though prominent in Zurich dadaist activities, soon sought to forget these earlier connections. In Cologne, Max Ernst, Hans Arp, and Johannes Theodor Baargeld in 1920 arranged one of the most famous of all dadaist exhibitions. For it they rented a glassed-in court which could only be reached through a public urinal. There a young girl, dressed as if for her first communion, recited obscene poems. One art work featured a skull emerging from a pool of blood-red liquid from which a hand projected. Another, made of wood, had a hatchet attached to it for the convenience of anyone who wished to attack it. The exhibition created such a scandal that it was closed by the police. The dadaist movement in Cologne came to an end in 1922 when Ernst and Arp left to take up residence elsewhere and Baargeld gave up painting. The most famous version of dada in Germany,

298

New Modes
of
Perception:
Expressionism,
Futurism,
Dadaism and
Surrealism

promoted by Kurt Schwitters in Hamburg, was called Merz, supposedly after a word fragment (part of *Kommerziale*) which appeared in one of Schwitters's collages. Schwitters promoted his version of dada as well through a periodical, also called *Merz*. But the German variations on dada, although lively for a time, contributed little to the theatre.

It was in France that dada most thrived. In 1919 Tzara became acquainted with a group of young men, including Louis Aragon, Philippe Soupault, and André Breton, who had founded the periodical *Litterature,* and soon afterward he moved to Paris. In January 1920, *Litterature* began to sponsor a series of dadaist "demonstrations," the first theatrical program of which was given in March 1920 at Lugné-Poë's Théâtre de l'Oeuvre. Composed of *The First Celestial Adventure of Mr. Fire-Extinguisher* by Tzara, *If you Please* by Breton and Soupault, a "Cannibal Manifesto" by Francis Picabia (read in total darkness), and *The Silent Canary* (in which a man who thinks himself to be Gounod teaches his compositions to a canary who is said to sing them "beautifully but silently") by Georges Ribemont-Dessaignes, the program used a setting made up of a bicycle wheel and signs hanging from a clothesline. It concluded in an exchange of mutual insults between audience and performers.

In May 1920, at the Salle Gaveau, the last significant dada program was given. Consisting of Tzara's *Mister Fire-Extinguisher's Second Celestial Adventure,* Breton and Soupault's *You Would Have Forgotten Me,* and Tzara's musical piece "Vaseline Symphonique" (described by one critic as a "cacophany of inarticulate sounds"), it provoked the public to throw eggs at the performers.

Despite a loss of vigor, the movement continued for a time. In 1923, Tzara's play *The Gas Heart,* in which actors impersonating various parts of the head—the neck, mouth, nose, ear, eyebrow—spoke disconnected dialogue in the tones of polite conversation, was performed at the Théâtre Michel and provoked a pitched battle between supporters and detractors of dadaism.

A scene from the sketch by Soupault and Breton titled *You Would Have Forgotten Me* (Salle Gaveau, Paris, 1920). Soupault is kneeling and Breton sits in the chair.

But by this time dadaism had lost its momentum. In 1922 Breton sought to convene an "International Congress to establish directives for the modern spirit and to defend it." Although this "Congress of Paris" collapsed, it provoked a definitive break between Tzara and Breton and led to the establishment of surrealism. With the publication of the first "Manifesto of Surrealism" in 1924, dada as a movement can be said to have ended.

~ VI ~

It is difficult to distinguish clearly between dadaist and surrealist art, for surrealism took over dada's emphasis on spontaneity, chance, and the juxtaposition of disparate elements. In fact, the principal difference between the movements lies in surrealism's attempt to define a specific course of action based upon stated principles, whereas dadaism was skeptical of all limitations. Thus, surrealism merely continued as its sole concern what had been one aspect (although a major one) of dadaism.

The principal spokesman for surrealism (indeed, he considered himself its near-owner) was André Breton (1896–1966). A former medical student, Breton served as an orderly in psychiatric wards during the war and developed a compelling interest in Freudian psychology, which was further deepened by a meeting with Freud in 1921. (It is often said that he was the first Frenchman to be well acquainted with Freud's writings.) Thus, psychoanalytic theory was probably the greatest influence on the manifesto with which Breton launched surrealism in 1924.

Breton defined surrealism as "pure psychic automatism, by which is intended to express, verbally in writing, or by other means, the real process of thought. Thought's dictation, in the absence of all control exercised by the reason and outside all esthetic or moral preoccupation." Thus, Breton makes the subconscious mind the source of the artist's most significant perceptions. Although Breton's statement about automatic writing and painting attracted more attention than did any other part of the manifesto, it was of little importance in the movement and was seldom practiced. In the *Second Manifesto of Surrealism* (1929) it was virtually ignored.

Because of the squabblings among the surrealists, it is difficult to pinpoint their major beliefs. Nevertheless, a few common principles emerge from their pronouncements. First, all seem to have believed in the primacy of the subconscious. Second, they attempted to distinguish between the subconscious and the conscious and to draw battle lines on this basis. They believed that truth is most apt to surface when the superego's censorship and the ego's logic have been neutralized. Third, they declared that in moments of truth life's contradictions are transcended. As Breton put it, "There is a certain point for the mind from which life and death, the real

300

*New Modes
of
Perception:
Expressionism,
Futurism,
Dadaism and
Surrealism*

and the imaginary, the past and the future, the communicable and the incommunicable, the high and the low cease being perceived as contradictions."

Surrealist artists and writers gained their effects most often by mingling the familiar and the strange. For instance, in Salvador Dali's paintings, probably the best-known examples of surrealist art, everyday objects are rendered with extreme care for detail but are placed in such unfamiliar surroundings (often in a "dream landscape"), or are put to such unfamiliar uses (a detached arm supports a boulder, an eye grows from a tree), or behave in such unfamiliar ways (a watch bends as if made of rubber) that they are invested with an air of significance in which the animate and inanimate worlds interpenetrate. In drama, familiar human situations occur in unusual surroundings or two seemingly unrelated scenes are juxtaposed. Such alogicality and discontinuity break the bonds of ordinary reality and create a "surreality" where associational patterns can lead the mind to novel but significant perceptions.

Surrealism was far less productive in drama than in the visual arts. In fact, a large number of the innovative theatrical productions later labeled surrealist had occurred before surrealism was launched as a movement. Furthermore, the term *surrealism* had been in use for some time before Breton issued his first manifesto.

As a descriptive term, *surrealism* seems to have been coined around 1917 by Guillaume Apollinaire (1880–1918), who had already done more than any other critic to explain the work of Jarry, the fauves, and the cubists. Between 1900 and 1917, Apollinaire was in the forefront of practically every important new artistic movement in France. In 1912 he published a near-manifesto in which he called for the abandonment of recognizable subject matter in painting and declared that proportion and vision can in themselves be the subjects of art. This is one of the first thoroughgoing defenses anywhere of purely abstract art. In 1913, Apollinaire began to champion futurism and, like Marinetti, called for a synthetic art in which special attention would be paid to the potential of motion pictures and recordings. In writing, Apollinaire valued two qualities above all others: musicality and plasticity. By musicality he meant a subjective state of mind under which (as in music) there is no concern for external appearances, and by plasticity he meant freedom to manipulate appearances. He also advocated simultaneity, or the attempt to capture the totality of an experience without sacrificing the lack of logical relationship among its components. Thus, it is clear that Apollinaire was spiritually allied with the futurists, dadaists, and surrealists.

It was as a subtitle (*"drame surrealiste"*) for his play *The Breasts of Tiresias* (begun, according to Apollinaire, under Jarry's influence in 1903 and completed in 1917) that the term *surrealism* was first used by an artist to describe his own work. This grotesque play, ostensibly set in Zanzibar, purports to contain a serious message about the repopulation of France, but

The original production of Apollinaire's *The Breasts of Tiresias* in 1917.
Scenery and costumes designed by M. Ferat.

it can probably more validly be considered a vaudevillesque spoof on the contemporary topic of women's emancipation. Early in the play, Thérèse, finding her life too confining, releases her breasts, which float away like balloons, and is transformed into Tiresias. Her husband, now forced to take over her functions, eventually discovers the means of creating children (sheer will power) and becomes the parent of more than forty thousand offspring. The inhabitants of Zanzibar, represented by a single actor, say nothing but occasionally provide music with pots and pans, castanets, and other instruments. Apollinaire's statement in the prologue about the kind of theatre he desires is of considerable interest: a circular structure with two stages, one in the middle and one surrounding the audience, where as in life itself "sounds, gestures, colors, cries, tumults, music, dancing, acrobatics, poetry, painting, choruses, actions, and multiple sets" may join.

Apollinaire also used the term *surrealist* to describe *Parade,* presented by the Ballets Russes in 1917, for which he wrote the program notes. For this ballet Jean Cocteau provided the script, Erik Satie the music, Pablo Picasso the settings and costumes, and Leonid Massine the choreography. It marks Diaghilev's first use of contemporary French painters as designers (a practice that, continued thereafter, brought new vitality to the Ballets Russes and made it as influential on postwar as it had been on prewar design, especially through the work of Picasso, Henri Matisse, Georges Braque, Juan Gris, and Marie Laurencin). *Parade* also marks the theatrical debut of Cocteau, who was to be one of the most important surrealist

Two variations by Pablo Picasso of the scene design for Cocteau's *Parade,*
staged by the Ballets Russes in 1917. (From Editions Cercle d'Art, Paris.)

dramatists. In *Parade,* Cocteau draws on the eighteenth-century practice
of using a short skit (a *parade*) outside a theatre to attract customers. But
in the ballet all the efforts fail, for the crowd mistakes the *parade* for the
play itself (suggesting in this way the human tendency to mistake outward
show for inner reality). Picasso's settings and costumes mingled characteristic devices from his Harlequin and cubist periods. The ballet was divided
into three parts, each featuring a different theatrical manager. The first
manager wore a ponderous cubist construction, the second (an American)
was dressed as a skyscraper, and the third was accompanied by a horse.
Overall, the work, with its fair barkers, acrobats, and Chinese conjurers,
seemed more nearly a sideshow, circus act, or music hall program than
a traditional ballet. It was a kind of collage, half-dance, half-pantomime,
in which the musical, visual, and choreographic elements seemed more
simultaneous than related. Perhaps the most startling ingredient was Satie's
music. His score was based on popular songs and jazz (in itself considered
outrageous) supplemented by such futurist devices as typewriters, sirens,
airplane propellers, telegraph tickers, and lottery wheels. Some outraged
patriots accused the artists of being on the side of the Germans (it was
performed in the midst of war); Satie wrote one critic an insulting postcard
and in return was sent to jail and fined 1,000 francs. Many historians have
credited this production with setting the tone for all postwar experimentation in France.

Cocteau went on to write other ballet-dramas. *The Ox on the Roof*
(1920), set in the "Nothing-Doing Bar" during the prohibition era in
America, was performed in part by the Fratellini family of circus clowns
in settings by Raoul Dufy and to a score by Darius Milhaud. *The Wedding
on the Eiffel Tower* (1921) was staged by the Ballets Suédois, which, under

The original production by the Ballets Suédois of Cocteau's
The Wedding on the Eiffel Tower. This scene shows the wedding feast,
while in the background is a panorama of Paris and the Seine
as seen through the girders of the Tower.

the direction of Rolf de Maré (1888–1964), between 1920 and 1925 was
perhaps even more willing to present novelties than was the Ballets Russes.
Like Diaghilev, Maré commissioned settings from contemporary painters,
among them Fernand Leger, Giorgio de Chirico, and Francis Picabia.

The Wedding on the Eiffel Tower had settings by Irène Lagut (a
painted backdrop showing a stylized bird's-eye view of Paris as seen through
the girders of the tower) and costumes by Jean Hugo. Two actors dressed
as phonographs and placed at the sides of the stage narrated the story and
spoke all of the dialogue. The most important set piece was an enormous
camera, from which the characters emerged when the shutter was clicked.
Out of it came such unlikely creatures as an ostrich, a lion, a hunter, and
a bathing beauty, in addition to the expected wedding party. Each character
and group had its own dance in this dreamlike fantasy that mingled the
commonplace with the magical. Though the public persisted in finding
his work strange, Cocteau declared: "The new generation will continue its
experiments in which the fantastic, the dance, acrobatics, mime, drama,
satire, music, and the word combine to produce a new form."

In 1924, Maré presented another ballet of some historical significance.
Relâche (*No Performance*), with scenario and settings by Francis Picabia
and music by Satie, featured dancers who smoked incessantly, a fireman

303

*New Modes
of
Perception:
Expressionism,
Futurism,
Dadaism and
Surrealism*

who wandered about the stage pouring water from one bucket to another, and two seemingly nude performers posed as Cranach's Adam and Eve. The setting was made up entirely of round metal discs which reflected bright light into the eyes of the spectators. As usual, Satie's music was considered scandalous. Its opening melody, taken from an obscene song, provoked many persons in the audience to roar out the lyrics and thereafter the heckling never ceased. But from the historical point of view the most important aspect of the production was its pioneering effort to integrate a film (*Entr'acte,* made by René Clair from Picabia's scenario) into a live performance.

Thus by 1924, when surrealism was launched as a movement, many productions later called surrealist (and just as often futurist and dadaist) had already been seen in Paris. The surrealists were not very active in drama, however, in large part because after about 1925 Breton and his trusted associates considered the theatre to be decadent and bourgeois. Consequently, two of their most productive colleagues, Artaud and Vitrac, were expelled from the movement in 1927, the year in which they (in association with Robert Aron) founded the Théâtre Alfred Jarry. Not only were Artaud and Vitrac subsequently attacked in pamphlets, their performances were often disrupted.

Antonin Artaud (1896–1948) was drawn to surrealism by his preoccupation with the unconscious and dreams. But his interests in occultism, mysticism, and Oriental religions brought him into conflict with more orthodox surrealists and contributed to his rupture with them. From about 1920 he was active in Parisian theatres as an actor for Lugné-Poë, Charles Dullin, Georges Pitoëff, and others. He also wrote a few plays during the 1920s: *Jet of Blood* (a short scene inserted in *The Umbilical Cord of Limbo,* 1925), *The Philosopher's Stone* (a speaking pantomime written about 1926), and *The Burnt Belly, or the Crazy Mother* (produced 1927). All are characterized by violent images juxtaposed in disconnected sequences which defy ordinary logic. They were virtually ignored at the time. Artaud was also interested in film, and, in addition to acting in several (among them *Entr'Acte*) wrote scenarios, of which only one, *The Seashell and the Clergyman* (1927), was produced. It is now considered the first true surrealist film. But Artaud's work of the 1920s was merely a prelude to that which made him one of the most influential figures of the postwar theatre—his theoretical writings of the 1930s. (That aspect of his career will be discussed at length in a later chapter.)

Closely associated with Artaud in the 1920s was Roger Vitrac (1899–1952), perhaps the best dramatist among the conscious surrealists and author of several vaudevillesque works characterized by mordant cynicism and brutal assaults on conformity. *The Mysteries of Love* (written in 1924 and first produced in 1927) treats the fantasies (most of them shocking) of a pair of lovers as they continually change their relationship and interact with other characters whose identities shift frequently. Among the characters are Mussolini and Lloyd George (who has a predilection for severing heads). Perhaps the most striking feature of the play is the interchanges between stage and auditorium. The opening scene occurs in a box; voices from the auditorium ask the actors questions; characters confide to the audience in asides; and eventually a character shoots a spectator seated in the auditorium. In *Victor, or Children in Power* (staged in 1928), Vitrac satirizes the follies of society through a world of fantasy in which a 7-foot-tall, nine-year-old child speaks and acts like an adult and dies of a heart attack. Through it, he also satirizes conventional drama in a cuckolded husband and a lover, both of whom commit suicide. In many ways Vitrac's works resemble Ionesco's, a fact which may account for their resurgent popularity during the 1960s.

But surrealism won its greatest popularity in the theatre through the plays of Jean Cocteau (1892–1963), never an acknowledged member of the movement. Following his experiments with ballet-drama, Cocteau next turned to classical myths for subjects, a truly important innovation, for this marks the beginning of a practice which was to become typical with modern French dramatists. Cocteau's first attempt to use classical myth, *Antigone* (1922), with music by Honegger and settings by Picasso, was not very successful. But with *Orpheus* (1926) he seemed on firmer ground. Here the story of Orpheus and Eurydice is transposed to a modern domestic setting. But the world of villas and bungalows is immediately given an air of the magical by a talking horse, in whose messages Orpheus sees great significance although Eurydice discounts them as meaningless. The glazier Heurtebise, who daily comes to repair a broken windowpane, adds to the air of fantasy when he remains suspended in midair after a chair on which he has been standing is removed. When Eurydice, through the machinations of the evil Bacchante Aglaonice, is poisoned, Death, dressed as a beautiful woman, enters through a mirror and, after a ritualistic ceremony which resembles a modern surgical operation, takes Eurydice back with her. Death forgets her glove, however, and Orpheus, on the advice of Heurtebise, returns it. He reenters almost immediately with Eurydice, who has been allowed to return with the stipulation that Orpheus never look at her again. But the domestic bickering, which has characterized the opening scenes, begins again, and Orpheus, forgetting his promise, looks at Eurydice, who once more dies. No longer caring to live, Orpheus goes to meet the Bacchantes, who are seeking to kill him, and a moment later his severed head is thrown through the window. Heurtebise places it on a pedestal, from which, when asked its name by the police inspector, it replies, "Jean Cocteau." After the inspector has left, Orpheus, Eurydice, and Heurtebise enter from the mirror, now apparently in the world of the dead, and sit down happily to lunch.

Through such interminglings, Cocteau made the everyday magical and the mythical familiar. He also achieved a simultaneity of vision (ancient Greece and modern France became coexistent) as Marinetti had done

306

*New Modes
of
Perception:
Expressionism,
Futurism,
Dadaism and
Surrealism*

with his association of Pegasus with a modern racing car. Perhaps of equal importance, Cocteau found in myth a means of overcoming the seeming randomness which made much surrealist drama seem incoherent. The received myth provides a basic framework but still permits considerable latitude of treatment within those broad outlines.

Cocteau's best-known play is *The Infernal Machine* (1932), a retelling of the myth of Oedipus. The title refers to Fate, an instrument of the gods, which, like a time bomb, goes on ticking away while man believes that he is free to determine his own destiny. Although Oedipus constantly proclaims his freedom to choose, like everyone else, he is powerless to stop the machine. In constructing the play, Cocteau seems to have been influenced as much by Shakespeare's *Hamlet* as by Sophocles' *Oedipus Rex*. The opening scene takes place on the ramparts of Thebes, where the ghost of the recently murdered Laius walks each night and where Jocasta comes to view it. But when it appears, the ghost is unable to make itself seen or fully understood. Act II shows the meeting between Oedipus and the Sphinx, a beautiful young woman who seeks to escape the god Anubis by running away with Oedipus. But once he learns her secret, Oedipus abandons her. Act III is also reminiscent of *Hamlet* (the bedroom scene between Hamlet and Gertrude). Occurring on the wedding night of Oedipus and Jocasta, it engenders a sense of impending doom, in part by mysterious warnings from Tiresias and in part because the bridal bed has the appearance of a sacrificial altar or funeral pyre. The final act, which takes place seventeen years later, parallels Sophocles' play: Oedipus learns of his heritage, Jocasta kills herself, Oedipus tears out his eyes, and Antigone leads her father into exile.

The fatalism so evident in all of Cocteau's classical plays is reminiscent of symbolism. Perhaps nothing more clearly sets Cocteau apart from the mainstream of surrealism and its preoccupation with the subconscious (Cocteau's truth is external, the surrealists' internal). Cocteau's relationship to surrealism is almost entirely one of literary devices rather than of philosophical outlook. That Cocteau was not committed to surrealism is further indicated in much of his later work, especially the realistic *The Terrible Parents* (1938) and the romantic *The Eagle Has Two Heads* (1946), although he returned to it often, perhaps with greatest success in such films as *The Blood of a Poet* (1932), *Beauty and the Beast* (1945), and *Orpheus* (1950), but also in his final stage work, *Bacchus* (1952). But if Cocteau was not a true surrealist, he did more than any other dramatist to popularize it.

By 1930 surrealism had begun to disintegrate as an organized movement, not only because of dissension among its adherents but because, like expressionism and futurism, surrealism had become increasingly politicized. In the late 1920s Breton sought to make commitment to Communism a tenet of surrealism. (In Germany many expressionists and dadaists also became Communists, although almost as many were Nazis; and in Italy, most of the futurists paid allegiance to fascism.) But though as a movement surrealism subsided, its achievements were lasting, especially in the visual arts (demonstrated definitively in the International Exhibition of Surrealist Art in 1938). That its influence is still potent is shown by the post-World War II French theatre.

~~ **VII** ~~

Surrealism was not confined to France, nor were all those whose works may be classified as surrealist even aware of Breton's views. For example, in Spain Ramón María del Valle-Inclán (1866–1936) was writing surrealistic plays before that label had been invented. Valle-Inclán began his career in the 1890s with novels that reflect an outlook not unlike that of the English aesthetes and French symbolists, but gradually these views were tempered by elements not unlike those found in the plays of Alfred Jarry. His earliest dramas (dating from 1899) are in verse, but the later ones, such as *The Farce of the True Spanish Queen* (1920), *Face of Silver* (1923), and *The Horns of Don Friolera* (1925), are in prose.

Valle-Inclán's dramatic method is probably seen at best advantage in *Divine Words* (1913), which embodies his concept of *esperpento* (usually translated, perhaps too conveniently, as "absurd"), defined by Valle-Inclán as a truthful vision arrived at "by a mathematics of concave mirrors" as in a fun house. He went on to say that the tragic reality of Spanish life can only be conveyed by a systematic deformation "because Spain is a grotesque deformation of European civilization." Valle-Inclán also labeled many of his plays "barbaric" because they present a ruthless and uncompromising version of reality.

In *Divine Words,* the action revolves around a deformed idiot, the object of contention among several persons who wish to display him as a sideshow attraction. The winner, an outwardly beautiful woman, is so callous that the idiot soon dies and is left in a wheelbarrow where his face is eaten away by pigs while she is involved in an adulterous affair. Incensed by her sexual activities, neighbors taunt her and strip her of her clothes, but when her husband, the church sexton, intones a Latin prayer, they slink away. The final stage direction reads: "Led by her husband's hand, the adultress takes refuge in the church, a sanctuary wreathed in a resplendent religious prestige which, in that superstitious world of rustic souls, is conjured up by the incomprehensible Latin of the DIVINE WORDS."

This grotesque story is set against the natural beauty of the Spanish countryside and given a poetic aura by intermingling the real and the surreal. In technique it is novelistic (or cinematic), for scenes shift rapidly and many touches difficult to realize on stage are freely inserted. But through it all comes the commentary on Spain—a beautiful exterior which

308

*New Modes
of
Perception:
Expressionism,
Futurism,
Dadaism and
Surrealism*

hides a callous and pagan soul kept in check by religious superstition. It was not seen in the theatre until 1933 and was not well known until after World War II. Valle-Inclán's worth as a dramatist is now being recognized outside of Spain, perhaps because of his affinity with absurdism and because such recent dramatists as Fernando Arrabal have acknowledged their indebtedness to him.

During the 1920s several Spanish artists were to come under the influence of surrealism. Of the dramatists, the most important is Federico García Lorca (1898–1936), who upon completing his university education came to Madrid in 1919 where he lived at a residential center associated with the Institución Libre de Enseñanza, the home of liberal thought in Spain. Here he joined a circle of brilliant young writers and artists, among them Salvador Dali (destined to become the best known of all surrealist painters) and Luis Buñuel (who was to be a pioneer of surrealist film). In 1925, Louis Aragon, one of Breton's most trusted associates, lectured in Madrid, and thereafter Lorca's group became increasingly interested in surrealism and other current artistic movements. But the key event of the decade was the celebration in 1927 of the three-hundredth anniversary of the death of Gongora, for it so effectively brought to focus the ideas of the young writers that they were thereafter called the Generation of '27. Their hallmark was the combination of traditional and native subjects with modernity of manner. In 1927 Lorca founded a magazine, *Gallo,* in which he published a statement by his group acknowledging their indebtedness to "Picasso, Gris, . . . Tristan Tzara, . . . Aragon, . . . Jean Cocteau, Stravinsky, . . . André Breton, etc., etc."

Lorca began writing about the time he went to Madrid, but for many years he devoted most of his effort to poetry. His first play, *The Butterfly's Spell* (1920), written while under the influence of symbolism, was a failure, and he avoided dramatic forms for some time. *Mariana Pineda* (1927) reflects the interests of the Generation of '27, for it is based on a popular ballad but is determinedly modern in its form. Each scene begins with a self-conscious atmosphere created out of allusive language, color, light, and music, and eventually these elements build to a climax all their own. The overall effect is more lyrical than dramatic. Nevertheless, it achieved a limited success when produced by Margarita Xirgu (one of Spain's finest actresses and the only one who truly appreciated Lorca), largely because audiences, probably mistakenly, found in it allusions to the contemporary political situation.

It was not until he returned to Madrid after a stay in New York and Latin America in 1929–30 that Lorca wrote the majority of his plays (although several may have been begun earlier). One of the characteristic works of this period is *The Love of Don Perlimplin and Dona Belisa in the Garden.* It uses the familiar situation of the middle-aged man cuckolded by a beautiful young wife. Out of such material, Lorca builds a distinctive work through poetic transformations. Part of the effect depends on exaggeration. Don Perlimplin is browbeaten into marriage by his servant, Marcolfa, and he is cuckolded not by one but five lovers almost instantly. But it is in the development after this point that Lorca's originality is most evident. When Marcolfa reports to Don Perlimplin that Belisa is now interested in a sixth young man, he seems delighted and his delight grows as Belisa's interest increases. Finally he declares that he will kill the young man to preserve him forever for Belisa; she frantically seeks some way to prevent the murder but the young man stumbles into her room mortally wounded. When she uncovers his face, she discovers Don Perlimplin, who dies happy, for he has made her fall in love with the man he has invented. Through his sacrifice Belisa at last comes to understand love and, as Marcolfa says, acquires a soul to inhabit what had been merely a beautiful body.

Lorca's major plays were written after he had worked closely with a theatrical troupe. The Spanish Republic, created in 1931, sought in several ways to increase educational opportunities, and as one part of those efforts the Ministry of Culture and Public Information established "cultural missions" to those areas most devoid of artistic activities. Two theatrical groups —the Teatro Universitario (more commonly known as La Barraca), headed by Lorca and Eduardo Ungarte, and the Teatro del Pueblo, headed by Alejandro Casona—were created.

Although La Barraca was subsidized by the government, it received funds sufficient to do little more than buy a truck and a few costumes and props. The actors were students who worked during vacations, and Lorca himself directed, acted, set up lights, and performed a variety of other tasks. For the most part, La Barraca performed works of the Golden Age for rural audiences in the squares of Castilian villages. The unabashed involvement of these unsophisticated spectators in the intensely dramatic situations deeply impressed Lorca and greatly influenced those works for which he is now best known: *Blood Wedding* (1933), *Yerma* (1934), and *The House of Bernarda Alba* (1936), for in all he takes familiar, even extreme, situations and lifts them to a near-mythic realm.

Lorca's *Yerma* at the Teatro Eslava, Madrid, in 1960. Directed by Luis Escobar and designed by José Cabellero.

310

*New Modes
of
Perception:
Expressionism,
Futurism,
Dadaism and
Surrealism*

Blood Wedding tells of a girl who, after her lover has married another woman, agrees to an engagement. But on the day of the wedding, Leonardo, her former lover, carries her away. Honor demands that the husband kill Leonardo. This much of the play occurs on a semirealistic though intensified plane. But the next section becomes symbolic and surrealistic through its chorus of woodcutters and the Moon, who comment on the action as the men kill each other. In the final scene, the bridegroom's mother, Leonardo's wife, and the bride lament their losses to the accompaniment of a semi-choral commentary by neighbors. Thus, *Blood Wedding* combines a story of overpowering love, honor, revenge, and loss with a poetic treatment, through which fate and blood are associated with the Spanish land itself.

The best known of Lorca's plays is *The House of Bernarda Alba,* in which, on the death of her husband, Bernarda decrees seven years of mourning for her household and so condemns her four daughters to an intolerable separation from all male companionship. The frustrations soon undermine the harmony of the family; then, Adela, the youngest daughter, escapes surveillance and slips out with Pepe el Romano, her elder sister's fiancé. Later, when Bernarda discovers Pepe in the barn, she shoots him with no more compunction than if he were a dog, and Adela commits suicide. Implacable, Bernarda demands that no one speak of what has happened so that the truth about her daughter can be concealed.

Lorca has done himself a disservice by describing the play as photographically realistic, for, though it is devoid of the obvious symbolic and surrealistic devices of his earlier works, it progresses on a level as near to Greek tragedy as to modern realism. The characters embody elemental forces that cannot be denied, and the clash between them leads inescapably to destruction. The surface may be realistic but the conception is archetypal.

Lorca's career was cut short when he was executed by Falangist forces at the beginning of the Spanish Civil War. The manner of his death has done much to spread his fame, for to many Lorca has become a symbol of a war they despise. Quite deservedly, Lorca is now almost universally considered the finest Spanish dramatist of the twentieth century.

A lesser figure, although once considered a major dramatist, is Alejandro Casona (1903–65), who, like Lorca, blended the traditional and the modern. Out of his experience with the Teatro del Pueblo, with which he toured more than three hundred villages in central Spain, he learned much about writing for unsophisticated audiences. He first won recognition as a playwright in 1933 when *The Siren Washed Ashore* won the Lope de Vega Prize. Thereafter he wrote regularly until the mid-1950s, when ill health interrupted his work. His most admired plays are three written while he was in exile (from the late 1930s until 1963): *The Lady of the Dawn* (1944), *The Boat Without a Fisherman* (1945), and *Trees Die Standing* (1949).

The most characteristic feature of Casona's work is the mingling of reality with fantasy, of the seen and the unseen, until it is difficult to tell where one ends and the other begins. For example, the title character of *The Lady of the Dawn* is Death, who appears in the guise of a beautiful and kind woman with all the feelings and sensitivity of a real person doomed to wander the earth and watch everything she touches die. Like Lorca, Casona achieves his effects by investing the familiar with previously unseen significance. But unlike Lorca, Casona builds upon the traditions of tragicomedy and views life with unquenchable optimism. Unfortunately, the promise represented by Lorca and Casona was negated by the coming of the civil war in 1936. By 1939 a rigorous censorship was being enforced and innovation was at a standstill.

~~ VIII ~~

In the years between 1910 and 1925, new modes of perception and expression came to the fore. The era is marked by numerous artistic movements, which, though most soon disappeared, contain the seeds of subsequent experiments down to the present day. Brecht's epic theatre is the direct descendant of expressionism, just as Artaud's theatre of cruelty is the offspring of dada and surrealism. Futurism, dadaism, and surrealism introduced many of the techniques which have been more fully exploited in "happenings" and recent theatrical production. The list of parallels between the artistic movements of the World War I era and those of our own day is so extensive that it is tempting to see in it evidence of more direct influence than can be clearly established. It seems likely that the trauma of World War I engendered doubts not unlike those which arose once more after World War II and that out of similar questioning came similar experiments and conclusions. But regardless of the specific line of development, it is clear that the attempts made by such men as Freud, Jung, and Einstein to redefine reality and our modes of perceiving it have had profound and lasting effects upon artistic forms.

The Soviet
Experiment

10

In 1917 revolution brought a new form of government to Russia and important changes to the theatre. The groundwork for theatrical innovation had already been laid by such men as Stanislavsky, Meyerhold, and Tairov, who continued as leaders in the postrevolutionary era. Most theatrical workers welcomed the release from stringent tsarist restraints and some, led by Meyerhold, saw the new state as a call to create comparable new artistic forms. Others merely sought to continue the ideals they had always championed. At first, the theatres were left relatively free to make their own decisions, but during the 1930s, after Stalin began to demand that art be subordinated to the needs of the state, socialist realism became the only accepted mode. Consequently, by the beginning of World War II, the

theatre had been almost completely subordinated to the will of the Communist party. During the 1920s, however, the Russian theatre was among
the most innovative in the entire world, although its drama was of little
worth. As Russian practices became known elsewhere, they made an enormous impact throughout the Western world.

In 1917 Russia underwent two revolutions, one in February (actually
March by the Western calendar, which was not adopted in Russia until
after the revolution) and the other in October (November). The first
revolt overthrew the tsarist regime and replaced it with a provisional government headed by Alexander Kerensky. The second brought the Bolshevik
branch of the Communist party to power, ended the Russian involvement in
World War I, and precipitated a civil war that continued until 1921.

During the eight months of the provisional government, the theatre
underwent many changes. First, the strict censorship which had for so
long been imposed by the tsarist government and the Orthodox church was
repealed. Consequently, many previously forbidden plays were produced.
These included works—such as A. K. Tolstoy's *The Death of Ivan the
Terrible* and Dmitri Merezhkovsky's *Paul I*—about royalty or official
institutions, or those—such as Wilde's *Salome* and Schnitzler's *Reigen*—
considered morally offensive. Second, the provisions against playing on
fast days and church holidays were repealed. Third, special privileges and
subsidies were canceled for the five imperial theatres of Moscow and
Petrograd. (In 1914 St. Petersburg was renamed Petrograd to rid it of any
Germanic taint; in 1924 it would become Leningrad.) All of these changes
were welcomed by the majority of theatrical personnel, who looked forward
to complete freedom for the arts.

The new political structure seemed to demand new organizational
patterns in the theatre and endless discussions about appropriate administrative structures were held. It became common to associate all managers
with the tsarist regime and to seek freedom from them. For example, Tairov,
in regulations he drew up for the Union of Moscow Actors, noted the
"class antagonism" between actors and managers, a theme pursued at
length by the All-Russian Conference of Theatrical Trade Unions, over
which Tairov presided in August 1917. Even the public became concerned
and it was not uncommon for spectators to make public speeches about art
and politics during intermissions at theatrical performances. Some theatres
were turned over to governing boards on which all personnel, ranging from
the janitors to the starring actors, were represented. There was also much

concern about making the theatre more appealing to the working classes. But despite much agitation, little had actually been done prior to the October Revolution.

In one sense the whole development of the Soviet theatre has been determined by one question: What form should the theatre take in a socialist society? In the years between 1917 and 1927, most theatrical personnel saw themselves as virtually able to pursue whatever answer seemed best. Almost everyone had an answer and almost everyone sought to make his plan prevail. It was this freedom to choose and this struggle for supremacy that gave the Russian theatre of the 1920s its peculiar character and enormous versatility.

Much that happened in the Russian theatre after 1917 went contrary to the wishes of the government. Lenin, for example, deplored the avant-garde experiments, preferring instead the continuation of romantic realism, into which there would merely be poured new ideological content. But such men as Meyerhold declared that a new society required wholly new theatrical forms and derided the very modes that Lenin and his friends supported. Still others wished to educate the masses through a classical repertory, and some declared that only those of working-class origins were capable of producing meaningful art for the proletariat. Since the ideas were many and contradictory, a struggle was inevitable.

Even though the rulers had firm ideas about the appropriate theatrical form, they were not as yet in a position to enforce them. Until 1923 they were concerned primarily with survival. Not only was there military opposition from both without and within, the economy was in shambles and the entire country on the verge of famine. Thus, close supervision of the theatre was not given high priority. Furthermore, the government was faced with a paradoxical situation: its most ardent supporters were members of the avant-garde, whereas the realists, whom the government favored, were at best neutral. Furthermore, the government itself had as yet formulated no clear program for the theatre. It wished to make art available to the masses and to have art assist in the socialization of Russian society, but it had no plan for bringing about these aims. For all these reasons, the theatre was left relatively free.

Between 1917 and 1921, theatrical conditions were almost chaotic in their bewildering variety and lack of clear direction. Perhaps the most remarkable feature of the Russian theatre in these years was its universal appeal. Amateur groups sprang up everywhere—in factories, in military barracks, in villages. The height of the craze came around 1920, but in 1926 there were still approximately twenty thousand rural dramatic circles with about 250,000 amateur actors. In 1920 the armed forces had more than eighteen hundred dramatic circles, and factories numbered them in the thousands. In addition there were about three thousand professional companies between 1918 and 1923. Everywhere, even in the midst of famine and deprivation, the theatres were filled nightly.

Evreinov's spectacular, *The Taking of the Winter Palace* in, November, 1919, the second anniversary of the Revolution.

In many ways the Russian theatre between 1917 and 1923 paralleled the "people's theatre" movement in the West before World War I. The Russians were conscious of the similarities, for they frequently quoted Rolland and compared their own productions with those of the French Revolution. Many enthusiasts spoke of transforming the theatre into an expression of all the people. For example, Andreyev, the major symbolist dramatist of the prerevolutionary era, declared that the old theatres would be replaced "by other theatres, perhaps theatres based on the entire nation. ... the walls of the theatres will fall, but the theatre will remain." Others argued that the theatre of the future would be entirely out-of-doors.

Such ideas reached their peak between 1919 and 1921 in a series of mass spectacles. The first—*The Mystery-Play of Liberating Toil*, staged by Yuri Annenkov and A. R. Kugel with a cast of more than two thousand— was performed in Petrograd in honor of May Day in 1919. But the most ambitious of the mass spectacles, *The Taking of the Winter Palace*, was given in November 1919 on the anniversary of the Revolution. Directed by Nikolai Evreinov, it required a cast of more than eight thousand soldiers, sailors, workers, and actors and utilized the site of the original event. There was an orchestra of five hundred and even the guns of battleships anchored nearby were brought into the action. At first glance, such a production might seem far removed from Evreinov's prerevolutionary work, but it is in keeping with his idealistic notions of the theatre as a tool for transforming life. It was the vision of a new era of humanitarian idealism which attracted practically all directors of the time, even if many were to become disillusioned later. But the mass spectacle never developed as many had envisioned. By 1922 it had virtually been abandoned. Thereafter, the people's theatre was largely restricted to amateur theatrical clubs.

A large number of dramatic productions in this period were propagandistic. The mass spectacles were essentially melodramatic glorifications of the Revolution and denunciations of the past. This approach was even more

315

prevalent in programs presented for peasants, soldiers, and factory workers, and in the numerous street demonstrations of the time. Immediate problems were treated in such skits as *The Fight Against Typhus, The Intrigues of Finance Capital,* and *The Plots of the Counterrevolution.* Mock trials—of the typhus louse, landowners, White Army officers, and others—were popular, as were staged debates and reports in which opposing points of view were illustrated through pantomimes, songs, dramatic skits, and choruses. Eventually such productions gave rise to more ambitious documentary forms—the "literary montage" and the "living newspaper." In the literary montage, some topic (such as the life of Lenin or Marx) or historical event (the Revolution of 1905 or of 1917) was developed through selections culled from memoirs, letters, official documents, poetry, and songs. Usually a narrator and chorus bridged the selections, which were given variety through the extensive use of pantomime, dance, dramatization, and comic episodes.

The living newspaper developed from the practice (which grew up immediately after the Revolution when newspapers were scarce) of reading actual news items from the stage. Soon such presentations were being supplemented by other devices designed to illustrate and interpret current events. Eventually the living newspaper was taken over by the "blue blouses" (named for the first professional living newspaper which featured performers wearing the workers' dress of the period). After a time the form palled, and disappeared around 1927.

By far the most radical version of a "people's theatre" was that championed by the Central Committee of Proletarian Cultural and Educational Organizations (more commonly known as the Proletarian Culture Movement or simply as Proletcult). Headed by Alexander Bogdanov, the Proletcult considered itself superior to both the Communist party and the government, since it was devoted to a "purely class organization of the proletariat." It was contemptuous of everything with bourgeois origins. In *Creative Theatre* (1919), Platon Kerzhentsev, Proletcult's major theoretician, declared: "Any effort to establish a socialist theatre with even the most brilliant bourgeois actors would be as fruitless as analogous efforts to organize, for example, a socialist magazine with the aid of bourgeois writers." He went on to insist that no distinctions should be made between proletarian artists and workers: "Only by standing at his machine, by remaining a worker, can the worker become the genuine creator of the proletarian theatre."

In 1918 the Proletcult began to establish its own theatres, which it hoped would soon replace all others. But in 1923, Proletcult was suppressed because it sought to make the industrial worker the sole repository of truth and creativity and sowed discord between the industrial workers and the peasants.

Although the people's theatre movement never completely disappeared, it was of little importance after 1923. But in the years immediately following the Revolution it was perhaps the greatest source of vigor, for the established theatres remained in old paths or were still wary of the new regime. For the most part, the major professional groups bided their time.

~~ II ~~

Unlike their predecessors, the Communists recognized the enormous potential of the theatre as a medium for education and propaganda. They also realized that it could just as easily work against them and consequently sought to maintain surveillance of it, if not full control. As part of their program to attain wide popular support, they sent hundreds of troupes to perform for the armed forces, in factories, and on the farms, and everywhere they encouraged the use of the theatre as a medium of party propaganda.

In 1917 much of the responsibility for the theatre was assigned to the Commissariat of Education and Enlightenment, headed by Anatoli Lunacharsky (1875–1932), a critic and dramatist who in the early years of the new regime sought through advice and cajolery to set the theatre on the path advocated by the party. His was not an easy task. In late 1917 he invited 120 leading artists to a conference devoted to the reorganization of the arts, but so cautious were artists about the new regime that only five attended, and these—among them Meyerhold, Alexander Blok (the symbolist poet, dramatist, and critic), and Vladimir Mayakovsky (1894–1930), leader of the Russian futurists—were prominent in the avant-garde. Thus, Lunacharsky was forced to work primarily with opponents of the romantic realism he favored. Consequently, when a Theatre Section was formed in early 1918, Meyerhold was appointed its Deputy Head (under O. L. Kameneva, Trotsky's sister). There were a number of subsections, each with its own chairman. Blok was put in charge of the subsection on repertory. Since he believed that the theatre could best serve the needs of the people through the classics, he published and distributed dramas from the past and made recommendations about those most suitable to particular kinds of companies. There was also a workers' and peasants' subsection concerned with amateur and mass spectacles, and a pedagogical subsection which sought to introduce drama in the schools and to establish theatres especially designed for children and young people. (This was a significant innovation, for Russia seems to have been the first country to give serious thought to children's theatre.) The directors' subsection was headed by Yevgeny Vakhtangov, who along with Meyerhold gave courses for directors.

To celebrate the first anniversary of the Revolution, Meyerhold staged the first Soviet play, Mayakovsky's *Mystery-Bouffe,* a parody of the biblical story of the ark ending with the arrival of the survivors in a Communistic promised land. Most theatrical personnel were still so uncertain about the permanence of Bolshevism that they hesitated to participate in the production and Meyerhold was forced to make a public appeal for actors. Lunacharsky also had reservations about the production, if not about the play, for before it was presented, he announced: "As a work of literature, it is most original, powerful and beautiful. But what it will turn out like in production I don't yet know. I fear very much that the Futurist artists have made millions of mistakes." His fears were well grounded, for it was not well received and in part because the setting was composed of geometrical designs painted on a blackcloth, a few cubes to indicate the ark, and a huge blue globe to represent the world. This was to be Meyerhold's last production for almost two years, for in early 1919 he went south for reasons of health.

The settings for *Mystery-Bouffe* were by Kazimir Malevich (1878–1935), one of the leading avant-garde painters of the day. Malevich belonged to a group of artists who around 1912 broke with the "World of Art" school and allied themselves with the cubists, futurists, and expressionists. Malevich launched his own movement, suprematism, which in a manifesto, written partly by Mayakovsky, he defined as the primacy of "pure feeling or perception in pictorial art. . . . The object in itself means nothing. Sensibility is the only thing that counts." Malevich seems to have believed, as did the expressionists, in the supremacy of inner vision, but unlike them favored pure abstractionism. In 1918 he exhibited a series of paintings called "White on White" that created a sensation in Russia.

The suprematists had much in common with the constructivists, led by Vladimir Tatlin, Naum Gabo, and Antoine Pevsner (who like Malevich were influenced by the cubists, expressionists, and futurists). Tatlin's sculptures were made of such industrial materials as glass, wire, and metal and were conceived as objects in space (a series of intersecting planes in depth) rather than as volume and mass (as in traditional sculpture). About constructivism, Gabo and Pevsner wrote in 1920: "In order to interpret the reality of life, art must be based upon two fundamental elements, space and time. . . . Kinetic and dynamic elements must be used to express the true nature of time. . . . Art must not be . . . imitative, but seek new forms." Thus, the major Russian artists of the period were concerned with those same qualities sought by cubists and futurists (dynamicism, geometrical forms, the sense of time) and by the expressionists (inner emotion and vision). To these schools belonged a number of artists who would make significant contributions to Soviet scenic design: Alexandra Ekster, Lyubov Popova, Ignaty Nivinsky, Nathan Altman, Georgy Yakulov, Marc Chagall, Mikhail Larionov, and others.

Parallel movements were underway in literature. The most important new outlook was futurism, which was strengthened by Marinetti's visit to Russia in 1914. The Russian futurists declared: "Set words free, destroy all grammatical structure, cultivate speed and modernity, be aggressive, repudiate all tradition, search for daring and startling forms of expression, and act as new barbarians in renovating creative life." The futurist manifesto, written in 1912 by Mayakovsky, was entitled "A Slap in the Face," and its signers sought to live up to the title. When the Revolution arrived, Mayakovsky declared that futurism was the form most suited to it and he urged his fellow artists to take to "the barricades of souls and hearts." In the early 1920s Mayakovsky joined with artists from other fields to create an integrated movement, the Left Front (LEF), which declared that art is to be judged by its service to the state—its ability to educate the masses, to provide them with revolutionary songs, uplifting slogans, and a vision of transformed society. There were, then, many strong parallels in the outlook, goals, and techniques of Soviet artists, German expressionists, and other Western artists. The important difference among them lay in the Russian political situation.

While Meyerhold was away from the capital, several important changes occurred. The most important of these was a reclassification of theatres, under which governmental financial support and protection were given a small group of "academic" theatres, while all others were required to be self-supporting and to submit to rather close scrutiny from the party. Ironically, the theatres designated as "academic" were the five former imperial theatres, the Moscow Art Theatre, and the Kamerny Theatre, none of which actively supported the new regime and all of which emphasized a classical repertory and, with the exception of the Kamerny, realistic production methods. To Meyerhold and the futurists, this decision seemed a negation of all that the Revolution stood for.

Another important force that came to the fore at this time was "Scythianism," a term derived from Blok's verses (published in 1918), "Yes, we are Scythians, we are Asiatics." Scythianism became a justification for breaking with the West (which was depicted as rapidly degenerating) and turning to the Asiatic heritage. The Revolution itself was seen as epitomizing the break, which was further strengthened in 1918 by moving the seat of government to the Slavic city of Moscow. Soon it was being argued that the theatre should seek out its folk origins, which had been obliterated by the influx of Western theatrical forms in the eighteenth century. A few attempts were made to revive ancient Slavic rituals and folk entertainments, but a more productive path was found in the theatre of the marketplace, the fairs, circuses, and other popular forms. This new direction received its fullest expression in Petrograd's Folk Comedy Theatre between 1920 and 1922. Headed by two of Meyerhold's former associates, Sergei Radlov and V. N. Soloviev, it sought to mingle improvisation with techniques borrowed from the silent motion picture and aspects of modern urban life. Most of its productions were based on simple melodramatic stories made eccentric through techniques borrowed from popular entertainments. These and other forms of Scythianism were to be important in Soviet production for many years to come.

In 1920 Meyerhold was invited by Lunacharsky to become head of the Theatre Section, a position which made him nominal head of the Russian theatre. He accepted, no doubt believing that through this position he could carry out his intention to revolutionize the Soviet theatre through an "October in the Theatre." He took over the section's periodical, *The Theatre Herald,* in the pages of which he launched bitter attacks on the "academic theatres" and provided support for the avant-garde proletarian companies. Thus, there arose the anomolous situation of the head of the Theatre Section attacking the theatrical policies of the government for which he worked. Friction was inevitable and was not long in coming to the fore.

The difficulties began in 1920 when Meyerhold took over a troupe and renamed it the RSFSR Theatre No. 1. After adding a number of actors and students, he prepared his first production, an adaptation of *The Dawns* (1898) by the Belgian symbolist Emile Verhaeren. The original play was a rather generalized treatment of imperialism and militarism in which the people were passive victims. Meyerhold reworked it into a play about a worldwide proletarian revolution in which the masses are active participants. His production style was borrowed from the political meeting. The auditorium and stage were stripped of all their theatrical trappings to give them the appearance of a meeting hall and the actors spoke as though delivering political orations; actors seated in the auditorium asked questions and made speeches of their own. A chorus, located in the orchestra pit, also commented on the action and provided clues to appropriate emotional responses. Leaflets were dropped on the audience from time to time and at one point a messenger arrived to read actual news dispatches from the front (the civil war was still in progress). Because the script made the divisions between supporters and opponents of the Revolution overly sharp and the issues overly simple, critics attacked the production as a distortion of political reality. On the other hand, ordinary spectators liked most of the production but were puzzled by the setting—an assemblage of red, gold, and silver cubes, discs, cylinders, and triangles by Vladimir Dmitriev. Although the production ran for more than one hundred performances, it was publicly denounced by Lenin's wife and other important party officials. Furthermore, Lunacharsky removed the "academic theatres" from administration by the Theatre Section, stating: "I can entrust Comrade Meyerhold with the destruction of what is old and bad and with the creation of what is new and good, but I cannot entrust him with preserving whatever is old and good, vital and strong, which must be allowed to develop in its own way in a revolutionary atmosphere." Since this change made Meyerhold's desire to

reform the theatres hopeless, in February 1921 he resigned his post as head
of the Theatre Section. Later in the same year the RSFSR Theatre No. 1
was closed, ostensibly for overspending, thus leaving Meyerhold without a
theatre.

The year 1921 was important for several other reasons. The civil
war was drawing to a close and reconstruction now began. Since the
state was on the verge of bankruptcy and financial collapse, Lenin sought
to encourage greater initiative through his New Economic Policy (NEP),
under which many earlier decrees were rescinded and limited private
enterprise was reinstated. Many theatres now reverted to private ownership
and Western plays began to find their way into the repertory. All theatres
were to enjoy considerable freedom of repertory and productional style from
1921 until Stalin assumed full control around 1927. But by 1921 it also
seemed clear that the Bolshevik regime was something more than a temporary phenomenon, and those theatres that had previously bided their time
now began to make accommodations with the government and began to
enlarge their programs. The next decade would be one of the most
fruitful in all Russian theatrical history.

~ **III** ~

The strange divisions within the Soviet theatre at this time are well illustrated by the appointment in 1921 of Meyerhold, despite his obvious
disaffection from official policies, as director of the State Higher Theatrical
Workshop, a major trainer of directors. In 1922, he also acquired a theatre
of his own, where he now began his best-known experiments—those with
biomechanics and constructivism.

Basically, biomechanics was an attempt to deal quasi-scientifically with
the motion of living bodies. But Meyerhold confounded and mingled it
with several other elements which have led to much confusion about its
meaning and nature. Since early in his career, Meyerhold had been concerned with movement, pantomime, and *commedia dell' arte* techniques,
and in the years just preceding the Revolution he had experimented at
length with rhythm, patterned movement, acrobatics, and circus and other
techniques. The new element added after the Revolution was the desire to
forge an art suited to a proletarian society in which the actor would be
merely one worker among many. Thus, Meyerhold began to think of the
theatre as a kind of factory and he came under the influence of "Taylorism"
(so called from the time-and-motion studies made by the American
Frederick Winslow Taylor), which was then being advocated in Soviet
industry. Meyerhold declared that it is "essential to discover those move-

ments in work which facilitate the maximum use of work time. If we observe a skilled worker in action, we notice the following in his movements: (1) an absence of superfluous, unproductive movements; (2) rhythm; (3) the correct positioning of the body's center of gravity; (4) stability." It was precisely these qualities that Meyerhold sought in his actors. His students were asked to study animal and human behavior and in rendering it to eliminate everything superfluous; they studied dance, acrobatics, fencing, and other physical disciplines until their bodies were as responsive as a machine in fulfilling its tasks. This in essence was biomechanics—thorough physical control. In this fundamental sense, there is nothing mysterious about it. Nevertheless, it was an innovation, for prior to this time no systematic physical training was required of Russian actors. Since Meyerhold's day, it has been a standard part of the programs offered by all acting schools, including those otherwise opposed to Meyerhold's methods.

Biomechanics seemed mysterious because it was associated by Meyerhold with other, more complex concepts. In addition to Taylorism, Meyerhold coupled a theory of psychological response with biomechanics. He declared that Stanislavsky's and other earlier systems of acting were mistaken because they asked the actor to base his stage behavior on internal psychological motivations, a waste of time and energy (thus anti-Taylorian) since the desired effects can be achieved more efficiently through purely physical means: "From a sequence of physical positions and situations there arise those 'points of excitation' which are informed with some particular emotion." Basically what Meyerhold proposes is a variation on the James-Lange theory: particular patterns of muscular activity elicit particular emotions. Consequently, the actor, to arouse within himself or the audience a desired emotional response need only enact an appropriate kinetic pattern; to go through a search for realistic internal motivations is not only wasteful of time but is wholly ineffective if it is not projected through appropriate muscular activity. Thus, Meyerhold sought to replace the earlier emphasis upon internal motivation with a new one on physical and emotional reflexes. He declared: "the actor must train his material (the body) so that it is capable of executing simultaneously those tasks which are dictated externally (by the actor, the director)." Consequently, to create a feeling of exuberant joy in both performer and audience, it may be more efficient for the actor to plummet down a slide, swing on a trapeze, or turn a somersault than to restrict himself to behavior considered appropriate by realistic social standards. Above all, it was the use of unusual physical behavior to express normal human responses that made biomechanics seem incomprehensible. (Meyerhold used such extremes only in his early experiments; thereafter he moved progressively toward more normal movement, although he never abandoned his basic theory about the relationship between physical and emotional reflexes.)

Biomechanics was further mingled with two other elements: Meyerhold's long-standing interest in *commedia dell' arte* and popular enter-

Model by L. Popova for Meyerhold's production of
The Magnificent Cuckold, 1922.

tainments of all sorts (many of the specific physical techniques used in his productions were taken over from these forms); and the futurists' concern for energy, speed, and vitality (associated with the new socialistic society and contrasted with the languid or merely frenetic rhythms of capitalistic society).

Constructivism was Meyerhold's attempt to achieve a setting which would be a "machine for acting" without any superfluous details, for he argued that the stage, like an industrial machine, should be practicable rather than decorative. In 1921, Meyerhold saw an exhibit of sculpture and painting by constructivists and invited one of the artists, Lyubov Popova, to join his teaching staff at the Theatrical Workshop and to design the setting for his first major production at his new theatre, *The Magnificent Cuckold* by the Belgian Fernand Crommelynck. It was with this play (presented in April 1922) that Meyerhold made his first important experiments with biomechanics and constructivism.

Crommelynck's cynical farce tells how the village miller Bruno, unable to believe that every man is not in love with his beautiful wife, seeks to discover his wife's lover (he cannot believe that she does not have one) by forcing her to submit to the advances of each man in the village. Eventually the previously virtuous wife, now disgusted with her husband's jealousy, runs away with a young man who seems more likely to trust her. Meyerhold rather lamely justified his choice of such a play in the midst of his proletarian theorizing by labeling it a universal statement about jealousy.

For the production, the stage, including the flies, was stripped of all machinery and laid completely bare. Popova's setting consisted primarily of steps, platforms, slides, and uncovered flats, behind which the unadorned brick walls of the stagehouse were clearly visible. There were two kinetic elements—a windmill sail and a large disc bearing the letters "CR ML NCK"—which turned at speeds that varied according to the emotional and rhythmic demands of a scene. Lighting instruments were exposed to view and no color filters were used. Costumes were the same for all characters— blue coveralls varied only by small accessories, such as a riding crop or eyeglasses. The costuming reflects Meyerhold's attempt to treat the actor as a worker. In a speech given in 1922, he declared: "One must not fritter away [time] in making up and putting on one's costume. The actor of the future will work without makeup and wear an overall." The acting was based on Meyerhold's biomechanical theories. For example, Igor Iliinsky, who played Bruno, is said to have delivered his long speeches in a monotonous tone and with set gestures, but to have commented on the impassioned moments by performing acrobatic stunts, "belching and comically rolling his eyes while enduring the most dramatic anguish." *The Magnificent Cuckold* was one of Meyerhold's most determinedly experimental productions.

Although he applied his theories in all subsequent productions, Meyerhold sought continuously to refine and perfect them. Consequently, each new production saw some alteration and an overall tendency to soften the original approach, which even Meyerhold came to consider extreme. Because his first constructivist settings were called mere extensions of futurist decorative art, he sought in *The Earth in Turmoil* (1923) to eliminate everything except purely utilitarian objects, such as trucks, machine guns, and field kitchens, and to use wholly naturalistic costumes. One important new feature was the use of captions projected on a screen, a device often employed by him thereafter.

In 1923, the centennial of Ostrovsky's birth, Lunacharsky declared "Back to Ostrovsky" to be a Soviet policy. In 1924, Meyerhold is said to have given his reply with Ostrovsky's play *The Forest*, a production that made nonsense of the government's position. At this time, Meyerhold stated what had long been his practice: "A play is simply the excuse for the revelation of its theme on the level at which that revelation may appear vital today." Consequently, he completely reworked the original text, separating and rearranging the episodes, inserting invented pantomimes, and giving each scene a title which was projected on a screen. Meyerhold conceived the play as a series of relationships among "social masks," and since he sought to reveal the essence of each "mask" upon its first appearance, character development was no longer important. For the uniforms worn in some earlier productions, he substituted period costumes selected and used, along with wigs, to capture a character's essence, which was further indicated by individualized rhythms in speech and movement. But he still used many of his biomechanical techniques: as the lovers become enthusiastic about their plan to run away, they soared higher and higher in their swings; a character's stupidity was shown by having him balance on two chairs while conversing; there were innumerable acrobatic tricks and much singing and dancing. The stage walls were now disguised with painted canvas, and many properties and pieces of furniture were placed about the stage and used as needed. But the major feature of the setting was a long curving ramp, included for its functional rather than its decorative value. Overall the production seemed an improvisation based on Ostrovsky's play, the original having almost completely disappeared. It was roundly denounced by traditionalists, but it was popular with audiences and eventually was given more than fifteen hundred performances. Furthermore, it led to many imitations, a contributing factor in Meyerhold's ultimate downfall.

By 1925, Meyerhold seems to have tired of his constructivist experiments and turned in new directions. In Faiko's *Bubus the Teacher* (1925), rhythm was the governing element. In several productions of this period, Meyerhold showed his concern for the rhythm inherent in materials. Here he suspended bamboo to create a semicircle and used a circular green rug to outline the acting area. These materials and their arrangement became part of an overall rhythmical pattern, almost orchestral in conception. Each scene was set to musical accompaniment, a few (those involving decadent and frenetic capitalists) to jazz, but most to works by Liszt and Chopin, played by a pianist placed in a visible alcove high above and at the rear of the stage. Each character also had his own individual rhythmic pattern. The actors were dressed in faultless fashionable dress and the whole had an air of refinement that had been completely missing from Meyerhold's rather crude productions of the preceding years. Perhaps the most controversial element in *Bubus the Teacher* was the "pre-acting"—long pauses between speeches during which pantomime was used to show transitions in thought and response and to prepare for what was about to come. Unfortunately the script was so thin that such drawing out of action and reaction only made its faults more evident.

By common consent, Meyerhold's finest production came in 1926 with *The Inspector General,* his reworking with Mikhail Korenev of Gogol's masterpiece. The original text was considerably altered through insertions of material taken from other works by Gogol, through invented pantomimes and tableaux, and through added characters and changed emphases. The script was divided into fifteen episodes, each with its own title. The provincial atmosphere of the original was abandoned in favor of an elegance, pomposity, and luxury more nearly that of St. Petersburg itself. In this way, the play was transformed into a judgment on the whole tsarist epoch.

The stage was surrounded by a semicircular arrangement of simulated mahogany screens in which there were fifteen doors. The back opened to permit wagons (approximately 16 by 20 feet in size) to glide forward or back in tracks. In his treatment of visual elements, Meyerhold seems to have relied on two sources: nineteenth-century engravings and the wax museum. The actors were dressed in elegant period costumes and the furnishings were authentic period pieces. At the beginning of each scene,

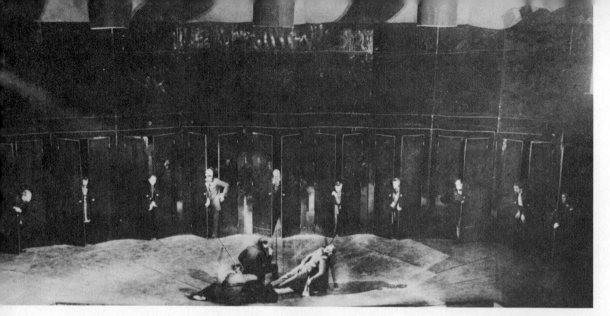

The "bribery" scene from Meyerhold's production of Gogol's
The Inspector General, 1926.

the wagon moved forward with the actors arranged in frozen wax-figure poses, which were held for a moment; at the end of scenes they froze once more and the wagon was taken away. Space on the platform was so restricted that all movement and business was carefully worked out and considerably stylized. At the end of the play, a screen, on which was projected the announcement of the real inspector's arrival, came down; when it rose again it revealed lifelike effigies of the characters captured forever in their wax-museum poses.

Rhythm played an important part in the production. Most of the action was accompanied by a musical score (much of it taken from nineteenth-century sources and the rest composed by Mikhail Gnesin, who arranged it all). In many scenes, characters spoke and gestured in unison, and a large proportion of the speech and action was worked out for its rhythmical values. The scenes were embellished throughout with highly inventive stage business. Perhaps the most famous example is that in which eleven hands extended simultaneously from eleven doors to offer bribes to the supposed inspector.

The production provoked a tempest throughout Russia and was widely discussed in the press. Some critics denounced the liberties taken with the text, Meyerhold's unorthodox political slant, and his "class-alien formalism." But it was one of the most popular productions of the era and remained in Meyerhold's repertory until his theatre was closed in 1938. But while *The Inspector General* was perhaps Meyerhold's greatest accomplishment, it also marks the beginning of his decline. Increasingly, and especially after

Stalin came to full power around 1927, he was accused of being out of touch with the needs of the people both in his choice of plays and in his production methods. Unfortunately, those new plays with which Meyerhold felt the greatest sympathy were often considered unacceptable.

By 1928 attendance at Meyerhold's theatre began to fall off, perhaps because there had been so few recent additions to the repertory. In 1929, seeking to remedy this situation, he presented Mayakovsky's *The Bed Bug,* a satire on the philistine Soviet society of the day set in perspective against the world of 1979. The contrast was sharpened by presenting the present-day scenes in semirealistic costumes and settings and the episodes from the future in constructivist style (no doubt indicating Meyerhold's and Mayakovsky's ideas about both society and art). This production was very popular with audiences, but Mayakovsky's *The Bath House* (1930), a satire on Soviet bureaucrats and red tape, seemed dangerously pointed. Here an inventor, held back by an inefficient bureaucracy, is able, through a time machine, to go forward to 2030 and bring back the Phosphorescent Lady, who comments acidulously on the conditions of 1930. Among other topics, the realism of the Moscow Art Theatre and conformity in all the arts were ridiculed. In a fashion somewhat reminiscent of his earlier productions, Meyerhold clothed the inventor and his friends in workers' coveralls and had them perform with great vitality, while he dressed the bureaucrats in business suits and had them sit about languidly in overstuffed chairs. Stalin is said to have been deeply offended by *The Bath House,* and it was viciously attacked by party spokesmen. Mayakovsky committed suicide shortly afterward.

These rebuffs were no doubt lessened for Meyerhold by the praise his company won on its foreign tour later that year. In Paris he received a standing ovation from an audience which included Cocteau, Picasso, Jouvet, Dullin, and Baty. But from then on, Meyerhold would fight a losing battle at home.

In the 1920s Meyerhold was without doubt the dominant figure in the Russian theatre, a fact even recognized by the government itself. Not only was Meyerhold named to head some of the country's most important training programs, he was the first director to be named "People's Artist of the Republic" (in 1923 on the occasion of his twentieth anniversary as a director). In 1928, his and Vakhtangov's companies represented Russia at an international festival in Paris (where Meyerhold's company presented his "class-alien" *The Inspector General*). At home, he was especially popular with young audiences and young directors, who spread his influence throughout Russia. If "formalism" was to be weeded out, Meyerhold necessarily became the foremost target.

Never a cautious man, Meyerhold supplied his enemies with plenty of ammunition to use against him. First, he had elevated his individual taste, ideas, and will above those of all the people with whom he worked.

His actors and designers were expected to carry out his ideas rather than to contribute their own (after 1924, even the settings and costumes were made to his specifications). Furthermore, Meyerhold reshaped plays as he saw fit (even contemporary plays and against the expressed wishes of the playwright). Thus, he could be accused of fostering the cult of the individual in an age of collectivism. Perhaps most damning in Soviet eyes, Meyerhold favored "formalism." The Russian leaders wanted orthodox political ideas presented in understandable (that is, traditional) form. This Meyerhold stoutly opposed. It is probably also true, as has often been charged, that Meyerhold's productions were not always polished (he often left detailed work to his assistants) and that he was more interested in new ideas than in perfecting old ones. Regardless of all charges that might be brought against him, his was one of the most inventive and fertile talents the theatre has known.

It is often said that Meyerhold's influence was not lasting because he created no "school" of followers as did Stanislavsky and Vakhtangov. In one sense this is true, for Meyerhold never developed a system that could be transmitted; his was a restless exploration of new means, and consequently if he had anything to teach it was the notion that each artist must find his own creative approach. Thus, he could bequeath only an attitude, not a method.

But in the 1920s, Meyerhold was clearly an inspiration to many young men. Of these, perhaps the most important was Sergei Eisenstein (1898–1948), an assistant to Meyerhold before he became director in 1922 of the Proletcult's Moscow theatre, to which he brought biomechanics and other of Meyerhold's ideas. Eisenstein's most important dramatic production was based on Ostrovsky's *Enough Stupidity in Every Wise Man,* which he completely modernized (even to the point of adding contemporary French and English generals). He treated the stage as an arena, above which characters balanced on tightropes while exchanging dialogue. Part of the action was shown on film. But probably the most important aspect of the production was Eisenstein's use of a "montage of attractions"—several unrelated events performed simultaneously in different parts of the theatre. By juxtaposing them, he could point up contrasts and make significant points. Montage was to become one of the most characteristic features of Eisenstein's masterful films, which he began to make in 1924.

Meyerhold and his followers were strong supporters of the Revolution (if not always of Soviet policies). Consequently, in the 1920s they believed that all productions should have some revolutionary import. Thus, it is ironical that in the 1930s they should fall victims to a politicalized theatre which they had helped to create, while the "academic" theatres that fought to keep the theatre free from tendentiousness survived. But before considering such results, it is necessary to trace other developments prior to the 1930s.

Next to Meyerhold, Tairov was the major antirealist of the 1920s, but unlike Meyerhold, he sought to keep the theatre free from ideological bias. In *Proclamations of an Artist* (1917), Tairov declared art's independence of politics and stated that the current turmoil had nothing specifically to do with the theatre. Later, in reference to Meyerhold's production of *The Dawns*, he said that to present plays about contemporary social and political events is like eating mustard after a meal. Tairov believed that the theatre, through esthetic and sensual experiences of great intensity, should lift audiences above the drabness of life. Consequently, his policies at the Kamerny Theatre after 1917 remained unchanged.

Tairov's first production after the Revolution was of Wilde's *Salome* (previously banned as immoral), with settings and costumes by Alexandra Ekster, a leading cubist-expressionist artist. Mme. Ekster's "dynamic costumes" for this play were to be extremely influential. For each character she sought to determine a basic rhythm and to capture it by combining various materials and colors in a single costume. She wrote of "delaying velvet, the speedy, agile silk, the heavy-paced brocade," and of "quieting and disquieting," "heavy and light" colors. She painted fabrics with pigment and fitted some costumes with rigid frameworks to ensure that they would function as she wished. Through the manipulation of fabric, texture, color, and line, she sought to create a "living, colorful sculpture" or "make-up for the body." The basic setting was an architectural arrangement of columns, steps, and levels, but it was made "dynamic" by draperies and curtains of various materials, colors, and designs which were raised or lowered, piled up on the floor, or torn. According to Tairov, they were intended to reflect emotional and esthetic values rather than to be representational. For example, at the beginning of Salome's dance, the backdrop was torn to reveal a red curtain that seemed to bleed. The entire production was a masterful handling of color, rhythm, music, dance, and intoned speech.

Tairov's production of Wilde's *Salome*, 1917. The costumes and setting are by Alexandra Ekster.

With his productions of Claudel's *The Exchange* and *The Tidings Brought to Mary,* Tairov encountered his first opposition from party officials, for Claudel, with his mystical Catholicism, was denounced as an "imperialist, reactionary bourgeois." Undeterred, Tairov, in the midst of famine, disease, and civil war, presented Scribe's *Adrienne Lecouvreur* in 1919. With its refined, colorful, and lyrical atmosphere, Tairov sought to provide a striking contrast with the realities of the moment. Any dissatisfaction with Tairov at this time did not prevent the Kamerny from being designated an "academic theatre" and provided a subsidy. But Tairov must have felt some need to justify his work, for in 1921 he published his *Notes of a Director,* which set forth his ideals and described his practice.

Tairov next turned to tragedy, presenting Racine's *Phaedra* in 1921 in settings and costumes by A. Vesnin, who, like Mme. Ekster, was a cubist-expressionist. The entire production was monumental, archaic, and mythic. Everything resembling modern life was cut away. The actors wore *cothurnoi,* which not only increased their height but restricted their movement to the absolutely essential. Costumes and gestures made the characters seem animated stone statues. The setting was composed of angular steps (which also suggested an ocean cliff), two enormous columns (which resembled the portals of some ancient temple), and geometrical forms suspended in the air. Three soldiers, static as the columns, were outlined against the limitless indigo background. Through such means, Tairov achieved a sense of complete timelessness.

Tairov then turned in 1922 to comedy and operetta with E. T. A. Hoffmann's *Princess Brambilla* and Charles Lecocq's *Giroflé-Girofla.* Here he utilized the contemporary concern for popular entertainments—music hall, harlequinade, circus—to achieve works of pure theatrical magic. *Giroflé-Girofla* was especially admired for its unrestrained gaiety and for its lighting effects, often said to be the finest ever seen in the Russian theatre.

Tairov's spirited production of Lecocq's *Giroflé-Girofla*
at the Kamerny Theatre in 1922.

In 1923 the Kamerny won great critical acclaim through its first foreign tour. (It was to undertake others in 1925 and 1930, as a result of which it became the best known of all Russian troupes, a factor often said to have prevented the Soviets from taking overly harsh measures against it.) But by this time Tairov was encountering increasing criticism at home for his seeming lack of commitment to the revolutionary cause. Perhaps as a result and to comply with Lunacharsky's "Back to Ostrovsky" policy, in 1924 Tairov mounted *The Thunderstorm,* the first realistic Russian drama he had ever staged. The single setting, by the constructivist-expressionist Sternberg brothers, was a wooden ramp and platform resembling a bridge. The costumes retained the lines of nineteenth-century garments, but all superfluous details were eliminated. The action was also freed from historical and localizing elements, and the actors recited their lines in the Kamerny's characteristic song-chant style. As a result, the action was removed from the regional and historical milieu with which it had always been associated, and lifted to the realm of the archetypal. By avoiding both naturalism and extreme formalism, Tairov achieved a style later to be designated "purism" or "neorealism," one to which he would often return thereafter.

In 1924, Tairov also presented his first play about contemporary life— although it was still foreign in setting—G. K. Chesterton's *The Man Who Was Thursday,* about a group of anarchists, each named for a day of the week, and how one outwits a number of detectives while he plans and carries out an act of terrorism. It marks a new phase in Tairov's work, the turn to the West in his repertory and to "urbanism" in his production style. The setting, designed by S. E. Krzhizhanovsky, outwardly resembled Meyerhold's "constructions," for it was composed of girders, turning wheels, elevators, and flashing signs, but it was used by Tairov to create a rhythmical "symphony of the big city." Still, with its realistic costumes and properties and its urbanistic effects, it moved Tairov much closer to the futurists.

Through the remainder of the 1920s, Tairov's major productions were of Western plays, of which his theatre was the principal purveyor in Russia. In his repertory were included Shaw's *Saint Joan* (1924), O'Neill's *The Hairy Ape* (1926), *Desire Under the Elms* (1926), and *All God's Chillun Got Wings* (1929), and Hasenclever's *Antigone* (1927). But by now Tairov was succumbing to the political pressures he had sought to resist, and both *The Hairy Ape* and *All God's Chillun Got Wings* were given strong anticapitalist slants much in the manner of Meyerhold. Tairov also capitulated to the demand that he include contemporary Soviet plays in his repertory, though with unfortunate results. In 1928, Bulgakov's *The Purple Island,* a satire on the propagandistic drama of the day and the party members who pass judgment on theatrical repertories, was viciously attacked and soon removed from the stage. In 1929, Mikhail Levidov's *Plot of the Equals,* a French revolutionary story of would-be reformers who degenerate into bloodthirsty dictators, was removed after a single performance. Thereafter, this production was always enumerated among Tairov's offenses.

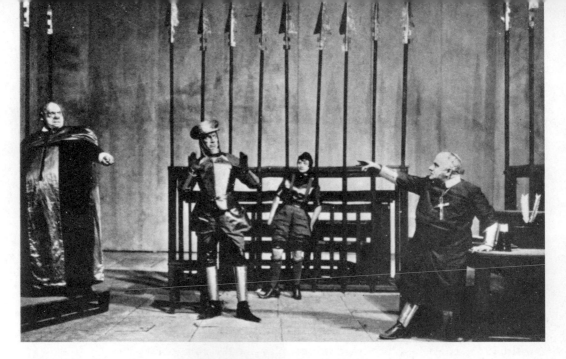

Scene from Shaw's *Saint Joan,* produced by Tairov at the Kamerny
in 1924. Note the mingling of elements from many periods.

Tairov, like Meyerhold, was tolerated throughout the 1920s. Though
he made many compromises with his desire to remain free from political
concerns and true to his esthetic ideals, he did not go far enough, according
to the party's officials, who after 1930 stepped up their attacks against
his "formalism" and his alienation from the needs of the state. For him,
too, the 1930s would be traumatic.

Another important director during the years immediately following the
Revolution was Yevgeny Vakhtangov (1883–1922), whose career was cut
short by his early death. By the time of the Revolution, Vakhtangov had
already established a reputation as a director and as head of the Moscow
Art Theatre's First Studio after 1916. Beginning in 1913, Vakhtangov
also worked with an independent student group, the Mansurov Studio,
which in 1917 became Vakhtangov's Studio and in 1921 the Third Studio of the Moscow Art Theatre. (Stanislavsky had created the Second Studio
in 1916 as a three-year actor-training course.) Thus, most of Vakhtangov's
significant work was done in subsidiaries of the Moscow Art Theatre.

The importance of Vakhtangov, however, lies in his successful blending of Stanislavsky's realism with Meyerhold's stylization. In the attempt to find an effective means of staging nonrealistic drama without denying the actor's creativity and the inner reality of characters, Vakhtangov succeeded where Stanislavsky had failed. Stanislavsky thoroughly approved of Vakhtangov's work and in him saw his potential successor.

Although Vakhtangov labeled his approach "fantastic realism," it most resembled expressionism, for in it external appearance and behavior were exaggerated, distorted, and reshaped to reflect inner realities (the mask behind the face, the psychological, social, or moral truth behind surface appearance). But if, like Meyerhold or Tairov, he distorted reality, like Stanislavsky, Vakhtangov believed that the director is bound by the playwright's text. Nevertheless, he declared that the director should "contemporize" scripts, keeping in mind his particular audience, time, actors, and theatrical situation, for what is effective in one context will not be suitable a decade later. Vakhtangov emphasized the director's need for creative actors. He declared that each production is the expression of a "theatrical collective at the given stage of its creative development," and in his actors he sought partners who could "fill form with content and find the necessary justification for conduct on the stage even though this justification had to be found not in the psychological but in the theatrical plan of the spectacle." Thus, to Stanislavsky's inner motivation Vakhtangov added theatrical motivation.

In practice, Vakhtangov began by deciding how he wished the audience to respond at each moment in a production. The actors, keeping in mind the desired results, then sought through improvisation to discover both the appropriate means and some justification for those means. From these "études," Vakhtangov eventually chose those which seemed most effective. Although time-consuming, it was a cooperative creative effort in which Vakhtangov avoided imposing his own preconceptions on the actors (as both Meyerhold and Tairov were accused of doing) and which resulted in emotionally convincing performances (for, even if he did not arrive at Stanislavskian inner motivations, each actor invented some theatrical justification for whatever he did). Nevertheless, it was Vakhtangov who made the crucial decisions—about which effects were desired and which of the many possible solutions would be used in performance—and it was his strong sense of fittingness that molded his actors' inventions into a unified production.

Although Vakhtangov's ultimate influence derived as much from his teaching as from his productions, his fame now rests primarily upon four productions done during the last two years of his life: *The Miracle of Saint Anthony, Erik XIV, The Dybbuk,* and *Turandot.* Vakhtangov had worked on Maeterlinck's *The Miracle of Saint Anthony* for almost four years before it was presented at the Third Studio in 1921 as a biting satire on bourgeois society. The play tells a simple story: upon the death of the rich

Hortense, relatives and hangers-on assemble to claim her wealth; then the tramplike Saint Anthony arrives and revives her, much to the chagrin of the relatives, who have him arrested; only the servant, Virginie, recognizes his saintliness. In Vakhtangov's production, all of the would-be heirs were conceived as a unit—dressed in black, given wooden gestures, and treated as living corpses seen against the white background of the setting and furniture. On the other hand, St. Anthony and Virginie, the representatives of virtue, were dressed in white and played with realistic vitality. Hortense was costumed as a large doll. The whole production was given such precise rhythms that some critics described it as geometric.

Erik XIV, one of Strindberg's late history plays, was presented at the First Studio in 1921. It tells the story of a near-pathological prince who yearns for the simple life of his subjects and seeks to marry the daughter of a poor soldier. Vakhtangov treated it as a struggle between the dying world of the nobility and the vital world of the proletariat. Consequently, the courtiers and aristocrats were presented as soulless automatons who spoke and moved mechanically, while the proletariat was treated as individuals, clothed and performed in lifelike manner. The scenery, designed by Ignaty Nivinsky, reflected the same pattern. Erik's throne room was composed of bent columns, rusty gold ornaments, distorted windows and doors, and angular shafts of light, while the settings associated with the common people were depicted realistically. But the great revelation of the production was Mikhail Chekhov's Erik, and thereafter he was considered one of Russia's foremost actors.

The Dybbuk by Solomon Rappaport (S. An-sky) was presented by the Habima Theatre in 1922. The Habima, composed of Jewish actors, was created in 1918 and headed by Alexander Granovsky (1890–1937). (During the 1920s it would tour widely to great critical acclaim. In 1931 it settled in Palestine and is now the national theatre of Israel.) Although he understood neither Hebrew nor Yiddish, the languages used by the Habima, Vakhtangov worked with the company from the beginning and was largely responsible for establishing its style.

The Dybbuk tells the story of two lovers, Leah (daughter of the wealthy Sender) and Channon (a poor struggling student). After Sender insists that Leah marry a rich man, Channon dies and his spirit (or dybbuk) enters Leah's body and takes control of it. At the urging of Sender, holy men exorcise the dybbuk, but Leah's spirit also leaves and she dies. Vakhtangov made of it a philosophical statement, summed up by Yuri Zavadsky (one of Vakhtangov's pupils who worked with him on the production): "It told of the monstrous injustice of life, of the poor and the rich, of the despair of the former and the smugness of the latter, and of love triumphant over death." The settings and costumes were by Nathan Altman, who also painted the actors' faces to integrate them into the total design. The vital and realistic Leah and Channon were surrounded by stylized and grotesque figures. Sender's dark, stifling, joyless house seemed to epitomize the oppressive Hassidic sect, which was further embodied in

Design by Nivinsky for Vakhtangov's production of Gozzi's *Turandot* in 1922.

the ten elders, who were dressed identically in grease-stained black robes and who moved in unison. At the wedding, a dance of beggars (a blind woman, a tubercular man, and a hunchback) with outstretched, clawing hands seemed a projection of Leah's torment and a prophecy of her death. Even those who could not understand the language were enormously impressed by the production's nightmarish oppressiveness.

Vakhtangov's final production, Gozzi's *Turandot,* presented at the Third Studio in 1922, is considered his masterpiece. Unlike the preceding productions, *Turandot* was a hymn of unalloyed joy. Although worked out in precise detail, it seemed mere spontaneous improvisation throughout. Gozzi's play tells of the cruel Princess Turandot, who beheads any suitor who cannot answer her three riddles, and how she is ultimately conquered by Prince Calaf. It is a *commedia dell' arte* script, the action of which supposedly occurs in China.

The setting, by Nivinsky, was a stylized, cubistic arrangement of ramps, platforms, balconies, and leaning walls. As the play opened, four *commedia* figures—Pantalone, Brighella, Truffaldino, and Tartaglia—came forward to tell the audience about the play, and while they spoke, the other actors, dressed in evening clothes, appeared and began to improvise their costumes. Prince Calaf made a turban from a towel; the Wise Man created a beard by tying a scarf about his chin; King Timur fashioned a scepter from a tennis racket. Music was also improvised by the actors with combs and tissue paper.

Thus, a thoroughgoing theatricality was established from the beginning. Thereafter, the actors seemed always to be improvising, changing their lines to suit their own tastes and commenting on their own and others' performances. Perhaps the combination of inner realism and theatrical irony that characterized the production are best suggested by the scene in which an actor cried real tears only to have another come from the wings, collect the tears in a bowl, and exhibit them to the audience as proof of the actor's talent. In *Turandot,* Vakhtangov sought no great message, declaring instead that in such troubled times "we need a festival." He fell ill on the night of the dress rehearsal and never saw a performance. He died three months later. This production of *Turandot* has been retained in the repertory ever since as a memorial to Vakhtangov's genius.

It is perhaps fortunate that Vakhtangov died early and did not live to suffer the fate of Meyerhold and Tairov, for like theirs, his work was "formalistic" and his major successes were gained with non-Soviet plays. Vakhtangov was even more fortunate in having created a "school" of directors who perpetuated his ideals. Among the major Russian figures of the period, only Vakhtangov and Stanislavsky left a strong heritage and Vakhtangov is unique in having created a school of directors, for Stanislavsky's following was largely among actors. Among Vakhtangov's disciples were Yuri Zavadsky (1894–   ), Boris Shchukin (1894–1939), Reuben Simonov (1899–1968), Boris Zakhava (1896–   ), Nikolai Akimov (1901–   ), and Alexander Popov (1892–1961), all major directors of the Soviet theatre. Through them, Vakhtangov's teaching was passed on to others, and since the end of the Stalinist era, when the hold of socialist realism began to weaken, the appeal of Vakhtangov's approach has greatly increased, for it avoids the extremes of both realism and formalism.

After Vakhtangov's death, both the Third Studio and the First Studio were separated from the Moscow Art Theatre. In 1926, the Third Studio

The production of *Turandot,* directed by Vakhtangov shortly before his death, at the Third Studio, 1922.

became the Vakhtangov Theatre and remains one of Moscow's leading companies. In 1924, the First Studio was renamed the Second Moscow Art Theatre and placed under the direction of Mikhail Chekhov (1891–1955), who had headed the studio since Vakhtangov's death. Chekhov soon established himself as one of Russia's leading innovators.

Nephew of the playwright, Chekhov became a member of the Moscow Art Theatre in 1910 at the age of nineteen, and was one of the young actors chosen for the First Studio when it was founded in 1911. At this time Chekhov was completely committed to Stanislavsky's system, but subsequently he moved steadily away from it and with his portrayal of Erik XIV declared his independence. Thereafter a break with the parent company became almost inevitable.

Chekhov explored his developing ideas in his own studio and later described them in *The Actor's Path* (1929), *The Problem of the Actor* (1946), and *To the Actor* (1951). He argued that creativity is aroused by a vision of what can be rather than by what is. Thus, he stressed imagination and inspiration over observation and psychological truth. He used yogalike exercises in concentration to liberate the actor from his surroundings and personal limitations so he might enter more fully into a world of fancy where stereotypes and common sense are left behind. Yet he taught the necessity of a fully developed stage technique and of the actor standing outside himself to observe and shape what he does. He made a sharp distinction between the actor and his creations: "The artist purifies and ennobles his characters without bringing them any useless features from his own personal nature." His method was in essence highly controlled fantasy making.

Chekhov himself played roles ranging from the comic and grotesque to the tragic. In his serious parts he seemed to lay bare the characters' inner torment in a kind of psychological expressionism, and his comic portrayals always had something of the grotesque in them. Although he devised many exercises and taught many students, no one else ever completely exemplified Chekhov's method.

Chekhov was without doubt one of the greatest actors of his time. His Hamlet at the First Studio in 1924 was considered a masterpiece. Following the production he was named "Honored Artist of the Soviet Union" and the First Studio was designated the Second Moscow Art Theatre and placed under his direction. But Chekhov's emphasis on the spiritual, ideal, and fantastic realms eventually laid him open to charges of mysticism and lack of sympathy with the Bolshevik cause. A conflict soon developed with Alexey Diky, a director at the Second Moscow Art Theatre and one of Vakhtangov's former students, who in 1927 led sixteen members of the company to secede and publicly to call Chekhov a mystic and political alien. Chekhov decided not to fight and left Russia. The remainder of his career was spent in films and stagework in Austria, France, Germany, England, and the United States. In 1936 he established a school in England and later moved it to America.

Chekhov's solution—flight to the West—had already been adopted by several others, among them Evreinov (who after his work with mass spectacles had gradually withdrawn from theatrical activities before departing in 1925 for Czechoslovakia and France) and Komissarzhevsky (who left in 1919 and thereafter worked in England, America, and France).

~~ VI ~~

Not all Soviet directors were interested in experimentation and innovation. Some theatres sought merely to maintain earlier standards and to educate the masses through realistic productions of the classics. Such troupes more nearly represented the tastes of Soviet leaders than did the experimenters. The most conservative companies were those at the former imperial theatres. In Petrograd, the Alexandrinsky at first performed a repertory which relied heavily on Ostrovsky, Fonvizin, and Turgenev. In Moscow, the Maly in some seasons devoted up to 98 percent of its performances to the classics. Its position was strengthened after 1923 when Lunacharsky proclaimed his "Back to Ostrovsky" campaign, for since the nineteenth century the Maly had been known as the "House of Ostrovsky." The government's attitude toward the company is indicated in part by its selection of Maria Yermolova (1853–1928) as the first artist to be honored by the state—in 1920 on the occasion of her fiftieth anniversary in the theatre. The company was also deeply involved in the struggle between the traditionalists and the innovators. When Meyerhold launched his attack against the academic theatres in 1921 and called for their liquidation, he was vigorously answered by Alexander Yuzhin (1857–1927), the Maly's director, who accused Meyerhold of sterile formalism. This was one of the first skirmishes in the long battle between two attitudes that would end in the triumph of socialist realism.

The Moscow Art Theatre also upheld tradition, although less rigidly than did the former imperial theatres. On the other hand, it did not play a very active role for several years after 1917. At first it depended entirely on its prerevolutionary repertory and did not add a new production until 1920. Furthermore, in 1919 it suffered a serious loss when a number of its actors, on tour in southern Russia, were cut off by the White Army and defected to the West. Several settled in Czechoslovakia, where they formed the "Prague Group of the Moscow Art Theatre," while others set up training schools in other countries. After 1919, the Moscow Art and the Maly theatres established a close relationship and often exchanged actors and sought to present a united front against their detractors.

Between 1917 and 1924, the Moscow Art Theatre mounted only two important productions, *Cain* and *The Inspector General*. Byron's *Cain* in 1920 was so unsuccessful that it was withdrawn after eight performances (although it was later played abroad). In this production, Stanislavsky sought to make his stage completely "sculptural," for he dispensed with painted scenery and created a wholly three-dimensional space to surround the actor. The production is best remembered for its awe-inspiring scene in Hell where the spirit of each departed Great Being was represented by a gigantic statue set against a hazy background. *The Inspector General,* staged in 1921, featured Mikhail Chekhov as Khlestakov in a production which freed the play from its historical milieu and concentrated on the universal truth of the satire. Stanislavsky also continued his exploration of spatial dimensions by beginning the play in a very restricted area and gradually enlarging it—suggesting thereby that the satire reaches out to encompass more and more of society. The production was a considerable success, although Chekhov was attacked by some critics for his near-pathological and grotesque characterization.

By 1922, the Moscow Art Theatre was playing such a small role in Soviet theatrical life that no objections were raised when the entire company (except for apprentices and the actors attached to the studios) left on a two-year tour of Europe and America. Not only did this tour increase the troupe's already considerable fame abroad, it resulted in one other major event: Stanislavsky was persuaded by Elizabeth Hapgood Reynolds to begin his writings about his work. The first result was *My Life in Art* (1924), available in English long before it was published in Russia. Mrs. Reynolds also worked with Stanislavsky on *An Actor Prepares* (1936), but because of the war she was unable to gain access to the remainder of the series—*Building a Character* and *Creating a Role*—until later. It is primarily through these works that Stanislavsky's ideas have been disseminated.

When Stanislavsky returned to Russia in 1924, he had to begin rebuilding his company. Not only had he lost many actors but some of the studios were alienated as well. The First Studio had already been designated the Second Moscow Art Theatre and soon the Third Studio would become the Vakhtangov Theatre. To strengthen the parent company, the Second Studio was now incorporated into it. There remained the Fourth Studio, established in 1921 to encourage a "healthy artistic realism based on simplicity and truth, depth and fullness of content, acting and production." But by 1924, it too was moving away from its sponsor and in 1927 would become the Realistic Theatre. The Moscow Art Theatre also retained its Musical Studio, established in 1920, to encourage effective acting in musical drama. Under Nemirovich-Danchenko's direction it would retain its strength well into the 1930s and present such notable productions as its adaptations of *Lysistrata* and of *Carmen*. But in 1924, the Moscow Art

Theatre was probably at its lowest point in terms of both its troupe and its prestige in Russia.

Having decided to rebuild, Stanislavsky set about demonstrating an effective alternative to Meyerhold's methods. His first major success came in 1926 with Ostrovsky's *The Burning Heart* (considered by many critics a calculated answer to Meyerhold's staging of *The Forest*). He played the text as written but, as in *The Inspector General,* muted the historical aspects and emphasized the universality of the satire. In this way he sought to demonstrate that a valid interpretation should arise from within a text rather than being superimposed upon it.

Like all the other companies, the Moscow Art Theatre now began to present Soviet plays, although before its foreign tour it had steadfastly refused to do so. Its first effort, Trenyov's *Pugachev's Rebellion* in 1925, was not a success, and, while Bulgakov's *The Days of the Turbins* in 1926 was extremely effective, its sympathetic portrait of the White Russians was denounced as counterrevolutionary. But with Ivanov's *Armored Train 14-69* in 1927 the Moscow Art Theatre achieved success. Here was an ideologically acceptable play performed with all the care for realistic and psychological detail admired by the Soviet leaders.

It was around 1925 that other companies also began to win recognition with Soviet drama. In 1926 the Maly had one of the greatest successes of the 1920s with Trenyov's *Lyubov Yarovaya.* Although unrecognized at the time, a turning point had been reached. The prototypes of socialist realism had been created and soon the campaign for its exclusive claims would begin. The fortunes of the Moscow Art Theatre would now steadily improve.

～ VII ～

The pressure to subordinate artistic to ideological ends was intensified around 1927 and increased thereafter. With the end of the New Economic Policy and the beginning of Stalin's first Five-Year Plan came the demand that everyone dedicate himself to realizing the party's goals. To bring artists into line, the government at first permitted the Russian Association of Proletarian Writers (RAPP) considerable latitude in its attacks on all nonproletarian art. The leaders of this group argued that, since Communist Russia represents the victory of the proletariat, its artists and writers should be proletarians who wholeheartedly serve its needs. It declared that no apolitical art should be tolerated and that the last bourgeois remnants should be stamped out. It denounced all the academic theatres: the Moscow Art Theatre was said to cater to the progressive bourgeoisie, the Maly to merchants and aristocrats, and Meyerhold and Tairov to bohemians and symbolists. To remedy this situation, it sought to gain control over criticism so that the right kind of plays and production methods would be praised or blamed. In 1927 RAPP also helped to found the Theatre of Working Young People (TRAM), which through amateur productions sought to indoctrinate workers about proletarian conceptions of art and to propagandize for governmental programs.

RAPP won many victories. After 1927 the administration of theatres was altered. Prior to this time there was no standard policy, perhaps because responsibility for theatres was divided among several governmental bodies. Many theatres were still privately owned and few of any type were headed by members of the party. In 1927 a concerted attempt was made to bring all theatres under stricter control and to establish clear-cut administrative procedures for them. Each theatre was placed under the control of a governing council presided over by a manager. Party members were now systematically trained and installed, wherever possible, as managers and given the task of ensuring the political orthodoxy of their troupes. A manager was in a position to influence the membership on the governing council and, since the council approved the repertory, budget, and production plans, he could do much to control both which plays would be presented and how they would be treated. In addition, a more stringent censorship was instituted after 1930. Not only did each play have to be approved before it could be placed in production, but no public performance could be given without a license, which could be obtained only after the dress rehearsal had been seen by the licensing officials. In other words, censorship was extended to include production methods as well as scripts, perhaps because Meyerhold had demonstrated that a well-known play might become unrecognizable in production.

Thus, governmental pressures gradually increased. In 1931, RAPP proposed establishing its own theatres to replace all those then existing. But by now RAPP and TRAM, like Proletcult, had made the error of elevating their views above those of the Communist party, for they argued that the transformation of the arts must arise out of the working class, whereas the party was seeking to impose a program from above. Consequently, in 1932, RAPP and TRAM were suppressed and the Union of Soviet Writers, which included all authors regardless of outlook, was created, and Maxim Gorky, a moderate, was appointed to head it. But this seeming rejection of extremism was illusory, for it soon became evident that the union merely made surveillance more efficient, since all authors were required to join it and since it began to establish policies for all Soviet writers.

The first major blow came in 1934 when the Union of Soviet Writers proclaimed "socialist realism" the appropriate style for all writing: "Socialist realism, being the basic method of Soviet literature and criticism, requires from the artists truthful, historically concrete representation of reality in its revolutionary development. Moreover, truth and historical completeness of artistic representation must be combined with the task of ideological transformation and education of the working man in the spirit of Socialism." Stalin more succinctly described it as "national in form and socialist in content" (by "national in form" he meant realistic). The official support of socialist realism was to last until the 1950s. Under it, not only were writers expected to reflect contemporary political realities but to include a positive hero who pointed the way toward the total triumph of communism.

In the theatre, socialist realism in effect required that all artists be subordinated to the dramatist, since it was the script that provided the primary ideological content and which was considered worthy of production by the censor (the assumption being that the play would not be seriously altered during rehearsal). Unfortunately, playwriting was the Soviet theatre's weakest element. (All the great achievements of the 1920s had been made with non-Soviet plays or with extreme stylistic treatments of Soviet scripts.) To insist that the theatre present ideologically correct messages in concrete material form was to insist that it be transformed. In its attempt to conform, it lost its distinctiveness and its vitality.

Few Soviet plays merit detailed attention. Most are melodramatic (characters who support the communist ideal are presented as heroes and those who oppose it are treated as villains; resolutions always point toward the ultimate triumph of communism and the discomfiture of its enemies). For this the playwrights cannot be blamed entirely, for those who sought to present complex characters and ideas were branded counterrevolutionaries or remnants of a decadent bourgeoisie. Since he was permitted little scope in characterization, idea, or style, the dramatist could only fall back on novelty of incident. Under the circumstances, it is not surprising that outstanding plays are rare.

Few prerevolutionary dramatists continued to write after 1917. Andreyev, probably the most popular of prewar writers, died in 1919. Blok headed the repertory subsection in the Commissariat of Education but championed the classics rather than new plays. Among the older writers, only Gorky played an important role under the Communists and even he was alienated from the regime for many years following the Revolution. Consequently, his plays were little performed until 1927, after which they soon came to be considered models of appropriate style, even if they did present rather outmoded pictures of a distant past. After Gorky was named head of the Union of Soviet Writers in 1932, his works came to be considered prototypes of socialist realism and his plays almost obligatory parts of each theatre's repertory.

After the Revolution, Gorky wrote only two plays, and these not until the 1930s—*Yegor Bulichev and Others* (1932) and *Dostigayev and Others* (1933)—and even these concern life before the Revolution. In the former, Yegor Bulichev, a merchant dying of cancer, is a kind of metaphor for the tsarist state, and his death coincides with the beginning of the Revolution.

Yet the metaphor is not precise, for Bulichev despises the corruption around him and would like to be free of it but can no more escape it than he can cure the cancer that is consuming him. The story is slight, for Gorky concentrates on re-creating the milieu and tone of the era. It is a loose collection of episodes given considerable strength by its fine characterizations. *Dostigayev and Others* is a continuation of the earlier play and includes many of the same characters. It takes place in the months between the two revolutions of 1917 and shows Dostigayev's attempts to use the political situation to his financial advantage. A far more partisan play than its predecessor, it satirizes those hostile to the Bolsheviks. Consequently, it lacks the complexity of the earlier work and never achieved a comparable popularity. Gorky's prerevolutionary works were also revived frequently. In numbers of productions during the 1930s, Gorky's plays ranked second only to those of Ostrovsky.

Except for Mayakovsky's *Mystery-Bouffe,* mass spectacles, and propaganda skits, few Soviet plays were written until the 1920s. The first playwright to make a strong impression was Vladimir Bill-Belotserkovsky (1885–   ), whose *Storm* (1925) was considered an important step forward for Soviet drama. Set in a provincial town during the civil war, it centers around an idealized district commander who overcomes all threats—from hunger, typhus, counterrevolutionaries, and the White Army—before he is killed. An episodic conglomeration of scenes in the realistic mode, its characters are divided into stereotyped supporters and opponents of the Revolution. It became a model for several subsequent plays. None of Bill-Belotserkovsky's later works ever matched the first in popularity. *Calm* (1927), a sequel, shows the attempts of many characters from *Storm* to adjust to the NEP, which at first they consider a betrayal of the ideals for which they have fought but to which they gradually adjust. The best of his later plays is *Life is Calling* (1934), in which a dying grandfather quicts the petty bickerings around him by showing his family that their quarrels are trivial beside the great challenge of Soviet life.

Another early Soviet playwright, Konstantin Trenyov (1884–1945), supplied the Moscow Art Theatre with its first contemporary play, *Pugachev's Rebellion* (1925), based on a peasant revolt of the eighteenth century and treated as a precursor of the Bolshevik Revolution. But Trenyov's attempt to show Pugachev's development from renegade to selfless leader was denounced, and the play had little success. In 1926, however, Trenyov achieved enormous success with *Lyubov Yarovaya* (also the Maly Theatre's first successful attempt to present contemporary drama). It tells the story of a schoolteacher whose husband has disappeared during the civil war; when the White Army comes to her region seeking to root out the Reds, whom she fully supports, she recognizes an officer as her husband; though she still loves him, she eventually betrays him. With its conspiracies, escapes, startling reversals, secondary comic figures, and double ending, *Lyubov Yarovaya* is so effective as melodrama that it was a favorite in Russian theatres during the next twenty years. Among Trenyov's later plays, perhaps the best is *On the Banks of the Neva* (1937), one of the many works of the period to glorify Lenin and Stalin.

Vsevolod Ivanov (1895–1963) supplied the Moscow Art Theatre with its first really successful Soviet play, *Armored Train 14-69* (1927), a dramatization of his novel. Set in Siberia against the final struggle of the Whites and Reds, it centers around the successful attempt of the Reds to capture the armored train which is essential to the Whites' survival. It skillfully builds resentment against the Whites and suspense about the outcome of the battle for the city. With this production, the Moscow Art Theatre returned to its most naturalistic style and, according to many historians, capitulated to the Soviet regime.

Leonid Leonov (1899–) wrote *The Badgers* (1927) at a propitious time—just as Stalin was seeking to root out peasant ownership of land and to institute collectivization. Primarily through two brothers—Semen (a peasant leader) and Paul (a Communist organizer)—the play traces the conflict between the peasants and the government. After his resistance has led to bloodshed, Semen confesses his errors and submits himself to the "will of the people." Of Leonov's later works, perhaps the best is *The Orchards of Polovchansk* (1939), written on the eve of World War II. Set against the background of a state orchard, it shows the director and his sons ready to smash any foreign invader just as they destroy the insects that threaten their fruit trees. The orchards not only serve as a microcosm of the state but also give a poetic aura to this optimistic patriotic statement. During the war, Leonov won additional fame with *Invasion* (1942), in which a Russian, embittered by several years of imprisonment, is gradually regenerated through his opposition to the German invaders. Captured, he passes himself off as the leader of the guerrilla forces which have so successfully harassed the Germans. After he is executed, his mother views the body and declares that it is that of the guerrilla leader. *Invasion* gave Russian morale a powerful lift when it was badly needed.

Mikhail Bulgakov (1891–1940), author of thirty-two plays, was one of Russia's finest playwrights, although more significant as a novelist. Nevertheless, he was never able to please the authorities. *The Days of the Turbins* (1926), based on one of his novels, treats the civil war from the viewpoint of the Whites. It was the first Soviet play (and perhaps the last) to give a sympathetic portrait of the enemy, and, though the protagonist acknowledges the defeat of his cause and declares his willingness to serve Russia's new leaders, Bulgakov was severely denounced. Nevertheless, *The Days of the Turbins* long remained one of the most popular of Soviet plays. Opposition to Bulgakov only increased following *Zoika's Apartment* (1926) and *The Purple Island* (1928), satires on contemporary Soviet problems. The latter was especially disliked, for it was directed against the committee on theatrical repertories and the propaganda plays it favored. Eventually silenced, Bulgakov ended his life as "theatrical editor" for the

Moscow Art Theatre. His most enduring theatrical piece has been an adaptation of Gogol's *Dead Souls* (1932), still in the Moscow Art Theatre's repertory.

Yuri Olesha (1899–1960) suffered much the same fate, and like Bulgakov was more significant as a novelist than as a dramatist. *Conspiracy of Feelings* (1929) treats the conflict between the optimistic builders of a new society and the anxieties of those who do not wish to be mere ciphers in a collectivist state. Although at the end the principal doubter is killed, critics recognized that Olesha was more concerned with the problem than with his overly facile ending. In *List of Good Deeds* (1931), an actress keeps a balance sheet showing the good and bad aspects of Soviet life and, deciding that the bad outweighs the good, she emigrates to the West. But there she finds all corrupted by materialism and is killed when she joins a public demonstration by French workers. Olesha was preoccupied with the conflict between freedom of conscience and the demand for conformity and never found a satisfactory solution. Undoubtedly one of the finest writers of his day, he was silenced in 1934 and later imprisoned. He was "rehabilitated" in 1956 shortly before he died.

The most successful playwrights of the 1930s were Afinogenov, Korniechuk, Pogodin, and Vishnevsky. Alexander Afinogenov (1904–41) in his early plays was, like Olesha, concerned with the problems of the intelligentsia under communism. For example, *Fear* (1931) centers around Professor Borodin, who argues that fear is a basic human motivation and that the Soviet regime is founded on it, a contention supported by several of his colleagues. But he eventually discovers that his colleagues are counter-revolutionaries and that, while they are motivated by fear, the Communists are fearless in their devotion to their just cause. Afinogenov later moved away from this concern. *Far Taiga* (1934) tells of a dying Red Army officer, who on his way to Moscow is forced to stay for a few days in a small village, where he becomes involved in local problems and convinces the people that all are important to the huge collective that is the Soviet state. Similarly, *On the Eve* (1941), produced after Afinogenov was killed in an air raid, shows a suburban Moscow family doing its part to stem the advance of the German army.

Alexander Korneichuk (1905–), a party official, was especially successful in treating the intelligentsia that had arisen from the proletariat. *Platon Krechet* (1934) shows a dedicated young doctor (formerly a stoker) being held back by bureaucrats until his worth is recognized by a wise party official and his detractors discomfited. It won many prizes and was presented throughout the Soviet Union. Korneichuk later joined the campaign to glorify Lenin. *Truth* (1937) tells how a Ukranian peasant in search of truth comes to Petrograd and encounters Lenin (and finds truth) just as the October Revolution begins. During the war Korneichuk was highly praised for *The Front* (1942), in which the young, innovative officer, Ognyov, opposes the outmoded methods of an old general, Gorlov, and how

A scene from Korneichuk's *The Front* at the Moscow Art Theatre during World War II. (From Komissarzhevsky, *Moscow Theatres*, Moscow, 1959.)

after Ognyov prevails the tide of battle turns against the Germans. Few dramatists have been so successful as Korneichuk in clothing party doctrine in dramatic form.

Nikolai Pogodin (1900–) began his playwriting career in 1929 and had written several works before achieving his first outstanding success with *Aristocrats* (1934), one of the finest Soviet plays. It is a half-comic, half-serious story about the building of a canal by thieves, bandits, and other "aristocrats" of crime. At first they work only under duress but gradually are transformed by their task. Like all of Pogodin's work, it is a loosely organized collection of diverse episodes held together by a common theme (a structure which was widely adopted by other dramatists because of Pogodin's success with it). Pogodin was also the most successful of the dramatists who glorified Lenin and Stalin. His most popular play, *Man With a Gun* (1937), tells of a soldier who guards the corridors of the Kremlin after the October Revolution and meets Lenin and Stalin before he goes to fight at the front. *The Kremlin's Chimes* (1942), set in 1920, shows Lenin hunting, talking to old people and children, and in general demonstrating his concern for the common people even as he deals with the most pressing problems of state. The title refers to an old Jewish watchmaker's attempt to repair the Kremlin's chimes and to make them play the "Internationale." Still later Pogodin wrote *The Third, Pathetic* (1955), which deals with Lenin's death and his great faith in the future. During the war Pogodin wrote several plays which boosted Russian morale and during the cold war a number of works that denounced the United States. Of these, perhaps the

346

Act I of Pogodin's *The Kremlin's Chimes* at the Moscow Art Theatre.
(From Komissarzhevsky, *Moscow Theatres*, 1959.)

best known is *Missouri Waltz* (1950), designed to ridicule President Truman.

Vsevolod Vishnevsky (1900–   ) began his career with *Final and Decisive* (1931), a play intended to counteract the romanticized versions of sailor life then prevalent on the Russian stage (Vishnevsky had been a sailor). The early scenes show the rather crude and immoral life of the sailors, but when war breaks out they prove their devotion to the Soviet Union. Twenty-seven defend their posts to the end and when the last is

Vishnevsky's *Final and Decisive,* directed by Meyerhold in the early 1930s.
(From Komissarzhevsky, *Moscow Theatres,* 1959.)

wounded he dies only after scrawling 162,000,000 (the population of Russia) minus 27—to show how many more will have to be killed before Russia will capitulate. By far the best-known work by Vishnevsky is *The Optimistic Tragedy* (1933), in which an anarchistic collection of sailors is molded into a disciplined fighting unit by a female commissar sent them by the party. At first they resent and oppose her, but eventually follow her into battle and to death. Although all are killed, the outcome is optimistic because the victory of the cause for which they have died is inevitable. Through the Narrator, who speaks the prologue in the name of the dead sailors and who interrupts the action throughout to comment on it, the play is given the quality of an epic saga. With this drama Tairov achieved one of his few successes with the party. Vishnevsky later contributed to the drama of war with *At the Walls of Leningrad* (1944) and to the glorification of Stalin with *The Unforgettable 1919* (1949), in which Stalin is depicted as Lenin's trusted advisor and as the person most responsible for breaking the White resistance.

Other playwrights could be added to this list but they would add little to the overall picture. Practically all those who won favor wrote on ideologically acceptable subjects and in the realistic mode. During the 1930s the classics were also "Sovietized" by interpreting them as supporting Communist positions or as showing the necessity of the Revolution because of the decadence of tsarist society. Many prerevolutionary playwrights (among them Chekhov) who had been downgraded were now "rehabilitated" and brought back into the repertory. But like that of the living, the work of dead writers had to be made conformable to Soviet ideology.

～ IX ～

It was to such drama that theatrical production was subordinated during the 1930s. Furthermore, the theatre was brought under increasingly strict controls in still other ways. In 1936 the Central Direction of Theatres was created to concentrate authority over all theatres (about nine hundred troupes) in a single agency. In 1938 a policy of "stabilizing companies" was proclaimed under which the size and personnel of all troupes were fixed; since any change had to be approved by the Central Direction, it became very difficult for anyone to change his job. These two developments brought all theatrical personnel under close surveillance and control.

Around 1936 the campaign to stamp out "formalism" also intensified. The major victims were Tairov and Meyerhold, even though both made many compromises with their earlier ideals. Beginning in the late 1920s, Tairov had presented a number of Soviet plays and in the 1930s declared his allegiance to socialist realism (although he interpreted it to include much that he had always done). In 1933 he seemed to have found the proper compromise when he presented Vishnevsky's *The Optimistic Trage-dy,* for in 1934 he was named a "National Artist of the USSR." But his success was short-lived and after his production of Demyan Bedny's *Heroes* (1936), a satire on the typical protagonists of Soviet literature, his troupe was merged with that of the Realistic Theatre. In 1939 he regained control of the Kamerny, which was then evacuated to Siberia during the war. For his wartime services, he was awarded the "Order of Lenin" in 1945, but this did not prevent him from encountering serious opposition upon his return to Moscow. After making a considerable hit with *The Sea Gull,* he was charged once more with formalism and in 1950 his theatre was liqui-dated.

Meyerhold's downfall was more rapid and final. During the early 1930s, Meyerhold seems to have sought a production style more acceptable to his critics, for his approach moved toward a stylized realism, labeled "impressionistic" by some critics. Perhaps the best of his late productions was Dumas *fils's The Lady of the Camellias,* presented in 1934. Although Meyerhold added material from novels by Dumas, Flaubert, and Zola and changed the period from the 1840s to the 1870s, he did not alter the dramatic values. The simple settings were arranged as though being viewed from a sharp angle, but all the furniture, properties, and costumes were historically accurate, and Meyerhold's wife, Zinaida Raikh, portrayed a realistically sensuous heroine. Although the production was a great popular success, its completely apolitical tone enraged the party. Nevertheless, Meyerhold used much the same approach in 1935 with Tchaikovsky's *The Queen of Spades,* his first operatic production since the Revolution. But the campaign against him only intensified and in 1938 his theatre was closed.

Paradoxically, even as Meyerhold was being attacked the government was financing a new theatre for his company. Designed by Mikhail Barkhin and Sergei Vakhtangov (son of Yevgeny Vakhthangov), it was remarkable for its time, since it had no proscenium; steeply raked, semicircular seating surrounded a deep oval playing area (about 80 feet deep by 25 feet wide) equipped with two revolving stages and lifts; there were also provisions for using motion pictures and projections. When Meyerhold's company was dissolved, the building was redesigned and opened in 1940 as a concert hall.

After his theatre was closed, Meyerhold was offered a position in the Moscow Art Theatre's Opera Studio, and when Stanislavsky died he was named artistic director of the studio. Then in June 1939 came the All-Union Conference of Stage Directors, at which he was scheduled to speak (on the assumption, it is said, that he would make a public confession of error). It has been reported that, contrary to expectation, Meyerhold roundly denounced socialist realism as the ruin of theatrical art. Although his alleged speech has been widely circulated, there is no clear indication of

Okhlopkov's Realistic Theatre in 1932. Note the various levels and the placement of the audience.

what actually occurred and some scholars have questioned whether the speech attributed to him is authentic. Whatever the content of the speech, Meyerhold was arrested immediately afterward. He was probably executed in 1940. Shortly after his arrest, Zinaida Raikh's mutilated body was discovered in their apartment. Almost twenty years would pass before Meyerhold would be "rehabilitated" and his pioneering work acknowledged once more in the Soviet Union.

But experimentation was not wholly missing from the Russian theatre of the 1930s. Perhaps the most significant work was that done by Nikolai Okhlopkov (1900–1966). Born in Siberia, Okhlopkov began his career there as a disciple of Mayakovsky and as a dramatist-actor-producer of mass spectacles. In 1925 he went to Moscow to study under Meyerhold and in 1932 became the director of the Realistic Theatre (until 1927 the Moscow Art Theatre's Fourth Studio). Here Okhlopkov applied many of Meyerhold's theories and adapted Eisenstein's "montage of attractions."

Okhlopkov's major innovation was his elimination of the proscenium stage and the relocation of all acting areas in the auditorium. Some scenes were played on a central platform but others at various spots around the periphery or on overhead ramps. The precise arrangement of acting areas and seating changed with each production. Okhlopkov favored scripts, many adapted from novels, which moved rapidly from one episode to another as in motion pictures. Short scenes, isolated bits of conversation, choral and instrumental music, and simultaneous events occurred in and around the spectators and placed them at the very center of the action as though they were participants. Although Okhlopkov enjoyed enormous popularity with audiences, he was denounced by Soviet critics as anarchistic. In 1936 he publicly confessed his errors and in 1937 his theatre was merged with Tairov's. Unable to work with the older man, Okhlopkov left in 1938 to join the Vakhtangov Theatre, where he directed until he was named head of the Theatre of the Revolution in 1943. Thereafter he continued to be one of Russia's finest directors, usually managing to inject novel touches into his productions no matter how rigid the supervision.

During the 1930s Vakhtangov's theatre, under Reuben Simonov and Boris Zakhava, seems to have been more successful than most companies in juggling freedom and conformity. But in 1936 Zakhava declared the theatre's repertory pernicious and set out to harmonize Vakhtangov's teachings with dialectical materialism. Nevertheless, many of the era's most imaginative productions were by Vakhtangov's pupils—Zavadsky, Popov, Akimov, and Simonov—who managed to keep his spirit alive.

The official policies of the 1930s tended to favor the traditional troupes, for it was they who most easily adjusted to the demands of socialist realism. Above all, it was the Moscow Art Theatre that gained in official esteem. In 1932 both Nemirovich-Danchenko and Stanislavsky denounced "formalism" and declared realism to be the only healthy approach. In the same year they announced that henceforth their theatre would be called the "House of Gorky" (thus renouncing Chekhov) and that they intended to stage a cycle of Gorky's plays. In 1937, the Moscow Art Theatre was awarded the "Order of Lenin" and after Stanislavsky's death in 1938 his "system" became virtually the only acceptable one for training actors. Thus, the Moscow Art Theatre came to set the standard for all Soviet theatres and to command the greatest official support of any troupe.

By the beginning of World War II, the Russian theatre had lost its independence and had become an instrument of the state. Its great creative urge was spent.

～ XI ～

But if it ceased to be innovative in the 1930s, the Soviet theatre had offered the world many ideas which strengthened or added to those already launched by the expressionists, futurists, dadaists, and surrealists. These include: Meyerhold's theories of biomechanics and constructivism; Eisenstein's "montage of attractions" and integration of motion pictures with live performers; Vakhtangov's use of improvization to discover effective means and motivations; Okhlopkov's interweaving of spectators with the dramatic action; Tairov's experiments with rhythm and Mme. Ekster's with "dynamic costume"; and numerous others. Many of these remain stimulating and yet to be fully explored.

Perhaps most characteristic of the Soviet regime has been its recognition of the theatre's power. Probably no state has assigned the theatre a higher role or supported it more fully. But it was the recognition of the potential that led the state to insist that the theatre be subordinated to political ends, although the demand was not enforced until the 1930s. In 1917 Russia seemed to be in a position to reshape the theatre along any lines it wished. During the next ten years the wide diversity of proposed goals and means gave the Soviet theatre enormous vitality and versatility. Then, the party gradually imposed political standards on it and snuffed out the diversity. Consequently, the Russian theatre, which between 1900 and 1930 was one of the world's most innovative, sank back into an obscurity from which it has only recently begun to recover.

The Inter-War Years
in
Italy, France, and Belgium

Italy, though its output was small during the interwar years, made a major contribution to modern drama through the work of Pirandello, whose preoccupation with "seeming" and "being" influenced virtually all subsequent playwrights. France, on the other hand, made its major impact through its "studio" theatres, most of which took their cue from the Vieux Colombier and Copeau, who sought to establish the highest artistic standards in both production and playwriting. The movement reached its peak in the work of Jouvet, Dullin, Baty, and Pitoëff. At the same time, however, quite contrary ideals—epitomized in the theories of Artaud—were gathering force. Similarly, playwriting in France was dominated by those, such as Romains, Vildrac, Lenormand, and (above all) Giraudoux, who emphasized

353

literary merit, even as the dominant role of language was being undermined by such writers as Achard and the Belgian playwright Ghelderode.

~ I ~

During those years when the futurists were seeking to transform the theatre in Italy, other equally powerful (and not wholly antipathetic) forces were at work in drama. They first became evident in the "theatre of the grotesque," a type of play that took its name from Luigi Chiarelli's (1884–1947) *The Mask and the Face* (1916), subtitled "a grotesque in three acts." Chiarelli's drama made such an impact that it was soon considered the pioneering work in a new school of writing. The protagonist of *The Mask and the Face,* Paolo, wishes to live by his country's code of honor, but is faced with a dilemma when he thinks his wife, Savina, has been unfaithful to him. Not wanting to kill her but unable to face possible ridicule, he sends Savina away and then declares that he has killed her and thrown her body into a lake. At his sensational trial, Paolo depicts himself as a husband acting to protect his honor; acquitted, he is given a civic welcome and receives many proposals of marriage. Then the public insists that a suitable burial service be arranged for Savina, who, unable to resist attending her own funeral, appears veiled in black. Paolo recognizes her, takes her home, and locks her in a room. Faced with the rampant gossip, he realizes that Savina is necessary to his happiness and decides to reinstate her as his wife regardless of what is said.

Chiarelli continued this vein in his later works. In *The Silken Ladder* (1917), for example, he combines grim humor with fantasy and allegory. Here a man without any qualifications except his popularity as a dancer rises to become minister of state. In his inaugural address, he mouths the most shopworn platitudes to the approval of the crowd and to the rhythmic accompaniment of his own dancing feet. On the other hand, *Chimeras* (1919) seems more bitter than satirical. It deals with a couple who profess the highest moral standards but, when they encounter financial difficulties, the wife, with the complete approval of her husband, gives herself to a banker in order to maintain their material position in the community.

By 1920 critics were conscious of a school of "grotesque" dramatists, which included in its ranks such writers as Luigi Antonelli (1882–1942), author of *The Man Who Met Himself* (1918) and *The Island of Monkeys* (1919), and Piermaria Rosso di San Secondo (1887–1956), author of *Marionettes, What Passion* (1918) and *The Sleeping Beauty* (1919). Among this group, critics at first also placed Luigi Pirandello (1867–1936), although the resemblance was largely superficial, for, though he too was concerned with appearance and reality, unlike the others he questioned whether a more reliable truth is to be seen when the mask is stripped away. Thus, though he employed some of the same means, he differed considerably from his contemporaries in his philosophical concerns. The plays which expressed his views were to have a profound effect on subsequent drama.

By birth a Sicilian, Pirandello had already earned an enviable reputation as novelist and short story writer before turning to short plays in 1910 and to full-length dramas in 1915. Thereafter he devoted himself almost entirely to the theatre. But if Pirandello wrote many plays, in all he developed the same set of related concepts. Unlike the dramatists who wrote in the "grotesque" vein and treated reality as clearly discernible behind the mask, Pirandello denied that reality can be grasped. He declared: "Each of us believes himself to be one, but that is a false assumption: each of us is so many, . . . as many as are all the potentialities of being that are in us. . . . We ourselves know only one part of ourselves, and in all likelihood the least significant." Thus, for Pirandello is it impossible to distinguish the mask from the face not only in others but in ourselves as well.

Pirandello believed that each person constructs his personality out of the various types of roles he is asked to play (family, social, religious, psychological), but that no one of these is the entire person, for each is like a separate mask put on for an occasion. Thus, it is virtually impossible to know the full truth about anyone. Furthermore, each person becomes so accustomed to playing his roles that he forgets he is doing so. Pirandello thought of his plays as mirrors in which people would be forced to view themselves more clearly: "A man lives . . . and does not see himself. Well, put a mirror before him and make him see himself in the act of living. Either he is astonished at his own appearance, or else he turns away his eyes so as not to see himself, or else in disgust he spits at his image, or, again, clenches his first to break it. In a word, there arises a crisis, and that crisis is my theatre."

Like Shaw, Pirandello was much influenced by Bergson's concept of creative evolution, according to which an instinctive urge within man seeks to move him toward a higher state of being. Thus, to be vital means to be forever changing. On the other hand, man also desires order, which can be gained only through fixity. Consequently, there is a fundamental conflict within him. Furthermore, man lives within a society which is subject to the same conflicts. Pirandello declares: "Society is necessarily formal, and in this sense I am antisocial, but only in the sense that I am opposed to social hypocrisies and conventions."

The search for fixity in a world of constant flux undergirds all of Pirandello's plays, which dramatize the evanescence of truth and proclaim that "the certainty of today . . . is not the certainty it was yesterday, and will not be the certainty of tomorrow." Though the specific situations change, the philosophical problem remains constant.

Pirandello's outlook and dramatic method were first clearly evidenced

A scene from Pirandello's *Right You Are—If You Think You Are,* as it was produced at the Teatro Quirino in Rome by the Emma Gramatica Company in 1957.

in *Right You Are—If You Think You Are* (1917), in which Signor Ponsa and his mother-in-law, Signora Frola, argue over the identity of Signora Ponsa. He declares that his first wife (the daughter of Signora Frola) has died and that he has remarried; because Signora Frola is emotionally disturbed, however, he has permitted her to think that his present wife is her daughter. Signora Frola, on the other hand, declares that it is Ponsa who is emotionally disturbed and that it is she who has permitted him to believe that his first wife has died and that he has remarried. Signora Ponsa, the only person who can resolve the issue, refuses to do so: "I am she whom you believe me to be" is her response. Thus, Pirandello establishes his thesis that truth varies according to the point of view.

Pirandello is most successful in meshing idea and action in *Henry IV* (1922). Twenty years before the play opens, the protagonist, while impersonating the eleventh-century Holy Roman Emperor Henry IV in a pageant, falls from his horse (goaded by Tito Belcredi, we later learn) and thereafter believes himself to be the emperor. Since he is wealthy, his whims are honored and he has been able to live in surroundings which re-create the eleventh-century milieu and has been served by retainers who enact the roles of his courtiers. But gradually he has regained his senses and recognizes that life has completely passed him by. Here the dramatic action begins. Suspecting that Henry may only be faking insanity, his relatives decide to test him. Consequently, Tito Belcredi, Donna Matilda (Henry's former mistress), and others disguise themselves as at the pageant and enter his world. But events get out of hand and, overcome by rage at his wasted life, Henry kills Belcredi. He now realizes that his deed has condemned him to go on playing the role of the madman for the rest of his life. Thus being and seeming are explored through a story of enormous emotional power.

Pirandello's concern for multileveled reality found its most complete and complex expression in his three plays about the theatre—*Six Characters in Search of an Author* (1921), *Each in His Own Way* (1924), and *Tonight We Improvise* (1930). It is here that his affinity with the futurists was most evident. In these works, Pirandello deliberately broke the fourth-wall convention so that he might explore varying levels of illusion. By including the theatrical milieu, he was able to depict self-conscious attempts to create an illusion of reality, which is itself already compounded of illusions. In these plays, Pirandello also explores another of his obsessions—the relationship of Art to Nature. Since truth means continual change and since "a finished work of art is fixed forever in immutable form," the theatre is the most satisfying form of art, for, since it ultimately depends on the actor (who can only partially assume the mask of a character and whose impersonation differs at each performance), drama is "not enduring creation. [It is a] thing of the moment. A miracle. A statue that moves." He shows how inadequate is realism, which can only produce a travesty of truth, and suggests that the only remedy lies in writing philosophical plays which show reality as ever-changing rather than trying to fix life itself on the stage.

In *Six Characters in Search of an Author,* fictional characters interrupt a rehearsal and plead to have their stories played out so they may take on full being. But when the actors seek to do so they present mere lifeless stereotypes. Even the characters cannot agree among themselves about the details of their rather melodramatic lives. But, because they are embedded in an art work, their fates are already sealed by the author; they may struggle against the inevitable but they are doomed by the artistic form.

Pirandello's *Tonight We Improvise,* directed by Silvio D'Amico, Royal Academy of Dramatic Art, Rome.

358

*The
Inter-War
Years in
Italy,
France and
Belgium*

By using the device of a rehearsal, Pirandello is able to explore reality as it appears on at least three different levels: in a written text, on the stage, and in life. *Each in His Own Way* takes the process one step further, for here the drama being presented in the theatre (the play-within-the-play) supposedly treats real events and persons, some of whom are in the audience watching it. Furthermore, some scenes are set in the lobby, where spectators discuss both the play and its real-life counterparts. Thus, the reality of the stage and the reality of life are intermingled. In *Tonight We Improvise,* Pirandello makes the Director announce that, in order that art may more nearly approximate life, the actors will improvise a play from a brief scenario. The performers then move in and out of the drama, commenting on it, the theatre, and life, but eventually get so caught up in their roles that they play out a conclusion which comes about contrary to their wishes. Despite Pirandello's attempts in his dramas about the theatre to present various levels of reality, however, one must ultimately recognize that it is he who has created all the levels and consequently that all is mere dramatic illusion.

If Pirandello's philosophical outlook was unusual for his day, many of his dramatic techniques were not. He made use of the extreme situations —adultery, murder, mistaken identity, and betrayals—and devices inherited from melodrama and the well-made play. Thus, for the most part he clothed philosophy in conventional dramatic form. His principal departure from tradition lay in breaking down the fourth-wall convention so that he might involve the audience more directly in a conflict of ideas. He was most revolutionary in his philosophical outlook, for he was the first major dramatist to treat all values as relative and truth as ultimately unknowable.

During the interwar years both Pirandello's ideas and the theatrical techniques of his theatre triology were sufficiently novel that they often baffled audiences and occasionally created minor scandals. For example, when *Six Characters in Search of an Author* was performed in Rome in 1921 (at the Teatro Valle under the direction of Dario Niccodemi) there was a near-riot, and when *Tonight We Improvise* was produced in Berlin in 1930 the audience became so unruly that the enraged director, Hans Hartung, shouted insults at them from the stage.

In 1924, Pirandello formed his own company, The Art Theatre of Rome, of which he was the director and Marta Abba (1906–   ) the principal actress. Between 1925 and 1927 the troupe toured widely in Europe and South America. By the time it was dissolved in 1928, it had done much to spread Pirandello's fame throughout the world. After this time Pirandello had little to do with dramatic production and lived abroad much of the time. In 1934 he was awarded the Nobel Prize.

Pirandello made a profound impression on his age. If his plays no longer seem as remarkable as they once did, it is because the ideas he championed have gained such wide currency that they no longer appear startling. Probably no other writer, however, was to be so instrumental in establishing the philosophical view espoused by dramatists of the post-World War II period.

~~ II ~~

In France, the years between 1914 and 1918 were extremely difficult ones for the theatre, since virtually every able-bodied man was conscripted. Many theatres closed altogether and even the august Comédie Française was reduced to using students from the Conservatoire in some of its productions. Most of those that remained open concentrated on productions designed to boost morale or to provide escapist entertainment. But when the hostilities ceased, the theatres rapidly regained vitality. In the revival, four men—Gémier, Lugné-Poë, Hébertot, and Copeau—were most important.

During the war years, Gémier continued to operate the Théâtre Antoine, though on a reduced scale. Nevertheless, he made a few innovations, the most important of which were the removal of the footlights and the installation of steps to bridge the stage and auditorium. His desire to break down the barriers between performers and spectators is further seen in one of his wartime patriotic pieces in which supernumeraries flooded through the auditorium and onto the stage.

When the war ended, Gémier, resuming his prewar efforts to create a "people's theatre," turned his attention to a circus-theatre. Here he could eliminate the division between audience and actor imposed by traditional architecture and could accommodate the masses he sought to attract. Furthermore, the circus seemed the nearest modern equivalent to the ancient Greek structure. Consequently, in 1919–20, with the financial backing of Serge Sandberg, Gémier mounted two plays in the Cirque d'Hiver in Paris. The first, *Oedipus, King of Thebes* by Saint-Georges de

Gémier's production of *Oedipus, King of Thebes* at the Cirque d'Hiver, Paris, in 1919. (From *L'Eclair*, 1919.)

360

*The
Inter-War
Years in
Italy,
France and
Belgium*

Bouhélier, was a chronicle play with major emphasis upon spectacle. Perhaps the most striking scene was that in which two hundred supernumeraries, many of them trained gymnasts, javelin throwers, and jumpers, staged an athletic contest. The second production, *The Great Pastoral,* a Provençal nativity play adapted by Charles Hellem and Pol d'Estoc, followed a similar pattern but the athletes were replaced by folk dancers, musicians, and trained animals.

In 1920, Gémier won a major victory in his struggle to establish a people's theatre when the government created the Théâtre National Populaire (TNP) and named Gémier its director. But it was a limited victory, for the TNP was merely a scheme under which productions from the national theatres would be played at the Trocadéro (a large exhibition hall located, incongruously for the TNP's purposes, in a fashionable area) at reduced prices for popular audiences and, when possible, taken on tour. It was given only token financial support, had no troupe of its own, and could not produce its own plays. It was partially out of his desire to serve the TNP that Gémier set out to attain the directorship of the Odéon, France's second state theatre, a campaign in which he succeeded in 1922. But, though Gémier continued to head the TNP until 1933, he was never able to develop it beyond the embryonic stage. Nevertheless, to him goes the credit of sustaining the organization and laying the groundwork for later developments. After 1951, when Jean Vilar became its head, the TNP would at last become the force Gémier had envisioned.

As an adjunct to the TNP, Gémier had hoped to organize festivals throughout France to provide an outlet for the people's dramatic instinct. In this, he did not succeed, but he did help to found an international organization, the Société Universelle du Théâtre, which sponsored international festivals annually between 1927 and 1938 and became a prototype for the similar endeavors which flourished after World War II.

Gémier sought to make the Odéon (which he headed until 1930) an experimental theatre capable of appealing to a wider audience than its traditional one, composed primarily of students and families. In his efforts, he was assisted by René Fuerst, an Austrian designer attuned to Appia's theories and thoroughly familiar with the German experiments of his time. Under Gémier, the Odéon became truly eclectic, reflecting all recent trends, including cubism, surrealism, and expressionism. Gémier was the French director who most nearly approximated Reinhardt's wide-ranging eclecticism.

Gémier's eclecticism is further illustrated by his interest in the intimate "studio" theatres so characteristic of postwar Paris. The studios were based on principles—primarily artistic—almost polar to those—primarily audience-centered—typical of Gémier's more characteristic endeavors. The directors of the studios believed that they—like dedicated painters—should never compromise their art in order to attract an audience. It is this ideal of the studio that gives the interwar French theatre its peculiar quality.

Gémier entered this field in 1920 with the Comédie Montaigne, which he placed under the direction of Gaston Baty. The season, composed of plays by Lenormand, Crommelynck, Shaw, Claudel, and Shakespeare, featured Gémier and Dullin as actors; it was a considerable critical success but a financial failure. Consequently, it was abandoned in 1921. Gémier also ran a school, the Conservatoire Syndical de Gémier, headed for a time by Dullin. Thus, his involvement in many and varied activities made him a major force in the postwar theatre. His career, extending from the 1890s to the 1930s, also represented a major link with the past.

Lugné-Poë provided a similar link but played a less prominent role than did Gémier in the theatre of the 1920s. With the coming of the war in 1914, Lugné-Poë had closed the Théâtre de l'Oeuvre, but in 1919 he reopened and continued to head it until 1929, when he turned it over to Paulette Pax and Lucien Berr. Lugné-Poë believed that the l'Oeuvre should serve a special function in Parisian theatrical life: to encourage young writers. He often derided Copeau's predilection for authors who had taken up playwriting in middle age and pointed out that the majority of his own programs were devoted to the works of unknown or unrecognized playwrights, among them Crommelynck, Salacrou, Achard, and Passeur. He was also the only producer in Paris to open his theatre to the dadaists. In addition to encouraging new authors, Lugné-Poë sought to familiarize the French public with plays by such foreign dramatists as Strindberg, Shaw, Chekhov, Kaiser, D'Annunzio, and Rosso di San Secondo. He also published the *Revue de l'Oeuvre,* through which, with articles on dramatists, ballet, architecture, and related subjects, he tried to keep audiences abreast of new developments.

Lugné-Poë's production of Crommelynck's *The Magnificent Cuckold,* Théâtre de l'Oeuvre, 1920. (From *Le Théâtre,* 1920.)

362

*The
Inter-War
Years in
Italy,
France and
Belgium*

After the war, Lugné-Poë was able for the first time to provide a permanent location for his productions, for he now acquired his own theatre, seating about 350 persons, still the home of the l'Oeuvre. He also became increasingly independent and irascible. He reserved the right to select his own subscribers, and, though they were admitted, critics were not invited. He also launched frequent and bitter attacks on Copeau's choice of plays and austere productions. For these and other reasons, Lugné-Poë came to be considered somewhat eccentric. But in the years between 1919 and 1929, he played an important role in promoting new playwrights, even if it was not so crucial as it had been in the 1890s.

Jacques Hébertot (1886–   ) contributed to the postwar theatre primarily as an entrepreneur. A poet, critic, and editor, Hébertot ran two adjacent theatres, the Théâtre des Champs-Elysées and the Comédie des Champs-Elysées from 1920 to 1926, and in 1923, in response to the growing interest in studios, added the Studio des Champs-Elysées. For these houses, he sought the best directors, plays, and companies, and was remarkably astute at recognizing talent. In 1922 he invited Georges Pitoëff to form a company, in the same year employed Jouvet as a director, and, when he established his studio, secured Baty to head it. He also employed Theodor Komissarzkevsky as a director. Furthermore, Hébertot sponsored many foreign troupes, among them the Moscow Art and Kamerny theatres, and it was in his theatres that the Ballets Suédois performed between 1920 and 1925. Hébertot gave up management in 1926 and thereafter edited a series of theatrical magazines. In 1940, he returned to directing, working in the theatre that now bears his name.

Above all, it was Jacques Copeau who set his stamp on the French theatre between the wars. After the Vieux Colombier was closed in 1914, he visited Gordon Craig in Florence (he had earlier gone to Switzerland to see Dalcroze and Appia) and with Suzanne Bing in 1915 opened a school for young amateurs, professionals, and children. In 1917, Copeau was sent by the French government on a cultural mission to New York, where he gave lectures and play readings. Otto Kahn, a banker and patron of the arts, was so impressed that he offered to subsidize Copeau's company in America. Consequently, with the blessing of his government, Copeau reconstituted his company and from 1917 to 1919 performed a repertory of plays in French at the Garrick Theatre. It is difficult to assess Copeau's impact on the American theatre, but undoubtedly it served along with several other forces to hasten the acceptance of new techniques.

In 1919 Copeau returned to Paris and to the Vieux Colombier, which was now remodeled by Jouvet along lines slightly different from those used in 1913–14. Forward of the proscenium there was an apron with three semicircular steps leading to a lower level and then to the auditorium. There were no footlights. Back of the proscenium there was virtually no wing space and access to acting areas could be gained only from stage right. At the rear of the stage, Jouvet erected a permanent structure which included

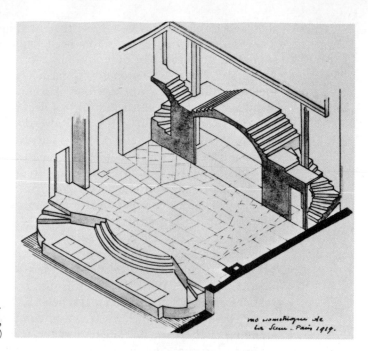

Interior of the Vieux Colombier
in 1919. (From Moussinac,
New Movement in the Theatre.)

an alcove below and a playing level above, reached by stairs. It could be
masked or altered in various ways. On this stage only the simplest, most
necessary, and expressive set pieces and properties were used, and its
appearance was only slightly altered from one production to the next. The
theatre's one luxury was lighting, which was used to create mood and to
emphasize the three-dimensionality of the performer. Copeau's was an
architectural stage intended to enhance but never to detract from the actor.

In 1919, Copeau's basic outlook had changed little since he had
launched the Vieux Colombier in 1913. He still declared his ultimate aim
to be the renovation of dramatic literature. Still, his choice of plays did not
always seem consistent with that aim, for while much of his repertory was
made up of plays by Shakespeare and Molière, he increasingly came to
select works (by such authors as Marivaux, Gozzi, and Musset) influenced
by *commedia dell' arte*—so much so that some critics accused him of
wishing to renovate the drama by reducing it to farce, pantomime, and
improvization. Somewhat inconsistently, his contemporary plays were by
such writers as André Gide, Georges Duhamel, Jean Schlumberger, and
Charles Vildrac, in whom it is difficult to perceive the seeds of a vital
dramatic tradition.

Copeau continued to demand complete respect for a text and unflinching integrity in production. But his interests gradually shifted from drama
to acting, as though he had come to believe that the renovation of performance had to precede a renaissance in writing. Thus, in 1924 he announced

363

364

*The
Inter-War
Years in
Italy,
France and
Belgium*

that he was closing his theatre so that he might concentrate on his school. The Vieux Colombier had never been financially profitable and had been supported in part by an organization of patrons, The Friends of the Vieux Colombier, but it was probably Copeau's conviction that there is a fundamental conflict between a schedule of regular performances and the pursuit of high standards that led him to this decision. Perfectionism was probably Copeau's strongest trait and it had already elicited many attacks upon his elitism, asceticism, and austerity. To pursue perfection without distractions, Copeau transferred his school to the small Burgundian village of Pernand-Vergelesses, where from 1924 to 1929 he devoted his full energies to it.

It is primarily as teacher-theoretician-reformer that Copeau made his great impact on the French theatre. In one sense, his whole mission depended upon education—of writers, actors, and public—and from the beginning he had considered a school necessary to his goals. Consequently, when he reopened the Vieux Colombier in 1920 he also established a school, although he placed it under the direction of Jules Romains, while he concentrated on the repertory. With the move to the country, however, he became the school's director and principal teacher.

The heart of Copeau's teaching continued to be a thorough understanding of the text, its milieu, and the techniques that would permit the actor to transpose to the stage all that he had found in the text. What seemed most remarkable about the training in the 1920s was its emphasis (then new) on the expressive power of mime and gesture. In Paris, the school's teachers had included the Fratellini family of circus clowns, as well as a mimist, Jean Dorcy. After the school moved to the country, Copeau

Shakespeare's *Winter's Tale* as produced by Copeau at the Vieux Colombier in 1920. Note the bareness of the stage. (From *Le Théâtre,* 1920.)

concentrated on improvisation. Much of the work centered upon a group of about ten type-characters that Copeau considered to epitomize the basic aspects of human behavior. Students learned to make masks which captured the essence of these types and, wearing them, to eliminate all actions, gestures, and motivations foreign to them. In this way, they were able to purge extraneous elements from a characterization and to rely entirely on the most essential and expressive means. They also improvised scenes based on such archetypal situations as war, famine, and lust. As the culmination of their work, they evolved scenarios, which they performed at the village festivals of Burgundy. In this way, the students, known as Les Copiaux, learned discipline, effective techniques, integrity, and selfless devotion to ensemble playing.

In 1929 Copeau abandoned his school when a powerful campaign was mounted to have him named head of the Comédie Française. It was unsuccessful, but Copeau now returned to theatrical production in Paris and elsewhere. Some of his most ambitious work in these years resembled that done by the "people's theatres" of the early twentieth century. In Florence, in 1933 he staged *The Miracle of Saint Uliva* in the cloister of Santa Croce, and in 1935 Rino Alessi's *Savonarola* in the Piazza della Signoria. In 1943 he produced his own religious spectacle, *The Miracle of the Golden Bread,* in a courtyard in Beaune. That Copeau now sought a larger audience is further suggested by his mounting of three plays—*The Only Napoleon* by Paul Raynal, *Jeanne* by Henri Duvernois, and *The Deceiver of Seville* by André Obey—in a large Parisian commercial theatre in 1936–37. Unfortunately, audiences remained sparse.

Molière's *Misanthrope* at the Vieux Colombier in 1922 with Valentine Tessier as Célimène and Copeau as Alceste. (From *Le Théâtre,* 1922.)

366

*The
Inter-War
Years in
Italy,
France and
Belgium*

In 1936, another effort was made to have Copeau named head of the Comédie Française, which had since World War I suffered a serious decline despite the inclusion in its ranks of such fine performers as Beatrix Dussane (1888–1969), Berthe Bovy (1888–   ), André Brunot (1879–   ), and Charles Grandval (1882–1943). Under the direction of Émile Fabré, it had undergone several crises because of inadequate subsidies and political interference. In 1936, Fabré resigned. Once more, however, Copeau was passed over, this time ironically in favor of Edouard Bourdet (1887–1945), a successful Boulevard dramatist. Fortunately, Bourdet recognized Copeau's worth and invited him to serve as his advisor. As a result, after 1936 Copeau (along with Jouvet, Dullin, and Baty) directed a number of productions at the Comédie Française; theirs were the first directors' names ever to be listed on that company's programs. In May 1940 Copeau was at last named head of the Comédie Française but was forced to resign in less than a year because of his son's participation in the resistance movement. Once more Copeau retired to the country, where he died in 1949.

III

Copeau's major contributions had been made by 1924. But, if he left Paris, his influence remained, for the most prestigious companies there were the studios he had inspired. None was so austere as the Vieux Colombier, but all elevated artistic above commercial motives, even though this meant playing to small audiences. Among Copeau's successors in the 1920s, the most important were Jouvet, Dullin, Baty, and Pitoëff, who composed the Cartel des Quatre ("Coalition of Four"—so called because of an agreement they made in 1926 to advise and assist each other). Between Copeau's departure from Paris and the beginning of World War II, they provided artistic leadership for the French theatre.

Of the four, Louis Jouvet (1887–1951) seems to have been most closely attuned to Copeau's ideals. When Copeau left Paris, he gave Jouvet much of his scenery and wardrobe and published an article in which he declared that Jouvet had agreed to carry out his program. Furthermore, Jouvet took into his company many of Copeau's best actors.

Jouvet had begun his theatrical career around 1907 while still engaged in pharmaceutical studies. At first he worked with groups seeking to bring more meaningful performances to working-class audiences. In 1911, while playing in *The Brothers Karamazov* at Rouché's Théâtre des Arts, he met Copeau, and in 1913 joined the Vieux Colombier to play minor roles and to serve as the company's technical director. In 1917, he rejoined Copeau and remained with him until 1922, when he went to work for Hébertot.

Jouvet as Knock in the play
by Jules Romains.

Jouvet's first major success came in 1923 with Romains's *Knock,* a play which he would revive fourteen times during the next twenty-five years. (Some critics maintain that there was something of Knock in every role that Jouvet played.) In 1924, Jouvet formed his own company, but at first had to rely for financial assistance on the Society of the Théâtre Louis Jouvet, formed in 1925 by Romains. The turning point in Jouvet's career came in 1928 when he staged Giraudoux's *Siegfried.* With this production, both director and playwright found his ideal collaborator and thereafter Jouvet devoted much of his energy to staging Giraudoux's works.

Another turning point came in 1934. Until this time, Jouvet had designed, directed, and performed in practically all his productions. But when he produced Cocteau's *The Infernal Machine,* he employed, at Cocteau's suggestion, Christian Bérard (1902–49) as designer, and thereafter retained him. In the same year, Jouvet decided that he could now command a larger audience and leased a Boulevard theatre, the Athenée, where he remained thereafter. Bérard's imaginative designs contributed significantly to Jouvet's success. In 1934, Jouvet was named to a teaching post at the Conservatoire and after 1936 he mounted a number of productions at the Comédie Française.

In 1940, the occupation government forbade Jouvet to perform the works of Giraudoux or Romains and in protest he closed his theatre. From 1941 to 1945 he toured in South America, but when the war ended, he returned to the Athenée, where he presented Jean Genet's *The Maids*, and Sartre's *The Devil and the Good Lord.* But most of Jouvet's postwar productions were of the classics. He died in 1951.

Like Copeau, Jouvet was a staunch believer in the sanctity of the text. He declared: "To direct a production means serving the playwright with a devotion that makes you love his work. It means finding the spiritual mood that was the poet's at the play's conception and during its writing, the living source and stream which must arouse the spectator, and of which even the author is sometimes unaware." Jouvet divided directors into two

367

368

*The
Inter-War
Years in
Italy,
France and
Belgium*

types: the one who expects everything from the play, and the one who expects everything from himself. The first seeks to illuminate the text; the second uses the play as a pretext for his own creation. The first admits spectacle only sparingly and never permits it to intrude on the text; with the second, "the work is swathed in personal contributions and inventions." It was the first type of director that Jouvet sought to be.

Jouvet believed that a director should work out of lucid understanding rather than enthusiastic feeling. He sought to immerse himself so completely in a play that his production would give the impression of being at one with the moment of the text's creation. He insisted that his actors also immerse themselves in the text until they comprehended every nuance of thought, every gesture and intonation, and that these be rendered with absolute precision. Above all, he was sensitive to language. In his productions, movement was restricted and vocal delivery slow so that every subtlety of idea and emotion could be projected. Jouvet's productions were noted for their lucidity, no doubt made possible by his devoted actors, especially Lucienne Bogaert, Valentine Tessier, Madeleine Ozeray, Romain Bouquet, and Pierre Renoir.

Jouvet was little concerned with scenic innovation. His settings can best be described as a combination of highly selective representational elements with an overall theatricalist quality. He believed that settings should always look like settings and never aspire to give the illusion of actuality. Thus the decor for his plays always established place and mood but had something of the fantastic about it.

Except with Molière's plays, Jouvet seldom ventured into the classics or into works by foreign authors. Such contemporary French playwrights as Romains, Achard, Cocteau, and Giraudoux provided him with his repertory. And he gave them impeccable productions, for perfect finish was Jouvet's trademark. He was probably the most successful of the Cartel.

Charles Dullin (1885–1949), like Jouvet, was a member of Copeau's company before establishing his own troupe. Dullin came to Paris in 1903 and played in many minor theatres and at the Odéon under Antoine before appearing in Copeau's adaptation of *The Brothers Karamazov* in 1911 and joining the Vieux Colombier in 1913. During the war he served in the army but was released after being wounded and went with Copeau to New York. After a misunderstanding with Copeau, Dullin went to work for Gémier, for whom he ran an acting school and performed at the Cirque d'Hiver and the Comédie Montaigne. But Dullin wanted his own company. In 1922 he created the Atelier, housed in a small theatre in the Montmartre district of Paris, where he was to remain for sixteen years. When he left he was as poor as when he began, in part because he refused to continue his successful productions for long runs.

Dullin was little interested in theory. But like his associates in the Cartel, he was opposed to naturalism. He was deeply interested in Oriental theatre and *commedia dell' arte* and sought in his productions to achieve a synthesis of dance, music, and plastic expression, which he associated with those forms. Nevertheless, he placed primary emphasis upon the text. He cautioned: "Never accept a play, saying: it is nothing, but when I have staged it it will be something." He was suspicious of any work that demanded the machinist's help. His preferences in art—Picasso in painting, Schoenberg in music, and Joyce in fiction—tell much about his theatrical approach, for he combined modernity of visual method with almost melodramatic intensity in acting. He declared that a production should lift the audience out of its commonplace existence through a theatricality compounded of dream and fantasy and composed of a homogeneous and harmonious synthesis of several concurrent elements: imaginative decors, subtle lighting, stylized costumes, ensemble movement, plastic groupings, mimed spectacle and dance, all set to a musical accompaniment which underlines and reenforces the other elements. Thus, though Dullin emphasized the primacy of the text, he never neglected the other elements. His designers—Jean Hugo, Picasso, Michel Duran, Lucien Coutaud, Louis Touchagues, Georges Valmier, and André Barsacq—were among the finest of the day, and he often commissioned music from such composers as Milhaud, Auric, Delannoy, and Sauguet. Music, dance, and mimed spectacle figured prominently in practically all of his productions. His approach is perhaps best exemplified in *Richard III,* in which the battle scenes were mimed and danced to rhythms created by a drum and the clash of weapons. It is also significant that Dullin admired Meyerhold above all foreign directors.

Dullin's production of Cocteau's adaptation of *Antigone,* the Atelier, 1922. (From *Le Théâtre,* 1923.)

370

*The
Inter-War
Years in
Italy,
France and
Belgium*

Dullin was probably the most eclectic of the Cartel in choice of repertory. He presented *The Birds, Peace,* and *Plutus* by Aristophanes; *Richard III* and *Julius Caesar* by Shakespeare; *The Silent Woman* and *Volpone* (his greatest success) by Jonson; *'Tis Pity She's a Whore* by Ford; *Life is a Dream* and *Physician to his Honor* by Calderon; *The Pleasure of Honesty* and *Right You Are—If you Think You Are* by Pirandello; and plays by such French authors as Molière, Cocteau, Achard, Salacrou, Romains, and Passeur. He ranged from farce to tragedy, but showed a predilection for the great classics. He performed in all of his productions, being especially effective in ambitious, cynical, and restless roles. Among his actors were Julien Bertheau, Raymond Rouleau, Tania Balachova, Madeleine Robinson, Jean Marchat, and Etienne Decroux.

Like Copeau, Dullin made a lasting impression through his school. He insisted that his students study ballet, music hall techniques, circus clowning and acrobatics, *commedia dell' arte,* music, and, above all, the text and its milieu. Little educated, he had a profound respect for knowledge and great contempt for the antiintellectualism of commercial producers (whom he called "grocers"). Dullin's legacy was to be most fully felt through such students as Jean-Louis Barrault and Jean Vilar, who after World War II would play dominant roles in French theatrical life.

Unfortunately Dullin always longed for a larger audience than he could command at the Atelier. Perhaps seduced by the success of his

Charles Dullin as Richard III, one of his most important roles.

productions at the Comédie Française after 1936, he gave up his theatre just before the beginning of World War II and after 1941 headed the large Théâtre de la Cité, which was subsidized by the city of Paris. Although his old audience remained faithful, he failed to attract a sufficiently large new one to remain financially solvent. After considerable conflict with civic authorities over his choice of repertory, Dullin gave up the theatre in 1947. He ended his career as director of the theatre section of the Maison des Arts in Geneva.

The other members of the Cartel, Baty and Pitoëff, never worked with Copeau but they shared his uncompromising devotion to the theatre as an art. Gaston Baty (1885–1952), the only member of the Cartel who was not an actor, was extremely well educated, having studied in Munich, where he became familiar with the work of Fuchs and Erler, and in Lyon, his home city. At first, although he wrote plays and criticism, he had no outlet for his interests in theatrical production. But in 1918, during the bombardment of Paris, Gémier came to Lyon to work, met Baty, and put him under contract for five years to assist him. Thus, in 1919, at the age of thirty-four, Baty entered the Parisian theatrical world as Gémier's assistant at the Cirque d'Hiver. In 1920, he made his debut as a director with *The Great Pastoral*; in the same year Gémier put him in charge of the Comédie Montaigne, where he directed plays by Lenormand, Crommelynck, Shaw, Claudel, and Shakespeare. In these early projects, Baty worked with both Gémier and Dullin.

But Baty wished to be independent and in 1921 founded the Chimère, with which he produced plays irregularly while completing his contract with Gémier. In 1924, his apprenticeship over, Baty was employed by Hébertot to take charge of his newly created Studio des Champs-Elysées. In 1928, he left that theatre and after playing in temporary locations settled in 1930 in the Théâtre Montparnasse, where he remained until he turned it over to Marguerite Jamois in 1947.

. Baty was the most philosophically inclined of the Cartel, so much so that it is difficult to understand his work without being aware of his views. Baty argued that since the Renaissance the French theatre had been primarily Cartesian and Jansenist in its orientation, for it had emphasized rationality and had reduced drama to dependence on the word; the result had been to deemphasize the totality of human existence, which includes the physical environment, states of feeling, spiritual experience, and all the invisible forces that lie beyond man's grasp. Since words can only express what can be conceptualized, they are inadequate for treating many facets of existence. Where the expressive power of the word ends, there "commences another zone, a zone of mystery, of silence, what one calls atmosphere, ambiance, climate, whatever you like. This it is the work of the director to express. We [his company] play all the text, all that can be expressed by the text, but we wish also to go beyond this margin into what the text cannot render."

372

*The
Inter-War
Years in
Italy,
France and
Belgium*

It was for these reasons that Baty placed great emphasis upon the visual aspects of production, so much so that he was often accused of subordinating everything to them.

Baty's outlook encompassed aspects of both naturalism and symbolism, for he recognized the importance of heredity and environment as well as that of a mysterious power which lies beyond the material realm. He sought to capture both. Consequently, his settings were always three-dimensional and representational but were imbued with symbolic qualities through the careful composition of the elements and through his masterful handling of lighting and color to create all-pervasive moods and strong emotional stimuli. Thus, his production style could probably best be described as a combination of realism and expressionism. So skillful was he that he came to be called "the magician of the mise-en-scène."

Baty's outlook also led him to consider the director the major artistic force in the theatre. "The man of letters, the painter, the composer, the actor all collaborate under the supervision of the director, who will be for them what the orchestral conductor is to musicians." He went on to say: "Painting, sculpture, the dance, prose, verse, song, music, these are the seven chords stretched side by side on the lyre of drama." But it is the director who plays the lyre. For all these reasons, Baty's productions were quite unlike those of other members of the Cartel. He was more nearly the descendant of Antoine and Lugné-Poë than of Copeau.

Baty's repertory was made up primarily of modern works, although occasionally he ventured into the classics, and his greatest successes were won with adaptations of novels. Perhaps his most famous production was

Baty's production of his own adaptation of Flaubert's *Madame Bovary* in 1936. The performers are Lucien Nat and Marguerite Jamois. (From *Theatre Arts,* 1936.)

that of *Madame Bovary* (1936) in his own adaptation. Although Flaubert's novel is usually considered a masterpiece of realistic writing, Baty declared that he was concerned primarily with showing a woman tortured by romantic dreams. Consequently, he added many expressionistic touches, such as a chorus of girls to reveal the heroine's romantic ideas. Comparable techniques were even more evident in the handling of visual details. For example, in an early scene showing Emma happy with her lover, the arbor in which the action occurs is covered with flowers and flooded with sunlight, whereas in a later scene when she is about to commit suicide the flowers are dead and withered and the light grey and harsh.

After 1930 Baty became increasingly interested in marionettes and his productions, especially in the gestures and movement of the actors, began to reflect this preoccupation. He eventually gave up his theatre so that he might concentrate more fully upon his experiments. In 1951, he became director of the newly created state-sponsored dramatic center in Aix-en-Provence, but died before he made any impact there. Of all French directors between the wars, Baty was most committed to "total theatre." His attack on the word and his concern for the expressive powers of nonverbal means form a bridge between the Cartel and Artaud's "theatre of cruelty."

Similarly, Georges Pitoëff (1884–1939) provided a bridge between the Parisian stage and foreign drama. Son of a theatre manager, Pitoëff was born in Russia and for a time lived in Moscow, where he became familiar with Stanislavsky's work. Following the Revolution of 1905, his family emigrated to Paris, but he returned to Russia shortly afterward and entered Vera Komissarzhevskaya's company, in which he worked under Meyerhold. Caught up in the ferment of the Russian theatre, he moved

The Pitoëffs in a production of Claudel's *The Exchange* in 1937.

374

*The
Inter-War
Years in
Italy,
France and
Belgium*

away from Stanislavsky's views toward those of the symbolists. In 1911, Pitoëff met Dalcroze, a great influence on his work, and it may have been this meeting which led him to move to Switzerland in 1914.

It was in Paris during the war that Pitoëff met his future wife, Ludmilla (1896–1951), a Russian student at the Conservatoire. When she completed her course, they were married and in 1918 formed their first company. This troupe, based in Switzerland, played short engagements in Paris each year, and in 1922 Hébertot invited Pitoëff to form a company and to perform regularly at his Théâtre des Champs-Elysées. After Hébertot gave up this theatre, Pitoëff's troupe played in a number of theatres in Paris and toured abroad before settling in the Théâtre des Mathurins in 1934, where they remained until Pitoëff's death in 1939. During the war, Mme. Pitoëff performed in America and from 1946 until her death in Paris.

Pitoëff was known above all for his productions of foreign plays, for French works made up only about one-third of his repertory. His was an important contribution, for the French were notoriously ill informed about the drama of other countries and complacently convinced of their own superiority. Pitoëff favored works which emphasized strong internal struggles, and won his greatest successes in plays by Chekhov, Pirandello, Lenormand, Ibsen, Schnitzler, Shaw, and O'Neill. Two productions of special importance were those of *Six Characters in Search of an Author,* which made Pirandello a major force in the French theatre, and of *Saint Joan,* the first successful presentation of a play by Shaw in France. In all his productions, Pitoëff sought to find the "secret truth" and the "invisible forces" in a script and to let them rise to the surface of the visible form.

Like Dullin, Pitoëff was little given to theorizing, but he placed

Pitoëffs' production of Pirandello's *Six Characters in Search of an Author* in 1923. (From *Le Théâtre,* 1923.)

primary emphasis upon the text and above all sought to isolate those
elements most capable of communicating with a contemporary audience.
"What does it matter if in Shakespeare's time Hamlet was played in a
certain way. What interests me is what contemporary spirit can be drawn
from it." He was extremely eclectic in taste and sought to let each play
dictate his approach to it. Nevertheless, his settings, which he designed,
suggest a marked leaning toward cubism and expressionism. Most were
strongly geometrical with a dominant central focus, often created by
radiating lines or concentric circles. His means varied from one production
to another—simple curtains, simultaneous settings or cross-sections of houses,
a revolving stage, set pieces changed within a basic unit—but all were
characterized by a radical simplicity in which only the most essential and
expressive elements were retained. Even when they are composed of
realistic elements, the settings seem endowed with symbolic significance.
Pitoëff also paid close attention to groupings and lighting, but above all
to rhythm. "For me, to play a role, to establish a mise-en-scène, to coach
the actors, to design the settings and costumes, to regulate the lighting is
only to find the 'line' that links all the diverse rhythms. And these lines can
be found only in the mysteries of rhythm."

Pitoëff's acting was hampered by his strong accent, but he was effective in ironical and bitter roles. His wife, much superior to him as a
performer, was noted for her spirituality, musical voice, and precise inflec-
tions. Despite Pitoëff's remarkable abilities as a director, as a foreigner he
was, as Hébertot remarked, the last of the Cartel to be honored.

If the Cartel was the most important artistic force in the French
theatre between the wars, it was not the most popular. All its members
dreamed of recapturing the glory that the theatre had enjoyed in Greece
and Elizabethan England, but all had to content themselves with much
less.

375

*The
Inter-War
Years in
Italy,
France and
Belgium*

~~~ **IV** ~~~

Around 1930 a new wave of activity, also owing much to Copeau, began.
Most directly related to Copeau was the Compagnie des Quinze (Company
of Fifteen), for it was composed of students from his school under the
leadership of Michel Saint-Denis (1897–1971), Copeau's nephew and his
assistant after 1919, who directed all of the plays and who acted in most as
well. At the Vieux Colombier, the Compagnie des Quinze presented eight
plays, four of them by André Obey, between January 1931 and May 1933.
Under the Compagnie, the Vieux Colombier, redesigned by André Barsacq,
was further simplified from the arrangement used by Copeau, for now it
was reduced to an unadorned large room with visible ceiling and walls.

376

*The
Inter-War
Years in
Italy,
France and
Belgium*

Only absolutely essential set pieces were permitted. The company's considerable impact was made almost entirely through its ensemble playing, stylized gesture and movement, and near-incantatory diction.

In 1934 the troupe made an enormous impression in London, and, when it dissolved for lack of funds, Tyrone Guthrie persuaded Saint-Denis to establish an acting school there. With the assistance of George Devine and the support of Laurence Olivier, John Gielgud, Edith Evans, Michael Redgrave, and others, Saint-Denis operated the London Theatre Studio from 1935 to 1939 and directed plays at the Old Vic and for Gielgud's company. After the war, Saint-Denis would establish and operate an acting school for the Old Vic. Thus, Copeau's methods were brought to England.

Léon Chancerel (1886–1965) also contributed to the new wave. After entering the Vieux Colombier in 1920, Chancerel remained with Copeau until 1926, when he went to work for Jouvet. In 1929 he founded the Comédiens Routiers, which until 1939 performed for boy scouts. In 1935, he established the Théâtre de l'Oncle Sébastien, a children's theatre. Through these organizations, Chancerel did much to raise the level of theatre for young people throughout France. Out of his troupes came a number of actors who have had significant careers, among them Maurice Jacquemont, Jean-Pierre Grenier, Olivier Hussenot, and Hubert Gignoux.

Analogous groups grew out of the work of Henri Ghéon (1875–1944), a friend of Copeau, who had presented Ghéon's first play in 1914. During the war, Ghéon was converted to Catholicism and thereafter wrote plays designed to increase faith and be performed by church groups. In 1924 he founded Les Compagnons de Notre Dame, a troupe of about thirty amateurs, who played a repertory of medievallike plays written by modern authors. They toured throughout France and Belgium until 1931. Their work was continued by the Compagnons de Jeux, under the direction of Henri Brochet, a friend and disciple of Ghéon.

Barsacq, Dasté, and Jacquemont also figured prominently in the theatre of the 1930s. André Barsacq (1909–   ) won fame overnight at the age of nineteen as the designer of Dullin's *Volpone*. He then worked with the Compagnie des Quinze and with Copeau on his mass spectacles in Florence before joining with Dasté and Jacquemont to found the Compagnie des Quatre Saisons in 1937. In 1940, Dullin offered the Atelier to Barsacq, who has run it since that time. Jean Dasté (1904–   ), Copeau's son-in-law, had been a student in Copeau's school and a member of the Compagnie des Quinze before joining Barsacq and Jacquemont. In 1940, he accompanied Barsacq to the Atelier and remained there until 1947, when he founded his own company in St. Etienne, which he still directs. Maurice Jacquemont (1910–   ) was trained by Chancerel in the Comédiens Routiers before joining Barsacq and Dasté. After they moved to the Atelier, he continued the Compagnie des Quatre Saisons until 1942. In 1944 he became director of the Studio des Champs-Elysées and continued in that post until 1960.

377

*The
Inter-War
Years in
Italy,
France and
Belgium*

Another important troupe was the Rideau de Paris, founded in 1929 by Marcel Herrand (1897–1953) and Jean Marchat (1902–1966). Herrand made his debut in 1917 in Apollinaire's *The Breasts of Tiresias,* studied with Copeau, appeared as one of the phonographs in Cocteau's *The Wedding on the Eiffel Tower,* and acted for various members of the Cartel before joining with Marchat in the Rideau de Paris. Marchat had also acted for members of the Cartel and had established his reputation as Mosca in Dullin's *Volpone.* In 1939, upon Pitoëff's death, they assumed control of the Théâtre des Mathurins, where they played until Herrand's death. They were especially noted for productions of plays by Lorca, Valle-Inclán, and Synge.

Though of a quite different kind, the work of Etienne Decroux (1898–) should also be noted. Decroux began his career in 1923 as a student in Copeau's school and then worked for Jouvet before becoming a leading actor and teacher at Dullin's Atelier from 1926 to 1934. Both Copeau and Dullin encouraged his interest in mime, which he taught at Dullin's school. In 1931 he gave his first independent program and from 1932 to 1939 devoted most of his time to the study of mime. In 1941 he founded a school which has done much to reestablish mime as a theatrical form. Practically all mime performers of the present day are indebted in some way to Decroux, although undoubtedly Marcel Marceau (1923–) is his most famous pupil and disciple.

Although it was Copeau who dominated theatrical art between the wars, another theorist—Artaud—then little heeded would surpass him in fame after World War II. Born in Marseilles, Antonin Artaud (1895–1948) had by 1915 already experienced his first bout with that mental disturbance that would plague him through the remainder of his life. In 1920 he came to Paris, where Lugné-Poë gave him his first role; in 1921 he joined Dullin and designed the settings for his first production, Calderon's *Life is a Dream.* He later acted for Pitoëff, Jouvet, and in films. Between 1924 and 1926, Artaud was deeply involved in the surrealist movement, but, along with many others, was expelled by Breton. Nevertheless, the surrealist influence remained strong in Artaud's work. In 1926 he founded, in association with Roger Vitrac and Robert Aron, the Théâtre Alfred Jarry and presented four programs before the group was disbanded in 1929. But it was not until 1931, when he saw a troupe of Balinese dancers at the Colonial Exposition in Paris, that he began to formulate the theories upon which his fame rests. Between 1931 and 1936 he wrote a series of essays and manifestoes, thirteen of which were collected in 1938 to form *The*

378

The
Inter-War
Years in
Italy,
France and
Belgium

Theatre and Its Double. In 1935, Artaud staged the only work on which he worked after formulating his theories, his own play *The Cenci* (based on works by Shelley and Stendhal). It was not well received and closed after seventeen performances.

In 1936 Artaud went to Mexico hoping to find there an authentic primitive culture which would provide him with clues about the relationship between art and ritual. But he came to believe that "international dark forces" were seeking to destroy him and he returned to France. In 1937 he was committed to a psychiatric hospital, where he remained until 1946. In 1947 he gave a lecture at the Vieux Colombier and recorded a work for radio, "To Have Done with the Judgment of God." In 1948 he died of cancer.

According to Artaud, the theatre in the Western world has been devoted to a very narrow range of human experience, primarily the psychological problems of individuals or the social problems of groups (in other words, the kind of experience that is related to the conscious mind). To Artaud, the more important aspects of existence are those submerged in the unconscious. Artaud calls the Western world's use of the theatre mistaken. Like the futurists, he declared that in the West the theatre is looked upon as a preserver of culture, something like a museum rather than a living experience; for this reason, the theatre has become the property of an elite group and has been cut off from the masses. But, adds Artaud: "I consider that the world is hungry and that it doesn't care about culture. . . . The most urgent thing is not so much to defend a culture whose existence never saved a man from the worry of living or of being hungry, as to extract from what we call culture some ideas whose living force is identical to hunger." Artaud considers all that is normally called "civilization" to be a numbing overlay of a deeper, more elemental culture. He argues that this form of civilization will eventually pass into oblivion "and that spaceless, timeless culture which is contained in our nervous capacities will reappear with an increased energy." He adds that we need a theatre "which does not numb us with ideas for the intellect but stirs us to feeling by stirring up pain."

Artaud considered man's important problems to be those buried in the subterranean reaches of the mind, those things that cause divisions within man and between men, those things that lead to hatred, violence, and disaster. For Artaud, then, the theatre should serve a near-psychiatric function, but for the whole society and not merely for the individual. The goal is something like a religious experience in which a true communion—the elimination of all divisions—is reached.

The theatre that Artaud envisions is akin to ritual and its subject matter mythic. But his view of myth is quite unlike that of Wagner, who tended to see it as uplifting and idealized. Artaud, on the contrary, states: "The great myths are dark, so much so that one cannot imagine, save in an atmos-

379

*The
Inter-War
Years in
Italy,
France and
Belgium*

phere of carnage, torture, and bloodshed, all the magnificent fables which recount to the multitudes the first sexual division and the first carnage . . . in creation." Artaud also states that we cannot return to the myths of the past—such as those of the Greeks and Christians—for these have lost their power to affect us sufficiently. Rather, new myths will arise out of something like a plague which destroys repressive social forms. "Order collapses, authority evaporates, anarchy prevails and man gives vent to all the disordered impulses which lie buried in his soul." But Artaud sees all this occurring in the theatre rather than outside it, for his theatre is to serve the function of cleansing society. According to Artaud, man, if given the proper theatrical experiences, can be freed from ferocity and can then express the joy which civilization has forced him to repress. The theatre will evacuate those feelings which are usually expressed in more destructive ways. "I defy that spectator [i.e., one who has been to Artaud's theatre] to give himself up, once outside the theatre, to ideas of war, riot, and blatant murder." Elsewhere, Artaud states: "For impelling men to see themselves as they are, [the theatre] causes the mask to fall, reveals the lie, the slackness, baseness, and hypocrisy of the world. . . ." Or, as Artaud put it most succinctly, "the theatre has been created to drain abcesses collectively." Artaud considered the world to be sick—a madman needing shock treatments. The theatre was to be the instrument of healing. And the cure was to consist of removing all those things which divide men. The goal is complete harmony.

To reach this goal, Artaud prescribed certain remedies. He was certain that it could not be done through appeals to the rational mind. Rather, it would be necessary to operate directly upon the senses, for the conscious mind has been conditioned to sublimate the most fundamental human impulses. Thus, it will be necessary to break down the audience's defenses. Artaud sometimes referred to his as a "theatre of cruelty," since in order to achieve its ends it would have to force the audience to confront itself. He declared that the theatre requires a force similar to that of a plague. "In the theatre as in the plague there is something both triumphant and vengeful." But the cruelty Artaud advocated is not primarily physical but moral. He says: "We are not talking about that cruelty which we can exert on one another by cutting up each other's bodies, by sawing on our personal anatomies." Rather, it is an extramoral identification which will take hold of us physically, kinesthetically. About his production of *The Cenci*, Artaud wrote that it is not a question of "purely corporal cruelty but a moral one; it goes to the extremity of instinct and forces the actor to plunge right to the roots of his being so that he leaves the stage exhausted. A cruelty which acts as well upon the spectator and should not allow him to leave the theatre intact, but exhausted, involved, perhaps transformed."

To achieve this transformation, Artaud sought what he called a new "language of the theatre." He was much impressed by Oriental art with

A scene from Artaud's *The Cenci* at the Folies-Wagram, Paris, 1935.

its symbolic, ritualistic elements, and he argued that the Western theatre could be reformed only by the use of comparable means, although he recognized that Eastern devices could not be taken over directly.

Part of his interest in the Eastern theatre stemmed from his discontent with the West's emphasis upon language and the consequent appeal to the rational mind. As he put it: "Whereas most people remain impervious to a subtle discourse whose intellectual development escapes them, they cannot resist effects of physical surprise, the dynamism of cries and violent movements, visual explosions, the aggregate of tetanizing effects called up on cue and used to act in a direct manner on the physical sensitivity of the spectators." Thus, "carried along by the paroxysms of a violent physical action which no sensitivity can resist, the spectator finds his overall nervous system becoming sharpened and refined."

Artaud's intention to operate directly on the nervous system, of evoking a kinesthetic response, led him to suggest many new devices for the theatre. Among these was the replacement of the traditional theatre building with remodeled barns, factories, or airplane hangars. He wished to locate acting areas in corners, on overhead catwalks, along the walls. Spectators, surrounded by the action, would be furnished with swivel chairs so they might turn in any direction. Artaud states: "There will be no decor. That will be adequately taken care of by hieroglyphic actors, ritualistic costumes, puppets thirty feet tall . . . , musical instruments as tall as a man, objects of unheard of form and purpose."

In lighting, he sought a "vibrating, shredded" effect. He called for "flashes of light whose nature changes, goes from red to a crude pink, from silver to green, then turns white, with suddenly an immense opaque yellow light the color of dirty fog and dust storms." Sound is treated in much the same way. He favors shrillness, staccato effects, abrupt in volume. In his script for *The Cenci,* he suggests that a scene set in a torture chamber should "give off the noise of a factory at peak production." When he staged the play, he used a screeching wheel which produced an almost intolerable sound. He also employed an electronic device (a forerunner of the Moog Synthesizer) that could vary volume from the softest tones to those louder than could be produced by a full symphony orchestra. There was also a great deal of vocal, nonverbal sound. Artaud used the human voice not so much as an instrument of discursive speech as for tonalities, prolonged modulations, yelps, barks, to create harmonies and dissonances. About language, Artaud declares: "Why is it that in the theatre, at least theatre as we know it in . . . the West, everything that is specifically theatrical, namely everything that . . . is not contained in dialogue, . . . is left in the background?" Again: "I say that the stage is a physical and concrete place that demands to be filled, and demands that one make it speak its own concrete language." This language should be "addressed first of all to the senses rather than to the mind, as is the case with the language of words," for "the public thinks first of all with its senses."

Thus, Artaud wanted to assault the audience, to break down its resistance, to purge it morally and spiritually. Unlike Wagner, who sought to transport the audience outside itself, Artaud sought to force the spectator to confront himself and through the process to cleanse himself and find harmony with his fellow man.

Like Appia and Craig, Artaud was a visionary rather than a wholly practical man, and like them he was at first little appreciated. Many of their ideas are similar, but Artaud differed drastically in his conception of the theatre's ultimate purpose. Appia and Craig (as well as Copeau and his followers) tended to value art for its own sake, whereas Artaud saw in it the salvation of mankind. Theirs is a world of transcendent beauty, his a region of cruel torment. Consequently, as the post-World War II view of man darkened, the influence of Appia and Craig declined and that of Artaud increased.

It is difficult to isolate immediate and certain influences from Artaud, but two directors who were to be significant in the post-World War II French theatre and who worked with Artaud on *The Cenci* have declared their indebtedness to him. One, Roger Blin, would not be important until after the war, but the other, Jean-Louis Barrault (1910–   ), had served his apprenticeship and won widespread fame before the war began.

Barrault had worked at several odd jobs by 1931 when he auditioned for Dullin, who was sufficiently impressed to admit him to his school without charge and let him sleep in the theatre. Not only did he perform in Dullin's troupe, he studied with Decroux and appeared in Decroux's first independent production in 1931. In 1935 he acted in Artaud's *The Cenci* and came under his influence. (Barrault has declared that *The Theatre and Its Double* is the most important work written about the theatre in the twentieth century.) Shortly afterward, he presented at the Atelier his own first production, a mime drama based on Faulkner's *As I Lay Dying*. After leaving Dullin, Barrault adapted and staged Cervantes's *The Seige of Numancia* (1937) and Hamsun's *Hunger* (1939). By this time he had also

382

*The
Inter-War
Years in
Italy,
France and
Belgium*

made a number of films and had married Madeleine Renaud (1903–   ), a leading actress with the Comédie Française. When the war began he served in the army but was demobilized when France surrendered. In 1940, he joined his wife as a member of the Comédie Française. Soon he would begin that series of productions that would make him the best known of postwar French directors.

~≈~ VI ~≈~

A number of French playwrights between the wars were highly regarded but few have withstood the test of time. One of the most controversial was Henri-René Lenormand (1882–1951), for he emphasized the power of the unconscious and the relativity of time and space, ideas then still novel. Lenormand was more successful than the surrealists, who treated similar themes, because he wrote in a form more accessible to ordinary theatregoers. Nevertheless, his work was at the time considered both unusual and puzzling.

Although Lenormand began writing in 1905, he attained little success until 1919, when Pitoëff presented *Time is A Dream,* still his best-known work. In its first scene, Romée has a "waking dream" in which a young man drowns in a lake. Then Nico, just returned from the Orient, enters and Romée discovers that he is the drowning man. Later they become engaged and he commits suicide exactly as she has foreseen. This clairvoyance and

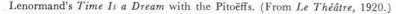

Lenormand's *Time Is a Dream* with the Pitoëffs. (From *Le Théâtre,* 1920.)

relativity of time is mingled with psychoanalytical material. Nico has been deeply affected by the climate and thought of the East, and the return to Holland and its mists precipitates a psychological and moral disintegration that leads to his death. *Time is A Dream* combines most of the interests that Lenormand would develop thereafter: metaphysical questioning, the interaction of personality and environment, the power of the unconscious, the relativity of time and space.

Some of these interests are reflected in *The Simoun,* directed by Baty at the Comédie Montaigne in 1920. Set in desert Africa, it shows how a father's willpower is so sapped by the climate that he cannot resist an incestuous desire for his daughter. When she is killed by a jealous half-caste, the father is both grieved and relieved. *The Eater of Dreams,* produced by Pitoëff in 1922, focuses on a psychoanalyst who feeds off his patients' weaknesses. The main line of action shows how a young woman is made to recognize that, through a fit of childhood jealousy, she was responsible for her mother's death. Unable to cope with this knowledge, she commits suicide.

Lenormand wrote many plays, but those just outlined are sufficient to show the major thrust of his drama. It was largely through his work that psychoanalysis became a dramatic subject in France. His techniques were also considered novel, although they were certainly far less extreme than those used by the dadaists or surrealists (but, then, those movements were seldom taken seriously). Lenormand abandoned the traditional division into acts in favor of scenes or tableaux (*The Simoun,* for example, has fifteen tableaux). Often he juxtaposed apparently unrelated scenes but these were ultimately unified through character, idea, or psychoanalytical problem. With such subject matter and techniques, Lenormand did much to popularize new perceptions and to encourage understanding of the more extreme devices employed by the surrealists and expressionists.

Interest in the unconscious was reflected in a somewhat different way by the "school of silence" or "drama of the unspoken," seen at its best in the works of Bernard and Vildrac. Jean-Jacques Bernard (1888–   ), in his article "Silence in the Theatre," published in the bulletin of Baty's Chimère in 1922, best sums up the outlook. He declares that literary drama has misrepresented truth by making characters openly express their inner feelings, whereas in reality people neither consciously analyze nor openly state their responses. Rather, in moments of crisis, inner emotion is more apt to take the form of a cliché, gesture, or glance than a well-articulated statement.

The play of silence is best exemplified by Bernard's *Martine,* presented by Baty in 1922. Bernard sums up his aim and his problem: "To tell the story of a young peasant girl who loves and who suffers, but who is unable to tell anyone about her love or her suffering, to seize this secret life, such has been my sole aim." He shows how Martine falls in love with

384

*The
Inter-War
Years in
Italy,
France and
Belgium*

a young man, sees him marry someone else while she is forced to wed an obtuse peasant. Her feelings are revealed almost entirely through indirection—small gestures, oblique remarks, looks; once the crisis is over, she resigns herself to her existence. In later works, Bernard made some attempt to broaden his approach, but it is for his "dramas of silence" that he is remembered.

Charles Vildrac (1882–   ) fits the same mold, although he was little interested in theory and had written his most significant play, *The Steamship Tenacity* (1920), before Bernard articulated the view which underlies the practice. *The Steamship Tenacity,* Vildrac's first play, was the most successful of the contemporary works presented by Copeau at the Vieux Colombier. It tells of two French workers, Bastien and Ségard, who have decided to emigrate to Canada aboard the *Tenacity,* the delayed sailing of which forces them to stay in a hotel where both are attracted to the maid, Thérèse. Although Thérèse prefers Ségard, she eventually goes away with Bastien because he is the more direct and outspoken. Ségard must go to Canada alone, even though he has never really wished to do so and has signed up only at Bastien's urging. The action is gripping despite Vildrac's determined avoidance of any surface conflict. None of his later plays ever quite matched the first in dramatic interest. The school of silence never made a deep impression, but it was significant for reviving and updating a major strain of French drama, the subtle revelation of internal psychological states, which can be traced from Racine through Marivaux and Musset to modern times.

A number of French dramatists of the interwar years were essentially satirists, and of these one of the most successful was Jules Romains (1885–1972). Extremely well educated, Romains early became interested in "unanimism," a philosophical concern for groups as entities with their own beliefs, wills, and consciences. This interest underlies practically all of his plays. His first dramatic work, *The Army in the Village,* produced by Antoine in 1911, treats a town's attempt to destroy an army (both conceived as groups more than as collections of individuals). Similarly, *Cromedeyre-le-Vieil,* produced by Copeau in 1920, shows how a group of young women who have been forcibly brought to a village are integrated into the group.

Today, Romains is remembered primarily for his satirical plays and above all for *Knock, or, The Triumph of Medicine* (1923), Jouvet's first major success. To a small village comes a new doctor, Knock, who, by implementing his slogan that every healthy man is a potential patient, is able to gain control over a group united through their common anxieties about health. Knock is enraptured by his vision of 250 villagers taking their temperatures and medicines at precisely the same time. Somewhat similarly, *Musse, or, The School of Hypocrisy* (1930) shows how an insignificant man who wishes to be honest discovers that the only way he can attain liberty is by joining other men in hypocrisy.

Romains was most active as a dramatist during the 1920s. He headed Copeau's school from 1920 to 1924 and then worked closely with Jouvet. But after 1930 he devoted most of his attention to the twenty-seven volumes of his "Men of Good Will" novels. Most of Romains plays seem contrived, for they are designed to illustrate ideas. As a result, few achieved genuine popularity, although several provided stimulating theatrical experiences.

Steve Passeur (1899–1966) also wrote in the satirical vein but his work more nearly resembles that of Strindberg or post-World War II "black comedy" than that of his contemporaries. His is a world turned upside down: parents fear their children, husbands their wives, love is only truly passionate when it is not returned. Most of his plays focus on duels between men and women, with one dominant (usually the woman) and the other dominated, often humiliated. His most characteristic work is *The Buyer* (1930), in which a spinster buys a young husband by paying off his debts. Her love turns to hatred almost immediately, for following the wedding her husband attempts to leave with his mistress. Thereafter she devises a thousand small tortures for him each day and he gradually becomes little more than a slave. But he also grows as fond of his masochistic role as she is of her sadistic one, and when he is finally freed he must be dragged away by his father. No longer having anything to live for, the wife commits suicide.

Passeur's characters are as addicted to direct and forceful statement as Bernard's are to indirectness. They exchange stinging charges, designed to wound, and seem always near the peak of emotion. They are also usually trapped by intermingled love and hatred, but are most aware of the desire for revenge. Their verbal fencing is clever but cynical in tone. Passeur's plays are marked by strong situation, keen intelligence, and pointed wit. During the 1920s Passeur was looked upon as one of France's most promising playwrights, but unfortunately he never fully developed his potential.

Marcel Achard (1899–   ) is almost opposite in outlook to Passeur, for his plays usually begin in a somewhat cynical atmosphere and end in romantic reconciliation. Achard is also noteworthy for capitalizing on the interest, so evident among the French intelligentsia of the 1920s, in *commedia dell' arte* and popular entertainments. Achard served as prompter at the Vieux Colombier under Copeau, but it was Lugné-Poë who presented his first play, *The Mass is Said* (1923)—which was hissed off the stage. Fortunately, in the same year, he achieved one of his greatest successes (at Dullin's Atelier) with *Will You Play With Me?*, written with the Fratellini family of circus clowns in mind and utilizing *commedia dell' arte* conventions. This self-conscious theatricality typifies most of Achard's plays prior to World War II. Perhaps the best is *Jean de la lune* (1929), in which Jef, a Pierrot figure, is married to a coquette who eternally flirts with other men. Eventually, however, his seeming ardent belief in her fidelity charms her into being the faithful woman he has imagined. After World War II,

Achard's *Will You Play With Me?* at the Atelier in 1923.
(From *Le Théâtre,* 1924.)

Achard achieved considerable popular success in Boulevard theatres with such works as *Beside My Blonde* (1946) and *Patate* (1957), which ran for seven years.

It is virtually impossible to categorize the works of Armand Salacrou (1899–   ), for they run the gamut from surrealist fantasy, comedy ballet, and satirical comedy to historical and psychological drama. They also mingle the most discordant elements: farce with anguish, lucidity with incoherence, romanticism with cynicism, melodrama with comedy of ideas. Perhaps as a result, he has never perfected any one approach and has enjoyed only erratic success, partially because he so often confuses his audiences.

Salacrou had studied medicine, philosophy, and law before turning to the theatre. His first produced work, *Turn to Earth,* was presented by Lugné-Poë in 1925, but he did not win success until 1934 with *A Free Woman.* Among his later plays, the most effective were *The Unknown Woman of Arras* (1935), *The World is Round* (1938), *Nights of Wrath* (1946), and *Boulevard Durand* (1960).

Many of Salacrou's plays are concerned with the suffering of the innocent and with the absurdity of the human condition (he used the term "absurd" long before Camus did). Some of his works are Pirandellian in their insistence that each man differs from one day to the next and that he cannot be judged today for his past deeds. Most of his plays are searches for answers to metaphysical questions about the meaning of life and one's own existence.

The Unknown Woman of Arras is one of Salacrou's most interesting experiments with techniques. It begins and ends with the same gunshot, as a man commits suicide, and the entire action occurs in the second between the firing of the bullet and the reaching of its target. In that time, the man relives incidents from the past, conversing with the living and the dead, searching for some meaning in his existence. Eventually he finds it in the unselfish assistance he once gave to an unknown woman on the battlefield at Arras. Now realizing that life has its compensations, he regrets his act of suicide, but nothing can change the destiny that man creates out of his own deeds.

Salacrou's finest play is perhaps *The World is Round,* set in Florence in the time of Savonarola, who has established a virtual dictatorship out of his desire to serve an ascetic God in a debauched age. The discovery that the world is round, a notion directly contrary to accepted belief, offers a challenge to his absolutism, and the people demand a miracle (that Savonarola submit to a trial by fire) to discredit the challenge. When he refuses, his downfall is assured, but it also arouses doubts within Savonarola about his past. While the play is set in the Renaissance, Salacrou is concerned with the cyclical nature of human experience (the circular motion of the world) which moves from submission to dictatorial absolutes and governments to libertinism and anarchy. Though the time, place, and participants may change, the pattern does not.

Nights of Wrath was perhaps Salacrou's most popular play, in part because of its topical treatment of resistance and collaboration during the German occupation. It begins with the killing of two collaborators for their part in the death of a resistance leader and then moves backward and forward in time to intermingle moments of friendship and betrayal among the same set of characters. It is also one of Salacrou's most optimistic dramas, for in it his people die not for themselves but "for the happiness of those yet to be born." In all his plays, Salacrou treats themes of enduring interest. He was clearly one of the most inquiring dramatists of his age, but his plays are of such uneven quality that he has often been judged overharshly.

André Obey (1892–   ) worked closely with the Compagnie des Quinze and wrote his early plays with their specific production methods in mind. As a result, it was many years before other French troupes felt they could present his works. *Noah* (1931), his first play, is composed of a series of episodes ranging from domestic comedy to epic grandeur. The animals, wiser than men, come to the ark of their own accord and ally themselves sympathetically with Noah during the trials and petty bickerings which plague him. When the flood recedes, the animals and Noah's own children desert him. At first discouraged, he regains his faith and sets about rebuilding his world.

388

The
Inter-War
Years in
Italy,
France and
Belgium

The Rape of Lucrece (1931), based on Shakespeare's poem, is indebted to Cocteau, for it depends primarily upon two narrators and mimed action. It provided an excellent opportunity for the Compagnie des Quinze to demonstrate its skills in mime and its adaptation of Japanese Noh techniques. Of Obey's later works, the most interesting is his play about Don Juan, of which there are three versions: *Don Juan* (1934), *The Deceiver of Seville* (1937), and *Man of Ashes* (1949). In them, Obey uses simultaneous settings grouped around a square representing Seville. Through complete fluidity of time and place, Obey is able to call up events out of Don Juan's life to illuminate his character. Obey wrote several additional plays and made a number of adaptations (among them *Richard III* for Dullin and the *Oresteia* for Barrault), but his reputation rests primarily on *Noah*. Outside of France, his influence is most evident in the work of Thornton Wilder.

Of all the French dramatists between the wars, it is now generally agreed that Jean Giraudoux (1882–1944) was the most important. Educated in France and Germany, Giraudoux had been a tutor in the household of the duke of Saxe-Meiningen and an instructor at Harvard University before entering the foreign service in 1910, after which he mingled his diplomatic and literary careers. Following World War I, he wrote a series of novels, and it was with an adaptation of one of these, *Siegfried*, that he made his debut as a dramatist at the age of forty-six in 1928. Encouraged by this success, he turned increasingly to dramatic writing. With the exception of two wartime works, Jouvet directed the first productions of all of Giraudoux's plays. The value placed on language by both made them ideal collaborators.

Giraudoux was not primarily interested in story. Most of his plays are based on well-known myths or legends, and only *Siegfried, Intermezzo* (1933), and *The Madwoman of Chaillot* (1944) use stories of his own invention. Furthermore, he was not deeply concerned with character. Most of his heroes are men of astonishing insight and are marked above all by intellectual acumen. Most are keenly interested in their own motives and ideas. The plays contain few unpleasant characters.

Giraudoux's was essentially a drama of ideas, but not in the sense of Brieux's plays, for Giraudoux was little concerned with social problems. Rather, his works turn on antitheses—peace and war, fidelity and infidelity, life and death, liberty and destiny, the absolute and the ephemeral—and their reconciliations. His dramas take place at the moment when men are faced with a choice between two contradictory positions; he explores the contradictions, even emphasizes them; his resolutions usually suggest means whereby the contradictions can be reconciled, often through some unusual perception. Thus, though the physical outcome of actions often seem fated (the use of myths and legends in part dictate the outcome), the protagonists still insist upon their intellectual independence from facts: "Nothing is true except what you accept as such; only logic is absurd and, since I am a man, I am god in my arbitrary rule."

Despite his interest in ideas, Giraudoux did not let his characters engage in direct arguments about philosophical positions. Rather, he sought to work through indirection and to let perceptions insinuate themselves into the mind through feeling and imagination. Consequently, Giraudoux had to disengage his characters from the world of everyday reality and lift them to a semimythic plane where the concerns of daily life are no longer immediately relevant.

Language is Giraudoux's primary means. He considered it to be the highest expression of human reason and man's major tool for escaping chaos. Writing at a time when the playwright had been subordinated to the director, Giraudoux sought to reaffirm the literary worth of drama. Therefore, literary style is perhaps the most distinctive element of his plays. He wrote in a euphonious and highly expressive prose with supple cadences and rhythms. At times his diction is overly subtle, almost precious; it shows a marked disposition for fantasy, irony, and humor. Through it, Giraudoux sought to unite the simple and complex, the homely and the eternal, and to arouse insight through its impact on the audience's sensibilities.

Among Giraudoux's plays, probably the best known are *Amphitryon 38, Judith, The Trojan War Shall Not Take Place, Ondine,* and *The Madwoman of Chaillot. Amphitryon 38* (1929), so called because Giraudoux considered it the thirty-eighth dramatic treatment of the myth, shows that true love is impervious even to the machinations of the gods. Jupiter desires Alcmene and uses all his wiles to trick her into an affair, but only when he transforms himself into a complete image of her husband is he successful and he never shakes her love for her husband or her belief in

Giraudoux's *The Trojan War Shall Not Take Place,* directed by Jouvet at the Théâtre Athénée in 1934. (From *Theatre Arts,* 1938.)

390

*The
Inter-War
Years in
Italy,
France and
Belgium*

marital fidelity. Thus, despite Alcmene's physical infidelity she remains absolutely unsullied.

In *Judith* (1931), based on the biblical story, the city of Bethulia can be saved only by the city's purest young woman. When she is named, Judith, overcome with pride, sets out to do what the army has been unable to accomplish: repel the invader. But when she meets Holofernes she is overcome by physical desire for a man who preaches the doctrine of joy without guilt. The next day, unable to face separation from him, she kills Holofernes, returns to Bethulia, and proudly proclaims her love in the face of the Elders' protests. Then, an angel (or perhaps only a drunken guard) orders her to accept the Elders' version of her deed, and she is proclaimed a virgin who has killed Holofernes to save her people.

The Trojan War Shall Not Take Place (1935, played in English as *Tiger at the Gates*) shows Hector's desperate attempts to avoid war—for he knows its horrors—in the face of a war party, who see in Helen a symbol of love and beauty for which men must be willing to die. All seems to go Hector's way until in a quarrel he wounds the leader of the war party, who, as he dies, declares that he has been treacherously killed by the Greeks. Despite Hector's protests, the Trojans swear to avenge this deed. As the play ends, war is inevitable. This is one of Giraudoux's darker works, for with it he seeks to show that behind the romanticization of war lie baser instincts which should be recognized and, hopefully, brought under control.

Ondine (1939), Giraudoux's most spectacular play, is based on a nineteenth-century story. It tells how the medieval knight Hans meets a water sprite, Ondine, who wishes to marry him despite a warning from the Old One (the King of the Sea) that she will not be happy. The Old One eventually consents to the marriage but decrees that Hans, if ever unfaithful to Ondine, will die. In the second act, the Illusionist (the Old One in disguise) speeds up time so that the audience sees in a series of rapid episodes the passage of ten years in the hypocritical court. Ultimately Hans is unfaithful and dies, and Ondine returns to her timeless world having forgotten him. Here Giraudoux seems to be concerned with man's (embodied in Hans) contradictory urges toward materialism (symbolized by Bertha, with whom Hans is unfaithful) and the timeless world of nature (symbolized by Ondine). Man is attracted to nonmateriality but is unequal to its demands; he dies, but nature lives on, little remembering that man ever existed.

The Madwoman of Chaillot is Giraudoux's least characteristic work. Written during the German occupation of France, it reflects Giraudoux's hope for the liberation of Paris, the symbol of all civilization. The barbarians, here represented by the materialistic exploiters, are lured by the Madwoman's tale of oil beneath her cellar into a pit, where they are entombed. At this moment, all the benevolent forces of nature are released and the world's beauty is renewed. Like *Ondine, The Madwoman of*

Madeline Ozeray and Louis Jouvet in the 1938 production of Giraudoux's *Ondine*. (Photo by Lipnitzki.)

Chaillot seems to suggest that man's welfare is closely linked to nature; to this it adds a plea for the elevation of humanitarianism above materialism. It was to be Giraudoux's final work.

It is not surprising that Giraudoux has come increasingly under attack since World War II, for his emphasis upon language places him at the opposite pole from Artaud's followers, who have so severely attacked the word. It is too early to predict Giraudoux's ultimate fate. Certainly his fame has declined, but it has not been eclipsed. Regardless of future estimates, he was, between the wars, the most respected of French dramatists, and his influence on such successors as Anouilh, Montherlant, Sartre, and Camus was marked.

During these years there were many other dramatists both avant-garde and traditional, but they either continued old trends or reflected the work of the playwrights discussed here. Interwar French theatre and drama, under Copeau's dominance, were on the whole probably the most ascetic and intellectual in the world. Although the surrealists and the Boulevard theatres extended the range considerably, to most critics the heart of French theatre and drama was located in Copeau's ideal and the work of the Cartel and its playwrights.

Two Belgian authors—Crommelynck and Ghelderode—are closely linked with the French theatre, for both wrote in French and owe their fame to French productions. Fernand Crommelynck (1888–1970), born in Brussels, began writing at an early age, and two of his plays, *We Will Go No More to the Woods* (1906) and *The Merchant of Regrets* (1911), had been presented in Brussels before he went to Paris in 1911. Crommelynck's reputation dates from 1921, when *The Magnificent Cuckold* was produced at the Théâtre de l'Oeuvre and *The Childish Lovers* at the Comédie Montaigne. By 1934, several other plays, among them *Golden Tripe* (1925), *Carine* (1929), *The Woman Whose Heart is Too Small* (1934), and *Hot and Cold* (1934), had been presented at the l'Oeuvre and the Comédie des Champs-Elysées. After 1934 Crommelynck wrote little.

Without doubt, Crommelynck's most popular work has been *The Magnificent Cuckold* (already discussed briefly in connection with Meyerhold's productions). Its method—pushing a banal situation to the edge of insanity—is typical of all of Crommelynck's work. In *The Magnificent Cuckold,* Bruno's love for his wife makes him boast of her beauty and charms, but when his praises arouse the interest of other men, he becomes insanely jealous. Seeking to quiet his anxiety, he forces his wife into the very infidelity he fears and eventually she runs away with another man in order to escape his unquenchable suspicions. Similarly, *Hot and Cold* tells of a wife who is completely indifferent to her husband and takes a series of lovers so casually that she cannot even remember their names. But when her husband dies, she learns that he has been adored by his young mistress, of whose existence she had been completely unaware. She now becomes obsessed with her husband's virtues, and she schemes until she gets her husband's mistress to take a new lover so that she can claim her dead husband entirely for herself. In such ways, Crommelynck pushes farcical situation into the realm of near-fantasy.

Michel de Ghelderode (1898–1962) was virtually unknown outside of Belgium until 1949, when *Chronicles of Hell* become the sensation of the Parisian season. Thereafter his fame spread rapidly and before he died his plays were being performed throughout the world. But if Ghelderode's fame is postwar, the plays are not, for virtually all were written between 1918 and 1937. Their popularity probably stems from their affinity with absurdist drama and Artaud's theories.

Although Ghelderode's plays were written in French, they are distinctively Flemish in flavor. They are often likened to the paintings of Bosch, Breughel, and Ensor, and indeed Ghelderode based some of his plays on the works of those painters. Throughout his more than thirty plays

393

*The
Inter-War
Years in
Italy,
France and
Belgium*

(some short, some long) runs his vision of man as a creature whose flesh overpowers his spirit. Corruption, death, and cruelty are always near the surface, although behind them lurks an implied criticism of degradation and materialism and a call to repentance. But Ghelderode studiously avoids didacticism, and in his works faith is apt to be approached through blasphemy and suffering through ludicrous farce. As one critic has put it, "Where most authors . . . attempt to discover rational explanations, Ghelderode discovers the demon."

Like Artaud, Ghelderode downgrades language in favor of spectacle. He has said, "I discovered the world of shapes before discovering the world of ideas." His visions are revealed through images, sound, color, light and shadow, and atmosphere. Place is apt to shift rapidly and unexpectedly; characters are usually exaggerated and many are descended from the clowns of the music hall, circus, and fair. Most of the plays were not written with production in mind but, as Ghelderode declares, only to please himself. They resemble the works of Jarry, the surrealists, and expressionists, but have their own quite distinctive flavor.

Ghelderode's earliest plays are little more than brief developments of a single episode, but in his first full-length play, *The Death of Doctor Faust* (1926), are found almost all the qualities that characterize his later work, as well as a compendium of the experimental tendencies of the age. In it, Faust emerges from his medieval study into a modern-day carnival, during which a performance of *Faust* is given in a tavern. Faust meets a young girl (Marguerite), seduces her, and then refuses to marry her on the grounds that he is both too old and from another age. Threatened by a crowd, he is saved by the Devil, who transforms the scene into a poster advertising the performance of *Faust*. When Marguerite commits suicide, the actors of *Faust* are accused of murder and, in seeking to escape, enter the study of the real Faust, where they come face to face with their counterparts. They merge sufficiently that when Faust seeks to kill his impersonator, he murders himself.

Ghelderode called this play "a music hall tragedy," and, like many French works of the period, it reflects the current interest in popular forms. It also reflects the concern for simultaneity—through its mingling of the sixteenth- and twentieth-century contexts, and through its use of multiple playing areas for concurrent scenes. It pursues as well the Pirandellian themes of appearance and reality, and of multiple levels of illusion. Furthermore, the script calls for such new technical devices as projections and titles flashed on a screen.

Something of a cross-section of Ghelderode's later work can be seen in *Pantagleize, Chronicles of Hell, Hop Signor!, School for Buffoons,* and *Red Magic. Pantagleize* (1929), "a depressing vaudeville," is set in Europe "on the morrow of one war and the eve of another." When the naïve protagonist, Pantagleize, adopts as his cliché of the moment, "What a

394

*The
Inter-War
Years in
Italy,
France and
Belgium*

lovely day," he is caught up in a revolution, for his greeting is the signal awaited by the insurrectionists. Innocent of his role, Pantagleize is spied upon by policemen disguised as palm trees, takes part in a raid on the national treasury, and is arrested and executed without realizing what is happening. Through this work, Ghelderode seems to suggest that all human endeavors—whether active or passive—are equally meaningless.

Chronicles of Hell (1929)—the work which, in Barrault's production, catapulted Ghelderode to fame in 1949—opens with the clergy blasphemously celebrating the funeral of Bishop Jan of Eremo. When an emissary from the pope arrives, Simon, the acting bishop, denies the rumor that he has been responsible for Jan's death, but he is answered with thunder and lightning and Jan's resurrection. Jan's mother extracts a poisoned wafer from her son's throat; now truly dying, Jan refuses to absolve Simon and is slapped by his mother, who is rewarded by being forced to eat the poisoned wafer herself. The final scene returns to the celebrating clergy. Simon joins them once more and now has a bowel movement, thus purging his body though unable to relieve his soul. It is perhaps not surprising that Parisians were scandalized. Still, no play illustrates so well Ghelderode's Rabelaisian strain or his approach to faith through blasphemy.

In *Hop Signor!* (1935), Marguerite, the chaste wife of Jureal, finds herself attracted to the handsome young executioner Larose, and eventually is so fascinated by the public killings he performs and so intermingles them with sexual fantasies that she can only be satisfied through her own execution by Larose on the headsman's block. Here, as in several others of Ghelderode's plays, carnal desire is not far removed from a lust for death. In *The School for Buffoons* (1937), Folial the clown (who appears in several of Ghelderode's plays) runs a school for deformed jesters. Before they graduate, he reveals to them the secret of "all art that deserves to endure"—cruelty.

But Ghelderode also had a lighter side, perhaps best seen in *Red Magic* (1931), which both in subject matter and tone reflects medieval farce. In it, the elderly Hieronymous is so miserly that he will not even give his body to his young wife. Then her lover gains entry to the house by pretending to be an alchemist who will reveal the secret of making gold. The lovers are so successful in their snares that when they run away together Hieronymous is accused both of witchcraft and of having murdered his wife. Here there is no condemnation, merely the lighthearted cynicism typical of medieval farce.

Ghelderode wished to reconcile man to himself by revealing his imperfections and spiritual longings. That he emphasized degradation over triumph only made him more attractive to a post-World War II generation mired in disillusionment.

~ VIII ~

The interwar years were ones during which earlier trends were consolidated and synthesized. Playwrights and directors were aware both of the spiritual and the physical realms, and consequently they avoided both actualism and marked abstractionism. Thus, the dominant mode might best be described as a theatricalized realism. For the majority of writers and producers, "art" still connoted beauty, humanitarianism, and a truth more elevated than that of daily life. But for some, such as Artaud and Ghelderode, the light could only be reached after a painful descent into darkness. And for Pirandello, truth had become wholly evanescent; for him, human realities, conceived as a series of roles in a state of constant flux, could only be contemplated compassionately, since they are beyond man's control or complete comprehension. But, on the whole, the interwar era was still essentially optimistic, even though the seeds of that darker view which would dominate the postwar theatre had already been planted.

Theatre and Drama in Central and Eastern Europe Between The Wars

12

In 1918, Germany and Austria were forced to accept harsh terms of peace after undergoing crushing defeats in World War I, but in both the theatre continued to be vital. A network of state-subsidized theatres kept tradition alive and a number of independent producers, of whom Max Reinhardt was the most important, encouraged experimentation. Until about 1924, expressionism dominated drama, but, as disillusionment grew, it was supplanted by neorealism. At the same time, significant innovations were being made in production by Piscator and Brecht and at the Bauhaus. Unfortunately, the rise of Hitler terminated almost all experimentation, for under National Socialism the theatre was subordinated to political ends. After 1933 the center of avant-grade theatre shifted to Czechoslovakia and

397

*Theatre and
Drama in
Central and
Eastern
Europe
Between
the Wars*

Poland, but the outbreak of World War II led to the suspension of all nontraditional theatrical practice. Vitality would not return anywhere in central and eastern Europe until after 1945.

In 1918, the German Empire collapsed. Although many saw this as the herald of a bright future, the immediate result was economic and political chaos. Until 1923, Germany would be embroiled in civil strife and plagued with rampant inflation. As a result, optimism gradually gave way to disillusionment.

Conditions between 1918 and 1923 affected the theatre in many ways. First, the strict wartime censorship was lifted and the previously suspect expressionist drama flooded the stage. Prior to 1919, expressionism was essentially a literary movement, since few of the plays had been produced, but from 1919 until 1924 it would be the dominant mode both in dramatic writing and theatrical production. Second, the former royal theatres were reconstituted to suit the new republican form of government. Fortunately, by this time Germans took it for granted that the state should support theatres just as it did educational and other cultural institutions, and so the network of state-subsidized theatres that had grown up under the German princes was preserved. Now freed from many former restrictions, some of these theatres took the lead in developing an expressionistic style of production. For example, it was at the Berlin State Theatre that Leopold Jessner set the tone for much theatrical work of the time. Nevertheless, the state theatres continued to provide a varied repertory in which the classics figured prominently. Third, the private theatres suffered most from the chaotic economic situation. Finding it increasingly difficult to subsist, many turned to works selected for their wide popular appeal. Even Reinhardt felt it necessary to give up his theatres in Berlin for a time. After 1923, as economic conditions improved, so did the lot of the private theatres, although most continued to provide popular entertainment, leaving the more varied repertory to the state theatres. Fourth, there was an upsurge of interest in the theatre among the working classes. Although the *Volksbühnen* movement had begun in the 1890s, the only really important groups prior to World War I were those in Berlin and Vienna. The increase in interest after the war was so great that by 1933 there were more than three hundred groups in Germany. Fifth, from 1918 until 1933 the German theatre reflected the great political, economic, and social conflicts which would eventually lead to the assumption of power by Hitler and the

*Theatre and
Drama in
Central and
Eastern
Europe
Between
the Wars*

suppression of all opposition. For the most part, however, the German theatre after World War I was socially conscious and deeply partisan.

Aside from the expressionists (already discussed in an earlier chapter), the dominant post-World War I director was Max Reinhardt, who continued to be eclectic both in choosing and producing plays. Beginning in 1917, he directed a number of expressionist dramas, the first—including Sorge's *The Beggar* and Hasenclever's *The Son*—for private viewing, and then several—among them works by Wedekind, Sternheim, Hasenclever, Toller, and Kaiser—for public presentation.

For the most part, Reinhardt merely continued his prewar practices, but a few of his post-World War I enterprises deserve special attention. Among the most significant was his conversion of Berlin's Circus Schumann into the Grosses Schauspielhaus (sometimes called the "Theatre of Five Thousand," although in actuality it seated around thirty-five hundred). Remodeled by Hanz Poelzig, the Grosses Schauspielhaus retained some of its circus qualities, for seating rose in tiers around three sides of the former ring, which now simulated the orchestra of an ancient Greek theatre. There were three acting areas: the orchestra; a raised platform forward of the proscenium and connected to the orchestra by steps; and, back of a proscenium arch, a fully equipped stage (with an enormous revolving stage and plaster skydome). Thus the Grosses Schauspielhaus combined the features of the open and proscenium stages. Here between 1919 and 1922 Reinhardt presented such plays as Aeschylus's *Oresteia*, Aristophanes' *Lysistrata,* Sophocles' *Oedipus Rex*, Shakespeare's *Julius Caesar*, Goethe's *Goetz von Berlichingen*, Rolland's *Danton*, Hauptmann's *The Weavers*, Hasenclever's *Antigone,* and Toller's *The Machine Wreckers.*

At the Grosses Schauspielhaus, Reinhardt made an effort to break down the barriers between audience and performers (in *Danton,* for example, he planted actors in the audience to increase the spectators' sense of involvement), but his retention of the proscenium stage indicates that he was not willing to break fully with tradition. He also sought to attract a wider audience by setting prices at approximately one-half those charged by other major theatres in Berlin. For a time he was successful, but gradually the theatre's popularity waned and in 1922 he abandoned it. For the most part thereafter it was given over to operettas and spectacular reviews. The major problem faced by Reinhardt here was probably the enormous size of the house, which encouraged dependence on spectacle, since acoustics were so poor that subtlety was virtually impossible.

Like other private theatre owners, Reinhardt was caught in the economic squeeze of the time and in 1920 he gave over the Deutsches Theater to Felix Holländer. Between 1920 and 1924, aside from the Grosses Schauspielhaus, Reinhardt's major enterprises were Austrian. In collaboration with Hugo von Hoffmannsthal, he founded the Salzburg Festival with the expressed aim of restoring Austria's cultural prestige and of preserving the best in the Austrian dramatic and musical heritage. Like other mani-

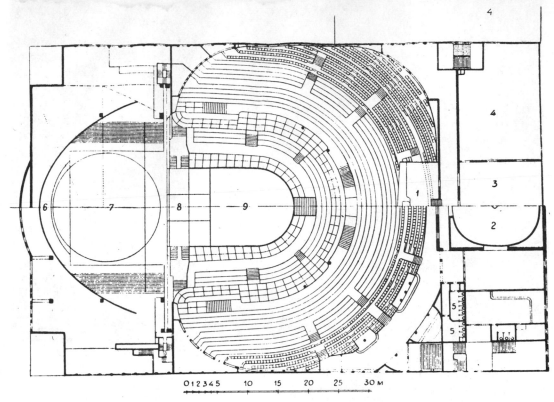

Floorplan and interior of Reinhardt's Grosses Schauspielhaus,
converted from the Circus Schumann in 1919.
(From Barkhin, *Teatra Architectura,* Moscow, 1947.)

Hoffmannsthal's adaptation of Calderon's *The Great World Theatre,*
produced at the Salzburg Festival in 1922 by Max Reinhardt.
(From Österreichische Nationalbibliothek.)

festations of the people's theatre movement, the Salzburg Festival sought to
coalesce the sentiments of a nation in an artistic endeavor. Consequently,
many of the theatrical offerings were of a special nature. Hofmannsthal's
adaptation of *Everyman,* staged in front of the Salzburg Cathedral, became
and remains the centerpiece of the festival. In 1922, Hosmannsthal's
adaptation of Calderon's *The Great World Theatre,* performed inside a
church and using medieval mansions as the basic scenic convention, was
added. Other plays were offered in theatres, riding schools, and other
locations. Everywhere Reinhardt's eclectic approach was evident. Here he
also began one of the first European training programs for directors. Soon
the Salzburg Festival was world-famous, and, except for wartime interruptions, has continued to be a major annual artistic event.

In Vienna, Reinhardt was granted permission in 1922 to create a
theatre in the ballroom of an eighteenth-century palace. This theatre, the
Redoutensaal, was almost opposite in nature to the Grosses Schauspielhaus,
for it was as intimate as the Berlin theatre was enormous. Since the
Redoutensaal was considered a national treasure, no major alterations were
permitted. There was no proscenium arch or front curtain. A platform
backed by a curving screen and balcony reached by stairways constituted
the stage. For the most part, scenery, designed by Alfred Roller, was
restricted to screens, although occasionally a few small set pieces and

Reinhardt's Redoutensaal theatre, Vienna, in 1922,
created in the ballroom of an eighteenth-century palace.
(From *Le Théâtre,* 1922.)

properties were introduced. The overall effect was that of a wholly
conventionalized and architectural stage (not unlike that of the Vieux
Colombier). The plays and chamber operas presented here were chosen
for their appropriateness to the background: works by Goethe, Beaumarchais, Molière, Mozart, and others. After 1924, Reinhardt also controlled Vienna's Josefstadt Theater, where he mounted a diverse repertory
in collaboration with his principal designer, Oskar Strnad.

When economic stability returned to Germany, Reinhardt resumed his
Berlin operations (after 1924 he sometimes managed as many as three
different theatres in Berlin) but continued his Austrian activities. In addition, he staged a number of productions elsewhere. Perhaps the most
famous of these was Vollmoeller's *The Miracle* in 1924. For this revival in
New York (Reinhardt had already presented the play in several European
cities), Norman Bel Geddes transformed the Century Theatre into a
simulated cathedral (by far the most effective of the simulations devised for
Reinhardt's various versions of the pantomime). Reinhardt also staged a
season of plays (including *A Midsummer Night's Dream, Everyman,* and
Danton's Death) in New York in 1927–28 and several plays in England in
1932–33.

When Hitler came to power, Reinhardt, as a Jew, was forced to give
up his theatres and leave Germany. Most of his final years were spent in

402

*Theatre and
Drama in
Central and
Eastern
Europe
Between
the Wars*

America, where he headed an acting school in Hollywood and directed films and plays. His last major stage production was Werfel's *The Eternal Road*, seen in New York in 1936.

By 1933, Reinhardt had produced 452 plays in Berlin for a total of 23,374 performances. But it was quality and variety more than volume that made him the dominant German director from 1905 until 1933. Still, by the time he left Germany Reinhardt was being accused of subordinating a script's meaning to some unifying visual motif or limited directorial concept and was being dismissed by some as a "mere popularizer." Even if the charges are true, he still performed an important service, for he kept audiences abreast of new movements and directed their attention to significant dramatists and production techniques that had appeared strange and obscure in other theatres.

❧ II ❧

Around 1923 both economic and political stability returned to Germany and continued until about 1929. The restoration of order coincided with the end of expressionism, and, though little drama of worth was written between 1923 and 1929, the plays exhibited a new outlook, usually labeled Neue Sachlichkeit (literally, "New Matter-of-factness") or neorealism. It was characterized by a return to more conventional dramatic techniques, both in writing and production, and by subjects dealing with ordinary people in everyday situations and settings. As at the end of the romantic era, there arose in the 1920s a demand that idealistic visions be abandoned in favor of down-to-earth fact. Some of the most rhapsodic of the expressionists now embraced neorealism fervently. For example, in *The Great Dream* (1923) Paul Kornfeld ridiculed the utopian ideal of the expressionists and in the following year demanded: "No more about war, revolution and the salvation of the world! Let us be modest and turn our attention to other and smaller things. Let us ponder on a human being, on a soul, or a fool."

But the neorealism of the 1920s differed considerably from the realism of the nineteenth century. The techniques were never so objective as those used by the realists and naturalists, for the many intervening antirealistic movements and the interest in the subconscious left their marks on it. Furthermore, it lacked the optimism of realism and naturalism (for in those movements there lurked behind any apparent degradation a belief in the perfectibility of man and society). In contrast, neorealism was characteristically pessimistic and disillusioned. Unfortunately, the movement lacked dramatists sufficiently strong to give it a sense of direction and it remained a diverse collection of secondary figures. The typical subjects were chosen from a wide range of contemporary problems: returning soldiers, adjustment to peacetime life, an overly rigid legal system, the traumas of adolescence and school life. Though the plays found ready audiences at the time, few now bear reading. Of the many playwrights, perhaps the best are Wolf, Bruckner, and Zuckmayer.

Friedrich Wolf (1888–1953) began as an expressionist with *That is You* (1918) and *The Absolute Man* (1919), but in 1923 turned to realism with *Poor Conrad,* based on a peasant revolt of the sixteenth century. More characteristic, however, is his *Cyanide* (1929), an attack on the laws against abortion, showing how a young girl dies because she is forced to seek help outside legitimate channels. Like many dramatists of the period, Wolf became increasingly committed to a leftist political position, one clearly evident in his best-known work, *The Sailors of Cattaro* (1930), a documentary play about an uprising in the Austro-Hungarian navy during World War I. Although Wolf sought to stick to documented fact (he even gave all the characters their real-life names), his sympathy with the revolt is clear, and at the end the last of the mutineers led away to execution declares: "This is not the end, this is only the beginning." When Hitler came to power, Wolf fled Germany but continued to write. In *Professor Mamlock* (1933) he tells the story of a Jewish doctor who becomes a victim of the Nazis, and in his last play, *Beaumarchais* (1945), somewhat prophetically shows how the French playwright, after helping to bring about the revolution, is unable to support its excesses. Similarly, Wolf returned to East Germany but under the communism he had advocated was never able to write another work.

Ferdinand Bruckner (1891–1958), an Austrian, had been an expressionist poet and the director of a theatre in Berlin before he wrote his first play, *The Malady of Youth* (1926), an overnight sensation and a major example of neorealism because of its treatment of the disillusionment of young people. The characters, mostly medical students, come to believe that the only alternative to corruption is death. As one sums it up: "Either one turns into a philistine, or one commits suicide. There is no other way out." *The Criminals* (1928) indicts the legal system and man's conscience. It is technically unusual, for Bruckner divides the stage into nine compartments in which he depicts a cross-section of German society involved in acts for which the participants are later brought to trial. By making injustice prevail in each case, Bruckner seeks to show that the legal system is so petrified that in following the letter of the law justice is subverted. But he also wishes to suggest that men use the legal system as a substitute for a rigorous conscience. As his *raisonneur* says: "We have set up a retributive authority in order to relieve our consciences. . . . In this escape from ourselves lies the indestructible power of public jurisprudence."

After this time, most of Bruckner's plays were based on historical sub-

404

*Theatre and
Drama in
Central and
Eastern
Europe
Between
the Wars*

jects treated to suggest contemporary relevance. The first of his works to achieve fame outside of Germany, *Elizabeth of England* (1930), is a collection of episodes (in the manner of a chronicle play) tracing Elizabeth's conflict with Philip of Spain and the treason of Essex. As in *The Criminals,* simultaneous scenes are used to great effect. One of the most striking episodes shows Elizabeth at church in England and Philip at church in Spain, each praying to God for assistance against the other. Ultimately the principal conflict is between fanaticism (represented by Philip and the Catholic Church) and reason (represented by Elizabeth and, especially, Sir Francis Bacon). *Elizabeth of England* is generally considered to be Bruckner's most successful play.

Bruckner continued to treat historical subjects in *Timon* (1931), based on Shakespeare's tragedy, *Napoleon the First* (1937), and *Heroic Comedy* (1942)—the last two designed to suggest parallels between Napoleon and Hitler. Like many of his countrymen, Bruckner spent the Nazi era in exile. After his return, he wrote a number of plays on historical, mythical, and contemporary subjects, but none was markedly successful.

Carl Zuckmayer (1896–   ), like many of his contemporaries, entered military service during World War I as a confirmed patriot and ended as a rebel. After the war he worked at several odd jobs, edited a revolutionary journal, and produced plays before turning to playwriting in 1920. At first he wrote in the expressionist vein but after two failures decided that another style was more suited to his talents. With *The Merry Vineyard* (1925) he won resounding success both for himself and for the emerging neorealistic mode. The play, set in Zuckmayer's native Rhineland, is written partially in the dialect of that region and reflects an earthy peasant humor throughout. The basic situation derives from a rich winemaker's determination that his daughter can only marry a man who has proved his worth both in drinking wine and making love. The action is set against a festival and its Aristophanic revelry, during which the young hero gains the favor of the winemaker and his daughter. A minor satirical strain treats the affectations of the townspeople, especially the self-satisfied "corps student" who also seeks the girl's hand. The lusty, earthy humor of *The Merry Vineyard* was enormously successful with a German public weary of the abstract flights of the expressionists.

Zuckmayer's most famous work, *The Captain of Köpenick* (1931), is a satirical treatment of Prussian bureaucracy and militarism. Based on a true incident, it shows how a poor cobbler who needs official documents in order to obtain work is continually frustrated by bureaucrats. Through a series of accidents, a captain's uniform falls into his hands and, now desperate, he dons the uniform, commandeers a company of soldiers, takes over the town hall, arrests the mayor, and attains the documents he needs. The satire is at first directed against the unfeeling bureaucrats but is gradually expanded to include the whole Prussian outlook which leads people to obey unquestioningly anyone in uniform. It has become one of the classics of the German stage and, with Hauptmann's *The Beaver Coat,* is perhaps the finest German comedy of the modern era. Hauptmann came to consider Zuckmayer his true literary successor, and Zuckmayer, perhaps flattered by the compliment, completed a play left unfinished by Hauptmann at his death.

When the Nazis came to power, Zuckmayer left Germany and eventually settled in America. After working on one film in Hollywood, he moved to a farm in Vermont, where he continued to write throughout the war. Of his late works, two are most significant. *The Devil's General* (1946), one of the first successful plays of the postwar period, indicated the future direction of German serious drama: the exploration of guilt and responsibility. *The Devil's General* is set in Germany at the height of Hitler's power. The protagonist is a charming man who, through political naïveté and misguided patriotism, has risen to become a general in the Luftwaffe. When it is discovered that saboteurs are at work in the airplane factory he supervises, he must seek out the culprits; in the process, he comes to self-awareness. He discovers that the principal saboteur is his chief engineer, who in contrast to himself has recognized the horror of nazism and has set out to disrupt it. The general seeks to protect the saboteurs but, when the Gestapo closes in, he takes to the air in one of the defective planes and dies. *The Cold Light* (1956) is based (though names and details are changed) on Klaus Fuchs's relaying of information about the atomic bomb to the Communists. The action takes place between 1939 and 1950 and shows how a German refugee scientist, almost without realizing it, becomes involved in espionage. Like the general in Zuckmayer's earlier play, the scientist comes to recognize his naïveté and guilt and seeks to atone for them. The play suggests that the main issue of our age is the need to choose between freedom and totalitarianism. Unfortunately, it

Zuckmayer's *The Devil's General,* directed by Heinz Hilpert and designed by Caspar Neher, produced in 1946 at the Schauspielhaus, Zurich.

406

*Theatre and
Drama in
Central and
Eastern
Europe
Between
the Wars*

was not an emotionally gripping play, although it was much admired for its moral stance. Most critics agree that Zuckmayer is at his best in earthy comedy and that he always falls short in dealing with intellectual and moral problems. Consequently, it is for his early plays, especially *The Captain of Köpenick*, that Zuckmayer continues to be most noted. And it was in these early plays that neorealism found its finest (though somewhat uncharacteristic) expression.

～ III ～

Although neorealism was the dominant mode after 1923, another—epic theatre—was also taking shape and would eventually surpass it in critical estimation, even though prior to World War II it would be considered a minor strain. Epic theatre combined features of expressionism and neorealism and added distinctive touches all its own.

In part, epic theatre grew out of the intense political awareness of the period. In some respects, the German theatre between 1918 and 1923 resembled its Russian counterpart, for in both many attempts were made to use drama as a weapon to bring about social change or to make specific programs prevail. In 1919 a Workers' Theatre League was established in Germany to assist in winning acceptance for working-class causes through troupes of amateurs who performed propaganda skits at meetings and in the streets. In several cities, mass spectacles were mounted. It was in this political and social ferment that epic theatre had its roots. In its formative stage, epic theatre owes most to Martin and Piscator.

In 1919, Karlheinz Martin (1888–1948), upon organizing a theatre, The Tribune, declared: "The urgent revolution of the theatre must start with a transformation of the stage. . . . We do not ask an audience, but a community, not a stage, but a pulpit." Through The Tribune he sought to establish a direct link between the theatre and the working class. During strikes his actors appeared at gatherings to read poems or to act out skits, but he also presented full-length plays, the most important of which was Toller's *Transfiguration*. He wished the audience to serve as a kind of judge of what was offered and to become as fully involved in the action as possible. The Tribune was run as a collective in which everyone had a voice. No names were given on the program, for Martin sought to discourage all tendencies toward stardom. Martin soon became wary of the overly political direction he had taken and abandoned The Tribune for a new group, the Proletarian Theatre, which was less communal and partisan in its approach. It was here that Martin met Piscator, who soon assumed control of the company. In 1920 Martin went to work for Reinhardt and thereafter had little to do with the emerging epic theatre.

Erwin Piscator (1893–1966) began his career in 1913 as an apprentice actor in Munich. He stated that it was during the war when, unable to accomplish a task on which his life depended and forced to admit with shame that in civilian life he had been an actor, he determined to make the theatre a profession of which he could be proud. After the war, Piscator went to Berlin, where he became part of the circle which included Richard Hulsenbeck, George Grosz, and others who had been dadaists but who were now becoming deeply involved in politics. In 1919–20, he established a theatre in Königsberg, which, like Martin's, was called The Tribune. When it failed because of financial difficulties and political pressures, Piscator returned to Berlin, where he met Martin and assumed control of the Proletarian Theatre.

At first Piscator was more concerned with sociopolitical goals than with theatrical techniques, and in the October 1920 issue of *The Antagonist* published a virtual manifesto for the proletarian theatre, one that parallels in many respects the outlook of the Russian Proletcult movement of the time. Among the points made by Piscator, these seem most important: (1) drama must be subordinated to revolutionary ends, even if this means altering scripts; (2) production style should be simple and direct so that the revolutionary aim remains clear to all; (3) new techniques should be used only insofar as they help to convey meaning; (4) productions should represent a collective effort of all workers; (5) actors should be recruited from the working class rather than being a separate professional group. Although Piscator would thereafter move increasingly toward greater professionalism, his political outlook changed little.

Piscator found the roots of the proletarian theatre in three earlier movements: naturalism, expressionism, and the *Volksbühnen*. He admired the naturalists' concern for social problems but considered them mistaken in confining themselves to objective reporting and in treating reality as fixed. Similarly, he admired the expressionists' desire to transform society, but considered it overly idealistic and abstract. And, while he supported the impulse that had established the people's theatres, he believed that the *Volksbühnen* had merely produced middle-class plays for the proletariat rather than creating a true proletarian theatre. Thus, Piscator wished to combine and reshape all these forces into something more useful and meaningful. His ideas and methods evolved throughout the 1920s.

In the Proletarian Theatre, all members of the company at first were amateurs and worked without pay (and even without having their names listed on programs). But Piscator seems to have realized early that highly developed skills are essential and gradually he induced professionals to contribute their services to the company. The troupe had no fixed home but played in assembly halls throughout Berlin. Piscator declares that it was through accident and necessity that he discovered the principle of "epic" scenery, for, unable to provide traditional settings, he had to rely on demonstration and explanation rather than representation. For example, instead of a painted backdrop depicting a street, a map might be used to show the

408

*Theatre and
Drama in
Central and
Eastern
Europe
Between
the Wars*

location of the town in which the action occurs. Unfortunately, the working-class audience wished to be entertained rather than harangued. The police came to consider the troupe a nuisance and, since it did not command wide popular support, denied its application for a renewed license in 1921. Piscator then leased the Central Theatre with the aim of making it into a true *Volksbühne,* since he considered the theatre that carried that name unsatisfactory. Again he was defeated by finances and was forced to close the theatre.

Ironically, it was the Berlin Volksbühne that gave Piscator his first real opportunity to display his talents. In 1924, he was invited to join the Volksbühne's directing staff and, perhaps believing this his chance to reshape that theatre's policies, he accepted. Here for the first time, Piscator had a first-rate stage and company at his disposal, in addition to a potential audience of thirty thousand members.

Earlier the Volksbühne, under the management of Friedrich Kayssler, had made a considerable impact with such productions as Toller's *Man and the Masses* as directed by Jurgen Fehling. But by 1924 the popularity of expressionism had waned and the management of the Volksbühne had passed to Siegfried Nestriepke and the repertory had reverted to prewar plays. Nestriepke seems to have counted on Piscator to enliven the theatre, but perhaps not to such an extent as he did.

Piscator's first production at the Volksbühne was of Alfons Paquet's play *The Flags,* which was based on the trial of the Chicago anarchists in 1888. This was the first production labeled "epic" by Piscator, and in it he tried to show through extratextual material, added by means of projections on screens, the social and economic background of the action. But Piscator's major work at the Volksbühne was Ehm Welk's *Storm over Gothland* in 1927. The play deals with Swedish fishermen in the Middle

Scene from Piscator's production of Welk's *Storm over Gothland,* produced in 1928. The ships are part of a motion picture projected on the background.

409

*Theatre and
Drama in
Central and
Eastern
Europe
Between
the Wars*

Ages, but Piscator made of it a contemporary work which recalled the Russian Revolution. The actors playing the leaders of the fishermen were made up to look like Lenin and Trotsky and the Russian parallels were forcefully drawn through motion pictures showing battleships at sea and ships in harbor. The production precipitated such a crisis that Piscator resigned his post.

By 1927 Piscator had built up a considerable following among the intelligentsia and the younger members of the working class, and he now decided to open his own theatre. Obviously Piscator had already been contemplating this move, for he had commissioned Walter Gropius to design a theatre for him. (Gropius's plans will be discussed later in this chapter.) Because he believed it essential to surround a text with documentary materials which would place it in the larger social and political context, Piscator found it necessary to rely heavily upon new technological means, especially motion pictures and projections. Consequently, at a time when most directors were championing simplicity, Piscator was seeking greater complexity. He declared: "The new dramatic principle with expansion of materials into space and time requires an enlargement and improvement of the apparatus," and went on to add that "it is not accidental that the spiritual metamorphosis of the theatre comes at the same time as the technical transformation of its equipment." By combining film and live actors, he hoped "to show that the problem of the individual's position in society does not have to be represented separate from it, but that his fate is imbedded in its political and social structure." It is perhaps not surprising, then, that Piscator would find traditional theatre architecture inadequate.

Unfortunately, he was unable to obtain the financial backing needed to build the theatre Gropius had designed for him, and instead he leased the Theatre-am-Nollendorfplatz and renamed it the Piscator Theatre. Nevertheless, he made many changes in the stage to permit the kind of staging he envisioned. Even this limited venture was made possible only through the good offices of Tilla Durieux, a retired actress, who helped raise the funds needed to finance a season of plays. (She also starred in *Rasputin*.) It is for three productions—*Hurrah, We Live!*, *Rasputin*, and *The Good Soldier Schweik*—all presented in the season of 1927–28, that Piscator is most famous.

The Piscator Theatre opened in 1927 with Toller's *Hurrah, We Live!*, the story of a revolutionary who is released from prison after ten years only to discover that all his former comrades have settled into comfortable lives; to him the world seems so bent on destruction that he commits suicide. The major feature of the production was the use of newsreel excerpts to review events of the ten years (1917–27) during which the protagonist has been in jail. The events range through the beginning of the Russian Revolution, the entry of the United States into the war, the end of the war, the founding of the League of Nations, the beginning of Prohibition in the United States,

Production of Tolstoy's *Rasputin* at the Piscator Theatre in 1927. (From Moussinac, *New Movement in the Theatre.*)

Mussolini's assumption of power, Hitler's beer hall *Putsch,* the Scopes trial, Lindbergh's flight, the execution of Sacco and Vanzetti, and Trotsky's expulsion from the Communist party. It was the most extensive attempt yet made to combine film and live performance.

Later in 1927, Piscator staged his version of Alexei Tolstoy's *Rasputin,* a melodrama which shows the power exerted by the monk Rasputin over the Russian royal family and the conspiracies of the court. Piscator was not interested in so restricted a subject, but, as he put it, "Our concern was world history: the destiny of Europe 1914 to 1917." Consequently, Tolstoy's play served merely as a starting point.

At the center of his stage Piscator erected a structure symbolically shaped like a globe and containing within it several acting areas. This structure could turn or open to reveal the interior, or its exterior white surface could serve as a screen for projections. Six thousand feet of film, assembled from libraries and archives, were projected on several surfaces. One screen at the side of the stage was used primarily to provide a running calendar and for commentaries and footnotes. At the beginning of the play, portraits of the successive tsars were shown on a large screen, while on the small screen at the side such comments as "Died insane," were projected. Then, when the line of tsars reached the present ruler, he stepped onto the stage and the action began. At times as many as three different events (for example, three battles) were shown on screens simultaneously while a dramatic episode was in progress on the stage. Captions were sometimes superimposed on the film to indicate the numbers killed in battle or the outcome of a campaign. Thus, *Rasputin* became a drama showing the clash of world powers in which the Russian royal family seemed rather petty participants. The production achieved added notoriety when the former Kaiser Wilhelm sued Piscator for showing films of him and for commenting on his actions.

Piscator's most famous production was *The Good Soldier Schweik,* **411**
based on an uncompleted novel by the Czech author Jaroslav Haček. Its
protagonist is that familiar comic figure, the seeming fool, who, through
naïve acceptance, shows up the pomposity and madness of the world. In
Haček's book, the peasant Schweik, wishing to serve his country, accepts
unquestioningly whatever happens, always rising above difficulties and never
losing his enthusiasm. His experiences and comments constitute a devastating satire on both the bureaucratic and militaristic Austro-Hungarian regime
and war in general.

*Theatre and
Drama in
Central and
Eastern
Europe
Between
the Wars*

The text used by Piscator was the work of several persons. Max Brod
and Hans Reimann had already dramatized the novel, but Piscator found
their version unsatisfactory and he, Bertolt Brecht, Leo Nania, and Felix
Gasbarra reworked it. The scenic conventions owed most to George Grosz,
who made innumerable cartoonlike sketches, from which many were chosen,
enlarged, and integrated into the action. The basic approach was established
immediately: on a bare stage nothing was visible except a screen; then, on
the screen a pen began to draw and gradually there took shape the caricatured figures of the emperor, a general, a lawyer, and a priest—the
major representatives of the power structure that Schweik will encounter.
This opening set the tone for the entire production—satirical caricature.

The other principal ingredients of the production were two treadmills
which moved in opposite directions. On one, Schweik seemed always on
the move although he never left the stage (the treadmills were stopped
while the brief episodes were being performed), while on the other were
mounted the set pieces (mostly cutouts of Grosz's caricatures) required by the
action. Many of the characters encountered by Schweik were also represented
by caricatures placed on the treadmill. But there were also motion pictures of
real places and events. For example, though Schweik boarded a cartoon
train, its travels were indicated by projections of real places on the back-

The Good Soldier Schweik
in 1927 at the Piscator
Theatre. The cartoon figures
were by George Grosz.

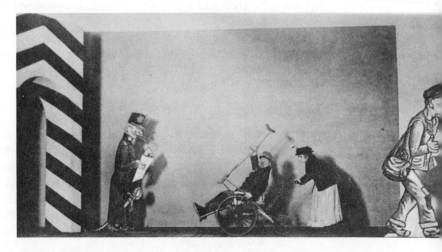

412

*Theatre and
Drama in
Central and
Eastern
Europe
Between
the Wars*

ground screen. Maps were also used to keep the audience informed of Schweik's progress (or lack of it) on his journey.

Every episode was designed to show the callousness, ineptness, and wastefulness of the Austro-Hungarian regime. But after laughing its target into oblivion, the play ended with Schweik's death. Then, projections showing row upon row of burial crosses seemed to move ever nearer the audience itself. The production was a great triumph, not only for Piscator but also for Max Pallenberg, the masterful actor who played Schweik.

Despite the critical success of this season, Piscator lost his theatre because he was unable to pay the taxes due on it. Thereafter he worked in a number of places before leaving Germany when Hitler came to power. He lived in Paris for a time and then went to America, where from 1939 to 1951 he headed the Dramatic Workshop at the New School for Social Research in New York and directed a number of plays on Broadway and elsewhere. (Piscator's postwar career will be discussed in a later chapter.)

Thus, it was Piscator who laid the foundations upon which Brecht built his version of epic theatre. But, though their ideas are similar in several respects, they also differ on major points. Both stated their desire to make spectators think and act, but they disagreed on the proper approach. The distinctions are few but crucial. First, unlike Brecht, who sought to "historify" his subjects, Piscator made all plays immediately contemporaneous (for example, *Storm over Gothland* seemed to suggest that there is no essential difference between medieval fishermen and Russian revolutionaries). Second, Piscator wished to involve his audience empathically in the action. He sought to place them at the center of world events and to make them respond emotionally to what was going on around them. Brecht's admirers would say that Piscator did not permit his audiences sufficient distance from the stage events to judge them. Rather, spectators were merely asked to respond emotionally to the events, much as in Wagner's theatre. Piscator, in effect, decided in advance what he wanted his audiences to feel, and he then structured his productions to arouse those feelings. Consequently, according to his critics, Piscator's audience, like that of any traditional theatre, came to substitute theatrical experience for practical action, for catharsis was achieved in the theatre rather than outside it. It is the immediacy and empathic qualities of Piscator's work that most distinguish it from Brecht's. A third difference can be seen in Piscator's emphasis upon complex technical means. Although Brecht adopted many of the same devices (for example, projections combined with live action), he always used them sparingly and sought to restrict them to those usable by any group. Brecht's theatre is technologically far simpler than Piscator's. Fourth, Piscator's was ultimately a director's theatre, Brecht's a playwright's.

It should also be evident that Piscator had much in common with Meyerhold. With Meyerhold he shared the predilection for new technical means, the insistence upon reworking texts to fit his needs, an autocratic approach, and the intention of influencing attitudes and behavior. But

413

*Theatre and
Drama in
Central and
Eastern
Europe
Between
the Wars*

Piscator was far less abstract in his production style than was Meyerhold, for most of Piscator's devices (newsreels, captions, and so on) were designed to increase the sense of reality rather than to abrogate normal perception. Even Grosz's caricatures sharpened insights by reducing things to essentials; consequently, rather than defying the audience's experience (as Meyerhold's devices sometimes did) they merely intensified them. Nevertheless, Piscator's approach was sufficiently novel that conservative theatregoers were often puzzled or repelled by it. Ironically, therefore, his audience tended to be composed of the intelligentsia rather than of the working classes, for whom his theatre was intended.

IV

In pre-Nazi Germany, Piscator was the best-known practitioner of epic theatre, for only later did Brecht overshadow him and come to be considered the major exponent of the epic approach. Bertolt Brecht (1898–1956), after studying medicine and serving as an orderly in a military hospital during the war, began his playwriting career in 1918 with *Baal,* a work which utilizes many expressionistic techniques to project a nihilistic view of man. Composed of twenty-two short scenes, it is held together by the

A scene from Brecht's first play, *Baal,*
produced in 1926 at the Deutsches Theater,
Berlin, by Brecht and Oskar Homolka.
Homolka, who played the title role, sits at left.
The setting is by Caspar Neher.

414

*Theatre and
Drama in
Central and
Eastern
Europe
Between
the Wars*

central figure, Baal, an ugly, sensually insatiable, bohemian poet who defies all of society's restraints. It includes a considerable amount of drunken revelry, sexual conquest, and bawdry, but these are intermingled with intimations of idealism, for Baal is poet as well as criminal, and passages of violence and obscenity alternate with others suggesting the beauties of nature and the freedom of the spirit. Thus, *Baal* seems more nearly related to Sorge's *The Beggar* than to Brecht's own mature work.

In the years immediately following the war, Brecht worked as a freelance writer, critic, and cabaret performer before winning the Kleist Prize in 1922 with *Drums in the Night,* his first play to be produced. In the following year *In the Jungle of Cities* was also produced in Munich and Brecht worked for a time at the Pocket Theatre there as a director. In 1924, he moved to Berlin, where until 1926 he served (along with Zuckmayer) as an assistant *Dramaturg* in Reinhardt's Deutsches Theater.

The first phase of Brecht's career ended in 1926. All the plays up to that time are seemingly anarchistic rejections of society and are indebted to expressionism for their techniques. In them, Brecht seems dissatisfied with his world but his discontent is without direction. A major turning point came with *Man is Man* (1926), for in it are found the seeds of that social consciousness and didacticism that would characterize his work thereafter. It is probably also significant that by this time expressionism had declined and that the Neue Sachlichkeit had begun to proclaim the need for

Brecht's *Man Is Man* at the Berlin State Theatre in 1931, directed by the author. Helene Weigel is at right in the role of Begbick; Peter Lorre (not pictured) performed the role of Galy Gay.

415

*Theatre and
Drama in
Central and
Eastern
Europe
Between
the Wars*

greater concreteness and sharper awareness of social realities. The protagonist of *Man is Man* is Galy Gay, a meek dockworker in the Indian port of Kilkoa, who is gradually transformed by three British soldiers into a "human fighting machine" through a kind of inversion of Kipling's imperialistic outlook. Brecht's earlier nihilistic vision has now been replaced by a dawning interest, still not fully articulated, in the exploitation of the working classes and in antimilitarism. It was also in 1926 that Brecht began his Marxist studies at the Berlin Workers' School. Thereafter his concern with social and political thought increased and his plays reflected a Marxist view, although it was not always sharply defined.

The years between 1927 and 1933 were productive ones for Brecht. In 1927–28, he worked with Piscator on *The Good Soldier Schweik* and became thoroughly familiar with Piscator's views and methods (he had seen most of Piscator's earlier work as well). In 1928, he achieved his first real fame with *The Threepenny Opera,* which ran for 400 performances. Thereafter until 1933, he had a theatre available to him. In 1928 he also married Helene Weigel (1900–1971), the actress with whom he worked closely thereafter. He now completed a number of works in rapid succession, including *St. Joan of the Stockyards* (1928), *The Rise and Fall of the City of Mahagonny* (1930), and a number of *Lehrstücke* or didactic plays.

To understand Brecht's work in this period, one needs to know something of contemporary music, for his contacts with composers influenced him greatly. Just as there was a movement toward a "new matter-of-factness" in drama, so too there was a similar trend in music. It arose during World War I when such composers as Stravinsky and Satie began to rebel against the complexities of Wagner, Richard Strauss, and Gustav Mahler who had written music which could only be played by highly accomplished professionals and thus had relegated it to recital halls and opera houses and divorced it from daily life. The revolt began around 1915 when Stravinsky wrote *Renard,* a chamber opera intended "to be played by clowns, dancers or acrobats, preferably on a trestle stage with the orchestra placed behind it." The intention was to bring music down from its pedestal and to encourage the kind of simplicity already evident in the visual arts. Stravinsky followed *Renard* with *The History of a Soldier* (1918), which required only seven musicians, narrators, dancers, and the simplest of stages. In 1917, Satie turned to popular and jazz music for themes in *Parade,* and later he introduced what he called "furniture music"—a background for other activities and only to be half-listened to. A number of Satie's disciples, most notably Darius Milhaud, joined this movement.

The trend toward simplicity soon reached Germany (where it was called the Neue Musik). In 1921 its adherents founded an annual festival at Donaueschingen to promote it, and here Stravinsky appeared annually after 1925 and Kurt Weill presented many of his early works. In 1927 the festival was moved to Baden-Baden, where Brecht was asked to stage some of the productions and later presented a number of his own works.

*Theatre and
Drama in
Central and
Eastern
Europe
Between
the Wars*

The leading spokesman for the Neue Musik in Germany was Paul Hindemith, who ran this festival. Hindemith believed that composers had gone astray by losing sight of how music is to be used. Thus, he tended to promote compositions of two kinds: functional music, which included scores for films and dances, and settings for poems and other texts; and music written for amateur performers. Hindemith sought to restore music in society by promoting works that could be played by nonprofessionals and was especially interested in compositions written for performance in schools. Out of this grew a number of "school" operas and *Lehrstücke,* or didactic musical plays, often likened to the school plays of the sixteenth-century humanists. The festivals at Baden-Baden and a Neue Musik festival held in Berlin in 1930 promoted such *Lehrstücke*. Hindemith was primarily concerned with artistic problems—making music more accessible to everyone—and he eventually came into conflict with Brecht, who was concerned with the *Lehrstücke* as a didactic medium. It was among the adherents of the Neue Musik that Brecht found all the composers with whom he worked thereafter: Weill, Hindemith, Hanns Eisler, Paul Dessau, and Rudolf Wagner-Regeny.

Music plays an important role in Brecht's drama from the very beginning. For the early works he composed his own music and only after 1927 did he collaborate with others. The first collaborative results were *The Threepenny Opera* and *The Rise and Fall of the City of Mahagonny,* with music by Kurt Weill. Of all Brecht's pre-Hitlerian works, *The Threepenny Opera* is the best known. It was motivated in part by the two-hundredth

Lotte Lenya in the Brecht/Weill collaboration, *The Threepenny Opera,* originally produced in 1928 at the Theater am Schiffbauerdamm, Berlin. (From *Theatre Arts,* 1939.)

anniversary of John Gay's *Beggar's Opera,* but also by Gay's satire on grand opera (against which the Neue Musik was also in rebellion) and on the ruling classes. Brecht relocated the action in nineteenth-century England, and through it sought to denounce the hypocrisy and resignation of the lower classes and through his thieves and whores to caricature middle-class values. But most critics agree that the satire remains ineffectual, for Brecht fails to provide any positive contrasts and seems to suggest throughout that "the world is poor and man is bad," thus making any change seem impossible. Consequently, audiences have tended to see the play merely as entertaining rather than as cautionary. Perhaps for that reason it has remained one of Brecht's most popular works.

The Rise and Fall of the City of Mahagonny approaches opera in its use of musical accompaniment throughout and in its score for forty instruments plus a stage orchestra of twenty-one pieces. (*The Threepenny Opera* used only eight instruments.) The play begins with the decision of three criminals to found the city of Mahagonny and enrich themselves by appealing to man's voluptuousness—his propensity to seek happiness in alcohol, sex, drugs, and money. Ultimately the protagonist concludes that everything bought with money is worthless and that anything gotten through force is ephemeral. Brecht seems to suggest that such a society will eventually die of its own contradictions, but he offers no positive alternative. Thus, like *The Threepenny Opera, Mahagonny* is somewhat unsatisfactory as social commentary.

In the *Lehrstücke,* Brecht was consciously didactic, although he did not escape ambiguities. The first, *Lindbergh's Flight* (1928–29), later revised as *Didactic Play for Baden-Baden on Acquiescence* (1929), argues that man has his reason for being in service to others and that he should be absolutely obedient to the needs of the masses. Of the several *Lehrstücke,* perhaps the best is *The Measures Taken* (1930). It uses four soloists and a chorus to tell the story of Four Agitators who have returned from a mission into China and report that they have liquidated a fifth agitator, the Young Comrade. The Control Chorus, representing the Communist party, asks the agitators to act out what has happened. They relate how the Young Comrade, by following his humanitarian instincts, has helped others and thereby has delayed the revolution. When he comes to see the errors of his ways, the Young Comrade asks to be killed. The Control Chorus weighs the evidence and approves "the measures taken"—the unfortunate necessity of sacrificing the individual for the good of the collective. This piece aroused a storm of controversy, especially within the Communist party (most orthodox members strenuously rejected it), and Brecht eventually forbade its presentation.

In 1933, Brecht fled Germany and for several years led a nomadic existence—in Austria, Switzerland, France, Denmark, Finland, and Russia —before settling in the United States between 1941 and 1947. Practically all of Brecht's pre-Hitlerian work had been damned by critics, who general-

418

*Theatre and
Drama in
Central and
Eastern
Europe
Between
the Wars*

ly considered him a minor though controversial writer. It was during his exile that he wrote those works upon which his reputation rests. Practically all that went into them had been sketched out by 1933, but it remained to be translated into mature accomplishment.

After 1933, Brecht matured both as dramatist and theoretician, and since his drama is illuminated by his theory, it will be helpful to examine the theoretical views first. Like his dramatic techniques, Brecht's theory evolved slowly. Nevertheless, by 1933 the basic outlines were clearly discernible in his postscripts and notes to various plays, especially those for *The Threepenny Opera, Mahagonny,* and the revised version of *Man is Man* (1931). Still, he did not use the term *alienation* until 1936 (although the concept is adumbrated in earlier writings), and he did not publish a fully integrated theory until 1948, when "Little Organon for the Theatre" appeared. Even then, he continued to modify his views up to the time of his death, and toward the end of his life declared his unhappiness at having ever written any theoretical works at all: "The whole debacle started when I wanted to have my plays staged properly and effectively and so—oh misery!—in order to define a non-Aristotelean dramaturgy I developed—oh calamity!—a theory of the epic theatre." He suggested that "dialectic" might better describe his work than "epic," and he came to favor a Hegelian approach in which thesis and antithesis are resolved into a new synthesis. Regardless of its evolutionary nature, there is a core of Brechtian theory which for better or worse has come to be called "epic," and which has precipitated arguments among Brecht's disciples not unlike those that rage among Stanislavsky's admirers.

Brecht's theory has many antecedents, both artistic and political. Among the artistic, the most important are the Sturm und Drang writers, Büchner, Hegel, the expressionists, Piscator, and the Neue Sachlichkeit, while clearly the most important political influence was Marxism.

Much of Brecht's theory amounts to a rebuttal of the Wagnerian outlook, which through the work of Appia and Craig had come to dominate European thought about theatrical practice. Brecht begins with the assumption that the hypnotic effect sought by Wagner is fundamentally mistaken, since it reduces the audience to a role of complete passivity. Although the ultimate purpose may be to make him a better human being by providing him with an idealized experience, only indirectly is Wagner's spectator expected to translate theatrical experience into practical action outside the theatre. Brecht wished to redefine this relationship among

spectator, theatre, and society. To identify his approach, he adopted the
term "epic" to distinguish it from the "dramatic" or "Aristotelean" theatre
against which he was in rebellion. He declared that the dramatic theatre
has outlived its usefulness because it has reduced the spectator to complete
passivity; in it, events are presented as fixed and unchangeable, for, even
when historical subjects are treated, they are couched in modern terms and
thus give the impression that things have always been as they now are.
Furthermore, illusionistic staging gives everything such an air of stability
that traditional values and modes of behavior seem permanently entrenched.
Since everything appears fixed, the spectator can only watch, for nothing
else is left for him to do.

*Theatre and
Drama in
Central and
Eastern
Europe
Between
the Wars*

Instead of this traditional approach, Brecht envisioned a new one in
which the audience would play a vital and active role. He insisted that the
spectator watch what he saw in the theatre critically. He added that, while
the theatre should be entertaining, it brings the greatest pleasure through
"productive participation," in which the spectator actively judges and
applies what he sees on the stage to conditions outside the theatre. But, if
the spectator is to watch in this active way, he must be assisted. Hence,
Brecht advocated techniques markedly different from those used in the
Wagnerian theatre.

Perhaps the most important term in Brecht's theoretical writings is
"alienation" (*Verfremdung*)—the process of making events or characters
strange, of sufficiently distancing the spectator from the play that he can
watch it critically. Whereas Wagner wanted a total empathic response,
Brecht sought to short-circuit empathy by breaking illusion and reminding
the audience that it is in a theatre watching a reflection of reality, not
reality itself—that the real problems lie outside the theatre, not on the stage.
At times Brecht approached alienation through "historification," a process
in which the "pastness" of events is emphasized so that not only can the
audience judge them but can be led to recognize that, since things have
changed, present conditions may also be altered.

Some critics have interpreted Brecht's concept of alienation to mean
that the audience should be in a continuous state of objective detachment.
In actuality, Brecht manipulated esthetic distance so as to involve the
spectator emotionally and then to jar him out of his empathic response so
that he might contemplate and judge what he has experienced. Thus, in
Brecht's plays there is a constantly shifting, dynamic relationship between
empathy and alienation.

All the elements of dramatic structure and theatrical production are
used by Brecht to achieve this constantly shifting relationship. His plays
are divided into a series of carefully separated episodes. As Brecht put it:
"Individual events must be tied together in such a way that the knots are
strikingly noticeable: the events must not follow upon one another imperceptibly, but rather one must be able to pass judgment in the midst of them.
. . . The parts of the fable, therefore, are to be carefully set off from one

420

*Theatre and
Drama in
Central and
Eastern
Europe
Between
the Wars*

another." Usually the episodes are separated by songs, brief speeches, or visual devices which serve much the same function as does the chorus in Greek drama, for they suspend the action so that the spectator can contemplate the implications of what he has seen. In structuring his plays, Brecht borrowed techniques from the epic poem, for he often alternated narration with dialogue, shifted time and place rapidly, and bridged gaps with narrative passages.

Brecht conceived of drama primarily as dialectic process—that is, as the exploration of problems or attitudes. Consequently, his plays are unified by thought. Furthermore, he reduced each scene to a basic *"gestus"*—a main point or argument—and often used this *gestus* as a title for the scene. Sometimes he even projected the title on a screen so that the episode's point was clear before it was viewed, for he was less concerned with story than with the interplay of social forces behind the story. Similarly, characters were conceived more in terms of social attitude than of individual psychology. Nevertheless, his plays seldom end with a neat solution to a problem; rather, they suggest the need to find an answer outside the theatre. Thus, the plays are constructed to lead the audience through a process of exploration and thought.

In production, Brecht employed analogous means. Unlike Wagner, who sought to hide the mechanics of production, Brecht flaunted them. He mounted lighting instruments where they would be seen, placed musicians on the stage with the actors, and changed scenery in view of the audience. Instead of full-stage, realistic settings, he used fragments or projections. To him, scenery should merely locate the action or comment on it; it should never seek to give the illusion of a place in its entirety, but should undercut the sense of permanence and unchangeability.

Brecht advised actors not to impersonate a character so much as to present the behavior of a kind of person in a type of situation. In rehearsals, he sometimes asked actors to speak of their characters in the third person and to recite speeches preceded or followed by "he said," so that, instead of trying to live a part, the actor would stand outside and comment on it.

Brecht rejected Wagner's conception of unified production, calling it redundant, since it sought to make music, scenery, lighting, costume, and acting all convey the same impressions. Brecht wanted each element to comment in a different way. In a satirical song, for example, the music need not be satirical since the words or acting might convey that quality. Rather, by contradicting expectations and by juxtaposing two contrary moods it could create conflict in the mind of the spectator and force him to reconcile the two elements. Thus, the audience must think instead of being lulled by the music. Similarly, a costume might be composed of disparate elements which give information about place and time but which also comment on the character and the issues. Unlike Wagner's theatre, in which the director has synthesized all elements prior to performance, in

Brecht's the audience is offered antithetical elements which it must synthesize
during the performance.

*Theatre and
Drama in
Central and
Eastern
Europe
Between
the Wars*

Ultimately the major differences between the views of Brecht and
Wagner are attributable to conceptions of how audiences should respond.
Wagner wished to transport the audience out of its mundane world; Brecht
wanted to make it more critically aware of its society. Wagner sought to
create a compelling illusion; Brecht sought to interrupt illusion and keep
the audience aware that it is in a theatre. Wagner was a sensualist (that is,
he wanted to appeal to the audience's senses so powerfully that it would
give itself up wholly to the artistic experience); Brecht was an intellectual,
for, though he did not deny the power of the senses, he saw them as
preliminary to thought. Brecht always assumed that man is capable of
reflection and of reaching wise decisions if he is provided with the proper
demonstrations.

Since the theories of Brecht and Artaud would be the major influences on the post-World War II theatre, a brief comparison of their goals
is also in order. Brecht believed that men need incentives to forge a new
society, Artaud that man's conscious defenses should be shattered so that
the anxieties buried in his subconscious mind might be relieved. In Jungian
terms, Brecht's theatre is extroverted, for it is concerned almost altogether
with societal forces, whereas Artaud's is introverted, for it emphasizes
internal and subterranean forces. In the postwar world, these strains—the
Brechtian concern for social forms, and the Artaudian concern for the
threatened psyche—would dominate drama and theatre.

～ VI ～

Critics are fond of pointing out that Brecht did not always follow his own
theory—that the poet often overcame the dialectician and the humanitarian
the Marxist. Nevertheless, there is always a relationship between the two,
even if not always precise. Several of the plays written in exile—*The Private
Life of the Master Race* (1935–38), *Mother Courage and Her Children*
(1938), *Life of Galileo* (1938–39), *The Good Woman of Setzuan* (1938–
39), *Herr Puntila and His Servant Matti* (1940), *The Resistible Rise of
Arturo Ui* (1941), and *The Caucasian Chalk Circle* (1944–45)—were
among his finest. Of these, the best known and most successful are *Mother
Courage, The Good Woman of Setzuan,* and *The Caucasian Chalk Circle.*

Mother Courage, set during the Thirty Years' War, focuses on the
itinerant trader Anna Fierling, who with her three children follows
the imperial and Swedish armies and sells liquor and other goods to the
soldiers. One by one the children are killed: the not-very-bright Swiss

422

Theatre and
Drama in
Central and
Eastern
Europe
Between
the Wars

Cheese is executed when he will not reveal the hiding place of the regimental cash box entrusted to him; the braggart Eilif, after being treated as a hero for stealing cattle, is shot as a looter; and the deaf-and-dumb Kattrin is killed as she beats a drum to warn a town of impending massacre. Nevertheless, at the end of the play Mother Courage sets off pulling the wagon (which during the action has symbolically become ever more dilapidated) all by herself. She never connects the loss of her children with the life she has made them lead, and indeed declares that she has taken up her trade for the sake of her children.

Brecht's protagonist is a powerful figure, who not only contributes to her own fate but who faces life's horrors with dogged courage. The admiration she arouses undercuts Brecht's own intention that she be viewed unsympathetically because of her complicity in the war and the deaths of her children. Perhaps the audience's judgment of her is softened by the play's overall impression that the world is a place in which human illusions are gradually eroded through a series of "little capitulations" to circumstance. Despite Brecht's use of such devices as disconnected episodes, captions, and songs, alienation is never very strong, and the overall impression is not so much that the world can be changed as that the human condition is permanently flawed. In terms of Brecht's theory, *Mother Courage* is probably a failure, but undoubtedly it is one of his finest achievements.

Helene Weigel as Anna Fierling in the 1949 production of *Mother Courage* at the Berliner Ensemble.
(Courtesy Berliner Ensemble.)

As epic drama, *The Good Woman of Setzuan* is much more successful.
Brecht subtitled it "A parable play, set in modern China," and declared: "The province of Setzuan is the symbol of all the places where man is exploited by other men." In it, three gods come to earth somewhat desperately seeking just one good person but eventually must settle for the prostitute Shen Te, who gives them shelter for the night. When upon leaving they caution her to be good, she replies: "I'd like to be good, it's true, but there's the rent to pay. . . . How is it done? Even breaking a few of your commandments, I can hardly manage." To this, one of the gods answers: "That's not our sphere. We never meddle in economics." This sets the problem Brecht has in mind—the relationship between morality and the economic system. How can Shen Te be good in a society that has forced her to become a prostitute in order to survive? Eventually the gods relent and give Shen Te a sum of money. The remainder of the play is taken up with Shen Te's attempts to live by the gods' commandments and with Brecht's demonstration of the impossibility of goodness under capitalism. When the other characters discover that Shen Te has money, they begin to make almost overwhelming demands on her. To survive, she assumes an alter ego, Shui Ta, a supposed cousin, who as an exploiting capitalist forces others to work for him if they are to receive help. Eventually Shen Te's love for an ungrateful man leads to pregnancy and, to disguise her state, she assumes the role of Shui Ta permanently only to be accused of her own murder. Put on trial, she is saved by the intervention of the gods. But once more they leave her as they found her—with the injunction to be good—and no nearer a resolution of her problem. In an epilogue, Brecht asks: "How could a better ending be arranged? / Could one change people? Can the world be changed?" Brecht clearly implies that the economic system should be changed, but he avoids saying so directly. Rather, he continues: "It is for you to find a way, my friends, / To help good men arrive at happy ends. / You write the happy ending to the play. / There must, there must, there's got to be a way." In terms of his theory, this is probably Brecht's most successful work, but as Marxist teaching it is not wholly successful, for it makes the proletariat seem so depraved that it is difficult to believe that the world would be transformed by a change in the economic system.

Brecht's last important work, *The Caucasian Chalk Circle,* is a play-within-a-play. The opening is set in Soviet Georgia just after it has been retaken from the Germans and involves a quarrel of goat breeders and fruit growers over who should possess the land. Eventually the Delegate from the State Reconstruction Commission decides that, since the greatest number of people would benefit, the land should go to the fruit growers' collective, even though historically the land has belonged to the goat breeders.

Then the Singer asks to tell a pertinent story. This introduces the play-within-the-play, but also establishes a rationale (the storyteller's presentation) for the combination of narrative and dramatic elements which follows.

424

*Theatre and
Drama in
Central and
Eastern
Europe
Between
the Wars*

At the end of the play-within-the-play, the Singer sums up the moral of both stories: "That what there is shall go to those who are good for it, / Children to the motherly, that they prosper, / Carts to good drivers, that they be driven well, / The valley to the waterers, that it yield fruit." Through this conclusion the two parts of the work are drawn together as parables illustrating similar lessons.

Most of *The Caucasian Chalk Circle* is devoted to the play-within-the-play, which illustrates that children should belong to the motherly. It begins with a revolution, during which the Governor's Wife abandons her child in her selfish desire to save herself. The child is saved by the servant girl Grusha, who at great personal peril takes him to the mountains, rears him, and for his welfare gives up her true love to marry a peasant. The second part of the play-within-a-play focuses on the crude, licentious, and corrupt Azdak, who, during the rebellion, at first harbors the Governor and then betrays him. The soldiers find him amusing and make him a judge. For two years, Azdak dispenses a peculiar kind of justice—on one level a travesty but on another strangely wise. As a result, he comes to be known as the poor man's friend. Another revolution returns the former ruler to power and the Governor's Wife now finds it essential that she have her child back. It is before Azdak that the trial is held. He draws a circle of chalk on the floor, places the child in it and tells the two women to pull the child out. Since Grusha loves the child too much, she will do nothing to hurt him and so the Governor's Wife pulls him out. But Azdak awards the child to the one who loves him most. He also annuls Grusha's marriage and restores her to her true lover.

But without the corruption and impulsiveness of Azdak there would have been no justice for Grusha, since by law the child belongs to the Governor's Wife and Grusha to the peasant. At the end, the Singer declares that the period of Azdak's judgment was long remembered "as a brief golden age, / Almost an age of justice." Through this ending and through the parables developed by the play, Brecht hoped to suggest that though perfection may not be possible, improvement is.

The Caucasian Chalk Circle, like several others of his works, reflects Brecht's interest in the Oriental theatre. (Some of the *Lehrstücke* were adapted from Oriental sources and Brecht wrote an essay on the acting of Mei Lan Fang, the celebrated Chinese actor.) Here he adapts some Oriental staging conventions. For example, in the episode entitled "Flight in the Northern Mountains," Brecht shows Grusha, pursued by soldiers, having to cross a rotting bridge over a deep ravine. The scene is set by the storyteller and the setting represented by a board placed across two chairs. Through such devices, Brecht was able to demonstrate action while avoiding illusionism and to present a sprawling story difficult to reduce to stage terms through traditional means.

The Caucasian Chalk Circle was to be Brecht's last major work. After he returned to Europe in 1947, he wrote *The Days of the Commune* (1948–

49), a rather undramatic and politically didactic account of the Paris Commune of 1871, and an opera, *The Trial of Lucullus* (1951), reworked from a radio play of 1939. His other postwar works were adaptations: Sophocles' *Antigone,* Shakespeare's *Coriolanus,* Goethe's *Urfaust,* Lenz's *The Tutor,* and Farquhar's *The Recruiting Officer.*

But if his dramatic output decreased, his fame soared. At the end of the war, he was still relatively unknown, but by the mid-1950s, he was one of the world's most admired playwrights. Similarly, in theatrical production Brecht was able to establish the validity of his ideas. After he returned to East Germany in 1948, he at first worked at the Deutsches Theater (where he had once been Reinhardt's assistant) and in 1949, with his wife, Helene Weigel, established the Berliner Ensemble. In 1954 the troupe was given its own home, the Theater-am-Schiffbauerdamm (where *The Threepenny Opera* had had its premiere in 1928). In the same year, the Berliner Ensemble, until then unknown outside of East Germany, won first prize at the World Theatre Festival in Paris. Thereafter, it was recognized as one of the finest troupes in the world and soon became the object of near-pilgrimages and one of East Germany's major cultural showpieces. The Russian Communists, who had ignored Brecht, at last acknowledged his worth in 1955 by awarding him the Stalin Prize. Thus, by the time of Brecht's death in 1956, epic theatre had become a major force in world drama and theatre. (The work of the Berliner Ensemble is considered in a later chapter.)

~ VII ~

Another major artistic force between the wars was the Bauhaus, which in the visual arts paralleled the Neue Musik and the Neue Sachlichkeit. Located in Weimar, the Bauhaus was created in 1919 by merging two earlier schools to form the Staatliches Bauhaus under the leadership of the architect Walter Gropius (1883–1969). The primary goals of the school were to reunite the arts, to break down the barriers between artists and craftsmen, and to make artistic products available to the common man and an integral part of daily life. In his manifesto for the Bauhaus, Gropius proclaimed: "Let us . . . create a new guild of craftsmen without the class distinctions that raise an arrogant barrier between craftsman and artist! Together let us desire, conceive, and create the new structure of the future, which will embrace architecture and sculpture and painting in one unity and which will one day rise toward heaven from the hands of a million workers like the crystal symbol of a new faith."

The Bauhaus arose out of problems and possibilities that had long been evident. During the nineteenth century, the artist had come increas-

426

*Theatre and
Drama in
Central and
Eastern
Europe
Between
the Wars*

ingly to be considered a creative and individual genius, while the crafts-man had suffered seriously from the industrialization of all the crafts. As a result, art works were largely confined to museums and the homes of the wealthy, while industrial products intended for the masses were manu-factured without regard for artistic design. At the same time, however, industrialization provided the potential to mass-produce well-designed articles that would be within the financial reach of the common man. Similarly, new building materials, especially steel and concrete, had provided the potential to revolutionize architecture, even though most builders continued to imitate the forms (especially Gothic and classical) of the past. The nineteenth century also popularized the notion of a *Gesamtkunstwerk* (Wagner was only one of many who dreamed of the "master art work") which would unite various arts in a higher form. In response to all these forces, many pioneers during the late nineteenth and early twentieth centuries began to reshape the arts, and it was in the Bauhaus that much of the earlier work came together.

The Bauhaus restructured artistic training so that each student had to learn the skills necessary for executing his designs. He also had to study all the related arts. (The Bauhaus's methods have now been adopted almost universally.) In this way, the Bauhaus sought to heal the rift between the arts and the crafts, and to insist that art is singular though its media are multiple. Ultimately, the Bauhaus tried to shape daily surroundings into a *Gesamtkunstwerk,* in which everything from the landscaping to the house, its furnishings, decorations, and even its kitchen utensils are conceived as parts of a total design for living. It sought to make the functional artistic, and the artistic functional. It wished to end the elitist status of art and to make it a part of daily life.

Throughout its existence, the Bauhaus was a source of controversy: because of its innovative methods and aims, it was opposed by tradition-alists in the arts; because of its concern for the masses, it was considered subversive by political conservatives; because of its often unusual artistic products, it met puzzlement and hostility from those it most wished to benefit. In 1925, the state of Thuringia, which had supported it, voted to dissolve the Bauhaus. The city of Dessau then became its home and from 1925 until 1932 provided it with funds. There the pressures became so great that Gropius resigned as head of the school in 1928. Hannes Meyer, who succeeded him, was in turn succeeded by Meis van der Rohe in 1930. When the National Socialists gained a majority in Dessau's government in 1932, the school was closed. It then moved to Berlin, where it continued as a private school until dissolved altogether when the Nazis came to power in 1933.

Despite its problems, the Bauhaus's accomplishments are impressive. Most were achieved in the visual arts, but from 1923 to 1929 it also in-cluded a Stage Workshop. Its contributions to the theatre fall into three main categories: the human figure in space; light in motion; and theatre architecture.

Bauhaus Dance by Oskar Schlemmer. (Courtesy Tut Schlemmer.)

The Bauhaus's stage work was at first under the direction of Lothar Schreyer (1886–1966), an expressionist writer and artist who for a time had directed the stage work done by Walden's Sturm group. But Schreyer's semireligious and emotionalist view of drama was at odds with the Bauhaus's concerns with form, and in 1923 he resigned. Thereafter until 1929, the Stage Workshop was headed by Oskar Schlemmer (1888–1943), who had joined the Bauhaus in 1920 as a sculptor, but whose interests in three-dimensional figures in space gradually led him toward the stage.

Schlemmer's conception of the theatre more nearly resembled the Oriental than the Occidental, and there was always something of the ritualistic in his attempts to reduce form and motion to a few basic shapes and movements. He early summed up his view of the fundamental problem of the stage: "Man, the human organism, stands in the cubical, abstract space of the stage.... Each has different laws of order. Whose shall prevail?" One answer is provided by the realistic stage which transforms space into an imitation of nature out of deference to natural man. Another is provided by the abstract stage, on which "natural man, in deference to abstract space, is recast to fit its mold." It was the abstract stage that Schlemmer chose to explore.

Because his interest was primarily visual, Schlemmer ignored the verbal element and devoted himself to formal experiments with space, shapes, and motion. He seems to have believed that eventually meaning would arise out of form. Thus, he systematically analyzed each element of his stage and explored its potentialities. For example, he declared: "We can imagine a curtain-play which would evolve literally from its own 'material' and reveal in an entertaining way the curtain's own secret nature." Similarly he explored empty space, the human figure, movement, light, and color, and the elements in various combinations. But his remained a dancer's theatre, for after four years of experimentation he was still stating:

428

*Theatre and
Drama in
Central and
Eastern
Europe
Between
the Wars*

"For the time being we must be content with the silent play of gesture and motion—that is, with pantomime—firmly believing that one day the word will develop automatically from it."

Schlemmer's experiments recall Craig's *Uebermarionetten* and the work of the futurists, for he sought to transcend the natural human shape through three-dimensional costumes that transformed the actors into "ambulant architecture," spinning tops, creatures with multiple limbs, or dematerialized forms, and to control their geometrical movements with mathematical precision. He was not concerned with inner psychology but with outer expressiveness. He treated properties as means for extending the body, movement, and gesture. His scenery was made up primarily of flats covered with unpainted canvas which could be altered dynamically by abstract and colored light from front or back.

Out of his experiments with space, shapes, motion, light, and color, Schlemmer evolved a number of stage productions ranging in tone from the comic to the mystic. The best known is *The Triadic Ballet,* which he began in 1912 and refined thereafter. It was first seen in its entirety in 1922 and was later repeated at the Neue Musik festival at Donaueschingen with music by Hindemith. It was *The Triadic Ballet* which established the direction the Stage Workshop would follow thereafter.

As the name suggests, *The Triadic Ballet* was divided into three parts: a burlesque section set against lemon-yellow curtains; a serious and festive part in a rose-colored setting; and a heroic and mystical finale played against a black background. It was subdivided into twelve parts, each danced by three performers whose shapes were altered by three-dimensional costumes made of padded fabrics and rigid frameworks. Schlemmer has stated that the costumes were conceived first; next the music was chosen to fit the shapes; then movement was evolved. "Thus, for instance, a dance moves only from downstage to the footlights along a straight line. Then the diagonal or the circle, the ellipse, and so on. There was no underlying definite 'intellectual' considerations. Rather, it was the inventive esthetic joy of fusing contrasts into form, color, and movement."

Schlemmer also developed a number of nonhuman "figural cabinets" in which mechanical figures were programmed to move into different configurations and act out a strange, grotesque drama. Thus, he achieved something like a drama performed by kinetic sculptures.

The Bauhaus stage made its greatest impact through its tour of several German and Swiss cities in 1929. The program was composed of several short pieces, the titles of which give some indication of their sources of inspiration: "Dance in Metal," "Dance of Hoops," "Game with Building Blocks," "Chorus of Masks." Some were humorous, others surrealistic, mysterious, or frightening. One reviewer wrote: "No feelings are 'expressed,' rather, feelings are evoked. . . . Pure absolute form."

When Schlemmer left the Bauhaus in 1929 the Stage Workshop came to an end. After Hitler came to power, Schlemmer was barred from all

teaching posts and had to subsist thereafter on odd jobs. His work at the
Bauhaus probably had little immediate influence on the theatre, but
interest in it revived in the 1950s, when the idea of total design for dance
became popular. Like much of the Bauhaus's work, Schlemmer's can *Theatre and
Drama in
Central and
Eastern
Europe
Between
the Wars*
probably best be viewed as "basic research," the possible applications of
which are almost infinite.

Paralleling the interests of Schlemmer were those of Laszlo Moholy-
Nagy (1895–1946) in light in motion. After a close association with the
Sturm group of expressionists, Moholy-Nagy joined the Bauhaus in 1923
as head of the Metal Workshop, but he became increasingly interested in the
problems of mobile, three-dimensional works of art, in the role of light, and
in spatial interrelationships. He was to make important contributions to
kinetic sculpture, photography, film, and advertising. His "Light-Space
Modulator," moved by electricity and using electric light to project the
ever-changing patterns, is considered a major pioneering work of art.

In 1925, Moholy-Nagy published a statement on "total theatre" (one
upon which Gropius and Piscator would build and which preceded Artaud's
theories by many years). In it, he begins by noting the characteristics of the
traditional theatre and by recognizing the contributions of the futurists,
dadaists, and the Bauhaus, all of which he finds partial and which he seeks
to absorb into a new totality. He acknowledges that the theatre's problem is
more complex than that of other arts because of the living actor. Most
arts "have discovered pure media for their constructions. . . . But how can
we integrate a sequence of human movements and thoughts on an equal
footing with the controlled 'absolute' elements of sound, light (color),
form, and motion?" The means suggested by Moholy-Nagy include the
amplification of voices and inner thoughts, close-up images of faces and
gestures, recordings, and films. He advocates directional sound and multiple
projections. About lighting, he writes: "We have not yet begun to realize
the potential of light for sudden or blinding illumination, for flare effects,
for phosphorescent effects, for bathing the auditorium in light synchronized
with climaxes or with the total extinguishing of lights on the stage." He
recommended that the barriers between stage and auditorium be removed
and that bridges be suspended overhead horizontally, diagonally and vertically, or that stages be extended far into the auditorium, that disklike
segments of the stage be swung forward to bring some scenes closer and
back to make others recede. But unlike many theorists of his time, Moholy-
Nagy did not wish to eliminate the text; he merely sought to place the
other elements on an equal footing with the spoken word. Moholy-Nagy's
ideas are of considerable importance as one of the earliest manifestoes for
"total theatre" and multimedia productions. His influence on the theatre
that Gropius designed for Piscator shortly afterward is clear.

After leaving the Bauhaus in 1928, Moholy-Nagy worked for Piscator
and designed scenery for operas in Berlin. His setting for *The Tales of
Hoffman*—an abstract composition of variously textured and shaped

430

*Theatre and
Drama in
Central and
Eastern
Europe
Between
the Wars*

panels suspended in the air, set on the floor, or attached to standing units, the whole varied endlessly and made opaque or transparent through light —still seems a marvel of inventiveness. It was such manipulations of light in space that most fascinated Moholy-Nagy, for as he later declared: "Vision in motion is a synonym for simultaneity and space-time."

In theatre architecture, the Bauhaus's most important work was done by Gropius, who in 1927 designed a "total theatre" for Piscator. According to Gropius, there are only three basic stage forms—the arena, thrust, and proscenium—and in his total theatre he sought to incorporate all three. To accomplish this, Gropius mounted a segment of seats and an acting area on a large revolvable circle forward of the proscenium. When the acting area was moved to a position contiguous with the proscenium, it formed a thrust stage, and when rotated 180 degrees it became an arena. Seats could also be mounted on it when the proscenium stage was to be used alone. From the wings of the proscenium stage ran an open platform which continued completely around the edge of the auditorium. It could be used as an acting area, and scenery could be shifted on it by means of wagons. A wide stage house also permitted rolling platforms to move horizontally. Spaced around the perimeter of the auditorium were twelve columns, between which could be mounted screens. A translucent cyclorama at the rear of the proscenium stage also provided a surface for projections, and other screens were mounted in the auditorium above the heads of the spectators.

Gropius declared that he wished to achieve a "unity of the scene of action and the spectator," and to use all available means to overwhelm viewers, to "stun them, and to force them to participate in experiencing the play." Thus, through the work of Gropius, Moholy-Nagy, and Piscator, the ideals of the Bauhaus and of epic theatre met. Unfortunately, Piscator

Gropius's Total Theatre (floorplan showing arrangements for, left to right, proscenium, thrust, and arena stagings). (Courtesy Walter Gropius.)

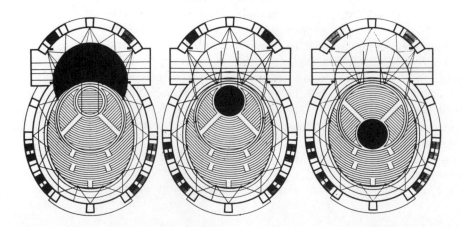

never found the funds to build Gropius's theatre. Nevertheless, Gropius's plans have remained an inspiration to others.

431

*Theatre and
Drama in
Central and
Eastern
Europe
Between
the Wars*

When Hitler came to power, the members of the Bauhaus dispersed, many to America. Gropius became head of Harvard University's Department of Architecture and a partner in some of the most influential architectural firms of the world. Moholy-Nagy served as head of the New Bauhaus, founded in Chicago in 1937, and, when it was dissolved in the following year, his own Institute of Design until his death. Mies van der Rohe became Head of the Department of Architecture at the Illinois Institute of Technology. The list could be extended many times.

There is scarcely an aspect of contemporary life that has not been influenced by the Bauhaus, often in quite unsuspected ways. Something of its enormous impact was conveyed by the commemorative exhibition of Bauhaus work mounted in 1969 to mark the fiftieth anniversary of its founding.

～ VIII ～

When the Nazis came to power in 1933 they effectively silenced liberalism in thought and experimentation in the arts. Many writers had little choice except to go into exile, some because they were Jews, others because their ideas made them targets of the Gestapo. In exile, several committed suicide, among them Toller and Hasenclever. After Austria was taken over in 1938, there remained no German-speaking areas except Switzerland to which exiles could go. Consequently, most were forced into an alienation from their own language. Cut off, many were unable to work, although a few, such as Brecht and Zuckmayer, were unusually productive. Hauptmann, by then more than seventy years old, was the only major dramatist to remain in Germany under Hitler, and his seeming acquiescence did much to destroy his reputation.

The plight of the writers who remained in Germany was not unlike that of their Russian counterparts in the same period. In both countries, authors were compliant or were silenced. Several German authors underwent what has been called an "inner emigration" by writing historical works or by deliberately distancing their work from the contemporary scene. In Germany and Russia an official style, in both instances variations on realism, was enforced. In Germany, the glorification of the Teutonic past and the Nietzschean superman (as interpreted by the Nazis) led to a grandiose, larger-than-life evocation of an all-powerful, all-Nordic world. The Russians, on the other hand, sought to dissociate themselves from the tsarist past and elevated the working man to the role of the hero who would bring about a world proletarian revolution with Soviet Russia at its head. Both versions of realism were equally sterile.

A production during World War II of Möller's *The Fall of Carthage* at the Darmstadt Hessisches Landestheater. The director was Franz Everth, setting by Caspar Neher. (From *Unbekanntes Theater*.)

The Nazis considered everything that had occurred since 1918 to be a mistake, and they set out to eliminate all vestiges of those years and to recapture the glories of the First Reich (the Holy Roman Empire) and the Second Reich (1870–1918) in their own Third Reich. Scarcely any drama written after the beginning of naturalism escaped their scorn, but the resulting emphasis upon the German classics partially masked the sterility of contemporary drama.

Nevertheless, a few writers accepted the Hitlerian ideal and sought to embody it in drama. Perhaps the most noteworthy of these were Friedrich Bethge (1891–   ), Eberhard Wolfgang Möller (1906–   ) and Hans Rethberg (1901–   ). It is perhaps significant that such dramatists as Hans Johst (1890–   ) and Arnolt Bronnen (1895–1959), who supported the National Socialists in their rise to power, ceased to write after 1933, although they were often honored by the state. Not a single play now considered worthwhile was written in Germany between 1933 and 1945.

Many theatrical workers also fled Germany. Reinhardt is the most prominent example. Most were seriously handicapped by the move, and some, such as Jessner, never adjusted to the change. But many remained in Germany and the quality of production (aside from the narrowed range of approved modes) was high. The state poured money into its theatres and sought to make of them showcases for Nordic culture. The heavy emphasis on the classics provided most with worthwhile challenges. Thus, such outstanding designers as Cesar Klein, Caspar Neher, Rochus Gliese, Wilhelm Reinking, and Karl Gröning and such major directors as Jürgen Fehling, Karlheinz Martin, Heinz Hilpert, and Berthold Viertel enjoyed a measure of freedom within the limits permitted by the Nazis.

Despite the exodus, the theatre remained prosperous and active until well into the war. Then, around 1942 conditions began to worsen, and in 1944 all theatres were closed. Thus ended the Nazi era.

IX

In the 1930s, as Germany and Russia yielded to totalitarianism and as other countries slipped into economic depression, Czechoslovakia came to the fore as an innovator in theatrical production. Until World War I, it had been a part of the Austro-Hungarian Empire and had had little opportunity to develop its theatrical resources, although steady progress had been made since 1883 when a Czech National Theatre was established in Prague with funds raised through national subscription.

After 1900 the general level of production at the National Theatre was raised by Jaroslav Kvapil (1868–1950), who introduced plays by Tolstoy, Ibsen, Chekhov, Wilde, Claudel, and others. In 1906 he sponsored the performances given in Prague by the Moscow Art Theatre and thereafter did much to implant Stanislavsky's ideals in his own company. Consequently, he is usually credited with creating a Czech school of psychological acting.

After Czech independence was gained in 1918, the direction of the National Theatre passed to K. H. Hilar (1885–1935), who was attuned to all the new artistic movements of his age. His productions, most of them designed by Vlatislav Hofman or A. Heythum, reflected the influence of expressionism, futurism, surrealism, neorealism, and other trends. Through the work of Hilar, Hofman, Čapeks, and others, the Czech theatre in the 1920s became an up-to-date and vital force.

Alongside the major theatres there grew up a number of "studios," among them Gamza's, the Dada, Proletkult, Devetsil, and Liberated theatres. It was out of these experimental troupes that E. F. Burian (1904–59) came just when experimentation was declining in other countries. In 1934, he founded the Theatre D34 (the name changed with the year), in which he sought to establish a creative partnership among writers, designers, actors, directors, and other stage personnel. Here with his principal designer Miroslav Kouril (1911–   ), he laid the foundations for work still underway in Czechoslovakia.

Burian worked in a small concert hall which seated only 383 persons and which had a stage only 20 by 12 feet in size. Perhaps because of his limited facilities, Burian placed special emphasis on light and music, out of which evolved three significant multimedia productions: Wedekind's *Spring's Awakening* in 1936; Pushkin's *Eugene Onegin* in 1937; and Goethe's *The Sorrows of Young Werther* in 1938. Burian seldom staged texts written for the stage, preferring to make his own adaptations, and even Wedekind's drama was transformed into "a voice crying out in times as terrible as those in which we are forced to live" against a society which deforms the spiritual growth of young people. The results were considered shocking by the audiences of 1936. Since the production of Wedekind's play

433

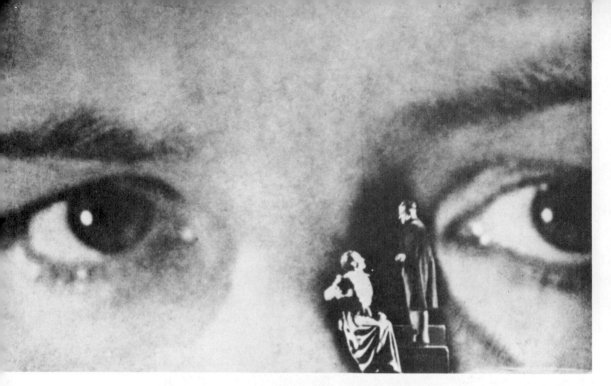

Burian's production of Wedekind's *Spring's Awakening*
at Theatre D37 1936. Setting by Kouril.
(Courtesy Professor F. Cerny, Charles University, Prague.)

may be taken as representative of Burian's work, it will be examined in some detail.

For it, Kouril made the stage a black void surrounded by black velvet drapes hung so as to permit characters to appear as if by magic. The acting area was composed of two connected platforms on which furniture and properties were placed as needed. The main feature of the stage was a narrow screen at the back, on which slides could be projected from the wings. More important, the entire proscenium opening was covered with a scrim through which the action could be seen and on which slides and films were projected from the front. Thus, the entire stage area was left free for use by the actors, and the scenic elements (except for properties) were created with projections and light.

Burian used light to emphasize his actors' three-dimensionality, to isolate them in space, to reveal a hand or face, or to make actors appear and disappear. The lighting also changed in color and intensity to reflect emotional and atmospheric qualities or to shift emphasis from one character to another.

The most remarkable feature of the production, however, was the overlapping of projected image with actor, for the performers were perceived within and through projections. Most of the slides showed enlarged or selective details. For example, a schoolroom setting was created by projecting on the scrim images of stuffed birds from the school museum, a meadow by close-ups of daisies in blossom, Melchior's room by a window, and a reformatory by bars. Often the actors related themselves to the projections. For example, in the meadow, the girl seemed to caress the daisies, in his room Melchior stared out of the window, and later in the reformatory he tried to break the bars. Most of the projections were chosen for their symbolic value: the deadness of school life, the confinement of the reformatory, the lyricism and freedom of nature. Thus, Burian's projections differed markedly from Piscator's.

A still more dynamic use was made of film. In the scene in which the girl is seduced, the entire action took place on film. It began with a close-up of the girl's face and then showed the boy's hand tearing away her dress to expose a breast; then the whole screen was covered with lily buds, which slowly opened into full flower. Similarly, the girl's death was conveyed by the fading of a rose. In some scenes, films of the actors were projected on the scrim while the actors read their lines into microphones backstage. A scene of accusation used rapid montage shots of faces accompanied by voices issuing from loudspeakers: "You are guilty," "You and your principles," "It was your crime," etc. Sometimes a picture of an absent person was projected on a screen as he was discussed by onstage characters. For example, as Melchior's parents discussed the girl, her face appeared and moved closer and closer until only her accusing eyes were seen.

Burian was extremely skillful in blending his media. The film and slides were always subordinated to the dramatic action and were meaningless without it. Thus, it did not compete with the main action, often the case in Piscator's productions. The overall impression was summed up well by a critic: "The rapid succession of images and settings, together with the use of light to model the characters on the stage, and the accompaniment of subdued music, accomplish true wonders here. The action seems to go on in a vision of budding, pulsing, blossoming spring, in waves of blossoms, through the apparition of accusing, terrifying eyes and faces, in an alternation of light and darkness, out of which scenes and images emerge one by one." Burian's were probably the most skillful multimedia productions seen prior to World War II.

When the Nazis came, the Czech theatre was soon reduced to mediocrity. In 1941 Burian's theatre was closed and he was confined to a concentration camp. Nevertheless, it is from the work of Burian and Kouril that the present-day Czech interest in multimedia, seen at its best in the work of Josef Svoboda, stems. In the 1950s, Kouril, with Svoboda, founded the Scenographic Institute in Prague and remains its head. But in the 1930s, the Czech experiments seemed merely the last flicker of originality before the holocaust of World War II engulfed all of Europe.

In the interwar years, the theatre in Poland also came to maturity. Although the Polish dramatic tradition can be traced back to the Middle

436

*Theatre and
Drama in
Central and
Eastern
Europe
Between
the Wars*

Ages, its first significant expression came during the romantic era in works by Poland's major poets—Adam Mickiewicz (1798–1855), Juliusz Slowacki (1809–49) and Zygmunt Krasiński (1812–59). Although their "dramatic poems" were not seen on the stage until the twentieth century, they then became the backbone of the national repertory. Of the three writers, Mickiewicz is usually considered the best, being accorded a place in Polish literature not unlike that of Goethe in Germany.

Mickiewicz's *Forefather's Eve* (in four parts, 1823–32) uses as a framework an ancient folk ritual in which the dead are invoked and offered food. Similarly, in Mickiewicz's play spirits of various kinds are summoned up and treated as representative of significant human experience. The heart of the poem is the third part, in which the hero, confined to a Russian prison (this portion was written shortly after an unsuccessful Polish uprising) gradually moves beyond his preoccupation with personal problems into the realm of political and humanitarian concerns. Eventually he assumes a moral stance superior even to that of God, for God sees misery and allows it to exist whereas Mickiewicz's hero resolves to destroy it. Overall, *Forefather's Eve* is a series of fragments unified by dream-vision.

Mickiewicz also influenced Polish thought in the twentieth century through a series of lectures on Slavic literature given in Paris during the 1840s. In them, he declared that Slavic drama continues the only valid theatrical tradition—ancient Greek and medieval religious drama in which saints and heroes are brought to life. He added that, through the Slavic gift for grasping the supernatural, Polish dramatists blend a concern for current problems with historical and spiritual awareness. Mickiewicz recognized that the kind of play he championed was impossible to stage in his day, but he called for a new theatre with resources sufficient to it.

The plays of Slowacki and Krasiński were also to be major influences on twentieth-century drama, and like Mickiewicz's they require theatrical means in excess of those in use when they were written. Slowacki's *Kordian* (1834) depicts the search of its hero for fulfillment, eventually found in the national cause. After an unsuccessful attempt to assassinate the tsar (foiled by Kordian's moral scruples), the hero is confined to an insane asylum, from which he is released after a daring feat of bravery, only to be condemned to death. But this outline cannot suggest the enormous scope of the action, the monumental visual effects, or the dematerializing thrust of the imagery. Krasiński's play *The Undivine Comedy* (1833) depicts the struggle between an entrenched aristocracy and a revolutionary proletariat. The protagonist views revolution as inevitable and foresees his own destruction, but at the moment when his premonitions prove true, a cross appears in the sky, thus suggesting that the ultimate answer lies in a synthesis of the old aristocratic view of Christianity and the new spirit of revolution. The overall action is conceived on such a scale and demands such large masses of characters that it was long considered wholly unsuited for the stage. These

437

*Theatre and
Drama in
Central and
Eastern
Europe
Between
the Wars*

romantic plays with their concern for national destiny were to have enormous appeal for twentieth-century Poles struggling to establish an independent state and a unique consciousness. The challenge of putting such works on the stage did much to shape the Polish theatre in the interwar years.

Of equal or greater importance was the drama of Stanislaw Wyspiański (1869–1907), usually considered to be Poland's greatest playwright and the founder of modern Polish drama. Wyspiański was well educated and widely traveled (in Italy and France, and in Germany, where he came under the influence of Wagner). A man of many talents, he worked in several artistic media and did not take up dramatic writing until 1898. He then wrote numerous plays of various types: classical tragedies on patriotic themes; dramas of peasant life; pieces based on contemporary events; and (above all) symbolic plays about the national character and destiny. In the last type, he was the direct heir of the romantic poets.

Wyspiański's most famous work is *The Wedding* (1901), often said to have begun a new era in Polish drama. In it Wyspiański uses a country wedding as an excuse for bringing together representatives of all ranks and professions who discuss literature, business, and politics. The characters come onto the stage one or two at a time and then return to the festivities in an adjoining room. But as time passes and drink flows more freely and music weaves a spell, characters of a quite different sort begin to appear, some of them historical or fictional personages, others fantastic creatures (such as a straw rosebush covering). At the end, all the characters join in a somnambulistic dance led by the straw creature and his fiddle. Thus Wyspiański mingles real persons and embodied dreams to create a cross-section of Polish society and ideas. Throughout there is a hint of some great revelation in the offing. But it never comes, and when the play ends there is a strong suggestion that the will of the Polish people is paralyzed and that they have become mere men of straw. *Akropolis* (1904) is also of considerable interest, in part because in recent years Jerzy Grotowski has featured it in his repertory (although in a much altered form). *Akropolis* is set in Cracow, the ancient capital of the Poles and thus the equivalent of the Greek Acropolis. During the action, biblical, classical, and historical figures from the tapestried walls come to life and enact scenes relevant to the contemporary situation. With these and other plays Wyspiański made a powerful impression on his countrymen, but his works do not translate well since they are so rooted in the Polish consciousness.

Wyspiański was also concerned with reforming the theatre. Like Wagner, he believed that the theatre should be a unified work of art composed of word, color, music, and movement. His plays were more nearly librettos for a director than self-contained literary works, and his stage directions call for effects beyond the capacity of the theatre technology of his time. He staged many plays himself and was the first to put the

Szyfman's production of Shakespeare's *Romeo and Juliet*
at the Polski Theatre, Warsaw in 1931. Scenery and costumes by K. Frycz.
(From Lorentowicz, *Teatr Polski w Warszawie, 1913–1938,* Warsaw, 1938.)

romantic works on the stage. But despite his imaginative genius, Wyspiański
was not able wholly to transcend his age and so, like most other directors
of the time, he thought it necessary to have a different setting for each
scene indicated in a script.

If Wyspiański marks the beginning of modern Polish drama, modern
Polish theatre can be said to begin in 1913 when Arnold Szyfman (1882–
) opened the Polski Theatre in Warsaw. Equipped with all the latest
technical devices (including a revolving stage), the Polski Theatre was the
first in Poland consistently to use specially designed sets and costumes for
each new production. The two principal designers, Karol Frycz and Win-
centy Drabik, among the best in Europe, were sympathetic to cubism,
expressionism, and constructivism, and both emphasized a polydimensional
space which could be transformed endlessly with light. After Poland became
independent in 1918, the Polski Theatre, named a state troupe, continued to
be a champion of innovative techniques.

After 1918, the attempt to create a truly national form of theatre was
avidly pursued by a host of talented directors and designers. Among these,
by far the most important was Leon Schiller (1887–1954), for it was he
who synthesized the major trends and gave them their most characteristic
expression. As a music student, Schiller had studied and traveled widely

in Europe before turning his attention to theatre after meeting Gordon
Craig. He then came under the influence of Wyspiański and eventually
evolved his own outlook during the time when he served as literary advisor
to the Polski Theatre. Schiller championed what he called "monumental
theatre" (based on ideas of Mickiewicz, Wyspiański, and Craig, in addition
to his own). He favored works with a large number of plots and with
moods and ideas that he could shape to give interpretations compatible
with his own artistic, social, and political views. He did not hesitate to
alter texts. Furthermore, he wholly ignored stage directions, seeking instead
to utilize modern technology (machinery, lighting, projections, and sound),
carefully orchestrated movement, and polydimensional, flexible space to
achieve effects comparable to those suggested by the authors but more
compatible with modern sensibilities.

Schiller did not begin to work as an independent director until 1924,
when he founded his own theatre—the Bogulslawski—in collaboration with
Wilam Horzyca. After this troupe was disbanded in 1926, he directed at
the Polski Theatre and later in Lvov. He made his greatest impact with
the dramatic poems of the Polish romantics, with dramatizations of novels,
and similar works. Among his most important productions were Krasiński's
The Undivine Comedy, Slowacki's *Kordian,* Wyspiański's *Achilleis,* an
adaptation of Zermoski's novel *The Story of Sin* (in forty-three scenes),
and Mickiewicz's *Forefather's Eve.* For Mickiewicz's play, Andrzej Pronaszko designed a permanent setting with three levels surmounted by three
crosses which remained visible through most of the action to symbolize the
Polish calvary. There were no interior settings; instead, generalized architectural forms and lighting were used in conjunction to define playing areas
for the multiple locales of the ever-shifting action. Ghosts, rather than

Leon Schiller's production of Mickiewicz's *Forefather's Eve*
at the Polski Theatre in 1934. Design by A. Pronaszko.
(From Lorentowicz, *Tear Polski w Warszawie, 1913–1938,* Warsaw, 1938.)

440

*Theatre and
Drama in
Central and
Eastern
Europe
Between
the Wars*

being played by actors, were depicted by such devices as a flame or pillar of smoke from which disembodied voices seemed to emanate. It was through his work with such "unstageable" plays that Schiller most firmly set his stamp on the theatre of his time.

During the 1930s Schiller became increasingly interested in politics and moved in the direction of German neorealism. He called his work of this period "composed realism." During World War II, he was confined to Auschwitz, but from 1945 to 1949 he once more became the most important director in Poland. When, under Russian domination, socialist realism became the only accepted mode, Schiller lost his privileged position. Nevertheless, there is scarcely a director in the postwar Polish theatre who has not been influenced by Schiller, not only through his productions but through his teaching (at the State Theatre Institute for directors) and writing (more than two hundred essays). During the interwar years, the Polish theatre probably reached its peak with Schiller's work, which both technologically and artistically equaled that to be seen anywhere in the world.

During this period one playwright—Stanislaw Ignacy Witkiewicz (1885–1939), or Witkacy as he called himself—could also claim true originality. Like Ghelderode, he was virtually ignored until after World War II, for of the approximately thirty plays he wrote, only eleven were produced during his lifetime and those primarily by amateurs. For the most part, Witkiewicz was considered by his contemporaries to be a prankster or a madman.

Son of a famous artist, Witkiewicz had by 1914 traveled widely in Europe (where he became familiar with cubism and futurism) and in Asia, Australia, and New Guinea (where unfamiliar cultural patterns made a deep impression on him). During World War I, he served as an officer in the Russian army and was elected political commissar of his regiment following the Revolution. By the time he returned to Poland in 1918 he had arrived at that vision of the world that was to inform his work thereafter. He considered Western civilization to be on the verge of collapse and about it he had mixed feelings: on the one hand, he saw revolution as essential to social equity, but, on the other, he was convinced that the aftermath would be a leveling in which all individuality would be lost. In this new world, he wrote, "ethics will devour metaphysics." About this he observed gloomily, "From a herd we came and to a herd we shall return."

To Witkiewicz, art was the only means of expressing and soothing the anxiety which results from the "metaphysical feeling of the strangeness of existence" under such circumstances. This view also affected his conception of artistic form. He declared that when religion and philosophy were still potent forces they gave to art a harmonious order which is no longer possible. The contemporary artist must seek to create a unity out of increasingly disparate and dissonant elements, for modern art tends toward perversity compounded of the strident, the ugly, and the jarring.

441

*Theatre and
Drama in
Central and
Eastern
Europe
Between
the Wars*

Witkiewicz wrote three books on esthetic questions, of which the most important here is *An Introduction to the Theory of Pure Form in the Theatre* (1923). In it he proposed the need for a kind of theatre which, rather than seeking to imitate life, would manipulate the theatrical elements for purely formal ends, as in painting or music. "The idea is to make it possible to define either life or the world of fantasy with complete freedom so as to create a whole whose meaning would be defined only by its purely scenic internal construction." Furthermore, he wrote, "our aim is not programmatic nonsense; we rather try to enlarge the possibilities of composition by abandoning lifelike logic in art, by introducing a fantastic psychology and fantastic action, in order to win complete freedom for formal elements." Yet Witkiewicz recognized that theatre is the most impure of the arts because of its composite nature, and that therefore it can never be as formally pure as painting or music. About the ultimate effect he sought, Witkiewicz wrote: "When leaving the theatre, one should have the impression that one wakes up from a strange dream in which the most trite things have the elusive, deep charm characteristic of dreams, not comparable to anything."

Witkiewicz felt it necessary to move beyond the realm of objective reality into the inner world of the unconscious, and he often used drugs to assist him in subverting the intellect. (He later described his experiences in *Nicotine, Alcohol, Cocaine, Peyote, Morphine, and Ether,* published in 1932.) In this realm beyond logic (comparable to that described by the surrealists), he was able to juxtapose several levels of reality and elements from various genres and styles. His pessimism about the future led him to write most often about madmen and misfits as specimens of a doomed world. They engage in violent actions in which sex and murder are the most common ingredients, although those killed usually come back to life. They are motivated by a fantastic psychology and speak a language bearing little relation to everyday speech; even the least educated are apt to discourse learnedly about literature and philosophy and to quote esoteric treatises. Often fictional and historical characters mingle with those of the present day, as time and space cease to exist as barriers; many have such constructed names as Dona Scabrosa Macabrescu, Countess Tremendosa, and Bageloff-Moltocockroachin. The plays, which Witkiewicz sometimes called "comedies with corpses," may be grouped with those of Strindberg, Jarry, Artaud, Ghelderode, and the surrealists.

Most of Witkiewicz's plays were written between 1918 and 1926. Perhaps the best are *They* (1920), *The Water Hen* (1921), *The Cuttlefish* (1922), *The Madman and the Nun* (1923), *The Crazy Locomotive* (1923), and *The Mother* (1924). They are difficult to describe because they are composed of such disparate elements and suggest much that defies logical explication. *The Mother* may be taken as representative. In it the protagonist, Leon, searches restlessly to discover his true calling, while his mother supports him by her ceaseless knitting. (There is throughout an

442

*Theatre and
Drama in
Central and
Eastern
Europe
Between
the Wars*

ironical and parodistic tone which passes over into direct references to such authors as Ibsen and Strindberg.) Against his mother's wishes, Leon marries, and then appears to find his destiny as an admired social reformer. Toward the end of the second act, all of the characters come together and under the influence of drugs speak the truth. It becomes clear that Leon derives his income from pimping for his wife and spying for foreign governments. His mother dies. The third act (called an epilogue) occurs in a kind of limbo. Leon's mother, now a woman of twenty-three (and pregnant with Leon) confronts her grown-up son even as her own corpse lies at her feet. She observes: "The whole thing [i.e., the play] has been brilliantly put on, although no one knows by whom." To comfort Leon, she declares the corpse to be a mannikin and she and others rip it apart. After they leave the broken-hearted Leon alone, a group of machinelike workers declare, "Well, and now, my friends, a little kangaroo court in the name of mealy-mouthed democracy," as they completely destroy Leon. Through such works Witkiewicz expressed his catastrophic view of civilization.

After 1926, Witkiewicz's interests turned away from the theatre, and thereafter he wrote only one important work, *The Shoemakers* (1934), his most conventional play. Shortly after World War II began, he committed suicide. When he died he was virtually unknown as a dramatist. His reputation did not begin to grow until *The Cuttlefish* was produced in Cracow in 1955. It spread rapidly thereafter, soon reaching outside of Poland into other countries where he came to be recognized as one of the most important of surrealist dramatists and as a significant forerunner of the absurdist school. Nevertheless, despite his important theoretical treatises and plays, Witkiewicz remains little known outside of European avant-garde circles.

After 1939 the theatre in Poland suffered much the same fate as that in Czechoslovakia. No country in Europe was more devastated by the conflict. But the Polish spirit was not broken and after the war it would be asserted once more through the theatre.

X

Although conditions in central and eastern Europe between the wars were often chaotic, the theatrical life was lively. Perhaps the major residue is epic theatre, although it was not fully appreciated until much later. It is difficult to tell if epic is actually a separate type of writing and production, for as conceived by Piscator and Brecht it has had few practitioners. Brecht's

443

*Theatre and
Drama in
Central and
Eastern
Europe
Between
the Wars*

epic theatre was compounded of four elements: a set of dramatic techniques, a set of theatrical devices, a didactic purpose, and a political content. If all are essential, then Brecht has had few successors. On the other hand, if epic is conceived more broadly, it seems legitimate to consider Aristophanes the first and several writers of the present the latest in a long line of epic dramatists. Certainly Brecht's dramatic techniques and theatrical devices can and have been employed for nondidactic purposes and without Marxist content. During the 1960s many elements from his practice were taken over and meshed with others borrowed from nonepic writers. Today Brecht's approach no longer seems strange because "theatricalism" is now so widespread that his particular form of it has come to seem restrained. But if epic is being absorbed into the larger stream, its part in that stream remains important.

The Bauhaus experiments in staging stemmed from the rebellion against realism in the visual arts that began in the late nineteenth century, when, to counteract the tendency to judge painting by its ability to render a likeness of reality, some artists began to insist that art is a manipulation of means and that subject matter is irrelevant—that a painting should be judged entirely on its color, line, and composition and not on its content. Thereafter came a steady movement toward abstraction until in the work of some artists recognizable subject matter disappeared altogether. It is against this background that Schlemmer's work must be seen, for, as he stated, he was concerned with an abstract stage, the elements of which he systematically explored to see what content would emerge from them rather than to discover how he might express preconceived ideas. His was opposite to the traditional approach, but for that reason free from preconceptions. The results were often illuminating. Nevertheless, because he had no precise goal in mind, Schlemmer's work tended to remain without focus and his influence small, even if the implications of what he did were great.

Although Burian's experiments with multimedia remain little known, they were very advanced for their time. He was able to mingle live actors with projected light images without destroying dramatic effectiveness or setting up competing attractions. In his work, the various media were truly integrated rather than merely juxtaposed. Few directors since his time have reached the level of sophistication with multimedia that marked his productions. Similarly, Witkiewicz is only now becoming widely known, although his are probably the most successful applications of surrealistic devices. With Ghelderode, he anticipated many elements that would become typical of postwar drama.

The work of these men is still relevant, for the potentialities they opened up have not yet been fully explored. Much in contemporary theatrical practice is a continuation of developments they began and which were interrupted before fully mature. After the war, their worth would gradually be rediscovered.

Theatre and Drama
in
The British Isles
Between The Wars

13

During World War I the actor-manager, who had dominated the English theatre for more than two hundred years, was superseded by commercial producers, more concerned with profit then with artistic excellence. Fortunately, however, a few groups in London—among them the Old Vic, the Lyric Theatre, and the Gate—and others in the provinces—including the Birmingham Repertory Theatre, the Oxford Playhouse, and the Cambridge Festival Theatre—followed a different path. Except for modified realism, there were no obvious styles of production or writing, perhaps because England has never been prone to follow artistic movements. Playwriting was not outstanding, although a number of writers—such as Maugham, Coward, Bridie, Priestley, and Eliot—placed English drama on a level not appreciably

444

below that then evident elsewhere. In Ireland, the theatre regained some of its former glory with the plays of O'Casey and the productions of the Dublin Gate Theatre. But overall it was a period of respectable rather than outstanding accomplishment.

World War I marked the end of an era in England, for with it came the virtual end of the actor-manager system. The change is summed up at His Majesty's Theatre, which under Tree had been the home of Shakespeare but which after Tree's retirement in 1915 was given over to 2,238 consecutive performances of Oscar Asche's *Chu-Chin-Chow,* a musical extravaganza based on *Ali Baba and the Forty Thieves. Chu-Chin-Chow,* with its emphasis upon escapist entertainment, set the tone for the war years as well as those that followed. A few actor-managers, such as Fred Terry, Matheson Lang, Frank Benson, Ben Greet, and John Martin-Harvey, continued to maintain companies, but they spent most of their time on the road and made little impact on London's West End, now dominated by businessmen like those who had gained control of the American theatre around 1900.

Chu-Chin-Chow at His Majesty's Theatre in 1916. This is the slave market scene. Oscar Asche, the author, is seated under the umbrella at right. (Courtesy Enthoven Collection, Victoria and Albert Museum.)

446

*Theatre and
Drama in
The British
Isles
Between
the Wars*

Actors were hired for the run of a play and scripts were chosen primarily for their potential to attract a mass audience. Thus, though there was no decline in the number of productions, quality suffered in the major houses. Fortunately, as in France, a few out-of-the-way theatres brightened this otherwise gloomy picture. Unlike the Parisian "studios," however, the English companies made few innovations in production and seemed little aware of theories or artistic movements. During the 1920s the most important of these groups were the Lyric Theatre, the Gate Theatre, the various Sunday evening clubs, the Barnes Theatre, and the Old Vic.

The Lyric Theatre, Hammersmith, was founded in 1918 by Nigel Playfair (1874–1934), who, after making his debut in 1902 and performing with Benson, Tree, and Barker, had failed to rise above the status of secondary performer. When he accidentally came across the Lyric Theatre (which after its opening in 1890 had been the home of melodrama and music hall entertainment before being closed during the war), he saw in it the opportunity to have his own company. With the assistance of Arnold Bennett, who served as his business manager for seven years, Playfair assumed control of this out-of-the-way building in one of London's western suburbs and remodeled it into an elegant resort.

The Lyric opened in 1918 with A. A. Milne's first play, *Make Believe,* a Christmas entertainment written especially for the occasion. A considerable success, it featured several young actors who would later become stars—among them Herbert Marshall, Hermione Baddeley, and Leslie Banks. The company's popularity increased with John Drinkwater's *Abraham Lincoln* (which in 1919 ran for 466 performances), but its real triumph came in 1920 with Gay's *The Beggar's Opera.* By the time its run of 1,463 performances had ended, the Lyric had become London's most fashionable theatre.

The Beggar's Opera was a significant production, for not only did it assure the company's success, it established its style and the direction its repertory would follow. The visual style of the Lyric owed most to Claud Lovat Fraser (1890–1921), often said to have inaugurated a new era in English scene design, for, despite Craig's theories and a few prewar productions by Rutherston, Wilkinson, and Charles Ricketts, English stage design had scarcely been touched by deviations from romantic realism. The enormous popularity of *The Beggar's Opera* focused attention on its visual style and marked the beginning of a change in English decor. For the production, Fraser designed a simple unit—an arrangement of columns and steps—within which smaller pieces could be changed rapidly. Fraser had a sure eye for the distinctive features of eighteenth-century architecture and was able to capture them with a few simple elements. Both settings and costumes were gay, bright, and stylish. In effect, he abandoned historical reconstruction for simplified realism. Though today Fraser's setting does not seem particularly novel, at the time it marked a distinct break with the cluttered, near-naturalistic settings typical of productions in London's West

The Beggar's Opera at the Lyric Theatre, Hammersmith, in 1920.
Setting by Claud Lovat Fraser. The unit in front remained throughout,
while pieces were changed behind the arches. (Courtesy Enthoven
Collection, Victoria and Albert Museum.)

End. Fraser died before *The Beggar's Opera* closed, but his work at the
Lyric was carried on by other progressive designers such as George Sher-
ingham, Norman Wilkinson, and Doris Zinkeisen.

The Beggar's Opera also reawakened interest in the drama of the
Restoration and eighteenth century, which, with the exception of Sheridan's
works, had long been dormant. Thereafter the majority of Playfair's
repertory was chosen from that era. Among his most significant productions
were *The Way of the World, The Beaux' Stratagem, Love in a Village,
Lionel and Clarissa, She Stoops to Conquer, The Critic, The Duenna,* and
The Rivals. Although he presented other types of plays—such as operas and
original scripts—all tended to be alike in tone.

Playfair's productions also tended to resemble each other in treatment.
He muted all harshness and sexual innuendo (even in *The Beggar's Opera*
and *The Way of the World*) and made of the scripts playful entertainments
verging on caricature. Nevertheless, they were completely unlike anything
else then to be seen in the English theatre, and therefore did much to create
a sense of style in production. Playfair always acknowledged the presence of
the audience and frequently employed costumed musicians and footmen

447

448

*Theatre and
Drama in
The British
Isles
Between
the Wars*

(who tended the footlights and moved furniture and properties on stage in full view of the audience). His productions were characterized by colorful costumes and settings, formalized compositions and stylized gestures, and a liberal use of dance and music. All were elegant and modish. Playfair's taste governed every detail, although much of the day-to-day work was done by Stephen Thomas, who staged the plays under Playfair's watchful eye.

Because of its narrow range, the Lyric's appeal eventually declined and in 1932 Playfair relinquished its direction. Still its influence was lasting, for here such major English performers as John Gielgud and Edith Evans gained an appreciation of the importance of style in acting, and Playfair began that trend toward a distinctive interpretation of scripts which would be more fully developed by others in the 1930s.

The Gate Theatre was as dilapidated as the Lyric was elegant. It was the creation of Peter Godfrey (1899–   ), who had been a magician in music halls as a child, a circus clown, a member of Ben Greet's Shakespearean troupe, and an actor in a number of repertory companies before he became interested in expressionistic drama and decided to found a theatre where he could present the works that he admired but which had found no outlet in England. Unfortunately he did not have the resources to rent a regular theatre and the only facilities he could afford did not pass fire regulations. Consequently, in 1925 he opened the Gate Theatre as a private club located in a loft near Covent Garden. Thus, it became the first of the theatre clubs that later would be numerous in London. Since the 1890s "private" performances had been used as a means of avoiding censorship, but unlike the Gate such organizations gave only one or two performances of each production and did not maintain a company or even continuity of production personnel. Godfrey, on the other hand, sought to establish a permanent group and to perform works for several weeks. He was not so much interested in avoiding censorship as in finding premises he could afford.

Godfrey's first theatre held only eighty persons and had only a tiny stage. In the beginning it attracted so few persons that it was on the verge of collapse when James Agate, one of London's most influential critics, published an extremely laudatory review of Georg Kaiser's *From Morn to Midnight*. As a result, the demand to see the play became so great that the production was moved to a West End theatre. It was the first fully expressionistic play seen on a public stage in London.

During the two seasons spent in his original theatre, Godfrey presented thirty-two plays by such authors as Strindberg, Wedekind, Toller, Evreinov, Čapek, Hauptmann, Ibsen, Maeterlinck, and Rice. Not all were expressionistic, but that mode was clearly favored. For most productions the stage was surrounded with black drapes in front of which were erected set pieces, often painted in distorted perspective and using nonrealistic color and line. Major emphasis was placed upon lighting and rhythmical effects.

Peter Godfrey's production of Kaiser's *From Morn to Midnight* at the Gate Theatre in 1928.
(Courtesy Enthoven Collection, Victoria and Albert Museum.)

450

*Theatre and
Drama in
The British
Isles
Between
the Wars*

In 1927 the Gate moved to a building which measured 55 by 30 feet and which Godfrey remodeled to suit his needs. Despite the small size of the structure, he reserved a generous area for the stage, which was raised only 18 inches above the auditorium floor and abutted directly onto the first row of seats. Its intimacy encouraged sincerity in acting. Here Godfrey presented plays by such authors as Pirandello, Cocteau, Lenormand, Bernard, O'Neill, and others. Because of the quality of the plays, Godfrey was able to attract a number of fine performers who were willing to work in them a few weeks for minimal pay. Among others, Flora Robson, Robert Speaight, Eric Portman, and Jean Forbes-Robertson appeared at the Gate. At Christmas time, Godfrey did burlesques of such plays as *Uncle Tom's Cabin, Ten Nights in a Barroom, Little Lord Fauntleroy,* and *Fashion* with outstanding comic performers, such as Hermione Gingold and Elsa Lanchester.

Like the Lyric, the Gate lost its appeal after a time and in 1934 Godfrey abandoned it. But if it failed, it had done a great service, for more than any other theatre it brought to London the best of Continental, English, and American drama. In nine years, Godfrey had produced approximately 350 plays and had demonstrated a simplified (often expressionistic) mode of production. His immediate influence on the public theatre probably was not great, but the Gate clearly served an important function by familiarizing audiences with new plays and techniques. In later years, Godfrey was a radio and film writer and a film director in Hollywood.

The work done by Godfrey was extended by that of several Sunday evening societies that presented minimally mounted productions acted by young professionals. Since rehearsals were few, the results were varied. Nevertheless, the societies kept their members in touch with new writing both domestic and foreign. The most important of the organizations continued to be the Incorporated Stage Society (founded in 1899), which between the wars presented plays by such authors as Toller, Kaiser, O'Neill, Vildrac, Romains, Bernard, Cocteau, Crommelynck, Pirandello, Afinogenov, Lorca, and Odets. It also gave such native authors as R. C. Sherriff, C. K. Munro, and Ashley Dukes their first hearings. But, largely because of the Gate Theatre, by the 1930s the Incorporated Stage Society had ceased to fulfill a truly important function. Nevertheless, it continued until 1939, when upon the advent of the war it was dissolved. The Phoenix, an offshoot of the Incorporated Stage Society founded in 1919, was devoted to works by Elizabethan and Restoration authors. Since of its twenty-six offerings only one was by Shakespeare, it did much to revive interest in neglected dramatists of the seventeenth century.

There were also a number of other societies. The Three Hundred Club, operated from 1923 to 1926 by Mrs. Geoffrey Whitworth and concerned with new plays not likely to attract a commercial producer, provided valuable assistance to developing authors. Other societies were founded by

451

*Theatre and
Drama in
The British
Isles
Between
the Wars*

actors. Some, such as the Fellowship of Players, were designed to give its members experience, such as acting in Shakespeare's plays, otherwise denied them. The Repertory Players and the Play Actors, on the other hand, staged plays as "showcases" for possible West End productions. The best of such societies was the Pioneers, headed by Edith Craig, sister of Gordon Craig and daughter of Ellen Terry. The Pioneers undertook a very ambitious program of plays—such as those by Claudel and Duhamel—that would not otherwise have been seen in England.

Valuable as the Sunday societies were, they could exert only limited influence on the English theatre. More than anything else they demonstrated how narrow was the range of offerings in London's West End.

Another venture of some importance in the 1920s was the Barnes Theatre, housed in a converted cinema in a suburb of London. Here in 1925–26 Theodore Komissarzhevsky, who had left Russia in 1919 and had worked in Paris for Hébertot, staged a season of plays which included Chekhov's *Uncle Vanya, The Three Sisters, The Cherry Orchard,* and *Ivanov*; Andreyev's *Katerina*; and Gogol's *The Inspector General.* These productions are significant for several reasons. They were the first effective presentations of Chekhov's works in England, for until this time they had seldom been produced and then so badly that they were found unintelligible by audiences who had come to admire the logic of Ibsen and Shaw. Komissarzhevsky's productions were considered revelations, for the plays were for the first time not merely understandable but deeply moving. Furthermore, Komissarzhevsky, through his subtle handling of tempo, pause, modulation, sculptural lighting, and simple and imaginative settings, gave a badly needed lesson in what directing at its best could achieve. According to Norman Marshall, Komissarzhevsky "had an enormous influence on the whole art of directing in the English theatre." The company included Charles Laughton, Claude Rains, Martita Hunt, Jean Forbes-Roberton, and John Giclgud (who has acknowledged his own great debt to Komissarzhevsky). Unfortunately the theatre was too small to pay its own way and had to be abandoned in 1926.

Ultimately the most important of the London theatres in the 1920s was the Old Vic, a theatre whose past history suggested little chance of glory. Built in 1818 as the Royal Coburg Theatre, it had in 1833 become the Royal Victoria and as such gradually descended on the theatrical scale until it was a very minor music hall. In 1880 it was acquired by Emma Cons, a social reformer who converted it into a "temperance music hall." With a program of musical entertainment and lectures, it became a family resort. In 1898, Miss Cons asked her niece, Lilian Baylis (1874–1937), to become her assistant. The daughter of musicians, Miss Baylis was a great lover of opera, which she soon began to present on a limited basis at the Old Vic. But it was not until World War I that she added plays.

The first dramatic performance—of *The Taming of the Shrew*—at the Old Vic was given in 1914 under the direction of Matheson Lang (1879–

Stage setting for a production of Shakespeare's
The Winter's Tale at the Old Vic in 1920.
(Courtesy Enthoven Collection, Victoria and Albert Museum.)

1948), who had acted in the companies of Irving, Benson, and Barker but who by 1914 was so identified with the role of Wu Li Chang (in *Mr. Wu* by Vernon and Owen) that he soon left the Old Vic to return to it. Ben Greet, just back from several years in America, then took charge from 1915 to 1918 and established the Old Vic as the home of Shakespeare in London. At this time, the theatre was so outmoded that it was still equipped with grooves and gas lighting (it was not modernized until 1919–20). Under Greet the Old Vic company performed three times a week (at prices ranging from three to thirty cents) and gave matinee performances for schoolchildren (the first professional productions in England intended for child audiences).

At the end of the war, the company came under the management of Robert Atkins (1886–1972), who after making his debut with Tree in 1906 had acted for Benson and Forbes-Robertson. But it was Poel's practices that most influenced him. Although he did not employ Poel's reconstructed Elizabethan stage, he kept scenery to a minimum so as not to interrupt the flow of scenes, and emphasized the rapid and incisive speaking of verse. Since he had to produce a new play every two weeks, there was no time for subtleties, but Atkins always managed to attain clarity of action and to make the plays understandable. With its presentation of *Troilus and Cressida* in 1923, the Old Vic became the first theatre in England to have produced all of Shakespeare's plays.

453

*Theatre and
Drama in
The British
Isles
Between
the Wars*

In 1925 the company came under the direction of Andrew Leigh (1887–1957), who followed Benson's workmanlike if not very imaginative lead. The period is noteworthy in part because Edith Evans, then still relatively unknown, joined the company so that she might gain experience in playing Shakespeare.

In 1929 leadership passed to Harcourt Williams (1880–1957), whose ideals had been formed under Granville-Barker. His productions were often disliked because he gave Shakespeare's plays new interpretations which emphasized psychological motivations and subtle new readings. Furthermore, his were probably the first productions since 1914 to follow Barker's principles. Williams's management is also of interest because for two seasons Gielgud was a member of his company. (More than anyone else Gielgud was to be responsible for gaining acceptance in West End theatres for the ideals championed by Barker and Williams.)

Williams's management was a watershed in still other respects. The changes that he had begun were to be extended in the 1930s and with them the character of the Old Vic would change. Furthermore, theatrical production in London's West End entered a new phase in the 1930s.

～ II ～

The major shift in the 1930s came with the gradual triumph of those principles which had been demonstrated by Barker (especially in his Shakespearean productions of 1912–14) in the decade preceding World War I. After Barker's retirement, the English theatre had settled once more into the practices popularized by Irving and Tree (indeed, except with Barker, it had never departed from them). These standards were continued, even extended, in the 1920s by Basil Dean (1888–   ), who with his photographically real productions set the standard for the West End. Consequently, despite the work done by Playfair and Godfrey, there was no marked change in the commercial theatre until the 1930s. The direction then taken owed most to a few persons: Tyrone Guthrie (and the Old Vic), John Gielgud, Michel Saint-Denis, and the circle of actors who clustered about them.

During the 1930s the Old Vic was beset by growing pains. It had built up its own special audience for a Shakespearean repertory performed in a straightforward manner and had never really attracted the West End playgoer. Now a series of innovations gradually changed the character of the Old Vic.

Although Shakespeare had been the Old Vic's mainstay, operas had also been presented regularly. In order to give them more scope, Miss Baylis

454

*Theatre and
Drama in
The British
Isles
Between
the Wars*

in 1931 bought the Sadler's Wells Theatre, located across town from the Old Vic in a northern suburb of London, and rebuilt it as an additional home for her companies. At this time she also acquired a ballet troupe when Ninette de Valois offered her company in return for a home for her ballet school. Thus, in 1931 the Old Vic was transformed into the Vic-Wells Company, divided into three subtroupes. Until 1935, the opera-ballet and drama programs alternated between the Old Vic and Sadler's Wells (the companies exchanged theatres at the end of each week). They also now increased the number of weekly performances to eight. It was an ambitious and tiring schedule, but not until 1935 were the opera-ballet programs restricted to Sadler's Wells and the dramatic productions to the Old Vic.

The Old Vic also changed in other ways, most of them attributable to Tyrone Guthrie. Miss Baylis had always insisted that Shakespeare be performed in a straightforward manner that stressed the human and humorous qualities. Furthermore, she expended very little on mounting the plays. In fact, Miss Baylis had become legendary for her penurious treatment of directors and actors, but she was also admired for her dedication to a mission, which she looked upon as a direct call from God to bring the best in drama and opera to an otherwise deprived audience. Thus, though she was often tactless and exasperating, her integrity was never questioned. Without her unswerving devotion, the Old Vic would not have survived. But over the years her protectiveness had tended to keep productions in a narrow path, even though she would have liked to attract a wider audience. Thus, there was something of a struggle between her and Guthrie, who never respected tradition. She employed him for one season, 1933–

Ralph Richardson as Iago and Edith Evans as Emilia in the Old Vic production of Shakespeare's *Othello* in 1932. (Courtesy Debenham Collection, British Theatre Museum, London.)

34, then let him go, only to bring him back in 1936. When Miss Baylis died
in 1937, it was Guthrie who became head of the Old Vic and Sadler's
Wells. The change is indicative of the direction taken by the Old Vic in
the 1930s.

Theatre and
Drama in
The British
Isles
Between
the Wars

Until Guthrie's first season as a director at the Old Vic, the acting
company had been composed almost entirely of competent but relatively
unknown performers—those on their way up, such as Edith Evans and
John Gielgud, or those who had never become stars. But in 1933–34,
four well-known actors, Charles Laughton, Flora Robson, Athene Seyler,
and Ursula Jeans, were employed. For the first time, the Old Vic began to
draw West End audiences. Many of the old patrons (and even some
critics) resented the change, for the Old Vic's audience in its own way had
became a coterie largely made up of those who were contemptuous of, or
aloof from, the commercial theatre. Now many of the old patrons defected
and when Guthrie departed after one season did not return. The Old Vic
seemed to hesitate between two paths and did not choose until Guthrie
resumed control.

After 1936 the Old Vic employed a nucleus company of fine actors—
almost every English performer of note passed through this troupe—and
added to it as needed for each production. Until that time it had also for
many years offered every production for three weeks regardless of popularity.
Now the length of runs might extend to eight weeks if the demand justified
it. In 1939, Guthrie devised a true repertory system under which a permanent company would alternate plays in regular rotation—a novelty at
the time, for such a scheme had not been tried in London since the nineteenth century, but one that would be taken up by several other permanent
troupes after 1950. Before the wisdom of the new policy could be tested,
however, the war caused the company to move its headquarters to
Burnley, where it remained until 1944, making only occasional forays into
London. But by the time the war began, the Old Vic was looked upon by
many as England's nearest equivalent to a national theatre. It would be
unfair to give too much credit to Guthrie, for it was Miss Baylis who
nurtured and sustained the company. Nevertheless, it was Guthrie who
transformed it from a workmanlike troupe into a major artistic force.

Tyrone Guthrie (1900–1971) had made his debut as an actor in 1924
in the Oxford Repertory Company but soon gave up acting in favor of
directing. In 1926–27 he became a director for the Scottish National
Theatre (the name of which reflects an ambition far in excess of its resources
or accomplishments) and in 1929–30 for the Cambridge Festival Theatre.
His debut in London, at the Westminster Theatre with Bridie's play *The
Anatomist,* was a considerable hit. Thereafter he was much in demand,
but his finest work before World War II was done at the Old Vic or with
Gielgud's company.

In London, Guthrie rapidly became known for those qualities which
thereafter characterized his work: his boldness in giving plays new and

startling (sometimes bizarre) interpretations, his disregard for tradition, his inventive and novel stage business, and restless, sometimes near-frenetic movement. His productions were often controversial because of novel directorial conceptions, but they were seldom boring. He made the director a major force in the theatre and perhaps did more than anyone else in the 1930s to provoke the common complaints of critics that directors were more concerned with original than with sound interpretations of plays. With Guthrie there arrived a new era in the English theatre.

The Vic-Wells Company was also instrumental in establishing English ballet, which prior to that time was virtually nonexistent. It built upon the work of two pioneering teachers, Ninette de Valois and Marie Rambert. Ninette de Valois (Edris Stannis, 1898–) was born in Ireland and trained in Diaghilev's Ballets Russes, which she left in 1926 to found her own school in London, the Academy of Choreographic Art. Thereafter she worked wherever she could to gain experience as a choreographer and to provide opportunities for her students. The turning point came in 1931 when Miss Baylis accepted her offer to provide a ballet troupe for the newly created Vic-Wells Company. In the face of considerable skepticism and much adverse criticism, Mlle. de Valois gradually but systematically built a ballet company almost wholly English in origin. At first she was the principal choreographer but soon added Frederick Ashton and then Robert Helpmann to her staff. By the beginning of the war, the Sadler's Wells Company was being recognized as a major troupe, a fact fully admitted with its reconstitution as the Royal Covent Garden Ballet Company in 1946. Since 1962, when Margot Fonteyn and Rudolf Nureyev became its principal dancers, the Royal Ballet has been acclaimed as one of the world's finest.

Another pioneer was Marie Rambert (1888–), also a dancer in Diaghilev's company before founding her own school in London. In 1931 she created the Ballet Club, where on Sunday evenings she presented performances by her company. Miss Rambert was considered by many to be a better teacher and a more astute judge of talent than was Mlle. de Valois, but she lacked the ability to make long-range plans and consequently her company never expanded. In fact, as the Sadler's Wells Ballet grew, it assimilated the best of her students. Consequently, the accomplishments of that troupe owe much to her. Together Miss Rambert and Mlle. de Valois wrought a virtual revolution in English ballet, but one that might never have taken place had it not been for the decision of Lilian Baylis in 1931 to accept Mlle. de Valois's offer of a ballet company.

Important as was the work of the Old Vic and Tyrone Guthrie, it did not at the time seem so significant as that of John Gielgud (1904–), for he prevailed in the West End theatres while the Old Vic remained on the fringe and outside the mainstream of the commercial theatre. A grand-nephew of Ellen Terry and a cousin of Gordon Craig, Gielgud made his debut as an actor at the Old Vic in 1921 and then performed with the Oxford Repertory Company, Komissarzhevsky, Playfair, and in various

London productions, including two seasons under Harcourt Williams at the Old Vic. Nevertheless, in 1930 he was still considered merely a promising actor. The turning point came in the season of 1932–33 when he directed and starred in Gordon Daviot's play about Richard II, *Richard of Bordeaux*. From this time on he was acknowledged to be both a major actor and the finest director of the new school. More than anyone else, Gielgud made Barker's principles acceptable to the English public, and with his work the English commercial theatre at last began to catch up with practices that had been common in most European countries since the beginning of World War I.

Gielgud's acceptance was probably aided by his belief in the integrity of the text. Unlike Guthrie, who sometimes imposed interpretations on plays, Gielgud sought only to bring out inherent meanings. In mounting productions, he favored simplified settings which captured the appropriate mood and atmosphere through line, color, and composition rather than through detailed historical reconstruction. Overall, Gielgud's visual style was a simplified realism, while his acting and directing stressed inner psychological motivations and stylistic appropriateness. He seems to have synthesized what he had learned from various directors, among them Komissarzhevsky, Playfair, and Williams. Although his approach differed markedly from that of earlier directors in the English commercial theatre, it won favor with West End audiences. Consequently, in the 1930s Gielgud was probably the most influential of all English directors.

Gielgud's successes in the 1930s were numerous. In 1934 he directed and starred in *Hamlet,* the most honored production of the decade. Like most of Gielgud's work, it was designed by Motley—a firm composed of Sophia Harris (1901–66), Margaret F. Harris (1904–   ), and Elizabeth Montgomery (1902–   )—who also played a significant role in altering

Gielgud's production of *Hamlet* at the New Theater in 1934. *Setting* by Motley. (Courtesy Mander and Mitchenson Theatre Collection.)

public taste. The setting was a semipermanent arrangement of steps and platforms which could be revolved and the appearance of which was altered with curtains, a few set pieces, and lighting. The costumes, inspired by Cranach, were made of canvas trimmed with silk and velvet and sprayed with paint. In 1935, Gielgud directed *Romeo and Juliet,* in which he alternated the roles of Romeo and Mercutio with Laurence Olivier and in which Edith Evans played the Nurse and Peggy Ashcroft played Juliet. In 1936, he starred in *The Sea Gull,* which, as designed and directed by Komissarzhevsky, was one of the finest productions of Chekhov's works ever seen in the West End.

Gielgud's prewar work reached its climax in a season of plays presented at the Queen's Theatre in 1937–38. It included *Richard II,* directed by Gielgud; *The School for Scandal,* directed by Guthrie; *The Three Sisters,* directed by Michel Saint-Denis, and *The Merchant of Venice,* directed by Gielgud and Glen Byam Shaw. All were designed by Motley, and the company included Peggy Ashcroft, Alec Guinness, Michael Redgrave, Anthony Quayle, Harcourt Williams, Glen Byam Shaw, and Athene Seyler. In quality and artistry, this season has seldom been surpassed in the English theatre. It set a standard for the whole era.

In 1936, Michel Saint-Denis (whose early career has already been discussed in a preceding chapter) at the urging of Guthrie and others opened the London Theatre Studio as a training school for actors. In addition, he directed at the Old Vic as well as for Gielgud. Consequently, in the period after 1936 there was an alliance among Guthrie, Gielgud, and Saint-Denis and around them gathered a whole new school of actors, including Edith Evans, Flora Robson, Peggy Ashcroft, Laurence Olivier, Maurice Evans, Michael Redgrave, Alec Guinness, Ralph Richardson, Anthony Quayle, and others.

Many outstanding performers, of course, were not associated with Gielgud and Guthrie in these years, among them Sybil Thorndike, Lewis Casson, Cedric Hardicke, and Donald Wolfit. Nevertheless, there were no marked schools of acting. The younger actors allied with Gielgud and Guthrie tended to be more concerned with inner psychology than were older performers, and, as in every period, some actors were more flamboyant and some more restrained than others. But for the most part English actors were devoted to a common ideal: convincing, lifelike impersonation. Consequently, they might differ about the approach to be used or the relative value of various techniques, but they argued little over goals.

The new atmosphere in the West End also owed much to the Westminster Theatre, opened in 1931 by Anmer Hall with Bridie's *The Anatomist* (Guthrie's first production in London). After Guthrie left, the principal director was Michael Macowan (1906–   ), whose productions included Pirandello's *Six Characters in Search of an Author,* O'Neill's *Mourning Becomes Electra,* and Barker's *Waste.* In 1938, Hall leased the Westminster to the London Mask Theatre, headed by J. B. Priestley and

Olivier as Romeo, Edith Evans as the Nurse, and Gielgud as Mercutio in *Romeo and Juliet* at the New Theatre in 1935. (Courtesy Debenham Collection, British Theatre Museum, London.)

Ronald Jeans. Macowan remained the principal director for the company, however, and for it staged such works as O'Neill's *Marco Millions* and *Desire Under the Elms,* Shaw's *Major Barbara,* Shakespeare's *Troilus and Cressida,* and several of Priestley's plays. One of London's most artistically successful theatres during the 1930s, the Westminster reenforced the approach followed by Gielgud.

Other theatres of note during this decade were the Mercury, the Gate, and the Open Air Theatre in Regent's Park. The Mercury Theatre was opened in 1933 by Ashley Dukes (1885–1959), husband of Marie Rambert, whose Ballet Club shared the theatre. Dukes, himself a playwright, was especially concerned with poetic drama, and it was at the Mercury that Eliot's *Murder in the Cathedral* was first seen in London. E. Martin Browne (1900–), who directed Eliot's work, was closely associated with the revival of religious as well as poetic drama. He would eventually take over the Mercury and play a significant role in the postwar development of poetic plays.

In 1934, Norman Marshall (1901–) assumed control of the Gate Theatre when Peter Godfrey left. He continued Godfrey's policy of offering unusual foreign and domestic plays, many of them—such as Lillian Hellman's *The Children's Hour,* Laurence Housman's *Victoria Regina,* and a play about Oscar Wilde—denied licenses for public performance. He also

459

460

*Theatre and
Drama in
The British
Isles
Between
the Wars*

raised such actors as Robert Morley and Vincent Price to stardom. But his major contribution was the revival of intimate musical revue. This form had been very popular during and immediately after World War I, especially as produced by C. B. Cochran (1873–1951) and André Charlot (1882–1956), but during the 1920s revues had become increasingly elaborate and lavish. For a time, the revue was perhaps the most vital theatrical form in England, but with the coming of the depression it virtually disappeared. It was the earlier, intimate revue that Marshall revived with sophisticated and satirical sketches written primarily by Herbert Farjeon and performed by Hermione Gingold and others. After some were moved successfully to West End theatres, a considerable revival of interest in the form followed. Under Marshall, the Gate did not serve as important a function as under Godfrey, but it still contributed much.

The Open Air Theatre in Regent's Park was begun in 1933 by Robert Atkins and Sidney Carroll. Since then each summer it has offered a program composed mostly of Shakespearean plays performed in a natural setting. Only essential properties are used to alter the permanent structure which incorporates (though it does not reproduce) the features of an Elizabethan public stage. As at the Old Vic, Atkins followed Poel's principles and gave clear, unpretentious, and straightforward renderings of the plays. It has always catered to schools, which supply a large proportion of the audience.

Thus, though the London theatre improved in the 1930s, it remained unimpressive in comparison with that of many other European capitals. It was clearly a conservative institution to which change came slowly. It was almost wholly devoid of the extreme experiments so common in Germany, France, and Russia between the wars.

III

This picture was brightened somewhat by organizations outside of London. But, as in the capital, the majority of professional productions catered to a mass audience. In 1919, there were 255 touring companies, most of them performing recent London successes or trying out plays for the West End. A few, however, were entirely provincial, and remained in the same town from six weeks to six months presenting a sizable repertory. Nevertheless, practically all the troupes took their standards from the commercial theatre of London.

In addition to the touring companies, there were a few resident troupes, some of which made outstanding contributions to the interwar theatre. Of these, the most important was the Birmingham Repertory

Theatre, founded by Barry Jackson (1879–1961) in 1913. Heir to a fortune and trained as an architect, Jackson's interest in the theatre was whetted by his participation in the Pilgrim Players, a group of amateurs who after 1907 met in Jackson's home. He soon became convinced of the need for a fully professional organization and in 1913 built a modern theatre with plaster skydome, advanced lighting system, apron stage, and a steeply raked auditorium which offered a good view from each of its 500 seats. Here between 1913 and 1935 Jackson produced approximately four hundred plays and operas. His taste was eclectic and his repertory extremely varied. With him, the play was the dominant element, and he sought to let each script dictate his approach to it. He valued good acting and had a flair for recognizing talent in the young. Those who passed through his company included Laurence Olivier, Ralph Richardson, John Gielgud, Felix Aylmer, Melville Cooper, Gwen Ffrangcon-Davies, and Cedric Hardwicke. His settings and costumes, most of them by Paul Shelving, were among the best to be seen in England.

Despite the high level of his work, Jackson received such little support that in 1924 he announced his intention of closing the theatre. Birmingham now seemed to feel that its reputation was at stake and the Civic Society guaranteed him sufficient subscribers to keep the theatre open. During the next ten years Jackson provided perhaps the finest repertory in England (for example, his was the first theatre in England to present Shaw's *Back to Methuselah*). But in 1934 the theatre was in trouble once more and Jackson refused to continue as sole financial backer of the company, for by

Birmingham Repertory production of Shaw's *Back to Methuselah* in 1924. (From *Le Théâtre,* 1924.)

462

*Theatre and
Drama in
The British
Isles
Between
the Wars*

this time he had lost 100,000 pounds. Consequently, in 1935 when he gave the building to the city of Birmingham, it became the first civic theatre in England. Jackson continued as the company's director, but with civic control came many curbs and a loss of adventurousness. The Birmingham Repertory Theatre's importance in England's theatrical life declined thereafter.

Jackson did not confine his activities to Birmingham. Between 1922 and 1934 he produced forty-two plays in London, many transferred from his Birmingham theatre. He soon gained a reputation in London for winning success with plays that commercial producers avoided, among them Pirandello's *Six Characters in Search of an Author*, Ibsen's *Rosmersholm*, Rice's *The Adding Machine*, Rudolf Besier's *The Barretts of Wimpole Street* (which had been refused by others on the grounds that the public would not go to see a play about literary figures), and Shaw's *The Apple Cart* and *Back to Methuselah* (which took five evenings to perform). Perhaps his most influential productions were modern-dress stagings of Shakespeare's *Cymbeline* (1922), *Hamlet* (1925), *Macbeth* (1928), and *The Taming of the Shrew* (1928), for they inaugurated a whole new trend. Thus, Jackson played an important role in London's theatrical life.

Jackson also founded the Malvern Festival. Its first season (1929), two weeks in length, was devoted entirely to works by Shaw: *Heartbreak House*, *Caesar and Cleopatra*, *Back to Methuselah*, and the world premiere

Modern dress production of Shakespeare's *Macbeth*
at the Birmingham Repertory Theatre in 1928.
Laurence Olivier is at far right.
(Courtesy Mander and Mitchenson Theatre Collection.)

of *The Apple Cart*. In 1930, once more all the works were by Shaw except for the premiere of *The Barretts of Wimpole Street*. The seasons of 1931–33, three weeks in length, were devoted to a survey of five hundred years of English drama, ranging from medieval plays to original works; each production was preceded by a lecture given by an eminent critic. Beginning in 1934 the seasons were four weeks in length but lacked coherence. Shaw always figured prominently in the programs (by 1939, twenty of his plays had been given, seven of them for the first time), but other works seem to have been chosen at random. Until 1937, when Jackson withdrew from the festival, the company was drawn from the Birmingham Repertory Theatre, as were many of the plays. After 1937 the festival was under the management of Roy Limbert and Cedric Hardwicke until closed by the war. By then the Malvern Festival had become one of the most popular annual events in England and its success did much to promote the idea of summer festivals, which were to flourish after the war.

Between the wars, few men played a larger role in English theatrical life than did Jackson. Next to Barker, he did more than any other producer to promote Shaw's plays, and his manifold activities extended into every aspect of the theatre. Nevertheless, because he was rich and chose plays to suit his own tastes, he was always considered an eccentric amateur by London's commercial managers.

The festival at Malvern was not England's first, for at Stratford-on-

Production by Bridges-Adams of *A Midsummer Night's Dream* in 1926. This was performed in a motion picture house while the Stratford theatre, destroyed by fire, was being planned and rebuilt. (From the Royal Shakespeare Theatre, Stratford-on-Avon.)

464

*Theatre and
Drama in
The British
Isles
Between
the Wars*

Avon one had been in operation since 1879, and between the wars it continued to be prominent. World War I marked a distinct break in the festival's history, for not only was it interrupted for two years but it brought an end to Frank Benson's domination (he had staged every festival except three since the 1880s). When productions were resumed in 1919, they were placed under the direction of W. Bridges-Adams (1889–1965), who worked under some of the most trying conditions imaginable. Benson had always performed plays already in his repertory and with his own company, but Bridges-Adams had to employ a new company each season and was permitted to engage it only a few weeks prior to the beginning of the festival. Furthermore, he was required to open six plays on six successive evenings, and consequently often had no more than four to six rehearsals for each play. Sometimes as much as a week elapsed between a dress rehearsal and opening night. Thus, it is not surprising that few established actors would risk their reputations by working at Stratford. Bridges-Adams was forced to depend on beginners or old-timers who insisted on following established traditions.

Furthermore, Bridges-Adams designed most of the settings and costumes. Faced with such a difficult problem, he adopted much the same solution as that used by Fraser at the Lyric Theatre: architectural units behind which or within which smaller pieces could be changed quickly. With his simplified settings, he achieved a rapid pace and visual unity.

In 1926 the Stratford theatre, an inadequate Gothic structure erected in 1879, was destroyed by fire. Bernard Shaw cabled the festival governors: "Congratulations. You must be delighted." A motion picture house then served as the festival's home from 1926 to 1931. Meanwhile, a drive for funds and a competition for architectural plans were launched. The governors specified that the auditorium should seat 1,000 persons, and that the stage should be 50 feet deep, unraked, and adequate for the presentation of plays in any style. The competition was won by Elizabeth Scott and the new building was opened in 1932.

Many of the structure's features were praised, but the stage was very unsatisfactory. A conventional proscenium arch and a large orchestra pit created a wide gulf between performers and spectators. Furthermore, attempts to include the newest in stage machinery were disappointing. The lifts could only sink 8 feet, making it impossible to lower anything except small units out of sight, and when the upstage lift was raised more than 3 feet above stage level the actors could no longer be seen from the balcony. Wing space was so restricted that the sliding stages could be moved out of sight only by hinging them so that one section ran up the stage wall (and thus became unusable for scenic units). In addition, there was no green room or rehearsal space, and the dressing rooms were inadequate for so large a company. There were other problems too numerous to catalogue. As a result, the theatre has been remodeled several times, most recently in 1971–1972.

465

*Theatre and
Drama in
The British
Isles
Between
the Wars*

The prospectus used to raise funds spoke of plans for a permanent company, and consequently Bridges-Adams assumed that with the opening of the new theatre many irksome policies would be altered. Unfortunately, the governors merely lengthened the season and added still more plays, thus increasing rather than easing the difficulties. Therefore, in 1934 Bridges-Adams resigned. Many critics of later years have disparaged Bridges-Adams's work at Stratford, but it is difficult to see how any one could have done better under the circumstances.

From 1935 until 1942, the festival was under the direction of B. Iden Payne (1881–   ), whose most characteristic productions followed the scheme popularized by Poel: an acting area simulating that of the Elizabethan public theatre (a deep forestage, backed by a curtained inner stage and balcony); costumed page boys to draw curtains and move the furniture and properties; and actors dressed in Elizabethan garments. Like Poel, Payne also placed primary emphasis upon clear and rapid speech and action. Although Payne often departed from this approach, it was used sufficiently often that critics soon began to complain of monotony.

Fortunately, when the new theatre opened in 1932, Bridges-Adams had been able to win one victory: he was permitted to employ additional directors, and after this time there was always one or more guest directors each season. Between 1932 and 1942 they included Robert Atkins, Tyrone Guthrie, Baliol Holloway, E. Martin Browne, John Wyse, H. K. Ayliff, Randle Ayrton, Donald Wolfit, Andrew Leigh, and Theodore Komissarzhevsky. Of these, Komissarzhevsky created the greatest controversy, for even before Guthrie won a reputation for eccentric interpretations, Komissarzhevsky was outraging traditionalists and delighting the avant-garde with novelties. His most controversial production was of *Macbeth* (1934), from which he completely eliminated the supernatural element. His setting, an arrangement of aluminum steps and platforms and entangled wire, gave the impression of a modern battlefield or of a modernistic building (depending upon the lighting). He treated the witches as battlefield scavengers who, when accosted by Macbeth, pose as fortune-tellers. Later scenes in which they appear were staged as Macbeth's nightmares. Thus, the prophecies merely supported Macbeth's unconscious wishes, which then rose to the surface in deeds. His *Merry Wives of Windsor* (1935) was almost as controversial, for he departed completely from earlier tradition (the play had always been staged as clearly Elizabethan and as farcical) by transforming it into something like a Viennese operetta—a lively, witty, sparkling comedy, with most of the action set to music and some of it passing over into dance. The setting was a colorful arrangement of small gingerbread houses, which remained unchanged until the final scene in Windsor Forest when it was transformed merely by removing a few elements. Though hated by purists, it was one of the most popular productions of the 1930s. Komissarzhevsky's *The Merchant of Venice* was enclosed within the framework of a Venetian carnival and the whole given a *commedia dell' arte* flavor. It

466

*Theatre and
Drama in
The British
Isles
Between
the Wars*

was the first new interpretation of the play since Irving had turned it into a vehicle for a sympathetic Shylock. Komissarzhevsky restored the comic balance and lifted the whole play to the level of romance. Many critics found it a very satisfactory reconciliation of the play's diverse elements (the intrigue centering around Shylock, the low comedy of Launcelot Gobbo, and the romantic aura of Portia's Belmont), but it too was heartily disliked by those who admired Irving's approach. Of all his productions, *King Lear* was undoubtedly the best and least controversial and it was almost universally admired. But on the whole, Komissarzhevsky's work at Stratford was little appreciated because it was so much in advance of its time. After the war, his approach would be considered appropriate rather than eccentric. He was one of the true pioneers of modern Shakespearean production in England.

Unfortunately, no major changes were made in the festival's organization until after the war, and consequently its potential was not fully realized. No director, however good, could be completely effective while restricted to fewer than six rehearsals for works so complex as Shakespeare's.

Two other provincial groups—at Oxford and Cambridge—were significant in the 1920s. The Oxford Playhouse, headed by J. B. Fagan (1873–1933) from 1923 to 1929, was located in a building that had once

Komissarzhevsky's production of Shakespeare's *Comedy of Errors* at Stratford in 1939. (From the Royal Shakespeare Theatre, Stratford-on-Avon.)

467

*Theatre and
Drama in
The British
Isles
Between
the Wars*

housed a museum of natural history. Its inadequate soundproofing, its tin roof, its lack of a foyer, and its wooden seats made the auditorium very uncomfortable. The stage was no better, for most of the space was taken up with a wide and deep apron backed by a small area behind the proscenium. Since Fagan used realistic scenery, the area behind the curtain served as a beginning point for most scenes, which then spilled onto the apron until near the end when actors were maneuvered upstage so the curtain could close.

Fagan's seasons followed the terms at Oxford. Thus, each was divided into three parts during which seven plays were presented, one each week to make a total of twenty-one plays during the school year. The repertory—which included works by Goldoni, Ibsen, Synge, Musset, Maugham, Sheridan, Shaw, Chekhov, Congreve, Strindberg, and others—was chosen with the student audience in mind. Lack of rehearsal time meant that performances were seldom polished, but the mood and dramatic thread were always clear and the acting spirited. The company came to be known for the excellent training it gave young actors—among them Guthrie, Gielgud, Flora Robson, Raymond Massey, Glen Byam Shaw, Robert Morley, and Alan Napier. Despite its poor facilities and adverse working conditions, for overall excellence it was probably second only to the Birmingham Repertory company among the provincial troupes.

The Cambridge Festival Theatre, operated by Terence Gray (1895–) from 1926 to 1933, was the most determinedly antirealistic company in England. Independently wealthy and trained as an Egyptologist, Gray early became interested in the theatre but found English practices very unsatisfactory in comparison with those he saw during his frequent visits to the Continent. Thus, he decided to open a theatre that would provide an alternative to the realistic mode then dominant in England. He acquired the Theatre Royal Barnwell near Cambridge and converted this regency structure into a theatre unlike any then to be seen in England. He removed the proscenium arch and linked the auditorium and stage with a broad flight of steps running the full width of the house. Several entrances for actors were provided forward of the old proscenium. On the stage he erected a 40-foot high plaster skydome, installed a turntable 15 feet in diameter and (upstage of it) a rolling platform that when moved opened up the basement for shifting furniture or properties or for entrances from below. The theatre also probably had the best lighting system in England, designed by Harold Ridge, Gray's partner during the first season and later one of England's major authorities on stage lighting. The auditorium was extremely comfortable and there was even a restaurant of the highest quality. In its decor and accommodations it was the most tasteful and elegant theatre in England.

Gray's repertory and audience differed little from Fagan's. The plays represented every period from ancient Greece to the present. The audience was drawn primarily from the university and the season followed the

468

*Theatre and
Drama in
The British
Isles
Between
the Wars*

Cambridge terms. Each year Gray presented twenty-four plays, eight each term. Of these, he directed approximately one-half, while the others were staged by two assistant directors. But here the similarities with the Oxford Playhouse ended. Gray's was a director's theatre dedicated to the destruction of realism. He declared that the audience is weary of "the old game of illusion, glamour, and all the rest of the nineteenth century hocus pocus and bamboozle. . . . We are the theatre theatrical. . . . We think the stage should be a raised platform . . . the levels and angles of which fulfill a function of emphasizing the dramatic relations. Beyond this platform all that is called for is a background against which the actors can be seen." This summarizes well Gray's approach, for practically every production was staged on an arrangement of steps and levels which could be turned or altered through lighting (though never for the sake of illusion). His settings were solid and decorative versions of Meyerhold's "machines for acting." He permitted very few properties, and made the actors pantomime stage business involving objects. This worked well in some plays, but in such works as Ibsen's *The Wild Duck,* with its domestic atmosphere, it could result in considerable confusion. Many entrances and exits were made through the auditorium and sometimes scenes were played there. Lighting was used imaginatively to assist emotional climaxes, to isolate figures in space, or to sculpture them three-dimensionally or reduce them to two-dimensionality.

Gray's productions of Greek tragedy were considered outstanding, but his interpretations of other plays were often unorthodox. Sometimes he sought to draw modern parallels, as in *As You Like It,* in which he dressed Rosalind as a boy scout and Celia as a girl scout when they went into the forest, or in *Twelfth Night,* in which he placed Sir Toby Belch and Sir Andrew Aguecheek on roller skates. At other times, he used staging to express his own feelings about scenes. For example, he found the trial scene in *The Merchant of Venice* boring and consequently directed all the actors to lapse into complete apathy and the judge to play with a yo-yo during Portia's oration. Some imaginative business (such as performing the wrestling scene in *As You Like It* in slow motion) was at the time considered unintelligible. One of his best productions was of Shakespeare's *Henry VIII,* which Gray viewed as transparent flattery of the English monarchy. Consequently, he dressed most of the characters as playing card figures, and raised Cardinal Wolsey on *cothurnoi* to indicate his dominant role. In one scene the cardinal moved listlessly back and forth in a swing as he delivered malicious speeches. In the final scene, in which the future Queen Elizabeth is christened, he used a doll dressed to recall the portrait of the grown-up queen; as the action progressed the stage began to revolve and everything became more and more frantic until at last the doll was flung into the auditorium among the spectators. Such touches delighted the Cambridge students but outraged conservative theatregoers.

In some respects, Gray's productions recall those of Meyerhold, and certainly he was the English director most attuned to Continental developments. But because he was a provincial and wealthy producer, he was

Terence Gray's production of Shakespeare's *Henry VIII*
at the Festival Theatre, Cambridge, in 1931.
(From Mousinnac, *New Movement in the Theatre.*)

seldom taken seriously and most often was considered a mere prankster.
Consequently, his immediate influence was slight. The incomprehension
with which he was greeted seems in turn to have made him cease listening
to all criticism and thus his productions deteriorated. Even more than
Komissarzhevsky, Gray seems to have been out of step with the mainstream.
Thus, it is now difficult to judge his work because so few persons of that
time wrote of it with understanding. Discouraged and disgusted, Gray gave
up his theatre in 1933 to make wine in France and to breed racehorses in
Ireland.

The repertory companies of Jackson, Fagan, and Gray were merely the
best of many. By 1938 there were seventy-five troupes outside of London,
although several played only during the summer months. Since most
presented a different production each week, many actors tended to depend
on surface polish, so much so that in London it was often said that an actor
who remained too long in a provincial troupe was ruined for life. One
marked exception to the typical practices was the Liverpool Repertory
Theatre, which under William Armstrong (1882–1952) from 1922 to
1940 maintained the highest of standards. Unadventurous in repertory or
staging techniques, it provided excellent experience for such actors as
Robert Donat, Rex Harrison, Diana Wynyard, Michael Redgrave, Robert
Speaight, and Robert Flemyng.

The British theatre was also given additional variety by amateur
groups. Some of these organizations could trace their origins back to the

470

*Theatre and
Drama in
The British
Isles
Between
the Wars*

nineteenth century, but most came into existence in the wake of the people's theatre movement at the beginning of the twentieth century. After World War I, the amateur theatre mushroomed, and by 1939 there were an estimated thirty thousand groups playing to approximately 5 million persons each year. In 1919, Geoffrey Whitworth (1883–1951) founded the British Drama League to assist these organizations. The League held annual conferences, organized workshops to train directors, maintained a library and information service, sent out props and costumes, aided in play selection and criticized original scripts, published *Drama,* and each year held a competitive Community Theatre Festival.

Most of these groups were of poor quality and most merely presented the latest hits from the London theatre. A few, however, were outstanding. The Leeds Civic Playhouse, inaugurated in 1925 by Charles F. Smith, had developed into a fully professional company by 1933. The most famous of the amateur groups, however, was the Maddermarket Theatre in Norwich, founded by Nugent Monck (1877–1958), who had been a stage manager at the Abbey Theatre and for Poel. In 1921, Monck built a replica of the Fortune Theatre inside an old building in Norwich's market area. Seating 250 persons, the Maddermarket Theatre offered one play each month, most of them by Shakespeare. Using amateurs entirely, Monck was soon known throughout England. Many critics considered his productions superior to most then being offered by professional companies.

It is to an offshoot of the amateur movement that one must turn to find the only attempt in this period to present politically conscious productions. This aim originated with the Rebel Players, who sought to counteract "the escapism and false ideology of the conventional theatre." In 1936 the group was reconstituted as the Unity Theatre, which with volunteer labor erected its own building in London. Calling itself "a people's theatre," Unity set out to "help in the vitally urgent struggle for world peace, and a better social and economic order, by establishing a drama which deals with realities, and reflects contemporary life, instead of plays which merely provide a dream world of escape." It presented works by O'Casey, Odets, Lope de Vega, Pogodin, and Afinogenov, and sought to encourage working-class dramatists by staging a number of plays about local problems written by local writers. It also converted the traditional Christmas pantomime into satirical social satire, and in 1937 adopted the "living newspaper" as a means of dramatizing a strike of busmen then underway. The plays were acted by amateurs under the direction of professionals.

Unity, with headquarters in London, set out to create similar groups throughout Britain. A Unity Theatre Society provided the same kinds of services as did the British Drama League. Ultimately it hoped to establish fully professional companies, but this goal would not be reached until after the war and then only for a brief time.

Thus, the provincial and amateur groups added considerably to the scope of the English theatre. But, except for the Cambridge Festival Theatre, here too there was little attempt to move outside traditional paths.

Today English drama of the interwar years does not seem particularly distinguished, although at the time it appeared impressive, perhaps more because of its civilized tone, wit, or skill than for truly lasting values. Much of the finest work was done by older dramatists who continued to write during and after the war. Shaw contributed such outstanding works as *Heartbreak House* (1919), *Back to Methuselah* (1919–20), and *Saint Joan* (1923) before writing a series of minor works, *The Apple Cart* (1929), *Too True to be Good* (1932), *On the Rocks* (1933), *The Simpleton of the Unexpected Isles* (1934), *The Millionairess* (1935), *Geneva* (1938), and *In Good King Charles' Golden Days* (1939). Barrie wrote *Dear Brutus* (1917), *Mary Rose* (1920), and *The Boy David* (1936), and Galsworthy *Loyalties* (1922), *Escape* (1926), and *Exiled* (1929). But these writers added little to their reputations with such post-World War I work, although their plays, both old and new, gave increased distinction to theatrical repertories of the time.

Perhaps the most characteristic form of the 1920s was a wordly-wise, satirical comedy, though by present-day standards it no longer seems so cynical as it once did. The most representative playwright of the type is Noel Coward (1899–   ), who after being on the stage as an actor since 1911 turned to dramatic and musical composition after the war. Although Coward is now remembered as a writer of comedy, it was with a serious play, *Vortex* (1924), that he first won fame. Treating a mother who loses her young lover to the fiancée of her son, a neurotic drug addict, the play was especially noted for its scene of confrontation between mother and son, during which, after mutual recriminations, they are reconciled. Today the ending seems overly simplistic, but in the 1920s it was considered sensational, and the entire play was viewed as an exposé of the decadent "smart set." As played by Lilian Braithwaite and Coward, it was a great popular success and began the vogue for Coward's work, which reached its peak in 1925 when five of his works—among them *Fallen Angels* (1925), *Hay Fever* (1925), and a musical revue, *On With the Dance* (1925)—were playing in West End theatres simultaneously.

Coward is probably at his best in *Private Lives* (1930), in which a divorced couple meet accidentally while on honeymoon with new mates and discover that they are still in love. It is a well-constructed, sophisticated, and witty comedy, although it seldom probes beneath the surface. *Design for Living* (1933) was somewhat more daring, for it treated a love triangle among a woman and two men, who are also involved with each other. It was such plays that won Coward the reputation of being a spokesman for the new generation of disillusioned men and unshockable women.

Coward's versatility is indicated by his musical plays, such as *This Year of Grace* (1928) and *Bittersweet* (1929); his sentimental and patriotic

Original production of Coward's *Private Lives* at the Phoenix Theatre in 1930. Left to right are Adrienne Allen as Sybil, Coward as Eliot, Gertrude Lawrence as Amanda, and Laurence Olivier as Victor. (Courtesy Mander and Mitchenson Theatre Collection.)

pieces, such as *Cavalcade* (1931) and *Peace in Our Time* (1947); and his one-act pieces which make up *Tonight at 8:30* (1935). Of his later works, the most popular was *Blithe Spirit* (1941), in which a medium creates havoc in a married man's life by calling up the spirit of his former wife. Since setting a new record for long runs in London, it has remained a perennial favorite.

After World War II, Coward's reputation declined rapidly and then rose once more. His plays cannot be considered profound, but several remain entertaining because of their surface polish and witty dialogue, which some critics have called the finest since Wilde.

The post-World War I comedy of manners is seen at its best in the plays of Somerset Maugham (1874–1965). After turning to drama around 1904, Maugham at first devoted himself primarily to light comedy deliberately designed to attract a wide audience, a goal in which he was so successful that in 1908 he had four plays running simultaneously in London. But it is for his later work—especially *Our Betters* (1917), *The Circle* (1921), *The Constant Wife* (1927), and *The Breadwinner* (1930)—that he is now remembered. *Our Betters* has sometimes been compared to the comedies of Wycherley, which like it are concerned with the sexual and social mores of the aristocracy. In Maugham's play, Lady Grayston rather casually pursues several affairs and even permits one lover to pay many of her bills. Her husband is quite content so long as a façade of respectability is maintained, but Lady Grayston grows careless and he is forced to confront the truth. In the climactic scene, all the flimsy social relationships seem about to collapse, when a way is found to preserve appearances. It is this ending which gives the play its ironic title.

The Circle is usually considered Maugham's masterpiece. The title refers to the recurrence of behavioral patterns in successive generations.

472

Maugham's *The Circle* at the Haymarket Theatre, London, in 1921.
Left to right are Holman Clark, Lottie Venne, and Allan Aynesworth.
(Courtesy Enthoven Collection, Victoria and Albert Museum.)

Thirty years before the play opens, Mrs. Champion-Cheney has deserted her
husband and small son to run away with Lord Porteus. Now back in
England for the first time, they are invited to the home of Mrs. Champion-
Cheney's son, whose wife is considering running away with another man.
The young wife is so disturbed by the unconscious vulgarity of the older
couple that she almost changes her mind, despite her husband's insensitivity
and her own lack of affection for him. She capitulates, however, when the
young man declares: "I don't offer you happiness; I offer you love." The
action is developed with such clarity and wit that it has often been compared with the comedies of Congreve, Sheridan, and Wilde.

Maugham was one of the finest craftsmen of the modern period. His
plays are soundly but unobtrusively constructed and demonstrate his keen
observation of manners and morals. Maugham was often accused of
cynicism, and after 1933 he gave up dramatic writing in disgust at the
public response to his plays. His reputation as a dramatist has declined
considerably. Nevertheless, his plays have greater depth than do Coward's,
whose works are kept alive primarily by sparkling and brittle wit.

The plays of Frederick Lonsdale (1881–1954) are often compared to
those of Maugham. Like the older dramatist, Lonsdale had written many
plays before the war but made his reputation with those produced during
the 1920s: *Spring Cleaning* (1923), *The Last of Mrs. Cheyney* (1925),
The High Road (1927), and *On Approval* (1927). Of these, *The Last of
Mrs. Cheyney* is the best known. It tells of a shop girl who is persuaded by
a gentleman crook that she is meant for a better life. He then involves her in
his scheme to rob a rich woman, in whose home he takes a job as butler.

474

*Theatre and
Drama in
The British
Isles
Between
the Wars*

When she is sent to the woman's room to steal a necklace, she finds it occupied by a man, Lord Dilling; after their lengthy and comic encounter, she gives up her life of crime to marry the nobleman. Lonsdale lacked Maugham's sense of dramatic structure, but had a flair for near-Wildean epigrammatic dialogue. It was his witty observations on manners that won Lonsdale his following in England, where his plays are still seen occasionally.

England produced a multitude of lesser writers. Among the authors of sentimental comedy, perhaps the most successful was A. A. Milne (1882–1956), now remembered more for his children's stories about Winnie-the-Pooh than for his plays. But between the wars his *Mr. Pim Passes By* (1919), *The Truth About Blayds* (1921), and *The Dover Road* (1922) were mainstays of the English repertory. Milne was Barrie's true successor, for like the older dramatist's his plays mingle sentiment, whimsy, and humor. For example, *The Dover Road* shows how a kindhearted millionaire through a number of humorous devices helps runaway couples recognize that the road to Paris, which to them symbolizes escape, involves more problems than they had imagined. Most of his other plays as well reconcile characters to lives they consider unhappy.

Emlyn Williams (1905–   ), now perhaps better known as actor than playwright, was comparably successful with melodramatic thrillers and plays of sentiment. *A Murder Has Been Arranged* (1930) and *Night Must Fall* (1935) were among the most suspenseful dramas of the period. In the second of these, Dan, a hotel bellboy, kills a woman and carries her severed head about in a hatbox while planning a second murder. The play is raised above the ordinary, however, by Williams's treatment of Dan as motivated by his sense of being mistreated by life. Williams's sentimental vein is best seen in *The Corn is Green* (1938), in which a Welsh schoolteacher struggles to save her prize pupil from a life of drudgery in the mines. Milne and Williams were probably equaled in quality by a score of other writers—among them R. C. Sherriff, John van Druten, Sutton Vane, Clemence Dane, and Dodie Smith—but the list only shows that English drama seldom rose above competence.

Of the serious writers, the best were probably Priestley, Bridie, and Eliot. J. B. Priestley (1894–   ) began his career as a playwright in 1931 with an adaptation of one of his own novels. In the following year, *Dangerous Corner,* directed by Guthrie and acted by Flora Robson, established Priestley's reputation, and during the remainder of the decade he was considered England's most significant dramatist of ideas.

Priestley's most characteristic works are concerned with the relativity of time, first fully developed in *Time and the Conways* and *I Have Been Here Before,* both written in 1937. *Time and the Conways* begins shortly after World War I during a birthday party, then switches forward twenty years to show what has happened to the characters since, and then goes back to the original time to point up the great disparity between their ambitions and their accomplishments. *I Have Been Here Before* relies on the idea of reincarnation. It tells the story of Walter Ormund, a rich industrialist who is haunted by a sense of futility and an urge to commit suicide. Then he meets a German professor who seems to be aware of his past existences, all of which have repeated the same pattern. Gradually Ormund comes to believe that through an act of will he can break out of the old cycle into a new one, and when the play ends he has gained new confidence. In this work, Priestley demonstrated his superb skill in establishing probability by gradually building up the characters' sense of having participated in similar events at some previous time. Like its predecessor, it was cast in three acts and utilized traditional dramatic techniques. In 1939, however, Priestley adopted expressionistic devices in *Johnson Over Jordan* and *Music at Night,* both of which he called "four-dimensional dramas." Of these, the better is *Johnson Over Jordan,* whose title character, a businessman, is a contemporary Everyman, with whom Priestley wishes his audience to identify as he moves through bureaucratic nightmares, memories, and regrets of things done and left undone. The action takes place after Johnson has died and while his spirit still lingers between life and death, in "a prolonged dreamlike state, in what may be called the fourth dimension of space, filled with hallucinatory visions." Time and place shift rapidly as Johnson recalls various incidents from his life. It ends on a poignant note, for Johnson concludes as he walks off into the unknown, "The earth is nobler than the world we have built on it." West End playgoers found it all very puzzling. In the 1930s, when Einsteinian conceptions of time and space were still novel, Priestley's plays seemed very "intellectual." Today his ideas appear merely devices used to make the dramatic action function rather than serious attempts to deal with significant concepts. Consequently, the plays, though skillfully written, are not profound. Priestley also wrote a number of successful farces and light comedies, such as *Laburnum Grove* (1933) and *When We Are Married* (1938). Of his post-World War II plays, the best is *An Inspector Calls* (1945), in which a family, after it hears an announcement on the radio of an unknown girl's death, is visited by an inspector who gradually manages to involve each of them in her fate. After he leaves, they call the police station only to discover that officials have no knowledge whatsoever of the incident.

A playwright of a quite different sort was James Bridie (Osborne Henry Mavor, 1888–1951), a Glasgow physician who continued to practice medicine throughout his playwriting career. Bridie was gradually drawn into the theatre first as a playreader and then as a dramatist for the Scottish National Theatre. His first play was not produced until 1928 (when he was forty years old), and he did not achieve critical success until 1931 when *The Anatomist,* directed by Guthrie (who had also staged his first works in Scotland), opened the Westminster Theatre in London. Set in the nineteenth century, *The Anatomist* focuses on Professor Knox, who for his experiments purchases cadavers from two men later discovered to be murderers.

Once launched on his playwriting career, Bridie pursued it indefatigably, turning out thirty-four full-length plays in twenty years, in addition to a number of adaptations, one-act, and radio plays. His works range through the serious and the comic, the historical, modern, and biblical. They are filled with well-conceived and challenging roles; most of his characters are talkative, articulate creatures who unwittingly reveal much about themselves and their world. Almost all the plays begin with striking dramatic situations, but Bridie's principal fault, and the one that kept him from becoming a major writer, was his inability to develop the potential suggested by his opening scenes. Thus, his work is both remarkable and disappointing.

One of Bridie's most admired plays was *A Sleeping Clergyman* (1933), a study of heredity as seen in three successive generations. One character, Dr. Marshall, follows the characters' progress throughout and suggests that, though the worst characteristics may be passed on to the next generation, the best may also reappear later. The first generation is represented by a young but completely amoral medical genius who dies of tuberculosis and leaves behind an illegitimate daughter who seems to have inherited all of his worst traits. She eventually kills her lover, but her children (the third generation) rise above their environment. The boy, also a medical genius, is able to achieve what was denied his grandfather, while the girl becomes a noted social reformer.

In sharp contrast, *Tobias and the Angel* (1931) is a whimsical domestic comedy based on the Apocrypha. It tells how the timid Tobias, with the assistance of the disguised archangel Raphael, is able to pass several tests, including killing a monster fish and frightening away a bandit, before marrying the rich Sara. Bridie also drew on biblical material for *Jonah and the Whale* (1932) and *Susannah and the Elders* (1937).

Bridie's versatility is further seen in such plays as *The King of Nowhere* (1938), a comic exploration of insanity and fascism; *Mr. Bolfry* (1943), in which the Devil is conjured up in the guise of a Protestant minister; and *Daphne Laureola* (1949), a study of a complex, capricious elderly woman. In these, as in most of his works, Bridie combines strong dramatic situation with philosophical inquiry. With all his strong points, it is unfortunate that Bridie was not able to perfect his dramatic technique.

This period also saw many attempts to revive poetic drama, which since the romantic era (and earlier) had languished. In the twentieth century, Yeats had written outstanding lyric dramas, but these had failed to find a receptive audience in the theatre. In England, Stephen Phillips (1868–1915), Gordon Bottomley (1874–1948), Lascelles Abercrombie (1881–1938), John Masefield (1875–1968), and John Drinkwater (1882–1937) had sought to revive the poetic tradition but had met with little success.

Then, for a time in the 1930s it appeared that the tide had turned. Part of the upsurge was due to the Group Theatre, founded in 1932 by young actors in the company at the Westminster Theatre who wished in their spare time to produce poetic drama. Fortunately, they were able to induce several well-known poets to write for them. The results included *Out of the Picture* (1937) by Louis MacNeice (1907–63), a play about a young artist who eventually is killed by a girl he abandons, and *The Trial of a Judge* (1938) by Stephen Spender (1907–), a denunciation of Nazi ideology. But the major works written for the Group were those by W. H. Auden (1907–) and Christopher Isherwood (1904–): *The Dog Beneath the Skin* (1935), *The Ascent of F6* (1936), and *On the Frontier* (1938). By far the most successful of all these plays was *The Ascent of F6,* in which the British government sends out an expedition to scale and lay claim to a mountain, designated on maps merely as F6. The protagonist, Michael Ransom, heads the mission, even though he is deeply opposed to England's imperialism, for the mountain also represents a challenge to gain spiritual control over himself. Intermingled with this is another theme concerning Ransom's relation to his mother. After many trials, he at last meets his spiritual daemon on the mountain, only to discover that it is his own mother, on whom he has had a fixation throughout his life. There is also a chorus in the form of a suburban couple who follow by way of the radio the daily accounts of the mission's progress, but who also serve to satirize the press and the sentimentality of the middle class. Since the diverse elements were never completely integrated, the play remained somewhat unsatisfactory. Nevertheless, its considerable power elicited widespread acclaim in the three professional productions it received during the 1930s.

The most impressive achievement in poetic drama was that of T. S. Eliot (1888–1965). Born in America, Eliot settled in London in 1914 and became a British citizen in 1927. After 1920 he was considered a major

Production of Auden's and Isherwood's *The Ascent of F6* by the Old Vic in 1939. (Courtesy Mander and Mitchenson Theatre Collection.)

478

*Theatre and
Drama in
The British
Isles
Between
the Wars*

poet, but he wrote no complete play until 1934, when he expanded an outline supplied by E. Martin Browne for a religious pageant, *The Rock*. Following this, he was commissioned to write a play for the Canterbury Festival. The result was *Murder in the Cathedral,* first performed in the Chapter House at Canterbury in 1935 and subsequently produced in London to great critical acclaim. (All the productions were directed by Browne and starred Robert Speaight as Becket.) Eliot's protagonist is a man beset by tempters who though real also symbolize his own inner torment. The play is little concerned with Becket's past life but concentrates instead upon his moment of decision, caught between his duty to Church and State. Thus, the principal emphasis is upon Becket's spiritual growth, while the context is supplied almost entirely by a Chorus of Canterbury Women.

Becket's triumph over his tempters is all the greater because he is not by nature ascetic. But once he has put them behind him there remains an even greater temptation—to become a martyr. The play is separated into two parts by Becket's Christmas sermon, which also sums up the play's message: martyrs are made by God for the good of the people. Once Becket has chosen the Church, nothing remains except for him to be killed. Significantly, the Four Tempters now become the Four Knights, who after they murder Becket step forward to tempt the audience with their rationalizations: "We have been perfectly disinterested." These speeches were

E. Martin Browne's production of T. S. Eliot's *Murder in the Cathedral* with Robert Speaight as Beckett at the Mercury Theatre, London, in 1935. (Courtesy Debenham Collection, British Theatre Museum, London.)

deliberately given a familiar ring to provide a link between Becket's death and modern man.

Murder in the Cathedral remains Eliot's finest drama, in part because in it he gave his lyric gift scope. In his later work he seems to have been overly influenced by those who, attuned to realism, attacked his poetic diction. Consequently, thereafter Eliot steadily pared down his verse until it was virtually indistinguishable from prose. Since he was not an accomplished constructer of plots, Eliot had given up his greatest gift (for poetic diction) to depend on others he had not mastered.

In his next play, *The Family Reunion* (1939), Eliot sought to recast Greek myth (here the story of Orestes) in modern domestic terms. It was not a very successful attempt, and Eliot later admitted that the supernatural elements (the Eumenides' torturing of Harry for some mysterious sin) and the choral element (the same characters were sometimes treated as individuals and sometimes as a chorus) had not been properly integrated into the domestic atmosphere. Nevertheless, it was significant as the first of his several similar attempts, some of which would meet with considerable success after the war. (Eliot's postwar poetic drama will be discussed in a later chapter.)

Fortunately, the English-language dramatists of Ireland helped to alter the rather disappointing record of British playwrights of the interwar period. Like many other parts of Europe, Ireland became embroiled in civil conflict during World War I, when the desire for national independence, increasingly evident since the nineteenth century, burst into rebellion in 1916. Put down, the fighting broke out again in 1919 when Ireland declared itself free. In 1921, Great Britain offered Ireland dominion status within the empire and the Irish Free State came into being, although internal strife continued until 1923. These years of unrest seriously interrupted theatrical life, but, when peace came, activities were quickly resumed. The Abbey Theatre, now provided with a subsidy by the state, became Ireland's national theatre. But with support came pressure to respect conventional taste and morality.

Nevertheless, with O'Casey's plays the Abbey for a time regained some of its old vigor. Sean O'Casey (1880–1964), reared in the Dublin slums, was virtually illiterate until he was fourteen years old. He then read voluminously, especially the works of Shakespeare, and attended the Abbey Theatre whenever he could. Although he soon began to write dramas of his own, he was more than forty years old before his first play was produced.

480

*Theatre and
Drama in
The British
Isles
Between
the Wars*

But upon its appearance, it was evident that a major new talent had emerged. *The Shadow of a Gunman* (1923), set in the Dublin slums in the midst of civil war, centers around a braggart whose pose as a revolutionary leads to the death of a young girl. It is filled with masterful and sympathetic portraits of Dubliners caught up in the atmosphere of anxiety and violence.

The promise seen in this first offering was more than fulfilled in the one that followed, *Juno and the Paycock* (1924), considered by many to be O'Casey's masterpiece. Also set in Dublin during the civil strife, it focuses on the Boyle family. Captain Boyle, the "paycock" father, is a lazy braggart who spends his days carousing with his likeable, ne'er-do-well friend Joxer, while his wife, Juno, works to support the family. There are also two children. A son, Johnny, who skulks about the house anxiously, is eventually killed by men who accuse him of having betrayed a comrade, while a daughter, Mary (perhaps symbolizing Ireland itself), is seduced and betrayed by an Englishman. Other residents of the tenement figure less prominently in the action. All the characters are treated with sympathy, but it is Juno who emerges as the dominant figure—a heroic woman fighting against overwhelming odds but refusing to capitulate. At the end, the patient Juno at last takes decisive action by leaving Boyle so that she can make a decent life for her daughter and the unborn child. Despite the grimness of the surroundings and the pathos aroused by several characters, there is much humor and gusto. It is a moving depiction of human frailties and, even more so, of human courage and endurance.

The action of *The Plough and the Stars* (1926) occurs during the Easter Rebellion of 1916, and recalls that week of fighting as it affects the dwellers of one tenement, especially the gossipy Mrs. Gogan, the ne'er-do-well Fluther, and the unhappy Nora Clitheroe and her young husband. Although he treats all sympathetically, O'Casey glorifies none and shows up the destructiveness of all war. The opening-night audience considered the play an insult to Irish patriotism, and a riot resulted the like of which had not been seen since the premiere of Synge's *The Playboy of the Western World*.

With *The Plough and the Stars*, O'Casey's realistic period came to an end. In these early works, O'Casey is little interested in story. Rather, he emphasizes character, especially strongly contrasted individuals who are brought into close contact by living conditions. It is the social unit—the family, the inhabitants of a tenement—which is most important, for not only does it provide the immediate and human context, it serves as a microcosm of contemporary Irish attitudes. His men usually talk about (and sometimes die for) ideals, whereas his women cope with the realities of daily life. The conflicts that result from the juxtaposition of contrasting individuals, ideals, and priorities lead to humor and violence. The tone of the plays shifts often and abruptly. Overall, the works are more concerned with creating the texture of life than with telling clearly structured stories.

The Silver Tassie (1929) marked O'Casey's break with his earlier

O'Casey's *The Plough and the Stars,* produced by the Abbey Theatre in 1926. Sara Allgood is at left. (From *Theatre Arts,* 1928.)

style as well as with the Abbey Theatre, which refused the work. As a result of this rebuff, O'Casey moved to England and thereafter remained aloof from the Irish scene for many years. With *The Silver Tassie,* O'Casey began to move toward expressionism, although in this play the new approach was only partially adopted. In the opening act, Harry Heegan, a man of powerful physique, is acclaimed by his friends for winning the "silver tassie," a football trophy, on the eve of his entrance into the army. This realistic scene is followed by an expressionistic evocation of life in the trenches and the horrors of war. The final act returns once more to the realistic vein and to Heegan, now incapacitated forever by wounds received while fighting.

In *Within the Gates* (1934), O'Casey uses the expressionistic mode throughout. The action, set within the gates of Hyde Park, is an allegory centering around the Young Whore, the Bishop, and the Poet Dreamer. As the play progresses, it is discovered that the Young Whore is the illegitimate daughter of the Bishop, but, on the point of death, it is to the Poet she turns for consolation rather than to the Bishop. Few have found this denunciation of the Church an entirely successful work, but its powerful scenes and rich language have won high praise.

From this time on, O'Casey favored expressionistic techniques. Of

482

*Theatre and
Drama in
The British
Isles
Between
the Wars*

his later plays, probably the best were *Purple Dust* (1940), in which the English and Irish temperaments are contrasted and an Irish peasant bests an Englishman, and *Red Roses for Me* (1943), in which the young poet Ayamonn Breydon is killed in a Dublin strike, which shows both the misery and the courage of the unemployed. In the latter's third act, a Dublin street at night is turned into a symbol of Ireland's sense of romance and of its sleeping greatness. As in most of O'Casey's late plays, however, there is an uneasy mingling of naturalistic and symbolic elements, a juxtaposition which became even more capricious in *Cock-a-Doodle-Dandy* (1949) and *The Drums of Father Ned* (1956). In his later years, O'Casey devoted little time to drama and concentrated instead on the volumes that make up his excellent autobiography.

It is difficult to judge O'Casey's career. His early plays are clearly among the finest of the age, but the later works are somewhat disjointed. No doubt his divorce from a theatrical troupe and from Irish life had some effect on his dramatic writing after 1930. Still, no playwright of his time had a finer ear for language, a sharper sense of character, or greater human compassion. Overall, he was probably the best of all the interwar British dramatists.

With its rejection of O'Casey, the Abbey Theatre lost much of its vitality and settled into its comfortable role as national theatre. It continued to encourage Irish authors, but few outstanding playwrights appeared. Perhaps the best was Paul Vincent Carroll (1900–   ), who came to prominence in 1932 when *The Things That Are Caesar's* won the Abbey Theatre's prize for the best new play. Treating the struggle between a strict religious mother and a free-thinking father over their daughter's upbringing, *The Things That Are Caesar's,* like most of Carroll's work, is ultimately concerned with the relationship of religion to Irish daily life and the friction between conservative and liberal ideas. This concern is also evident in Carroll's best-known play, *Shadow and Substance* (1934), in which the narrow, reactionary attitude of Canon Skerritt come into conflict with the broad-minded idealism of the teacher O'Flingsley. Here the action centers around a simple country girl, Brigid, who sees visions, the authenticity of which becomes a source of controversy. The reactions of Skerritt and O'Flingsley illuminate their personal qualities and attitudes, while their feud eventually contributes to Brigid's death. Over her dead body they achieve humility if not reconciliation. It is a moving drama if the audience can accept the girl's visions as credible.

Similar themes are developed in Carroll's later works, *The White Steed* (1938), *The Strings My Lord Are False* (1942), *The Wise Have Not Spoken* (1944), and *The Wayward Saint* (1955). In all there is evident a disparity between the Church's ideal of love and the actuality, in which inefficiency, poverty, and narrow-mindedness transform the potential to love into hatred and destruction. In many instances, however, Carroll's plays are so rooted in the Irish milieu that they lose their effectiveness outside their native country.

The conservatism of the Abbey Theatre during the 1920s motivated Micheál MacLiammóir (1899–   ) and Hilton Edwards (1903–   ) to found the Dublin Gate Theatre in 1928. Unlike the Abbey, which continued to emphasize plays of Irish life, the Gate sought to include works from all periods and countries and to establish a standard of production comparable to that found on the Continent. In both goals it was very successful, and when it toured abroad during the 1930s won universal praise. Most of the credit belongs to MacLiammóir, who, after being a child actor in London, had studied art and had had his work exhibited widely in Europe, where his travels acquainted him with contemporary theatrical practices. His outstanding talents as designer, director, and actor resulted in a high artistic standard at the Gate, where he continued to work until 1956.

The Gate also developed its own school of playwrights distinct from those of the Abbey. Of these, the best was Denis Johnston (1901–   ), whose first play, *The Old Lady Says No!* (1929), was an expressionistic mingling of elements drawn from Irish life, thought, political history, and literature which satirized and exposed the sentimental attitudes underlying them. Although successful with the Gate's audiences, it depended so much on allusion and association that it is virtually indecipherable by anyone not Irish.

Johnston's best play, *The Moon in the Yellow River* (1931), centers around an idealistic revolutionary who has fought for Ireland's liberation and now seeks to keep his country free from the blight of industrialism, symbolized by the plan to build a power plant near Dublin. In it, Johnston captured the mood of the 1920s with its conflict between conservatives and liberals. It is a rather free-wheeling mixture of zany humor and philosophical inquiry, of irresponsible and idealistic characters. The mood is probably best captured in one speech: "This is no country! It's a damned Debating Society!" But the seemingly endless stream of consequential and inconsequential talk eventually leads to the death of the revolutionary, who is shot while singing a song which includes the line, "He tried to embrace a moon in the Yellow River."

Johnston never again was completely successful, for like O'Casey, he mingled realism and symbolism without finding a way to reconcile the two convincingly. Perhaps the best of his later works is *The Dreaming Dust* (1940), an evocation of the life of Jonathan Swift.

Thus, the Irish theatre between the wars was lively but lacked the ferment that made the early years of the Abbey Theatre so memorable. Furthermore, it failed, except with the works of O'Casey, to make a strong impact outside its own country. Its accomplishments were considerable but not pace-setting, for it tended merely to naturalize trends already established elsewhere.

The interwar theatre and drama of the British Isles was mixed in quality. Not till the 1930s did the commercial theatre begin to accept approaches that had been widely practiced on the Continent since before the war. Even then, the triumphs were for the most part restricted to selective realism, for the English and Irish were unreceptive to other modes. Similarly, they shied away from new techniques in writing. A few dramatists dabbled in expressionism, but the majority remained in traditional paths.

The accomplishments of the period were those of individuals working more or less in isolation from each other rather than as members of an organized movement. Nevertheless, in the 1930s, such men as Gielgud, Guthrie, and Saint-Denis began to synthesize earlier trends and to lay the foundations for postwar developments. But, on the whole, the interwar British theatre was more competent than adventurous.

American
Theatre and Drama
Between The Wars

14

With World War I, the United States became a major global power, and soon afterward its theatre and drama for the first time began to win international recognition. In the 1920s significant contributions were made by such groups as the Theatre Guild and the Provincetown Players and by such producers as Arthur Hopkins; in the 1930s the Group Theatre, the Federal Theatre, and others consolidated these gains. American dramatists, among them O'Neill, Anderson, Rice, and Wilder, also won high praise both at home and abroad. As in England, there were no marked movements, for the major mode was a simplified realism, although there was much borrowing from other styles. By the time America entered World War II in 1941, its theatre and drama had reached maturity, even if its accomplishments were not great in comparison with those of most European countries.

By 1915, the foundations of an "art" theatre had been laid in America: the "people's theatre" movement had engendered considerable enthusiasm, the study of theatre and drama had been introduced into a few colleges and universities, a number of Americans had observed foreign developments and returned to write of them, exhibits of "new stagecraft" designs had been shown, many foreign troupes and productions had been seen in America, and several little theatres had been founded to implement the new spirit. But prior to 1915 such harbingers of change had been few and sporadic. Now the pace accelerated.

The crucial developments began outside the commercial theatre and only gradually affected it. Although the grip of the Syndicate was broken around 1916, its power merely passed to the Shuberts, who retained supremacy until after World War II. Generally conservative, such producers adopted new approaches only after their viability had been established by others. Thus, the pioneering work was left to a few groups operating on the fringes of the commercial theatre. Most of those persons involved in the struggle for change were cultivated and well educated; many were university-trained and widely traveled. They deplored the poor literary quality of the typical Broadway fare and the photographically real production style of Belasco, who still set the standard for the professional theatre. In 1915, the romantic realism that dominated European theatres in the late nineteenth century remained almost universal in American productions.

Much of the incentive for change came from foreign sources. Such authors as Hiram Moderwell, Clayton Hamilton, Kenneth Macgowan, Oliver Sayler, and Sheldon Cheney wrote voluminously of the work going on in Europe and of the artistic principles upon which that work was based. In 1917, Cheney founded *Theatre Arts Magazine,* which between the wars was a focal point for the new movement and a disseminator of ideas. Much of the writing by these men now seems vague, often near-precious in its invocation of beauty, art, spirit, and the ideal. Often it is so abstract as to defy translation into concrete terms, but at the time it was inspirational in its incitement to build a theatre quite unlike that of Broadway.

Concrete examples were provided from time to time, however, by foreign visitors. In this the New York Stage Society played a large role, for in 1915 it imported Barker to stage several plays (now said to mark the true beginning of the "new stagecraft" in America), and it was Otto Kahn, a philanthropist and leading spirit of the society, who subsidized Copeau's two seasons in New York between 1917 and 1919. Other significant visits included the Ballets Russes in 1916, the Moscow Art Theatre in 1923–24 (with performances of thirteen plays in twelve cities), the Musical Studio of the Moscow Art Theatre in 1925–26 (with seven productions in eight cities), the Habimah in 1926–27 (playing among other works Vakhtangov's production of *The Dybbuk*), and Reinhardt's production of *The Miracle* in 1924 and his season of plays in 1927–28.

But all of this had to be translated into native effort if the American theatre was to change. A major step had already been taken around 1912, when "little theatres" began to appear in several cities. Taking their inspiration from European independent theatres, these groups offered their subscribers seasons of plays mounted with care for artistic principles. By 1917, there were about fifty such organizations. It was out of a few of these—especially the Provincetown Players, the Neighborhood Playhouse, and the Washington Square Players—that the major impulse for change came.

The Provincetown Players was founded in the summer of 1915 by artists and writers vacationing in Provincetown, Massachusetts. At first they staged short plays on the porches of their homes, but in 1916 they remodeled a wharf into a theatre seating 150 to 200 persons. More important, they encountered Eugene O'Neill and produced his first plays. Thus, they early made a major contribution to the American theatre. In the fall of 1916, the Provincetown group decided to continue its work in New York during the winter months. Consequently, it acquired a theatre in Greenwich Village in New York City, where it continued under various guises until 1929.

The Provincetown Players differed from virtually all the other "little theatres," for it sought to encourage new American dramatists. (Others tended to present European works or classics, and were interested above all in production methods.) According to a statement of purpose issued in 1916, the Provincetown intended to encourage sincere playwrights who were unable to get their plays produced elsewhere. It sought to assist actors, designers, directors, and technicians in experiments with simple resources, but it added: "Elaborate settings are unnecessary to bring out the essential qualities of a good play."

Under the inspirational leadership of George Cram Cook, the Provincetown presented programs composed of three or four one-act dramas. At first it gave a new program every two weeks for three nights each week. As its popularity grew, the number of performances was increased to five each week and the runs extended to three weeks. Occasionally a full-length work was included. By 1925, ninety-three new plays by forty-seven writers had been presented.

Like several other little theatres, the Provincetown soon encountered difficulties. At first novelty and enthusiasm had been sufficient to carry it along, but soon both the members and the public were demanding higher standards, and professionalism began to undermine the camaraderie that had originally characterized the group. The trend was crystallized in 1920, when O'Neill's *The Emperor Jones* became such a hit that it was moved to Broadway. In the flush of success, the Provincetown faltered, and in 1922–23 Cook declared a year of rest in which to re-evaluate its purpose.

In 1923, a new phase began when a reorganization led to the adoption of the Experimental Theatre, Inc., as the group's name and to a triumvirate leadership under O'Neill, Robert Edmond Jones (1887–1954), and Kenneth Macgowan (1888–1963). Emphasis now shifted to greater professionalism in production, and the repertory was altered to include works by Strindberg, Gozzi, Molière, and other Continental playwrights, as well as those works by O'Neill that Broadway producers would not accept. Here Jones was able to design settings for plays which were not likely to be produced on Broadway, and he even directed some. New American playwrights were not ignored, but they no longer were the group's major concern.

In 1925, another reorganization resulted in two branches and two theatres, one continuing the triumvirate's policies, the other seeking to recapture the original spirit. But by now the spark was dim and problems with unions and production costs made survival difficult. It stumbled along, with frequent help from Otto Kahn, but with the coming of the depression in 1929 it had to be abandoned.

On one level the accomplishments of the Provincetown were not great, but on another they were very significant. The number of important playwrights it discovered were few, but O'Neill alone would justify its fame. Even after O'Neill was accepted by Broadway audiences, the Provincetown provided him an outlet for his most experimental works, a luxury denied most playwrights. It also permitted Jones an outlet for talents not in demand in the Broadway theatre and it promoted the career of Cleon Throckmorton, another talented designer of the time. Perhaps most important, it was instrumental in building an audience for a kind of play not previously seen on Broadway and in gaining acceptance for serious American playwrights and new approaches to production.

O'Neill's *All God's Chillun Got Wings,*
produced by the Provincetown Playhouse, New York, in 1924.

The Neighborhood Playhouse, founded in 1915 at the Henry Street Settlement House in New York, also contributed to the new spirit, although less significantly. The initiators of this theatre program were Irene and Alice Lewisohn, wealthy, well-educated, and widely-traveled sisters who went to the settlement house to teach dancing and ended by building and endowing one of the best-equipped small theatres in America (for example, it was the first to have a plaster skydome). The technical director, Agnes Morgan, had been one of George Pierce Baker's students and under her guidance the productions were noted for their variety of approach and for the artistic unity of all the elements.

The pattern at the Neighborhood Playhouse paralleled that of the Provincetown. At first the actors were unpaid amateurs, but by 1920 the demand for higher quality had led to the employment of a small professional company supplemented with amateurs. Like the Provincetown, it too began to transfer successful productions to Broadway theatres, and it took a season's rest in 1922–23. In 1923–24, a professional troupe of ten was employed and Richard Boleslavsky (who had been prominent in the Moscow Art Theatre's First Studio before he emigrated) was engaged to direct some of the productions. But rising costs, difficulties with unions, and other problems led to the closing of the theatre in 1927. In 1928, the Neighborhood School of Theatre was formed and soon became and long remained one of the major professional schools in America.

The Washington Square Players, founded in 1915, came into being after a group of artists, writers, and theatre enthusiasts staged Dunsany's *The Glittering Gate* in the back room of a bookstore. This experience was sufficiently exhilarating that they rented the Bandbox Theatre in Greenwich Village and began giving weekend performances of one-act plays. Soon the group was playing four times a week and in 1917 moved to the

Andreyev's *The Life of Man* as produced by the Washington Square Players. (From *Stage Yearbook,* 1918.)

490

*American
Theatre and
Drama
Between
the Wars*

Comedy Theatre in the Broadway area. Now having to compete with commercial productions, the group began to hire professional actors. Numerous difficulties led to its dissolution in 1918. By that time it had presented sixty-two short and six long plays and had provided valuable experience to such young actors as Katherine Cornell, Rollo Peters, and Roland Young and to the designer Lee Simonson.

The experience of the Provincetown Players, the Neighborhood Playhouse, and the Washington Square Players demonstrated that enthusiasm and high ideals were not sufficient. To change the theatre, the transition to professionalism had to be made, but was difficult to accomplish. All of these early groups eventually faltered and then failed. Nevertheless, they pointed out the direction of change, and it was out of the ashes of the Washington Square Players that the first truly successful group—the Theatre Guild—would rise.

~~~ II ~~~

The Theatre Guild was the cooperative creation of several persons who made up its board of managers: Lawrence Langner, Helen Westley, Rollo Peters, Philip Moeller, Lee Simonson, and Justus Sheffield. To this list Theresa Helburn and Maurice Wertheim were soon added. So many persons had difficulty agreeing upon a statement of purpose, but eventually declared their intention "to produce plays of artistic merit not ordinarily produced by the commercial managers." They drew their principal inspiration from Continental models and sought to attract that intellectual and cultured audience which had been ignored by commercial producers in their attempts to win mass popularity.

The Theatre Guild rented the Garrick Theatre in New York (just vacated by Copeau's Vieux Colombier company) and opened in April 1919 with Benavente's *The Bonds of Interest*. The play was not popular with audiences or critics and the Guild was on the verge of financial collapse when in May it offered St. John Ervine's *John Ferguson*. Fortunately, the new work's success was sufficient to restore stability and to ensure the company's continuance.

For the first few years the Guild depended almost entirely on foreign plays. It gave the world premieres of Shaw's *Heartbreak House, Back to Methuselah,* and *Saint Joan,* and presented works by such authors as Kaiser, Lenormand, Claudel, Andreyev, Toller, Pirandello, Gorky, Ibsen, Strindberg, Goethe, Schnitzler, Turgenev, Tolstoy, and many others. Its first notable American piece, Rice's *The Adding Machine,* was given in 1923, but it was not until the season of 1927–28, when it began its association with O'Neill, that it paid much attention to native authors.

By 1925, the Guild's policy of presenting several productions each year

Production of St. John Ervine's *John Ferguson* at the Theatre Guild in 1919.
(From *Stage Yearbook,* 1920.)

for its subscribers had brought it sufficient security to build its own theatre in the Broadway area. The result was a well-equipped building seating 930 (the Garrick held only 550), although there was little remarkable about it, since it was a traditional proscenium-arch structure. At the time, the Guild's acquisition of its own theatre seemed a major triumph, but when the depression came it would become an overwhelming financial burden.

After 1925, the Guild also made other innovations. The visit of the Moscow Art Theatre in 1923–24 had demonstrated the desirability of a permanent company and in the season of 1926–27 the Guild employed a nucleus troupe of ten players (Helen Westley, Alfred Lunt, Lynne Fontanne, Dudley Digges, Henry Travers, Claire Eames, Margalo Gillmore, Edward G. Robinson, Earle Larimore, and Philip Loeb), and hired other actors as needed to fill out casts. At this time, the Guild also rented a second theatre and mounted four plays at a time, alternating them weekly. Thus, briefly the Guild accomplished what many had long advocated for America: a permanent troupe with a repertory of plays alternated with some regularity. But in 1927–28, the great success of O'Neill's *Marco Millions* and *Strange Interlude* led to the abandonment of the scheme so that the profits from the long runs could be reaped.

492

*American
Theatre and
Drama
Between
the Wars*

By 1926–27, the Guild had twenty-three thousand subscribers and now began to consider extending its work to other cities. In that season, *Pygmalion* played in Philadelphia and in 1927–28 some of the Guild's productions (but not the original casts) were sent on the road. Then, in 1928–29, it offered subscription series in six cities—Baltimore, Boston, Cleveland, Pittsburgh, Philadelphia, and Chicago—and employed two hundred actors who played for seventy-five thousand subscribers. But so many productions put a major strain on the Guild's resources and quality began to suffer.

With the coming of the depression, the Guild's fortunes began to decline. It had to abandon its seasons in other cities, and it soon began to depart from the adventurousness that had marked its programming in the 1920s to depend increasingly on new plays by American authors. Such changes in policy, combined with financial difficulties, led to a breakup of the group that had run the organization, and eventually only Lawrence Langner and Theresa Helburn were left. The theatre building now became a liability and was lost around 1935, although the Guild continued to rent it until about 1943. (It became the ANTA Theatre in 1950.) By 1940, the Theatre Guild was scarcely distinguishable from the commercial producers against which it had originally rebelled.

Between 1919 and 1935, however, the Guild set a high standard of artistic excellence. Not only was its repertory wide-ranging and outstanding, the quality of its production was also high. The majority of the plays were directed by Philip Moeller (1880–1958)—he staged thirty-two of the first sixty-two productions—but such outstanding European directors as Jacques Copeau and Theodore Komissarzhevsky also staged works for the Guild. Its usual designer was Lee Simonson (1888–1967), who after studying at Harvard and traveling in Europe had been one of the principal naturalizers of the "new stagecraft" in America. His most characteristic settings utilized basic units (often framed by a false proscenium) within which smaller pieces could quickly transform the appearance of the whole. Simonson adopted this solution both out of a desire for simplicity and out of the need to economize on costs and storage space. Through a few basic architectural forms, simple set pieces, projections, and lighting, Simonson created effective settings out of limited means. Perhaps the most important contribution of the Guild was its example to the entire American theatre, for it was able to compete successfully with the commercial theatre even while adopting a repertory and practices usually associated with "art" theatres. Consequently, its influence was considerable.

The Theatre Guild was not alone in seeking to establish a permanent organization providing productions of high quality. During the 1920s, two other producers—Hampden and Le Gallienne—also achieved considerable success with these goals.

Walter Hampden (1879–1955) was born in America and trained in England, where he had played in several troupes, including Benson's and Barker's, before returning to America in 1907, after which he was Alla

493

*American
Theatre and
Drama
Between
the Wars*

Nazimova's leading man and worked for Henry Miller, the Shuberts, and several other producers. But Hampden's ideals had been formed in the actor-manager tradition of England and he desired a company of his own. His first opportunity came in 1918–19, when, with several other actors, he presented a series of matinee performances of Shakespeare's plays in New York. These were sufficiently well received that in 1919 he created Walter Hampden, Inc., and began to tour widely with a repertory which included *Hamlet, Romeo and Juliet, The Merchant of Venice, Othello, The Taming of the Shrew,* and Charles Rann Kennedy's *Servant in the House* (a play with which Hampden was associated for almost twenty years). In 1923 he added *Cyrano de Bergerac,* probably his finest production and certainly the mainstay of his company for the next ten years. In 1925 he leased the Colonial Theatre in New York, rechristened it Hampden's Theatre, and performed there until 1930. To his earlier productions, he now added *An Enemy of the People, Henry V, The Bonds of Interest, Richelieu,* and *Caponsacchi* (an adaptation of Browning's *The Ring and the Book*). But like many other troupes, Hampden's was unable to survive the depression. After giving up his theatre in 1930, he toured for a time and then presented his last play in New York in 1934. Thereafter he played in other companies and in films. He was a member of Le Gallienne's American Repertory Theatre in 1946–47 and made his last Broadway appearance in 1953 in Arthur Miller's *The Crucible.*

In some ways Hampden's efforts paralleled those of the Theatre Guild, but unfortunately he was more backward- than forward-looking, for he aimed to revive the actor-manager system and produced plays in the romantic vein. The only modern work of note in his repertory was Ibsen's *An Enemy of the People,* and that probably appealed to him because of Dr. Stockmann's quasi-romantic rebellion against great odds. The company revolved around Hampden and included no other actors of the first rank (except for Ethel Barrymore during part of one season). Nevertheless, his was an important departure from the typical practices of the time. Furthermore, his designer, Claude Bragdon, working in a simplified realistic mode, reenforced the movement away from naturalistic detail. Hampden's was a distinguished, if conservative, repertory, and its success over a period of ten years added much variety to the American theatre.

Eva Le Gallienne (1899–   ) was born in England and attended the Royal Academy of Dramatic Art before coming to America and making a considerable hit in the early productions of the Theatre Guild. In 1926 she decided to begin her own company—the Civic Repertory Theatre—with which she hoped to attract an audience of students, workers, and low-income playgoers. Consequently, she rented the decrepit, out-of-the-way Fourteenth Street Theatre (which seated about one thousand), and established a price range of fifty cents to $1.50. With a company of thirty-three (mostly young actors but also Nazimova), she utilized a true repertory system under which the bill was changed from three to five times each week

Production by Eva
LeGallienne's Civic Repertory
Theatre in 1926 of Chekhov's
The Three Sisters. Pictured
is Miss LeGallienne, who
played Masha.

and productions of merit were retained for several seasons. She also instituted an apprentice program which included from thirty to fifty students.

The theatre opened in the fall of 1926 with Benavente's *Saturday Night* and Chekhov's *The Three Sisters.* Thereafter it continued for seven seasons (until 1933) with thirty-four plays by such authors as Shakespeare, Molière, Goldoni, Ibsen, Tolstoy, Martínez Sierra, Dumas, Schnitzler, Barrie, and Chekhov, for a total of 1,581 performances. Many of the productions accumulated impressive records over the years—Martínez Sierra's *Cradle Song* was given 164 times, Barrie's *Peter Pan* 129 times, and Chekhov's *The Cherry Orchard* 108 times. Attendance was excellent: 79 percent of capacity in the first season and 96 percent in the second. Still the prices were so low that financial difficulties never disappeared. Le Gallienne was often rescued by Otto Kahn, and in 1928–29 she sought to raise an endowment fund but only managed to accumulate $50,000. Like many other troupes, the Civic Repertory Theatre became a victim of the depression and closed in 1933.

Le Gallienne's company was noteworthy for its wide-ranging selection of fine plays, its permanent troupe, and its use of a true repertory system. On the other hand, practically all of her plays were by foreign authors and she made few innovations in staging. Nevertheless, it was probably second only to the Theatre Guild in importance in the late 1920s.

Not all the progressive work was done by those working away from Broadway. In fact, Arthur Hopkins (1878–1950) probably did as much as any of the dissidents to naturalize European practices. Born in Cleveland, Hopkins began his career as a reporter and entered the theatre as a vaudeville press agent, talent scout, and producer of vaudeville acts before presenting his first play in New York, Eleanor Gates's *The Poor Little Rich Girl,* in 1912. He then went to Europe to visit the major theatres of England, France, and Germany, and, greatly impressed by Reinhardt's work, determined to apply in his own productions what he had seen. Upon his return to New York, he produced Elmer Rice's first play, another work starring Mrs. Fiske, and a series of Ibsen's plays featuring Nazimova before he began that series of productions for which he is now remembered.

In 1918, Hopkins leased the Plymouth Theatre from the Shuberts, intending to produce at least two new works each year and gradually build up a repertory. For this, he engaged John Barrymore (1882–1942) as his principal actor and Robert Edmond Jones as his designer. The first production was of Tolstoy's *The Living Corpse* (retitled *Redemption*). Cooly received, it had begun to attract an audience when its run was interrupted to open the second production, *The Jest* by Sem Benelli, in which Lionel Barrymore (1878–1954) starred with his brother. After this successful run came *Richard III,* which established John Barrymore's reputation as a classical actor. In the midst of the engagement, however, Barrymore suffered a breakdown and Hopkins's original scheme had to be abandoned. Nevertheless, these three productions established Hopkins as a major force in the Broadway theatre, for with works of considerable literary merit he had been able to compete successfully with the usual popular fare. Much of the credit belongs to Jones, who now won his first triumphs on Broadway. His setting for *Richard III* employed a single unit throughout (the Tower of London), while changes were suggested by curtains or by small pieces placed within an opening or in front of the main structure. Lighting played a major part in creating the appropriate moods and atmosphere. These productions, done in 1918–20, coincided with the beginnings of the Theatre Guild and with them served to indicate the direction of change.

In 1921, Hopkins presented *Macbeth* with Lionel Barrymore, who made of the protagonist a tortured, near-mad creature. Jones's settings added to the nightmarish quality by emphasizing the all-pervasive power of witchcraft. The style of this production is usually labeled expressionistic, and it does seem to have reflected trends then underway in Germany. (Jones had recently returned from Europe, where he had seen the work of Fehling and Jessner.) In Jones's setting, figures seemed to appear from and

Robert Edmond Jones's design for Hopkins's production of *Macbeth* in 1921, with Lionel Barrymore. (From *Theatre Arts,* 1921.)

disappear into a black void. The basic architectural units were Gothic arches which according to some accounts tilted ever more precariously as the action progressed. During some scenes, three large masks, which symbolized the witches and fate, were suspended above the stage. In many ways this was a crucial production, for it was so controversial that it seems to have turned Jones and others back to a simplified realism as the basic mode, from which they seldom departed thereafter. Furthermore, the reactions so disturbed Barrymore that he soon left the stage for films.

In 1922, Hopkins presented *Hamlet* with John Barrymore (perhaps the first actor to make the Oedipus complex a major ingredient in his performance of the role). Jones's settings were now clearly in the tradition of Craig. (When the production was moved to London, critics there declared that the settings embodied Craig's ideas adapted to the practical needs of the stage.) Perhaps as much as any other production, *Hamlet* made it clear that a new era had arrived. Nevertheless, it was a very uneven production, for Barrymore was an erratic performer and like his brother he soon deserted the stage.

Hopkins also presented Ethel Barrymore (1879–1959) in a series of plays (including Hauptmann's *Rose Bernd,* Pinero's *The Second Mrs. Tanqueray,* and Shakespeare's *Romeo and Juliet*), and began as well to produce distinguished modern works. He took over O'Neill's *The Hairy Ape* from the Provincetown and then directed *Anna Christie.* These were followed by Stallings's and Anderson's *What Price Glory?,* the first modern

497

*American
Theatre and
Drama
Between
the Wars*

serious play on war to win wide popular success. Its profanity and anti-romantic stance were often said to have set the tone for a whole new school of writers. Hopkins went on to produce plays by Sidney Howard, Robert E. Sherwood, George S. Kaufman, and Philip Barry—some of the best playwrights of the age. Furthermore, he promoted the careers of such actors as Pauline Lord, Katherine Hepburn, Hope Williams, Barbara Stanwyck, Louis Wolheim, and Clark Gable.

Hopkins continued to direct until World War II, but his significant work was done between 1918 and 1925, for it was then that he helped to establish new productional approaches. Hopkins always placed primary emphasis upon the text. As he put it, "The rest can only be echo." Thus, he sought to make the actors and settings unobtrusive so that the inner meaning of the plays might shine through without interference. He admired Jones for his insistence upon eliminating everything not essential to or expressive of the text's mood and action. Hopkins sought creative actors, of whose feelings he was always extremely considerate. He never criticized them in the presence of others, and he offered suggestions about interpretation only if he believed that an actor had misconceived his role. Because he permitted so much freedom, those used to the minute and constant supervision of a Belasco often declared that Hopkins did nothing as a director. Nevertheless, he seems to have achieved results that compared favorably with the best to be seen in Europe.

Hopkins was not the only commercial producer who forwarded the new practices. Winthrop Ames (1871–1937) continued to present works of high quality until he retired in 1932, by which time he had produced about sixty plays, mostly English or Continental. One of Ames's assistants, Guthrie McClintic (1893–1961), also made important contributions, especially after 1925 with productions—among them *The Green Hat, Candida, The Barretts of Wimpole Street, The Doctor's Dilemma,* and *The Three Sisters* —starring Katherine Cornell, whom he had married in 1921. After the mid-1920s, as their appeal was established, the new modes were gradually taken over by such producers and directors as William A. Brady, Jed Harris, Herman Shumlin, Gilbert Miller, Sam Harris, John Golden, and Brock Pemberton.

Much of the credit for the triumph of the "new stagecraft" belongs to the designers, for the most readily apparent changes were visual. The major leaders in the interwar years were Jones, Simonson, and Norman Bel Geddes (1893–1958). Geddes's designs often resembled Appia's but they were conceived on the scale of Craig's. Geddes's unproduced project for staging Dante's *Divine Comedy* (1921) was one of the most remarkable works of its age. Composed of a series of concentric rising levels, the appearance of which was changed through skillful lighting, it was too monumental for an ordinary stage but awe-inspiring in its grandeur. Later he staged such plays as *Lysistrata* and *Hamlet* on unadorned steps and platforms and used actors and hand-carried properties (such as banners and

Norman Bel Geddes's project for staging Dante's *The Divine Comedy*.
This scene is entitled "Dante Meets Beatrice."
(Courtesy Hoblitzelle Theatre Arts Library, University of Texas.)

weapons) to create changes through "living scenery" and light. But he could also work effectively in the realistic mode, as clearly demonstrated by his settings for Reinhardt's *The Miracle* (for which he transformed the Century Theatre into a cathedral) and for Kingsley's *Dead End* (for which he designed a naturalistic East River pier). Geddes, although probably the most inventive of all the American designers, seems to have been the most atypical, since he had so few followers. After 1943 he gave up the stage for industrial design.

Other important designers included Cleon Throckmorton (1897– 1965), who won recognition with his designs for O'Neill's *The Emperor Jones* and *The Hairy Ape;* Mordecai Gorelik (1899–   ), who was especially noted in the 1920s and 1930s for designing social-problem plays and left-wing drama; and Jo Mielziner (1901–   ), who began as Jones's assistant, became an independent designer in 1924, won great acclaim through his poetically realistic settings for such works as *Winterset,* and eventually was recognized as the most influential American designer of the post-World War II period because of his settings for such works as *A Streetcar Named Desire* and *Death of a Salesman.* Livingston Platt, Rollo Peters, Donald Oenslager, Aline Bernstein, Howard Bay, Boris Aronson, and Stewart Chaney also contributed significantly to stage design in the interwar years. So effective were they that by 1930 the previously dominant romantic realism had virtually disappeared.

America also had many talented actors in the interwar years, among them Helen Hayes, Katherine Cornell, Jane Cowl, Pauline Lord, Laurette Taylor, Ina Claire, Ruth Gordon, Lynne Fontanne, Alfred Lunt, the Barrymores, Frederic March, Florence Eldridge, Tallulah Bankhead, Walter Huston, Winifred Lenihan, and Alice Brady. Still, these actors belonged to no particular school. Like their English counterparts in the same period, they tended to accept the notion that good acting is synonymous with impersonation, and they tended to place greater emphasis upon inner motivations than had their predecessors. On the other hand, two groups, the American Laboratory Theatre and the Group Theatre, were consciously committed to a particular approach, the Stanislavsky system, which they sought to introduce into the American theatre.

The American Laboratory Theatre came into being in the wake of the enthusiasm aroused by the visit of the Moscow Art Theatre, when two former members of the Russian troupe—Richard Boleslavsky (1889–1937) and Maria Ouspenskaya (1881–1949)—were persuaded to head the school. Opened in late 1923, the American Laboratory Theatre offered training in ballet, interpretive dance, eurythmics, fencing, mime, phonetics, diction, voice production, theatre history, art, music, and literature, development of the imagination and memory, improvisation, concentration, and characterization. Beginning in 1923, Boleslavsky published a series of essays in *Theatre Arts Magazine* (collected in 1933 as *Acting: The First Six Lessons*) which constituted the first American version of the Stanislavsky system.

The American Laboratory Theatre also included a performing company, in connection with which some students studied directing. As time passed, Boleslavsky became increasingly concerned with staging and Ouspenskaya with actor training. Among the plays presented were *Twelfth Night*, *Much Ado About Nothing*, *Martine*, *The Three Sisters*, *Dr. Knock*, Cocteau's *Antigone*, Scribe's *A Glass of Water*, and *The Trumpet Shall Sound* (Thornton Wilder's first full-length play).

Like so many other organizations, in 1930 the American Laboratory Theatre was forced by the depression to close. Fortunately, such former students as Harold Clurman, Lee Strasberg, and Stella Adler were to carry on its work in the Group Theatre.

The Group Theatre evolved slowly. In 1928, several actors, among them Harold Clurman (1901–), Lee Strasberg (1901–), Morris Carnovsky (1898–), and Sanford Meisner (1905–), had begun to rehearse plays in their spare time and to perform them for invited audiences. In 1929, several future members of the Group participated in a studio project at the Theatre Guild—for which Cheryl Crawford (1902–) was then casting director and Clurman a play reader—a production of Kirshon's *Red Dust*. Out of these beginnings developed the idea for a new organization.

American Laboratory Theatre production of Jean-Jacques Bernard's
Martine in 1928. Setting by Robert Edmond Jones. (Courtesy Ronald A. Willis.)

In part, members of the Group Theatre were protesting against the Guild itself, which, according to them, had no program other than rather vague "cultural" and "artistic" aims. The Group, on the other hand, was committed to the Stanislavsky system in acting and to leftist sentiments in politics. Nevertheless, the Theatre Guild gave the budding organization considerable help: not only did it contribute $1,000, it released Clurman, Crawford, Carnovsky, and Franchot Tone (1904–   ) from their contracts and gave up its option on Paul Green's *The House of Connelly*, which was to be the Group's first play.

In the summer of 1931, the three directors—Clurman, Strasberg, and Crawford—took their twenty-eight actors to the country to study and rehearse, and in the fall, with further assistance from the Theatre Guild, opened their first season. For the next ten years it was to be one of America's most influential companies.

The Group Theatre was a close-knit unit which lived and worked together while seeking to create an ensemble like that of the Moscow Art Theatre. Among its actors were Carnovsky, Tone, Meisner, Stella Adler (1904–   ), Luther Adler (1903–   ), J. Edward Bromberg (1903–51), Elia Kazan (1909–   ), Alexander Kirkland (1908–   ), John Garfield (1913–52), and Lee J. Cobb (1911–   ). Its principal designer was Mordecai Gorelik, whose work was supplemented by that of Donald Oenslager and Boris Aronson.

In the early years, Strasberg was the dominant figure, but his authority began to be challenged in 1934 when Stella Adler and Clurman, who had

Odets's *Awake and Sing!* as produced by the Group Theatre in 1935.
(Photo courtesy Alfredo Valente.)

spent some time with Stanislavsky in France, returned with the message
that Strasberg had been placing too much emphasis on "emotion memory"
and too little on "given circumstances" and the "magic 'if.'" In 1935,
Clurman and Crawford went to Russia, saw many productions, and
visited with Meyerhold, with whose productions they were greatly impressed.
By this time, Michael Chekhov was also appearing in America and many
members of the Group were much interested in his variations on Stanislavsky's work. The shift away from Strasberg was hastened when Odets's
Awake and Sing! (1935) was produced with resounding success but over
Strasberg's strong objections. From that time on, Clurman became dominant. In these years can be found the seeds of that endless American debate
over the proper interpretation of Stanislavsky's system.

Other factors also contributed to rifts in the company. The desire to
maintain a complete and permanent troupe while operating a full-fledged
Broadway theatre kept it in constant financial straits. Profits from successes
usually went to pay off the debts accrued with failures, and most of the
members lived in virtual poverty for several years. Franchot Tone was the
first to give in to the lure of Hollywood, but he was not to be the last.
By 1936–37 the internal problems had become so great that all the directors
resigned.

In 1937–38, Clurman reorganized the Group and changed many of
its earlier policies. His decision not to pay members who were not working
in a current production removed the one factor that had made the Group
distinctive—its integrity as a company. Thus, it soon differed little from

502

*American
Theatre and
Drama
Between
the Wars*

other commercial theatres. After the failure of Odets's *Night Music* in 1940, Clurman was so dissatisfied with the rapidly disintegrating troupe that he threatened to cast outside the membership in the future. This provoked a revolt, and in 1941 Strasberg returned to direct Odets's *Clash by Night*. (Strasberg has said that he was recalled to revive the original spirit.) But the Group was now doomed, and it ceased to exist when Odets's play closed.

Despite its problems, the Group Theatre was the most important artistic force in the American theatre during the ten years of its existence. With its plays by socially conscious dramatists such as Paul Green, John Howard Lawson, Sidney Kingsley, Irwin Shaw, Robert Ardrey, and Clifford Odets, it sought to counteract the idea that deep social concern is antipathetic to art. It also provided the finest ensemble acting to be seen in America, especially in the early plays of Odets, which were to the Group what Chekhov's dramas were to the Moscow Art Theatre. It came along at an especially crucial time, when both the Theatre Guild and the Civic Repertory Theatre were declining. But above all, the Group's influence was to be felt through its legacy to acting and directing, for after the war not only was its version of the Stanislavsky system to triumph (especially through the work of the Actors' Studio), but such former members as Kazan and Clurman were for many years to be the most prestigious of American directors.

The social consciousness evident in much of the Group Theatre's work was widespread during the 1930s, for the country was in the grip of a deep economic depression. One significant result was the Federal Theatre Project, inaugurated in 1935 as a part of the Works Progress Administration (WPA) program to provide jobs for the unemployed. The project was headed by Hallie Flanagan (1890–1969), one of Baker's students who after 1925 had won a considerable reputation with her experimental productions at Vassar College. Miss Flanagan saw in the Federal Theatre an opportunity to create something like a national theatre with many branches. Consequently, she set up five regional centers to provide leadership in each part of the country. Each center was expected to establish its own patterns and to build "grass roots" support for its work. Regionally oriented playwrights were also encouraged, as was experimentation in writing and staging.

Eventually the Federal Theatre had branches in forty states. It published its own journal, *Federal Theatre Magazine,* and maintained a play and research bureau to assist school, church, and community theatres throughout the country. But above all, it was a producer of plays. In its four seasons, the Federal Theatre financed over twelve hundred productions of 830 major works, 105 of which were performed for the first time. At the height of its activity, it employed twelve thousand persons, of whom nine-tenths had been on federal relief rolls. During the four years, Congress appropriated $46 million to support the project. Most of the money went for wages, for in other respects the Federal Theatre was financed by admissions, even though 65 percent of the performances were free and no more than one dollar was ever charged for entrance.

Predictably, the project ran into difficulties. The great concentration of its work in New York (where unemployment among theatre workers was the greatest) led to many complaints, as did the apparent incompetence of many who found their way onto the payroll. But, it was the liberal political views, especially those expressed in the "living newspapers," that created the greatest problems, for they aroused the suspicions of conservative legislators, and, following an investigation, Congress in 1939 refused to appropriate the funds required to continue the project.

Nevertheless, the Federal Theatre accomplished much. It helped to revive the theatre in parts of the country from which professional productions had almost wholly disappeared. It provided ambitious programs of classical and modern works, children's plays, religious dramas, outdoor productions, musical comedies, dance plays, and works by both distinguished and unknown authors. But the best-known works of the Federal Theatre were the "living newspapers," which explored major contemporary social, economic, or political problems. Supposedly the idea for such productions originated with Elmer Rice, and the principal writer was Arthur Arents, but most of the "living newspapers" included segments by many different authors. The first, *Ethiopia* (1935–36), was never produced because, dealing as it did with the Italian invasion of Ethiopia, it included among its characters several living foreign rulers, whom officials of the Federal Theatre thought it unwise to offend. Most of the subsequent examples centered on American problems: *Triple-A Plowed Under* (1936) treated the plight of farmers, *Power* (1937) electrical utilities and the TVA, *One-Third of a Nation* (1938) housing. Most used the "little man" as a unifying character, an average citizen whose curiosity has been aroused by controversy over a problem. He begins to ask questions, and is then led through the background of the problem, its human consequences, and the possible solutions. Much of the dialogue was extracted from speeches, newspaper stories, and public documents. Dramatic scenes, often showing the desperate plight of individuals affected by the problem, alternated with film clips, projections of statistical data, and other devices which illustrated the problem and provided information. Many of the techniques resembled those used earlier by Piscator and Meyerhold. Most of the living newspapers advocated strong government action to solve problems, but, though quite liberal in outlook, never exceeded the position taken by

Setting by Howard Bay for *One-Third of a Nation* in 1938 at the Federal Theatre. (From *Theatre Arts,* 1938.)

President Roosevelt's administration. But this in itself was sufficient to make the form seem overly partisan and it was largely the living newspapers which brought an end to the Federal Theatre Project. By far the most extensive involvement of the American government with the theatre, this project has been used ever since as an example both of what might be accomplished with government assistance and the dangers of federal involvement in the arts.

The Federal Theatre also gave rise to other groups, the most important of which was the Mercury Theatre, established in 1937 by John Houseman (1902–) and Orson Welles (1915–). Houseman headed the Negro People's Theatre, a unit of the Federal Theatre, housed at the Lafayette Theatre in Harlem. Here in 1935–36, Welles had staged an all-Black version of *Macbeth,* in which the setting had been changed to Haiti and in which the witches were transformed into witch doctors. It starred Edna Thomas as Lady Macbeth, Jack Carter as Macbeth, and Canada Lee as Banquo. It was one of the most successful productions of the Federal Theatre. Welles won additional fame with a production of *Doctor Faustus* (1937), in which he played the leading role and the Black actor Jack Carter played Mephistopheles. Later in 1937, when Houseman and Welles mounted Marc Blitzstein's *The Cradle Will Rock,* a prounion, witty, and derisive musical play about the opposition of steel companies to unionization, the WPA ordered the postponement of the production on the grounds that it was too explosive. Welles and Houseman defied the order, and out of the conflict came the Mercury Theatre.

At first, the Mercury was housed in the Comedy Theatre (once the home of the Washington Square Players), but its 622 seats were considered too few and it was moved to the National Theatre. Welles and Houseman intended to provide a repertory of classical plays which had some specific relevance to the contemporary scene. Their most famous production was of *Julius Caesar,* done in modern dress, mostly military uniforms, to suggest parallels with the rise of Mussolini and Hitler. The text was cut, rearranged, and changed in various ways to bring out contemporary parallels. It was starkly and simply mounted; the stage's back wall was visible throughout, and effects were gained primarily through banners, groupings, and lighting. It was both highly controversial and popular. It was followed by an abbreviated version of Dekker's *The Shoemaker's Holiday* and Shaw's *Heartbreak House.* The second season was much less successful. Büchner's *Danton's Death* closed after twenty-one performances, and a condensation of Shakespeare's history plays into a single work, *The Five Kings,* also fared badly. Welles and Houseman then moved to Hollywood, where they intended to continue the Mercury. But in 1940, after they presented Richard Wright and Paul Green's *Native Son* in New York, the Mercury came to an end.

The venture cannot be counted a success. Welles and Houseman had intended to form a permanent repertory company and most of the original actors were made shareholders and promised long-term engagements. But none of the goals was reached, in part because Welles would not plan sufficiently far in advance. Nevertheless, the Mercury presented a few exciting productions and demonstrated that imaginative and gripping work could be done without elaborate mounting.

The Federal Theatre, Welles, and Houseman also promoted Black theatre, which though not widespread during the interwar years was laying the foundations for later and more extensive developments. Despite the importance of Blacks in American life from the beginning, they were long permitted little part in the theatre, except to be depicted in drama from time to time as servants or as comic caricatures. Nevertheless, there were a few exceptions. In 1821, the African Company of Black actors opened a theatre in New York under the leadership of James Hewlett, who among other roles played Othello and Richard III. Unfortunately, White rowdies soon brought the closing of the theatre. Later Ira Aldridge (1807–67) was decorated by several foreign rulers and acclaimed throughout Europe as one of the most celebrated tragic actors of his age. America, however, never availed itself of his genius, for its theatrical interest in the Black man was largely confined to Negro minstrels.

After 1890 some progress was made. Musical plays were written occasionally for Black casts and a few stock companies performed sporadically in New York and elsewhere. After 1910, a Black performer—Bert Williams (1876–1922)—won stardom on Broadway in several editions of *Ziegfeld's Follies* and even in one of the Shuberts' musical comedies, *Under the*

Bamboo Tree. Such productions, however, were carefully tailored to avoid offending White sensibilities.

After World War I, a few dramatists began to write sympathetically of Blacks. The first serious plays for Black actors to be seen on Broadway were Ridgely Torrence's *Three Plays for a Negro Theatre* (1917), designed and directed by Robert Edmond Jones. This production did not have a long run, but it marked a turning away from the stereotyped treatment of Blacks and, equally important, Blacks were for the first time welcomed into Broadway audiences. There followed a number of sympathetic treatments of Blacks, among them O'Neill's *The Emperor Jones* (in which a Black actor played the leading role in a serious American play for the first time), *The Dreamy Kid,* and *All God's Chillun Got Wings,* DuBose and Dorothy Heyward's *Porgy* (later adapted into Gershwin's opera *Porgy and Bess*) and *Mamba's Daughters,* Marc Connelly's *The Green Pastures,* Paul Green's *In Abraham's Bosom,* Paul Peters' and George Sklar's *Stevedore*, and John Wexley's *They Shall Not Die,* all by White dramatists. There were as well several Black authors, but they were given little encouragement by producers and most had their works presented under circumstances that permitted only brief runs. Among the best of these dramas were Willis Richardson's *The Chipwoman's Fortune,* Frank Wilson's *Sugar Cane,* Ernest Culbertson's *Goat Alley,* Mary Hoyt Wiborg's *Taboo* (in which Paul Robeson made his debut as an actor), Hall Caine's *Run Little Chillun,* and Langston Hughes's *Mulatto.* There were as well a large number of musical plays, among the most successful of which were Noble Sissle and Eubie Blake's *Shuffle Along, Chocolate Dandies,* and *Runnin' Wild.* Unfortunately, most Black theatres had difficulty in remaining open and consequently both Black playwrights and Black actors seldom were able to perfect their art. For example, Charles Gilpin, the star of *The Emperor Jones* and one of the best actors of the day, had to take a job as an elevator operator after that play closed. For the most part, it was only those performers who were singers, dancers, or comedians who found ready acceptance in major theatres and then only in vaudeville and musical comedy. Nevertheless, Richard Harrison, Frank Wilson, Rose McClendon, and Abbie Mitchell demonstrated that they could compete with the best actors of the period.

Black theatre received a major boost from the Federal Theatre Project, for in several cities it established Negro units which in four years presented seventy-five plays. Some productions, such as Welles's *Macbeth* and *The Swing Mikado* (an adaptation of Gilbert's and Sullivan's operetta), became nationally famous. There were as well a number of original works by Black authors, such as Frank Wilson's *Walk Together Children* (a detective story), J. A. Smith and Peter Morrell's *Turpentine* (about labor troubles in Florida), and W. E. B. Du Bois's *Haiti* (about Toussaint L'Ouverture). Unfortunately, most of the hopes raised for Black theatre were dashed when the project ended in 1939.

By World War II, many plays about Black life had found their way onto the stage, but few showed the ugly side. Such works as *Stevedore, They Shall Not Die,* and *Turpentine* had ventured into this area but they were usually dismissed as left-wing political tracts. By far the most disturbing play was *Native Son,* Paul Green's and Richard Wright's adaptation of Wright's novel, which showed the terrible effects of social evils on the life of the protagonist. Furthermore, only a few Black actors—most notably Ethel Waters, Paul Robeson, and Canada Lee—had won true fame. But, if there was still a long way to go, at least the situation had improved since 1915. The Black theatre artist had made his presence felt, even if he had not yet been permitted to demonstrate his full potential.

The social consciousness seen in the work of the Group Theatre, the Federal Theatre, and the Mercury Theatre was even more evident in that of the "workers' theatre" movement, which began in the 1920s and flourished after the depression began in 1929. The movement had its beginnings in 1926 with the Workers' Drama League, founded by John Howard Lawson, Ida Rauh, Jasper Deeter, and Michael Gold. This group was never very active, however, and its productions attracted little attention. In 1927, the New Playwrights' Theatre was organized by Lawson, Gold, John Dos Passos, Emjo Basshe, and Francis Farragoh (with the financial assistance of Otto Kahn). Seeking to advance the cause of the working class, it presented Lawson's *Loud Speaker* (a farce on political themes) and *International* (a history of communism), and Basshe's *Earth* (about the plight of the Black man) and *The Centuries* (about Jewish immigrants). Like several similar groups elsewhere, however, the New Playwrights' Theatre offended more than it attracted a working-class audience, for it was overintellectual and depended too much on unusual dramatic techniques. It was disbanded in 1930.

Meantime several foreign-language groups—German, Hungarian, Finnish, Yugoslavian, Swedish, and Yiddish—were also performing in New York. At first they operated in isolation from each other, but in 1929 twelve of them formed the Workers' Dramatic Council. Soon the council began to attract those outside of New York and by 1931 had a membership of twenty-one groups, some as far away as Oregon, and had begun publishing a periodical, *Workers' Theatre.* In 1932 the first National Workers' Theatre Festival and Conference was held in New York and at that time a national League of Workers' Theatres was formed and affiliated with the International Workers' Dramatic Union. Thereafter the movement grew rapidly. By 1934, there were an estimated four hundred groups in the United States and *Workers' Theatre* had been replaced by a more ambitious publication, *New Theatre,* with a monthly circulation of ten thousand.

The most important of the workers' theatre groups was the Theatre Union, which was founded in 1933 and performed in the Fourteenth Street Theatre, just vacated by Le Gallienne. There, it sought to attract a working-class audience with admission prices ranging from fifty cents to

508

*American
Theatre and
Drama
Between
the Wars*

$1.50. Its principal playwrights were George Sklar, Albert Maltz, and Paul Peters, and its major successes were won with Sklar's and Maltz's *Peace on Earth* (1933), about the interconnections between big business and war; Sklar's and Peters's *Stevedore* (1934), a stirring plea for justice for and unionization among southern Blacks; and Maltz's *Black Pit* (1935), about coal mining. The Theatre Union, which had begun as an amateur organization, became fully professional in 1935. It now presented Brecht's *Mother,* Victor Wolfson's *Bitter Stream,* Lawson's *Marching Song,* and Albert Bein's *Let Freedom Ring.*

The workers' theatre movement reached its peak in the years between 1935 and 1937. In 1935, the League of Workers' Theatre was reconstituted as the New Theatre League, ostensibly to indicate its enlarged position in the life of the country and its growing professional stance. But with professionalism came troubles. Most groups outside of New York came increasingly to depend on the Theatre Union for their plays and local inspiration quickly dried up. By late 1936, *New Theatre* had ceased publication. (It was replaced from time to time by other short-lived periodicals until 1941.) In 1937 the Theatre Union had to disband and other groups rapidly crumbled. In 1940, when the final conference of the movement was held, only twelve delegates appeared. With the war, the movement virtually came to an end.

The causes of this rapid decline were several. Most groups had communist leanings, and with the Spanish Civil War and the Soviet purges disillusionment set in. Furthermore, as the American economy began to recover, much of the stimulus behind the movement disappeared as well. In addition, the Group Theatre and the Federal Theatre were doing many plays of the type favored by the workers' theatre and doing them much more effectively. Perhaps most ironically, many of the groups upon becoming professional adopted policies that differed little from the capitalist organizations against which they were ostensibly rebelling. But, if they failed to build a lasting movement, they added considerable variety to the theatrical life of the time, and they reflected dynamically the social, economic, and political tenor of the era.

VI

The economic forces which motivated the workers' theatre movement affected the theatre in many other ways as well, for the interwar years brought many financial problems. The theatre in New York continued to expand steadily until about 1927–28. The number of theatres increased from forty-three in 1900 to about eighty in the late 1920s. Similarly, the number of productions reached a peak of 302 in 1927–28. Then the decline began. By 1937 there were only forty-four theatres, and in 1939–40 the number of new productions had dwindled to eighty. The theatre outside of New York was even more adversely affected. In 1920 there were still about fifteen hundred theatres across the country. By 1930 the number had been reduced to about five hundred and by 1940 there probably were no more than two hundred in the entire nation.

The causes of this decline were several. One of the most important was competing attractions. Spectator sports, which grew steadily in popularity during the twentieth century, siphoned off many former theatregoers. But their effect was probably minor in comparison with motion pictures, which with the development of full-length feature films after World War I became ever more attractive. The introduction of radio in the early 1920s was another blow, but one not nearly so heavy as the rapid progress of sound motion pictures after 1928. Their appeal, plus the low admission fees at a time when the depression was being felt, made it almost impossible for the theatre to compete effectively.

Unfortunately, just when the theatre needed most to lower admission prices in order to compete with other media, it was driven to raise them because of rapidly expanding production costs. Every industry of the period was plagued by sharp inflation, but few were as vulnerable as the theatre. The situation was further complicated by the rise of theatrical unions. Most theatrical personnel long resisted the idea of unionization, for they considered themselves artists rather than workers. That they eventually succumbed is probably due more to the high-handedness of such organizations as the Syndicate and the Shuberts than to any interest in unions as such. The first union to win recognition was the International Alliance of Theatrical Stage Employees (the stagehands' union), which came into being in 1893 but did not gain any real power until it undertook a long and bitter strike in 1910–11. Similarly, the actors formed an association in 1896 but did not seriously consider unionization until 1913, when Actors Equity Association was formed, and did not win recognition until 1919, following the first strike of actors in American history. Even then, the privileges it gained were few, and they had to be increased thereafter from time to time: in 1924 Equity became a "closed shop"; in 1928 it gained control over foreign performers in America; in 1933 it negotiated its first minimum-wage agreement; and in 1935 it won payments to actors for rehearsal expenses. A dramatists' club formed in 1891 became the Dramatists' Guild (a section of the Authors' League of America) in 1912, but did not exert any power until 1926, when it was recognized as the bargaining agent for all playwrights and established a standard contract. In 1918 came the United Scenic Artists, and in 1938 the Association of Theatrical Press Agents and Managers. All of these organizations provided important services for their members and helped to correct legitimate grievances. Nevertheless, each also contributed to rising production costs.

Another factor which has adversely affected the theatres of New York

510

*American
Theatre and
Drama
Between
the Wars*

is the building code. At the beginning of the twentieth century, in the wake of several disastrous fires, a number of restrictive laws, designed to protect the public, were passed. One required every theatre to be able to cut off the stage from the auditorium by means of a fireproof curtain. At the time, this was no handicap, but later it was to be a major deterrent to changes in theatre architecture. Similarly, the law forbade any structure above a theatre. Consequently, in New York, where land values are astronomical, a theatre had to justify taking up space that might be occupied by a skyscraper. Under these circumstances rents necessarily were extremely high. These regulations did not apply to motion picture theatres, thus giving films still another advantage in the competition for audiences. (The laws were finally altered in the 1960s.)

Under such conditions, most managers were forced to cater to popular taste in order to survive. Thus, most were not very adventurous either in programming or in production methods. When new trends began to be accepted, they were adopted, but experimentation remained minimal in the commercial theatre. Financially, the most successful productions were probably that spectacular series of musical extravaganzas *The Ziegfeld Follies,* of which Florenz Ziegfeld (1869–1932) provided a new version each year from 1907 until 1931, and the equally lavish musical comedies presented by the Shuberts.

After 1930, theatrical production became increasingly risky. Large profits could still be made with long-run hits, but the number of such successes decreased. Most of the adventurous groups had to disband, and commercial producers, increasingly wary of taking chances, often demanded changes in plays to eliminate anything that seemed unusual. It was out of this situation that the Playwrights' Theatre grew in 1938, when several leading dramatists—Maxwell Anderson, Elmer Rice, Sidney Howard, Robert E. Sherwood, and S. N. Behrman—banded together to produce their own plays, as well as those by other writers. In this way, not only could they preserve the integrity of their scripts, but also they could retain the profits that normally went to producers. Fortunately, they immediately had a series of successes with Sherwood's *Abe Lincoln in Illinois,* Anderson's *Knickerbocker Holiday,* and Behrman's *No Time for Comedy.* By the time the war began, the Playwrights' Theatre was firmly established. It was to remain a major producer in New York until it was dissolved in 1960.

If the commercial theatre shrank after 1930, the amateur theatre prospered. Following World War I, the community theatre movement mushroomed. By 1925 there were some nineteen hundred groups registered with the Drama League of America and the number continued to grow. Similarly the theatre was increasingly introduced into the curricula of colleges and universities. The University of North Carolina, Cornell University, Yale University, the University of Iowa, and others established outstanding programs. Several schools encouraged new playwrights and experiments in theatrical production. At the University of Washington, for example, the first American theatre-in-the-round was opened in 1932. The movement was given added strength and greater focus in 1936 by the formation of the American Educational Theatre Association.

Still, amateurs can seldom compensate for the lack of a truly professional theatre, and by 1940 there were vast reaches of America, which alone is almost as large as all of Europe, that were wholly devoid of theatrical fare.

∼ VII ∼

The interwar American theatre successfully naturalized many techniques and approaches already well established in Europe, but it did not make any major innovations. Thus, it was more derivative than original. Much the same might be said of American drama in the period, for, though it probably equaled that of any other country, it made its impact through excellence rather than through originality. American dramatists borrowed freely from almost every European artistic movement but paid allegiance to none. Thus, an author might mingle diverse elements in a single play or write successive works in contrasting styles. The major dramatists were united primarily by their opposition to romantic realism in writing and staging and by their desire to raise American drama to literary excellence. Except for the left-wing playwrights, few set out to change the attitudes of audiences and most seemed content merely to explore commonly held views and their effects upon characters. Thus, instead of attacking conventional values, most authors reenforced them. Consequently, if audiences objected to plays, it was usually because of unfamiliar techniques rather than because of startlingly new ideas. The increased interest in high quality for American drama is also indicated by the establishment in 1918 of the Pulitzer Prize for the best new American drama performed in New York and in 1936 of the Drama Critics Circle Award for the best American play of the season.

Between the wars, America produced a remarkable number of superior dramatists, although many no longer seem so outstanding as they once did. Without doubt, the most important was Eugene O'Neill (1888–1953), son of the popular actor James O'Neill. A problem child, O'Neill dropped out of Princeton University after one year and then worked at various odd jobs between bouts of prolonged drunkenness and debauchery. In 1912, a brush with tuberculosis seems to have marked a turning point, for during his illness he developed a consuming interest in playwriting. In 1914, five of his one-act plays were published at his father's expense and in the same year he began to attend Baker's class in playwriting at Harvard. In 1915, he met members of the Provincetown Players, who gave him his first production. They then induced him to go to New York, where others of his one-act

Robert Edmond Jones's design for O'Neill's *Desire Under the Elms*. (Photo by Bruguiere; courtesy of the Theatre Collection, New York Public Library at Lincoln Center; Astor, Lenox, and Tilden Foundations.)

plays were produced before his first full-length work, *Beyond the Horizon,* was presented on Broadway at matinee performances in February 1920 and won that year's Pulitzer Prize. Shortly afterward *The Emperor Jones* was moved from the Provincetown Playhouse to a Broadway theatre, and in 1921 Hopkins presented *Anna Christie.* Soon O'Neill was being looked upon as the leader of a new school of writers, a position accorded him until the mid-1930s.

O'Neill was a prolific writer, eventually turning out about twenty-five full-length works. In addition to those mentioned above, the best known of his early plays are *The Hairy Ape* (1922), *Desire Under the Elms* (1924), *The Great God Brown* (1926), *Marco Millions* (1928), *Strange Interlude* (1928), and *Mourning Becomes Electra* (1931). After *Days Without End* (1934), O'Neill withheld his works from production, although he continued to write regularly, devoting himself especially to a cycle of plays that was never completed. In 1936, he won the Nobel Prize in literature, but by that time his reputation was declining steadily under strong critical attack. It suffered further after *A Moon for the Misbegotten* (1943) and *The Iceman Cometh* (1939) failed when first presented in the 1940s. It was not until the latter play was revived successfully in 1956 and *Long Day's Journey Into Night* (1939–41) was produced shortly afterward that O'Neill's reputation began to revive. Since then, he has steadily regained his earlier position as America's foremost dramatist.

The revolutions in critical opinion about O'Neill's work are explained in large part by the uneven quality of the plays, for as many are failures as are successes and even in many of the best there is a sense that more is intended than actually achieved. O'Neill once declared that in all his plays he had been concerned with man's relations to God—by which he meant man's search for some set of values to which he might commit himself. O'Neill was almost obsessed by the conviction that man has lost faith in his old gods but has been unable to find a new set of values on which to build a meaningful life. Consequently, he saw man as adrift without faith in a materialistic world, a lost creature searching for some way to escape despair. In some plays, the search is explicit, in others merely implied. O'Neill is at his worst when he is most obviously concerned with philosophical ideas, for then he usually ends by championing some new-found but ill-conceived answer to the human dilemma. Furthermore, language is one of O'Neill's weakest points and he uses it least effectively when he seeks most to be profound. O'Neill's strength lies in his ability to create character and situation. The concern of his characters with fundamental, often metaphysical questions gives his work a sense of high seriousness, but when he permits idea to override character and situation the plays falter. His faults were most evident in his middle years—from around 1924 to 1934—and it is perhaps significant that it was during the same period that he was most concerned with novel technical devices (the use of masks, extended asides, excessive length, expressionistic elements), as though in them he sought the same kind of magic he pursued in philosophy. In the early plays, before he became overconcerned with metaphysical questions, and in the late ones, where ideas are integral parts of characterization, he is at his best. In the other works, he is almost always challenging, but in them he often fails to mesh idea and dramatic action, with the result that "message" often seems imposed upon action rather than growing out of it. Still, no American playwright has been concerned more deeply with significant problems or, overall, has been more successful in dealing with them in dramatic form.

O'Neill's early one-act plays, most of them about the sea, are well-constructed pieces in the realistic vein and create a strong sense of character and mood. Much the same approach was used in *Beyond the Horizon,* in which Robert Mayo, a dreamer and idealist who longs for what lies "beyond the horizon," marries Ruth and stays on the farm while his down-to-earth brother Andrew goes to sea. Too late Robert realizes that Ruth has bought his life with her youth but that her soul is barren. Here is the theme that would be developed variously thereafter—frustration of the search for some ideal.

With *The Emperor Jones,* O'Neill began a new phase, for now he partially departed from the realistic mode. Written in eight short scenes, it tells of a Pullman porter who, having made himself emperor of a West Indian island, is faced with a rebellion. The first scene is rather straightforwardly expository. Then the Emperor, seeking to escape the rebels, sets off into the jungle. The scenes that follow reflect the Jungian racial unconscious, for the the Emperor's fears gradually drive him deeper and deeper into the past—at first into his own personal anxieties and deeds, but then into racial memories of the auction block, the slave ship, and the voodoo gods of the Congo. Eventually, having traveled in a circle, he comes back to where he started and is killed. Throughout the action a steady tom-tom beat sounds and accelerates, giving the whole a strong rhythmic sense

514

*American
Theatre and
Drama
Between
the Wars*

of increasing excitement. In this play, O'Neill seems to suggest that the Black man, uprooted from his native culture, has lost his sense of identity and has substituted for it the worst aspects of the White man's culture. It remains one of O'Neill's most interesting dramas.

The Hairy Ape, a related work, focuses on Yank, a stoker on a luxury liner, who in the beginning is convinced that he is the most important person on the ship, for it is he who makes it run—that unlike others "he belongs." His confidence is shattered by a rich girl who, horrified by his appearance, calls him a "hairy ape." Like many expressionistic plays, the remainder is devoted to a search for some meaning in life. Having lost his faith, however, Yank goes progressively back through the evolutionary scale until he arrives outside an ape's cage and is crushed to death. As Yank's alienation from the present increases, the visual background becomes ever more nightmarishly distorted. Through this play, O'Neill comments on the plight of modern man, who, having placed his faith in materialism (the machine), has only his physical and primitive instincts to fall back upon when his faith is shattered.

The Great God Brown is a more ambitious but less successful work. Here O'Neill uses masks to distinguish the characters' public and private roles—external appearance and inner reality. The main character is Dion Anthony (a compound of Dionysus and Saint Anthony—or, in Nietzchean terms, Dionysus and Apollo), but since there is in his world nothing to nourish either a Dionysian ecstacy or to encourage a saintly asceticism, he merely becomes cynical and dons a mask to hide his suffering as a sensitive genius who can find no fulfillment in life or faith in God. For comfort he turns to the prostitute Cybele ("Mother Earth"), but he dies knowing only that he has "loved, lusted, won and lost, sung and wept." Ironically, after Dion has died, his wife takes his mask and, unaware that it is not really he at all, promises that it shall live forever in her heart. Though intriguing, the play cannot be called successful, for O'Neill's intention is clear only because he later supplied an explanation of it.

Strange Interlude was the first of O'Neill's monumental works. Written in nine acts and requiring five hours for performance, its major technical innovation is the use of lengthy asides (or, as O'Neill called them, "interior monologues") in which characters reveal their inner feelings, which contrast strongly with their public statements and external manner. It tells the story of Nina Leeds and the men in her life. Prevented from marrying the man she loves before he is killed in the war, she weds another, but, since there is a history of insanity in his family, she takes a lover so she may have a son. She also develops a close platonic relationship with a novelist. Eventually her husband dies, the passion for her lover fades, her son goes away, and she is left with the novelist. The play is concerned above all with the psychological nature of the characters, each of whom is caught in the toils of his own psyche, concealed from the others but revealed to the audience through the monologues. It expresses the characters' desires and shows how

O'Neill's *Strange Interlude,* produced by the Theatre Guild in 1928. Left to right are Glenn Anders, Lynn Fontanne, Tom Powers, and Earle Larimore. (From *Theatre Arts,* 1929.)

they fail because of their own spiritual aridity. Nevertheless, since the characters are never given any strong sense of direction, there can be no satisfactory resolution. Furthermore, there is no culminating revelation. The play remains essentially an in-depth study of character, but what is revealed no longer seems to justify the play's excessive length, although at the time psychoanalysis was still sufficiently novel that the exploration of the unconscious mind was compelling.

In *Mourning Becomes Electra,* O'Neill reshapes Aeschylus's trilogy the *Oresteia* into three connected plays with a total of fourteen acts requiring six hours to perform. He transfers the action to New England in the nineteenth century, an almost Godless universe in which fate and the supernatural have been eliminated, but in which human motivations, conceived entirely in Freudian terms, are invested with a fatalistic aura. For many years it was one of the most admired of O'Neill's works, though now it is more often derided. On the other hand, *Days Without End* was from the beginning considered by most critics a failure, in part because here the perennial search for the meaning of life ends rather disappointingly at the foot of the cross, where after a lifetime of doubt the protagonist finds peace.

Days Without End marked an eclipse in O'Neill's fame. Though he was eventually to overcome the doubts, those works upon which he most prided himself—those written between 1925 and 1934—never recovered the high esteem originally accorded them. Today critics value O'Neill primarily for the early plays and for those written after 1934—*A Moon for the Misbegotten, A Touch of the Poet* (1935–42), the unfinished *More Stately Mansions* (1935–41), and, above all, *The Iceman Cometh* and *Long Day's Journey Into Night.*

516

*American
Theatre and
Drama
Between
the Wars*

O'Neill's greatness was first strongly reaffirmed with *The Iceman Cometh,* which though of great length otherwise utilizes the realistic techniques characteristic of the earliest plays. Despite this realistic surface, however, the play treats Harry Hope's saloon as a microcosm of the world and its inhabitants, for their dreams sum up the human condition and the various forms that man's illusions take—political, racial, domestic, intellectual, psychological, and religious. The derelicts gathered in the saloon are happy until Hickey forces them to test their illusions, for he believes that then they will be able to face life without guilt. On the other hand, Larry argues that happiness is based on "the lie of a pipe dream." Eventually, O'Neill shows that both Hickey and Larry are merely offering still other variations on illusion, for in a world without faith man must construct phantoms to protect him from the abyss of nothingness.

Many critics consider *Long Day's Journey Into Night* O'Neill's finest achievement. Like *The Iceman Cometh,* it is realistic in method and much longer than the average play. Here the action is confined within a very restricted framework: it takes place in a single room on one day and focuses on four characters (the elder Tyrones and their two sons, transparent disguises for O'Neill's own family as they were in 1912). All of the characters are caught in a hell created by their own psychological and spiritual failures. All seek to evade an unpleasant present—through drugs, alcohol, dreams, and memories—but there can only be a temporary escape backward to a time before faith and hope were shattered, for, as in the earlier plays, here O'Neill suggests that life without faith can only be a delayed journey into night. Thus, in his own distinctive way, O'Neill pursues the same theme that preoccupies the existentialists and Samuel Beckett.

O'Neill wrote many other plays and left several unfinished works, but practically all are variations on a single concern: man's place in the scheme of things. They are a record of O'Neill's search for some larger meaning in life and of his eventual resignation to an existence without God. It is this fundamental metaphysical concern that sets O'Neill's work above that of his American contemporaries and makes it retain its appeal even as theirs has been made distant by time.

~ VIII ~

O'Neill was surrounded by a number of lesser figures who together made it a most notable era in American playwriting. In the 1920s the most esteemed of these dramatists were Rice, Howard, Kelly, Barry, and Kaufman.

Lee Simonson's setting for Elmer Rice's *The Adding Machine,*
as it was produced by the Theatre Guild in 1923.
(Photo by Vandamm; courtesy of the Theatre Collection,
New York Public Library at Lincoln Center; Astor, Lenox, and Tilden Foundations.)

Elmer Rice (1892–   ) began his career in 1914 with *On Trial,* a courtroom drama noted primarily for its introduction in America of the "flashback" to show earlier incidents and for its dependence on the revolving stage to move the action rapidly from the present into the past. But today Rice is remembered primarily for two works, *The Adding Machine* and *Street Scene. The Adding Machine* (1923), the first notable American drama produced by the Theatre Guild and one of several plays of the 1920s to adopt expressionistic techniques, is a commentary on materialism, symbolized by the adding machine, and its dehumanizing effects. When its principal character, the accountant Mr. Zero, little more than an automaton, is dismissed because he is to be replaced by an adding machine, he goes berserk, kills his employer, is tried, condemned, and executed. This part of the play arouses considerable sympathy for the oppressed protagonist and his revolt, but the later scenes, set in an afterlife, dissipate this response by making Mr. Zero so puritanical that he spurns the Elysian Fields, preferring instead to operate a gigantic adding machine, and eventually proving so unworthy that he is sent back to earth to begin the whole cycle over again. In fact, the final scenes suggest that persons like Mr. Zero are condemned to the same petty existence throughout eternity. Consequently, both rebellion and attempts to reform society become irrelevant. Nevertheless, *The Adding Machine* has remained Rice's most popular work, largely because of its attack on materialism and because of its skillful handling of mood. It is also considered one of the most successful American experiments with expressionism, the techniques of which it uses throughout:

Setting designed by Jo Mielziner for the production of Elmer Rice's
Street Scene in 1929. (Photo by Vandamm; courtesy of the Theatre Collection,
New York Public Library at Lincoln Center;
Astor, Lenox, and Tilden Foundations.)

visual distortion, telegraphic dialogue, schematic characters, and semi-allegorical situations.

Street Scene (1929), in sharp contrast, is naturalistic in tone and treatment. The setting shows the sidewalk, steps, and façade of a tenement building, while sound effects evoke the life of the streets themselves. The families who live in the building are introduced and gradually the problems of one become the focus of interest: the wife's unhappiness and infidelity; the husband's jealousy, which leads him to murder his wife and her lover; and, especially, the effects of events on the daughter. Throughout, the play creates a sense of real persons caught up in the swirl of city life. Although the characters are not basically different from those of *The Adding Machine*, here they are treated sympathetically and invested with a dignity which suggests that were their environment changed they might have lived a full and happy life. *Street Scene* is not only one of Rice's most striking works but also one of the most successful attempts in American drama to use naturalistic techniques.

Rice's later plays (of which there are many) fall into two principal categories: the propagandistic—such as *We the People* (1933), which attacks practically everything in modern society, and *Judgment Day* (1934), a fantasy based on the Reichstag fire; and the popular—such as *Dream Girl* (1945), about the daydreams and romance of a working girl. The first type suffers from overschematization of ideas and the second from

Production in 1924 by the Theatre Guild of Sidney Howard's
They Knew What They Wanted.
Pictured are Richard Bennett and Pauline Lord.

overconcern with popular appeal. During the 1920s, however, these faults were not yet evident and Rice ranked high in critical esteem both at home and abroad.

Sidney Howard (1891–1931) had his first play presented on Broadway in 1921 and first won wide critical renown with *They Knew What They Wanted* in 1924. This work centers upon three characters: a middle-aged Italian-American vineyard owner; a lonely waitress; and a young, itinerant farm worker. The waitress, after becoming pregnant by the worker, marries the vineyard owner, who is fully aware of what has happened, and the worker goes away. Each has gotten what he wanted (the owner a wife and child, the waitress security and someone to look after her, the worker his freedom) but only at the expense of considerable compromise. The play suggests that though life often fails to meet expectations, it does not necessarily end in catastrophe. It is also significant because it helped to establish the antiromantic stance of American drama between the wars.

Although Howard was prolific, only two others of his plays—*The Silver Cord* and *Yellow Jack*—now seem noteworthy. *The Silver Cord* (1927) treats a mother's excessive attachment to her two sons, the younger of whom remains at home and becomes increasingly enslaved, and the elder of whom returns home with a wife after a period abroad. The action, most of it taken up by the struggle between the mother and the wife, no longer seems startling, but originally *The Silver Cord* shocked many because

519

520

*American
Theatre and
Drama
Between
the Wars*

nothing in American life had been considered more sacred than a mother's love for her children. *Yellow Jack* (1934), a semidocumentary play about the search to discover the cause of yellow fever, is set in Panama during the building of the canal and centers around the doctors and soldiers who are plagued by the disease and who eventually triumph over it. Like Howard's other plays, it is written in the realistic mode and demonstrates that technical skill which made him one of the most successful playwrights of his age.

George Kelly (1890–   ) was essentially a moralist who most often used satire as his medium. His earliest success was won with *The Torchbearers* (1922), a lighthearted treatment of the little theatre movement and its pretensions, but he is now best remembered for *The Show Off* (1924), a satirical portrait of Aubrey Piper, a liar and untrustworthy braggart who speaks in clichés, dreams only of material success, and never loses his optimism or self-confidence. With *Craig's Wife* (1925), Kelly adopted a serious tone to show how a woman's obsession with her physical surroundings destroys her marriage. Like *The Silver Cord*, it reverses one of the firmest of American sentiments—that good housekeeping is an unquestionable virtue. Thereafter, Kelly became increasingly uncompromising and his popularity diminished correspondingly. After 1931 he virtually gave up writing, making one brief return in 1946 with *The Fatal Weakness*.

Philip Barry (1896–1949) won his first success in 1923 with *You and I* and soon established the pattern that was subsequently to characterize his career—the alternation of success with failure and of sophisticated comedy with plays of idea. Ironically, he cared little for the comedies, with which virtually all of his successes were won, and valued his serious plays, which were usually damned. Of the serious works, perhaps the best

George Kelly's *Craig's Wife* as it was produced in 1925. (From *Stage Yearbook*, 1926.)

521

*American
Theatre and
Drama
Between
the Wars*

is *Hotel Universe* (1930), set in a house on the French Riviera where a number of world-weary sophisticates have gathered. Through the special powers of a physicist, who has become disoriented during work on the space-time continuum, each is transported back to some traumatic experience, relives is, and comes away purged. At the end, all are ready to face life anew while the physicist is found to be dead. In its broad outlines it resembles Barrie's *Dear Brutus*. As to the play's significance, Barry seems to have nothing in mind more complex than that one should not let the past weigh one down. Nevertheless, during the 1930s it was considered a profound and puzzling work.

Barry was much more at home with sophisticated comedy, best exemplified in *Philadelphia Story* (1939), in which a rich and spoiled socialite realizes on the eve of her second marriage that she is still in love with her first husband and returns to him. If lacking in profundity, it is nevertheless highly entertaining in its skillful manipulation of incident, character, and witty dialogue. It was to be one of Barry's last works, for with the coming of the war he virtually gave up writing.

George S. Kaufman (1889–1961), noted primarily for his farces, gained his first success with *Dulcy* in 1921, written in collaboration with Marc Connolly (1890–   ). Of their many works, the most famous is *Beggar on Horseback* (1924), a comedy in the expressionistic mode, in which a young musician views his impending marriage to a wealthy girl as a prelude to the serious pursuit of his art. When he falls asleep there follows a series of dream episodes in which he finds himself enslaved to the materialist system epitomized by his fiancée's father and even placed in a cage and forced to turn out popular songs to meet the never-ending demand. Now realizing the danger of selling his soul in return for financial security, upon awakening he decides to marry the poor girl across the hall, whom he has really loved all along.

Of Kaufman's other collaborative works, the most successful were written with Moss Hart (1904–60) between 1930 and 1941. Especially outstanding is *You Can't Take it With You* (1936), which treats an eccentric household, each member of which follows his own whims despite the regimentation and bureaucracy with which each is surrounded. The play probably owes its continuing popularity to its celebration of the joys of nonconformity.

Kaufman was never able to form another productive partnership, although he won occasional success, the last with *The Solid Gold Cadillac* (1953), written with Howard Teichmann. Nevertheless, for thirty years Kaufman, through his mastery of topical humor and comic dialogue, was America's leading farceur. His strength lay in his ability to perceive the comic possibilities in a situation, even though he seems to have had virtually no talent for conceiving situations themselves. Significantly, his collaborators won little success without his help. For example, after leaving Kaufman, Connolly wrote only one important work, *The Green Pastures* (1930), a

522

*American
Theatre and
Drama
Between
the Wars*

retelling of Old Testament stories within the context of southern Black culture. Similarly, Hart wrote little by himself: *Lady in the Dark* (1941), a musical play in collaboration with Kurt Weill; *Light Up the Sky* (1948), a farce about theatre people; and a few other minor pieces. After 1950 he devoted himself primarily to directing.

∼ IX ∼

During the 1930s the richness of American drama increased, for most of the playwrights of the 1920s continued to be productive even as a new group came to the fore. At the time, the most significant of the new writers seemed to be Maxwell Anderson (1888–1959), for as O'Neill's reputation declined, Anderson was often championed as his successor and superior. Anderson's career had actually begun considerably before the 1930s, for he first won fame as Laurence Stallings's collaborator on *What Price Glory?* (1924), which, with its antiromantic treatment of war and its liberal use of profanity, was considered a landmark in the American theatre. It treats Captain Flagg, a tough professional soldier, and his company as they drink and carouse in their off-duty hours. Most of the play is taken up with the rivalry between Flagg and his sergeant, Quirt, over the favors of a French girl, for whom neither has any romantic feelings but over whom they eventually come near to fighting a duel. The call to duty interrupts the rivalry, which will probably be resumed when the next battle ends. The enormous success of this play initiated a trend toward greater freedom in subject matter and language which reached its peak around 1927 when a

Anderson's and Stallings's *What Price Glory* with Louis Wolheim and William Boyd in 1924.

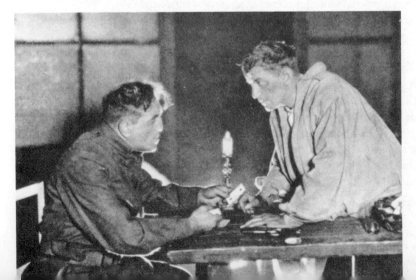

number of works treating homosexuality and other previously forbidden subjects led to the formation of several committees to investigate the need for stronger censorship. In many ways, the situation paralleled that of the 1960s, except that during the 1920s the forces of repression won.

Despite this initial success, Anderson wrote no other important works until the 1930s and consequently it is as a writer of that decade that he is now best remembered. His fame depends primarily upon his efforts to revive poetic drama, with which he seemed for a time destined to succeed, for such works as *Elizabeth the Queen* (1930), *Mary of Scotland* (1933), *Valley Forge* (1934), *The Masque of Kings* (1937), and *Anne of the Thousand Days* (1948), though written in blank verse and Shakespearean in construction, were able to attract a wide following. They are perhaps most significant as having changed public attitudes about poetic drama, for by the 1930s it had come to be assumed that no play could win popular success unless it was written in prose and in the realistic mode. In other respects, however, Anderson's plays are not remarkable, for they merely retell familiar stories in familiar form and neither offer new interpretations of the characters or events nor provide a new vision of human destiny. Thus, they are essentially traditional dramas somewhat elevated by diction.

Anderson's most adventurous works are *Winterset* (1935) and *High Tor* (1937), for here he abandoned historical for contemporary subjects but retained the poetic dialogue which many skeptics considered unacceptable in modern situations. Most critics consider *Winterset* Anderson's greatest achievement. Based on the Sacco-Vanzetti case, which, with Harold Hickerson, Anderson had already treated more directly and journalistically in *Gods of the Lightning* (1928), *Winterset* keeps the actual events at a distance by focusing upon Mio, the son of a man who has been executed for a crime he did not commit. Seeking revenge, Mio comes to a tenement seeking Garth Esdras, whom he thinks can throw some light on the case, but he is followed by the gangsters who were actually responsible for the crime. Falling in love with Miriamne, Garth's sister, he realizes too late that he has wasted his life in hatred, and both he and Miriamne are killed by the gangsters. It is a compelling story, but Anderson's seeming message, that only through death can innocence be retained, is neither convincing nor integral to the dramatic action. Thus, despite the great claims made for Anderson in the 1930s, it now seems clear that he is more skillful than penetrating as a dramatist.

Anderson continued to write until 1958, but such postwar works as *Joan of Lorraine* (1946), *Barefoot in Athens* (1951), and *The Golden Six* (1958) added little to his reputation. Just as his fame had risen as O'Neill's declined, so in turn it waned as O'Neill's revived once more. Between 1930 and 1950, however, Anderson was usually considered America's leading playwright, and, though that estimate is no longer tenable, his skill and his service in changing attitudes about poetic drama cannot be denied.

524

*American
Theatre and
Drama
Between
the Wars*

Of the other playwrights of the 1930s, some of the most important are Sherwood, Behrman, and Hellman. Robert E. Sherwood (1896–1955) began his career with *The Road to Rome* in 1927 and until World War II wrote prolifically, turning out such works as *Reunion in Vienna* (1931), *The Petrified Forest* (1935), *Idiot's Delight* (1936), *Abe Lincoln in Illinois* (1938), and *There Shall Be No Night* (1940). Of these, perhaps the best are *The Petrified Forest* and *Idiot's Delight*.

A melodrama with allegorical overtones, *The Petrified Forest* is set in the restaurant of a filling station located at the edge of the Petrified Forest where a cross-section of American society is assembled through the accidents of travel. Then, a group of fleeing gangsters invades the restaurant, holds everyone captive for several hours and induces crises which lead to reassessments of motives and values. Among the characters are an unsuccessful playwright (who represents the failure of civilized men to solve society's problems), a banker (who epitomizes the materialist outlook), an American Legion commander (who symbolizes blind patriotism), and the gangsters (who stand for raw violence). The forest itself represents something once alive and vital until overtaken by disaster and serves as a warning of what may happen to America unless it remedies the failures in its values. On this allegorical level, *The Petrified Forest* is a gloomy work, but on the realistic level it is an enjoyable and suspenseful melodrama with a happy outcome.

Idiot's Delight pursues similar concerns, this time in semifarcical form and with the issues enlarged to include the entire world situation. Set in a resort hotel in the Alps, it focuses upon Harry Van, the head of a vaudeville troupe, and Irene, the mistress of an international munitions magnate and (as it is eventually revealed) Harry's former love. All the possibilities of farce and vaudeville are used to keep the action entertaining, but behind them lies a preoccupation with war (the "idiot's delight") which men seem unable to abandon. Consequently, the desperate gaiety ends with Harry and Irene clinging together as bombs fall on a neighboring airfield.

As these plays suggest, Sherwood became increasingly concerned with world affairs and the drift toward war. In *Abe Lincoln in Illinois* he took a more positive stance, seeking through Lincoln's early life to remind Americans of the ideals upon which their country was founded. It is probably not surprising, therefore, that when the war came Sherwood gave up playwriting for government service. After the conflict ended he produced three additional works—*The Rugged Path* (1945); *Miss Liberty* (1949), a musical written in collaboration with Irving Berlin; and *Small War on Murray Hill* (produced after his death)—but none added to his stature. It is upon his perceptive works of the 1930s that his reputation rests.

After achieving success in 1927 with *The Second Man,* S. N. Behrman (1893–   ) was for the next decade looked upon as America's leading exponent of high comedy because of such works as *Biography* (1932), *Rain from Heaven* (1934), *End of Summer* (1936), and *No Time for Comedy* (1939). In some ways, Behrman's work parallels Sherwood's,

but unlike Sherwood, Behrman could not commit himself to the patriotic
ideal. A witty, urbane, and (above all) tolerant man, he found the world
increasingly divided into camps, each demanding allegiance; it is this
conflict which informs most of his plays.

525

*American
Theatre and
Drama
Between
the Wars*

Biography has as its protagonist a successful portrait painter whose
biography is about to be written when she becomes entangled with two
men: one a successful politician who through compromise has gradually
risen to a position of power, the other a revolutionary who blames the world
situation on the failures of such persons as the painter to accept responsibility. Although sympathetic to each, she eventually rejects both, for she
places her faith in grace, charm, wit, and tolerance. In *Rain from Heaven,*
the protagonist makes much the same decision, even though it is pointed out
to her that while she is being charming and tolerant her enemies will
destroy her. Similarly, *End of Summer* discusses with wit and insight many
of the world's problems but resolves nothing.

With the coming of the war, Behrman virtually gave up original composition, turning instead to adaptations—among them *Jacobowsky and the
Colonel* (1944) and *Jane* (1947)—until 1958 when he fashioned *The Cold
Wind and the Warm* from a volume of his own reminiscences and later
added *But for Whom Charlie* (1962). None of these contributed appreciably
to his reputation. Behrman is one of the most witty and urbane writers
America has produced, but he seems to have been paralyzed by the horror
of World War II.

Lillian Hellman (1905–   ) is primarily a moralist preoccupied with
the evil in man, usually that within the individual but sometimes that in
society. She came to prominence in 1934 with *The Children's Hour,* in
which a girls' school is destroyed by malicious stories spread by a child.
Yet, since the child could not have been effective were there not hidden
fears and motivations upon which she could play, she merely serves as a
catalyst who activates submerged anxieties and desires.

Miss Hellman's best-known play is *The Little Foxes* (1938), which
exposes the greed of the rising industrial class in the South at the turn of
the century. The characters, mostly members of a single family, fall into
two groups: those willing to sacrifice everyone in order to gain control,
and those who are merely passive observers. Although Miss Hellman
displays compassion for the second group, she makes it clear that both are
equally guilty, for the despoilers could not prosper without the acquiecence
of the bystanders. Many of the same characters are treated in *Another Part
of the Forest* (1946), which further illuminates the Hubbard family's
motives by showing them twenty years before the time of *The Little Foxes.*
Miss Hellman wrote little after the war, devoting most of her time to such
adaptations as Emmanuel Robles's *Montserrat* (1949) and Anouilh's *The
Lark* (1955). Her most recent play is *Toys in the Attic* (1960), in which a
sister deliberately seeks to destroy her brother when his business success
threatens to end his dependence on her.

526

*American
Theatre and
Drama
Between
the Wars*

Miss Hellman's plays, in which situations are powerful and the characters well drawn, are essentially melodramas without the traditional melodramatic ending, for rather than showing virtue rewarded and villainy punished they depict goodness so weak that it is trodden underfoot by evil. But she also suggests that such an outcome is possible only because the morally upright have failed to assert themselves. Hers is a world overrun by materialistic connivers and cheats who meet little resistance from those who could build a better world.

To these dramatists, many others might be added, for in the 1930s there were many competent writers. Among the best were Paul Green (1894–), author of *In Abraham's Bosom* (1926), which shows a Black man's hopeless struggle to help his race, *The House of Connelly* (1931), in which a southern aristocratic family gains new strength through a marital alliance with "poor white trash," and *Johnny Johnson* (1937), an expressionistic, antiwar play; Sidney Kingsley (1906–), author of *Men in White* (1933), a glorification of the medical profession, and *Dead End* (1935), a naturalistic play about the kind of environment that leads to gangsterism; and William Saroyan (1900–), author of *My Heart's in the Highlands* (1939), *The Time of Your Life* (1939), and *The Beautiful People* (1941), all of which celebrate the simple joys of poor but eccentric characters.

❦ X ❦

Most major American playwrights of the interwar years were concerned with the individual—his psychological or familial relationships—or with rather generalized social conditions. Many denounced conformity or tradition, but few suggested any need for a revolutionary change in the American way of life. Those who did received little encouragement.

Of the politically conscious dramatists, perhaps the best was John Howard Lawson (1895–), who made his debut in 1923 with *Roger Bloomer,* an expressionistic evocation of the problems of an adolescent growing up in an insensitive environment. His first major work was *Processional* (1925), hailed by some critics of the time as the most important drama of the post–World War I period because its approach—a combination of expressionistic devices, vaudeville techniques, and jazz music with serious, comic, and burlesque episodes—seemed so innovative. Based on the conflict between workers and owners in the West Virginia coal mines, it treats only the protagonist realistically and reduces the other characters to caricatures: the top-hatted owner; the banjo-playing Negro; the jazz-age dancing girl. Members of the Ku Klux Klan shout "God's will be done"

527

*American
Theatre and
Drama
Between
the Wars*

when the tar and feathers are ready for a victim and break up their meeting in a fox-trot. Much of the action is set to jazz accompaniment. It was such devices and the overall sense of vitality which most attracted critics, who in general ignored the underlying story: the protagonist's degrading and destructive experiences which foreshadow the eventual rebellion of the working class. Lawson also wished to suggest that the enormous energy of America, which he saw epitomized in jazz, was being used for destructive rather than for constructive purposes. Thus, *Processional* mingles admiration for America's potential with revulsion at its failures.

In *Loud Speaker* (1927), Lawson adopted many of Meyerhold's constructivist and biomechanical devices. Clownlike performers caricatured such familiar figures as the journalist, the politician, and the flapper and made their entrances down chutes or tumbled about on the series of platforms that made up the setting. To most critics it seemed merely a confused and disconnected commentary on modern life. *International* (1928), using techniques already explored in Lawson's earlier works, presented a kaleidoscopic vision of communism's eventual triumph over capitalism and imperialism.

During the 1920s Lawson made the most extensive use of nonrealistic techniques of any American playwright. Rather surprisingly, therefore, after 1930 he abandoned his earlier approach and turned to the "well-made play" to express his growingly explicit political concerns. *Success Story* (1932) shows how a Jewish radical betrays his political ideals to become the head of a corporation, while *Gentlewoman* (1934) suggests that fulfillment can be found only by allying oneself with the aspirations of the working class. Lawson's last important play, *Marching Song* (1937), treats a family which has been turned out of its home by capitalists because of the father's radical ideas. When the workers go on strike, the father is offered a secure position if he will betray the cause, but the strike spreads and the capitalists are brought to their knees. After this time, Lawson spent most of his time in Hollywood.

Lawson's career suggests that he was closely attuned to Russian developments, for his works of the 1920s seem to reflect Meyerhold's approach, just as his plays of the 1930s are related to socialist realism. And like that of the Russians, his work seems to decline from vitality and promise to lifeless propaganda.

Nevertheless, Lawson obtained a much fuller hearing than did such left-wing writers of the interwar years as Sophie Treadwell, Albert Maltz, George Sklar, Paul Peters, Albert Bein, Emjo Basshe, John Dos Passos, John Wexley, and Michael Gold, for most were dismissed as mere propagandists and were encouraged only by workers' theatre groups. One of the most effective works to come out of this movement was *Stevedore* (1934) by Paul Peters and George Sklar. A stirring melodrama about injustices done to Blacks in Louisiana, it ends with a mob about to attack the Black settlement when unionized White workers, recognizing at last the necessity for proletarian solidarity, arrive to rout the mob. Although in

528

*American
Theatre and
Drama
Between
the Wars*

many ways crude, its power to arouse sympathy and emotional fervor for a cause cannot be denied. For the most part, this kind of play tended to disappear after the Theatre Union was disbanded in the late 1930s and as economic stability returned to America.

The drama of political and social consciousness found its finest expression in the work of Clifford Odets (1906–63), even though he followed a path opposite to that of Lawson, for he became steadily less interested in propaganda even as Lawson was becoming more concerned with it. Odets began his career as an apprentice actor in the Group Theatre before turning to playwriting in 1935 with *Waiting for Lefty,* one of America's most effective agit-prop plays. Set on a bare platform of a union hall, it ostensibly begins in the midst of a meeting during which taxi drivers will decide whether or not to go on strike. Speakers rise to present their views and vignettes of life among the taxi drivers and their families illustrate the workers' plight. But since the union's leadership has been taken over by racketeers who are in league with the owners, the workers feel that they can depend only on Lefty, whose arrival they await before making a decision. Outrage at the workers' treatment is skillfully built and when it is discovered that Lefty has been treacherously murdered because he is on the side of the workers, they rise as one with shouts of "Strike, Strike!" This is Odets's most committed play, in which one of the characters praises *The Communist Manifesto* and recommends it to all workers.

Odets soon became the resident playwright of the Group Theatre, for whom he wrote in rapid succession *Awake and Sing!* (1935), *Till the Day I Die* (1935), *Paradise Lost* (1935), *Golden Boy* (1937), and *Rocket to the Moon* (1938). Of these, the best is probably *Awake and Sing!,* the story of a close-knit Jewish family whose dreams of happiness are gradually shattered: the grandfather commits suicide, the daughter Hennie is condemned to a loveless marriage, and the son Ralph sees his romance broken. Yet throughout there is a sense of dignity as the characters struggle to get more out of life than it will ever give them. In general approach, it has been compared to the works of Chekhov and O'Casey, for it is rich in the texture of a life that undermines bright hopes. The ending, in which Ralph decides to leave home and fight for the rights of all workers, is obviously tacked on, but it is not a fault sufficient to destroy the warm and rich portraiture which constitutes the play's enduring strength.

Of the other plays, the best is *Golden Boy,* the story of Joe Bonaparte, who dreams of being a violinist but becomes a prize fighter because the world values brute force more than it does music. Increasingly involved with gangsters (who represent the parasitic and corrupting forces of capitalism), his disillusionment grows and reaches a crisis after he kills a man in the ring. Now trapped, he wrecks his automobile, killing both himself and the girl he loves. Yet it is clear that any decision Joe could have made would have led to despair, for the indifference of society to his musical talents could only have generated poverty and frustration, just as boxing has led to his brutalization.

Odets's *Golden Boy,* as it was produced by the Group Theatre in 1937
with Luther Adler. (Photo courtesy Alfredo Valente.)

In the late 1930s after Odets moved to Hollywood, the vitality of
his work disappeared. The failures of *Night Music* (1940) and *Clash by
Night* (1941) were major factors in the demise of the Group Theatre.
After the war, Odets regained some of his earlier strength with *The Country
Girl* (1950), which depicts the psychological conflicts of a wife and her
alcoholic husband, and *The Flowering Peach* (1954), a retelling of the
story of Noah. Both are competent and effective plays, but they add little
to Odets's reputation, which continues to depend upon his dramas of the
1930s.

～ XI ～

Of all the American playwrights of the interwar years, Thornton Wilder
(1897–   ), with the possible exception of O'Neill, now enjoys the greatest
international reputation. Not only are his dramas well known in Europe,
they have been acknowledged by numerous contemporary writers, among
them Frisch and Duerrenmatt, as major influences on their work.

530

*American
Theatre and
Drama
Between
the Wars*

Wilder began writing plays while still a student at Yale University, but his first production did not come until 1927 when the American Laboratory Theatre staged the four-act allegory about God's capacity for forgiving sinners, *The Trumpet Shall Sound* (1919–20). In 1928, after his first novels had aroused wide interest, sixteen of Wilder's short plays (some of them written before 1920) were published in *The Angel That Troubled the Waters and Other Plays.* Because of their brevity, Wilder labeled them "three-minute plays." They demonstrate Wilder's penchant for compression, for, like the futurists, he disliked conventional exposition, complication, and denouement. Consequently, most of these early plays merely treat a climactic moment, a feeling, or perception. Furthermore, the stage directions are often reminiscent of Artaud's, as when Wilder writes that Judas's thirty pieces of silver are thrown upward and "hurtle through the skies, flinging their enormous shadows across the stars and continue falling forever through the vast funnel of space." Thus, from the beginning Wilder was unwilling to be bound by the conventions of realistic staging.

The direction his drama would ultimately take is first clearly seen in *The Long Christmas Dinner and Other Plays in One Act* (1931), a collection of six short pieces. The title work once more shows Wilder's affinity with futurism, for in it ninety years pass without any break in the action as three successive generations enjoy a Christmas dinner. Newborn babies are wheeled in by nurses; old age is indicated by the donning of white wigs; and those who die merely exit through a "death door." In both *Pullman Car Hiawatha* and *The Happy Journey to Trenton and Camden,* the Stage Manager, using a few chairs or simple properties, sets a bare stage and supervises the performance. Because Wilder does not define the physical limits of his settings, he is able to suggest that they continue to the ends of the universe. Similarly, time is treated as the unbroken, never-ending flow of life itself. (His practice contrasts sharply with that of expressionist drama, in which the action is usually divided into many short, discontinuous scenes.) Through such techniques, Wilder adapts his essentially narrative bent to the limitations imposed by the stage.

The techniques employed in these short plays were further refined in *Our Town* (1938), now one of the best known and most popular of all American dramas. Set in a small town in New Hampshire between 1901 and 1913, *Our Town* tells the simple story of a girl who falls in love, marries, and dies while giving birth to a child. The first act, which re-creates the small-town milieu, is entitled "The Daily Life," the second "Love and Marriage," and the third "Death." On a bare stage, the Stage Manager manipulates a few chairs, a ladder, and two trellises as needed by the episodes, which his narration introduces and links. He also assumes numerous roles, ranging from small children to aging adults, and comments on the events and their significance. On one level, *Our Town* treats a very specific time and place, but it does so in order to capture in miniature that which is universal and eternal in human experience. As Wilder wrote: *"Our Town*

The wedding scene of Thornton Wilder's *Our Town* as produced originally in 1938. (Photo by Vandamm; courtesy of the Theatre Collection, New York Public Library at Lincoln Center; Astor, Lenox, and Tilden Foundations.)

is not offered as a picture of life in a New Hampshire village. . . . It is an attempt to find a value above all price for the smallest events in our daily life." Or, as the Stage Manager says: "We all know that *something* is eternal," and, he adds, "that something has to do with human beings." Above all, Wilder tries to point out that if men are unhappy it is not because they have failed to achieve fame or material reward but because they have not taken delight in everyday, ordinary experiences.

Later in 1938 Wilder's *The Merchant of Yonkers* (directed by Max Reinhardt) was also produced in New York but, unlike *Our Town*, was a dismal failure. In 1954, with a few revisions, a new title (*The Matchmaker*), and the direction of Tyrone Guthrie, it was to be a resounding success, at first in Great Britain and later in New York; in 1964, as *Hello, Dolly*, it would become one of America's longest-running musical plays. *The Merchant of Yonkers* is derived from two earlier dramatic treatments of the same story, one by Nestroy (written in 1842), the other by Oxenford (written in 1835). But the central character, Dolly Levi, is based on Frosine, the matchmaker of Molière's *The Miser*. It is she who manipulates events in her desire to marry the rich Horace Vandergelder, and it is she who brings to a happy conclusion the madcap adventures of the young people. Wilder

Frederic March as Antrobus and Tallulah
Bankhead as Sabina in Thornton
Wilder's *The Skin of Our Teeth,*
produced originally in 1943.

has said that in this play he parodies the kind of stock piece that was popular
in his youth. But he is also concerned with the simple pleasures of man as
embodied in an almost archetypal form of farce with its disguises, artificial
complications, surprise encounters, and asides—all fully exploited and
called to the attention of the audience. Or, as Wilder has put it: "My play
is about the aspirations of the young (and not only the young) for a fuller,
freer life."

In *The Skin of Our Teeth* (1943), Wilder seeks to summarize the
experience of man in the face of disaster (the ice age, the flood, and war)
and to show how each time we have escaped by "the skin of our teeth."
Produced in the midst of World War II, it was intended as a reminder of
man's resilience. As in his earlier works, Wilder here uses many theatricalist
devices, such as having performers seemingly step out of their roles to speak
to the audience or to backstage personnel and to comment on the play
and its ideas. Anachronisms abound (in the ice age, Mr. Antrobus lives in
New Jersey and commutes to his office; at the time of the flood, the characters are on a boardwalk; and so on), for Wilder wishes to emphasize the
continuity of experience. Consequently, not only is the audience never
permitted long to forget that it is watching a play, it is also reminded that
the subject matter reaches out to encompass the entire human race.

Since 1943 Wilder has written little for the theatre. In 1948 his
translation of Sartre's *Morts sans Sépulture* (which he called *The Victors*)

533

*American
Theatre and
Drama
Between
the Wars*

was presented in New York. In 1955, his *Alcestiad* (also called *A Life in the Sun*) was produced at the Edinburgh Festival. Not well received, only one part of it has been published in English, although it has been translated and performed with success in Germany. Wilder has also stated his intention of writing two series of short plays, one to be called *The Seven Deadly Sins* and the other *The Seven Ages of Man*. Three plays from these series were presented at the Circle in the Square in 1962 but the cycles have yet to be completed.

Wilder has made his impact in part through a theatricalism compounded of devices taken over from many sources, including vaudeville, expressionism, futurism, and surrealism. Much in his approach resembles that of André Obey (whose *The Rape of Lucrece* he adapted for Katherine Cornell in 1932). Unlike most of his nonrealist contemporaries, however, Wilder has been able to make his theatricalism acceptable to ordinary theatregoers, for he couples it with subject matter clearly understandable to the most unsophisticated spectator. Furthermore, he avoids discontinuity, for, though he telescopes both time and space more drastically than does almost any other major playwright, he is always careful to point out that he is doing so and makes it seem wholly justified. Such simplicity and clarity, coupled with an optimistic faith in humanity, have led some critics to describe Wilder as a mere purveyor of clichés, just as they have prompted others to praise him for cutting through the bewildering surface of experience to reveal its eternal patterns. Regardless of the ultimate worth of his perceptions, Wilder's importance cannot be questioned, for perhaps more so than any other dramatist he has demonstrated how utter simplicity of subject and means may be fashioned into a compelling theatricality.

ᨏ XII ᨏ

In many ways, American theatre and drama reached their zenith between the wars, when, for the first time, outstanding native dramatists won international esteem for American drama. But, as in England, there were in America no conscious artistic movements or true innovations. The playwrights viewed their role seriously and sought to create works with both literary and artistic merit, but most remained within the limits of traditional values and of modified realism. A few ventured outside this pattern to explore metaphysical questions (as did O'Neill) or to attack the American system (as did Lawson) and many borrowed techniques from expressionism and other movements, but for the most part, American playwrights, compared with their continental European counterparts, were revolutionary neither in outlook nor approach. Nevertheless, both in quality and quantity, American drama probably was at its best during the interwar period.

Similarly, theatrical producers also naturalized many European ideals, although the dominant commercial outlook was never seriously challenged. During the 1920s the number of productions reached its highest point before the depression brought a marked decline. By 1940, the theatre was largely an institution confined to New York City, from which a few satellite companies were sent out to serve the rest of the country.

The coming of World War II seems to have sapped the vitality which had undergirded the interwar dramatic impulse. Virtually every major playwright either gave up writing or failed to progress beyond a point already reached. Recovery had to await new talent, but it is questionable whether America has yet been able to equal the level reached during the quarter-century which separated the two global conflicts.

War
and
Recovery

15

Like the First, the Second World War interrupted or slowed theatrical activity almost everywhere. In some places production virtually ceased and elsewhere it turned increasingly toward entertainment intended to build morale or to provide diversion. When peace returned in 1944–45, the process of rebuilding began. The major goal in the immediate postwar years was to revive and extend earlier methods and standards. In many countries, most notably England, Germany, and France, governmental agencies played an active role in the revival. A few significant new practitioners— among them Felsenstein, Barrault, Vilar, Kazan, and Strehler—and several new dramatists—among them Fry, Frisch, Duerrenmatt, Anouilh, Montherlant, Williams, Miller, and Betti—emerged in this era to give it vitality.

But essentially it was a period of recovery rather than of innovation, for not until the mid-1950s did significant new directions become evident.

~ I ~

Of all European countries, England was among the hardest hit in the early years of the war. Subjected to heavy German aerial attacks, London during 1940–41 had only one theatre in operation, the Windmill (a variety house). Except for a series of lunchtime performances of Shakespearean plays given by Donald Wolfit, the legitimate drama was completely silenced in London.

This situation motivated a truly significant event—the British government for the first time in its history provided direct financial support to the arts. This began in 1940 with the formation of the Council for the Encouragement of Music and the Arts (CEMA), for which Parliament appropriated 50,000 pounds. At first in collaboration with the Pilgrim Trust and after 1942 alone, CEMA sponsored entertainment for the wartime population and assisted artists in all fields. Between 1942 and 1946 CEMA was especially concerned with sending theatrical productions to the many hostels that had been established throughout England to house factory workers. By 1945, sixty-nine hostels were being visited regularly by companies offering such plays as *Medea, Twelfth Night, Hedda Gabler, Arms and the Man, The Importance of Being Earnest,* and *The Shoemaker's Holiday.*

Following the end of the war, CEMA was reorganized and renamed the Arts Council. The royal charter issued it in 1946 stated its purposes as follows: to promote greater understanding of the arts; to raise standards of practice; and to make the arts more accessible to the public. To avoid direct government involvement (and possible interference) with the arts, the council was made an independent body which received governmental funds and decided how they would be allocated. It was (and continues to be) composed of representatives from all artistic fields, some appointed by the government and others by organizations representing the various arts. Since it has never had large sums at its disposal, it has sought to assist most those organizations or individuals with the greatest potential. By the 1960s it was giving at least token support to more than forty theatrical companies throughout Britain.

The changed attitude toward governmental subsidies for the arts was further indicated in 1948 when Parliament authorized local governments to allot a part of their revenue for this purpose. Although not all have done so, many municipalities have taken advantage of this act to subsidize resident

Lewis Casson and Sybil Thorndike in the CEMA production of *Medea,*
which toured mining villages in England in 1941.
(Courtesy Mander and Mitchenson Theatre Collection.)

companies. The Greater London Council has been especially generous with
its assistance to such groups as the Old Vic, the Royal Covent Garden
Opera and Ballet troupes, Sadler's Wells, the National Theatre, and the
English Stage Company (at the Royal Court Theatre). The central
government has also given indirect support to many theatres by exempting
from the rather heavy entertainment tax those concerned with more than
mere diversion. This provision has encouraged the production of classics,
unusual new plays, and other works not considered purely commercial.
Much of the high quality of postwar British theatre must be attributed to
such governmental subsidies.

One of the first organizations to benefit from the change in governmental policy was the Old Vic. When the war began, this company's
headquarters were moved to Burnley and later to Liverpool. In 1940, in
association with CEMA, it undertook its first wartime tour—*Macbeth,* with
Sybil Thorndike and Lewis Casson—to Welsh mining towns. Subsequently,
it sent out nine other companies, with plays ranging from Greek and
Shakespearean tragedy to Victorian drama and modern plays, to all parts
of England and Scotland.

Laurence Olivier as Richard III in the Old Vic production of 1945. (Photo by John Vickers.)

In the fall of 1944, the Old Vic returned to London, but had to play in the New Theatre, for its own home had been bombed. It now entered the era of its greatest glory. The management passed from Tyrone Guthrie to Laurence Olivier, Ralph Richardson, and John Burrell, who presented a series of brilliant productions, among them *Richard III, Love for Love, Oedipus Rex, The Critic, Peer Gynt, King Lear, Cyrano de Bergerac,* and *Henry IV, Part I.* As a result, by the late 1940s the Old Vic was one of the most admired companies in the entire world.

In 1946, the Old Vic also established a theatre school under the direction of Michel Saint-Denis, assisted by George Devine and Glen Byam Shaw. Here Saint-Denis applied the concepts (primarily those he had learned from Copeau) which he had followed in his London Theatre Studio before the war. Auditions for entry were very strict and the daily criticism rigid. Each teacher was required to participate in several areas of the training to ensure that the total program was directed toward commonly understood goals. It was probably the best acting school in England at that time. Closely allied with the school was a company—the Young Vic, under the direction of George Devine—which performed for children. Both were housed in the patched-up Old Vic Theatre building.

After 1946 the Old Vic also had a second branch. In 1942, CEMA had acquired the Theatre Royal, Bristol (built in 1766 and the oldest theatre building in England), then in danger of being converted into a warehouse. After the war, the Arts Council requested the Old Vic to assume control of the theatre and to establish a company there—the Bristol Old Vic. Thus, in the late 1940s, the Old Vic, with its two branches, school, and Young Vic troupe, reached a peak of activity and of excellence.

Unfortunately, after 1948 it began to decline. Olivier and Richardson, now in demand everywhere, devoted increasing time to films and other outside engagements. Considerable conflict arose and in 1949 they resigned. The management then passed to Hugh Hunt (1911–   ), who had headed the Bristol Old Vic since its formation. Hunt mounted a number of fine productions—the best with Michael Redgrave in such plays as *Hamlet, Love's Labour's Lost,* and *She Stoops to Conquer*—but new troubles came when the company returned to its home theatre, now fully repaired, in 1950. Saint-Denis and Devine had requested a theatre of their own in which students from the school would gain further training in the Young Vic troupe. With the return of the parent company to the Old Vic, however, their work was seriously hampered for lack of space; when it became evident that they would not get their own quarters, they resigned in 1952, and both the school and the Young Vic came to an end.

From 1953 to 1958 the Old Vic was headed by Michael Benthall (1919–   ), during whose management all of Shakespeare's plays except *Pericles* were staged. The company was still good, although now relatively young—the leading players were John Neville (1925–   ), Barbara Jefford (1930–   ), and Paul Rogers (1917–   )—but it necessarily suffered from comparisons with the preceding era. Some critics welcomed the change, arguing that the Guthrie-Olivier-Richardson years had deflected the Old Vic from its true mission. But the days of greatness were over and the company declined rather steadily after 1958, although it momentarily regained some of its former glory in 1960 with Franco Zeffirelli's brawling, lusty production of *Romeo and Juliet*. In 1963, the Old Vic was dissolved and its headquarters became the home of the National Theatre, its true successor.

As the Old Vic declined, the Stratford Festival company gained in prestige. During the war, the seasons at Stratford had continued on a much reduced scale. Then, between 1946 and 1948, while Barry Jackson was director of the festival, significant reforms were undertaken. Jackson was the first person to gain control over both productions and festival plans and consequently he was able to change many of the practices which had previously made it virtually impossible to maintain high standards in production. Not only did he use a different director for each play, he staggered the openings so that each production could be adequately rehearsed. Furthermore, he was able to make the theatre self-contained by

Zeffirelli's production of *Romeo and Juliet* at the Old Vic in 1959.
(Photo by Houston Rogers.)

enlarging the workshops and storage spaces for scenery and costumes. He also imported young and vigorous personnel, among them Peter Brook (1925–), who directed *Love's Labour's Lost* and *Romeo and Juliet,* and Paul Scofield (1922–), who acted in *Cymbeline, Love's Labour's Lost, Romeo and Juliet, Twelfth Night,* and *Pericles.*

Once his reforms were accepted, Jackson resigned and was replaced in 1949 by Anthony Quayle (1913–), joined between 1953 and 1956 by Glen Byam Shaw (1904–), who then managed the company alone until 1959. It was in this Quayle-Shaw decade that the Shakespeare Festival attained its considerable international reputation, largely because, beginning in 1950, actors, directors, and designers of the first rank began to work there. Among them were John Gielgud, Peggy Ashcroft, Michael Redgrave, Diana Wynyard, Laurence Olivier, Margaret Leighton, Ralph Richardson, Vivien Leigh, Edith Evans, Charles Laughton, Tyrone Guthrie, Tanya Moiseiwitsch, Leslie Hurry, and James Bailey. For the first time, London's critics attended the performances regularly and Stratford was soon being elevated in their reviews above the Old Vic. During this decade, novel interpretations also came to be accepted as the norm rather than as aberrational. It was out of this atmosphere that still other developments would come in the 1960s.

Michael Redgrave and Peggy Ashcroft
in the 1953 Stratford production of
Antony and Cleopatra. (Angus McBean
Photograph, Harvard Theatre Collection.)

Laurence Olivier (at right) in the 1955 Stratford
production of Shakespeare's *Titus Andronicus*.
(Angus McBean Photograph, Harvard Theatre Collection.)

In London, Gielgud continued his prewar practices as actor and director. In 1944–45 at the Haymarket Theatre he staged an outstanding season which included Maugham's *The Circle,* Congreve's *Love for Love,* Shakespeare's *Hamlet* and *A Midsummer Night's Dream,* Webster's *The Duchess of Malfi,* and Wilde's *Lady Windermere's Fan.* Like much of Gielgud's postwar work, this season was partially supported by Tennent Plays, Inc., a subsidiary of H. M. Tennent, Ltd., England's largest producer. But though Gielgud remained a major actor and director, his influence never again equaled that which he had exerted in the 1930s.

Gielgud's work was paralleled in part by the Company of Four, which between 1945 and 1956 used the Lyric Theatre, Hammersmith, as a base for trying out revivals. Most of the major stars of the time appeared in their productions, which often toured throughout England before opening in the West End. The high point of its operations probably came in 1952, when Gielgud acted in *Venice Preserv'd, Richard II,* and *The Way of the World.*

After 1946, the English commercial theatre encountered major difficulties as production costs soared. Many of the problems stemmed from a trend toward monopolistic control. The dominant figure was Prince Littler (1901–   ), a provincial manager who in 1942 acquired the Stoll Theatre Corporation. By 1947, his associates, usually called the Group, controlled 75 percent of England's theatres and were the largest stockholder in H. M. Tennent, Ltd. With this control, they could demand 30 to 40 percent of each producer's gross earnings and the right to close any play that fell below a stated weekly income. Thus, they came to exert enormous pressure on producers to select popular works and to cast well-known stars. The power of the Group did not diminish until after 1956, when the new wave of dramatists lessened its influence, but it still controls practically every major commercial theatre in England and has invested as well in commercial television, recording studios, and song-publishing firms.

The real sufferers were the new dramatists, for the Old Vic, the Stratford Festival, and the Company of Four presented classics and revivals, while the commercial producers favored established dramatists. Thus, the British theatre suffered most from a lack of new playwrights.

The most successful writer of the postwar period was Terence Rattigan (1911–   ), who had already gained prominence in 1936 with *French Without Tears,* a light comedy which ran for more than one thousand performances, as did a wartime farce, *While the Sun Shines* (1943). He continued to win success in this light vein with *Love in Idleness* (1944), *Who is Sylvia?* (1950), and *The Sleeping Prince* (1953), but he now wrote more serious works as well. In *The Winslow Boy* (1946) he treated the well-known Archer-Shee case in which a schoolboy is unjustly accused of stealing; in *The Browning Version* (1948) he created a moving portrait of a thwarted schoolmaster plagued with a faithless wife; and in *Separate Tables* (1954), two linked short plays, he treated girls dominated by their

mothers. Rattigan later achieved considerable success with *Ross* (1960),
based on the life of T. E. Lawrence, and *A Bequest to the Nation* (1970),
which deals with Lord Nelson and Lady Hamilton. In all these works,
Rattigan remained firmly within the realistic mode. But, though he is one
of the best craftsmen of the age, handling situation and character with
admirable skill, Rattigan seldom rises above competence, perhaps because
no strong vision underlies his work.

During the 1940s and 1950s, Peter Ustinov (1921–   ) was constantly hailed as a promising playwright. After studying acting with Saint-
Denis, Ustinov made his first impression as a dramatist in 1942 with *The
House of Regrets,* a study of elderly White Russian exiles. This was followed
by *The Banbury Nose* (1944), which traced backward through time the
fortunes of the Hume-Banbury family, contrasting present disappointments
with the shining hopes of earlier times. Ustinov's major successes were won
with *The Love of Four Colonels* (1951), which shows the differing attitudes of Americans, French, English, and Russians about love, and *Roman-
off and Juliet* (1956), in which the love of an American girl and a
Russian boy are set against the background of the cold war. But, though
Ustinov always seemed on the verge of important insights, he never passed
beyond humor and charm.

In the 1950s, Graham Greene (1904–   ), already an established
novelist, came to the fore as a dramatist. After collaborating with Basil
Dean in 1950 on a dramatization of his novel *The Heart of the Matter,*
Greene wrote his first original play, *The Living Room,* in 1953. Its protagonist is a young Catholic girl who falls in love with a married man and
eventually commits suicide. Through it Greene seems to suggest that had
the girl received the proper love from her family she would not have
fallen into the trap of sensuality; above all he shows that adultery, rather
than being a solution, only leads to increased unhappiness. Greene continued
his interest in moral and religious questions in later plays, of which *The
Potting Shed* (1957), a drama about the recovery of faith, and *The Com-
plaisant Lover* (1959), a comedy about the failure of adultery, are the best.

Other writers might be mentioned, but they would only show that
English dramatists, though groping toward mature expression, were for the
most part mired in the earlier tradition of drawing-room comedy and
realistic drama.

Two organizations—the Arts Theatre Club and the Mercury Theatre
—were instrumental in encouraging new writers. The Arts Theatre Club,
with its well-equipped building seating 339, was begun in 1927 but
remained unimportant until taken over in 1942 by Alec Clunes (1912–   ).
Although he presented many foreign works and revived many older
English plays, Clunes also actively sought new works, for the best of which
he offered prizes. It was he who presented Ustinov's first play, and who for
a time employed Christopher Fry as resident dramatist. From 1947 until
1953 the Arts Theatre was run by Norman Marshall, who continued

Clunes's policies, and after that time by Campbell Williams (1906–   ), who imported such Continental works as *Waiting for Godot* in 1955 and *Waltz of the Toreadors* in 1956.

The Mercury Theatre is noted primarily for promoting poetic and religious drama. In 1945, E. Martin Browne (1900–   ) took over the Mercury as a home for his Pilgrim Players, with whom he had toured England from 1939 to 1945. (His was the first troupe to tour under the auspices of CEMA.) Originally its repertory was composed of such poetic religious dramas as Norman Nicholson's *The Old Man of the Mountains,* a transposition of the story of Elijah to an English setting; Ronald Duncan's *This Way to the Tomb,* which combines a masque about Saint Anthony with an antimasque in which the saint is attacked in his tomb when he appears to a group of modern fundamentalists; and Anne Ridler's *The Shadow Factory,* which intermingles the conflicts of a modern factory with a nativity play. After 1946, Browne turned to more secular works, such as Fry's *A Phoenix too Frequent,* and Donagh McDonagh's *Happy as Larry* (1947), based on a story by Goldsmith and the first postwar poetic drama to attract a large audience, eventually being transferred to a West End theatre. These beginnings fostered by the Arts and Mercury theaters blossomed in 1949 when Fry's play *The Lady's Not for Burning,* starring John Gielgud, Pamela Brown, Richard Burton, Claire Bloom, Harcourt Williams, and Esme Percy, became the hit of the season and established Fry as England's most respected writer of the postwar period.

Christopher Fry (1907–   ) had been an actor, director, and librettist before he turned to playwriting in 1938 with *The Boy with a Cart,* a poetic religious drama, a type that he continued in *Thor with Angels* (1948) and *A Sleep of Prisoners* (1951). He first attracted favorable attention in 1946 with *A Phoenix too Frequent,* a one-act comedy about a widow whose interest in life is reawakened by a soldier who guards her husband's tomb.

Fry was catapulted to fame in 1949 with *The Lady's Not for Burning,* a medieval story of witchcraft made comic by the twentieth-century perspective on such superstition. When the heroine, Jennet Jourdemayne, is accused of being a witch and of causing a death, Thomas Mendip, a soldier of fortune, demands that he be hanged as the murderer so that Jennet can be saved. Much of the play's charm stems from the rhythmic verse, but this element also tends to obscure the story line, since it draws attention to the witty dialogue and characterizations and away from the developing action. Nevertheless, the plot is worked out carefully and all is brought to a happy conclusion.

The success of *The Lady's Not for Burning* led Laurence Olivier to commission another work, *Venus Observed* (1950), which Fry called his autumn play just as he labeled the earlier comedy a spring play. It focuses upon a duke who is addicted to stargazing and is searching among his earlier loves for a wife, to be chosen by his son. The search is interrupted when he falls in love with the young Perpetua, but when she deserts him he

Christopher Fry's *The Lady's Not for Burning,* produced in London
in 1949. At center are Pamela Brown, who played Jennet,
and John Gielgud, who played Thomas Mendip.
(Angus McBean Photograph, Harvard Theatre Collection.)

resigns himself to the pleasures of growing old with Rosabel, the most
devoted of his former mistresses.

Fry's winter play, *The Dark is Light Enough* (1954), is set in Austria
during the uprisings of 1848–49 and centers on an aging countess, played
in the original production by Edith Evans. But by this time Fry's inspiration
seemed to be waning and the vogue for poetic drama to be passing.
During the 1950s, Fry also did a number of adaptations, such as *Ring
Around the Moon* (based on Anouilh's *Invitation to the Chateau*) and
Tiger at the Gates (based on Giraudoux's *The Trojan War Shall Not Take
Place*). In 1962 Fry turned once more to original composition with
Curtmantle, a play which seeks to illuminate the character of Henry II of
England and the relationship among various kinds of law—civil, moral,
canon, esthetic, and divine. In 1970, Fry at last completed his cycle of
seasonal plays with his summer work, *A Yard of Sun,* a seriocomic drama
set in Siena in 1946 when three brothers return from the war and seek to
come to grips with peace. These late works met little success, however, and
Fry's reputation continues to rest primarily on *The Lady's Not for Burning*
and to a lesser extent on *A Phoenix Too Frequent* and *A Sleep of Prisoners.*

The turn toward poetic drama was strengthened by T. S. Eliot, who
in 1949 returned to dramatic composition with *The Cocktail Party,* first
presented at the Edinburgh Festival and later in London and New York. By

T. S. Eliot's *The Cocktail Party,* as produced originally
at the Edinburgh Festival in 1949. Rex Harrison, at center,
played Sir Henry Harcourt-Reilly. (Photo by Anthony Buckley.)

now Eliot had pared down the poetic imagery found in his earlier plays
and had turned toward a more conventional dramatic structure. Ostensibly
The Cocktail Party is a comedy of manners about contemporary sophisticates, but on the deeper level it concerns the search for spiritual fulfillment
in a world that has lost its faith. Eliot uses a psychiatrist, Sir Henry Harcourt-Reilly—the modern equivalent of the priest or confessor—as a center
around which the other characters cluster and to provide a point of view
about them and their lives. Ultimately Eliot is most interested in the
spiritual destiny of Celia Coplestone, who after an unhappy love affair
chooses martyrdom in preference to the spiritual aridity of her earlier
existence.

This wedding of worldly surface detail with religious concern characterized Eliot's subsequent dramas as well, although both the texture of the
verse and the saintly nature of his protagonists lessened progressively. In
The Confidential Clerk (1954), Colby Simpkins eventually settles down as
the organist of a parish church and the other characters also become reconciled to their roles in life. In *The Elder Statesman* (1958), Lord Claverton,
who has retired to a nursing home after a lifetime of public service, comes to
acknowledge his past misdeeds before going off to a mysterious death on the
grounds of the sanitarium.

In all of these late works, Eliot sought increased dimensions by drawing upon Greek drama and the conventions of modern genres. Thus *The Cocktail Party* disguises Euripides' *Alcestis* as drawing-room comedy, just as *The Confidential Clerk* recasts Euripides' *Ion* as brittle farce, and *The Elder Statesman* reshapes Sophocles' *Oedipus at Colonus* as modern realistic drama. But as with Fry, it is the earliest of Eliot's works that have remained the most respected. After 1955, what had seemed a renaissance in poetic drama faded rapidly.

Throughout the period between 1940 and 1955, the dominant mode in English production was a simplified realism. Guthrie's penchant for novel interpretation of the classics gained ground, however, as it was taken up by Brook, Quayle, Benthall, and others. One important innovation came in 1948 at the Edinburgh Festival (which since its foundation in 1947 has been an important annual event) when an open stage was erected in the Assembly Hall for Guthrie's production of the sixteenth-century *Satire of the Three Estates*. Guthrie found this arrangement so satisfying that thereafter he was to promote it throughout the English-speaking world.

But, though the English theatre made a remarkable recovery after its virtual demise in 1940, it failed to move in significant new directions. By 1955 it seemed at a standstill. Soon, however, a new era was to begin.

~~~ **II** ~~~

The wartime German theatre followed a path almost opposite to that of Britain, for at first it remained active and prosperous, and then, after 1942, rapidly declined as almost one hundred theatre buildings (about 85 percent of the total) were destroyed. In 1944 all theatres were closed. In 1945 the Ministry of Education and Propaganda, which during Hitler's regime had controlled all cultural activities, was abolished. Since that time there has been no federal supervision of the theatre in West Germany, although individual states have sometimes exerted pressure.

At the end of the war Germany was divided into two parts, but in both parts the reestablishment of resident companies was given high priority and in both theatrical activity resumed almost immediately after peace arrived. Since the prewar pattern (under which each sizable city subsidized a permanent troupe) was revived, the theatre continued to be distributed throughout the country rather than being concentrated in a few urban areas.

Beginning around 1950 West Germany embarked on a vast program of rebuilding. As a result, no other country in the world has so many new theatre plants. In most of the new structures, there is a large house for operas, ballets, and traditional drama, and a small theatre for experimental works (or those not expected to attract large audiences). The large houses are relatively traditional in design, for the stages are framed by proscenium arches and equipped with complex machinery. For example, the Schiller Theater, opened in West Berlin in 1951, has a revolving stage, elevators, rolling platforms, and a cyclorama designed for use with rear projections. Most of the stages have aprons which are adjustable in extent, and with some, such as the theatre at Bochum, the proscenium opening can be varied in width. But for the most part, tradition reigns. On the other hand, the small houses are more apt to depart from past usage, for many have apron or thrust stages, and others are completely flexible in audience-actor relationship. In both large and small houses, considerable attention has been given to optimum vision and hearing. Both beauty and functionalism have been emphasized. By the late 1960s, there were about 175 professional theatres in West Germany, of which 120 were publicly owned, either by municipal or state governments. East Germany has done much less new building and consequently its companies are less well housed, many of them functioning in converted structures. Its new theatres tend to be even more traditional than those of West Germany. In East Germany there are about 135 companies, all operating in state-owned buildings.

In the subsidized theatres (both East and West), the government, as owner of the facilities, appoints a managing director (*Intendant*), who hires the company and other personnel. He is assisted by a literary advisor (*Dramaturg*), who recommends plays, provides translations and adaptations, and encourages high artistic standards. In the East, there is as well an advisory board (composed of representatives drawn from each branch of theatrical personnel and from the audience) which helps to determine policy and repertory. This arrangement (taken over from Russia) also serves, through the manipulation of the board's composition, to keep the theatres within the bounds favored by the government. All the subsidized companies—dramatic, operatic, and ballet—in a city (both in East and West Germany) are usually under a single *Intendant,* whose staff of directors and designers serves all the troupes. Since they also have personnel and space to construct and store scenery and costumes, they are self-contained units.

In West Germany the *Volksbühnen,* outlawed by Hitler, were revived after the war. By the late 1960s there were more than 150 local groups with over a half-million members. West Germany also has a few privately owned and operated theatres, most of them devoted to long runs of popular works. But, for the most part, the German theatre (both East and West) is a subsidized institution which each season presents a diverse program of plays drawn from many periods and styles. So many resident companies, however, has meant that few are truly outstanding. The strength of the German theatre stems from its diversity, eclecticism, and dispersal rather than from its virtuoso personnel.

Among the best of the postwar German troupes have been those at West Berlin, Dusseldorf, Dresden, Hamburg, Weimar, Darmstadt, Cologne, Munich, Leipzig, and Bochum. But the most famous have been two in East Berlin—the Komische Oper and the Berliner Ensemble.

The Komische Oper was founded in 1947 by Walter Felsenstein (1901–   ), also largely responsible for building the company's reputation. Unlike most other opera troupes, the Komische Oper rehearses a new production daily for several weeks or even months. Each moment of the action is polished. Primary emphasis is placed on acting and dramatic story rather than upon a series of arias. There are no stars and the singers are not always of the highest quality, but the ensemble effect far surpasses that normally encountered in operatic productions. Felsenstein has worked with a number of designers—most often Rudolf Heinrich but also Caspar Neher and Heinz Pfeiffenberger—who typically have used a simplified but evocative realism created by set pieces surrounded by a cyclorama and projections. The means are simple but the effect is always tied to reality. The major concern, however, is with the singing actor. Not only has Felsenstein's company become famous in East Germany, it has won world-wide renown through appearances at international festivals.

But the best known of all postwar German companies is the Berliner Ensemble, Brecht's troupe. After Brecht returned to Germany in 1948, he worked for a time at the Deutsches Theater (Reinhardt's former headquarters), where in 1949 he staged *Mother Courage* with the assistance of Erich Engel as director, Teo Otto as designer, and Helene Weigel as the protagonist. Later that year the Berliner Ensemble came into being. Helene

The Theater am Schiffbauerdamm, which, after 1954, housed the Berliner Ensemble. (Courtesy Berliner Ensemble.)

Weigel was named director, and Brecht was listed modestly as a member of the artistic advisory board (although he almost always directed his own plays, the majority of the troupe's repertory). At first the company shared the Deutsches Theater with another troupe and spent much of its time on tour. Not until 1954 did it gain its own permanent building, the Theater am Schiffbauerdamm (in which *The Threepenny Opera* was originally staged in 1928).

The troupe's first production in its permanent home, *The Caucasian Chalk Circle*, directed by Brecht, was to be significant in many ways. For setting, a concave white curtain was hung at the rear of the stage, and a convex white curtain at times swept across the front; between them a revolving stage turned to bring fragmentary set pieces into position as needed, while billowing silken cloths, on which Oriental landscapes were painted, were lowered from above. It epitomized the ensemble's emphasis on beauty as well as functionalism. Not only was this one of the company's greatest triumphs at home, it catapulted the ensemble to international fame when it was presented at the Théâtre des Nations in Paris in 1954 (where it won a prize as the best production of the year). By the time Brecht died in 1956, he was recognized as one of the truly important figures of the modern theatre, a position attained not only through his plays and theoretical writings but through the work of the Berliner Ensemble as well, for it established the effectiveness of much that he had advocated.

As with the Komische Oper, the Berliner Ensemble's results are in large part attributable to its care in staging plays. Rehearsals normally consume from two to six months, and productions are shown only after the desired effects are found and perfected. A large mirror is placed at the front of the stage so that the actors may observe themselves, and photographers take innumerable pictures so that the company may study what they have been doing. This slow process keeps the company's repertory correspondingly small. During its first ten years the troupe staged only about twenty-five plays. The majority of the repertory has always been composed of Brecht's plays, but it also includes many lesser works, most never shown outside of East Berlin.

The Berliner Ensemble is a completely self-contained organization. By the time of Brecht's death it consisted of about sixty-two actors, and a staff of designers, musicians, stagehands, electricians, and others for a combined total of almost three hundred persons. As one of East Germany's major cultural showpieces, it was also being handsomely subsidized. (In the late 1950s it received about 3 million marks annually.)

Many thought that the Berliner Ensemble would disintegrate after Brecht died, but it was held together by persons steeped in Brecht's theories and practices, many of them trained by Brecht. At first Erich Engel (1891–1966) and Helene Weigel (1900–1971), who had worked with Brecht since the 1920s, provided the major leadership, but they were strongly seconded by Manfred Wekwerth (1929–   ), assisted by Joachim Tenschert and (until he moved to West Germany) Peter Palitzsch. The company has also had the services of Paul Dessau and Hanns Eisler as composers, and Caspar Neher and Karl von Appen as designers.

In addition to its performances in East Berlin and throughout Europe, the Berliner Ensemble's work has also become widely known through its publications. *Theaterarbeit* (*Theatre Work*, 1952) described the first six productions, and such later productions as *Mother Courage* and *Galileo* have been recorded in *Modellbücher* ("sample books"), each of which includes from six hundred to eight hundred photographs. These have served as inspirations for many who have never seen an actual production by the troupe.

Although less famous, a number of other companies also helped to raise postwar production to a high level. Of the directors, perhaps the best were Gustav Gründgens (1899–1963), also one of Germany's finest actors; Fritz Kortner (1892–1970), who had won fame in the 1920s with his performances in Jessner's productions; Oscar Fritz Schuh (1904–   ); Karlheinz Stroux (1908–   ); Boleslaw Barlog (1906–   ); Heinz Hilpert (1890–1967); Rudolf Sellner (1905–   ); Günther Rennert (1911–   ); Hans Schalla (1904–   ); Harry Buchwitz (1904–   ); and Erwin Piscator, who returned to West Germany in 1951 and staged plays for numerous companies as well as being *Intendant* of the Freie Volksbühne in West Berlin until his death in 1966.

The dominant visual mode underwent a marked change. During Hitler's regime the officially sanctioned approach had been a grandiose realism. After the war, partially because of material shortages, full-stage representation gave way to suggestion. The dominant figures in stage design were Otto and Neher, both attuned to Brecht's approach. Teo Otto (1904–68) was educated at the Bauhaus and began his career as a designer at the Kroll Opera House in Berlin in 1927. In 1931 he was appointed chief designer at the Berlin State Theatre, but he left Germany for Zurich in 1933. After the war, he worked with practically all the great directors of the time—Brecht, Gründgens, von Karajan, Strehler, and others. He was a master of "selective decor," using scanty means in such a way as to be impressive but unostentatious. More than any other designer, Otto shaped postwar German practices. Caspar Neher (1897–1962) began his career in 1923 and worked for Jessner, Martin, and the Berlin Volksbühne before becoming principal designer at the Deutsches Theater from 1934 to 1944. He was a childhood friend and lifetime collaborator of Brecht, working closely with him both before and after Hitler's regime. By the time he died he had mounted more than six hundred productions in theatres throughout the world.

Both Otto and Neher moved design in the direction of theatricalism—the frank manipulation of stage means. Although they often used realistic elements, they normally suggested place through decorative screens, projections, a few architectural details, and lighting which created mood and atmosphere. Their settings were functional and beautiful, and often commented on the drama in an epic manner. It was their approach that came to dominate the postwar German stage. There were as well many other fine designers, among them Max Fritzsche, Karl Gröning, Helmut Jürgens, Rudolf Heinrich, Wilhelm Reinking, and Karl von Appen.

In addition to normal theatrical activity, festivals were also revived after the war and have continued to increase in number. In Austria, the Salzburg Festival, reopened in 1946, has produced von Hofmannsthal's *Everyman* and a host of other attractions each summer. In 1960, it opened a new theatre seating 2,158 persons and containing a stage which is one of the world's largest (the proscenium opening may be varied from 50 to 100 feet in width) and best equipped (with revolving, sliding, and elevator sections). At Bayreuth, the Wagnerian festival was reestablished in 1951 under the direction of Wieland Wagner (1917–1966), who outraged traditionalists with his simple settings composed primarily of a few set pieces, projections, and atmospheric lighting. (It was often charged that the action was practically invisible because of the near-darkness.) For the first time at Bayreuth, the operas were staged in symbolic settings reminiscent of the plans Appia had championed as early as the 1890s, and thus for the first time were brought into touch with modern theatrical developments. Among other festivals perhaps the most important have been the Ruhr Festival at Recklinghausen (since 1947), and the Berlin Festwochen (since 1951).

Wagner's *Götterdämmerung,* Act I, as it was produced in 1964 at Bayreuth. (Courtesy Bayreuther Festspiele.)

But if the theatre recovered rapidly, drama did not, for, except for
those older writers who now returned to Germany, there was something of
a cultural vacuum. During the Nazi era, Germany had been isolated from
the rest of the world and after that time Nazi playwrights were no longer
acceptable. Thus, Germany had to await the arrival of a new generation of
dramatists. Meantime the stage was flooded with foreign works that had
been forbidden in Germany since 1933 and with classics or works by
writers who had begun their careers before Hitler came to power. For
example, Georg Kaiser's last play, *The Raft of Medusa,* was a considerable
hit when produced in 1945, as was Zuckmayer's *The Devil's General* in
1948. These dramas, dealing with personal and social morality, did much
to establish the tone of postwar German drama. But the major figure from
the pre-Hitlerian period was Brecht. Even before the war ended, his plays
were being presented in the German-language theatres of Switzerland, and
when the hostilities ended they rapidly found their way into Germany,
where their popularity has steadily grown. Between 1950 and 1968 there
were 15,920 performances of Brecht's plays in the German-language
theatres of Europe. By 1957–58 he trailed only Shakespeare, Schiller, and
Goethe in numbers of productions and by 1967–68 he was second only to
Shakespeare. Nevertheless, Brecht wrote no important new works after he
returned to Germany.

The first new dramatist to attract widespread attention was Wolfgang
Borchert (1921–47), although because of his early death he produced only
one play. *The Man Outside* (1947) is reminiscent of numerous works of
the post-World War I period, for like them it shows the difficulties of a
returning soldier seeking to adjust to civilian life, and depends heavily on
expressionistic techniques. Despite its derivativeness, it struck a responsive
chord with its treatment of a man's failure to reestablish human contacts,
and for several years it was one of the most popular works in the repertory.

Fritz Hochwalder (1911–   ), an Austrian writer, also came to prominence in the postwar period. His most famous play, *The Holy Experiment*
(1943), deals with the expulsion of the Jesuits from Paraguay in 1767 and
centers on the father provincial, who has sought to set up a utopian state
only to be told that what he is doing conflicts with the higher needs of the
Church. Thus he is faced with a dilemma—to obey orders he considers
immoral, or to resist through violence. Since he considers neither proper,
he decides that religion provides no answer for the world's problems. No
doubt it was the moral question, which recalled that faced by many Germans under Hitler, that accounted for its considerable appeal.

Most of Hochwalder's later plays are based upon historical subjects
chosen to illuminate timeless moral issues. For example, *The Public Prosecutor* (1949) shows a prosecutor during the French Revolution diligently
and heartlessly preparing a case against an unknown enemy of the state
only to discover that he is the victim. Another group of Hochwalder's
plays shows how inquiries into minor problems lead to revelations about

the past and the human propensity for evil. For example, in *The Command* (1968) a routine investigation gradually uncovers a man's criminal Nazi past. In every case, it is the moral dilemma that interests Hochwalder. A traditional writer in his techniques, he usually observes the three unities and utilizes many devices borrowed from the well-made play.

The vacuum in the postwar period was partially filled by two Swiss playwrights, Frisch and Duerrenmatt. Both came to the fore in the 1940s through productions at the Zurich Stadttheater, which under Oskar Walterlin and Kurt Hirschfeld was probably the best German-language theatre in the world during the war years.

Max Frisch (1911–), born in Zurich, was trained as an architect but turned to playwriting in 1944 with *Santa Cruz,* a symbolic play about the conflict between the claims of domesticity and freedom. He has written regularly since that time, but is best known for *The Chinese Wall* (1946, 1955), *Biedermann and the Firebugs* (1953, 1958), and *Andorra* (1961). (Frisch is notorious for revising his plays, some of which are available in several versions.)

The Chinese Wall is set in medieval China just before the building of the Great Wall. Happy at having rid his country of the last barbarians, the emperor gives a party in celebration, and to it come real and fictional persons from times ranging over thousands of years. The play is held together by the Man of Today, who also points up the basic ideas. The characters embody the mistakes of the past, just as the play demonstrates that man learns nothing from his errors. Frisch's immediate concern is the atomic bomb, which he obviously believes will be used and then rationalized as necessary. Thus, in Frisch's view the contemporary attempt to avoid barbarism is as useless as was that of the Chinese when they built the Great Wall.

Biedermann and the Firebugs is more restricted in scope but more pointed in its criticism. In this semiallegory, Biedermann takes arsonists into his home in the belief that they will spare him if he does not oppose them. Eventually, however, he, along with his family, home, and city, is consumed. A mock-serious chorus of firemen repeatedly declares its readiness to protect the city, for, according to Frisch, people now trust in the fireman instead of God. In an epilogue (which Frisch later removed as being overly explicit), Biedermann declares his complete innocence in the catastrophe, thus pointing up man's inability to learn from his mistakes. This is probably Frisch's most popular work, having been offered in sixty-one different German theatres in 1961.

Andorra, about anti-Semitism and the rationalizations that undergird it, shows how a supposed Jewish boy is killed as pressures from a neighboring state grow. Many scenes are devoted to testimony given years later and emphasize the rationalizations of those involved. Most excuse themselves by declaring that they thought the boy actually to be Jewish, again demonstrating Frisch's contention that men do not learn.

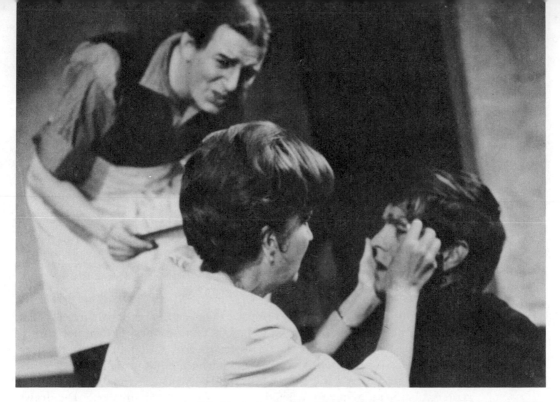

Frisch's *Andorra* at the National Theatre, London, with, left to right,
Trevor Martin, Diana Wynyard, and Tom Courtenay.
(Courtesy National Theatre, London.)

All of Frisch's work suggests that he longs for a better world, one in which men would love one another and live together happily, but it also implies that his dream is impossible to realize. Through techniques borrowed from Wilder, Strindberg, Brecht, and others, he embodies his search and disillusionment in symbolic and nightmarish fantasy.

Friedrich Duerrenmatt (1921–   ), the son of a Protestant minister, was a theology student before turning to drama with *It is Written,* produced in Zurich in 1947. Since that time he has written extensively for the theatre, including *Romulus the Great* (1949), *The Marriage of Mr. Mississippi* (1952), *Frank the Fifth* (1959), *The Meteor* (1966), and *Play Strindberg* (1969). But his international reputation rests primarily on two works— *The Visit* (1956) and *The Physicists* (1962). *The Visit* deals with the corrupting force of materialism. (Titled *The Old Lady's Visit* by Duerrenmatt, it is known to English-speaking audiences primarily through Maurice Valency's adaptation, in which among other alterations the name Alfred Ill has been changed to Anton Schill.) In it, Claire Zachanassian, the richest woman in the world, returns to her native and bankrupt village with an offer to give the townspeople $1 billion, half to go to the town and the other half to be divided among the residents, if they will kill Alfred Ill, who seduced her and had her branded a whore when she was a young girl.

Duerrenmatt's *The Old Lady's Visit,* as produced in 1956 at the Düsseldorf Schauspielhaus, directed by Leo Mittler with Hermine Körner as Claire.

Seemingly outraged, the people declare their determination to reject such an offer. But gradually they begin to buy on credit things they cannot afford, and eventually they acquiesce to Ill's death and rationalize their deed as an act of justice. Not only has a crime been committed, it has been sanctioned by the democratic process. In this way, Duerrenmatt suggests the corruptibility of mankind when its own interests are involved. He draws heavily on Wilder and Brecht for his techniques and at times on Pirandello for his outlook, but to these he adds his own disillusionment about the human spirit.

The Physicists deals with the problem of scientific knowledge under political control. Set in an asylum, it focuses on three ostensibly insane men who have assumed the identities of world-famous physicists. Eventually it becomes clear that all are sane, that one, Mobius, has made a discovery which opens up such possibilities for political misuse that he has decided to hide his discovery behind his mask of madness, and that the other two are agents of world powers seeking to gain control of his secret. In order to protect humanity, they all agree to stay where they are, only to find that the keeper of the asylum has stolen the secret and intends to use it to control the world. In addition to exploring the moral dilemma of the modern scientist, Duerrenmatt also seems to imply that the fate of the world hangs on chance. Here, as in several of his plays, Duerrenmatt draws on the detective story and traditional dramatic structure.

Duerrenmatt is much more detached than is Frisch. He emphasizes the grotesqueness of the human condition which he expresses through a rather "dark comedy," for, according to him, tragedy "presupposes a formed world. Comedy . . . supposes an unformed world, a world being made and turned upside down, a world about to fold like ours." Although he is concerned with moral dilemmas, he shows the human instinct for good corrupted either by power and greed or by chance. He avoids bitterness by standing at a distance and viewing events sardonically. "The universal for me is chaos. The world (hence the stage which represents the world) is for me something monstrous, a riddle of misfortunes which must be accepted but before which one must not capitulate."

These playwrights—Zuckmayer, Brecht, Borchert, Hochwalder, Frisch, and Duerrenmatt—turned the postwar German theatre toward questions of guilt and responsibility and the role of the individual in the body politic. This moral search has been the most characteristic feature of postwar German drama. It was to become even more evident in the 1960s.

III

In France, practically all entertainments were interrupted briefly in 1939–40 during the fighting with Germany, but, after France's capitulation, the theatre, under the German occupation between 1940 and 1944, was relatively prosperous. It was never deprived of materials, and some productions were truly sumptuous. Because of the midnight curfew, curtain time was moved to 6:30, but houses were usually crowded. As elsewhere, most producers catered to a wartime audience seeking diversion.

During the war Jean-Louis Barrault came to the fore as a director at the Comédie Française, where between 1940 and 1946 he and his wife were leading performers. Here he mounted some of the most admired productions of the decade: *The Suppliants, The Dead Queen, Phèdre, Le Cid,* and *The Satin Slipper*. With these, he established himself as a major force in the theatre comparable to that exerted earlier by the Cartel.

In his work, Barrault synthesized most of the major interwar trends. He had studied with Dullin and Decroux and had worked with Artaud. From the Cartel he learned respect for a text and for precise workmanship, from Decroux the power of mime, and from Artaud the importance of subterranean impulses and of nonverbal means. He sought to incorporate all of these lessons both in his acting and in his directing.

Few directors have been more eclectic than has Barrault in the choice of plays. He has produced works ranging in time from ancient Greece to the present and in form from tragedy to farce. In staging, he has sought to create a "total theatre" (as opposed to the earlier partial theatre that had grown up around realistic psychological drama). He does not reject realism, for he has declared that, as an art of sensuality, flesh, and blood, the theatre is at its base realistic. But it is also an art in which the text is only a small part. "A script is like the upper and visible part of an iceberg, representing only about one-eighth of the whole; the other seven-eighths are the invisible roots, that is to say, that which creates poetry or the signification of reality." His productions have always been noted for their technical perfection and complexity—sometimes puzzling in their attempt to embody multiple meanings simultaneously. Some of his most popular productions have been of such light works as Feydeau's *Look After Amélie,* but his most respected productions have been of such complex works as Claudel's plays, an adaptation of Kafka's novel *The Trial,* and his own adaptation of Rabelais's works.

Barrault's greatest wartime triumph came in 1943 with Claudel's *The Satin Slipper,* designed by Lucien Coutaud, and acted by Marie Bell, Madeleine Renaud, Pierre Dux, Aimé Clairond, Jean Yonnel, André Brunot, and Barrault. Like most of Claudel's works, *The Satin Slipper* is concerned with the conflict between human and divine love, sensuality and spirituality. Set against the background of Spain's American empire, the action is spread over a century in time and much of the globe. Furthermore, much of it is symbolic, as when the hemispheres converse and the earth is represented as one bead on a rosary. Barrault's success with a work that had previously been considered unstageable established his reputation. It was also considered the first significant example of "total theatre." Claudel later permitted Barrault to stage others of his works, the success of which were largely responsible for Claudel's current position of honor in the French theatre.

Barrault's production of Claudel's *The Satin Slipper* in 1943; design by Lucien Coutaud. (Photo by Pic.)

At the end of the war, the Comédie Française entered a period of stress. When Pierre Dux (1908–   ), appointed administrator in 1944, sought to institute a number of reforms, many motivated by the actors' increasing outside commitments, a large number of the leading performers resigned. Among those who left were Barrault and his wife, who in 1946 established their own troupe, the Compagnie Madeleine Renaud–Jean-Louis Barrault, into which they took many of those who had left the Comédie Française, including Jean Desailly, André Brunot, Jacques Dacqmine, Edwige Feuillère, and Pierre Brasseur. Until 1956 the company performed at the Théâtre Marigny in a repertory which included *The Oresteia* (adapted by Obey), *Hamlet* (in Gide's translation), Molière's *Scapin* and *Amphitryon,* Marivaux's *False Confessions,* Claudel's *Break of Noon* and *Christophe Colomb ,* and Kafka's *The Trial* (as adapted by Gide and Barrault). In the *Cahiers* (*Notebooks*) published by the troupe, the problems posed by each production were explored at length. They provide valuable insights into the company's working methods and artistic principles. Forced to give up the Marigny in 1956, the troupe toured widely until 1959, when Barrault became manager of the state-subsidized Théâtre de France (about which more will be said later). But by 1956 Barrault was generally looked upon as France's most important director.

The war years also brought to the fore two major playwrights— Montherlant and Anouilh. Henry de Montherlant (1896–1972) had been a leading novelist since the 1920s, but, though interested in drama, he had done little playwriting before 1941, when Jean-Louis Vaudoyer, the administrator of the Comédie Française, requested him to translate a Spanish drama. Instead, Montherlant decided to write an original work. The result was *The Dead Queen* (1942), which in Barrault's production was considered a major artistic triumph. Since that time Montherlant has written with some regularity. Among the best of his many plays are *The Master of Santiago* (1948), *Malatesta* (1950), *Port-Royal* (1954), *The Cardinal of Spain* (1960), and *The Civil War* (1965).

The Master of Santiago is often considered Montherlant's most characteristic work because of its simple external action, complex psychology, and elevated style. Set in Spain in 1519, it focuses on Alvaro, head of the Order of Santiago, and his daughter Mariana. Early in the play it is learned that members of the order are to go to the New World, where they will be able to make a fortune; as a result of Alvaro's improved finances, Mariana will then be able to marry the man she loves. But when she learns that all these plans have been made to assist her father who considers the Spanish incursions in America evil temptations, Mariana reveals the truth to him, although it condemns her to a life in the convent. Through it all runs the motif of sacrifice: Mariana gives up her chances for happiness because of love for her father, and he sacrifices everything to his conception of the ideal man. In his ascetic and harsh rejection of all mediocrity, Alvaro is often considered to be a reflection of Montherlant himself.

Montherlant's *The Master of Santiago* at the Théâtre Hébertot in 1948.
Directed by Paul Oettly, designed by Mariano Andreu.
(Photo by Bernand.)

Port-Royal is Montherlant's most austere play, for, like Racine's works, it reduces the action to internal conflict. It takes place on a single day in 1664 after Jansenist nuns at the Convent of Port-Royal have refused to sign articles of faith dictated by the Church. The principal characters are the archbishop of Paris (the representative of orthodoxy) and Sisters Angelique and Françoise (the dissenters). Since the nuns are defeated from the start, the play concentrates upon their inner struggle. The interest resides as much in their intellectual positions as in their characterizations and actions.

Montherlant has said: "A play interests me only if the exterior action, reduced to the utmost simplicity, is only a pretext for the exploration of man; if the author has taken on himself the task not of imagining and constructing mechanically an intrigue, but of expressing with the maximum of truth, intensity and profundity a certain number of movements of the human spirit." His work as a whole illustrates the large role that philosophical concerns have played in postwar French drama.

Jean Anouilh (1910–   ) was a law student when he saw Giraudoux's first play in 1928 and decided that he wished to be a playwright. He worked for a time as Jouvet's secretary, had his first play produced in 1932, and married the actress Monelle Valentin before he achieved his first success in 1937 with the Pitoëffs' production of *Traveller Without Baggage*. He then

Anouilh's *Antigone,* directed and designed by André Barsacq at the Théâtre de l'Atelier in 1943. Left to right are Elisabeth Hardy, Lucien Barjon, Paul Mathos, and Marcel Peres. (Photo by Bernand.)

formed an association with Barsacq, who between 1939 and 1948 produced Anouilh's plays at the Atelier. The production there of *Antigone* in the midst of the war raised Anouilh to the forefront of living French dramatists, especially after Giraudoux's death in 1944.

Anouilh has now written about thirty-five plays, among the best of which are *Antigone* (1943), *Waltz of the Toreadors* (1952), *The Lark* (1953), *Poor Bitos* (1956), *Becket* (1959), *Dear Antoine* (1970), and *Do Not Awaken Madame* (1971). He has divided his plays into *pièces noires* (the black or serious) and *pièces roses* (the rose or happy). But all pursue the same basic theme—the conflict between integrity and compromise. It is with the noncompromisers that Anouilh seems to sympathize. The action of his plays usually focuses on the protagonist's struggle to maintain his purity, even as it becomes clear that compromise can be avoided only in death. *Antigone* shows the pattern at its best. Unlike Sophocles, Anouilh is not concerned with the gods or the supernatural. When asked why she has buried her brother, Antigone replies, "For myself." This adherence to a self-imposed standard is contrasted with Creon's compromises, dictated by his views of what is best for others. Antigone dies rather than accept Creon's accommodations with a morally corrupt world.

561

In the "happy plays," Anouilh often suspends final judgment to permit happy endings. For example, in *Thieves' Carnival* (1938) two young lovers seem to find happiness, but most of Anouilh's plays suggest that ultimately betrayals are inevitable. Anouilh also often mingles the serious and the comic, as in *Becket* and *Waltz of the Toreadors*.

Anouilh has declared that the greatest influence on his work has been Pirandello, especially through *Six Characters in Search of An Author*. This influence can be detected in many of his plays, which are often concerned with illusion and reality, but, unlike Pirandello, Anouilh seems to believe that truth can be uncovered. The influence is more evident, however, in his manipulation of illusion, as in *Antigone,* which begins in frank theatricality and gradually builds a sense of intense reality.

There is also in Anouilh's work an element of romanticism, seen especially in his protagonists' rejection of compromise and in their revolt against philistinism. In his late works, however, youthful rebellion is pushed to the background and disillusionment brought to the fore. Anouilh has as well a classical bent, for he develops simple and clearly defined actions which involve only a few characters. A realistic vein is also evident in the straightforward, forceful prose spoken by the characters and in the psychological motivations assigned them. On the other hand, his disgust with life and its compromises has served as a kind of bridge between the older school of drama and the absurdists. Anouilh's wide appeal is perhaps due to his skillful blending of so many modes. Although his reputation has declined since the absurdists came to the fore, he remains one of the most popular dramatists in the world. Probably no modern play has been produced more often than has *Antigone*.

Most of the other significant playwrights of this period had won fame before the war, as had Achard, Salacrou, and Obey—or were existentialists or absurdists (movements which will be discussed in the next chapter). Until the mid-1950s, however, Anouilh and the traditionalists remained dominant.

After the war ended, the French theatre entered a period of readjustment. To ease the stresses, the newly reconstituted central government took a number of measures. It reduced the state theatres (which since Napoleon's time had numbered four) to two managements: the Opéra and Opéra-Comique were placed under one director, and the Odéon was absorbed into the Comédie Française. Now having two theatres, the Comédie Française sought to confine classics to its traditional home and to present more recent and popular works at the former Odéon. This policy became too difficult to maintain, however, and eventually distinctions between the two virtually disappeared. Furthermore, the company was at a low point, from which it only gradually recovered under the administrations of Pierre-Aimé Touchard (from 1947 to 1953) and Pierre Descaves (from 1953 to 1959).

The Ministry of Fine Arts took a number of other actions designed to strengthen the French theatre. It sought to improve the overall quality by encouraging new companies, directors, and playwrights. In 1946 it established an annual festival at which substantial prizes were awarded the best production by a new company and the best work by a new director. At the same time, the government began to subsidize the first productions of promising young playwrights. The state also sought to prevent a few managers from dominating the commercial theatre by requiring a separate license for each theatre and limiting the number of licenses that could be held by an individual or organization. Furthermore, several of the Parisian studios were granted subsidies to help them survive the hardships created by rapidly rising production costs. Nevertheless, few of the studios could any longer afford permanent companies and in Paris only the Comédie Française and Barrault were able to hold a troupe together throughout an entire season.

Perhaps the most important governmental program, however, was that designed to decentralize the theatre. Between the wars the provincial theatre had dwindled steadily so that by 1944 there were only fifty-one theatres outside of Paris, while in the capital there were fifty-two. Thus, despite the government's commitment to assist the theatre, benefits were confined almost entirely to Paris. To remedy this situation, the central government, in cooperation with departmental and municipal authorities, began in 1947 to establish a series of "dramatic centers" distributed throughout France. Each company had its headquarters in a large town, where it performed for several weeks at a time and then toured to others within an approximate radius of 100 miles. The first was the Théâtre de l'Est, founded in 1947, and now based at Strasbourg. Originally headed by Roland Pietri and André Clavé, it passed to Michel Saint-Denis in 1953 and to Hubert Gignoux in 1958. There in 1957 the first new theatre built in postwar France was opened. Designed by Pierre Sonrel (in collaboration with Saint-Denis) and financed by the central government and the city of Strasbourg, it seats 754 persons and houses a company of about twenty-five actors, four directors, and a technical staff of fifteen. Admission charges are kept low by subsidies and subscriptions, of which there are more than twenty thousand in Strasbourg. The company also tours to about seventy towns with two kinds of productions, one intended for large and the other for small stages. Since 1954 the dramatic center has also operated a training school, headed by Pierre Lefevre but organized along the lines used by Saint-Denis in his earlier ventures.

A second center was created in 1947 at St.-Etienne from a troupe which Jean Dasté, Copeau's son-in-law, had begun in 1942, playing first at Grenoble and then in the mining center of St.-Etienne, where it presented works by Shakespeare, Brecht, and others for an audience drawn primarily from the working classes. Similarly, in 1949 another dramatic center was created in Toulouse out of a troupe, Le Grenier, begun there in 1945 by Maurice Sarrazin, Daniel Sorano, and Jacques Duby. In 1964 it was provided a new theatre seating 600. In 1949 a center was also created at

Rennes to serve Brittany and western France. The Dramatic Center of the Southeast, based in Aix-en-Provence, was founded in 1952 under the direction of Gaston Baty, who died on the day of the first production. He was succeeded by Georges Douking until 1956, then by René Lafforgue until 1966, and after that by Antoine Bourseiller. Other centers include the Théâtre de la Cité at Villeurbanne (a suburb of Lyon) under the direction of Roger Planchon (about whom more will be said in a later chapter); at Tourcoing, under the direction of André Reybaz; and at Bourges, under the direction of Gabriel Monnet. Others will probably be created in the future.

In addition to the dramatic centers, there are as well a number of "permanent troupes," which tour widely to fill the gaps between centers. The first of these dates from 1952, but most were created in the 1960s. The number fluctuates, but in the late 1960s there were nine. In such ways, the French theatre has made considerable progress toward decentralization since the war.

The national and local governments have also encouraged and subsidized the many annual festivals which have sprung up. The first appeared in 1947 at Avignon and Strasbourg, and they were soon followed by others at Besancon, Aix-en-Provence, Bordeaux, and Toulouse. There are now well over fifty each year.

Of the festivals, the most prestigious is that at Avignon, directed by Jean Vilar (1912–71), who during the 1950s was second only to Barrault as a major force in the French theatre. Vilar was a university student in French literature when in 1933 he auditioned for and was admitted to Dullin's school, where he was a fellow student of Barrault. He then toured with a company throughout France before directing his first play, Synge's *The Well of the Saints,* in 1943. He next formed his own troupe, the Company of Seven, which in a series of small Parisian theatres presented such plays as Strindberg's *The Dance of Death* and Eliot's *Murder in the Cathedral.*

With his appointment as director of the Avignon Festival in 1947, Vilar had to make a great leap from small- to large-scale productions. He was so successful with such works as Shakespeare's *Richard II* and Büchner's *Danton's Death* that in 1951 he was asked to head the Théâtre National Populaire (TNP), then an insignificant scheme under which a few productions staged by other organizations were presented each season at reduced prices. Given a subsidy of 52,000 francs, Vilar was expected to employ a company of his own and to provide a minimum of 150 performances in Paris and others on tour. After some initial setbacks, the TNP grew steadily in stature. The company included the enormously popular film star Gerard Philipe, along with such outstanding performers as Vilar, Daniel Sorano, Georges Wilson, Philippe Noiret, Lucien Arnaud, Maria Casarès, Germaine Montéro, Genevieve Page, and Monique Chaumette. With such productions as *Le Cid,* Kleist's *The Prince of Homburg,* Brecht's

Jean Vilar (foreground) as
Robespierre in his production
of Büchner's *Danton's Death*
in 1953 by the TNP
(Photo by Agnès Varda.)

Mother Courage, and Molière's *Dom Juan* and *The Miser,* the TNP soon
became the most popular of all the state-subsidized troupes. Under Vilar
it divided its time between Paris, tours throughout France, and Avignon.
Its accomplishments were recognized in 1959 when it was placed on an
equal footing with the Comédie Française.

More so than Barrault, Vilar was the heir of Copeau, Dullin, and
Jouvet, and was the first French director to gain a wide following with
productions utilizing the principles championed by Copeau and the Cartel.
He upheld the integrity of the text and placed primary emphasis upon
clarity of interpretation, diction, and movement. At the TNP most typically
he used a near-bare stage without a front curtain. Scenic pieces were introduced sparingly, although as time went by they increased in number. Vilar's
principal designer was Léon Gischia (1903–   ), who often used platforms
to model the floor, but gained most of his effects through costumes,
lighting, carefully selected furniture and properties, projections, and occasional set pieces.

Vilar was especially concerned with making the theatre meaningful
to the masses. He established a price scale that could compete with the
movies and did away with such practices as tipping ushers so as to make
theatregoing less forbidding. He also selected plays he thought relevant to
a popular audience. His repertory was about evenly divided between French
and foreign works.

Vilar remained head of the TNP until 1963, when he resigned, but he continued to manage the Avignon Festival up to the time of his death. Although he went on directing and acting in Paris, his influence lessened considerably in the late 1960s. Thus, it is upon his work of the 1950s that his reputation rests.

After the war, the Cartel slowly faded from the scene. Dullin left Paris in 1947, Baty in 1951; Jouvet died in 1951. The Cartel's ideals survived through various groups, however, such as the Atelier under Barsacq, the Studio des Champs-Elysées under Maurice Jacquement, the Rideau de Paris under Marcel Herrand and Jean Marchat, and the Théâtre Montparnasse under Marguerite Jamois. To these prewar figures should be added Jean-Pierre Grenier (1914–   ) and Olivier Hussenot (1913–   ), whose Compagnie Grenier-Hussenot between 1945 and 1957 presented outstanding productions of Feydeau's *Hotel Paradiso,* an adaptation of Dumas *père*'s *The Three Musketeers,* Courteline's *Follies of the Squadron,* and Duerrenmatt's *The Visit.* But by the mid-1950s this group of directors was beginning to be replaced by a new wave, most of whom were attuned to absurdism or to Artaud.

～ IV ～

In the United States, as elsewhere, the theatre during the war was devoted primarily to diversionary entertainment, although occasionally it reached a higher level through such productions as Margaret Webster's staging of *Othello* with Paul Robeson, José Ferrer, and Uta Hagen. Following the war, when the price controls that had been in effect were removed, production costs skyrocketed. At the beginning of the war about $25,000 was needed to produce a straight drama and about $100,000 to produce a musical on Broadway. By 1960 these costs had risen to $150,000 and $600,000 respectively. Similarly, the minimum weekly salary for actors rose from $40 during the war to $85 in 1953 and to $100 in 1957. Ticket prices reflected these increases. In 1944 the maximum price at dramas was $3.50 and at musicals $4.85; by 1955 these had risen to $5.50 and $7.00, and by 1960 to $7.15 and $8.60. Despite such constant increases in entrance fees, by 1959 75 percent of all productions failed to regain their initial investments.

Under these circumstances, it is not surprising that the theatre continued to decline. In 1940 there were still about forty-three Broadway theatres, but by 1956 the number had dropped to thirty. New productions on Broadway reached a low point in 1949–50 when there were fifty-nine. Between 1950 and 1960 the number averaged sixty-two. This figure could not rise significantly until additional theatres were available, and none was built between 1927 and 1960.

Such problems were compounded by the introduction of television broadcasting, which in some areas began as early as 1945. By 1948 there were forty-eight stations in twenty-five cities, and by 1958 there were 512 stations and over 50 million receivers. To compete with this free entertain- ment, theatrical producers resorted to well-known stars, lavish mounting, and plays calculated to exert the widest possible appeal. Scripts were shaped to fit public taste, which was gauged through a series of out-of-town tryouts prior to a Broadway opening. Under such conditions play-writing did not flourish.

The most popular form was the musical, often said to have reached maturity during World War II. Musical drama has always been a favored form, but it has flourished especially during the twentieth century and above all in America. The conventionalized stories and the emphasis upon songs, dances, and beautiful girls, which characterized most musical comedy until after World War I, began to change around 1928 with *Showboat,* by Jerome Kern and Oscar Hammerstein II, in which the story became as important as the music. This innovation was strengthened during the 1930s by such works as *Of Thee I Sing* (1931), a satire on American presidential campaigns by George S. Kaufman, Morris Ryskind, and Ira and George Gershwin, which was also the first musical play to win a Pulitzer Prize; and in the 1940s by *Pal Joey* (1940) by John O'Hara, Lorenz Hart, and Richard Rodgers, the first musical to avoid sentimentality, and *Lady in the Dark* (1941), by Moss Hart and Kurt Weill, which explored a woman's deep-seated psychological problems.

All of these advances were synthesized in *Oklahoma!* (1943) by Oscar Hammerstein II (1895–1960) and Richard Rodgers (1902–   ). Based on Lynn Riggs's *Green Grow the Lilacs,* it was the first musical to use all the theatrical elements in a fully integrated manner so that all shared in telling the story. Its success (2,248 performances) and that of such subsequent works by Rodgers and Hammerstein as *Carousel* (1945), *South Pacific* (1949), and *The King and I* (1951) established the pattern which still dominates musical drama in America. Among their successors, some of the best have been Alan Jay Lerner and Frederick Loewe with *Brigadoon* (1947) and *My Fair Lady* (1956), Frank Loesser with *Guys and Dolls* (1950) and *Most Happy Fella* (1956), Jules Styne with *Gentlemen Prefer Blondes* (1949) and *Funny Girl* (1964), Jerry Herman with *Hello, Dolly* (1964) and *Mame* (1966), and Leonard Bernstein and Arthur Laurents with *West Side Story* (1957). Such works have dominated the Broadway stage.

Nevertheless, authors of nonmusical plays made considerable impact in the postwar American theatre. Among the older dramatists who continued to write were Maxwell Anderson with *Joan of Lorraine* (1946), *Anne of the Thousand Days* (1948), and *Barefoot in Athens* (1951); Clifford Odets with *The Country Girl* (1950) and *The Flowering Peach* (1954); Lillian Hellman with *Another Part of the Forest* (1946), *Autumn Garden* (1951), and *Toys in the Attic* (1960); Thornton Wilder with

Design by Jo Mielziner for the original New York production of Williams's *The Glass Menagerie* in 1945. (Courtesy Jo Mielziner; photo by Peter A. Juley and Son.)

The Skin of Our Teeth (1943) and *The Matchmaker* (1954); and William Saroyan with *The Cave Dwellers* (1957). Perhaps most important, O'Neill's works gradually returned to the stage. Although *The Iceman Cometh* failed when it was first presented in 1946, it became a great success in 1956 (in an off-Broadway production) and led to the production of previously unknown plays, *Long Day's Journey Into Night* in 1956 and *A Touch of the Poet* in 1957. Thereafter, O'Neill's reputation steadily revived.

In addition, two major new dramatists—Williams and Miller—appeared. Tennessee Williams (Thomas Lanier Williams, 1914–   ) had earned a university degree and had worked at various odd jobs before *Battle of Angels* was produced in 1940. His first success came in 1945 with *The Glass Menagerie* and was consolidated with *A Streetcar Named Desire* (1947), *The Rose Tattoo* (1951), *Cat on a Hot Tin Roof* (1954), *Orpheus Descending* (1957), and *Sweet Bird of Youth* (1959). But by the late 1950s Williams was being accused of repeating himself and thereafter both his critical stature and his output declined, although he later produced *Period of Adjustment* (1960), *Night of the Iguana* (1961), *The Milk Train Doesn't Stop Here Anymore* (1962), *The Seven Descents of Myrtle* (1968), and others.

The Glass Menagerie is both Williams's most popular and least characteristic work. A "memory play" in which Tom Wingfield calls up scenes from his youth, it shows his mother Amanda seeking in the midst of poverty to maintain a past gentility and to cajole her children into happiness. Most of Amanda's concern is for her daughter, Laura, a shy, crippled girl who for comfort turns to her menagerie of glass figurines. After one abortive attempt to find her a suitor, Tom runs away from home but cannot escape his sense of guilt. In some ways, *The Glass Menagerie* sums up the major modern experiments in drama. In it symbols are used much in the manner of Ibsen and Chekhov, time and place are manipulated as in Strindberg's plays, frank theatricality is employed in the manner of

Wilder and Brecht, inner psychology and hidden motivations are explored as in post-Freudian drama, and many touches are reminiscent of those in realistic and naturalistic drama.

Although in many ways *The Glass Menagerie* foreshadowed Williams's subsequent works, it did not provide any clue to the violence and sex—rape, cannibalism, castration, promiscuity, homosexuality, drug addiction, and so on—which figure so prominently in them. But Williams is interested in sensationalism only as part of his inquiry into "what place can be found in the modern world for 'lost souls'—the artist, the natural man, the aristocrat, the non-conformist." His protagonists are almost always out of tune with accepted norms, which are usually represented in one or more of three ways: the dull and vulgar; the hypocritical and complacent; or the ugly and violent. Williams's sympathy lies with the misfits—the "fugitive kind" —who usually combine sensitivity and imagination with some form of corruption—often sex, drugs, or alcohol. Occasionally they are merely withdrawn, but in almost every instance they are seeking to escape an unfriendly present or to recover a dead past. The action usually shows the protagonist progressively forced to face the truth—usually after he is subjected to physical or moral degradation by "normal" characters. In a few plays (such as *The Rose Tattoo* and *Cat on a Hot Tin Roof*), the protagonist is able to come to terms with himself and his society, but more often he resorts to some extreme form of escape—insanity, violence, or death.

Williams relies rather heavily on antitheses to divide his characters into the sensitive and the complacent. It is the former who suffer, the latter who prosper. In the early plays, the protagonists are usually left in a kind of living death, but in such later works as *Orpheus Descending* and *Suddenly Last Summer* (1958) they become sacrificial victims. Thus their

Original production of Williams's *A Streetcar Named Desire* in 1947 with Kim Hunter, Marlon Brando, and Jessica Tandy. (Photo by Eileen Darby.)

suffering takes on meaning, even if it is not always given an entirely satisfactory explanation.

But Williams is not basically a "thinker," for he is concerned primarily with feeling, inner desires, and attempts to find some accommodation with an unfriendly world. To achieve his effects, he has used theatrical means imaginatively, manipulating them, sometimes quite obviously, to focus attention upon the inner truth of character and situation. No American playwright commanded such a wide audience as did Williams between 1945 and 1960. The worth of his early plays remains unchallenged, although the later ones have found little favor. His vision of the isolated individual surrounded by a hostile universe has won him a sympathetic hearing throughout the world.

Arthur Miller (1915–   ) studied playwriting in college and began to write plays in the 1930s, but did not win success until 1947 with *All My Sons,* a "well-made," didactic drama about Joe Keller, a manufacturer whose defective airplane engines have caused the deaths of many pilots, perhaps even his own son. He comes to realize that he should have considered all members of the air force to be his sons. This moral consciousness (somewhat like that which dominated postwar German drama) was to inform much of Miller's subsequent work, although he was to abandon such conventionalized dramatic structure.

Death of a Salesman (1949) is usually considered Miller's finest work. Its hero, like that of *All My Sons,* is drawn from the world of business and subscribes to the same materialistic ideals. But, whereas Joe Keller has been successful, Willy Loman has not. The gap between his accomplishments and his ambitions leads Willy to the verge of a breakdown and to inquire into the reasons for his failure. Willy also wants to be loved, but he unconsciously believes that he does not deserve esteem if he is financially unsuccessful. It is only when he comes to see that his son loves him in spite of his failures that a change is possible. Eventually Willy commits suicide so that his family will receive his insurance. Thus, though he does not wholly escape materialism, he subordinates it to selfless concern for others.

In *Death of a Salesman,* Miller abandons the well-made play for a much freer structure. As the action moves from the present external world to Willy's internal memories, events from various past times are called up to illuminate Willy's character and values. Few plays have captured better the conflict between materialism and moral integrity.

The Crucible (1953) is set in Massachusetts in the seventeenth century during a witchhunt. Miller explores the hysteria which accompanies the search but he also shows how both a supporter (the Revered John Hale) and a doubter (John Proctor) are forced to reexamine their own values. When it was first produced, many saw in it a commentary upon Senator Joseph McCarthy's communist "witchhunt," and certainly it provided striking parallels and strong warnings against accepting mere accusation as proof of guilt. But the play was more than topical, for it has continued to be one of Miller's most popular works.

A View from the Bridge (1955, revised 1956) focuses on Eddie Carbone, a Brooklyn longshoreman, who is killed by his former friends after he informs on an illegal immigrant. Eddie acts largely because he is unable to accept his attraction to both his niece and the young immigrant with whom she falls in love. Thus, he sacrifices himself to the guilt he feels but does not fully understand. Miller uses a lawyer, Alfieri, to introduce and to conclude the play and to draw rather unconvincing parallels between Eddie and the heroes of classical drama who violate the moral code and are struck down by relentless forces.

After a long silence, Miller produced two new plays, *After the Fall* (1964) and *Incident at Vichy* (1964). Neither was very successful. Of the first, Miller has said that he was concerned with the Cain or destructive instinct in man. He shows his protagonist's relationship with a series of wives and draws parallels between the ruinous results and the Nazi extermination camps. He was trying to suggest that the cruelty we condone in daily life is merely violence in miniature, and that, like Adam and Eve after their fall from innocence, we must come to grips with domestic destructiveness if we are to avoid a more extreme holocaust. Unfortunately, Miller did not sufficiently dramatize his vision, and audiences have seen in it merely a rather tasteless autobiographical work about Miller's own marriage to Marilyn Monroe.

Miller regained some of his earlier appeal with *The Price* (1968), a compact play that harks back to *All My Sons* in its structure. It treats two middle-aged brothers (a policeman and a successful lawyer) who meet after many years to dispose of their dead father's belongings. The policeman, who as a young man gave up all his ambitions in order to look after his father, accuses his brother of winning success at his expense. Ultimately the play is concerned with the price to be placed on love. Why do we serve others? Should we expect to be paid for making voluntary sacrifices? If they are not made willingly, are they truly based on love? Out of the recriminations and revelations, the men come to a better understanding both of themselves and of the nature of love.

Through all of Miller's plays run the same ideas. His characters stray because of overly narrow (often materialistic) values and find peace in some more meaningful understanding both of themselves and of their roles in society. Miller is often called a "social" dramatist, but his interests have always been moral. Though society may encourage false values, it remains the individual's responsibility to sort out the true and the false. Miller clearly implies that it is possible to maintain one's integrity within the framework of society. Thus, he is far more traditional in his outlook than is Williams, who always places the blame on society for forcing men to become misfits.

For a time, William Inge (1913–   ) seemed to be following in Williams's footsteps. He first came to prominence in 1950 with *Come Back, Little Sheba,* a play about an alcoholic husband and his slatternly, daydreaming wife, for whom the loss of happiness is represented by her dog,

Ralph Meeker and Janice Rule (at center) in the original production of
Inge's *Picnic* in 1953. (Photo courtesy of Alfredo Valente.)

Little Sheba, who disappeared long ago but whom she still calls each day.
Inge's reputation increased with *Picnic* (1953), in which an attractive
drifter acts as a catalyst in the life of a small town, and *Bus Stop* (1955), in
which a group of characters, marooned in a small cafe, work out their
frustrations. Inge's last major success came with *The Dark at the Top of
the Stairs* (1957), after which he entered a period of decline with such
works as *A Loss of Roses* (1959) and *Where's Daddy?* (1966).

Inge's resemblance to Williams stems primarily from his predilection
for "misfit" characters and sexual themes. But Inge is a sentimentalist,
for he implies that all problems can be solved merely by facing up to
them. Thus, once the characters come to understand themselves, happiness
seems to lie ahead. Unlike Williams, Inge seems to have no vision of a
world order, and consequently his work is more limited in its import.

Other playwrights might be mentioned. Robert Anderson (1917–   )
first won acclaim with *Tea and Sympathy* (1953), a work about the
tensions in a boys' school, especially after one is accused of homosexuality.
After a period of obscurity, he reemerged in the 1960s with *You Know I
Can't Hear You When the Water's Running* (1967), a group of one-act
plays; *I Never Sang for My Father* (1968), which explores the relationship
between a father and son; and *Solitaire/Double Solitaire* (1971), two
one-act plays on the theme of loneliness. All are competent works but
unlikely to survive the test of time. Much the same might be said of
Paddy Chayefsky (1923–   ), who after a striking debut in television turned
to the theatre with *Middle of the Night* (1956), which treats an affair
between a young woman and an aging manufacturer. He went on to *The
Tenth Man* (1959), which tells in comic terms much the same story as
The Dybbuk—how a young girl is freed from an evil spirit by the power of
love—and *Gideon* (1961), an adaptation of the biblical story.

Until the mid-1950s, American drama seemed vigorous. Then, as prewar writers began to die, as Williams and Miller lost their vitality, and as no significant new dramatists appeared, a decline became evident. By 1960, old impulses seemed spent and new ones not yet clear.

Theatrical production followed a similar pattern. The dominant style in the American theatre from the late 1940s until about 1960 was a theatricalized realism compounded of acting which emphasized intense psychological truth and of visual elements which eliminated nonessentials but retained realistic outlines. It combined near-naturalism in performance with stylization in settings. This mode was popularized by the director Elia Kazan and the designer Jo Mielziner through such productions as *A Streetcar Named Desire* (1947) and *Death of a Salesman* (1949). As this approach gained wide acceptance in the 1950s, settings increasingly moved away from full-stage representation to a few pieces which suggested the whole. This trend has yet to be reversed. As its leading exponent, Mielziner remained the dominant designer throughout the 1950s.

The style of acting derived from Stanislavsky and the Group Theatre, as embodied in the productions of Kazan, and to a lesser extent in those of Harold Clurman and Robert Lewis (1909–). Above all, it came to be associated with the Actors' Studio. Founded in 1947 by Kazan, Cheryl Crawford, and Lee Strasberg (the artistic director and dominant figure), the Actors' Studio sought to develop talent in isolation from public criticism by freeing actors from psychological inhibitions and by encouraging imagination through "emotion memory," improvisation, and other exercises derived from Stanislavsky. It seems to have placed primary emphasis, however, on leading the actor to self-understanding. Consequently, it was often accused of caring nothing for technical skills and of encouraging self-indulgence.

Much of the public's conception of the Actors' Studio was based on the work of Marlon Brando (1924–), who was catapulted to fame by his

Jo Mielziner's design for Miller's *Death of a Salesman* (1949). (Courtesy Jo Mielziner; photo by Peter A. Juley and Son.)

performance as Stanley Kowalski in *A Streetcar Named Desire*. The novelty of serious acting based on substandard speech, untidy dress, and boorish behavior captured the public fancy and soon became associated with the Actors' Studio. Since Kazan's subsequent productions were the most prestigious of the 1950s, they too directed attention to the Studio and its methods. Many actors who sought to adopt the new mode mumbled their speeches and invented endless mundane stage business. Such distortions were soon thought typical of the Actors' Studio, and Strasberg's attempts to counter them largely went unheeded. The controversy further increased the Studio's prestige, however, and made it the dominant force in actor training, just as it motivated endless debates over the authenticity of Strasberg's interpretation of Stanislavsky.

In 1956 the Actors' Studio added a Playwrights' Unit, in 1960 a Directors' Unit, and in 1962 a Production Unit. For a time, it staged its own productions, among them O'Neill's *Strange Interlude* and June Havoc's *Marathon '33* (1963). But by the early 1960s the tone of the American theatre was changing and the psychological realism of the studio soon came to seem too limiting. Thereafter the studio's influence waned rapidly, although it still commands a devoted (though much reduced) following. But during the 1950s, it was perhaps the most potent force in the American theatre.

As in France, so too in postwar America there were several attempts to diversify the theatre. Unfortunately in the United States the government offered virtually no assistance. One exception came in 1943 when the city of New York acquired the Mecca Temple on 55th Street and converted it into the City Center, where productions (primarily of opera, musical comedy, and ballet) were offered for short runs at low prices. Under the direction of Jean Dalrymple (1910–   ), it built an enviable record, which was recognized in 1966 when its ballet and opera companies were given permanent homes in the newly constructed Lincoln Center for the Performing Arts. The City Center continues to provide space and assistance to promising ventures.

Another admirable attempt to diversify the theatre was made in 1946 when Eva Le Gallienne, Margaret Webster, and Cheryl Crawford established the American Repertory Theatre and produced a season of plays composed of *Henry VIII, What Every Woman Knows, John Gabriel Borkman, Androcles and the Lion,* and *Alice in Wonderland.* After suffering a loss of $250,000, however, the venture came to an end in 1947.

The American National Theatre and Academy (ANTA) also put forth several schemes for diversification. ANTA was created in 1935 by a congressional charter which listed as its goals to stimulate and rejuvenate the theatre throughout the country and to establish and operate a training school. Prior to the war, however, little was done to implement these aims. In 1945, ANTA was reorganized to include on its board of directors representatives from all regions and fields of interests. Since then it has from time to time sponsored series of productions, such as Experimental Theatre, Inc., which between 1947 and 1949 sought to encourage new playwrights. In 1950 it acquired the Guild Theatre and renamed it the ANTA Theatre. Because of its tax-exempt status, ANTA has been able to use this theatre for nonprofit projects or for those of unusual cultural interest. As recently as 1969–70 it organized a "Showcase Series" which brought various regional companies to New York for limited engagements. But, for the most part, ANTA has remained a forum for ideas, and virtually none of its original goals have been realized.

More important accomplishments were to come from the off-Broadway theatres, descendants of such interwar groups as the Provincetown and Washington Square Players. Like their predecessors, the off-Broadway producers rented quarters removed from the midtown theatrical center so that production and ticket costs could be kept low. Since many operated in buildings never intended for theatrical purposes, experimentation with such audience-actor spatial arrangements as arena and thrust stages were inevitable. Because most of the theatres seated a maximum of 199 persons (theatres with 200 seats are subject to more stringent city regulations), they could be sustained by a limited audience interested in a more eclectic repertory than that provided by Broadway. Thus, in some ways they resembled the studios that had dominated the Parisian theatre between the wars.

The off-Broadway theatre received its first important impetus in 1947–48 when New Stages, under the direction of David Heilweil, offered Sartre's *The Respectful Prostitute* to such acclaim that it was moved to a Broadway theatre. In 1950, New Stages rented the ballroom of the midtown Hotel Edison where it operated the first professional arena theatre in New York. Unfortunately this venture survived only about six months.

But by 1950 off-Broadway was gaining strength. In 1949, the League of Off-Broadway Theatres was formed to deal with common problems. It was able to negotiate favorable terms with various unions and to establish a more professional attitude among its members.

A major upturn in the critical fortunes of off-Broadway came in 1952 when Williams's *Summer and Smoke,* a failure on Broadway, achieved enormous success at the Circle in the Square. Not only did this production bring José Quintero to prominence as a director and raise Geraldine Page to stardom, it suggested that some off-Broadway theatres might be superior to many of their commercial rivals. Furthermore, by the mid-1950s off-Broadway had far outdistanced Broadway in the number and diversity of its offerings.

During the 1950s the most influential of the off-Broadway theatres were the Circle in the Square and the Phoenix Theatre. The Circle in the Square was opened in 1951 by José Quintero and Theodore Mann. In this former nightclub, the actor-audience relationship was entirely flexible, although spectators were normally seated around three sides of a rectangular acting area. Here such performers as Geraldine Page, Jason Robards, Jr., George C. Scott, and Colleen Dewhurst came to prominence. After his triumph with *The Iceman Cometh* in 1956, Quintero was asked to direct the Broadway production of *Long Day's Journey into Night*. Its cumulative record made the Circle in the Square one of the most respected theatres of the 1950s. But, though it has continued to play an important role, it has since lost much of the vitality it displayed in the first decade of its existence.

The Phoenix Theatre was founded in 1953 by Norris Houghton (1909–   ) and T. Edward Hambleton (1911–   ). In the 1930s Houghton had been associated with a group of young actors known as the University Players and had won considerable esteem with his *Moscow Rehearsals* (1936), a first-hand account of the Russian theatre. Hambleton had been responsible for ANTA's productions. When they founded the Phoenix, Houghton and Hambleton were able to rent an out-of-the-way but well-equipped conventional theatre seating 1,172. The Phoenix presented a diverse program of plays by such authors as Aristophanes, Shakespeare, Turgenev, Ibsen, Shaw, Pirandello, and Montherlant. Out of a desire to use a different director for each play, it turned to Tyrone Guthrie, Michael Redgrave, John Houseman, and others, and it frequently attracted outstanding actors, such as Siobhan McKenna and Robert Ryan. Although most of its repertory was composed of well-known pieces, it occasionally produced works by controversial newcomers. For example, it did much to establish Ionesco's reputation in America with an excellent production of *The Chairs* and *The Lesson,* directed by Tony Richardson and starring Joan Plowright and Eli Wallach. Beginning in the late 1950s, the Phoenix employed a permanent acting company, which under the direction of Stuart Vaughan presented a series of plays each season. This arrangement lasted until the early 1960s, when Houghton and Hambleton formed a liaison with the Association of Producing Artists (APA) and thereafter became primarily producers of that company's offerings.

For the most part, off-Broadway theatres in the 1950s were little concerned with experimentation in staging except for their use of arena or thrust stages. They were most interested in repertory. Thus, they differed from Broadway primarily in taste and resources. Their goals were essentially artistic. Not till the 1960s did the off-Broadway and off-off-Broadway theatres experiment extensively with new techniques in writing and staging.

After the war there were also a number of attempts to decentralize the theatre. ANTA set forth a number of schemes, but all had to be abandoned for lack of support. Ultimately progress came only through the work of a few dedicated individuals. One of the first to attract wide attention was Margo Jones (1913–55), who in 1947 established in Dallas her Theatre 47 (the theatre's name changed with the year). With a resident troupe, she mounted on an arena stage a series of varied plays each season. After her death, the venture was kept alive until 1959. Other pioneering regional companies include the Alley Theatre, founded in

Houston in 1947 by Nina Vance; the Arena Stage, founded in Washington, D.C., in 1949 by Zelda Finchandler and Edward Mangum; and the Actors Workshop, founded in San Francisco in 1952 by Jules Irving and Herbert Blau. These groups began with unpaid performers and worked on arena stages or in cramped quarters while gradually building support. A turning point came in 1959, when the Ford Foundation began to make large grants to those troupes which seemed most likely to survive and grow. Thus, although the accomplishments of the 1950s were not great, the foundations were laid for more ambitious projects in the 1960s.

Summer festivals also added diversity. At Stratford, Ontario, a Shakespearean Festival was inaugurated in 1953. Here Tyrone Guthrie, who at first was the guiding spirit, introduced the kind of open stage he had originally used in Edinburgh. The success both of the festival and of its spatial arrangements were to be influential throughout North America. An American Shakespeare Festival was instituted at Stratford, Connecticut, in 1955; since then it has annually offered a fifteen-week season of plays, the best of which have often been sent on tour or to Broadway. The New York Shakespeare Festival was established in 1954 by Joseph Papp, and since 1957 has played free of charge in Central Park, where the municipally owned Delacorte Theatre (seating 2,263) was inaugurated in 1962 primarily to accommodate it. Other Shakespearean festivals are held annually at Ashland (Oregon), Boulder (Colorado), San Diego, and elsewhere. Summer theatres, most of them located in resort areas, have also steadily increased in numbers, as have amateur community groups. Additionally, by the 1960s approximately fifteen hundred colleges and universities were offering courses in theatre. Thus, various groups sought to compensate for the concentration of the professional theatre in New York.

Despite these endeavors, however, the American theatre between 1940 and 1960 took most of its cues from Broadway. In terms of its size and resources, the United States, in comparison with European countries, did little to support the theatre. By 1960 however, improvement seemed to be in the offing.

Activities elsewhere can be summarized quickly, for important developments were few. In wartime Russia, troupes were dispatched throughout the country to perform for members of the armed forces and for factory workers. Since censorship was relaxed during the conflict, many thought the end of the war would bring still further freedom. Instead, socialist realism and the needs of the state were enforced as strenuously as ever. The government still sought to make the theatre available to all the people, but in turn it expected adherence to the guidelines it laid down. There would be no significant change until after Stalin's death in 1953 and Khrushchev's denunciation of Stalin in 1956.

In Italy, the war made little impact on the theatre since there was no strong tradition to affect. After the war, a few persons sought to remedy the lack of permanent troupes. The most important attempt came in 1947 with the foundation of the Piccolo Teatro in Milan by Giorgio Strehler (1921–) and Paolo Grassi (1919–). It was given a rent-free theatre by the city of Milan and later became the first dramatic company in Italy to receive a governmental subsidy. By the time Strehler resigned in 1968, it had presented well over one hundred plays, about evenly divided between Italian and foreign works. Partially because of its several foreign tours, it came to be considered not only Italy's finest troupe but one of the best in the world.

The Piccolo Teatro is a self-contained organization with a company of twenty to thirty actors, two directors, and a designer, plus technical and maintenance personnel. In addition, it operates a school for actors and other theatrical workers. It attracts a predominantly young audience, about one-fifth drawn from the working class. While he was its head, Strehler directed about three-fourths of all productions, but for others he imported a number of outstanding directors from other countries. Strehler leaned heavily toward Brechtian techniques, as did his designers—Gianni Ratto (1916–) until 1954, and Luciano Damiani (1923–) after that time.

In the postwar period, two Italian playwrights—Betti and de Filippo —achieved international recognition. Ugo Betti (1892–1953) began writing in 1927, but all of his major works came after the war: *Corruption in the Palace of Justice* (1948), *The Crime on Goat Island* (1950), *The Queen and the Rebels* (1951), and *The Burnt Flower Bed* (1953). The most important influences on Betti's work were his own judicial background and Pirandello's plays.

All of Betti's dramas treat crises of conscience among the powerful, who usually have gained their positions through party or governmental influence. In the beginning, his protagonists usually set themselves up as arbiters of morality (his representative heroes are judges), but gradually they are forced to reassess their values as sordid events from the past are brought to light. Betti dwells upon the deceptiveness of appearances and upon the way past deeds determine present ones. But Betti also treats evil and guilt as instruments for good, since they lead to compassion and mercy. No doubt it was his preoccupation with guilt and responsibility, a favorite theme with postwar dramatists, that won Betti his wide following throughout the world. His plays are traditional in structure, most of them melodramas given a philosophical turn. Ultimately Betti seems more derivative than original.

Eduardo de Filippo (1900–) was born into a Neapolitan theatrical family and between the late 1920s and 1946 was associated with his brother and sister in their own troupe, for which he wrote all of his early works. His plays demonstrate the sound theatrical experience he gained there as actor, director, and writer. Most of his work is deeply rooted in the Neapolitan background and written in the dialect of that region. But his characters and situations are universal in their concern with the pressures of poverty, ignorance, disease, war, and strained family relationships. His characters are usually passive beings who manage to survive by adapting themselves to circumstances. The plays mingle pathos and humor with closely observed local color.

De Filippo began writing around 1930. Among his best works are *Christmas in the Cupiello* (1931), *Naples' Millionaires* (1946), *Filumena* (1955), *Saturday, Sunday and Monday* (1959), and *The Boss* (1960). *Naples' Millionaires* tells the story of a man who returns from prison camp to discover that his family has prospered through prostitution and black-marketeering. After his initial shock and remonstrations, however, he settles down to enjoy the fruits of wealth. *Filumena* concerns a former prostitute who tricks a lover into marrying her by pretending to be dying. After the marriage, she quickly recovers, and when he threatens to leave her tells him that he is the father of one of her three children. Since she refuses to identify the child, he eventually settles down with her and accepts all the children as his own. The warmth, humor, and deep human sympathy of de Filippo's plays and film scripts have endeared him to audiences both at home and abroad.

In Spain, theatrical activity was seriously interrupted during the 1930s by the civil war and was subsequently kept isolated from the rest of the world until the 1960s by heavy censorship. Nothing that was thought likely to conflict with "the fundamental principle of the State" was permitted. The censors, a large proportion of whom were priests, had no fixed guidelines, and consequently their rulings were often capricious and contradictory.

Nevertheless, around 1950 a revival of Spanish drama began as new authors appeared and as such veterans as Benavente and Martínez Sierra died. The turning point is usually dated from the production of *The Story of a Stairway* by Antonio Buero Vallejo (1916–   ) in 1949, the first time after the civil war that a new play was judged worthy of the prestigious Lope de Vega Prize. The drama traces the story over a period of twenty-eight years of four lower-class families who live on the same floor of an apartment house. It shows friendships, conflicts, and marriages, but most of all it creates a sense of tragic waste as the illusions and hopes of youth are eroded by time.

Since 1949, Buero Vallejo has written about twenty plays and has come to be considered Spain's leading dramatist. Until 1958 he wrote about contemporary subjects and primarily in the realistic vein, although occasionally, as in *The Weaver of Dreams* (1952), he made forays into fantasy and symbolism. He then turned to historical subjects, often taking his primary inspiration from paintings. (Buero Vallejo began his career as

Buero Vallejo's *The Weaver of Dreams* at the Teatro Español, Madrid, in 1952. Design by Vincente Viudes, directed by Cayetano Luca de Tena. The performers are María Jesús and Guillermo Marín.

a painter.) Of these later works, the best is probably *The Concert at Saint Ovide* (1962), based on an eighteenth-century engraving of the Parisian fair of Saint Ovide, where untrained, blind musicians were made to play for a public who came to be amused or to jeer at this ridiculous spectacle. Buero Vallejo uses this situation as the basis for a "parable in three acts" about man's struggle to overcome the forces of darkness, cruelty, and prejudice.

Alfonso Sastre (1926–) also made considerable impact, as much through his essays about the theatre as through his dramas. He objected to the predominance in Spain of a "theatre of magic" which encourages the public to evade problems even as ever more efficient means of destruction are being invented and as the working class vainly cries out for improved conditions. As an alternative, Sastre advocates a "theatre of anguish" designed to meet squarely the problems of modern life. He was also one of the founders of the Teatro Populaire Universitario, a pioneer in theatrical reform and the producer of Sastre's first play, *The Condemned Squad* (1953). Divided into twelve scenes, the action of this play occurs during some future war and focuses on the six members of a squad who are sent on a deadly mission. The first part of the play ends with a Christmas celebration during which four of the men kill their leader. The second part shows the effect of this deed on the others. By the end of the play, the killers have come to accept their guilt and to see its relationship to the whole concept of war. Sastre implies as well that citizens in general must recognize their responsibility for the kind of world in which they live. Because of his concern with social, moral, and political questions, many of Sastre's more pointed works have never been seen in Spain, although they are widely read and admired. Among the best of these later works are *Every Man's Bread* (1957), *Gored* (1960), *In the Net* (1961), and *The Business of Utter Darkness* (1967).

As Sastre suggests, most recent Spanish drama has been escapist and comic. Occasionally, however, a comic writer has risen above the ordinary, as did José López Rubio (1903–   ), who after winning fame as a writer in the 1920s became a filmmaker before turning to the theatre in 1949 with *Alberto*. Like most of López Rubio's plays, *Alberto* uses fantasy and comedy for semiserious purposes. Here he shows how the lives of boardinghouse residents are affected when they create an imaginary person to help solve their problems. His work is perhaps seen to best advantage in *The Other Side* (1955), in which three persons who have died violently linger at the scene and watch the disillusioning behavior of the survivors. It is a witty, sophisticated, cynical, sometimes malicious view of humanity. López Rubio was extremely prolific during the 1950s, but then largely gave up writing plays to do research for a history of the Spanish theatre.

During the 1950s, the Spanish theatre slowly became more aware of the work going on in other countries. As censorship gradually eased, the works of such authors as Williams, Wilder, O'Neill, Claudel, Anouilh, and Montherlant began to be presented. Even so, the Spanish theatre remained conservative in outlook and production techniques until well into the 1960s.

One other aspect of the postwar theatre—the formation of international organizations—also deserves mention. Most of these associations have been promoted by the United Nations and its subsidiaries, especially the United Nations Educational, Scientific and Cultural Organization (UNESCO), which in 1947 sponsored the International Theatre Institute (ITI). Although it has a charter of its own, the ITI receives a yearly subsidy from UNESCO and has its headquarters in the UNESCO building in Paris. Each member country maintains a national center (in the United States, ANTA serves this function) which undertakes activities of four kinds: the collection and dissemination of information, the publication of books and periodicals of international interest, the exchange of persons, and the exchange of companies. The ITI also holds congresses every two years and other meetings less frequently. In addition, it sponsors the Théâtre des Nations, which annually since 1954 has presented a season of productions in Paris by companies from all over the world. Furthermore, the ITI has assisted in the formation of other organizations, among them the International Association of Theatre Technicians, the International Association of Theatre Critics, and the International Society for Theatre Research. Together these groups have done much to promote greater understanding and closer cooperation among theatrical personnel throughout the world.

~~ VI ~~

World War II marked a pause more than a drastic change in theatrical life. In England and France, it motivated the government to reassess its role in the arts and to assist them in surviving, recovering, and expanding. In Germany, where so many theatrical facilities were destroyed, vast sums were expended in rebuilding. Almost everywhere the postwar theatre underwent a period of stress as the extensive demands on materials and labor in a peacetime economy caused production costs to soar. But after 1950, the theatre also participated in the general prosperity, even if to a lesser extent than did most endeavors.

During the war and afterward until the mid-1950s, theatre and drama for the most part continued along lines that had been established earlier. It was more a time of recovery than of change, for neither theatrical practice nor dramatic composition was innovative. A few exceptions to this pattern could be cited in Germany and in the work of Barrault, but Germany was catching up after the strictures of the Nazi era, and Barrault was synthesizing a number of earlier trends. These were important accomplishments, but the norm almost everywhere could best be characterized as an extension of practices already underway.

Nevertheless, in the postwar years there also gradually came to the fore new directions, the most innovative being those championed by the absurdists and the followers of Artaud. They appeared first in France but did not attract wide attention until the mid-1950s. By then the recovery from wartime conditions seemed complete, but apathy had also begun to set in and consequently change was welcomed. The time when new directions became evident varied in each country: in France it came about 1953 with the production of Beckett's *Waiting for Godot;* in England about 1956 with the appearance of Osborne's *Look Back in Anger;* in Russia and Eastern Europe about 1956 with Khrushchev's denunciation of Stalin; in Germany about 1963 with the emergence of such writers as Peter Weiss; and in America about 1959 with the appearance of Edward Albee and with the Living Theatre's production of Gelber's *The Connection.* Other events might serve as signs of change, but these seem to have been those that drew wide public attention to new directions. Soon the relative quiet of the immediate postwar years had given way to some of the most frenetic experimentation the theatre has known.

Absurdity
and
Anger

The patterns that dominated theatre and drama during and immediately following World War II began to alter in the late 1940s and to be almost completely disrupted by the late 1950s. As during the decade between 1910 and 1920, changes resulted in part from altered perceptions. New directions first became evident in the work of such writers as Sartre and Camus, whose existentialist vision was embodied in their own dramas, and, in attenuated versions, in the plays of the absurdists—especially Beckett, Ionesco, Adamov, and Genet—as well as those of many other writers both in France and elsewhere. In England, a more socially conscious outlook gave rise after 1956 to a new generation of writers—of which the most prominent were Osborne and Wesker—usually called the "angry young men." The new wave in England produced as well playwrights such as Arden and Pinter whose works are not easily classifiable. By 1960, both countries had revivified their dramatic traditions.

The horrors of World War II, especially the systematic displacement and extermination of vast numbers of persons, created a crisis of conscience among many of the world's intellectuals. Traditional values seemed incapable of coping with such dilemmas and, more significantly, to rest on no solid foundation. As the implications of a Godless universe, first suggested by late-nineteenth-century thought, at last became fully evident, the search for absolute values gave way to fundamental questioning about man and the universe in which he lives.

Perhaps the most compelling force in immediate postwar thought was existentialism, with its focus on "What does it mean 'to be' or 'to exist'?" Existentialism is not a twentieth-century innovation, for it can be found as early as the Greeks, but it remained a relatively minor strain in philosophy until the mid-nineteenth century (beginning with Kierkegaard) and especially the twentieth century. Historically, philosophy has been "essentialist" —that is, concerned with defining the norms and essences of species or generic traits. Existentialism, on the other hand, sees existence as prior to essence. Thus, while an essentialist might inquire into what it means to be a man—or, what the normative or essential traits of man are—the existentialist begins by asking what it means "to be." For the latter, just to be alive is not sufficient in itself to define "being"; rather, being depends upon the quality of existence. Modern existentialists argue that each individual is responsible for making himself what he is, since his being is defined by his choices and actions, and that unless a man acts only after choosing consciously and freely he cannot truly be said "to exist." Thus, they shift the emphasis away from the essentialists' concern for species and norms to a focus on the individual's definition of himself.

Existentialism struck a responsive chord during and after the war, for the world had seemingly gone mad through the abdication of personal choice in favor of blindly following national leaders and policies, even when this meant condoning almost unbelievable cruelties. In part, then, existentialism posed fundamental moral questions—about the source of standards (internally or externally generated) and about freedom and conformity. It strongly argued that each man must define his own values if he is "to exist" as a human being; it sought to cut the individual free from external authority and to force him to discover within himself the conditions for choosing and acting.

The most prominent of the postwar existentialists is Jean-Paul Sartre (1905–   ), for, although he has not always commanded the highest respect from other philosophers, it was through his work that existentialism was brought to public consciousness. Furthermore, Sartre, through his own plays, bridged the gap between philosophy and drama. After studying in France and Germany (where he became thoroughly familiar with the work of the philosophers Heidegger and Husserl), Sartre taught in various French schools between 1931 and 1944. After 1936 he also wrote a number of philosophical treatises, of which the best known are *Being and Nothingness* (1943), *Existentialism is a Humanism* (1946), and *Critique of Dialectic Reason* (1960). He early turned as well to fiction, in which his most famous works are *Nausea* (1938) and a series of three novels under the general title *The Ways of Liberty* (1945–49). In 1943 he wrote his first play, *The Flies,* and then went on to *No Exit* (1944), *Death Without Burial* (1946), *The Respectful Prostitute* (1946), *Dirty Hands* (1948), *The Devil and the Good Lord* (1951), *Nekrassov* (1955), *The Condemned of Altona* (1959), *The Cobweb* (1969), and several adaptations and screenplays.

Although Sartre's view of the human condition is complex, its broad outlines may be summarized briefly. He has declared that all his work is an attempt to draw logical conclusions from a consistent atheism. Since God does not exist, "all possibility of finding values in an intelligible heaven" disappears also. Furthermore, Sartre rejects as guides the state and other man-made institutions. Thus, there are no higher authorities to whom man owes allegiance. "Man is condemned to be free." Some men refuse to accept this freedom, but those who do must come to grips with the terrible consequences. The realization that they live in a meaningless universe inspires in them a growing anguish which eventually culminates in

Sartre's *The Flies,* directed by Dullin at the Théâtre de la Cité in 1943.

"nausea"—a desperation born out of a sense of futility. Such feelings throw them into the abyss of despair, out of which they can rise only by accepting the necessity of creating their own "being" through choice and action, for ultimately "man is only what he does. Man becomes what he chooses to be." Therefore, in accepting his freedom, each man must find a set of values by which he can live, and he becomes moral by adhering to those standards despite all opposition or danger. Since being is defined by choice and deeds, man must accept the necessity of "engagement" in social, moral, and political action, through which he not only defines himself but (insofar as it is possible for one person to do so) his world as well.

These are the ideas which Sartre's plays illustrate. In *The Flies,* based on the *Oresteia,* Sartre shows Orestes asserting his independence both of Jupiter (god) and Egisthus (the state), the primary representatives of externally imposed order. He demands that men rid themselves of the sense of guilt which traditionally has been induced by defying authority so that, through "engagement," they may correct the errors of the past. Thus, Orestes becomes an exemplar of Sartre's ideal man. Contrarily, *No Exit* depicts the results of failing to choose properly. One of the three principal characters remarks, "Hell is other people." But the concept of Hell as depicted here also includes all external pressures which urge conformity. So long as man is alive, he may choose to change, but death fixes his identity for all time. Hell is the torture of looking back on one's failure to choose when the opportunity arose. The necessity and danger of engagement are treated in *Dirty Hands,* which suggests that the social and political choices men are faced with are seldom ideal and that many are sometimes wholly unacceptable. Therefore, to participate in political action inevitably means that one's hands will get dirty, even bloody. But to refuse for that reason to become engaged is merely to let others make the choices which will determine the direction of our world.

Sartre's early plays are still the best known. They fit a formula that he described in the 1940s: "Dramas which are short and violent . . . , dramas entirely centered on one event—usually a conflict of rights, bearing on some very general situation—written in a sparse, extremely tense style, with a small cast not presented for their individual characters but thrust into a conjunction where they are forced to make a choice—in brief this is the theatre, austere, moral, mythic, and ceremonial in aspect, which has given birth to new plays in Paris during the occupation and especially since the end of the war." He might have added that the plays were classical in structure and in their adherence to logic and traditional concepts of unity. In his later works, Sartre departed from this formula. Both *The Devil and the Good Lord* and *The Condemned of Altona* are very prolix, requiring about three hours to perform. Although it is doubtful that Sartre belongs in the first rank of dramatists, he remains a major figure because of his key role in popularizing a philosophical position which was to undergird much of postwar drama.

The original production of Sartre's *The Devil and the Good Lord* in 1951.
(Photo by Pic.)

Sartre's influence was reenforced by that of Albert Camus (1913–60). Born in Algeria into a greatly impoverished family, Camus was nevertheless able to obtain an excellent education. He early developed an interest in the theatre which led him at the age of twenty-two to found an amateur company. By the beginning of the war, he had worked at various jobs, including journalism, a profession which he pursued in Paris during the occupation. Camus began writing in the late 1930s, but it was in the war years that he made his first strong impact with a novel, *The Stranger* (1942), and an essay, "The Myth of Sisyphus" (1942), which set forth the doctrine of the "absurd," a term later used to describe a whole school of dramatists.

Camus wrote only a few plays: *The Misunderstanding* (1944), *Caligula* (produced in 1945 but written in 1938), *State of Seige* (1948), and *The Just Assassins* (1949). Thereafter he wrote no original dramas, but he made a number of adaptations, of which the best are of Faulkner's *Requiem for a Nun* (1956) and Dostoevsky's *The Possessed* (1959). He published as well a number of essays and novels before his untimely death in an automobile accident in 1960.

Although Camus and Sartre eventually quarreled and Camus greatly disliked being called an existentialist, his thought parallels that of Sartre. In "The Myth of Sisyphus" Camus seeks to define the human condition and concludes that it has no rational foundation. "A world that can be explained even with bad reasons is a familiar world. But, on the other hand, in a universe suddenly divested of illusions and lights, man feels an alien, a stranger. His exile is without remedy since he is deprived of the memory of a lost home or the hope of a promised land. This divorce between man and his life . . . is properly the feeling of absurdity." Camus declares that absurdity results from a gap between an inborn human desire for clarity and order on the one hand and the irrationality of the world into which man is thrown on the other. "What is absurd is the confrontation of this irrational and wild longing for clarity whose call echoes in the human heart. . . . The absurd is born of this confrontation between the human need and the unreasonable silence of the world." Camus rejects suicide as an answer and argues that the urge to live is in itself an argument that life is valuable. He then goes on to argue that, since life is valuable, man should not capitulate to absurdity but should go beyond it by creating his own order out of the chaos of his surroundings. Thus, like Sartre, Camus concludes that, even though there are no absolutes, man must shape his own destiny through choice and action.

Also like Sartre, Camus embodied his ideas in dramatic form. His first two plays dramatize the "absurd condition" and the "absurd man." For example, after he discovers that "men die and they are not happy," Caligula becomes obsessed with the need for some absolute, and he decides to seek it in power without limit since "everything is permitted." He then embarks on a deliberate and systematic tyranny over his subjects, making them submit to the most outrageous demands and even to murder and the perversion of all traditional values in order to make them recognize the world's absurdity. But he comes to see that some things are more humanly valid than others and, now lacking the will to live, gives himself up unresisting to his assassins. Nevertheless, Caligula has performed a valuable function—"He forces everyone to think. Insecurity, that is what leads to thought"—for only when people re-evaluate their existence can they decide what is worth living or dying for (that is, what they choose "to be").

Although from the beginning Camus suggests that absurdity must be overcome, the early plays do not show characters progressing beyond absurdity except in a negative way: by denying its power. But in the late 1940s, Camus began to emphasize revolt more than absurdity. This shift seems to have stemmed in part from his increased alienation from Sartre. In *Dirty Hands* and elsewhere Sartre insisted upon the necessity of engagement even if it meant accepting and using means of which one did not always approve, and he, along with many other intellectuals of the time, turned to communism as the best available (though admittedly imperfect) means of building a better future. Camus could not accept the party's position and the disagreement eventually led to a prolonged and bitter debate following the publication of "Man the Rebel" in 1951. In this essay and elsewhere, Camus denied the validity of choosing between two immoral positions, insisting instead that the individual should create his own alternatives and refuse to destroy others for the sake of abstract principle and an uncertain future. He declared that the only rule of life today is "to learn to live and to die, and, in order to be a man, to refuse to be a god."

Camus's ideas about the limits of revolt form the basis of *The Just Assassins*, in which he uses as concrete examples the activities of idealistic Russian terrorists in 1905. When the protagonist, Kaliayev, fails to throw a bomb into the carriage of the Grand Duke Serge because he would also have killed two small children, he is severely chastised by Stepan, a fanatical revolutionary: "What do the two nephews of the Grand Duke matter beside the millions of Russian children who will die during the years to come? When we decide to forget the children, that day we will be the masters of the world and the revolution will triumph." But Kaliayev refuses to be unjust in the name of some unknowable future. "It is for those who are living today that I strike and for whom I agree to kill. And for some future city, of which I am not sure, I will not strike the face of my brothers." He declares that a just cause is defined by just means as well as by just ends. Eventually he does kill the Grand Duke, but he does so openly and insists upon accepting both the responsibility and the consequences of his deed. Thus, Kaliayev acts positively whereas Camus's earlier protago-

Original production of Camus' *The Just Assassins* at the Théâtre Hébertot in 1949. Directed by Paul Oettly, setting and costumes by Rosnay. (Photo by Bernand.)

nists react negatively, just as the emphasis shifts to revolt and away from absurdity—from contemplation of the human condition to action which seeks to redefine the individual's role in his world.

Nevertheless, because his late protagonists ultimately fare little better than the early ones, Camus has often been accused of nihilism. But he was concerned with discovering some ground for positive action that might create a better and more humane world (but one which did not require a leap of faith). Furthermore, he never lost his love for mankind: "If there is one thing that can always be hoped for and sometimes obtained, it is human tenderness."

Camus was also attempting to create a "modern tragedy." But though he posed important moral questions and wrote incisive and dignified dialogue, ultimately his plays remain more nearly demonstrations of ideas than convincing portraits of human experience. As a playwright, he is probably less successful than Sartre.

Despite their shortcomings as dramatists, Sartre and Camus are of unquestioned importance to postwar drama, for they defined the human condition for a generation whose faith in a logical universe had been destroyed. Their influence was more ideological than artistic, for both still employed traditional forms and a dialectical process which led through logical argument to a definite conclusion. They differed ideologically in one crucial way from their successors, however, for, even though they depicted man as adrift in an unfriendly universe, they still retained their faith in the capacity of the human mind to forge a way out of the chaos. Both still believed man capable of shaping his own destiny. Their successors—the absurdists—merely accepted from them the notion of a quixotic universe and abandoned all faith that a path out of absurdity might be found. Consequently, the absurdists rejected traditional dramatic techniques as well as traditional values. But if the playwrights of the 1950s seem to have been paralyzed by looking into the abyss of nothingness, those of the 1960s accepted the challenge to create the conditions for meaningful action. Thus, in one sense, the writers of the 1960s were more truly the successors of Camus and Sartre than were the absurdists.

The influence of Camus and Sartre was ultimately strengthened by another postwar event—the Nuremberg war crimes trials. Here German officials were tried and convicted for obeying the laws and policies of Hitler's state. Prosecutors argued that there is a higher law—a kind of universal moral code—that takes precedence over man's laws. While on the surface this position may seem to contradict that of the existentialists on moral codes, it nevertheless implies that each man should decide which laws he will obey and which he should defy and that his private conscience should determine choice and action. This concept, consistent with those of Camus and Sartre, was to underlie much of the protest and civil disobedience of the 1960s.

If Camus and Sartre were in the 1940s considered novel, puzzling, or nihilistic, before 1960 they were thought by many to be too obvious. Their place of preeminence had been usurped by the absurdists, who rejected the logic and rationalism of the two earlier writers. As Ionesco puts it: "Cut off from his religious, metaphysical, and transcendental roots, man is lost; all his actions become senseless, absurd, useless."

This vision led to several results in drama. First, the traditional pattern of cause-and-effect relationship among incidents—exposition, complication, and denouement—is abandoned or reduced to a minimum. Rather than developing linearly, action tends to be circular, to concentrate upon exploring the texture of a condition rather than telling a connected story. Problems or situations are seldom resolved. Second, characters tend toward the typical or archetypal rather than the specific and individual. Often they exchange roles or metamorphose into other characters. Some are given only generic or numerical designations. Third, time and place are generalized. Most of the plays occur in some symbolic location, or in a void or limbo cut off from the concrete world. Time is flexible as in dreams. Fourth, language is for the most part downgraded. Although the characters often talk as volubly as in traditional drama, they themselves usually recognize that they are indulging in a game. Language is also frequently ridiculed by distorting it or exaggerating its mechanical aspects. Fifth, spectacle is usually used symbolically or metaphorically to compensate in part for the demotion of language as a means. Sixth, traditional distinctions among dramatic forms disappear. The serious often becomes grotesque and the comic takes on tragic overtones. The world is "demystified" by deriding everything that in the past has been taken seriously, just as the traditionally ludicrous may be turned into the pathetic, ominous, or violent. Seventh, despite their rejection of logic, the plays are ultimately conceptual, for they seek to project intellectualized perceptions about the human condition, although they do so indirectly rather than, like Sartre and Camus, discursively.

Many of these characteristics can be found in varying degrees and combinations in earlier nonrealistic drama from symbolism onward. The absurdists were especially attuned to the work of Jarry, Apollinaire, Ghelderode, Pirandello, and the futurists, dadaists, and (perhaps most of all) the surrealists. Their attitude toward language and the need to use all theatrical means reflects Artaud's ideas, although virtually all the absurdists stopped short of Artaud's ultimate aims. It is sometimes forgotten that Artaud has his rational side, for behind his work lies a vision of a world based on knowable values, where happiness is frustrated merely by the divisions which the right kind of theatre would eliminate so that a utopia of love and harmony could emerge. Artaud does not seem to have doubts about the possibility of knowing truth, he merely denounces its enemies. Thus, what most distinguishes the absurdists from their predecessors is their vision rather than their techniques. Their subject is man's entrapment in an illogical, hostile, impersonal, and indifferent existence.

Each of the major absurdists conceived this subject somewhat differently. Behind the work of all, however, lies a common conclusion: the world is irrational and truth unknowable. Many writers both in France and elsewhere were attracted to the absurdist view, but by common consent four—Beckett, Ionesco, Genet, and Adamov—are the primary exponents and popularizers of absurdist drama, although Adamov's reputation has now declined considerably. They represent as well important variations on the type.

Samuel Beckett (1906–   ), although not the earliest of the absurdist dramatists, was the first to win international fame, and it was his *Waiting for Godot* which in 1953 brought absurdism its first popular attention both in France and elsewhere. Born and educated in Ireland, Beckett went to Paris to teach in 1928 and there became the friend and translator of James Joyce, one of the major influences on his work. In 1930 he returned to Ireland, where he taught for a short time before traveling widely and settling permanently in France. He began writing around 1930 and published his first novel in 1938. Not until 1950 did he complete his first play, *Waiting for Godot,* a work not easily placed, but which in Roger Blin's production in 1953 became a sensation, running for about four hundred performances. By 1958 approximately 1 million spectators had seen it. After this initial success, Beckett went on to write *Endgame* (1957), *Krapp's Last Tape* (1958), *Happy Days* (1961), *Play* (1963), and *Come and Go* (1966). Beckett has written as well two short silent plays, both called *Act Without Words,* a few works for radio, television, and film, and several novels.

In many ways, Beckett seems the characteristic dramatist of the 1950s, a decade made anxious by the threat of the cold war and of total destruction in an atomic holocaust. In fact, Beckett's characters often seem to be set down in a world that has already undergone the ravages of disaster and in which man's very existence is in question. Beckett is not so much concerned with man as a social or political creature as with the human condition in a metaphysical sense.

Waiting for Godot is undoubtedly Beckett's most characteristic and finest work. Its story is slight. Two tramps—Vladimir and Estragon—wait in a desolate place by the side of a road for Godot to arrive. The play's two acts are virtually identical in structure and content. Vladimir and Estragon improvise diversions to pass the time. As Estragon observes: "Nothing happens, nobody comes, nobody goes, it's awful." In each act, two other men—Pozzo and Lucky—appear briefly. In the first act, Pozzo is in fine health but his slave, Lucky, is weakening. Nevertheless, Pozzo forces Lucky to show off his tricks: a grotesque dance and his power to think (a stream of disconnected, erudite, but ultimately meaningless words

Original Paris production of Beckett's *Waiting for Godot* in 1953, directed by Roger Blin at the Théâtre de Babylone. (Photo by Pic.)

and phrases). In the second act, Pozzo is blind and Lucky dumb. Each act ends with a message, delivered by a boy, saying that Godot cannot come today but may come tomorrow. Estragon asks, "What shall we do?" and Vladimir replies, "Wait for Godot."

When first produced, *Waiting for Godot* provoked endless and heated discussions about its meaning. Many ingenious interpretations were suggested and several were quite enlightening. Most suffered, however, from being overspecific and confined to the religious or psychological realms. The play will bear several interpretations because it is concerned with the human condition—man's endless and fruitless search for something or someone who will give meaning and direction to his life and to his day-by-day endurance despite the disappointment of his hopes. As the play demonstrates, those who like Pozzo and Lucky rush about in their search fare no better than those who remain stationary. It has also been suggested that Lucky represents the intellect and Pozzo the senses, both of which decay and come to naught. Certainly man is depicted as a derelict adrift in an impersonal universe, improvising dialectical exchanges and other diversions to pass the time. The form matches the content, for both are essentially circular and repetitive. There are no revelations, no true climaxes or resolutions. Rather than telling a story, the play explores a condition.

Nell and Nagg, Hamm's senile parents, in Beckett's *Endgame,*
directed by Roger Blin. (Photo by Pic.)

Endgame seems to occur at a still more advanced stage in the world's
decay. It is set in a cell-like room from which one may glimpse the outside
world only after climbing a ladder. Of the four characters, only one is
able to move about. Hamm, the master, is blind and confined to a chair.
His senile parents are kept in garbage cans, from which they peek out
occasionally to demand attention or to mumble a few remembered phrases.
Only Clov, the slave, is left to look after them in this shelter that seems
to be the only remains from some unmentioned holocaust. Like the characters in *Waiting for Godot,* they cling to life even though there seems to
be little to hope for. Hamm says, "The end is in the beginning, but nevertheless one continues."

In *Happy Days,* Winnie, the protagonist, sits beneath a burning sun
buried in sand to her waist. Not far away, her husband sleeps and groans.
The sand gradually grows deeper and all life seems to be drawing to a close.
But throughout Winnie remains hopeful and busies herself with her makeup,
with the treasures in her handbag, with scolding her husband, and
recalling the happy days of her youth as she reads from her diary. Thus,
despite the progressive mounting of the sand, she maintains her serenity
and gains dignity by refusing to be dismayed by her situation. Critics have
variously interpreted her behavior as a comment on the unwillingness of

men to face up to disaster and as a positive statement about human endurance.

All of Beckett's plays show man in much the same light. Isolated from others, he survives even though he has little to look forward to in a world without faith. The limbo in which man is caught is symbolized by the virtually bare stage for which Beckett calls. Although his characters recognize the need for human contacts, they demonstrate little compassion in their relationships. The only comfort left to them is words, with which they play games and improvise, but in a senseless universe the word too loses its power and only serves to increase the sense of absurdity and desolation. But if Beckett's outlook is pessimistic, it nevertheless struck a strong responsive chord throughout the world. His accomplishments were recognized in 1969 when he was awarded the Nobel Prize in literature.

Eugène Ionesco (1912–   ) was born in Roumania but grew up in France, and learned Roumanian only after he returned to his native country in 1925. There he attended the University of Bucharest and taught before going back to Paris in 1938, where he has since lived. For a time he worked for a publishing firm and only accidentally took up playwriting. He has declared that the inspiration for his first play came from a phrase book he was using while studying English. Its simple statements of the most commonplace facts struck his imagination and from them he fashioned *The Bald Soprano*. Produced in 1950, it was a failure. Nevertheless, he persisted, even though *The Lesson* (1951) and *The Chairs* (1952) fared

Paris production of Ionesco's *The Chairs* in 1956 at the Studio des Champs-Elysées, directed by Jacques Mauclair, who played the Old Man. (Photo by Pic.)

little better. The turning point in Ionesco's career came in 1953, when Anouilh wrote glowingly of *Victims of Duty*. Thereafter Ionesco's public steadily grew as he presented *Amedée* (1954), *Jack, or the Submission* (1955), *The Future is in Eggs* (1955), *The New Tenant* (1957), and *The Killer* (1958). In 1960 Ionesco's work began to be brought into the repertory of the major theatres when Barrault presented *Rhinoceros* (1960) and *A Stroll in the Air* (1962). In 1966 *Hunger and Thirst* was taken into the repertory of the Comédie Française, and in 1970 Ionesco was elected to the French Academy.

Unlike Beckett, Ionesco is concerned primarily with man's social relationships, most typically those of middle-class characters in family situations. Two themes run through most of his work: the deadening nature of materialistic, bourgeois society, and the loneliness and isolation of the individual. Perhaps ultimately his vision of man's condition differs little from Beckett's, but it is conceived in more domestic terms.

Ionesco's earliest works (*The Bald Soprano* through *The Future is in Eggs*) are the most detached, using puppetlike characters and parodistic and exaggerated speech and action. For example, in *The Bald Soprano* the characters speak only in clichés and espouse only received values which have become meaningless. The aura of a machined existence is reenforced by the ending, when the action begins all over but with the couples now interchanged. It is a satirical commentary on the petite bourgeoisie about whom Ionesco has written: "For me the *petit bourgeois* is just a man of slogans, who no longer thinks for himself but repeats the truths that others have imposed upon him, ready-made and therefore lifeless." He labeled *The Bald Soprano* "an antiplay" because he was aware that his work, with its lack of connected story, its circularity, and solemn absurdity, was quite unlike traditional drama.

In *The Chairs*, Ionesco's characters are somewhat more humanized. In this "tragic farce" two old people have announced their intention to deliver a message about the meaning of life. This promise attracts many persons (all invisible) and as the Old Woman brings a chair for each new arrival the stage becomes ever more crowded. At the climactic moment, the couple jump from the window leaving the Orator to proclaim their secret. Unfortunately he is a deaf-mute. According to Ionesco, the play's theme is "the chairs, that is to say the absence of people, . . . the absence of God, the absence of matter, the unreality of the world, the metaphysical void; the theme of life is nothingness."

Further movement away from the early pieces is evident in *Rhinoceros*. Here the inhabitants of a village one after another turn into rhinoceroses. Only Berenger resists. "I am the last man, I will hold out to the end. I will not capitulate." Through this work Ionesco sought to show how ideologies, like diseases, infect people and dehumanize them. Berenger's refusal to follow the herd constitutes Ionesco's most positive dramatic treatment of human values.

Original production of Ionesco's *Rhinoceros* at the Odéon, Paris, in 1960.
Barrault, second from left, played Berenger and directed the production.
(Photo by Pic.)

Exit the King also uses Berenger as protagonist, but now he is a king instead of a working man and the play seeks to show the necessity of reconciling oneself to death and the nothingness which it represents. As the action progresses, the stage is gradually denuded of furnishings and characters, just as the king gradually loses his strength and control, until at last he is left alone on his throne. Then the throne also disappears and Berenger is forced to face and accept the void. *Exit the King* is Ionesco's most metaphysical work, for in it death becomes a symbol of man's loneliness and his ultimate nothingness. It is in this play that Ionesco most nearly approaches Beckett.

Although one can distinguish something resembling a progressive humanization in Ionesco's work, all of the plays seek to discredit clichés, ideologies, and materialism; indirectly they argue the need for each man to live his own life free from tyranny and without vain hopes. His characters for the most part are the products of a conformity imposed from without and they are often dominated by material objects. Thus, his people tend to be unthinking automatons oblivious to their own mechanical behavior and speech, just as material objects tend to proliferate and take over the space that should be occupied by people. Among the clichés that Ionesco seeks to undermine is the theatre itself and all its accumulated traditions and techniques. He is especially antipathetic to the notion that drama should be didactic and his greatest scorn is reserved for Brecht and his followers. To Ionesco truth means the absence of commitment, either ideologically or esthetically, for commitment involves a fatal step toward conformity.

Jean Genet (1910–   ), an illegitimate child abandoned by his mother and reared in a foster home, early turned to crime and until the late 1940s spent most of his adult years in prison or as an itinerant criminal. Around 1940 he began writing—at first poems, then prose poems (or novels), and finally drama. *The Maids* (in Jouvet's production of 1947) was his first work to reach the stage. Although it won critical favor in some quarters, it was generally considered scandalous. In 1949 *Deathwatch* (a work written earlier than *The Maids*) was produced by the Rideau de Paris with much the same result. Genet then declared his intention of giving up drama and it was not until 1957 that *The Balcony* was produced. Since then he has written *The Blacks* (1959) and *The Screens* (1961). Thus, his output has been relatively small, but since the late 1950s he has been considered one of France's major postwar dramatists.

Genet celebrates evil, investing it with metaphysical significance, for in it he sees total negation. Any attempt to give it rational explanation merely makes evil an aspect of some structure that men have created to give their lives a sense of direction. Thus, Genet's hero-criminals are comparable to saints in refusing to admit limits on their actions and in accepting their special fate. Similarly, he sees society as being created out of a series of ritualized ceremonies, none of which has any ultimate validity. Therefore, his characters wear masks, assume identities and various disguises, but when they remove one there is always another beneath it, for it is impossible ever to arrive at some final, truthful revelation. Genet has suggested that the theatre should be like a "hall of mirrors" in which man is "inexorably trapped by an endless progression of images that are merely his own distorted reflection." Thus, Genet combines subjects usually considered perverse with ritualized action not unlike that recommended by Artaud.

Deathwatch depicts the "saintly criminal" Green Eyes, who without a motive and without wishing to do so has committed a murder, as a result of which he stands near the top of that heirarchy which prevails in the prison where the action occurs. He is contrasted with Lefranc, who covets Green Eyes's prestige and, in order to gain it, murders another prisoner out of malice. But he is then rejected by his fellows, for the "sacred sign of the monster" cannot be gained through such means.

The Maids blends ritual and subject more successfully than does *Deathwatch*. Here, two maids and sisters, Claire and Solange, take turns impersonating their mistress and enacting their hatreds both for her and for themselves. When Madame's lover, who has been arrested because of a letter written to the police by Claire, is released, the maids decide to poison their mistress to prevent her from discovering their duplicity. But Madame leaves without drinking the poisoned tea, and Claire assumes her role and makes Solange force her to drink it. Thus Claire sacrifices her life so that Solange may have the glory of being a murderess. *The Maids* is a ritualization of impotent rebellion, for, since they accept Madame's contempt for servants as a class, Claire and Solange can find no outlet for their resentment except in criminal dreams.

The Balcony moves beyond the claustrophobic world of the first two plays. As it opens, a Bishop dressed in ceremonial robes is delivering an elevated speech. But it soon becomes clear that the Bishop is a gasman and that the scene is a brothel where Mme. Irma caters to men's fantasies by letting them dress up and act out their dreams of power and sex (which are always intertwined in Genet's world). Everywhere there are mirrors so that the participants may watch themselves, even as they in turn reflect those they impersonate. Soon another element is introduced: a real revolution is underway outside the brothel, and when the Queen, Bishop, and other authoritarian figures are killed, their impersonators in Mme. Irma's establishment are asked to take their places temporarily in order to quiet the anxieties of the populace until the revolution is put down. The real manipulator of the political events is another of Mme. Irma's customers, the Chief of Police, who, believing that no one has won popular acceptance until someone comes to the brothel and asks to dress up and assume his role, anxiously hopes that he will become an object of envy. Eventually his wish is granted when the young leader of the defeated revolutionaries arrives. But, once dressed in the uniform, the young man emasculates himself, thus symbolically punishing the Chief of Police as an authoritarian figure and himself for wishing to break into the magic circle of power. The entire play is dominated by the motifs of domination-submission and oppressor-oppressed, and society itself is reduced to a ritualized enactment of roles. Though the revolutionaries seek to break out of the pattern, their failure only serves to reconfirm the ritual.

Nevertheless, *The Balcony* does suggest that Genet was here more concerned with societal forces than he had been in his earlier works. This implication is even greater in *The Blacks,* an elaborate structure of ceremonies. On stage, Blacks act out a ritualized murder before a group of masked figures—the Queen, her valet, a governor, a judge, and a missionary—who represent White colonialists. But when these characters come down to punish the murderers, they are themselves massacred. All of this, however, is merely a mock ceremony designed to distract the White audience from an offstage trial and execution of a Black for betraying his people. Overall, the play urges the need for independence, freedom, and self-respect among all oppressed groups. It is less successful than *The Balcony,* nevertheless, because too many important events occur offstage and too much of the onstage action is puzzling or prolix.

Genet's most ambitious work is *The Screens,* a panoramic spectacle divided into seventeen scenes and utilizing 104 characters. At first denied production in France because it is based on the Algerian rebellion and treats the French as oppressors of the Arabs, it became an enormous success in 1966 when staged by Roger Blin at the Théâtre de France. The title refers to the movable screens used to indicate changes in place as actors push them about and sketch on their surfaces the objects required by each scene. The major source of unity is the character Said, the soul of outcastness, in which he revels. In this play, Genet seems to sum up all the

Genet's *The Screens*, directed by Roger Blin at
the Théâtre de France in 1966. (Photo by Pic.)

themes of his earlier work. Though he is still concerned with the insubstantiality of truth, the saintly criminal, and ceremonials, here, as in his
other dramas, reality asserts itself and recalls more conventional theatrical
works, since behind the ritualized action there is always evident a commentary on colonialism and the need for dignity among oppressed peoples.

Nevertheless, Genet does not think of his works as being ideologically
committed, for he is more concerned with the question of "being" than
with programmatic action. Perhaps ultimately he is most interested in
imposing order on an unfriendly world by converting it into a series of
elaborate ceremonies.

Arthur Adamov (1908–71) was born in Russia of a wealthy Armenian
family but was educated in western Europe—in French—as a member of
the European international set. After his father committed suicide, Adamov
moved to Paris, where he was associated with several of the surrealists,
including Artaud. Although he began writing in the 1920s, he later gave
it up because of deep spiritual and psychological crises. Then, around 1945,
he began to write plays, at first extremely subjective ones through which
he sought to cope with his own anxieties. These early works (by dates of
first production) include: *The Large and the Small Maneuver* (1950),
The Invasion (1950), *Parody* (1952), *Professor Taranne* (1953), *The*

Direction of the March (1953), *All Against All* (1953), and *As We Were* (1953).

These early pieces are divided into numerous short tableaux, in which the characters are near-archetypal (often with letter or generic names) and condemned to be eternal failures by their inability to communicate with each other; they are often persecuted by such authority figures as parents, teachers, police, or military officers, or, if they are delivered, become persecutors themselves. Time and place are usually indefinite, as in dreams. The plays are influenced by several writers whose works were deeply admired by Adamov at this time: Artaud, with his violent images designed to affect the nerves and sinews and the theatrical devices of the "theatre of cruelty"; Strindberg, with his taste for symbols and multiple identity; Kafka, with his nightmarish dream world; and Chekhov, with his indirect dialogue.

Parody is a typical early work. In it two young men, N. and the Employee, desire the same girl, although she pays no attention to either. N. remains completely passive, but the Employee conceives one frantic scheme after another to attract her notice. Eventually N. is run over and swept up as garbage, while the Employee is blinded and imprisoned. About it, Adamov writes: "the refusal of life (N.) and its beatific acceptance (the Employee) both end in inevitable failure and total destruction."

A change is evident in Adamov's work beginning with *Ping Pong* (1955). Now there are fully developed characters, Arthur and Victor, who become interested in a Ping-Pong machine and thereafter obsessively devote their lives to schemes involving it. The machine probably represents materialism (or perhaps any ideology) and the play shows how life is wasted by an unquestioning pursuit of false ideals. Although there is still much of the absurdist mode in it, the action tends toward social commentary.

Shortly after completing *Ping Pong*, Adamov declared that to understand the small machine one needs to analyze the large machine—society—as well. Consequently, he disavowed all of his earlier work and turned to the Brechtian mode of dialectic drama and embraced communism. The

A scene from Arthur Adamov's *Ping Pong*, as produced originally at the Théâtre des Noctambules in 1955.
(Photo by Bernand.)

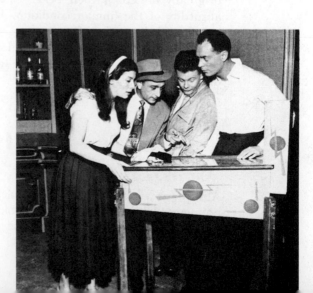

first result was *Paolo Paoli* (1957), a work which seeks to show the relationship between a society grounded in material profit and the destruction which grows out of this grounding in the years between 1900 and 1914. Despite its large subject, it is a very economical play, for it uses only seven characters to provide a cross-section of society and twelve scenes to show the progress of events during this fifteen-year period. Of the two principal characters, one is a dealer in rare butterflies and the other a dealer in ostrich plumes, trades which are not only essentially useless but dependent upon war and a harsh penal system. (The butterflies are obtained from Devil's Island and China and the ostrich plumes from South Africa.) Each scene is preceded by projections which establish the larger context of the events and accompanied by popular tunes which set the mood.

Spring '71 (1961) is much more complex, for here Adamov uses numerous characters and divides the work into twenty-six scenes, nine interludes, and an epilogue which trace the rise and suppression of the Paris Commune of 1871. Unfortunately, Adamov's political commitment seems to cause him to make all those on the side of the commune good and all those opposed to it evil. The interludes are the most successful elements, for in them historical and allegorical figures are mingled symbolically and grotesquely to clarify Adamov's arguments without the obviousness which characterizes the principal episodes. In his succeeding works—*The Politics of Leftovers* (1963), *Sainte Europe* (1966), and *M. le Moderé* (1968)—Adamov continued both his political and Brechtian commitments.

In some ways, Adamov's career indicates the direction drama has taken since World War II: a period of personal anxieties and introspection followed by social commitment and the demand for change. He bridges the Artaudian and the Brechtian modes, those that have dominated much of postwar theatrical practice.

These four dramatists—Beckett, Ionesco, Genet, and Adamov—were most responsible for winning absurdism its international recognition. Although they differed markedly in their immediate preoccupations, all were originally united by their belief in the irrationality of the world and the absurdity of the human condition. In Jungian terms, they are essentially introverted dramatists, for they are concerned primarily with the "self" in a threatening and unfriendly world. Although they often show characters of unquenchable endurance, they hold out little hope for a better or different world.

III

Absurdism was never a conscious, clearly defined movement. The label was popularized by Martin Esslin's book *The Theatre of the Absurd* (1961) rather than being chosen by those now considered its prime exponents.

Since it was not a conscious movement, it is therefore difficult to specify those authors who should be included within its ranks. Nevertheless, a number of French dramatists of the 1950s share certain characteristic outlooks and techniques with Beckett, Ionesco, Genet, and Adamov, and consequently may be treated with them. Of these writers, perhaps the most important are Tardieu, Vian, and Pinget. Jean Tardieu (1903–) has made his mark primarily through his endless experimentation with new techniques. Prior to World War II, Tardieu had won some renown as a poet, and after the war he became head of the experimental workshop of the French Radio and Television Service. In 1947, he began to write plays, a great number of which have been produced in Paris since 1951. Most have been published in two collections: *Chamber Theatre* (1955) and *Poems for Acting* (1960). Almost all are short and all are resolutely opposed to tradition.

Tardieu sought in music inspiration to help him "discover for drama some new rules, which will substitute, for example, for those traditional ones of intrigue." This musical influence is especially evident in *The Sonata and the Three Gentlemen* (1955), in which three characters (A, B, and C) converse about a subject that remains undefined. It is divided into three movements (largo, andante, and finale), each with its distinctive tempo and mood. Tardieu often treats language much in the manner of Ionesco. For example, in *Who is There?* (1952), while a family is seated at the dinner table, the father asks questions to which he also supplies the answers since he can predict them so easily. Like Ionesco, Tardieu also suggests here that men must avoid bourgeois conformity and look within themselves for standards.

Tardieu frequently evokes a nightmarish world, as in *The Information Window* (1956), in which a man seeks to inquire about train schedules but is not permitted to pose his questions until he has filled out a lengthy form. The attendant then casts his horoscope and declares that he has only a few minutes to live. When the man rushes away in disgust, he is killed. The play summarizes in brief, semistatistical form man's life and its senselessness.

Tardieu's determined experimentation is evident in such works as *A Voice Without Anyone* (1956), in which the stage remains empty while a voice from offstage recalls memories of the room as the lights change in accordance with the varying moods. Tardieu's strength lies in his considerable range and his continuing exploration of dramatic means. It is also perhaps the source of his weakness, for he has perfected no strain and established no particular direction in his work. Thus, he reflects most of the trends of his time but fails to project a distinctive individuality.

Boris Vian (1920–59) was educated as an engineer but then pursued such multiple activities as jazz trumpeter, dancer, actor, critic, and journalist. He began writing novels in 1946 and made his debut as a playwright in 1948 with an adaptation of one of his own works, *I Will Spit on Your Graves.* His first original play, *Horsebutchering for Everyone,* was presented in 1950. Like his posthumously produced drama, *The Taste of Generals,* it is an antiwar tract. Set in a horse butcher's establishment in 1944 at the time of the Allied invasion of France, it indiscriminately mingles soldiers from all nations (including Oriental ones) and shows them all to be much the same. Eventually the horse butcher's entire family is killed and his home blown up to make way for a new building scheme. Perhaps Vian's anti-militaristic attitude is best summed up in a line from *The Taste of Generals*: "What is the plural of general? Degenerates."

Vian is remembered above all for one play, *The Empire Builders, or the Schmurz* (1959). Divided into three acts, it shows a family seeking to escape some unspecified horror, represented by a mysterious noise. During the play, the family moves into progressively higher and more cramped quarters and as they do so the family decreases in size until at last no one is left except the father. With no place to flee, he dies. Throughout there is as well another character, the Schmurz, bandaged, bleeding, and ugly, who appears not to be seen by the others even though they continuously and cruelly beat him. He has been variously interpreted as a symbol of man's conscience, of death, of pain, and of man's mortality. The title of the play suggests that man vainly tries to construct a future even as he is progressively hemmed in by the approach of death (or some other disaster). It is one of the most successful plays of its type.

Robert Pinget (1920–   ) is noted primarily for his novels but he has also written a few plays: *Dead Letter* (1960), *Architruc* (1962), *La Manivelle* (translated by Beckett as *The Old Tune*, 1962), and *The Hypothesis* (1965). Of these, the best known are *Dead Letter*, in which an old man awaits year after year a letter from his dearly beloved son, who possibly exists only in his imagination, and *La Manivelle*, in which two old men recall a common past, although their memories never quite agree. Pinget is often compared to Beckett, who is a close friend, because of his depiction of man as isolated in a universe where everything is repeated with unending monotony.

~~~ IV ~~~

Not all postwar French experimentalists were absurdists. Several departed markedly from earlier techniques without accepting the philosophical views of the existentialists or their successors. For this reason, some critics have preferred to avoid the label absurdism altogether and to group all postwar innovators under a single heading, avant-garde. Among this more inclusive group, two important playwrights—Audiberti and Schehadé—clearly cannot be called absurdists.

Jacques Audiberti (1899–1965) was a poet, critic, novelist, and journalist before he turned to playwriting after World War II. His first play, *Quoat-Quoat,* was produced in 1946 and his last, *The Doll,* in 1968 after his death. Altogether he wrote about fifteen plays.

Audiberti's work often resembles Ghelderode's in its mixture of the saintly and the blasphemous, fantasy and realism, the serious and the farcical. The result is sometimes amusing, sometimes frightening, sometimes thought-provoking. He writes out of what he calls an "accepted delirium" and elaborates on themes rather than clear-cut ideas; his imaginatively conceived characters speak a brilliant and expansive dialogue. The plays also mingle love of nature and humanity with strong dislike for modern life and its loss of faith and standards. Good and evil are usually at war, and Audiberti implies that man does know the difference between the two, even if he has lost direct contact with God. Thus, Audiberti shares with the absurdists only his defiance of traditional notions of drama and his view of man as isolated and alienated.

Audiberti's nearest approach to absurdism is probably found in *Knight Alone* (1963). Set in the eleventh century, it traces the exaggerated and often sacrilegious adventures of the knight Mirtus on his way to the Holy Sepulchre. But despite all his attempts to unite himself with a higher being, he cannot free himself from an anguished sense of his own nothingness. *The Hobby* (1956) shows man's alienation from nature. In it, the peasant Garon, who plays a bear in a troupe of traveling players, is gradually overcome by a sense of loss. "My bear's head is a wooden head. My claws are made by the shoemaker. I can no longer understand the reeds, the firs." Here as elsewhere, Audiberti tends to see nature as good and man as corrupter.

Audiberti also writes of man's alienation from himself. In *The Black Feast,* the frustrations of Felicien, an attractive but somehow unlovable man, give rise to a monster who ravishes and kills women. With the encouragement of the Church, the men of the region set out to kill the monster, but, unwilling to recognize that they are seeking something within man, they kill a goat and name it the monster. Felicien himself is finally slain by a man who discovers his niece in Felicien's embrace. Audiberti's intentions in this play are not entirely clear, but he seems to have in mind the conflict between the sexual instinct and the demand for purity. Since Felicien idolizes women, approaching one sexually becomes for him an act of violence. Thus, the failure of man to reconcile himself with what is natural leads to alienation and disaster.

Audiberti's plays mingle so many diverse elements and are so uncontrolled in their richness that critics have tended either to praise them extravagantly or to despise them. Unlike that of the absurdists, his is a pagan and sensual world in which man is still richly endowed and still in touch with the supernatural.

Georges Schehadé (1910–) is even further removed from the absurdist dramatists, although he too uses some of the same techniques. Born in Egypt of Lebanese parents, Schehadé was educated in France.

Schehadé's *The Soirée of Proverbs,* produced originally by Barrault
at the Petit Théâtre Marigny in 1954.
(Photo by Bernand.)

Recognized first as a poet, he wrote his first play, *Monsieur Bob'le,* in 1951.
It was followed by *The Soirée of Proverbs* (1954), *The Story of Vasco*
(1956), *Narrative of the Year Zero* (1956), *The Voyage* (1961), *The
Violets* (1966), and *The Brisbane Emigrant* (1967).

Schehadé has often been compared with Giraudoux because of his
sensitivity to language and its nuances, but his outlook is more nearly
related to Anouilh's, since he emphasizes the difficulty of remaining
innocent in a corrupt world. In *The Soirée of Proverbs,* the protagonist,
Argengeorge, an idealistic young man, while at an inn overhears travelers
speak of a magical place where a soirée of proverbs is to be held. Hoping to
see this wonderful thing, he follows them but when he arrives discovers only
ridiculous old men who, having lost their faith, are seeking desperately to
recapture the spirit of their youth. Then, a hunter, Alexis, arrives. It is
Argengeorge grown old. Preferring to die rather than submit to the
disappointments which lie ahead, Argengeorge unresistingly allows himself
to be killed by Alexis. Now the soirée of which he dreamed can take place,
for he has discovered the secret of remaining young: a poetic conception of
life.

Similarly, in *The Story of Vasco,* a young barber is chosen by General
Mirador to carry a message through enemy territory because he thinks the

young man's fright will make him wary. Instead, Vasco's innocence makes him an easy prey to the machinations of others and eventually he is captured and killed because he will not reveal the message. As in his other works, Schehadé treats this situation lightly, sometimes ludicrously, as when two mustachioed soldiers disguise themselves as flirtatious women or when others equally obviously disguise themselves as trees. Schehadé's is a fairy-tale world in which innocence is endangered by the corruption that sets in with the loss of childhood faith, enthusiasm, and awe. His heroes search for truth and wonder and, though they find death instead, they remain unaware of its imminence until it arrives. The dreamlike quality of Schehadé's plays perhaps resembles the work of the surrealists more than that of the absurdists, for though melancholy is evident despair is not. His universe is still filled with magic, even though it sometimes turns dark.

There were, of course, many other French playwrights of the 1950s, but these were the most important. Although varying widely in outlook, they share a predilection for experimentation in form and techniques. During that decade they made French drama seem the most vital in the world.

The triumph of postwar French drama owed much to directors, many of whom had to struggle against public resistance to the new dramatic modes. Although a few of the well-established directors assisted the new writers, their record is not impressive. Dullin produced Sartre's first play, *The Flies,* in 1943; Jouvet gave Genet his first hearing in 1947 with *The Maids*; Herrand and Marchat were the first to produce a work by Camus (*The Misunderstanding* in 1944) and they presented Genet's *Deathwatch* in 1949. Barrault has tended to assist writers only after they have been introduced by others. For example, he presented Camus's last two plays, Schehadé's second and third plays, Ionesco's late works, and Genet's latest play. But for the most part, new writers had first to struggle for recognition and only afterward were they accepted into the established houses.

In promoting the avant-garde drama of the 1940s and 1950s, a few theatres, somewhat like the studios of the interwar years, played a crucial role. Although most had no established policy, as did those of the Cartel, they were characterized by adventurousness in choice of plays and by experimentation in staging. The most important were Les Noctambules, the Théâtre de la Huchette, the Théâtre de Babylone, the Théâtre de la Bruyère, and the Théâtre de Poche. Because they were small (some miniscule), they could mount plays economically and perform them for restricted audiences. Like their predecessors, most fell victim to success, for, as they won acceptance for new authors and methods, both their playwrights and directors were wooed away by the larger houses.

The directors associated with avant-garde drama shared many aims, often collaborated with each other, and passed easily from one theatre to another. The most important were Blin, Serreau, Vitaly, Reybaz, Bataille, and Ré.

Roger Blin (1907–) upon leaving the Sorbonne was a film critic in the late 1920s and at that time became acquainted with Artaud, with whom he was subsequently closely associated and with whom he worked on *The Cenci*. Through Artaud he also met Barrault, in whose productions he acted in the 1930s. He performed as well in Dullin's production of *Richard III*. Blin did not begin directing until 1949, when with Christine Tsingos he took over the Gaîté-Montparnasse and presented such works as Büchner's *Woyzeck*, Strindberg's *The Ghost Sonata,* and Johnston's *The Moon in the Yellow River*. In 1950 he acted in the first production of Adamov's work done in Paris, and in 1952 he directed *Parody*. But Blin's fame as a director dates from 1953 when he staged Beckett's *Waiting for Godot* at the Théâtre de Babylone, which he then ran in conjunction with Serreau. This production also marked the turning point in public response to absurdist drama. Blin then directed the play in Austria, Switzerland, and Holland before staging *Endgame, Krapp's Last Tape,* and *Happy Days*. Blin has also worked closely with Genet, having mounted *The Blacks* in 1959 and *The Screens* in 1966. By the 1960s Blin, now considered one of France's major directors, was working in such major theatres as the Odéon, where he staged a number of works for Barrault's company. Because he refuses to direct any play in which he does not believe, Blin has had a limited career. Nevertheless, he has exerted considerable influence and is probably Artaud's most devoted disciple.

Jean-Marie Serreau (1915–) had been educated as an architect before he went to study in Dullin's school. After the war he founded his own company and soon became one of the most active of avant-garde directors. Serreau's tastes were rather broad, for not only did he give the first postwar production of Brecht's work in France, he was also the first to present Adamov, and, in association with Blin, he produced plays by Beckett, Ionesco, Genet, Arrabal, and many others. By the 1960s he too had won acceptance by the major theatres and in 1966 was named the best director of the year for his production of Ionesco's *Hunger and Thirst* at the Comédie Française.

Georges Vitaly (1917–) was born in Russia but moved to France at an early age. In 1947 his production of Audiberti's *Evil at Large* won the grand prize offered for young companies. From 1948 until 1952 he headed the Théâtre de la Huchette and since 1953 the Théâtre de la Bruyère, both major homes of avant-garde drama. Nevertheless, he has been very eclectic in his taste, for, in addition to discovering Schehadé, he has also presented works by Feydeau, Montherlant, Strindberg, Duerrenmatt, and others.

André Reybaz (1922–   ) began his career in 1941 as an actor. In
1946, with his wife, Catherine Toth, he founded the Compagnie de Myrmidon, which in that year gave Audiberti his first production. In 1947 he also
introduced Ghelderode's work in Paris. In 1949 his troupe won the prize
for young companies and in 1950 he gave the first production of a play
by Vian. Throughout the 1950s Reybaz increased his reputation, and in
1960 he was given official blessing by being appointed director of the
Dramatic Center of the North, located at Tourcoing.

Nicolas Bataille (1926–   ) after the war formed a troupe which in
1948 won the prize for avant-garde works staged by young companies. In
1950 he produced Ionesco's first play and later became especially well
known for his mounting of works not originally intended for the stage.
Michel de Ré (1925–   ) won the prize for avant-garde productions by
young companies in 1946 and in the 1950s was known above all for his
productions of Tardieu's plays. He also did much to forward the cause of
new drama by organizing festivals of avant-garde works. Other outstanding
postwar directors included Jacques Mauclair (1919–   ), Guy Retoré
(1924–   ), Jacques Fabbri (1925–   ), and Marcel Cuvelier (1924–   ).

So many vital and adventurous directors and playwrights gave the
French theatre of the 1950s a sense of ferment and vigor which infected
other countries as well.

~ **VI** ~

The absurdist tradition eventually was to affect the theatre and drama of
almost every country. In some, however, it did not flourish until the 1960s.
This is especially true of Eastern Europe, where socialist realism (because
of Soviet influence) was the dominant mode until the late 1950s. (Since it
did not prosper until the 1960s, absurdism in Eastern Europe will be
treated in a later chapter.) In West Germany, absurdism had a considerable
vogue, for it was here that plays of this school (especially those by French
writers) received the greatest number of productions. Nevertheless, few
native authors wrote in this vein. Of those who did, the best were Hildesheimer and Grass.

Wolfgang Hildesheimer (1916–   ) spent the war years in exile and
later became a citizen of Israel, although he resides in Switzerland. Originally a painter, he began his playwriting career with radio dramas, primarily fantastic stories of social or artistic fraud placed against some
exotic background. Probably the best of these is *The Dragon Throne*
(1955), a retelling of the Turandot legend. He then adopted the absurdist
mode, which he has championed both in essays and in his own practice. In
1958 he published a collection of three plays under the general title, *Plays*

in Which Darkness Falls. Of these, *The Clocks* may be taken as representative. A man and wife, somewhat in the manner of Ionesco's old people in *The Chairs,* relive their past. Then a salesman arrives and from him they buy clocks of almost every conceivable kind. As darkness falls at the end of the play, they are inside the clocks ticking away. Hildesheimer seems to suggest that man is both the victim and a part of time, although it is perhaps unsafe to speculate about any intention on his part since he has stated that absurd drama "becomes a parable of life precisely through the intentional omission of any statement. For life, too, makes no statement."

Hildesheimer's later works include *The Delay* (1963) and *Nightpiece* (1963). The latter is probably his best play. It utilizes only two characters, The Man Who Wants to Sleep and The Burglar. The Man has two compelling fears: of sleeplessness, and of burglars. Thus, each evening he undertakes an elaborate ritual designed to induce sleep (including taking several narcotics) and virtually seals himself off from the outside world. But on this occasion he has forgotten to lock the front door, and the Burglar enters boldly and gradually takes over the house as the Man falls deeper and deeper into his drugged state. At the conclusion, the Burglar is in complete charge, answering the phone and eating his breakfast at ease. Hildesheimer seems to have in mind a parable about the intellectual who seeks to escape the troublesome world only to find himself at the mercy of unlawful forces because he has withdrawn from the struggle and has left himself no defenses.

Günter Grass (1927–   ) grew up in Nazi Germany and was for a time an American prisoner of war. When peace returned, he worked first as a stonemason and then studied painting and sculpture and traveled widely. He began writing poetry in 1954 and since 1959 has devoted himself primarily to the novel, for which he is now best known. Most of his plays were written between 1954 and 1958, although he has continued to revise his early dramas. His first production, however, did not come until 1957. His short plays include *Rocking Back and Forth* (1954, first produced in 1959), *Only Ten Minutes to Buffalo* (1957, produced in 1959), and *Thirty-two Teeth* (1958). His long plays include *The Flood* (1955, produced in 1957, revised in 1962), *Mister, Mister* (1956, produced in 1958, revised in 1965), *The Wicked Cooks* (1957, produced in 1962), *The Plebeians Rehearse the Uprising* (written and produced in 1966), and *Beforehand* (written and produced in 1969).

Except for the final two, Grass's plays belong to the absurdist tradition, and are even vaguer in intention than are Hildesheimer's. The best are *Mister, Mister* and *The Wicked Cooks.* The former focuses on Bollin, a murderer who fails in three successive attempts to kill his victims and is himself killed by two children who steal his revolver. It is filled with black humor, grotesque imagery, and commentary on modern life (an actress, for example, is willing to be killed for the publicity). The older and the younger generations are contrasted: the older kills deliberately, the younger without knowing what it is doing. The play also suggests that there are always people who submit willingly, even eagerly, to their destroyers.

The Wicked Cooks is Grass's most poetic (and most obscure) play. In it two factions of cooks try to obtain the recipe for a mysterious soup known only to the Count (who is not a count). The cooks allow him to marry the nurse, Martha, on the condition that he give them the recipe. After living with Martha for two months, however, the Count can no longer remember the recipe and the couple commit suicide. The play has been given many interpretations, but the central idea seems to be the human propensity for wishing to mass-produce and commercialize any valuable experience (whatever its nature) even though that which raises an experience above the ordinary is something so mysterious and ineffable that it cannot be reproduced on demand. As the Count declares, the soup is "not a recipe, it's an experience, a living knowledge, continuous change."

With *The Plebeians Rehearse the Uprising,* Grass abandoned the absurdist for the Brechtian vein. Set in East Berlin in 1953 during the uprising of German workers, the action takes place on the stage of a theatre (presumably that of the Berliner Ensemble) where actors are rehearsing the Boss's (Brecht's?) version of *Coriolanus*. Workers arrive and ask the Boss to formulate their petition to the government, but he vacillates until it is too late. The events of *Coriolanus* and of the uprising in Berlin are used as parallels, while the device of the rehearsal serves to distance the events somewhat in the manner of Brecht's own drama. Grass's conception has generally been admired but his execution of it faulted. Grass subtitled the play "A German Tragedy," by which he meant to suggest something in the German character which makes any true revolution impossible. It is this with which he is primarily concerned—especially with the German intellectual's divorce from the workers—and he merely chose Brecht as a prototype rather than meaning the play as a personal attack on him. Perhaps Grass convinced himself, for since the mid-1960s he has devoted much of his time to politics.

Grass has also declared himself interested in a "dialectic theatre" designed to place situations before an audience and to let them participate in the complex issues of justice and injustice. *Beforehand,* a dramatization of a chapter from one of his novels, falls into this category. The title refers to a time before 1967, when the Berlin student Benno Ohnesorg was killed and German students became increasingly radical. Its thirteen scenes involve a seventeen-year-old boy's plan to burn his dog alive outside an exclusive restaurant in order to make its complacent customers aware of the cruelty of the war in Vietnam. His girl friend urges him on, but he is eventually persuaded that reasoned dialectic is the better path and he becomes the editor of his school newspaper. The play was severely criticized for its structure and mixture of modes. Grass defended himself by declaring that he was seeking to get away from the foreground of action so that he might "clarify dialectically what happens, before it either gets as far or fails to get as far as becoming fact." In 1970 Grass joined the advisory staff of the state theatre in Frankfurt and declared his intention of working for reforms. Thus, somewhat like Adamov, Grass has moved from the absurdist vision to a more socially engaged position.

The work of Witold Gombrowicz (1904–69) also parallels that of the absurdists, although he is descended from the Polish tradition of Wyspianski and Witkiewicz and owes little to French influences. Gombrowicz began his literary career in the 1930s and by the time the war broke out was recognized as a leading figure in Polish avant-garde circles. Abroad when the conflict began in 1939, he went to live in Argentina, where he supported himself by working in a bank. There he continued to write and in 1957 his collected works were published in Poland. Shortly afterward they began to be translated into French and then into other languages, and soon his plays found their way to the stage. In 1964, Gombrowicz settled in France, where he lived until his death. Two of his plays—*Yvonne, Princess of Burgundy* (1935) and *The Marriage* (1946)—were written before any major French absurdist drama had appeared. After moving to France, he wrote only one play, *Operetta* (1966).

Gombrowicz was preoccupied with the conflict between freedom and form and tended to see life as a set of interacting deformations. "The process of deformation is a reciprocal one, a constant struggle between two forces—one internal, the other external—each imposing limitations upon the other." Elsewhere he wrote: "People impose upon one another this or that manner of being, speaking, behaving. . . . Each person deforms other persons while being at the same time deformed by them." He was inclined to view anything that destroys "form" as good, but at the same time he recognized the inevitability of submitting to various formative pressures. He often wrote about adolescents because he saw in them a mass of contradictions with endless possibilities which when they enter the adult world will be molded to fit preexisting norms. Thus, men are constantly adapting to what is expected of them, for even if they rebel they merely fall into another pattern.

These ideas run through all of Gombrowicz's plays. *Yvonne, Princess of Burgundy,* a four-act tragifarce, shows the effect of a deviant pattern of behavior on those who have adapted themselves to accepted forms. Prince Philip, bored with the convention that young men must pine after beautiful and vivacious girls, meets the ugly, lethargic Yvonne and decides that he will declare his freedom by announcing his betrothal to her. In order to avoid a scandal, the King and Queen accept his pronouncement and consequently so must the entire court. Soon, however, everyone finds himself revealing long-repressed secrets and impulses, and, recognizing in Yvonne the disruptive force, they decide that she must be eliminated, though in a way that will not outrage civilized tastes. Therefore, she is fed fish containing so many bones that she chokes to death. To maintain propriety, the King and Queen proclaim a suitable period of mourning.

Scene from Gombrowicz's *Operetta,* as produced at the TNP in 1966.
(Photo by Pic.)

The Marriage (first performed in Paris in 1964) is a much more complex play, for it mingles simultaneously several levels of reality in a dreamlike, ritualized sequence of events. At the opening the protagonist, Henry, stands with his friend Johnny before a ruined church somewhere in France during World War II. Soon the church also becomes Henry's childhood home in Poland, and thereafter the action occurs in both the present and the past and in both France and Poland. Henry's father and mother are at once innkeepers and King and Queen, and his fiancée a prostitute and an Ophelia-like gentlewoman. Everything is both degraded and alive with some former glory, and even in the midst of squalor the rituals of religion and court manners are attempted. Urged on by the Drunkard, Henry deposes his father and becomes a despotic ruler. His wedding is arranged, but, fearing that his fiancée has deceived him with Johnny, he hints that his friend should prove his loyalty by committing suicide. When in the midst of the wedding Johnny complies, the celebration turns into a funeral. Though Henry is now king and insists that he is innocent of Johnny's death, he still feels trapped by form and ends by ordering his own arrest. All of this is brought about through an enormously complex process of interacting pressures and conventions which deform both the individual and society. Henry asks: "What does it matter if, taken separately, each of us is lucid, sensible, balanced, when altogether we are nothing but a gigantic madman?"

Operetta depicts the struggle between aristocrats and revolutionaries to gain control of history through fashion, for as Master Flor, who dictates vogues, says: "Fashion is history." Unfortunately, Flor has lost the power either to control fashion or to predict what turn it will next take. It is decided, therefore, that a party will be held to which each person will wear his proposed new fashion, but kept concealed under a wrap until the moment of judgment. Each faction hopes to manipulate the verdict and so to gain power. But the two warring sides do not take into account the youthful Albertinette and her followers, who insist that all clothing be abandoned in favor of nudity. Faced with this solution, most of the guests become so disoriented that they lose even the power of speech. At the end, Albertinette's followers proclaim: "It's us now! It's us now! It's us now!"

This play has been interpreted as a rejection of all partisan ideologies (symbolized by various fashions in clothing), but it also shows Gombrowicz's interest in the conflict between potentiality and fixity as seen in the adolescent-adult relationship. It is illuminated by Gombrowicz's questions: "What writer has felt more violently than I the dependence of the Higher on the Lower? Who has gone so far as I in the feeling that Creation, beauty, vitality, and all the Passion, all the poetry of the world is situated precisely at the point at which the Higher, the elder, the most mature, is under the sway of the Lower, the younger, the junior?"

Gombrowicz's rapid rise in fame since 1960 is probably accounted for by such themes as distorting social forms, the multiplicity of psychological roles played by each person, and the superiority of pliable adolescence over petrified age in combination with a compelling surreality. Perhaps he should not be considered a member of the absurdist school; nevertheless, his outlook and his techniques reenforce those typical of Gombrowicz's contemporaries in France.

~ VII ~

While Continental authors were winning acceptance for the absurdist mode (a relatively lengthy process because of the initial unfamiliarity of audiences both with the outlook and the techniques), the British theatre was entering a new phase as well. English playwrights were accepted more quickly because both their views and their methods were more readily understandable, since the works that made the immediate impact were concerned with social issues treated straightforwardly. But plays of a quite different sort—many resembling absurdist drama—also soon appeared. Consequently, the British revival encompassed many outlooks and dramatic types.

The malaise into which the British theatre had fallen after the war was interrupted in 1956 by the production of John Osborne's *Look Back in*

Anger. But this occasion might never have arisen had it not been for the English Stage Company, founded in 1956 and headed by George Devine (1910–66), who had earlier worked with Saint-Denis at the London Theatre Studio and in the Old Vic School and the Young Vic Company. Tony Richardson (1928–) was assistant director. The company took a thirty-four-year lease on the Royal Court Theatre, which earlier in the century had housed the Barker-Vedrenne troupe. Devine intended to devote himself primarily to new English works or to foreign plays not previously seen in London. But like Grein in the 1890s, he soon found that there was no backlog of good but unproduced works. It was in response to an advertisement which Devine had placed in *The Stage* that Osborne submitted *Look Back in Anger,* the production of which in May 1956 (it was the company's third offering) marked a turning point both in the fortunes of the Royal Court and of the English stage in general. The play was not an instant hit, but within a few months it had found its audience. It came at a crucial time, just when a number of novelists were voicing similar dissatisfactions. Furthermore, the Hungarian uprising, with which it almost coincided, and the Suez crisis, which followed shortly, forcefully directed attention to the kind of social and political realities against which Osborne objected but which had been wholly ignored by such popular dramatists as Rattigan and Priestley.

John Osborne (1929–) began his theatrical career as an actor but between 1949 and 1956, in collaboration with others, wrote several plays, although none was seen in London. Only one of these early works, *Epitaph for George Dillon* (written with Anthony Creighton in 1954 and produced at the Royal Court in 1958) ever became widely known. Thus, it was as an unknown writer that Osborne burst upon the scene in 1956.

Look Back in Anger is conventionally structured and has only five characters. It focuses on Jimmy Porter and his dissatisfactions with the

The original production of John Osborne's *Look Back in Anger* in 1956 at the Royal Court Theatre, London. Mary Ure as Alison, Alan Bates as Cliff, Helena Hughes as Helena, and Kenneth Haigh as Jimmy. (Photo by Houston Rogers.)

world: "There aren't any good, brave causes left. If the big bang comes, and we all get killed off, it won't be in aid of the old-fashioned, grand design. It'll just be for the Brave New Nothing-very-much-thank-you. About as pointless and inglorious as stepping in front of a bus." Thus, Jimmy, like many of the French absurdists, sees life as essentially meaningless, but unlike them, he seems to believe that difficulties could be righted were it not for the class system and other frustrations created by modern society. His disaffection extends as well to the intellectual inertia found in all classes and perhaps in the whole world. Because his wife Alison comes from the upper middle class (his primary target), Jimmy rather sadistically baits her throughout the play. He seems to have no positive solution to suggest as an alternative and contents himself with what Alison describes as guerrilla warfare as he looks back angrily upon a long list of moral, social, and political betrayals by those who go on mouthing Edwardian platitudes. Although the play is essentially negative in tone, it caught the contemporary rebellious mood so well that Jimmy Porter soon became a symbol of all the "angry young men," a category into which such widely differing kinds of protest were soon being placed that the term became meaningless.

Although he has written regularly since 1956, Osborne has never completely recaptured the appeal of this early play. For the most part his subsequent works deal either with rebels or with failures. For example, *Luther* (1961) treats the great church reformer, with his protest against eccleciastical stultification, as another version of the angry young man. Here Osborne uses the chronicle form to trace Luther's development (dwelling especially upon the psychological influences on his early life), his progress through suffering and doubt, and his determination to restore faith in the church. In addition, Osborne has treated rebels, though less successfully, in *Time Present* (1968), which explores but does not pinpoint the heroine's sense of the world's and her own imperfections, and in *Hotel Amsterdam* (1968), which shows a group of people seeking to escape their tyrannous employer only to discover that the real problems lie within themselves.

With the exception of *Look Back in Anger,* most of Osborne's greatest successes have been won with plays about human failure. *The Entertainer* (1957) has as its protagonist a disintegrating music hall performer (originally played by Laurence Olivier). Here England's progressive decline in vigor and values is symbolized in three generations of the Rice family of entertainers: Billy, the respected figure of the preceding era; Archie, the tasteless failure of today; and Archie's children, one dead at Suez, the others no longer interested in the profession. In this play, Osborne also seems to have been influenced by Brecht, for he alternates realistic scenes with Archie's vaudeville routines.

Inadmissible Evidence (1965) is one of Osborne's most powerful dramas. It deals with the outwardly successful, middle-aged lawyer, Bill Maitland, who has come to view his life as a failure. Now on trial for some unnamed sexual offense, he recalls the experiences which have led him to despair. It is this evidence, inadmissible at the real trial but essential to understanding what it represents, that makes up the play. The structure is determined by Maitland's thoughts as (onstage throughout) he recalls his past with family, mistresses, clients, and business associates. A moving evocation of a wasted life, it offered Nicol Williamson an opportunity in the leading role to display his enormous talent.

Osborne continues to write and consequently the direction of his work may yet alter. Although his techniques have changed somewhat (perhaps most noticeably in the freer handling of time and place), Osborne's approach remains essentially discursive, just as his interests continue to cluster around moral and social issues. Despite the critics' fondness for declaring that he has failed to live up to his early promise, Osborne must be considered one of the most important of postwar dramatists.

Next to Osborne, the Royal Court's most important dramatist of the early years was John Arden (1930–   ). Trained as an architect, Arden had written a prize-winning radio play before his *The Waters of Babylon* was presented on one of the Sunday evening programs used by the Royal Court to try out new works. Then, *Live Like Pigs* was given a full production in 1958. Since then Arden has written many plays, among them *Sergeant Musgrave's Dance* (1959), *The Happy Haven* (1960), *The Workhouse Donkey* (1963), *Armstrong's Last Goodnight* (1964), *Left-handed Liberty* (1966), and *The Hero Rises Up* (1968).

Arden's plays have been both highly praised and judged confused. Because he treats contemporary problems but does not seem to take sides, audiences have found it difficult to decide what he intends. But practically all of the plays pursue the same themes—the conflict between order and anarchy, between conformity and freedom, between those who wish to impose some pattern or principle and those who resist such efforts.

In *Live Like Pigs,* a group of gypsylike characters is forced by the government to move into a housing project where it is surrounded by neighbors with rigid ideas about cleanliness and propriety. Eventually the conflict leads to violence and the gypsies are forced to conform. Arden plays down neither the filth of the gypsies nor the narrow-mindedness of the neighbors, although he obviously admires the lustiness of gypsy life. He justifies neither position, but because the play is set against the background of the welfare state, audiences and critics seem to have concluded that it must contain some intended message and, when it escaped them, they judged it puzzling or unsuccessful.

In *Sergeant Musgrave's Dance,* Arden's best-known work, the title character and his companions arrive in a town with the intention of teaching the residents a lesson about the wastefulness of all aggression and military power by taking twenty-five lives for the five they were forced to take in the colonies. When he is in danger of being distracted by love from his fanatical scheme, Musgrave declares: "If you come to us with what

Arden's *Sergeant Musgrave's Dance* at the Royal Court in 1959.
(Photo by Dominic.)

you call your life and love. . . and you scribble all over that plan, . . . there's anarchy." But later, after his scheme has failed, he is told: "We'd got life and love. Then *you* came in and did your scribbling where nobody asked you. . . . It's still anarchy, isn't it?" This complex play has often been interpreted as an antiwar tract (though admittedly not a wholly successful one), but Arden seems to be suggesting that, though life has its ugly aspects (and that war is perhaps the ugliest), to force peace (or any pattern) on people is merely another form of aggression, for there is a fundamental conflict between anarchy and order which almost inevitably leads to violence.

The Happy Haven embodies the conflict in still another way. Here the setting is an old people's home where a doctor performs experiments on his patients in an attempt to make them young again. The struggle is between the old people, who want merely to be themselves, and the doctor, who sees youth as the ideal pattern. The play also differs markedly in tone from *Sergeant Musgrave's Dance,* for it ends in farcical fantasy as the patients force the doctor to drink his own elixir until he is reduced to childhood.

Armstrong's Last Goodnight deals with the conflict between a Scottish chieftain, Armstrong, who wishes to retain his freedom, and King James, who is seeking to establish a strong central government. Armstrong, in pursuing anarchical freedom, and the king, in his attempts to impose

618

Albert Finney in Arden's
Armstrong's Last Goodnight
at the National Theatre. (Photo courtesy
the National Theatre.)

order, are equally cruel and unjust. Here, as elsewhere, it is the contraries that interest Arden. If he offers no solutions, it is probably because he does not see any as possible, for both the urge to freedom and the desire for order are omnipresent and ineradicable.

Arden has covered a wide range of subjects and has used diverse means. In *The Happy Haven,* the characters wear caricatured masks, and in most of the plays ballads, songs, and dance are important. Arden's diction is also varied, for it is composed of realistic dialect and figurative and lyrical speech (a combination which has led to charges that Arden is self-consciously literary). In the works written since 1965, Arden appears to have moved toward greater social and political commitment, but this direction is so tentative that it remains uncertain. Arden is both one of the most perceptive and one of the least understood of contemporary British playwrights.

The Royal Court also introduced the work of Norman Frederick Simpson (1919–   ), who helped to acclimatize absurdism in England. In 1956, his *A Resounding Tinkle* won a prize offered by the Royal Court and later it was presented there on a double bill with *The Hole.* He then won considerable commercial success with *One Way Pendulum* (1959), and went on to write *The Form* (1961), *The Cresta Run* (1965), and *How Are Your Handles?* (1970). Simpson's work is reminiscent of Ionesco's but without the darker side. He takes the life of suburbia and reduces it to absurdity through non sequitur and exaggeration.

The Royal Court produced classics and foreign plays as well as new

619

works. Among its productions were *Lysistrata, The Country Wife, Major Barbara, The Good Woman of Setzuan, Endgame, The Blacks, Rhinoceros,* and *Orpheus Descending.* It has continued this policy of mingling new, old, and foreign plays. As the importance of the company was established, it won increased support. At first it received a small subsidy from the Arts Council (about 5,000 pounds annually), but in 1963 this was increased to 30,000 pounds and it was also granted some financial assistance by the Greater London Council as well. By the time Devine retired in 1965, the English Stage Company had become one of the most potent forces in the British theatre.

~~ **VIII** ~~

In addition to the English Stage Company, a second group—the Theatre Workshop—played an important role in the theatrical renaissance of the 1950s. The guiding spirit of this company was Joan Littlewood (1914–   ), who began her theatrical career in Manchester in the 1930s when she and Ewan MacColl, a folksinger and playwright, established the Theatre of Action, a politically committed organization. In 1945 she founded the Theatre Workshop with the idea of producing plays, both old and new, with contemporary relevance for working-class audiences. Until 1953 the company toured, especially in the north of England, and then settled permanently in the East London suburb of Stratford, a working-class district. The first production in its new home, MacColl's version of *The Good Soldier Schweik,* was followed by *Volpone* and *Edward II,* a repertory with which the troupe won its first (and considerable) international reputation at the Théâtre des Nations in Paris in 1955 and 1956.

By 1956 the company's style and working methods were well established. Of all English directors, Miss Littlewood has been the one most addicted to Brechtian techniques, although these have been considerably altered in her usage by other influences, perhaps above all that of the music hall. But she has also drawn heavily on Stanislavsky. She asked each actor in the Workshop to determine the objective of his character in each scene and in the play as a whole, and she placed special emphasis upon "through lines" of action. She made extensive use of improvisation as well. While keeping objectives and through line of action in mind, the actors were encouraged to seek ways of improving scenes through cooperative improvisations. The Workshop seems to have been one of the first postwar groups to work directly with authors on developing scripts. Of its productions, a number were "Cockney improvisations," such as *Fings Ain't Wot They Used T'Be,* a musical with book by Frank Norman (1930–   ) and music by Lionel Bart (1930–   ), which is said to have evolved out of an eighteen-page outline. Some of the company's most controversial productions were classics reshaped by Miss Littlewood to give social or political slants not readily apparent in the original texts. Her ultimate aim was to create a theatre to which the working classes would go with the same regularity and enthusiasm as to fun palaces or penny arcades. Thus, she sought to imbed within a framework of techniques borrowed from popular entertainments some lasting message or significant content. She wished her productions to be "grand, vulgar, simple, pathetic—but not genteel, not poetical."

The Theatre Workshop contributed to the dramatic renaissance primarily through its work with two playwrights—Behan and Delaney. Brendan Behan (1923–64) was born in Ireland and early became involved with the IRA (Irish Republican Army, an organization dedicated to reuniting Ireland), as a result of which he spent much of the time between 1939 and 1948 in prison. It is these two influences—the IRA and prison life—which are most evident in Behan's plays, *The Quare Fellow* and *The Hostage.*

When *The Quare Fellow* was presented by the Theatre Workshop in 1956 it aroused almost as much excitement as had *Look Back in Anger,* in part because of its subject matter but even more for outlook and vitality. It provides a cross-section of prison life (both inmates and wardens) on the eve of an execution. A loose but skillfully handled mixture of serious and comic vignettes, it slowly builds recognition of the essential humanity of the inmates and horror at legalized murder. There is little in the way of story but tension builds steadily as the time of the execution approaches. In many ways *The Quare Fellow* resembles such naturalistic dramas as *The Weavers* and *The Lower Depths,* although it has considerably greater variety in tone.

The Hostage (1958) is said to have begun as a short work and to have been expanded through the Workshop's improvisations. Like *The Quare Fellow,* it shows varying attitudes to a central event, this time the impending execution of an IRA agent. But now the action is set in a brothel to which a young British soldier is brought as a hostage to be killed in reprisal if the IRA agent dies. Although Behan is sympathetic to all his characters, he is critical of the IRA, which, though perhaps once useful, now encourages Ireland to look backward instead of inciting it to construct a more meaningful future. The degeneration of the organization is symbolized in part by the setting itself, once the haunt of heroes but now a place of prostitution. This idea is further reenforced by the play's ending, in which the hostage is accidentally killed during a raid on the hideout by secret agents. The whole scheme is shown to have been an empty and wasteful gesture. These central ideas are stated rather directly, but the action relating to them consumes only a small portion of the total play, much of which is taken up with various diversions—songs, dances, comic routines, and discussions only tenuously related to the main action. The overall effect is more that of a music hall entertainment than of a play of ideas. Still, it was these additions that made the play popular, not only in Britain but in other countries where the Irish question was almost totally unfamiliar. Behan never completed another play. If they cannot be called great, his works nevertheless exerted a tonic effect on the theatre of the time.

Shelagh Delaney (1939–   ) made her impact largely through one play, *A Taste of Honey* (1958), which she is said to have written in reaction to Rattigan's dramas. Its protagonist is a teenage girl, who, after being virtually abandoned by her slatternly mother, has an affair with a Black sailor and becomes pregnant. Taken in by a homosexual boy who looks after her, their relationship is relatively happy until the mother reappears and forces the boy to leave. The play stresses closely observed life and character rather than ideas. There is no anger in it, for each character accepts his fate without complaint. The story is slight, the social comment indirect; the play's strength lies in its sense of immediate life and its compassion. Miss Delaney has written little else for the stage. Her only other major attempt, *The Lion in Love* (1960), a diffuse study of several characters grouped around an unsatisfactory marriage, had little success.

Many critics have credited Miss Littlewood with the success of both Behan and Delaney. She and her company certainly worked closely with the authors and provided considerable help in reworking scripts, but there is no

Joan Littlewood's production of *Oh What a Lovely War!* in 1963 at the Theatre Workshop; design by John Bury. (Photos courtesy of Romano Cagnoni.)

evidence to suggest that the plays were changed by anyone other than their authors. Nevertheless, the failure of Miss Delaney to develop after leaving the Workshop suggests how salutary Miss Littlewood's advice must have been.

The Theatre Workshop, like many earlier groups, was eventually weakened by success. Since it received no outside financial assistance, it succumbed to the temptation of moving its hits to the West End where it could reap greater profits. But as a result, the close-knit company, upon which the Workshop's style really depended, began to disintegrate. In 1961 Miss Littlewood resigned as director. She returned in 1963 to stage *Oh, What a Lovely War!*, the Workshop's greatest popular success, an evocation and bitingly satirical commentary on World War I as put together by Miss Littlewood, Charles Chilton, and the company. Then, after directing for the Theatre Workshop a combined version of both parts of Shakespeare's *Henry IV* in 1964, she devoted herself for a time to establishing a theatre school in Tunisia and to plans for a series of "fun palaces" in England. Although the Workshop has continued its training program, it has presented plays only occasionally since 1965, usually when Miss Littlewood is available to stage them. Nevertheless, it can no longer be considered the vital force which it unquestionably was during the years between 1955 and 1965.

If the Theatre Workshop was England's most prominent politically oriented company, Arnold Wesker (1932–) was its most politically oriented playwright. Born in London of immigrant parents, Wesker worked for a time as a plumber's assistant and as a pastry cook. He then attended a film course, during which he wrote his first play, *Chicken Soup With Barley,* produced in 1958 at the Belgrade Theatre, Coventry, with the assistance of the Royal Court, where it later played. This was the opening work in a trilogy, of which the other two parts are *Roots* (1959) and *I'm Talking About Jerusalem* (1960).

Chicken Soup With Barley is perhaps the most complex of the plays, since it covers a period of twenty years (from 1936 to 1956) and provides a history of the Kahn family, around whom the trilogy centers. The mother, Sarah, believes unquestioningly in the socialist ideal and spends her time working to achieve it, while her husband, Harry, retreats more and more from political concerns. The children, Ada and Ronnie, at first follow in their mother's footsteps, but by the end of the play are disillusioned. (Wesker suggests that the welfare state has in part removed the clear-cut issues upon which the socialist movement had originally thrived and that the violent supression of the Hungarian uprising in 1956 had raised disturbing doubts about communism.) Because of various experiences the children have come to believe that people do not really want to be helped and that the world is not worth saving. Thus, though Sarah's faith is unshaken, that of Ada and her husband, Dave, is, and they go off to the country to pursue the idyllic dream of being self-supporting craftsmen, while Ronnie strikes out on his own.

Roots revolves around Beatie Bryant, a young farm girl who has met Ronnie in the city and has returned home for a visit, during which Ronnie is expected to arrive. Most of the play is devoted to showing the stupidity and indifference of Beatie's parents, who resent her new interests; when Ronnie decides not to marry Beatie, they taunt instead of comfort her. Up to this crucial point, Beatie has merely parroted ideas she has picked up from Ronnie, but now she begins to think for herself and decides that the working class has set its sights too low. "We want the third-rate—we got it." As the curtain falls, she resolves to change the life around her.

I'm Talking About Jerusalem takes up the story of Ada and Dave after they have moved to the country, where they soon find that their schemes are economically unfeasible. Eventually they decide to return to the city because "machinery and modern techniques" have made Dave "the odd man out." He concludes, "Maybe you can't build on your own," but Ronnie suggests an alternative idea: "Maybe by coming here you've purified yourselves, like Jesus in the wilderness."

As a whole, the trilogy traces the declining sense of purpose in the socialist movement and seeks to show that workers have settled for too little and have chosen the wrong paths in seeking to remedy ills. Wesker seems to suggest that one cannot run away from problems (as Ada and Dave try to do) or solve them through individual effort. The needs are for collective action and higher standards.

With the early works belongs *The Kitchen* (written in 1958 but later expanded), in which working-class conditions are explored through the microcosm of a kitchen in a large restaurant. It implies that violence and other forms of socially unacceptable behavior are almost inevitable under the tensions created by adverse working conditions. All four of these early plays are essentially realistic (perhaps even naturalistic) in their attempt to impart a sense of life as it is lived by workers and to depict their disappointments.

Chips With Everything (1962) moves toward greater schematization of ideas. Set in a Royal Air Force training camp, it uses the military establishment as an exemplar of the English class system. The main character, Pip Thompson, a young man from the upper class, chooses to throw in his lot with the enlisted men, who, he believes, are exploited and systematically deprived of all that is best in entertainment, art, and living conditions. Wesker seems to use Pip as his spokesman, but he also casts doubts on Pip's ideas by letting him be broken by the accusation that he has joined the enlisted men only because he fears that he cannot compete within his own class for the power he desires.

That many of Wesker's own ideas are expressed by Pip seems reasonably certain, since shortly after completing the play he became the leader of a working-class artistic organization, Center 42 (so named from the Trades Union Congress resolution number 42 which in 1961 called for the popularization of the arts among workers). With Center 42 Wesker intended to supply plays and music of high quality for festivals throughout the country. But after a brief burst of energy in 1962 the movement subsided, and since 1966 has receded to the Roundhouse, a converted railroad shop located in northern London. Though intended as a cultural center for workers, it has in recent years been devoted increasingly to avant-garde productions, and Wesker has now severed his connection with it.

Since 1962 Wesker has written little. *Their Very Own and Golden City* (1966), which shows an architect's dream of building a number of cooperatively owned model cities gradually dissipate, is near in spirit to the earlier works, though it does not equal them in power. A marked change can be seen in Wesker's work beginning with *The Four Seasons* (1966), a two-character play about the varying aspects of marriage as seen in the cycle of a year. It is by far Wesker's most introspective and psychologically oriented drama. A few critics praised it, but most seemed disturbed by Wesker's departure from his political stance and some accused him of "expressionistic vagueness." Even more negative critical response greeted *The Friends* (1970), in which the death of one of their number leads the six characters to reexamine their lives and values. All six have come from working families and, like the characters in Wesker's early plays, originally had dreams of serving their class. Instead, they have gradually become a part of the world they had wished to change. (The crises they undergo during the play constitute a critique of Wesker's own earlier views and activities.) With their newly acquired self-knowledge, they seem at the end to be headed for a brighter future. The London production, directed by Wesker, seems not to have done full justice to the script, but Wesker responded bitterly to the generally unfavorable critical response, charging that the critics were more concerned with defending their image of him, based on the early works, than with responding to his new play. Whatever the basis of the disagreement, it seems clear that Wesker is moving toward a more complex view of art, man, and society.

Wesker's reputation, nevertheless, still rests primarily on the early plays, which, more positive in stance than Osborne's, attracted a wide following among the politically inclined. In combination with *Look Back in Anger,* they also did much to revive the realism of an earlier period, especially the type popular in the 1930s. Though Wesker probably cannot be considered a major playwright, he did much to reawaken interest in a drama seriously concerned with political and social action.

Several other playwrights—among them John Whiting, Ann Jellicoe, Bernard Kops, Alun Owen, and John Mortimer—also came to prominence after 1956, but, though their achievements are considerable, most have now receded in critical estimation. In marked contrast, one writer—Pinter—has risen steadily in fame and is now considered the best of all contemporary English dramatists.

Harold Pinter (1930–) began his career as an actor, turned to playwriting in 1957 with *The Room,* and has since written regularly for the theatre, television, and films. His stage works include *The Dumb Waiter* (1957), *The Birthday Party* (1958), *The Caretaker* (1960), *The Collection* (1962), *The Lover* (1963), *The Homecoming* (1965), *Landscape* (1968), *Silence* (1969), and *Old Times* (1971). Although there is much variety among them, almost all the plays have in common a few characteristics: everyday situations which gradually take on an air of mystery or menace; unexplained, unrevealed, or ambiguous motivations or background facts; and authentic, seemingly natural, though carefully wrought dialogue.

Pinter's plays are always grounded in ordinary reality, for almost everything that happens in them lies within the realm of everyday possibility. Sometimes action and dialogue even suggest naturalism. Nevertheless, the overall impression is one of ambiguity and mystery, in large part because the background, motivations, and sometimes even the identity of characters are unstated or only partially revealed. Pinter has argued that traditional drama goes astray because of its assumption that everything can be verified, whereas in actuality little can be definitely known. Consequently, he rejects the idea that an author should be expected to know everything about his characters, since he cannot be sure even about what goes on within his own mind; all he can do is record a situation as it appears at its beginning and note the changes that take place subsequently. Pinter encloses his characters in a confined space (usually a single room) and confronts them with a crisis (most often created by quite ordinary events) which forces them to define their existential being. His characters speak a dialogue that re-creates the rhythms and effect of daily speech but in which controlled silences and an unspoken "subtext" are as important as what is verbalized. Pinter has said of people in general that "most of the time we're inexpressive, giving little away, unreliable, elusive, evasive, obstructive, unwilling. But it's out of these attributes that a language arises. A language . . . where, under what is said, another thing is being said." Thus, with Pinter silence is an integral part of language and he treats all speech as one type of stratagem whereby characters seek to cover their psychological nakedness as they attempt to avoid the difficulties and pitfalls of communication, for it is a terrifying thing for anyone either to reveal too much about themselves to others or to have others reveal too much to them. In Pinter's plays everything may at first appear amusing or pleasantly ambiguous, but gradually the tone changes to anxiety, pathos, or fear as the characters confront some predicament and seek to defend themselves against some menace—created by themselves or others, or by some unknown, often undefined danger from outside the all-too-vulnerable room in which they are seeking refuge.

The Birthday Party, Pinter's first full-length play, may be taken as representative of the early works. In it, Stanley has settled down in a seaside boardinghouse where he is mothered by Meg, the proprietress. Then, two men—McCann and Goldberg—arrive. Ostensibly looking for rooms, in actuality they have come for Stanley. They organize a birthday party for him, even though he insists that it is not his birthday, and subject him to a grueling cross-examination during which he is accused of a wide range of misdeeds (many of them contradictory). Stanley is reduced to such a state of desperation that during the party he tries to strangle Meg. The next morning, Stanley, wearing formal clothes, is brought in silently and taken away. It is unclear what Stanley has done, who McCann and Goldberg are, who has sent them, or what they intend to do with Stanley. The play has been variously interpreted as an allegory about conformity, death, guilt, or retribution. Pinter has denied any philosophical intent but has said that he considers all men to be surrounded by the unknown and that "the unknown leads us to the next step. . . . There is a kind of horror about and I think that this horror and absurdity go together."

In Pinter's early works, especially in the climactic moments of the one-act plays, there is a tendency for realistic action to pass over into fantasy or symbolism, although these moments are always treated as projections of the characters' dreams or anxieties. Beginning with *The Caretaker,* his second full-length play, Pinter is able to merge more completely the symbolic with the realistic. Consequently, in most of the plays written thereafter the sense of menace no longer stems from some power outside the room, but is now usually embodied in the characters themselves or in forces existing within the room. *The Caretaker* depicts three characters: Aston, a handyman; Mick, his brother; and Davies, an old man whom Aston has befriended. Pinter provides much more specific (or unambiguous) information about these characters than about earlier ones. We learn that Aston, because of hallucinations, has been given shock treatments, as a result of which his brain has been damaged; that Mick, who owns the house in which Aston lives, watches over his brother somewhat distantly; that the irascible Davies, who vacillates between assertiveness and obsequiousness, has been fired from his job and rescued from an altercation by Aston. There is little forward movement in the action. Davies, sensing the possibility of driving a wedge between the brothers and supplanting Aston as caretaker, misjudges the situation and is evicted—that is, thrown back into the hostile world from which he has been rescued momentarily. Though Davies's plight may ultimately differ little from Stanley's, he seems more clearly to embody within himself the weaknesses that explain (it has been suggested) man's expulsion from the Garden of Eden.

Pinter's next full-length play, *The Homecoming,* is usually considered his best. In it, Teddy, an Englishman who is now a professor of philosophy in an American university, and his wife Ruth return to visit his family: his father Max; his two brothers, Joey and Lenny; and his cabdriver uncle, Sam. Eventually Lenny, who is a pimp, suggests that he set Ruth up as a prostitute; she calmly acquiesces and Teddy cheerfully returns to America without her. Near the end of the play, Sam collapses after revealing that the boys' mother used his cab for an adulterous assignation, and Max grovels before Ruth begging for her sexual favors.

On one level, the play proceeds realistically enough. Some critics have objected that the characters agree too calmly and readily to Lenny's proposition, but they tend to ignore several clues that the family may have a history of involvement with prostitution: it is implied that the dead mother was either a true or near-prostitute, and it seems likely that before her marriage the same might be said of Ruth. Furthermore, the marriage between Teddy and Ruth is not entirely happy and he may be glad of an opportunity to be rid of her. At any rate, on the realistic level any

Michael Craig as Teddy and Vivien Merchant
as Ruth in Pinter's *The Homecoming* at
the Aldwych Theatre in 1965,
directed by Peter Hall. (Photo courtesy
the Royal Shakespeare Company.)

sense of mystery is due almost wholly to inexplicitness about the past and
about the characters' motivations in the present. As in the earlier plays,
the audience must rely on ambiguous clues and the rich but imprecise
subtext. Because of this inexplicitness, a certain air of mystery surrounds
the characters, to each of whom "homecoming" probably has a different
significance in the action. On the symbolic level, *The Homecoming* has
been interpreted variously: as a wishfulfillment of the Oedipus complex
(with the sons taking possession of Ruth, their surrogate mother); as a
conflict between the mental, moral, and physical instincts, with the physical
an easy winner over its weaker competitors; as Ruth's recognition that
woman must play many and contradictory roles and the discovery of all
these possibilities within herself; as a reworking of the parable of the
prodigal son; and as an adaptation of the biblical story of Ruth. So many
diverse (though not mutually exclusive) views indicate the richness of
connotation aroused by the drama and the many chords struck by its
allusiveness.

The short plays *Landscape* and *Silence* mark something of a change
in Pinter's method. In both, characters alternate speeches but do not seem
to hear each other or even necessarily to be talking of the same things. In
Silence, Pinter's most abstract play, the three characters, rather than being
in a room, exist in some indefinite place—perhaps the interior world of
memory, perhaps some afterlife. Sometimes each seems to be alone, at
others with one or both of his fellows. At times each appears to have
returned to a period in life different from that then being inhabited by the
others. Both *Landscape* and *Silence* show the ambiguity of memory and
the way the mind reshapes the past. When produced in 1969, they were
seen by critics as marking a new direction in Pinter's work.

Pinter's *Old Times,* staged by Peter Hall at the RSC in 1971. Left to right, Colin Blakely as Deeley, Vivien Merchant as Kate, and Dorothy Tutin as Anna. (Photo courtesy the Royal Shakespeare Company.)

Old Times, however, suggests that the change is only partial, for in method it is related to *The Homecoming,* although its subject, like that of its immediate predecessors, is memory. To the isolated country home of Deeley (a filmmaker) and his wife Kate comes Anna, Kate's roommate before she married Deeley some twenty years ago. Their conversation deals almost exclusively with memories of the past and eventually becomes an unacknowledged struggle between Deeley and Anna for proprietary claims on Kate, who says little until near the end of the play, when she forcefully reasserts her independence. But there is no victor, for through memory all are inextricably intertwined, though for each in a different way. The truth about the past remains unknown, almost irrelevant, for as Anna says: "There are some things one remembers even though they may never have happened. There are things I remember which may never have happened, but as I recall them so they take place."

As a dramatist, Pinter seems to fall somewhere between Beckett and Chekhov. Like the former, he isolates characters and lets them wrestle with their anxieties in an unverifiable universe; like Chekhov, he creates a realistic texture of background and dialogue in which surface act and speech are merely evasions or disguises of deeper conflicts and anxieties. Working within a relatively narrow range of subject and method, Pinter is a master dramatist—one who hopefully still has many years in which to develop his talents even further.

XI

Dissatisfaction with the human condition was common among many dramatists of the 1950s. But they tended to react in two different ways: by depicting all human endeavor as absurd, or by angrily denouncing the social or political conditions which had created problems. Of these, the notion of absurdity was the first to appear, and in many ways it seems the characteristic response of the 1950s, when the cold war and the threat of atomic warfare created the aura of a hostile universe in which all values were under attack. To retreat from the fray, "not to get involved," was perhaps the most frequently expressed desire of the time.

By the late 1950s, however, this mood of retreat had begun to give way to anger—perhaps the dominant note of the 1960s. The advice of Sartre and Camus to establish one's own standards and to act forcefully on them—not to be paralyzed by the world's absurdity—seemed to come to the surface once more. The work of such playwrights as Osborne and Wesker offered merely a foretaste of what the 1960s would bring. Martin Luther King, Jr.'s demonstrations of the power of group effort to publicize wrongs and to effect change also had a releasing effect. While the outlook of the 1960s was probably no more positive than that of the 1950s, it replaced the passive contemplation of absurdity with action designed to deride absurdity and to champion change. If the position of the absurdists was not wholly rejected, it was at least subordinated to another which implied that standards are clearly understandable and that they can be realized if men fight together strongly for them.

Thus, though absurdity and anger existed simultaneously during the 1950s, there is something of a linear movement—from absurdity to anger. The 1960s brought a combination of the two in which the past was depicted as absurd and the future as a time when all mistakes might be overcome, in which absurdity might be transcended through anger. It was out of the questioning of the 1940s and 1950s that these still newer efforts grew in the 1960s.

Continental
Theatre and Drama
Since 1960

17

Although there was much experimentation in theatre and drama during the 1960s, there was also much pressure to retain tradition and to resist innovation, or to accept it warily. Consequently, many countries on the European continent were little affected by new directions, even though most showed an increase in vitality over the preceding decade. Spain and Italy remained conservative, in part because of censorship and other restraints, although Italy suffered as well from the lack of a strong theatrical tradition. Meanwhile, Eastern Europe was seeking to break the hold of socialist realism. But Soviet Russia, though it welcomed some changes, remained attuned to the realistic mode and, by Western standards, reactionary. In Poland and Czechoslovakia, on the other hand, the desire for

632

change led to imaginative, semi-allegorical drama in the absurdist vein and to productions which could rank among the world's finest. In Germany documentary drama brought new vigor to the theatre, but in France the great creative surge of the 1950s seemed to wane. In general, it was a decade of increased prosperity for the theatre almost everywhere. Around 1968, however, many previously submerged conflicts burst into the open and disrupted the seeming satisfaction with tradition. There followed a time of hesitation, reassessment, and change—a phase still evident in the early 1970s.

During the 1960s, Spain's theatre continued to be one of the most conservative in the world despite the relaxation of censorship after 1963. At that time, guidelines were at last established and most of the churchmen removed from their posts as censors. Nevertheless, prohibitions remained against anything considered inimical to either church or state. The plays of Lorca, Casona, and Valle-Inclán began to find their way onto the stage once more and Casona returned to live in Spain. The upsurge of interest in the work of Valle-Inclán was especially instrumental in turning attention to absurdism and other recent European drama.

Valle-Inclán's *Divine Words,* as it was produced at the Teatro Bellas Artes, Madrid, in 1961. Directed by José Tomayo. (Courtesy *World Theatre.*)

Despite the relaxation of strictures on subject matter and techniques, authors remained wary, for at times censorship was still harsh. Among the best of the new writers was Lauro Olmo, who first came to prominence in 1961 with *The Shirt,* a play about the plight of the Spanish worker who must migrate because he cannot earn enough at home. In *The Decoration* (1965) Olmo uses the conflicting ideologies within a family as a microcosm of all Spain; and in a group of short plays with the overall title *The Fourth Estate,* he shows how the press is manipulated to keep Spanish affairs under control. Considering his subjects, it is not surprising that Olmo has had difficulty in getting his plays produced and that he remains little known among the general public of his own country.

José-María Bellido has adopted a more indirect approach and perhaps for that reason has fared better. His most famous play is *Football* (1963), an allegorical fantasy about modern Spain. Set in an imaginary village, it deals with a conflict precipitated by a football (soccer) game some thirty years before the action begins. The outcome has left the losers enslaved to the winners, who lord it over them and keep them in close check. Another strand of action shows the attempts of two world powers (Soviet Russia and America) to gain control of a star football player. A peacemaker seems on the verge of healing the breach between the two rival teams when he is killed by a shot that comes from "the direction of the church." At the end, having lost all faith in their leaders, the two world powers, and the Church, the rival teams unite. This thinly disguised parable is clothed in a form which links it to both the absurdist and Brechtian strands of European drama. It has become one of the most popular of recent Spanish plays both at home and abroad. But despite the work of Olmo and Bellido, most Spanish drama remains relatively conservative and the Spanish theatre largely isolated from contemporary foreign developments.

There are now about twenty theatres in Madrid. Since most give two performances each evening, they exert considerable pressure on writers to keep their works short. Probably for this reason, the majority of plays are in two acts. There are two national theatres in Madrid: the Teatro Espagñol, devoted to Spanish and foreign classics; and the Teatro María Guerrero, specializing in more recent Spanish and foreign works. The state has also recognized the inevitability of change and, both to control and to give it order, in 1965 established the National Experimental Theatre to try out new plays and techniques. Compared with the innovations to be seen in most Western European countries, however, this theatre's offerings are mild indeed. Until Spain enjoys greater freedom, its theatres are not apt to move far outside traditional paths.

As in Spain, censorship was relaxed in Italy in 1963, and as a result works by a number of foreign authors, among them Brecht and Sartre, were seen for the first time. Nevertheless, many restrictions remain, especially in Rome, for a treaty with the Vatican forbids anything there which might offend "the sacred nature of the Eternal City." Consequently, the plays of such authors as Genet and Hochhuth remain unwelcome, and in 1969 the Living Theatre was expelled from the country allegedly for performing in the nude.

But it is not censorship so much as the lack of a strong theatrical tradition which has most plagued Italy. The postwar struggle to build permanent resident companies has been partially successful, for Strehler's pioneering work at Milan had led by the 1960s to the establishment of subsidized companies in each of the ten major cities. In addition to Milan, the most prestigious of the troupes were those in Turin (under the direction of Gianfranco de Bosio), Genoa (under the direction of Luigi Squarzina), and Rome (under the direction of Orazio Costa).

Most of Italy, however, has continued to depend on touring companies featuring well-known stars. Two have become virtually permanent, although without any fixed base: the Compagnia Proclemer-Albertazzi, headed by the actor-directors Anna Proclemer and Giorgio Albertazzi; and the Compagnia DeLullo-Falk, a cooperative venture of Giorgio DeLullo (as leading man and director), Rosella Falk (as leading lady), Romolo Valli, and Elsa Albani (both character actors). In addition, Vittorio Gassman has from time to time organized troupes to tour throughout Italy in productions of classics.

Besides Strehler, the directors with the greatest international reputations are Visconti and Zeffirelli, both of whom have from time to time assembled companies in Italy. Luchino Visconti (1906–   ) was one of the originators of the neorealism that won Italian film much of its postwar fame, and the same stylistic qualities have distinguished his stage productions as well. His best-known work has been done in opera, above all *La Sonnambula* and *La Traviata,* both of which starred Maria Callas. Franco Zeffirelli (1923–   ) began his career as a designer for Visconti, from whom his most typical approach is derived. He turned to directing in 1953, at first primarily in opera. Around 1958 he began receiving invitations to direct in other countries and soon built a reputation for bringing classics down to earth. Among his best-known productions are *Romeo and Juliet* (both at the Old Vic and in film), *Hamlet* (presented by his own company in Rome), and *Much Ado About Nothing* (at the National Theatre in London). In most of his productions (which he also designs), Zeffirelli has used neorealistic settings and business (always more picturesque than sordid), an approach which has led on the one hand to accusations that the text has been swamped with visual detail, and on the other to praise for bringing a sense of concreteness to works which all too often remain remote from audiences.

Of all European countries, Italy is probably the one most dedicated to the idea of theatre as a place for virtuoso performers, even as it provides few places where an actor can receive sound technical training. These two conditions have made it difficult to achieve ensemble playing. As a result, outside of a few companies, the general level of acting tends to be poor.

Franco Zeffirelli's production of Shakespeare's *Much Ado About Nothing* at the National Theatre, London, in 1965. At center, Maggie Smith and Robert Stephens as Beatrice and Benedick. (Photo by Dominic.)

Virtually no contemporary Italian playwrights have been able to win international recognition. Two principal problems stand in their way: the overwhelming demand for plays with popular appeal, and regional dialects. If playwrights avoid one of the many dialects, they are usually accused of remoteness or literariness, but if they write in dialect, their plays have difficulty in appealing to audiences outside the immediate region. Today Italy has a number of competent dramatists—among them Diego Fabbri, Carlo Terron, Federico Zardi, Franco Brusati, Giuseppe Patroni-Griffi, and Luigi Squarzina—but most remain virtually unknown elsewhere.

In the late 1960s, Italy, like most other countries, was rent by dissatisfactions, many of which had considerable effect on the theatre. The resident companies were among the hardest hit. In 1968 Strehler resigned his post as director when the Piccolo Teatro in Milan failed to get the new building it had been seeking for years and when it was not named a national theatre, as had seemed likely. (Strehler has since returned as a guest director.) In the same year, de Bosio resigned his post at Turin, where an overambitious program had led to economic difficulties. The DeLullo-

Goldoni's *Servant of Two Masters* at the Teatro Piccolo, Milan;
directed by Giorgio Strehler, designed by Ezio Frigerio.
(From *Scene Design Throughout the World Since 1950*.)

Falk company was installed in his theatre in Turin, while he went to Milan
to fill Strehler's post. By the end of 1968 only eight of the resident companies remained, and of these only Squarzina's troupe in Genoa seemed
able to achieve a truly permanent company, in part because he employed
young actors and instilled in them a sense of loyalty, whereas elsewhere
actors were avoiding long-term commitments so they might work in films
and television.

More fundamental questions were being raised by young actors, many
of whom looked for their standards to such radical groups as the Living
Theatre. By 1969 there were at least two young companies with promise:
the Nuova Scena, directed by Dario Fo and Franca Rame, who were
presenting pantomimed or improvised works on current problems for
working-class audiences in Italy's small towns; and the Community Theatre,
directed by Giancarlo Cobelli, which was presenting such plays as *The
Birds* by Aristophanes and following each performance with a debate
carried on with the audience.

Multimedia productions also arrived in Italy during the 1960s. As
early as 1966 the Piccolo Teatro of Milan staged Weiss's *The Investigation*

in sports arenas throughout Italy using closed-circuit television, stereo-phonic sound, and other devices to illustrate the evidence given about the extermination camps. It drew extremely large audiences, many of whom had never attended a theatre before. "Environmental theatre," through such productions as *1789* and *Orlando Furioso* (both of which will be discussed in a later chapter), also made a considerable impact after 1968.

But, though Italy's theatre has shown some signs of vitality and fer-ment, its problem remains much the same as at the end of World War II— the need to establish a climate which will encourage work beyond the purely popular or merely exhibitionistic.

~~ II ~~

In Soviet Russia the theatre also remains essentially conservative, but not for lack of support or of a strong tradition, for in few countries does it have a wider following or a firmer foothold. Rather the principal problem stems from governmental pressures of various kinds.

At the beginning of World War II, there were approximately 950 theatres in the Soviet Union, of which some 450 were destroyed during the conflict. This number was further reduced after 1948 when the govern-ment ended most subsidies. By the time of Stalin's death in 1953 only about 250 were left. Between 1945 and 1953, socialist realism was also imposed as stringently as in the late 1930s. With Khrushchev's assumption of power, restrictions began to be eased, especially after his denunciation of Stalin in 1956, although since that time there has been a tendency to alternate periods of relative freedom with demands for conformity. Under Khrushchev, censorship prior to production also lessened, but restraints were still applied through the governing councils of theatres, most of whose members had Communist party approval.

Playwrights also began to depart from the earlier type of socialist realism and to criticize the distortion of true Communist ideals that had taken place under Stalin. For example, *The Factory Girl* (1957) by Alexander Volodin (1919–   ) interweaves a love story with another plot about the unjust expulsion of a girl from her factory job. Eventually she is vindicated and returned to her position, thus suggesting that officials are not always right. Similarly, Alexander Pogodin, one of the most faithful of Soviet playwrights, shows in his *Sonnet of Petrarch* (1957) how a middle-aged married man is harassed by a party leader because he falls in love with a young girl. After accusing the official of trying to regulate even love, the man seems at the end to have won a victory and to be headed for happiness. Victor Rozov (1913–   ) won a considerable following with

Pogodin's *Sonnet of Petrarch* at the Mayakovsky Theatre in 1957.
Directed by Y. Zotova. (From Komissarzhevsky, *Moscow Theatres,*
Moscow, 1959.)

such works as *The Unequal Struggle* (1960), which stresses the conflict
between generations. Thus, there was a trend away from the depiction of
social and economic realities to greater concern for the individual and for
personal problems.

Nevertheless, playwrights did not give up dramatizing current official
policies. For example, Konstantin Simonov in *The Fourth* (1963) defends
international coexistence and the necessity of peace in an atomic age, while
Alexander Korneichuk in *Over the Dneiper* (1963) reflects the concern
for higher agricultural productivity. As in earlier years, practically all the
plays end on an optimistic note, showing either a reconciliation or pointing
toward some future solution to problems. The plays differ from their earlier
counterparts, however, in creating characters with both good and bad
traits and in reflecting greater independence of thought. Nevertheless,
by Western standards most of these Soviet plays still seem overly didactic.

The easing of restrictions also meant that many previously forbidden
foreign plays now came into the repertory. In 1960 Brecht's works were
introduced, and plays by Miller, Osborne, and Williams were given with
some frequency. Except for Ionesco's *Rhinoceros*, however, absurdist drama
was virtually ignored. A number of Soviet writers and producers long out
of favor were rehabilitated as well. Shortly after Stalin died, Mayakovsky's
plays were presented by Valentin Pluchek at the Moscow Theatre of Satire
in a style not unlike that used in Meyerhold's original staging. (Although
Mayakovsky had been read and praised as a revolutionary poet, his plays

639

had not been produced since the early 1930s.) They were enormously successful and remain so. Soon afterward the Theatre of the Revolution was renamed the Mayakovsky Theatre. Meyerhold's contributions also began to be acknowledged and in the 1960s a complete edition of his writings was issued and exhibits of his and of Tairov's work were organized. As socialist realism relaxed its hold on production, Vakhtangov's prestige rose, for his methods provided a mean between the extremes of realism and formalism. In 1962, on the occasion of its fortieth anniversary, Vakhtangov's *Turandot* was lovingly re-created.

Several survivors from the prewar era of experimentation also revived earlier techniques. For example, in the 1950s Okhlopkov presented Pogodin's *Aristocrats* with the audience surrounding the playing area (as in the 1930s). Several directors who had been associated with Vakhtangov—among them Alexei Popov, Yuri Zavadsky, Reuben Simonov, and Nikolai Akimov—continued to work well into the 1960s and to display much of their earlier originality.

There was as well a trend away from the politicalization of the classics and toward letting the plays rest on their own dramatic merits rather than serving as conveyers of propaganda. For example, a considerable furor was created in 1965 when Chekhov's *The Cherry Orchard* was presented at the Central Theatre of the Soviet Army without the traditional Soviet emphases on the decaying aristocracy, the promise of future progress, and naturalistic settings.

The lot of theatrical personnel also improved after 1956 with the abandonment of the concept of fixed companies, under which since the 1930s the wages and ranks of actors had been regulated and under which any change in personnel had to be approved by a central office. Abolishment of these regulations allowed greater interchange of personnel among troupes and lessened a major cause of unhappiness—the impossibility for younger actors to rise in rank or to attempt certain roles because of senior players.

All these relaxations, however, served primarily to increase the range of Soviet theatre rather than to alter it in any fundamental sense. The Moscow Art Theatre continued to set the standard for the entire Soviet theatre. Stalin had declared its methods those best suited for Russian troupes everywhere, and, after the war, when virtually all subsidies were abolished, the Moscow Art Theatre continued to be given generous financial support. By the late 1950s, however, this troupe was considered a bastion of conservatism and more nearly a museum than a vital force. Nevertheless, its actors continue to be the highest paid and most privileged in the Soviet Union. As part of the celebrations of the Moscow Art Theatre's seventieth anniversary in 1968–69, it received a new building (erected on the site of the original) with an auditorium seating 1,800, as well as a rehearsal theatre and two recording theatres. Nevertheless, its productions, determinedly realistic, were still considered the most old-fashioned in Moscow, although this may change under its new director, Oleg Yefremov, appointed in 1970.

The Maly Theatre ranks only slightly lower than the Moscow Art Theatre, being the only other dramatic theatre in Moscow still subsidized, but it is no more adventurous in repertory or approach. Fortunately, Moscow's other theatres (of which there are about twenty) are more flexible. Of the well-established troupes, the best are those of the Vakhtangov Theatre, the Mayakovsky Theatre, the Mossoviet, the Moscow Theatre of Satire, and the Central Theatre of the Soviet Army. In Leningrad, the Pushkin Theatre occupies a position comparable to that of the Maly in Moscow, but the finest work, at least by Western standards, is that done by the Gorky Theatre, headed by Georgi Tovstogonov (1915–   ).

The visual style of settings seen in most theatres has changed markedly since 1956. Instead of the detailed representationalism almost universal during the Stalinist era, suggestion is now common. In place of a full stage setting for each place called for in a script, one fixed background representative of a play's overall mood or locale is often provided and supplemented with small realistic set pieces as needed. Nevertheless, the overall effect is a simplified realism.

Two companies—the Contemporary and the Taganka—have been the major champions of innovation. The Contemporary Theatre (directed by Oleg Yefremov until 1970 and then by Oleg Tabakov) was founded in 1957, the first new troupe to be authorized since the 1930s. Its personnel was drawn primarily from dissatisfied members of the Moscow Art Theatre or its school. Until 1961 it had no home of its own but shared a concert hall with various other groups. Except in its use of simplified settings, its approach has differed little from that of its parent company. It has made its considerable impact almost entirely by presenting plays relevant to con-

Setting by Nisson Chifrine for a dramatization of a novel by Sholokhov at the Central Theatre of the Soviet Army, Moscow, in 1957. (From *Scene Design Throughout the World Since 1950.*)

temporary preoccupations. The appointment of Yefremov to head the Moscow Art Theatre is perhaps the clearest evidence of the high regard, both official and popular, in which the company is held.

The Contemporary Theatre has also done much to revive the reputation of Yevgeny Schwarz (1897–1958), whose fairytales and legends transmuted into satirical parables about modern life had been removed from the repertory during World War II. Among his plays, which include *The Snow Queen* (1929), *The Naked King* (1933), *The Shadow* (1941), *The Dragon* (1943), and *Two Maples* (1953), *The Shadow* may be taken as representative. It tells the story of a young scholar who falls in love with a princess, only to have his shadow, an evil force, separate itself from him and seek the princess for itself. Through various machinations, the shadow also gains power over government officials and uses them for its own ends. Then the scholar begins to wonder if the shadow could survive if he died. Told with considerable wit and irony, this fantasy also raises questions about the relationship of power to those being governed. Could it survive without their acquiescence? It is the ambiguity of Schwarz's work—on one level, dramatized fairytales suitable for children, on another possible political commentary—that has led Soviet authorities alternately to allow and forbid its presentation. Since about 1960, the plays have also won widespread fame outside of Russia and Schwarz has become one of the most respected of Soviet dramatists.

The second new troupe, the Moscow Theatre of Drama and Comedy (usually called the Taganka after the suburb in which it is located), was founded in 1964 by Yuri Lyubimov, a former teacher in the Vakhtangov Theatre's training school. It is now considered the most adventurous of all Russian troupes, and significantly both its actors and the majority of its audience are young. Its approach to production is essentially presentational. It makes liberal use of mime, of scenes isolated in space by light, of projections on the walls of the auditorium, and of musical accompaniment. Its production of Gorky's *Mother* was highly praised for its crowd scenes and its brilliant use of about twenty soldiers: sometimes as living scenery (as when they surrounded a character to create a prison), at others as a curtain or scene-changing device (as when they swept a disorderly crowd from the stage), and at times as themselves. Lyubimov has also presented an evocation of the life of Mayakovsky, using such devices as slides, masks, dances, puppets, special lighting effects, and direct address to the audience —and with the implication that Soviet bureaucracy drove the poet-dramatist to commit suicide. Lyubimov is often in trouble with officials. In 1969 his *Tartuffe* was publicly attacked as unorthodox, and in 1970 Voznesenski's *Save Your Face* was ordered closed because of "ideological inadequacies." Additionally, in 1970, at the first congress held in four years of the All-Union Society of Theatre Workers, the Taganka was the only theatre singled out for censure.

Another director often in trouble with authorities is Anatoly Efros, who has been moved from one theatre to another. For a time he worked at the Komsomol Theatre (for young people), where he won a reputation for modernity of approach; more recently he has been attached to the Moscow Theatre for Drama, where in 1967 his production of Chekhov's *The Three Sisters* attracted considerable attention because it played up the sexual relationships and treated ironically the prophecies about a glorious future for Russia. Although the production was highly praised when it opened, it was removed from the repertory in 1968. Such arbitrary and capricious actions serve as reminders that the theatre is still subordinate to the needs of the state. Nevertheless, officials seem more interested in controlling than forbidding the work of Lyubimov and Efros, perhaps because they are so popular with young audiences.

If the Soviet theatre is essentially conservative, it remains a respected and popular institution with the Russian people. There are now about five hundred troupes, all but a few of which are self-supporting (although the buildings in which they operate are owned by the state). There are as well about one hundred companies who play exclusively for children and adolescents. Russian theatrical personnel are also perhaps the most systematically trained in the world.

Despite all its strengths and despite its increased freedom since 1956, Russian theatre still remains closer to its Stalinist outlook than to that of contemporary Western Europe. Probably in no other country of the world is the theatre quite so conservative.

III

Since World War II practically all of Eastern Europe has been dominated by Soviet Russia, and consequently until 1956 socialist realism was the accepted mode there. Once restrictions were eased, however, most countries set out on paths far more adventurous than that followed by Russia. Absurdist drama, especially, won favor, perhaps because its ambiguities could suggest implications unsafe to voice directly. But though Eastern European dramatists adopted many absurdist techniques, their ultimate purposes differed markedly from those of their French counterparts, since for the most part they used absurdist devices to explore (or disguise) social and political subject matter. Their audiences, long used to searching between the lines of official communiqués, proved themselves adept at perceiving hidden meanings and oblique references.

Of all the Eastern European countries, two—Czechoslovakia and Poland—have exerted the greatest influence on the theatre outside their own borders. Czechoslovakia has made its greatest impact through technology and design, especially through the work of Josef Svoboda (discussed in a later chapter). Scenography, in turn, has drawn attention to the generally lively Czech theatrical scene. In the late 1960s there were about twenty theatres in Prague, all subsidized by the state or city. Outside of Prague there were thirty-six theatres housing seventy-six ensembles. The most prestigious of all the groups is the Prague National Theatre with its large company and staff and its two auditoriums operating simultaneously. Svoboda is head designer. It is generally agreed that the productions have been better mounted than acted since Otomar Krejča, the artistic director from 1956 until 1961, resigned under pressure from the older actors.

Much of Czechoslovakia's best work has been done since 1962, when the Ministry of Culture created the State Theatre Studio to assist new experimental groups, of which two—the Gate and Činoherní—have been most outstanding. The Theatre Behind the Gate, founded in 1965 by Krejča, shares its 435-seat theatre with the Laterna Magika, for both of which Svoboda is designer. Because he insisted on a long and painstaking rehearsal schedule, Krejča mounted only about two new productions each year. The Gate rapidly built an enviable reputation with works by Nestroy, Schnitzler, Chekhov (especially an exuberant production of *The Three Sisters*), and its resident dramatist, Josef Topol (1935–), who after beginning his playwriting career at the age of eighteen became Krejča's protégé. (It was Topol's *Their Day* which in 1959 marked Svoboda's first venture into multimedia theatrical production.) Topol's most popular work is probably *Cat on the Rails* (1967), which has as its main characters two young people (a waitress and a furniture mover) who have for a long time been carrying on an affair. She wishes to marry and he does not. The action takes place in the country as they await a train to return to town. Symbolically, the two sit on parallel rails that can never converge. At the end, they are deadlocked as the train is heard thundering toward them. Although Topol is now considered one of Czechoslovakia's leading dramatists, he is little known elsewhere, perhaps because his works depend so much on subtleties of Czech language and life that they cannot be fully translated.

The Činoherní (Actor's Club), founded in 1965, is headed by Jaroslav Vostry and performs in a theatre seating only 220 persons. Its principal directors are Vostry, Ladislav Smoček, and Jan Kačer, who like most of the actors in the company work in films as well. Most are young. The emphasis is upon acting and upon the ensemble, probably the best in Czechoslovakia. Considerable stress is placed on realistic detail, which in the tiny theatre becomes extremely expressive. It has presented plays by Camus, O'Casey, Albee, Gogol, and Machiavelli, and adaptations of Dostoevsky's novels. It has also produced a number of Czech plays, especially those by Smoček.

The Cinoherní opened with Smoček's *Picnic* (1965), a nonpolitical play about American soldiers in the South Pacific during World War II. Here he is concerned primarily with exploring human character, with all its strengths and weaknesses, as seen in men under stress. Smoček's best-known play is *The Labyrinth* (1967), in which a group of people enter a maze (with all the jollity and anticipation of entering a funhouse). An onlooker soon becomes worried because no one ever seems to come out. When at last emaciated figures do appear at the opening, they are brutally shoved back inside by an attendant, who points to the sign which designates this as an entrance (and therefore not to be used as an exit). The spectator then decides that he will leave, but the attendant forces him to enter the maze. The play clearly suggests that bureaucratic systems devour all those who come into contact with them, even those who think they can remain mere onlookers.

A third important small company, the Theatre on the Balustrade, is subsidized by the city of Prague and operates in a house seating only 200 persons. Founded in 1958, it was headed from 1962 until 1969 by Jan Grossman, the principal promoter of absurdist drama in Czechoslovakia. Until recently the resident dramatist was Václav Havel (1936–   ), generally considered Czechoslovakia's leading contemporary playwright. His first play, *The Garden Party* (1963), introduced the characteristics for which he has since been known— biting political satire, zany humor, and nightmarish atmosphere, all directed against attempts to reduce men to cogs in some impersonal bureaucratic machine. Set in a country which has decided to liberalize its policies, the play shows the conflict between the Department of Inauguration and the Department of Liquidation, which it has been instructed to do away with. The latter refuses to cooperate, however, since it is the only bureau authorized to liquidate anything. By manipulating this absurd situation, Hugo, the protagonist, is able to survive within the official hierarchy.

The Memorandum (1965), usually considered Havel's best work,

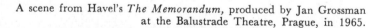

A scene from Havel's *The Memorandum,* produced by Jan Grossman at the Balustrade Theatre, Prague, in 1965.

also deals with officialdom, this time faced with a new language intended to be so precise that no misunderstandings will be possible. But because of the convoluted procedures laid down, when the first memorandum in the new language arrives, Gross, the head of the bureau, can find no one to translate the message. His assistant, Ballas, takes advantage of the situation and gradually gains ascendance over his boss, who is saved only because his secretary goes outside the prescribed channels to get the message decoded, though at the cost of her own job. The memorandum declares the new language no longer acceptable and says that for it another language, so simple that words may mean several different things, is to be substituted. The play ends with Gross speaking at length about the alienation of man from man and from himself, and of his own determination to resist the deterioration in human values caused by men such as Ballas.

The Increased Difficulty of Concentration (1968) is a satire on computer technology and its attempts to measure and predict human behavior. In it, a computer being used to analyze human responses counterpoints the experiences of Dr. Eduard Huml, a social scientist involved in a number of amorous relationships even as he seeks to write a book on happiness. As in his earlier plays, Havel discredits the computerized society. Here he denies the validity of such a mechanical approach, since human behavior is unpredictable because people act differently with each person they know. As Huml concludes: "The fundamental key to man lies not in his brain but in his heart."

In addition to new works, the Balustrade has been noted for its productions of *Ubu Roi,* an adaptation of Kafka's *The Trial,* and other similar works. It shares its quarters with the troupe of Ladislav Fialka, Czechoslovakia's leading mime. Much less restricted in scope than Marceau's, Fialka's mime uses whiteface only sparingly and employs a troupe of about ten performers who enact stories of considerable complexity set to carefully timed music and sound effects. His troupe has been seen throughout Europe and during 1969–70 played in about seventy-five American cities.

Of those dramatists not attached to a specific theatre, Ivan Klíma (1931–   ) is perhaps the best known. His major work, *The Castle* (1966), derives much of its inspiration and tone from Kafka's novel of the same title. In Klíma's play, Joseph Kan joins a distinguished group who are permitted by the state to live and work in a feudal castle. Very quickly he becomes disturbed both by the isolationism of the residents and by a series of mysterious murders. Eventually an investigation reveals that the crimes have been committed by those among the residents who cannot tolerate anyone still committed to helping others. The murderers, however, are considered too eminent to arrest, and when the inspector leaves they surround and kill Joseph Kan because of his attacks on the castle's sterility.

In 1968, the Soviet-directed invasion of Czechoslovakia dealt a sharp blow to the Czech theatre. Most companies showed their resentment by removing from their repertories all works by non-Czech Eastern European authors (except Chekhov). Many took refuge in the classics, but audiences greeted enthusiastically any passage that might be considered a reference to repression. After a time, however, resignation set in, and most theatres gradually and cautiously returned to their earlier practices.

Klíma's *The Jury* is one of the few post-invasion plays to treat (though still semiallegorically) the Czech situation. The ostensible subject of *The Jury* is the trial of a man on charges of murder, but the ultimate issue is justice in a state where all standards are manipulated by those who hold power. Although the trial is ultimately made useless when the prisoner is "guillotined while trying to escape," the prosecutor insists on a verdict—of guilty. At the end, the Historian declares: "The real murderers are still walking among us."

At first those in authority took no direct action against theatres, but, beginning in September 1969, censorship was imposed, especially on works with political implications. At the Balustrade, Grossman and Havel had already resigned. In late 1969, the Činoherní, charged with decadence, was forced to change its artistic policies, and in 1971 Krejča was removed from his post as director of the Gate. Such actions have created much anxiety about the future. But even if it declines, the theatre in Czechoslovakia must be counted among the liveliest, most productive, and most advanced anywhere in the world during the 1960s.

~ IV ~

If Czechoslovakia's influence stems primarily from technology and design, Poland's depends upon actor training and, to a lesser extent, drama. Poland's theatrical renaissance is especially remarkable considering that during World War II virtually every theatre building in the country was destroyed. When the conflict ended, Poland, like other Eastern European countries, came under Soviet domination. But it was also the first of the satellite countries to ease restrictions, and from 1956 until 1968 official political ideology exerted little direct influence on the theatre.

As in Czechoslovakia, the playwrights who have made the greatest impact are those allied with the absurdist or surrealist traditions. As soon as the thaw began, *Waiting for Godot* was produced in Warsaw to enthusiastic acclaim, and soon the works of Witkiewicz were being revived and championed as forerunners of absurdism. In 1962 an edition of his works was published and shortly afterward his plays began to find their way

A scene from Rósewicz's *The Card Index,* as it was produced in Warsaw in 1960.

into foreign repertories. The Poles also rediscovered Gombrowicz, whose complete works were published in 1957. Since something of a native tradition already existed, it is probably not surprising that plays in the absurdist vein found a ready audience in Poland.

Of the new authors, the best were Rósewicz and Mrozek. Tadeusz Rósewicz (1921–   ), one of Poland's leading poets since the late 1940s, did not turn to playwriting until 1960. By that time his vision of a chaotic world in search of some order had established him as the Polish writer most attuned to Sartre and Camus, although he considered those writers overly optimistic about the human condition. In his first and best-known play, *The Card Index* (also translated as *Personal File* or *The Dossier,* 1960), memory, like the postmortem tribunal of a medieval morality play, sits in judgment on the hero's life. As it begins, the protagonist (whose name shifts often) is lying in bed; there follows a series of encounters with himself (under various guises) at various times in his life, as one identity fades rapidly into another. Each of these personae makes a different demand on him and all are rejected. At the end, asked what he is doing to prevent an atomic war that may wipe out humanity, he laughingly replies: "Nothing." Rósewicz's hero seems to be searching for a self (filed away somewhere in his card index), although he recognizes that life is so fluid that fixed being and fixed standards are impossible. "An empty place I hoped to find, the place I had left. Now I know: there are no gaps. Life like flowing water fills cracks and crannies more than enough." This play set a pattern for much subsequent Polish drama, in which the most common theme is the search for a lost order even as the notion of absolutes is being rejected.

Many of Rósewicz's preoccupations are found in *He Left Home*

(1964), a series of counterpointed scenes about a man's attempt to escape a meaningless, mechanized world. He disappears, is found, and is brought home suffering from an amnesia so complete that he does not understand so simple a question as, "What does 'father' mean?" His daughter wants to leave him without a past, for she thinks this will make him free and therefore happy, but his wife insists: "He must be what he was in order to be what he is." Therefore, she reminds him of everything in his unhappy past. Once more he becomes aware of life's absurdity, and at the end bandages his head and leaves the room. It is not clear whether he has now accepted life, or has chosen to flee from it once more. Nevertheless, it is apparent that Rósewicz considers both the past and the present unsatisfactory.

Rósewicz has also sought to destroy traditional literary forms, since he sees them as contrivances to cover man's brutality. His dissatisfaction with drama, even his own, is suggested by *The Interrupted Act* (1965), in which an author tries unsuccessfully to complete a play while he ruminates on the major trends in the modern theatre and concludes that it is impossible to write for the contemporary stage.

Although Rósewicz is perhaps the best-known avant-garde dramatist within Poland, his international reputation cannot compare with that of Slawomir Mrozek (1930–   ). It is perhaps significant that Mrozek began his career as a cartoonist, for caricature plays a large part in his drama. His first play, *The Police* (1958), illustrates this trait well. In it, the secret police have been so successful that, when the last revolutionary recants, they are in danger of losing their jobs. Rather than run this risk, the chief orders one of his own men to assume the role of enemy agent. *The Police* is also Mrozek's most traditional work in terms of structure and technique, for thereafter he turned toward absurdism, although his plays continued to be political and moral satires. A typical short play is *Charlie* (1961), which introduces an old man obsessed with the idea that he must shoot an as yet unidentified man named Charlie, who poses some unspecified threat. To make certain that he will be able to recognize Charlie, he goes to have his feeble eyesight corrected by an opthalmologist, who ultimately points out someone named Charlie for him to shoot. Its implied commentary, both about killers and betrayers, is clear and powerful.

Above all, Mrozek writes parables about man adrift in a moral vacuum. For example, his first full-length play, *The Turkeycock* (1961), is set in a run-down tavern where the patrons have lost all sense of purpose: a writer has stopped writing, a military officer considers the army meaningless, three farmworkers no longer farm, and a hermit sleeps all the time. There is virtually no story beyond occasional quibbling over who should drive away the turkeycock that is threatening the hens. But no one acts, and eventually the turkeycock ceases his threats, for, like the tavern's patrons, he too loses interest. In a world without purpose, all action has become meaningless.

Mrozek's most famous play is *Tango* (1965), which many critics have hailed as the best Polish play written since World War II. It was soon being widely produced throughout Europe to great critical acclaim and Mrozek rapidly achieved the status of major dramatist. Artur, the protagonist of *Tango,* rebels against the disorder of his bohemian family (usually thought to represent the interwar generation): his father is an ineffectual avant-garde writer who seems not to notice that his wife sleeps with the boorish proletarian Edek; his grandmother wears a jockey's cap and plays cards constantly, except when ordered to lie down in her late husband's coffin; his uncle Eugene is an aristocratic but ineffectual gentleman. This moral chaos has also affected the younger generation, for Artur's cousin Ala, whom he wishes to marry, is quite willing to sleep with him but sees no reason for a marriage ceremony. Disgusted with this disorder, Artur stages his own revolution and forces his family, at gunpoint, into order and tidiness. But he is too humane to believe in naked power and eventually is killed by Edek, who has no scruples about assuming the role that Artur has been unable to fill. As the play ends, the family submits to Edek, as he and Uncle Eugene dance the tango around Artur's dead body.

Artur fails in large part because the values needed to undergird the order he wishes to restore are gone. "I ask you: when there is nothing left and even revolt has become impossible, what can we then bring into being out of nothingness?. . .Only power!. . .All that matters is to be strong and resolute." The tango of the title is the symbol of the older generation's prewar revolt against traditional standards and behavior, one which has destroyed all values but has left nothing to fill the vacuum except power; consequently, those most willing to exercise power, ruthlessly and without regard for humanitarian principles, become the rulers of the world. The play has had wide appeal because not only is it a parable of political power but of the decline of values in the Western world as well.

Because of their relentless logic, Mrozek's plays are more readily comprehensible than those of Rósewicz, Gombrowicz, or most of the French absurdists. They usually begin with some basically fantastic, ludicrous, or exaggerated situation, but once this situation is established, the rest follows inexorably from it.

Poland has also been outstanding in theatrical production. Probably no director in the world is now more famous than Grotowski (whose work will be discussed in a later chapter). Within Poland, however, two other directors—Swinarski and Axer—are much better known than is Grotowski. Konrad Swinarski began his directing career at Warsaw's Dramatic Theatre (the Polish Army Theatre before it was renamed and given handsome new quarters in 1955). This company has attained its greatest successes with foreign plays by such authors as Duerrenmatt (Poland's favorite foreign playwright), Brecht, Anouilh, Fry, Miller, Sartre, and Ionesco. It was also the first to stage works by Rósewicz and Mrozek and to give professional productions in Poland of Witkiewicz's plays. Swinarski's international reputation dates from 1964, when he directed the premiere of Weiss's *Marat/Sade* at the Schiller Theater in West Berlin. Since then he has been in wide demand in Germany, Turkey, Israel, and elsewhere.

Erwin Axer (1917–   ) is the most admired director in Poland, even if he is not the most famous internationally. Axer began his career just before the war but had little chance to pursue it until 1945, when he established the Chamber Theatre in Lodz, soon considered the best company in Poland. In 1949 he took most of his actors with him to Warsaw, where he opened the Contemporary Theatre, which he still heads. Axer stresses that his is a "chamber" theatre—one that seeks intimate rapport both among the actors and between performer and spectator, and one that elevates the text above pageantry, setting, or sound. He is sometimes called the "invisible director" because he elevates the text to a position of primacy and resists all temptations to reshape plays in accordance with some subjective vision. Nevertheless, as the name of his theatre implies, he has favored works which reflect contemporary concerns. In his productions, he emphasizes clarity of thought and action, and discourages all extraneous detail. This simplicity is seen most clearly in crowd scenes, in which a few symbolic characters stand for larger groups.

In many ways the Contemporary Theatre resembles the Dramatic Theatre, for both have promoted foreign and new Polish drama. (Axer directed the premiere of Mrozek's *Tango*.) The two have also attracted similar audiences, although the Contemporary tends to appeal most to the middle-class intelligentsia and the Dramatic to avant-garde enthusiasts. Axer's company has considerably greater range, however, for it, unlike its rival, performs as effectively in classics as in modern works. Thus, Axer's reputation rests in part upon his eclecticism and range.

In 1968 the theatre in Poland underwent a crisis when Czechoslovakia was invaded, for many liberal Polish critics, dramatists, and theatrical workers protested their country's participation in suppressing Czech liberalization. Many made public protests and as a result either had to leave Poland or to give up their positions. Mrozek, who had not lived in his native country for some time, lost his citizenship. Jan Kott, Poland's best-known critic, went to teach in America; Adam Tarn, editor of the monthly dramatic journal *Dialog*, which had done much to promote the dramatic revival, was removed from his post and emigrated to Canada. Grotowski, as always, studiously ignored current events.

In 1970–71 internal problems brought Poland a change in political leadership, and the policies of the new leaders toward the theatre are not yet clear. Regardless of the future, however, during the 1960s the Polish theatre made considerable international impact, the results of which are still being felt, especially through the work of Grotowski and Mrozek.

By the 1960s, German-language areas had largely overcome the shortage of good contemporary plays which had characterized the immediate postwar era. In number of German performances, Brecht was during the 1960s the most popular of all modern dramatists, and several playwrights of the 1950s—among them Hochwalder, Frisch, Duerrenmatt, Hildesheimer, and Grass—continued to write, although less frequently. But the most characteristic form of the decade was "documentary drama" or the "theatre of fact," as seen in the plays of Hochhuth, Weiss, and Kipphardt.

Documentary drama took much of its inspiration from Piscator, who after his return to Germany in 1951 had at first been tolerated as a relic from the past but who through outstanding productions of such plays as *The Crucible, War and Peace, Don Carlos,* and *The Robbers* had reestablished his reputation. In 1962 he was named *Intendant* of the Freie Volksbühne in West Berlin, where, in collaboration with his designer, Hans-Ulrich Schmuckle, he revived many of the techniques he had used in the 1920s and experimented with many new ones. For example, in Kirst's *The Officers* he returned to the globe stage he had introduced in *Rasputin* in 1927. But whereas such devices had met with misunderstanding and hostility earlier, they now gained eager acceptance.

Piscator also did much to establish the vogue for documentary drama when in rapid succession he presented Hochhuth's *The Deputy,* Kipphardt's *In the Case of J. Robert Oppenheimer,* and Weiss's *The Investigation.* In these writers Piscator found the kind of dramatist he had vainly sought in the 1920s, and they in turn were aware of their indebtedness to him. In a tribute published shortly after Piscator's death in 1966, Kipphardt wrote: "The hour has come to tell you, dear Erwin Piscator, that we all stem from your...theatre of the Nollendorfplatz....You showed us what a powerful political institution the theatre could become in a *de facto* democracy.... We all stem from your Political Theatre."

Documentary drama came into being in part because Germans seemed to be settling into a comfortable existence and forgetting the Nazi era and its horrors. As Piscator put it: "By refusing to confront this past, they are evading the necessary consequence, that is: learning a lesson from the past." It is for this reason that all of the documentary dramas focus on issues of wide ethical import.

The first of the documentarians to achieve prominence was Rolf Hochhuth (1931–   ) with *The Deputy,* produced by Piscator in 1963. It concerns the efforts of the young priest Riccardo and the SS officer Gerstein to persuade Pope Pius XII to take a decisive stand against the extermination of the Jews. All their attempts fail, and ultimately they are themselves killed. The play seeks to place much of the blame for the fate of the Jews on the pope, and to support this view Hochhuth appends

Scene from *The Deputy* by Rolf
Hochhuth, directed by Erwin Piscator,
designed by Leo Kerz at the Theater
am Kurfüstendamm, Berlin, in 1963.
(Photo by Ilse Buhs.)

many documents to the printed text (although, as it has been pointed out,
other documents considerably modify those he has chosen). This accusation
made the play so notorious that only eight theatres in Germany were
willing to produce it. (It is still banned in Italy and has generally had a
stormy reception in heavily Catholic areas throughout the world.) The
play's fame is largely attributable to its subject, for it is a diffuse, rambling,
repetitious, and overlong work. (The full text would take up about ten
hours in performance.) It most resembles the plays of Schiller in its attempt
to wed history, moral and philosophical viewpoint, and melodramatic story.
Ultimately, the distinction between it and the historical dramas of earlier
eras lies in the relative contemporaneity of the events treated in it. Many
of Hochhuth's critics argue that he has passed over into libel by assigning
motives to real persons and offering them as factual. In this claim of truth
to fact lies Hochhuth's greatest weakness, for, despite his references to documents and his use of real names, he has still written a work of fiction, and
consequently to insist upon its "documentary" nature can only lead to confusion.

Hochhuth aroused almost as much controversy with *The Soldiers*
(1967), which would require about six hours to perform in its entirety.
(Most productions have used less than half the original text.) The major
character is Winston Churchill, whom Hochhuth has called the most

653

important figure of the twentieth century. By far the most controversial part treats the death of General Sikorski, President of the Polish government-in-exile, which, according to the play, was deliberately carried out in an air crash with Churchill's consent because Sikorski threatened the Anglo-Russian alliance. Hochhuth intended Churchill to emerge as a tragic hero caught in the web of circumstance and the death of Sikorski to parallel the destruction of Dresden through air raids so that he might raise important moral questions: What is the difference between exterminating a man whom you know and thousands of nameless enemy citizens? Can such deeds be justified by national interest? Most critics have found the play better as read than as performed because the staged cuttings have so distorted the original text.

The Guerrillas (1970) departs from the pretense of being factual, but is still unusually long. Here Hochhuth begins with the premise that the only revolutionary with a chance to succeed must be one who is above suspicion. His protagonist is David Nicolson, an American millionaire and member of the ruling oligarchy, who sets out to stage a *coup d'état*. In the lengthy preface to the play, Hochhuth vehemently denies that he is anti-American and declares his opposition to both capitalism and orthodox communism. Although many critics voiced relief that Hochhuth had given up his insistence that he is presenting fact, they still found the play highly unsatisfactory and sensationalistic. Hochhuth has yet to write a work which seems designed primarily for the stage, but he has succeeded in raising fundamental ethical questions about the desirability of transferring recent events and living persons to the stage.

Peter Weiss (1916–   ) has won more wholehearted acceptance. Born into a Jewish family which left Germany in 1934, Weiss lived successively in England, Czechoslovakia, and Sweden. Originally a graphic artist, film-maker, and journalist, he did not win fame as a playwright until the 1960s. His first drama to be produced—*The Tower*—was presented on radio and published in 1962 (although it was written in 1948). Its protagonist is Pablo, who in a series of dreamlike events imagines himself to be an escape artist in a circus which is located in a tower. In semiallegorical manner, the action shows Pablo seeking to free himself from all bonds (family, tradition, love). He seemingly succeeds but then a disembodied voice announces, "The rope dangles down from him now like an umbilical cord," suggesting that the ultimate attachment is to the mother and the womb. *The Tower*, with its concern for the human condition, seems more nearly related to the absurdist tradition than to Weiss's own subsequent documentary plays.

Weiss was then catapulated to international fame with *The Persecution and Assassination of Jean-Paul Marat as Performed by the Inmates of the Asylum of Charenton Under the Direction of the Marquis de Sade*, first presented in 1964 at the Schiller Theater in West Berlin under the direction of Konrad Swinarski and with the close collaboration of Weiss.

Marat/Sade by Peter Weiss at the Schiller Theater, West Berlin, in 1964.
(Photo by Ilse Buhs.)

Marat/Sade is a play-within-a-play. The main action takes place in 1808 in the Asylum of Charenton, where the Marquis de Sade is confined. Here he composes plays which are presented by the patients for the amusement of a fashionable audience from nearby Paris. On this occasion, de Sade presents his play about the assassination in 1793 of Jean-Paul Marat, a leader of the French Revolution, by Charlotte Corday. The inmates, attendants, director of the asylum, and his family are on stage (treated as a large room), while the audience is supposedly separated from them by bars. Several levels of reality are present simultaneously, as the inmates display various forms of disorientation, are watched closely by the attendants, are prodded into their roles, and prevented from doing harm to each other and to the director's family. Thus, it is not always easy to know when they are doing what is demanded by de Sade's play and when they are following their own impulses. A "presenter" introduces the scenes in de Sade's production and Brechtian songs are used to comment on the action. At the end of the play, the inmates get out of hand, overcome the attendants, and reduce all to total chaos. But the heart of the play resides in the dialectic exchanges between de Sade, the anarchistic individualist, and Marat, the champion of revolution as a means of achieving a just social order. Weiss has said: "So far as I am concerned the essence of the play is not the chaos that develops towards the end but the constant pull and tug of the arguments, which are intended to see through the humbug of society and to provoke the audience to think." Nevertheless, Weiss seems to have used the asylum as a metaphor for the world and through the ending to have shown what happens when the sensual and anarchistic outlook of de Sade is given full rein.

Later in 1964 the play was presented by the Royal Shakespeare Company under the direction of Peter Brook and became the sensation of the London (and later of the New York) season. Despite the power of the production, however, it obscured the argument between de Sade and Marat and emphasized the insane asylum as context. Critics were most impressed by the production's use of devices from Artaud's "theatre of cruelty." As one reviewer put it: "It hypnotizes the eye and bruises the ear. It shreds the nerves; it vivisects the psyche." Weiss declared that the spectacle had inundated his primary concern, and he later rewrote the ending to give Marat greater force. It seems only fair to point out, however, that the dialectic exchanges are the least interesting parts of the play and that it is the context, with its uneasy tensions, which most rivets an audience's attention. Thus, it is almost inevitable that the spectacular and sensational elements stand out above the argument. Even if it violated Weiss's intentions, Brook's production was of enormous importance, for it attracted widespread attention for the first time in England and America to the theatre of cruelty (though not a wholly authentic version of it), it established Weiss's reputation as a major contemporary dramatist, and it offered a model upon which many playwrights would build by imbedding social and political argument within a swirling context of visual and aural effects.

While *Marat/Sade* mingled fact and fiction, spectacle and dialectic, with his next play, *The Investigation,* Weiss moved into a fully developed documentary drama. In 1965 it was produced simultaneously by fourteen theatres in East and West Germany. It is composed entirely of extracts from official hearings concerning the Auschwitz extermination camp. The setting is a courtroom; there is virtually no physical action other than the entrances and exits of witnesses; the defendants are identified by actual name, the plaintiffs by number. But, though it is based on a document, it employs considerable selectivity, for only a small portion of the total testimony is included. Of the work, Weiss has said: "I see Auschwitz as a scientific instrument that could have been used by anyone to exterminate anyone. For that matter, given a different deal, the Jews could have been on the side of the Nazis." He adds: "It is capitalism, indeed the whole Western way of life, that is on trial." He considers the play much superior to *Marat/Sade,* a verdict in which most critics probably would not concur.

With *The Investigation,* Weiss seems to have made his commitment both to documentary drama and to socialism (although he admits reservations). In 1968 he published "Fourteen Propositions for a Documentary Theatre," in which he set forth his understanding of the type. Among his many points, these seem most important. (1) Documentary theatre is based on factual reports and shuns all invention. (2) It selects its material so that it may focus on a precise political or social theme. (3) Its quality is determined by the viewpoint and the editing. (4) It is superior to journalistic reporting because it can cut through the camouflages erected by official sources of information. (5) It adopts the attitude of an observer and submits facts to appraisal. (6) It "makes use not of domestic characters or of evocations of atmosphere, but of groups, of magnetic fields, of tendencies"; it caricatures personalities and drastically simplifies situations in order to make them more striking; it uses such devices as songs, choruses, pantomime, masks, music, sound effects, and commentary. (7) It takes sides; "the only possible epilogue of many of its themes is a condemnation." (8) To be truly effective, it ought to move outside the traditional theatrical framework, which is too subject to official control, and "gain entry into the factories, the schools, the sports grounds, the public halls." (9) It is possible only in the context of "a stable working-group, possessing a political and sociological formation." (10) It is opposed to the absurdist view; "the documentary theatre affirms that reality, whatever the obscurity in which it masks itself, can be explained in minute detail." In these points, nevertheless, it is readily apparent that Weiss leaves considerable leeway for slanting material, even while he maintains that documentary theatre is wholly factual.

Weiss has written several documentary plays, although none has yet equaled the impact made by *The Investigation. The Song of the Lusitanian Bogey* (1967) treats the suppression of native Africans by the Portuguese in Angola. *A Discourse on the Previous History and Development of the Long War of Liberation in Vietnam as an Example of the Necessity for the Armed Fight of the Suppressed Against their Suppressors as well as on the Attempt of the United States of America to Destroy the Foundations of the Revolution* (usually called *Vietnam Discourse,* 1968) is divided into two parts: the first, in eleven scenes, presents the history of Vietnam; the second treats developments since the withdrawal of the French during the 1950s. *Trotsky in Exile* (1970) is divided into fifteen scenes which trace Trotsky's career from his imprisonment in 1901 to his expulsion from Russia in 1927 and his assassination. It is not organized entirely chronologically, however, for events from many parts of his life are brought together associationally. Weiss treats Trotsky as an exile not only in the literal sense but in the way his visions and prophecies have been rejected by capitalists and communists alike. Weiss has stated his concern for demonstrating through this play the difficulty of realizing revolutionary ideals; "I have tried to create a perspective which leads on to our present-day situation." As a result he was accused by communists in both Eastern and Western Europe of having sold out to capitalism.

In recent years, some of Weiss's earlier works—such as *The Assurance* (written in 1958, produced in 1969) and *How Mr. Mackinpott Was Cured*

Heiner Kipphardt's *In the Case of J. Robert Oppenheimer,*
directed by Erwin Piscator at the Freie Volksbühne, West Berlin, in 1964.
(Photo by Heinz Köster.)

of Suffering (1963, produced in 1968)—have for the first time been performed. They demonstrate how Weiss has moved from a position not unlike that of the absurdists to one of full political commitment. In many ways his career is indicative of a widespread trend away from the search for personal identity toward involvement with political and social action designed to reshape society.

Heinar Kipphardt (1922–) wrote a number of plays between 1950 and 1959 while he was *Dramaturg* at the Deutsches Theater in East Berlin, but he is known for those which appeared after he moved to West Germany and above all for *In the Case of J. Robert Oppenheimer,* produced by Piscator in 1964. This play is based on the 3,000-page published proceedings of an inquiry made during the early 1950s by the U.S. government into the loyalty of Oppenheimer after he resisted the development of the hydrogen bomb. Kipphardt reduces the original forty witnesses to six and combines much of the testimony. Although Oppenheimer, then still alive, objected that the play did not accurately reflect the original context, Kipphardt insisted upon its faithfulness to fact: "The author deliberately confined himself to drawing only upon historical data for all the facts presented in the play. The author exercised his freedom only in the selection, the arrangement, formulation, and condensation of the material." (Such a statement might have been written by Zola, and indeed the whole documentary drama movement seems to have much in common with naturalism.) Kipphardt was ultimately interested in the conflict between a scientist's responsibility to his country and his responsibility to humanity at large, and the right of a citizen to express opinions at odds with those of his government. These issues had pervaded much of German postwar drama and obviously were still potent, for the play was the most popular of the year, being presented by twenty-seven different theatres.

Kipphardt's next play, *Joel Brand* (1965), also treated actual events.
Its title character had during World War II acted as a go-between in
negotiations in which Germany proposed to exchange 1 million Hungarian
Jews for 10,000 Allied trucks. Unfortunately, Brand was unable to convince
the Allies that the offer was being made in good faith and consequently
the Jews perished. Although its moral implications are many, the play had
little success. Kipphardt has written little since. In 1968 he made an
adaptation of Lenz's play *The Soldiers* (written in 1767), and in 1970
he became chief *Dramaturg* at the Munich Kammerspiele and announced
his intention of seeking authors interested in the "burning questions of our
time."

The documentary drama initiated by Hochhuth, Weiss, and Kipphardt
has gained currency throughout the world, although it has not been pursued
so diligently elsewhere as it has been in Germany. In France in 1965, Jean
Vilar, unhappy with Kipphardt's play, countered with *The Oppenheimer
Dossier;* in 1966, a Belgian company presented *Dallas, 22 November 1963,*
about the assassination of President Kennedy; in England in 1967, the
Royal Shakespeare Company, working under Peter Brook, produced *US*
(about Vietnam); in America in 1970 Donald Freed's *Inquest,* dealing with
the Rosenberg trial of the early 1950s, and in 1971 Daniel Berrigan's *The
Trial of the Catonsville Nine* were given. Many other examples could be
cited, for it has become increasingly common to bring recent events—such
as the war in Vietnam or the trial of the "Chicago Seven"—onto the stage,
even though in many cases the documentary treatment advocated by the
German playwrights has given way to highly partisan, impressionistic approaches in which factual presentation is clearly abandoned in favor of
agitation for a point of view. Thus documentary theatre has been imperceptibly blended into the drama of political and social commitment. By the
early 1970s the vogue for documentary drama seemed on the wane in
Germany, although this trend remains to be confirmed.

Of course not all German playwrights of the 1960s wrote documentary
drama. Of those who did not concentrate on this mode two of the most
prominent were Dorst and Walser. Tankred Dorst (1925–　) has won
several literary prizes since he began writing dramas in the 1950s, although
his most popular plays, most of them short, have appeared since 1960.
Among the best is *Freedom for Clemens* (1961), whose protagonist is
thrown into jail on unspecified charges. While awaiting an answer to his
petition to be released, he learns to communicate with the warden's daughter
by tapping on the walls of his cell. Gradually he comes to believe that he
is as free in as out of prison, and when the order for his release arrives,
he decides to remain where he is. This allegory about human freedom,
treated with great theatricality, is extremely effective on the stage and has
enjoyed continued popularity.

Among Dorst's more recent works, perhaps the best is *Toller* (1968),
a lengthy and complex play treating that brief period in 1919 when the
playwright Ernst Toller, at the age of twenty-six, became chairman of the

revolutionary government set up in Munich. Dorst has marked some of the scenes "obligatory" (that is, ones that must be performed) and others (ones which merely provide more detailed information about the characters and events) "optional." He has denied any attempt to write a documentary play; rather, somewhat like Grass in *The Plebeians Rehearse the Uprising,* he is concerned with the relationship of the artist to political realities. Like most of Dorst's work, *Toller* is ultimately concerned with human freedom and the need to define one's being from within, especially when faced with unpleasant external circumstances.

Martin Walser (1927–   ) is a well-known novelist who, in addition to writing plays, has been a director in radio and television. His early dramas, like those of many contemporary German writers, deal with guilt or complacency about the Nazi era. Among these works, the best are perhaps *Oak and Angora* (1962) and *The Black Swan* (1964). In the latter, an innocent but emotionally disturbed young man imagines that he has been an assassin for the Gestapo, while his doctor and his father, who actually were involved in such activities, lead quiet, seemingly respectable lives. Walser is here concerned with the contrast between generations—the older with its complacency and rationalizations, the younger with its exaggerated sensitivity. Walser's more recent work has taken a different turn, as may be seen in *The Battle of the Bedroom* (1967), a Strindbergian treatment of a marriage under the stresses of boredom, routine, misunderstandings, shallowness, and deception.

Of those German-language playwrights who came to prominence in the late 1960s, perhaps the best are Handke and Sperr. Peter Handke (1942–   ), an Austrian, has written his plays under the influence of the structural linguist Ludwig Wittgenstein. In them he explores the relationship of language to behavior, for he believes that what one can think is controlled by what one can say. He is also much opposed to traditional, storytelling drama and even to the use of fiction in the theatre. His Wittgensteinian and antifictional biases have made him the most controversial of today's German-language avant-garde dramatists.

Handke began his playwriting career in 1966 with *Offending the Audience,* in which four actors face the audience and in a series of statements seek to disrupt all the expectations with which spectators come to the theatre. The pronouncements aim to encompass all possibilities, and ultimately they insist that a theatrical performance is itself the reality and not some substitute for an event which has occurred elsewhere (the usual fictional approach). Handke labels *Offending the Audience* (as well as three other similar short pieces) a *Sprechstück* (a "piece for speaking" or, punningly, "a play on words").

In his first full-length work, *Kaspar* (1968), Handke approaches more nearly traditional drama, although here also his concern is with words as controllers of thought. He uses as a starting point the historical Kaspar Hauser, who one day in 1828 appeared in a Nuremberg street bearing a

Masked actors in a scene from Peter Handke's play without dialogue,
The Ward Wants to Be Warden.

note which stated that he had been wholly isolated from human contact
up to that time. At first unable to speak, Kaspar is assailed by a barrage
of voices from unidentified sources until he has mastered the clichés which
transform him into a man so conventional that at the end he is indistinguishable from the host of identical figures who surround him. Through
language his thought and behavior have been wholly mechanized. In this
way, Handke seeks to make of Kaspar a figure symbolic of us all. It has
been suggested that Handke here is criticizing the social forms which lie
behind the words, but he denies any constructive intention.

In his next long play, *The Ward Wants to Be Warden* (or *My Foot
My Tutor,* 1969), Handke uses no dialogue but explores those patterns of
behavior which lie beyond language. "A mimed allegory of subjection," it
shows, in the course of nine scenes of daily routine, how a peasant boy is
forced to submit to a patterned existence, even as he learns the devices
whereby others may be subjugated. In *The Ride Across Lake Constance*
(1971), Handke returns to his preoccupation with language. In it five people, upon becoming aware of the way language determines their daily
actions, are soon reduced to stuttering and finally to complete silence.

Since Handke is the most consistently experimental of all contemporary
German-language writers, it is difficult to predict what turn his future
work will take, although it will probably continue to illustrate his declaration: "The only thing that preoccupies me as a writer...is nausea at
stupid speechification and the resulting brutalization of people."

Martin Sperr (1944–   ) is much more traditional than Handke both in his techniques and in his outlook. Most of his plays are biting commentaries on the weakness and moral failures of humanity. He is noted above all for a trilogy of plays that together treat a cross-section of society: the peasantry, small-town life, and city dwellers. The first, *Hunting Scenes from Lower Bavaria* (1966), depicts village life within the framework of a manhunt. In this rural setting men are vital and inarticulately instinctive but hate-filled in their thoughtless cruelty. The second, *Tales of Landshut* (1967), centers around the pigheaded struggle of two businessmen for supremacy in a small town. In the third, *Munich Freedom* (1971), a building scandal reveals the flagrant disregard by authorities of the rights of the majority; but the protestors, after occupying a brewery for a time, eventually give up, for the banality of the situation gradually corrupts everyone, both those on the left and those on the right. In all these plays, Sperr depicts man as selfish, corruptible, and cruel.

A similar view is found in *Koralle Meier* (1970). Set in Nazi Germany, it has as its protagonist a prostitute who, after helping a Jew, is confronted with a choice between upholding her idea of right and being punished and of violating it and benefitting thereby. She chooses the former course, but, after a period spent in a concentration camp, becomes an informer. Unable to continue in this path, she denounces the system and is shot. Like Sperr's other plays, *Koralle Meier,* in its directness, owes much to the morality and folk drama traditions. It is probably this forthrightness, coupled with moral and social questioning, which has made Sperr one of the most popular young authors in Germany.

Among numerous other playwrights, some of the best are Leopold Ahlsen, Jochen Zeim, Hartmut Lange, Hans Gunter Michelsen, Rainer Werner Fassbinder, Karl Wittlinger, Siegfried Lenz, and Wolfgang Bauer (whose *Magic Afternoon* was the most performed new play of the 1969–70 season).

In East Germany few dramatists have won wide renown. Most still adhere to socialist realism, although a few have sought to follow in Brecht's footsteps. Perhaps the best is Peter Hacks (1928–   ), who moved to East Berlin from West Germany in order to work with the Berliner Ensemble, on whose governing board he served for a time. He has had a checkered career, for he has been in and out of favor with the authorities. His *Cares and Power* (1960) generated so much adverse criticism when it was produced at the Deutsches Theater that the *Intendant,* Wolfgang Langhoff, resigned. On the other hand, his next play, *Moritz Tassow* (1965), won high praise for its orthodoxy. Perhaps for these reasons (or in imitation of Brecht), Hacks has in recent years taken his subjects from other writers, myths, or history. But he has also moved away from social and political themes and toward more personal concerns. For example, *Amphitryon* (1968) explores concepts of love and marriage, while *Omphale* (1970)

shows Heracles seeking to break out of the myths that have grown up
around him so that he may find his true identity.

Helmut Baierl (1927–   ) is more typical of East German writers. Party chairman of the Berliner Ensemble, he has written very orthodox plays. He won special praise for *Frau Flinz* (1961), which has been likened (rather unconvincingly) to *Mother Courage*. Set in 1945, the play shows its title character caught up in the quarreling factions of the time. Finally perceiving the political needs of the age, however, she saves the state by reconciling the various parties and rallying them to the communist cause. Other East German dramatists who have won acceptance elsewhere include Rolf Schneider and Heiner Müller, both followers of Brecht.

The basic patterns of the German theatre have changed little since 1960. Both East and West Germany continue to be served by a network of subsidized companies which seek to provide a balanced season of new and old, foreign and domestic plays. The theatre also continues to be popular: there are around 25 million paid admissions each year in West Germany (whose total population is only about 60 million).

Nevertheless, since the late 1960s there have been many signs of change. Some have involved personnel as the directors and *Intendanten* who had dominated the theatre since World War II retired or died. At the beginning of the season of 1968–69, for example, no fewer than twenty-five municipal theatres had new *Intendanten*. This merely reflected the peak of a process that had been going on throughout the 1960s and which still continues as veterans (such as Gustav Gründgens, Oscar Fritz Schuh, Erwin Piscator, Fritz Kortner, Heinz Hilpert, and Harry Buchwitz) have been replaced by younger men (such as Egon Monk, Peter Palitzsch, Ulrich Erfurth, Kurt Hubner, Hans Lietzau, Hansjorg Utzerath, and August Everding).

Perhaps more important, however, has been the dissatisfaction in West Germany among young directors, actors, and theatregoers. Some problems have been acknowledged by West German officials and steps taken to overcome them. For example, in 1966 an annual Experimental Theatre Festival was inaugurated; conferences have also been held to deal with the problems of dramatists, and an attempt has been made to recognize outstanding work by bringing the best productions of each year to West Berlin.

Such measures, however, could not cope with the most significant objection: the bureaucratic organization and control of the theatre. This is an important issue in West Germany, where about nine-tenths of all productions are given in state-owned and subsidized theatres. Some complaints centered on political pressures involved in the appointment of *Intendanten*. (Contracts are renewable every few years and are issued by the governmental bodies that subsidize theatres.) Others focused on the power of an *Intendant* to make practically all decisions relating to repertory and working conditions without consulting the members of his company.

The issues began to come to a head in 1969, when the actors at Frankfurt demanded a voice in decision making, and in Bremen, where actors, instead of playing their roles, read their lines and interspersed them with remarks about working conditions. Such occurrences soon became common throughout Germany.

There was as well a marked increase in militancy and political commitment in West Germany. At a production of Weiss's *Vietnam Discourse* in Munich, the directors Peter Stein and Wolfgang Schwierdzik sent the actors into the audience at the end of the play to collect money with which to buy arms for the Vietcong. This raised such a storm of protest that the two directors were fired. On the other hand, in a seeming counterreaction, a number of directors increasingly turned away from any involvement with contemporary issues and adopted a detached, esthetic stance. In the ensuing conflict, many directors resigned. Although issues were widely discussed, no one seemed to have a solution to them.

Out of this has come one important development. In 1970 West Berlin agreed to subsidize a theatre collective for a trial period of two years. The leaders of this group were Peter Stein (one of the most militant supporters of total democracy and political commitment) and Claus Peymann (who was to leave the troupe in 1971). The theatre has a directorate of six and a company of twenty actors, a "codeterminant ensemble" who must agree to all artistic and economic plans. Operating in the Playhouse at the Halle Embankment—an out-of-the-way, poorly equipped house seating about five hundred—the troupe seeks to create a model which can be followed by others.

Such collective leadership seems to be growing in popularity. In 1971, the Theater am Turm in Frankfurt became the second theatre to replace its manager with a three-man directorate who consult with the entire staff on all major decisions. Similarly, in Cologne a three-man directorate began working with the *Intendant* in 1972. Others seem likely to follow a similar path.

～ VI ～

When General de Gaulle came to power in France in the late 1950s, his minister of culture, André Malraux, set out to reorganize and revitalize the arts. In 1959 he removed the Odéon from the control of the Comédie Française, renamed it the Théâtre de France, and installed Barrault and his company in it. The Théâtre National Populaire (TNP) was elevated to an equal rank. Under the rules established for both theatres, the director was appointed for a limited period, although he might be reappointed so

long as his work was judged satisfactory. (The Comédie Française is largely
controlled by the actors, but an administrator with a renewable contract
carries out most of the managerial tasks.) Barrault continued to head the
Théâtre de France until 1968, but Vilar resigned his post at the TNP in
1963. He was succeeded by Georges Wilson, who had been a member of
Vilar's acting company from the beginning. Wilson still heads the troupe.

In 1959 Malraux also authorized two experimental theatres, one to
be directed by Camus, the other by Vilar. Unfortunately, Camus died
before his theatre got underway, and Vilar's never thrived. The need for
"studios" became increasingly evident, however, and in 1966 both the
Théâtre de France and the TNP opened small theatres. At the Odéon,
Barrault converted a corridor into a small auditorium seating 118, while
at the TNP a more fully equipped theatre, the Salle Firmin Gémier, seating
500 persons, was constructed. The Théâtre de France was the most experimental of the French state theatres both in terms of repertory and production techniques. It also became a focus for new ideas because it served as
host each spring to the Théâtre des Nations (to which leading companies
from throughout the world came for limited engagements) and to provincial troupes from within France.

The Gaullist government also continued the earlier policy of sub-
sidizing promising new dramatists and young companies, and it sought to
extend the decentralization of the theatre begun in the late 1940s. In addition to the dramatic centers, it championed as well the concept of municipal
cultural centers (*maisons de la culture*) and announced plans to open twenty
of them. The first was inaugurated in 1962; by 1966 there were six, and
others are still being completed. These centers include facilities for films,
music, dance, the visual arts, and public lectures, as well as for theatrical
productions. Some now serve as homes for "dramatic centers," and others
have troupes of their own. After 1965, the concept of cultural centers was
also extended to include the suburbs of Paris, for it became increasingly
clear that the residents of these areas were too far removed from the center
of the capital to benefit from its cultural resources. In the outlying areas
of Paris, unsubsidized "theatres on the periphery" also began to appear,
as adventurous directors discovered the untapped audiences of the suburbs.
By 1968 there were about twenty such companies. Thus, during the de
Gaulle years the trend toward decentralization accelerated.

Most of the directors who came to prominence during the 1950s—
Blin, Serreau, Vitaly, Reybaz, Bataille, Ré, Vilar, and others—continued
to work throughout the 1960s. Among new figures, the most influential
was Roger Planchon (1931–   ), who began his career in the 1950s as a
director of the 100-seat avant-garde Théâtre de la Comédie in Lyons before
founding in 1957 the Théâtre de la Cité in the industrial town of Villeurbanne, a suburb of Lyons. Taking over a 1,300-seat auditorium, he set
out to build a company that would attract a working-class audience with
no previous experience of theatregoing. He spent much time building up

Roger Planchon's production of *The Three Musketeers*
at the Théâtre de la Cité, Villeurbanne, in 1957. (Photo by Pic.)

friendly relations with various industrial and workers' organizations and
made surveys to find out what plays his potential audience would most
like to see. Since Dumas *père*'s *The Three Musketeers* received the most
votes, Planchon had an adaptation made. Not only has it been very popular
in Villeurbanne but almost everywhere the company has played on its many
tours.

Since 1957 Planchon has built a repertory that he considers of particular relevance to his audience. He has also encouraged attendance by
providing free transportation from outlying areas. (His bus bears the
inscription "Theatre is a privilege to be shared so there may be no more
privilege.") But Planchon has never patronized his audiences. Rather he
has given them works by Molière, Marivaux, Shakespeare, Kleist, Marlowe,
Racine, and Brecht. He was also able to persuade Arthur Adamov to
become the company's resident playwright.

Planchon has likened the theatre to soccer (with which his audience is
thoroughly familiar), for it depends on a set of clearly understood conventions. Consequently, in trying to reach his audience, he has utilized conventions or established new ones which are readily comprehensible to them. He
has drawn heavily on film (since this is the artistic medium most familiar
to his spectators) and on Brecht. He makes frequent use of turntables
which, like multiple camera angles, permit the action to be shown from
various views. He also introduces captions and projected commentaries
to provide the appropriate context, and always gives a clear indication of
place (though almost always through suggestion rather than full-stage
settings). Stage business establishes a social context of great richness. In
this work, Planchon has been assisted by his excellent designer René Allio
(1921–   ), also a great admirer of Brecht.

666

Planchon has stated that his audiences in Villeurbanne readily accept his productions but that whenever he plays in Paris (usually at least once each season) there is always an uproar. The Parisian response is attributable to the novel interpretation given by Planchon to classical texts. In his version of Molière's *Georges Dandin,* for example, the title character is no longer the traditional cuckold of farce but a rich peasant who has betrayed his class. To emphasize this social slant, the stage is divided down the middle, showing on one side Dandin's elegant house and on the other the farm, while the whole action is filled out with realistic details of seventeenth-century farm life. Perhaps his most controversial production has been of *Tartuffe,* for Planchon interprets the relationship between Orgon and Tartuffe as homosexual. Thus, Tartuffe is young and handsome, rather than middle-aged and obese (as suggested by Molière). Some of Planchon's finest work has been done with the plays of Brecht, which he has helped to popularize in France. The liveliness, richness, clarity, and novelty of the productions have won Planchon one of the largest followings, both at home and abroad, commanded by any French director.

Despite many offers of prestigious posts in Paris, Planchon remains faithful to his audience in Villeurbanne, where during the first ten years he was able to increase the average attendance at each production from five thousand to fifty thousand. On the strength of its appeal to working-

Planchon's production of Molière's *Georges Dandin* at the Théâtre de la Cité. (Photo by Pic.)

class audiences, the Théâtre de la Cité has been made a dramatic center and given a subsidy by the central government.

Another influential young director is Antoine Bourseiller (1930–   ), who first came to public notice in 1960 when he won the prize offered annually for the best production by a young company. On the strength of this award, he was named head of the Studio des Champs-Elysées (the post from which Maurice Jacquemont was then retiring). There, between 1960 and 1963, he mounted several critically acclaimed productions of works by Pirandello, Brecht, Villiers de l'Isle-Adam, Billetdoux, and others. He then staged an adaptation of Kafka's *America* for Barrault's company, and for a time ran the Théâtre de Poche (where among other works he presented LeRoi Jones's *Dutchman* and *The Slave*). In 1966 he was appointed director of the Dramatic Center in Aix-en-Provence, a post which he still holds.

Bourseiller's most famous and controversial production is Molière's *Dom Juan,* produced at the Comédie Française in 1967. In Oskar Gustin's copper and brass decors (which suggested gnarled roots, enormous waves, and paneled rooms), the action seemed to occur in a vast, abstract echo chamber. The actors were dressed in varying shades of blue leather and all wore high leather boots. Bourseiller does not see Dom Juan as a romantic seducer: "My own personal belief is that Dom Juan is a phantom tottering towards death and we are not told where he comes from. He could very well

Bourseiller's controversial production of Molière's *Dom Juan* at the Comédie Française in 1967. Georges Descrueres as Dom Juan. (Photo by Bernand.)

be coming back from the concentration camps." The play was further removed from its traditional Christian and moral framework by the ending, in which, rather than being engulfed by flames from Hell, Dom Juan was destroyed by what appeared to be a large sun.

Bourseiller has stated his wish as a director to provoke the public—to provide an emotional shock, "a blow with the fist"—which will make them think and reassess their preconceptions. Thus, he favors novel interpretations which confound expectation. In settings he leans toward the abstract and geometrical, while his directing mingles elements drawn from many sources, of which the most obvious are Artaud, the surrealists, the expressionists, and Brecht.

Another important director, even though his primary interest has been in dance, is Maurice Béjart (1927–), whose eclecticism probably owes much to his upbringing by a philosopher-father much attuned to Eastern thought. Most of Béjart's efforts have been directed toward reestablishing the prestige of dance, which he believes has declined in estimation because it has been separated from its religious and ritualistic origins and because it has been restricted to a narrow range of means and techniques. At the same time, he believes that dance is uniquely equipped to bridge the gulf between men of varying outlooks and nationalities because it does not depend on language.

The turning point in Béjart's career came in 1959, when he was invited by the Théâtre de la Monnaie in Brussels to settle there with his Twentieth Century Ballet Company. The troupe's membership reflects Béjart's belief in diversity, for it includes dancers from all over the world who are trained in varying traditions. His emphasis is upon the ensemble rather than upon stars. His work is often denounced by purists, for he has sought to make of dance a form of "total theatre" by mingling elements drawn from traditional ballet, modern dance, Oriental forms, spoken texts, music from diverse sources (such as Indian, classical, and jazz), contemporary themes, and subtle visual effects.

Some of Béjart's most controversial work has been done with opera. In 1963 his staging of Berlioz's *The Damnation of Faust* became the center of a critical storm because Béjart emphasized totality of effect (in which each moment was composed with infinite care for its visual and aural values) rather than bravura singing. It was one of the few outstanding productions at the Paris Opéra in recent times. Béjart has also worked in dramatic theatres. In 1967 he staged Flaubert's *The Temptation of Saint Anthony* at the Théâtre de France in Paris. In a stunning metallic setting of spiraling scaffolding (which symbolized the progressions in Saint Anthony's thought), Béjart used his dancers to embody the temptations of the flesh and the spirit which afflict the saint (a role which allowed Barrault to use his enormous skill in mime), while other roles were played by members of Barrault's troupe. Like most of Béjart's work, this too created enormous controversy. At the same time, however, it perhaps typifies his

Béjart's staging of Flaubert's *The Temptation of Saint Anthony* at the Théâtre de France, Paris, 1967. (Photo by Pic.)

approach, which cuts across traditional barriers among the performing arts. It also suggests the nature of Béjart's influence—the broadening of theatrical means, the attempt to involve the total sensory apparatus, and the meticulous execution of every detail in a complex conception.

~ VII ~

A number of dramatists who had gained prominence in postwar France continued to write during the 1960s. Among the most important were Anouilh, Montherlant, Ionesco, Beckett, Adamov, Pinget, Audiberti, Schehadé, and Sartre. A few other outstanding playwrights appeared as well. Among these, the best were Obaldia, Arrabal, and Billetdoux.

René de Obaldia (1918–   ) was born in Hong Kong and educated in France, where he was an editor, poet, and novelist before turning to playwriting in 1960 with *Genousie*, presented with considerable success by Vilar at the TNP. After *The Satyr of la Villette*, produced by Barsacq at the Atelier in 1963, won a comparable response, Obaldia went on to write *The Unknown General* (1964), *The Agricultural Cosmonaut* (1965), *The Wind in the Sassafras Branches* (1965), and *In the End the Bang* (1968).

Obaldia has been compared to Jarry because of the way he mingles satire and farce, to Giraudoux because of his poetic diction, to Audiberti because of his verbal torrents and baroque inventions, to Ionesco because of his sense of the absurd, and to Beckett because of his derelict characters.

Obaldia's subject is the inanities and concealed lies of life, which he brings to the surface and treats as wholly logical. For example, in one of his several brief "impromptus" a couple is in bed, the husband trying to complete a lecture while his wife interrupts him with readings from her magazine. Then a burglar arrives, shoots the wife, and is thanked by the husband, who can now work uninterruptedly. Because he seems so detached from his characters, Obaldia is often accused of cruelty and corrosiveness. His aim, however, is to free his audience from the horror of modern life by lifting them above it imaginatively so they may see it more clearly and learn to cope with it. One of his most characteristic plays is *In the End the Bang,* in which a young man feels so oppressed by a world under the threat of atomic disintegration that he decides to avert the wrath of God by imitating Saint Simeon the Stylite, who retreated to the top of a column. Rather than recalling the world to its senses, however, he merely becomes a tourist attraction, and eventually both he and his column are disintegrated by the sonic boom of a passing aircraft. Thus, Obaldia suggests that it is not apocalyptic disasters that we need fear so much as jaded sensibilities and modern technology.

Of all contemporary French playwrights, Fernando Arrabal (1932–   ) is probably the most prolific and best known. Like many other of France's leading dramatists—among them Ionesco, Beckett, Adamov, and Schehadé—Arrabal is not French by birth. Born in Spanish Morocco, he was reared in Spain, where he studied law before moving to Paris in 1955. Like the others too, his plays are written in French. Although he took up playwriting in 1952, his works remained unproduced until the late 1950s and did not achieve wide fame until the 1960s. Arrabal has now written more than forty plays (of which about half have been printed or performed) and about five novels.

Arrabal's work can be divided into two principal stages. The first, up to about 1962, emphasizes a childish, thoughtless cruelty embodied in techniques not unlike those of the absurdists. Of the plays from this period, some of the most characteristic are *Picnic on the Battlefield* (1952), *The Automobile Graveyard* (1958), and *Fando and Lis* (1958). In the first, a young soldier is alone in a foxhole at the front lines when his father and mother, oblivious of the dangers, arrive with a picnic hamper and insist that he join them. After an enemy soldier is taken prisoner, they invite him to the party and all proceeds happily until suddenly all are killed by a burst of gunfire. As in most of Arrabal's plays, there is here both a childlike unawareness of danger (the parents treat war as though it were merely a game) combined with a kind of fascination with violence.

The Automobile Graveyard, one of Arrabal's few full-length plays, is set in a junkyard run as though it were a luxury hotel. This background serves as a framework for several loosely related episodes, the most important of which concerns Emanou, a musician, and his two companions. Emanou expresses his desire to be good and tries to serve others by providing free

Arrabal's *The Automobile Graveyard,* directed by Victor Garcia
at the Théâtre des Arts, Paris, in 1967. (Photo by Bernand.)

concerts, but he is forbidden to play by the authorities, who constantly
seek to arrest him. A bicycle racer, Tiossido, and his elderly woman trainer,
Lasca, cross the stage from time to time and are eventually revealed to be
secret police when they pay one of Emanou's friends to betray him (for
money and with a kiss). Emanou is captured, beaten, and spread out on
the bicycle and bound as though on a cross. Thus, Emanou's story parallels
Christ's, but his sacrifice has no meaning, for the world into which he has
appeared is merely the rusty remains of a technological nightmare. Here,
as in most of Arrabal's plays, are intermingled the religious and the sacrilegious, the erotic and the sadistic, innocence and corruption, tenderness
and cruelty.

Fando and Lis is representative of Arrabal's treatment of love. Lis,
who is paralyzed, is pushed in her wheelchair by Fando as they try to
reach the town of Tar. But, though they travel constantly, they always
come back to the same place. Fando resents Lis because she is so dependent
on him, but he also loves her and is proud of her beauty, so much so that
when two men arrive he insists on showing her off, lifting her skirts and
even leaving her naked in the open all night so that others may admire
her. As a result, Lis becomes very ill, and when she falls and breaks Fando's
beloved drum, he beats her so cruelly that she dies.

Since 1962 Arrabal has demonstrated a concern for theatre as a
"ceremony—partly sacrilegious, partly sacred, erotic and mystic, a putting
to death and exaltation of life, part Don Quixote and part Alice in Wonderland." He labels this *théâtre panique*— "a literary manifestation of the

Great God Pan's gifts." He adds: "This infinitely free type of theatre which
I envisage has nothing to do with anti-theatre or with the Theatre of the
Absurd. It's a vast domain, shrouded in ambiguities, and patrolled very
carefully by the mad hound which stalks the night." In still another context
he has written: "In our time various people throughout the world are trying
to create a new form of theatre which will extend its range to the utmost. . . .
We are all aiming at a festive theatre, a tightly organized ceremonial.
Tragedy and the Punch-and-Judy show, poetry and vulgarity, comedy and
melodrama, love and eroticism, the happenings and theories of total theatre,
bad taste and paeans to life, the sordid and the sublime quite naturally
find their place in this festive act, the panic ceremonial."

Of Arrabal's numerous later works, which include *Solemn Communion*
(1966), *Impossible Loves* (1966), and *And They Handcuffed the Flowers*
(1970, perhaps the best known is *The Architect and the Emperor of Assyria*
(1967). Set on a desert island which has only a single inhabitant (the
Architect) until out of the sky parachutes the survivor of an airplane
crash (the Emperor of Assyria), it is essentially a series of ritualized human
relationships: master and slave, judge and criminal, mother and child,
male and female, confessor and penitent, sadist and masochist, and many
others. Eventually the Emperor decides that, because he has hated and
tried to kill his mother, he must be punished, and he asks the Architect
to kill and eat him. The Architect complies, even cracking open the skull
and sipping out the brains. But when he dives under the table to retrieve
a bone, out comes the Emperor, now in the guise of the Architect. Something like a symbiosis has occurred. Now alone, he hears a frightening
noise and down parachutes a figure who looks like the Emperor, and the
process begins over again.

One critic has called the play "Godot seen through the eyes of Genet."
Another declares: "By means of ceremony Arrabal tries to exorcise his
private obsessions, to shatter the tabus that weighed upon his Spanish
childhood, to liberate himself through blasphemy, humor, cruelty, black
poetry, and demonstrations of an eroticism at once innocent and premedi-
tated." A third writes: "Here we encounter all of Arrabal's themes and
obsessions, exposed with stunning verve and invention: Oedipus complex,
sense of sin, narcissism, megalomania, thirst for humiliation, metaphysical
unease, need for tenderness, sado-masochism, instinct to murder, betrayal,
remorse, etc." All of these comments are instructive, but underlying the
action there are as well two polar types of humanity: the Architect with
his animal energy, and the Emperor with his civilized knowledge. Primitive
man gradually absorbs the knowledge of the more sophisticated, who then
becomes useless, although in the process primitive man loses much of his
original power. Once the symbiosis has taken place, a new confrontation
between unlike quantities begins. It is the unending process of life. Thus,
though undoubtedly Arrabal dramatizes his own anxieties and neuroses,
he also comments on the human condition in general.

Arrabal is still relatively young and so may alter once more the trend of his drama. At the moment, however, he is looked upon in France as the playwright who has pushed to their limits many of the themes introduced by the absurdists (who in comparison have come to seem tame). Arrabal not only challenges all values, he ferrets out all the concealed corners of the human psyche.

François Billetdoux (1927–   ) was educated at the Sorbonne, studied with Dullin for a short time, recited poems in cafes, and worked in radio before making his first literary impression as a novelist. As early as 1951, Billetdoux had a short play performed in one of Michel de Ré's festivals of avant-garde works, and in 1955 his *Night by Night* was presented at the Théâtre de l'Oeuvre. His reputation as a dramatist, however, did not flower until *Tchin-Tchin* (in which Billetdoux also acted) won the Lugné-Poë Prize in 1959. Since that time he has written, among other plays, *The Bredburrys' Behavior* (1960), *Chez Torpe* (1961), *How Goes the World, Mossieu? It Turns, Mossieu* (1964), *It is Necessary to Pass Through the Clouds* (1964), and *Silence, the Tree is Still Moving* (1967).

Billetdoux might best be described as a postabsurdist, for, though to him the world seems mysterious, it is not wholly unknowable or hostile. "In my eyes, there are merely some things that we have not yet understood." He sees the world in itself as neither good nor bad. "To gain the region of light, it is necessary to pass through the clouds. Some stop there, but others know to go beyond." Thus, Billetdoux's outlook resembles Camus's in some respects, although it is ultimately more mystical, since Billetdoux considers truth to be something intuited by the spirit rather than apprehended through logic. Like Camus, Billetdoux also has far greater respect for language than do most of the absurdists. His plays are essentially monologues or duologues in which all the resources of diction are exploited. He has said that a play is a "series of scenes for two people, of dialogues where two wills confront each other until one of them wins." Nevertheless, in practice Billetdoux's plays resemble those of the absurdists, for like them they are often ironical, disconcerting, and roundabout.

Most of Billetdoux's characteristic concerns are found in *Chez Torpe*, in which the rational conception of life, as espoused by Inspector Karl, is set in opposition to the dreams and evasions which lead the clients of the mysterious Ursula Torpe toward suicide. His most positive work is *It is Necessary to Pass Through the Clouds*, in which Claire Verduret, after a career of considerable success, is led by an unhappy love affair to reassess her life. She eventually decides that all of her earlier experiences have been mere evasions, and, passing beyond the clouds, she achieves a kind of saintliness. *Silence, the Tree is Still Moving* is described by Billetdoux as "the adventure of a simple man who's trying to live for love. It's a dream, a lyrical score, a questionnaire." Throughout, a village carpenter tries to relive, even as he tries to forget, his murder of his wife. As he digs his own grave, he recalls his childhood, his mother, his wife, and his loss of love.

Paris production of Billetdoux's *Chez Torpe* in 1961. (Photo by Pic.)

It mingles psychoanalytic themes about mother-son and love-hate relationships with tender longings for happiness and fulfillment. In this and others
of his works, Billetdoux seems to synthesize many of the postwar trends in
drama.

Other dramatists who might be mentioned include Romain Wein-
garten (1926–), in whose best-known play, *Summer* (1966), childhood
experience is counterpointed with the quarrels of two lovers and the comments of two cats on humanity and life; Françoise Sagan (1935–),
whose *Castle in Sweden* (1960), *The Vanishing Horse* (1966), and *The
Piano in the Grass* (1971) are characterized by penetrating psychological
insight, bittersweet lyricism, and elegance of diction set within the framework of traditional drawing-room drama; and Marguerite Duras
(1914–), who after a notable career in films and as a novelist turned
to drama of minute internal dissection, usually of female characters, in
such plays as *Entire Days in the Trees* (1965), *Yes, Peut-être* (1968), *La
Shaga* (1968), and *A Place Without Doors* (1969). But while France continued to produce writers of note, the overall impression was one of decline
in vigor since the 1950s, when French drama was perhaps the most vital
in the world.

Like many countries, France was afflicted with considerable unrest in the late 1960s. In May 1968 dissatisfaction culminated in uprisings by students and workers which virtually paralyzed the country. Though outwardly the rift was healed, President de Gaulle soon retired and with him went much of the stability that he had imposed during the preceding decade. Along with other aspects of French life, the theatre was also deeply affected.

Perhaps the most publicized of the immediate results was the resignation of Barrault as director of the Théâtre de France. This meant as well that the Odéon lost its troupe, which was under contract to Barrault rather than to the theatre. This led the newly appointed minister of culture, Edmond Michelet, to revise the rules which governed the Odéon and the TNP so that in the future the director of each theatre would be appointed for a period of three years and the actors contracted separately. The roles of the two troupes were also reassessed. It was decided that the Odéon should be devoted to research and experimentation and the TNP to works likely to attract a large and diversified public. To make both theatres more responsive to the public, a commission, composed of representatives of the government and of cultural organizations, was appointed to review at three-month intervals the work of the theatres.

In practice, these regulations were not fully implemented. Barrault's post was never filled. The Odéon served for a time as host to visiting companies—either young or provincial French troupes or foreign groups appearing at the Théâtre des Nations (headed by Felix Giacomi)—but in 1971 it was assigned once more to the Comédie Française. The Théâtre de France, as Barrault's troupe at the Odéon was called, no longer exists. Barrault has continued his work elsewhere, most notably with *Jarry* and *Rabelais* (to be discussed in a later chapter). In 1971, he was reappointed director of the Théâtre des Nations, which the present minister of culture, Jacques Duhamel, is seeking to enlarge both in scope and length of season. Madeleine Renaud has performed at the TNP and with her own company in a limited repertory composed of such works as Duras's *A Place Without Doors* and Witkiewicz's *The Mother*.

The TNP seems to have taken over the Théâtre de France's former role as the state-subsidized company most concerned with experimentation. In the Salle Firmin Gémier (the TNP's small theatre), Wilson has presented the work of many young writers and has invited young companies and controversial directors to present productions there. In the main theatre, Wilson has also adopted a more avant-garde stance than in the past. For example, in 1969 he gave the world premiere of Gombrowicz's *Operetta*. He also continues to champion Brecht, several of whose plays have been staged at the TNP by Jacques Rosner, one of Planchon's associates.

By the late 1960s, the Comédie Française was undergoing another of

The Madeleine Renaud Company in a production of Witkiewicz's
The Mother, Paris, in 1970. Madeleine Renaud is at left.
(Photo by Pic.)

its periodic declines. In 1970 Maurice Escande, who had served as administrator since 1959, was replaced by Pierre Dux, who has reduced the number of annual performances (of which there were 532 in 1969–70) so that overall quality may be improved. More important, Dux is seeking to revise the image of the company (which has come to be viewed as overly conservative) by introducing a series of new and avant-garde works to be performed at the Odéon.

The Ministry of Cultural Affairs has departed little from policies established by Malraux starting in the late 1950s. New dramatic centers continue to be opened (the latest in Nice in 1969), as do *maisons de la culture*. But to the disaffected all such official programs seem mere tinkering and a waste of time. They have rejected established practices and have sought elsewhere for answers. During the 1960s, many groups began to stage programs in cafes, artists' centers, and other nontheatrical environments. Cafe owners often permitted their premises to be used because performances increased the sale of food and drink, and the actors accepted as pay whatever they could collect from the patrons. Some sought unsophisticated audiences in outlying urban areas. As one director has said: "We are not bringing a pre-established culture to the public, but together, we are creating a new language." The uprising in 1968 also saw agit-prop plays being presented in the streets. This kind of activity has continued. Nowadays, almost any place may serve as the scene of theatrical events.

A number of young directors have sought to alter older practices. Patrice Chereau, working in the Parisian suburbs, has won a considerable following through a series of startling productions. (In 1971, he was named codirector of Planchon's troupe.) Jerome Savary and Jorge Lavelli, both Argentinians, have gained widespread fame for innovative productions, especially with the works of Arrabal. Perhaps the best of the young directors, however, are Garcia and Mnouchkine.

Victor Garcia (1934–), like Savary and Lavelli, was born in Argentina, and had studied psychiatry, architecture, drama, and modern dance before moving to Paris in 1961 to work as author and director for France's national television service. In 1962–64 he was associated with Serreau's company, for whom he staged plays by Lorca and Valle-Inclán. The turning point in his career came in 1966 when he made a montage of four of Arrabal's plays using the title of one, *The Automobile Graveyard.* The production ran for two years. In 1969 he directed the first production of a play by Genet to be seen in Spain—*The Maids*—which ran for 500 performances, won the first prize at the international festival in Belgrade, toured Austria, Italy, France, and Iran, and later played in London. His most revolutionary work has been done with Genet's *The Balcony,* presented in São Paulo, Brazil, in 1970. For it the entire interior of a traditional proscenium-arch theatre was gutted and rebuilt. The audience was distributed on seven circular balconies inside a 60-foot-high tubular structure, while the action took place on transparent circular platforms (that moved up and down on elevators) or on transparent spiral constructions. Thus, in Mme. Irma's "House of Mirrors" the activity in all the rooms could be seen at once in an arrangement which recalls Dante's *Inferno.* It constitutes perhaps the most radical restructuring of theatrical space yet attempted; it combines at once elements of environmental theatre and of the most advanced technology. Garcia is now in wide demand. Among his commissions has been one from England's National Theatre to stage Arrabal's *The Architect and the Emperor of Assyria.*

Ariane Mnouchkine (1940–) has followed a wholly different, though no less influential, path. Born in Paris of Russian parents, she attended the Sorbonne, where she demonstrated her great potential with a production of Lorca's *Blood Wedding.* Upon leaving the Sorbonne, she formed the Théâtre du Soleil, a commune of about forty members. Working at first in the Cirque d'Hiver, the company created a sensation with Wesker's *The Kitchen,* in which the entire circular structure was utilized for the microcosm suggested by Wesker's text. It also permitted the troupe considerable scope for expressing its political commitment as well. Its production of *A Midsummer Night's Dream* made an equal impact, for in it the fairy world was inhabited by writhing, crawling, frightening creatures who slithered among the seats and over all available surfaces. When the Cirque d'Hiver was torn down in 1968, the troupe had to leave Paris, for it was unable to find another suitable home. Then the Piccolo Teatro invited it to create a program in Milan. The result was *1789* (to be discussed in a later chapter), an extremely successful example of environmental theatre as well as a statement of the company's political outlook.

The Théâtre du Soleil has worked almost entirely outside traditional theatre buildings. As a commune, its members also seek in their own lives to embody the company's ideals. Nevertheless, the members do not live together as a group, for their commitment is to a working rather than to a familial arrangement. Furthermore, they have high esthetic standards. Among the young, the Théâtre du Soleil is now probably the most admired company in France.

Despite these examples, the extent and range of experimentation by new groups is not great. Perhaps it will increase, for France has traditionally been the cradle of new artistic movements. At the moment, however, the French seem more interested in variations on trends begun in the 1950s than in striking out in radically new directions.

~ IX ~

As this survey indicates, many European countries are caught between the twin urges toward freedom and toward control. Indecision about which path to take, with the consequent alternation of laxity and firmness, were probably the most characteristic traits of the 1960s. The reasons are several. First, the tensions which had existed since the 1930s and which had kept all Europe on edge during the cold war of the early 1950s were eased in the late 1950s, after Soviet Russia adopted a policy of coexistence with the West. Thereafter the internal repressions which had been justified in the name of national security were gradually relaxed if not wholly removed. Second, the worldwide upsurge in prosperity removed many of the pressures which had elevated Freud's "reality principle" above his "pleasure principle." Third, the intense questioning of all values which had been under way since World War II began to affect increasing numbers of people and to undermine the convictions upon which values ultimately rest. The combination of reduced financial and political pressures and of weakened convictions led to relaxed boundaries of acceptability in morals and artistic taste.

The trend toward increased leniency was evident everywhere during the 1960s, even though its extent varied considerably. Both rightist Spain and leftist Soviet Russia, the most puritanical of the countries, acceded to pressures for greater freedom, although both demonstrated their uneasiness by alternating concessions with renewed restraints. The widespread disturbances of 1968 seem to have aroused fears in almost every country that too many concessions had been made, and consequently there was a general tightening of the reins, although no real solution to the conflict between freedom and conformity was found.

Throughout Europe the theatre's problems were intensified by the relationship of the state to the arts, for almost everywhere the government subsidized the theatre. Although direct control was seldom exerted by the governmental units providing assistance, there was indirect pressure, since the theatres were semiofficial institutions and therefore limited in the degree to which they might depart from accepted channels without risking loss of support or incurring political reprisal. Thus, while subsidy decreased financial risks, it carried with it certain implied obligations. Under these circumstances, the theatres followed a pattern not unlike that of the governing bodies, for they often vacillated between defiance and conformity. On the other hand, independent companies, of which there were relatively few, had to contend with different pressures, for if they struck out on new paths they often failed to attract a sufficiently large public to support their programs. Thus, both subsidy and independence had pitfalls.

Attacks on tradition had the beneficial effect of making theatrical groups reassess their policies, and there was growing recognition that the theatre had come to cater primarily to the middle class, the intelligentsia, or avant-garde enthusiasts. Consequently, many changes were introduced in the attempt to make the theatre more appealing to the working classes, to the artistically unsophisticated, and to all those who for one reason or another had avoided it. This trend was part of a worldwide reassessment of rights and privileges, of the nature of power and subjugation. Although it was generally acknowledged that conditions should be improved, a struggle developed between those who advocated radical changes—some so great that it would mean a complete break with the past—and those who merely wished to make a few gradual adjustments. When around 1968 the issues became clear, the polar groups took up rigid positions, while those between vacillated, hoping for some compromise. Beginning around 1968, prosperity also seemed to recede. Consequently, the expansion which had been under way since the 1950s stalled. The theatre, like other institutions, entered the 1970s in a state of considerable uncertainty.

The Theatre
in
England and America
Since 1960

18

During the 1960s the basic patterns of the English and American theatre differed little from those found on the Continent. Prosperity and expansion characterized most of the decade, while reassessment and hesitation were clearly evident after 1968. The English theatre was dominated by a few subsidized organizations, all of which were concerned with both tradition and change. Not until the end of the decade did dissident groups make an impression, and then to a much lesser extent than in America. A substantial number of new playwrights—such as Bond, Orton, Storey, and Stoppard—also enlivened the scene. Overall, the English theatre displayed a healthy mixture of the old and the new. In America, Broadway remained relatively unchanged, but the theatre as a whole underwent considerable expansion, largely because of the off-off-Broadway movement and the development of resident theatres outside of New York. It was also strengthened considerably by the emergence of Black writers and companies. Playwrights were numerous, but few were truly outstanding. Perhaps nowhere else in the world, however, were there so many or so varied attempts to reassess the theatre's role and means.

The renewed vitality of the English theatre after 1956 continued throughout the 1960s. During that decade it was sustained above all by three organizations: the Royal Shakespeare Company, the National Theatre, and the English Stage Company.

After World War II, the Stratford Memorial Theatre gradually grew in critical estimation, but it remained a seasonal venture—an annual festival held in a small town—until it was transformed into a diverse, year-round organization by Peter Hall (1930–   ), who became its head in 1960. Educated at Cambridge University, Hall first attracted attention at the Arts Theatre, where in 1955–56 he was instrumental in acclimatizing absurdist drama in England through productions of *Waiting for Godot* and plays by Ionesco. His association with Stratford began in 1957; by 1960 he was considered one of its most effective directors. Thus, when it became obvious that the Stratford troupe was in need of new ideas and more forceful leadership, Hall seemed the logical choice.

The major problems faced by the company were the lack of continuity in personnel and the restriction of the repertory to the works of a single author. Since the season at Stratford consumed only about six months of the year, actors had to find employment elsewhere during the remaining months and often were not free at the beginning of the next festival season. Consequently, an ensemble could not be built. To overcome the difficulties, Hall took a lease on the Aldwych Theatre in London. This permitted him to put actors under contract for the entire year and also to vary the repertory by offering non-Shakespearean plays at the Aldwych. In 1961, the troupe received a government charter and a new name: the Royal Shakespeare Company (RSC). It had now made the transition from annual festival to permanent producing organization. Soon, instead of five productions the troupe was presenting about twenty-five each season. Since Hall found it difficult to handle these increased responsibilities alone, the management was expanded in 1962 to include Peter Brook and Michel Saint-Denis.

The RSC now began further to expand its activities. In 1962 it took over the Arts Theatre in London for a season of experimental works, and

Scene from Peter Brook's production of Weiss's *Marat/Sade*
at the RSC in 1964. Left to right, Glenda Jackson as Charlotte Corday,
Patrick Magee as the Marquis de Sade, Ian Richardson as Marat,
Susan Williamson as Simone Everard, and Clive Revill as the Herald.
(Photo by Morris Newcombe.)

in 1963, under the direction of Brook and Charles Marowitz, a season
entitled "Theatre of Cruelty" was given at the LAMDA Experimental
Theatre. The latter included Artaud's *Jet of Blood,* scenes from Genet's
The Screens, two "collages" by Brook, a "collage" *Hamlet* by Marowitz,
and a number of improvisations. Out of this experience came Brook's
production of Weiss's *Marat/Sade* in 1964—one of the company's greatest
hits and the production which made Brook internationally famous. Furthermore, with it many techniques of the theatre of cruelty—at least, as conceived by Brook—were assimilated by the RSC. By the time Pinter's *The
Homecoming* was produced in 1965, the RSC was considered not only the
primary producer of Shakespearean drama but one of the world's leading
avant-garde troupes as well.

Although its experimental work attracted most attention, the RSC
offered a wide-ranging repertory in London. Shakespearean productions
were transferred there from Stratford and mingled with works by Brecht,
Chekhov, Giraudoux, Hochhuth, and numerous old and new British writers.
The RSC also established Theatregoround (originally under the direction
of Terry Hands and later under Gareth Morgan and Peter Kemp), a company of young actors who tour throughout England and who play occasionally at Stratford, in London, and abroad. Additionally, the RSC
inaugurated a training program for actors under the direction of Saint-

Denis. Furthermore the Aldwych became host for a "World Theatre Season."
This grew out of the efforts of Peter Daubeny (1921–   ), a theatrical producer who after the war had sponsored a number of foreign companies
in England. It was he who imported a Peking opera troupe in 1955, the
Berliner Ensemble in 1956, and the Moscow Art Theatre in 1957. In 1964
the RSC and Daubeny jointly launched an annual World Theatre Season,
during which several companies appear successively for limited engagements
each spring. This venture has done much to keep the English public aware
of work going on elsewhere and has provided considerable stimulation to
British producers.

But, if by 1965 the RSC had been almost totally transformed from its
pre-1960 state, it was not free of problems. The Arts Theatre had had to
be abandoned as too costly. Saint-Denis was away for increasingly long
periods helping to establish acting schools (among them, the national
theatre school of Canada and Juilliard's acting program in New York).
Brook too was much in demand elsewhere. Other issues were raised by a
trend toward politicalization (as in Brook's *US*) and rising production costs.
For these and other reasons, the directors resigned in 1968. After some
initial reshuffling, the leadership passed in 1969 to Trevor Nunn, assisted
by an advisory board composed of Brook, Hall, and Peggy Ashcroft. Saint-
Denis and Daubeny were named "consultant directors." Thus, the basic
approach has changed little.

Despite its fine work, the RSC was by 1970 faced with a severe financial crisis. During the 1950s the Stratford company had built up a large
reserve fund, and this was used to underwrite the troupe's expansion into
London. But, even though the RSC had received a sizable subsidy from
the Arts Council (in 1968–69, £200,000), its treasury was gradually
depleted. In 1969, even with a record attendance of over 1 million, it
suffered a deficit of £160,000, partially made up by an emergency grant
from the Arts Council of £100,000. Its subsidy for 1970–71 was £250,000,
but this was still too small to meet its needs. This crisis has raised important
issues about the whole approach to subsidies in England, for, unless funds
are increased, the RSC may have to curtail its programs or give up its
London venture altogether (probably unlikely since the Corporation of the
City of London has offered the troupe a new theatre in the Barbican Arts
Center due to be opened in 1973–74). But if it has financial worries, the
RSC has not as yet ceased to pursue its multiple activities.

During the 1960s the RSC included in its company some of England's
finest actors: Paul Scofield, Peggy Ashcroft, Ian Richardson, David Warner,
Ian Holm, Judy Dench, David Waller, Eric Porter, Norman Rodway, and
many others. But the RSC was above all a director's theatre. Among those
who have done most to shape its image are (in addition to Hall and Brook)
Clifford Williams, John Barton, Terry Hands, and Trevor Nunn.

Without doubt, however, the most important of the RSC's directors

during the 1960s was Peter Brook (1925–   ). He began directing while
still in his teens and then worked with Barry Jackson, first at Birmingham
and (beginning in 1946) at Stratford. In the late 1940s he was for a time
Director of Productions at Covent Garden, where his *Salome,* with designs
by Salvador Dali, created a sensation. During the 1950s he continued to
build his reputation for novel and forceful productions with such works as
Fry's *The Dark is Light Enough,* Anouilh's *The Lark, Titus Andronicus*
(with Olivier and Vivien Leigh), a season of plays starring Paul Scofield
(*Hamlet, The Power and the Glory,* and *The Family Reunion*), and Duerrenmatt's *The Visit* (starring the Lunts). In 1956 he directed his first play
in Paris, where he has since worked often on such plays as Genet's *The
Balcony.* In France he developed an interest in Artaud and the theatre of
cruelty, first fully evident in the RSC's season at LAMDA in 1963 and
his production of *Marat/Sade* in 1964. Brook's renown has also been enhanced by *The Empty Space* (1968), in which he describes the theatre
as an area which may be filled to create one of four principal results: deadly
(traditional commercial fare), holy (best exemplified by Grotowski), rough
(Brechtian), or immediate (presumably Brook's own approach).

In recent seasons Brook has staged two extremely influential productions: *The Tempest* and *A Midsummer Night's Dream.* The first grew out
of sessions which Barrault requested Brook to conduct at the Théâtre des
Nations in 1968 and which Brook later continued. The final results were
shown in late 1968 at the Roundhouse in London.

Brook's approach to Shakespeare's text seems an extension of Marowitz's collage of *Hamlet* as done for the "Theatre of Cruelty" in 1963.
Taking for granted the audience's familiarity with the original text, Marowitz sought to explore and illuminate certain aspects of it by juxtaposing
lines from widely separated scenes, by rearranging and intermingling
elements from different scenes, by treating short, discontinuous fragments
as emanations from Hamlet's subconscious, by interchanging male and
female roles, and by other devices. Somewhat similarly, Brook did not set
out to perform the original text of *The Tempest* so much as to explore the
motifs of violence normally obscured by romanticized interpretations of the
play. He also wished to see how traditional techniques might be enlarged
by working with actors and conventions from many nations. (His performers, as in Paris, were from all over the world, including the Orient.)
For the production, seating in the large, open space of the Roundhouse
was arranged to surround three sides of a central area, in which were
erected scaffolding, platforms of varying heights, pipes, and ladders. Some
portions were flexible so they might be rocked or moved during the performance. The action elaborated or improvised on selected scenes, motifs,
and implications in the text. Shakespeare's lines, when spoken, were used
primarily for rhythmical effect. The opening shipwreck was staged entirely
through nonverbal sound and mime in which the actors became the ship.

Mirror images or contradictions played a large part in almost every scene. For example, the love scenes between Ferdinand and Miranda were mirrored in couplings of every conceivable kind. One section of the production explored what might happen were Caliban to become master: the result was a vast orgy, during which Prospero was captured, bitten, and chewed as the scene descended further and further into animality. As might be expected, the production aroused widely divergent responses.

Brook's *A Midsummer Night's Dream,* first performed at Stratford in 1970, used a completely different approach and was the most radically new interpretation of the play since Barker's production in 1914. Brook wished to divest the play of the romantic aura of fairies and haunted woodlands and to make it more immediately relevant to today's audiences. The stage was enclosed on three sides by white, unadorned walls broken only by two nearly invisible doors at the rear. At the downstage corners, fire ladders ran up to a visible catwalk on which musicians in modern

Peter Brook's production of Shakespeare's *A Midsummer Night's Dream,*
first performed at Stratford in 1970. Design by Sally Jacobs. Alan Howard
as Oberon and John Kane as Puck are on the trapezes. Below are
Sara Kestelman as Titania and David Waller as Bottom. (Photo courtesy
the Royal Shakespeare Company.)

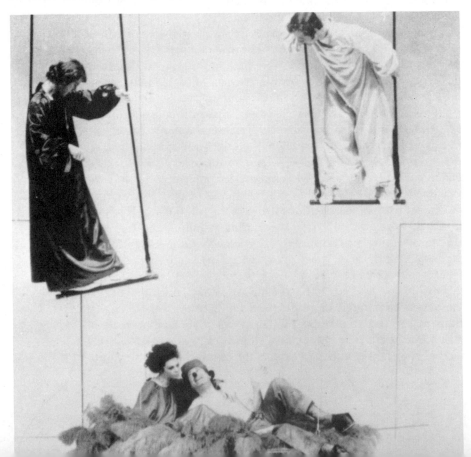

dress were placed and on which actors appeared frequently. The forest was suggested by loosely coiled metal springs attached to fishing rods. Trapezes lowered and raised to varying heights within the setting served as perches for actors. The performers wore a kind of coverall or "mod boutique" clothing, varied by a sprinkling of *commedia dell' arte* and circus costumes. Many acting devices, as well as the setting and costumes, were reminiscent of Meyerhold's experiments with biomechanics and constructivism, influences readily admitted by Brook. The text was interpreted as an exploration of love in which the fantasy scenes become a series of dreamlike illustrations designed to show the royal pair the near-cosmic effects of misunderstandings between lovers or about love. Consequently, the same pair of actors played both Theseus and Hippolyta and Oberon and Titania. (There was other doubling as well.) The whole production breathed a spirit of freedom and exhilaration which swept audiences along, while it retained Shakespeare's text and gave the verse its full value. As usual, such a novel approach found many detractors, but admirers seem to have been greatly in the majority. Regardless of critical response, the production was revolutionary in its abandonment of the traditions with which the text had become encrusted.

In 1971 Brook assumed direction of the International Center for Theatre Research, housed in Paris in a large hall about 300 feet long originally designed for showing Gobelins tapestries and made available to the center by the Ministry for Cultural Affairs. The center is a continuation of the project out of which *The Tempest* came. Financed by American and Portuguese foundations and the government of Iran, it permits about twenty professional actors from several countries to experiment together. In the summer of 1971 the group performed at the Persepolis Festival in Iran and present plans call for it to appear in the United States in 1973.

Brook now enjoys an enormous international reputation. It is perhaps above all through his work that the RSC has come to be such a potent force both at home and abroad. Few subsidized troupes anywhere could boast a more impressive record during the 1960s.

~ **II** ~

Some of the RSC's problems in the late 1960s stemmed from unavoidable competition for subsidies, actors, and audiences with the National Theatre, which came into existence just as the RSC was expanding its scope. With the exception of Italy, Great Britain was the last major European country to create a national theatre. Although concrete proposals for

All male cast for the National Theatre's production of Shakespeare's *As You Like It* in the late 1960s. (Photo by Dominic.)

such an organization had been seriously forwarded as early as 1848, it was not until 1949 that a parliamentary bill approved such a scheme, and even then the date of implementation was left up to the chancellor of the exchequer. A cornerstone for a building was laid in 1951, but the plan was abandoned and it was not until 1962 that a workable scheme for establishing a company was approved. At that time there was talk of making the RSC the nucleus of a national theatre, but eventually the choice fell on the Old Vic, whose troupe was liquidated and its building acquired in 1963. Only the Bristol branch, which passed to the city of Bristol, survived. Under the direction of Val May, the Bristol Old Vic remains one of the finest of provincial troupes.

When plans for the National Theatre became final, Laurence Olivier was named director and Kenneth Tynan (1927–) literary consultant. The nucleus of a troupe was assembled and given a trial run at the Chichester Festival (begun by Leslie Evershed-Martin in 1962). The National Theatre opened in October 1963 with *Hamlet* (a new production), followed by four productions from Chichester (of which the best were Shaw's *Saint Joan* and Chekhov's *Uncle Vanya*). Before the season ended, the repertory ranged from Sophocles' *Philoctetes* to Beckett's *Play*. This eclecticism in choice of plays also extended to production, for from the beginning Olivier invited outstanding English and foreign directors and designers to stage productions. Consequently, the company has favored no single or distinctive approach and instead has sought excellence in a broad range of styles.

Many of the directors in the early years—such as George Devine, Lindsay Anderson, and Peter Wood—were from the Royal Court, and both William Gaskill and John Dexter, two of the National's associate directors, made their reputations there. Other English directors who have worked at the National Theatre include Brook, Guthrie, Clifford Williams, Anthony Quayle, Glen Byam Shaw, and Jonathan Miller. Outstanding foreign directors include Franco Zeffirelli, Jacques Charon, Ingmar Bergman, and Victor Garcia. This variety extends as well to designers: Motley, Jocelyn Herbert, Sean Kenny, Julia Trevelyan Oman, Ralph Koltai, Josef Svoboda, René Allio, Rudolf Heinrich, André Levasseur, and Lila de Nobili.

Unlike the RSC, however, the National Theatre is essentially an actor's theatre. Consequently, it has sought to build a permanent ensemble, and in order to attract leading performers it has adopted liberal policies concerning outside work in films and television and with other troupes. Its company has included such fine actors as Michael Redgrave, Maggie Smith, Robert Stephens, Colin Blakely, Albert Finnie, Joan Plowright, Max Adrian, Derek Jacobi, Geraldine MacEwan, Robert Lang, John Stride, and Paul Scofield.

For the most part the National Theatre has made its mark with classics. Some of the best productions of the decade were of *Othello, The Merchant of Venice,* and *The Dance of Death,* all starring Olivier. It has produced as well such recent works as Brecht's *Mother Courage,* Frisch's *Andorra,* and Arrabal's *The Architect and the Emperor of Assyria.* In its

Shakespeare's *The Merchant of Venice* at the National Theatre in 1970. Joan Plowright, standing left, played Portia, while Olivier, seated right, played Shylock. (Photo by Anthony Crickmay.)

second season it also began to present new English plays. The first was Peter Shaffer's *The Royal Hunt of the Sun,* while later ones include Arden's *Armstrong's Last Goodnight,* Tom Stoppard's *Rosencrantz and Guildenstern Are Dead,* and Peter Nichols's *The National Health.*

Until recently, however, the National Theatre has shown little interest in the kind of experimentation which was so much a part of the RSC during the 1960s. Its reputation has resulted primarily from the generally high quality of its productions rather than from innovations. There are indications, however, that the National Theatre would like to avoid the charge of conservatism. In the spring of 1969 it mounted a season of experimental works at the Jeannetta Cochrane Theatre, and later two of the plays—John Spurling's *Macrune's Guevara* and Maurine Duffy's *Rites*—were presented at the Old Vic. This experiment was repeated in 1970. The company expanded its program in other ways as well. In 1969 its long-awaited permanent home was authorized. (The completion date is now set at 1973.) It will include two auditoriums, one (with an open stage) seating 1,165, and the other (with a proscenium stage) seating 895. In anticipation of the demands created by two theatres, the troupe transferred some productions to the Cambridge Theatre in the West End in 1970, and in 1971 it operated both the New Theatre and the Old Vic. In 1970 it also reinstituted the Young Vic to play for young audiences. Headed by Frank Dunlop, formerly administrative director of the National Theatre, it performs in a temporary building equipped with a completely open stage and stadium seating. Its repertory ranges from *Oedipus Rex* to *The Taming of the Shrew,* Molière's *Scapin,* Gozzi's *King Stag,* and Beckett's *Waiting for Godot.* It hosts visiting productions by other young companies as well. Ticket prices are set at approximately one dollar.

The enlargement of the theatre's program has led to increased staff. Associate directors now include Paul Scofield, Frank Dunlop, John Dexter, and Michael Blakemore, while as literary consultant Kenneth Tynan has been joined by Derek Granger.

The National Theatre receives the highest subsidy of any English dramatic troupe, about £260,000 from the Arts Council and an additional £90,000 from the Greater London Council. It is in the struggle for financial support that the National Theatre and the Royal Shakespeare Company are placed in direct competition, for otherwise they have been more complementary than competitive. Commercial producers have long complained that together the two companies have so many of the best actors under contract that it is difficult to mount a play in the West End with major stars.

In less than ten years the National Theatre has taken its place alongside the best troupes of Europe. It was in part this accomplishment that was recognized in 1970 when Olivier became the first actor in British history to be raised to the peerage.

The English Stage Company, housed in the Royal Court Theatre, also continued to play an important role, although the quality of its work after 1960 was erratic. Upon George Devine's retirement in 1965, the management passed to William Gaskill (1930–   ), who had first joined the company in 1957 and was the company's associate director from 1959 until 1963, when he left to take a similar post at the National Theatre. Gaskill, who acknowledges Brecht as the greatest influence on his work, is an excellent analyst of texts and is noted for his restrained and clear direction, achieved in large part through emphasis on diction. (He dislikes the trend toward downgrading language.) Since he believes it necessary that actors have some sense of tradition, he mingles classics with new works in the Royal Court's repertory, although he considers the promotion of new writers the company's primary mission. In 1969–70, for example, of the seventeen plays presented by the troupe twelve were new. Furthermore, in recent years the company seems once more to have recovered its eye for important writers—among them Edward Bond, Joe Orton, and David Storey.

The English Stage Company's concern for new playwrights was strengthened in 1969 by the opening of the Theatre Upstairs, a small area in the attic of the Royal Court. Eventually it will have its own company and be devoted almost entirely to brief runs of plays by new writers. At that time the Royal Court's staff was also enlarged. In addition to Gaskill, the management now includes Lindsay Anderson, Anthony Page, and Peter Gill, with Jonathan Hales as literary advisor. Of these directors, the best known in recent years has been Lindsay Anderson (1923–   ), widely acclaimed for his films, especially *If*. He first came to the Royal Court in 1960 after having worked in films since 1949. Perhaps the best of his productions have been Arden's *Sergeant Musgrave's Dance* and the plays of Storey. He has also directed at the National Theatre.

The Royal Court serves a function unlike that of either the RSC or the National Theatre, since it is essentially the champion of new writers. Consequently, it takes much greater chances than do the other two and has a far more checkered career. It has also had to subsist on much less support, although its subsidies grew from £30,000 in the early 1960s to almost £100,000 in 1968–69. Its role in the continued renewal of English drama has been significant.

Another of London's subsidized theatres is the Mermaid, inaugurated in 1951 by Bernard Miles (1907–   ), who in collaboration with C. Walter Hodges reconstructed an Elizabethan theatre within a hall in suburban London. In 1953 it was moved to the quadrangle of the Royal Exchange, and in 1959 it settled in a converted dock on the Thames River, thus becoming the first new theatre to be opened in the City (that portion of London bounded by the original walls) in over three hundred years. It was also the first professional theatre in modern London to have an open stage. The Mermaid has devoted much of its effort to Elizabethan drama, for which it was originally conceived, but since the advent of the RSC and the National Theatre it has broadened its selection and has had its greatest successes with musicals based on Restoration and eighteenth-century texts (such as Miles's *Lock Up Your Daughters,* adapted from Fielding's *Rape upon Rape*). It also produces original works (of which the most profitable has been Peter Luke's *Hadrian VII*) and classics from many periods. In 1968–69, Miles's contributions were recognized with a knighthood.

Another organization of some importance is the National Youth Theatre (NYT), founded in 1956 by Michael Croft. Working with non-professional adolescent actors, Croft attained such fine results that soon he was touring throughout England and on the Continent. By the summer of 1969 he had six separate companies with a combined total of more than five hundred members. Croft had also induced several dramatists—most notably Peter Terson and David Halliwell—to write for his company. Not until 1971, however, did the NYT have a permanent home. At that time, the just-completed Shaw Theatre became its headquarters, as well as that of the Dolphin Company, the NYT's newly organized professional troupe. No group has done more than Croft's to provide both excellent training and outstanding productions for England's youth, whose needs have otherwise been little recognized.

Outside of London, the number of resident companies increased from twenty-eight to fifty-two during the 1960s. Perhaps the best are those at Bristol, Birmingham, Manchester, Nottingham, Coventry, and Glasgow. Subsidized by local governmental units, most provide a varied repertory of old and recent plays and an occasional premiere. During the same period the commercial theatres outside of London declined from 130 to 33. How far the prewar scale had shifted may be judged from a government-sponsored report which in 1970 recommended that a Theatre Investment Fund be created to support a circuit for touring shows from London.

English companies have been able to attract a substantial audience in part because of low admission fees. In the provinces the maximum admission price in 1970 was about $1.80, and even in London the maximum seldom rose above $4.00. Much of this was accomplished at the expense of theatre workers, however, for in 1970 provincial actors were paid only about $25.00 per week, and British Actors Equity's proposal to seek a raise to $55.00 elicited a response of outrage from both producers and critics.

If the English theatre was productive in the 1960s, it remained within rather conservative limits, especially until 1968 when, after more than two hundred years, censorship was abolished. Since 1737, any play intended for public performance had had to be licensed by the lord chamberlain prior to production. There was no appeal from his decisions. Although censorship could be evaded by forming private theatre clubs open only to members, licensing had served nevertheless to keep many potentially objectionable plays off the public stage. The Theatres Act of 1968 abolished the lord chamberlain's role and invested the right to license theatres in local authorities. It did not affect a number of existing laws relating to obscenity and public indecency, however, and consequently potential restraints remain.

As soon as the new law come into effect in September 1968, a number of plays were immediately produced that had previously been forbidden by the lord chamberlain for a variety of reasons: *Hair,* forbidden because of nudity and obscene language; Osborne's *A Patriot for Me,* because it portrays homosexuality; Hochhuth's *The Soldiers,* because it was considered offensive to Churchill's family and to others; and some of Edward Bond's plays, because they were thought offensive to public morality. Since 1968 there has been a general trend toward greater freedom in subject matter and treatment. As in America, nudity received its widest publicity with the production in 1970 of *Oh, Calcutta* (which, ironically, owed its existence to Kenneth Tynan, the National Theatre's literary consultant). Like their American counterparts, Actors Equity became sufficiently concerned to institute regulations designed to protect its members from exploitation and legal prosecution.

Removal of censorship seems also to have encouraged experimentation outside traditional paths, for since 1968 "underground theatre" (the English equivalent of America's off-off-Broadway) has burgeoned. Prior to 1968 there were few groups of this type, but in 1970 twenty appeared at the Royal Court's *Come Together,* a "festival of new theatre," and in 1971 *Theatre Quarterly*'s guide to "underground theatre" described thirty-one. Much of the inspiration for the British underground has come from the various La Mama troupes (which since the mid-1960s have appeared regularly in London), the Open Theatre (which made its first appearance in London in 1967), and the Living Theatre—all American companies. Americans residing in London have also played a large role. For example, Charles Marowitz inaugurated the Open Space in 1968 as a home for avant-garde plays and techniques. He has presented mime performances, his own "collages" of *Hamlet* and *Macbeth,* and many new works, especially by American authors. Even more important is Ed Berman, who in 1968 founded Inter-Action, a multifaceted organization dedicated to making the arts relevant in urban community life. Inter-Action operates a massive program of street drama for children, a lunchtime theatre (the Ambiance), and a professional company, along with a host of other activities. It has been called the most successful community arts program in Europe. Among the other groups, some of the best are the Freehold (an ensemble headed by Nancy Meckler and Tony Sibbald), the Portable Theatre (directed by David Hare and Tony Bicat), and the People Show (an improvisational troupe). Many of the companies perform in pubs, playgrounds, meeting halls, and other nontheatrical spaces, and at lunchtime, late at night, or other times not normally associated with theatrical performances. The "underground theatre" in England is still relatively new and still growing. It is also less extensively developed than in America, and, perhaps for this reason, the English theatre as a whole gives the impression of being strongly tied to tradition.

～ IV ～

The renaissance in English drama begun in 1956 has continued. Many dramatists discussed in earlier chapters—among them Terence Rattigan, Christopher Fry, John Osborne, John Arden, Arnold Wesker, and Harold Pinter—are still writing. In addition, others came to prominence or began their careers after 1960. Of these, two—Shaffer and Bolt—have been most successful in bridging the gap between tradition and innovation.

Peter Shaffer (1926–) has written in a variety of modes, in all of which he has shown a masterful control of his medium. His first success came in 1958 with *Five Finger Exercise,* a conventionally structured play about a German tutor's effect on a household as each member seeks to make of him either a lover or an ally in psychological warfare with the others. From this vein, Shaffer seemed to move easily to comic absurdity in two one-act plays, *The Private Ear* and *The Public Eye* (1962), and to historical drama in *The Royal Hunt of the Sun* (1964). About the last, which deals with Pizzaro's conquest of Peru and the death of the Inca ruler Atahualpa, Shaffer has said that it is "about the relationship, intense, involved and obscure between these two men, one of whom is the other's prisoner: . . . in many ways . . . they are mirror images of each other. And the theme which lies behind their relationship is the search for God. . . . In fact, the play is an attempt to define the concept of God." This historical and spectacular chronicle was followed by a foray into pure farce, *Black Comedy* (1965), which shows a young man's attempts to juggle his complex relationships with two mistresses, irate or frightened neighbors, a potential father-in-law, an art dealer, and others, as one misunderstanding leads to another in the darkness (caused by a power failure) during which virtually all the action transpires. Shaffer essayed still another type in *The Battle of Shrivings* (1970), a play of ideas. In it, two writers, about to receive a joint award for "humane letters," indulge in a game designed to prove which of their conflicting notions of man is more accurate: that he has the capacity for improvement, or that he is essentially imperfectible. Eventually they are brought together by the cruel suffering both undergo as a result of their "battle." It is one of Shaffer's least successful works, perhaps because its realistic framework does not seem appropriate to its rather schematic separation of ideas and characters into opposing camps. On the whole, however, Shaffer is one of the best craftsmen and most versatile dramatists writing today.

Robert Bolt (1924–   ) was a teacher before making the transition to writing for radio, television, stage, and film. His first work to be seen in London, *The Flowering Cherry* (1957), is a quasi-Chekhovian study of self-deception and failure. In his most successful play, *A Man for All Seasons* (1960), based on the life and martyrdom of Sir Thomas More, Bolt contrasts his protagonist, a man who can be pushed only so far before he takes a stand, with Richard Rich, a man who knows no limits in treachery, especially when the fall of another means elevation for himself. Since Bolt is most concerned with those moral and personal conflicts which recur in all ages, he does not stress the sixteenth-century context but seeks rather to link More's time with the twentieth century. To do this, he relies heavily on the Common Man, a choruslike figure who addresses the audience, introduces characters, assumes the roles of many different persons, and comments on the action. Bolt has said: "The style I eventually used was a bastardized version of the one most recently associated with Bertolt Brecht." Unlike Brecht, however, Bolt uses presentational techniques to draw the audience into the play rather than to alienate them from it. As a result, in production the Common Man often assumed a prominence equal to or greater than that of the protagonist. Obviously this did not diminish the play's appeal, for it amassed one of the longest runs of the decade in London.

Bolt's next two plays—*The Tiger and the Horse* (1960) and *Gentle Jack* (1963)—were not well received, but *The Thwarting of Baron Bolligrew* (1965), a fairytale story about how the bumbling, naïve hero triumphs over the scheming, comic villain, has been called one of the best plays written for children in modern times. With *Vivat! Vivat Regina!* (1970), a sympathetic treatment of Elizabeth I's struggle with Mary of Scotland, Bolt regained some of the popularity he had won with *A Man for All Seasons,* even if in depth of insight it did not equal that earlier work.

Two slightly younger writers—Terson and Nichols—may be likened to both Shaffer and Bolt in writing plays which fall somewhere between the traditional and the innovative. Peter Terson (1932–   ) turned to drama around 1957 but had no work performed until 1964. Since then he has composed two kinds of plays. For the Victoria Theatre at Stoke-on-Trent (directed by Peter Cheeseman), he has written about rural areas and about characters who resist the onslaughts of industrialization and other outside pressures. These include *A Night to Make the Angels Weep* (1964), *I'm in Charge of These Ruins* (1966), and *The Affair at Bennett's Hill* (1970). The last of these tells how a village in Worcestershire rejects a neo-Fascist paramilitary group. It shifts rapidly and often from the comic to the threatening, from caricature to realistic portraiture, and provides striking insights into violence of various kinds. For the National Youth Theatre Terson has written works that emphasize groups and which can be performed convincingly by adolescents. These include *Zigger Zagger* (1967), *The Apprentices* (1968), *Fuzz* (1969), and *Spring-heeled Jack* (1970). Of these, *Zigger Zagger* is representative. A musical play about youthful football fans and their wild enthusiasm which can easily pass over into vandalism, it also follows the story of one boy who is caught between loyalty to the superfan, Zigger Zagger, and a relative who tries to interest him in good music. Terson's rare ability to capture the spirit of youth has made him a favorite author both in England and on the Continent.

Peter Nichols (1929–   ) had been writing television plays for almost ten years before his first stage work, *A Day in the Death of Joe Egg,* was presented in 1967. It deals with the attempts of a schoolteacher and his wife to cope with their spastic child, whom they treat as a joke played on them by life. Despite his initial light tone, the husband eventually tries to kill the child and when he fails leaves his wife. Ultimately, then, the child serves merely as a catalyst who brings to the surface latent anxieties and frustrations. The play won wide acclaim because of its successful mingling of humor with deep compassion for human suffering. *The National Health* (1969) is set in a hospital where elderly patients drag out their lives. The bleakness of the ward contrasts sharply with the romanticized programs about medical life which the patients eagerly watch on television. It is a sympathetic and sometimes comic treatment of the horrors of growing old in a welfare state. Parody of popular culture, so evident throughout *The National Health,* is also a major ingredient in *Forget-Me-Not Lane* (1971), in which Frank, the middle-aged protagonist, in the midst of marital and

Peter Nichol's *The National Health,* produced at the National Theatre in 1969. (Photo by Reg Wilson.)

A scene from the production of Stoppard's *Rosencrantz and Guildenstern Are Dead* at the National Theatre in 1967. Actors in the foreground, left to right, are John Stride, Edward Petherbridge, and Graham Crowden. (Photo by Anthony Crickmay.)

family crises recalls (through associational flashbacks) growing up during World War II. Patriotic music hall acts (performed by enthusiastic amateurs) and songs of the 1940s mingle with Frank's recollections of family conflicts, in which the ineffectual father is the usual loser. The play suggests that most children come to resemble their parents, especially in those things they disliked most about them. It also shows how children may be a divisive force in a marriage. Like Nichols's other works, it is humorous, compassionate, and insightful.

During the 1960s a few British playwrights made use of devices and views popularized by the French absurdists. Apart from Pinter, the most successful of these was Tom Stoppard (1937–), who had written a novel and several plays for television before winning fame in 1967 with *Rosencrantz and Guildenstern Are Dead*. Here Stoppard takes two attendant lords from Shakespeare's *Hamlet* and makes their perspective central. They sense that important events are going on around them, but their attempts to interpret or to become part of them remain tentative. Eventually they are killed without understanding anything about the events of which they have been a part. The overall result is a more readily accessible (and therefore somewhat popularized) version of Beckett's vision of man, for, like Vladimir and Estragon, Rosencrantz and Guildenstern can only improvise games to pass the time while waiting for a revelation which never comes.

Stoppard has not been able to recapture this original success. *The*

Real Inspector Hound (1968) uses the theatricalist device of mingling the onstage performance of a murder mystery with the comments of two critics in the audience; eventually the critics find themselves on stage while the characters watch them from the auditorium. Similarly, *Magritte* (1970) mingles conventions drawn from the murder mystery with the device of shifting identities. Stoppard insists that in his plays he is not concerned with ideas, and, with the possible exception of *Rosencrantz and Guildenstern Are Dead,* this seems borne out, for apparently he is attracted to multiple levels of reality and shifting identities more for their dramatic possibilities than for their philosophical implications.

None of these writers was truly controversial, for though they often employed nontraditional techniques, they did not stray far outside moral perspectives acceptable to a popular audience. On the other hand, a few writers gained considerable notoriety because of their subjects, the ethical implications of which audiences and critics often failed to perceive. Of these writers, perhaps the best are Joe Orton and Edward Bond.

Joe Orton (1933–67) began his playwriting career in 1964 with a work for television. He wrote only three plays for the stage: *Entertaining Mr. Sloane* (1964), *Loot* (1966), and *What the Butler Saw* (produced in 1969). In the first of these, the title character, a murderer, insinuates himself into the household of a middle-aged woman, her businessman brother, and doddering old father. Sloane considers them easy prey, but gradually the brother and sister encourage him to rid them of their father, and after he does so finds himself completely in their power. Since they each desire him sexually, the brother and sister decide to divide Sloane's time equally between them in six-month segments. Despite its seeming amorality, the play suggests much about the disparity between surface propriety and deeper values, a contrast made especially evident through the juxtaposition of the decorous speech and manners with the motives of the brother and sister. Implied commentary is less evident in Orton's later plays. *Loot* parodies the conventions of the detective thriller through a story about robbery, murder, and machination in which the criminals and police eventually agree to share the loot. Similarly, *What the Butler Saw* travesties the conventions of farce through a series of complex sexual relationships. In these later works, Orton seems more concerned with following up the possibilities of amoral situations than with commenting on them. But his firm grasp of dramatic technique makes his plays clear and entertaining, even to those who dislike his perspective. More so than any other contemporary English playwright, Orton has achieved commercial success with subjects almost wholly amoral.

If Orton at times seems merely to exploit sensationalism, Edward Bond (1935–) has been more uncompromising, for the shocking is an integral part of his vision. Bond made his debut as a playwright with *The Pope's Wedding,* presented by the Royal Court on one of its Sunday evening programs in 1962. Then, in 1965, when *Saved* was given "privately" at the same theatre, Bond achieved overnight notoriety with a work depicted

"Private" production of Edward Bond's *Saved* at the Royal Court in 1965.
This is the scene in which Pam's baby is stoned to death.
(Photo by Dominic.)

by many critics as the epitome of decadence and sensationalism. In it, Len picks up Pam, goes home with her, and takes up lodgings with her family, even though she rejects him and has a baby by Fred, whom she follows about adoringly. Resenting the baby, Pam keeps it drugged, and, when she leaves it alone in its pram, Fred and his friends try to rouse it, then smear its face with its own excrement, and eventually stone it to death. (It is this scene that aroused the greatest hostility.) Sent to prison and later released, Fred rejects Pam. Though Len decides that he will go away, he never does. At the end there appears to be a complete impasse. Some critics saw in this work a total rejection of all moral values. But behind the surface lies a moral fable about the spiritual emptiness of people such as Pam and Fred and the violence engendered by their inability to imagine how others feel; there is as well an implied commentary on such affable but weak-willed persons as Len, whose potential for goodness is thwarted by the callousness surrounding them.

Bond's outlook is perhaps most clear in *Early Morning* (1968), a devastating evocation of Victorian society under the guise of surrealistic horror-farce. Although he assigns historical names to many of the characters, Bond is concerned with the attitudes they embody rather than with truth to historical fact. Consequently, the royal household is shown as a nest of intriguers and murderers; Queen Victoria is involved in a lesbian relationship with Florence Nightingale, and eventually virtually all the characters participate in a cannibalistic feast in Heaven. In fact, the entire play may be viewed as a work about the symbolic cannibalism of our times, the inheritor of Victorian attitudes so narrow and selfish that they caused the soul to wither, leaving only material gratifications for consolation. As one of the characters says: "Most people die before they reach their teens. . . . Hardly anyone lives on into their twenties. . . . Bodies are supposed to die first and souls go on living. That's not true. Souls die first and bodies live."

Bond's first play to receive public performance was *Narrow Road to the Deep North* (1968). On the surface it seems totally unlike the earlier works, for it is set in Japan and uses stylized, poetic diction. In it, Basho, a priest on his way to the North to seek enlightenment, finds a baby but leaves it to die. Thirty years later he returns to discover that a city has been built on the spot by the bitter and evil Shogo (who may have been that baby). With the help of Basho, an English commodore and his sister (or is she his concubine?) overthrow Shogo. Then Kiro, who had become a follower of Shogo after being refused as a pupil by Basho, commits hara-kiri as a drowning man calls out for help. After Kiro dies, the man crawls ashore, having saved himself. Again, some critics interpreted the play as a complete rejection (or inversion) of all moral values, although it can be seen as a parable about the violence engendered by inability or unwillingness to offer love and compassion to those in need of it. Those who survive without help from others see no reason to repay callous neglect with kindness.

Although Bond has been denounced by many as a mere sensationalist, he might more accurately be viewed as a moralist who often uses surrealistic or shocking devices to project his disgust for and despair over a world in which the potential for good is swamped by selfishness, greed, and callousness. A more significant dramatist than Orton, Bond is unlikely to win wide popular acclaim because of his uncompromising views about contemporary man.

David Storey (1933–   ), another playwright who recently has garnered high praise from critics, shares many of Bond's ideas about modern man but has avoided his sensationalism. Stylistically, Storey's work often resembles Chekhov's or Pinter's. A teacher before he began to write novels in the late 1950s, Storey had his first play produced in 1967, when Lindsay Anderson, with whom he was working on a film, directed *The Restoration of Arnold Middleton* at the Royal Court. In rapid succession, Storey then composed *In Celebration* (1969), *The Contractor* (1970), and *Home* (1970).

In Celebration takes place on the fortieth wedding anniversary of a coal miner and his wife, for which their three sons return home. Andrew, the least successful, tries to make his brothers look more closely at themselves and see that their mother has enslaved them all because she married beneath her station. But at the end of the play nothing has really changed, and when the sons depart the couple settle back into their old ways. *The Contractor,* in addition to its concern with psychological pressures, displays considerable concern for class divisions. On the surface little happens. The rhythm of the action is largely controlled by the physical process of erecting

A scene from Storey's *The Contractor,* as produced at the Royal Court in 1970. (Photo by Tom Murray.)

(during the first part) and taking down (during the second part) a tent, used for the wedding of Ewbank's daughter (which takes place between the parts). The characters are divided into two groups: Ewbank's family and the workmen. From the first there emanates a sense of lost illusions and shattered ideals, from the second an undercurrent of hostility and potential violence. Ewbank is a self-made contractor on the verge of alcoholism; his daughter is leaving with her husband; his son is so alienated that they cannot communicate. The workers verge on open defiance, although they indulge in considerable raillery among themselves. Much is revealed, nothing resolved.

The situation and many of the characters in *The Contractor* are taken directly from Storey's novel *Radcliffe* (1963), probably the key to all his work and especially relevant to *Home*. In *Radcliffe*, Storey implies that the problems of contemporary man are attributable in large measure to the division that has grown up between the spiritual-mental (also associated with idealism and the governing classes) and the physical-emotional (associated with materialism and the working classes). This alienation is manifested not only internally within the individual, but externally in society (especially through asceticism vs. materialism) and in politics (above all in idealism vs. imperialism). In all cases, the effects have been debilitating, as man has become confused about his goals and as England has declined as a world power. This outlook underlies *Home*. In the opening scene, two apparently refined gentlemen meet on a terrace furnished only with two chairs and an empty flagpole. They talk pleasantly, though seldom is there any sense of true communication. When they leave, their places are taken by two rather bawdy women who obviously are from a lower social class. Gradually it becomes clear that all are inmates in some kind of asylum. The second part merely elaborates on the first. A few revelations are made. One of the men is said to have molested young girls, the other to be a pyromaniac; one of the women cannot control her kidneys, the other is sexually promiscuous. But the overpowering effect is of loneliness, of people on parallel paths which never converge.

The divisions suggested in *Radcliffe* have in *Home* been translated into a metaphor—the insane asylum, a concrete manifestation of alienation. As the dialogue indicates, this alienation exists on several planes—England from its former glory and ideals; class from class; men from women; the individual from himself. Even the title (which may mean one's country, a family dwelling, or a sense of belonging) strengthens the image. In *Home,* Storey enters a universe not unlike Beckett's, for he treats the existential plight of modern man. His method, however, more nearly resembles Pinter's, for all that occurs might happen in real life. The play is rich in concrete detail, the dialogue seemingly natural, though rambling. Story line is virtually nonexistent, motivations only hinted at. Ultimately *Home's* power resides in its multiple implications and its deep compassion.

A number of other playwrights deserve mention. Henry Livings (1929–   ), in such works as *Stop It, Whoever You Are* (1961), *Big Soft Nellie* (1961), *Nils Carborundum* (1962), *Eh?* (1964), and *Honour and Offer* (1969), has written farces of character which comment on working-class conditions. David Mercer (1928–   ), in *Ride a Cock Horse* (1965), *The Governor's Lady* (1965), *Belcher's Luck* (1966), and *After Haggerty* (1970), treats social alienation as reflected in the psychological alienation of his characters. Charles Wood (1932–   ), in *Cockade* (1963), *Dingo* (1967), and *H, or Monologue at the Front on Burning Cities* (1969), uses antiheroic military themes to show the great gap between idealistic statement and violent day-to-day reality. Others—such as David Campton, David Rudkin, Christopher Hampton, and Frank Marcus—might be added, but enough have been treated to show that during the 1960s England produced a relatively large number of good writers, although few were markedly original. Nevertheless, England entered the 1970s with the promise of continued theatrical vigor.

The American theatre since 1960 has continued along paths that were opened earlier. In New York the theatre remains divided between the commercially oriented Broadway and the smaller, out-of-the-way houses. On Broadway the offerings still mingle musicals, light comedy, occasional works of some weight, and plays already proven successful abroad, especially in London. The earlier pattern of "smash hit" or dismal failure has intensified. For example, in 1970, *Hello, Dolly* closed after setting a new record with 2,844 performances, while another musical about the early life of the Marx brothers, *Minnie's Boys,* closed almost immediately with a loss of $800,000. This situation led during the 1960s to a gradual decrease in new productions each season. (In 1970 there were only thirty-eight.) Production costs also drove up the price of admission until in 1970 tickets for some musicals were as much as $15.00 and for dramatic shows $9.50. Thus, play production on Broadway had more than ever become a risk and theatregoing increasingly a luxury.

As in the past, new schemes were proposed to ease Broadway's ills. One of the most promising was the Theatre Development Fund, launched in 1968 with $400,000 raised from several sources. It is headed by a board of directors to whom Harold Clurman recommends the productions to be supported. The fund seeks to assist plays which the directors consider worthy by purchasing at box-office prices blocks of tickets for performances during the first five weeks of a run. These tickets are then sold at discount prices to selected groups (primarily students) who might otherwise find it difficult to attend the theatre. No direct assistance is given any production, for the aim is to help worthy plays find audiences by permitting them to remain open during the first crucial weeks. By 1970 it had assisted twenty-four shows in the total amount of $365,000. Another, quite different scheme was initiated in early 1971, when the starting time for evening performances was moved forward from 8:40 to 7:30 in the hope that playgoing would increase if audiences could get home earlier.

During the 1960s New York also made an attempt to overcome its lack of a permanent repertory company like those found in practically all major European cities. Around 1960 plans were announced for the Lincoln Center for the Performing Arts, with facilities for ballet, opera, concerts, and drama. In 1963 a repertory company was formed, with Elia Kazan and Robert Whitehead as directors and Harold Clurman as "executive consultant." Since the company's permanent home was not yet completed, it performed at first in a temporary building erected in Greenwich Village. The first season began in 1964. Expectations were high, for Kazan was still considered America's finest director, and Arthur Miller and S. N. Behrman had been induced to provide new plays for the company. But disappointment rapidly ensued, reaching a peak with Kazan's production of *The Changeling*. No doubt audiences expected too much, for an ensemble cannot be built overnight. But *The Changeling* also pinpointed the weaknesses of American "method" acting, which had concentrated almost entirely on modern, realistic drama. The failure of this production was crucial in the widespread disenchantment with the "method" during the late 1960s. In the wake of critical attacks, Kazan and Whitehead resigned.

They were replaced by Herbert Blau and Jules Irving, who had been outstandingly successful at the Actors' Workshop in San Francisco. In

October 1965, Blau's production of *Danton's Death* inaugurated the newly completed Vivian Beaumont Theater at Lincoln Center. Seating about eleven hundred, the Vivian Beaumont has a regular proscenium stage but forward of it a 12-foot apron which can be extended to create a thrust stage. Its first season, which included works by Wycherley, Sartre, and Brecht, was only marginally successful, and when the second season encountered serious difficulties, Blau resigned.

Since 1967 Irving has sought to rebuild the company's reputation, but, though there have been signs of improvement, the productions have seldom generated any real excitement. There is still a long way to go before the company can compare favorably with major European troupes. Many of Irving's problems are related to the heavy financial burden imposed by the theatre, the expenses of which his company has had to meet on a year-round basis, even though its season lasts only thirty-two weeks. In 1971 a new arrangement was announced. The building is now to be administered by the New York City Center, which will attempt to keep it filled throughout the year, while the resident company will merely pay rent and reduce its season to twenty-eight weeks. This will also permit a lowering of admission prices, until now among the highest in New York. Whether the new arrangement will stimulate increased quality, however, remains to be seen.

It is probably worth noting as well that Lincoln Center is also the home of the Juilliard School's actor-training program, inaugurated in 1969 under the direction of John Houseman and Michel Saint-Denis. Since it follows much the same plan used by Saint-Denis since the 1930s, it provides a link with acting schools in England, France, and Canada and a tradition going back to Copeau.

In addition to Lincoln Center, it seemed for a time that New York might have a second permanent company in the Association of Producing Artists (APA). Founded in 1960 by Ellis Rabb, the APA gave its first performances in Bermuda and had toured widely before appearing in New York in 1962. In 1964 it formed a liaison with the Phoenix Theatre, which after this time acted as its producer. In 1965 the Phoenix abandoned its off-Broadway home to present the APA in a Broadway theatre and on tour. The APA, unlike the Vivian Beaumont, was soon garnering almost universal praise with its company of about thirty-three actors, among them Helen Hayes, Rosemary Harris, Nancy Marchand, Clayton Corzatte, Donald Moffat, Will Geer, Richard Easton, and Rabb. In 1967 it was selected as America's official representative at Expo 67 in Montreal. Then in 1968 the troupe began to encounter difficulties, partially created by the cessation of grants upon which it depended and partially by the defection of members. In 1969 it had to cease performing in New York and in 1970 it was dissolved.

The repertory of the APA was impressive, for it included Shaw's *Man and Superman*, Chekhov's *The Sea Gull*, Pirandello's *Right You Are*,

If You Think You Are, Giraudoux's *Judith,* Sheridan's *The School for Scandal,* Ibsen's *The Wild Duck,* George Kelly's *The Show Off,* Ghelderode's *Pantagleize,* Ionesco's *Exit the King,* Molière's *The Misanthrope,* Shakespeare's *Hamlet,* Eliot's *The Cocktail Party,* and others. It was sometimes accused of conservatism because it did not present new works and seemed more concerned with preserving past tradition than with creating a new one. Nevertheless, for a time it provided the most impressive cross-section of drama to be seen in America.

~ VI ~

The greatest lack in the Broadway theatre during the 1960s was significant drama. There was, of course, a steady stream of diverting plays, of which the most successful were those by Neil Simon (1927–   ), who, after a somewhat tentative beginning with *Come Blow Your Horn* (1961), hit his stride with a stream of hits: *Barefoot in the Park* (1963), *The Odd Couple* (1965), *Plaza Suite* (1968), *The Last of the Red Hot Lovers* (1970), *The Gingerbread Lady* (1970), and others. All combine zany humor and eccentric characters. The recent plays, however, suggest that Simon may be moving toward a concern for ideas as well as for diversion.

The most important American playwright during the 1960s was Edward Albee (1928–   ), whose first four plays, all short, reached off-Broadway in 1960–61. *The Zoo Story* (1958) includes only two characters —the conventional Peter and the near-derelict Jerry. During the first half of the play Jerry needles Peter about his family and middle-class way of life. Then the tone becomes more ominous, and Peter, feeling threatened, is moved to pick up a knife, upon which Jerry impales himself. Through this play Albee seems to suggest that each of us is caged—cut off from others by various restraints—and that in extreme cases, like Jerry's, the barriers can be broken down only through violence.

The Sandbox (1959) and *The American Dream* (1960) are closely related works with absurdist affinities. Both include husbands who have been emasculated by overbearing wives; both introduce a grandmother (in one she is left to die in a sandbox; in the other, like an animal, she is merely permitted a box behind the stove); both have a muscular, narcissistic young man (in one he is the "angel of death," in the other the "American dream"). These works imply that American life is mother-dominated, insensitive or ineffectual, and attuned primarily to the physical (sexual, materialistic, sensually gratifying) ideal, even though such an ideal is a disguised death wish. On the surface, *The Death of Bessie Smith* (1959) relates the story of how the great blues singer Bessie Smith dies because a

Scene from Albee's *Who's Afraid of Virginia Woolf?* in 1962 with
Uta Hagen as Martha, George Grizzard as Nick, and Arthur Hill as George.
(Photo by A. Jeffry.)

Memphis hospital for Whites will not admit her. But Bessie's black skin is
merely a metaphor for the human condition, in which we are all trapped.
As an hysterical nurse says: "I am tired of my skin.... I WANT OUT!"
On the basis of these short plays, Albee was in the early 1960s usually
considered an American exponent of absurdism.

With *Who's Afraid of Virginia Woolf?* (1962), his first full-length
play and first Broadway success, Albee demonstrated an alliance with
Strindberg and Williams in his exploration of painful psychological relationships. The principal characters, George and Martha (a college professor and
his wife), like Strindberg's couples, are held together by an intense love-hate
relationship which is painfully abrasive both to themselves and to those
around them. The other couple, Nick and Honey (a younger college
professor and his wife), are outwardly polite and optimistic. During a night
spent in drinking and playing sadomasochistic games, they strip each other
bare of illusions and hopefully achieve a more realistic view of themselves.
But it is not a rosy future they look forward to so much as acceptance of
each other's shortcomings and the knowledge that life will not give them
what they had hoped for.

Who's Afraid of Virginia Woolf? reshapes material used earlier in
The American Dream. George is the emasculated man, Martha the dominating wife; their son, though imaginary, is a perfect physical specimen
who represents for them a dream. Honey and Nick are mirror images of
Martha and George: Honey is as introverted as Martha is extroverted;
Nick as assured as George is self-denigrating. Honey aborts babies so she
will not have to face reality; Martha invents a child as a means of coping

706

with an unsatisfying reality. All are crippled by dreams of success that are essentially materialistic or sexual. In leading the characters to see themselves more clearly, the play passes through three stages, entitled by Albee "Fun and Games" (the cruel playfulness of the first act), "Walpurgisnacht" (the sadomasochistic revelations of the second act), and "Exorcism" (the dispelled false illusions of the third act). Albee shows how men create hells for each other through inability to accept weaknesses, which instead of seeking to heal they use as psychic blackmail. Though Albee seems to imply that a brighter future lies ahead for his characters, it is difficult to imagine the psychologically crippled George and Martha achieving peace of mind.

Tiny Alice (1964) is a far less successful and a far more puzzling play, for it is a parable which must be translated into concepts before it can be fully appreciated. It begins in a scene of witty insults between a lawyer and a cardinal before it settles into haggling over the terms under which Brother Julian will be delivered up to Miss Alice (she will give the Church $100 million annually for twenty years). Thereafter interest shifts to Brother Julian's path toward martyrdom. The dominant motif is of one thing inside another (perhaps going on infinitely). Even Alice herself takes on different guises and attributes as the play progresses. Albee seems to have in mind the human propensity to invest unpleasant events with significance. As the lawyer says: "Face the inevitable and call it what you have always wanted. How to come out on top, going under." Thus, man reconciles himself to his fate by constructing systems to explain why he has been martyred by life. Because explanations may take so many forms, it is perhaps not surprising that various critics have seen the play's concerns as essentially religious, sexual, moral, or existentialist.

A Delicate Balance (1966) shows a middle-aged, suburban couple, Tobias and Agnes, seeking to cope with Agnes's drunken sister, Claire; their neurotic daughter, Julie, who has returned home from her fourth marriage; and their oldest friends, Harry and Edna, who arrive without

Scene from the production of Albee's *A Delicate Balance* at the RSG in 1967. (Photo courtesy the Royal Shakespeare Company.)

warning, fleeing some unexplained terror. It is Agnes who through half-truths is most instrumental in preserving the delicate balance between sanity and the stresses of familial relationships, but Tobias is the most crucial character, for it is he who, through the harrowing experiences he endures, comes to perceive that friendship is more important than self-protectiveness.

Albee's most experimental work has been done in *Box and Quotations from Chairman Mao Tse-tung* (1968). When the production begins, only an empty box is visible, as a voice ruminates about all the things a box can hold or be. There follows a playlet in which speeches by Mao Tse-tung are interlarded with stanzas from "Over the Hill to the Poorhouse" and a story told by an affluent woman. Then the phrases about the box begin to dominate once more as the others gradually fade away. The play was generally praised for its "musical" structure and faulted for lack of clear intention. Albee seems to have in mind the dangers of triviality and boredom, of conflicts in ideologies, and disparities between rich and poor which, if not corrected, may reduce the world to something like an empty box.

All Over (1971) is closely related to *Box/Mao* since it is a parable told abstractly. In it, the imminent death of a "great man" brings together several characters: the Wife, the Mistress, the Daughter, the Son, the Best Friend, the Doctor, and the Nurse. It is clear, then, that Albee is not concerned with particular persons but with a condition reflected in domestic and personal relationships and ultimately applicable to mankind as a whole. Precisely what he is trying to say remains uncertain, but it appears to involve the "death of God," the bleakness of existence in which love has been replaced by selfishness, betrayal, and hate, in which blame is always placed on others. Though the characters seek to define themselves, they do not look within but only without and especially to the dying man. Having no inner being, no integrity, what will support them when he is gone? Albee seems to suggest that if we do not develop inner strengths (which must include self-knowledge, compassion, and the will to act upon conviction), it will soon be all over with mankind, for external authoritarian guides are dying. But, if this was Albee's message, it remained too obscure and dramatically ineffective, and the play was accorded a hostile response.

In some ways Albee's career parallels O'Neill's. During the 1960s he established himself as America's leading playwright through his complex characterizations, compelling situations, and excellent command of diction. Like O'Neill, Albee has faltered most when he has sought to be profound. Also like O'Neill, after being highly praised, he is now being downgraded. Nevertheless, both at home and abroad he is probably still the most respected of contemporary American dramatists.

In discussions of promising young writers during the early 1960s, Albee was often paired with Arthur Kopit (1938–   ), but whereas Albee rapidly consolidated his reputation, Kopit developed more erratically. Kopit came to prominence in 1960 with *Oh, Dad, Poor Dad, Mama's Hung You in the Closet and I'm Feeling So Sad,* subtitled "A Pseudoclassical Tragifarce in a Bastard French Tradition." As this subtitle suggests, Kopit's play derives from absurdism, but it also contains much parody of Williams's dramas, especially their more bizarre and decadent elements. In it, a domineering mother, Mme. Rosepettle, keeps her husband's stuffed body hanging in the closet like a trophy, and seeks to insulate her son, Jonathan, from the world. The impression that she is a "man-eating" woman is enhanced by the piranhas and Venus's-flytraps she keeps. Then a babysitter, who seems merely a younger version of Mme. Rosepettle, tries to seduce Jonathan and to replace his mother in his life. As a result of the ensuing struggle, Jonathan chops down the plants, breaks the fishbowl, kills the babysitter, and frees himself from his mother's restraints. Despite the exotic exterior, the figures are the familiar ones of earlier drama (the adolescent escaping an oppressive parent). Only the manner seems new, and that is more parodistic than truly original. Nevertheless, the play won considerable success both in New York and Paris.

Kopit's next play, *The Day the Whores Came out to Play Tennis* (1965), raised doubts about his talents, for it was a decided failure. But with *Indians* (1968) he realized much of the promise shown by his first work. Produced originally by the RSC, it was later revised and restaged in New York in 1969. It depicts American relations with the Indians as seen through the distorted perspective of Buffalo Bill's Wild West Show. Before the action begins, figures of Indians are exhibited in glass cases as though stuffed animals; then Buffalo Bill appears on his horse and begins his showman's attempt to arouse interest in this vanishing race. He sees himself as the champion of the Indians, but fails to recognize his own role in their

Scene from the original production of Kopit's *Indians,* performed by the RSC in 1968. (Photo courtesy the Royal Shakespeare Company.)

decline. From the framework of the tent show, the action moves freely backward in time to scenes showing both the dignity of the Indians and the duplicity of the White man, who uses any complaint or rebellion against mistreatment as an excuse for additional encroachments. Throughout, the Indians are treated in the "noble savage" tradition, while the White men are depicted as either hypocritical or uncomprehending. At times the action passes over into farcical burlesque with such figures as the President and Wild Bill Hickok. The play's greatest fault lies in its treatment of the central character, for Buffalo Bill never comes to recognize that it is he who has done most to divert attention from the true plight of the Indian by converting him into a mythical figure in his own Wild West Show (an image continued and reenforced by such succeeding forms of entertainment as the movie Western). Buffalo Bill remains merely puzzled about why his intentions have led to his present sense of uneasiness. "I had a dream that I was gonna help people, great numbers of people." He perhaps never quite emerges as the tragic figure Kopit seems to have intended. *Indians* is another variation on the by-now familiar theme of the American dream gone awry. If not wholly successful, it remains one of the most ambitious and interesting of recent American plays.

~~ VII ~~

During the 1960s, off-Broadway fared little better than Broadway, for it succumbed to many of the same adverse pressures. When unions began to withdraw the concessions made in the 1950s, producers had to pay actors a prescribed minimum wage and hire union technicians. Consequently, by the early 1960s it cost up to $20,000 to produce a dramatic show off-Broadway and thereafter continued to increase. This has been reflected in higher admission prices and greater caution in the choice of plays. The extent to which off-Broadway has been affected by financial problems is reflected by the loss of $400,000 in 1970 on a production of Brecht's *Mahagonny*. Thus, though off-Broadway has continued to play an important role in New York's theatrical life, the distinctions between it and Broadway have steadily eroded.

The role played by off-Broadway in the 1950s passed during the 1960s to off-off-Broadway, a name coined in 1960 by Jerry Tallmer, critic for the *Village Voice*. Off-off-Broadway is usually dated from 1958, when Joe Cino opened the Café Cino, a coffeehouse which served also as an art gallery and as a place for poetry readings and dramatic productions. At first, plays were given only occasionally, but from 1961 on they formed a regular part of the program. Soon Cino was beseiged by young playwrights seeking a hearing for their plays. By the time Cino died in 1967, his willingness to assist young artists had made him one of the most beloved figures in Greenwich Village.

As the kind of program instituted by Cino was taken up by others, plays were soon being presented almost anywhere. Off-off-Broadway, in the beginning, was essentially an amateur movement in which enthusiasm substituted for professional skill. Most participants were unpaid, the budgets for productions were infinitesimal, and financial returns slight, often what could be gathered by taking up a collection. Nevertheless, it has been estimated that between 1960 and 1965 off-off-Broadway groups presented about four hundred new plays by over two hundred new playwrights.

By far the most influential of the off-off-Broadway producers has been Ellen Stewart, a clothing designer who began her theatrical work because she had tired of hearing young people complain about lack of opportunity in the theatre without taking any steps to remedy the situation. Without any previous theatrical experience whatsoever, she began in 1961 to present plays in a converted basement room. Since then, like several other producers, she has encountered setbacks from municipal authorities (usually on charges that fire regulations have been violated). To avoid problems both with fire inspectors and unions, Miss Stewart established her La Mama Experimental Theatre Club (ostensibly a private organization, although

A scene from the La Mama production of Leonard Melfi's *Birdbath*.
(Photo courtesy James D. Gossage.)

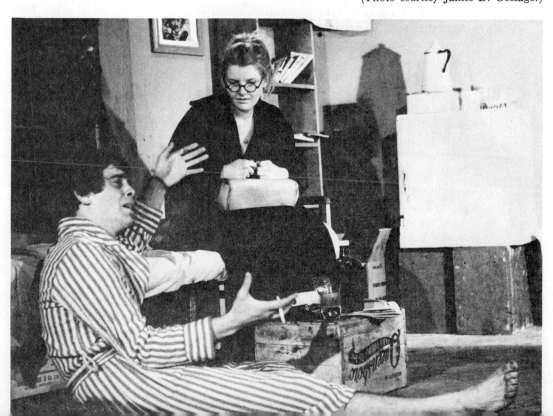

membership is easily available). Here she produced the works of young writers (by 1967, 175 plays by 130 writers) and acted as host to productions by other groups, such as the Open Theatre. After moving several times, the La Mama organization in 1969 at last acquired its own building, which includes two theatres and meets all fire regulations. By that time, it had also become one of the most potent forces in the New York theatre, for during the season of 1969–70 it alone produced more plays than were seen on Broadway that year.

The influence of La Mama is not restricted to the United States. In 1964 Miss Stewart began taking her groups abroad, where they were greeted with such enthusiasm that she gradually established branches in such cities as Copenhagen, Bogotá (Colombia), and Tokyo. Her companies have performed so frequently at foreign festivals in Europe that La Mama has become a label for free-ranging experimentation. Along with the Living Theatre, La Mama has been one of the greatest sources of inspiration for those young people seeking to escape the patterns they associate with the state-subsidized troupes.

Miss Stewart considers La Mama to be a playwright's theatre. She seeks to nourish talent without imposing any mold on it, although she admits her preference for abstract or nonrealistic plays. The encouragement of open-ended experimentation has meant, of course, that much of the work is amateurish, some of it abysmal. But the right to fail is essential when new paths are being sought. In fact, the greatest pitfalls of off-off-Broadway have been the determined pursuit of novelty and the lack of standards by which to judge it. Consequently, inanities have often been greeted with the same enthusiasm as minor masterpieces. Miss Stewart has gradually developed a more professional attitude about the work of La Mama and has sought to raise the level of acting and production, although the quality is still erratic. But whatever La Mama's shortcomings, it has perhaps done more than any other contemporary producer to encourage new writers.

Since most of La Mama's writers are somewhat Artaudian in seeking to approach the brain through the nerves and sinews, a new directorial approach has also been required. The result is best seen in the work of Tom O'Horgan, who worked at La Mama before winning wide renown around 1968 with his productions of *Hair, Futz,* and *Tom Paine.* In O'Horgan's productions, manner tends to be more important than matter, since primary emphasis is placed not on story, character, or idea but on picturesque physical activity (writhing pantomimes, subtextual business, human pyramids, and sexual semiexhibitionism), tableaux, bold antiillusionistic devices, frantic light effects, amplified music and sound, and gimmickry of various sorts. O'Horgan's strength lies in his ability to achieve seeming spontaneity from not-very-gifted actors, whom he uses as kinetic and aural elements in a dynamic whole designed in part to conceal the inadequacies of individual performers. For his work, he does not need actors trained in

Kevin O'Connor in the title role of *Tom Paine* by Paul Foster,
directed by Tom O'Horgan for Ellen Stewart's La Mama troupe in 1968.
(Photo by Friedman-Abeles.)

traditional techniques but ones who can dance, sing, play musical instruments, perform acrobatics, and interchange roles. His productions are colorful, unabashedly frenetic and joyful, but they also tend to obscure story and idea. It was probably his tendency to subordinate scripts to directorial manner that led to O'Horgan's rupture with La Mama. O'Horgan then suffered a decline in reputation but made a forceful return in 1971 with productions of *Lenny* and *Jesus Christ Superstar,* although in both cases critics pronounced his directing contrived and distracting. But though O'Horgan's image is tarnished, many of the techniques he popularized remain, perhaps because so many new plays are verbally inarticulate and require the kind of "physicalization" he utilizes so liberally.

La Mama is merely the most important of the numerous off-off-Broadway groups. Of the others, two of the most effective have been the Judson Poets' Theatre and Theatre Genesis. The Judson Poets' Theatre came into existence in 1961, when the Judson Memorial Church on Washington Square allocated $600 to subsidize an arts program, including dance and theatre. The assistant pastor and director of the program, Al Carmines, has built it into one of the finest organizations in New York. He has directed about half of the theatrical productions and Lawrence Kornfeld the rest. Carmines is also a composer and has done much to create a vogue for small-scale musicals in off-off-Broadway theatres. For example, in 1969 he made a musical adaptation of Aristophanes' *Peace,* and later that year, with Maria Irene Fornes, wrote *Promenade.* Judson's program has been wide-ranging, extending from plays by Strindberg and Gertrude Stein to "happenings" and the pop-art perversities of *Gorilla Queen.* Theatre Genesis, housed in the church of St. Mark's in the Bowery, was established

713

in 1964 and is headed by Ralph Cook, who has staged most of the plays. Like La Mama, this is a playwright's theatre which seeks above all to assist new writers.

Of off-off-Broadway groups, one of the most distinctive was the inspiration of Ronald Tavel, who, after working as a film scenarist for Andy Warhol, wrote his first play in 1965 and in 1966, with John Vaccaro, Bill Walters, and his brother, Harvey Tavel, created the Theatre of the Ridiculous. The manifesto declared: "We have passed beyond the absurd. Our position is absolutely preposterous." Tavel and Vaccaro soon came into conflict because Vaccaro's direction seemed to smother Tavel's scripts. Consequently, in 1967 Tavel left the group and presented *Gorilla Queen* at the Judson Poets' Theatre. Since that time productions have been offered by rival factions, one using the name Theatre of the Ridiculous and the other Ridiculous Theatrical Company. In addition to Tavel, other playwrights associated with the movement are Charles Ludlam (with such plays as *Big Hotel, Conquest of the Universe,* and *When Queens Collide*) and Bill Vehr (with *Whores of Babylon* and—in collaboration with Ludlam—*Turds in Hell*). Tavel's works include *The Life of Lady Godiva, Screen Test, Kitchenette,* and *Vinyl Visits an FM Station.*

The plays of these authors have much in common. Practically all are fantasies based on "popular culture" myths, many drawn from old movies, and they ludicrously exaggerate the notion that happiness lies in a life of sexual gratification. They transcend pornography because there is in them no sense of furtiveness, guilt, or abnormality (no matter how extravagant the occurrences). The principal roles are usually taken by female impersonators who invest everything with an air of indiscriminate sexuality or homosexuality. The scripts show as well a delight in outrageous puns and plays on words. Tavel says that he aims "to hit you in the subconscious," and clearly in his sexual-fantasies-gone-wild there are strong implied comments on the spiritual aridity of that physical ideal which underlies much popular culture (including, most of all, television advertising).

One of the best known of "Ridiculous" plays is Tavel's *Gorilla Queen,* which parodies Maria Montez's jungle films. The title character is Queen Kong, a fat, homosexual ape, who makes its appearance to the sound of obviously fake thunder and flashes of lightning. Eventually it is killed by Clyde Batty, who rapes the corpse, which is then resurrected in a "Deus Sex Mattachine" (a pun on *Mattachine Society,* the organization which seeks to protect the rights of homosexuals), as all the characters are brought together in every conceivable type of coupling so that the ending may be happy for everyone. The uninhibited verbal and sexual exuberance of such works, in combination with their strong implications about modern life, makes them simultaneously both outrageous and insightful. They are merely the most extreme form of the current ambivalent interest (part amusement, part condemnation) of popular cultural forms, especially those of the 1920s and 1930s.

Other groups which have played an important role in New York's theatrical life but which do not fit easily into the off-off-Broadway category include the American Place Theatre and the Public Theatre. The American Place Theatre, founded in 1964 by Wynn Handman and Sidney Lanier, was housed until recently in St. Clement's Church. In 1971 it moved into its present home, one of the several new theatres being included in mid-Manhattan skyscrapers because of tax incentives which the city is offering builders. The American Place Theatre has been supported almost entirely by subscriptions and by grants from foundations. Its repertory is restricted to new plays by exceptionally gifted American authors, many of them primarily poets or novelists. Consequently, it has favored writers such as Robert Lowell, Paul Goodman, and Joyce Carol Oates, although it has also produced works by such playwrights as Sam Shepard, Ed Bullins, and Jack Gelber. Ultimately it seeks to reform the American theatre by encouraging writers of exceptional talent.

A more extensive and varied program is offered by Joseph Papp (1921–) at the Public Theatre. Papp began his work in the 1950s with the New York Shakespeare Festival, out of which grew a liaison with the municipal authorities, who eventually permitted and subsidized free Shakespearean performances in Central Park and who in 1962 built there the Delacorte Theatre, an outdoor amphitheatre seating 2,236. In 1964 Papp began to take some of his productions on tours of New York's neighborhoods, performing in playgrounds for local audiences. He has consistently argued that the renewal of the theatre depends upon attracting a new audience, for otherwise it will be impossible to escape the middle-class biases which have created most of the problems. Thus, one of his major goals has been to reach the unsophisticated and to show them that the theatre is both relevant and entertaining.

In 1967 Papp further enlarged his activities when the Astor Library was transformed into the Public Theatre with five auditoriums suited to different kinds of productions. It opened with *Hair,* which after its initial run was revived for a time at a discotheque before being restaged on Broadway by O'Horgan. Since then Papp has offered a varied and often controversial program, ranging through such works as Havel's *The Memorandum,* Charles Gordone's *No Place to Be Somebody, Stomp* (a communally conceived musical reminiscent of *Hair*), *Mod Donna* (a women's liberation musical), *Hamlet as a Happening,* and David Rabe's *The Basic Training of Pavlo Hummel* (considered by many the best play yet written about the Vietnam war).

Papp has constantly been dogged by financial crises because much of his support has come from foundations and the city of New York, uncertain sources from year to year. For example, in 1969, though he received a large grant from the Rockefeller Foundation, it was earmarked for the production of new plays and a low-cost ticket program at the Public Theatre and could not be used for the performances in Central Park, which came near to being canceled for lack of municipal funds. In 1970, all of Papp's enterprises seemed on the verge of collapse, not only for lack of operating funds but because the Public Theatre was unable to pay a lien of $400,000. In 1971 the city came to his rescue by agreeing to buy the Public Theatre, to renovate it, and to lease it back to him for one dollar per year. Although this will not solve his financial problems, it will do much to ease them. Despite all difficulties, Papp persists in his determined effort to make the theatre a truly popular institution.

Another group of increasing importance is the Chelsea Theatre Center, headed by Robert Kalfin and housed in the Brooklyn Academy of Music. Until 1970 many of its productions were free; though it now charges for all programs, admission is low in comparison with other groups in New York. Nevertheless, it maintains a permanent staff of twelve, employs about twenty actors, and redesigns its playing area for each production. Much of its support comes from grants, the continuance of which cannot be assured. It has presented an adventurous program, including the American premiere of Genet's *The Screens,* Witkiewicz's *The Water Hen,* Bond's *Saved,* Jones's *The Slave Ship,* and many new works and classics. By 1971 it had come to be one of the most exciting theatres in the New York area.

~~~ **VIII** ~~~

The playwrights of the off-off-Broadway theatre have been numerous indeed and perhaps more important as a group than individually, since together they have done much to shift American drama toward short forms, experimentation, and disaffection from the mores and values of the past. As in production, the absence of clear artistic standards has encouraged toleration of works ranging from the most amateurish, muddled, and self-indulgent to the incisive and insightful. On the other hand, these conditions have also meant that much could be attempted that would not have been permitted in more traditional or commercially oriented theatres. Some of the best work has been done by Shepard, Owens, Foster, and McNally.

Sam Shepard (1943–   ) is the most prolific and successful of the new writers. By the time he was twenty-three he had already written around one hundred plays. One of the first to be performed in New York, *Chicago* (1965), concentrates on Stu, a young man who sits in a bathtub in the middle of the stage reflecting on life as his friends bustle about in various activities. For a time his girl friend gets into the tub with him, but soon she goes off to a job in Chicago. At the end, all of the characters line up across the front of the stage and stare at the audience. Then Stu gets out of his tub and comes forward to tell of the joys of just breathing and being alive. As he demonstrates, all the other characters begin to follow his example (self-consciously but happily breathing in and out) as Stu says: "Once you get the taste of it. The hang of it. . . . Ladies and Gentlemen, it's fantastic!" Thus, he seems to suggest that the bustle of daily activity is a distraction from the true joys of life.

Operation Sidewinder (1970) is one of Shepard's most ambitious plays. Divided into twelve scenes separated by rock music, it takes its title from the $2 billion computer shaped like a snake that is let loose in the desert from a nearby airbase. There it wraps itself around a female tourist and has its head cut off by passing Indians. Later reattached, the head is severed once more by soldiers from the base. All this is related to a Hopi Indian legend about how the severing of a snake's head leads to mistrust and hatred, which are healed by the rejoining of head and body and followed by cataclysm when the head is severed once more. In addition to this line of action, there are several others—one, for example, showing a White carhop trying to radicalize Black Panthers, and another about a plan to drug the airbase's water supply so the pilots will all fly off to Cuba. Through this complex play Shepard attacks materialism and moral blindness and suggests that America is disintegrating because of its concern for technological progress and warfare and its neglect of love and the simple life of the Indians. By 1970 Shepard's numerous plays had made him the best known of the playwrights who began their careers in the off-off-Broadway theatre.

Rochelle Owens is noted primarily for *Futz* (written in 1961, first produced in 1965, and restaged in 1967 by O'Horgan). It treats inhabitants of a rural community near-mad from repressed sexual longings who in order to maintain their inhibitions destroy Cyrus Futz when he develops a passion for his sow. Miss Owens suggests that Futz's passion is more natural than that of the puritans, one of whom strangles a girl when he hears Futz making love to his sow. The play demonstrates the author's considerable gift for imagery, dialect, and surrealistic devices. It epitomizes as well the tendency of off-off-Broadway playwrights to thumb their noses at the mores of "Middle America."

In *Beclch* (1969) the title character is a tribal queen who goads men into painful acts and then destroys them if they seem to hold back. Finally she meets a man whom she cannot intimidate, and when the play ends she herself is about to be killed. There are as well several subplots and diversions, among them (according to the stage directions) the onstage slaughter of a goat. Although Miss Owens has said that she is interested here with the social upheaval brought about by the gulf between active and passive temperaments, she appears to conceive her theme in purely sadomasochistic terms. Similar ideas underlie *Homo* (1969) and *The Queen of Greece* (1969), both of which show the chronic conflict between East and West, masochists and sadists, and other polar adversaries, all of them linked through behavior which blends cruelty and supplication. In all her work, Miss Owens is concerned with the never-ending conflict between the simple people of the world (who merely want to be natural and peaceful) and the violent and repressive (who refuse to accept or allow simple pleasures). Though often disturbing and violent, the plays are also among the most imaginative and imagistic of the decade.

Paul Foster has written many plays, among them *The Recluse, Hurrah for the Bridge,* and *The Hessian Corporal,* but he is probably best known for *Balls* (1964) and *Tom Paine* (1968). In *Balls,* the stage remains completely empty throughout except for two pingpong balls which swing back and forth while amplified voices, sounds, and lighting effects evoke both the memories of the dead who lie buried in a cemetery and the living who engage in love making and other activities over their graves. It implies that life is too fleeting to waste in unnecessary repressions. *Tom Paine,* in O'Horgan's production, became one of New York's hits of 1968. In it, actors clad in black, anonymous garb arrived, played eighteenth-century musical instruments, introduced themselves to the audience, and elected to enact the story of Tom Paine. Since Foster wished to differentiate between Paine as a man (arrogant, conceited, and drunken) and Paine's ideal (the equality of mankind), his protagonist was played by two different actors, around whom the rest of the cast swirled, little differentiated and used primarily to suggest Paine's agony. The actors dropped out of the action to comment on it and at one point sought to engage the audience in political discussion. Many sections were left for the actors to improvise. (In 1970–71, it was presented with considerable success by the TNP in Paris.)

Terrence McNally displays a much keener sense of irony and humor than do most of the off-off-Broadway writers. Most typically he tells a rather clear and connected story ending in some unexpected bit of black humor. For example, in *Witness* a psychopath has captured and tied up an encyclopedia salesman so he will have a witness to prove that it was he who assassinated the President, due shortly to pass beneath his window in a motorcade. The arrivals of a window washer and a neighbor at first seem to threaten his arrangement, but neither pays any attention whatsoever to the salesman's plight. Ultimately, however, the psychopath's plan is foiled, because several other persons shoot the President before he gets a chance. *Sweet Eros* (1968) created a considerable stir because in it a kidnapped girl is stripped naked and tied to a chair, where she remains throughout the action. The kidnapper, another of McNally's psychopaths, seeks to force the girl into the kind of meaningful relationship that he has never been able to achieve. But the girl is so passive that, after some initial anxiety, she comes to enjoy her role and thwarts his desire by her unresisting submission. McNally's numerous works also include *And Things that Go Bump in the Night* (1964), *Next* (1969), and *Where Has Tommy Flowers Gone?* (1971).

Other noteworthy off-off-Broadway writers include Maria Irene Fornes, who not only has written such plays as *The Successful Life of Three* (1965) and *The Office* (1966) but the scripts for several musicals by Al Carmines; Adrienne Kennedy, with such multilayered, ritualistic fantasies as *The Owl Answers* and *A Rat's Mass*; Tom Eyen, who has exploited the mock-epic vein of "pop culture" in *Caution, A Love Story,* and *The Dirtiest Show in Town;* Lanford Wilson, with *The Madness of Lady Bright, Balm in Gilead, The Rimers of Eldritch* and *Lemon Sky;* Leonard Melfi, with *Birdbath, Halloween,* and *Times Square;* Israel Horovitz, with *The Indian Wants the Bronx, It's Called the Sugar Plum,* and *Line;* Ronald Ribman, with *Harry, Noon and Night, The Journey of the Fifth Horse,* and *The Ceremony of Innocence;* and Julie Bovasso, with *Gloria and Esperanza* and *Shubert's Last Serenade.* The list could be extended almost endlessly.

But if off-off-Broadway has been generous in offering these playwrights a hearing, it has been less so in supporting them financially, for most have earned little from their work. Thus, most are faced with the dilemma of not yet being welcome in the established theatres but of being unable to support themselves on what they can earn in the permissive atmosphere of off-off-Broadway. On the other hand, there are signs that off-off-Broadway is beginning to change, for by 1970 it was being subjected to many of the same pressures from Actors Equity and other unions which a decade earlier had driven off-Broadway to retreat from its stance of indifference to commercial success. Soon there may have to be an off-off-off-Broadway if the casual and freewheeling experimentation of the 1960s is to survive.

IX

One of the most encouraging developments in the American theatre since 1960 has been the emergence of a Black theatre movement. The promising advances of the interwar years had largely faded after 1939 with the demise of the Federal Theatre Project and the coming of World War II. A few efforts in the late 1940s—such as the Manhattan Arts Theatre and the American Negro Theatre—were abortive, in large part because Black writers and artists had not yet built support for their work among Blacks and were treated by Whites as expendable (that is, as persons to be used for an occasion and then abandoned when it passed). Thus, momentary encouragement typically ended in bitter disappointment.

The Black arts movement of the 1960s differed from its forerunners in accepting the integrity and dignity of the Black experience and in its unwillingness to compromise with White sensibilities as the price for success or to depend for its support on a fickle White audience. Ultimately, however, the difference was due to a change in the consciousness of Black people. Herein lies both the strength of the movement (firm belief in the fundamental worth of "Blackness" and all that it entails) and most of its difficulties (largely due to differences of opinion among Blacks about the goals and means most likely to insure success). Thus, though all groups are united in the struggle to increase Black pride, differences on means have often led to bitter in-fighting.

The Black theatre movement received its first important impetus in 1964 when LeRoi Jones, Clarence Reed, Johnny Moore, Charles and William Patterson, and others founded the Black Arts Repertoire Theatre School in New York. This group produced a number of plays and gave poetry readings and concerts, some of which were taken into the streets. It came to an end when congressmen became concerned over the radical tone of some work done by the school, which was partially supported by funds from the Office of Economic Opportunity.

But though this group was dissolved, a spark had been lighted and Black arts organizations were soon springing up throughout the country. For a rationale, many looked to Maulana Ron Karenga, who had suggested seven requisites for a Black culture: unity, self-determination, collective work and responsibility, cooperative economic policies, sense of common purpose, creativity, and faith. By 1968 there were about forty groups scattered throughout the United States, of which the most important were Black Arts/West (in San Francisco), Concept East (in Detroit), the Spirit House (in Newark), and the Negro Ensemble Company and the New Lafayette Theatre (both in New York). For the theatre, the last three have been most important.

The Negro Ensemble Company (with financial support from the Ford Foundation) was established in 1968. Douglas Turner Ward was named artistic director, Robert Hooks executive director, and Gerald S. Krone administrative director. Its headquarters are in the St. Marks Playhouse. It began with a permanent company of thirteen, who worked together for three months before opening the first season. Both to assist its own future growth and Black theatre in general, it instituted as well a training program for actors, directors, and playwrights. Since 1968 the Negro Ensemble Company has performed a varied repertory of works considered meaningful to Blacks, though not necessarily written by Blacks. It is one of the least militant of Black organizations and has often been accused by more radical groups of being anxious not to offend Whites or middle-class Blacks. In general, the quality of its work has been high. (It won much praise for its appearances at the World Theatre Season in London in 1969.)

The New Lafayette Company, headed by Robert Macbeth, was founded in 1967 and serves as something of a cultural center for Harlem. At first it was given rather tentative assistance by the Ford Foundation, but in 1969 it was granted $529,350 to support the company and a workshop (especially for plays about contemporary Black life). This company is

more fully dedicated to the notion of an exclusively Black theatre than is the
Negro Ensemble Company.

But neither is sufficiently radical to please LeRoi Jones, who after his total disaffection from Whites founded the Spirit House in Newark to serve as headquarters for a Black arts movement completely removed from a White context. Jones is vehement in his denunciation of most other groups as insufficiently dedicated to a separatist Black culture.

The demand for actors created by these and other groups has led to the emergence of many fine Black actors and directors. (It should also be noted that several White playwrights have come to write more often and more sympathetically about Blacks, and that federal legislation and Actors Equity have sought to reduce the discrimination in casting formerly practiced on Broadway and elsewhere.) Among the best Black actors are James Earl Jones, Ruby Dee, Diana Sands, Claudia McNeill, Ossie Davis, Roscoe Lee Brown, Moses Gunn, Robert Hooks, and John O'Neal, and of the directors Michael Schultz, Robert Macbeth, and Robert Hooks. The list is constantly growing.

Perhaps more important has been the emergence of a sizable number of Black dramatists. Among them, some of the best are Baldwin, Hansberry, Jones, Ward, Elder, Bullins, and Gordone. Of these, Baldwin and Hansberry stand somewhat apart, for they wrote during a period before the Black arts movement was fully underway.

James Baldwin (1924–   ) first won literary fame as a novelist during the 1950s. At this time he also wrote his first play, *The Amen Corner* (produced in 1954–55 at Howard University and professionally in 1964), a rather conventional play about growing up. In it, a son is torn between his revivalist mother (who denies life) and his jazz musician father (who affirms life). At the end, the son has decided to follow neither but to go his own way, while the mother gives up her church and kneels by the bed of her dying husband. *Blues for Mister Charlie* (1964) was written out of Baldwin's rage over the Emmet Till case (in which a young Black was killed in Mississippi for whistling at a White woman and his accused murderer acquitted). Baldwin's play moves freely in time and place while tracing several intertwined stories relating to the sickness of racism. Its strength lies more in its fervor than in its characterization or story. Despite Baldwin's evident talent, he has written no more for the stage.

Lorraine Hansberry (1930–65) completed only two plays, *Raisin in the Sun* (1959) and *The Sign in Sidney Brustein's Window* (1964). The first deals with a hard-working family living in Chicago in crowded quarters presided over by the matriarch, Lena Younger. Miss Hansberry very skillfully builds up a strong sense of the individual members of the family, both their strengths and weaknesses, their squabbles and wry humor. Then, all the family's dreams seem near fulfillment when Mrs. Younger gets money from her husband's insurance. Unfortunately, most of the money is lost, but if the dreams fade, the family is compensated by an

Scene from the production of Lorraine Hansberry's *A Raisin in the Sun,* Ethel Barrymore Theatre, New York, in 1959. The cast included Sidney Poitier, Claudia McNeil, Ruby Dee, and Diana Sands. (Photo by Friedman-Abeles.)

increased sense of pride and love. It is a warm, rich, moving study of family relationships and maturing values. *The Sign in Sidney Brustein's Window* is less successful, perhaps because it seems more concerned with moral concepts than human portraiture. It treats a well-meaning Greenwich Village idealist who is too busy campaigning for a reform candidate to recognize the problems that exist within his own family. But when his sister commits suicide and his candidate turns out to be worthless, he, like the characters in *Raisin in the Sun,* is forced to reassess his values. Unfortunately, Miss Hansberry's great promise was cut short by her early death. Since 1965, two other works have appeared. *Les Blancs,* a play about the impossibility of two men of different color maintaining a close friendship in an era of racial conflict, was produced in 1970. It was adapted by Robert Nemiroff (Miss Hansberry's husband), who also put together *To Be Young, Gifted, and Black* (1971), a "portrait" of Miss Hansberry made up entirely of selections from her letters, diaries, notebooks, and plays.

In many ways, LeRoi Jones (1934–   ) is the most important of Black dramatists, for not only is he one of the most effective, but he demonstrates as well through the successive stages of his career most of the major attitudes of Black artists during the 1960s, ranging from an original interest in integration to a demand for full separation. In his early plays, Jones is concerned with Black-White love-hate relationships, which, though abrasive and destructive, seem not yet beyond resolution. Perhaps the most poignant treatment is found in *The Toilet* (1964), in which a group of students round up a White boy, Jimmy, and beat him unmercifully because he allegedly has indicated an attraction to a Black boy, Ray. After the attackers leave, Ray stealthily returns and cradles Jimmy in his arms. Here Jones has used homosexuality as a metaphor for the barrier erected by society between Whites and Blacks, one which makes it shameful to admit mutual love and respect. A much less sympathetic view of the relationship is seen in *Dutchman* (1964). Set in a subway car, it shows a young White woman, Lulu, accosting a young Black, Clay, and needling him about all the things that mark him out as middle-class—that is, for his failure to live up to her notion of the debased figure that a Black man should be. When he is finally provoked into a show of violence, she stabs him to death and at the end is ready to advance on another prey. Here Lulu is used to represent the tendency of Whites to categorize the Black man, to humiliate and insult him, and then to use any show of resentment or rebellion as an excuse for destroying him. Such imaginative and powerful treatments of Black-White relations (along with other plays—*The Baptism, The Slave,* and *Dante*) had by the mid-1960s made Jones the best known of all Black dramatists.

Since then Jones has steadily become more militant in his dislike for anything White. Among his later works are *Great Goodness of Life (A Coon Show), The Death of Malcolm X,* and *Home on the Range.* Some of this later work seems rather crude in comparison with his earlier plays, but in others, especially *The Slave Ship* (1967), his power remains undiminished. *The Slave Ship* is composed of a series of vignettes designed not only to denounce actual slavery but enslaving social forms and attitudes as well. We see African Blacks thrown into a ship's hold, one on top of the other; they are beaten, raped, driven to suicide and madness. In America they are sold and become completely ineffectual because of the brute force of their oppressors or because of betrayals by other Blacks. The play does not seek to analyze a condition so much as to provoke solidarity among Blacks and rejection of White society. Music underscores the play's rhythms, and spectacle is used imaginatively to incite revolt against Whites. Here as elsewhere in his recent work, Jones seems to champion a puritanical, simple, separatist, near-tribal existence as the answer to Black problems.

Two recent writers—Ward and Elder—are closely connected with the Negro Ensemble Company. Douglas Turner Ward, artistic director of the NEC, usually writes in a comic vein showing Blacks besting Whites. In *Happy Ending* (1967), two Black women bemoan the breakup of their White employers' marriage. This seeming "Uncle Tomism" is soon dispelled, however, for the sorrow is caused by the loss of their source of scavenged food and clothing. But it is also clear that they are driven to outwit their employers by the treatment and wages they receive. Eventually all is resolved happily when the impending divorce is canceled. Somewhat similarly, *Day of Absence* (1967) shows a Southern town totally paralyzed when all its Blacks disappear. *The Reckoning* (1969), billed as "a surreal Southern fable," shows a governor's attempts to stop a march on his capital by a young Black militant and his followers. Dressed all in white (including a mane of white hair), the governor is addicted to such speeches as: "Never will we prepare the bridal chamber for a mating of the baboon with little white Goldilocks." Then a Black pimp confronts the governor with pictures of him in bed with a Black whore and threatens to circulate them throughout the state. The governor decides not to oppose the march. Because of his humor, Ward tends to be one of the least abrasive of Black dramatists in his treatment of Black-White relationships.

Lonne Elder III, director of the playwrights' program of the NEC, is known primarily for *Ceremonies in Dark Old Men* (1969). Set in Harlem, it focuses on the Parker family: the father (a former vaudeville dancer), his two unemployed sons (Theo and Bobby), and his daughter Adele (who supports the family). The men are persuaded by Blue Haven to use their home and unpatronized barbershop as a blind for various illegal activities (numbers and dart games, the sale of corn liquor, and burglary), all in the supposed interest of the Harlem Decolonization Association, whose goal is to run "you know who" out of Harlem. Although for a time they seem to prosper, their dreams of happiness collapse when Bobby is killed while participating in a robbery. More compassionate than bitter, the play is concerned with Black identity and the ceremonies the characters enact to escape the world they inhabit.

Ed Bullins (1935–), one of the finest and most prolific of contemporary dramatists, is now resident playwright at the New Lafayette Theatre. He has also done much to promote Black drama by publishing anthologies of plays, both his own and others, by writing about the movement, and by editing *Black Theatre Magazine,* published by the New Lafayette Theatre. One of Bullins's best plays is *The Pig Pen* (1970), the action of which takes place in 1965 at a party given by Len, a Black liberal, and his White wife. Although sympathetic to Black nationalism, Len has contented himself with discussions and with recommending books, such as those by Frantz Fanon. Then, news arrives that Malcolm X has been killed. As a result, a Black girl rejects her White boyfriend and the various Whites who are present become overeager to please the Blacks. The play then passes over into fantasy as a white-helmeted policeman with an American flag plastered on his enormous belly whirls about the stage beating everyone in sight, while those at the party remain oblivious both to him and to the gunfire in the background. The play seems to indicate that the death of Malcolm X marked the point after which Black intellectuals could no longer remain aloof. The false Black intellectual, more interested in words and parroted ideas than in life around him, is one of Bullins's most frequent targets, seen at its best in *The Electronic Nigger* (1968). But Bullins is interested as well in many other facets of Black life. For example, *Clara's Old Man* (1965) is set in a household where Clara, an attractive young girl, lives with Big Girl (her "old man"). Clara has invited Jack, another of Bullins's pseudointellectuals, to visit her, thinking that Big Girl will be away. Not understanding the relationship between the two women, Jack increasingly arouses Big Girl's hostility and when three neighborhood toughs arrive, she takes Clara to the movies (which Jack had intended to do) and the young men give Jack a vicious beating. It is a powerful evocation of frustration and loneliness, but also a commentary on various kinds

Ed Bullins' *Clara's Old Man,* performed
at the American Place Theatre,
New York, in 1968.
(Photo by Martha Holmes.)

of responsibility. Among Bullins's other plays, some of the best are *Goin' a
Buffalo* (1968) and *A Son Come Home* (1968). Bullins has also announced
his intention of writing a twenty-play cycle about the "life of black people
in the industrial North and West," of which two, *In the Wine Time* and
In New England Winter, have already been produced with considerable
success.

Like Elder, Charles Gordone (1926–   ) is known for one play, *No
Place to Be Somebody* (1969), first produced at the Public Theatre and
winner of a Pulitzer Prize. Set in a Greenwich Village bar, it shows the
Black, illiterate owner, Johnny Williams, trying to start his own version
of the Mafia as a way of getting back at the White world. Despite objections from others, he persists and the action ends in four deaths onstage
and a suicide offstage. The main interest of the play, however, resides in
its characters, all Blacks or misfit Whites: an unemployed author and actor,
part-Black, part-White, who cannot fit into either world; an effeminate
Black ballet dancer; a near-mad White helper; several Black and White
prostitutes; and White representatives of the Mafia. The interaction of
these characters, along with their colorful and imaginative diction, keeps
interest high and everything seemingly casual until it suddenly and unexpectedly explodes into violence. Not only is the play skillfully constructed,
it avoids the clichés and stereotypes which afflict much contemporary drama.

Other playwrights include Ben Caldwell, Ron Milner, Frank Cucci,
Ossie Davis, Marvin X, Kingsley B. Bass, Jr., J. E. Franklin, Adrienne

Kennedy, John Scott, Melvin van Peebles, and Ted Shine. That virtually all these writers have emerged since 1965 suggests the enormous potential and vitality of the Black theatre movement.

Despite their considerable diversity, these writers are united in their aim of building Black consciousness. Most typically this means as well the denigration of Whites. Thus, White spectators at the plays often find themselves forced to accept a masochistic role. (No doubt the reverse is often true for Blacks attending White plays.) Although many persons (both Black and White) find this unsettling, it is probably a necessary phase. Ultimate harmony requires that each race not only be convinced of its own worth but that of the other as well. Consequently, Whites would do well not only to respect and encourage plays that contribute to a sense of dignity among Blacks but also those that encourage respect for Blacks among Whites. Meanwhile, it appears that, for the first time in American history, Black theatre and drama may succeed in sustaining themselves, largely because they have created the conditions necessary for continuing support.

Just as increased consciousness among Blacks has led to significant creativity in the arts, so too political and social concerns have given rise to a number of "radical theatre" groups who are seeking to change society. Among the most important of these have been the Bread and Puppet Theatre, the San Francisco Mime Troupe, El Teatro Campesino, and the Free Southern Theatre.

The Bread and Puppet Theatre was founded in 1961 by Peter Schumann, who came to New York from Germany with the intention of forming a dance troupe. The organization's title reflects both its philosophy and major productional device. Schumann is concerned with overcoming the perennial subversion of love, charity, and humility by political and materialistic deceptions. His theatre seeks to remind us of certain simple and eternal values and to incite us to return to them. "Theatre is not . . . the place of commerce . . . where you pay and get something. Theatre . . . is more like bread, more a necessity. . . . It preaches sermons and it builds up a self-sufficient ritual where the actors try to raise their lives to the purity and ecstacy of the actions in which they participate." At most performances this purpose is reaffirmed by the ritual offering of bread to the audience. All of the group's plays utilize puppets or "moving sculptures" of various sizes. Some can be manipulated by single actors but others, as large as 12 feet tall, require several operators. Building on fairytales, legends, myths, biblical or other familiar material, Schumann seeks through puppets to

Outdoor performance in 1970 by the Bread and Puppet Theatre on the University of Kansas campus. (Photo courtesy Ronald A. Willis.)

create gestures that are larger, simpler, and more profound than would be possible with the human figure alone. The Bread and Puppet Theatre is a "poor" company. It works with limited means and makes all of its figures and properties from "found" materials—old clothes, burlap, newspapers, scrap wood, and clay.

The Bread and Puppet Theatre has now presented about seventy shows of various kinds in Harlem, the Bronx, at Papp's Public Theatre, and on tour both in America and abroad. It begins each performance with a striking and entertaining parade of puppet figures and players. Then comes a parablelike drama. One of the best is *The Cry of the People for Meat*. It begins with the mating of the archcapitalist Uncle Fatso (representing Uranus) with Mother Earth, as a result of which Kronos is born with sword in hand and immediately kills his father. From this context, in which from time immemorial capitalism has sired violence, the play moves into biblical mythology, beginning with the Creation and going forward to the Crucifixion. Many contemporary references are introduced, as when the Massacre of the Innocents is treated as an air raid in Vietnam. Bread is distributed during the recitation of the beatitudes. At the end of the production, a stunning tableau of the Last Supper is shattered by warplanes which destroy the bread eaters. Thus, it seeks to provoke rejection of capitalism and violence and acceptance of true Christian virtues. The Bread and Puppet Theatre is perhaps the most artistically sophisticated of the radical theatre groups, as well as the one most attuned to traditional humanistic values.

The San Francisco Mime Troupe giving a puppet show
on the campus of Colorado State University in 1969.
(Photo courtesy Ronald A. Willis.)

The San Francisco Mime Troupe was founded in 1959 by R. G. Davis, a member of the Actors' Workshop, under whose auspices its first performances were given. Originally, it did silent plays but later introduced speech because silence seemed to dampen the response of audiences. In 1962 it began to perform in parks and other outdoor locations. In these early years, the Mime Troupe was still closely attuned to *commedia dell' arte* and to plays (such as Molière's *Scapin*, Goldoni's *The Servant of Two Masters*, and Jarry's *Ubu Roi*) which lent themselves to presentational techniques. Not until 1966, with *A Minstrel Show, or, Civil Rights in a Cracker Barrel* (an attack on racism and naïve integrationism), did the troupe commit itself to radical agitation. At that time it also began to tour widely in the United States and Canada. Since then it has devised such works as *The Independent Female* (a women's liberation play) and *Seize the Time: The Story of Chairman Bobby Seale and the Black Panther Party*. In 1969, when Davis left the company, it was collectivized and since then all important decisions have been made by the group as a whole. About its aims, a spokesman for the Mime Troupe has said: "We are committed to change, not to Art. We have tried to cut through the aristocratic and square notion of what theatre is, and risk our egos to keep the search open for better ways of making the theatre, in content and style, a living radical force." In doing so, it has adopted a broad acting style which ridicules all that it dislikes and lauds all that it favors. Its productions are skillfully performed agit-prop plays.

El Teatro Campesino was founded in 1965 by Luis Valdez in conjunction with the National Farm Workers Association to dramatize the issues of the grape picker's strike in Delano, California, and to urge workers to join the union. It is now a bilingual troupe which seeks to create pride in the heritage and accomplishments of Mexican-Americans. Through its work in California and on tour, it has been extremely successful in calling attention to the problems of Mexican-Americans and in serving as a cohesive force within its own community.

The Free Southern Theatre, based in New Orleans, was founded by Gilbert Moses and John O'Neal in 1963–64 as an extension of the civil rights movement. Its original prospectus declared: "A combination of art and social awareness can evolve into plays written for a Negro audience, which relate to the problems within the Negro himself, and within the Negro community. Through theatre, we think to open a new area of protest." Originally it performed standard plays, among them works by Beckett, Brecht, O'Casey, and Ionesco, for it was primarily interested in promoting integration. The members soon began to suspect, however, that they were trying to bring culture to an audience not interested in the kind of drama they were presenting. There were also conflicts among members about the relative importance of art and social change. Consequently, since the late 1960s the Free Southern Theatre has moved progressively toward concern with Black problems and toward promoting Black consciousness and support.

There are as well many other radical theatre groups in America. In 1967 several joined in creating the Radical Theatre Repertory, headed by Oda Jurges and Saul Gottlieb, and in 1968 held the first radical theatre festival. The radical groups are held together not only by similar political views, but by their common belief that theatre should be an integral part of daily life rather than a commodity to be sold to the affluent. As Gottlieb has said: "Art as a pursuit in itself doesn't mean anything anymore. We just believe that the human body, and the human voice, and the human soul can create works of theatre that further the revolution."

Those who elevate political and social change above art have tended to gravitate toward "guerilla theatre," a term proposed by R. G. Davis in 1966 in pointing out how the theatre might be adapted for uses analogous to guerilla warfare. Consequently, as most typically practiced, guerilla theatre seizes the opportunity provided by a gathering or occasion to present a brief, pithy, unscheduled dramatization of some issue.

One of the most active groups is the American Playground, headed by Marc Estrin, who has published a number of pieces suitable for guerilla theatre. A typical example is called *Military Execution of the Bill of Rights*. In it, a drummer dressed in army uniform appears and strikes up a funeral beat, as a black-draped stake is carried in by two soldiers in dress uniforms, followed by three others with machine guns. The stake is set up, the gunners take their positions, and the drape is pulled away to reveal the Bill of Rights nailed to the stake; then, as they are read one by one, the articles are executed by the machine gunners. Estrin adds: "This piece is a simple, effective way of getting attention . . . in a way which will attract the media, . . . the point being to get the message into sixty million homes." Guerilla theatre is a form of aggression which borrows certain techniques from art to use in a battle over political, social, or moral issues.

Practically all the radical and guerilla theatre groups are allied ideologically with the New Left (to be discussed in the next chapter). Although much the same might be said about many of the writers and workers in off-off-Broadway, the latter seldom put ideology and social action first, whereas the former almost always do.

XI

The 1960s saw the greatest expansion of the American theatre since the nineteenth century, even though it remained relatively restricted in comparison with that of many European countries. In addition to the great number of off-Broadway and off-off-Broadway companies, resident troupes, scattered throughout the country, also were established. The major impetus for regional companies came in 1959 when the Ford Foundation made large grants to a number of existing troupes that seemed likely to survive. This financial boost permitted many organizations to become fully professional for the first time. Among the most important of these early groups were the Alley Theatre in Houston, the Actors' Workshop in San Francisco, and the Arena Stage in Washington.

The movement was further strengthened when Tyrone Guthrie announced his decision to found a theatre in Minneapolis, since the example of a major director seeking a home outside of New York gave much needed

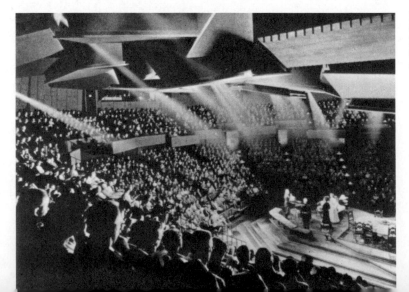

Interior of the Tyrone Guthrie Theatre, Minneapolis. (Courtesy the Minnesota Theatre Company.)

Exterior of the Arena Stage, Washington, D.C. (Photo courtesy Arena Stage.)

prestige. The Tyrone Guthrie Theatre, home of the Minneapolis Theatre Company, opened in 1963. Its design derives from the Stratford (Canada) Festival Theatre, although it has a fully equipped proscenium stage as well as a thrust stage, around which the 1,400 seats are wrapped. Guthrie remained with the company for three years, by which time it was well underway. Unfortunately, after he left, internal bickering soon led to a decline in quality and in 1968 Guthrie's successor, Douglas Campbell, resigned. After a period of hesitation, the troupe began to build once more after Michael Langham took charge in 1970.

The favorable publicity received by Minneapolis in 1963 motivated many other cities to build art centers with facilities for resident companies. It is in these regional theatres (and in universities) that most of the innovations in theatre architecture in America can be found. Most have thrust or arena stages, although some include proscenium stages as well. Among the innovative buildings are those at the Alley Theatre, Theatre Atlanta, the Arena Stage (Washington), and the Playhouse in the Park (Cincinnati). One of the most elaborate has been built in Los Angeles, where the new Music Center includes a large concert hall and two theatres, one seating 750 and the other 2,100.

By 1966 the regional theatres had so burgeoned (there were about thirty-five permanent troupes) that for the first time in the twentieth century more actors were working outside of than in New York. Practically all the resident companies were presenting a season of plays (part classics, part recent hits) for limited runs. Thus, they resembled European subsidized troupes more than they did Broadway theatres. In the late 1960s one of the best known of the regional companies was the American Conservatory Theatre (ACT), founded in 1965 by William Ball. After beginning

A scene from Dolores Sutton's adaptation of the Thomas Wolfe novel,
The Web and the Rock, directed by Davey Marlin-Jones at the Washington
Theatre Club in 1971. Left to right are Stephen McHattie as
George Webber, Miss Sutton as Esther Jack, and Ruth Maynard as
Julia Webber. (Photo courtesy the Washington Theatre Club.)

in Pittsburgh, it played in several cities before settling in San Francisco,
which had been without a major resident company since the Actors'
Workshop had folded after Irving and Blau left for Lincoln Center. By
1969 the ACT was running two theatres simultaneously and producing as
many as thirty-two plays a season.

But the resident companies were for the most part rather conservative
institutions more concerned with presenting the best from the past than in
championing innovation. There were a few exceptions, such as the Washington Theatre Club (founded in 1965 and headed by Davey Marlin-Jones),
which has emphasized new plays.

All the resident companies, however, were haunted by the same
problem—the lack of assured continuing support—for unlike their European
counterparts, which are assured of governmental subsidies, they are dependent upon box-office receipts and the good will of private donors. A somewhat hesitant step toward governmental subsidy for the arts was taken,
however, in 1965 when federal legislation established the National Endowment for the Arts, which, somewhat like England's Arts Council, makes
grants to projects which seem to have considerable potential. Money has
also been made available to the arts councils of individual states, most of
which are still in the formative stage, to assist them in planning programs
for the arts. But federal appropriations have been relatively small, although
they have steadily increased. Unfortunately, there is no firm assurance
that they will be continued from one year to the next. Thus, though a

beginning has been made, there is as yet no recognition, as there is in Europe, that an enlightened state should commit itself to continuing assistance for the arts.

During the 1960s many universities reassessed their roles and sought to bridge the gap between their training programs and the professional theatre. The University of Minnesota established a link with the Tyrone Guthrie Theatre, as did the University of Michigan with the APA. Other universities, among them Stanford, Yale, and Princeton, formed resident professional companies. Still others created troupes composed of talented students. In 1969 the University Resident Theatre Association (URTA) was formed by companies associated with universities. By 1971 it included twenty-two member groups and was a division within the American Theatre Association (which in 1971 superseded the American Educational Theatre Association).

Despite the gains made during the preceding decade, the American theatre entered the 1970s in a state of disarray, for financial, political, and social anxieties were beginning to curtail the liberal support which had made expansion possible. Many of the regional companies were undergoing crises, and some universities were cutting back on their programs. How long caution will last or how far retrenchment will go remains to be seen, but the growth which characterized the 1960s had definitely slowed by 1971.

~ XII ~

As in Europe, the theatre in England and America has since 1960 been caught up in a struggle between those seeking to maintain tradition and those championing continuous innovation and change. This conflict was especially strong in the late 1960s. If the battle sometimes became bitter, it at least served to broaden the theatre's range and appeal, even though in the process it sometimes alienated former patrons. It also provoked much soul-searching about the nature and function of theatre in a world under stress. The conception of art as detached contemplation or as a pursuit of some superior beauty and order was seriously challenged by those who wished to make of it a reflection of immediate social and political pressures and an instrument for change. Out of this struggle came many significant attempts to redefine the theatre both for our time and for the future.

Reassessment and Revolution: Reshaping the Theatre for the Future

19

Few periods have been subjected to so many conflicting demands as has our own, during which no sphere of human activity has escaped stress. Perhaps the most far-reaching challenges have been posed by the "New Left," whose adherents have largely rejected tradition in favor of immediate relevance. But challenges have not come solely from the New Left. During the past decade persons of varying outlooks have challenged earlier conceptions of theatre and drama and have proposed new ones. Nevertheless, the degree and direction of the revolt have differed widely among would-be reformers. Perhaps the most radical has been the Living Theatre, with its commitment to anarchy, direct confrontation, and communal creation. A quite different direction has been taken by Grotowski in his attempt to

734

create a ritualized, semireligious experience; another by devisers of "happenings," who have sought to break down the barriers between the arts and between performers and spectators; and still another by "environmental theatre," which synthesizes elements drawn from virtually all contemporary innovations. By the 1970s, these varied attempts had gone far toward redefining "theatre."

~~~ I ~~~

As in past eras, so, too, many of the conflicts since 1960 have arisen because new perceptions have posed serious threats to accepted points of view. By far the most forceful challenge has been thrown down by the New Left (so called because, unlike the "old left," it is post-Marxian and post-Freudian in outlook). Although many writers have contributed to the New Left's vision, the most influential have been Marcuse, Laing, and Brown.

Herbert Marcuse (1898–), in such works as *Eros and Civilization* (1955), *One Dimensional Man* (1964), and *An Essay on Liberation* (1969), does not reject Freud and Marx but seeks to update their concepts. He declares that we have passed beyond the era when manual labor defined the proletariat and that today it is the engineers and technicians who are the workers. But mass production and specialized tasks have deprived them of any sense of pride in their work, since no one person makes a product in its entirety. Furthermore, although technology has enormously increased leisure time, it has also led to automated activities (which are stupefying instead of enlarging) to fill up the free hours and to condition workers to accept the status quo. Consequently, the proletariat has become the chief support of middle-class values. It acquiesces to oppression by materialistic forces because it fails to recognize that "totalitarianism need not be terroristic."

Marcuse also sees as no longer valid Freud's notion that the "pleasure principle" should be held in check by the "reality principle" (that is, that the unrestrained pursuit of pleasure is made impossible, and indeed undesirable, by the practical demands posed by daily life). According to Marcuse, Freud's view may have been applicable in the past, but in advanced technological civilizations, such as those of most contemporary Western countries, it is irrational to hold people in "exhausting, stupefying, inhuman slavery" merely because work is considered a good. "Bodies should be instruments of pleasure rather than labor."

Nevertheless, according to Marcuse, the modern proletariat neither accepts the pleasure principle as desirable nor is it prepared to demand that technology's potential be used to correct social injustice. Consequently, some social evils will be overcome only by the abandonment of democratic

736

Reassessment
and
Revolution:
Reshaping
the Theatre
for the
Future

procedures and probably will be effected only through the efforts of students or minority groups. Marcuse argues, however, that true revolution is seldom possible in sated societies. Rather, utopian thought comes to the fore and the demand for its instant fulfillment is acted out through such devices as demonstrations and sit-ins. Thus, Marcuse offers a rationale for radical reform and for the pursuit of the pleasure principle instead of the reality principle.

Ronald David Laing (1927–), in such works as *The Divided Self* (1960), *Interpersonal Perception* (1966), *The Politics of Experience* (1967), and *The Politics of the Family* (1969), has also sought to revise Freudian thought. He is an advocate of "existential psychoanalysis," which is grounded in the belief that sexually based anxieties constitute only one small area of man's problems and that successful therapy must be concerned with a patient's entire social context, his total existence. Laing has gone one step further than most existential analysts, however, in declaring that the behavior we normally label schizophrenic or paranoid is merely a form of role playing in which a "self" is constructed in order to cope with disturbing realities and to protect the "inner self," which usually remains wholly intact beneath the disguise. He goes on to draw an analogy with theatre, which he defines as a situation in which someone pretends to be himself. Such "elusion" permits a person to avoid making decisions, for, if he is pretending to be himself, he can project a reality and be faithful to it without ever actually believing in it.

Laing is as critical of society as he is of traditional psychiatry, which he has called a "degradation ceremonial." In Freudian psychoanalysis, it has usually been taken for granted that society provides a norm to which a patient is to be adjusted—that the sickness is within rather than without. Laing, on the other hand, has argued that parents and teachers, out of motives of love, are almost fated to destroy a child's potential as an individual by forcing him to conform to ideals which they had earlier absorbed from their parents and teachers. "By the time the new human being is fifteen or so, we are left with a being like ourselves, a half-crazed creature more or less adjusted to a mad world. This is normality." Thus, children are made into nonthinking tools of the group (the "we," a "demonic group mysticism") and despisers of all those (the "they") outside the magic circle. As Laing sees it, society needs treatment as badly as does the individual, for a "cure" depends upon some successful alignment between external circumstances and internal response.

Norman O. Brown (1913–), in such works as *Life Against Death* (1959) and *Love's Body* (1966), opposes technocratic society, competitive activity, tradition, and rationality. He also seeks to discredit the idea that "character" means the acceptance of restraints which delay the gratification of desires until some future time. He argues instead that happiness depends upon freedom from restraints. Consequently, he elevates feeling and instinct above reason, and the id above the ego and superego. He blames many contemporary problems on the wedge that has been driven between man's physical and spiritual urges, a division which he likens to being expelled from the Garden of Eden and which can be bridged only by abandoning competitive struggle for harmonious coexistence.

Brown also deplores the tendency to associate pleasure primarily with the sexual organs and sees competition among parts of the body and between the sexes as another source of unhappiness. In his ideal scheme there is little place for the family, monogamy, discrete sexuality, or other social forms, for all put restraints on feeling, impulse, and pleasure. Ultimately, Brown seems to envision a psychological utopia where every wish would be gratified (although he does admit that his view disregards the reality principle). About Brown, Leslie Fiedler has written: "His post-Freudian program for pan-sexual, non-orgasmic love rejects 'full genitality' in favor of a species of indiscriminate bundling, a dream of unlimited subcoital intimacy which Brown calls . . . 'polymorphous perverse.'" It is Brown who has most clearly set forth the rationale upon which those who have rejected the past have erected a new "life style." His position also undergirds the recent trend of theatrical groups to abandon the traditional emphasis upon individual artists—especially playwrights and starring actors —in favor of noncompetitive, collective, often near-anonymous creativity.

In pursuing the reforms envisioned by Marcuse, Laing, and Brown, three paths are open: to adjust society until it fits the needs of man; to adjust the human psyche and thereby ultimately transform society; or, to follow both paths simultaneously. It is the last course which most members of the New Left seem to have taken. In many ways the current situation is reminiscent of the late nineteenth century, when the naturalists were championing social change while members of the art-for-art's-sake school were devoting themselves to intense personal pleasure and fulfillment. One was extroverted, the other introverted; one was selfless, the other hedonistic. The principal differences between those times and our own lie in the current joining of the two strains and in the intensity of the commitment to them.

Not all significant recent views have come from the New Left, although most are interrelated in various ways. For example, in psychology "sensitivity training"—the attempt to break down barriers between human beings by building trust, sympathy, and understanding—has achieved an enormous vogue in recent years among both those with and without strong political views. It seeks to stimulate awareness of others as human beings rather than as mere objects through a number of techniques: by exploratory touching, by intense visual examination, by attentive listening, and by other devices designed to induce recognition of how we and others experience reality. Conversely, by letting oneself be touched and examined, and by revealing one's repressed thoughts, impulses, and hostilities, one becomes vulnerable but at the same time lays the foundation for trust and meaningful relationships. Such techniques have been used not only for therapeutic purposes, but for increasing the sensitivity of "normal" persons in all sorts of daily situations—family, racial, and business. They have been used as well by theatre groups to build a sense of trust and understanding among performers (and therefore a more effective ensemble) and for ridding actors of inhibitions that handicap them.

In a somewhat different vein, social psychologists have depicted all human behavior as role playing or as a kind of game. Erving Goffman in *The Presentation of Self in Everyday Life* (1959) states, "Ordinary social intercourse is itself put together as a scene is put together, by the exchange of dramatically inflated actions, counteractions, and terminating replies." Similarly, Eric Berne, in *Games People Play* (1964), treats social relationships as ritualized encounters. In both views, personality, rather than being fixed, is composed of a series of "roles" which are assumed according to the situation and the participants; during the course of each day, a person plays many roles, one flowing into another in a series of gradual transformations.

These ideas were to be of considerable importance to theatre, for they form the basis of theatre games" and "transformational acting." The "games" theory also implies that most human behavior falls into semi-archetypal patterns, another notion favored by many theatre workers since 1960. Advocates of this view have gained considerable inspiration from the writings of Claude Lévi-Strauss (1908–   ), especially *The Elementary Structures of Kinship* (1949, revised in 1967) and *The Savage Mind* (1962). Lévi-Strauss rejects the long-accepted classification of societies into "advanced" and "primitive," arguing that it is more accurate to describe those which make rapid technological advances as mobile (or "hot") and others as static (or "cold"). He goes on to declare that, while mobile societies may be superior in technology, static societies are often preferable in other respects, such as imbuing its members with a sense of belonging. Lévi-Strauss has also explored human thought and social organisms in various societies through a structural analysis of their myths and has concluded that cultural patterns are based on universal principles of thought. Thus, similar patterns are found in the myths of all cultures. Lévi-Strauss, then, joins others in questioning the superiority of technocracy and suggests that a common bond between all men can be found in myth, ritual, and archetypal patterns. Consequently, he has given new impetus to Jung's conception of the racial unconscious and has spurred on those who would make of the theatre a communion among men.

Another strong influence on contemporary thought has been the writings of Marshall McLuhan (1911–   )—among them *The Gutenberg Galaxy* (1963), *Understanding Media* (1964), and *The Medium is the*

739

*Reassessment
and
Revolution:
Reshaping
the Theatre
for the
Future*

Massage (1967)—with their theories about the relationship of media to thought and perception. According to McLuhan, the invention of movable type made the printed page (with its linear arrangement) the primary medium for communicating ideas. This in turn led to serial thinking in the sciences and sequential organization in drama. McLuhan also suggests that books, dependent as they are on the eye, induce self-centeredness in individuals and chauvinism in nations. With the coming of the electronic age, however, communication reverted once more to multisensory appeals. Consequently, there was a revival of something resembling old tribal ways, since, due to the rapidity of modern communication, the whole world has been converted into a global village. Furthermore, according to McLuhan, electronic media, by conditioning the perceptual apparatus, have enormously reduced the time lapse between thought and action within individuals, for they have become increasingly adept at assimilating both multiple and concurrent stimuli. Therefore, rather than serial thought and orderly sequence, man is now more concerned with heightened sensitivity and simultaneity, with discovery rather than instruction, with roles rather than goals. Thus, McLuhan provides a rationale for downgrading language, for employing multimedia devices and multiple focus, and for attempting to involve the entire sensory apparatus rather than merely the eye and the ear.

The effect of all these new ideas has been to focus attention upon the needs of the present or upon shaping a future quite unlike the past. Even when the past is not wholly rejected it has usually been drastically reinterpreted in light of present preoccupations. Not only have political and social history been reexamined, so have the great plays of the past. One of the most influential figures in this trend has been the Polish critic Jan Kott (1914–   ), especially through *Shakespeare Our Contemporary* (1962), which discusses several of Shakespeare's plays in relation to current interests, problems, anxieties, and motifs, so that they are made to seem immediately relevant rather than works about some distant past. Though Kott did not begin the vogue for "contemporizing" plays, relocating the action in time and place, or rearranging scenes and changing emphases, his book nevertheless seems to have epitomized the spirit that underlay that trend.

It should be clear that most of the ideas so influential since 1960 are reworkings of those familiar from past conflicts: the rejection of materialism, regimentation, and conformity; the need to redefine goals and means; the separation of the old and new into divisions more clear-cut than is perhaps warranted in order to dramatize the issues. They probably differ most from their earlier manifestations in the degree to which they reject the reality principle, elevate the pleasure principle, and eschew competitive goals. Perhaps most of all, they differ in the impact they have made, for not only have they been embraced by large numbers of persons, they have, through mass media, been widely disseminated throughout the world.

Of all those groups dedicated to altering society and the theatre probably the most militant has been the Living Theatre. Furthermore, its considerable influence on the young of America and Europe makes it especially significant in charting the directions of change since 1960.

The Living Theatre was founded in 1946 by Judith Malina (1926–), one of Piscator's students, and Julian Beck (1925–), to whom she was married in 1948. Their original purpose was (in their own words) "that of encouraging the modern poet to write for the theatre, and of bringing interest and stimulation to an art medium which tends to become repetitive in its form rather than creative." Their first production, a bill of one-act plays by Brecht, Lorca, Gertrude Stein, and Paul Goodman, was presented in their own living room. In 1951 they moved to the Cherry Lane Theatre, a small house in Greenwich Village, where they produced plays by Eliot, Picasso, Goodman, Stein, Jarry, and Kenneth Rexroth before the theatre was closed by fire inspectors in 1952. Not until 1954 were they able to find another home, this time a loft. They now decided to rehearse plays until they considered them ready, to charge no admission and merely to take up a collection. Here they performed works by W. H. Auden, Strindberg, Cocteau, Pirandello, Racine, and William Carlos Williams. This theatre too was pronounced unsafe in 1956. They then found a building where they could use two entire floors and set about renovating it. It was not ready until 1959.

Up to this time the Becks had been primarily interested in poetic drama and in nonrealistic productional approaches. They had from time to time tried to include the audience within the play's framework and had often experimented with multiple levels of reality. They also had discovered Artaud and had become deeply interested in his theories.

The turning point in the Becks' work came in 1959, when they presented *The Connection* by Jack Gelber (1932–), a work which pretends that the audience is being allowed to watch a group of real dope addicts who have agreed to be the subject of a documentary film, parts of which are supposedly being shot as the audience watches. While the addicts await a connection so they may get a fix, the time is passed in small talk, in performances of jazz music, in arguments, interferences from the supposed producer of the film, and in other ways designed to create a sense of complete spontaneity. Finally, the connection arrives, the addicts get their fix, and one nearly dies. Gelber seems to be suggesting that we are all waiting for some kind of fix that will release us from our humdrum existence. The overall effect of the production was that of a naturalistic slice of real life. With it the Living Theatre won a number of awards in New York, and later in Paris where in 1961 it was given the Critics Circle Award as the finest company to appear at the Théâtre des Nations that year.

Production by the Living Theatre of Gelber's *The Connection* in 1959.
Directed by Judith Malina, designed by Julian Beck, music by Cecil Payne
and Kenny Drew. (Photo courtesy the Living Theatre.)

Although after 1959 the Living Theatre for a time continued its work with poetic drama, it became increasingly interested in improvisation and chance. In 1960, it presented Jackson MacLow's *The Marrying Maiden,* for which the author chose a text and five hundred verbs relating to action and the delivery of lines. The order of the lines and their combination with the verbs were then determined at each performance by chance. Thus, though the basic ingredients were the same each time, the overall effect varied considerably. In 1963 the company produced Kenneth Brown's *The Brig,* which is set in a U.S. Marine prison and follows the activities of the inmates through a day from the time they arise until they go to bed. There is virtually no story: the men go to the latrine, make beds, take exercises, and are rigidly regimented by sadistic guards. Most of the business was improvised. As in *The Connection,* the effect was documentary, but here it depended in large part upon the repetitive and senseless ritual of a routine day.

Out of elements in *The Connection* and *The Brig* the Living Theatre was to shape its characteristic style. *The Connection* was crucial, for the group turned increasingly thereafter to improvisation. The principal difference between it and later productions is owing to the abandonment of the deceptive framework found in *The Connection* (that is, the attempt to convince the audience that the actors are real dope addicts) in favor of ritualized situations (such as those in *The Brig*), in which the actors do not pretend so much to be other people as to present through themselves archetypal states of being or societal conditions. (Only two of the Living Theatre's productions after 1963 were of scripts originating outside the group, and these are wholly free of Gelber's deceptive conceit.)

742

*Reassessment
and
Revolution:
Reshaping
the Theatre
for the
Future*

In 1963 the troupe's theatre was forcibly closed once more, this time for failure to pay taxes, and the following year it went into voluntary exile. By this time it had proven itself one of the best of off-Broadway companies and was virtually the only one with a strong sense of purpose and dedication. Had it ceased to exist at this point, however, it would have made little lasting impact. It is significant because of what was yet to come. Still, its development, when viewed in retrospect, seems consistent. After beginning with an interest in poetic drama, it went on to champion freedom from esthetic restrictions and then freedom from social and political restraints. The Becks have declared that from the beginning they have been confirmed anarchists but that during the 1950s they acceded to the arguments of those around them that art and politics are inimical. No doubt their many difficulties with the authorities in New York hastened their radicalization. At any rate, after 1964 they moved steadily toward an activist political stance which strongly affected their theatrical work, although admiration for Artaud and Genet also kept alive their interest in ritualized action, nonverbal means, and devices of the theatre of cruelty.

Of the twenty-six persons who went abroad with the company in 1964, sixteen were still with it when it returned four years later. In Europe the group entered upon a nomadic and communal existence and sought to implement the ideal of communal creation. Both their life style and their working methods held a powerful attraction for the young of Europe. They now developed a new repertory, consisting of Genet's *The Maids, Antigone* (based on Sophocles' and Brecht's versions), *Frankenstein* (their own variations on the man-monster created by technology), *Mysteries and Smaller Pieces* (a series of short works, also of their own creation), and *Paradise Now* (a collectively conceived incitement to revolution).

With Genet's work the Living Theatre continued its interest in ritual, but the play did not remain long in its repertory. *Antigone* was conceived as a work about the necessity of civil disobedience and was given a strong political slant. But the productions for which the company became best known were those which it created without the aid of a playwright.

Mysteries and Smaller Pieces is, according to the Becks, concerned with the good and bad qualities in life and the potentials for good and evil in contemporary society. It is organized around affinities and oppositions between the body and the mind and the individual and the group. Mysticism, stemming from Zen Buddhism, and a generalized notion of love among all men, alternates with frenetic, violent, hate-filled scenes. At the beginning of the performance, an actor comes to the front of the stage and for six minutes looks unmovingly at the audience, thus providing it with a kind of mirror or screen onto which it may project its own feelings and responses. Other sections are entitled "Incense and Light Show," "Give and Take Exercise," "Soldier at Attention," "Mass Burial," "The Plague," and "The Dollar Bill." In all these ritualized or archetypal situations, total freedom emerges as the good, conformity as the evil.

"The Plague" section of *Mysteries and Smaller Pieces,* performed by the
Living Theatre at Avignon, 1968. The image of piled bodies relates
to Artaud's statements in "The Theatre and the Plague" in *The Theatre and
Its Double.* (Photo courtesy the Living Theatre.)

Frankenstein provides an anarchistic view of history in which, though
each generation re-creates man, the product is so deformed as to be a
monster. Cruelty and inhumanity are emphasized throughout most of the
scenes. Then, when at last the faults of the past are recognized and rejected,
a new man, free from the old restraints, can be created, now no longer a
monster but a vital being. This basic outline is filled out with almost
endless variations on the central idea. The total performance requires
about three hours.

Perhaps their experiences while traveling in Europe, where they were
welcomed by the young and politically committed but opposed by
established authority, tended increasingly to radicalize the group. At any
rate, *Paradise Now* (first performed in 1968) is primarily a series of
provocations to revolution and anarchy (denunciations of the necessity of
wearing clothing, of having a passport, of having money, and demands that
one be indifferent to economics and to moral strictures). It requires four to
five hours to perform. In the program, the action is broken into twenty-
four scenes arranged into eight triads (a rite, a vision, a contemporary
example) which form an order of ascent, each moving closer to the present
situation. At the end, having reached the present, it is envisioned that the
audience will move into the streets to continue the work begun in the
theatre. It is intensely aggressive throughout. During performances the actors
came into the audience, confronted individuals directly, met objections
with insults and obscenities, spat in their faces, and sought to humiliate or
intimidate them in various ways. Frequently the barriers between performers
and spectators were broken down completely and both roamed stage and

Program design used by the Living Theatre during its tour of the United States in 1968: the silhouette of the "Creature" in *Frankenstein*. Built of human figures on a scaffold, the enormous figure moves, changes color, and flashes lights. (Courtesy the Living Theatre.)

auditorium freely. The overall effect was more that of an inflammatory political meeting than of a theatrical event.

In all of these late works, the Living Theatre performed half-nude or used everyday work clothing instead of theatrical costumes. Similarly, scenery was reduced to scaffolding (often elaborate) and essential properties; there was little speech but much use of vocal and other sound for aural effect; acrobatic and frenetic movement abounded but was varied with occasional moments of quiet spirituality. Nevertheless, the dominant effect was aggressiveness, especially with bourgeois audiences, for whom the actors openly expressed contempt. Despite the company's professed interest in eliciting direct audience participation, they strongly discouraged any response that did not agree with their own point of view.

The Living Theatre reached the peak of its influence in 1968–69, when its production of *Paradise Now* reenforced student agitation and the May uprisings in France. Both the content and the techniques of the Living Theatre's productions seemed geared to the mood of that moment. Wherever it went it stirred up controversy and thereby gained additional fame and notoriety.

Consequently, it was almost as a legend that the Living Theatre returned to the United States in late 1968. It played in various cities in New England, in Brooklyn, San Francisco, and elsewhere, always accompanied by enormous controversy and publicity—in part because of its refusal to differentiate between life style and theatrical performance, for it wished to uphold the idea that theatre and life should not be separated. Nevertheless, 1968–69 seems to have marked a downward turn in the group's fortunes, for not only did the tour lose considerable money, the Living Theatre was accused by several radical groups in America of having lost touch with realities. Furthermore, by this time many of those most concerned with change were beginning to suspect that the aggressively insulting approach used by the Living Theatre had become "counterproductive."

After leaving America in 1969, the troupe played in London and then returned to the Continent. In 1970, it split into three groups. The Becks took their contingent to Brazil, where it began work on *The Legacy of Cain* (which takes up where *Paradise Now* leaves off). This still-uncompleted piece is conceived as a street spectacle composed of about 150 different plays, each to be performed at a different place in the same city and over a period of two to three weeks. It seeks to demonstrate man's enslavement of man and the need for throwing off restraints. When portions of this work were performed in 1971, Brazilian authorities were sufficiently disturbed that fifteen members of the company (including the Becks) were jailed. After being held for several months, they were expelled from the country in late 1971 and returned to New York. They then outlined a number of plans for the future, which remain to be implemented.

Even if the Living Theatre were to disband, its importance during the 1960s cannot be questioned. It exerted an enormous influence in America and even more in Europe, where through continuous touring it became well known almost everywhere and provided an example so unlike that of staid established groups that it became a rallying point for the disaffected. This, in turn, gave added prestige to its attitudes and practices: denigration of any text that cannot be transformed into an argument for anarchy, downgrading language in favor of Artaudian techniques, athleticism, insistence upon confronting and overriding audiences, evangelical tone, and life style. To many, the Living Theatre came to personify commitment and change.

III

An equally potent (and now perhaps even greater influence) has been exerted by Jerzy Grotowski (1933–   ), director of the Polish Laboratory Theatre, which he established in 1959 with the critic Ludwig Flaszen as literary advisor. At first the group worked in the small town of Opole, but in 1965 moved to Wroclaw (Breslau), where it became the Institute for Research into Acting. Thus, Grotowski's is not a performing company in the usual sense but a laboratory devoted to experimentation with theatrical techniques. Its productions (of which there have only been about ten) grow out of the Laboratory's work. The permanent members also act as instructors in the

746

*Reassessment
and
Revolution:
Reshaping
the Theatre
for the
Future*

training program. Of these, the most important is Ryszard Cieslak, now acknowledged to be one of the world's finest actors. Jerzy Gurawski, an architect, is also essential to the group's work, since it is he who designs the space used in each production.

Grotowski did not become widely known until after 1965. During the first few years of its existence the Polish Laboratory Theatre worked in relative isolation, even within Poland, where, though subsidized from the beginning, it was tolerated more than encouraged. Its elevation to the status of an institute came about primarily as a result of its international fame, which the Polish government has used as cultural propaganda (much as East Germany has used the Berliner Ensemble) even while it has continued to be wary of Grotowski's approach. Grotowski was first championed abroad by Eugenio Barba, an Italian who worked with Grotowski during the early years of the Laboratory and who wrote the first book about his work, *In Search of the Lost Theatre* (1965). In 1964 Barba founded his own troupe, the Odin Teatret, modeled on Grotowski's. At first it performed in Norway but in 1966 was invited to settle in a municipally owned and subsidized theatre in Holstebro, Denmark, where it has built an enviable reputation while acknowledging its indebtedness to its Polish counterpart. Barba has continued to champion and publicize Grotowski, and in 1969 organized an international seminar for actors and directors, to which Grotowski came as observer and commentator.

Around 1965 Grotowski began to be invited abroad. In 1966 his production of *The Constant Prince* was seen at the Théâtre des Nations in Paris, and in the same year he and Cieslak spent some time working with members of the Royal Shakespeare Company. (Peter Brook has long been one of Grotowski's most ardent admirers.) Such foreign tributes made Grotowski's position in Poland much easier and for the first time Polish magazines began to print accounts of his work. Grotowski's reputation was further enhanced by the publication in 1968 of a collection of essays by and about him, *Towards a Poor Theatre,* and by the subsequent appearances of the Polish Laboratory Theatre in London, New York, and elsewhere. By 1970, Grotowski had attained a position of preeminence in acting theory not unlike that of Stanislavsky. There were the same kinds of debates over the elements of his "method" and the emphasis to be given each. Like Stanislavsky, Grotowski vainly denied that his was a method and denounced those who wished to treat his approach as fixed and rigid. But, as usual, such warnings had little effect.

As in the case of Stanislavsky, it is important to remember that Grotowski did not arrive at his ideas all at once and that his approach is still developing. He began his career in a rather conventional company but came to believe that the theatre can survive only if it ceases competing with films and television and concentrates on that which makes it unique—the direct interaction between actor and spectator, a "collective introspection." Consequently, two central concepts have dominated Grotowski's work: the notion of the theatre as a ritualistic and communal experience, and the belief that theatre should be reduced to its essential elements.

Grotowski views the theatre as a secular rite, the modern equivalent of the primitive tribal ceremony which united a community. Of theatre in its earliest form, Grotowski has stated that it "liberated the spiritual energy of the congregation or tribe by incorporating myth and profaning or rather transcending it. The spectator thus had a renewed awareness of his personal truth in the truth of the myth, and through fright and a sense of the sacred he came to catharsis." This seems to sum up Grotowski's own aims as well, although he recognizes that today the community of belief which underlay ancient ritual is missing. Therefore, to replace it he seeks a nonreligious equivalent in archetypal human experiences, actions, and images—things deeply imbedded in the human psyche quite independent of religion or faith. Consequently, in working with a text, he first searches out its archetypes. "Ordinarily there are several archetypes in a text. They branch out and intermingle. One is chosen as the pivot of a play." Thus far all of his productions have been based on familiar material (such as the Bible) or well-known Polish plays. But he reshapes the original texts to suit his needs. "We eliminate those parts of the text which have no importance to us, those parts with which we can neither agree nor disagree." Once a new text is refashioned from the old, the actors treat it with complete respect.

The ultimate aim, however, is not so much to interpret a text as "to confront ourselves" in a kind of psychospiritual experience during which both performers and audience come to deeper intuitions. What Grotowski seeks is not an introverted, self-indulgent response, but a communion which brings order and meaning to existence. According to Grotowski, "What is achieved is a total acceptance of one human being by another." Like the tribal theatre, it aims at purification. Thus, it is religiomystical and psychological in its orientation.

But if Grotowski's aims resemble Artaud's, his means differ considerably. Whereas Artaud emphasized spectacle and technological devices, Grotowski seeks to eliminate everything not entirely essential. To him, "total theatre" borrows too much from films and television and fails to exploit the uniqueness of the theatre. He seeks to replace the "rich theatre" with the "poor theatre": "Ours then is a *via negativa*—not a collection of skills but an eradication of blocks."

This process of elimination extends to all aspects of production. First, the traditional proscenium-arch theatre is abandoned in favor of an undivided, completely flexible space which can be rearranged to create "the proper spectator-actor relationship for each type of show." Second, elaborate lighting effects are avoided in favor of fixed sources, although there may still be bright and dark areas, candlelight or glaring floodlights according to the demand of the particular production. Usually, the spectators as well as the actors are lighted. Third, makeup is forbidden and the

748

*Reassessment
and
Revolution:
Reshaping
the Theatre
for the
Future*

actor must transform himself as needed through posture, movement, facial expression, or improvisation with whatever garments he may be wearing. Fourth, costume is restricted to the entirely functional and no actor is permitted to change dress in order to indicate a change of role or in a character's state; he may use only what he wears when the performance begins or what he can fashion from what he finds on himself or on the stage. Fifth, properties are treated as extensions of the actors' movements and gestures; all are chosen for their functionalism and for their multiple potentialities. Sixth, scenery in the traditional sense does not appear. A few functional objects—such as wheelbarrows, pipes, and platforms—may be used and rearranged in different patterns but seldom are they treated representationally. Seventh, all music must be produced by the actors. Occasionally a musical instrument is introduced, but more typically "music" is created by vocal sound or the rhythmic clash of objects.

Thus, the actor is thrown back on his own resources, for external means have been reduced to a minimum. And it is the actor who is at the heart of Grotowski's theatre, since in his search to answer the question, "What is theatre?" he came to the conclusion that its essence resides in "the actor-spectator relationship of perceptual, direct, 'live' communion." Consequently, his major energies have been devoted to exploring the actor's potential. In his approach to actor training, Grotowski admits his indebtedness to many influences, among them Stanislavsky, Meyerhold, Vakhtangov, Dullin, Delsarte, Jung, Lévi-Strauss, Yoga, Kathakali, and others. But he has transformed most of his borrowings and made them his own.

Physical training plays a large role in his program. Originally he emphasized yoga, but he later came to believe that yoga's aims (to achieve negation through total concentration) are foreign to acting. Nevertheless, he has retained many of the exercises. But he insists that physical exercises are useless unless they extend into the psychological realm so that, through a process of associations, inner impulses are released and pursued. The goal is the elimination of all blocks, both physical and psychic, so that in performance the actor may give himself totally and not stop short of complete truth at the crucial moment. Grotowski insists, however, that there must be nothing exhibitionistic or narcissistic in the actor's "giving" of himself but that it must be wholly honest and unselfconscious. It is here that Grotowski remains most obscure and most open to those charges of mysticism often leveled at him.

Grotowski also declares that the magic of the theatre consists in the actor doing what is normally considered impossible. Therefore, his actors are urged to "surpass" themselves, and to do so they train almost beyond the limits of endurance so they may transform their bodies, faces, and actions in ways demanded by performance and without the external aids of makeup and costume. Similarly, the voice is stretched so that it may be used as an instrument far exceeding the needs of speech. In addition to developing strengths, actors are also trained to utilize limitations. For example, an old man might be able to play Romeo if he translates the situation into the right context—an old man recalling his youth. Similarly, rather than seeking to disguise perspiration, the actor should find a way of making it part of the situation. In their training, actors are asked to exchange roles, to metamorphose one character into another, to play the same role on different levels of reality or in different styles. The ultimate aim is absolute physical control and the development of capabilities that exceed those of the audience so far that a sense of wonder is aroused in spectators.

In performance, the actor seeks, through actions, speech, sound, and gestures, to awaken associations in the audience's unconscious. Sometimes archetypes are evoked so they may be contradicted and prejudices confronted. In this process, everything has been carefully planned and perfected. Grotowski considers improvisation during performance an evasion. "Creativity in theatre does not exist if there is no score, a line of fixed elements. . . . That's why a search for discipline and structure is as inevitable as a search for spontaneity. Searching for spontaneity without order always leads to chaos, a lost confession because an inarticulate voice cannot confess." Thus, each moment in a production must be executed with absolute precision and in accordance with a fixed plan.

Given the demands made upon the actor, it is not surprising that it takes years for a performer to master Grotowski's approach. Nor is it surprising that Grotowski has expressed his contempt for those who think they can assimilate his approach almost overnight, even during rehearsals for a single production. His is a long process fraught with considerable danger of psychological trauma and physical damage. It is not a regimen to be undertaken lightly.

The other essential ingredient in Grotowski's theatre is the audience, and perhaps no other feature of his approach has created more puzzlement than his attempt to control the audience and its participation. Grotowski's own theatre in Wroclaw seats from forty to one hundred and on tour the number of spectators are restricted to that for which each production was originally designed.

Grotowski does not consider those who attend his theatre as audiences in the traditional sense but rather as privileged participants in a ritual. In the beginning, he attempted to involve the spectator rather directly but soon came to believe that he was forcing him to play a role for which he was not equipped. About such attempts he has said: "Direct audience participation has become a new myth, a miraculous solution. . . . I have never come across direct participation. The Theatre Lab seeks a spectator-witness, but the spectator's testimony is only possible if the actor achieves an authentic act." He argues that the kind of audience confrontation sought by such groups as the Living Theatre does not reduce but rather increases psychic distance because it merely makes the audience self-conscious. "But if the spectators play the role of spectators and that role

Axiometric view of Grotowski's arrangement of the audience-performer
relationship for the production of Slowacki's *Kordian* in 1962,
Dark figures are actors, the others are audience members.
(Courtesy *World Theatre.*)

has a function within the production, the psychic curtain vanishes." Thus, for each production Grotowski seeks to place the audience in the proper relationship to the action so that it may play its role unselfconsciously.

Grotowski's work can probably be understood better by considering a few of his productions. Those works done for public performances include adaptations of Byron's *Cain,* Kalidasa's *Shakuntala,* Mickiewicz's *Forefather's Eve,* Slowacki's *Kordian,* Wyspiański's *Akropolis,* Shakespeare's *Hamlet,* Marlowe's *Doctor Faustus,* Calderon's *The Constant Prince,* and an original work, *Apocalypsis cum Figuris* (with spoken passages drawn from the Bible, Dostoevsky, Eliot, and Simone Weil).

In *Doctor Faustus* Marlowe's text is reworked so that the audience members become guests who have been invited by Faustus to a banquet. It is the night on which Faustus's soul is to be claimed by the Devil and Faustus uses the occasion to analyze and explain what has happened to him. The spectators are seated at two long tables (on which much of the action takes place) and Faustus at a third. Thus, the audience is cast as friendly listeners for whom scenes are conjured up as Faustus tells his story. The image of the Last Supper runs throughout, as does the notion of Faustus as a martyr who accepts damnation as the price of seeking knowledge.

Akropolis is one of the Laboratory's best-known productions. The action of Wyspiański's original text is set in the Royal Palace of Cracow (which for Poland is the equivalent of the Greek Acropolis) on the night of the Feast of the Resurrection. Figures from the tapestries on the walls

come to life and enact what amounts to a history of Europe, at the end of
which the resurrected Christ leads them all in a procession which sets out
to liberate Europe from its past errors. Grotowski saw *Akropolis* as treating
the "cemetery of our civilization," and, seeking a contemporary equivalent,
settled on the extermination camp at Auschwitz. Therefore, the actors are
treated as inmates of the camp and during the play build an elaborate
system of pipes—which represent the ovens in which prisoners are to be
cremated. Their work is interrupted from time to time by the fantasies of
tortured souls dreaming in the midst of their agony. These dreamlike
sequences are Grotowski's version of the original tapestry figures, now
considerably distorted. For example, in the episode between Paris and
Helen, both participants are male and this homosexual love scene is played
to the snickers of the voyeur-inmates. Similarly, at the end of the play, the
Savior is a headless corpse and the march is into the ovens, which have now
been completed. After the procession disappears, a voice declares: "They
are gone and the smoke rises in spirals." The actors wore frayed and torn
burlap bags, heavy shoes, and berets; this uniform made both men and
women lose their sexual identity as they moved in and out of the dream
sequences. The action was set to the rhythms of the work. Since the inmates
were treated as though already spirits or ghosts, they ignored the audience
completely. In *Akropolis,* the spectator is less directly involved and the
original text more severely altered than in any other of Grotowski's productions.

    The Constant Prince is based on Calderon's play about a nobleman
so faithful to the Christian ideal that he transcends bodily suffering and
achieves spiritual fulfillment by overcoming all the temptations and
tortures of temporality, enduring and accepting his fate as an offering made

751

*Reassessment
and
Revolution:
Reshaping
the Theatre
for the
Future*

Scene from Grotowski's production of *The Constant Prince*—
the Pietà—in which the Prince, played by Cieslak,
is embraced by one of his persecutors.

752

*Reassessment
and
Revolution:
Reshaping
the Theatre
for the
Future*

to God. Grotowski abandoned the Christian framework and concentrated on a hero who suffers and ultimately acquiesces to a death which is a direct result of the evil in men. In opening himself up to all the destructive acts of others, he achieves detachment and accepts evil and annihilation. After this central figure has died, others are then tortured in his name. The Prince was played by Cieslak, who underwent various forms of attack and torture from the other performers; but as he was gradually destroyed he reached ever-increasing peaks of spiritual ecstacy. The performance demanded such physical endurance and psychical engagement that it was generally considered one of the great performances of our time. Grotowski thought the level of psychophysical energy demanded by the production to be so great that it would make an audience uncomfortable. Therefore, he and Gurawski designed a physical arrangement that cast the audience in the role of voyeurs watching a prohibited spectacle. Some critics likened it to a bullring or boxing ring, but Grotowski has called it an operating room for "psychic surgery." Like much of Grotowski's work, *The Constant Prince* seems to suggest that liberation is to be reached only through humiliation of the spirit and torture of the body (or even through death itself). Thus, his outlook seems essentially Christian but without any belief in immortality.

Grotowski's work has been appraised variously. Some consider it the most significant contribution of the age or as a synthesis which will prove the salvation of the contemporary stage; others see it as pseudomystical, ascetic, pretentious, elitist, and as indifferent to socioeconomic problems. All, however, acknowledge the technical excellence of Grotowski's actors and the perfection of his ensemble. Although it seems doubtful that other groups will be able to duplicate his working conditions, Grotowski's ideas and practices are seminal and have stimulated theatre workers almost everywhere.

～ IV ～

Another group which has played a significant role since 1960 is the Open Theatre, an organization that resembles Grotowski's in some ways but which differs on many crucial points. The Open Theatre was founded in New York in 1963 by Peter Feldman and Joseph Chaikin, the latter previously an actor with the Living Theatre. With a membership composed of actors, choreographers, musicians, and playwrights, the Open Theatre has been more nearly a workshop than a producing theatre, for it has shown the results of its efforts only at irregular intervals.

Somewhat like Grotowski, Chaikin began the Open Theatre out of dissatisfaction with established modes. He was especially unhappy with the

753

*Reassessment
and
Revolution:
Reshaping
the Theatre
for the
Future*

Stanislavsky method as it was then being taught in New York and wished to explore other possibilities in movement, speech, pantomime, and improvisation. He sought also to build an ensemble "without the pressures of money, real estate, and other commercial considerations which usurp creative energy." Thus, he withdrew from the demands of immediate production so that he might experiment at leisure.

Also like Grotowski, Chaikin wished to explore and capitalize on those qualities which are peculiar to the theatre as a medium. He has said that "the only thing that makes the theatre different from movies and TV is this encounter with mortality—your own and everyone else's. . . . The sense of being alive now in this room, in this place. . . . I think one of my reasons for rejecting naturalism is because it corresponds to social order, certain kinds of emphasis, and certain kinds of repression. . . . Naturalism corresponds to the programmed responses of our daily life. . . . To accept naturalism is to collaborate, to accept society's limits."

It is at this point that Chaikin and Grotowski begin to part ways, for Chaikin is attuned to the New Left (although in his productions this commitment is not always readily apparent) and most of his work constitutes an indirect comment on contemporary political and social problems. Furthermore, the primary basis for the Open Theatre's work can be found in "games" and "role playing" theories of human behavior, especially as adapted to the theatre by Viola Spolin and Paul Sills. Thus, it is concerned with "transformations"—that is, a reality which is constantly shifting and in which the same person takes on and discards roles as demanded by the changing context. As Feldman has put it: "What may change are character and/or situation and/or time and/or objectives, etc. Whatever realities are established at the beginning are destroyed after a few minutes and replaced by others. Then these are in turn destroyed and replaced. These changes occur swiftly and almost without transition, until the audience's dependence upon any fixed reality is called into question." He adds: "The transformation, besides questioning our notion of reality in a very graphic way, also raises certain questions about the nature of identity and the finitude of character. At the Open Theatre we tend to define character by what a person does that we can see, not by what society or his childhood experiences have produced in him."

Working out of this "transformational reality," the Open Theatre has adopted a number of techniques that resemble those used by Grotowski, but which owe nothing to him. Like the Polish Laboratory Theatre, the Open Theatre is "poor" in the sense that it abandons everything not absolutely essential. The actors wear rehearsal or everyday garments which remain unchanged throughout a performance. They use no makeup and often no properties. Scenery is usually nonexistent and lighting simple. The emphasis is almost entirely on the actor, who moves easily from one role to another in a series of transformations. Thus, a small troupe can perform a complex work with many characters but without any of the traditional aids to

754

*Reassessment
and
Revolution:
Reshaping
the Theatre
for the
Future*

assist in changes of role. Unlike the Polish Laboratory Theatre, the Open Theatre has made no attempt to control the audience and it has worked primarily with new texts which it has helped to evolve, which leave considerable leeway for improvisation during performance, and which have immediate social or political relevance.

The relationship between the Open Theatre and its playwrights is close. Typically a writer supplies an outline, scenes, situations, or motifs; working from this base, the actors begin an exploratory process, through improvisation, discussion, metaphorical associations, and other techniques, during which they seek to discover the multiple possibilities imbedded in the playwright's conception. Gradually movement, dialogue, and sound effects emerge, from among which the dramatist selects those which seem to him most effective. Many of the experiments have come to nothing, but others have resulted in fully developed texts, although all retain portions to be improvised during performance.

The Open Theatre's work can probably be seen at its best in Jean-Claude Van Itallie's *The Serpent* (1969), which was worked out in collaboration with the company. When the audience enters, the actors are warming up in all parts of the theatre and on stage and continue to do so until time for the performance to begin. Then comes a procession, which is accompanied by a kind of percussion music beaten out rhythmically by the actors on their own bodies. Occasionally they freeze and prefigure things that will come later in the play. This procession is transformed into an autopsy, followed by a pantomime intended to recall the assassinations of John F. Kennedy and Martin Luther King, Jr. Next the scene becomes the Garden of Eden, and the temptation, fall, and expulsion are enacted. This is followed by a series of statements, many of them highly personal, others philosophic. Then comes the Cain and Abel story, followed by "Blind Man's Hell," during which the actors grope their way about the stage and continue to do so through a second set of statements. Next comes a reading of a lengthy passage from Genesis (enumerating the various generations who followed Adam) accompanied by pantomimes of meetings, matings, births, child bearing, and so on. Eventually all grow old and line up across the front of the stage. The play ends with this direction: "The actors move about freely on the stage. Each is overtaken by a slow kind of dying, not so much a physical one as an 'emptying out,' a living death which soon slows them to a complete stop. Each actor has a final small physical tremor. Then, as if ghosts, the actors begin to sing a sentimental popular song from twenty or thirty years ago. No longer as ghosts but as themselves they continue singing the song as they leave the theatre, walking out through the audience."

In this production there was no scenery or properties; the actors established through pantomime whatever was needed. All roles were played by the same group of actors, none of whom ever left the stage. Chaikin has

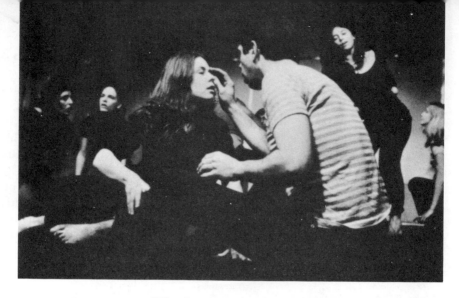

"The Creation of Eve" in the Open Theatre's production of Jean-Claude van Itallie's *The Serpent*. (Photo by Richard Bellak.)

said: "The Method Actor gets tied up in the character's psychological knots, but in the new theatre he keeps up his awareness that he's an actor on a stage. Instead of portraying an individual, he's a universal man." In keeping with these ideas, the actors in *The Serpent* did not pretend to be characters so much as to present the essence of roles without ever losing their own identities. Primary emphasis was placed on the significant experiences of mankind rather than on the personal stories of individuals.

Ultimately *The Serpent* is a parable which uses biblical material and well-known recent events to suggest lessons for the present. The Serpent is that impulse within man that makes him violate the limits set on him, whereas God is an idea man has invented in order to set limits on himself. Thus, God equals conformity, the Serpent freedom. The play as a whole suggests that, since the rules established by contemporary society have led to so much violence, we need to break those limits and make new choices which will lead us out of the morass.

The same basic approach is followed in another of the Open Theatre's recent productions, *Terminal* (1969–70), codirected by Chaikin and Roberta Sklar and written by Susan Yankowitz. *Terminal* is composed of about two dozen scenes, all of which relate in some way to death or the death-in-life to which most of us have consented. The recurrent motif is: "The judgment of your life is your life." Special emphasis is placed on those moments when it might have been possible to make different choices and to have escaped death-in-life. It seeks to remind the spectator not only of his mortality but of the necessity of living life while he has it and of making those choices which will keep life from becoming merely another form of death. In late 1970 the Open Theatre was reconstituted as a collective with

Scene from the Open Theatre's production of *Terminal,*
titled "The Dying Imagine Their Judgment." (Photo courtesy Michael Kirby.)

twelve members. It reworked *Terminal* and since then has performed
primarily for university and prison audiences—those it considers most attuned to its ideas and techniques.

As should be evident, the Open Theatre reflects recent ideas, both in
its conception of reality and in its concern for political and social problems.
In techniques it has certain affinities with the Polish Laboratory Theatre
and in outlook with the Living Theatre. Yet it has avoided the kind of
direct confrontation with audiences which the Living Theatre has championed, and in general its texts have been superior to those performed by
that group. There is also a note of optimism in the Open Theatre's work
that is missing from that of most contemporary groups. This is perhaps
attributable to the company's conception of reality as transformational, for
this means that, since reality is constantly shifting, it may be improved if
men will make the right choices. The Open Theatre has also contributed
significantly to the ideal of communal creation (and a consequent deem-
phasis upon virtuoso artists). Through its appearances both in America and
Europe (where it is much admired), it has exerted considerable influence
on new directions in theatrical production.

A number of playwrights have been associated with the Open Theatre,
but the most prominent are Van Itallie and Terry. Both have worked
closely with the group (as well as outside it). In addition to *The Serpent,*

Jean-Claude Van Itallie (1936–) is best known for a group of short plays performed in 1966 under the collective title *America, Hurrah!* Two of the plays, *Interview* (performed earlier as *Pavane*) and *TV*, utilize transformational techniques. In *Interview*, "the actors walk straight forward toward the audience and then walk backwards to the rear of the stage. Each time they approach the audience, they do so as a different character." In *TV*, "after each television segment, the People involved in it will freeze where they are until it is time for them to become another character." Both employ a series of vignettes to comment on the conformity of contemporary life. The best known of the three plays, *Motel*—"A Masque for Three Dolls"—is a commentary on the mindlessness of American civilization as embodied in a motel and its insensitive manager with her enumeration of its creature comforts. Like a recorded message, her paean of praise drones on as the other characters become increasingly frantic, write obscene words on the wall, tear things apart, and eventually dismember the manager herself. The performers are encased in large puppet forms to enhance the idea that the materialist ideal turns men into robots, while the suggestion that civilization is courting death can be seen in the motel manager's description of plans for an underground-shelter motel. Most of Van Itallie's plays (among them *War, I'm Really Here, The Hunter,* and *The Bird*) are short, and all develop similar themes about the horrors of modern life.

Megan Terry (1932–) has written plays with similar qualities. Her first work, *Ex-Miss Copper Queen on a Set of Pills* (1965), not produced by the Open Theatre, is rather conventionally structured. It shows a former beauty queen, now turned prostitute and dope addict, seeking to make human contact in the city's jungle. Its message seems to be that competitiveness and selfishness lead to such dilemmas as hers and that only through openness and love can they be avoided. In her next play, *Keep Tightly Closed in a Cool Dry Place* (1965), Miss Terry adopted transformational techniques. In it, three actors play out the main story (about a man who has had his wife murdered and who eventually accepts his guilt) as well as several parallel ones about historical figures, as time, place, and identity metamorphose freely and often.

Miss Terry's best-known play is *Viet Rock* (1966). Using a company of about fifteen, it shows the induction of a squad of soldiers and their subsequent experiences in Vietnam as a framework for a series of transformations dramatizing the horrors of war. Drawing heavily on stereotypes and elements of popular culture, it employs music, dance, and rhythmical sound. At the end, all of the characters are blown up. Then, after a long pause, all come to life and go into the audience, where they reach out to others in the wonder of being alive. It pursues many of the same themes developed in *Terminal* but here specifically directed against the war in Vietnam.

Megen Terry's *Viet Rock,* as produced at Yale University.
(Photo courtesy Yale Drama School.)

In *Approaching Simone* (1970), which she evolved with students at Boston University, Miss Terry traces the life and thought of the French philosopher and mystic Simone Weil from 1914 to 1943. Here the central figure runs throughout, while transformational techniques are used to show the life around her. The agitational tone, evident in Miss Terry's earlier work, is here muted. These and other works have proven her one of the most able writers to have adopted the transformational approach.

Techniques like those used by the Open Theatre have become very popular and have been mingled with others derived from various sources. One closely related approach is through "theatre games," which, as outlined by Viola Spolin in *Improvisation in the Theatre* (1963) and practiced by her son Paul Sills, has exerted considerable influence on the Open Theatre's work. In her book, Miss Spolin describes a series of improvised games designed to induce greater freedom and spontaneity in the actor by leading him to become thoroughly familiar with the theatrical space, with his fellow actors, and with himself. Her exercises require close attention to the movements, moods, and motivations of others and continuous transformation of situations, responses, and roles. They seek also to create mutual understanding and trust among actors and thereby to encourage ensemble work. As Sills has said: "Playing is communion. . . . Play is also mutual. You can't play alone." Furthermore, for Sills games and improvisations are ways of knowing and communicating. He has declared that meaning is not cognitive. "It's not known in the head. It's known all through you. It's body knowledge."

Most of Sills's work has been done in Chicago. There in 1956 he founded Compass, the first professional improvisational theatre in America.

In 1959, with Bernard Sahlins and Howard Alk, Sills formed Second City, a company soon widely known for its topical sketches and its versatile performers, among them Mike Nichols, Elaine May, Barbara Harris, and Shelley Berman. Sills ultimately became dissatisfied with Second City because of its limitations: "All these things are failures in terms of real organic theatre." Consequently, he developed Story Theatre, which in 1970, upon its first appearance in New York, was hailed by many critics as the theatrical breakthrough they had long awaited.

This first program was composed of ten stories, most of them taken from fairytales by the brothers Grimm. Using third-person narrative, a limited amount of dialogue and improvisation, and a great deal of mime, eight performers enacted the stories on a bare stage, although there were numerous slide and light projections on the rear wall and folk-rock musical accompaniment. In 1971 Sills added to his repertory Arnold Weinstein's adaptation of Ovid's *Metamorphoses*. Although both productions used the same basic techniques, critics were less enthusiastic about the second and some voiced doubts about the potential of Story Theatre to project complex ideas and characterizations. Even if it is not yet fully developed, Sills's approach nonetheless suggests means whereby almost any literary work might be brought to the stage. Furthermore, his practice and Miss Spolin's book have made an enormous impact on theatrical training throughout America, for no one has done more to popularize the use of theatre games and improvisation.

Despite the differences among them, the techniques utilized by Sills, the Open Theatre, and Grotowski are now often intermingled by other groups. An especially skillful synthesis (although it is more than that) can be seen in *Alice in Wonderland* as staged in 1970 by André Gregory and the Manhattan Project (an outgrowth of work done at New York University). The text followed Carroll's rather faithfully, but it was given strong contemporary overtones through imaginative improvisations and stage business. The performers created all essential properties out of their own bodies: an actor's back became a table, four actors formed a mushroom, and so on. Critics pronounced it one of the most brilliant productions of the season. Though seldom so well done as Gregory's, similar work is becoming increasingly popular throughout America, especially among young companies and student groups.

The confrontation between Orestes and Clytemnestra after the killing of Aegisthus in an improvisationally derived student production of Aeschylus' *The Oresteia,* University of Kansas Experimental Theatre, 1971. Directed by Peter Clough, setting by Harry Silverglat. (Photo courtesy Michael Pandzik.)

Both the Polish Laboratory Theatre and Open Theatre are antimaterialistic in outlook and consequently they deemphasize complex means, especially those involving advanced technology. At the same time, however, other groups have been moving in a contrary direction by exploiting such electronic means as motion pictures, recorded and amplified sound, complex lighting effects, and similar devices. These practices are not new, for they were pioneered by the futurists, dadaists, surrealists, and the Bauhaus, by Meyerhold, Eisenstein, Piscator, Brecht, Burian, and others. During the 1950s, the earlier techniques were revived and considerably extended to create what have come to be called multimedia productions.

The reasons behind the increased acceptance of multimedia devices are several. First, wartime and space research led to significant advances in electronics and consequently opened up many new possibilities in theatrical practice. Second, escalating costs of production created a demand for means less expensive than full-stage, three-dimensional settings. Third, and most important, the expectations and perceptual capabilities of audiences changed. Prior to World War II, skeletal settings were associated almost entirely with highly stylized drama, while illusionism remained the norm (even if less detailed than in the late nineteenth century). In the postwar period, however, as playwrights such as Brecht came to the fore, audiences were conditioned to accept suggestion in the place of representation. The rapid development of television also played a key role, for, as McLuhan has argued, it helped to speed up the rate at which stimuli are absorbed. In fact, the whole tempo of life accelerated, and simultaneous claims for attention became ever more common, making multiple focus a familiar part of daily life. Furthermore, as response was speeded, audiences grew impatient with anything (especially pauses to shift scenery) that slowed the pace of performance.

For these and other reasons, traditional scenery was gradually abandoned. Appia's and Craig's insistence upon three-dimensionality now came for postwar designers to seem as outmoded as nineteenth-century painted settings had to those earlier reformers. Consequently, settings began to consist of sound and light more than of flats, and three-dimensionality to be restricted to furniture, properties, and a few set pieces. Playwrights began to take it for granted that time and place can be transformed instantaneously and that multiplicity of place is no barrier to production. Thus, the transformationalism associated by the Open Theatre with role and situation came to be applied by others to setting.

Although it is usual to say that multimedia productions involve some combination of stereophonic sound, elaborate lighting effects, motion pictures, projected still images, dance, and music (and possibly other media), in actuality the distinguishing element for most commentators is the liberal use of slides or motion pictures.

In the development and popularization of multimedia, a key role has been played by the Czech designer Josef Svoboda (1920–   ). After graduating from the School of Applied Arts in Prague, Svoboda served from 1945 to 1948 as designer at the Fifth of May Opera House before moving to the Prague National Theatre, where since 1950 he has been head designer. Although from the beginning Svoboda has been a fine artist, he is known for his work since 1956, for until that time the Czech theatre was subordinated to the Russian demand for socialist realism. Following the denunciation of Stalin in 1956, however, the Czech theatre rapidly became one of the most advanced in the world.

Much of Svoboda's work is an extension of earlier experiments by Burian and Kouril. It has also been deeply indebted to the Prague Institute of Scenography, founded in 1957 and headed by Kouril. The institute has four divisions, each devoted to a different range of problems: theory and history, theatrical space, sound and light, and stage means. Its permanent staff is involved in continuing experiments with new materials, equipment, and techniques, the results of which have given Czechoslovakia world preeminence in theatre technology.

The crucial change in Svoboda's career came in 1958, when in collaboration with the director Alfred Radok he began work on two projects: Polyekran and Laterna Magika. Polyekran ("Multiple Screen") used filmed images projected on seven screens of varying sizes and hung at varying distances from the audience. Rather than deemphasizing the screens (as in movie theatres), it called attention to them. On these screens were projected black-and-white and color images (some still, others moving at different rates, some showing close-ups and others distant views). According to its creators, Polyekran aimed to overcome the "visual paralysis" of traditional theatre by giving the spectator a choice of things to watch. Performances were also accompanied by stereophonic sound. The first version (that shown at the Brussels World's Fair in 1958) centered around the Prague Spring Music Festival. The techniques of Polyekran were later extended in the Diapolyekran, which was featured at Expo 67 in Montreal. Both, however, are more nearly related to film than to theatre.

The Laterna Magika was also begun in 1958. Here live actors were combined with still and moving projections. Since it was intended as an exploration of new techniques, the episodes were short and varied. For example, one segment featured an excerpt from opera, while another showed a skater on film and then the same skater, now in person, seeming to come out of the screen and onto the stage. There were eight mobile screens which could move in any direction, and with which treadmills and trapdoors were coordinated so that filmed and live action might interact and flow into each other. Laterna Magika was also first seen at the Brussels

Svoboda's setting for Shakespeare's *Romeo and Juliet* at the Prague
National Theatre, directed by Otomar Krejca, in 1963.
(Photo copyrighted by Jaromír Svoboda.)

World's Fair in 1958 and since then has been exploited primarily for
propaganda purposes. It would be many years before its theatrical possibilities were followed up, perhaps because in its original form the technical
apparatus enslaved the live actor (that is, since the filmed portions were
inflexible, the actor had to be adapted to them).

In 1959 Svoboda began to carry over certain features of these experiments into his stage work. For Josef Topol's *Their Day,* his first attempt
to adapt the new techniques to the theatre, Svoboda mounted nine screens
on overhead tracks and coordinated them with movable stage wagons,
which carried plastic elements. Most scenes were accompanied only by
still projections (some showing objects close-up, some at a distance, but all
designed to suggest place, associations, or mood), but occasionally moving
pictures were introduced.

Since that time Svoboda has championed a completely flexible stage.
"I want to have a kinetic scene, where movement becomes a law, a stage
which can change form and structure in the course of a play depending on
the needs and naturally in accordance with the contents of the play." Thus,
in addition to working with projected images, he has also experimented
with movable three-dimensional elements. He found much traditional stage
machinery, especially the revolving stage, too dictatorial and replaced it
with moving treadmills, multiple movable platforms, and screens and panels
that could be shifted in any direction. All of these devices played a part in
one of his most ambitious settings—for *Romeo and Juliet* (1963) as

Adaptation of Gorky's novel *The Last Ones* at the Prague National Theatre in 1966. Designed by Svoboda, directed by Alfred Radok. (Photo copyrighted by Jaromír Svoboda.)

directed by Otomar Krejca. Here the platforms, steps, and architectural units moved vertically, horizontally, and laterally to create a dynamic, kinetic place which altered in size, shape, and general appearance according to the needs of the action.

Throughout the 1960s Svoboda continued his experiments. For example, he worked with extremely diverse projection surfaces: lengths of rope hung side by side, fishnet, wire, plastic, and other materials. In 1966, he further adapted the principle of the Laterna Magika to stage use for an adaptation of Gorky's novel *The Last Ones,* staged by Alfred Radok, the director of Laterna Magika. Gorky's text depicts the deterioration of a family as seen against the background of a disintegrating society. In the production, three live scenes were placed on stage simultaneously but at varying depths, while still other scenes were shown on the screens, thus creating a collage of family life and of the society which surrounds it. In 1969, he adapted the Polyekran for stage use in an opera, *The Soldiers.* The multiple screens were used to show scenes of war from Roman times to the present (often scenes from widely separated eras simultaneously) while live scenes were performed on stage. At the end, all the screens disappeared and a terrifying new war machine advanced toward the audience amidst flashing lights and ear-splitting noise.

Although Svoboda is best known for his multimedia productions, these constitute only a small percentage of his work. But his other designs have also been characterized by experimentation, though of a different sort. For example, he has introduced many nontraditional materials into his settings.

Svoboda's setting for *The Insect Comedy* by Čapek in 1965 at the Prague
National Theatre. (Photo copyrighted by Jaromír Svoboda.)

For a production of *Hamlet* (1965), the director, Krejca, wished to treat
the Ghost as a trick conceived by Hamlet to win support in his fight against
Claudius. To project this idea, Svoboda suspended at an angle above the
stage a large plastic mirror, in which the audience saw much of the action
as if from above and behind the actors, and it was in this mirror that Hamlet
pretended to see the Ghost (actually his own reflection), while speaking
both his own lines and those of the spirit. Still more extensive use was
made of mirrors in *The Insect Comedy* (1965), for which two large
reflecting surfaces (each about 25 by 25 feet and honeycombed) were hung
at 45-degree angles to the stage floor. Few scenic elements were used,
though each act displayed a different floorcloth, which was reflected in the
angled mirrors. The actors, portraying insects, moved about the stage,
sometimes crawling, and were reflected in the honeycombed surfaces above
them.

Even when he uses traditional elements, Svoboda has usually given
them some new imaginative twist. For example, his setting for *Oedipus Rex*
is composed entirely of broad steps which stretch from the orchestra pit to
the back of the stage and out of sight overhead. But Svoboda has designed
settings in almost every conceivable style from socialist realism to complete
abstractionism, for he is extremely eclectic. He has declared that style is

merely a solution to the problems posed by a work, and therefore that it must vary according to the dramatist, director, stage facilities, and actors. Consequently, he does not consider himself committed to any particular mode. He has also said that technology must not become an end in itself but should be constantly refined so it may aid in solving problems posed by dramatic texts. Svoboda has now designed approximately four hundred productions for companies throughout the world and is probably the best known and most influential of all contemporary designers.

Above all, however, it is in the field of multimedia that Svoboda's work has been influential. Nevertheless, he has not been alone in developing this approach, for since 1960 many other designers have pursued similar goals. Consequently, it has become increasingly common to see productions which incorporate rapidly changing projections of still pictures on multiple screens, stereophonic and directional sound (which may vary from the loudest to the softest in volume, from the realistic to the purely abstract, from the atmospheric to the psychologically jolting), and "strobe" lights (with their rapid on-off changes from darkness to intense brightness and shifts in color). Through such devices the theatre has come closest to realizing the effects envisioned by Artaud.

The potentials of electronic devices continue to increase. Consequently, no doubt our multimedia productions, which now seem so technologically advanced, will someday seem as primitive as those of the 1920s do to us.

～ VI ～

A related development led in the late 1950s to "happenings," which grew out of dissatisfactions with the traditional boundaries placed on the individual arts. The results were extensions of earlier experiments by the futurists, dadaists, and surrealists, especially their use of multiple focus, simultaneity, chance, and discontinuity, and their mingling of elements drawn from collage, kinetic sculpture, "noise music," dance, and film. In fact, happenings seem to have borrowed from almost every avant-garde movement of the twentieth century. Although not specifically theatrical, they have exerted considerable influence on the theatre, for they have raised many significant questions about the relationship between creator and consumer, about organizational patterns, visual perception, and other perennial problems common to all the arts.

The key figure in the early stages was the composer John Cage (1912–   ), who in 1952 created a considerable sensation with his composition *4' 33"*, in which a pianist came on stage and merely sat at the piano for four minutes and thirty-three seconds. According to Cage, all the sounds

766

*Reassessment
and
Revolution:
Reshaping
the Theatre
for the
Future*

heard by the audience during that time, no matter the source, made up the piece. He has said that the "obligation . . . of the arts today is to intensify, alter perceptual awareness and, hence consciousness . . . of the real, material world." Thus, he is more concerned with stimulating the audience's awareness of its surroundings than with creating a lasting art work. He considers any specific intention by the artist to be irrelevant, since life itself is nonintentional (that is, what each person makes of an experience should be his own business), and he labels "police work" any attempt to make an audience respond in a particular way or to receive a particular message. He declares that all traditional criticism is misguided, since the only legitimate criticism is what one is stimulated to do by the experience.

Cage also organized what was probably the first American happening. In 1952 at Black Mountain College (North Carolina), he arranged a 45-minute program which included either at intervals or simultaneously the "paintings of Bob Rauschenberg, the dancing of Merce Cunningham, films, slides, phonograph records, radios, the poetries of Charles Olson and M. C. Richards recited from the tops of ladders, and the pianism of David Tudor," as well as a lecture by Cage. The audience, seated in the center, was surrounded by the activities. Much of the program was improvised, although controlled by time brackets. For example, Cage says that within a particular segment of time, "I knew that Merce would be dancing but I didn't know what he'd be dancing." Many of those who were to be involved in happenings were students or admirers of Cage, but most were not so devoted as he to the concept of nonintention or to total freedom for audiences.

Despite Cage's work, those events now generally labeled "happenings" did not begin until the late 1950s and grew primarily out of trends in painting. Such artists as Allan Kaprow, Robert Rauschenberg, and Jim Dine became dissatisfied with the two-dimensionality of painting and sought ways of transcending the limitations. As Kaprow put it: "Not satisfied with the *suggestion* through paint of our other senses, we shall utilize the specific substances of sight, sound, movement, people, odors, touch." Rauschenberg began to incorporate three-dimensional objects (such as a stuffed goat and a radio) into his canvases. "Action painters" and "abstract expressionists" sought to capture through brush strokes the feeling and the sense of movement at the moment of creation. These and other attempts sought to make painting either three-dimensional or kinetic.

In the development of happenings, the key figure was Allan Kaprow (1927–   ), a painter and art historian (but also a student and admirer of Cage) who gave the new form its name. Kaprow's work grew in part out of his interest in "environments" (that is, the extension of the concept of art to include the entire setting in which it is seen or in which it occurs). The dadaists had first championed this idea and it had been used as well for the great Parisian exhibition of surrealist art in 1938. During the 1950s, Kaprow came to believe that all those who attended an exhibit became a part of the environment, and consequently he gradually began to give them things to do. Then, in 1959 he published an outline for an artistic event which he labeled a "happening," because he considered the term neutral. Later that year he gave the first public showing of the form he had proposed—*18 Happenings in 6 Parts,* seen at the Reuben Gallery in New York.

For this presentation, the gallery, located in a large loft, was divided into three compartments by transparent plastic walls; in each segment, the floors and walls were decorated differently and each contained a number of chairs. Those who attended were given sheets of directions telling them in which room to sit during each of the parts. (Each person was in at least two different compartments during the course of the event.) Instructions were passed out at random so that no one would know in advance who would be where. The instructions also included directions about things to do at specific times during the program. Different actions occurred in each of the compartments and were accompanied by tape recordings of sound, music, voices, and abstract noise—often several simultaneously but dysynchronously and at varying volumes. There were as well some moments of total silence. Slides of paintings, familiar objects, and collages were projected on screens, the plastic walls, and people. At the same time, a number of performers carried out rigidly prescribed, often gymnastic or machinelike movements: some painted on canvas; a girl sliced oranges, squeezed them, filled glasses, and drank the juice; a man rolled up his trousers; a girl bounced a ball. In each compartment, there were usually several things going on simultaneously.

This and Kaprow's subsequent happenings were much more highly

Eat, an "environment" by Allan Kaprow, presented in 1964 in a cave in the Bronx, New York. A performer, seated at left, serves fried bananas to two visitors. (Photo by Peter Moore.)

768

*Reassessment
and
Revolution:
Reshaping
the Theatre
for the
Future*

organized and intentional than were Cage's. Everything was carefully planned and rehearsed. All those present were assigned specific tasks to do within clearly defined time periods (though precisely when or how the tasks were to be carried out was left open). Kaprow was not interested in wholly improvised, spontaneous events. He later came to dislike intensely the term *happenings,* especially after his attempt to restrict its use to his original conception failed.

But if Kaprow invented the label, he was only one of many persons working along similar lines. Nor were painters the only ones interested in such events. Dance, for example, witnessed parallel developments. Merce Cunningham (1922–   ), long one of Cage's collaborators, believes that any kind of movement may become dance and has presented works made up of common everyday activities (such as combing hair). He has also made dance independent of musical rhythms (that is, his dancers do not try to fit their movements to music) and of any necessary sequence (sometimes he determines the order by chance selection). Furthermore, he usually avoids a single focus (so that each dancer is more or less independent of the others) and connected story.

Ann Halprin (1921–   ) has worked along similar lines but in recent years has sought to involve all those present and to increase awareness (somewhat in the manner of Cage). "I have come back to the ritualistic beginnings of art as a sharpened experience of life, extending every kind of perception. I want to . . . involve people with their environment so that life is lived as a whole. . . . I am coming to see the artist . . . no longer [as] a solitary hero figure, but rather a guide who works to evoke the art within us all. This is the true meaning of a seminal theatre." She often uses archetypal situations or motifs (such as creation, atonement, maze) as a basis around which the participants improvise and evolve a collaborative experience.

Some filmmakers have also produced works with characteristics similar to those of happenings. For example, in *cinema verité* ordinary persons are often filmed as they go about everyday tasks. A quite different approach was used in Milton J. Cohen's "space theatre," in which images of many types were projected on surfaces of all sorts, including persons, so that those present were completely enmeshed in sensory stimuli (the projections were usually combined with music and sound, and sometimes with odors).

There were many other variations as well, but, as the vogue spread, the movement lost definition. Eventually "happening" was used to describe any event in which improvisation or chance played a significant part— even demonstrations, sit-ins, and "be-ins." No doubt this extension of the term until it became meaningless contributed to the decline of happenings, although since the late 1960s there has been a resurgence of interest in the form.

As this brief survey suggests, happenings are not directly theatrical. Nevertheless, several of their characteristics were carried over into the theatre during the 1960s (although it should be emphasized that happenings were not the only source for many of the innovations). First, as "institutionalized" art came under attack, there were attempts to transcend the confines of the museum, the concert hall, and the theatre auditorium. There were also attempts to enlarge the audience for art by removing it from the stultifying atmosphere of fixed places and of fixed attitudes which had made it the preserve of a privileged class. Second, emphasis was shifted from observation to participation—from the product to the process—as event and spectator were brought into closer relationship. Sometimes the audience and the performers were the same. Third, emphasis was shifted to awareness and away from the artist's intention. Guideposts suggesting meanings became correspondingly scarce. Fourth, simultaneity and multiple focus tended to replace orderly sequence and cause-and-effect arrangement. Usually there was no pretense that everyone could see and hear the same things at the same time. Fifth, since happenings were essentially nonverbal, they promoted the retreat from the conceptual and the exploration into the perceptual. Thus, they tended to be multimedia events appealing to the total sensory apparatus. Sixth, they largely ignored characterization and story. Participants carried out tasks rather than assuming roles; in most instances, they did not pretend to be someone else but remained themselves enmeshed in a novel experience.

No doubt other characteristics might be listed, but these seem the ones most related to theatrical developments. They have exerted considerable influence on virtually all attempts made since 1960 to redefine the theatre.

⇜ VII ⇝

Many elements from various innovations were brought together during the 1960s to form "environmental theatre," a label popularized by Richard Schechner (1934–   ), editor of *The Drama Review* (earlier called *Tulane Drama Review*), one of the most influential theatrical journals of the time. For Schechner, environmental theatre includes the work of the Living Theatre, Grotowski, the Open Theatre, the Bread and Puppet Theatre, and several other groups, for it is primarily "a new way of dealing with theatre space and audience relationships" and a rebellion against the orthodox theatre, which is "scenically characterized by (1) segregation of audience from performers; (2) fixed and regular seating of audiences; (3) construction of scenery situated in one part of the theatre only."

Schechner's clearest statement concerning environmental theatre is that published in 1968 in which he sets forth six "axioms" that define the characteristics and limits of this approach. The first of his axioms—"The theatrical event is a set of related transactions"—provides the general

770

*Reassessment
and
Revolution:
Reshaping
the Theatre
for the
Future*

context. Schechner declares that events may be placed on a continuum with "Pure"/"Art" at one end and "Impure"/"Life" at the other, and extending from traditional theatre at one pole through environmental theatre to happenings and ending with public events and demonstrations at the other pole. Thus, he locates environmental theatre somewhere between traditional theatre and happenings. Second, in environmental theatre, "All the space is used for performance; All the space is used for the audience." Spectators are both "scene-makers" and "scene-watchers," for, as in a street scene from daily life, those who watch are part of the total picture, even when they consider themselves to be mere spectators. Third, "The event can take place either in a totally transformed space or in a 'found' space." In other words, space may be converted into an "environment" suited to a particular theatrical production, or a place may be accepted as it is and the production adapted to it. In the latter instance, presumably a place (for example, a playground) would be found which had characteristics suited to the play to be performed there (for example, a work which treats war as a game). Fourth, "Focus is flexible and variable." Fifth, "All production elements speak their own language" rather than being mere supports for words. Sixth, "A text need be neither the starting point nor the goal of a production. There may be no text at all."

The key concept here is an extension of Kaprow's idea of environments, so that the site of a performance is made an integral part of the whole, encompassing both actors and spectators so that all may interact as an entity. Such an attempt almost automatically means abandoning traditional theatre architecture in favor of places already suitable as "environments" or which can be easily converted. Furthermore, focus almost of necessity becomes multiple or variable. On the other hand, Schechner's sixth axiom—concerning the text—does not seem essential to environmental theatre. Nevertheless, in his view the text is subordinate to the total environment rather than environment growing out of the text. About a production based on Ionesco's *Victims of Duty,* he writes: "We confronted it, searched among its words and themes, built around and through it. And we came out with our own thing. That is the heart of the environmental theatre." In this production, the performers, through several devices, also tried to involve the audience. For example, near the end of the play as the detective forces the protagonist to eat bread, several actors repeated his actions using spectators as subjects.

There are in Schechner's outlook elements derived from numerous sources: Grotowski (of whom he is a great admirer), cultural anthropology, Jung, Lévi-Strauss, Laing, and many others. He is sympathetic to much recent social and political agitation but not to many of its more radical manifestations. He has said that "the new art and most of our rebellious behavior is a reaction against existing rotten cultural forms and not a self-sustaining new culture." It was perhaps his desire to create something more permanent and positive than mere protest that led him to form his own company, the Performance Group. About its first production, *Dionysus in 69*, he also said that he wished through it to "warn the New Left of its leaders."

The Performance Group, founded in 1968, undertook about six months of exercises and experiments prior to presenting *Dionysus in 69*, a reworking of Euripides' *The Bacchae*. Performances took place in a converted garage, to which the audience was admitted as though to a secret rite comparable to the Eleusinian mysteries. Upon entering, spectators found themselves in a large room, essentially bare except for platforms and towers made of unpainted lumber. There were no seats in the traditional sense, and the audience dispersed, sitting on the floor, platforms, or towers as they wished. When the performance began, the actors were scattered throughout the room, but gradually formed into groups and couples. Some moved among the spectators, caressing or addressing them privately, almost secretly. Lines were barely audible, sometimes becoming mumbled chants, as Euripides' lines were often replaced by modern paraphrases. But the text was secondary to the enactment of rituals, most of them relating to the flesh or sex, and all concerned with themes of repression or freedom. The actors often exposed their own psyches as well. Dionysus was equated with a total lack of conflicting impulses, whereas Pentheus was eventually destroyed by violence-begetting repressions. Overall the play became a plea for greater freedom coupled with a warning against the dangers of blindly throwing off restraints. Because so much of it was improvised and because the group tended to change its outlook as time went by, the production underwent many changes during the course of its run. Among the revisions was the adoption of total nudity for some scenes, whereas originally the actors remained partially clothed throughout.

The Performance Group had little success with its next production, *Makbeth* (based on Shakespeare's *Macbeth*), but aroused considerable controversy with *Commune* (1970), a work created by the company out of its discussions and improvisations. *Commune* is a montage of events from the American past and present in which the rationale behind the new youth culture is seen to be merely a continuation of those motives that brought America into being: evasion of the past and rejection of boundaries. From the beginning people have come to America expecting to find community (the "melting pot") but instead have been faced with competitiveness. When their dreams of fulfillment are denied, they respond by moving on, "dropping out," or, in resentment, turning to violence. Thus, *Commune* is about the American dream of community/interdependence/love and its subversion by individualism/competition/hatred. It suggests, nevertheless, that a better future can be built only by accepting the past in its totality rather than by seeking to ignore some parts of it. In many ways, *Commune* sums up the preoccupations of American playwrights during the 1960s.

In this production, the entire theatrical space was used by both the

The Performance Group in *Commune*, 1970, directed by Richard Schechner. (Photo courtesy Richard Schechner.)

actors and the spectators. The dominant structure, a platform which rose in undulating curves, was used as a hill, ocean, or gathering place in times of disaster. Other platforms (and towers) were scattered about the room. The actors borrowed articles of clothing from the audience, used spectators as victims in massacres, and invited them to write slogans in chalk on the walls. Many critics found the work wholly incomprehensible; only a few seemed to comprehend its intentions.

The Performance Group has met a mixed reception. Many commentators consider Schechner to be far better as a critic and theorist than as a practitioner. Whatever his shortcomings as a director, however, Schechner's overall influence has been great, for few others have been able to perceive and synthesize so many of the preoccupations and trends of our age.

In one guise or another, environmental theatre has been pursued in several countries. One of the most successful examples has been *Orlando Furioso,* conceived by the director Luca Ronconi and the writer Edoardo Sanguineti of the Teatro Libero di Roma and first performed at the Festival of Two Worlds in Spoleto in 1969. The text was adapted from Lodovico Ariosto's sixteenth-century work with its forty-six cantos (each with 1,000 lines) and its multitude of characters and diffuse events involving mythical creatures, enchanted castles, sorcerers, captive maidens, and chivalric adventures. In making his adaptation, Sanguineti abridged the text and changed some narrative to dramatic passages, but added nothing.

In his staging, Ronconi sought to combine aspects of environmental theatre with medieval devices. Thus, instead of playing the episodes one after another, two or more progressed simultaneously in different parts of the theatrical space. In the original text, the various narrative strands are

Ronconi's and Sanguineti's *Orlando Furioso*, first performed at the Festival of Two Worlds, Spoleto, in 1969. (Photo by Pic.)

taken up singly, pursued for a time and then dropped, while other, wholly unconnected ones are developed. Characters come to the foreground for a time and then recede, often never to reappear. To have played the original work as written would have required an excessive amount of time. Ronconi believed that to play several parts simultaneously achieved the same effect of discorder and fantasy as is gained from a reading of the poem. The medieval element was introduced through the use of about fifty wheeled wooden platforms (reminiscent of pageant wagons), sometimes surmounted by stylized metal horses or fantastic creatures (such as the hippogriff), sometimes bare. The production was designed for a large open space of about 120 feet by 45 feet with a stage at either end. The area between the stages was occupied both by the moving platforms and the audience, who moved about, choosing what they wished to watch, mingling with the events and dodging the rapidly moving wagons. Near the end of the play, most of the spectators were surrounded by cages composing a labyrinth. The forty-five actors required for the production also propelled the platforms when not directly involved in the action. The overall effect was something like a street pageant and parade, a happening, and several playlets all proceeding simultaneously.

After playing at Spoleto, *Orlando Furioso* was revived at the Festival of Belgrade, in Milan and elsewhere in Italy, in Paris, and New York, where, billed as "theatre in the surround," it played under a plastic bubble-dome in a park. The publicity which it engendered did much to spread knowledge of its novel approach, even if some critics denounced it as all noise and empty-headedness.

In 1971, Ronconi staged a new work, *XX,* as part of the Théâtre des

773

Nations in Paris. For it, the auditorium of the Odéon was transformed by a structure of two stories, each divided into ten rooms. At the beginning of the performance about twenty-five persons were shut into each of the cubicles (measuring about nine by twelve feet). Occasionally an actor burst into a compartment with a warning or announcement, and sounds (such as a piano, gunshot, or scream) were audible elsewhere. Then the division between two cubicles was removed and the spectators could watch each other. Gradually more and more walls were withdrawn and the spectators witnessed scenes of interrogation, humiliation, and torture. Finally, when all of the divsions were gone, a coup d'état was announced and the audience was ordered to disperse. Of *XX*, Ronconi said: "I wanted to show how a system of oppression can take over a society, almost unnoticed, how in our time a neo-fascism could be born." He argues that individuals are usually only vaguely aware of what goes on outside their immediate surroundings and that by the time they become conscious of dangers it is often too late to resist them. "Closely intermingled with the actors, the audience is invited to a greater awareness of the oppressive relation which already exists in society." In comparison with *Orlando Furioso, XX* was generally considered less exciting but more relevant to contemporary life.

Jean-Louis Barrault has also turned to environmental theatre in two recent productions. *Rabelais,* first presented in 1968 at the Elysée-Montmartre, a Paris sports arena, is a three-hour adaptation of the five books devoted by Rabelais to Gargantua and Pantagruel. Some portions of the story were narrated and others acted out, sometimes several simultaneously, in a central ring and on ramps forming a cross extending into the audience. Around the hall hung portraits of Rabelais, Francis I, Molière, LaFontaine, Ubu Roi, and Kafka.

Through this production, Barrault sought to point up parallels between our times and those of Rabelais—an era of expansion in knowledge but of repression in society. But if Rabelais fought for freedom and against a stifling scholasticism, he also championed good sense and rational restraint. It was this balanced view of life that Barrault sought most to project, although he also wished to lead the audience to recognize that each of us is responsible for that "dry time" which Rabelais hoped to overcome.

In *Rabelais* Barrault drew on practically all contemporary trends, but unlike many producers of the day he did not subordinate his superb text to his own improvisations. The production won awards from the Parisian critics both as the best dramatic production and as the best musical production (because of its score by Michel Polnareff) of the year. It was later performed in Brussels, London, Berlin, New York, and elsewhere.

In 1970, Barrault, using techniques similar to those of *Rabelais,* presented his evocation of Jarry's life and works, *Jarry sur la Butte.* Its almost total failure was blamed by most critics on the incompatability of

Barrault's production of *Rabelais,* first performed
at the Elysée-Montmartre in 1968. (Photo by Pic.)

treatment with material. It is said to have cost Barrault his entire life
savings.

Another significant example of environmental theatre may be seen in
*1789—The revolution must stop only at the perfection of happiness—Saint-
Just,* created by the company-cooperative directed by Ariane Mnouchkine
and first performed in Milan under the auspices of the Piccolo Teatro in
1970 before being moved to Paris. A communal creation, it traces the
French Revolution from 1789 until the flight of Louis XVI. Ultimately it
seeks to show how the uncompleted revolution was stopped by those who
wanted to safeguard the rights of property. Parallels with the events of May
1968 are made clearly apparent.

The production is designed for a large open space. (In Milan it was
presented in a gymnasium and in Paris in a disused munitions factory.)
Platforms about 4 feet high are placed around all four sides and the
unseated audience in the middle. As in *Orlando Furioso,* several scenes
take place simultaneously and the spectators are free to choose which they
will watch. But in *1789* the audience plays a more integral part, since it is
cast as the mob—those who can make the revolution succeed. The production employs extremely varied devices: puppets, mime, sideshow entertainments, musical scenes, conventional dialogue. After the Bastille has
been stormed, the lights go out and each actor gathers a small group of
spectators around him while he at first whispers, as though telling a dangerous secret, his version of what has happened; gradually the tempo and

775

Ariane Mnouchkine's production of 1789 for the Théâtre du Soleil,
staged in an old cartridge factory just outside Paris in 1970.
(Photo by Bernand.)

sound build to a loud swell of triumph, and the lights come on to a joyous
carnivallike celebration. In another striking scene, a huge puppet figure of
Louis XVI is destroyed, revealing that it is only made of rags, scraps, and
paste. Critics were almost unanimous in their praise of the production, for
here was an innovative work in which intention and realization seemed one.

It is too early to predict the future of this kind of production, but its
popularity seems to be growing. Because it brings together so many strands
of experimentation, it holds the promise of a workable synthesis.

~~~ VIII ~~~

The continuing and insistent demands made since 1960 for the relaxation
of all restraints in the theatre have resulted in the gradual lessening of
strictures on subject matter, behavior, and language in theatrical productions. For the general public, the results have perhaps been best epitomized
in nudity and obscenity.

The first notable use of nudity came in 1968 in the Broadway production of *Hair,* a popularized version of the work with which Papp opened his Public Theatre. *Hair* (subtitled "An American Tribal Love-Rock Musical"), with book and lyrics by Gerome Ragni and James Rado and music by Galt MacDermot, has little story line. Rather it elaborates on themes and anxieties of our time (such as the military draft, the war in Vietnam, mismatched couples, the conflict between generations), many expressed through song and music. Most of all, it is a good-natured attempt to justify a new life style and it ends with a plea for understanding and for happiness and peace. Throughout the work obscenity is introduced freely, and, at the end of the first part, the performers for one brief moment remove their clothes. Both innovations created a furor. *Hair* was destined to go on creating similar crises around the world: in England, France, Japan, Yugoslavia, and elsewhere.

Other productions soon followed *Hair's* example. In late 1968 off-Broadway saw the opening of Terrence McNally's *Sweet Eros,* in which a nude actress remains on stage throughout. In 1969, *Geese* by Gus Weill brought both nude and homosexual love scenes on stage. Then, *Che!* by Lennox Raphael provoked the prosecution and eventual conviction of four actors, the playwright, producer, and lighting man on charges of obscenity. In this work, Che Guevara was treated as a hero who is envied by all those who seek to thwart him. One of the envious characters, called the President, was dressed in an Uncle Sam hat and little else. The envy seemed primarily sexually motivated, as Che became the object of desire to all

The "Black Boys/White Boys" number from *Hair,* the American Tribal Love-Rock Musical by Gerome Ragni, James Rado, and Galt MacDermot, 1968.

*Reassessment
and
Revolution:
Reshaping
the Theatre
for the
Future*

the other characters. According to the court's ruling: "The stage directions permitted actual sex on stage," and "ran the gamut" indiscriminately from heterosexual to homosexual. The judges added: "It cannot be said that . . . standards of public acceptance and morality so sharply different and shocking can be established by a few commercially inspired producers who try to see how far they can go."

Nevertheless, producers continued to introduce nudity, although most sought to avoid police action. In 1969, *Oh! Calcutta!*, "an entertainment with music" devised by Kenneth Tynan (literary advisor to England's National Theatre) and directed by Jacques Levy, opened in New York. Composed of short sketches purportedly written by famous authors, it was essentially a revue in which all the parts were related through sex. Many were performed in their entirety by nude actors, thus considerably extending the innovation somewhat tentatively introduced by earlier productions. *Oh! Calcutta!* was labeled sophisticated pornography by many and a bore by others, but it rapidly won a reputation as a daring show and became a great hit. In 1970 it opened in London, where it also failed to provoke action by the public prosecutor.

By the early 1970s, although the limits of permissibility were still vague, almost any sexual theme or obscenity had become potential material for stage use. The actors' unions in both America and England obviously were unhappy with developments but contented themselves with laying down certain conditions (clear notice to the actor of what would be required, and indemnification in case of public prosecution) to protect its members. In no area has the theatrical revolution been more complete than in the attitudes toward sex, nudity, and obscenity. To many, the new direction seemed a clear indication that moral fiber had disappeared, but to others it marked only a relaxation of restraints that never should have been imposed. Perhaps nothing so encapsulated the wide gulf that existed between traditionalists and innovators in the late 1960s.

Most productions that have employed nudity and obscenity have done so in a spirit of defiance or bravado. Consequently, though they have thrown off restraints, the results have often seemed not so much joyful as semi-pornographic and prurient. The ideals championed by Norman O. Brown and advocates of sensitivity training have for the most part been missing. A few groups, however, have sought to move beyond defiance into the more positive realms of freedom and trust. Of these, the most successful has been The James Joyce Memorial Liquid Theatre, founded in 1969 by Steven Kent. A company of twenty-eight, it worked in Los Angeles until mid-1971, when the troupe was disbanded. Kent then brought eighteen of his associates to New York, added another eighteen, and prepared a program which opened at the Guggenheim Museum in October 1971.

The Liquid Theatre is essentially a tactile experience—a theatre of touch. It uses no script, although there is an overall plan. Upon entering, those who attend are asked to close their eyes, and, as they are led through

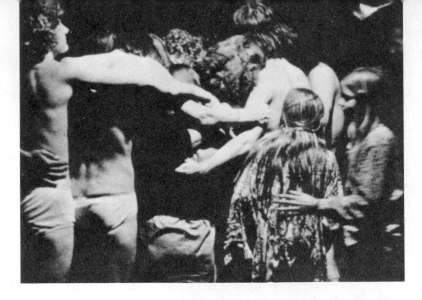

The James Joyce Memorial Liquid Theatre in performance in Los Angeles in 1971, shortly before the troupe was disbanded and reconstituted in New York at the Guggenheim Museum.

a maze, voices whisper soothingly, "Trust us." They are stroked, embraced, rocked gently. The experience is sensory, essentially asexual, a surrender of self to tenderness and love. Later, with eyes open, participants play all sorts of games that induce a sense of togetherness. Then they form groups and, moving in harmony, they begin to chant. Voices blend, become louder and louder and, when the sound can increase no further, a band bursts into music, thus providing a final sense of liberation.

One critic has said that the Liquid Theatre "leaves the cleanest after-taste you've ever brought from a theatre." Kent calls it an unhostile *Paradise Now* which seeks to create an environment "where people can be free and open and happy." It is perhaps the nearest theatrical equivalent of Norman O. Brown's ideal yet achieved. Where such work will lead remains to be seen, but it clearly marks a new direction.

IX

The views championed by the New Left and other innovative thinkers have made a considerable impact on the theatre since 1960. Similarly, the Living Theatre, the Polish Laboratory Theatre, the Open Theatre, and numerous other groups and individuals have opened up new directions in theatrical practice. Together these forces have gone far toward redefining the theatre: its function, content, and techniques. But the 1970s have brought consid-

780

*Reassessment
and
Revolution:
Reshaping
the Theatre
for the
Future*

erable doubt about much that has happened in the recent past. Even the New Left is in considerable disarray. Hesitation and reassessment seem almost universal. How all this will affect the theatre is unclear, but we may be certain that it will affect it in some way.

Nevertheless, it would be idle to predict the future of theatre and drama, for to do so one would have to foresee the course of world events and thought. Western theatre has always reflected changing views about man and events in the world at large. Thus, as our conceptions of human psychology, morality, society, and politics alter in the future, so too will theatre alter.

During the past century changes in theatre and drama have been legion, but behind them all can be seen a few basic patterns. Practically all innovations have stemmed from changes in perceptions about man and his world. But such changes have seldom been welcomed immediately. New views have nearly always been greeted by bafflement, resentment, or outrage, and only gradually accepted. But eventually the new is imperceptibly absorbed until it too becomes entrenched and therefore part of a new orthodoxy.

Since altered outlooks require altered techniques, the history of theatre and drama is in large part a record of the search for means adequate to express changing perceptions. During the past century, revolutions in perception have been many, just as their frequency has accelerated. Nevertheless, innovation in itself is unimportant, for much of it leads nowhere. Whether it is significant is determined not so much by immediate response as by subsequent developments, for only then can one tell whether a novelty was a forerunner of a new phase in theatre or merely an isolated and still-born experiment. Many recent innovations which now seem important will no doubt in the future fade into oblivion because they were false starts, whereas others, perhaps unnoted in this book, will in retrospect be seen as harbingers of major changes. History must constantly be rewritten because it is from present perspectives that we must view the past, and, because our values and interests change, so too must our estimates of the past.

We seem now to be in the midst of a period of questioning, doubt, and agitation even more intense than that which a century ago gave rise to the "modern" theatre. That "art" should be caught up in the stresses of our time is lamented by many, but unless theatre and drama are to stagnate and become irrelevant they must reflect (or even create) conflicts, for if drama is an "imitation of man in action," it must be of man as we know him now and not as conceived in some earlier time. Consequently, it is present and future conceptions of man—what sort of creature he is, what kinds of appeals must be made to his sensory apparatus, what kind of personal, moral, social, and political ideals he is capable of sustaining—that will determine the direction to be taken by theatre and drama. And that only the passage of time can tell.

Bibliography

This bibliography lists books selected from among the most helpful studies of modern theatre and drama. It is divided according to chapters and is restricted primarily to works in English.

GENERAL

ALTMAN, GEORGE, et al. *Theatre Pictorial*. Berkeley, 1953.
BENTLEY, ERIC (ed.). *The Theory of the Modern Stage*. Baltimore, 1968.
BROCKETT, OSCAR G. *History of the Theatre*. Boston, 1968.

781

CHENEY, SHELDON. *The Theatre*. Rev. ed. New York, 1952.

CLARK, BARRETT H. (ed.). *European Theories of the Drama*. Rev. ed. New York, 1965.

CLARK, BARRETT H., and FREEDLEY, GEORGE. *A History of Modern Drama*. New York, 1947.

COLE, TOBY (ed.). *Playwrights on Playwriting*. New York, 1960.

COLE, TOBY, and CHINOY, HELEN K. (eds.). *Actors on Acting*. Rev. ed. New York, 1970.

————. *Directors on Directing*. Indianapolis, 1963.

DUERR, EDWIN. *The Length and Depth of Acting*. New York, 1962.

Enciclopedia dello Spettacolo. 9 vols. Rome, 1953–65.

FERGUSSON, FRANCIS. *The Idea of a Theatre*. Princeton, 1949.

GASCOIGNE, BAMBER. *Twentieth-Century Drama*. London, 1962.

GASSNER, JOHN. *Directions in Modern Theatre and Drama*. New York, 1965.

————. *Masters of the Drama*. 3d ed. New York, 1954.

————. *The Theatre in Our Times*. New York, 1954.

GASSNER, JOHN, and ALLEN, RALPH (eds.). *Theatre and Drama in the Making*. Vol. 2. Boston, 1964.

GORELIK, MORDECAI. *New Theatres for Old*. New York, 1940.

HEWITT, BARNARD. *History of the Theatre from 1800*. New York, 1970.

KRUTCH, J. W. *"Modernism" in Modern Drama*. Ithaca, N.Y., 1953.

LAMM, MARTIN. *Modern Drama*. Translated by Karin Elliott. New York, 1953.

LUMLEY, FREDERICK. *Trends in Twentieth Century Drama*. 2d ed. London, 1960.

MACGOWAN, KENNETH, and MELNITZ, WILLIAM. *The Living Stage*. Englewood Cliffs, N.J., 1955.

MELCHINGER, SIEGFRIED. *The Concise Encyclopedia of Modern Drama*. Translated by George Wellwarth. New York, 1964.

NICOLL, ALLARDYCE. *The Development of the Theatre*. 5th ed. London, 1966.

————. *World Drama*. London, 1949.

RISCHBEITER, HENNING. *Art and the Stage in the Twentieth Century*. Greenwich, Conn., 1968.

SELTZER, DANIEL (ed.). *The Modern Theatre: Readings and Documents*. Boston, 1967.

SIMONSON, LEE. *The Stage is Set*. New York, 1932.

STYAN, J. L. *The Dark Comedy*. 2d ed. Cambridge, 1968.

WILLIAMS, RAYMOND. *Drama from Ibsen to Brecht*. London, 1968.

CHAPTER 1

ARVIN, NEIL E. *Eugène Scribe and the French Theatre, 1815–60*. Cambridge, Mass., 1924.

BANCROFT, MARIE EFFIE. *The Bancrofts*. New York, 1909.

BARZUN, JACQUES. *Darwin, Marx, Wagner*. Boston, 1941.

BRUFORD, W. H. *Theatre, Drama, and Audience in Goethe's Germany*. London, 1957.

COLE, J. W. *The Life and Theatrical Times of Charles Kean*. London, 1859.

Downer, Alan S. *The Eminent Tragedian: William Charles Macready.* Cambridge, Mass., 1966.

Droz, Jacques. *Europe Between Revolutions, 1815–1848.* Translated by Robert Baldick. New York, 1967.

Fitzgerald, Percy. *The World Behind the Scenes.* London, 1881.

Kindermann, Heinz. *Theatergeschichte das Europas.* Vol. 7: *Realismus.* Salzburg, 1965.

Klenze, Camillo von. *From Goethe to Hauptmann.* New York, 1926.

Lacey, Alexander. *Pixérécourt and the French Romantic Drama.* Toronto, 1928.

Mammen, Edward W. *The Old Stock Company School of Acting.* Boston, 1945.

Matthews, Brander. *French Dramatists of the Nineteenth Century.* 5th ed. New York, 1914.

Melcher, Edith. *Stage Realism in France Between Diderot and Antoine.* Bryn Mawr, Pa., 1928.

Rowell, George. *The Victorian Theatre.* London, 1956.

Savin, Maynard. *Thomas William Robertson: His Plays and His Stagecraft.* Providence, R.I., 1950.

Schwarz, Henry S. *Alexandre Dumas fils, Dramatist.* New York, 1927.

Smith, Hugh A. *Main Currents in Modern French Drama.* New York, 1925.

Southern, Richard. *Changeable Scenery: Its Origins and Development in the British Theatre.* London, 1952.

Talmon, Jacob L. *Romanticism and Revolt: Europe, 1815–1848.* New York, 1967.

Taylor, Frank A. *The Theatre of Alexandre Dumas fils.* Oxford, 1937.

Vardac, A. N. *Stage to Screen: Theatrical Method from Garrick to Griffith.* Cambridge, Mass., 1949.

Watson, Ernest B. *Sheridan to Robertson: A Study of the Nineteenth-Century London Stage.* Cambridge, Mass., 1926.

Weinberg, Bernard. *French Realism: The Critical Reaction, 1830–1870.* Chicago, 1937.

Wellek, René. *A History of Modern Criticism.* Vols. 3 and 4. New Haven, 1965.

Witkowski, Georg. *German Drama of the Nineteenth Century.* Translated by L. E. Horning. New York, 1909.

CHAPTER 2

Barzun, Jacques. See Chapter I.

Brereton, Austin. *The Life of Henry Irving.* 2 vols. London, 1908.

Felheim, Marvin. *The Theater of Augustin Daly.* Cambridge, Mass., 1956.

Grube, Max. *The Story of the Meiningen.* Translated by Ann Marie Koller. Coral Gables, Fla., 1963.

Gutman, Robert W. *Richard Wagner: The Man, his Mind, and his Music.* New York, 1968.

Hart, Jerome A. *Sardou and the Sardou Plays.* London, 1913.

Irving, Laurence. *Henry Irving.* London, 1951.

KINDERMANN, HEINZ. See Chapter I.

MACKAYE, PERCY. *Epoch: The Life of Steele Mackaye.* 2 vols. New York, 1927.

MELCHER, EDITH. See Chapter I.

NEWMAN, ERNEST. *The Life of Richard Wagner.* 4 vols. New York, 1933–60.

ODELL, G. C. D. *Annals of the New York Stage.* Vols. 8–15. New York, 1936–49.

QUINN, ARTHUR H. *A History of American Drama from the Civil War to the Present Day.* 2d ed. New York, 1949.

RANOUS, DORA KNOWLTON. *Diary of a Daly Debutante.* New York, 1910.

ROWELL, GEORGE. See Chapter I.

RUGGLES, ELEANOR. *Prince of Players: Edwin Booth.* New York, 1953.

SHATTUCK, CHARLES H. *The Hamlet of Edwin Booth.* Urbana, Ill., 1969.

SKELTON, GEOFFREY. *Wagner at Bayreuth.* New York, 1965.

SOUTHERN, RICHARD. See Chapter I.

STEBBINS, G. *The Delsarte System of Expression.* 5th ed. New York, 1894.

STEIN, JACK M. *Richard Wagner and the Synthesis of the Arts.* Detroit, 1960.

VARDAC, A. N. See Chapter I.

WAGNER, RICHARD. *Opera and Drama.* Translated by Edwin Evans. London, 1913.

———. *Richard Wagner on Music and Drama.* Edited by Albert Goldman and Evert Sprinchorn. New York, 1964.

WELLEK, RENÉ. See Chapter I.

CHAPTER 3

BENTLEY, ERIC. *The Playwright as Thinker: A Study of Drama in Modern Times.* New York, 1946.

BJORKMAN, EDWIN A. *Voices of Tomorrow.* New York, 1913.

BRADBROOK, MURIEL. *Ibsen the Norwegian.* London, 1946.

BRANDES, GEORG. *Henrik Ibsen; Bjornsterne Bjornson.* London, 1899.

BRUSTEIN, ROBERT. *The Theatre of Revolt.* New York, 1964.

CARTER, LAWSON A. *Zola and the Theatre.* New Haven, 1963.

CHANDLER, FRANK W. *The Contemporary Drama of France.* Boston, 1920.

CLARK, B. H. *Contemporary French Dramatists.* Cincinnati, 1915.

DOWNS, BRIAN W. *A Study of Six Plays by Ibsen.* Cambridge, 1950.

———. *Ibsen: The Intellectual Background.* Cambridge, 1946.

GRANT, ELLIOTT M. *Emile Zola.* New York, 1966.

HEMMINGS, FREDERIC. *Emile Zola.* Oxford, 1953.

HOLTAN, ORLEY I. *Mythic Patterns in Ibsen's Last Plays,* Minneapolis, 1970.

HUNEKER, JAMES G. *Iconoclasts.* London, 1905.

JOHNSON, WALTER. *Strindberg and the Historical Drama.* Seattle, 1963.

JOSEPHSON, MATTHEW. *Zola and His Time.* Garden City, N.Y., 1928.

KINDERMANN, HEINZ. *Theatergeschichte das Europas.* Vol 8: *Naturalismus und Expressionismus.* Salzburg, 1968.

KLAF, FRANKLIN S. *Strindberg: Origin of Psychology in Modern Drama.* New York, 1963.

KOHT, HALVDAN. *The Life of Ibsen.* 2 vols. New York, 1931.

LAMM, MARTIN. *August Strindberg.* Translated and edited by Harry G. Carlson. New York, 1971.

LAVRIN, JANKO. *Ibsen: An Approach.* London, 1950.

LEWISOHN, LUDWIG. *The Modern Drama.* New York, 1916.

McFARLANE, JAMES W. *Ibsen and the Temper of Norwegian Literature.* London, 1960.

McGILL, V. J. *August Strindberg: The Bedevilled Viking.* London, 1930.

MADSEN, BORGE G. *Strindberg's Naturalistic Theatre: Its Relation to French Naturalism.* Copenhagen, 1962.

MORTENSEN, B. M. E. and DOWNS, B. W. *Strindberg: An Introduction to His Life and Works.* Cambridge, 1949.

NORTHAM, JOHN. *Ibsen's Dramatic Method.* London, 1953.

SHAW, GEORGE BERNARD. *The Quintessence of Ibsenism.* London, 1913.

SMITH, HUGH A. See Chapter I.

SONDEL, BESS. *Zola's Naturalistic Theory with Particular Reference to the Drama.* Chicago, 1939.

SPRIGGE, ELIZABETH. *The Strange Life of August Strindberg.* New York, 1949.

TENNANT, P. F. D. *Ibsen's Dramatic Technique.* Cambridge, 1948.

VALENCY, MAURICE. *The Flower and the Castle: An Introduction to Modern Drama.* New York, 1963.

WITKOWSKI, GEORG. See Chapter I.

ZUCKER, A. E. *Ibsen: The Master Builder.* New York, 1929.

ANTOINE, ANDRÉ. *Memories of the Théâtre Libre.* Translated by Marvin Carlson. Coral Gables, Fla., 1964.

BABLET, DENIS. *Esthétique Générale du Décor de Théâtre de 1870 à 1914.* Paris, 1965.

BENTLEY, ERIC. See Chapter III.

CARPENTER, CHARLES A. *Bernard Shaw and the Art of Destroying Ideals: The Early Plays.* Madison, Wis., 1969.

CHANDLER, FRANK W. *Aspects of Modern Drama.* New York, 1914.

———. See Chapter III.

CLARK, B. H. *The British and American Drama of Today.* New York, 1921.

———. See Chapter III.

CORDELL, RICHARD. *Henry Arthur Jones and the Modern Drama.* New York, 1932.

CROMPTON, LOUIS. *Shaw the Dramatist.* Lincoln, Nebr., 1969.

DICKINSON, T. H. *The Contemporary Drama in England.* Boston, 1931.

ERVINE, ST. JOHN. *Bernard Shaw.* New York, 1956.

FYFE, H. HAMILTON. *Sir Arthur Pinero's Plays and Players.* London, 1930.

GARTEN, HUGH F. *Gerhart Hauptmann.* New Haven, 1954.

HUDSON, L. A. *The English Stage, 1850–1950.* London, 1951.

INCORPORATED STAGE SOCIETY. *Ten Years: 1899 to 1909.* London, 1909.

JONES, HENRY ARTHUR. *The Renascence of the English Drama.* London, 1895.

KNIGHT, K. G., and NORMAN, F. (eds.). *Hauptmann Centenary Lectures.* London, 1964.

MASON, A. E. W. *Sir George Alexander and the St. James' Theatre.* London, 1935.

MEISEL, MARTIN. *Shaw and the Nineteenth-Century Theater.* Princeton, 1963.

MELCHER, EDITH. See Chapter I.

MILLER, ANNA IRENE. *The Independent Theatre in Europe, 1887 to the Present.* New York, 1931.

NEWMARK, MAXIM. *Otto Brahm: The Man and the Critic.* New York, 1938.

NICOLL, ALLARDYCE. *A History of Late Nineteenth Century Drama.* Cambridge, 1946.

ORME, MICHAEL. *J. T. Grein: The Story of a Pioneer.* London, 1936.

SCHIEFLEY, W. H. *Brieux and Contemporary French Society.* New York, 1917.

SHAW, GEORGE BERNARD. *Our Theatre in the Nineties.* London, 1932.

———. *Shaw on Theatre.* Edited by E. J. West. New York, 1958.

SHAW, LEROY R. *Witness of Deceit: Gerhart Hauptmann as Critic of Society.* Berkeley, 1958.

SINDEN, MARGARET. *Gerhart Hauptmann: The Prose Plays.* Toronto, 1957.

SMITH, HUGH A. See Chapter I.

SMITH, JOSEPH P. *The Unrepentant Pilgrim: A Study of the Development of Bernard Shaw.* Boston, 1965.

WAXMAN, SAMUEL. *Antoine and the Théâtre Libre.* Cambridge, Mass., 1926.

WILSON, COLIN. *Bernard Shaw: A Reassessment.* New York, 1969.

CHAPTER 5

BECKSON, KARL E. (ed.) *Oscar Wilde: The Critical Heritage.* London, 1970.

BITHELL, JETHRO. *The Life and Writings of Maurice Maeterlinck.* London, 1913.

BLOCK, HASKELL. *Mallarmé and the Symbolist Drama.* Detroit, 1963.

CHANDLER, FRANK W. See Chapter III.

CHIARI, JOSEPH. *The Poetic Drama of Paul Claudel.* New York, 1954.

———. *Symbolism from Poe to Mallarmé.* 2d ed. New York, 1970.

CLARK, B. H. See Chapter III.

CLAUDEL, PAUL. *Claudel on Theatre.* Coral Gables, Fla., 1971.

CORNELL, KENNETH. *The Symbolist Movement.* New Haven, 1951.

COOPERMAN, HASYE. *The Aesthetics of Stephane Mallarmé.* New York, 1933.

DUPONTAVICE DE HEUSSEY, ROBERT. *Villiers de l'Isle Adam.* Translated by Lady Mary Loyd. New York, 1894.

ELLMANN, RICHARD (ed.). *Oscar Wilde: A Collection of Critical Essays.* Englewood Cliffs, N.J., 1969.

FOWLIE, WALLACE. *Age of Surrealism.* Bloomington, Ind., 1960.

———. *Mallarmé.* Chicago, 1953.

———. *Paul Claudel.* New York, 1957.

GRAY, RONALD D. *The German Tradition in Literature, 1871–1945.* Cambridge, 1965.

HALLS, W. D. *Maurice Maeterlinck: A Study of His Life and Thought.* Oxford, 1960.

HAMMELMANN, HANNS A. *Hugo von Hofmannsthal.* New Haven, 1957.

HELLER, OTTO. *Prophets of Dissent: Essays on Maeterlinck, Strindberg, Nietzsche, and Tolstoy.* New York, 1918.

HOLLINGDALE, R. J. *Nietzsche: The Man and his Philosophy.* London, 1965.

JASPER, GERTRUDE. *Adventure in the Theatre: Lugné-Poë and the Théâtre de l'Oeuvre to 1899.* New Brunswick, N.J., 1947.

LEHMANN, ANDREW. *The Symbolist Aesthetic in France, 1885–1895.* Oxford, 1950.

LOVE, FREDERICK R. *Young Nietzsche and the Wagnerian Experience.* Chapel Hill, N.C., 1963.

OJALA, AATOS. *Aestheticism and Oscar Wilde.* 2 vols. Helsinki, 1954–55.

QUENNELL, PETER. *Baudelaire and the Symbolists.* New York, 1929.

SAN JUAN, EPIFANIO. *The Art of Oscar Wilde.* Princeton, 1967.

SHATTUCK, ROGER. *The Banquet Years: The Arts In France, 1885–1918.* New York, 1961.

SMITH, HUGH A. See Chapter I.

SYMONS, ARTHUR. *The Symbolist Movement in Literature.* Rev. ed. New York, 1919.

WEINTRAUB, STANLEY. *The Literary Criticism of Oscar Wilde.* Lincoln, Nebr., 1968.

CHAPTER 6

AGATE, JAMES. *A Short View of the English Stage, 1900–26.* London, 1926.

BELASCO, DAVID. *The Theatre Through Its Stage Door.* New York, 1919.

BERNHEIM, ALFRED L. *The Business of the Theatre.* New York, 1932.

BLAKE, BEN. *The Awakening of the American Theatre.* New York, 1935.

BOURGEOIS, MAURICE. *J. M. Synge and the Irish Theatre.* New York, 1965.

BROWN, J. A. C. *Freud and the Post-Freudians.* Baltimore, 1961.

BRUSTEIN, ROBERT. See Chapter III.

BYRNE, DAWSON. *The Story of Ireland's National Theatre: The Abbey.* Dublin, 1929.

CHANDLER, FRANK W. See Chapters III and IV.

CLARK, B. H. See Chapters III and IV.

COXHEAD, ELIZABETH. *Lady Gregory: A Literary Portrait.* New York, 1961.

DAHLSTROM, C. E. W. L. *Strindberg's Dramatic Expressionism.* Ann Arbor, Mich., 1930.

DICKINSON, T. H. See Chapter IV.

DOWNER, ALAN S. *Fifty Years of American Drama, 1900–1950.* Chicago, 1950.

DUNBAR, JANET. *J. M. Barrie.* New York, 1970.

ELLIS-FERMOR, UNA. *The Irish Dramatic Movement.* London, 1939.

FAY, GERARD. *The Abbey Theatre.* London, 1958.

GARTEN, HUGH F. *Modern German Drama.* London, 1959.

GITTELMAN, SOL. *Frank Wedekind.* New York, 1969.

GREENE, DAVID H., and STEPHENS, E. M. *J. M. Synge, 1871–1909.* New York, 1959.

GREGORY, (LADY) ISABELLA AUGUSTA. *Our Irish Theatre*. New York, 1913.

HEWITT, BARNARD. *Theatre USA, 1668–1957*. New York, 1959.

HUDSON, L. A. See Chapter IV.

ISHIBASHI, HIRO. *Yeats and the Noh*. Edited by Anthony Kerrigan. Dublin, 1966.

JAMESON, STORM. *Modern Drama in Europe*. London, 1920.

JONES, ERNEST. *The Life and Work of Sigmund Freud*. 3 vols. New York, 1953–60.

JOURDAIN, ELEANOR F. *The Drama of Europe in Theory and Practice*. New York, 1924.

KLAF, FRANKLIN S. See Chapter III.

LAMM, MARTIN. See Chapter III.

LE GALLIENNE, EVA. *Mystic in the Theatre: Eleanora Duse*. New York, 1966.

LIPTZIN, SOL. *Arthur Schnitzler*. New York, 1932.

LUCAS, F. L. *The Drama of Chekhov, Synge, Yeats, and Pirandello*. London, 1963.

MacCLINTOCK, LANDER. *The Contemporary Drama of Italy*. Boston, 1920.

McLEOD, ADDISON. *Plays and Players in Modern Italy*. London, 1912.

MOORE, JAMES R. *Masks of Love and Death: Yeats as Dramatist*. Ithaca, N.Y., 1971.

MORGAN, MARGERY M. *Drama of Political Man: A Study of the Plays of Granville Barker*. London, 1961.

NATHAN, LEONARD E. *The Tragic Drama of William Butler Yeats*. New York, 1965.

O'NEILL, MICHAEL J. *Lennox Robinson*. New York, 1964.

PEAK, J. HUNTER. *Social Drama in Nineteenth-Century Spain*. Chapel Hill, N.C., 1965.

PEARSON, HESKETH. *The Last Actor-Managers*. London, 1950.

PENUELAS, MARCELINO. *Jacinto Benavente*. New York, 1968.

POGGI, JACK. *Theater in America: The Impact of Economic Forces, 1870–1967*. Ithaca, N.Y., 1968.

PURDOM, CHARLES B. *Harley Granville Barker: Man of the Theatre, Dramatist, and Scholar*. London, 1955.

QUINN, ARTHUR H. See Chapter II.

REICHERT, H. W., and SALINGER, H. (eds.). *Studies in Arthur Schnitzler*. Chapel Hill, N.C., 1963.

ROBINSON, LENNOX (ed.). *Ireland's Abbey Theatre: A History, 1899–1951*. London, 1951.

ROWELL, GEORGE. See Chapter I.

SKELTON, ROBIN. *J. M. Synge and His World*. London, 1971.

SKINNER, CORNELIA OTIS. *Madame Sarah*. Boston, 1967.

SMITH, HUGH A. See Chapter I.

STRINDBERG, AUGUST. *Open Letters to the Intimate Theatre*. Translated by Walter Johnson. Seattle, 1966.

URE, PETER. *Yeats the Playwright*. London, 1963.

VALENCY, MAURICE. See Chapter III.

VENDLER, HELEN H. *Yeats' Vision and the Later Plays*. Cambridge, Mass., 1963.

WALBROOK, HENRY M. *J. M. Barrie and the Theatre*. London, 1922.

WHYTE, LANCELOT L. *The Unconscious Before Freud*. Garden City, N.Y., 1962.

WINTER, WILLIAM. *The Life of David Belasco*. 2 vols. New York, 1918.

WINWAR, FRANCES. *Wingless Victory: A Biography of Gabriele D'Annunzio and Eleanora Duse*. New York, 1956.

WOLMAN, BENJAMIN B. *The Unconscious Mind: The Meaning of Freudian Psychology.* Englewood Cliffs, N.J., 1968.

YEATS, WILLIAM BUTLER. *Autobiography. New* York, 1938.

————. *Plays and Controversies.* London, 1923.

CHAPTER 7

APPIA, ADOLPHE. *Music and the Art of the Theatre.* Translated by R. W. CORRIGAN and M. D. DIRKS. Coral Gables, Fla., 1962.

————. *The Work of Living Art* and *Man is the Measure of All Things.* Translated by H. D. ALBRIGHT and BARNARD HEWITT. Coral Gables, Fla., 1960.

BABLET, DENIS. *Edward Gordon Craig.* Translated by Daphne Woodward. New York, 1966.

————. See Chapter IV.

BLAKE, BEN. See Chapter VI.

BUCKLEY, REGINALD R. *The Shakespeare Revival and the Stratford-upon-Avon Movement.* London, 1911.

CARTER, HUNTLY. *The Theatre of Max Reinhardt,* New York, 1914.

CHENEY, SHELDON. *The Art Theatre.* New York, 1917.

————. *The New Movement in the Theatre.* New York. 1914.

————. *The Open Air Theatre.* New York, 1918.

CRAIG, EDWARD GORDON. *Index to the Story of My Days.* New York, 1957.

————. *On the Art of the Theatre.* Chicago, 1911.

————. *The Theatre—Advancing.* Boston, 1921.

DOWNER, ALAN S. See Chapter VI.

DUKORE, BERNARD F. *Bernard Shaw, Director.* London, 1971.

ELLIS, RUTH. *The Shakespeare Memorial Theatre.* London, 1948.

FISCHEL, OSKAR. *Das Moderne Bühnenbild.* Berlin, 1923.

FRANK, WALDO. *The Art of the Vieux-Colombier.* New York, 1918.

FUCHS, GEORG. *Revolution in the Theatre.* Translated by C. C. Kuhn. Ithaca, N.Y., 1959.

FUCHS, THEODORE. *Stage Lighting.* Boston, 1929.

FUERST, RENÉ, and HUME, S. J. *Twentieth Century Stage Decoration.* 2 vols. London, 1928.

GOLDIE, GRACE. *The Liverpool Repertory Theatre.* London, 1922.

GORELIK, MORDECAI. *New Theatres for Old.* New York, 1940.

GRANVILLE BARKER, HARLEY. *The Exemplary Theatre.* London, 1922.

GRIFFITH, RICHARD. *The Movies.* New York, 1957.

HEWITT, BARNARD. See Chapter VI.

HUDSON, L. A. See Chapter IV.

JAQUES-DALCROZE, EMILE. *Rhythm, Music, and Education.* London, 1921.

KINNE, W. P. *George Pierce Baker and the American Theatre.* Cambridge, Mass., 1954.

KNAPP, BETTINA L. *Louis Jouvet, Man of the Theatre.* New York, 1958.

790   KNIGHT, ARTHUR. *The Liveliest Art: A Panoramic History of the Movies.* New York, 1957.

Bibliography   LEEPER, JANET. *E. Gordon Craig: Designs for the Theatre.* Harmondsworth, England, 1948.

MacCARTHY, DESMOND. *The Court Theatre, 1904–1907.* London, 1907.

MACGOWAN, KENNETH. *The Theatre of Tomorrow.* New York, 1921.

MACKAY, CONSTANCE D. *The Little Theatre in the United States.* New York, 1917.

MACKAYE, PERCY. *The Civic Theatre and Its Relation to the Redemption of Leisure.* New York, 1912.

———. *Community Drama.* Boston, 1917.

MARCH, HAROLD. *Romain Rolland.* New York, 1971.

MODERWELL, HIRAM. *The Theatre of Today.* New York, 1914.

PEARSON, HESKETH. See Chapter VI.

PICHEL, IRVING. *Modern Theatres.* New York, 1925.

POEL, WILLIAM. *Shakespeare in the Theatre.* London, 1913.

POGSON, REX. *Miss Horniman and the Gaiety Theatre, Manchester.* London, 1952.

PURDOM, CHARLES B. See Chapter VI.

QUINN, ARTHUR H. See Chapter II.

RISCHBIETER, HENNING. *Art and the Stage in the Twentieth Century.* Greenwich, Conn., 1968.

ROLLAND, ROMAIN. *The People's Theatre.* Translated by B. H. Clark. New York, 1918.

SAYLER, OLIVER M. *Max Reinhardt and His Theatre.* New York, 1936.

SHAW, G. B. *Letters to Granville Barker.* Edited by C. B. Purdom. New York, 1957.

SPEAIGHT, ROBERT. *William Poel and the Elizabethan Revival.* London, 1954.

STERN, ERNST. *My Life, My Stage.* London, 1951.

TREWIN, J. C. *Benson and the Bensonians.* London, 1960.

———. *Shakespeare on the English Stage, 1900–1964.* London, 1964.

TREWIN, J. C., and KEMP, T. C. *The Stratford Festival: A History of the Shakespeare Memorial Theatre.* Birmingham, 1953.

VOLBACH, WALTHER R. *Adolphe Appia, Prophet of the Modern Theatre.* Middletown, Conn., 1968.

CHAPTER 8

ALEXANDER, ARSÈNE. *The Decorative Art of Leon Bakst.* Translated by Harry Melville. New York, 1971.

BABLET, DENIS. See Chapter IV.

BAKSHY, ALEXANDER. *The Path of the Modern Russian Stage.* Boston, 1918.

BORRAS, F. M. *Maxim Gorky the Writer.* Oxford, 1967.

BRAUN, EDWARD. *Meyerhold on Theatre.* New York, 1969.

BRUFORD, W. H. *Chekhov.* London, 1957.

EVREINOV, NIKOLAI. *The Theatre in Life.* Translated by A. I. Nazaroff. New York, 1927.

FUERST, RENÉ, and HUME, S. J. See Chapter VII.

GORCHAKOV, NIKOLAI A. *The Theatre in Soviet Russia.* Translated by Edgar Lehman. New York, 1957.

GREGOR, JOSEPH, and FÜLOP-MILLER, RENÉ. *The Russian Theatre.* Translated by Paul England. Philadelphia, 1930.

GRIGORIEV, S. L. *The Diaghilev Ballet, 1909–1929.* Harmondsworth, England, 1960.

KAUN, ALEXANDER. *Maxim Gorky and His Russia.* New York, 1931.

KOCHNO, BORIS. *Diaghilev and the Ballets Russes.* Translated by Adreinne Foulke. New York, 1970.

KOMMISARJEVSKY, THEODORE. *Myself and the Theatre.* New York, 1930.

KOMISSARZHEVSKII, V. *Moscow Theatres.* Moscow, 1959.

KOTELIANSKY, S. S. *The Life and Letters of Anton Tchekov.* New York, 1925.

LAVRIN, JANKO. *Pushkin to Mayakovsky.* London, 1948.

LEVIN, DON. *Stormy Petrel: The Life and Work of Maxim Gorky.* New York, 1965.

LEVINSON, ANDRÉ I. *Bakst: The Story of the Artist's Life.* New York, 1971.

MAGARSCHACK, DAVID. *Chekhov the Dramatist.* London, 1952.

———. *Stanislavsky.* New York, 1951.

MELIK-ZAKHAROV, S., and SOLNTSEV, N. *Konstantin Stanislavsky, 1863–1963.* Moscow, 1963.

NEMIROVICH-DANTCHENKO, VLADIMIR. *My Life in the Russian Theatre.* Translated by John Cournos. Boston, 1936.

SLONIM, MARC. *Russian Theater from the Empire to the Soviets.* Cleveland, 1961.

STANISLAVSKY, KONSTANTIN. *An Actor Prepares.* Translated by Elizabeth R. Hapgood. New York, 1936.

———. *Building a Character.* Translated by Elizabeth R. Hapgood. New York, 1949.

———. *Creating a Role.* Translated by Elizabeth R. Hapgood. New York, 1961.

———. *My Life in Art.* Translated by J. J. Robbins. New York, 1924.

———. *Stanislavsky on the Art of the Stage.* Translated by David Magarschack. New York, 1952.

———. *Stanislavsky's Legacy.* Translated by Elizabeth R. Hapgood. New York, 1958.

STYAN, J. L. *Chekhov in Performance.* Cambridge, 1971.

TAIROV, ALEXANDER. *Notes of a Director.* Translated by William Kuhlke. Coral Gables, Fla., 1969.

VALENCY, MAURICE. *The Breaking String: The Plays of Anton Chekhov.* New York, 1966.

VARNEKE, BORIS. *History of Russian Theatre, Seventeenth through Nineteenth Centuries.* Translated by Boris Brasol. New York, 1951.

CHAPTER 9

BALAKIAN, ANNA. *André Breton, Magus of Surrealism.* New York, 1971.

BATES, SCOTT. *Guillaume Apollinaire.* New York, 1967.

BRETON, ANDRÉ. *Manifestoes of Surrealism.* Translated by Richard Seaver and Helen R. Lane. Ann Arbor, Mich., 1969.

———. *What is Surrealism?* Translated by David Gascoyne. London, 1936.

CARRIERI, RAFFAELE. *Futurism.* Milan, 1963.

CARTER, HUNTLY. *The New Spirit in the European Theatre, 1914–1924.* New York, 1926.

CHENEY, SHELDON. *Expressionism in Art.* Rev. ed. New York, 1948.

———. *Stage Decoration.* New York, 1928.

CLOUGH, ROSA T. *Futurism—The Story of a Modern Art Movement.* New York, 1961.

COCTEAU, JEAN. *Journals.* Edited and translated by Wallace Fowlie. Bloomington, Ind., 1964.

DAVIES, MARGARET. *Apollinaire.* Edinburgh, 1964.

DRY, AVIS M. *The Psychology of Jung.* New York, 1961.

DURAN, MANUEL (ed.). *Lorca: A Collection of Critical Essays.* Englewood Cliffs, N.J., 1962.

EISNER, LOTTE. *The Haunted Screen.* London, 1969.

FOWLIE, WALLACE. *The Age of Surrealism.* Bloomington, Ind., 1960.

FUERST, RENE, and HUME, S. J. See Chapter VII.

GARTEN, HUGH F. See Chapter VI.

GOLDING, JOHN. *Cubism: A History and an Analysis, 1907–1914.* 2d ed. London, 1968.

GORELIK, MORDECAI. See Chapter VII.

GROSSMAN, MANUEL L. *Dada: Paradox, Mystification, and Ambiguity in European Literature.* New York, 1971.

HONIG, EDWIN. *Federico García Lorca.* Norfolk, Conn., 1944.

ILIE, PAUL. *The Surrealist Mode in Spanish Literature.* Ann Arbor, Mich., 1968.

INFELD, LEOPOLD. *Albert Einstein: His Work and Its Influence on our World.* New York, 1950.

JACOBI, JOLANDE. *Complex, Archetype, and Symbol in the Psychology of C. G. Jung.* Translated by Ralph Manheim. New York, 1959.

KENWORTHY, B. J. *Georg Kaiser.* Oxford, 1957.

KINDERMANN, HEINZ. See Chapter III.

KIRBY, MICHAEL. *Futurist Performance.* New York, 1971.

KRAKAUER, SIEGFRIED. *From Caligari to Hitler.* London, 1947.

KRISPYN, EGBERT. *Style and Society in German Literary Expressionism.* Gainesville, Fla., 1964.

LEMAITRE, GEORGES. *From Cubism to Surrealism in French Literature.* Cambridge, Mass., 1941.

LEVY, JULIAN. *Surrealism.* New York, 1936.

LIMA, ROBERT. *The Theatre of García Lorca.* New York, 1963.

MACGOWAN, KENNETH, and JONES, R. E. *Continental Stagecraft.* New York, 1922.

MACKWORTH, CECILY. *Guillaume Apollinaire and the Cubist Life.* London, 1961.

MIESEL, VICTOR H. (ed.). *Voices of German Expressionism.* Englewood Cliffs, N.J., 1970.

MOUSSINAC, LEON. *The New Movement in the Theatre.* London, 1931.

NADEAU, MAURICE. *The History of Surrealism.* New York, 1965.

OXENHANDLER, NEAL. *Scandal and Parade: The Theatre of Jean Cocteau.* New Brunswick, N.J., 1957.

REICHENBACH, HANS. *From Copernicus to Einstein*. Translated by Ralph B. Winn. New York, 1942.

RICHTER, HANS. *Dada: Art and Anti-Art*. New York, 1966.

RISCHBIETER, HENNING. See Chapter VII.

SAMUEL, RICHARD, and THOMAS, R. HINTON. *Expressionism in German Life, Literature, and the Theatre*. Cambridge, 1939.

SHATTUCK, ROGER. See Chapter V.

SOKEL, WALTER H. *The Writer in Extremis: Expressionism in Twentieth Century German Literature*. New York, 1964.

TOLLER, ERNST. *I Was a German*. New York, 1934.

VERKAUF, WILLY, et al. (eds.). *Dada: Monograph of a Movement*. New York, 1957.

WILLETT, JOHN. *Expressionism*. New York, 1970.

CHAPTER 10

BOWERS, FAUBION. *Broadway USSR*. New York, 1959.

BRADSHAW, MARTHA. *Soviet Theatres, 1917–1941*. New York, 1954.

BRAUN, EDWARD. See Chapter VIII.

CARTER, HUNTLY. *The New Spirit in the Russian Theatre, 1917–1928*. London, 1929.

CHEKHOV, MICHAEL. *To the Actor*. New York, 1953.

DANA, H. W. L. *Handbook of Soviet Drama*. New York, 1938.

ERLICH, VICTOR. *Russian Formalism*. The Hague, 1955.

FUERST, RENÉ and HUME, S. J. See Chapter VII.

GORCHAKOV, NIKOLAI A. See Chapter VIII.

GORCHAKOV, NIKOLAI M. *The Vakhtangov School of Stage Art*. Moscow, 1961.

GORELIK, MORDECAI. See Chapter VII.

GREGOR, JOSEPH, and FÜLOP-MILLER, RENÉ. See Chapter VIII.

HOUGHTON, NORRIS. *Moscow Rehearsals*. New York, 1936.

KOHANSKY, MENDEL. *The Hebrew Theatre: Its First Fifty Years*. New York, 1969.

KOMISSARZHEVSKII, V. See Chapter VIII.

LAVRIN, JANKO. See Chapter VIII.

MAGARSCHACK, DAVID. *Stanislavsky*. New York, 1951.

MARKOV, P. A. *The Soviet Theatre*. London, 1934.

MARKOV, VLADIMIR. *Russian Futurism*. Berkeley, 1968.

MELIK-ZAKHAROV, S., and SOLNTSEV, N. See Chapter VIII.

MOUSSINAC, LEON. See Chapter IX.

NEMIROVICH-DANTCHENKO, VLADIMIR. See Chapter VIII.

SAYLER, OLIVER M. *Inside the Moscow Art Theatre*. New York, 1925.

———. *The Russian Theatre*. New York, 1922.

SETON, MARIE. *Sergei M. Eisenstein*. New York, 1952.

SIMONOV, REUBEN. *Stanislavsky's Protégé, Eugene Vakhtangov*. Translated by Miriam Goldina. New York, 1969.

SLONIM, MARC. See Chapter VIII.

STANISLAVSKY, KONSTANTIN. See Chapter VIII.

SYMONS, JAMES. *Meyerhold's Theatre of the Grotesque: The Post-Revolutionary Productions, 1920–1932.* Coral Gables, Fla., 1971.

TAIROV, ALEXANDER. See Chapter VIII.

VAN GYSEGHEM, ANDRÉ. *Theatre in Soviet Russia.* London, 1944.

WEIL, IRWIN. *Gorky: His Literary Development and Influence on Soviet Intellectual Life.* New York, 1966.

WEINER, LEO. *The Contemporary Drama of Russia.* Boston, 1924.

WOLFE, BERTRAM D. *The Bridge and the Abyss: The Troubled Friendship of Maxim Gorky and V. I. Lenin.* New York, 1967.

WOROZYLSKI, WIKTOR. *The Life of Mayakovsky.* Translated by Boleslaw Doborski. New York, 1970.

YERSHOV, PETER. *Comedy in Soviet Russia.* New York, 1956.

CHAPTER 11

ARTAUD, ANTONIN. *The Theatre and Its Double.* Translated by M. C. Richards. New York, 1958.

BISHOP, THOMAS. *Pirandello and the French Theatre.* New York, 1960.

BREDEL, OSCAR. *Pirandello.* New York, 1966.

BRUSTEIN, ROBERT. See Chapter III.

CHANDLER, FRANK W. *Modern Continental Playwrights.* New York, 1931.

CHIARI, JOSEPH. *The Contemporary French Theatre: Flight from Naturalism.* New York, 1958.

COHEN, ROBERT G. *Giraudoux: Three Faces of Destiny.* Chicago, 1968.

DANIELS, MAY. *The French Drama of the Unspoken.* Edinburgh, 1953.

DICKINSON, T. H. *The Theatre in a Changing Europe.* New York, 1937.

FUERST, RENÉ, and HUME, S. J. See Chapter VII.

GREENE, NAOMI. *Antonin Artaud: Poet Without Words.* New York, 1970.

GUICHARNAUD, JACQUES. *Modern French Theatre from Giraudoux to Beckett.* New Haven, 1961.

INSKIP, DONALD P. *Jean Giraudoux: The Making of a Dramatist.* London, 1958.

KNAPP, BETTINA L. *Antonin Artaud, Man of Vision.* New York, 1969.

———. See Chapter VII.

KNOWLES, DOROTHY. *French Drama of the Inter-war Years, 1918–39.* New York, 1967.

LESAGE, LAURENCE. *Jean Giraudoux, Surrealism and the German Romantic Ideal.* Urbana, Ill., 1952.

MACCLINTOCK, LANDER. *The Age of Pirandello.* Bloomington, Ind., 1951.

MOUSSINAC, LEON. See Chapter IX.

PALMER, JOHN. *Studies in the Contemporary French Theatre.* New York, 1927.

PRONKO, LEONARD. *Avant-Garde: The Experimental Theatre in France.* Berkeley, 1962.

PUCCIANI, ORESTE F. *The French Theatre Since 1930.* Boston, 1954.

SAINT-DENIS, MICHEL. *Theatre: The Rediscovery of Style.* New York, 1960.

SELLIN, ERIC. *The Dramatic Concepts of Antonin Artaud.* Chicago, 1968.
STARKIE, WALTER F. *Luigi Pirandello.* New York, 1926.
VITTORINI, DOMENICO. *The Drama of Luigi Pirandello.* New York, 1957.

CHAPTER 12

BRAUN, HANNS. *The Theatre in Germany.* Munich, 1952.

Bertolt Brecht on Stage. Frankfort on the Main, 1968.

BRECHT, BERTOLT. *Brecht on Theatre.* Translated by John Willett. New York, 1964.

CSATO, EDWARD. *The Polish Theatre.* Warsaw, 1963.

DEMETZ, PETER (ed.). *Brecht: A Collection of Critical Essays.* Englewood Cliffs, N.J., 1962.

ESSLIN, MARTIN. *Brecht: The Man and His Works.* New York, 1960.

FENCL, OTAKAR. *The Czechoslovak Theatre Today.* Prague, 1963.

FUERST, RENE, and HUME, S. J. See Chapter VII.

GARTEN, HUGH F. See Chapter VI.

GROPIUS, WALTER (ed.). *The Theatre of the Bauhaus.* Middletown, Conn., 1961.

HAAS, WILLY. *Bert Brecht.* Translated by Max Knight and Joseph Fabry. New York, 1970.

KRIDL, MANFRED. *A Survey of Polish Literature and Culture.* New York, 1956.

LEY-PISCATOR, MARIA. *The Piscator Experiment.* New York, 1967.

LYONS, CHARLES R. *Bertolt Brecht: The Despair and the Polemic.* Carbondale, Ill., 1968.

MILOSZ, CZESLAW. *The History of Polish Literature.* New York, 1969.

MOHOLY-NAGY, LASZLO. *Vision in Motion.* Chicago, 1947.

SAYLER, OLIVER M. See Chapter VII.

SPALTER, MAX. *Brecht's Tradition.* Baltimore, 1967.

WEIDELI, WALTER. *The Art of Bertolt Brecht.* New York, 1963.

WENGLER, HANS M. *Bauhaus.* Cambridge, Mass., 1969.

WILLETT, JOHN. *The Theatre of Bertolt Brecht.* New York, 1959.

WITKIEWICZ, STANISLAW. *The Madman and the Nun and Other Plays.* Translated, edited, and with an Introduction by Daniel C. Gerould and C. S. Durer. Foreword by Jan Kott. Seattle, 1968.

CHAPTER 13

BENSTOCK, BERNARD. *Sean O'Casey.* Lewisburg, Pa., 1970.

BISHOP, G. W. *Barry Jackson and the London Theatre.* London, 1933.

BRIDGES-ADAMS, W. *The Irresistible Theatre.* London, 1957.

BROWNE, E. MARTIN. *The Making of T. S. Eliot's Plays.* London, 1969.

CLUNES, ALEC. *The British Theatre.* London, 1964.

DENT, EDWARD J. *A Theatre for Everybody: The Story of the Old Vic and Sadlers Wells.* London, 1946.

796

Bibliography

DICKINSON, T. H. See Chapter IV.

DONOGHUE, DENIS. *The Third Voice: Modern British and American Verse Drama.* Princeton, 1959.

ELLIS, RUTH. See Chapter VII.

EVANS, GARETH L. *J. B. Priestley: The Dramatist.* London, 1964.

GIELGUD, JOHN. *Early Stages.* New York, 1939.

GUTHRIE, TYRONE. *A Life in the Theatre.* London, 1960.

———. *In Various Directions.* New York, 1965.

HOGAN, ROBERT G. *After the Irish Renaissance: A Critical History of the Irish Drama Since "The Plough and the Stars."* Minneapolis, 1967.

———. *The Experiments of Sean O'Casey.* New York, 1960.

HUDSON, L. A. See Chapter IV.

KRAUSE, DAVID. *Sean O'Casey: The Man and His Work.* New York, 1960.

LEVIN, MILTON. *Noel Coward.* New York, 1968.

McFALL, HALDANE. *The Book of Claud Lovat Fraser.* London, 1923.

MACLIAMMOIR, MICHAEL. *Theatre in Ireland.* Dublin, 1950.

MARSHALL, NORMAN. *The Other Theatre.* London, 1949.

MILLER, ANNA IRENE. See Chapter IV.

MOUSSINAC, LEON. See Chapter IX.

PEACOCK, RONALD. *The Poet in the Theatre.* New York, 1946.

PLAYFAIR, NIGEL. *Story of the Lyric Theatre, Hammersmith.* London, 1925.

ROBINSON, LENNOX. See Chapter VI.

SAINT-DENIS, MICHEL. See Chapter XI.

TREWIN, J. C. See Chapter VII.

———. *The Birmingham Repertory Theatre, 1913–1963.* London, 1963.

WHITWORTH, G. A. *The Making of a National Theatre.* London, 1951.

WILLIAMS, E. HARCOURT. *Old Vic Saga.* London, 1949.

CHAPTER 14

ALEXANDER, DORIS. *The Tempering of Eugene O'Neill.* New York, 1962.

ATKINSON, BROOKS. *Broadway Scrapbook.* New York, 1947.

BAILEY, MABEL D. *Maxwell Anderson: The Playwright as Prophet.* New York, 1957.

BERNHEIM, ALFRED L. See Chapter VI.

BOND, FREDERICK. *The Negro and the Drama.* Washington, D.C., 1940.

BRONSSARD, LOUIS. *American Drama: Contemporary Allegory from Eugene O'Neill to Tennessee Williams.* Norman, Okla., 1962.

BRUSTEIN, ROBERT. See Chapter III.

BURBANK, REX. *Thornton Wilder.* New York, 1961.

CARGILL, OSCAR, et al. (eds.). *O'Neill and His Plays: Four Decades of Criticism.* New York, 1961.

CHENEY, SHELDON. *The Art Theatre,* Rev. ed. New York, 1925.

———. *Stage Decoration*. New York, 1928.

CLURMAN, HAROLD. *The Fervent Years: The Story of the Group Theatre in the Thirties*. New York, 1957.

DAVIS, HALLIE FLANAGAN. *Arena*. New York, 1940.

DEUTSCH, HELEN, and HANAU, STELLA. *The Provincetown*. New York, 1931.

DICKINSON, THOMAS H. *Playwrights of the New American Theatre*. New York, 1925.

DOWNER, ALAN S. See Chapter VI.

EATON, WALTER P. (ed.). *The Theatre Guild: The First Ten Years*. New York, 1929.

ENGEL, EDWIN. *The Haunted Heroes of Eugene O'Neill*. Cambridge, Mass., 1953.

FALK, DORIS V. *Eugene O'Neill and the Tragic Tension*. New Brunswick, N.J., 1958.

GEDDES, NORMAN BEL. *Miracle in the Evening*. Garden City, N.Y., 1960.

GELB, ARTHUR, and GELB, BARBARA. *O'Neill*. New York, 1962.

GORELIK, MORDECAI. See Chapter VII.

GREBANIER, BERNARD. *Thornton Wilder*. Minneapolis, 1964.

HEWITT, BARNARD. See Chapter VI.

HIMELSTEIN, MORGAN Y. *Drama was a Weapon: The Left-wing Theatre in New York, 1929–1941*. New Brunswick, N.J., 1963.

HOPKINS, ARTHUR. *Reference Point*. New York, 1948.

ISAACS, EDITH J. R. *The Negro in the American Theatre*. New York, 1947.

KRUTCH, JOSEPH W. *The American Drama Since 1918*. Rev. ed. New York, 1957.

MACGOWAN, KENNETH. *Footlights Across America*. New York, 1925.

MERSAND, JOSEPH. *The American Drama, 1930–1940*. New York, 1941.

MESERVE, WALTER J. *Robert E. Sherwood: Reluctant Moralist*. New York, 1970.

MILLER, JORDAN Y. *Playwright's Progress: O'Neill and the Critics*. Chicago, 1965.

PENDLETON, RALPH. *The Theatre of Robert E. Jones*. Middletown, Conn., 1958.

POGGI, JACK. See Chapter VI.

QUINN, ARTHUR H. See Chapter II.

RABKIN, GERALD. *Drama and Commitment: Politics in the American Theatre of the Thirties*. Bloomington, Ind., 1964.

SIMONSON, LEE. *Part of a Lifetime*. New York, 1943.

Theatre Arts Magazine. 32 vols. Detroit and New York, 1916–48.

TORQVIST, EGIL. *A Drama of Souls: Studies in O'Neill's Supernaturalistic Technique*. New Haven, 1968.

TUISANEN, TIMO. *O'Neill's Scenic Images*. Princeton, 1968.

WEALES, GERALD. *Clifford Odets, Playwright*. New York, 1971.

YOUNG, STARK. *The Theatre*. New York, 1927.

CHAPTER 15

ANDREWS, JOHN. *International Theatre*. London, 1949.

BARRAULT, JEAN-LOUIS. *Reflections on the Theatre*. London, 1951.

———. *The Theatre of Jean-Louis Barrault*. Translated by J. Chiari. New York, 1961.

BENTLEY, ERIC. *In Search of Theatre.* New York, 1954.

BOWERS, FAUBION. See Chapter X.

BRAUN, HANS. See Chapter XII.

BRECHT, BERTOLT. See Chapter XII.

BRONSSARD, LOUIS. See Chapter XIV.

BROWN, IVOR. *Shakespeare Memorial Theatre.* 4 vols. London, 1951–59.

BROWNE, E. MARTIN. See Chapter XIII.

CHIARI, JOSEPH. See Chapter XI.

CLUNES, ALEC. See Chapter XIII.

CLURMAN, HAROLD. *Lies Like Truth.* New York, 1958.

COHN, RUBY. *Currents in Contemporary Drama.* Bloomington, Ind., 1969.

DONOGHUE, DENIS. See Chapter XIII.

DOWNER, ALAN S. *Recent American Drama.* Minneapolis, 1961.

EDWARDS, CHRISTINE. *The Stanislavsky Heritage.* New York, 1965.

Five Seasons of the Old Vic Theatre Company..., *1944–1949.* London, 1949.

FOWLIE, WALLACE. *Dionysus in Paris: A Guide to Contemporary French Theatre.* New York, 1960.

GARDNER, R. H. *The Splintered Stage: The Decline of the American Theatre.* New York, 1965.

GARTEN, HUGH F. See Chapter VI.

GASSNER, JOHN. *Theatre at the Crossroads: Plays and Playwrights of the Mid-Century American Stage.* New York, 1960.

GORCHAKOV, NIKOLAI A. See Chapter VIII.

GROSSVOGEL, DAVID. *The Self-conscious Stage in Modern French Drama.* New York, 1958.

GUICHARNAUD, JACQUES. See Chapter XI.

HAINAUX, RENÉ (ed.). *Stage Design Throughout the World Since 1935.* New York, 1956.

HARVEY, JOHN E. *Anouilh: A Study in Theatrics.* New Haven, 1964.

HEWITT, BARNARD. See Chapter VI.

HOBSON, HAROLD. *The French Theatre of Today.* London, 1953.

JACKSON, ESTHER. *The Broken World of Tennessee Williams.* Madison, Wis., 1965.

JONES, ROBERT EMMETT. *The Alienated Hero in Modern French Drama.* Athens, Ga., 1962.

KERNAN, ALVIN B. (ed.). *The Modern American Theatre: A Collection of Critical Essays.* Englewood Cliffs, N.J., 1967.

LEWIS, ALLAN. *American Plays and Playwrights of the Contemporary Theatre.* New York, 1965.

MIELZINER, JO. *Designing for the Theatre.* New York, 1965.

MOSS, LEONARD. *Arthur Miller.* New York, 1967.

NELSON, BENJAMIN. *Arthur Miller.* New York, 1970.

———. *Tennessee Williams.* New York, 1961.

PEPPARD, MURRAY. *Friedrich Duerrenmatt.* New York, 1969.

PRICE, JULIA. *The Off-Broadway Theatre.* New York, 1962.

PRONKO, LEONARD. *The World of Jean Anouilh.* Berkeley, 1968.

———. See Chapter XI.

PUCCIANI, ORESTE F. See Chapter XI.

Roy, Emil. *Christopher Fry.* Carbondale, Ill., 1968.

Smith, Cecil M. *Musical Comedy in America.* New York, 1950.

Speaight, Robert. *Drama Since 1939.* London, 1947.

Strasberg, Lee. *Strasberg at the Actor's Studio.* New York, 1965.

Tischler, Nancy. *Tennessee Williams: Rebellious Puritan.* New York, 1961.

Trewin, J. C. See Chapter VII.

———. *Dramatists of Today.* London, 1953.

Weales, Gerald. *American Drama Since World War II.* New York, 1962.

Weisstein, Ulrich. *Max Frisch.* New York, 1967.

Welland, Dennis. *Arthur Miller.* Edinburgh, 1961.

CHAPTER 16

Allsop, Kenneth. *The Angry Decade: A Survey of the Cultural Revolt of the 1950s.* London, 1958.

Armstrong, William A. (ed.). *Experimental Drama.* London, 1963.

Bentley, Eric. *What is Theatre? Incorporating the Dramatic Event and Other Reviews, 1944–1967.* New York, 1968.

Bree, Germaine. *Camus.* New Brunswick, N.J., 1961.

Brown, John Russell (ed.). *Modern British Dramatists: A Collection of Critical Essays.* Englewood Cliffs, N.J., 1968.

Brustein, Robert. See Chapter III.

Burkman, Katherine H. *The Dramatic World of Harold Pinter.* Columbus, Ohio, 1970.

Champigny, Robert. *Stages on Sartre's Way, 1938–52.* Bloomington, Ind., 1959.

Chiari, Joseph. See Chapter XI.

Coe, Richard. *Ionesco.* Edinburgh, 1961.

Cohn, Ruby. See Chapter XV.

Cunliffe, William G. *Günter Grass.* New York, 1969.

Driver, Tom. *Jean Genet.* New York, 1966.

English Stage Company. *Ten Years at the Royal Court, 1956–1966.* London, 1966.

Esslin, Martin. *The Peopled Wound: The Work of Harold Pinter.* New York, 1970.

———. *The Theatre of the Absurd.* Rev. ed. London, 1968.

Fowlie, Wallace. See Chapter XV.

Garten, Hugh F. See Chapter VI.

Grossvogel, David. *Four Playwrights and a Postscript: Brecht, Ionesco, Beckett, Genet.* Ithaca, N.Y., 1963.

———. See Chapter XV.

Guicharnaud, Jacques. See Chapter XI.

Hainaux, René (ed.). *Scene Design Throughout the World Since 1950.* New York, 1964.

Hayman, Ronald. *Harold Pinter.* London, 1968.

Ionesco, Eugène. *Notes and Counter Notes.* Translated by Donald Watson. New York, 1964.

800

JACOBSEN, JOSEPHINE, and MUELLER, WILLIAM R. *Ionesco and Genet: Playwrights of Silence*. New York, 1968.

————. *The Testament of Samuel Beckett*. New York, 1964.

JAMESON, FREDRIC. *Sartre: The Origins of a Style*. New Haven, 1961.

JEFFS, RAE. *Brendan Behan: Man and Showman*. London, 1966.

JONES, ROBERT EMMETT. See Chapter XV.

KENNER, HUGH. *Samuel Beckett*. Carbondale, Ill., 1961.

KITCHIN, LAURENCE. *Drama in the Sixties*. London, 1966.

————. *Mid-Century Drama*. 2d ed. London, 1962.

McMAHON, JOSEPH H. *The Imagination of Jean Genet*. New Haven, 1963.

MAROWITZ, CHARLES, and TRUSSLER, SIMON. *Theatre at Work: Playwrights and Productions in the Modern British Theatre*. New York, 1968.

POPKIN, HENRY (ed.). *The New British Drama*. New York, 1964.

PRONKO, LEONARD C. See Chapter XI.

————. *Eugène Ionesco*. New York, 1965.

RIBALOW, HAROLD U. *Arnold Wesker*. New York, 1965.

SARTRE, JEAN-PAUL. *Literary and Philosophical Essays*. London, 1955.

————. *Saint Genet, Actor and Martyr*. Translated by Bernard Frechtman. New York, 1964.

SHAW, LEROY R. *The German Theater Today*. Austin, Tex., 1963.

SIMPSON, ALAN. *Beckett, Behan, and a Theatre in Dublin*. London, 1962.

STYAN, J. L. *The Dark Comedy*. 2d ed. Cambridge, 1968.

TAYLOR, JOHN RUSSELL. *The Angry Theatre: New British Drama*. New York, 1969.

TRUSSLER, SIMON. *The Plays of John Osborne*. London, 1969.

TYNAN, KENNETH. *Curtains: Selections from Drama Criticism*. London, 1961.

WELLWARTH, GEORGE E. *The Theater of Protest and Paradox*. New York, 1964.

CHAPTERS 17, 18, AND 19

BENTLEY, ERIC. See Chapter XVI.

BIGSBY, C. W. E. *Confrontation and Commitment: A Study of Contemporary American Drama, 1959–66*. Columbia, Mo., 1967.

BREINES, PAUL (ed.). *Critical Interruptions: New Left Perspectives on Herbert Marcuse*. New York, 1970.

BROCKETT, OSCAR G. *Perspectives on Contemporary Theatre*. Baton Rouge, La., 1971.

BROOK, PETER. *The Empty Space*. New York, 1968.

BRUSTEIN, ROBERT. *Revolution as Theatre: Notes on the New Radical Style*. New York, 1971.

BURIAN, JARKA. *The Scenography of Josef Svoboda*. Middletown, Conn., 1971.

CAGE, JOHN. *Silence*. Middletown, Conn., 1961.

COHN, RUBY. See Chapter XV.

CRANSTON, MAURICE (ed.). *The New Left: Six Critical Essays*. New York, 1970.

CSATO, EDWARD. See Chapter XII.

DAY, BARRY. *The Message of Marshall McLuhan.* London, 1967.

DEBUSSCHER, GILBERT. *Edward Albee.* Brussels, 1967.

DENT, THOMAS O., et al. (eds.). *The Free Southern Theatre.* Indianapolis, 1969.

ENGLISH STAGE COMPANY. See Chapter XVI.

ESSLIN, MARTIN. See Chapter XVI.

FAIRWEATHER, VIRGINIA. *Cry God for Larry: An Intimate Memoir of Sir Laurence Olivier.* London, 1969.

FENCL, OTAKAR. See Chapter XII.

FINKELSTEIN, SIDNEY W. *Sense and Nonsense of McLuhan.* New York, 1968.

GOODWIN, JOHN (ed.). *Royal Shakespeare Theatre Company, 1960–63.* New York, 1964.

GROTOWSKI, JERZY. *Towards a Poor Theatre.* New York, 1968.

HAINAUX, RENÉ. See Chapter XVI.

HANSEN, AL. *A Primer of Happenings and Space/Time Art.* New York, 1966.

HAYES, EUGENE N. (ed.). *Claude Lévi-Strauss: The Anthropologist as Hero.* Cambridge, Mass., 1970.

HOUGHTON, NORRIS. *Return Engagement: A Postscript to "Moscow Rehearsals."* New York, 1962.

KAPROW, ALLAN. *Assemblage, Environments, and Happenings.* New York, 1966.

———. *Some Recent Happenings.* New York, 1966.

KERNAN, ALVIN B. See Chapter XV.

KIRBY, MICHAEL. *Happenings.* New York, 1966.

KITCHIN, LAURENCE. See Chapter XVI.

KOSTELANETZ, RICHARD. *The Theatre of Mixed Means.* New York, 1968.

LAHR, JOHN. *Up Against the Fourth Wall: Essays on Modern Theater.* New York, 1970.

LEACH, EDMUND R. *Claude Lévi-Strauss.* New York, 1970.

MAROWITZ, CHARLES, and TRUSSLER, SIMON. See Chapter XVI.

MILOSZ, CZESLAW. See Chapter XII.

MITCHELL, LOFTEN. *Black Drama: The Story of the American Negro in the Theatre.* New York, 1967.

NATIONAL THEATRE (GREAT BRITAIN). *Some Facts and Figures, 1963–1967.* London, 1968.

NEFF, RENFREU. *The Living Theatre USA.* Indianapolis, 1970.

NOVICK, JULIUS. *Beyond Broadway.* New York, 1968.

PASOLLI, ROBERT. *A Book on the Open Theatre.* New York, 1970.

POGGI, JACK. See Chapter VI.

ROBINSON, PAUL A. *The Freudian Left.* New York, 1969.

ROSTAGNO, ALDO. *We, the Living Theatre.* New York, 1970.

RUTENBERG, MICHAEL. *Edward Albee.* New York, 1969.

SCHECHNER, RICHARD. *Public Domain: Essays on the Theatre.* Indianapolis, 1969.

SLONIM, MARC. See Chapter VIII.

TAYLOR, JOHN RUSSELL. See Chapter XVI.

WEALES, GERALD. *The Jumping Off Place: American Drama in the 1960s.* New York, 1969.

802 Information about recent developments must still be sought primarily in periodicals. Some of the most helpful are:

Bibliography

> *Comparative Drama*
> *Drama Survey*
> *Educational Theatre Journal*
> *Modern Drama*
> *Plays and Players*
> *Theatre Crafts*
> *Theatre Quarterly*
> *The Drama Review (TDR)*
> *Village Voice*
> *World Theatre*

Index

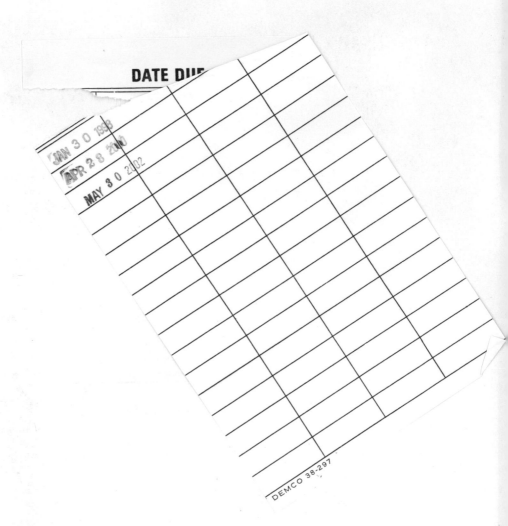